EDITION

4

W9-CMO-903

# Principles of Everyday Behavior Analysis

## L. Keith Miller

**University of Kansas**

WADSWORTH
CENGAGE Learning

Australia • Brazil • Japan • Korea • Mexico • Singapore • Spain • United Kingdom • United States

WADSWORTH
CENGAGE Learning

**Principles of Everyday Behavior Analysis, Fourth Edition**
L. Keith Miller

Publisher: Vicki Knight

Psychology Editor: Marianne Taflinger

Assistant Editor: Dan Moneypenny

Editorial Assistant: Lucy Faridany

Technology Project Manager: Darin Derstine

Marketing Manager: Chris Caldeira

Marketing Assistant: Nicole Morinon

Marketing Communications Manager: Laurel Anderson

Art Director: Vernon Boes

Print Buyer: Rebecca Cross

Permissions Editor: Stephanie Lee

Production Service: Matrix Productions

Photo Researcher: Connie Gardner

Copy Editor: Lauren Root

Illustrator: Integra

Compositor: Integra

Cover Designer: Ark Stein

Cover Image: Ryan McVay/Getty Images

For product information and technology assistance, contact us at
**Cengage Learning Customer & Sales Support, 1-800-354-9706**

For permission to use material from this text or product, submit all requests online at **www.cengage.com/permissions**
Further permissions questions can be emailed to
**permissionrequest@cengage.com**

Library of Congress Control Number: 2005922293

ISBN-13: 978-0-534-59994-2

ISBN-10: 0-534-59994-X

**Wadsworth**
10 Davis Drive
Belmont, CA 94002-3098
USA

Cengage Learning is a leading provider of customized learning solutions with office locations around the globe, including Singapore, the United Kingdom, Australia, Mexico, Brazil, and Japan. Locate your local office at: **www.cengage.com/global**

Cengage Learning products are represented in Canada by Nelson Education, Ltd.

To learn more about Wadsworth, visit
**www.cengage.com/wadsworth**

Purchase any of our products at your local college store or at our preferred online store **www.ichapters.com**

Printed in the United States of America
7  8   11

*To my wife, Ocoee Lynn Miller, my dear children Marty and Kieru Miller, and my beloved colleagues at the University of Kansas*

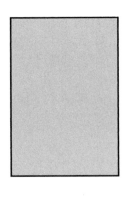

# Contents

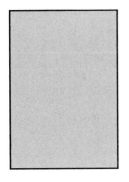

# Preface

I am happy to offer the new, updated Fourth Edition of *Principles of Everyday Behavior Analysis*. I have maintained the carefully programmed format of earlier editions, while updating the text and adding web-based learning resources.

The most powerful change in the Fourth Edition is the opportunity for students to use a "virtual teaching machine," so-called because students access it via the Web. This virtual teaching machine contains the same text, examples, illustrations, and questions as the printed version of the book. However, it acts as a guide throughout the book, providing instant feedback, frequent evaluations, and opportunities to skip sections that the student has already mastered. It prevents peeking at answers and skipping material not mastered. I have developed, tested, and revised the program over a 12-year period. Students give it exceptionally high ratings. Every student who buys a new printed book receives a password that permits unlimited access to the virtual teaching machine until all 25 lessons have been completed.

I have modified the structure of the printed book somewhat as a result of experience with the virtual teaching machine. Each of the programmed lessons starts with a reading section that presents the core concepts for that lesson, along with examples, illustrations from the literature, notes, helpful hints, and additional readings. The Programmed Reading section offers the student additional instruction on these concepts. This section contains 5–10 modules covering a specific idea from the Reading Section. Each module is preceded by a 1- to 5-item pre-test permitting the student to judge whether they need to study that module or whether they can skip to the next one. After finishing the Programmed Reading section, the student can then get detailed instruction on the core concepts in the Programmed Examples section. As in previous editions, each lesson also continuously reviews concepts from earlier lessons. The book contains three tear-out quizzes for each lesson as well as detailed answer keys.

Notably, I have extensively restructured Lesson 6 on Visual Analysis, creating more than 100 instructional graphs to replace the data tables of the Third Edition and providing simple graphical tools so that students can analyze the graphs in an intuitive way. The result is a lesson that is much easier to understand.

Throughout the text, I have improved the obscure observation forms, reliability tables, and data tables of the Third Edition.

In addition, I have added more than 125 references covering new research findings. Most of these date since the year 2000.

Finally, the Instructor's Manual for this text has four review exam forms for Lessons 7, 15, 21, and 25, and it also comes with a diskette that will generate random forms of the review exam from a pool of over 1,000 items. You can obtain the manual from the publisher. This free supplement is available to qualified adopters. Please consult your local sales representative for details.

I would like to thank the many people who have made this book possible. I owe a boundless debt to my wife, Ocoee. She supported my efforts over these many years to revise this book. She has discussed every important change once, if not many times. She helped me more than I can ever repay.

I also owe an enormous debt to Nathan Smith, who has served as my teaching assistant the last five years. He has helped find many of the interesting and relevant advancements in behavior analysis newly added to the book. He has helped identify and test revisions to weak programming sequences. He has been a wonderful colleague.

I owe a great debt also to Darwin Eakins. Darwin has developed the computer program that eventually turned into the virtual teaching machine. He has been a wonderful person to work with not only because of his computer skills but also because he has a master's degree in behavior analysis and thus understands what I am trying to accomplish.

I want also to thank Greg Madden for his interest in the book and his helpful comments on some portions of the revision, particularly Lesson 6.

I am grateful for the participation of the following reviewers: Michael Clayton, Jacksonville State University; Susan Claxton, Floyd College; Bradley Donohue, University of Nevada, Las Vegas; Phillip Duncan, West Chester University; Sigrid Glenn, University of North Texas; Timothy Kelly, Portland State University; Robert Madigan, University of Alaska, Anchorage; Gerald Mertens, St. Cloud State; and W. Scott Wood, Drake University.

I hope that students and faculty will find this book of personal value and easy to use. I trust that readers finding errors will inform me of them. I invite readers to tell me about their favorite examples of both research and everyday life.

*L. Keith Miller*

# Introduction: The Science of Learning and the Technology of Education

(Note to the student: The book uses **boldface** to emphasize basic concepts and <u>underlining</u> to highlight key words. I will ask you questions about these terms in the Quiz later. Please pay careful attention to those terms that are boldfaced or underlined.)

This book introduces you to the science of <u>behavior analysis</u>. Behavior analysis studies how the events in your daily life affect your behavior. This science has three branches: experimental, applied, and conceptual. The experimental analysis of behavior studies the basic principles that determine people's behavior. It conducts "basic research." Applied behavior analysis studies the application of those principles to behavioral problems. It conducts "applied research." Conceptual behavior analysis discusses theoretical issues. It conducts "theoretical research." The name given to the basis, applied, and conceptual branches together is <u>behavior analysis</u>. This book focuses on applied behavior analysis while drawing on elements of the other two branches. (Notice that I underlined the important words *behavior analysis*.)

1. This book introduces you to the science of behavior ＿＿＿＿＿＿＿＿＿＿. (Note: Answers are found on pages 493–505.)

## Behavior Analysis and Learning

Behavior analysis studies how people <u>learn</u> the rich variety of behaviors that mark their lives. It examines how children learn new skills as they grow up, how adults learn to work and love, and how older people learn to adjust to retirement. It studies how people learn both rational and emotional behavior. It investigates how we can help people with retardation learn to run their own lives. It studies how normal people can learn to live cooperatively. These studies enable behavior analysts to help troubled people learn new, better-adapted behaviors. (I have emphasized the word *learn* because behavior analysis is the science of learning.)

2. Behavior analysis studies how people ＿＿＿＿＿＿＿＿＿＿ the rich variety of behaviors that mark their lives.

Behavior analysis helps people with many kinds of <u>problems</u> improve their lives. In particular, it has developed numerous ways to help people overcome disabilities. It has helped college students to overcome learning problems. It has assisted all kinds of people in dealing with problems in social relationships. It has helped parents handle problems in raising their children. (Notice what behavior analysis helps people with.)

3. Behavior analysis helps people with many kinds of ＿＿＿＿＿＿＿＿＿＿ improve their lives.

This book in not only <u>about</u> behavior analysis; it is also an <u>example</u> of behavior analysis. In writing it, I have used many of the discoveries behavior analysis has made about learning. You will probably find that you are learning more material with less effort. Because the book is an example of behavior analysis, you will be learning about behavior analysis simply by using it. If you like using it, then you can appreciate what behavior analysis has to offer. (Notice the words emphasized in this paragraph.)

4. This book is not only <u>about</u> behavior analysis; it is also a(n) _____ of behavior analysis.

The book differs from most other introductory textbooks by inviting you to actively <u>respond</u> to it throughout. It invites you to respond by answering questions about what you have just read, by extending that understanding to everyday situations, and by applying your understanding to examples. By answering, extending, and applying your understanding, you will be actively responding to the book. You will thereby participate in the process that is at the very heart of behavior analysis: modifying behavior! (Did you notice?)

5. The book differs from most other introductory textbooks by inviting you to actively _____ to it throughout.

## Lesson Section

The book divides each of the 25 lessons into four <u>sections</u>. Each section prompts your active responses to its ideas. The sections of each lesson appear in the following order: Reading Section, Programmed Reading, Programmed Examples, and Class Quizzes. I will explain what you can expect to learn from each of these sections in the following paragraphs.

6. The book divides each of the 25 lessons into four _____.

### *Reading Section*
You begin each lesson by reading about one or more behavioral concepts in the <u>Reading Section,</u> which defines each concept, gives examples of research that uses it, and illustrates how it can help you understand everyday situations.

7. You begin each lesson by reading about one or more behavioral concepts in the _____ section.

After a lesson introduces you to one or more concepts, it then provides Behavior Analysis Examples of research exemplifying how that concept can be used to help someone. The examples provide more of the details of the research than the short references in the Reading Section. You learn about the behavioral problem, how it is observed, how it was solved, and a graph illustrating the change.

The Notes section refines or extends discussion of a concept in the Reading Section. It comes after the Examples.

The Helpful Hints section helps you apply the concepts to examples by clarifying the definitions of concepts. These hints will help you prepare for quizzes and exams on your readings. I have included questions based on the hints in the Programmed Reading section. I have also included questions in the Class Quizzes and Review Exams to test you on some of the Helpful Hints. This section follows the Notes section.

Finally, each lesson gives a list of additional readings for the students who wish to pursue their understanding beyond this book. This section comes after the Helpful Hints section.

### *Programmed Reading Section*
The book then invites you to answer questions about your reading in the Programmed Reading section. The quiz questions help you identify and remember the most important points from the Reading Section. I have added extra questions to help you remember and learn the correct answers. These extra questions make this section into a program on the ideas in the lesson. The answers to the quiz questions appear at the end of the book.

8. The book then invites you to answer questions about your reading in the _____ _____ Reading section.

After you answer the questions in the Programmed Reading section, you should check your answers. This is very important. If you make a mistake and don't check your answer, you will end up practicing that mistake! If you find a mistake, you should also consider rereading the corresponding part of the Reading Section.

9. After you answer the questions in the Programmed Reading section, you should _____ your answers.

### Programmed Examples Section

The book next invites you to apply your new skills to short stories about everyday events in the Programmed Examples section. I call the section Programmed Examples because each story gives you an example to analyze using the concepts you have learned in the Reading Section. Your analysis of the examples is guided by a series of questions. The questions help you decide whether you can use one of the concepts from the lesson to analyze the situation. If not, the questions lead you to a concept from an earlier lesson that can help you analyze the example.

10. The book next invites you to apply your new skills to short stories about everyday events in the Programmed _____ section.

To help you answer the questions in the first few examples, the Programmed Examples section gives hints that draw your attention to the most important parts of the examples. The book provides many hints to help you learn to use the basic ideas. After the first few examples, the number of hints decreases until you get no hints at all for the last ten examples. By slowly reducing the number of hints, the book gradually puts you on your own. The answers to all of the questions appear at the end of the book.

11. To help you answer the questions in the first few examples, the Programmed Examples section gives _____.

### Class Quiz

The last part of each lesson is the Class Quiz. For most lessons, at the back of the book there are three class quizzes, keyed to the Reading (Form A), Programmed Reading (Form B), and Programmed Example (Form C) sections. Normally, your teacher will give you these quizzes in class. You can prepare for them by trying to answer the Class Quiz questions without writing on the forms themselves.

After you answer the questions in the Programmed Examples section, you should check your answers to see if they are correct.

12. After you answer the questions in the Programmed Examples section, you should _____ your answers to see if they are correct.
13. The last section of each lesson is the Class _____.

You now know that each lesson consists of four parts. The first part is the Reading Section, in which you read about different aspects of behavior analysis. The second part is the Programmed Reading section, in which you answer questions about what you just read. The third part is the Programmed Examples section, in which you analyze stories in terms of behavior analysis concepts. The fourth and last part of each lesson is the Class Quiz, based on the ideas in the lessons.

14. The four sections of a lesson are the part you read, called the _____ _____; the part that tests you on the your reading, called the Programmed _____ _____ section; the part with the short fictional stories, called the Programmed _____ section; and the part that tests you on the whole lesson, called the Class _____ section.

### Practice Review Sections

In addition to the regular lessons, the book contains four Review lessons. Each Review lesson includes a Practice Review section. The questions in this section are drawn from everything that you have learned up to that point, to help you study for your review exam. If you can answer these questions correctly, you will be able to answer similar questions on your review exam correctly.

15. In addition to the regular lessons, the book contains four _____ lessons.

## How to Study for Review Exams

After you study a Review lesson, your instructor will probably give you a <u>Review Exam</u>. This 25-item exam will contain questions from every lesson that you have already studied. Your instructor will probably base your course grade primarily on your scores on the four Review Exams.

16. After you study a review lesson, your instructor will probably give you a major exam called a Review _____ _____.

Don't confuse the Class Quiz and the Review Exam. The Class Quiz is a minor test that appears as a section of each lesson. You can look at it ahead of time and make sure you know the answers. The Review Exam is a major test that is not a section of the book. You will not be able to look at it ahead of time.

17. Don't confuse the Class Quiz and the Review Exam. A minor test included in the book is a _____ Quiz. A major test not included in the book is a _____ Exam.

If you can answer 90% or more of the questions in a Class Quiz, you should have little trouble scoring well on the Review Exam covering all the material previously presented. If you answer fewer correctly, then consider changing the way you prepare for the quizzes. I recommend three practices that I will call the <u>read-write-check</u> method.

18. If you do not score 90% on the Class Quizzes, I recommend the read-write-check method: First, you _____ every section of the lesson; second, you _____ _____ answers to every question; and third, you _____ every one of your answers.

First, <u>read</u> every section of the lesson. Read every sentence of the Reading Section—the text, the boxes, the examples, as well as the notes, and helpful hints. Read all the Programmed Reading section, which will help you determine whether you have read the Reading Section carefully enough to remember the major ideas. Then, read the Programmed Examples section. It will help you learn how to apply the behavioral concepts you have read about to real-life situations. You cannot learn everything you need to know just by reading the Reading Section.

19. First, you _____ every section of the lesson.

Second, <u>write</u> your answers to the Programmed Reading section and to the Programmed Examples section in the book. Many students just *think* their answers without writing them down. Others simply look up the answers, perhaps without even reading the Reading Section. Educational research has demonstrated that writing down your answers is likely to improve your learning (e.g., Holland, 1965; Tudor & Bostow, 1991).

20. Second, you _____ your answers to the Reading Quiz and to the Examples in the book.

Third, <u>check</u> to see if all of your responses are correct by looking them up. If you make an incorrect response and don't check it, you will be practicing making the wrong response. Checking your responses can help you correct misunderstandings that may have developed. This will prepare you for tests given by your teacher.

21. Third, you _____ to see if all of your responses are correct by looking them up.

## Summary

This book introduces you to the science of behavior analysis. I designed it using the behavior analysis of learning. It differs from most other introductory textbooks by inviting you to actively respond to it throughout. Basically, each lesson is divided into a Reading Section, Programmed Reading section, Programmed Examples section, and Class Quiz section. In addition, the four review lessons have Practice Review sections. If you have trouble scoring 90% on the class quizzes, consider using the read-write-check method. First, read every section of the lesson. Second, write your answers to every question. Third, check all of your answers.

## Helpful Hints

### Helpful Hint #1
Words referring to basic concepts initially appear in boldface type. You will encounter them throughout the book. Key words crucial to understanding a concept are underlined. These key words often answer questions posed by the book.

22. Basic concepts appear in _____ _____ type. Key words are _____.

### Helpful Hint #2
Some of the questions on the Class Quiz will come from the Programmed Reading section you completed after the Reading Section. This means that one way to study for the Class Quiz is to make sure you can correctly answer every question in the Programmed Reading section.

23. One way to study for the Class Quiz is to make sure you can correctly answer every question in the Programmed _____ _____ section.

### Helpful Hint #3
I include references to behavior analysis books and articles. You can look up more details by going to the source for my statements. I put these references in the standard form for behavior analysis. They appear in parentheses, with the names of the authors first, followed by the year of publication. For example, a reference to this book would look like this: (Miller, 2006). You could then go to the References section of the book to find

the title, where it was published, and what pages I refer to. When you do not wish further details, you will be safe ignoring these references.

24. If you wish further details, look up the reference in the _____ section.

### Helpful Hint #4
Some of the questions on the Class Quiz will be shortened forms of examples from the Programmed Examples section. Being familiar with the original version is helpful. This means that a second way to study for the Class Quiz is to make sure you can correctly answer questions about the examples.

25. A second way to study for the Class Quiz is to make sure you can correctly answer questions about the _____.

### Helpful Hint #5
I have adopted an unusual way of numbering quiz questions. For example, I might label the first question 14, the second 5, and so on. I have scrambled them so you won't accidentally see the answer to the second question while checking the first one to see if your response is correct. Seeing the second answer would prevent you from recalling that answer on you own. You may check the answer to the first question labeled 14, by looking at the Answer section at the end of the book and finding 14.

26. Scrambling the answers in this way prevents you from seeing the answer to other questions while _____ to see if your response is correct.

### Helpful Hint #6
I have changed some of the Class Quiz questions that are based on the Programmed Reading and the Programmed Examples enough to make a different answer correct. Be sure to read the Class Quiz questions closely even if they look familiar. I have made these changes so that you must read each question carefully to determine your answer. By doing so, I have ensured that students can't simply memorize answers.

27. You can't memorize answers, because I have sometimes changed Class Quiz questions that are based on the Programmed Reading and Programmed Examples enough to make a(n) _____ answer correct.

### *Helpful Hint #7*

Pay special attention to sentences with underlined words, but read <u>every</u> sentence in the Reading Section. In this lesson, I have made the questions by simply copying those sentences with an underlined word and leaving out the underlined word. This makes your reading quiz simple; in future lessons, I will gradually make things harder. I will often reword the question so that it in no longer identical to the Reading Section sentence. I will also ask questions based on sentences without underlined words.

28. Pay special attention to sentences with underlined words, but still read _____ _____ sentence.

### *Helpful Hint #8*

One final hint: Make sure you have a calculator for the two lessons that require computations. The lesson on reliability and the lesson on visual analysis both require computations. Many students make errors because they can't divide 3 by 8 without a calculator.

## Additional Readings

Holland, J. G. (1965). Research on programming variables. In R. Glaser (Ed.), *Teaching machines and programming learning II: Data and directions*. Washington, DC: National Education Association.

Tudor, R. M., & Bostow, D. E. (1991). Computer-programmed instruction: The relation of required interaction to practical application. *Journal of Applied Behavior Analysis, 24,* 361–368. This article describes recent research on the importance of actively responding to questions.

## Programmed Reading

I have provided a set of questions about the ideas that you have just read. They may help you learn those ideas. Some of the questions are designed to teach you. They may have obvious clues, be extremely easy to answer, or have several possible answers listed. These questions lead up to harder questions that I have labeled Review questions. Pay particular attention to the Review questions. I urge you to write out and check your answers to these questions. If you don't always get them right, then you should write out and check your answers to the more obvious teaching questions as well.

29. This book introduces you to the science of behavior _____ .

30. Students sometimes decide that the name of the field is *behavioral analysis*. It is not! It is incorrect to add *–al* to *behavior*. The correct term is *behavior analysis*. Your answer is wrong unless you call it _____ analysis.

25. Review: The name of the field applies to all three of its branches taken together. Thus, the name for the basic, applied, and conceptual branches together is _____ _____ analysis.

5. Behavior analysis studies how people _____ the rich variety of behaviors that mark their lives.

4. Behavior analysis helps people with many kinds of _____ improve their lives.

34. This book is not only about behavior analysis, it is also a(n) _____ of behavior analysis.

30. The book differs from most other introductory textbooks by inviting you to actively _____ to it.

31. The book divides each of the 25 lessons into four _____ .

27. Review: You begin each lesson by reading about one or more behavioral concepts in the _____ section.

23. Review. The book then invites you to answer questions about the reading in the _____ Reading section.

1. After you answer the questions in Programmed Reading, you should _____ _____ your answers!

22. Review: The book next invites you to apply your behavior analysis skills to stories about everyday events in the Programmed _____ section.

33. To help you answer the questions in the first few examples, the Programmed Examples section gives you _____ _____.

2. After you answer the questions in the Programmed Examples section, you should _____ your answers to see if they are correct!

24. Review: The last section of each lesson is the _____ Quiz.

28. Review: You review groups of regular lessons with four special lessons. I call these special lessons _____ lessons.

3. After you study a review lesson, your instructor will probably give you an exam called a Review _____, containing questions from every lesson you have already studied.

13. If you can answer 90% or more of the questions in a Class Quiz, you should have little trouble scoring well on the _____ Exam that reviews all the material previously presented.

21. Review: If you are not able to answer 90% of the questions correctly on the Class Quiz, first be sure that you _____ _____ every section of each lesson from then on.

17. Review: If you are not able to answer 90% of the questions correctly of the Programmed Reading, second, you should _____ down your answers to the Reading Quiz and to the Examples.

18. Review: If you not able to answer 90% of the questions correctly on the Class Quiz, third, you should _____ to see if all of your responses are correct by looking them up.

32. The Class Quizzes and Review Exams test you on the Helpful _____ _____.

14. Remember to read the Helpful Hints section. From Hint #1: Words referring to basic concepts initially appear in _____ type.

6. From Hint #1: Key words crucial to understanding a concept are _____ _____.

7. From Hint #2: Some of the questions on the Class Quiz will come from the section that asks you questions about the reading:

the _____ Reading section.

8. From Hint #4: Some of the questions on the Class Quiz will be shortened forms of stories from the section called the Programmed _____ section.

9. From Hint #5: I have scrambled question numbers so you won't accidentally see the answer to the second question when you _____ the first one to see if your response is correct.

10. From Hint #6: I have changed some of the Class Quiz questions that are based on the Programmed Reading and the Programmed Examples enough to make a/the _____ (different, same) answer correct.

11. From Hint #7: Pay special attention to sentences with underlined words in this book, but read _____ sentence in the Reading Section.

12. From Hint #8: If you can't divide 3 by 8 without a calculator, then you should be ready on two lessons to use a _____ _____ (calculator, friend).

26. Review: When you have finished answering the questions in the Programmed Reading, you should _____ _____ your answers.

19. Review: If you have trouble scoring 90% on the Class Quizzes, consider three practices. First, _____ every section of the lessons. Second, _____ _____ down your answers to every question. Third, _____ all of your answers.

20. Review: Some of the questions of the Class Quiz will come from the Programmed _____ section you have already completed; others will be shortened forms of _____ from the Programmed Examples section.

16. Review: I have changed some of the Class Quiz questions that are based on the Programmed Reading and the Programmed Examples enough to make a(n) _____ answer correct.

15. Review: Carefully note sentences in the Reading Section with underlined words, but be sure to _____ every sentence, whether or not it contains an underlined word.

# LESSON 1

# Introduction to Everyday Behavior Analysis

## Reading Section

## Introduction to Unit 1

The purpose of this book is to introduce you to the dynamic new science of applied behavior analysis. Applied behavior analysis solves a wide variety of human problems from autism to zoophobia. Let me give you two examples.

The first example involves children with a severe behavioral disorder. Applied behavior analysis is so effective with children with autism that parents around the country seek it out whenever possible. I saw the power of this new science when a group of parents sued to force the local school board to offer a behavior analytic program for their children with autism—and won. I then saw parents from around the country quit their jobs, sell their houses, and move to Lawrence, Kansas, so that their children with autism could benefit from this program.

The second example involves college students living in a cooperative dormitory. Kansans fresh from the Depression had founded a cooperative dormitory in 1940 where students with little money could afford to live by sharing the chores. The dorm had failed when I came to Kansas in 1968 because students had stopped sharing the chores. My students and I created a behavior analytic system for sharing chores from cleaning toilets to managing the finances. That system is now run entirely by the residents and still uses that chore-sharing system in 2005.

I hope to convince you that this new science can revolutionize not only the way we help people with severe behavioral disorders but also the way that we conduct our everyday lives. By the way, you will learn more about the treatment of autism and about the cooperative dormitory later in the book.

As you study the book, you will learn four broad strategies for solving human problems, involving behavior analysis, reinforcement, stimulus control, and aversive control. In this unit you will explore the behavioral strategy. You will learn that the simple act of gathering information about the role of behavior in a human problem will often lead to its solution. You will also learn five specific tactics for using this approach. Let us first take a quick look at its historical roots.

Behavior analysis is the modern form of the philosophy of <u>behaviorism</u>. Behavior analysis was born in the 1930s and started to grow rapidly in 1970. Since 1970, it has helped people solve many behavioral problems. It has launched new fields such as behavioral medicine. It has become the most successful approach to understanding human behavior. It has found a way to use the methods of natural science. Behavior analysis has succeeded because it has solved many problems that plagued the study of human behavior. One such problem is understanding the role of private events in causing behavior.

1. Behavior analysis is the modern form of the philosophy of _____.

## Modern Behaviorism

The historical roots of behavior analysis lie in the philosophy of <u>behaviorism</u>. Behaviorism first appeared on the American scene around 1900. It took an approach to human conduct that looked for <u>facts</u>. It tried to find out

*1*

what people do and why they do it. It favored natural science methods to discover the causes of human behavior. It aimed to use this information to solve the many social problems of that time. It appeared in economics, political science, and sociology even before psychology (Samelson, 1985). (You can look up the title and location of the Samelson comments by finding *Samelson* in the References section, followed by the year *1985* in parentheses.)

2. The philosophy of behaviorism took an approach to human conduct that looked for _____.

Most people interested in the study of human behavior in 1900 resisted the philosophy of <u>behaviorism</u>. They stuck with the approach to human conduct going back to ancient times. They engaged in theories, guesses, and much learned debate. They favored spending many hours in the library reading what other "experts" had to say. They remained philosophers, not scientists. They used logic to explain human behavior, not facts. They gathered data through people's reports of their own thoughts. They assumed that thoughts cause behavior.

John B. <u>Watson</u> argued passionately that psychology should adopt the philosophy of behaviorism (Watson, 1914). He was the first widely known psychologist to do so. He based his approach on the laws of reflex behavior (Pavlov, 1927). Reflex behavior is responding caused by a stimulus. It is responding that you cannot avoid. It is involuntary. For example, the eye blink is a reflex caused by an object moving toward the eye. Blinking your eye is involuntary. Watson argued that simple reflexes combine to form complex behavior. He proposed the first <u>stimulus-response</u> behaviorism. His behaviorism accounts for much behavior in primitive organisms, but it only accounts for a small amount of human behavior. Its most important weakness is that it cannot explain voluntary behavior. Behavior analysts argue that this kind of behaviorism cannot explain complex human behavior.

B. F. Skinner laid the basis for modern behaviorism in 1938. That is the year he formulated the law of <u>reinforcement</u>. This

***Figure 1-1.*** John B. Watson urged psychology to adopt a form of stimulus-response behaviorism in 1914. (Source: Archives of the History of American Psychology)

law had its roots in earlier observations, particularly those of Thorndike. A major finding of behavior analysis, it seems simple yet it explains much. The law says: A behavior followed by a reinforcer will increase in probability. The law means that a person is more likely to behave in a way that works. People learn from experience.

Skinner applied the term *operant* to behavior affected by reinforcement. He thereby set it apart from reflex behavior, which is involuntary. He argued that operant behavior is <u>voluntary</u> behavior. In fact, he argued that "operant behavior is the field of intention, purpose and expectation" (Skinner, 1986: p. 716). He argued that the laws of operant behavior can explain complex human behavior.

Skinner founded <u>modern</u> behaviorism. He added operant behavior to Watson's and Pavlov's reflex behavior to get a rounded picture of the causes of behavior. In doing so, he

*Figure 1-2.* B. F. Skinner founded the science of behavior analysis in the 1930s. (Source: Bettmann Archive)

## The Growth of Behavior Analysis

Skinner did not gain instant recognition for his formulation of the law of reinforcement. Instead, his work caused a few other researchers to study reinforcement, who made additional discoveries. The number of behavior analysts grew slowly from this start in the 1930s. Their numbers had grown large enough to found their first journal by 1958. They studied basic laws of reinforcement during those early years, but they did not try to apply these basic laws to practical problems.

Behavior analysts found variables that strongly affected behavior. These variables were the basis for the first laws of voluntary behavior. The laws allowed this new field to begin solving practical behavioral problems. Behavior analysts called this practical application of behavioral laws to solve behavioral problems <u>applied behavior analysis</u>. The first examples of such application occurred in the

went beyond the stimulus-response behaviorism advocated by Watson. Skinner's approach has been much more successful because so much of human behavior is voluntary. He called his brand of behaviorism <u>behavior analysis</u>.

Many people have ranked Skinner's work next to other <u>major</u> advances in science. Vaughan (1984) argues that it is one of three major advances. The first was to stop seeing Earth as the center of the universe. The second was to stop seeing humans as totally different from animals. The third was to give up the idea that private events cause behavior.

Many people view Skinner as the world's <u>greatest</u> psychologist (Haggbloom et al., 2002). The American Psychological Association cited his work as "unparalleled among contemporary psychologists" (Graham, 1990). It gave him an award for his lifetime contribution to psychology. It has never honored another psychologist in this way.

*Figure 1-3.* Charles Ferster was the first editor of the first journal devoted to behavior analysis. It published basic research. (Source: Courtesy of Marilyn Gilbert)

***Figure 1-4.*** Montrose Wolf was the first editor of the first journal devoted to applied behavior analysis. It published applied research. (Source: Montrose Wolfe)

early 1960s. They created a sensation among students of human behavior.

3. When behavior analysts first <u>applied</u> behavioral laws to solve behavioral problems they called it _____ behavior analysis.

Applied behavior analysts first used these laws to help people with only the most <u>severe</u> problems. They often used them on problems that were so bad that all other approaches had failed. They taught long-term mental patients to take care of themselves (Ayllon & Azrin, 1968). They helped people with severe retardation learn how to talk (Guess, 1969). They got children with devastating autism to stop hurting themselves (Lovaas, Schaeffer, & Simmons, 1965). Such triumphs with severe problems convinced many students of human behavior that behavior analysis was a major breakthrough. You will have the chance to judge for yourself as you read this book.

Behavior analysts drew strength from these triumphs. They used behavioral laws to help people with <u>moderate</u> problems. They helped adults change their stuttering (James, Ricciardelli, Hunter, & Rogers, 1989). They helped people with mild retardation prepare their own meals (Sanders & Parr, 1989). They helped troubled teens learn better social and academic skills (Phillips, Phillips, Fixsen, & Wolf, 1971). They had thousands of similar successes. They found that their methods worked not only with severe problems but with a wide range of moderate problems.

Behavior analysts use these laws to improve the lives of <u>everyday</u> people. They help children form healthy sleep habits (Durand & Mindell, 1990). They help college students learn (Kulik, Kulik, & Cohen, 1979). They help low-income children learn more in school (Bereiter & Midian, 1978; Bushell, 1978). They help motorists learn safer driving behaviors (e.g., Van Houten & Retting, 2001). They help parents and classroom teachers learn to effectively manage children with problem behaviors (e.g., Papatheodorou, 2000). They help drug treatment counselors learn to effectively implement interventions (e.g., Andrzejewski, Kirby, Morral, & Iguchi, 2001). They even help groups learn to cooperate more fully (Los Horcones, 1986; Miller, 1976). You will find many other examples of everyday applications in this book.

4. Applied behavior analysts started helping people with severe or moderate problems that you don't run into <u>everyday.</u> They have finally begun improving the lives of people with _____ problems.

Behavior analysts are opening up whole new fields of study with the power of these laws. <u>Behavioral medicine</u> has replaced psychosomatic medicine (Pattischall, 1989). This new field is becoming a major part of medicine because people's behavior causes as much as half of all disease (Dush & Spoth, 1988). Behaviors that cause disease include overeating, careless sex, smoking, lack of exercise, drinking alcohol, using drugs, poor driving, and fighting. Other new fields include behavioral pediatrics, which improves the care of infants (Gross & Drabman, 1990); behavioral gerontology, which helps keep older people active and healthy

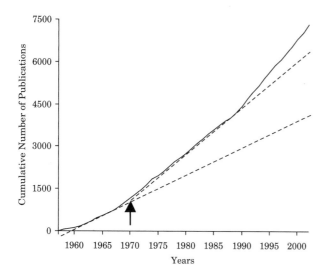

***Figure 1-5.*** The solid line shows the growing number of behavior analysis publications since 1958. The dotted lines show that the rate of growth doubled in 1970 and again in 1990. The increase in 1970 marks the explosion of applied behavior analysis on the American scientific scene. (Graph shows papers published in 14 behavioral journals. Articles published before 1973 are cited in Wyatt, Hawkins, & Davis, 1986. Articles published after 1973 were counted from the PsychLit database.)

(Carstensen, 1988; Gallagher & Keenan, 2000); behavioral dentistry, which helps improve self-care like toothbrushing and flossing (Melamed & Bennett, 1985); and behavioral sports psychology, which improves the performance of athletes (e.g., Ward & Carnes, 2002).

Behavior analysts believe behavioral laws provide a foundation for all <u>behavioral</u> sciences. They are the basis of "behavioral sociology" (Burgess & Bushell, 1969; Kunkel, 1975), of "behavioral economics" (Hursh, 1984; Kagel & Winkler, 1972), of "behavioral social work" (Thyer, 1988), and of "behavioral anthropology" (Lloyd, 1985). Glenn has suggested that the concept of the *operant*, upon which behavior analysis is based, is the "gene" for all of the social sciences (Glenn, 1986). Thus behavior analysis may be more than just another approach to human behavior (Kazdin, 1975).

Behavior analysis exploded on the American scientific scene about <u>1970</u>. Figure 1-5 shows the growth of scientific papers from the inauguration of the first journal devoted exclusively to behavior analysis in 1958. The growth rate of these publications doubled in 1970 when the application of behavior analysis exploded

on the American scientific scene. The growth rate doubled again in 1990. This explosive growth reflected the unparalleled success with which behavior analysis developed effective solutions to a wide range of human problems.

5. Behavior analysis exploded on the American scientific scene about _____.

As you might expect, behavior analysts view B. F. <u>Skinner</u> as the founder of their field. Skinner discovered many of the basic laws of behavior analysis. He foresaw the possibility of applying these laws to solving practical problems. He also laid out the basis for the methods and philosophy of behavior analysis (e.g., Skinner, 1945; Skinner, 1950).

## What Is Behavior Analysis?

Just what is behavior analysis? Here is your first definition. Behavior analysis is the science that studies <u>environmental</u> events that <u>change</u> behavior (Baer, Wolf, & Risley, 1968).

6. **Behavior analysis**: The science that studies <u>environmental</u> events that do what to behavior: they _____ it.

Now you know how to define *behavior analysis*, but just what are *environmental events*? Environmental events are any events outside the person. The physical world provides many such events. Rain is an environmental event that changes the way you dress and what you do. The presence of a cliff is an environmental event that changes the direction of your walking. The social world of other people provides innumerable environmental events. When your Mom tells you to stop teasing your brother, she creates an event that may change how you play. When your boss gives you a raise, she may influence how well you do your job. Environmental events are all of those events in your world that may influence your behavior.

Here is an example of behavior analysis. Suppose Tom is having trouble in fifth-grade spelling. We might guess that studying does not lead to any environmental events that are an obvious benefit for Tom. His parents may not praise him, the teacher may not notice his effort, and his friends may like other things about him. We might help Tom change by arranging for some benefits. The easiest place to start might be with the teacher. We might induce the teacher to pay attention to Tom when he studies. His teacher might praise him whenever he is studying, which is an observable behavior. Praise is an environmental event. If Tom's studying increases, then we have found an environmental event that seems to change behavior. If Tom's studying does not increase, then we might look at other events. Behavior analysis is the science that studies environmental events like praise. It studies whether these events can change behaviors like studying.

Notice that praise is an environmental event. Also notice that we can observe studying. We can experiment with praise to see if it changes Tom's studying. The defining feature of behavior analysis is this focus on environmental events that change behavior.

## The Problem with Using Private Events to Explain Behavior

Skinner invented a natural science method for the study of behavior. His method was to focus on environmental events that change behavior. He focused on environmental events rather than private events as causes of behavior.

People often explain behavior with private events. Private events include thoughts, feelings, emotions, attitudes, and other similar events. They are private because only the person who has them can observe them. Following are some examples of explanations based on private events.

"I ate vegetables because I decided I needed more vitamins." You are explaining the behavior of eating vegetables by the thought that you need more vitamins. Your decision is private because you are the only person who can observe your thoughts.

"I went to a movie because I felt like laughing." You are explaining the behavior of going to the movie with the feeling of wanting to laugh.

"I voted for Dole because I like his sense of humor." You are explaining the behavior of voting for Dole by your attitude toward his sense of humor.

"I hit him because I was angry." You are explaining your behavior of hitting the person by your emotion of anger.

These explanations have a problem. The problem is that we need to explain the private events just as much as we need to explain the public behavior. For example, we might say, "Joe decided to do his homework." This invites the next question, "Why did Joe decide to do his homework?" If we cannot answer that question, then we cannot increase the chances that Joe will do his homework. Common sense suggests that Joe decided to do his homework for a reason. Perhaps he has a test coming up. Perhaps his allowance depends on doing his homework. Perhaps he has some free time. Notice that these causes are environmental events, not private events. If we can find an environmental event that explains his decision, then we can use it to increase his chances of doing his homework. As long as we find only private events, we can't do anything that will help Joe. Thus when we use private behavior, like Joe's decision, to explain doing his homework, we still need to explain his decision.

7. The problem with using private events to explain behavior is that we still need to _____ the private events!

## The Principle of Public Events

Skinner advocated the **principle of public events**, which seeks the causes of behavior in environmental events, not in private events such as thinking or feeling. This approach required Skinner to establish two facts: (1) the observed behavior and (2) the state of the environment. He looked for an environmental event that causes Ann's swearing and yelling. Maybe Ann's Dad usually helps her when she swears and yells. Getting Dad's help is a reasonable explanation for Ann's swearing and yelling. It is an event in Ann's environment that we might be able to observe. Skinner did not have to use unexplained causes to explain Ann's behavior. He sought the explanation in environmental events.

8. **The principle of public events**: Seeking the causes of behavior in _____ _____ events.

Notice that Skinner did <u>not</u> deny the existence of private events. He did not deny that Ann had feelings of anger. He simply argued that the study of public events, like Dad's offer to help, permits a natural science approach to behavior. You will learn in the next chapter that behavior analysts regard private events as behavior. Ann's feelings of anger are complex and subtle behaviors that only Ann can observe. They are private. Skinner argued that Ann's feelings are caused by the same kind of public events that caused her yelling and cursing.

Many people still explain behavior by private events. However, Skinner's arguments convinced many researchers to reject the use of private events as causes. Skinner and his colleagues call this approach *behavior analysis*. It seeks causes of behavior in the environment rather than in private events.

---

*A Leading Anthropologist's View of Private Events*

"The human intuition concerning the priority of thought over behavior is worth just about as much as our human intuition that the earth is flat" (Harris, 1979). In other words, Marvin Harris thinks that thought does <u>not</u> have priority over behavior; he does <u>not</u> think that thought causes behavior. Remember, behavior analysts do not deny the existence of thoughts. In fact, they claim that thoughts are a form of behavior. They seek environmental causes of our thoughts just as they seek environmental causes of all behavior.

10. Do you think behavior analysts agree with Marvin Harris that thoughts do <u>not</u> cause other behavior? _____ (yes, no)

---

*Skinner on Feelings*

Skinner asserts that, according to critics, "behaviorists are not supposed to have <u>feelings</u>, or at least to admit that they have them. Of the many ways in which behaviorism has been misunderstood for so many years, this is perhaps the commonest" (Skinner, 1989: p. 3).

9. Skinner calls this a misunderstanding because he has never asserted that people have no _____. In fact, he calls them private events.

---

## The Behavioral Strategy

As noted earlier, the book presents four strategies for changing behavior, and it introduces them in the order in which you, as an analyst would usually try them. If the first doesn't work, then you would try the second. If the second doesn't work, you would try the third.

I call the first strategy for changing behavior the *behavioral strategy*. The behavioral strategy is the simplest of the four strategies. Its core idea is that people will often be able to solve their problems if they clearly define them as behavioral problems. People often require nothing more. The **behavioral strategy** is a way of defining human problems as <u>behavioral</u> problems. Again, this is the easiest strategy to use.

11. The first strategy for solving human problems is defining them as <u>behavioral</u> problems. I will call this strategy the _____ strategy.

I will teach you five tactics in applying the behavioral strategy. I will devote one lesson to each of these tactics.

Remember, if the behavioral strategy doesn't work, then you, as an analyst, could try the reinforcement strategy, which you will learn in Unit 2. If that doesn't work, then you could try the stimulus control strategy, which you will learn in Unit 3. Finally, if all else failed, you could try the aversive control strategy, which you will learn in Unit 4.

## Summary

Behavior analysis is modern behaviorism. It differs from stimulus-response behaviorism because it studies "voluntary" behavior. It started in the 1930s. It built a foundation of basic knowledge until its explosive growth in the 1970s. Behavior analysis is the science that studies environmental events that change behavior. Its most important contribution may be avoiding the problem with private events. It seeks the causes of behavior in environmental events rather than in private events. The behavioral strategy for solving human problems is a way of defining them as <u>behavioral</u> problems. You will learn about that strategy in Unit 1.

## Notes

I have put a section entitled "Notes" in most lessons. You will find it at the end of the reading and just prior to the Helpful Hints and the Programmed Reading. These notes expand on some of the ideas presented in the lesson. They may help you prepare for quizzes and exams on your readings. I have included questions based on the notes in the Programmed Reading section. I have also included questions in the Lesson Quizzes and Review Exams to test you on some of the notes.

### Note #1

Place (1993) asserts that advances in behavior analysis may lead to methods for measuring <u>private</u> events. He argues that we may learn when self-reports are accurate and when they are not. Some studies have begun exploring the conditions under which people make accurate reports (e.g., Critchfield & Perone, 1990). Other studies have shown ways to teach children to report public events accurately (e.g., Baer & Detrich, 1990). Perhaps we can teach people to report private events accurately. We may then discover how to predict when people will report private events accurately.

13. Such advances may lead to methods for accurately measuring _____ events.

## Helpful Hints

### Helpful Hint #1

When asked for a person's name, give only their last name. Do not include their first name or initials.

14. For example, when asked who is the founder of the science of behavior analysis, give only the single name _____.

---

### *Why the First Part of This Book Is about Scientific Methods*

Astrophysicist Carl Sagan asserts that we live in a society deeply influenced by science, but most of us know little about it. "Virtually every newspaper in America has a daily astrology column. How many have a daily science column? Science is much more than a body of knowledge. It is a way of thinking. This is central to its success. Science invites us to let the facts in, even when they don't conform to our preconceptions. It counsels us to carry alternative hypotheses in our heads and see which ones best match the facts. It urges on us a fine balance between no-holds-barred openness to new ideas and established wisdom. We need wide appreciation of this kind of thinking. It works" (Sagan, 1989, cited in *Behavior Analysis Digest*, December, 1989). In other words, science is a <u>method</u> for understanding. Therefore, I have placed first in this book the scientific methods used by behavior analysis.

12. I have placed first in this book the scientific _____ used by behavior analysis.

### Helpful Hint #2

The first time that I present a question in this lesson I will use exactly the same wording as in the text. Each time I repeat that question, I will change some of the words. I do that to encourage you to learn the idea, not some mechanical formula. Notice, however, that I insist that you use the exact term or the exact underlined key words as your answers. I do this so you will learn technical terms.

For example, here is the initial definition of *behavior analysis*: "Behavior analysis is the science that studies <u>environmental</u> events that <u>change</u> behavior."

I use the exact same wording the first time I ask you about behavior analysis: "Behavior analysis is the science that studies environmental events that (blank) behavior." To make the question a little easier, I omit only one key term.

When I ask you about behavior analysis the second time, I change "the science that studies" to "the science of" and leave out two key terms: "Behavior analysis is the science of (blank) events that (blank) behavior." Notice that this time I left out two key terms.

When I ask you about behavior analysis the third time, I change a few words and I change the order. This time I ask for the term being defined. "What science looks at environmental events to find ways to help people change their behavior: (blank)?"

When I ask you about behavior analysis the fourth time, I reword further. "The name of the science that studies external events that change people's behavior is (blank)."

Much later I change wording still further: "If you wanted to develop techniques that used external events to change behaviors what behavioral science would you use: (blank)."

15. To recap: The first time I ask about a term I often use the exact <u>same</u> words as appear in the readings. The next time I ask about that term I use somewhat _____ _____ words.

### Helpful Hint #3

When asking the first question about an idea, I will sometimes give you a multiple-choice instead of a fill-in question. When I give you multiple choices, I will always list them alphabetically.

16. If the choices are "same" and "different," which word would I list second? _____ _____

### Helpful Hint #4

I will ask you to define the major terms in the book in many different places and in many different ways. You can help yourself by memorizing each definition. The simplest way to do that is to memorize the key terms in the definition. For example, I have defined *behavior analysis* as "the science that studies <u>environmental</u> events that <u>change</u> behavior." I have underlined the key terms in the definition. If you learn only them you will probably be able to recite the whole definition. So, to memorize the definition of *behavior analysis* you need to remember that the two key terms are *environmental* and *change*. You will help yourself further if you will repeat the full definition of the term without looking at it several times during each lesson. Thus, after you read the definition of *behavior analysis*, try closing your eyes and reciting the definition. Try it now!

17. I have defined *behavior analysis* as "the science that studies <u>environmental</u> events that <u>change</u> behavior." To memorize the definition of behavior analysis you need to remember that the two key terms are _____ and _____.

## Additional Readings

Bandura, A. (1969). *Principles of behavior modification*. New York: Holt, Rinehart, and Winston. This book gives an overview of behavior modification. It shows the broader meaning of the term *behavior modification* in psychology.

Goodall, K. (1972, November). Shapers at work. *Psychology Today*, p. 6. This is an extremely well-written, popular introduction to the founders of behavior analysis.

Moore, J. (1980). On behaviorism and private events. *Psychological Record*, 30, 459–475. This paper presents an extensive discussion of the behavior analysis of private events. Many examples. A classic.

Pryor, K. (1984). *Don't shoot the dog*. New York: Bantam Books. This book was written by one of the original porpoise trainers. She used behavioral procedures that worked so well she became an advocate of behavior analysis. This is a wonderfully readable book that will help you reach a better understanding of behavior analysis.

Skinner, B. F. (1989). *Recent issues in the analysis of behavior*. Columbus, OH: Merrill. This is the most recent collections of Skinner's papers. He discusses a variety of misunderstandings about behavior analysis. He includes an analysis of feeling, cognitive thought, the role of genes in behavior, and behavior therapy.

Ullman, L. P., & Krasner, L. (1965). *Case studies in behavior modification*. New York: Holt, Rinehart, and Winston. This book is an early sample of research on specific behavioral problems.

Willis, J., & Giles, D. (1976). *Great experiments in behavior modification*. Indianapolis: Hackett. This book provides brief accounts of 100 great experiments in behavior analysis. It is a good book from which to get an overview of behavior analysis research.

## Programmed Reading

You are about to begin your first Programmed Reading section. This section is designed to help you apply the terms <u>behavior analysis</u>, the <u>principle of public events</u>, and the <u>behavioral strategy</u>. This Programmed Reading section is divided into four "modules." The first module helps you with the term *behavior analysis,* the second with the principle of public events, the third with the behavioral strategy, and the fourth is an integrated review of all three.

Each module begins with a "pre-test." The pre-test asks you questions about the term for that module. The questions are designed to find out whether you understand and can apply that term. If you miss any questions, then you should study that module carefully. If you do not miss any questions, then you have a choice: you can skip to the next module or you can study the module.

I recommend that you study the module regardless of your pre-test. By doing so, you will practice applying your understanding of each term. You will be able to use the terms more quickly and for a wider range of examples. Further, you are more likely to remember the term much later during your major exams. Unless you are an extraordinary student, you will need the extra practice to get an A or a B instead of just passing. If you are a poor student, you will need the extra practice to even pass the major exams.

#### ♦ Very Important ♦

When asking the first question about an idea, I will sometimes give you a multiple-choice instead of a fill-in question. If the choices are "good" and "bad," I will list "bad" first because "b" is earlier in the alphabet than "g." If two choices of a multiple-choice question are: "multiple choice" and "fill-in," which choice would I list last?_____

#### ♦ Very Important ♦

The first time I ask about a term I often use the exact <u>same</u> words as appear in the readings. The next time I ask about a term I will usually use _____ (different, identical) words.

### 1. Defining Behavior Analysis

34. Pre-test: The science that studies environmental events that change behavior is called _____.

21. Pre-test: Applied behavior analysis exploded in popularity in the year _____.

22. Pre-test: As you might expect, behavior analysts view _____ as the founder of their field. (Give last name only—do not give initials.)

24. Pre-test: Behavior analysis studies such private events as thoughts and feelings as a form of _____.

25. Pre-test: Behavior analysts view most behavior as _____ behavior.

26. Pre-test: Behavior analysis is the study of _____ events that _____ behavior.

14. I will teach you the basic facts about behavior analysis in this module. First, be sure you are spelling behavior analysis

correctly. The science is not called behavioral analysis. It is called _____ _____ analysis.

18. Next, I want to make sure you are correctly spelling a word crucial to defining behavior analysis. *Environmental* is a word that many students rarely use. Behavior analysts use it to refer to events in the world outside of a person's body as opposed to the world inside the person's body. Copy *environmental* to become familiar with its spelling: _____.

13. I will start with the definition of behavior analysis. By now you should know that the name of the science that studies <u>environmental</u> events that <u>change</u> behavior is behavior _____.

45. The definition of behavior analysis includes two key words: *environmental* and *change*. Behavior analysis is the science that studies <u>environmental</u> events. It seeks to discover those environmental events that _____ behavior.

55. The science of behavior analysis is the study of _____ events that change behavior.

61. What is the name of the science that studies environmental events that change behavior? _____

69. You will be able to define behavior analysis if you remember that it is the science that studies _____ events that _____ behavior.

12. Here is the first important fact you should know about behavior analysis. B. F. Skinner made many of the important discoveries that created the foundation for behavior analysis. Therefore, you can guess that most behavior analysts consider the founder of their field to be _____.

56. The second important fact is that behavior analysts started applying the laws of behavior to solve behavioral problems in about 1970. You need to remember that applications of behavior analysis to solve practical problems began in the year _____.

49. The following information may help you remember the year. The roots of behavior analysis appeared about 1900 in America. Skinner's discoveries started about 35 years later, in 1935. Applications of his discoveries appeared another 35 years later, in the year _____.

58. The third fact you should know is how behavior analysts view their subject matter. They view most behavior as a tool to get useful results from the environment. According to this view, people repeat behaviors that "work" and don't repeat behaviors that don't work. Clearly, behavior analysts view these behaviors as _____. (involuntary, voluntary)

10. Early behaviorists dealt only with a tiny portion of behavior. They dealt with reflex behavior. Reflex behavior is <u>involuntary</u> behavior like the blink of your eye when an object flies at it. Early behaviorists argued that even complex behavior is caused by combinations of such reflexes. Therefore, early behaviorists, unlike behavior analysts, viewed all behavior as _____. _____ (involuntary, voluntary)

70. You will correctly understand an important assumption of behavior analysis if you know that it views most behavior as _____ behavior.

50. The fourth fact is how behavior analysts regard thoughts and feelings. They insist that thoughts and feelings are a form of behavior even though they are inside the person and therefore private. They argue that such private events are just as much behavior as is public behavior that others can also observe Bottom line: Behavior analysts view thoughts and feelings in the same way they view moving or walking, that is, as a form of _____.

67. You need to keep these last two facts separate. Behavior analysts view most behavior as _____ behavior. Behavior analysts view private events like thoughts and feelings as a form of _____.

68. You need to remember four facts. The founder of behavior analysis is _____. Applied behavior analysis began in the year _____. Behavior analysts view most behavior as _____. _____ Behavior analysts view private events like thoughts and feelings as a form of _____.

66. You also need to remember the two key terms that define behavior analysis: it is the study of _____ events that _____ behavior.

46. The field that studies environmental events that change behavior is _____. _____.

64. Who founded behavior analysis? _____ _____

4. Behavior analysis is the study of _____ _____ events that _____ behavior.

6. Behavior analysis views private events like thoughts and feelings as a form of _____.

2. Applied behavior analysis exploded onto the American scientific scene in the year _____.

7. Behavior analysts view most behavior as _____ behavior.

## 2. Principle of Public Events

31. Pre-test: The principle of public events seeks the causes of behavior in _____ _____ events.

33. Pre-test: The problem with using private events to explain behavior is that you still have to _____ the private events.

28. Pre-test: Seeking the causes of behavior in environmental events is called the principle of _____ events.

41. Skinner took a new approach to private events. Thoughts, feelings, emotions, and attitudes are all examples of what he called _____ (private, public) events.

65. Why did Skinner call events like thoughts, feelings, emotions, and attitudes private events? Notice that the person who has a thought or experiences a feeling _____ (is, isn't) the only person who can observe it. Therefore, these events are private.

40. Skinner called thoughts, feelings, and emotions _____ events.

20. People often argue that public behavior is caused by these private events. For example, they might explain John's running by saying he is afraid. Unfortunately, to fully explain why John ran, we still need to explain what caused his fear. In other words, the problem with using private events to explain what caused behavior is that we still must _____ what caused the private events.

11. For example, someone might try to explain that Mary hit Ted because she was mad at him. They are explaining the behavior of hitting by the private event of feeling mad. Skinner argued that the problem with this explanation is that we still need to _____ _____ why Mary feels mad!

42. Skinner would look for environmental events to explain why Mary hit Ted. He might guess that Ted's stealing a kiss caused Mary to hit Ted (and become mad). This explanation does not point to an event inside of Mary's skin like anger. It points to an event outside of her skin like Ted's stolen kiss. This explanation points to the cause of Mary's hitting in a(n)_____ _____ (environmental, private) event.

3. As another example, someone might try to explain why Mozart composed such beautiful music. They might assert that Mozart was creative. The problem is that we can't explain Mozart's composing behavior any better as a result. In order to explain his composing behavior we still need to _____ why Mozart was so creative.

1. A behavior analyst might explain Mozart's musical creativity by pointing out the encouragement of his father as a young child. This explains the cause of Mozart's creative compositions in terms of a(n) _____ (environmental, private) event.

15. In general, when someone states that a private event causes a behavior, we are still left with the need to _____ _____ the cause of the private event.

62. When I ask students for the name of the approach that looks for causes of behavior in public, environmental events, they often make the mistake of calling it the principle of environmental events. The correct label is the principle of _____ events.

63. When people try to explain behavior by pointing to private events, you might say they are using the principle of private events. When behavior analysts explain behavior by pointing to environmental events that are public, you might say they are using the principle of _____ events.

39. Skinner advocated the principle of public events. Students are often tempted to say

that this approach seeks the causes of behavior in public events. Unfortunately, that doesn't tell you very much. A better answer is that this approach seeks the causes of behavior in _____ events.

38. Remember, the problem with using private events to explain what caused behavior is that we still need to _____ what caused them.

51. The principle of public events seeks the causes of behavior in _____ _____ events.

52. The problem with explaining the cause of behavior in private events is that you still must _____ the private events.

17. Looking for the causes of behavior in environmental events is called the principle of _____ events.

### 3. The First Strategy for Solving Human Problems

35. Pre-test: The strategy for solving human problems that defines the problem as behavioral is the _____ strategy.

30. Pre-test: The field that studies environmental events that change behavior is _____.

48. The first <u>strategy</u> for solving human problems is to define them as behavioral problems. Note that I do not call this the behavior strategy, but rather I call this the behavior<u>al</u> _____.

19. Notice that the correct name for the science is *behavior analysis*, but the correct name for the strategy of defining human problems as behavioral problems is the _____ *strategy*.

43. The <u>behavioral</u> strategy is a way of defining human problems as _____ problems.

57. The strategy for solving human problems that defines the problem as behavioral is the _____ strategy.

47. The field that studies environmental events that change behavior is _____.

### 4. Review

23. Pre-test: Behavior analysis is the science that studies _____ events that _____ behavior.

27. Pre-test: I call defining human problems as behavioral problems the _____ _____ strategy.

29. Pre-test: Seeking the cause of behavior in environmental events is called the principle of _____ events.

36. Pre-test: What science looks at environmental events to find ways to help people change their behavior? _____ _____

32. Pre-test: The principle of public events is to look for the causes of behavior in _____ _____ events.

37. Publication of applied behavior analysis became widespread about _____.

53. The problem with private events is that we must still _____ the private events.

8. Behavior analysts view _____ as the founder of their field (last name).

5. Behavior analysis sees most behavior as _____ behavior.

9. Does behavior analysis deny the existence of such private events as thoughts and feelings? _____ (yes, no)

44. The behavioral strategy is defining human problems as _____ problems.

54. The problem with using private events to explain behavior has led behavior analysts to use environmental events to explain behavior. I call this the principle of _____ (private, public) events.

16. Let's review the earlier module. The science that studies environmental events that change behavior is _____ _____. Using environmental events to explain behavior is called the principle of _____ events.

## Programmed Examples

You are about to begin your first Programmed Examples section. This section is designed to help you apply the term <u>behavior analysis</u>, the <u>principle of public events</u>, and the <u>behavioral strategy</u> to actual examples. Doing so will help you move beyond simply memorizing definitions and terms. By learning how these ideas apply to actual examples you will be deepening your understanding of them.

### 1. *Programmed Examples*

9. Pre-test: Suppose Dad taught Kenny how to clean his room and then showered him with praise and fun when he did. Dad would find out if this approach works. In a way, he would be "studying" whether teaching plus praise and fun can change Kenny's cleaning behavior. Therefore, Dad would be using an informal approach to the science of _____ _____.

7. Pre-test: Dad defined Kenny's problem as stemming from being a slob. Dad's approach defines the problem as being inside of Kenny. Mom defined Kenny's problem as not cleaning his room. Because she defined Kenny's problem in terms of his room-cleaning behavior, she was using the _____ strategy to solve his problem.

8. Pre-test: Ms. Snow claimed that Gary was doing well in second grade because his parents supported his efforts. They asked him questions when he came home from school, encouraged his homework, and showed an interest when he brought home drawings and other classwork. By explaining Gary's success in school by his parents' support, Ms. Snow was using the principle of _____ events.

3. Dr. Ward helped Willie become a better listener for Queen, his wife. Dr. Ward did this by praising Willie for paraphrasing any important point that Queen made. Dr. Ward studied whether his praise increased Willie's paraphrasing. I will ask you to decide whether Dr. Ward is using behavior analysis. You must ask first, did Dr. Ward study an environmental event that might change Willie's behavior? Dr. Ward's use of praise is outside of Willie. Therefore his praise is a(n) _____ (environmental, private) event. You must ask second, did Dr. Ward try to change Willie's behavior? Because Dr. Ward praised Willie when he paraphrased Queen, Dr. Ward was trying to _____ (change, understand) Willie's behavior. Because Dr. Ward was studying the use of praise to increase Willie's paraphrasing, he was applying the science of _____.

10. Willie consulted Dr. Corey before seeing Dr. Ward. Dr. Corey explained Willie's poor listening of Queen's points as the result of feeling coldness toward his wife. Since the feeling of coldness is inside of Willie, Dr. Corey was explaining Willie's poor listening by pointing to _____ (environmental, private) events. The problem with using the feeling of coldness to explain Willie's poor listening behavior is that you still have to _____ Willie's feelings of coldness.

4. Dr. Ward took a different approach. He guessed that Willie had not learned good listening skills. He guessed that Willie's father had not taught such skills. Father's teaching would consist of demonstrating good listening, explaining good listening, and praising Willie when he listened well. Because these events are outside of Willie, Dr. Ward is using the principle of _____ events to explain Willie's poor listening.

1. Dad claims little Kenny has a messy room because he is a slob. Dad is claiming that being a slob is causing Kenny to not clean his room. Ask yourself if being a slob is outside or inside of Kenny? You should conclude that Dad is explaining Kenny's lack of cleaning with a(n) _____ (environmental, private) event. The problem with Dad's approach is that he still needs to _____ why Kenny is a slob.

5. Mom claims that Kenny doesn't clean his room because Dad never taught him to. She told Dad to teach Kenny how to maintain a clean room and to shower him with attention and fun when he does any cleaning. Mom is explaining Kenny's lack of cleaning as due to no one teaching him to. Teaching consists of _____ (environmental, private) events. Therefore Mom is using the principle of _____ events.

2. Dr. Gordon suspected that Dwayne did poorly in school because his parents did not reward him for his homework. Dr. Gordon convinced the parents to reward Dwayne for schoolwork. Dwayne started doing much better in school. Dr. Gordon improved Dwayne's schoolwork by using the science of _____ _____.

6. Norman was a rotten employee. He came late, left early, and did sloppy work when he was there. A non–behavior analyst might define Norman's problem as a "bad attitude." A behavior analyst would define it as three behaviors: coming late, leaving early, and doing sloppy work. Such a definition suggests finding ways to change those behaviors. The behavior analyst would be using the _____ strategy to solve Norman's work problems.

# 2 Definitions of Everyday Behaviors

## Reading Section

You will learn in this lesson the first tactic in solving human problems by using the behavioral strategy. The first tactic in using the behavioral strategy is to develop a <u>behavioral definition</u> of the problem. You may help people solve a problem with this tactic alone. You will focus their attention on their behavior rather than on inner causes. But that doesn't mean that you will be restricted to superficial or trivial problems. Indeed, behavior is not a trivial or superficial aspect of human conduct. It is all of human conduct. You can apply the idea of behavior to everything that people do. You can define everything that people do in terms of behavior. You can define every problem that people have in terms of behavior.

When you learn how to define problems in terms of behavior, you will see that many vague terms such as *bad attitude* ultimately refer to behaviors. You will see that self-reports such as questionnaires and interviews usually do not let you get accurate information about behaviors (see Moran & Tai, 2001). The alternative is to use the principle of direct observation. The great value of studying behavior is that it permits direct observation. Direct observation is the most important tool in changing behavior.

## What Is Behavior?

Behavior analysts study behavior. However, many students of human behavior believe that studying only behavior leaves out the most interesting human phenomena. They believe that behavior analysis deals with only trivial and mechanical aspects of human activity. They believe that focusing on behavior is limiting. Therefore, I will start by showing you what behavior analysts mean by behavior.

**Behavior** is anything that a person <u>does</u> (cf. Catania, 1998). Behavior is <u>physical</u>, and it <u>functions</u> to do something. The best test of whether it is physical is whether you can observe it. You might use your unaided senses or you might use electronic instrumentation. Running is an obvious example of behavior because you can observe the action of the legs as they move the body somewhere. I will describe four broad categories of human activity that behavior analysts consider behavior, starting with examples that are clear to most people. I will then progress to examples that confuse most people, such as many activities that people usually call *mental*. I will help you understand why behavior analysts refer to such activities as *behavior*.

1. Behavior is anything that a person _____ _____.

Clear examples of behavior for most people involve <u>obvious</u> body actions. You would

---

***A Leading Philosopher's View on Mental Events***

"Mental events are identical with physical events" (Davidson, 1974: p. 209). Behavior analysts view anything that people do, including mental and physical activities, as forms of behavior.

2. Behavior analysts view anything that people do, including mental and physical activities, as forms of _____.

---

**Figure 2-1.** Everyone considers athletes jumping hurdles as a form of behavior. This is obvious behavior. (Source: © S. Carmona/CORBIS)

probably label biting into an apple as behavior. You might also label hitting a ball, walking a mile, and jumping over a ditch as behavior. You would probably label shouting as behavior. Behavior analysts label such actions as behavior because they are physical and they function to do something. Everyone agrees that the obvious movements of major muscles are behavior.

Less clear examples of behavior for most people involve subtle body actions. You might waver before you labeled talking, looking, and reading as behaviors. Behavior analysts argue that affecting someone's behavior by talking to them is behavior. Talking involves small physical movements of speech, mouth, and tongue muscles to produce sounds. Moving these small muscles to say something is as much behavior as moving the bigger muscles of the body. These movements don't require a different label just because the muscles are small and hard to observe. Behavior analysts also label reading that teaches you facts and skills as behavior. Reading involves small physical movements of head, eye, and neck muscles to face the book and to focus on the page. Reading functions to change what you can say or do after reading. Talking and reading are behaviors because they are physical and they function to do

something. Behavior analysts regard the subtle movement of small visible muscles as behavior because they are physical and they function to do something.

Unclear examples of behavior for most people involve internal body actions. You might not label secreting stomach acids to digest a steak as a behavior. Behavior analysts argue that secreting stomach acid is behavior. They point out that valves must open in tiny stomach glands to release the acid into the stomach. Electronic equipment can detect the stomach acids coming from these glands (Whitehead, Renault, & Goldiamond, 1975). Again, these movements don't require a different label just because they are tiny and hard to see. They are physical because we can observe their movement with proper equipment. They function to digest food. We cannot now measure all, or even most, internal body actions. However, we will be able to measure more and more of them as our instruments improve. Behavior analysts consider internal movements as behavior because they are physical and produce results.

Murky examples of behavior for most people involve private events. Behavior analysts use the term *private events* to refer to complex human actions that people often see as mental.

People usually regard thinking as mental activity and assert that it is not physical (e.g., Chaplin, 1985). They assert that mental activity occurs in a world parallel to the physical world of the brain. Their approach reflects the old idea that the world is divided into two realms: physical and mental.

As you already know, behavior analysts do not deny that thinking exists. They argue that it exists in the physical world. They argue that we do not need to call upon a hypothetical mental world that we can never observe directly. They propose that it is a form of behavior that is very private. You will see in this lesson that they can observe such "cognitive" activities as learning and creativity. You will see additional examples throughout the book. Interpreting private events as complex, hard-to-observe behavior has led to a great deal of misunderstanding. Insisting that private events must themselves be explained may have led to even more. Denying that private events <u>cause</u> behavior must convince many people that behavior analysts deny the existence of thinking. They are wrong! Behavior analysts simply claim that private events are a type of behavior.

You might resist labeling *silent reading* as behavior. Many people experience reading as saying the words in a book to themselves. One idea is that those words occur in their minds. However, another idea is that the words may occur in their speech muscles. People may use the same muscles when saying words to themselves as when saying them aloud (Hardycke, Petrinovich, & Ellsworth, 1966). They may be silent only because the silent reader does not expel the <u>air</u> required to sound the word out loud. Of course, silent reading also involves moving the head, focusing the eyes, turning pages, taking notes, and ultimately describing what you have read to someone else. By viewing silent reading as something that people do, behavior analysts have been able to help people improve their reading. For behavior analysts, the most important aspect of silent reading, saying words to yourself, is an example of private behavior.

Problem solving as a form of thinking may also be private behavior. Most people regard "saying things in your head" as what happens when you problem solve. They regard it as mental activity occurring in one's mind. Yet "saying things in your head" may simply be silent talk and therefore similar to silent reading. Suppose you say "I could improve my grade by studying more for tests" to yourself. That seems to involve doing everything you do when you say it out loud except that you don't expel air to make an audible sound. Try saying "ouch" to yourself. Notice the slight tension in your throat as you say it. If you don't notice anything, try humming "The Star Spangled Banner" and saying "ouch" to yourself at the same time. Chances are that using the vocal cords to hum will interfere with the tiny movements of thinking. Similar tiny movements may account for other forms of thinking. They may also account for "seeing images in your imagination" in the same way (Skinner, 1953).

Behavior analysts regard thinking, imagining, and feeling as something that people do. They call human conduct of this kind *private events* and consider it behavior. Most private events involve complex activities that we don't know how to observe yet (see Lamal, 2000). Often they also involve complex functions such as those involved in conveying meaning to other people.

You may have read about behavior analysis in another course. You may have been told that behavior analysts deny that thinking and visualizing exist. That is not the case! Behavior analysts argue that thinking is private behavior. In their view, private behavior does not cause behavior, although it often precedes it (see Moore, 2000). They argue that students of human behavior must analyze the causes of private behavior just as they must analyze the causes of public behavior. They assume that people's experience with past environments determines what they think as well as what they do. Behavior analysts see private events simply as additional <u>behavior</u> for them to explain.

Behavior analysis has been very successful in helping people change many behaviors. Some of those behaviors have been very complex, very subtle, and even very private, such as irrational self-talk. I hope you will notice from the examples you have just read how broadly the term *behavior* applies. I hope you will end up concluding that behavior refers to more than the trivial or mechanical "doings" of human beings.

---

### Skinner on Awareness

Instead of taking awareness as a given, Skinner views the act of becoming aware . . . as another learned behavior" (Bry, 1991: p. 9). Awareness involves looking and listening. It involves noticing the differences between things. It involves acting differently under different conditions. In short, awareness is something that people do. We learn to look, listen, notice, and act differently.

3. Because it involves people doing things, behavior analysts like Skinner view awareness as a form of _____.

---

In summary, behavior analysts study everything that people <u>do</u>. They study actions that are physical and produce a result. They study obvious, subtle, internal, and private behaviors. Although they focus on behavior, their research does not limit their study of human activity.

## Behavioral Definitions

Remember that I defined behavior analysis in the first lesson as the study of <u>environmental</u> events that <u>change</u> behavior. Applied behavior analysts apply the principles of behavior to solve human problems. Their goal is to <u>modify</u> human behavior that causes suffering. A lonely teenager may wish to increase her social skills to get more dates. A harassed parent may wish to decrease a child's crying or nagging. A concerned teacher may wish to increase the amount of time that a student spends studying. An annoyed university student may want to increase his roommate's neatness. An overweight person may wish to alter his eating patterns to lose weight.

Behavior analysts often help solve problems like these. They first try to specify the exact behavior causing the problem in a way that allows clear and precise observation. Behavior analysts call such a specification a *behavioral definition*. A **behavioral definition** is a statement that specifies exactly what behavior to <u>observe</u>.

4. A behavioral definition is a statement that specifies exactly what behavior to _____.

A behavioral definition specifies the included behavior. It also specifies the <u>excluded</u> behavior. For example, suppose that Fred's father complains to Dr. South that Fred punches other children. Dr. South would have little trouble defining punching. It is an obvious behavior. Her first attempt might be: a punch is any blow that Fred gives to another child with his hand. That leaves open the question of how hard the contact must be. A better definition might be "A punch is any blow by Fred hard enough to move any part of the other child's body." This helps Fred's father, Dr. South and even Fred to know what counts as a punch. Punching is not hard to define because it is an obvious behavior.

For a slightly harder example, suppose that his mother complains that Fred cries when put to bed at night. Dr. South would interview Fred's mother to find exactly what she means by "crying." Her definition might include obnoxious and loud crying and exclude talking and other soft noises. Dr. South might define crying as "any vocal noise made by the child that the parents can hear outside the child's room and that does not involve recognizable words." The definition <u>specifies</u> exactly what behavior everyone has agreed to call crying. Therefore it is a behavioral definition.

Crying is not hard to define because it refers to an easily heard behavior. However, many terms refer to more subtle behavior. For example, suppose that Mr. Teller, Fred's fourth-grade teacher, complains of his bad attitude. While most of us would guess that Fred must be doing something that annoys Mr. Teller, we don't have a clue what it is. In fact, Fred may be doing more than one thing. To avoid punishment Fred is probably being pretty subtle. The term *bad attitude* doesn't begin to specify this complex, subtle behavior.

Dr. South must interview Mr. Teller to find out what he means by "bad attitude." She might find that Mr. Teller doesn't like Fred whispering to friends, talking back to

***Figure 2-2.*** Many people would pause before considering reading a form of behavior. Yet reading involves the behavior of using the muscles of the eyes to focus on the words. This subtle behavior. (Source: Elizabeth Crews/Stock, Boston)

him, or rattling papers in his desk. She now knows that Mr. Teller uses the vague term *bad attitude* to mean these three behaviors. She would probably use a more descriptive term like *disruptive behavior* to label them. Dr. South's task of defining disruptive behavior requires defining these three behaviors.

You benefit in two ways by talking about specifically defined behaviors. You have <u>clearer communication</u> with others and you have <u>consistent observations</u>.

First, behavioral definitions produce <u>clearer communication</u> with others about the behavioral problem. You could badly misunderstand the complaints of Fred's father, mother, and teacher. If you do not specify the behaviors, you might not be talking about the same behavioral problem as they are. You may even find that many nonbehavioral terms they use, such as *bad attitude*, refer to subtle behavior, once you have discovered what they mean by it.

Second, behavioral definitions produce more <u>consistent observations</u>. People often let their hopes influence their observations when they are unsure of what they are observing. Suppose Mr. Teller tries to change Fred's "bad attitude" by being more loving

and accepting. Fred's whispering, back talk, and paper rustling might originally have upset Mr. Teller. However, his hopes of changing Fred's bad attitude might change his definition. He might ignore whispering and paper rustling because they are minor problems. He would end up observing fewer instances of "bad attitude" even if Fred's behavior did not change. Mr. Teller's observations would show that Fred's attitude had changed for the better even if it had remained exactly the same. Only Mr. Teller's definition of what constituted a bad attitude would have changed. Maintaining consistency of observations is an important benefit of using specific behavioral definitions.

5. Two advantages of behavioral definitions is that they make communication _____ _____ and they produce more consistent _____.

## The Problem with Self-Reports

Once you decide exactly what behavior you want to observe, you have to decide what approach you will take to observe it. The most common approach used by non–behavior analysts is called *self-report observations*, which you are undoubtedly more familiar with. After describing the approach, I will explain why it usually does not produce data that help behavior analysts discover laws. I will then describe, in the following section, how behavior analysts use this approach.

Many people interested in human behavior rely heavily on self-report observations made by *informants*. Informants are simply people who report from memory their own behavior or someone else's behavior. You might say they are "untrained observers." I am sure you frequently read or hear findings based on the most common forms of self-reports: questionnaires and interviews. Here's a definition. **Self-report observations**: The observer relies on their memory of the behavior.

6. **Self-Report Observations**: The observer relies on their _____ of the behavior.

Behavior analysts usually avoid questionnaires and interviews because of the problem with self-reports. The problem is that they are usually inaccurate or of unknown accuracy. They are inaccurate in three ways.

7. The problem with self-reports is that they are usually _____ or of unknown accuracy.

First, self-reports usually lack detail. You may find out from asking a person that they often study. However, you usually will not find out the details of their studying. You are not likely to find out exactly when they start, how long they study, or when they stop. You are unlikely to find out exactly when they are distracted or for how long. You are unlikely to find out how many pages they read or how many questions they answered. In other words, you will not find out precisely what happened. The behavior analyst faced with such global data can learn little about what causes studying. The situation is similar to physicists trying to learn about gravity by someone telling them that an object falls pretty fast.

Second, self-reports often cannot be checked. When people report on internal events, we usually cannot check their accuracy. The same goes for reporting of events with no one else present, events that happen rarely, and events that people hide from others, such as crime, deviant acts, or behavior they feel guilty about. We probably should not rely on the information contained in self-reports that cannot be verified.

Third, self-reports are often wrong. Even when self-reports provide sufficient detail, we may find that they are simply not accurate. When we can check up on them, we often find that they are not correct reports of what happened. The errors sometimes arise because memory is imperfect, but they also often occur because people want to present a particular image to others. We should never simply assume that self-reports are correct. We should verify that they are accurate.

Over the years I have collected a number of examples of problems with self-reports. These examples do not prove that all self-reports lack detail, are wrong, or cannot be checked. But they can give you a feeling for some of the problems they entail.

For example, Mertz and his colleagues asked 266 people how many calories they usually eat (Mertz, Tsui, Judd, Reiser, Hallfrisch, Morris, Steele, & Lashley, 1991). He then fed them only the amount of calories they claimed to be eating. They lost weight! He concluded that most of his informants had been eating 25% more than they reported. This study clearly shows the dangers of relying on the self-report observations of informants.

Mertz's findings are not unusual. La Pierre wrote a letter in 1934 to 128 owners of restaurants and motels. He asked whether they would accept Chinese guests. Over 90% of them said no, yet every single one of them had served La Pierre and his Chinese friend on a recent cross-country trip (La Pierre, 1934). La Pierre did this study before most Americans felt ashamed of discriminating. The owners probably feared that La Pierre didn't like the Chinese and that they would lose his business if they admitted serving them. If he had drawn conclusions from these self-report observations, he would have been seriously wrong.

Brickman asked college students walking on a college campus if they would pick up litter. Ninety-four percent of them said yes. The researchers made sure that only 20 feet after they answered the question, the students passed some litter near a trash can. Only 1% of the students picked it up (Brickman, 1972). Based on the self-report observations, he would have drawn conclusions exactly counter to reality.

Hoelscher and his colleagues studied 21 anxiety patients. The researchers lent the patients a relaxation tape recorder and asked them to practice using it. Later, the researchers asked how much time each patient practiced (Hoelscher, Lichstein, & Rosenthal, 1984). They also secretly observed how much time each patient practiced. The secret observations used a hidden timer that recorded how long the patients turned the tape recorder on. The patients reported that they practiced 26% longer than the time found from the hidden timer. In addition, the researchers made an even more important discovery. When they used the patients' self-report observations, they found no correlation with anxiety. However, when they used the time from the hidden timer, the researchers found an inverse correlation with anxiety. The more the patients practiced, the less anxiety they had. Thus, if the researchers had relied on self-report observations, they would have drawn the wrong conclusion. They would have concluded that relaxation practice had no effect, when in fact it did.

Many similar studies exist. Wicker reviewed 31 studies showing that what people say and do differ (Wicker, 1969). Lloyd reviewed additional studies concluding that self-report observations are not accurate (Lloyd, 1980).

Much research shows just how inaccurate untrained observers are. For example, studies of rumor illustrate how inaccurately people report events (Allport & Postman, 1945). Likewise, studies of eyewitness testimony show how inaccurately untrained observers report events (see Wells & Olsen, 2003). Read for yourself how about how nearly 2,000 eyewitnesses can be wrong! (See box.)

Self-report observations, such as answers given to questionnaires and interviews, are based on memory. As we have seen, people giving self-report observations may report inaccurately for many reasons. They may not want to admit how much they eat. In the 1930s they may not have wanted to admit serving minorities. In modern times they may not want to admit not serving minorities. They may want to claim concern about litter without having to pick it up. They may not remember what really happened. They may be using a different behavioral definition than you use. They can seldom provide detailed descriptions of the behavior. The problem with self-reports is that they are usually <u>inaccurate</u> or of unknown accuracy. Behavior analysts usually do not trust informants as a primary source of data.

Although behavior analysts usually do not rely on self-report observations, let me hasten to add that self-reports can sometimes be useful. People often answer questions from

---

### Nearly 2,000 Witnesses Can Be Wrong

Robert Buckhout (1980) staged a mock crime consisting of a mugging and a purse snatching. He showed a videotape, in which the "criminal" was clearly visible, to 2,145 people. Afterwards, he asked each viewer to pick the "criminal" out of a lineup from memory. Only 301 identified the correct person, while 1,844 were unable to do so. This experiment shows the problem of remembering even the most important aspects of situations. It probably also illustrates the importance of training. A trained police officer would probably have little difficulty identifying the "criminal." Police officers are trained to immediately write down a criminal's outstanding features. They would note such details as hair color and style, face, scars, and clothing. Similar training might have helped the "eyewitnesses" pick the "criminal" out of the lineup. Only a few viewers were able to correctly identify the "criminal."

8. The problem with such self-reports is that they are usually _____ _____ or of unknown accuracy.

a census taker accurately. They often answer questions about political preferences accurately. Businesses often gain useful consumer information. All of us learn a great deal about other people from their reports. Self-reports can be useful under some conditions.

In fact, because self-reports are something that people do, behavior analysts sometimes study them as a form of <u>behavior.</u> Behavior analysts might study people's statements about a situation. When studying self-reports, behavior analysts would describe their results very carefully. For example, suppose we ask Mrs. Smith how many calories she usually eats. She might claim that she ate 1,300 calories per day. Behavior analysts would not say, "Mrs. Smith eats 1,300 calories a day." Rather they would state that she "reported" eating 1,300 calories a day, which permits them to remain neutral about whether she really did eat only 1,300 calories!

While behavior analysts sometimes study self-reports as a form of behavior, they do not rely on them as basic data because they are unreliable. Because self-reports are usually inaccurate or of unknown accuracy (Boyce & Geller, 2001b), behavior analysts rely on a different approach to observing behavior. That approach will be the subject of the next section.

## The Principle of Direct Observation

The second approach to observing behavior is to directly observe the behavior of interest, which prevents reliance on the recall of untrained observers. Behavior analysts may be interested in obvious behaviors like punching or crying or in subtle behaviors like whispering or talking back to a teacher. They may be interested in internal behavior like a stomach ache or in private events like thoughts and feelings. Whatever behaviors might interest them, behavior analysts avoid the problem with self-reporting by directly observing them.

Behavior analysts arrange to be present so that they can directly observe obvious and subtle behaviors. They use biofeedback instruments to observe stomach acidity and other

***Figure 2-3.*** Many people do not consider the forehead tension that this device is measuring a form of behavior. However, behavior analysts point out that this form of biofeedback amplifies the tiny amount of tension in the forehead muscles so that the person can learn to relax those muscles. In other words, this person is engaging in "relaxing their forehead muscles." This is internal behavior that we can observe only with special instruments. (Source: Ray Ellis/Photo Researchers)

***Figure 2-4.*** This famous sculpture is called *The Thinker*. Few people consider thinking a form of behavior. Thinkers may not call what they are doing *behavior*, but they are doing something. They may be rehearsing conversations, solving problems, remembering meetings, or pondering the meaning of life. Because thinkers are doing something, behavior analysts consider thinking to be one form of behavior that others cannot see. They call such behavior *private behavior*. They assert that private behavior follows the same laws of behavior as more obvious behavior. (Source: Vanni/Art Resource, NY)

internal events, and they sometimes even find ways to directly observe such private events as self-talk and pain. Behavior analysts usually find a way to directly observe whatever behavior they are interested in.

**The principle of direct observation** involves the use of trained observers for the <u>direct observation</u> of behavior. Behavior analysts require the observers to immediately record what they see in order to avoid the factor of memory. They carefully formulate and test behavioral definitions for these observers

to use and then train them to use the definitions correctly. Further, they spot-check the observers to ensure correct use of the definitions. These steps ensure highly accurate behavioral observations. Observations based on the principle of direct observation are called *direct observations*. They provide a second approach to observing behavior that reduces the problem with self-reports.

9. The principle of direct observation involves the use of trained observers for the _____ of behavior.

Let us further define our terms. **Direct observation**: The observer personally <u>sees</u> and immediately <u>records</u> behavior.

10. **Direct observation**: The observer personally _____ and immediately _____ behavior.

Notice the differences between the approach used for self-report observations and that used for direct observations. Self-report observations are made from memory by observers untrained in the use of a consistent definition. Direct observations are made by observers who personally see (or hear) the behavior and immediately record it. The observers are trained to use an explicit behavioral definition.

There are two exceptions to the requirement that the observer see the behavior. One exception is for sounds, such as talking or shouting, which the observer may listen for, without having to witness their source. In this case, the requirement is that the observer personally <u>hear</u> the behavior and immediately record it.

The other exception involves the presence of a physical <u>result</u> that enables the observers to decide whether the behavior occurred. For example, they might look for a clean floor to decide if someone swept the floor. I will describe this method, called *outcome recording*, in a future lesson. Notice that even in this case, the observer must be personally present to see or hear the result of the behavior.

If behavior analysts have taken steps to ensure that the data are <u>accurate</u>, they sometimes ask people to observe their own behavior. Behavior analysts can increase accuracy by insisting that people use a behavioral definition and write their observations immediately. This eliminates the failings of memory. If Mrs. Smith kept a diary of meals and snacks written as she was eating, her accuracy would be greater. Behavior analysts can increase accuracy further by having someone else make an independent report. For example, accuracy would be greater if Mr. Smith openly checked up on one of his wife's meals each week. Accuracy would be greater if the behavior analyst told Mrs. Smith about disagreements. These and other steps can improve the accuracy of such observations. Observing your own behavior is a form of direct observation when these safeguards are followed.

When people use a behavioral definition and write their observations immediately, and when someone else makes an independent report, behavior analysts call this a <u>direct observation</u>. When people do not use a behavioral definition, when they report from memory, or when no one makes an independent report, then behavior analysts call this a <u>self-report</u>.

## Summary

This lesson teaches you the first tactic in using the behavioral strategy to solve human problems: to develop a behavioral definition that specifies exactly how to observe the behavior. Observing behavior is not a limitation,

because behavior is anything that people do. You can observe obvious, subtle, internal, or private behavior. One approach to observing behavior is through self-reports. Unfortunately that leads to problems: self-reports are usually inaccurate or of unknown accuracy. You can solve this difficulty by using the principle of direct observation to observe behavior. Using direct observations is usually a more accurate approach to observing behavior.

## Behavior Analysis Examples

I will outline examples of behavioral definitions below. They show how behavior analysts define behaviors that are subtle, internal or private. These are only a few of many creative behavioral definitions devised by behavior analysts.

### *Tension*

I am sure you have been in situations where you felt "tense." You may have thought of your tension as a mental problem. However, you might look at it as a behavioral problem instead. Your tension may have consisted entirely of muscles in your body becoming tight. In particular, your forehead muscles may have become so tight that they hurt. Tension is usually associated with tight forehead muscles. But this tightness occurs inside the muscles and often cannot be observed by others. Luckily, these muscles

---

### *Is Attention a Behavior? Part 1*

Do you think of attention as something that goes on in the hidden recesses of the mind? One dictionary defines it as "applying the mind to an object of sense or thought . . . a selective narrowing or focusing of consciousness and receptivity" (Woolf, et al, 1977: p. 72). Behavior analysts view it as something that people do. They view it as behavior! Jim Holland found one way to observe it. He placed a U.S. Navy recruit in a dark room with a button. When the recruit pressed the button, a light came on

showing the pointer on a dial for a moment. The recruit's task was to report any time that the pointer was deflected. Holland could tell when the recruit looked by observing when he pressed the button. He could tell whether the recruit was attending by whether he correctly reported deflections of the pointer (Holland, 1958).

11. Holland turned the concept of attention from a private event into one that can be directly _____.

produce electrical activity when they are tightened. Researchers use this fact to define "tension as a high level of electrical activity in the forehead muscles." They measure it with a sensitive electronic device.

Many researchers have used this behavioral definition to treat tension as an internal behavior needing change rather than as a mental event. They provide people with immediate electronic feedback to help them learn how to relax their forehead muscles. Note that if a person can reduce the electrical activity, they are no longer "tense." The electrical activity is the same thing as "tension." This approach is called *biofeedback*. It is widely used as an alternative to medication.

Biofeedback provides a strategy for observing human activity that is otherwise difficult to observe. Clearly, tension does not involve the obvious movement of major muscles. It often does not involve easily visible movements, but rather subtle movements of muscles. Nor is it so private that it cannot be directly observed. The strategy for observing tension is based on the fact that it consists of tiny changes in electrical activity within the muscles. This same approach can be applied to any internal activity that involves tiny changes in muscles or glands that can be detected with specialized equipment. Such behavior can be observed as directly as obvious or subtle behavior. (Based on Budzynski & Stoyva, 1969.)

12. The statement "tension is a high level of electrical activity in the forehead muscles" specifies exactly what internal behavior to observe if you are interested in tension. Behavior analysts call that statement a behavioral _____.

### Creativity

Creativity is mysterious. We know so little about what it is. We know even less about how to encourage it in ourselves and others. Some people seem wildly creative whereas others seem to have no creativity at all. Most people regard creativity as the result of mental process deep inside a person.

Goetz and Baer studied the creativity with which 4-year-old preschool children use building blocks. They defined creative block building

as "building a form that the child hadn't used before." They found that complex structures were made up of 20 basic forms. For example, one basic form is a "story." A story is "any two or more blocks placed one on top another, the upper block(s) resting solely upon the lower." Another form is a "balance." A balance is "any story in which the upper block is at least four times as wide as the lower." The researchers found that the children built almost no new forms until reinforced by the teacher for doing so. When reinforced, the children produced many novel forms. The children built structures that were far more creative than they had built before. Goetz and Baer helped these children become more creative by treating creativity as an observable behavior instead of an unobservable mental activity.

Notice that the researchers were interested in the behavior itself. They wanted the children to use new forms. They were not inferring some internal creativity from the children's use of novel forms. Rather, being creative was identical with using the new forms.

When a child, let's call her Mary, builds two different forms, she uses similar motions. She usually does not use obvious movements of major muscles. Clearly Mary's creative behaviors are not so tiny or internal that they require electronic instruments to measure. Nor are her creative behaviors so private that we need to infer them from other behaviors. Rather, Mary's creative behaviors involve the smallest muscles of her fingers and hands as she stacks, turns, or rotates the blocks. Only if you watch very closely would you notice a difference between novel and repetitive forms. (Based on Goetz & Baer, 1973.)

13. Because building creative forms is something that Mary does, it is a subtle form of _____.

### Learning

Learning is often regarded as a magical process occurring deep within the mind. But if you think about it, you only know if someone has learned a fact if they state the fact. You only know if they have learned to identify a species of tree if they point to the tree. All learning eventually must be displayed at an appropriate time and place. Whereas learning

**Figure 2-5.** This is a picture of a fanciful block structure built by preschool children. Goetz and Baer studied ways to increase children's creative behavior. (Source: Greg Mancuso/Stock, Boston)

may be displayed privately so that only the learner can observe it, learning in the classroom must be displayed publicly. No teacher will credit a student with having learned the answer to a question if they cannot produce that answer. Thus learning cannot be separated from behavior.

Skinner (1954) went a step further. He argued that learning is the development of new behaviors. He defined learning in the classroom as "giving correct answers to increasingly difficult questions."

The behavioral definition of learning eventually led to a new approach to learning. Skinner developed written programs that presented small units of information. He posed frequent questions to determine student mastery over the small units. He then revised the programs until most students answered the questions correctly He did not use tests to find out which students learned and which did not. Rather, he sought to

ensure that all students could learn. He changed the emphasis from dumb students to dumb teaching. This book uses Skinner's definition of learning.

Notice that Skinner was interested in the behavior of giving correct answers itself. He was not interested in inferring that something was going on inside of the person that he might call learning. Learning consists essentially in acquiring correct answers to questions. You learn American history by acquiring answers to questions about dates, persons, and events. You learn even more by acquiring answers to questions about trends, epochs, and related world conditions. You learn still more by acquiring answers to questions that compare different epochs. Learning does not exist somewhere apart from the answering behavior. Learning is acquiring the behavior of answering questions.

Skinner's definition of learning did not focus on movements of major muscle groups. It did not involve electronic detection of tiny internal events. It did not involve behavior so private you can't observe it. Writing a correct answer involves only slightly different movement of the fingers and hand from writing a wrong answer. Skinner specified that if you wanted to observe the subtle behavior of learning you must observe "writing correct answers." (Based on Skinner, 1954.)

14. Because it specifies exactly what to observe if you're interested in learning, the statement "learning is writing correct answers" is called a behavioral _____ _____.

### Pain

You might imagine that the pain of cancer is far from being a behavior of any kind. It may seem like something that the cancer patient must endure alone. It may seem that no one else could know anything about it. It seems to be totally private. The doctor can see the tumor, but only the patient can experience the pain.

Behavior analysts maintain that anything that a person does is behavior. Therefore, the action of a person feeling pain must be behavior. Ahles and his colleagues found a way to measure some components of this behavior. They found that cancer patients emit subtle pain behaviors that most of us could easily overlook. These pain behaviors correlate with the patients' experience of pain. The patients "guard" painful parts of their body when moving. They "brace" themselves to reduce pain. They "express" pain through sighing, sobbing, and cursing. They "rub" or hold sore areas. They "grimace" and make terrible faces. As a result, Ahles and his associates defined pain behavior as "guarding, bracing, expressing, rubbing, or grimacing." They inferred the private experience of pain from these behaviors, justifying their conclusions by showing that the total number of the pain behaviors they observed correlated with the patient's own rating of their pain.

This example is interesting because it illustrates a method for observing private behavior. Pain is largely private behavior, but it is accompanied by subtle but observable behaviors like "guarding, bracing, expressing, rubbing, or grimacing." By observing these subtle behaviors, we can infer when the more private aspects of pain are also likely to be occurring. We are not interested in the observable pain behaviors so much as the private experience of pain. To put it another way, eliminating the pain behaviors would not necessarily eliminate the pain! This approach to pain is quite different from the earlier examples of tension, creativity, and learning in which the researchers were interested in the observed behavior alone. The approach to pain that Ahles and his colleagues developed can be used to observe any private events that are accompanied by observable behaviors.

Ahles's method provided an objective measure for when to give terminal cancer patients narcotic drugs to ease their pain. Similar studies have sought to find ways to help patients ease their pain without recourse to drugs, including meditation, relaxation, and "cognitive restructuring."

Ahles and his colleagues observed cancer patients guarding, bracing, rubbing, expressing, and grimacing so that they could infer their pain. Clearly, such behaviors as bracing and grimacing do not involve obvious movements of major muscles. Nor are they internal actions detectable only with electronic devices. Even though they observed subtle behaviors, the researchers were interested in something more than those behaviors. They inferred from the subtle behaviors the feeling of pain itself. (Based on Ahles, Coombs, Jensen, Stukel, Maurer, & Keefe, 1990.)

15. Because the private behavior of feeling pain is something that a person does, feeling pain is a form of _____.

## Notes

### Note #1

Psychologists use the term *operational definition*. They define it as "the operations used to measure the concept being defined." They often use it to refer to a concept involving a private event. This term differs from *behavioral definition*. Because behavioral definitions always refer to some aspect of behavior. the two terms are not synonymous (Moore, 1975; Skinner, 1945).

16. Remember, an operational definition _____ (is, isn't) the same as a behavioral definition.

### Note #2

Behavior analysts emphasize that all behavior involves the whole body. The most obvious aspect of running is movement of the legs. However, running also involves moving the arms and upper body. It also involves breathing, pumping blood, and looking. It also involves the coordination of looking and moving. Thus running involves legs, arms, lungs, heart, and brain. The behavior analysis of thinking points to saying words to yourself "under your breath." However, thinking also involves breathing, sitting, and looking. Thus thinking involves the vocal cords, lungs, spine, eyes, and brain. We may readily label running as behavior because of the obvious movement. We may incorrectly label thinking as mental because of the lack of obvious movement.

17. Whether a behavior is obvious, subtle, internal or private, it involves the _____ body.

# Helpful Hints

### Helpful Hint #1

A person can make direct observations of their own behavior. If they use a behavioral definition and record their behavior as soon as it occurs, they are using direct observation. Be careful not to confuse direct observations whereby people record their own behavior immediately with self-reports that depend on people's memory!

18. Behavior analysts call the use of a behavioral definition by someone to immediately record observations of their own behavior _____.

### Helpful Hint #2

I will <u>always</u> refer to a statement that specifies the focus of observation as a *behavioral definition*. By using this term, I emphasize its reference to behavior. I will consider your answer wrong if you refer to a statement that specifies the subject of behavioral observation simply as a *definition*.

19. When you are answering questions, you should always refer to a statement that specifies exactly what to observe as a(n) _____.

### Helpful Hint #3

I will <u>always</u> refer to personally seeing and immediately recording an observation as *direct observation*. By doing so, I will distinguish direct observation from self-report observations. I will consider your answer wrong if you refer to personally seeing and immediately recording an observation simply as an *observation*. You must take a stand on whether it is a *self-report observation* or a *direct observation*.

20. When you are answering questions, you too should always refer to personally seeing and immediately recording an observation as _____.

### Helpful Hint #4

Students sometimes conclude that both approaches to studying behavior involve <u>reports</u> to someone else. If a researcher asks informants about their behavior, the informants clearly "report" their memories to the researcher. But a researcher who directly observes a person's behavior records what he or she just saw. Do not assume that researchers ever report their observations to anyone else. Even if they do eventually report them to other behavior analysts, they do not do so immediately. I have used the word *record* to stress that researchers write their observations as soon as they make them.

21. Define direct observation as "the use of a trained observer who personally sees and immediately _____ their observations."

### Helpful Hint #5

Here is a hint that will help you understand some of the questions, I will ask you later. If you understand the questions, you are more likely to answer them correctly! When I want to ask you about self-report observations or direct observations, I will ask you what <u>approach</u> the observers took to observing behavior.

22. You can be sure that I am asking you about either self-report observations or direct observations if my question concerns observations and it uses the specific word _____.

# Additional Readings

Danskin, D. G., & Crow, M. A. (1981). *Biofeedback: An introduction and guide*. Palo Alto, CA: Mayfield. These authors give a very brief rationale for biofeedback. In addition, they have an interesting chapter on the use of biofeedback in education.

Hatch, J. P. (1990). Growth and development of biofeedback: A bibliographic update. *Biofeedback and Self-Regulation*, *15*(1), 37–46. Hatch charts the recent growth of biofeedback research. He found that research began in the early 1970s and averaged over 200 articles per year since 1976.

Hatch, J. P., Fisher, J. G., & Rugh, J. D. (1987). *Biofeedback: Studies in clinical efficacy*. New York: Plenum.

Irwin, D. M., & Bushnell, M. M. (1980). *Observational strategies for child study*. New York: Holt, Rinehart, and Winston.

Mager, R. F. (1962). *Preparing instructional objectives*. Belmont, CA: Fearon. This book explains how to prepare sound behavioral definitions, particularly in educational settings.

Skinner, B. F. (1945). The operational analysis of psychological terms. *Psychological Review, 52*, 270–277. Skinner gives his rationale for behavioral definitions. He also argues that behavior analysis can study both overt and covert activities.

Sackett, G. C., Rupenthal, G. P., & Gluck, J. (1978). *Observing behavior: Data collection and analysis methods* (Vol. II). Baltimore: University Park Press.

Von Bozzay, G. D. F. (1984). *Projects in biofeedback: A text/workbook*. Dubuque, IA: Kendall/Hunt. This is an elementary introduction to biofeedback. It covers instruments, relaxation, and how to conduct a biofeedback project.

## Programmed Reading

This Programmed Reading section contains five modules: (1) What Behavior Analysis Studies, (2) Specifying What to Observe, (3) Approaches to Observing Behavior, (4) The First Tactic of the Behavioral Strategy, and (5) Review.

### 1. What Behavior Analysis Studies

46. Pre-test: Behavior analysts call anything that a person does _____.

48. Pre-test: Behavior refers to activities that are obvious, subtle, _____ or _____.

47. Pre-test: Behavior is anything that a person _____.

15. Behavior analysts regard anything that a person does as a form of <u>behavior</u>. Because looking at a snowcapped mountain is something that a person does, behavior analysts regard it as a form of _____.

16. Behavior analysts regard remembering the directions to a friend's house as a

form of behavior because it is something that a person _____.

1. "Anything that a person does" defines the term _____.

74. The definition of behavior is: anything that a person _____.

32. Human activities can be <u>obvious</u>, <u>subtle</u>, <u>internal</u>, or <u>private</u>. Because these four types of activities are something that people do, behavior analysts regard all of them as a form of _____.

71. The <u>obvious</u> movement of big muscles used in scoring a touchdown is a clear example of behavior because it is something that a person _____.

5. Because it is something that a person does, the <u>subtle</u> movement of eye muscles used in watching a movie is a form of _____.

70. The <u>internal</u> action of secreting stomach acid needed to digest dinner is a form of behavior because it is something that a person _____.

20. Behavior includes activities that are obvious, subtle, _____ (like secreting stomach acid), or private.

72. The <u>private</u> event of daydreaming about a vacation is an example of behavior because it is something that a person _____.

21. Behavior includes activities that are obvious, subtle, internal, or, like daydreaming, _____.

80. The most important idea in this lesson is that behavior analysts regard anything that a person does as a form of _____.

36. Let me put that point another way: behavior does not refer just to obvious or subtle activities but also to activities that are _____ or _____.

31. Finally, the definition of behavior is "anything that a person _____."

### 2. Specifying What to Observe

41. Pre-test: A behavioral definition tells you exactly what behavior to _____.

49. Pre-test: Mom told Jim what she meant by eating everything on your plate. She meant that he would not leave anything that could be picked up with a fork. Her statement of what she meant is called a(n) _____.

42. Pre-test: A behavioral definition makes communication _____ and it maintains consistency of _____ _____.

54. Pre-test: The field that studies the effect of environmental events on behavior is called _____.

44. Pre-test: A statement that describes exactly what behavior to observe is called a(n) _____.

12. Behavior analysts label a <u>definition</u> that tells you exactly what behavior to observe a behavioral _____.

90. You will make fewer errors in this lesson if you notice that the first word in the term *behavioral definition* ends with the two letters: ___.

64. So remember that a statement that specifies exactly what behavior to observe is called a(n) _____ definition.

88. When students first learn the term *behavioral definition*, they sometimes start adding –*al* to the name of the field to make it *behavioral analysis*. That is wrong! The name of the field is _____ _____ analysis.

77. The label for a statement that specifies exactly what to observe is _____ _____ definition; the name of the science that studies environmental events that change behavior is _____ analysis.

13. Behavior analysts label the statement "eye contact occurs whenever Tommy looks directly in your eyes" as a behavioral _____.

6. Because the statement "eye contact occurs whenever Tommy looks directly in your eyes" tells you exactly what behavior to observe when looking for eye contact, behavior analysts call it a(n) _____ _____ definition.

65. Sometimes students get lazy and refer to a behavioral definition as simply a "definition." But that doesn't say whether it's a dictionary definition, a qualitative definition, or a semantic definition! Therefore you should <u>always</u> refer to a statement that specifies exactly what to observe with the full name: _____.

30. Dr. South might define *understanding*" as "being able to fill in the key words left out of a definition." Because this statement specifies what behavior she has decided to call understanding, it is a(n) _____.

29. Dr. Barnes found out what Mrs. Jones wanted from Mr. Jones when she spoke of "affection." She wanted to be hugged more often. "Being hugged more often" is a behavioral definition because it specifies exactly what behavior Dr. Barnes would have to _____ to find out if Mr. Jones were showing more affection.

7. Because you are more likely to <u>clearly</u> talk about the same behavior, an advantage of using a behavioral definition is _____ communication.

4. Because it helps you consistently <u>observe</u> the same behavior, another advantage of a behavioral definition is that you have more consistent _____.

22. Behavioral definitions have two advantages. First, when people are talking about a behavioral problem, using a behavioral definition leads to _____ communication. Second, when an observer is observing a behavior over a long period of time, using a behavioral definition leads to more consistent _____.

2. "Disruptive behavior includes whispering in class, leaving your desk, or hitting other children" tells you what behavior to look for if you are looking for "disruptive behavior." Behavior analysts call a sentence of this kind a(n) _____ _____.

23. Behavioral definitions make communication _____, and they help maintain consistent _____.

3. A statement that describes the exact behavior to look for is called a(n) _____.

### 3. Approaches to Observing Behavior

57. Pre-test: The problem with self-reports is that they are usually _____ or of unknown accuracy.

50. Pre-test: The approach to observation that relies on people's memory is called _____ observation.

53. Pre-test: The direct observation approach is being used when the observer personally

_____ the behavior and immediately _____ it.

51. Pre-test: The approach to observing someone's behavior in which they immediately write down what they did is called _____ observation.

38. Non–behavior analysts often try to learn about a particular behavior by asking people to remember facts about that behavior. Because they are based on memory, behavior analysts call a person's answers about behavior *self-reports*. Questionnaires and interviews are examples of the approach called self-_____ _____ observations.

39. Non–behavior analysts rely heavily on people reporting their memory of behavior. This approach is called _____ report observations.

62. Reliance on the memory of behavior after it has occurred is characteristic of the approach called _____ observation.

63. Self-reports usually lack detail, they can be wrong, and they often can't be checked. I summarize these three problems by saying that the problem with self-reports is that they are usually _____ _____ (accurate, inaccurate) or of unknown accuracy.

40. Observations that rely on memory of the behavior are usually inaccurate or of unknown accuracy. I refer to this as the problem with _____ observations.

83. The problem with self-reports is that they are usually _____ or of unknown accuracy.

26. Direct observation has two features: The observer must personally _____ (or hear) the behavior, and they must immediately record it.

17. Behavior analysts solve the problem with self-reports by having observers personally <u>see</u> the behavior and immediately <u>record</u> what they saw. Behavior analysts call this approach *direct* _____.

28. Direct observation involves seeing and recording: The observer must personally <u>see</u> (or hear) the behavior, and they must immediately _____ the behavior.

10. Behavior analysts call the approach to observation in which an observer personally sees the behavior and immediately records it _____ observation.

27. Direct observation has two features: an observer personally _____ the behavior and immediately _____ it.

37. Many students confuse *record* and *report*. Be sure to define *direct observation* as "the use of a trained observer who personally sees and immediately _____ their observation."

67. Students sometimes refer to the approach of personally seeing and immediately recording an observation simply as "observation." Doing so doesn't specify whether the approach is direct observation or self-report observation. You should be specific by <u>always</u> referring to personally seeing and immediately recording an observation as "_____ observation."

33. If I ask what "approach" is being used, you can be sure that the question is asking you about either _____ _____ observation or _____ observation.

8. Behavior analysts almost always use the approach called _____ observation with the behaviors of interest.

86. When behavior analysts use trained observers who personally <u>see</u> and immediately <u>record</u> behavior, they are using the principle of _____ observation.

81. The principle of direct observation is using trained observers for the _____ _____ of behavior.

14. Behavior analysts make one exception to the requirement that an observer personally see or hear the behavior. They permit the observer to personally see the <u>result</u> of a behavior if it proves that the behavior occurred. For example, washing a window produces a clean window. If an observer sees a clean window, that proves that it was washed. If an observer sees the result of washing a window and immediately records it, behavior analysts call the approach _____ observation.

66. Students sometimes confuse direct observation and behavioral definition. A statement specifying what to observe is called

a(n) _____; personally seeing and immediately recording observations is called a(n) _____ _____.

69. Suppose Mary observes how often her son plays with other children. If she immediately writes down her observations, then she is using the approach called _____ _____ observation.

68. Students sometimes think that any observation by a person of their own behavior must be a self-report observation. You will miss many exam questions if you think that! If a person observes their own behavior and immediately <u>records</u> it, they are using the _____ observation approach.

9. Behavior analysts ask a person to directly observe their own behavior by personally seeing and immediately recording it. They call this approach *direct observation*. If they let the person write their observations from memory, then they would call this the _____ observation approach.

73. The approach to observation in which a person observes their own behavior and immediately records it _____ (is, isn't) called *self-report observation*.

87. When Joe records his own behavior immediately after it occurs, behavior analysts call his approach a(n) _____ _____ observation. When Paul records his own behavior from memory, behavior analysts call his approach a(n) _____ _____ observation.

### 4. The First Tactic of the Behavioral Strategy

52. Pre-test: The behavioral strategy is a way of defining a human problem as a(n) _____ problem.

55. Pre-test: The first tactic in using the behavioral strategy is to develop a(n) _____.

25. Developing a behavioral definition is the first tactic in using the _____ _____ (behavior, behavioral) strategy.

75. The first tactic in using the behavioral strategy is to specify the problem in terms of what behavior to observe. To use the term you learned in this lesson, the first tactic is to develop a(n) _____ _____ of the problem.

### 5. Review

59. Pre-test: The science that studies environmental events that modify what a person does is called _____.

61. Pre-test: You benefit in two ways by talking about specifically defined behaviors. Your communication is _____, and you increase the consistency of your _____.

58. Pre-test: The problem with self-reports is that they are usually _____ _____.

56. Pre-test: The principle of direct observation is using trained observers for the _____ of behavior.

43. Pre-test: A behavioral definition clearly states what behavior to _____ _____.

45. Pre-test: Behavior analysts call everything that a person does _____.

60. Pre-test: When an observer personally sees a behavior and immediately records it, behavior analysts call the approach _____ observation. When an observer relies on memory, behavior analysts call the approach _____ _____ observation.

11. Behavior analysts call a statement of exactly what behavior to observe a(n) _____; they call personally seeing and immediately recording their observations _____ _____.

24. By describing exactly what everyone has agreed to call yelling, Dr. North has created a(n) _____ _____.

79. The most accurate approach to observing behavior is usually _____ _____.

82. The principle of direct observation is using trained observers for the _____ _____ of behavior.

18. Behavior analysts solve the problem with self-reports by using the principle of _____ _____.

89. When the observer immediately records observations that they personally see (or

hear), behavior analysts call the approach
_____.

76. The first tactic in using the behavioral strategy for solving human problems is to develop a(n) _____
_____.

85. When an untrained observer reports observations from memory, we call the approach _____ observation.

78. The label for statements that specify exactly what to observe is _____
_____ definition; the name of the science that studies environmental events that change behavior is _____
_____ analysis.

84. When a person observes their own behavior using a behavioral definition and records instances of the behavior at the time they occur, they are using what approach? _____ observation

34. If you do not observe a behavior but do observe its result, can this be a direct observation? _____ (yes, no)

19. Behavior analysts view private events like "thinking" simply as a form of
_____.

35. In summary, behavior analysts study everything that a person _____
_____.

## Programmed Examples

I have developed a set of examples based on the ideas in this lesson. The four pre-test examples help you diagnose your need for more instruction. If you need more instruction, the first few examples after the pre-test teach how to analyze everyday situations in terms of behavior, direct observations, and other forms of behavior analysis. These examples include clues and show you how to analyze situations in a step-by-step manner. I then present examples that do not give clues. You will find that some examples include terms from prior lessons. Be sure to focus on these examples carefully. Write out and check your answers. If you have trouble with review examples from the Programmed Reading or if you have trouble with Lesson Quizzes, then you should also write out and check your answers to the easier examples.

### 1. Programmed Examples

7. Pre-test: Because Andy felt depressed he went to see Dr. Shaw. After Dr. Shaw talked with Andy, he guessed that Andy's depression involved a cluster of related behaviors. First, it involved the obvious behavior of poor social skills that resulted in people ignoring him. Second, it involved the subtle behaviors of speaking in a whisper, slumping, and looking down. Third, it involved internal behaviors such as shallow breathing. Fourth, it also involved the private behavior of telling himself that he wasn't likable. Dr. Shaw kept track of Andy's progress by observing the postural behaviors and by noting what Andy said about himself. Because Dr. Shaw saw and heard these behaviors himself and promptly noted them, he used the principle of _____
_____. Dr. Shaw helped Andy to learn more positive ways to talk about himself. Dr. Shaw also taught him the skills to participate in social activities. Dr. Shaw's help is an environmental event that could change Andy's behavior. Dr. Shaw's treatment was therefore an example of the science of
_____.

8. Pre-test: Dave decided that Vince was "mad at him" because someone told him that Vince thought he was a mean guy. Is Dave's conclusion based on direct observation of Vince's behavior? _____

6. Pre-test: Ann decided that Vince was mad at her. By "mad" she meant that Vince made negative comments about her. Vince told her that she must be eating too much because she had gotten fat. She immediately wrote the comment down in her notebook. Is Ann's conclusion based on direct observation of Vince's behavior? _____

9. Pre-test: John measured the littering behavior of his family on a picnic. He observed this behavior by measuring its result—namely, the amount of litter. He carefully picked up all litter as his family was leaving the area, weighed it, and wrote the weight down. He also was careful to completely clean the area before the picnic started. He defined litter as "human-made objects bigger than a quarter inch across that were not permanent parts of the picnic area." The principle that John followed to measure litter is called _____
_____.

4. Mrs. James observed the amount of time that Fred spent studying. She recorded Fred as studying when "He had a book in front of him and was looking at it." Her statement of when to record studying is a(n) _____ definition of studying. By using that definition to personally look for studying and then immediately recording it, Ms. James was using the principle of _____ observation.

2. Dorm members complained that Sarah cleaned the lounge poorly. Bob disagreed. He made a checklist of tasks such as (a) floor cleaned, (b) furniture returned, (c) surfaces dusted, (d) rugs vacuumed, (e) ashtrays emptied, (f) picked up, (g) trash emptied. Bob inspected for two weeks. He found that Sarah was a good cleaner who completed 85% of the tasks. Bob used direct observation because, even though he didn't see Sarah actually cleaning, he personally saw the physical _____ _____ of Sarah's cleaning behavior. Further, because the checklist of tasks is a kind of statement that specified the exact results to observe, it is a(n) _____ of cleaning behavior.

5. Ms. Thompson read a book on acting assertively. The book stated that it is assertive to openly accept praise. She decided to count each time that she looked directly at anyone who praised her and said "thank you." She used a wrist counter to immediately record her successes. Ms. Thompson's use of the wrist counter to record her own behavior is an example of the approach called _____ _____ observation. If Ms. Thompson waited till the end of the day to record the number of times she had accepted praise that day, she would have been using the approach called _____ observation.

1. Bill's son, Don, was in fifth grade. Don had often been "aggressive" in the past and had gotten into a lot of trouble. Bill decided to visit Don's class to see if he was being aggressive. However, Bill knew that the word *aggressive* is vague and could actually refer to many different behaviors. He decided to limit the term to times when Don hit or pushed another child. He specifically ruled out yelling or talking in an angry way at another child. The statement "aggression refers only to hitting or pushing another child" describes what Bill should observe to measure Don's aggression. Therefore, it is called a(n) _____ .

3. Frank thought he was selfish. He said "no" to any request by his son for a favor, such as letting him have extra ice cream, giving him a ride to the movies, and playing games with him. Then Frank read a book by Skinner. He decided that "selfish" was something that he did, not something that he was. Every time he said "no," he pushed a button on a wrist counter, and every time he said "yes," he pushed a button on another counter. By using the counters, Frank recorded his observations when they occurred. He said "no" 17 times and "yes" 3 times the first day. By the tenth day his behavior had changed to the extent that he said "no" only 4 times and "yes" 12 times. Frank recorded what he heard himself saying when he heard it. Therefore, he was using the approach called _____ _____ observation. Because the counts of "yes" and "no" are environmental events that changed his behavior, Frank's use of the counters to change his selfish behavior is a good example of what science? _____ _____

10. Rob set his watch alarm to go off every 15 minutes. When it did, he noted what he was saying to himself. At the end of the day, he found that he was thinking about sex 93% of the time. Because Rob immediately recorded instances of his self-talk when he noticed them, he was using the approach called _____ observation.

# 3 Methods for the Observation of Everyday Behaviors

## Reading Section

You have learned that the first tactic in using the behavioral strategy to solve human problems is to develop a behavioral definition. You can gather information about when and how often the behavior occurs. This information will sometimes motivate people to change the behavior. Other times it will provide enough information to let others help them make the change. With this tactic, you will build on your behavioral definition. The behavioral definition gives you the basis for observing the problem behavior. However, when the resultant focus on a behavior does not solve the problem, you can use a second tactic, which is the subject of this lesson.

The second tactic of using the behavioral strategy is to use direct observation to gather information about the problem behavior. This lesson teaches the four most common methods you can use to directly observe behavior. These methods are also the most commonly cited methods in leading behavior analysis journals. Each of these methods is useful for different situations. You can use *outcome recording* when the behavior leaves a unique result. You can use *event recording* when instances of the behavior are uniform. You can use *interval recording* when the behavior is nonuniform. You can use *time sample recording* when you wish to sample the behavior. You will learn how and when to use each of these methods.

## Outcome Recording for Behaviors That Leave Unique Results

Here is the first idea you will need to help you analyze examples of different methods of observation. Some behaviors are uniform in length while others are nonuniform. For example, consider saying a syllable. Every syllable takes about the same length of time to say—the responses of saying them are relatively uniform in length. Compare saying a syllable with speaking. You may speak only long enough to say "hello." You may speak long enough to ask a friend how she is feeling. Or you may speak long enough to tell a story. You might even make a speech taking one hour! Clearly, you may speak for vastly different lengths of time. The occurrences of speaking are nonuniform in length.

Behavior analysts use two methods to observe behaviors that are uniform. If a uniform behavior produces a unique result, they use outcome recording. If a uniform behavior does not produce a unique result, they use event recording.

You can use outcome recording with behaviors that leave unique results. Many behaviors produce unique results. Writing with a pencil leaves marks on the paper. Washing a window leaves the window clean. Cooking food produces a meal. Filling out a form leaves a form with writing on it. Driving a car leaves the odometer (mileage meter) with a new number on it. It may also leave the car in a new spot. All of these behaviors leave some unique result that proves the behavior took place. Notice that the durability of the result may vary from one behavior to the next. The form may stay filled out for years. Meals that I cook stay around for only a few minutes!

Observing a behavior that leaves a unique result is easy. Observers can look for the result at their convenience. They can even look for it long after the behavior occurred. Further, it may take them only a moment to see the

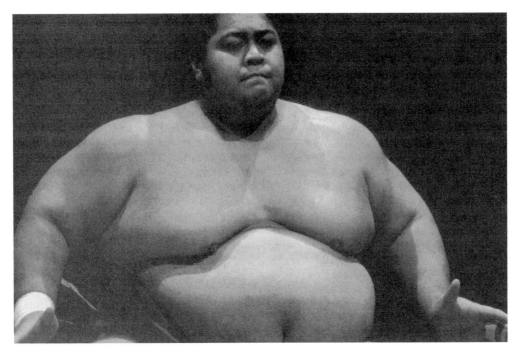

***Figure 3-1.*** You might measure how much someone eats by weighing them. Because you are measuring the result of eating rather than the act of eating, you would be using outcome recording. (Source:  Petit/Photo Researchers, Inc.)

result, but it may have taken hours to create it. Thus, looking at the result is much quicker. Observing the result of a behavior is the easiest method of observation when feasible. It is the simplest instance-type method. Behavior analysts call this method *outcome recording.*

### Outcome Recording

For *outcome recording,* you record a response when you see the <u>result</u> of the behavior. You use a behavioral definition to state the result to look for. You select a result that is a good indicator of that behavior. Behavior analysts use this method with behaviors that leave a unique change in the environment. Because they look for the result, they do not have to watch the behavior itself.

1.  For outcome recording, you record a response when you see the _____ of the behavior.

A mark of outcome recording is that the observation takes place <u>after</u> the response, possibly long after. This is because the result occurs after the response and continues to exist after the response has ended. Sometimes you may have trouble deciding if an observer looked

at a response or a result. If observers look after a response ends, you can conclude that they looked at its result. You always can be sure that observers are using outcome recording if they observe after the response has ended.

An example of outcome recording might involve Ann's dish-washing behavior. Washing dishes leaves the unique result that dirty dishes are now clean. They can't get clean any way other than by someone washing them. Therefore, you can define dish washing in terms of whether the dishes are clean. You needn't watch Ann's dish-washing behavior. Rather you can check to see if the dishes are clean. If they are clean, then you can conclude that she washed them. Notice that you check for the result of washing dishes—clean dishes—rather than the actual dipping of a dish in soapy water and scrubbing. How do you know that checking dishes is outcome recording? Because you can check for clean dishes only <u>after</u> the dish washing has been done.

You must be able to see the results of a behavior for them to be useful. For example, suppose you wanted to observe whether Tom was making nasty comments to Martha. One result of Tom's nasty comments might be

Martha's hurt feelings. But you can't observe hurt feelings, so you can't use that result to observe whether Tom makes nasty comments.

Likewise, you must be sure that the result is unique to the behavior for it to be useful. Suppose you wanted to observe how often Ken does favors for other people. One result of Ken doing favors might be that he will tell you how often he does them. But his report is based on memory, and it does not use a behavioral definition. Further, he might lie to make himself look good. So his reports do not have a known relation to actually doing favors. You could not use them with any confidence to observe Ken's favors.

Observers can use outcome recording to observe a <u>variety</u> of behaviors. You can count the number of written mathematical problems correctly answered to observe their understanding (e.g., Mayfield & Chase, 2002). You can observe plaque deposits on the teeth of children to determine the frequency of their flossing (Dahlquist & Gil, 1986). You can count workbook pages completed for public school pupils to observe their studying (Jones, Fremouw, & Carples, 1977). You can weigh litter deposited in a trash bin to observe cleanup behavior (O'Neill, Blanck, & Joyner, 1980). You can build a special cassette recorder that plays only a relaxation tape and that has a built-in time meter. The meter will let you observe the duration that someone listens to the tape at home (Hoelscher, Lichstein, & Rosenthal, 1984). You can ask students diagnosed with sexually transmitted diseases to tell their partner to seek treatment. You can observe whether they do by whether the partner shows up at the clinic (Montesinos, Frisch, Greene, & Hamilton, 1990). These observations focus on the result of a behavior rather than on the behavior itself.

You may use outcome recording to observe a <u>complex</u> behavior. One way is to use a checklist to observe a series of behavioral results. One research team used a checklist to measure the quality of teaching behaviors. They checked quizzes scored, worksheets scored, computer printouts posted, student records updated, and daily instructions (Bacon, Fulton, & Malott, 1982). Another research team used a checklist to observe self-care by a memory-impaired person with diabetes. They checked off whether the woman completed each step necessary to measure her own glucose level (Wong, Seroka, & Ogisi, 2000). You might observe whether a person washed all the tableware dirtied at dinner by making up a list of all types of utensils used. These might include plates, glasses, silverware, pots, and serving spoons. If you found all the plates clean, you would check them off. If you found the glasses clean, you would check them off. You would continue with each type of utensil. This approach permits very detailed observation of dish-washing behavior. Of course, it would still be an example of outcome recording, even though a list of behavioral results is being observed.

Classify a method as outcome recording only if it looks for a <u>result</u> of the behavior. Do not consider it outcome recording if it looks at the behavior itself. This result must occur

---

### Learning Simple Arithmetic Takes 50,000 Responses!

People often explain the differences between how easily children learn math by saying that some children are "smart" and others are "dumb." Skinner explains it differently. He guesses children make about 50,000 responses to learn arithmetic. Teachers, parents, and books help children with some of these responses. But they don't help all children equally. Skinner explains differences between children in terms of the amount of help they get. He invented a "teaching machine" that provides help on every single response! He showed that almost all children learn well with the machine. The children wrote their answers directly on paper in the machine. Skinner used <u>outcome</u> recording because he looked at the result of their writing behavior: their written answers on the paper (Skinner, 1954).

2. Because Skinner looked at the result of their writing, he was using what method of observing? _____ recording

after the behavior. If you are observing a result of behavior rather than the behavior itself, then always label the method as outcome recording.

To decide whether a method of observation is outcome recording, start by asking the question, "Does the behavior occur as uniform instances?" If the answer is "yes," then ask, "Does the behavior leave a result?" If the answer is "yes," then the method is outcome recording.

## Event Recording for Uniform Behaviors

If a behavior does not leave a unique result, you must observe it <u>during</u> the occurrence of the response. Many behaviors do not leave unique results. Waving your hand at someone, saying thank you, and reading a book do not leave a result. They occur, and then they are gone. Your hand is back in your pocket, your voice has died away, or the book is back in its place. You must observe these behaviors when they are performed.

Some behaviors that do not leave unique results are <u>uniform</u>, while others are nonuniform. A behavior is uniform if each instance of the behavior takes about the same length of time as every other instance. For example, stuttering is uniform because each stutter involves only the brief moment. Solving math problems is uniform if students take about the same time for each problem. Even long sequences of behaviors like swimming laps can be uniform. A swimmer usually takes about the same time to complete each lap. For uniform behaviors that do not leave a result, you can use a second instance-type method of observation. This method is called *event recording.*

### Event Recording

For *event recording,* you record a response when you see an <u>instance</u> of the behavior. Behavior analysts use this method when they observe behavior that is relatively uniform in length. You observe the behavior during the response.

3. For event recording, you record a response when you see an _____ of the behavior.

***Figure 3-2.*** Umpires call balls and strikes. Because they are observing instances of uniform behaviors, they are using event recording. (Source: Streeter Leeka/Getty Images)

An example of event recording might involve counting each time that a student raises his hand in class. You would record hand raising when you see someone raise their hand. You can use event recording because each hand-raising response takes about the same amount of time. Usually the whole episode takes only a few moments to complete.

You can use event recording to record many <u>simple</u> behaviors. You might observe the number of times a third-grade peer tutor praised the spelling efforts of the pupil they were tutoring (Kohler & Greenwood, 1990). You might observe the number of correct tags by a competitive roller speed skater (e.g., Anderson & Kirkpatrick, 2002). You might observe the number of children engaging in disruptive behavior on a playground (White & Bailey, 1990). You might even count the number of

### The Making of an Observation System

David Lombard studied whether people protect themselves against skin cancer from the sun. His behavioral definition of "safe sunning" included: wearing a shirt, being in the shade, wearing a hat, wearing sunglasses, wearing zinc oxide, using sun screen lotion. He went to a private pool every day at 2:00 P.M., walking the same path around the pool each day, and he counted the number of people using each of those steps. He found that the lifeguards used about 25% and patrons 19% of the steps. He then asked lifeguards to model safe sunning. They increased their use to 65%. The patrons increased their use to about 25% as a result. The observation system made it possible to see the effect of using lifeguards as models. (Lombard, Neubauer, Canfield, & Winett, 1991).

4. Because Lombard recorded each instance of safe sunning behavior that he observed, he was using what method of observation? _____
recording (event, outcome)

---

curve balls hit well by players trying out for the college team (Osborne, Rudrud, & Zezoney, 1990). Behavior analysts usually use event recording to find out how many times the behavior occurs. The observer counts praises, disruptive acts, or well-hit balls.

You can also use event recording to observe the performance of complex behaviors. You would break the complex behavior down into its parts. You would then use event recording to fill out a checklist of the parts. For example, you might wish to observe a public speech that a friend makes to see if it is complete. You might list the major parts of a speech. This might include opening comments, the main body of the speech, closing comments, and inviting questions (Fawcett & Miller, 1975).

Then, you would record the occurrence of each category when it occurred.

Classify a method as event recording only if it involves observing uniform instances of a behavior. The observer must watch the behavior during its occurrence. Be very careful when trying to decide between event recording and outcome recording. Suppose you are observing the "result" of an "instance" of behavior after the behavior occurs. You are not using event recording. Behavior analysts always call the observation of "results" by the name *outcome recording*. They call the observation of instances of a behavior *event recording* only if those instances are behaviors, not results. Be careful not to look only for the word *results* or the word *instances*.

### Delinquent Children Learn through Thousands of Parental Conflicts

Some people explain gang violence by an inner mechanism such as a violent personality or identity crisis. But Gerry Patterson wouldn't. He spent a lifetime studying the causes of delinquent behavior. He gathered data on families in their own homes. He observed instances of conflicts that children have with their parents. Children who become delinquent have twice as many conflicts as do normal children. Delinquents have up to 10 times as many conflicts! Children have the opportunity to conflict with their parents as many as one million times before they leave home. The parents have that many chances to teach their children kindness or violence. Patterson has developed classes to teach parents of potential delinquents how to reduce conflict. (Based on Patterson, 1993.)

5. By observing instances of conflict, Patterson uses what method of observation? _____
recording (event, outcome)

To decide whether a method of observation is outcome recording, start by asking the following question: "Does the behavior occur as uniform instances?" If the answer is "yes," then ask, "Does the behavior leave a result?" If the answer is "no," then the method is event recording.

## Interval Recording for Nonuniform Behaviors

This section introduces you to the first of the *interval-type* methods of observation. If you decide that you cannot use an instance-type method of observation, then you will probably need to use an interval-type method.

Many behaviors are <u>nonuniform</u> in length. For example, study behavior is nonuniform. Often you may study for a few minutes and then look out the window, get a drink, or think about something else. Studying for an hour may mean studying on and off like that for an hour. It might mean studying for an hour straight. Other similar (that is, interrupted) behaviors might be reading, talking, listening to music, or even walking. Behavior analysts use different methods to observe uniform and nonuniform behaviors.

For example, you might think of using event recording with a nonuniform behavior to count how often it occurs. However, if you count nonuniform behaviors, you will probably produce <u>meaningless</u> results. Suppose Deb starts watching TV football at 3:00 P.M. If Deb watches straight through to a commercial at 3:15, you might call her viewing one TV-watching response. Suppose you also observe Tom. Tom takes his first commercial break at 3:12. He returns at 3:13 and watches until the next commercial at 3:15. Should you count his viewing as two TV-watching responses? The trouble is that Tom watches less of the program than Deb, but you count him as having twice as many responses. Doesn't make much sense, does it?

I can imagine an even worse case. Suppose that Ann starts watching the same program at 3:00. She may have told her 5-year-old son, Dan, to stay in the yard. She might stop watching the program after every play to see if Dan is still in the yard. Should you count each time she checks on Dan as the end of a watching response? If the teams made 15 plays, then you would count Ann with 15 TV-watching responses. However, she might spend more time checking on Dan than she spends watching the plays. So you would count Ann as having more responses than Deb or Tom, even though she spent the least time watching. This result makes even less sense than the result in the previous case.

The problem with nonuniform behavior is that each response can take very different amounts of time. With our TV-watching examples, we found that people may look at the screen for different lengths of time. Deb looked once for 15 minutes. Tom looked twice for 12 and 2 minutes. Ann looked 15 times for less than a minute each time. The different people watch TV for widely varying times. Even one person can watch TV for times that vary widely.

Behavior analysts observe nonuniform behaviors by dividing the overall observation time into short <u>intervals</u>. For example, you might divide the football game into intervals 1 minute long. You would divide the time from 3:00 to 3:15 into 15 intervals. You would then look to see if Deb appears to be watching TV at any time during each 1-minute interval. If so, you would record a response. You would end up with a count of how many intervals contained some watching. You would have a crude measure of the amount of time spent watching TV during the 15 minutes. This method would probably show that Deb, Tom, and Ann each watched for 14 or 15 intervals. You could get an even more accurate measure by dividing the time between 3:00 and 3:15 into smaller intervals. For example, if you are concerned about the frequent glances out the window by Ann, you could use 30-second intervals. That might show Deb with 30 intervals, Tom with 28 intervals, and Ann with 15.

Using a series of continuous intervals gives a rough estimate of the amount of <u>time</u> for that behavior. You observe during each interval and count the number of intervals during which you saw the behavior. This number gives you an idea of what percentage of the time the behavior occurs.

### Interval Recording

For interval recording, you record a response if the behavior occurs in one of a series of <u>continuous</u> intervals. *Continuous* just means

| How to use interval recording on singing musical notes | | | | | | | | | | | |
|---|---|---|---|---|---|---|---|---|---|---|---|
| Seconds: | 1 | 2 | 3 | 4 | 5 | 6 | 7 | 8 | 9 | 10 | Singing? |
| Interval: 01–10 | - | - | - | - | - | - | - | - | - | - | No |
| Interval: 11–20 | - | - | - | - | G | - | - | - | - | - | Yes |
| Interval: 21–30 | - | - | - | - | - | - | - | F | F | - | Yes |
| Interval: 31–40 | - | - | - | - | A | A | A | A | A | A | Yes |
| Interval: 41–50 | A | A | A | A | - | - | - | - | - | - | Yes |
| Interval: 51–60 | E | E | E | - | E | E | - | E | E | E | Yes |
| Interval: 61–70 | B | B | B | B | B | B | B | B | B | B | Yes |
| Interval: 71–80 | - | - | - | - | - | - | - | - | - | - | No |

***Figure 3-3.*** Each row shows whether Mary was singing during each second of a 10-second interval. Each cell shows the note if Mary was singing during that second or a dash if she was not singing. The last column shows whether an observer would record "Yes" that Mary was singing during that 1-second interval, or "No" if she was not.

that each additional interval starts right after the end of the prior interval. The observer divides the entire observation period into intervals that follow one another. Note that the behavior doesn't have to occur in each interval. However, the observer has to look for it throughout each interval. You can also say that the observer looks continuously.

6. For interval recording, you record a response if the behavior occurs in one of a series of _____ intervals.

Behavior analysts use this method to observe occurrences of a <u>nonuniform</u> behavior that vary greatly in length. Because such behavior is "unstructured," you must use a structured observational method. You create the structure by dividing the observation period into a series of short intervals. Sometimes the response will fit into one interval because it is short. Other times it will cover more than one interval because it is longer. Sometimes there will be no response during an interval in which you have observed. Your job is to decide whether any part of these nonuniform responses occurs within each of the intervals.

For example, all of the following behavioral events would be considered an occurrence of a behavior in interval recording. (1) The behavior starts within the interval. (2) The behavior ends within the interval. (3) The behavior starts before the interval and continues past the end of the interval. (4) The behavior starts and ends during the interval. (5) The behavior starts and stops more than once during the interval. In this last case, you

would not record that the response occurred more than once. You are interested only in whether any part of a response occurs within the interval. To summarize, a behavior is scored as occurring in interval recording if any part of the behavior takes place within the interval. Figure 3-3 illustrates these different cases when observing Mary's humming.

7. Figure 3-3 shows how interval recording records one behavioral episode that overlaps more than one interval. For example, Mary sang an A-note for 10 seconds starting in Interval 31–40. But Mary got credit for singing that A-note in how many intervals? ___

Interval recording is used to observe occurrence of behaviors that are nonuniform in length. The overall observation period is then divided into a series of intervals of a convenient length. The intervals are continuous because each interval immediately follows the prior interval.

For example, you might use interval recording to determine whether Jay's TV show spends more time telling funny stories in the monologue than David's. You would first divide each show's monologue into a series of short intervals. If you picked 15-second intervals and if each monologue is 30 minutes long, then you would have a series of 120 continuous intervals. You can then observe during each interval and record whether the host was telling any part of a funny story during the interval. A long joke might cover 6 intervals. A very short joke might take just one interval. At the conclusion of Jay's and David's shows, you could easily determine which show spent more time telling funny stories in its monologue by comparing the number of intervals with the number of funny stories. However, because different jokes take different lengths of time, you would not know how many jokes occurred in each show.

Notice three aspects of interval recording. First, you use interval recording to observe <u>nonuniform</u> behavioral episodes. Funny stories can last a few seconds or a few minutes. Five of Jay's stories might take a couple of minutes to tell, whereas five of David's might take 10 minutes to tell. If you counted stories, you would score them both as five stories. Second, you divide the overall observational period into continuous <u>intervals</u> that follow right after one another. You then observe during each interval to determine whether or not the behavior occurs during some portion of the interval. A long story might occur in many intervals. Two short ones might occur in one interval. Remember, recording that a response occurred during an interval does not indicate whether the response covered the entire interval or only a moment of it. Nor does it indicate the number of occurrences. Third, note that the overall record indicates the amount of <u>time</u> the behavior occurred.

Consider another example. Interval recording would be an ideal method for observing the study behavior of a child. Suppose you want to watch the child from 4:00 to 5:00 in the afternoon. You divide the hour into a series of continuous time intervals of a convenient length, perhaps 30 seconds. You then record for each of those 30-second intervals whether or not the child studies during any part of that interval. You do not record whether the behavior occurs for all or part of the interval. Your objective is to discover what percentage of intervals contains some studying.

You might also observe the behavior of a group of children with interval recording. For example, you might be interested in how much of the time the children are playing quietly. You might observe them during 20-second intervals. If all of them are playing quietly, then you would score them as quiet. If any of them are screaming or yelling, you would not score them as quiet. In this example, you are not observing each child but the group as a whole.

You might also use interval recording to observe the occurrence of off-task behavior within classroom settings (e.g., Flood, Wilder, Flood, & Masuda, 2002). You might use it to observe the level of positive behavior such as smiling or looking at toys emitted by an infant (Derrickson, Neef, & Cataldo, 1993). You might use it to observe the activity level of preschool children after consuming cola drinks (Baer, 1987). You might use it to measure the amount of time that junior high students study or socialize appropriately (Ninness, Fuerst, Rutherford, & Glenn, 1991). You might use it to measure on-task behaviors among preschool children (e.g., Morrison, Sainato, Benchaaban, & Endo, 2002).

Be very careful when trying to distinguish between interval recording and outcome recording! Suppose you look every 30 minutes for the result of some behavior. Behavior analysts would call this outcome recording because you are looking for a result after the behavior occurs. Looking for a result is always considered outcome recording. Looking every 30 minutes is simply a systematic way to look for the result.

Be very careful when trying to distinguish between event recording and interval recording! Looking for instances of a nonuniform behavior during a series of continuous 30-second intervals is not event recording. You may record a particular instance in more than one interval. You find out about how much of the time this nonuniform behavior occurs. You do not find out how many times the behavior occurs. Therefore, this method would be interval recording.

Classify a method as interval recording only if the intervals are <u>continuous</u>. Remember, the response does not have to fill the interval. Not only that but the response may extend over more than one interval. Many of the intervals will contain no response. Also, you record only one response per interval.

## Time Sample Recording for Sampling a Behavior

Time sample recording is a variation of interval recording. Behavior analysts use it when they can't continuously record one behavior.

Instead, they <u>sample</u> a behavior—that is, observe it only part of the time. You may wish to observe Tom's peculiar habit of reading while watching TV. You might have trouble accurately recording both behaviors at the same time. Behavior analysts handle this problem by sampling one behavior and then sampling the other. In other words, they switch back and forth between the two behaviors. First, they look for reading, then they look for TV watching. This same approach can be used with more than two behaviors.

Interestingly enough, you can use the same approach to observe a "single" behavior when it is not convenient to observe it continuously. For example, you may wish to observe Tom's study behavior over an 8-hour day. But you may not be able to observe every moment of that 8 hours. You can estimate the amount of his study behavior throughout the day by sampling a 15-second interval once every half hour.

### Time Sample Recording

For *time sample recording* you record a response if one behavior occurs within one of a series of <u>discontinuous</u> intervals. Behavior analysts use this method to sample one or more behaviors during an observation period. The name comes from observing the behavior during a sample of the total time period rather than during all of it.

8. For time sample recording, you record a response if the behavior occurs within one of a series of _____ intervals.

Time sample recording differs from interval recording by using discontinuous intervals. *Discontinuous* means that the beginning of each time interval does not start at the end of the prior time interval. Rather there is an interruption between intervals. If the intervals used to observe one behavior are <u>discontinuous</u>, then the method is time sample recording. If the intervals used to observe one behavior are <u>continuous</u>, then the method is interval recording.

For example, you might use time sample recording to observe Tom watching TV and reading. Suppose you use 15-second intervals. You might observe TV watching during the first interval and reading during the second interval. You would continue switching from one

| Observing two behaviors with time sample recording | | | | | | | | | | |
|---|---|---|---|---|---|---|---|---|---|---|
| 15-second intervals: | 1 | 2 | 3 | 4 | 5 | 6 | 7 | 8 | 9 | 10 |
| Is Tom watching TV? | Y | - | N | - | Y | - | Y | - | Y | - |
| Is Tom reading book? | - | N | - | Y | - | N | - | N | - | N |

***Figure 3-4.*** During odd-numbered intervals, the observer records a "Y" for "yes" when Tom is watching TV, an "N" for "no" when he is not watching TV. The observer records a "–" for "no observation" during the even-numbered interval. During the even-numbered intervals, the observer uses the same code to record when Tom is reading a book. Notice that the observer looked for TV watching during the first but not the second interval and then looked for TV watching again during the third interval.

behavior to the other. You would observe Tom's TV watching during the odd-numbered intervals: 1, 3, 5, etc. You would observe Tom's reading during the even-numbered intervals: 2, 4, 6, etc. Notice that you would observe TV watching during discontinuous intervals. The beginning of a TV-watching interval does not immediately follow the end of the previous TV-watching interval. Rather, a reading interval intervenes. Figure 3-4 illustrates the way an observer switches back and forth between these two behaviors.

9. Figure 3-4 shows a case in which a new interval devoted to looking for TV watching does not follow immediately after the last interval devoted to looking for TV watching. Therefore, the intervals devoted to looking for TV watching _____(are, aren't) continuous.

One variation of time sample recording involves observing multiple <u>people</u> one after the other. For example, suppose that a teacher checks for 20 seconds to see if Willie is studying, then shifts to observe Diane for 20 seconds, and then returns to observe Willie again. Notice that she checks on Willie's behavior for 20 seconds and then doesn't check on his behavior again for another 20 seconds. She observes his behavior every other interval. Thus, she would be using time sample recording because she is observing Willie's behavior during discontinuous 20-second intervals. Likewise, she is observing Diane's behavior during discontinuous

| Observing two persons with time sample recording | | | | | | | | | | |
|---|---|---|---|---|---|---|---|---|---|---|
| 20 second intervals | 1 | 2 | 3 | 4 | 5 | 6 | 7 | 8 | 9 | 10 |
| Is Willie studying? | Y | - | N | - | Y | - | N | - | Y | - |
| Is Diane studying? | - | N | - | Y | - | Y | - | Y | - | Y |

**Figure 3-5.** During odd-numbered intervals, the observer records whether or not Willie is studying. The observer records a "–" for "no observation" during the even-numbered intervals. During the even-numbered intervals, the observer uses the same code to record whether Diane is studying. Notice that the observer looked at Willie during the first but not the second interval and then looked at Willie again during the third interval. Notice that a new interval devoted to looking at Willie does not follow immediately after the last intervals devoted to looking at Willie.

intervals. Figure 3-5 illustrates the switching back and forth between two people.

10. Figure 3-5 shows that the intervals devoted to looking at Willie are _____ _____ (continuous, discontinuous).

Notice that you might observe a group of individuals as a group and not be using time sample recording. Remember the example of interval recording involving children playing quietly. In that example, you observed to see if all the children were quiet during each 20-second interval. You were observing for quiet behavior during continuous intervals. You didn't switch from child to child, thus creating discontinuous intervals. You didn't switch from behavior to behavior. You observed only one behavior, even though it was the behavior of a group. You observed it for continuous intervals. Therefore it was interval, not time sample, recording.

Another variation on time sample recording is to observe only <u>one</u> behavior during discontinuous intervals. This variation is often used to sample the behavior over a long period of time. For example, you might want to see if Dan is

really studying during most of his "all-nighter." To find out, you might look in his room for 5 seconds every 30 minutes all night. Each 5-second interval is discontinuous because there is a gap of almost 30 minutes before the next 5-second interval of observation. Therefore, you would be using time sample recording. Similarly, you might want to find out how much of the time elderly patients in a nursing home were moving instead of sitting. You could observe for a brief interval every 40 minutes during the day (Burgio, Burgio, Engel, & Tice, 1986). This is time sample recording because each brief interval is separated by almost 40 minutes. The arrangement of observational intervals is illustrated by Figure 3-6.

11. Figure 3-6 shows that the first interval during which the observer is supposed to observe begins at 20 seconds and ends at 24 seconds. If the next interval of observation began at 25 seconds, then the intervals of observation would be continuous. However, the next interval of observation is discontinuous because it begins at _____ seconds.

Time sample recording is also used by applied behavior analysts when they simply need more time to record their observations. Researchers observed a child for a 1-second interval every 10 seconds to see how he was playing (Esposito & Koorland, 1989). This approach gave them 9 seconds to write down the result and prepare for the next observation.

Another variation of time sample recording is to observe one behavior during <u>randomly</u> selected observational periods. For example, suppose that a professor checked for 5 seconds to see whether a particular student was awake. The professor might check after 5 minutes, 9 minutes, 17 minutes, and 25 minutes. The 5-second intervals are discontinuous because

| When is the observer looking during time sample recording of one behavior? | | | | | | | | | | | | | | |
|---|---|---|---|---|---|---|---|---|---|---|---|---|---|---|
| Begins: | 0:00 | 0:05 | 0:10 | 0:15 | 0:20 | 0:25 | 0:30 | 0:35 | 0:40 | 0:45 | 0:50 | 0:55 | 1:00 | 1:05 | 1:10 |
| Ends: | 0:04 | 0:09 | 0:14 | 0:19 | 0:24 | 0:29 | 0:34 | 0:39 | 0:44 | 0:49 | 0:54 | 0:59 | 1:04 | 1:09 | 1:14 |
| Observing? | 👁 | 👁 | 👁 | 👁 | 👁 | 👁 | 👁 | 👁 | 👁 | 👁 | 👁 | 👁 | 👁 | 👁 | 👁 |

**Figure 3-6.** When observers use time sample recording for just one behavior, they don't look for long periods of time and then they look for a brief period of time.

the next interval is not observed immediately after the prior interval. Therefore, the professor would be using time sample recording. Likewise, researchers sampled staff performance in a hospital for a brief interval on the average of every 12 minutes to find out how much of the time they were doing their job (Burgio, Whitman, & Reid, 1983). The researchers used time sample recording because the brief intervals of observation were separated by an average of 12 minutes.

Classify an observational method as time sample recording only if the intervals for one behavior are <u>discontinuous</u>. Be very careful when trying to distinguish between time sample recording and outcome recording! If you observe every hour whether the behavior has produced a result, then you are not using time sample recording, you are instead using outcome recording.

## Summary

This lesson showed you the second tactic in using the behavioral strategy for solving human problems. The second tactic is to use the approach of <u>direct observation</u> to gather information about the problem behavior. It showed you the four most commonly used and cited methods of direct observation. You can use outcome recording to observe the <u>result</u> of a behavior. You can use event recording to observe <u>instances</u> of a uniform behavior. You can use interval recording to observe nonuniform behavior during <u>continuous</u> intervals. You can use time sample recording to observe a sample of a behavior during <u>discontinuous</u> intervals.

## Behavior Analysis Examples

This section gives you some examples of how behavior analysts actually use the four methods of direct observation. (Hint: The examples of the methods do not necessarily appear in the same order that you learned them.)

### *Study Behavior*

Studying is mental activity, right? Behavior analysts couldn't possibly study it, right?

| Recording sheet for interval recording | | | | | | | | | | |
|---|---|---|---|---|---|---|---|---|---|---|
| Intervals: | 1 | 2 | 3 | 4 | 5 | 6 | 7 | 8 | 9 | 10 |
| Studying | | x | x | x | x | x | | | | x |

**Figure 3-7.** This is the recording sheet for observing Phillips's studying behavior. The sheet permits recording whether Phillip was studying during each of 10 intervals, each 10 seconds long. The observer placed an "x" in boxes corresponding to intervals where Philip studied. You can see that he did not study during the first interval, but he did during the second, third, fourth, fifth, and sixth. (Based on Walker & Buckley, 1968.)

Walker and Buckley were among the first to find a way. They analyzed the study behavior of Phillip, a bright fourth grader. Phillip did very little work in school so he was not getting good grades. They defined study behavior as "looking at the assigned page, working problems, and recording responses." They divided their 10-minute observation period into 10-second intervals. Figure 3-7 shows a sample of their observation form. The authors found that Phillip studied during about 40% of the intervals. They then let him work toward a model airplane by studying. They found that his study behavior increased to more than 90% of the intervals. (Based on Walker & Buckley, 1968.)

12. Because they observed study behavior during <u>continuous intervals</u>, Walker and Buckley used what observational method? _____ recording (event, interval, outcome, time sample)
13. Figure 3-7 shows that the number of the last interval during which Phillip studied was _____.

### *Self-Recording*

You might think that behavior analysts can't study behavior emitted by an isolated individual. There is no one else around to observe their behavior. Lindsley suggested using people to observe their own behavior directly. Direct observation requires that they use a behavioral definition and that they immediately record the behavior. Lindsley suggested that people use golf wrist counters to easily record their own behavior. These counters can be operated by a button press that doesn't interfere with other

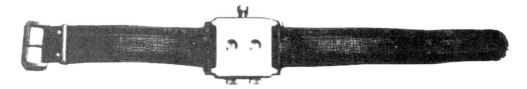

**Figure 3-8.** People can use a wrist counter to directly observe such behaviors as smoking, smiling, and complaining. Wrist counters are widely available in the golf section of sports departments. (Adapted from "A Reliable Wrist Counter for Recording Behavior Rates," by O. R. Lindsley, *Journal of Applied Behavior Analysis*, 1968, 1, 77. Copyright 1968 by the Society for the Experimental Analysis of Behavior, Inc. Used by permission.)

activities. Figure 3-8 shows a wrist counter. People use wrist counters to record a variety of discrete behaviors including smoking, smiling, making positive comments to others, and even anxious thoughts. Note that *self-recording* is not another method of recording behavior. Note also that it is not self-report if people use a behavioral definition and record their observations immediately. (Based on Lindsley, 1968.)

14. Because Lindsley suggests using a wrist counter to count <u>instances</u> of uniform behaviors, he is suggesting what method of observation? _____ recording (event, interval, outcome, time sample)

### Cooperative Dormitory

One approach to helping people be more cooperative may be to define cooperation behaviorally. Then, we could observe it and make sure everyone acts fairly. Feallock and Miller developed the checklist of behaviors shown in Figure 3-9. The members of a cooperative dorm used it to observe their own lounge cleaning. The behavior analysts gave

| Cleaning Checklist | | | |
|---|---|---|---|
| | Lounge | | Phone Room |
| x | Pick up trash | x | Pick up trash |
| x | Sweep lounge | x | Sweep up dirt |
| x | Vaccum rugs | x | Mop floor |
| x | Clean ashtrays | x | Get clean paper |
| | Empty trash | x | Provide fresh pen |
| x | Mop tile floor | | Replace dead bulbs |
| x | Return items | x | Return items |

**Figure 3-9.** This is the inspection checklist for lounge cleaning in a cooperative dorm. The observer writes an "x" for each task completed. (Based on Feallock & Miller, 1976.)

each of the entries, such as "pick up trash," a careful behavioral definition. That way the members knew exactly what results to record. Members appointed one of themselves as inspector, who then used the checklist after another member cleaned the lounge. The inspector used similar checklists for the results of all basic housework. The data clearly revealed that members did very little cleaning. However, by giving a rent reduction to members who did their share of the cleaning, they were able to get everyone to clean. (Based on Feallock & Miller, 1976.)

15. Because the inspector observed the <u>results</u> of lounge cleaning, they used what method of observation? _____ recording (event, outcome, interval, time sample)

16. Figure 3-9 shows an example where the lounge cleaner did not empty the trash. Nor did they _____ dead bulbs.

### Positive Interactions

Could we observe whether interacting with normal children improves the behavior of children with retardation? If so, maybe we could find ways to improve their interactions. Beckman and Kohl studied positive interactions by children with mild retardation. They compared the amount of positive interactions when only children with retardation were grouped together with the amount of positive interactions when normal children were also in the group. Examples of positive interaction are saying something nice, hugging, waving, sharing toys, and smiling. They observed each of six children every 10 seconds. During the first 10 seconds, they recorded whether the first child was engaging in positive interaction; then a timer went off, and they observed the second child for 10 seconds; then a timer went off again, and the process was repeated for the remaining children. After the six children had been observed once, they again observed the first child, repeating the process with all six children. They observed 30 intervals per day.

Beckman and Kohl found that children with retardation engaged in positive interactions about 6 times out of 30 when in segregated groups consisting only of children with retardation. They found that children with retardation engaged in positive interactions in integrated groups about 9 times out of 30. Thus, the children with retardation engaged in about 50% more positive interactions when normal children were around. (Based on Beckman & Kohl, 1987.)

17. Because they observed the children in <u>discontinuous</u> intervals, what method of observation did Beckman and Kohl use? _____ recording (event, interval, outcome, time sample)

## Notes

### Note #1
In the remainder of the book, I will make a distinction between behavior and response. When referring to a <u>type</u> of activity, I will use the word *behavior*. When referring to a single <u>occurrence</u> of a behavior, I will use the word *response*.

18. When referring to a single <u>occurrence</u> of a behavior, I will use the word _____.

### Note #2
This lesson provides an introduction to the four most commonly used methods of observation. Kelly (1977) reported that these four methods accounted for about 90% of the cases reported in the *Journal of Applied Behavior Analysis*. More precisely, 8% used outcome recording, 50% used event recording, 15% used interval recording, and 15% used time sample recording. For information on additional methods of observation, consult the additional readings at the end of this lesson.

19. The most widely used method was _____ recording. These four methods accounted for about _____ % of the cases.

### Note #3
Behavior analysts have found that when the frequency of behaviors is high, interval recording and time sample recording underestimate them (Repp, Roberts, Slack, Repp, & Berkler, 1976). Event recording, on the other hand, does not produce either an overestimate or underestimate.

20. When the frequency of a behavior is high, which method will produce the most accurate estimate of the frequency of the behavior? _____ (event, interval, time sample)

### Note #4
Behavior analysts have found that interval recording and time sample recording are inaccurate when intervals are long compared to duration of responses (Mann, Ten Have, Plunkett, & Meisels, 1991). Event recording, on the other hand, does not produce either an overestimate or underestimate.

21. Therefore, when the intervals are longer than the behavior, which method will produce the most accurate estimate of the frequency of the behavior? _____ (event, interval, time sample)

## Helpful Hints

### Helpful Hint #1
To figure out what method of observation is being used, you need ask only two questions. First, you need to establish whether or not the presence of a behavior during an interval is being observed. If the presence of a behavior during an interval is not observed, then the method has to be either outcome or event recording. If the presence of a behavior during an interval is observed, then the method has to be either interval or time sample recording. So by establishing whether the presence of a behavior during an interval is observed, you eliminate two of

Method of Observation Decision Tree

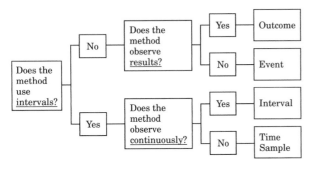

**Figure 3-10.** Questions to figure out what observational method is being used. First, ask if the method uses intervals. If the answer is "no, it does not use intervals," then ask if it observes results. If it does, it is outcome; if it doesn't, it is event. If the answer is "yes, it does use intervals," then ask if it observes continuously with the intervals. If the answer is "no, it does not use continuous intervals," then you know that the recording method is time sample recording.

the four methods. One follow-up question will then determine the method. The second question depends on the answer to the first question. If the presence of a behavior during an interval is not observed, then you need only find out whether a result is being observed. If the presence of a behavior during an interval is observed, then you need only find out whether the intervals are continuous or not.

I want you to remember these questions because I will use them as a prompt many times in the rest of this lesson. First, you ask about <u>intervals</u>. Then, depending on the answer, you ask about either <u>results</u> or <u>continuous</u> (intervals). So, remember this sequence: intervals: results/continuous, where the "/" means "or." Can you remember those three words? Let's repeat: intervals/results/continuous. Figure 3-10 shows a flow diagram of these questions. Can you remember those three words: intervals/continuous/results? Figure 3-10 shows a flow diagram of these questions.

22. Figure 3-10 asks you to answer two questions. Suppose your answers are "Yes" and "No." You then know that the recording method is _____ (event, interval, outcome, time sample) recording.

### Helpful Hint #2

The behavior does not have to occur during each consecutive interval in interval recording. The only requirement is that the observer look for it during each interval. You will encounter examples in which an observer uses 15-second intervals. The behavior will usually not occur during every single interval. Some students have reasoned that because the behavior did not occur during continuous intervals, the observer did not look for it during continuous intervals. Therefore, they must have looked for it during discontinuous intervals. They concluded that the observational method was time sample recording. This is incorrect. The definition requires only that you <u>observe</u> the person during continuous intervals. It does not require that the behavior <u>occur</u> during each of those intervals.

23. For example, suppose you observe Fred during 100 intervals. Suppose each interval is 15 seconds long. Suppose that each new interval starts when the old interval ends. If you find that Fred listens to music during some but not all intervals, would you be using interval recording or time sample recording? _____ recording

### Helpful Hint #3

Normally when I am asking you to distinguish between self-report and direct observation, I will ask you what <u>approach</u> to observation is used. This is the same term I used in the prior lesson. When I am asking you to distinguish between the four methods of observation, I will ask you what <u>method</u> of observation is used. I will also place the word *recording* after the blank so that you don't have the busywork of writing that out.

24. When I want you to distinguish between the different methods of observation, I will ask you what _____ of observation was used.

### Helpful Hint #4

I have underlined the key words in the definition of each method of observation to call your attention to a major idea. Be careful not to look only for those words, however, as they may appear in an example of another method. To answer a question, you must understand the concept rather than just memorize a key word. For example, suppose that you count the number of words that someone says in one minute to measure their speed of talking. Clearly, that is event recording. It is not interval recording because you are not looking for the presence or absence of talking in that interval. It is not interval recording just because you are counting for one minute. It would not be interval recording even if you were to start a new count for each new minute. You still would be counting instances of saying a word rather than whether or not talking occurs in the interval. So cuing in on the presence or absence of an interval is a very helpful clue, but you need to look at every aspect of the method.

25. Counting the number of consecutive one-minute intervals in which words are spoken is an example of what method of observation? _____ recording

### Helpful Hint #5
You should have access to a calculator for the next lesson unless you are very good at math.

## Additional Readings

Bass, R. F., & Aserlind, R. (1984). Interval and time sample data collection procedures: Methodological issues. In K. D. Gadow (Ed.), *Advances in learning and behavioral disabilities* (Vol. 3, pp. 1–39). Greenwich, CT: JAI Press. A brief discussion of the history and prevalence of direct measures is presented, as well as a critique of the comparability of interval and time sample. Note also the discussion of the variables affecting observer records. Finally, a case is put forth for the development of an observer technology that emphasizes the strength of observational procedures.

Bijou, S. W., Peterson, R. F., & Ault, M. H. (1968). A method to integrate descriptive and experimental field studies at the level of data and empirical concepts. *Journal of Applied Behavior Analysis, 1,* 175–191. This article discusses the use of objective direct observation procedures in the description and analysis of everyday behavior.

Brandt, R. (1972). *Studying behavior in natural settings.* New York: Holt, Rinehart, and Winston. This book describes a variety of observational procedures that can be used in the study of everyday behavior; narrative data, ratings, and data from simulated situations are described.

Hartmann, D. P., & Peterson, L. (1975). A neglected literature and an aphorism. *Journal of Applied Behavior Analysis, 8,* 231–232. This article cites 12 references to discussions of observational technology in social psychology, education, and child psychology.

O'Leary, K. D. (Ed.) (1979). Behavioral assessment (Special issue). *Journal of Applied Behavior Analysis, 12*(4). A special issue of JABA devoted to behavioral assessment that includes articles on behavioral assessment, the functions of assessment, various graphic aids, and various commentaries related to these issues.

Rosenthal, R., & Rosnow, R. L. (1969). *Artifact in behavioral research.* New York: Academic Press. This book discusses the effect that being observed has on people's behavior. Because people may act differently when they know they are being observed, the resulting data can be misleading. This phenomenon is known as *reactivity* and is an important issue in behavior analysis.

Wright, H. (1960). Observational child study. In P. Mussen (Ed.), *Handbook of research methods in child development* (pp. 71–139). New York: Wiley. The application of "ecological" psychology to direct observation is described. The article contains explanations of methods that have been adopted by behavior analysts. Many are documented in this reading as early as the 1920s.

## Programmed Reading

This section presents the following modules: (1) Recording Based on Results, (2) Recording Instances of Behavior, (3) Recording Behavior during Continuous Intervals, (4) Recording Behavior during Discontinuous Intervals, (5) Another Tactic, and (6) Review.

### 1. Recording Based on Results

56. Pre-test: Observing Mary's paper grading by seeing whether a stack of graded papers exists is an example of _____ recording.

54. Pre-test: If you record a response when you see the unique result of a behavior after the response takes place, you are using what method of observation: _____ recording

65. Pre-test: Tom had a date with Beautiful Barb. The result of the date was that afterwards he bragged to his friends about the date. Of course, Tom could have lied about his date. Could an observer use the result that his friends "knew" he had a date to prove that Tom had a date with Barb? _____

48. Pre-test: Classify a method as "outcome recording" only if it looks for a unique and observable _____ of the behavior.

24. I will use a simple convention to help you answer questions in this section. I will ask you to distinguish between self-report and direct observation by asking you which <u>approach</u> to observation was used. I will ask you to distinguish between the <u>methods</u> of event recording, interval recording, outcome recording, and time sample recording by asking you which _____ of observation was used.

83. The first method of observation is called *outcome recording*. You look at the unique results of a behavior to find out if it happened. If you use a method of observations that looks at such unique results of a behavior, then you know that you are using _____ recording.

43. Observing a behavior that leaves unique results is easy. At their convenience, even long after the behavior occurs, observers can look for that unique _____ _____ of the behavior.

1. A mark of outcome recording is that the observation of the result takes place _____ (after, before, during) the response.

32. If you record a response when you see the unique result of a behavior after the response takes place, you are

using what method of observation? _____ recording

44. Observing Ann's dish-washing behavior by checking to see if the dishes are clean is an example of outcome recording because you are checking the _____ of her dish washing.

108. You cannot use every kind of result to make an outcome observation. For example, if you can't observe the result because it is a feeling inside of someone, in a different location, can be caused by other behaviors, or just doesn't last long enough, you _____ (can, can't) use it to prove that the behavior occurred.

22. Fran might yell at Jane. The result might be that Jane felt bad. However, an observer could not directly observe whether Jane feels bad. Therefore, the observer _____ (could, couldn't) use that result to observe Fran yelling at Jane.

38. Juan got a haircut. The result of the haircut is that Juan's long locks were reduced to a short crewcut. Could an observer use the short crewcut to directly observe whether Juan had a haircut? _____ (yes, no)

96. When Mom bakes chocolate chip cookies, they disappear in a few hours. Could an observer look for chocolate chip cookies this evening to see how many Mom had baked at noon? _____ (yes, no)

19. Do not count on seeing the word *result* in the description of an example of outcome recording. For example, Skinner's teaching machine recorded every answer that a student wrote. Afterwards, Skinner looked at their written answers on paper. Clearly, Skinner was not watching the students write their answer. Rather he was looking afterwards at the answers they had written. This is an example of outcome recording because the written answer _____ (is, isn't) the result of their writing behavior.

34. In analyzing descriptions of observing methods, you must ask if the method involves observing a result of the behavior rather than the behavior itself. For example, Dad observed Ken's car washing behavior by looking to see if all

the dust had been removed after Ken supposedly washed the car. You must notice that Dad didn't observe Ken while he was washing the car. Rather he observed what Ken changed by washing the car. What method of observation did Dad use to observe Ken's car washing behavior? _____ recording

13. Classify a method as outcome recording only if it looks for a unique and observable _____ of the behavior.

73. Some students get confused and think that when an observer records the occurrence of a behavior, their record is a result of the behavior. They then label the method as outcome recording. Since every method of observation requires an observer to record the occurrence of the behavior, these students usually get the _____ (right, wrong) answer.

23. I make a distinction between *behavior* and *response*. When referring to a <u>type</u> of activity, I will use the word *behavior*. When referring to a single <u>occurrence</u> of a behavior, I will use the word _____ _____.

72. So, remember to distinguish between behavior and response. When you want to refer to a single <u>occurrence</u> of a behavior, use the word response. When you want to refer to a <u>type</u> of activity, use the word _____.

37. John sees a beer. John chugalugs the beer. You should call that particular chugalugging a(n) _____ _____. You should call the type of activity known as chugalugging a(n) _____.

### 2. Recording Instances of Behavior

66. Pre-test: Using a checklist to observe instances of a complex behavior, such as whether Jose remembered every part of his speech, would be an example of what method of observation? _____ _____ recording

49. Pre-test: Classify a method as event recording only if it involves observing _____ of a behavior during their occurrence.

69. Pre-test: You should classify a method as outcome recording only if it looks for a(n) _____ of the behavior.

58. Pre-test: Remember, if you look for an instance of the behavior, you are using _____ recording. If you look for a result of the behavior, you are using _____ recording.

87. The second method of observation is called *event recording*. Outcome recording occurs after the behavior has occurred because it looks at the result of the behavior. Event recording is a way of observing behavior that does not leave a result. If a behavior does <u>not</u> leave a unique result, then you must observe it _____ (before, during, after) its occurrence.

115. You use event recording with relatively uniform instances of behavior. I will describe later methods of observation that can be used with nonuniform behavior. If you are observing uniform instances of behavior while they are occurring, you are using the method called _____ recording.

100. When using event recording, you record a response when you see a(n) _____ _____ (result, instance) of the behavior.

21. Each time that Martha raises her hand would be called an <u>instance</u> of that behavior. Counting how many times Martha raises her hand in class would be observing how many instances of that behavior occurred. Therefore, counting how many times Martha raises her hand is what method of observing? _____ _____ recording

110. You might count how often Barry interrupts Charlie. You would be using event recording because each time that Barry interrupts Charlie is a(n) _____ _____ of that behavior. (Do not answer with the word *example;* use the exact term used to define event recording.)

95. Using a checklist to observe instances of a complex behavior, such as whether Jose remembered every part of his speech, would be an example of what method of observation? _____ recording

80. Suppose you use a checklist of the different kinds of tableware to observe

whether Don washed all the tableware dirtied at dinner. If you check the results after Don was supposed to wash them to see if every item of each kind is clean, you would be using what method of observation? _____ recording

74. Suppose I ask you what method of observation is involved if you observe someone saying "ain't." First, ask yourself whether "ain't" is an instance of the behavior or whether it is a result of the behavior. You would no doubt conclude that it is a(n) _____ of the behavior.

4. Ann counted the instances when Bob put on zinc oxide sun block. What method of observation did she use? _____ recording

14. Classify a method as event recording only if it involves observing _____ _____ of a behavior during their occurrence.

114. You should classify a method as outcome recording only if it looks for a(n) _____ of the behavior.

71. Remember, if you look for an instance of the behavior, you are using _____ recording. If you look for a result of the behavior, you are using _____ recording.

6. Be very careful when trying to decide between event recording and outcome recording. If a method involves observing a result, always call the method outcome recording. For example, when the observer looks for the "result" of an "instance" of behavior after the behavior occurs, they are using the method of observation? _____ recording

3. Also, do not look only for the key word "instance." Make sure you read to understand what is being observed. Suppose that Mom is observing Danny while he tugs on weeds to produce the result of pulling the roots out. In this case, Mom observes the weed pulling while it is happening. She sees the result, but she watches and records the weed pulling. The best label for Mom's method of observing weed pulling is _____ recording. If Mom did not watch weed pulling but came back

later to count weeds pulled, then the best label would be _____ recording.

18. Do not count on always finding the word *instance* in the description of event recording. Instead, decide whether the observer is looking for a relatively uniform res-ponse. Suppose you count how often Lew says "thank you" when his parents pass him some food. You should label the method of observation as event recording because each "thank you" that Lew says takes about the same amount of time. Therefore, you are observing an _____ (instance, result) of behavior.

111. You observe each time Ted hits another child in preschool. Because each hit takes about the same amount of time, you are observing instances of the behavior. You are using what method of observation? _____ recording

89. Time for a review: Louise immediately recorded every time that Pablo said a new word. She learned that Pablo was saying new words at the rate of 2 a week. She was using what method of observation? _____ recording

41. More review: Dad saw that the gas gauge was now half empty rather than full. He knew that his son had driven the car while he was away on vacation. Dad was using what method of observation? _____ recording

94. Use the terms for specific methods of direct observation when possible. A question may ask you to name the <u>method</u> of observation whereby the observer immediately records all behavioral instances. It is _____ recording. The name of the <u>approach</u> to observation is _____.

### 3. Recording Behavior during Continuous Intervals

68. Pre-test: You observe Larry in preschool to see how much time he spends playing with other children. To do so, you break a 30-minute play period into 60 half-minute periods. You record during each interval whether Larry is playing with another child. You are using _____ recording.

50. Pre-test: Classify a method as interval recording only if the intervals are _____.

63. Pre-test: Tom and Sue observe the behavior of Joe, a bright fourth grader. They divided their 30 minute observation period into 20-second intervals. They made a check mark in each interval that they observed Joe studying. The name of the observational method is _____ _____ recording.

55. Pre-test: Interval recording: You record a response if the behavior occurs in one of a series of _____ intervals.

   The third method of observation is called *interval recording*. It is a method for observing nonuniform behaviors.

46. People normally don't engage in studying, reading, or watching TV steadily. They look away, go get a snack, or talk to someone at random times. Therefore, studying, reading, and watching TV are examples of behaviors that occur for _____ (uniform, nonuniform) periods of time.

86. The problem with nonuniform behavior is that each response can take _____ (different, identical) amounts of time.

105. You can produce meaningless data if you use event recording to observe nonuniform behavior. A better approach is to observe nonuniform behavior by dividing the observation period into intervals and using what method of observation? _____recording

10. Behavior analysts use <u>interval</u> recording to observe nonuniform behaviors by dividing the overall observation time into a series of <u>continuous</u> _____ of time.

101. When you observe using interval recording, you divide the observation period into a series of continuous intervals. Students often make errors when answering questions about interval recording because they misspell the word *continuous*. Copy the word here: _____.

36. Interval recording: You record a response if the behavior occurs in one of a series of _____ intervals.

92. To use interval recording, divide the overall observation period into a series of <u>continuous intervals</u>. Continuous intervals follow one another immediately. For instance, you divide an hour into 15-second intervals. When interval #1 stops, interval #2 immediately begins, and so on for the entire hour. If the intervals in an observation period follow one another immediately, they are _____ intervals.

113. You record an occurrence of a behavior in interval recording in four situations: (1) when the person starts the behavior within the interval, you record an occurrence; (2) when the person doesn't start the behavior within the interval but does finish it within the interval, you record an occurrence; (3) when the person starts the behavior prior to the interval and continues it past the end of the interval, you record an occurrence; and (4) when the person makes the complete response during the interval, you record an occurrence. A behavior is scored as an occurrence of a behavior in interval recording if any part of the behavior takes place within the _____.

116. You use interval recording to observe behaviors that are nonuniform in length. The overall observation period is then divided into a series of _____ (continuous, discontinuous) intervals of a convenient length.

78. Suppose you divide Jay's TV show into 15-second intervals to see how much time he spends telling funny stories in the monologue. Because the intervals are continuous, you would be using what method of observation? _____ _____ recording

77. Suppose you are observing the study behavior of a child. Suppose you want to watch the child from 4:00 to 5:00 in the afternoon. You divide the hour into a series of time intervals of a convenient length, perhaps 30 seconds. The 30-second intervals follow one another immediately. You then record for each of those 30-second intervals whether or not the child studies during any part of that interval. You are using interval

recording because the intervals are _____.

112. You observe Larry in preschool to see how much time he spends playing with other children. To do so, you break a 30-minute play period into 60 half-minute periods. You record during each interval whether Larry is playing with another child. You are using _____ recording.

15. Classify a method as interval recording only if the intervals are _____ _____.

7. Be very careful when trying to distinguish between interval recording and outcome recording! Suppose an observer looks for the "results" of a behavior every 30 minutes. Because the observation takes place after the behavior occurs, the observer is using what method of observation? _____ recording

82. The definition of interval recording requires only that you look for the behavior during continuous intervals. Does it also require that the behavior occur during each of those intervals? _____ (yes, no)

25. If an observer checks for a behavior during a series of 15-second intervals but the behavior does not occur during every interval, what method of observation is the observer using? _____ _____ recording The reason this is interval recording is that the observer looks for the behavior during each 15-second interval. The behavior does not have to occur during each interval.

12. Call the method of observation that looks for instances of a behavior _____ _____ recording. Call the method that looks for behavior during continuous intervals _____ recording. Call the method that looks for the results of a behavior _____ _____ recording.

### 4. Recording Behavior during Discontinuous Intervals

57. Pre-test: Recording behavior during discontinuous intervals is called _____ _____ recording.

52. Pre-test: If we observe Jane's aerobic exercising during a series of 15-second intervals, we are using _____ _____ recording.

53. Pre-test: If we observe John's lawn mowing during a series of randomly selected intervals, the method of observation is _____ recording.

62. Pre-test: Time sample recording: You record a response if the behavior occurs within one of a series of _____ _____ intervals.

85. The fourth method of observation is called *time sample recording*. It uses discontinuous intervals to observe nonuniform behavior. You may observe more than one behavior during discontinuous intervals by using the method called time _____ recording.

70. Recording behavior during discontinuous intervals is called _____ recording.

90. Time sample recording: You record a response if the behavior occurs within one of a series of _____ intervals.

97. When the beginning of one time interval does not begin at the end of the prior time interval, we call the intervals _____.

26. If the intervals used to observe one behavior are discontinuous, then the method is _____ recording. If the intervals used to observe one behavior are continuous, then the method is _____ recording.

79. Suppose you observe Tom watching TV and snacking with 30-second intervals. You observe TV watching during the first interval and snacking during the second interval. You return to observe TV watching during the third interval and then snacking during the fourth interval. You continue switching from one behavior to the other. During intervals 1, 3, 5, and 7 you observe TV watching. Thus, the intervals for observing TV watching _____ (are, aren't) continuous.

40. Let's talk more about observing two behaviors during 10-second intervals. You observe Behavior A during the odd

intervals such as 1, 3, 5, etc. You observe Behavior B during the even intervals such as 2, 4, 6, etc. Notice that overall you are observing continuously. The end of interval 1 is the beginning of interval 2 and so on. Because the intervals are continuous overall, you might be tempted to label this method interval recording. You would be wrong. Because the intervals for each behavior are discontinuous, the method of observing each behavior is called _____ recording.

99. When the method involves observing two behaviors (or two people) by switching back and forth between them, I will usually ask a very specific question. I will not ask "what is the method of observation" but rather "what is the method of observation for Behavior A." I will do that to call attention to the fact that the intervals for Behavior A in this situation are _____ (continuous, discontinuous).

76. Suppose you are answering a question about observing two or more behaviors. Suppose the intervals for Behavior A are discontinuous while the intervals overall are continuous. What method of observation is used to observe Behavior A? _____ recording

42. Mrs. Hobbs checks for 30 seconds to see if Willie is studying, then shifts to observe Diane for 30 seconds, and then returns to observe Willie again. Because she observes each of them for discontinuous 30-second intervals, she is using _____ recording to observe multiple people at the same time.

5. At another time, Mrs. Hobbs observes during each 30-second interval to see if Willie and Diane are both studying. So she observes one behavior, "group study behavior," for continuous 30-second intervals. Therefore, she is using _____ recording to observe a group during the same interval.

75. Suppose we observe John's lawn mowing for one interval, then do not observe him for four intervals while we observe other

individuals. Suppose we observe him again. This is an example of time sample recording because the intervals of observing John are _____.

29. If we observe John's lawn mowing during a series of randomly selected intervals, the method of observation is _____ recording.

20. Do not count on the word *interval* appearing in the description of time sample recording. Suppose a question reads: "You look for a few seconds every hour to see if Mary is partying." A few seconds makes up an "interval" even though the description may not say that. You look only during those few seconds every hour so that the periods of looking are _____ (continuous, discontinuous). Because you are looking for the partying behavior during intervals that are discontinuous, this is an example of time sample recording.

109. You look at Van's playing for a period of 20 seconds, then at Ann's playing, and finally at Jan's playing. What method of observing are you using to observe Van's playing? _____ recording

39. Let's do some review. Suppose we observe John's lawn mowing for one minute and then continue to observe his lawn mowing during the next minute and the next 30 one-minute intervals. What method of observation are we using? _____ recording

103. You are curious how often Verna eats. You briefly check on her eating every 30 minutes during the day. She's eating 76% of the times you check. What method of observation are you using? _____ recording

104. You are curious how much Verna eats. You give her a total of exactly 6 pounds of food each day. You weigh how much is left over three times a day (after each meal). You subtract to find out how much she eats. You find she eats an average of 5.8 pounds of food each day! What method of observation are you using? _____ recording

8. Be very careful when trying to distinguish between time sample recording

and outcome recording. Suppose an observer records "every hour" whether the behavior produced a "result." Because the observation takes place after the behavior occurs, the method of observation being used is _____ _____ recording.

35. In summary, behavior analysts use four methods of observation. When they record nonuniform behaviors during contitinuous intervals, we call it _____ _____ recording. When they record results after the behavior, we call it _____ recording. When they record nonuniform behavior during discontinuous intervals, we call it _____ recording. When they record instances of uniform behavior, we call it _____ _____ recording.

### 5. Another Tactic

60. Pre-test: The second tactic in using the behavioral strategy is to use the approach of _____ to gather information.

107. You can use the behavioral strategy to help change a problem behavior by (1) specifying what to observe by developing a behavioral definition and (2) gathering information by using the approach to observing called _____.

93. To use the behavioral strategy, (1) specify the behavior by creating a behavioral definition, then (2) gather information about the behavior by using the approach of _____ (direct observation, self-report observation).

88. The second tactic in using the behavioral strategy is to gather information by using the approach of _____ _____.

### 6. Review

51. Pre-test: Classify a method as interval recording only if the intervals are _____.

64. Pre-test: Tom and Sue observe the behavior of Joe, a bright fourth grader. They divided their 30-minute observation period into 20-second intervals.

They make a check mark in each interval they observe Joe studying. The name of the observational method is _____ recording.

61. Pre-test: The second tactic in using the behavioral strategy is to use one of the four methods based on the approach of _____.

47. Pre-test: Ben uses a golf wrist counter to record thoughts of sex. He was counting instances of uniform behaviors. He used what method of observation? _____ recording

67. Pre-test: When referring to a type of activity, I will use the word _____ _____. When referring to a single occurrence of an activity, I will use the word _____.

59. Pre-test: Suppose you observe once an hour whether the behavior produced the result. You are using what method of observation? _____ recording

98. When the beginning of one interval does not begin at the end of the prior interval, we call the intervals _____ _____.

16. Classify a method as event recording only if it involves observing _____ _____ of a behavior while the person is making them.

81. The behavior is observed while it happens for which three methods of observation? _____ recording, _____ recording, and _____ recording

11. Behavior is recorded during either continuous or discontinuous intervals for what two methods? _____ _____ recording and _____ _____ recording

17. Classify a method as outcome recording only if it looks for a _____ _____ of the behavior.

9. Behavior analysts observe nonuniform behaviors by dividing the overall observation time into short _____ _____.

45. One form of time sampling involves observing behavior during a series of _____ time intervals.

31. If you observe a behavior during a 30-minute observation period divided into sixty 30-second intervals and the behavior occurs only during some of those intervals, what method of observation are you using? _____ recording

102. Which of the following behavioral events would be scored as an occurrence in interval recording? (a) The person starts the behavior within the interval; (b) the person doesn't start the behavior within the interval but does finish it within the interval; (c) the person starts the behavior prior to the interval and continues it past the end of the interval; (d) the person makes the complete response during the interval; (e) all of the above. _____

27. If the observer records a response only when she sees the result of an instance of some behavior, what method is she using? _____ recording

84. The first tactic in using the behavioral strategy to solve human problems is to create a(n) _____ of the problem behavior.

33. If you score a response occurrence each time an instance of behavior has been observed, what method are you using? _____ recording

28. If we observe John for 10 minutes in 40 intervals each 15 seconds long, what method are we using? _____ recording

30. If we observe one individual for brief intervals separated by a considerable amount of time, what method is being used? _____ recording

91. To find out what method of observation is being used, you need to remember three words. First, you ask: "Does this method involve time _____?" If it does involve intervals, ask, "Does this method involve _____ time intervals?" If it doesn't involve intervals, ask: "Does this method involve the _____ of a behavior?"

106. You can use the behavioral strategy to help change a problem behavior by (1) developing a(n) _____ and (2) using the approach to observing called _____ to gather information about the behavior.

2. A statement that specifies exactly what to observe is called a(n) _____ definition; the science that studies environmental events that change behavior is called _____ analysis.

## Programmed Examples

### 1. Programmed Examples

14. Pre-test: It's time to mix in some review questions from earlier lessons. Fran observed Professor Young to see how arrogant he was. She decided that she would record every time that the professor said to a student "No, you're wrong." The statement "arrogant behavior is saying 'No, you're wrong'" is a(n) _____.

15. Pre-test: Mary was concerned about the rampant sexism appearing in TV shows. She wanted to write a paper about it containing specific numbers showing how much sexism was occurring. Since she did not have time to watch every show all the way through, she arranged to observe for 10 randomly scheduled intervals of 10 seconds each during each program. She was using what method of observation? _____ recording

12. Pre-test: Al wanted to find out how much of the class period his child spent studying in math class. He went to school and observed whether his child was studying during each 20-second period of the math class. He used what method of observation? _____ recording

13. Pre-test: Fred was interested in the extent to which people were positive and supportive of one another in casual interactions. His sociology professor suggested that he use a questionnaire approach and ask people how often they were positive toward other people. Fred wanted better information than that, however, so he recorded only what he personally heard and saw at the time of the observation. Because Fred immediately recorded what he personally heard and saw, he was using what approach to observation? _____

3. David took English 159 from Professor McNault. He wanted a discussion course. David divided the class into one hundred 30-second intervals. He observed all intervals and noted

those in which the professor talked. The professor talked during 65% of the intervals. You can analyze David's method of observation by asking two questions. Remember the first question by the key word *interval*. That word reminds you to answer the question, "Does David's method involve looking for the behavior during intervals?" _____ (yes, no) Once you've answered the first question, then remember "continuous/result." If your first answer was "yes," then your key word is "continuous." That reminds you to answer the question, "Does the method use continuous intervals?" ___ (yes, no) Since your answer was "yes," you can conclude that he used _____ recording.

8. John was terrible in spelling. Mr. Wilson counted the number of correct answers in John's book. You can analyze Mr. Wilson's method of observation by asking two questions. Remember the first question by the key word *interval*. That word reminds you to answer the question, "Does Mr. Wilson's method involve looking for the behavior during intervals?" ___ (yes, no) Once you've answered the first question, then remember "continuous/result." If your first answer was "no", then your key word is *results*. That reminds you to answer the question, "Does the method observe the result of behavior?" ___ (yes, no) Since your answer was "yes," you can conclude that he used _____ recording.

16. Ted felt that the cooperative dorm should not buy a new couch because nobody ever used the living room. To prove this, Ted visited the living room for a brief time every 15 minutes to observe whether anyone was sitting there. You can analyze Ted's method of observation by asking two questions. Answer the first question that the key word *interval* reminds you of: ___. Once you've answered the first question, then remember "continuous/result." Pick the correct key word based on your answer. Answer the second question that the key word reminds you of: ___. The intervals of observation are not continuous because you look for a brief time and then you don't look again for 15 minutes. You can conclude that Ted used _____ recording.

7. John got a B on his essay paper because he had used one split infinitive. The professor told him that the essay was excellent but that his incorrect English had cost him an A. John counted the number of times that he heard the professor use a split infinitive during his lectures. He found that the professor had split his infinitives seven times during five class periods. John gave him a C. You can analyze John's method of observation by asking two questions. Answer the first question that the key word *interval* reminds you of: ___. Once you've answered the first question, then remember "continuous/result." Pick the correct key word based on your answer. Answer the second question that the key word reminds you of ___. You can conclude that John used _____ recording.

17. The Bales wanted to teach their 5-year-old daughter to make her bed and clean her room every day. She was supposed to do this right after school. To find out if she cleaned her room, the Bales checked her room every day to see whether the bed was made, the floor swept, the trash taken out, and all toys put away. You can analyze the Bales's method of observation by asking two questions. First, remember "interval: continuous/result." Answer the first question the key word reminds you of: ___. Once you've answered the first question, pick the correct key word for the second and answer it: ___. You can conclude that the Bales used _____ recording.

6. Heddy observed littering in a local park. She began by watching four families at the same time. She observed family #1 for 15 seconds. Then, she switched to family #2 for 15 seconds. Then, she observed family #3. Finally, she observed family #4. After she watched each family once, she started over again. You can analyze Heddy's method of observation by asking two questions. First, remember "interval: continuous/result." Answer the first question the key word reminds you of: ___. Once you've answered the first question, pick the correct key word for the second and answer it: ___. You can conclude that Heddy observed Family #1 by what method of observation? _____ recording

11. Mary and Rex decided that Ronny dominated the meetings of their committee. They decided to measure his domination and report their results at a future meeting of the committee. They recorded when Ronny talked during a 15-second interval of the meeting. They found

that he spoke during 76% of the intervals. You can analyze Mary and Rex's method of observation by asking two questions. First, remember "interval: continuous/result." Answer the first question that the key word reminds you of: _____. Once you've answered the first question, pick the correct key word for the second and answer it: _____. You can conclude that Mary and Rex used _____ recording.

4. Dee worried that Alice was bullying her son at school. She recorded whether Alice bullied her son in the classroom during a series of 15-second intervals while they were on the playground. She found that Alice bullied her son about 23% of the time. You can analyze Dee's method of observation by asking two questions. First, remember the clue. Answer the first question that the key word reminds you of: _____. Once you've answered the first question, pick the correct key word for the second and answer it: _____. You can conclude that Dee used _____ recording.

18. The Cooperative Dorm had successfully set up programs for keeping the dorm clean, but they hadn't been very successful in keeping the house repaired. They decided to pay cash for each repair job completed. They decided on the amount of pay for each job by inspecting to see how well the damaged area had been repaired. Analyze their method of observation by remembering the clue and then asking the questions. What method of observation did they use to decide on payments? _____ recording

5. Don went to counseling because he constantly got his feelings hurt by others. Dr. Barton decided that Don was an expert at seeing every situation from the point of view of how the other person might not like him. However, he was poor at seeing other aspects of the situation. Dr. Barton taught Don how to seek out other aspects of situations in which his feelings got hurt. He then suggested that he count each time that he could describe other aspects of a situation that caused him to have hurt feelings. What method of observation was Don using? _____ recording

2. Being a bit of a gossip, you want to know how often John has his girl friend in his room, so you make a note every time that you see her visit. You would be using what method of observation? _____ recording

19. To decide whether the public areas of a dorm have been cleaned well enough, you might make a checklist of things that should be clean (such as floors, ashtrays, trash baskets, and so on) and check once a day to see whether they are clean. You would be using what method of observing? _____ recording

20. Your living group is having trouble with Selma griping during the dinner hour. You sit at the dinner table and note whether she is griping during each 30-second interval. You would be using what method of observing? _____ recording

10. Martha wants to determine the actual amount of violence on prime-time TV. She decides to record every scene in which there is a weapon (gun, knife, and so on) present, every scene that involves physical assault on a person, and all scenes in which one person is yelling in anger at another as constituting "violence." By describing exactly what she is going to observe, Martha is stating a(n) _____.

1. Barb was a new student senator. She was very concerned that parliamentary procedure was not being followed when the chairperson's friends wanted to get something done. She counted the number of times that a motion was passed without fully observing correct procedure. She noted an average of about three per meeting. What method of observation was Barb using? _____ recording

9. Maria got reports each Friday from Mrs. Green about how sociable her daughter Lucy was at school. Maria did not tell Mrs. Green exactly what she meant by sociability. She simply asked Mrs. Green to describe Lucy's sociability for the whole week as well as she could remember. What approach to observation did Maria use to observe Lucy's sociability? _____ observations

# Reliability and Validity of Everyday Observations

## Reading Section

You've learned the first two tactics in using the behavioral strategy to help solve human problems. First, you create a behavioral definition of what you want to study. Second, you use a method of direct observation to study it. When those tactics don't solve the problem, you may need to use the third tactic. The third tactic is to check the <u>reliability</u> and <u>social validity</u> of your observations. Reliability is a measure of the accuracy of your observations. Social validity is a measure of whether you are observing what you are really interested in. If your observations are not reliable and socially valid, you may be getting inaccurate or useless information. Improving your information may lead to a solution for the problem.

1. The third tactic in using the behavioral strategy is to check the reliability and social _____ of your observations.

(If you have trouble dividing 3 by 8 or 91 by 20, you should borrow a calculator for this lesson.)

## Repeated Observations

The most basic question about an observation is whether you can <u>repeat</u> it. By repeat it, I mean get the same value. Suppose you measure the length of a table and find it is 36 inches long. You would have little trust in that length if you measured twice more and got 35 and then 38 inches. Suppose you measure the amount that a child studies during one hour and find 90%. You would have little trust in that amount if you measured two more days and found 25% and 99%. While a certain amount of change is OK, large changes undermine your trust.

Behavior analysts measure people's behavior for many days until it reaches a <u>stable</u> level. If a person is learning a new task, their skill may improve for days before it becomes stable. For example, Kate, a 12-year-old girl with retardation, almost never responded to questions. Behavior analysts gave her special training. She learned very slowly to respond to more questions. She took over 35 days to reach her maximum level (Krantz & McClannahan, 1993). Normal adults may also take time to learn new behaviors. Teachers were still improving their performance 10 days after learning an innovative teaching method (Ingham & Greer, 1992). Police were instructed to ticket parents who failed to put their infants in car safety seats (Lavelle, Hovell, West, & Wahlgren, 1992). They were still increasing the rate of ticketing six months after adoption of the new procedure.

These examples suggest that many factors may influence behavior in a complex situation. A clear picture of the total effect of these factors may take days and weeks to emerge. Thus, behavior analysts often observe behavior for long periods of time. Behavior analysts get data they can trust by repeating their observations many times.

This practice contrasts with the methods often used by other approaches to human behavior. They often involve interviewing a person for an hour to learn about that person's behavior. They often ask a person to take a few minutes answering a questionnaire. People are far too complex for this approach to work very well. Measurements taken for a few minutes don't deal with this complexity.

Researchers may find it easier to make only one observation. They may find it easier to observe people for a short period of time. However, the result will be that they won't get data that they can <u>trust</u>.

## Reliability and Accuracy

Applied behavior analysts use direct observations made by human observers to learn about behavior. Can observations made by human observers be trusted? Are they accurate? Behavior analysts have found no way to measure the <u>accuracy</u> of their data directly. To understand why, suppose that you want to observe how often Don says "ain't" in a conversation. You might observe Don for an hour and count 27 "ain'ts," but how can you be sure that Don said "ain't" 27 times? You might record what Don says. You might then count the "ain'ts" from the tape. Surely, you think, that would be exact. But suppose that you count 23 "ain'ts" on the tape. Which count is correct? Don might have said four "ain'ts" too softly for the tape. You could ignore soft responses and have another observer count from the tape recording. If she counts 25 "ain'ts," which of you is right? She might hear Don say "She ain't it" where you heard "She ate it." There is no way to find out exactly how many times Don said "ain't." You can never compare your count with the "real" count to find your accuracy.

Behavior analysts have solved this problem by measuring accuracy indirectly. They compare observations of the same responses made by two independent observers using the same behavioral definition. They assume that the more the observers agree, the more accurate the observations. In other words, agreement between two observers is evidence of accuracy. Behavior analysts call this agreement *reliability*. **Reliability** is the <u>agreement</u> between two independent observers.

2. Reliability is the _____ between two independent observers.
3. The agreement between two independent observers is called their _____.

Measuring reliability requires two conditions. The two observers must use the same behavioral definition. They must observe the same <u>responses</u>.

First, both observers must use the same <u>behavioral definition</u> of the behavior. Suppose that Carl and Jane agree on the following behavioral definition of reading: "John looks at the book and makes eye sweeps from one side of the page to the other." Perhaps they both note that John reads during the first interval. Their agreement suggests that John was really reading. On the other hand, suppose that Carl used his behavioral definition whereas Jane used a different behavioral definition. Jane's definition might be "John sits in front of an open book." Agreement between Carl and Jane doesn't suggest that John was making eye sweeps during the first interval. Maybe Carl made a mistake while Jane noted that John was sitting in front of the book! Their agreement would no longer be evidence that they were both carefully observing.

Second, both observers must observe the same <u>responses</u>. Suppose Carl and Jane use the same behavioral definition. Perhaps Carl finds John reading at 9:00 A.M. Perhaps Jane finds John reading the next day at 9:00. Perhaps not. Either way, Jane's finding doesn't help us guess whether Carl's finding is accurate. Their agreement does not tell us anything about what John was really doing.

4. Measuring reliability requires that the observers use the same _____ _____ and that they observe the same _____.

Reliability comes in two forms (Martin & Pear, 1999). I will call one form <u>trial reliability</u> and the other form <u>frequency reliability</u>. Behavior analysts use trial reliability when they can compare each observation of two observers. They use frequency reliability when they can only compare the total observations.

## Computing Trial Reliability

*Trial reliability* compares <u>each</u> observation of the two observers. The name arises because we call every chance to observe the behavior a *trial*. One example of a trial is every time a pitcher throws a ball to the batter. We have

**Figure 4-1.** Even skilled craftsmen have to measure and remeasure their work to get it right. Hence the old saying, "Measure twice, cut once!" Accurate, repeatable measurement is important in all fields. (Source: Addison Geary/Stock, Boston)

**Figure 4-2.** Two umpires huddle to discuss a call. Believe it or not, players and coaches sometimes disagree with their observations! Huddling with another umpire provides a check on reliability. (Source: Bob Daemmrich/Stock Boston)

the chance to observe whether the batter hits it well (e.g., Osborne & Himadi, 1990). Another example is every question directed at a student. We can then see whether the student can answer the question (e.g., Secan, Egel, & Tilley, 1989). The pitch and the question create a "trial" of the person's behavior. Each trial permits two observers to use the same behavioral definition on the same responses. They can then compare their observations to find out if they agreed. Trial reliability is the most rigorous form of reliability.

5. Trial reliability compares _____ observation of the two observers.

You find trial reliability by counting the number of agreements and disagreements between the two observers. Trial reliability is the percentage of the total number of trials that are agreements between two independent

observers. Here is the formula. Use "A" to stand for the number of agreements. Use "D" to stand for the number of disagreements. Use "x" to stand for "times." Then the formula for reliability is $\underline{100\% \times A/(A+D)}$ (Araujo & Born, 1985). In other words, you multiply 100% times the agreements. You divide by the sum of the agreements and disagreements. Note that agreements plus disagreements equal the total number of trials. Note also that the parentheses require that you add agreements and disagreements before dividing.

6. Trial reliability is the percentage of the total number of trials that are _____ between two independent observers.

You cannot use trial reliability with outcome or event recording of simple behaviors. These methods lead to a total count, but they don't produce a trial-by-trial record. You can

| Reliability of interval observations | | | | | |
|---|---|---|---|---|---|
| Interval | 1 | 2 | 3 | 4 | 5 |
| Johnathon | R | Ⓡ | R | R | N |
| MaryEllen | R | Ⓝ | R | R | N |

***Figure 4-3.*** Johnathon's and MaryEllen's agreement on whether they saw Juan reading his history book during five continuous intervals of 30 seconds each. "R" means that the observer saw Juan reading. "N" means that the observer saw that Juan was not reading. This figure exemplifies how the observations made by two observers can be compared in order to compute reliability.

use trial reliability with these methods only when observing complex behaviors with a checklist. You can then compare each item on the checklist as though it were one trial.

You can always use trial reliability with <u>interval</u> and <u>time sample</u> recording. That is because each interval defines a trial. You can compare the records of two observers interval by interval. The only complication is that the two observers must start each interval at the same time. Researchers do this with a signal that both observers can hear.

For example, suppose that Johnathon and MaryEllen observe how much Juan reads his history book while the TV is on. They define reading as "Juan looks at the book and makes eye sweeps from one side of the page to the other during 15-second intervals." Figure 4-3 shows their first five observations.

7. Both sets of observations shown in Figure 4-3 agree that Juan read in the first, third, and fourth intervals. They agree that he did not read in the fifth interval. Their observations agree for these four intervals. However, they disagree on whether Juan read during the second interval. Johnathon recorded that Juan was reading while MaryEllen recorded that he was not. Notice the circle around the observations that _____ (agree, disagree). (Researchers find it helpful to circle observations on which they differ when asked to compute reliability—you might do the same.)

8. The reliability of observations in Figure 4-3 equals 100% times the number of agreements (4) divided by agreements and disagreements (4+1). In algebraic form

| Reliability of outcome checklist | | | | | |
|---|---|---|---|---|---|
| Items | Knife | Fork | Spoon | Plate | Glass |
| Ann | yes | yes | not | yes | not |
| Bob | not | yes | not | yes | not |

***Figure 4-4.*** Ann and Bob's agreement on whether items were set on the table. "Yes" indicates that the table setter placed the item. "Not" indicates that the table setter did not place the item.

that is: $100\% \times A/(A+D) = 100\% \times 4/(4+1)$. That formula equals 100% times 4 divided by the sum ____. Finally, 4/5 equals 80% reliability.

You can also use trial reliability with complex outcome data involving a checklist. For example, suppose that two members of a cooperative dorm observe how well the table setter does their job. They might observe five outcomes: placement of a knife, 2 forks, spoon, plate, and glass. Figure 4-4 shows an example of using trial reliability with a <u>checklist</u> of these five outcomes.

9. Figure 4-4 lets you compute trial reliability. Circle the pairs of observations that do not agree. Then use the formula for reliability, $100\% \times A/(A+D)$ to get $100\% \times 4/(4+1)$. That formula equals 100% times ____ divided by the sum ____. Thus the reliability is 80%.

You can also use trial reliability for an event-recording checklist. Suppose two observers record whether a tutor did each task on a checklist. Professor Sloan may have told the tutor to greet students, smile, probe them with questions, praise their correct answers, record their score, and then tell them their grade. This simple list of chores may yield better tutoring than leaving tutors on their own (Weaver & Miller, 1975). Figure 4-5 shows what the record for the two observers might look like.

10. Figure 4-5 lets have you analyze this case yourself by circling and then counting disagreements. Use the formula $100\% \times A/(A+D)$ to compute reliability. The formula for these observations equals 100% times ____ (enter number of agreements) divided by ____ (enter number of agreements plus disagreements). Thus reliability equals 50%.

| Reliability of an event checklist | | | | | | |
|------|--------|--------|--------|--------|--------|-------|
| Chores | Greets | Smiles | Probes | Praise | Record | Grade |
| Mark | not | yes | yes | not | yes | not |
| Jan | not | not | yes | yes | yes | yes |

***Figure 4-5.*** Mark and Jan's agreement on whether a tutor emitted each of six behaviors needed to correctly tutor a student. "Yes" means that the observer saw the tutor emit the behavior and "not" means that the observer saw that the tutor did not emit the behavior.

## Computing Frequency Reliability

You cannot use trial reliability when using outcome or event recording with a simple behavior. Both methods yield a count of frequency of the behavior. For example, you might find that the Fat Lady left 753 candy bar wrappers in her dressing room on Wednesday morning. Even if Tom reports exactly 753 wrappers, we have no way of knowing whether he counted the same wrappers. We do not know if you and he agree on each wrapper.

In the same way, you might observe that Hal smiled 50 times on Monday. Suppose Ann reports 40 smiles. You both might have observed the same 40 smiles, with Ann missing 10 smiles. On the other hand, Ann might have observed 40 smiles that you did not observe. Since this is extremely unlikely, we usually assume that she simply missed some of the ones that you saw.

"Frequency reliability" compares the total count between two observers. It is used when each observation cannot be compared, such as with simple outcome or simple event recording. You can't find the exact agreement between the observers when you work only with the total count. Therefore, we assume that the overlap in the two counts represents agreement. We assume that nonoverlap represents disagreement. In the case of the observations of the Fat Lady, reliability would be 100%x753/(753+0) or 100%. In the case of Hal and Ann, reliability would be 100%x40/(40+10) or 80%. Behavior analysts assume that the 40 observations that you and Ann report are agreements. They assume that the 10 smiles that you reported and Ann didn't are disagreements.

11. Frequency reliability compares the total _____ between two observers.

The formula for frequency reliability is the same as trial reliability: 100%xA/(A+D). Notice that this amounts to dividing the larger number into the smaller number. This form of reliability is less rigorous. You do not compare the observers as closely.

## Goal for Reliability

Most researchers aim for a reliability of <u>90%</u> or more. However, they may accept less with a new behavioral definition for subtle or complex behavior. This book accepts a figure of 80% or more for such "new" behavioral definitions. Be sure to read each example to find out if the behavioral definition is "new" or whether it is "old." You may assume that an example involves an "old" behavioral definition unless otherwise specified.

12. Most researchers aim for a reliability of _____% except for new behavioral definitions for which they usually accept 80%.

Suppose you observe whether 4-year-old Dave engages in anxious behavior when the dentist works on his teeth. You might define "anxious" as "he moved his head or body more than a half inch or cried or complained." If you made this behavioral definition yourself, then it would be a new behavioral definition. This behavioral definition is fairly complicated. It requires the observer to notice three different aspects of Dave's behavior. The observer must notice movements of Dave's head, his crying, and his complaining. Therefore, you can be satisfied with 80% or greater reliability. However, suppose you got this behavioral definition from the work of Stark, Allen, Hurst, Nash, Rigney, and Stokes (1989). Then, it would be an old behavioral definition. You would have the benefits of their experience in developing a workable behavioral definition. If you used their behavioral definition, then you should seek a 90% reliability or greater. Remember, if you're inventing it, seek 80%; if you're adapting from someone else, seek 90%. If it's old, seek 90%; if it's new, seek 80%.

Behavior analysts often do not attain the goal on their first try. Often, they must refine their behavioral definition before observers can reliably agree. Sometimes they must train their observers longer or give more examples. If you don't attain the goal, you must revise your observational system until you do.

## Social Validity of Behavioral Definitions

Applied behavior analysts often observe complex and subtle aspects of human behavior. The resulting behavioral definitions are not always obvious to the average person. Wolf (1978) suggested that behavior analysts measure the "social validity" of such behavioral definitions (cf. Kazdin, 1977a; see Bosch & Fuqua, 2001). **Social validity** is the correlation between ratings by outside judges and observations by trained observers. By correlating the ratings of a behavior by outside judges with the observations of trained observers, we can see if the common meaning of the behavior matches our behavioral definition. We call them outside judges because they view the behavior from "outside" the behavioral definition. They help us understand what normal adults mean by a word.

13. Social validity is the _____ between ratings by outside judges and observations by trained observers.
14. The correlation of rating by outside judges and observations by trained observers is called social _____.

Imagine that an observer trained to use a particular behavioral definition observes a trial. They either record a response, or they record a nonresponse according to the behavioral definition. Meanwhile, an outside judge observes the same trial. They report whether they saw an example of that behavior. Since they are not using the behavioral definition, their report would reflect the common understanding of what is an example of that behavior. If the observer and the outside judge observed many trials together, we could find out whether or not their observations correlated. If they

did, then the behavioral definition would have social validity. If they did not, then the behavioral definition would lack social validity.

For example, suppose that you defined smiling as "lips parted with teeth showing and the edges of the mouth upturned." You might train an observer to look at a photo of Mary and use the behavioral definition to decide if she were smiling. You might have an outside judge do the same without the behavioral definition. You could repeat this with many photos of Mary. I am sure you can imagine many facial expressions that meet the behavioral definition but that someone not using it would not judge to be smiles. Certainly the lips can be parted, the teeth showing, and the edges of the mouth upturned while showing disdain, superiority, perhaps even hatred. The trained observer and the outside judge might well disagree on photos of such expressions. We might expect the trained observer and the outside judge to agree on some smiles, agree on some nonsmiles, but to disagree on at least some photos. If their observations mostly did correlate, then we would conclude that the behavioral definition has pretty good social validity. If their observations mostly did not correlate, then we would conclude that the behavioral definition has poor social validity.

Researchers usually use a modification of this procedure to measure social validity (e.g., Feldman, Condillac, Tough, Hunt, & Griffiths, 2002). They try to create a "low behavior situation" and a "high behavior situation." They train their observer to observe the behavior in both situations according to the behavioral definition. However, they do not ask the outside observer to report on each instance of the behavior. Rather they ask the outside judge to give an overall rating of the behavior in both situations. They then correlate the detailed count by the observer with the overall rating by the outside judge.

For example, the researchers might find someone who didn't smile very often because they were depressed. They would have their trained observer look for smiles from this person during an observation period. They would have the outside judge rate how often the person smiled during that same period

***Figure 4-6.*** Wine tasters judge the characteristics and acceptability of a batch of wine. They are judging its social validity. (Source: Jean Claude LeJeune/ Stock, Boston)

of time. Then they would help the person solve their depression, perhaps over many days, weeks or even months. They would then again have the trained observer look for smiles while the outside judge rated how often the person smiled.

The researchers might find that the observer saw three smiles during an hour of observation before helping with the depression. The outside judge might give a rating of "few smiles" during the same period. After treating the person for depression, the observer might see 29 smiles during an hour of observation. The outside judge might give a rating of "many smiles" during the same period. Although this approach does not show a smile-by-smile correlation, it does show a correlation between the trained observer's observations and the outside judges' ratings. It provides evidence that the behavioral definition captures much of the meaning of "smile" held by everyday people. It provides evidence of social validity.

Fawcett and Miller (1975) provide a real example of this approach. They developed a behavioral definition of "good public speaking." Their behavioral definition of public speaking

had several parts. They guessed that good public speaking takes a high rate of eye contact with the audience. It takes animated gestures. It takes a central position on stage. It takes greeting the audience. The researchers specified these and a number of other behaviors. As you can see, their behavioral definition is debatable. Maybe it misses some very important but subtle aspects of being a good public speaker. This raises the question of social validity. The researchers answered the question by measuring the social validity of their behavioral definition.

The researchers used two steps to validate their behavioral definition. First, they had someone who they thought was low in good public-speaking behaviors talk to an audience. Their trained observer found that the speaker performed few of the good public-speaking behaviors. The researchers then asked the members of the audience to serve as outside judges. These outside judges rated the person as a "poor" speaker. Second, they trained the speaker to engage in the good public-speaking behaviors. They had the person speak to another audience, during which time the observer found that the person engaged in more of the required behaviors. They found that the audience now rated the speaker as "good." Thus they found a correlation between the amount of the speaking behaviors found by the observers and the ratings given by the audience. This correlation suggests that the behavioral definition caught the audiences' more subjective and unspecified meaning. Note that the members of each audience were "outside judges"— they were not behavior analysts.

You know that behavior analysts rely on direct observation. They rarely use questionaires. One of the rare times they use questionnaires is to measure social validity (see Kennedy, 2002). They use questionnaires to find out how outside judges rate their behavioral definition. They regard the ratings as a sample of what the outside judges say about the behavior (e.g., Elliott & Fuqua, 2002). If the ratings agree with the observations, then the behavioral definition is socially valid. The behavior analyst does not study the rating to infer an inner cause.

Social validity has found a permanent place in behavior analysis (Fuqua & Schwade, 1986). It provides evidence that the behavioral definition is or is not reasonable.

## Summary

This lesson taught you the third tactic in using the behavioral strategy to help solve human problems. The third tactic is to check for reliability and social validity. This lesson taught you how to check for accuracy by measuring reliability. Reliability assumes that two observers use the same behavioral definition to observe the same responses. You can use trial reliability to compare two observers' reactions to the same trial. You can use frequency reliability when each observer produces only a total count. Both forms multiply 100% times agreements over agreements plus disagreements. You can write the formula as $100\% \times A/(A+D)$. You should seek 90% agreement with old behavioral definitions and 80% with new ones. This lesson taught you how to check the social validity of your observations. Social validity is the extent that ratings by outside judges correlate with observations based on your behavioral definition.

## Behavior Analysis Examples

### Social Skills

Some people seem born with smooth social skills. We often wish our own skills were better. Too often we assume that our present level is "just the way we are." Behavior analysts have tried to define many of these skills behaviorally. If they can define them behaviorally, then they can help people learn them. For example, Quinn and his colleagues defined the parts of "accepting criticism." Nonverbal parts include facing the critic, not moving away from them, keeping eye contact,

---

### Thinking May Involve Tiny Muscular Movements

Delprato (1977) had people hold a pendulum above three words and think about one of them. They usually swung the pendulum toward that word without being aware of it! "Thinking" involved "making tiny movements toward the selected word." It may also involve tiny movements of the speech apparatus, looking toward the word and focusing on it, and activation of brain responses. All of these responses, and more, are involved in thinking about the selected word. No single one of them, such as the brain response, is by itself "thinking" about the selected word. Behavior analysts label thinking as a behavior because it involves these active and potentially observable responses. Is this a reasonable label?

15. Suppose you found that when these responses are present, people report "thinking" about the word. You would be using these people as outside judges to measure the social _____ of calling these responses thinking.

keeping a neutral expression, and having a straight posture. Verbal parts include paraphrasing the criticism, apologizing when appropriate, asking for suggestions, and accepting feedback. Other parts include using a normal voice, not making angry statements, and not interrupting.

Most people are tempted to ask, "Can you define a subtle skill like accepting criticism with such simple behaviors?" Quinn and colleagues decided to find out. They videotaped scenes in which one roommate criticized the other. Sixty-one adult judges rated "how well the person handled the situation." When the roommates performed all the behaviors well, the outside judges rated them as quite acceptable (6 on a 7-point scale). When the roommates performed all the behaviors poorly, the outside judges rated them as unacceptable (1.5 out of 7). When the roommates performed only one area badly, like the nonverbal parts, the outside judges gave a moderate rating (about 4 out of 7). Thus, the outside judge's ratings correlated with the performance of these behaviors. This means that these behaviors do indeed define the subtle skill of accepting criticism.

16. The correlation between the performance of the behaviors and the ratings by <u>outside judges</u> shows that Quinn's behavioral definition of skilled acceptance of criticism has _____ validity. (Based on Quinn, Sherman, Sheldon, Quinn, & Harchik, 1992.)

### *Cooperation with Dentists*

Children seldom want to visit the dentist. During visits they may be very uncooperative. Williams and his colleagues set up a way to observe this behavior in 1983. They observed uncooperative behavior during 15-second intervals. They defined four types of uncooperative behavior: head movements, body movements, complaining, or any behavior that led the dental assistant to restrain the child. They found that two observers agreed 84% of the time. This was good for a new behavioral definition. Researchers refined the behavioral definition in 1987 and found 85% agreement. Other researchers revised it again in 1992 and found 93% agreement. This was good for an old behavioral definition. Many behavioral definitions are revised many times before observers reach high reliability.

17. When Williams compared the <u>agreement</u> between two observers on noncooperative behavior, he was measuring the _____ (reliability, social validity) of the observations. (Based on articles by Williams, Hurst, & Stokes, 1983; Allen & Stokes, 1987; and Allen, Loiben, Allen, & Stanley, 1992.)

### *Conversational Skills*

Conversing in a skillful way might seem even more difficult to define behaviorally than accepting criticism. Minkin and his colleagues studied a group of 12- to 14-year old girls with poor conversational skills. They defined three parts of skilled conversational behavior. One part is asking many conversational questions. Another is providing positive conversational feedback. The last one is talking a reasonable amount. They defined each component carefully. For example, they defined "providing positive conversational feedback." It is "three or fewer words that approve, concur with, or understand what the other conversant is saying." They tested whether this behavioral definition captured what most people regard as skilled conversation. They videotaped conversations showing high or low rates of the three behaviors. They showed these videotapes to a cross section of adults and asked them to rate the conversational skills of the girls. When the three behaviors were high, the ratings were high. When the behaviors were low, the ratings were low.

18. The <u>correlation</u> between the observed amount of three conversational behaviors and the ratings of conversational skill by outside judges shows that their behavioral definition has _____ (reliability, social validity). (Based on Minkin, Braukmann, Minkin, & Timbers, 1976.)

## Notes

### *Note #1*

This lesson provides only a brief introduction to reliability. It is a critical issue in behavior analysis. Kelly found that 94% of all articles published in one journal report <u>reliability</u> (Kelly, 1977). Most behavior analysts see it as a major aspect defining behavior analysis (e.g., Kazdin, 1975). Part of the spring 1977 issue of the *Journal of Applied Behavior Analysis* discusses additional aspects of reliability.

19. Kelly found that 94% of all articles published in one journal report _____ _____ among observers.

### Note #2
Sometimes you must provide added information about reliability. Sometimes you must compare the obtained reliability with chance reliability (Harrop, Foulkes, & Daniels, 1989). Sometimes you must compute the reliability of the intervals in which at least one observer records the behavior (e.g., Hopkins & Hermann, 1977).

20. Sometimes you must provide added information about _____.

### Note #3
Behavior analysts may use <u>social validity</u> to validate more than the behavioral definition. They may use it to evaluate the social appropriateness of intervention procedures. They may also use it to evaluate the social importance of the effects of behavioral procedures (e.g., Twohig & Woods, 2001). Schwartz and Baer (1991) argue that the most important use of social validity is to ensure survival of behavioral programs.

21. Behavior analysts may evaluate the social appropriateness of intervention procedures by asking outside judges to rate the intervention. They would be evaluating the _____ of the intervention.

### Note #4
Social validity is becoming a routine part of behavior analysis. Schwartz and Baer (1991) report that 29% of behavior analysis articles surveyed used some measure of social validity.

23. Although reliability is reported by more than 90% of research articles, social validity is reported by only _____%.

---

### Social Validity of Different Treatments

Alan Kazdin invented a clever way to find the social validity of different treatments. He described a normal 5-year-old who didn't follow mom's instructions, and he described a 10-year-old child with mental retardation who was disruptive in class. He asked students to read his descriptions and then to act as outside judges of the acceptability of four treatments. He found the order of acceptability to be reinforcement, isolation, drugs, and shock. This suggests that the behavioral procedures are more acceptable than psychiatric drug treatments (Kazdin, 1980).

22. The ratings by the outside judges are a measure of the _____ _____ (reliability, social validity) of the treatment.

---

## Helpful Hints

### Helpful Hint #1
Remember, when you are answering questions, you must assume that the behavioral definition is old. The questions will have two exceptions. One exception is when the question tells you that the behavioral definition is new. Another is when the question tells you that the observers developed it. Never assume that the observers developed it unless the book tells you. I will give many examples where the reliability is 80% or 85%. The correct answer to questions about these examples will depend on whether the behavioral definition is old or new. So be ready!

24. Remember, when analyzing examples and quizzes, always assume that the behavioral definition is _____. You must assume that the behavioral definition is old unless the question or example clearly states that it is _____.

### Helpful Hint #2
Here's a hint about how to tell reliability from social validity. If an example involves

agreement between two observers, that agreement is called *reliability*. The goal is to find out whether the observers can use the same behavioral definition to score the same responses in the same way. On the other hand, if the example involves the correlation between one observer and one or more outside judges, the correlation is called *social validity* The goal is to find out whether the observer's behavioral definition points to the same responses as does the outside judge's commonsense definition.

25. If an example involves the correlation between one trained observer and one or more outside judges, that correlation is called _____. If an example involves agreement between two observers, that agreement is called _____.

Remember, agreement between two observers is reliability. Correlation between outside judges and an observer is social validity.

### Helpful Hint #3

The formula for reliability is 100%x A/(A+D). The formula has only two parts. First, the "100%" means simply that you are converting the fraction that follows to a percentage. The uncapitalized letter "x" stands for multiplication. It means you are multiplying the fraction times the 100% to make it into a percentage. Second, the fraction "A/(A+D)" means you are dividing the number of agreements by the sum of the agreements plus the disagreements. If you have one agreement and one disagreement, then you multiply 100% times the fraction "1 divided by (1 plus 1)." Of course you can simplify that by adding (1 plus 1) to get 2. Then you have 100% times 1 divided by 2, or 1/2; 100% times 1/2 is 50%. You may need a calculator for bigger numbers, but the idea is simple.

You might easily make five mistakes in writing or using this formula. First, you might omit the percent sign after 100. Be sure to write "100%." Second, you might not use the small "x" for the multiplication sign. Some students insist that the asterisk on their computer is the multiplication sign. Do not use it! Use the uncapitalized letter "x." Third, you might omit the parentheses. If you omit them,

then you incorrectly make the formula 100%xA/A+D. This means that you divide A by A and later add D instead of dividing by A+D. So be sure to include the parentheses. Fourth, you might type the backward slash "\" instead of the forward slash "/." The backward slash does not stand for division. So be sure to use the forward slash. Fifth, you might put spaces between the characters. Do not add any spaces when writing the formula.

26. Write the whole formula for reliability (without looking if possible): _____ _____ .

### Helpful Hint #4

You should assume that two observers use the same definition and observe the same responses unless you are told otherwise. If you are told, even indirectly, that the observers do not use the same definition on the same responses, you cannot compute reliability. For example, suppose that the example states that you observe Beth on Wednesday and find that she hits Paul 5 times. The example might go on to say that your friend observes Beth on Thursday and finds that Beth hit Paul 10 times.

27. If you observe Beth on Wednesday and your friend observes Beth on Thursday, agreement between their observations is not an example of reliability because you and your friend _____ (did, didn't) observe the same responses.

### Helpful Hint #5

If you are not good at arithmetic and percentages, borrow a calculator before you go any further. Otherwise, you will get many of the questions requiring computation of reliability wrong. Why be frustrated? Another point: the book lists answers using only two digits when asking for decimals or percentages (unless the answer is 100%).

### Helpful Hint #6

Throughout the course you will be repeatedly tested on reliability. You will be required to compute reliability and decide whether the result is an acceptable level. You will be asked for the formula for reliability. Many students ignore both of these and simply guess. You stand to lose almost 5% of your grade if you ignore reliability.

### Helpful Hint #7

This hint is for those answering on a computer. You will sometimes be asked to list the tactics in Unit 1: "The first tactic is to specify the behavior using a (blank); the second tactic is to gather information about the behavior using the approach of (blank); the third tactic is to check for (blank) and (blank)." Because of a limitation in the computer book, you must enter your answers in the order learned (i.e., "reliability" then "social validity").

28. Answer this question with both answers in the correct order: "The third tactic is to check for _____ and

_____."


## Additional Readings

Baer, D. M. (1977). Reviewer's comments: Just because it's reliable doesn't mean that you can use it. *Journal of Applied Behavior Analysis, 10,* 117–119. This article argues that statistical estimates of reliability are not functional for behavior analysis.

Bass, R. F. (1987). Computer-assisted observer training. *Journal of Applied Behavior Analysis, 20,* 83–88. Although direct observation techniques continue to be the most used method of data collection procedures reported in JABA, there are also a number of problems involved. Consequently, Bass found that training students on a computer to observe resulted in accurate observational repertoires that met or exceeded current standards for interobserver accuracy.

Fuqua, R. W., & Schwade, J. (1986). Social validation of applied behavioral research: A selective review and critique. In A. Poling & R. W. Fuqua (Eds.), *Research methods in applied behavior analysis: Issues and advances* (pp. 265–292). New York: Plenum. A review of the role of social validation in the selection of target behaviors, intervention procedures, and judgment of effects.

## Programmed Reading

This section presents the following modules: (1) Measuring Observer Agreement, (2) Assumptions about Reliability, (3) Two Types of Reliability, (4) New versus Old Behavioral Definitions, (5) Does Your Behavioral Definition Make Sense? (6) A New Tactic, and (7) Review.

### 1. Measuring Observer Agreement

42. Pre-test: Behavior analysts call the agreement between two observers _____

_____.

59. Pre-test: The exact formula for reliability is: _____.

51. Pre-test: Reliability is the _____ _____ between two independent observers.

You can learn two ideas from this module. First, you can learn to define reliability. Second, you can learn the formula for reliability. Remember, even if you can answer questions about these two ideas, this section can help you answer them faster. Be sure to remember what I said about being asked to give the formula for reliability in all future major exams.

1. *Reliability* and *agreement* are almost synonyms. Behavior analysts define reliability in terms of a certain kind of agreement. Reliability is the _____ _____ between two independent observers.

8. Behavior analysts call the agreement between two observers _____

_____.

76. Reliability is the _____ between two independent observers.

99. The formula for reliability is $100\% \times A/(A+D)$. This means that you multiply 100% times (x) the agreements (A) between two observers and divide by the agreements (A) plus disagreements (D). Agreements are symbolized in this formula by the letter _____. Disagreements are symbolized by the letter _____.

98. The first term in the formula refers to the maximum agreement that two observers can reach: 100%. You can symbolize the formula for reliability with: _____ x A/(A+D).

102. The second term in the formula for reliability uses the symbol "(A+D)." That

stands for "agreements plus disagreements." If two observers agree on one observation and disagree on one observations, then this (A+D) would equal the number ____.

103. The second term in the formula for reliability is the fraction "A/(A+D)." That fraction refers to the number of agreements out of all the observations made. If two observers agreed on one observation and disagreed on one observation, the fraction would be 1 divided by ____.

104. The second term is the fraction of total observations on which the two observers actually agree. Therefore the formula is 100%x_____. (Be sure to include the division sign and the parentheses.)

39. Now put it all together. If two observers agree on one observation out of two, the formula 100%xA/(A+D) would mean multiplying 100% times (represented by the "x") the fraction 1/(1+1), or 1/2. Their reliability according to the formula equals "100% times 1/2," or ____%.

120. You should now be able to write out the formula for reliability from memory. It is _____. (Be sure to include the percent sign, the uncapitalized letter "x" as the symbol of multiplication, the division sign, and the parentheses!)

77. Reliability is the _____ between two observers.

28. I know this is getting to be repetitious, but see if you can type the whole formula with no hints from me: _____ ____.

## 2. Assumptions about Reliability

65. Pre-test: Tom and Sue both use the same behavioral definition to observe Jimmy's studying. Tom found that Jimmy was studying every moment between 9 A.M. and 9:15 A.M. on Tuesday. Sue found that Jimmy was studying every moment between 9 A.M. and 9:15 A.M. on Wednesday. Is this evidence that the observations of Tom and Sue are reliable? _____ (yes, no)

48. Pre-test: Mom and Dad agreed on what polite dinner behavior should be. Mom found that Ken was 100% polite during Thursday night dinner. Dad also found that Ken was 100% polite during Thurs-

day night dinner. Is this evidence that the observations by Mom and Dad were reliable? _____ (yes, no)

43. Pre-test: Dr. Fawcett found that John did every chore his mother asked of him the first week in June. Dr. White, using the same definition of chores, found that John did only a few chores during the second week in June. Is this evidence that the observations by Fawcett and White are unreliable? _____ (yes, no)

41. Pre-test: A measure of reliability makes sense only when two requirements are met. Both observers must use the same _____, and they must observe the same _____ _____.

You can learn a single idea from this module. You can learn the two conditions under which observations can be compared to measure reliability. This idea is a major cause of students getting wrong answers on tests about reliability. It is not a hard idea, you simply need to understand it and have practice applying it to different situations.

114. Would you expect that the observations of two observers using different behavioral definitions would agree? Of course not! Therefore, the first requirement for reliability is that both observers must observe the behavior while using the same _____.

105. Would you expect that two observers looking at entirely different responses, for example, responses occurring at different times, would agree? Again, the answer is obvious. Therefore, the second requirement for measuring reliability is that the observers must use the same behavioral definitions while observing the same _____.

29. I told you, the idea is simple: measuring reliability requires two conditions. The first requirement is that the two observers must use the same _____ _____ of the behavior. The second requirement is that they must observe the same _____.

20. Here's an example of the first requirement. Suppose one observer defines play

as "all activity outside the classroom" and the other observer defines play as "all fun activity." They would not be able to measure the reliability of their observations because they were using different _____.

7. Before I can give you an example of the second requirement, I need to explain what observing the "same responses" means. Suppose I am observing Janie's play behavior. That means I am observing instances of that behavior. For example, she might get on the swing at 10:15 A.M. on Tuesday. That would be one play _____ (response, behavior).

11. Both observers of Janie's play behavior must be observing the same responses. Suppose one person observes Janie swinging at 10:15 A.M. on Tuesday and the other is observing Janie swinging at 3:15 P.M. Are they observing the same response? _____ (yes, no)

34. In any examples where you read that one observer observes at one time and the other observer observes at another time, can they possibly be observing the same responses? _____ (yes, no)

86. Suppose one observer observes Freddy's yelling in the morning and the other observer observes his yelling in the afternoon. They would not be able to measure the reliability of their observations because they are observing different _____.

83. Suppose Betty observes Kim's cooperative play on Friday and Ted observes it on Monday. Did the observers meet the requirement that they observe the same responses? _____ (yes, no)

110. Vern was trained to use the behavioral definition of depressed behavior. Ben was not. They observe Marie's depressed behavior during the afternoon. Do their observations meet the requirement of using the same behavioral definition? _____ (yes, no)

89. Suppose that Jim observes that Patty smiles 25 times in the morning while Kim observes that Patty smiles 25 times in the afternoon. You might say that they "agreed" on 25 smiles. However, because they observe the 25 smiles at different times, they have not agreed on particular responses. Measuring reliability requires agreeing on particular smiles. Therefore, you _____ (can, can't) measure reliability in this case.

18. Here is the way I will often ask questions about reliability. Bob observed 15 murders on the TV show *Manic* on January 15. Shiela observed 14 murders on the TV show *Manic* on January 22. Is this evidence that Bob and Shiela's observing is reliable? The answer is a definite "no," because they are not observing the same _____. Notice that you are not concluding that they are unreliable. You are only saying that you can't draw any conclusions about their reliability because they are not observing the same responses.

17. Here is a slight variation on the same question. Harry reads the *New York Times* on Sunday and finds 75 column inches devoted to the Republican candidate for president. Marsha read the *Times* on Monday and finds only five column inches devoted the Republican candidate. Is this evidence that their observations are unreliable? First you must notice that they are not observing the same responses. Therefore, you _____ (can, can't) measure their reliability. If you can't measure their reliability, can you conclude that they are unreliable? _____ (yes, no) Notice that you can't know whether they are unreliable unless they both observe the same day's paper!

10. Bob observed that Professor Brainbuster smiled 15 times during Monday's lecture. Ann observed that he smiled three times during Wednesday's lecture. Is their disagreement evidence that their observations are unreliable? _____ (yes, no) Notice that their disagreement does not relate to observations of the same responses. Therefore their disagreement is not evidence for either reliability or unreliability.

92. Ted observed that Gary had 15 hot dogs at the ball game on Saturday. Mary also observed that Gary had 15 hot dogs at

| Carol | N | W | N | N | N |
|-------|---|---|---|---|---|
| Johan | N | N | N | N | N |

**Figure 4-9.** The agreement between Carol and Johan's observations of Dave's weightlifting exercises.

| Task | Greet | Smile | Look | Loud | Thank | Leave |
|------|-------|-------|------|------|-------|-------|
| Tim | not | yes | yes | not | yes | not |
| Ann | yes | yes | yes | not | yes | yes |

**Figure 4-10.** Tim and Ann's agreement on observations of good public speaking.

the ball game on Saturday. Can you conclude that the observations by Ted and Mary were reliable? _____ (yes, no)

113. Willie saw Jerome goofing off 10 times on Saturday afternoon. Queen saw Jerome goofing off nine times on Sunday afternoon. Can you conclude that the observations by Willie and Queen are reliable? _____ (yes, no)

73. Randy found 15 mentions of behavior analysis ideas in *Time* magazine for June 4. Juanita found only three mentions of behavior analysis ideas in *Time* for the same date. Can you conclude that the observations by Randy and Juanita were unreliable? _____ (yes, no)

6. Be sure that you can answer the following kind of question correctly. Pete observed that his Dad buckled his seat belt only three times during May. His sister, Karen, observed that Dad buckled up 27 times during June. Can you conclude that the observations by Pete and Karen are not reliable? _____ (yes, no)

2. A measure of reliability makes sense only when two requirements are met. Both observers must use the same _____ _____ and they must observe the same _____.

### 3. Two Types of Reliability

62. Pre-test: Figure 4-9 shows Carol and Johan's observations of Dave's weightlifting exercises, where "W" stands for "weightlifting" and "N" stands for "not weightlifting." Their reliability is _____%.

| Obs# | 1 | 2 | 3 | 4 | 5 |
|------|---|---|---|---|---|
| Dave | S | N | S | S | N |
| Ann | S | N | N | S | S |

**Figure 4-11.** The agreement between Dave and Ann's observations.

67. Pre-test: When used to observe a simple behavior, you cannot use trial reliability with either _____ or _____ _____ recording.

64. Pre-test: Figure 4-10 shows the observations of Tim and Ann of good public speaking behaviors. What is the reliability of their observations? _____% (Round to the nearest number.)

69. Pre-test: You can use trial reliability with _____ recording and with _____ recording.

55. Pre-test: Suppose Observer A records 4 instances of the behavior and Observer B records 6. What is their reliability? _____% (Round to the nearest number.)

You can learn two ideas in this module. You can learn how and when to compute trial reliability, and you can learn how and when to compute frequency reliability. This module will introduce you to the actual measurement of reliability. It will give you the chance to practice using reliability.

Sometimes two observers can look for a behavior during defined periods called *trials*. For example, suppose two observers are looking for a batter to swing at a pitch. The batter may swing when a pitch is thrown but will not swing when a pitch has not been thrown. Each pitch defines a "trial." You use trial reliability by comparing the observation of each trial. I will not test you on the definition of trial reliability, but you will have to know how to use it.

9. Behavior analysts use trial reliability with the two methods of observation that use intervals. Because each interval defines a trial, you can always use trial reliability with interval recording and with _____ recording.

16. Figure 4-11 shows a simple example of trial reliability with time sample recording. The table shows Dave and Ann's

| Carl | R | R | R | R | N |
|------|---|---|---|---|---|
| Jane | R | N | R | R | N |

**Figure 4-12.** Carl and Jane's agreement on observations.

| Item | Knife | Fork | Spoon | Plate | Glass |
|------|-------|------|-------|-------|-------|
| Ann | yes | yes | not | yes | not |
| Bob | not | yes | not | yes | yes |

**Figure 4-13.** Ann and Bob's observations of table setting.

| Task | Greet | Smile | Probe | Praise | Record | Grade |
|------|-------|-------|-------|--------|--------|-------|
| Tom | not | yes | yes | not | yes | not |
| Ken | not | not | yes | yes | yes | yes |

**Figure 4-14.** Observations by Tom and Ken of teaching behaviors.

observations of Gloria's studying, where "S" stands for "studying" and "N" for "not studying." They agreed on observations #1, #2, and #4. Thus, A=____. They disagreed on observations #3 and #5. Thus, D=____.

75. Reliability equals 100% times A/(A+D). If A=3 and D=2, reliability equals 100% times ____ divided by the sum ____. When you divide 3 by 5, you get the decimal ____. You then multiply 100% times the decimal. The result equals ____%. (You only have to enter the number. If you enter the number followed by "%," the program will count it wrong—the question already says "percent.") If you got the wrong number, use a calculator next time!

21. Figure 4-12 shows an example of trial reliability with interval recording. The table shows Carl and Jane's observations of Ken's reading where "R" stands for "reading" and "N" stands for "not reading." Count agreements to get the value of "A" and disagreements to get the value "D." Then, add to get (A+D). Then, divide A by (A+D) to get the decimal ____. Multiply 100% by the decimal to find the percentage of agreement. The result equals ____%. (Be sure not to write "%.") If you got the wrong number, use a calculator!

118. You can also use trial reliability when observing a complex behavior using a checklist. For example, a salesperson should perform four steps when a customer enters their sales area. They should promptly approach the customer. They should greet the customer. They should ask if they need help finding anything. They should accompany the customer to the item they seek. Because each step in a complex behavior defines a trial, you ____ (can, can't) compute trial reliability.

22. Figure 4-13 shows an example of computing trial reliability with a complex behavior. Ann and Bob observed table setting. Compute the reliability of these observations made by Ann and Bob. Find A and D. A/(A+D)=____ (give fraction). The reliability of Ann and Bob's observations equals ____%.

12. Figure 4-14 shows Tom and Ken's observations of good teaching behaviors. In this case reliability equals ____%.

40. Outcome and event recording with simple behaviors do not produce a trial-by-trial record. Rather they produce a total count of the behavior. Therefore, when used to observe a simple behavior, you cannot use trial reliability with either ____ ____ or ____ recording.

81. Remember, when used to observe a simple behavior, you cannot use trial reliability with either ____ or ____ recording.

14. Frequency reliability assumes that two observers agree on all overlapping observations. For example, you might observe that Meg smiled three times. However, Lettie might observe that Meg smiled four times. Frequency reliability assumes that Lettie agrees with all of the smiles that you counted. It assumes that you disagree on the one extra smile that Lettie observed. Therefore, in this case A=____. Also D=____. And (A+D)=____.

24. Here's another example of frequency reliability. You might observe that Hal smiled 50 times. Ann might observe

| Obs# | 1 | 2 | 3 | 4 | 5 | 6 | 7 | 8 | 9 | 10 |
|------|---|---|---|---|---|---|---|---|---|----|
| Vern | C | C | C | N | C | N | N | C | C | N |
| Carl | C | C | C | N | C | N | C | N | C | N |

**Figure 4-15.** Observations by Vern and Carl.

40 smiles. Frequency reliability assumes that you agree with Ann on each of the smiles that she observed. In this case, A=___, D=___, (A+D)=___.

105. It is time to compute a frequency reliability. You and Ken observe Ted littering with candy wrappers. Suppose you observe 10 candy wrappers, but Ken sees only 8. In this case A=___, (A+D)=___. A divided by (A+D) equals the fraction ___. Multiply 100% times the decimal equivalent of the fraction to find that frequency reliability is: ___%.

19. Here's a simplification of the formula for reliability. Remember that in the previous example, you observed 10 wrappers and Ken observed 8. Agreement was 8 and (agreement plus disagreement) was 10. Notice that the smaller number equaled the agreements and the larger number equaled the agreements plus disagreements. Therefore, the formula for frequency reliability amounts to multiplying 100% times the result of dividing the smaller number by the _____ _____ number.

32. If Gene counted Mary solving 10 problems in class whereas Fred counted only 8, their reliability would equal ___%.

### 4. New versus Old Behavioral Definitions

47. Pre-test: Luis and Anna observed how often Maria flirted with a customer. Luis observed 8 flirtations and Anna observed 10. Their reliability is ___%. Is it acceptable? ___ (yes, no)

66. Pre-test: Figure 4-15 shows the resulting observations when Vern and Carl developed a behavioral definition to observe Ted's cooperative playing (where "C" stands for "cooperative playing" and "N" for "not cooperative playing"). What is their reliability? ___%. Is it acceptable? ___(yes, no)

52. Pre-test: Remember, if an example does not tell you that the behavioral definition is new, or that the researchers developed it, then acceptable reliability is ___% or more.

49. Pre-test: Patty observed that the talk show host insulted women 25 times on Thursday. Ann observed that the same talk show host also insulted women 25 times on Friday. Can you conclude from this that the observations by Patty and Ann were reliable? ___ (yes, no)

68. Pre-test: When using a new behavioral definition, reliability is acceptable if it reaches ___%. When using an old behavioral definition, reliability is acceptable if it reaches ___%.

You can learn one very crucial idea in this lesson. You can learn how large reliability should be to be acceptable. Observations based on old, established behavioral definitions should reach 90% or more to be acceptable. Observations based on new, less well-developed behavioral definitions need reach only 80% or more to be acceptable. To use this idea, you need to learn how to distinguish between old and new behavioral definitions.

25. How large should reliability be? Most researchers aim for a reliability of 90% or more with <u>old</u>, well-established behavioral definitions. However, for new behavioral definitions, most researchers accept a figure of only ___% or more.

79. Remember, if you're using a new behavioral definition, seek 80%; if you're using an established, old behavioral definition, seek the higher figure of ___%.

116. You and Bob use a new behavioral definition to observe relaxation. You make a checklist and get 85% reliability. Since your reliability is greater than the 80% required for new behavioral definitions, you ___ (can, can't) conclude that your behavioral definition is acceptable.

35. Jan and Ted use an old behavioral definition to observe how often Flora greets customers. They find that the reliability of their observations is 86%. Since their reliability is less than the 90% required for old behavioral definitions, they

_____ (can, can't) conclude that their behavioral definition is acceptable.

5. Barb and Fred use a new behavioral definition to observe how often Nicole glances in her rearview mirror. They find that the reliability of their observations is 73%. Since they used a new behavioral definition, they _____ (can, can't) conclude that their behavioral definition is acceptable.

111. Wendy and Mel use an old behavioral definition to observe how often Sam tells Bobby he loves her. They find that the reliability of their observations is 88%. Since they used an old behavioral definitions, they _____ (can, can't) conclude that their behavioral definition is acceptable.

112. When using a new behavioral definition, reliability is acceptable if it reaches _____%. When using an old behavioral definition, reliability is acceptable if it reaches _____%.

91. Suppose you develop a new behavioral definition that produces 81% reliability. Is that reliability acceptable? _____ (yes, no)

33. If the researchers or observers developed a behavioral definition, then obviously it is new. If the question does <u>not</u> tell you that the observers developed a behavioral definition, you should assume that the behavioral definition is _____.

84. Suppose I tell you that two observers developed a behavioral definition for "thoughtfulness" and that they agreed on 82% of their observations. Is their reliability acceptable? _____ (yes, no)

31. If a question tells you that two observers used an established behavioral definition, the level for acceptable reliability is _____%. If it tells you that they developed the behavioral definition, then the level for acceptable reliability is _____%. If the question doesn't tell you anything about the behavioral definition, then you should assume that the acceptable reliability is _____%.

38. Let me put this another way. When analyzing examples and quizzes, always assume that the behavioral definition is old. You must assume that the behavioral

| Obs# | 1 | 2 | 3 | 4 | 5 |
|------|---|---|---|---|---|
| Joe | B | S | B | B | S |
| You | B | S | B | S | S |

*Figure 4-16* Observations by Joe and you.

| Obs# | 1 | 2 | 3 | 4 | 5 | 6 | 7 | 8 | 9 | 10 |
|------|---|---|---|---|---|---|---|---|---|----|
| Ali | G | G | G | P | G | P | G | G | P | P |
| Mary | G | G | P | P | G | P | G | G | G | P |

*Figure 4-17* Observations by Ali and Mary.

definition is old unless the question or example clearly states that it is _____.

117. Figure 4-16 shows the results when you and Joe make observations about baseball pitches where "B" is a "ball" and "S" is a "strike." What is your reliability? _____%. Is it acceptable? _____ (yes, no)

4. Barb and Carlos develop a behavioral definition of kindness. Barb observes that their friend Tony is kind 10 times on Tuesday while Barb observes that Tony is kind only 8 times on Tuesday. Their reliability is _____%. Is their reliability acceptable? _____ (yes, no)

3. Figure 4-17 shows the results when Ali and Mary observe Mom's parenting behaviors, where "G" stands for "good parenting behaviors" and "P" stands for "poor parenting behaviors." Their reliability is _____%. Is it acceptable? _____

30. If a question gives you no clue about whether the behavioral definition is old or new, you should assume that it is old. So if I tell you that two observers agreed on 88% of their observations and ask you if that is an acceptable level, you will answer _____.

13. Costas saw Ken wink at 20 women on Thursday. Maria saw Ken wink at 19 women on Friday. Is this evidence that the observations made by Costas and Ken are reliable? _____ (yes, no) (Remember to always evaluate whether the observations are made on the same behaviors.)

## 5. Does the Behavioral Definition Make Sense?

58. Pre-test: The correlation between the ratings by outside judges of a behavior

and the observations of a trained observer is called _____.

56. Pre-test: The agreement between two observers is called _____.

53. Pre-test: Social validity is the _____ _____ between the ratings by outside judges of a behavior and the observations of a trained observer.

You can learn two ideas in this module. You can learn how to define social validity. And you can learn how to recognize examples of social validity. In particular, you can learn how to tell the difference between social validity and reliability.

94. The agreement between two observers is called reliability. The correlation between ratings of a behavior by <u>outside judges</u> and the observations of that behavior by an observer is called _____ _____ (reliability, social validity).

82. Social validity is the _____ _____ (agreement, correlation) between ratings of a behavior by outside judges and the observations of that behavior by a trained observer.

27. I have used the word *correlation* with a particular meaning. It means that if a trained observer counts <u>many</u> responses, outside judges will rate the behavior as occurring <u>frequently</u>, *and* if the observer counts <u>few</u> responses, outside judges will rate the behavior as occurring <u>rarely</u>. So there is a correlation if a high count occurs when there is a high rating and if a low count occurs when there is a _____ rating.

23. Here's an example. Suppose Fred, the observer, is using a behavioral definition to record smiling by Butch. Suppose that Fred counts only three smiles in an hour and outside judges rate the smiling as "very rare." Suppose that Butch undergoes therapy. Fred might count 29 smiles, and the outside judges might rate the smiling as "frequent." The correlation between the counts and the ratings provides evidence that the behavioral definition has _____ (reliability, social validity).

85. Suppose Jerry, another observer, uses a different behavioral definition to record Butch's smiling. Suppose that Jerry counts five smiles in an hour and outside judges rate the smiling as "very rare." Suppose that after Butch's therapy Jerry counts 29 smiles, but the outside judges still rate the smiling as "very rare." In this case there is no correlation between the counts and the ratings. Whether the count is high or low, the rating is always "very rare." This lack of correlation suggests that the behavioral definition _____ (does, doesn't) have social validity.

97. The correlation between the observations of a trained observer and the ratings of outside judges is called _____ _____.

87. Suppose that Jane observes that Ken acts sensitively only a few times before he undergoes sensitivity training and many times afterward. Suppose that five friends rate Ken as insensitive before and "fairly sensitive after" training. The correlation between Jane's observations and the friends' ratings indicate that Jane's behavioral definition has _____.

88. Suppose that Jane observes 9 instances of sensitivity before Ken's training, whereas Joe observes 10 instances. The agreement between Jane's observations and Joe's observations indicate that Jane's observations have an acceptable level of _____.

108. To summarize, the agreement between two observers is called _____ _____. The correlation between ratings by outside judges and observations based on a behavioral definition is called _____.

100. The key word to look for is *correlation*. If an example involves the correlation between an observation and one or more ratings, then you can be sure that the examples is measuring _____ _____.

37. Jose wants to find out how interested John is in Mary, so he observes how often John asks Mary questions about herself. If Benny also observes John's

questions to find out if his observations are about the same as Jose's, Benny is measuring the _____ of their observations.

36. Jose observes how often John asks Mary questions about herself to find out how interested he is in her. Is this a good measure of "interest"? To find out, he asks five friends of Mary to rate how interested John is in Mary. They find that when John asks a lot of questions the friends rate him as very interested, but when he asks few questions, they rate him as not very interested. By comparing his observations and their ratings, Jose is measuring the _____ of his behavioral definition of interest.

80. Remember, reliability is the _____ between two observers. Social validity is the _____ between observations of an observer and the ratings of one or more outside judges.

### 6. A New Tactic

57. Pre-test: The behavioral strategy is to define human problems as _____ _____ problems.

70. Pre-test: You can use the behavioral strategy to help solve a human problem. First, you specify the behavior with a(n) _____.

71. Pre-test: You can use the behavioral strategy to help solve a human problem. First, you specify the behavior with a behavioral definition. Second, you gather information using the approach called _____.

72. Pre-test: You can use the behavioral strategy to help solve a human problem. First, you create a behavioral definition of what you want to study. Second, you use the approach of direct observation to study it. Third, you check the _____ _____ and _____ of your observations.

This module teaches you to summarize all of the lessons up to this point. The behavioral strategy points to the overall core of the unit: define human problems as behavior. Each tactic in that strategy points to the focus of each lesson: behavioral definition, method of direct observation, and reliability/social

| Obs# | 1 | 2 | 3 | 4 | 5 | 6 | 7 | 8 | 9 | 10 |
|------|---|---|---|---|---|---|---|---|---|----|
| Henry | W | W | W | W | N | N | N | W | W | W |
| Pablo | W | W | W | W | W | N | N | W | W | N |

**Figure 4-18.** Observations by Henry and Pablo.

validity. You probably know these four concepts already. All I am going to do in this module is drill you on each one of them.

96. The behavioral strategy is to define human problems as _____ problems.

106. To remember the first concept, you only need to remember the first tactic you learned. You have to <u>specify</u> the behavior before you can do anything else. So all you need to remember is how you specify what behavior to observe. To use the behavioral strategy, (1) you specify the problem behavior with a(n) _____.

107. To remember the second tactic, you need to remember how behavior analysts observe behavior. They use a particular approach to observing behavior. To use the behavioral strategy, (1) create a behavioral definition of the problem behavior and (2) gather information by using the approach called _____ _____.

119. You learned in this lesson how to check those observations to make sure they are accurately measuring something that people consider valid. To use the behavioral strategy, (1) specify the problem behavior with a behavioral definition, (2) gather information using the approach called direct observation, (3) check the _____ and _____ _____ of your observations.

### 7. Review

54. Pre-test: Social validity is the extent of the _____ between ratings by outside observers and observations based on your behavioral definition.

44. Pre-test: Figure 4-18 shows the results when Henry and Pablo observe Jenny's aerobic workout, where "W" means "working out" and "N" means "not working out."

| Obs# | 1 | 2 | 3 | 4 | 5 | 6 | 7 | 8 | 9 | 10 |
|------|---|---|---|---|---|---|---|---|---|----|
| Penny | N | N | N | N | N | N | N | N | N | N |
| Ann | N | N | N | N | N | N | N | S | N | S |

**Figure 4-19.** Observations by Penny and Ann.

What is their reliability? ____% Is it acceptable? ____ (yes, no)

45. Pre-test: Juanita and Carlos were trained to use a complex behavioral definition to observe the gracefulness of ballet dancing. Juanita observed Doris on Tuesday and found that she danced gracefully during all 50 of the intervals. Carlos observed Doris on Friday and also found that she danced gracefully during all 50 of the intervals. Is this evidence of reliability?____ (yes, no)

46. Pre-test: Ken observed Fran's looks at the TV news as a measure of her interest in that news. He found that she looked 10 times at the news about the environment but only 1 time at the news about the election. Three of his friends also watched Fran. They rated how interested she was in news of the environment and how interested she was in news of the election. The relationship between their ratings and his own observations provide a measure of the _____ _____ of his behavioral definition of interest.

50. Pre-test: Figure 4-19 shows the observations when Penny and Ann developed a behavioral definition of smiling. They observed Gina's smiling at others as a measure of depression, where "S" stands for "smile" and "N" for "no smile." What is their reliability? ____% Is it acceptable? ____ (yes, no)

78. Reliability requires two conditions. The two observers must use the same _____. They must observe the same _____ _____.

95. The agreement between two independent observers is called _____.

90. Suppose that Ted observed that the Millers recycled 10 pieces of plastic on Monday while May observed only 3 pieces on Tuesday. You might conclude that their reliability is 30% and that

it is not acceptable. Can you conclude that their observations are unreliable? _____ (yes, no)

74. Recording a behavior during a series of discontinuous intervals is called _____ recording; recording a behavior during a series of continuous intervals is called _____ recording.

121. You should seek _____% agreement with old behavioral definitions and _____% with new ones.

109. To use the behavioral strategy, first specify the behavior using a(n) _____ _____. Second, gather information about the behavior using the approach of _____ _____. Third, check the _____ _____ and _____ _____ of your observations.

101. The name of the science that studies environmental events that change behavior is _____.

15. Frequency reliability is used when observers produce only a total count, such as with _____ and _____ recording of simple behaviors.

26. I am asking this question again to emphasize how important it will be on your tests. What is the formula for reliability? _____

93. Ted observed that Professor Brainbuster asked 10 tough questions on Thursday. Ned observed that he asked 8 tough questions also on Thursday. What is the reliability of observations by Ted and Ned? ____% Can you conclude that they are reliable? ____ (yes, no)

## Programmed Examples

### 1. Programmed Examples

9. Pre-test: Figure 4-22 shows the first 10 observations Barb and Gary made after developing a behavioral definition to find out how much time the children at the Yellow

| Barb | S | S | N | N | N | N | N | N | N | N |
|------|---|---|---|---|---|---|---|---|---|---|
| Gary | S | S | S | N | N | N | N | S | N | N |

**Figure 4-22.** Observations by Barb and Gary

| Observer 1 | A | A | A | O | A | O | A | O | A | A |
|---|---|---|---|---|---|---|---|---|---|---|
| Observer 2 | A | A | A | A | A | O | A | O | A | A |

*Figure 4-23.* Observations by two observers.

| Alice | H | H | N | H | N | H | H | H | N | H |
|---|---|---|---|---|---|---|---|---|---|---|
| Janet | H | H | H | H | N | H | H | H | H | H |

*Figure 4-24.* Observations by Alice and Janet.

| Sammy | S | S | A | S | A | S | S | A | S | A |
|---|---|---|---|---|---|---|---|---|---|---|
| Marge | S | A | A | S | A | S | A | A | S | A |

*Figure 4-25.* Observations by Sammy and Marge.

| Chore | Floor | Walls | Table | Trash | Chair |
|---|---|---|---|---|---|
| Tam | yes | not | yes | not | yes |
| Fay | yes | not | not | not | not |

*Figure 4-26.* Observations by Tam and Fay.

Brick Road Alternative School were spending learning to read, write, and do arithmetic. They observed in 30-second blocks of time (S=studying basics; N=not studying basics). Compute the reliability of their observations: ____%. Is it acceptable? ____ (yes, no)

8. Pre-test: Figure 4-23 shows the first observations made when Alice was chairperson of the local Wilderness Society. She worried that she dominated monthly meetings. She asked two other members to observe the number of 10-second intervals during which she talked (A=Alice talked; 0=others talked). Compute the reliability: ____%. Does this evidence permit you to conclude that the observations are reliable? _____ (yes, no)

7. Pre-test: Figure 4-24 shows the observations that Alice and Janet made when they watched 10 commercials shown on late-night TV to determine how many of them were advertising products that were ecologically harmful (H=harmful; N=not harmful). Compute the reliability: _____%. Is it acceptable: _____.

13. Figure 4-25 shows the first 10 observations when Sammy and Marge used a new and complicated behavioral definition of sleep to see if their new baby was sleeping. They observed every half hour (S=sleep; A=awake). First, does the example let you assume that the observers used the same behavioral definition and observed the same responses? ____ Second, A=____, D=____, (A+D)=____. A/(A+D) equals the decimal ____. Multiply the decimal by 100% to find that its reliability is ____%.

3. Fred and Charlie counted the number of beers that Murray drank on Saturday. Fred counted 10, but Charlie counted only 9. Decide whether their observations are reliable. First,

does the information given in the example let you assume that the observers used the same behavioral definition on the same responses? ____ (yes, no) Second, compute reliability using 100%xA/(A+D). In this case, you should assume that Fred agrees with all of Charlie's observations. Thus, the number of agreements is A=____. Likewise, you should assume that Charlie disagrees with the extra beer that Fred counted. Thus the number of disagreements is D=____. (A+D)=____. Thus A/(A+D) equals the decimal ____. Multiply that decimal by 100% to find that reliability equals ____%.

12. Roger counted the number of times that Terry threw his clothes down on Saturday rather than putting them away. He counted 8 times. Bunny, his friend, counted 10 times on Sunday. First, does the example let you assume that Roger and Bunny used the same behavioral definition and observed the same responses? ____ (yes, no) Please notice that if one observer counts on Saturday and the other counts on Sunday, they are not observing the same responses!

14. Figure 4-26 shows the observations made by Tam and Fay after they developed a behavioral definition of cleaning behavior. They made their observations at 8:00 P.M. at their co-op dorm (yes=pass; not=fail). First, does the example let you assume that they observed using the same behavioral definition with the same responses? ____ (yes, no) Second, count how many observations agree and how many disagree. Then, use the formula 100%xA/A(A+D) to find that their computed reliability is ____%. Third, notice that they developed their own behavioral definition, which means that it is new. To be acceptable, their reliability must be at least ____%. Is their

| Sue | N | N | N | U | N | N | N | N | N | N |
|-----|---|---|---|---|---|---|---|---|---|---|
| Tom | N | N | N | U | U | N | N | N | N | N |

**Figure 4-27.** Observations by Sue and Tom.

| Fran | U | U | U | U | N | U | N | U | U | U |
|------|---|---|---|---|---|---|---|---|---|---|
| Will | U | U | U | U | U | U | N | N | U | U |

**Figure 4-28.** Observations by Fran and Will.

reliability high enough for a new behavioral definition? _____ (yes, no) Enter the letter indicating the conclusion reached: (a) No conclusion is possible because the same responses were not observed; (b) the observations are reliable; (c) the observations are unreliable. _____

6. Owen was appointed to obtain an objective measure of the number of gripes made during dinner at the dorm. Mary was appointed to record the gripes once a week to measure Owen's reliability. On Thursday, when they were both observing, Owen counted 9 gripes and Mary counted 10 gripes. First, can you assume that they used the same behavioral definition on the same responses? _____ (yes, no) Second, their reliability is _____%. Third, decide what level of reliability they must meet to be acceptable. Are their observations reliable enough to be acceptable? _____ (yes, no)

4. Joan and Al feel that Professor Brainbuster says "uh" too often during lectures. Joan counted 48 "uh's" during Monday's lecture. To make sure Joan was accurate in her counting, Al counted "uh's" during the Tuesday's lecture and found 50. They decided that their counts were so close that Joan's count must have been correct. Should you assume in this case that the observers used the same behavioral definition and observed the same responses? _____ (yes, no) Is their high agreement evidence of acceptable reliability? _____ (yes, no)

20. You and a friend observe the amount of time that the *Tonight Show*'s host talks in a sexist way to his women guests. You develop a behavioral definition of "sexist talk." You find 67% of the intervals on Monday's show contain sexist talk. On Tuesday, a well-known feminist guest told the host to stop being a sexist. You find that only 5% of the intervals in Wednesday's show contain sexist talk. Suppose you asked a local women's group to rate a videotape of Monday's and Wednesday's show. Suppose the local women's group rates Monday's show as "highly sexist" and Wednesday's as "slightly sexist." The correlation between your observations and the women's ratings suggests that

your behavioral definition has _____ _____.

15. Figure 4-27 shows observations made to help the church members consider whether to continue using some of their space for private worship. There were differing opinions on how often the private worship room was used, so the members appointed Sue to measure its use. She asked Tom to help test the reliability of her observations. She noted that the room was used during only one of those times. Tom noted two uses of the room (U=used; N=not used). Is reliability meaningful (same time and behavioral definition)? _____ (yes, no) Their reliability equals _____%. Does the reliability meet the goal? _____ (yes, no)

17. Figure 4-28 shows some observations to help the co-op dorm members know how much their sauna was used before agreeing to buy a second one. Fran and Will agreed to observe its use once an hour (U=use; N=nonuse). What is the reliability of these observations? _____% Is it acceptable? _____ (yes, no)

5. Marie was using behavioral methods to teach a group of women how to be more assertive. She had a behavioral definition of assertiveness. Some of her students questioned her behavioral definition, so she took videotapes of her students' performance before and after training and showed them to a cross section of adults, asking them to rate how assertive the taped individuals were acting. They rated the students as more assertive after training than before, just as the behavioral definition did. Marie was attempting to establish the _____ of her behavioral definition.

11. Figure 4-29 shows the results when Rob and Jan observed Professor Brainbuster to find out whether he was looking at students when he lectured. They used 15-second intervals. Compute the reliability: _____%. Is this an acceptable level? _____ (yes, no)

| Rob | O | O | O | O | X | O | O | X | O | O |
| Jan | O | X | O | O | O | O | O | X | O | O |

*Figure 4-29.* Observations by Rob and Jan.

18. It is time to include some review questions on concepts introduced in lessons. Marc sometimes thought of himself as Sultan. He made up a checklist of 15 services that he expected of Anna every day. He watched to see if she served him breakfast in bed, brought him his clothes, poured his bath, and so on. His plan was to immediately record when she performed each service. During the first day of his system, he asked Anna to bring him breakfast in bed. She looked at him kind of funny but did it. He then marked it down on his checklist. Next he asked her to pour his bath and to be sure to put cologne in it. She looked real funny at him this time, went into the kitchen, and then threw a pot of water on the Sultan. What method of observation was the Sultan hoping to use? _____ recording

1. Dave observed the study behavior of each of 16 pupils in the fifth grade for 10 seconds before moving on to the next pupil. Every four minutes, he started over again with the first pupil. What method of observation was he using with the first pupil? _____ recording

2. Dom observed each story on the evening news for a week. He found that 50 of the news items were biased toward the status quo. John wanted to see if Dom was correct, so he watched the evening news the next week using the same behavioral definition. He found that 46 of the items were biased toward the status quo. Enter the letter of your conclusion: (a) No conclusion is possible because the same responses were not observed; (b) the observations are reliable; (c) the observations are unreliable. _____

16. The coach diagrammed a football play that showed exactly what the fullback should do. The coach assigned an assistant coach to observe whether the fullback made the right play according to the diagram. Behavior analysts would call the diagram a(n) _____ of "made the right play."

19. Two members of NOW counted the number of shoppers going into Nick's store before NOW started its boycott over the wages of Nick's women employees. One member counted 18 shoppers, the other member counted 20 shoppers. They used the same behavioral definition. Compute the reliability: _____% . Is it acceptable? _____ (yes, no)

# Experimental Designs for Studying Everyday Behavior

## Reading Section

You have learned the first three tactics in using the behavioral strategy to solve a problem: you develop a behavioral definition, use a method of direct observation, and check the reliability and social validity of your observations. When those tactics don't solve the problem, you can use a fourth tactic, which is to design a <u>single-subject experiment</u>. You can use single-subject experiments to find out if a particular "treatment" for the problem behavior works. Treatments involve environmental events like praising or giving tangible items.

1. The fourth tactic in using the behavioral strategy to solve a problem is to design a single-subject _____.

Behavior analysts speak of "designing" these experiments. The design is a plan for presenting and withholding the treatment. The simplest design compares the rate of the behavioral variable before and after treatment. If the rate is higher after treatment, then this suggests that the treatment caused the change. As you will see, there are several more complex designs.

The most important aspect of an experimental design is whether it can rule out <u>alternative</u> explanations of the results. You might use any one of three widely used designs. Behavior analysts use these three designs so that they can discover laws of behavior. These designs use the principle of single-subject experiments. You will learn about the three single-subject designs commonly used by behavior analysts.

## Alternative Explanations

You can use behavioral <u>experiments</u> to find out whether a particular treatment works. For example, you might wish to increase the amount of chores done by children. Most parents give their children an allowance whether or not they do chores. I will call this *free allowance*. You might guess that an earned allowance would produce more chores than free allowance. You might get interested in whether that is true. You can find out in only one way: you must design an experiment that compares the effects of giving earned allowance with the effects of giving free allowance.

You might find that children do more chores with earned allowance. However, your results might be subject to alternative explanations. They might be subject to two types of alternative explanations in particular: <u>individual differences</u> and <u>time coincidences</u>.

Consider two examples of time coincidences. Suppose you decide to compare chore behavior using free allowance during November with chore behavior using earned allowance during December. You might find the children did more chores during December. Maybe this means that earned allowance works better than free allowance. But maybe it doesn't. Can you think of an alternative explanation? Sure, Christmas. Most children are on their best behavior just before Christmas. They might increase their chore behavior to get more presents. Another alternative explanation is that their mother might have given them a lecture about neatness in the beginning of December. Both these alternative explanations involve a coincidence between when you switch from free allowance to earned allowance and some other factor such as Christmas or Mom's lecture. The number of possible coincidences is endless. They prevent you from being sure that your results mean that an earned allowance works better.

Consider two examples of individual differences. Suppose you observe the amount of chores done by Tom and Tracey, two children getting earned allowances. Suppose you also observe the amount done by Bob and Becky, two children getting free allowances. You might find that Tom and Tracey do more chores than Bob and Becky. Can you conclude that earned allowance works better? Can you think of alternative explanations? For example, Tom and Tracey may have held real jobs prior to the experiment. Those jobs may have taught them to do what is asked of them. Bob and Becky may never have held real jobs. The result might appear to favor earned allowances, but the real cause of Tom and Tracey doing more chores may be their job experience. Other individual differences such as age, IQ, or cooperativeness might also explain any differences. In fact, the possible alternative explanations based on individual differences are endless. They prevent you from being sure that your results mean that earned allowance works better.

Until you can rule out all alternative explanations, you can't be sure that the increased chores are the result of earned allowance. You must rule out time coincidences. You must also rule out individual differences. The more alternative explanations that an experiment rules out, the more sure you can be about what caused any change in a behavioral variable.

## Experimental Conditions

I will describe three experimental designs in this lesson. I will discuss the ability of each one to rule out alternative explanations. First, I need a few terms to help talk about experimental designs.

Behavior analysts seek methods of changing behavior that can help solve problems. They call these methods *treatments*. The **treatment** is the method introduced to modify the rate of a behavior. The treatment may be designed to either increase or decrease the behavior. Thus,

giving an earned allowance for chores is the "treatment." Behavior analysts call the period of time during an experiment when they are delivering the treatment the *treatment condition*. Thus, the period of time when the children receive an earned allowance is the "treatment condition."

2. The treatment is the method introduced to _____ the rate of a behavior.
3. The method introduced to modify the rate of a behavior is called the _____.

Behavior analysts usually compare the effect of using a treatment with the effect of not using it. They call absence of the treatment the *baseline*. The **baseline** is the period of an experiment without the treatment. In your experiment with chores, the period of time when you observe chores with free allowance would be called the baseline or the baseline condition.

4. The period of an experiment without the treatment is called the _____.

Behavior analysts run experiments to find out whether a treatment modifies a behavioral variable. Their experiments have at least a baseline condition and a treatment condition. They compare the rate of the behavior in each condition. The rate during treatment might be similar to baseline or it might be different from baseline. Finding a similar rate suggests that the treatment did not modify the behavior. Finding a different rate suggests the obvious explanation that the treatment modified behavior. However, the obvious explanation may not be the correct one. The correct explanation for the change may be an *alternative* explanation.

## Ruling Out Alternative Explanations

**Ruling out alternative explanations** means "showing that events other than the treatment did not cause an observed difference." For example, you might be able to show that Christmas didn't cause the children to do their chores. You might be able to show that Mom didn't just have a talk with them. If so, you have ruled out those alternative explanations.

5. *Ruling out alternative explanations* means "showing that events other than the treatment did not _____ an observed difference."
6. Showing that events other than the treatment did not cause an observed difference is called "ruling out _____ explanations."

Suppose that you found a difference in behavior with and without treatment. Suppose you ruled out all alternative explanations. You are left with the treatment as the only explanation of the difference. You have designed an experiment that proves that the treatment causes the difference! The remainder of this lesson will introduce you to designing such experiments.

## The Principle of Single-Subject Experiments

Single-subject experiments provide a powerful way to establish causality. These experiments involve one person at a time. You observe the behavior of one person before treatment. You then observe the same person during treatment. This simple step immediately rules out individual differences between baseline and treatment. Since you use only one individual, there can be no individual differences. As you will see, behavior analysts have additional ways to rule out time coincidences as alternative explanations. When you have ruled out alternative explanations, you are left with the treatment as the only remaining explanation for changes in that single person's behavior. If you find the same result with additional individuals, then you have evidence that it is true in general. **The principle of single-subject experiments** is to expose the <u>same person</u> to the baseline and treatment.

7. The principle of single-subject experiments is to expose the _____ person to the baseline and treatment.

An experiment is "single subject" if it exposes the same subject to both the baseline condition and the treatment condition. However, "single subject" does not refer to how many subjects there are in the experiment. Rather it refers to the minimum number of subjects—one—needed to compare baseline and treatment. Most single-subject experiments use more than one subject (e.g., Ryan, Ormond, Imwold, & Rotunda, 2002), but each subject is exposed to both the baseline and the treatment condition. In other words, the individuals in the baseline condition are the same individuals as those in the treatment condition. Single-subject experiments use more than one subject to see if their findings apply to one person or to many persons. They use more than one subject to assess the generality of their findings.

For example, suppose you want to find out if teaching relaxation can help people reduce their tension headaches. You might start by teaching Ken a simple method of relaxation. Perhaps you find that pain behaviors linked to headaches decrease by half. By comparing Ken's pain before relaxation with his pain after relaxation, you have ruled out individual differences. If you rule out other alternative explanations, then you can conclude that relaxation caused the reduction of Ken's pain. If you want to see whether this finding applies to many people, you could repeat your comparison of baseline and treatment with other people suffering from tension headaches. Suppose you repeat the experiment with 8 people. If you find that they all improve, then you can conclude that relaxation causes a reduction in headache pain. Your results would be similar to those obtained in a similar study (Applebaum, Blanchard, & Nicholson, 1990). Notice that the design is single subject even though it involves more than one person. It is a single-subject experiment because you expose the same subjects to baseline and treatment.

Behavior analysts argue that single-subject experiments are powerful designs (e.g., Barlow & Hersen, 1984). They have used single-subject experiments to discover many laws of behavior. Skinner's discovery of the law of reinforcement was only the first. You will read about additional laws throughout this book. Single-subject experiments let behavior analysis discover many <u>causes</u> of behavior.

Behavior analysts most often use three experimental designs suitable for single subjects (see Foster, Watson, & Young, 2002). I will describe and illustrate the comparison design first. Then I will introduce you to the reversal design and the multiple-baseline design.

## Comparison Design

Behavior analysts call the simplest design a *comparison design*. A **comparison** design is an experimental design comparing the <u>baseline</u> condition with the <u>treatment</u> condition. It observes the behavior for the same person (or persons) in both conditions. You would use this design by first observing a behavior prior to the start of treatment while the "normal" conditions are still in effect. You call this your baseline. You would then observe the behavior during the treatment. Figure 5-1 shows the baseline condition of Sarge's "rational leadership" behavior. Suppose you wished to study the effects of leadership training as a treatment to improve his leadership behavior. You would train Sarge and then observe his rational leadership behavior with training.

8. Comparison design: An experimental design comparing the baseline condition with the _____ condition.
9. The design that involves comparing the baseline condition with the treatment condition is called the _____ design.

As a more serious example, let's return to the chore behavior of children. You wish to compare free allowance with earned allowance. You would select a specific child for your experiment. Let's say you pick Terry. You would start by observing Terry's chore behavior during a "baseline" period when you used free allowance rather than earned allowance. Let's say you find that he did about 25% of his chores for the 15 days of baseline. Then, you would observe his chore behavior during the following 15 days. During that period, you would give Terry the "treatment" of earned allowance. Let's say you find that Terry's chore behavior improved so that he did about 75% of his chores for those 15 days. Figure 5-2 shows a graph of this result.

Can you rule out alternative explanations of this finding? You can rule out individual difference because you have studied only Terry. However, you cannot rule out time coincidences (Parsonson & Baer, 1978). For example, Terry may have started inviting a playmate home at the same time that you started earned allowance. If so, Terry may have improved his chore behavior to impress the friend, not because of your earned allowance. Or Terry may have had a decrease in schoolwork, job, or other duties that interfered with chore behaviors during baseline. Or maybe, he simply wanted to please you. You can imagine many events that might have coincided with the start of your treatment. This design does not rule any of them out. Therefore, you can't have complete confidence in the effect of the treatment. The change may have simply been a coincidence.

***Figure 5-1.*** Observing Sarge "before" and "after" leadership training would be a comparison design. (Source: Cartoon copyright 1973 King Features Syndicate. Reproduced by permission.)

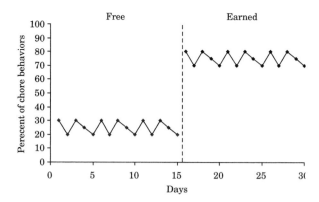

**Figure 5-2.** Comparison design: A hypothetical experiment to increase Terry's chore behavior through using earned allowance. This is a comparison design because it observes one behavior with just baseline and treatment conditions. The first condition is free allowance. The second condition is earned allowance.

Sometimes you might use a "backward" comparison design. You might start by introducing the treatment rather than the baseline first. Your experiment would have the same two conditions as with any comparison design. The first condition would be treatment and the second would be baseline. The logic of the design is identical to the standard comparison design.

You can always tell whether a single-subject experiment uses a comparison design by asking one question. Does the experiment compare the treatment with only one baseline? If so, it uses a comparison design.

Comparison designs do not rule out alternative explanations based on time. However, behavior analysts have developed two experimental designs that do rule out alternative explanations based on time coincidences. These designs provide strong evidence about whether or not a treatment works. They are called the *reversal design* and the *multiple-baseline* design. Because they rule out alternative explanations, I will call these *strong* designs.

## Reversal Design

Behavior analysts call one strong design a *reversal design*. The reversal design is similar to the comparison design. You start with a comparison of behavior during the baseline and treatment conditions. In other words, you start

with a comparison design. You then go one step further and "reverse" from treatment back to baseline (e.g., Roane, Fisher, & McDonough, 2003). This creates a third condition, which behavior analysts call *reversal to baseline* or simply the *reversal*. The **reversal design** is an experimental design that looks at a behavior during <u>baseline</u>, <u>treatment</u>, and <u>reversal</u>.

10. The reversal design looks at a behavior during baseline, treatment, and _____ _____.

11. The design that looks at a behavior during baseline, treatment, and reversal is called the _____ design.

You could use this design to determine the effect of earned allowance on the chore behavior of Terry. You would start the same way you did with the comparison design. Let's say the percentages are the same. You find that Terry did 25% of his chores during an initial 15 days of baseline (with free allowance). Terry did 75% of his chores during the following 15 days of treatment (with earned allowance). You then create the reversal design by adding a third condition, which is a reversal to the baseline condition: you once again give Terry a free allowance. Let's say you find that Terry's chores decreased to 25% during the 15 days of this condition. You would have conducted a reversal design on earned allowance for chores. Figure 5-3 shows a graph of this experiment.

Can you rule out alternative explanations for your finding? Your results make alternative explanations for Terry's changed behavior very unlikely. First, you have ruled out individual differences because you are comparing Terry to himself. Second, you have made a time coincidence with some other event very unlikely. The other event would have to begin when you started using earned allowance and cease when you stopped using it. The coincidence is too great to be very realistic. So you can conclude that the earned allowance caused the change.

Suppose the experiment had come out differently. If Terry had persisted in his chore behavior during the reversal, then you could not have ruled out alternative explanations. Suppose that Terry's chores stayed at 75% during the reversal. You should suspect that

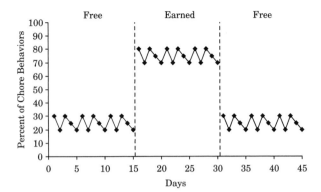

**Figure 5-3.** Reversal design: A hypothetical experiment to increase Terry's chore behavior by using earned allowance. This is a reversal design because it observes one behavior with three conditions. The first condition is the baseline of free allowance. The second condition is the treatment of earned allowance. The third condition is the reversal to free allowance again.

some unknown event began when you started to use earned allowance and was still working when you were no longer using earned allowance. In other words, you should suspect that some unknown event, rather than earned allowance, explains Terry's improved chore behavior. The failure of Terry's chore behavior to decrease during the reversal would mean that you could no longer rule this possibility out.

You can use more than one reversal if the results are ambiguous. For example, suppose that chores didn't reverse back to baseline levels. Maybe chores decreased to only 55% when you stopped giving Terry an earned allowance. In other words, you saw a decrease of 20% (75%–55%) when you stopped earned allowance. That compares to an increase of 50% (25%–75%) when you started earned allowance. The difference suggests that another factor coincided with earned allowance to cause the initial increase. To clarify this alternative explanation, you could try the treatment a second time. You might find that Terry once again did 75% of his chores. This observation suggests that some coinciding factor helped produce the first increase and is still operating. However, with this additional reversal, you would be much more confident that earned allowance produced part of the difference.

Sometimes you might use a "backward" reversal design. The first two conditions would be identical to a backward comparison design. You would start with the treatment rather than the baseline. You would have three conditions: treatment, then baseline, then reversal to treatment. For example, one researcher started by helping old people with a memory aid (Bourgeois, 1993). She then took away the aid. Finally, she returned the memory aid. The logic of the design is identical to that of the forward reversal design.

The reversal design permits you to rule out alternative explanations of any change in behavior associated with the treatment. It is a very convincing and powerful design.

You can always tell whether a single-subject experiment uses a reversal design by asking one question: Does the experiment have a third condition that is the same as the initial condition? If so, it uses a reversal design.

## Multiple-Baseline Design

Behavior analysts call a second strong design the "*multiple-baseline* design. The **multiple-baseline** is an experimental design that introduces the treatment at <u>different times</u> for two or more behaviors (e.g., Neef, Nelles, Iwata, & Page, 2003). You might think of the simplest multiple-baseline design as two comparison designs. The only difference is that you start the treatment at different times for each of the comparison designs.

13. A multiple-baseline design introduces the treatment at _____ times for two or more behaviors.
14. The design that introduces the treatment at different times for two or more behaviors, persons, or situations is called the multiple _____.

For example, suppose that Terry not only doesn't do his share of chores but he also doesn't answer the phone very often. Suppose you obtain a baseline for both of these behaviors. Maybe Terry does 25% of his chores and 25% of the phone answering. After 15 days, you might give him earned allowance based only on doing his chores whether or not he answers the

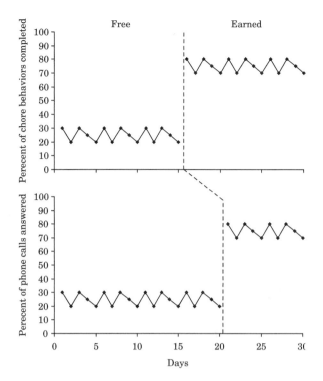

***Figure 5-4.*** Multiple-baseline design: A hypothetical experiment to increase Terry's chore and phone behavior by using earned allowance. This is a multiple-baseline because you started requiring Terry to earn his allowance at different times for chore behavior and phone answering.

***Data from Well-Designed Experiments Outlive Theories***

"The investigator is . . . faced with a dilemma. Shall he follow the lead of sophisticated theoreticians and design experiments whose data may be of interest only in reference to the theory in question? Or shall he perform experiments that he believes will yield data of general interest, irrespective of whether current theories have been designed to handle them? . . . Good data are notoriously fickle. They change their allegiance from theory to theory, and even maintain their importance in the presence of no theory at all" (Sidman, 1960: pp. 6–7).

12. Data from single-subject experiments are likely to be of lasting interest because they rule out _____ _____ explanations.

phone. In other words, you introduce the treatment for chores but not for phone answering. You might find that Terry's chores increase to 75% while his phone answering stays at 25%. After 20 days, you might give him earned allowance based on both chores and phone answering. In other words, you introduce the treatment for the phone answering as well as for the chores. You might find that chores stay at 75% and that phone answering now goes up to 75% also. Figure 5-4 shows a graph of these results. What is unique about this design is that you introduced the treatment at different times for the two behaviors.

Figure 5-4 also illustrates a convention used in graphing multiple-baseline experiments. Remember, first of all, that the vertical line in the top graph divides the condition of free allowance from the condition of earned allowance for chore behavior. The convention is to use a slanted line to connect the line in the top graph to the line in the bottom graph to show that the same allowance conditions are applied to phone answering—although the start of earned allowance is 5 days later.

You now want to know if you can rule out alternative explanations of the difference.

Restricting your study to Terry rules out individual differences. Starting earned allowance at a different time for each behavior makes a coinciding event very unlikely. Such an event would have to occur by coincidence after 15 days for chores. It would also have to occur after 20 days for phone answering. Two such coincidences are very unlikely. You can be pretty sure that a time coincidence does not give an alternative explanation for the difference in chores and phone answering.

If you had found that chores increased but phone answering did not, you could not conclude that the change in chores was a result of the earned allowance. In this case, a coincidence with the introduction of the treatment for chores is possible.

One variation on the multiple baseline uses the same behavior with two or more people (e.g., Lavie & Sturmey, 2002). For example, suppose that you have two lazy children, Bob and Sue, instead of only one.

You might start by measuring Bob and Sue's chore behavior during a baseline. Next, you might begin treatment for Bob's chores but not for Sue's on the tenth day. Third, you might begin treatment for Sue's chores while continuing the treatment for Bob's on the twentieth day. If the treatment is effective for both Bob and Sue, the chances are slim that some unknown alternative explanation was responsible for the change. Notice that you have used two persons instead of two behaviors. What is unique here is that you introduce the treatment at different times for the two persons.

Be careful not to confuse a multiple baseline that uses two persons with a simple comparison design using two persons. For example, you might measure a baseline for Ted and Ann. Next you might introduce earned allowance for both of them on the tenth day. This is a comparison design because you are introducing the treatment at the same time for both persons. The example with Bob and Sue differs because you introduced the treatment at different times for each person.

Sometimes you might use a "backward" multiple-baseline design. You would start with the treatment first and then introduce the baseline. You would have two conditions for each person. You would start with treatment and then change to baseline.

Multiple-baseline designs are used when a behavior change will not reverse. For example, if your treatment teaches a child that 2 and 2 equals 4, you can't unteach him. By using a multiple baseline, you simply use the same treatment on a different behavior. You can still rule out time coincidences. The earliest known use of a multiple-baseline design was almost 40 years ago, in 1967 (Marks & Gelder, 1967).

You can always tell whether a single-subject experiment uses a multiple-baseline design by asking one question: "Does the experiment introduce the treatment condition at different times for two (or more) behaviors (or persons)?" The key fact to look for is starting the treatment at different times. If the treatment starts at different times, you can be sure the experiment uses a multiple-baseline design.

## One-Time Treatments

Most treatments continue until stopped. For example, if you give your children earned allowance, that remains the treatment only until you stop it. We know when treatment started and when treatment ended. Other treatments occur only once. Once you teach Barb how to do long division, you have delivered the treatment. Now she knows how to do it. I will consider one-time treatments as though they are ongoing. Thus, the treatment period starts when you teach Barb long division. It never ends. The treatment may be over but its effects continue. Therefore, the treatment period continues.

You can't use a reversal design with a one-time treatment because you can't undo your treatment. For example, you can't eliminate your friend's knowledge of how to do long division. You can use a comparison design or a multiple baseline. But you must be looking for this kind of situation to identify it. The experiment might involve comparing your friend's accuracy after teaching her the skill. Your baseline would be the period before you teach her. Your treatment would be the period after you teach her. That period would have no ending.

## Summary

The fourth tactic in using the behavioral strategy is to design a single-subject experiment. The principle of single-subject experiments is to expose the same person to all conditions in the experiment. The comparison design involves a comparison between baseline and treatment. This design rules out individual differences, but it does not rule out time coincidences. Reversal and multiple-baseline designs rule out both individual differences and time coincidences. A reversal design uses the sequence of baseline, treatment, and reversal to baseline. A multiple baseline compares the baseline and treatment conditions, introducing the treatment condition at different times for each behavioral variable. Single-subject experiments expose at least one person to all the conditions.

# Behavior Analysis Examples

This section presents several examples taken directly from the research literature. The examples show actual uses of all three experimental designs. (Hint: They are not in the same order as you learned them.)

### *Coaching Football*

Behavior analysis doesn't always deal with earth-shaking problems. One study reported a method for coaching football with 9- and 10-year-old boys in a Pop Warner League. Komaki and her colleagues applied their method to three plays: quarterback option, power sweep, and counter. Their method involved four steps. First, the coaches told each boy his assignment on each play. Second, they rehearsed each play. Third, they recorded the boys' performance during practice scrimmages and games. They used a checklist to record the plays as they occurred. Fourth, they told the boys how they did. They praised those who carried out their assignments. They hoped to improve the performance of each boy by using these four steps. Thus, these four steps are the treatment they used. I will call their treatment *praise.*

The baseline condition for all three types of plays was the old coaching method before the coaches started using the praise treatment. The researchers introduced the treatment condition for each play at different times. They introduced it for the quarterback option first. They left the power sweep and counter plays in the baseline condition of no praise. They then introduced the treatment for the power sweep. They left the counter play in baseline. This condition lasted four games. They then introduced the treatment condition for the counter play for 8 games. At that point they had all three plays in the treatment condition. Figure 5-5 shows this design. Correct performance was about 60% for all plays before praise and over 80% during praise.

15. Because they introduced the treatment at <u>different times</u> for <u>two or more</u> behaviors, what design did they use? _____ (comparison, multiple baseline, reversal) (Based on Komaki & Barnett, 1977.)

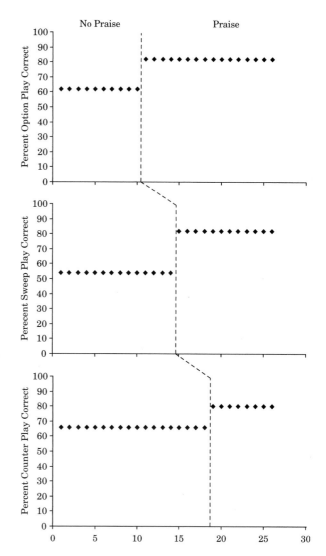

**Figure 5-5.** An experiment to analyze the effect of praising the player's execution of three football plays. This is a multiple baseline because praise was started at different times for each of the three plays. (Based loosely on Komaki & Barnett, 1977, except only the average for each condition is shown to keep the graph easy to read.)

16. Refer to Figure 5-5. The coach started praising correct execution after game 10 for the option play, after game 14 for the sweep play, and after game ____ for the counter play.

### *Energy Conservation*

Here's another example of a behavioral approach to conservation. Palmer and his associates studied a treatment to reduce electrical usage. First, they observed the Smiths' daily

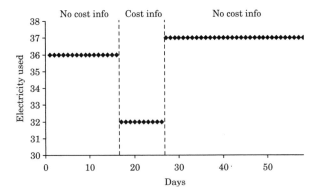

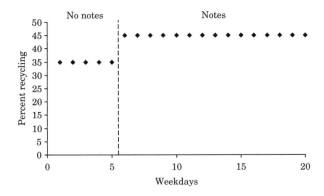

**Figure 5-6.** Results of an experiment to reduce electrical usage. This is a reversal design because it starts with a baseline, then a treatment, and finally a reversal to baseline. (Based loosely on Palmer, Lloyd, & Lloyd, 1977, except that only the average for each condition is shown to keep the graph easy to read.)

**Figure 5-7.** Results of an experiment to increase the percentage of families recycling. This is a comparison design because the treatment was compared to the baseline condition. (Based loosely on Keller, 1991, except that only the average is shown for each condition to keep the graph easy to read.)

usage of electricity for 16 days during baseline. Second, they observed the Smiths' usage during treatment for 10 days. The treatment was telling the Smiths the cost of the electricity they used each day. Third, they observed usage for 30 days during a reversal to baseline. During the reversal, they stopped telling the Smiths how much their electricity cost. Figure 5-6 shows this design. The researchers found that providing cost information reduced usage more than 10%. They studied three other families and found similar results. Because the researchers studied each family during baseline and treatment conditions, they used a single-subject experiment. (Based on Palmer, Lloyd, & Lloyd, 1977.)

17. Because the researchers returned to the baseline condition of no feedback after treatment, the researchers used what type of design? _____
(comparison, multiple-baseline, reversal)
18. Refer to Figure 5-6. This is a reversal design because the families were initially given no cost information, then cost information, and, finally, they were again given no cost information starting on day ____.

### Recycling

Conservation of global resources is critical to our world. Jacob Keller invented a simple way to increase recycling. What is so unique

about this example is that he was only 10 years old when he did the study. Jacob wrote notes to the 44 families on his street. He told them how many families on their street had put out material to recycle the week before. He found that the notes increased the number of families recycling. He studied each family during baseline and treatment. Therefore he used a single-subject experiment. (Based on Keller, 1991.)

19. Because he observed recycling only during baseline and treatment, what design did he use? _____
(comparison, multiple-baseline, reversal)
20. Refer to Figure 5-7. The baseline condition was "No notes" and the treatment condition was _____.

## Notes

### Note #1

Behavior analysts use the single-subject designs outlined in this lesson to find the effect of a particular treatment on the behavior of one individual. They test the generality of the treatment by repeating the experiment. If it works with a second individual, you have proved some generality. You can try it on more or different types of individuals. If it works, you've shown more generality. Sidman discusses the issue of generality extensively (Sidman, 1960).

21. Behavior analysts test the generality of the treatment by repeating the _____ _____.

### Note #2
Behavior analysts sometimes use group designs instead of single-subject designs. They often use them when they are interested in statistical information. For example, they might want to know how a behavioral treatment compares with a standard treatment. Does it increase studying and lead to higher achievement than standard classroom approaches? They would then try the behavioral treatment with one group and the standard treatment with another. They might find that the behavioral treatment produced an advance of 1.2 grade levels a year. If the standard treatment produced 0.7, they would conclude that the behavioral treatment worked better (Bushell, 1978). This is not a question of what causes the improvement. It is a question of how much improvement the treatment produces compared to other treatments.

22. I don't want you to conclude from my book that behavior analysts always use single-subject designs. Sometimes they use _____ designs.

### Note #3
Behavior analysts call another experimental design the *multi-element design*. It involves alternating the experimental conditions frequently, often every day. Treatment effect shows up as different rates of behavior under the two conditions. This design also rules out alternative explanations. Behavior analysts compared third-grade studying with and without a teacher's aide in the room (Loos, Williams, & Bailey, 1977). To determine if an aide was helpful, they alternated randomly between having an aide and not having an aide. When the aide was present, the students completed 28% more units.

23. The multi-element design involves _____ the experimental conditions many times, often every day.

## Helpful Hints

### Helpful Hint #1
As you have seen, the single-subject experiment is designed around the presentation and withdrawal of the treatment condition. When you are asked questions about what modifies a behavior, you may be tempted to answer "experiment." However, the experiment only studies the causes that may change behavior. The correct answer would be "treatment" because that is the part of the experiment that has modified or changed the behavior.

24. Therefore, when asked a question about what has modified a behavior, you should answer _____ (experiment, treatment).

### Helpful Hint #2
You can identify each experimental design by asking key questions. First, ask if the treatment condition is introduced at different times for two or more behaviors. If so, it is a multiple-baseline design. Second, ask if the third condition returns to the initial condition. If so, it is a reversal design. Third, ask if the design involves only a baseline and a treatment condition. If so, it is a comparison design.

25. Remember, the very first question to ask is whether the treatment condition is introduced at _____ times for two or more behaviors.

### Helpful Hint #3
If you have trouble with simple division, such as dividing 3 by 8 or 19 by 20, then you should use a calculator for the next lesson.

## Additional Readings

Baer, D. M., Wolf, M., & Risley, T. R. (1968). Some current dimensions of applied behavior analysis. *Journal of Applied Behavior Analysis*, pp. 91–97. This is a classic statement of the methods and goals of applied behavior analysis.

Barlow, D. H., Hayes, S. C., & Nelson, R. O. (1984). *The scientist practitioner: Research* accountability in clinical and educational settings. New York: Pergamon Press. This book discusses various experimental designs that can be used in clinical and educational settings. It also discusses the ethics of using these designs.

Barlow, D. H., & Hersen, M. (1984). *Single case experimental designs: Strategies for studying behavior change* (2nd. ed.). New York: Pergamon Press. A text on the history, issues, and use of single-case designs, including statistics and replication procedures. A good text for determining the pros and cons of this sort of design.

Campbell, D. T., & Stanley, J. C. (1963). *Experimental and quasi-experimental designs for research*. Chicago: Rand McNally. This book is the best exposition of complex comparison designs available. It outlines methods by which many alternative explanations of differences can be eliminated.

Pennypacker, H. S., & Johnston, J. M. (1993). *Strategies and tactics of human behavioral research*. Hillsdale, NJ: Erlbaum. Introduction to research methods for the advanced student.

Kazdin, A. E. (1977). Assessing the clinical or applied importance of behavior change through social validation. *Behavior Modification, 1*, 427–452. Kazdin provides a thorough overview of social validation techniques for assessing the importance of behavior change.

Risley, T. R., & Wolf, M. M. (1972). Strategies for analyzing behavior change over time. In J. Nesselroade & H. Reese (Eds.), *Lifespan developmental psychology: Methodological issues*. New York: Academic Press. This is an advanced statement of the methodological ideas underlying the two complex designs taught in this lesson.

Sidman, M. (1960). *Tactics of scientific research*. New York: Basic Books. This book is a classical statement of the logic underlying single-subject research designs. It was written prior to the widespread use of such designs with applied human research, and so it focuses on basic research.

# Programmed Reading

This section presents the following modules: (1) Fundamentals of Experimental Design, (2) Making a Useful Experiment, (3) The Simplest Design, (4) Using a Third Condition, (5) Using Many Behaviors or Persons, (6) Telling the Difference between Designs, (7) Another Tactic, and (8) Review.

## 1. Fundamentals of Experimental Design

59. Pre-test: The period of time when you are using an environmental event to modify someone's behavior is called the _____ condition.

60. Pre-test: The period of time when you are not using a treatment is called the _____ condition.

62. Pre-test: The treatment is an environmental event used to _____ the rate of a problem behavior.

68. Pre-test: You might praise Becky when she studies in hopes of increasing the amount of time that she studies. A behavior analyst would call this a(n) _____.

This is a really simple module. It teaches you how to define two concepts: baseline and treatment.

15. Behavior analysts use environmental events to modify behavior. The use of such events to modify a problem behavior is considered a *treatment*. Therefore, the use of an event like praising to get Nancy to study more would be called a(n) _____.

107. The treatment can either increase or decrease the rate of the behavior. To include both possibilities, we define it as the method introduced to _____ _____ (increase, decrease, modify) the behavior.

120. When called upon to define *treatment*, remember to choose the key word that includes both increasing and decreasing the behavior. Define it as the method introduced to _____ the rate of a behavior.

104. The period of time when the treatment is in effect is called the _____ (baseline, treatment) condition.

113. To find out whether a treatment works, you must compare the rate of the behavior when the treatment is being used and the rate of the behavior when the treatment is not being used. Scientists call the period of time when the treatment is not being used the *baseline* condition. For example, suppose you want to find out if you can use praise to increase the rate of Nancy's studying. To find out, you must compare her rate of studying when you use praise with her rate when you do not use praise. The condition where you do not use praise is called the _____ condition.

99. The baseline is the period of an experiment without the _____.

108. The treatment is the method introduced to _____ the rate of a behavior.

119. When asked what modified a behavior, students often answer "experiment." Can you see why that is wrong? Every experiment includes a baseline. The baseline does not modify the behavior. Therefore part of every experiment does not modify the behavior. The correct answer is the _____ condition.

### *2. Making a Useful Experiment*

75. Pre-test: Exposing one person to both the baseline and the treatment is the principle of _____ experiments.

54. Pre-test: Showing that individual differences and time coincidences did not cause a behavior is called *ruling out _____ explanations.*

76. Pre-test: You use the principle of single-subject experiments by exposing the same person to both the baseline condition and the _____ condition.

74. Pre-test: *Ruling out alternative explanations* means "showing that events other than the treatment did not _____ any change in the rate of behavior."

This module teaches a more complicated set of ideas. You will learn (1) what an alternative explanation is, (2) how to define two kinds of alternative explanations, (3) what it means to rule out alternative explanations, and (4) how single-subject designs help rule out alternative explanations. The concept of alternative explanations is the basis of all scientific experiments, so you will benefit throughout the course from learning the ideas presented in this module.

9. All experimental designs compare the rate of behavior during two conditions. They compare the _____ condition with the _____ condition.

8. A scientist may favor one way to explain the results of an experiment. But often other scientists can see <u>alternative</u> explanations for the same result. The most important aspect of an experimental design is whether it can rule out such _____ explanations of the results.

102. The first type of alternative explanation is that another cause started affecting the behavior at the same time as the cause that the scientist is studying. This is called a *time coincidence* because of the coincidence of the other cause starting at the same time. I will not quiz you on this term. However, you should recognize that a time coincidence is one kind of _____ explanation.

21. Here's an example of a time coincidence. Your son might start dating a new girlfriend at the same time that you started praising dressing more neatly. You might explain the neatness by your praise. However, the time coincidence permits the alternative explanation that the neatness is caused by the new _____ _____.

106. The second type of alternative explanation is that a difference between individuals explains why they behave differently. This is called *individual differences*. I will not quiz you on this term, but you should recognize that individual differences may provide a(n) _____ explanation for experimental results.

20. Here's an example of *individual differences.* You praise both Tony and Ann for studying. Tony's rate increases, but Ann's does not. You might conclude that praise doesn't work for everyone. However, the explanation for Ann's studying not increasing may be that she doesn't have basic studying skills. If true, you could teach her how to study and then use praise to increase her rate of studying. The individual difference here is that only _____ (Tony, Ann) has study skills.

1. *Individual differences* and *time coincidences* are two types of _____ explanations of experimental results.

24. If the results of your experiment have alternative explanations, then you have not learned anything. The goal of scientists is to design experiments so you can be sure that events other than the treatment did not <u>cause</u> the result. This is known as *ruling out _____ explanations.*

2. *Ruling out alternative explanations* means "showing that events other than the treatment _____ (did, didn't) <u>cause</u> an observed change in behavior."

37. Poorly designed experiments permit alternative explanations of the <u>cause</u> of any change in the rate of behavior. Well-designed experiments "rule out alternative explanations," which means "showing that events other than the treatment did not _____ any change in the rate of behavior."

3. *Ruling out alternative explanations* means showing that events other than the treatment did not _____ any change in the rate of behavior."

82. Showing that events other than the treatment did not cause any change in the rate of behavior is called *ruling out _____ explanations.*

25. If you can't rule out alternative explanations of behavior, you can never prove that your _____ caused any observed difference in behavior.

14. Behavior analysts use what are called <u>single-subject</u> designs to rule out alternative explanations of their results. I will show you how they do that in the rest of this module and the next few modules. Keep in mind that the importance of single-subject designs is that they rule out many _____ explanations of behavioral changes.

136. You use the principle of single-subject experiments by exposing the same person to both the baseline condition and the _____ condition.

17. Exposing <u>one</u> single person to both the baseline and the treatment is the principle of _____ subject experiments.

18. Exposing many people to both the baseline condition and the treatment condition also follows the principle of single-subject experiments. "Single subject" doesn't refer to how many people are in the experiment. It refers to whether each person is exposed to both the baseline and the _____ condition.

121. When behavior analysts use the principle of single-subject experiments, are the individuals in the baseline condition the same individuals as those in the treatment condition? _____ (yes, no)

16. By comparing Ken's pain before he knew how to relax with Ken's pain after he knew how to relax, you have ruled out _____ explanations based on individual differences between Ken and someone else. (There is no one else!)

### 3. The Simplest Design

51. Pre-test: Mom observed how often Teddy complied with her requests to pick up his toys. Then, she observed how often he complied when she gave him a little hug for complying. Mom used a(n) _____ design to study the effect of her little hug.

43. Pre-test: How many conditions does a comparison design use? _____

40. Pre-test: Because a comparison design exposes one person to both the baseline and the treatment, it uses the principle of _____ experiments.

57. Pre-test: The design in which you examine whether the treatment condition produces a higher rate of behavior

than the baseline condition is called a(n) _____ design.

56. Pre-test: The comparison design eliminates individual differences as causes of experimental results. The comparison design therefore is a design that rules out _____ explanations.

You can learn how to define and identify the simplest single-subject design in this module—the comparison design. You will learn why this design can rule out individual differences but not time coincidences.

83. Some experiments <u>compare</u> the rate of a person's behavior during baseline condition with the rate of the same person's behavior during the treatment condition. Such an experiment is the simplest form of single-subject design that involves only two conditions. Behavior analysts call such a design a(n) _____ design.

86. Suppose Jerry does 25% on his spelling tests when he cannot earn extra allowance and 75% when he can. You can rule out individual difference because you have studied only Jerry. You _____ (can, can't) rule out time coincidences.

5. A design that rules out individual differences (but not time coincidences) is the _____ design.

100. The comparison design eliminates individual differences. It therefore rules out some _____ explanations.

28. If you observe your weight loss without going to the weight loss center and then observe your weight loss when going to the center, you are using a(n) _____ design to study the effect of the center.

84. Sometimes behavior analysts start their experiments with the treatment rather than the baseline first. Such designs observe the two conditions <u>backwards</u> to their usual order. Therefore, an experiment in which you start by introducing the treatment rather than the baseline first is called using a(n) _____ comparison design.

124. When you use a "backward" comparison design, you start by introducing the _____ condition first.

127. You can always tell whether a single-subject experiment uses a comparison design by asking one question: "Does the experiment involve only the two conditions: baseline and _____?"

22. How many conditions do you use in a comparison design? ___

### 4. Using a Third Condition

52. Pre-test: Professor Brainbuster found that Ted averaged 50% when given quizzes every two weeks, 90% when given quizzes every class, and 50% when again given them only every two weeks. The prof used a(n) _____ design to study the effect of daily quizzing.

66. Pre-test: When you study baseline, then treatment, and then return to baseline, you are using a(n) _____ design.

64. Pre-test: When you observe treatment first, baseline second, and then return to treatment third, you are using a(n) _____ reversal design.

53. Pre-test: Professor Quenton found that Ann studied 50% of the study period when he used a standard sociology textbook but 90% when he used a comic book style sociology textbook. The prof used a(n) _____ design to study the effect of different textbooks.

You will learn in this module about an experimental design that is a little more complicated than the comparison design. The reversal design observes behavior during the baseline, treatment, and reversal conditions. By adding the third condition, the reversal condition, it rules out alternative explanations based on time coincidences. It is therefore a stronger single-subject design than the comparison design.

109. There are three single-subject experimental designs that rule out alternative explanations based on individual differences: the reversal design, the multiple-baseline design, and the _____ design.

13. Behavior analysts have invented two strong experimental designs called the *reversal design* and the "*multiple-baseline design* that not only eliminate individual differences but also eliminate time coincidences. Thus, the reversal design is stronger because it rules out more _____ explanations than the comparison design.

101. The first strong design is the reversal design. A <u>reversal</u> design is an experiment that looks at one behavior during baseline, during treatment, and during _____ to baseline.

11. Behavior analysts call a single-subject experiment that looks at one behavior during baseline, treatment, and reversal to baseline, a _____ design.

87. Suppose Jerry does 25% on his spelling test with no hugs, 75% with hugs, and 25% when returned to no hugs. The name for this experimental design is the _____ *design*.

88. Suppose Jerry's scores increase from 25% to 75% when you introduce hugs. Suppose that they decrease from 75% to 25% when you return him to no hugs. Notice that Jerry's scores change every time you change the hugging. Because it is unlikely that some other cause would twice just happen to change by coincidence at the same time that you change the hugging, this experiment rules out such _____ explanations.

89. Suppose Jerry's scores increased from 25% to 75% when you hug but then stayed at 75% when you stopped hugging. You should suspect that some unknown event caused Jerry to increase his scores at the same time that you started hugging. You should suspect that this unknown event continues to keep Jerry getting good scores even after you stopped hugging. The failure of Jerry's scores to decrease during the reversal means that you _____ (can, can't) rule out this possibility.

122. When you cannot rule out an alternative explanation for a change in behavior, then you _____ (can, can't)

conclude that the treatment caused the change.

85. Sometimes behavior analysts start with the treatment condition rather than the baseline. When using a reversal design, they will then end up reversing to their first condition, which is now the _____ condition.

123. When you start with treatment (rather than baseline), change to baseline, and then reverse to treatment, you are using a reversal design called a(n) _____ reversal design.

125. When you use a backward reversal design, you start with the _____ condition.

81. Remember, to figure out if you have a comparison design, you ask if the experiment involves only baseline and treatment. To confirm a reversal design, ask, "Does the experiment involve a third condition that is the same as condition number ___ (1,2)?"

138. You will more accurately identify experimental designs if you ask the right questions. The design that studies only baseline and treatment is the _____ design; the design that has a third condition that is the same as the first condition is the _____ _____ design.

### 5. Using Many Behaviors or Persons

45. Pre-test: If you introduce the treatment for Ann and Marie at the same time, you are using a(n) _____ design.

41. Pre-test: Bonnie argues and cries a lot during her first two years. When Bonnie is 2 years old, Mom reassures her when she isn't crying. Bonnie stops crying but keeps arguing. When Bonnie is 3, Mom continues to reassure her when she isn't crying and also reassures her a lot when she isn't arguing. Bonnie now doesn't cry or argue. Mom used a(n) _____ design.

39. Pre-test: A multiple-baseline design introduces the treatment for two or more behaviors at _____ times.

46. Pre-test: If you observe a behavior during baseline, treatment, and reversal, you are using a(n) _____ design.

55. Pre-test: Suppose you start with the treatment for one behavior and then later observe baseline for that behavior. Suppose you start with treatment at a different time for another behavior and then later observe baseline. You are using a(n) _____ multiple-baseline design.

65. Pre-test: When you observe baseline for two behaviors, introduce treatments for each behavior at different times, you are using a(n) _____ design.

You will learn about the other strong single-subject design in this module. You will learn to define it and identify examples of it. The multiple baseline can also rule out time coincidences by observing two behaviors. By introducing the treatment at different times for each behavior, you rule out time coincidences.

105. The second strong experimental design is the multiple-baseline design. It studies the introduction of treatment at different times to two or more behaviors. The key feature of the multiple-baseline design is that it begins treatment at _____ _____ times for two or more behaviors.

10. Because you obtain a baseline for <u>more than one</u> behavior, you call such a design a(n) _____ baseline design.

12. Behavior analysts call the experimental design that begins treatment at <u>different times</u> for <u>two or more</u> behaviors the multiple _____ _____ design.

98. The *multiple* in *multiple baseline* refers to at least two behaviors. A design is called a multiple baseline if it begins treatment at different times with at least _____ behaviors. The design could have three or four or even more behaviors!

80. Remember what <u>multiple</u> means. A multiple-baseline design involves introducing the treatment at different times for ____ or more behaviors.

92. Suppose Wally does 25% of his spelling homework and 50% of his math homework during the first month of school when Dad ignores both of them. Suppose he does 75% of his spelling and 50% of his math when Dad praises his spelling (but not his math) during the second month of school. Suppose, finally, that he does 75% of his spelling and 100% of his math when Dad praises both during the third month of school. Notice that Dad started treatment in different months for each behavior. Therefore, Dad is using a(n) _____ design.

90. Suppose that Wally's spelling increases when Dad praises it. Suppose, a month later, his math also increases when Dad praises it. Each behavior increased only when Dad praised it. Some other event probably did not cause the increase because it would have had to appear after one month for spelling and then after another month for math to coincide with Dad's use of praise. Two coincidences are very unlikely. Because Dad studied the same person for baseline and treatment, you can also rule out individual differences. Therefore, Dad's design rules out _____ explanations of the sudden improvement in Wally's homework.

93. Suppose you observe Tom's politeness and manners. After a month, you smile at him anytime he's polite. After another month, you also smile at him any time he shows some manners. Have you introduced treatment at different times for two behaviors? _____ (yes, no) Therefore, you used what single-subject design? _____ design

94. Suppose you observe Tom's politeness with no treatment. After a month you smile when he is polite. After another month you stop smiling when he is polite. Have you introduced the treatment at two different times? ____ (yes, no) Because the third condition returns to the first condition of no treatment, this is what single-subject experimental design? _____ design

110. There are several variations of multiple-baseline designs. Researchers may introduce treatment at different times for two people instead of two behaviors. This is a variation of which single-subject design? _____ design

91. Suppose this week you observe Tom's and Ann's studying for math. Next week you introduce treatment for Tom's studying math. The third week you introduce treatment for Ann's studying math. Have you introduced treatment at different times? ____ (yes, no) Therefore, this is what single-subject design? _____ _____ design

26. If you introduce treatment for one behavior and then, later, for another behavior, you are using what single-subject design? _____ design. If you introduce treatment after baseline and then return to baseline after treatment, you are using what single-subject design? _____ design

27. If you introduce treatment for three behaviors at the same time, you are using what single-subject design? _____ _____ design If you introduce treatment for three behaviors at different times, you are using what single-subject design? _____ design

95. Suppose you observe the number of dates that Ted and Bob get during March. You then teach them some good pick-up lines and observe their number of dates during April. You are using a(n) _____ design.

96. Suppose you observe the number of dates that Ted and Bob get during March. You then teach Ted some good pick-up lines and observe their number of dates during April. Finally, you teach Bob some good pick-up lines and observe their number of dates during May. You are using a(n) _____ design.

130. You have already learned about a backward comparison design and a backward reversal design. When you use a "backward" multiple-baseline design, you start with the _____ condition.

128. You can always tell whether a single-subject experiment uses a multiple-baseline design by asking one question, "Does the experiment introduce the treatment condition for each behavior at _____ (different, identical) times?"

129. You can identify each experimental design by asking key questions. The best question to start with is whether the treatment condition is introduced at _____ times. If so, it is a multiple baseline.

### 6. Telling the Difference between Designs

71. Pre-test: You should call a design that introduces the treatment at different times for two or more behaviors, a(n) _____ design.

47. Pre-test: Maria observes Davey's studying spelling with no special attention from her. She then gives him lots of praise whenever he studies spelling. Finally, she stops giving him praise. Maria is using a(n) _____ design.

48. Pre-test: Maria observes Davey's studying spelling with no special attention from her. She then gives him lots of praise whenever he studies spelling. Maria is using a(n) _____ design.

49. Pre-test: Maria observes Davey's study of spelling and English with no special attention from her. She then gives him lots of praise whenever he studies spelling. Finally, also gives him lots praise when he is studying English. Maria is using a(n) _____ design.

50. Pre-test: Maria observes Davey's studying spelling and English with no special attention from her. She then gives him lots of praise whenever he studies spelling and whenever he studies English. Maria is using a(n) _____ design.

72. Pre-test: You should call a design where you observe treatment, baseline, and reversal to treatment a backward _____ design.

73. Pre-test: You should call a design that introduces the treatment at the same time for two or more behaviors a(n) _____ design.

This module simply gives you some more practice telling the designs apart.

112. There are two single-subject experimental designs that rule out alternative explanations based on time coincidences: the _____ design and the _____ design.

111. There are three single-subject experimental designs that rule out alternative explanations based on individual differences: the _____ design, the _____ design, and the _____ design.

135 You should call a single-subject design that compares the same person's behavior during baseline and treatment a(n) _____ design.

79. Remember, though, if you observe baseline for two people and introduce the treatment at the <u>same</u> time you are still using a(n) _____ design. Only if you introduced the treatment at <u>different</u> times would you be using a(n) _____ design.

134. You should call a design that compares one person's behavior during baseline, treatment, and reversal to baseline a(n) _____ design.

7. A multiple-baseline design introduces the treatment to two behaviors at _____ times.

78. Remember the rule for one-time treatments like teaching someone long division. The rule is that the treatment period _____ (does, doesn't) end.

97. Suppose you observe John's long division and find he gets most of them wrong. Suppose you then teach him how to do it, and he gets most problems right. You might argue that this is a reversal design because you observed baseline, then you introduced the treatment of teaching him how to do long division, and then you observed after teaching. Three conditions! The trouble is that the condition after teaching is not a reversal to baseline. He now knows how to do long division. You can't reverse that. Therefore this is an example of a(n) _____ design.

33. Mom observes Kenny's cooperative playing with no special attention from her. She then gives him lots of praise whenever he plays cooperatively. Finally, she stops giving him praise. Mom is using a(n) _____ design.

34. Mom observes Kenny's cooperative playing and smiling with no special attention from her. She then gives him lots of praise whenever he plays cooperatively and whenever he smiles. Mom is using a(n) _____ design.

35. Mom observes Kenny's cooperative playing and smiling with no special attention from her. She then gives him lots of praise whenever he plays cooperatively. Finally, also gives him lots praise when he is smiling. Mom is using a(n) _____ design.

36. Mom observes Kenny's cooperative playing with no special attention from her. She then gives him lots of praise whenever he plays cooperatively. Mom is using a(n) _____ design.

### 7. Another Tactic

63. Pre-test: To use the behavioral strategy: (1) specify the problem behavior using a(n) _____, (2) gather information about it using the approach of _____, (3) check the _____ and _____ of your observations, (4) design a(n) _____ experiment.

I'll keep this simple by just giving you some simple drill on the tactics.

114. To use the behavioral strategy, (1) specify the problem behavior using a(n) _____.

115. To use the behavioral strategy, (1) specify the problem behavior using a behavioral definition, (2) gather information about it using the approach of _____.

116. To use the behavioral strategy, (1) specify the problem behavior using a behavioral definition, (2) gather information about it using the approach of direct observation,

(3) check the _____ and
_____ of your
observations.

117. To use the behavioral strategy: (1) specify the problem behavior using a behavioral definition, (2) gather information about it using the approach of direct observation, (3) check the reliability and social validity of your observations, (4) design a(n)_____ experiment.

77. Remember, if you are using the Web Book to answer questions about the tactics, you must enter your answers in the order learned. Thus, if you are asked to list the tactics in Unit 1, enter first "reliability" and then "social validity." Answer this question with both answers in the correct order: "The third tactic is to check for _____ and _____."

## 8. Review

67. Pre-test: You count the number of times Karen talks to you when you don't make eye contact with her. You then count the number of times that she talks to you when you do make eye contact with her. You are using a(n) _____ design.

61. Pre-test: The third tactic in using the behavioral strategy is to check the _____ and _____ of your observations.

58. Pre-test: The formula for reliability is: _____.

38. Pre-test: A design in which two (or more) behaviors are subjected to the same treatment at different times is called a(n) _____ design.

44. Pre-test: If an experimenter starts the treatment of two of Terry's behaviors at the same time, it is the single-subject design called a(n) _____ design.

70. Pre-test: You observe Ken's smiling without smiling back for 5 days. Then, you smile back for 10 days. You observe Ali's smiling without smiling back for 5 days. Then, you smile back for 10 days. You have used a(n) _____ design.

42. Pre-test: For one week, Alice smiles when Willie flirts. For another week she stops smiling. Finally, she smiles for a week. She is using a(n) _____ design to determine the effect of her smiling.

69. Pre-test: You might show that events other than the treatment did not cause an observed difference between baseline and treatment. Behavior analysts call this *ruling out* _____ *explanations*.

30. Infant Emily cries when you put her to bed. You have been comforting her when she cries. You stop comforting her on the advice of your doctor. You call the period of time when you stop comforting her the _____ condition.

137. You use the principle of single-subject experiments by exposing the _____ person to the baseline and treatment condition.

32. List three single-subject designs that can rule out individual differences: _____ design, _____ design, and _____ design.

6. A method designed to modify the rate of a behavior is called a(n) _____.

23. If experimenters compare a baseline condition with the treatment condition using the same person, they are using which single-subject design? _____ design

118. To use the behavioral strategy, (1) create a behavioral definition, (2) use a method of direct observation, (3) check the reliability and social validity of your observations, and (4) design a(n) _____ experiment.

29. In an experiment, a baseline is the record of a behavior prior to the use of a(n) _____ designed to modify that behavior.

126. With time sample recording, the observer records during a series of _____ intervals.

133. You observe Ken's smiling without smiling back for 5 days. Then, you smile back for 10 days. You observe Ali's smiling without smiling back for 10 days. Then, you smile back for 5 days. You

have used a(n) _____
_____ design.

19. Exposing the same person to both the baseline and the treatment is the principle of _____
_____ experiments.

103. The period of time before starting the treatment is called the _____
_____ condition. The period of time when the treatment is in effect is called the _____ condition.

31. List two single-subject designs that can rule out time coincidences: the _____ design and the _____ design.

131. You observe how many sales Clem makes when you pay him a straight salary for four weeks. Then, you pay him on commission for eight weeks. You also observe how many sales Ann makes when you pay her a straight salary for eight weeks. Then you pay her on commission for four weeks. You are using a(n) _____design to see if commissions produce more sales.

4. A design in which a behavior is measured before treatment, during treatment, and during a return to baseline is called a(n) _____ design.

132. You observe Juanita's smiling without smiling back for five days. Then you smile back for five days. Finally, you stop smiling back. You have used a(n) _____
_____ design.

## Programmed Examples

### 1. Programmed Examples

12. Pre-test: Dave had two friends, each of whom complained a lot about life. Dave listened to them for years, but he finally decided that he was only encouraging their complaints rather than helping them by listening. So he decided to do an experiment to see if ignoring them would be a help to them. He first recorded the number of complaints that they each made for a month. Then, he ignored his first friend while continuing to listen to his second friend's complaints. After another month, he ignored the complaints of both. He found that ignoring their complaints did reduce the amount of complaining without any other evidence of problems. Ask yourself the three questions. What single-subject experimental design did Dave use? _____
_____ design

13. Pre-test: Forgetful Fred always brought his books back to the library late. The library committee had charged only $.05 a day for overdue books. When they realized they had many patrons like Fred, they increased the fine to $.25 a day. Forgetful Fred became Fast Fred, always returning his books promptly. What single-subject experimental design did the library committee use to see if the increased fine would work? _____ design

14. Pre-test: Sarah normally weighed 130. She tried a new quick diet to find out how well it worked and lost 13 pounds. She then stopped using the diet, and her weight returned to 130. What experimental design was she using to determine the effectiveness of her new diet? _____ design

11. Pre-test: Dad defined "friendly" as "smiles, offers to do favors, and always stopping to talk." He observed his daughter Sally's behavior and found that she rarely engaged in those behaviors. He discussed his ideas with her, and she decided to work hard to increase those behaviors. Dad found that she now engaged in them frequently. He was not sure other people would agree that these behaviors made Sally friendly. He asked five family friends to rate Sally's friendliness before and after his talk with her. By comparing how the friends rated her friendliness with his observations, he was trying to determine the _____ of his behavioral definition of "friendly."

16. Regan wanted to be a more effective teacher. She decided to investigate the effect of praising her second-grade students when they were working hard. She measured Tony's study time before using praise and during using praise. Behavior analysts call the period before using praise the _____
_____ condition. They call the period of using praise the _____ condition. To find out what experimental design she was using, ask questions. Did she start treatment at different times? _____ (yes, no) Did she use a third condition that returned to the first

condition? _____ (yes, no) Did she study only baseline and treatment? ____ (yes, no) Therefore, she was using what single-subject design? a(n) _____ design

3. From January to June Ms. Murray politely listened to everything that Mr. James said when he interrupted her work. He interrupted her about 17 times a week. In July she started to ignore him. His interruptions decreased to less than twice a week. In September she began to feel sorry for him. She began listening to him again. His rate of interruptions increased to more than 16 a week. Behavior analysts call the initial period of listening the _____ condition. They call the period of ignoring him the _____condition. They call the period of once again listening to him the reversal to _____. To find out what experimental design she was using, ask questions. Did she start the treatment of ignoring him at different times? ____ (yes, no) Did she use a third condition that returned to the first condition? _____ (yes, no) Did she study only baseline and treatment? _____ (yes, no) Therefore, she was using what single-subject design? a(n) _____ design

17. Roger was not a socially skilled person. He never greeted friends or even smiled at them. Carol observed greeting and smiling for two weeks before trying to change them. After two weeks she started praising him when he greeted her. Two weeks later she started praising him when he smiled at her. Roger became a new, and friendlier, man! Notice that after two weeks she started praising greeting. Then after another two weeks she started praising smiling. So when you ask if she started treatment at different times, the answer is ____ (yes, no) Therefore, she was using what single-subject design? a(n) _____ design

10. Mrs. Green usually fixed a meat and potatoes kind of meal. Mr. Green kept track for six months and found that she prepared a vegetarian meal an average of once a week. Then, he started telling her how much better he felt every time that she fixed a vegetarian meal. She slowly increased the number of such meals so that after six months she was preparing an average of five a week. To find out what design Mr. Green was using, ask: did he introduce the treatment at different times? ____

(yes, no) Did he use a third condition identical to the first? ____ (yes, no) Did he use only baseline and treatment? ____ (yes, no) You can conclude that he used what singlesubject design? _____ design

18. Sonny had asked Ann and Patsy out for a date each week for two months with no success. Then Sonny put on some Rut Aftershave and asked Patsy out for a date each week for a month, with more success. He still asked Ann, but he never remembered to wear Rut. Finally, he started wearing Rut when asking both Ann and Patsy out. You want to figure out what design Sonny was using to find out how effective Rut was at changing both women's behavior. Ask: Treatment at different times? A third condition same as the first, or only baseline and treatment? The answers show that Sonny was using what single-subject design? a(n) _____ design

8. Mary seems to start talking most often in the middle of Fran's studying. Fran decided to record the interruptions for several days before discussing the situation with Mary. Notice that a discussion is a one-time treatment. That means that the treatment never ends. The period of time starting with the discussion is called the _____ _____ condition. Ask: Treatment at different times? A third condition, or only baseline and treatment? The answers show that Fran was using what single-subject design to find out if discussion changed Mary's interrupting? a(n) _____ design

2. Freda wore a wrist counter and found that she was critical of other people's ideas an average of 89 times per day for a two-week period. Then, she started meditating on being more accepting at the start of every day. Her rate of critical reactions dropped to less than eight per day for two weeks. Then she forgot to meditate for the next two weeks and found the rate of critical reactions increased to an average of 56 per day. You can ask three questions to figure out what design Freda used (by accident) to find out if meditating reduced her critical reactions. Ask: Treatment at different times? A third condition, or only baseline and treatment? The answers show that Freda was using what single-subject design to find out if meditating changed her

critical reactions? a(n) _____
_____ design

6. Let's see if you still remember ideas from prior lessons. Marie and Harry observed the frequency with which Steve played his new record. The agreement between their observations would be called _____.

19. Vern and his friend counted the number of times that Dee hit the tennis ball with a good level swing and immediately told her the results. Vern counted 100 level hits, whereas his friend counted only 87. What is the reliability of their observations? _____? Is this acceptable? _____

5. Jimmy counted the number of headaches that he got prior to enrolling in a transcendental meditation class. He got an average of five per week. His record of headaches before enrolling in the class would be called a(n) _____.

1. Bob was excited about the new audiovisual material he had for teaching his junior high social studies class. He found that the students' grades averaged 85% compared with only 78% last year. The problem with Bob's experimental design is that it cannot rule out _____ explanations for the observed increase (such as better students this year!).

9. Mom observed Sally's little-league batting average by recording each hit and at-bat immediately. After five weeks, she was delighted to find Sally usually got at least one hit per game. What method of observation did mom use? _____ recording

7. Marvin gradually became aware that he talked about the circumstances of his life in a negative and self-defeating manner. He decided to go to a class in self-actualization. Because the class might change his way of talking, it would be called a(n) _____.

| Calls | Hal | Fry |
|-------|------|------|
| throw | out | out |
| steal | out | safe |
| slide | safe | safe |
| catch | out | out |
| homer | safe | safe |

*Figure 5-8* Observations by Hal and Fry.

15. Professor Brainbuster was actually a very kindly old guy. He did everything that he could to help any student who was really trying in his courses. He considered a student to be trying if "they came to class regularly, asked questions, did their assignments, and asked for help when they needed it." The words in quotes would be called a(n) _____ of "trying."

20. When Billy nagged her for cookies just before dinner, Mom usually ended up giving him one. Billy nagged her every day as a result. Finally, one day she got tired of this routine and vowed to resist giving Billy any cookies before dinner. She found that he eventually stopped asking. After this had been going along well for six months, Billy asked for a cookie again one day, quite by surprise. Mom without thinking gave him a cookie. Now Billy nags her for a cookie every day. Mom ended up using a strong experimental design to discover the effect of giving Billy a cookie before dinner. This design effectively rules out _____ explanations of Billy's nagging.

4. Figure 5-8 shows the calls by Hal and Fay after they had been appointed umpires for the annual softball game. They decided to keep track of how they called action plays. What is their reliability? _____% Would a behavior analyst consider it acceptable? _____

# LESSON

# 6 Visual Analysis of Behavioral Experiments

## Reading Section

You have learned four tactics in using the behavioral strategy. You know how to develop a behavioral definition. You know how to use methods of direct observation. You know how to check for reliability and validity. You know how to design a single-subject experiment. This lesson will teach you a tactic for analyzing the results of that experiment.

The fifth tactic in using the behavioral strategy is to do a <u>visual analysis</u> of the data. Your analysis must result in drawing a conclusion about a simple question: "Did the treatment cause the behavior to change?" Drawing that conclusion requires four steps. I will teach you in this lesson how to take each step.

Behavior analysts usually use <u>visual analysis</u> to decide if their treatment caused a behavioral change. They usually use visual analysis in preference to statistical, the most common alternative method of analysis (see, Smith, Best, Stubbs, Johnston, & Archibald, 2000; Wainer & Velleman, 2000). I will describe the principle of visual analysis and show you how behavior analysts use it. I will show you how to use it with each single-subject design to decide if the treatment caused a difference.

## The Principle of Visual Analysis

**The principle of visual analysis** is to decide whether observed differences in behavior between baseline and treatment look <u>convincing</u>. That is, do they convince you that the level of behavior has changed as a result of the treatment? Do they convince you

---

> ### Who Needs Statistics?
>
> "It is not the obligation of the research worker to bow to the dictates of statistical theory until he or she has conclusively established its relevance to the technique of inquiry. On the contrary, the onus lies on the exponent of statistical theory to furnish irresistible reasons for adopting procedures which still have to prove their worth against a background of three centuries of progress in scientific discovery accomplished without their aid" (Hogben, 1957: p. 344, cited in Parsonson & Baer, 1978).
>
> 1. In other words, for three centuries scientific progress _____ (did, didn't) need statistics.

that the treatment actually helped? Scientists need more than simple differences to be convinced. They ask whether additional data would continue to show the difference. Most scientists find differences convincing if the observed behavior in baseline and treatment are "divided" and "stable." I will give you a brief introduction to using the criteria of *divided* and *stable* to decide whether convincing differences exist.

2. **The principle of visual analysis** is to decide whether differences between baseline and treatment look _____.

(To keep the treatment of visual analysis at an introductory level, I will ask you to visually analyze only the last three observations in each condition. Often examples will show many more observations. However, I will ask you to consider only the last three observations. I will base my definitions of *divided* and *stable*, as well as my examples of their use on the last three observations. Use the last three observations to determine both division and stability.)

The first criterion for convincing differences is whether the ranges of observed behavior in two conditions are divided. **Divided conditions** are when the ranges of the last three points of two conditions are <u>mutually exclusive</u>. (Note that you must look only at the last three points in each condition to find out if this is true.)

3. **Divided conditions**: The ranges of the last three points of two conditions are mutually _____.

Consider what *divided* means. *Divided conditions* means that the range of observed behavior in two conditions are mutually exclusive. The numbers are mutually exclusive if one condition consists only of low numbers while the other condition consists only of higher numbers. For example, suppose that baseline is 2, 3, and 1. Suppose that treatment is 7, 9, and 8. None of the baseline numbers are as large as even the smallest of the treatment numbers. These conditions are divided. Divided conditions help convince scientists that additional observations will continue to show differences.

By contrast, *not divided* means that one condition has a range that includes values from the other condition. A condition consisting mostly of high values but one low value might not exclude the values of the other condition. For example, suppose baseline consists of 4, 1, and 0. Suppose that treatment consists of 7, 3, and 9. Clearly the treatment numbers tend to be higher than the baseline numbers. However, treatment includes a value lower than the "4," the highest value observed during baseline. These conditions are not divided. Their failure to mutually exclude values from the other condition raises a doubt that added observations in treatment would still show a difference. For example, added observations might be numbers like 3, 5, and 2. Such num-

bers are hardly different from baseline. Observations that are not divided are not convincing!

The second criterion for convincing differences is whether the behavior in each condition is stable. Here is the definition for a **stable condition**: The last three numbers of one condition are <u>not moving closer</u> to the numbers in the other condition. (Note that you must look only at the last three points in both conditions to determine stability.)

4. A **stable condition**: The last three numbers of one condition are not moving _____ to the numbers in the other condition.

You might ask what *not moving closer* means. *Moving* refers to the way that the numerical values in a sequence of observations change. Suppose that the value of the first observation is 3. If the second value is 4, then the sequence *moves* from 3 to 4. The sequence "*moves* closer to larger values because 4 is a larger value than is the 3. If the third observation is 1, then the sequence *moves* from 4 to 1. The sequence is *not moving closer* to the larger values—in fact it is moving away. If the fourth observation is another 1, then the sequence is also not moving closer to the larger values.

Consider what *stable* means. A *stable condition* involves observations that are *not moving closer* to the values of the other condition. For example, suppose that baseline consists of 3, 3, 3. These values are not moving closer to larger values from observation to observation away from low numbers. You might be willing to guess that additional observations would continue to be low numbers, perhaps even the same number. Consider a second example. Suppose baseline consists of 2, 1, 2. These values also are not moving closer to larger values. You might guess that more observations would also be low. Stable rates are more likely to convince scientists that additional observations would still show a difference between the conditions.

By contrast, a *not stable* condition consists of observations that are moving closer to the values of the other condition. For example, suppose that baseline consists of 1, 2, and 3. Every new observation is larger than the one before it. You might guess that the next observations would be 4, 5, and 6. In that case, baseline observations might eventually increase until they showed no difference with the higher values of treatment. If that happened, then the conditions would no longer show a difference. Observations that are not stable are not convincing!

Please understand one very special consideration: a stable condition can consist of values that are changing as long as they are changing <u>away</u> from the values of the other condition. For example, baseline might consist of 3, 2, and 1. These low numbers are staying low—not getting larger. You might guess that the next observations might even stay at "1." Or perhaps they would vary from 3 to 1 as in 3, 1, 2, 3, 2, 1, etc. In any event, these baseline observations are showing no signs of approaching the higher values of treatment. Thus, these value are considered stable.

## The Four Steps of Visual Analysis

You must take four steps to decide if the treatment caused an observed difference between baseline and treatment. Each step requires asking and then answering a question. First, ask if the ranges of behavior in the two conditions are <u>divided</u>. Second, ask if the rates of behavior in the two conditions are <u>stable</u>. Third, ask if the differences are <u>convincing</u> in terms of the first two questions. Fourth, ask if the treatment <u>caused</u> the differences. I will explain how to do each of these steps in the rest of this lesson.

5. Start your visual analysis with two questions. First, ask if the ranges of behavior in the two conditions are _____ _____. Second, ask if the rates of behavior are _____.

The third step is to ask the question, "Are the differences convincing?" Answering the question depends on your answers to the first two questions. On the one hand, you might have found that the rates of behavior are both divided and stable. If so, you can predict that added observations would probably continue to show a difference. Because added observations would probably continue to show a difference, you can answer the question by concluding

that the differences are convincing. Here is the definition. **Convincing differences**: Every pair of adjacent conditions must be <u>divided</u>; every condition must be <u>stable</u>.

6. Convincing differences: Every pair of adjacent conditions must be _____, and every condition must be _____ _____.

On the other hand, you might have found in the first two steps that the rates of behavior fail to be either divided or stable. If so, you can't predict a continued difference. Remember, your data must meet both criteria to show a convincing difference. If they are divided but not stable, they do not show a convincing difference. If they are stable but not divided, they do not show a convincing difference. In either case, you would answer the third question by concluding that the differences are not convincing.

The fourth step is to ask the question, "Did the treatment cause the difference in behavior?" You should conclude that it did only if you have convincing differences and if you have ruled out alternative explanations. As you recall, only an experiment that uses a reversal or a multiple-baseline design rules out both time coincidences and individual differences. So you can conclude that the treatment caused the difference only if the difference is convincing and if you used either of these designs. You must conclude that the treatment did not cause the behavior to change if you do not have convincing differences or if you did not use one of these designs. Specifically, you cannot conclude that treatment caused behavior change if you use a comparison design even if you have convincing differences.

In summary, you must take four steps to complete a visual analysis. First, you must ask whether the behavior in treatment and baseline is divided. Second, you must ask if the behavior in each condition is stable. Third, you must ask if the differences are convincing. Fourth, you must ask if the treatment caused the differences.

### *How to Learn Visual Analysis*
Visual analysis involves looking at the results of an experiment. The results are expressed as numbers displayed in a graph.

Many people do not like numbers because math classes are often taught poorly. Many people react by shunning numbers. If you are one of those people, you can do yourself a huge favor by making an exception in this lesson. I strongly suggest that you read this lesson carefully and tune into the numbers and their graphs. If you do, you will find visual analysis quite easy. You will find that it does not involve computations of any kind. You simply need to look at the graph of the size and direction of the numerical results. Visual analysis is very important in this course. I estimate that as much as 10% of your grade depends on visual analysis.

◆ **Very Important** ◆

I will keep the first few examples simple by using only three numbers per condition. Later, I will give examples in which conditions consist of more than three numbers. No matter how many numbers are included in a condition, you will always look only at the last three to determine whether conditions are stable.

### Step #1: Are Conditions Divided?

Let's start with the first step. Ask, "Are the rates of behavior in the two conditions <u>divided</u>?" If the ranges of the last three points in each condition are mutually exclusive, the conditions are divided.

For example, suppose you run an experiment to see whether Mom's tutoring improves the scores that Annie earns on her weekly spelling test. Suppose you find that Annie gets low spelling test scores when Mom doesn't tutor her. Suppose you also find that Alice scores higher when Mom does tutor her. You would conduct a visual analysis to find out whether the differences in Annie's tests scores with and without tutoring are convincing. Figure 6-1 graphs the data from this experiment that you must visually analyze.

I have drawn a box in Figure 6-1 to help you understand the idea of mutually exclusive ranges. I have drawn the top line of the box through the highest No Tutoring observation of 60%. The box visually represents the range of No Tutoring observations because it includes all of those observations. The box

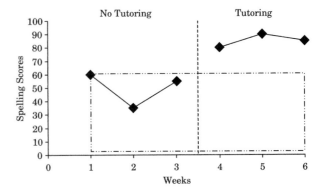

***Figure 6-1.*** First step in the visual analysis of a comparison design to analyze the effect of tutoring on Annie's spelling scores. The box gives you a simple way to decide if the conditions are divided. (This is a hypothetical experiment.)

makes it very easy to see that none of the observations in the Tutoring condition are within the range of the No Tutoring condition. In other words, the ranges of numbers in the two conditions are mutually exclusive. Therefore, you conclude that the ranges for the two conditions are divided.

7. Refer to Figure 6-1. The box clearly shows that the two conditions are divided because the No Tutoring scores are inside the box and the Tutoring scores are _____ (inside, outside) the box.

Here's another example. Suppose that you run an experiment to find out if Mom can raise Tom's math scores through tutoring. Suppose that you find that Tom's math score are low without tutoring and higher with tutoring. You would conduct a visual analysis to find out whether the differences in Tom's test scores with and without tutoring are convincing. Figure 6-2 graphs the data from this experiment that you would visually analyze.

I have drawn a box in Figure 6-2 to simplify deciding whether the conditions are divided. Again, I drew the top line of the box through the highest No Tutoring observation of 75%. The box makes it very easy to see that one of the observations in the Tutoring condition is within the range of the No Tutoring condition. You can conclude that the two conditions are not divided.

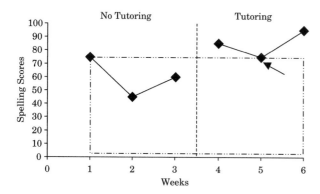

**Figure 6-2.** First step in the visual analysis of a comparison design to analyze the effect of tutoring on Tom's math scores. The box gives you a simple way to decide if the conditions are divided. (This is a hypothetical experiment.)

8. Refer to Figure 6-2. Because one of the tutoring observations is inside the box, we say that the conditions _____ (are, aren't) divided.

In summary, to see if the ranges of behavior in baseline and treatment are divided, draw a box around the last three points in the lowest condition. Make sure the top of the box goes through the highest point. Make sure that top line is parallel with the bottom line of the graph. Extend the box into the other condition. The conditions are divided if none of the points in the other condition are in the box.

### Step #2: Are Conditions Stable?

Let's move on to the second step. Ask, "Are the rates of behavior in the two conditions stable?" To the extent that the last three observations in baseline and treatment are stable, you can conclude that the differences would still exist if you made more observations. How do you know if the observations are stable?

Here is a simple definition: The numbers in a condition are stable if they are *not* <u>moving closer</u> to the values in the other condition.

For example, suppose you are looking at a sequence of low numbers in a baseline condition and wish to decide if the sequence is moving closer to the larger numbers in treatment. If the three numbers are 3, 3, and 3, then they are not moving closer in value to the larger treatment values. Clearly they are stable. If the three numbers are 4, 3, and 1, then they are not moving closer to the larger treatment

values—in fact they are moving further away from those values. Clearly, they are stable. However, if the three numbers are 0, 2, and 5, then they are moving closer to the larger treatment values. Clearly, they are not stable. You can easily decide stability in these cases because the three numbers are changing in the same direction. Such cases are easy to decide!

But suppose you are looking at a sequence of observations moving in different directions. For example, suppose the three baseline numbers are 1, 3, and 2. Suppose the treatment numbers are larger. Let's apply the definition. The second number moves the sequence closer to the larger treatment numbers. But then the third number does not move closer to the larger values because it decreases from 3 to 2. Thus the sequence of numbers first moves closer to the larger treatment numbers and then it moves away from them. Nevertheless, the sequence started at 1 and ended at 2 so that overall it moved closer to the treatment values by one. If future observations continued this pattern, they would slowly draw closer to the larger treatment numbers. Thus, they are *not* stable.

The last example suggests a more precise definition of stability. If the sequence ends with a value that is not moving closer to the treatment values compared to the value with which it starts, then the sequence is stable.

Let's look at a simple example of stability. Suppose you wanted to run an experiment to see if Mom's tutoring would improve the scores Lisa earns on her weekly spelling test. Again suppose that you find lower scores when Mom is not tutoring and higher scores when she is tutoring. You want to conduct a visual analysis to see if the differences are convincing. Let's assume you already decided the scores are divided. Figure 6-3 shows the results of the experiment.

I have drawn an arrow on Figure 6-3 to help you understand the idea of stability. I have started the arrow on the first point of baseline and drawn it through the last point of baseline. The arrow visually represents the overall movement in the value of these three numbers. The arrow makes it very easy to see that these points are not moving closer to the larger treatment numbers. Therefore, you conclude that the baseline condition is stable.

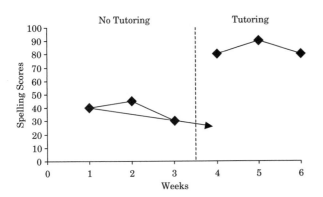

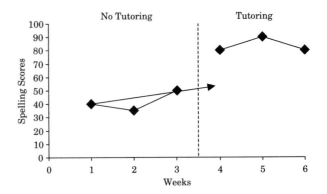

***Figure 6-3.*** Second step in the visual analysis of a comparison design to analyze the effect of tutoring on Lisa's spelling scores. The arrows give you a simple way to decide if the conditions are stable. (This is a hypothetical experiment.)

***Figure 6-4.*** Second step in the visual analysis of a comparison design to analyze the effect of tutoring on Paul's math scores. The arrows give you a simple way to decide if the conditions are stable. (This is a hypothetical experiment.)

9. Refer to Figure 6-3. The arrow clearly shows that the No Tutoring condition is stable because it points _____ (away from, toward) the values in the Tutoring condition.

Here's an example of an unstable condition. Suppose you run an experiment to see if Mom's tutoring will improve Paul's math scores. You find that his math scores are lower when Mom doesn't tutor and higher when she does. You want to conduct a visual analysis to see if the differences are convincing. Let's assume you already decided the scores are divided. Figure 6-4 shows the results of the experiment.

I have again drawn an arrow on Figure 6-4 to help you analyze stability. I have started the arrow on the first point of baseline and drawn it through the last point of baseline. The arrow visually represents the overall direction of change in these three numbers. The arrow makes it very easy to see that these points are moving toward the larger treatment numbers. Therefore, you conclude that the baseline condition is not stable.

10. Refer to Figure 6-4. Because the arrow points toward the larger values of the Tutoring condition, we say that the numbers in the No Tutoring condition _____ (are, aren't) stable.

In summary, the easiest way to decide if the numbers in a condition are stable is to

draw an arrow through the first and last numbers. If the arrow either points straight ahead or away from the values in the other condition, then the condition is stable.

### Step #3: Are Differences Convincing?

Let's move on to the third step. Ask, "Do convincing differences exist?" Consider only the last three observations. Ask if the rates of behavior for each set of adjacent conditions are divided. Ask if the rates of behavior for every condition is stable. If you find divided and stable data, then conclude that the data show a convincing difference between conditions. If you find data that fail to meet even one of the criteria in even one condition, conclude that they do *not* show a convincing difference. I will show you how to apply these criteria to the three basic single-subject experimental designs.

### Step #4: Did Treatment Cause the Differences?

Finally, you arrive at the fourth step, where you ask, "Does the design rule out alternative explanations?" You can answer this question easily. You can automatically answer "no" to this question if you do not have convincing differences. You can answer "yes" if you have convincing differences and you used a single-subject design that rules out both individual differences and time coincidences. Thus, you can answer "yes" only if you used a reversal design or a multiple-baseline

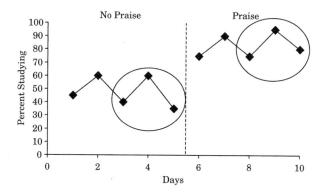

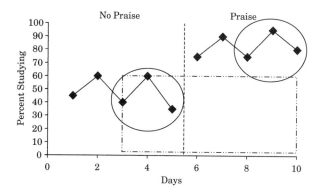

**Figure 6-5.** Graph of the effect of praise on Tommy's studying. The circles remind you to conduct your visual analysis using only the last three points of each condition.

**Figure 6-6.** First step in the visual analysis of a comparison design to analyze the effect of praise on the percentage of scheduled studying that Tommy does. Apply the box only to the last three points of each condition. (This is a hypothetical experiment.)

design. You must answer "no" if you used a comparison design or any kind of group design with statistics.

## Visual Analysis of Comparison Designs

The visual analysis of comparison designs is simple. First, you determine if rates of behavior for baseline and treatment are divided. Second, you look for stability for both the baseline and treatment. Of course, you restrict your attention to the last three observations in each condition. I will give you examples of data in a comparison design that are both convincing and unconvincing. I will start with an example that might convince you that a clear change of behavior occurred.

Suppose that Teacher wants to know if praising Tommy will increase the percentage of time he studies during study hall. You might select a comparison design. You might observe Tommy's studying for 5 days without praise and then for 5 days with praise. You would graph these 10 observations so you can visually analyze them. I have made the graph for you in Figure 6-5.

This is the first example that shows more than three observations per condition. I suggest you draw a circle around the last three points of each condition as a reminder to base your decision about both divided and stable on only those last three points. Notice that I have added circles to Figure 6-5.

You would then take the first step: decide if the conditions are divided. The first step is to draw a box around the last three points in the baseline condition, extending it into the treatment condition. Make sure the top line goes through the highest of those last three points. Extend the box through the treatment condition. If none of the last three points in treatment are in the box, then the conditions are divided. I have shown the box in Figure 6-6.

11. Refer to Figure 6-6. The last three points of each condition _____ (are, aren't) divided.

You would then take the second step: decide if the observations in each condition are stable. The second step is to draw an arrow through the first and third (of the last three points) in each condition to see which way they are pointing! I have added the arrows to Figure 6-7.

12. Refer to Figure 6-7. The last three points of the No Praise condition _____ (are, aren't) stable. The last three points of the Praise condition _____ (are, aren't) stable. Decide whether you agree that a convincing difference exists between the conditions.

You would then take the third step: decide if the differences are convincing. To do that you

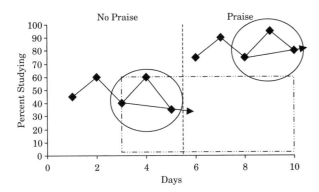

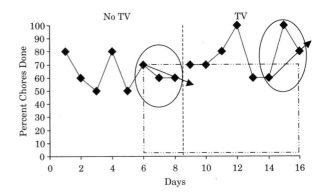

**Figure 6-7.** Second step in the visual analysis of a comparison design to analyze the effect of praise on the percentage of scheduled studying that Tommy does. Apply the arrows only to the last three points of each condition. (This is a hypothetical experiment.)

**Figure 6-8.** Visual analysis of a comparison design to analyze the effect of permission to watch TV on the percentage of chores that Alice does. (This is a hypothetical experiment.)

must decide whether the rates of behavior in the two conditions are *both* divided and stable.

You are now ready to take the fourth step. If your experimental design rules out alternative explanations, then you can conclude that your praise made a difference. You ruled out individual differences because you studied only Tommy. Unfortunately, as you already know, comparison designs do not rule out time coincidences. Some event may have happened at about the same time that you introduced praise. That event might have had a powerful effect on studying. This design gives you little confidence that such a coincidence did not occur. Even though you can confidently conclude that Tommy's studying changed, you can't be sure that praise was the cause of the change.

13. Even though the differences are convincing, you can't conclude that the treatment caused the differences because you used a(n) _____ design.

Before going on to more effective designs, let me show you an example of results with a comparison design that is not as clear. Suppose Mom wants to know if letting Alice earn the right to watch TV will increase the percentage of chores she does. You select a comparison design. You observe Alice's chore behavior for 5 days without being able to earn TV and then for 5 days when able to earn TV.

You graph these 16 observations so you can visually analyze them. Remember to draw circles around the last three points in each condition.

Step #1: Decide if the conditions are divided. Draw a box around the last three points in the baseline condition, extending it into the treatment condition. Make sure the top line goes through the highest of those last three points. Extend the box through the treatment condition. If none of the last three points in treatment are in the box, then the conditions are divided.

Step #2: Decide if every condition is stable. Draw an arrow through the first and the last points (of the last three points) of each condition. Decide if the baseline arrow is pointing toward or away from the values of the treatment. Decide if the treatment arrow is pointing toward or away from the values of the baseline.

Step #3: Decide whether the differences between the conditions are convincing. Remember, the conditions are convincing if you found that the conditions are divided and if every condition is stable. Figure 6-8 shows the graph with the points circled and the box and arrows added.

14. Refer to Figure 6-8. Step #1: Are the conditions divided? _____ (yes, no) Step #2: Are all conditions stable? _____ (yes, no) Step #3: Are the differences convincing? _____ (yes, no) Step #4: Did the treatment cause the differences? _____ (yes, no)

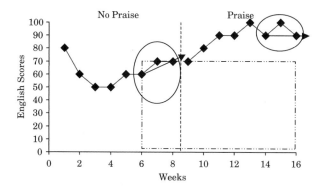

***Figure 6-9.*** Visual analysis of a comparison design to analyze the effect of praise on Danny's English scores. (This is a hypothetical experiment.)

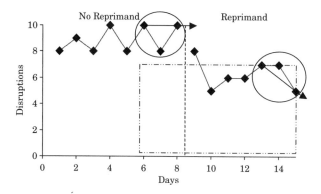

***Figure 6-10.*** Visual analysis of a comparison design to analyze the effect of reprimands on Tommy's disruptions. (This is a hypothetical experiment.)

In summary, Alice's data show conditions that are not divided although they are stable. We cannot be sure that the level of Alice's studying has permanently changed because the differences are not convincing. You would conclude that the treatment did not cause differences in Alice's chore behavior.

Now let's consider an example of differences that are not convincing because they are not stable. Suppose you analyze the effect of praise on Danny's studying.

You visually analyze Danny's data. The first step is to decide whether the last three points of the conditions are divided. The second step is to decide if every condition is stable. The third step is to decide if the conditions show convincing differences. The fourth step is to decide whether treatment caused a difference. Figure 6-9 shows the graph complete with points circled, with the box to determine divided conditions, and the arrows to determine stable conditions.

15. Refer to Figure 6-9. Step #1: Are the conditions divided? _____ (yes, no) Step #2: Are all conditions stable? _____ (yes, no) Step #3: Are the differences convincing? _____ (yes, no) Step #4: Did the treatment cause the differences? _____ (yes, no)

Analyzing a treatment that reduces behavior is no different from analyzing one that increases behavior. You take the four steps of visual analysis in both cases. See if you can take these steps using the data in Figure 6-10.

16. Refer to Figure 6-10. Step #1: Are the conditions divided? _____ (yes, no) Step #2: Are all conditions stable? _____ (yes, no) Step #3: Are the differences convincing: _____ (yes, no)? Step #4: Did the treatment cause the differences? _____ (yes, no)

In summary, here's how you visually analyze data from a comparison experiment. First, you ask whether the range of behavior in baseline and treatment are divided. Second, you ask if the rates of behavior in both conditions are stable. You consider only the last three points in each condition. Third, you ask if the differences are convincing. If the data meet both criteria, you conclude the differences are convincing. If the data fail to meet both criteria even once, you conclude the differences are not convincing. Fourth, you can never conclude that the treatment caused a difference when using a comparison design.

## Visual Analysis of Reversal Designs

As you recall, reversal designs start out as comparison designs. You make a comparison design into a reversal design by adding a reversal-to-baseline condition. To do a visual analysis of a reversal experiment, you follow the same four steps but with several small changes.

### Modifying Cartoonists' Behavior

Cartoons can be very influential. Two researchers noticed that many cartoonists showed their characters in cars without seatbelts. They found that only 15% showed seatbelt usage. They set out to change that. They wanted cartoonists to set a good example for children by showing seatbelt usage. They wrote a letter to each of eight cartoonists, asking them to do so. They sent the letter after differing amounts of time. This created a multiple-baseline design. After their letter, 41% of the cartoons showed seatbelt usage. Thus, cartoonists showed 26% more seatbelt usage after the letter. (Based on Mathews & Dix, 1992.)

17. To see if the difference was real would require a(n) _____ analysis.

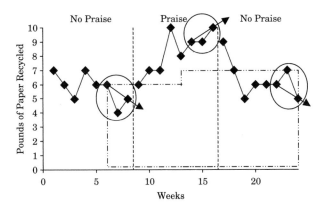

**Figure 6-11.** Visual analysis of a reversal design to analyze the effect of praise on the pounds of paper that Jill recycles. (This is a hypothetical experiment.)

18. Refer to Figure 6-11. Step #1: Are the conditions divided (including treatment and reversal)? _____ (yes, no) Step #2: Are all conditions stable (including treatment)? _____ (yes, no) Step #3: Are the differences convincing? _____ (yes, no) Step #4: Did the treatment cause the differences? _____ (yes, no)

As you will see in the following example, you must follow the same four steps used in conducting a visual analysis of this experiment, but you must also consider data in the reversal-to-baseline condition. Your first step is to ask, "Are the last three points in baseline and treatment divided?" The change in this step is that you must also ask whether the last three points in treatment and reversal are divided. Your second step is to ask, "Is each condition stable?" You analyze baseline and treatment as in a comparison design. The change in this step is that you must also analyze stability of the reversal to baseline. The third step is the same. The fourth is the same, but with a reversal design, you can conclude that the treatment caused convincing differences.

Suppose that you run an experiment to see if Dad's praise can improve Jill's recycling. You start the experiment by having Dad ignore Jill's recycling. You then have him praise her recycling to see whether that increases recycling. Finally, you have him stop praising her recycling to be sure that any increase really is caused by his praise.

Let's look at one more reversal design. Suppose that Mom is trying to get Jim to leave the TV and exercise more often. Suppose that she uses "pep talks" about health as her treatment. You might run an experiment using a reversal design. For baseline, Mom doesn't require Jim to exercise in order to see TV. For treatment, Mom does require Jim to exercise. Finally, for reversal to baseline, she again lets Jim freely watch TV. Figure 6-12 shows the data complete with circles, boxes, and arrows to help you analyze the results.

19. Refer to Figure 6-12. Step #1: Are the conditions divided (including treatment and reversal)? _____ (yes, no) Step #2: Are all conditions stable (including treatment)? _____ (yes, no) Step #3: Are the differences convincing? _____ (yes, no) Step #4: Did the treatment cause the differences? _____ (yes, no)

Jim's data illustrate an important point about the third step in visual analysis. Failure of the data to meet one criterion in even one condition means that you can't conclude the

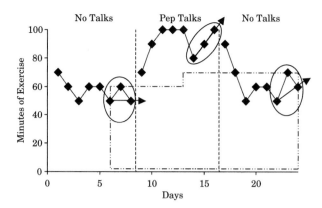

***Figure 6-12.*** Visual analysis of a reversal design to analyze the effect of pep talks on the amount of time Jim exercises. (This is a hypothetical experiment.)

data show convincing differences. With Jim's data, the division between baseline and treatment and between treatment and reversal was clear. Also, both the baseline and treatment were stable. But the reversal was not stable. Even though reversal was the only condition not stable, you must conclude that the differences are not convincing. That in turn makes a point for the fourth step. It means you can't conclude that the pep talks caused an increase in exercising even though you have a design that rules out alternative explanations.

In summary, here's how you visually analyze data from a reversal experiment. First, you ask whether the last three observations in baseline and treatment are divided. You also ask whether the last three observations in treatment and reversal are divided. Second, you ask whether the last three observations in baseline, treatment, and reversal are stable. Third, you conclude that you have convincing differences if both criteria are met. Fourth, if you have found convincing differences, you conclude that treatment caused the differences because the reversal design rules out alternative explanations.

## Visual Analysis of Multiple-Baseline Experiments

Multiple-baseline designs also start out as comparison designs. You make them into multiple-baseline designs by adding a second comparison. This involves repeating the

experiment with a second behavior, person, or situation. You must also start treatment for the second comparison at a different time from the first comparison. You have ruled out coincidences if the behavior changes only after treatment for both behavioral variables.

One way that you could make a comparison design into a multiple baseline is simply by adding a second person and starting treatment at a different time. You would visually analyze each person's data separately, using the same approach that you used with comparison designs. Suppose you found convincing differences for both persons (and you started treatment at different times for each on them). Then, you could conclude that treatment caused the differences.

Let's look at an example. Suppose Teacher wants to help Robby and Marie study more. She decides to use praise. You help her design a multiple baseline to find out if praise works. You observe the percentage of each day that each student spends studying. You must then visually analyze the resulting data.

How do you do a visual analysis of the experiment with Robby and Marie? You essentially do the first two steps on the data for each person separately. First, ask if the conditions are divided for Robby. Then, ask if they are divided for Marie. You conclude that the conditions are divided for the whole experiment only if they are divided for each person. Second, ask if the conditions are stable for Robby. Then, ask if they are stable for Marie. Again, conclude they are stable for the whole experiment only if they are stable for each person. Third, consider the results of the first two steps for both Robby and Marie. The experiment shows convincing differences only if the differences for both Robby and Marie are convincing. Do your analysis with Figure 6-13.

20. Refer to Figure 6-13. Step #1: Are the conditions divided (for Robby and for Marie)? _____ (yes, no) Step #2: Are all conditions stable (for Robby and Marie)? _____ (yes, no) Step #3: Are the differences convincing? _____ (yes, no) Step #4: Did the treatment cause the differences? _____ (yes, no)

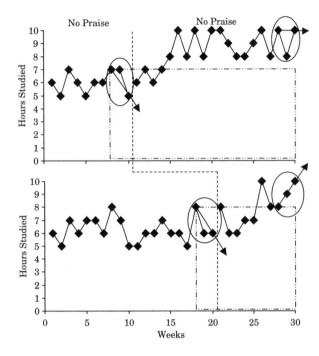

***Figure 6-13.*** Visual analysis of a multiple baseline design to analyze the effect of praise on Robby's and Marie's studying. (This is a hypothetical experiment.)

---

---

In taking step #3, you note that the data for Robby meet both criteria. However, the data for Marie are not divided because the last three points in each condition include a score of 80%. Because the data for one person, Marie, are not convincing, you must conclude that the data for the experiment as a whole are not convincing. Since you don't have convincing differences, you cannot draw a conclusion about whether praise caused Robby and Marie to study more in the fourth step.

In summary, here's how you visually analyze data from a multiple-baseline experiment. First, you ask whether the last three observations in baseline and treatment are divided for the first person (or behavior or setting). Second, you ask if the last three observations for baseline and treatment are stable for both conditions for the first person. Then, you repeat the same questions for the second person. Third, if both behavioral variables meet both criteria, then you can conclude that you have convincing differences for the overall experiment. If you find even one place for either person where the data do not meet the criteria, then you can't conclude that you have convincing differences.

Fourth, if you have convincing differences in a multiple-baseline design, you can conclude that the treatment caused the differences.

## Summary

In this lesson, you learned that the fifth tactic in using the behavioral strategy is to visually analyze the data. The principle of visual analysis is to look for convincing differences. First, you ask if the last three observations in each condition are divided. Second, you look to see if the last three observations in all conditions are stable. Third, if the observations are divided and stable, then the results convincingly show a difference. Fourth, if you use an experimental design that rules out alternative explanations, then you can conclude that the treatment caused the difference.

## Behavior Analysis Examples

### Changing Police Behavior

Police in Greeley, Colorado, were reluctant to give tickets for not using child safety seats. They felt it unfair if the parents were obeying the law in every other way. Lavelle and her colleagues knew that safety seats could save children from serious injuries.

Lavelle and her colleagues convinced the police to change procedures. This new procedure permitted the police to give a coupon

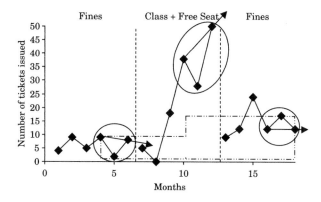

**Figure 6-14.** Visual analysis of a reversal design to analyze the effect of permitting police to substitute a milder punishment than fines for parents driving with infants not in a safety seat.

when they issued a ticket. Drivers could use the coupon to attend a one-hour class on child safety and to get a child safety seat. If they did, then the courts would waive the $50 fine. This way the parents could learn why safety seats are important. Also, they could get a safety seat even if they could not afford one. Police apparently found this mild punishment more socially valid than a monetary fine.

Lavelle and colleagues designed a reversal experiment. The baseline consisted of observing the number of tickets that police issued when the tickets led to a monetary fine. Treatment consisted of issuing tickets that led to the milder punishment of attending a class and being eligible for a free safety seat. The reversal returned to the monetary fine. Figure 6-14 illustrates the experiment.

22. Refer to Figure 6-14. Step #1: Are the conditions divided (including treatment and reversal)? _____ (yes, no) Step #2: Are all conditions stable (including treatment)? _____ (yes, no) Step #3: Are the differences convincing? _____ (yes, no) Step #4: Did the treatment cause the differences? _____ (yes, no)

Successful visual analysis of this example requires remembering to include the reversal condition in your analysis. If you did that, then you concluded that the conditions were divided and stable. You concluded that the data show convincing differences. Finally, because the reversal design rules out alternative

explanations, you can conclude that other alternative explanations are unlikely and the coupon did cause the difference. You can be pretty sure that the coupon procedure caused the police to write more tickets. (Based on an article by Lavelle, Hovell, West, & Wahlgren, 1992. The data are rounded off to values consistent with the grid used in this figure.)

### *Helping the Elderly Remember*

Talking with your aging relatives can be hard. They tend to ramble on. They say confusing things and ignore what you have said. Bourgeois guessed that helping their memory might improve their conversations. She made a memory booklet for six elderly people suffering from Alzheimer's. Each page of the booklet contained one fact and a relevant photo. Some pages contained facts like "My name is Anna" and other facts such as relatives, birthplace, and dates. Other pages of the booklet contained the daily schedule and the names and photos of people who helped bathe and feed Anna. Booklets contained 20–40 facts. Bourgeois gave the booklets to the elderly people to use during conversations.

Bourgeois designed a (backward) reversal design. For baseline, she observed how often the elderly person made comments relevant to a conversation when they had access to the memory aid. For treatment, she removed the memory aid. Finally, for the reversal she again gave the elderly person access to the memory aid. Figure 6-15 illustrates this experiment.

23. Refer to Figure 6-15. Step #1: Are the conditions divided (including treatment and reversal)? _____ (yes, no) Step #2: Are all conditions stable (including treatment)? _____ (yes, no) Step #3: Are the differences convincing? _____ (yes, no) Step #4: Did the treatment cause the differences? _____ (yes, no)

Notice that this design is "backward." The first condition involves the treatment. The second condition involves no treatment and is thus the baseline. The third condition is the reversal and returns the person to the treatment condition. Your visual analysis followed the same four steps as a "forward" reversal design.

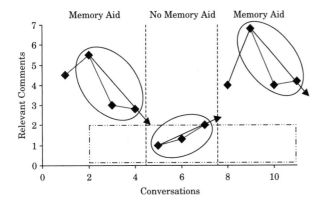

**Figure 6-15.** Visual analysis of a (backward) reversal design on the effect of memory aids on the conversational behavior of elders with Alzheimer's disease.

These conditions are divided, but they are not stable. The number of comments in the initial baseline and reversal condition are both decreasing toward the smaller values of baseline. Likewise, the values in the baseline are also increasing toward the values of the treatment condition. None of them are stable! These results suggest that the memory aid produced an increase in relevant comments at first but then started to lose its power. It appears that had the researchers made more observations they would have seen the differences disappear altogether. In any event, you cannot conclude that the differences are convincing. The use of a reversal design rules out alternative explanations, but since you don't have convincing differences, you can't conclude that the treatment caused any difference (based on Bourgeois, 1993).

## Notes

### Note #1
Most behavior analysts argue that the use of statistics has not helped find strong causal relationships. It rewards researchers for finding weak relationships. After earning a Ph.D. in sociology with a minor in mathematical statistics, I examined the strength of statistically significant relationships reported in the most prestigious sociological journal. I examined all 100 significant relationships for one full year. I found that, on the average, the relationship explained about 7% of the data (Miller, 1968a). In other words, they left 93% unexplained! I soon stopped using statistical research in favor of the visual analysis of single-subject experiments.

Statistics have not been helpful for a second reason. Researchers often use statistics to analyze correlations between variables. When they find a relationship, even if it were to be strong, they do not know if it is causal. If boys are more assertive than girls, we have a correlation. But the correlation doesn't provide evidence that male genes cause assertive behavior. The correlation could come from most adults encouraging assertive behavior in males and discouraging it in females. In other words, the correlation could come from other variables that the researcher has not measured. Single-subject experiments provide much stronger evidence of causality. When the researcher introduces the treatment and the behavior changes, we can be much more confident that the treatment caused the change. We can continue to turn the effect on and off until we are satisfied that the treatment is the causal agent.

24. All natural science recognizes the superiority of _____ (experiments, correlations).

### Note #2
The problem with statistics comes from what is called *inference statistics*. Researchers use inference statistics to infer whether two sets of data show a real difference. Descriptive statistics consist of methods to describe large amounts of data simply. These methods include means, correlations, and percentage of explained variance. Behavior analysts rarely use inference statistics, but they often use descriptive statistics (see O'Donohue & Buchanan, 2001).

### Note #3
There are additional considerations in evaluating graphical data beyond division and stability. They include variability within and between conditions, number of data points, and trends within conditions, changes in trend between conditions, comparison of similar conditions, and the overall pattern of the data. Parsonson and Baer (1978) describe many of these considerations. They also present additional information on how to create and present graphical data.

25. Are division and stability the only considerations in visual analysis? ____ (yes, no)

### Note #4

Sometimes behavior analysts use inferential statistics to analyze their data (see Fisch, 2001). These statistics can help them tease out very subtle or very complicated relationships. Other behavior analysts object to using inferential statistics even in these rare cases.

# Helpful Hints

### Helpful Hint #1

Deciding whether data support the conclusion that a treatment causes a change in behavior involves four steps. I will abbreviate the questions defining these four steps. First, "Divided?" asks you to decide whether the last three points in neighboring conditions are divided. Second, "Stable?" asks you to determine whether the last three points in all conditions are stable. Third, "Convincing?" asks you to decide whether the data show a convincing difference between conditions. Fourth, "Caused?" asks you to decide whether the treatment caused a change in behavior. You should answer each question as "yes" or "no." On exams I will give you credit only if you answer all four questions correctly.

26. In order to save space in some questions, I will abbreviate the question about whether conditions are divided with the single word "Divided?" followed by an answer blank. I will abbreviate the question about whether conditions are stable with the single word "Stable?" followed by an answer blank. So if you see the abbreviated question "Convincing?" you know it means "Are the differences between conditions _____?" Following this pattern, I will abbreviate the fourth question about whether the treatment caused a change in behavior as "_____".

### Helpful Hint #2

Use the same approach to analyze backward designs as you would use to analyze standard designs. You still must ask if the conditions divide and if the conditions are stable.

27. Thus you use a(n) _____ (different, identical) approach for backward designs as for standard designs.

### Helpful Hint #3

Remember to base your visual analysis on the last three observations in each condition. I have made your job easy up to this point by circling the last three points in graphs. I will not help you in this way on tests!

28. Remember to base your analysis on the last ____ points of each condition.

# Additional Readings

Baer, D. (1977). Perhaps it would be better not to know everything. *Journal of Applied Behavior Analysis, 10,* 167–172. An excellent description of the reasons that most applied behavior analysts do not rely on statistical inference to determine whether they have found an important treatment effect.

Bailey, J. S., & Burch, M. R. (2002). *Research methods in applied behavior analysis.* Thousand Oaks, CA: Sage. This book provides the nuts and bolts of applied behavior analysis research methods. Pages 213–224, in particular, address the nature of visual analysis in single-subject designs.

Jones, R. R., Weinrott, M. R., & Vaught, R. S. (1978). Effects of serial dependency on the agreement between visual and statistical analysis. *Journal of Applied Behavior Analysis, 11,* 277–283. This article gives the other side of the story. It suggests that visual interpretation of data is unreliable.

Kratochwill, T. R., & Brody, G. H. (1978). Single-subject designs: A perspective on the controversy over employing statistical inference and implications for research and training in behavior modification. *Behavior Modification, 2,* 291–307. A discussion of trends in the use of statistical inference in behavior modification. The authors argue that statistical inference is used even in the *Journal of Applied Behavior Analysis* (but by less than 20% of the articles) and that it should be used more often.

Michael, J. (1974). Statistical inference for single-subject research: Mixed blessing or curse? *Journal of Applied Behavior Analysis, 7*, 647–653. A discussion of the implications of using statistical inference in conjunction with single-subject designs.

Miller, L. K. (1968). Determinancy versus risk: A critique of contemporary statistical methodology in sociology. *Kansas Journal of Sociology, 4*, 71–78. This paper describes a method for assessing the strength of relationships. It reports on all statistically significant findings in one year's *American Sociological Review*. The average strength of relationship was about 7% of the variance explained.

Parsonson, B. S., & Baer, D. M. (1978). The analysis and presentation of graphic data. In T. R. Kratochwill (Ed.), *Single-subject research: Strategies for evaluating change* (pp. 101–165). New York: Academic Press. This article provides detailed consideration of how to conduct visual analysis. The authors consider factors in addition to trend and overlap.

Smith, L. D., Best, L. A., Stubbs, D. A., Archibald, A. B., & Roberson-Nay, R. (2002). Constructing knowledge: The role of graphs and tables in hard and soft psychology. *American Psychologist, 57*, 749–761. This article reviews the function of graphs and tables in psychology. The authors suggest that the use of graphs highly correlates with the "hardness" of scientific fields. The authors suggest that the use of visual graphing among psychologists could contribute to the progress of psychological science as an alternative to significance testing and therefore facilitating communication across subfields.

## Programmed Reading

This section presents the following modules: (1) Principle of Visual Analysis, (2) Are the Conditions Divided?, (3) Are the Conditions Stable?, (4) Visual Analysis of Comparison Design, (5) Visual Analysis of Reversal and Multiple-Baseline Designs, (6) Another Tactic, and (7) Review.

### 1. *Principle of Visual Analysis*

68. Pre-test: Finding differences that look <u>convincing</u> is the principle of _____ _____ analysis.

81. Pre-test: To conduct a visual analysis requires four steps. First, you decide whether the conditions are _____ _____. Second, you decide if the conditions are _____. Third, you decide whether the differences between conditions are _____. Fourth, decide whether the treatment _____ _____ behavior to change.

You will learn two ideas in this module. First, you will learn how to define visual analysis. Second, you will learn the four steps of doing a visual analysis.

29. Behavior analysts decide if their treatment makes a difference by using ____ _____ (statistical, visual) analysis.

103. The principle of visual analysis is to find differences that look _____ (convincing, interesting).

30. Behavior analysts often take the following four steps. First, decide whether the conditions are divided. Second, decide if the conditions are stable. Third, decide whether the differences between conditions are convincing. Fourth, decide whether the treatment caused behavior to change. Doing these four steps is called a(n) _____ analysis.

117. Visual analysis is looking for _____ _____ differences.

91. Step #1 in visual analysis is to ask if the last three observations in each condition are _____.

92. Step #2 is to ask if the last three observations in each condition are _____ _____.

94. Step #3 is to ask whether the differences are _____.

34. Differences are convincing to most scientists only if the conditions are _____ _____and _____.

95. Step #4 involves deciding whether the treatment _____ the behavior to change.

98. The first three steps in using the principle of visual analysis involve looking for

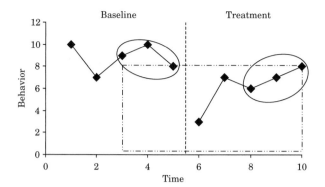

**Figure 6-20.** An experimental analysis of unspecified behavior.

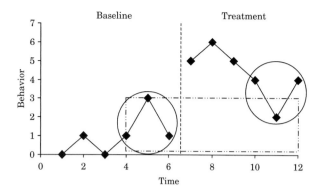

**Figure 6-22.** An experimental analysis of unspecified behavior.

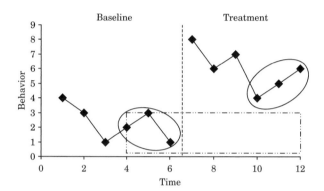

**Figure 6-21.** An experimental analysis of unspecified behavior.

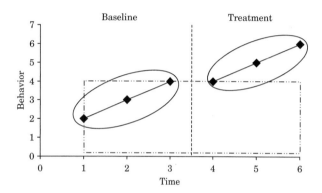

**Figure 6-23.** An experimental analysis of unspecified behavior.

divided and stable conditions to decide if differences between conditions look _____.

108. To conduct a visual analysis requires four steps. First, you decide whether the conditions are _____. Second, you decide if the conditions are _____. Third, you decide whether the differences between conditions are _____. Fourth, decide whether the treatment _____ _____ behavior to change.

33. Deciding whether differences look convincing is called a(n) _____ analysis.

### 2. Are the Conditions Divided?

58. Pre-test: Figure 6-20 shows the results of a simple experiment. Are the conditions divided? _____ (yes, no)

59. Pre-test: Figure 6-21 shows the results of another simple experiment. Are the conditions divided? _____ (yes, no)

60. Pre-test: Figure 6-22 shows the results of another simple experiment. Are the conditions divided? _____ (yes, no)

You will learn how to do step #1 of visual analysis in this module. That step is to decide if two conditions are <u>divided</u>. You will learn to start by finding the ranges for the last three numbers of both conditions. Then, you decide if the ranges are mutually exclusive. Finally, based on your findings, you can decide if the conditions are divided.

90. Step #1 in a visual analysis is to decide whether the conditions are _____ _____.

119. When you are looking for divided conditions, look only at the last _____ (how many?) observations in each condition.

97. Figure 6-23 shows the results of a simple experiment. Start your analysis by examining the box to see if the ranges for each condition overlap. If any points

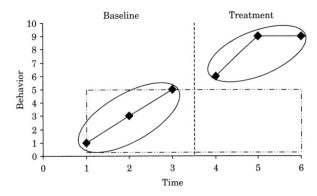

**Figure 6-24.** An experimental analysis of unspecified behavior.

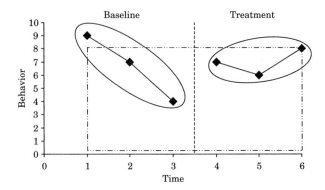

**Figure 6-26.** An experimental analysis of unspecified behavior.

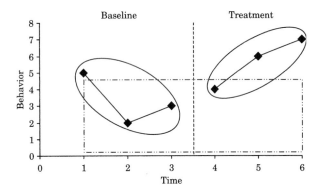

**Figure 6-25.** An experimental analysis of unspecified behavior.

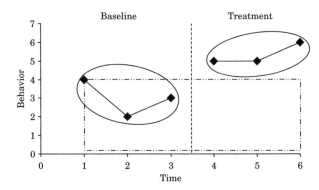

**Figure 6-27.** An experimental analysis of unspecified behavior.

in the treatment condition enter or touch the box, then the ranges overlap and the conditions are not divided. In the present example, the first point in treatment touches the box, showing that the numbers are not mutually exclusive. Therefore, the two sets _____ (are, aren't) divided.

1. Figure 6-24 shows another simple experiment. Because no treatment points touch the box, the ranges do not overlap. Thus, the conditions are mutually exclusive. The conditions _____ (are, aren't) divided.

2. Figure 6-25 shows another simple experiment. Look at the box to determine whether any treatment points touch or enter the box to see if the two conditions are divided. Are the conditions divided? ____ (yes, no)

3. Figure 6-26 shows a simple experiment. Look at the box to see if any treatment points touch or enter the box. Are the conditions divided? _____ (yes, no)

4. Figure 6-27 shows another simple experiment. Use the box to decide if the points overlap. Are the conditions divided? ____ (yes, no)

5. Figure 6-28 shows an experiment to reduce a high rate of an undesirable behavior. Notice that the box is drawn around the lower set of points that occur in the treatment condition and that it extends backwards into the baseline. The principle is the same. You must now look to see if any of the baseline points enter or touch the box. Are the two sets divided? ____ (yes, no)

6. Figure 6-29 shows an experiment with more than three observations per condition. Remember to look only at the last three numbers in each set. I have circled them as a reminder. Divided? _____ (yes, no)

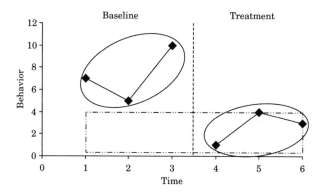

**Figure 6-28.** An experimental analysis of unspecified behavior.

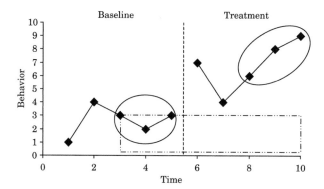

**Figure 6-29.** An experimental analysis of unspecified behavior.

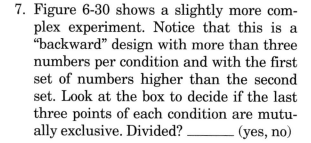

**Figure 6-30.** An experimental analysis of unspecified behavior.

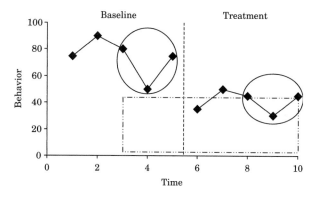

**Figure 6-31.** An experimental analysis of unspecified behavior.

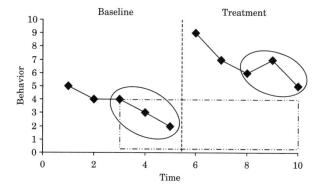

**Figure 6-32.** An experimental analysis of unspecified behavior.

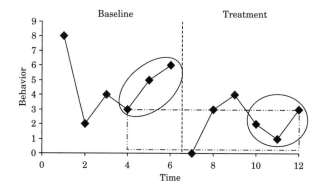

**Figure 6-33.** An experimental analysis of unspecified behavior.

7. Figure 6-30 shows a slightly more complex experiment. Notice that this is a "backward" design with more than three numbers per condition and with the first set of numbers higher than the second set. Look at the box to decide if the last three points of each condition are mutually exclusive. Divided? _____ (yes, no)

8. Figure 6-31 shows another experiment. Use the box to decide whether the conditions are divided. Are they _____?

9. Figure 6-32 shows another experiment. Use the box. Divided? _____ (yes, no)

10. Figure 6-33 shows yet another experiment. Divided? _____ (yes, no)

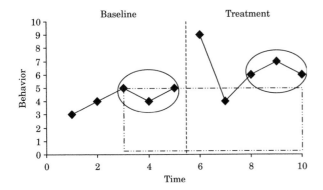

**Figure 6-34.** An experimental analysis of unspecified behavior.

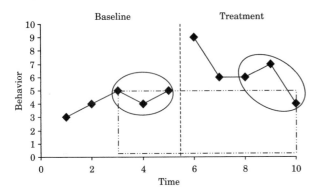

**Figure 6-35.** An experimental analysis of unspecified behavior.

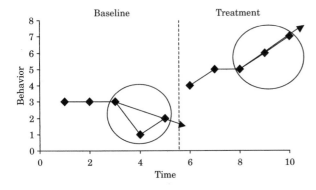

**Figure 6-36.** An experimental analysis of unspecified behavior.

11. Figure 6-34 shows another experiment. Divided? _____ (yes, no)
12. Figure 6-35 shows another experiment. Divided? _____ (yes, no)

### 3. Are the Conditions Stable?

57. Pre-test: Figure 6-36 shows an experiment. Are all conditions stable? _____ (yes, no)

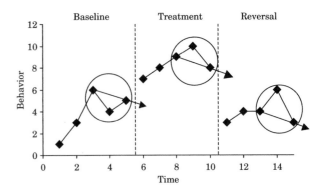

**Figure 6-37.** An experimental analysis of unspecified behavior.

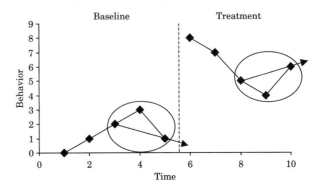

**Figure 6-38.** An experimental analysis of unspecified behavior.

62. Pre-test: Refer to Figure 6-37. Is baseline stable? _____ (yes, no) Is treatment stable? _____ (yes, no) Is reversal stable? _____ (yes, no)
63. Pre-test: Refer to Figure 6-38. Are all conditions stable? _____ (yes, no)

You will learn how to do step #2 of a visual analysis in this module. You will start by deciding whether the condition you are analyzing has values higher or lower than the values of a second condition. You will then decide whether the last three observations are or are <u>not moving closer</u> to the values in the other condition. If they are not moving closer, then the numbers in that condition are stable. If the last number is moving closer to the other values, then the condition is not stable. You must remember to look only at the last three numbers in each condition.

52. Look for stability by looking only at the last _____ (how many) numbers in a condition.

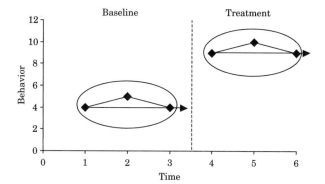

**Figure 6-39.** An experimental analysis of unspecified behavior.

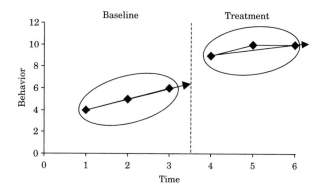

**Figure 6-41.** An experimental analysis of unspecified behavior.

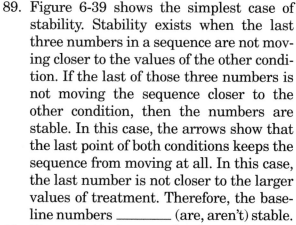

**Figure 6-40.** An experimental analysis of unspecified behavior.

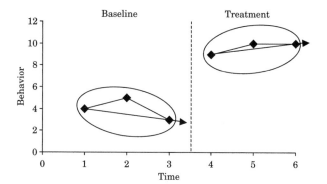

**Figure 6-42.** An experimental analysis of unspecified behavior.

89. Figure 6-39 shows the simplest case of stability. Stability exists when the last three numbers in a sequence are not moving closer to the values of the other condition. If the last of those three numbers is not moving the sequence closer to the other condition, then the numbers are stable. In this case, the arrows show that the last point of both conditions keeps the sequence from moving at all. In this case, the last number is not closer to the larger values of treatment. Therefore, the baseline numbers _____ (are, aren't) stable.

13. Figure 6-40 shows a simple experiment. I have drawn an arrow showing the direction of the last point compared to the first point. In this case the baseline arrow points down toward lower values. This means that overall the sequence of numbers is <u>not moving closer</u> to the larger treatment values. Can you conclude from this that the baseline numbers are stable? _____ (yes, no)

14. Figure 6-41 shows a baseline with the arrow pointing up. This means that overall the sequence of numbers is moving closer to the larger treatment values. Can you conclude from this that the baseline numbers are stable? _____ (yes, no)

15. Figure 6-42 shows a baseline arrow that again points up even though the middle number is down. In spite of the middle number decreasing, the overall sequence of numbers is moving closer to the larger treatment values. Can you conclude from this that the baseline numbers are stable? _____ (yes, no)

16. Figure 6-43 shows the baseline arrow pointing down toward smaller numbers. Decide if the arrow means that the sequence of numbers is or is not moving closer to the larger treatment values. Can you conclude from this that the baseline numbers are stable? _____ (yes, no)

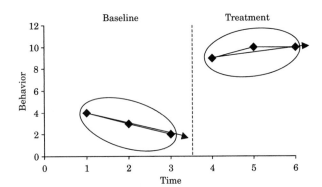

**Figure 6-43.** An experimental analysis of unspecified behavior.

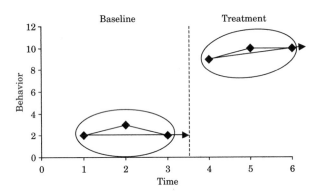

**Figure 6-44.** An experimental analysis of unspecified behavior.

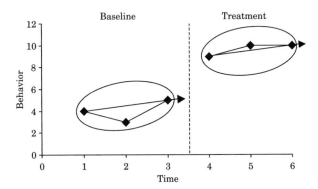

**Figure 6-45.** An experimental analysis of unspecified behavior.

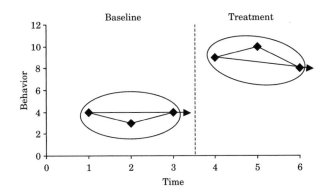

**Figure 6-46.** An experimental analysis of unspecified behavior.

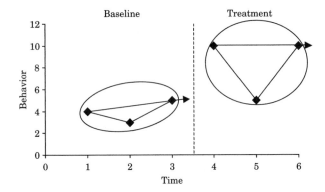

**Figure 6-47.** An experimental analysis of unspecified behavior.

17. Figure 6-44 shows that the arrow for the baseline is pointing level. This means that the sequence of numbers is neither increasing nor decreasing. Thus, the sequence of baseline numbers is not moving closer to the larger treatment values. Can you conclude from this that the baseline numbers are stable? _____ (yes, no)

18. For Figure 6-45, I want you to analyze the stability of the treatment condition. The treatment arrow is pointing away from the lower baseline values. Are the treatment numbers moving closer to the lower baseline values? _____ (yes, no) Can you conclude from this that the treatment numbers stable? _____ (yes, no)

19. For Figure 6-46, analyze whether the treatment is stable. The arrow is pointing down. This means that the sequence of numbers is decreasing. Thus, the sequence of treatment numbers is moving closer to the smaller baseline values. Can you conclude from this that the treatment numbers are stable? _____ (yes, no)

20. For Figure 6-47, analyze whether the treatment is stable. The arrow is pointing level. This means that the sequence of numbers is neither increasing nor decreasing. Thus, the sequence of treatment numbers is not moving closer to the smaller baseline values. Can you conclude

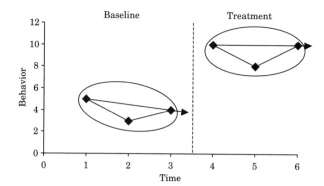

**Figure 6-48.** An experimental analysis of unspecified behavior.

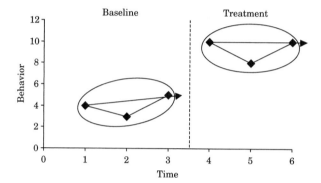

**Figure 6-49.** An experimental analysis of unspecified behavior.

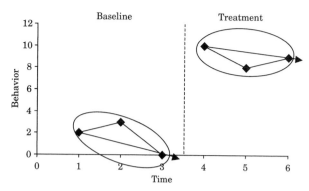

**Figure 6-50.** An experimental analysis of unspecified behavior.

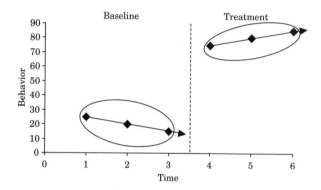

**Figure 6-51.** An experimental analysis of unspecified behavior.

from this that the treatment numbers are stable? _____ (yes, no)

107. To complete step #2 of a visual analysis, you have to decide whether every condition in the experiment is stable. If all of them are, then you conclude that the data are stable. If even one condition is not stable, then conclude that the data _____ (are, aren't) stable.

21. For Figure 6-48, analyze whether both baseline and treatment are stable. Can you conclude from the baseline arrow that the baseline numbers are stable? _____ (yes, no) Can you conclude from the treatment arrow that the treatment numbers are stable? _____ (yes, no) Finally, decide whether both conditions are stable. If so, conclude that the data are stable. If not, conclude the data are not stable. Are the data stable? _____ (yes, no)

22. For Figure 6-49, analyze whether both baseline and treatment are stable. Can you conclude from the baseline arrow that the baseline numbers are stable? _____

(yes, no) Can you conclude from the treatment arrow that the treatment numbers are stable? _____ (yes, no) Finally, decide whether both conditions are stable. If so, conclude that the data are stable. If not, conclude the data are not stable. Are the data stable? _____ (yes, no)

23. For Figure 6-50, I will ask you to take all the steps on your own. Look at whether the arrow for each condition is showing the points moving closer to or further from the values of the other condition. Finally, decide whether the data for every condition are stable? _____ (yes, no)

24. For Figure 6-51, are the data stable? _____ (yes, no)

88. Figure 6-52 shows the results of modifying an unwanted behavior that occurs too often. In such a case, the baseline may consist of large numbers and the treatment of low numbers. The definition of stability applies just as well. Use the same approach to decide whether the last number of baseline shows the sequence

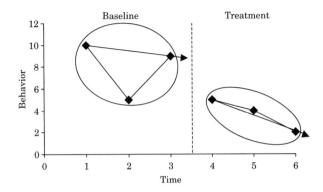

**Figure 6-52.** An experimental analysis of unspecified behavior.

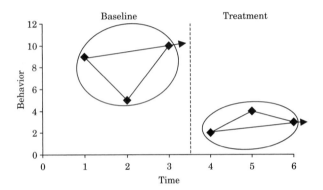

**Figure 6-53.** An experimental analysis of unspecified behavior.

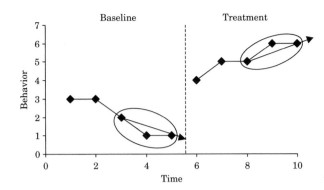

**Figure 6-54.** An experimental analysis of unspecified behavior.

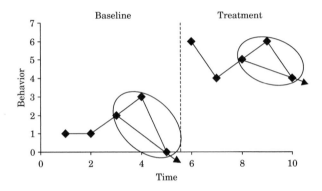

**Figure 6-55.** An experimental analysis of unspecified behavior.

moving closer to the smaller values of treatment. Are the baseline numbers stable? _____ (yes, no) (If you got this one wrong, you may have been asking if the last number of baseline is decreasing rather than if it is moving closer to *smaller* treatment values.)

25. Figure 6-53 shows another experiment to reduce a high rate behavior. Decide whether the last number of baseline shows the sequence moving closer to the smaller values of treatment. Are the baseline numbers stable? _____ (yes, no) (If you got this one wrong, you may have been asking if the last number of baseline is decreasing rather than if it is moving closer to *smaller* treatment values.)

45. Figure 6-54 requires you to remember one last detail. Experiments often make more than three observations in a condition. So you will need to remember to look only at the last three numbers in each condition. Are the last three observations in both conditions stable? _____ (yes, no)

26. Analyze the stability of Figure 6-55. Stability? _____ (yes, no)

61. Is baseline in Figure 6-56 stable? _____ (yes, no)

41. Here is a review. Step #1 of a visual analysis is to decide if the conditions are _____.

93. Step #2 of a visual analysis is to decide if the data in each condition are_____ _____.

### 4. Visual Analysis of Comparison Design

77. Pre-test: Figure 6-57 shows Steve's minutes of pumping iron each day. Do a visual analysis. Divided? _____ Stable? _____ Convincing? _____ Caused? _____ (yes, no)

64. Pre-test: Figure 6-58 shows Alice's studying data. Do a visual analysis. Divided? _____ Stable? _____ Convincing? _____ Caused? _____ (yes, no)

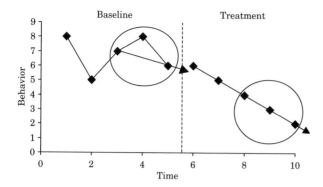

**Figure 6-56.** An experimental analysis of unspecified behavior.

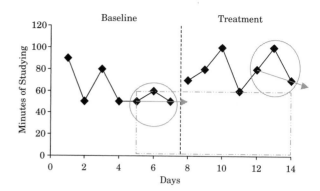

**Figure 6-58.** An experimental analysis of studying.

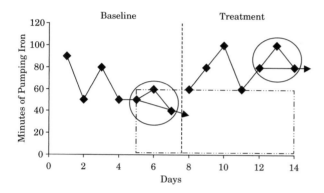

**Figure 6-57.** An experimental analysis of pumping iron.

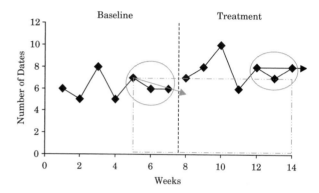

**Figure 6-59.** An experimental analysis of Amy's dates.

65. Pre-test: Figure 6-59 shows Amy's number of dates per week. Do a visual analysis. Divided? _____ Stable? _____ Convincing? _____ Caused? _____ (yes, no)

You can learn how to apply visual analysis to a comparison design in this module. You will learn to apply the four steps of visual analysis to comparison experiments.

42. Here's how you visually analyze a comparison design. First, decide whether the conditions are _____. Second, decide if the conditions are _____. Third, decide whether the differences between conditions are _____. Fourth, decide whether the treatment _____ _____ behavior to change.

86. Remember, your analysis of comparison designs always consists of looking only at the last _____ (how many?) observations in each condition.

120. You will often look at comparison experiments where both conditions are divided

and stable. You will save yourself a lot of trouble if you remember that the use of a comparison design in these cases means that you _____ (can, can't) conclude that treatment caused behavioral change. The reason is because a comparison design does not rule out alternative explanations!

96. Suppose that a comparison design experiment shows divided and stable conditions so that you find convincing differences. You can *never* conclude that the treatment caused the differences because a comparison design doesn't rule out _____ _____ explanations.

114. Figure 6-60 shows Tommy's studying data. The first step in a visual analysis is to look for divided conditions. Remember to look at the box to see if the last three points in the baseline and treatment are mutually exclusive. If they are, then the conditions are divided. In this case, are the conditions divided? _____ (yes, no)

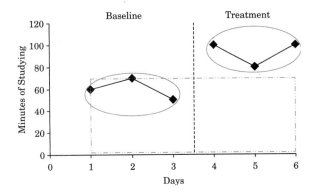

**Figure 6-60.** An experimental analysis of studying.

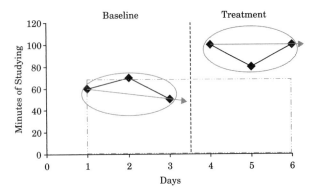

**Figure 6-61.** An experimental analysis of studying.

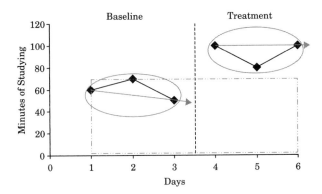

**Figure 6-62.** An experimental analysis of studying.

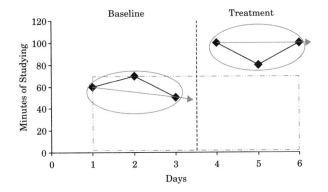

**Figure 6-63.** An experimental analysis of studying.

115. Figure 6-61 shows Tommy's studying data. The second step in a visual analysis is to look for stable behavior in each condition. Look at the baseline arrow to see if the last observation is moving the sequence closer to the values of treatment. Repeat for treatment condition. Only if all conditions are stable can you conclude that the data are stable. Stable? _____ (yes, no)

113. Figure 6-62 shows Tommy's studying data. The first two steps of your visual analysis found divided conditions and stable data. The third in a visual analysis is to decide whether the data show convincing differences. Remember, the data must pass every test. Convincing? _____ (yes, no)

116. Figure 6-63 shows Tommy's studying data. Step #1 in the visual analysis found divided conditions; Step #2 found stable data. Step #3 concluded convincing differences. For step #4, you must decide whether you can conclude that

the treatment caused the increase in Tommy's studying. Caused? _____ (yes, no) Remember, this is a comparison design.

50. Figure 6-64 shows Lonnie's consumption of broccoli per week. Do each step in a visual analysis of Lonnie's data. Divided? _____ Stable? _____ Convincing? _____ Caused? _____ (yes, no)

56. Figure 6-65 shows Ollie's percent of truthful answers on the witness stand. Do a visual analysis of this experiment. Remember to use only the last three observations. Divided? ____ Stable? ____ Convincing? ____ Caused? ____ (yes, no)

118. Figure 6-66 shows the percent of class time that Rita stays awake. Visually analyze her data. Divided? ____ Stable? ____ Convincing? ____ Caused? ____ (yes, no)

49. Figure 6-67 shows the percent of intervals during which Larry engages in disruptive behavior. Perform a visual analysis of his data. Divided? ____ Stable? ____ Convincing? ____ Caused? ____ (yes, no)

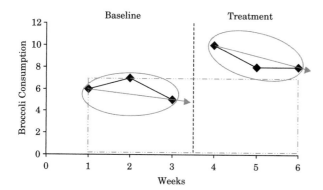

**Figure 6-64.** An experimental analysis of broccoli.

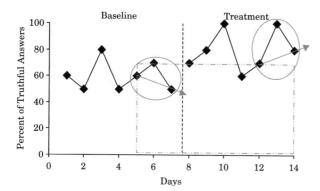

**Figure 6-65.** An experimental analysis of truthtelling.

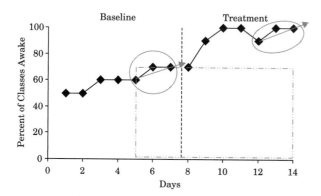

**Figure 6-66.** An experimental analysis of staying awake.

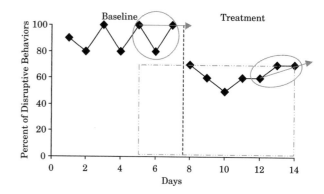

**Figure 6-67.** An experimental analysis of disruptive behavior.

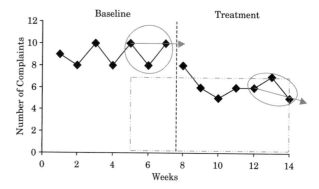

**Figure 6-68.** An experimental analysis of complaining.

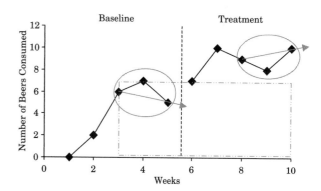

**Figure 6-69.** An experimental analysis of drinking.

102. Figure 6-68 shows the number of complaints that Ann makes each week. Conduct a visual analysis of this experiment. Divided? ____ Stable? ____ Convincing? ____ Caused? ____ (yes, no)

51. Figure 6-69 shows Lonnie's consumption of beer per week. Do a visual analysis of the experiment. Divided? ____ Stable? ____ Convincing? ____ Caused? ____ (yes, no)

43. Here's how you visually analyze a comparison design. First, decide whether the conditions are _____. Second, decide if the conditions are _____. Third, decide whether the differences between conditions are _____.

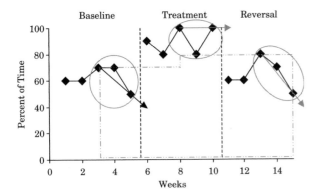

**Figure 6-70.** An experimental analysis of housework.

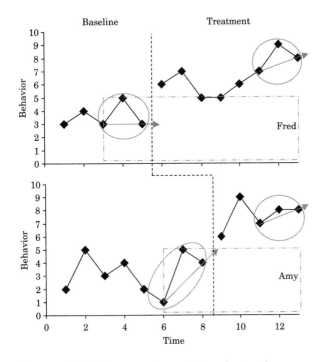

**Figure 6-71.** An experimental analysis of unspecified behavior.

Fourth, decide whether the treatment _____ behavior to change.

## 5. Visual Analysis of Reversal and Multiple-Baseline Designs

66. Pre-test: Figure 6-70 shows the percent of time that Bev does her share of the housework. Do a visual analysis of the data. Divided? _____ Stable? _____ Convincing? _____ Caused? _____ (yes, no)

69. Pre-test: Figure 6-71 shows the behaviors of Fred and Amy. Do a visual analysis.

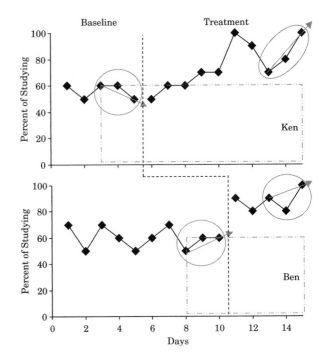

**Figure 6-72.** An experimental analysis of unspecified behavior.

Divided? _____ Stable? _____ Convincing? _____ Caused? _____ (yes, no)

74. Pre-test: Figure 6-72 shows the behavior of Ken and Ben. Do a visual analysis. Divided? _____ Stable? _____ Convincing? _____ Caused? _____ (yes, no)

You can learn how to apply visual analysis to both reversal and multiple-baseline designs in this module. You will take the same four steps that you have already learned. The only difference is that you will apply those steps to more conditions. Thus, for reversal designs, you must also decide if treatment is divided from reversal. You must also decide whether the reversal condition is stable.

Likewise, in multiple-baseline designs you must take the same four steps. You must apply the steps to the first person to see whether the conditions are divided and stable. You must then also apply the steps to the second person to see if the conditions are divided and stable.

39. Here are some points to remember. First point: Remember that you look only at the last ____ observations of each condition.

87. Second point: Remember that every test of divided conditions must be met to

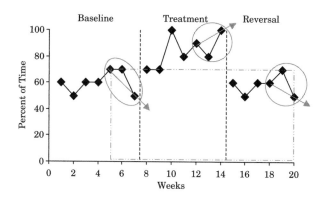

**Figure 6-73.** An experimental analysis of working hard.

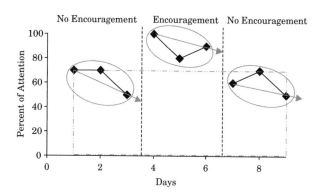

**Figure 6-74.** An experimental analysis of attention.

conclude that the conditions are divided. Suppose that you are analyzing a reversal design in which baseline and treatment are divided but treatment and reversal are not divided. You must conclude that the conditions _____ (are, aren't) divided.

104. If you are analyzing a multiple-baseline design in which the conditions for Mary are divided but the conditions for Paul aren't divided, you conclude that the conditions _____ (are, aren't) divided.

106. Third point: Remember that every condition must be stable to conclude that the data are stable. If you are analyzing a reversal design in which baseline and treatment are stable but reversal is not, you would conclude that the data _____ (are, aren't) stable.

105. For example, if you are analyzing a multiple-baseline design in which baseline and treatment for Mary are stable whereas the baseline for Paul is stable but not the treatment for Paul, then you would conclude that the data _____ (are, aren't) stable.

75. Figure 6-73 shows the percentage of time that Len is working hard on the job. Step #1 requires you to compare baseline and treatment to see if they are divided. You must also compare treatment and reversal to see if they are divided. Only if both are divided can you conclude that the data meet the criterion of being divided. Step #2 requires you to decide if all three conditions are stable. You can conclude that the data are stable only if all three conditions meet the criteria.

Step #3 requires you to decide if the differences are convincing. They are convincing only if all the neighboring conditions are divided and if all are stable. Finally, if the differences are convincing, you can conclude that the treatment caused the changes in Len's work only if your experimental design rules out alternative explanations. Do a visual analysis. Divided? _____ Stable? _____ Convincing? _____ Caused? _____ (yes, no)

27. Figure 6-74 shows the percentage of intervals during which Karen is paying attention to her baby before, during, and after Grandma used encouragement to increase Karen's attention to her baby. Step #1 requires you to compare baseline and treatment and then also to compare treatment and reversal to see if they are divided. Step #2 requires you to decide if all three conditions are stable. Step #3 requires you to decide if all the neighboring conditions are divided and if all are stable. Finally, if the differences are convincing, you can conclude that the treatment caused Karen's change in attention to her baby only if your design rules out alternative explanations. Divided? _____ Stable? _____ Convincing? _____ Caused? _____ (yes, no)

54. Figure 6-75 shows the percentage of the time that Dave is studying. Mom used access to computer games to increase his studying. Remember to look only at the last three observations in each condition. Divided? _____ Stable? _____ Convincing? _____ Caused? _____ (yes, no)

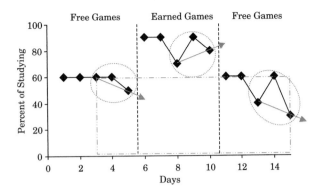

**Figure 6-75.** An experimental analysis of studying.

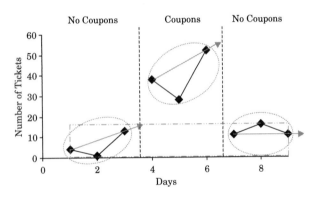

**Figure 6-76.** An experimental analysis of issuing tickets.

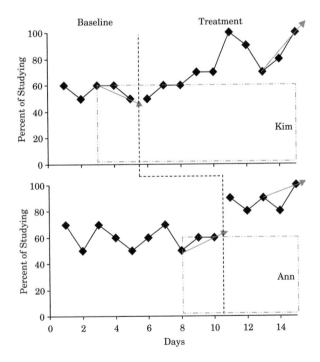

**Figure 6-77.** An experimental analysis of unspecified behavior.

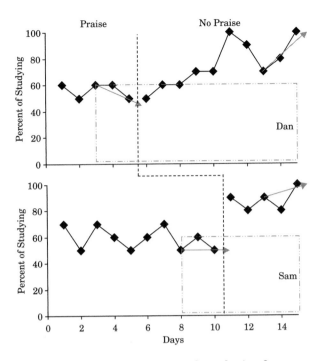

**Figure 6-78.** An experimental analysis of studying.

36. Figure 6-76 shows the number of tickets police issued for child safety seat violations with and without letting police issue educational coupons that parents could use instead of paying a fine. Divided? _____ Stable? _____ Convincing? _____ Caused? _____ (yes, no)

48. Figure 6-77 shows the behaviors of Kim and Ann during baseline and treatment. Remember to look only at the last three observations in each condition. Remember to find if both Kim and Ann show divided and stable conditions. Conclude convincing differences only if all tests for divided and stable conditions are positive. Finally, conclude that treatment caused behavior change if you have convincing differences. You can do so because multiple-baseline designs rule out alternative explanations. Divided? _____ Stable? _____ Convincing? _____ Caused? _____ (yes, no)

32. Figure 6-78 shows the percent of time studying for Dan and Sam without and with praise. Divided? ____ Stable? ____ Convincing? ____ Caused? ____ (yes, no)

46. I will now give you some practice with all three designs to help you remember how to work with each one. Remember,

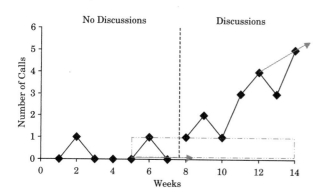

**Figure 6-79.** An experimental analysis of phone calling.

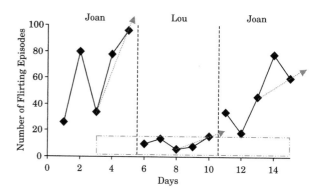

**Figure 6-81.** An experimental analysis of flirting.

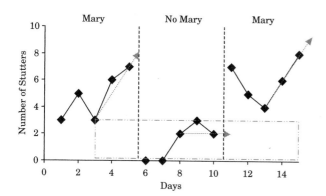

**Figure 6-80.** An experimental analysis of stuttering.

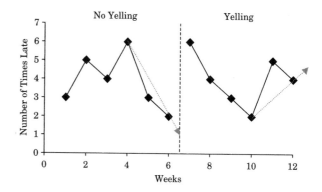

**Figure 6-82.** An experimental analysis of being late.

no matter if you have divided conditions and stable data, you _____ (can, can't) conclude the treatment caused a behavioral change with comparison designs.

53. Figure 6-79 shows the number of calls Harry made to find a date before and after Mom helped Harry figure out the best way to ask for a date. Divided? _____ Stable? _____ Convincing? _____ Caused? _____ (yes, no)

85. Figure 6-80 shows the number of times that Professor Brainbuster stuttered when Mary was and when she was not in class. Divided? _____ Stable? _____ Convincing? _____ Caused? _____ (yes, no)

37. Figure 6-81 shows the number of times that Frank flirted when he was around Joan and when he was around Lou. Divided? _____ Stable? _____ Convincing? _____ Caused? _____ (yes, no)

38. Figure 6-82 shows the number of times that Gabe's daughter was late when

he didn't yell at her and when he did. Divided? _____ Stable? _____ Convincing? _____ Caused? _____ (yes, no)

55. Figure 6-83 shows the number of favorable votes for Head Start made by Senators Nixon and Regan when Mr. Walters did and did not bribe them. Divided? _____ Stable? _____ Convincing? _____ Caused? _____ (yes, no)

35. Figure 6-84 shows the number of relevant comments Mr. Jones made when Dr. Bourgeois did and did not supply him with a memory book. Note that this is a backward reversal design. Divided? _____ Stable? _____ Convincing? _____ Caused? _____ (yes, no)

### 6. Another Tactic

82. Pre-test: To use the behavioral strategy, tactic #5, do a(n) _____ analysis of your data.

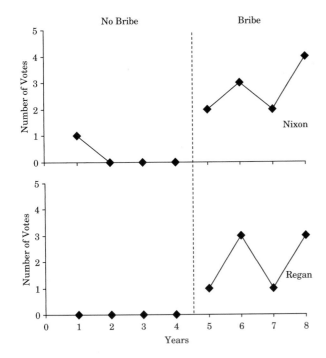

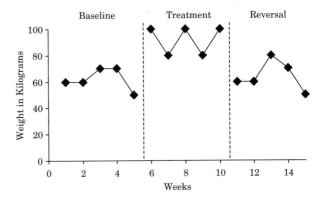

**Figure 6-85.** An experimental analysis of dieting.

**Figure 6-83.** An experimental analysis of voting.

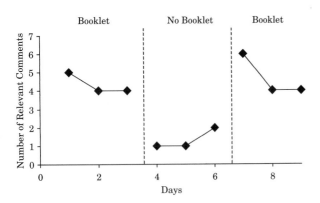

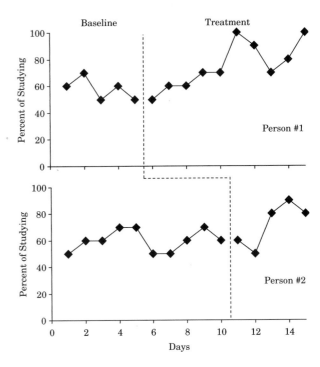

**Figure 6-84.** An experimental analysis of relevant comments.

**Figure 6-86.** An experimental analysis of studying.

You can learn tactic #5 of the behavioral strategy in this module.

109. To use the behavioral strategy you must (1) specify the behavior with a behavioral definition, (2) gather information using the approach of direct observation, (3) check the reliability and social validity of your observations, (4) use a single-subject experiment to test your treatment, (5) do a(n) _____ (statistical, visual) analysis of your data.

110. To use the behavioral strategy (5), do a(n) _____ analysis of your data.

### 7. *Review*

76. Pre-test: Figure 6-85 shows Mom's weight in kilograms before, during, and after treatment. Divided? _____ Stable? _____ Convincing? _____ Caused? _____ (yes, no)

70. Pre-test: Figure 6-86 shows the effect of treatment on the percentage of time spent studying by person #1 and person #2. Divided? _____ Stable? _____ Convincing? _____ Caused? _____ (yes, no)

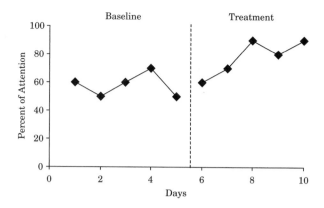

**Figure 6-87.** An experimental analysis of attention.

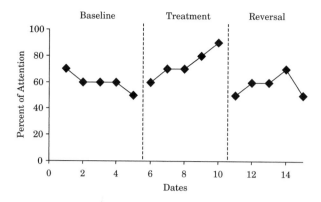

**Figure 6-88.** An experimental analysis of attending.

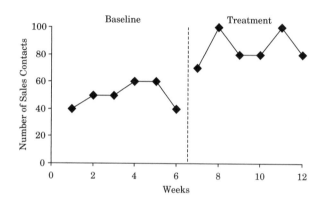

**Figure 6-89.** An experimental analysis of making sales contacts.

67. Pre-test: Figure 6-87 shows the percent of intervals during which Dad paid attention to his kids. Divided? _____ Stable? _____ Convincing? _____ Caused? _____ (yes, no)

This module contains review questions over this and prior lessons.

44. Here's how you visually analyze any experiment. First, decide whether the conditions are _____. Second, decide if the conditions are _____ _____. Third, decide whether the differences between conditions are _____. Fourth, decide whether the treatment _____ behavior to change.

111. To use the behavioral strategy, you must (1) specify the behavior with a behavioral definition, (2) gather information using the approach of direct observation, (3) check the reliability and social validity of your observations, (4) use a single-subject experiment to test your treatment, (5) do a(n) _____ analysis of the results.

101. The name of the science that studies environmental events that change behavior is _____; the label for a statement that specifies exactly what to observe is _____ _____.

28. An experiment contains convincing differences if the conditions are _____ and if the data are _____.

100. The fourth tactic in using the behavioral strategy is to use a(n) _____ experiment to test your treatment.

47. Figure 6-88 shows the percentage of Jerry's attention to Adeline when they are out on a date. Divided? _____ Stable? _____ Convincing? _____ Caused? _____ (yes, no)

99. The formula for reliability is: _____ _____.

112. To use the behavioral strategy: (4) use a(n) _____ experiment to test your treatment; and (5) do a _____ analysis of the data.

31. Figure 6-89 shows the number of Bob's sales contacts per week during baseline and treatment. Divided? _____ Stable? _____ Convincing? _____ Caused? _____ (yes, no)

40. Figure 6-90 shows the percent of intervals studying for Ted and Ann during baseline

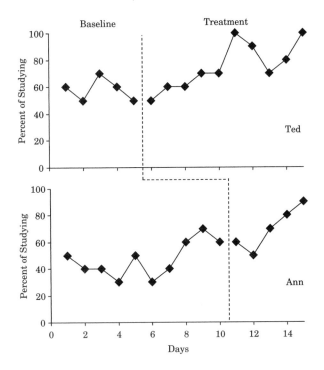

**Figure 6-90.** An experimental analysis of studying.

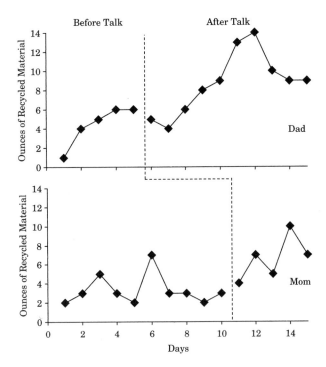

**Figure 6-94.** An experimental analysis of recycling.

and treatment. Divided? _____ Stable? _____ Convincing? _____ Caused? _____ (yes, no)

## Programmed Examples

### 1. Programmed Examples

11. Pre-test: Figure 6-94 shows the ounces of material that Ben's Mom and Dad put into the recycling bins before and after Ben had a talk with them about the importance of recycling. Divided? _____ Stable? _____ Convincing? _____ Caused? _____ (yes, no)

13. Pre-test: Figure 6-95 shows the number of pages that Tom studied in spelling and math before and after Mom decreed that Tom must study a half hour before watching TV. Divided? _____ Stable? _____ Convincing? _____ Caused? _____ (yes, no)

12. Pre-test: Figure 6-96 shows the times that Bob spent with his son Bill before and after Bev asked him every day to spend more time with Bill. Divided? _____ Stable? _____ Convincing? _____ Caused? _____ (yes, no)

14. Figure 6-97 shows how many minutes late Sue was in waking up when Mom did not wake her and when Mom did. Divided? _____

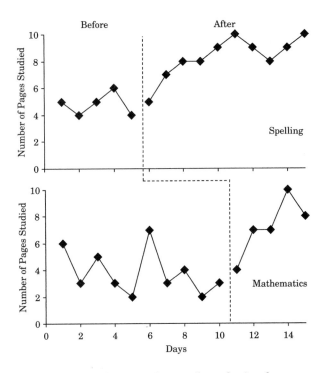

**Figure 6-95.** An experimental analysis of studying.

Stable? _____ Convincing? _____ Caused? _____ (yes, no)

21. Figure 6-98 shows the number of portions of fatty food you eat each day before and after you resolve to have no more than three portions of fatty food a day. Remember to look

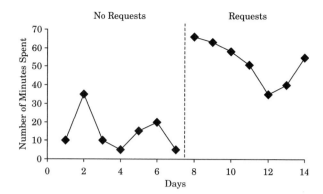

**Figure 6-96.** An experimental analysis of Bob spending time with his son.

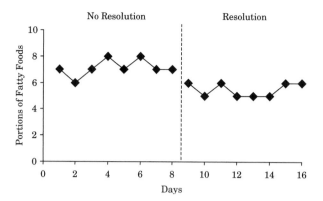

**Figure 6-98.** An experimental analysis of eating.

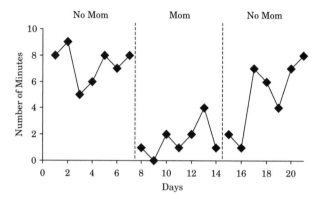

**Figure 6-97.** An experimental analysis of waking up.

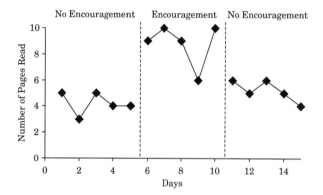

**Figure 6-99.** An experimental analysis of reading.

only at the last three numbers of baseline and treatment. First, look for divided conditions. They are divided only if they are mutually exclusive. (Tip: Imagine drawing a box like you saw in earlier parts of this lesson, or make your own graph and draw the box!) Divided? _____ Second, look for stable behavior in each condition. (Tip: Imagine drawing arrows like you saw earlier to see if the last observation shows the sequence moving closer to the values in the other condition, or actually draw them. If not, then that condition is stable.) Only if all conditions are stable can you conclude that the data are stable. Stable? _____ (yes, no) Third, decide whether you have convincing differences. Remember, the data must pass every test. Convincing? _____ (yes, no) Fourth, decide if treatment caused a behavioral change. Caused? _____ (yes, no) (Remember, your design must rule out alternative explanations.)

19. Figure 6-99 shows how many pages Tom read every day when Dad did and did not encourage his reading. Look only at the last three points of each condition. Step #1: See

whether baseline and treatment are divided and if treatment and reversal are divided. If both pairs of conditions are divided, conclude that the data are divided. Step #2: See whether each condition is stable. Conclude that the data are stable if all three conditions are stable. Step #3: Decide whether the differences are convincing. They are if the conditions are divided and stable. Step #4: If you find convincing differences, then decide if the treatment caused Tom's change in reading. Decide that it did only if you used a design that rules out alternatives. Divided? _____ Stable? _____ Convincing? _____ Caused? _____ (yes, no)

17. Figure 6-100 shows how many laughs Sam gets from Mom and Ron for his 10 daily jokes when he tells his own jokes and when he tells jokes from a joke book. (Remember to analyze Mom's and Ron's conditions separately. Don't compare Mom's and Ron's conditions.) Find whether both Mom and Ron show divided and stable conditions. Conclude differences are convincing only if both Mom's and Ron's conditions are divided and stable. Finally, if you

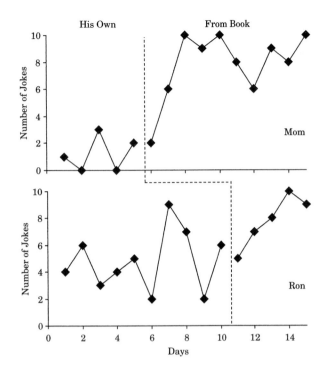

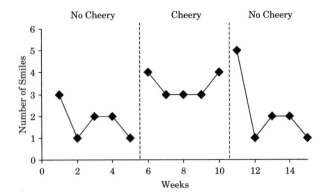

**Figure 6-100.** An experimental analysis of joke telling.

**Figure 6-102.** An experimental analysis of smiling.

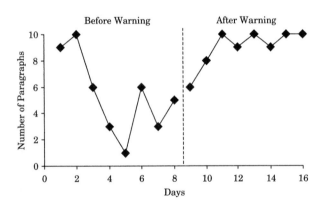

**Figure 6-101.** An experimental analysis of writing.

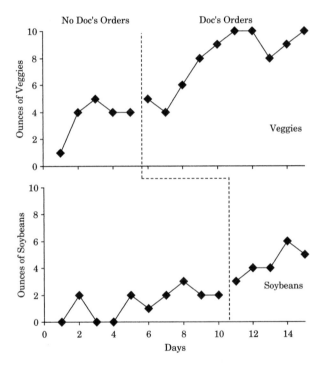

**Figure 6-103.** An experimental analysis of healthy eating.

have convincing differences, conclude that treatment caused behavior change only if you used an experimental design that rules out alternative explanations. Divided? _____ Stable? _____ Convincing? _____ Caused? _____ (yes, no)

20. Figure 6-101 shows how many paragraphs you write for your term paper each day before and after your professor warns you that the paper counts as half your grade. Check for divided and stable conditions. Conclude convincing differences only if all conditions are divided and stable. Finally, if you have convincing differences, conclude that treatment

caused behavior change only if you used an experimental design that rules out alternative explanations. (Remember to use only the last three observations in each condition.) Divided? _____ Stable? _____ Convincing? _____ Caused? _____ (yes, no)

6. Figure 6-102 shows how many days per week Jan gives you a big smile in the morning when you don't give her a cheery greeting and when you do. Divided? _____ Stable? _____ Convincing? _____ Caused? _____ (yes, no)

3. Figure 6-103 shows how many ounces of veggies and soybeans Bob ate each day before and after Doc ordered him to eat more.

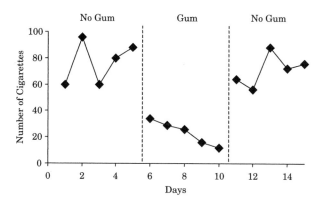

**Figure 6-104.** An experimental analysis of smoking.

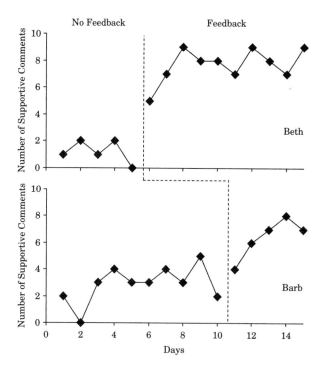

**Figure 6-105.** An experimental analysis of making supportive comments.

Divided? _____ Stable? _____ Convincing? _____ Caused? _____ (yes, no)

8. Figure 6-104 shows how many cigarettes Kay smoked each day when she was and wasn't substituting gum for cigarettes. Divided? _____ Stable? _____ Convincing? _____ Caused? _____ (yes, no)

1. Be prepared for review questions! Louise observed the interrupting behavior of Archie while she was being her usual polite self. She continued to observe his interrupting behavior after she began ignoring him. She was using a design that couldn't rule out _____ explanations for any change in his interrupting behavior. She used what type of single-subject experimental design? _____ design

9. Kim was fighting off depression. She tried to see friends but didn't do it very often. She got counseling from Dr. Hale. He taught her why seeing friends was important. He taught her some skills to make seeing friends more fun. He taught her how to record data about seeing friends. She started seeing friends much more often. Even when she discontinued counseling, she continued to use her new skills and to see friends often. She felt much less depressed. The condition before she got counseling is called the _____ _____. Counseling is called the _____ _____. The condition after she stopped counseling is called the _____ _____ to baseline. Her experiment with counseling uses what single-subject experimental design? _____ design This is a strong design because it rules out _____ explanations.

16. Sam checked every 15 minutes to see whether any of his students were studying. He was using what method of direct observation? (Do you still remember the questions that help you pinpoint the method?) _____ recording

15. Professor George noticed that Paul rarely talked in his classes. Starting in October, he reacted to every comment that Paul made in Sociology. Paul started making more comments, but only in Sociology. Starting in November, Professor George reacted to every comment that Paul made in Political Science. Paul started making more comments in that class, too. Professor George used what kind of single-subject experimental design? (Do you remember the questions?) _____ design.

10. Melodie wrote down each time Tim attended class prior to the strike at Reagan College. If the strike is considered the treatment condition, the period before the strike is called the _____ condition.

5. If a teacher is having trouble with his children hitting each other, an observer might note whether anyone was hitting during each 30-second period of the class. The observer

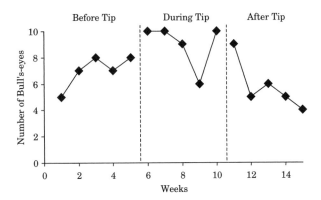

***Figure 6-106.*** An experimental analysis of dart throwing.

would be using what method of observing? _____ recording

4. Figure 6-105 shows how many supportive comments you make to Beth and Barb each day when Fred did not and then did give you feedback. Divided? _____ Stable? _____ Convincing? _____ Caused? _____ (yes, no)

7. John decided that good interview behavior is "looking the interviewer in the eye and answering each question clearly and politely." The words in quotes would be called a(n) _____.

18. Figure 6-106 shows many bull's-eyes Tim throws in darts when he gets or doesn't get a tip from Ann. Divided? _____ Stable? _____ Convincing? _____ Caused? _____ (yes, no)

2. By way of final review: Here's how you visually analyze any experiment. First, decide whether the conditions are _____. Second, decide if the conditions are _____. Third, decide whether the differences between conditions are _____. _____ Fourth, decide whether the treatment _____ behavior to change.

# LESSON 7

# Review of Behavioral Methods

## Reading Section

Behavior analysis is the modern form of behaviorism. It retains many beliefs of early behaviorism: that we can study human action by natural science methods, that such a science must study behavior rather than mental events, that such a science can help us solve our problems. Behavior analysis has kept the optimistic and forward-looking aspects of the old behaviorism.

At the same time, it has taken a direction that has revolutionized behaviorism. It has cast off narrow behaviorism by defining behavior very broadly. It has cast off the mechanical stimulus-response approach by looking at the context of behavior (e.g., Morris, 1988; Klatt & Morris, 2001; Hayes, 1988). It has cast off the involuntary reflex as the building block of complex behavior. Behavior analysis has broadened behaviorism to deal with the entire range of human activities.

Skinner's formulation of reinforcement in the 1930s let behavior analysts study voluntary "operant" behavior. As a result, the practical use of behavior analysis has exploded since 1970, helping to solve behavioral problems from shyness to lack of creativity to autism. Behavior analysis has spawned such new fields as behavioral gerontology (see Derenne & Baron, 2002), behavioral medicine, and behavioral social work. This modern form of behaviorism has enjoyed widespread success.

This success comes partly from enlarging the meaning of the term *behavior*. Behavior analysts refer to obvious movements as behavior just as everyone else does. However, they extend the meaning of behavior beyond obvious movement to include more subtle activity, such as talking, looking, listening, and reading. They extend it still further to include internal events measurable by electronic devices—muscle tension, brain waves, stomach acidity, and so forth. Finally, they extend it radically to include private events such as thinking and feeling. In short, they apply *behavior* to anything that people do.

You have read in this book about many examples of this broader meaning of behavior. Behavior analysts have found useful ways to observe many obvious, but complex, behaviors. They have observed carrying out football assignments, doing cooperative household chores, recycling, disrupting dental treatment, conserving electricity, and giving traffic tickets. They have observed many subtle behaviors, such as accepting criticism and conversing skillfully, and others that involve what many would call cognitive functioning: learning, creating, studying, and remembering. They have observed internal behavior such as tension. They have found ways to get at private behaviors such as pain, attention, and thoughts. Behavior analysts have observed these behaviors in order to help people change them (see the box on Sleeping as Behavior). Examples in this book often report the success of the behavior analysis approach at doing just that. Can anyone familiar with its richness and depth call it narrow or mechanical?

The success of behavior analysis also comes from other sources. It has solved some major problems that plagued researchers studying human behavior, such as seeking the causes of behavior in private events. The

*Sleeping as Behavior*

You may think of sleep as "markedly reduced consciousness" (Chaplin, 1985: p. 430). How would you measure that? You might not think of observing sleep as behavior, yet that is exactly what two researchers did. They provided older insomniacs with a simple device to measure sleep. The device sounded a very soft tone for 1 second every 10 minutes. It then tape-recorded whether the insomniac said "I'm awake" within 10 seconds. Obviously, if the insomniacs replied, they were not asleep. If they did not reply, they were probably asleep. Thus, the researchers defined consciousness in terms of whether the insomniacs were responsive to their environment. That's just common sense! (Based on Lichstein & Johnson, 1991.)

1. By observing briefly every 10 minutes and not observing the rest of the time, what method of observation did these researchers use to observe sleep?
_____ recording

problem with using private events to explain behavior is that they must still be <u>explained</u> (see Calkin, 2002, for a review of empirical investigations of private events).

Behavior analysis solves this problem by using the *principle of public events*. You use this principle when you seek the causes of behavior in <u>environmental</u> events. You can study these causes with the methods of natural science. You thereby avoid the problem of causes that must themselves be explained.

The behavior analysis approach has allowed methods of inquiry to be applied to human behavior. The result is that human behavior is now a respected field of scientific endeavor. In fact, the role of natural science in the study of human behavior cannot be underestimated. Already you have learned about five tactics that enable you to apply scientific methods in the form of the behavioral strategy to solving human problems.

## The Five Tactics of the Behavioral Strategy

Behavior analysis helps you find treatments for changing socially important behavior. Finding such treatments involves at least five tactics. Let's review them: First, you create a behavioral definition of the problem. Second, you use a method for the direct observation of the behavior. Third, you check the reliability and social validity of your observations. Fourth, you use a single-subject experiment that rules out alternative explanations. Fifth, you do a visual analysis of your data. Each of these tactics is a part of the behavioral strategy for solving human problems.

The first tactic in using the behavioral strategy is to create a behavioral definition of the problem behavior. This often requires that you translate everyday talk into behavioral language. Sometimes, everyday talk is explicitly behavioral. In this case, all you have to do is specify the details of your behavioral definition. "Crying" already has a clear behavioral referent. To define crying, all you have to do is specify when a vocal sound is a cry, which might involve specifying loudness. Other times, everyday talk is only implicitly behavioral. "Studying" obviously describes what a person is doing. However, you must specify aspects of the behavior that are a valid part of studying. These might be as simple as the student looking at the book or answering questions about the book. Making behavioral definitions when everyday talk is already behavioral is easy.

Often, however, everyday talk is vague. It may not seem to refer to behavior at all. For example, *understanding* seems to refer to thoughts rather than to behavior. However, common sense dictates that if someone understands an idea, they can explain it. For example, you might want to find out whether Tom understands the concept of *reliability*. You can ask Tom to apply it to a set of behavioral observations. If he can, then you know that he understands the concept. In this way, *understanding* is no longer just an unobservable event but a behavioral event.

When you get interested in a human problem, you can search for the behaviors involved.

They may be obvious, subtle, internal, or private. You can find good behavioral definitions through this search. Researchers have defined such complex behaviors as aggression (Borrero, Vollmer, & Wright, 2002), creativity (Goetz & Baer, 1973), nervous tension (Budzynski & Stoyva, 1969), and cooperative living (Miller & Feallock, 1975). Researchers will continue to look at human actions not now considered behavioral. You can be sure that they will find ways to translate them into behavioral terms.

Once you have created a behavioral definition, you move on to the next tactic of the behavioral strategy: You can apply a method of direct observation to gather information about the problem behavior. Using the principle of direct observation, you can enlist trained observers to record people's <u>observable behavior</u>. You can get accurate and detailed data and avoid the problems that come from people reporting their own behavior.

Direct observation solves the problem of relying on self-reports, which tend to be <u>inaccurate</u> or of unknown accuracy (e.g., Ardoin & Martens, 2000). You will find that when you can check up on people's self-reports, they are often wrong. Too many times, you can't even check up on them because they are about mental events that no one else can see.

You can use any of the four methods of direct observation: (1) You can use outcome recording if the behavior leaves a result. (2) You can use event recording if the behavior is uniform. (3) You can use interval recording if the behavior occurs for nonuniform episodes. (4) You can use time sample recording to observe a sample of the behavior. Each method allows you to observe the behavior directly.

In using the third tactic of the behavioral strategy, you first find out if the data are reliable. If they are not, then the data have no meaning or use to other people. If they are, then you can use them to devise a solution to the problem. You must also find out if your observations are socially valid. You do this by correlating the ratings of outside judges with observations of trained observers.

If the behavioral observations are not reliable, you have several options. You can give more training to the observers. You can revise the behavioral definition so that it is clearer. Likewise, if your behavioral definition is not socially valid, you can revise it to agree with the meaning used by your judges.

In using the fourth tactic of the behavioral strategy, you design a single-subject experiment to find out if the treatment works. You use this tactic when you have found a treatment that seems to change the behavior. Your treatment can be anything capable of objective specification. It might be a reward, a new training method, or even meditation. If you can specify the treatment, you can test to see if it really works.

Finding out whether a treatment works requires ruling out alternative explanations.

---

### *Inner versus Outer Causes in Everyday Language*

Hineline (1992) analyzed how people talk about the causes of behavior in everyday life. He suggested that people point to an inner cause when explaining unexpected behavior. When John rejects a $25,000 promotion, people say he is "a man of principle." Those people are pointing to an inner cause. Hineline suggested that people sometimes point to external causes when explaining expected behavior. If John turns down a promotion that would prevent him from helping his terminally ill wife, he is likely to say that his wife needs his help. John is pointing to an external cause. Note those times when the behavioral approach of pointing to an external cause doesn't sound right to you because the behavior is unexpected.

2. The behavioral approach may sound right to you when it uses an external cause to explain an expected behavior. However, it is likely to sound wrong to you when it uses an external cause to explain a(n) _____ (expected, unexpected) behavior.

You can do this by using the principle of single-subject experiments. Single-subject designs, such as comparison, reversal, and multiple baseline, look at the behavior of <u>one person</u> at a time. The two most powerful designs are the reversal design and the multiple-baseline design. Both designs not only rule out individual differences by studying one person at a time, but they also rule out time coincidences by observing behavior change at least twice. In contrast, the comparison design rules out only individual differences.

Single-subject designs solve the problem of alternative explanations, which don't allow us to pinpoint what actually caused any of the observed behavioral differences. Designs that don't rule out alternative explanations have not helped discover the <u>causes</u> of individual behavior.

Finally, you perform a visual analysis of your data—the fifth tactic—to decide whether the effect of the conditions is different. You must look to see if the conditions are divided and stable. If you find both divided and stable conditions, then you can conclude that the conditions differ. You may have ruled out alternative explanations with a single-subject design. If so, you can then conclude that the treatment caused the change in behavior. This approach finds important causes of behavior change. Called the principle of visual analysis, it requires that you look for <u>convincing</u> effects.

Visual analysis solves the problem of finding weak effects. It finds powerful treatments that cause large and important differences in behavior. Such treatments have important theoretical and practical implications.

## Summary

Behavior analysis uses a natural science approach to studying human activity. It has broadened behaviorism to deal with voluntary behavior. It has solved major problems that often plague researchers wishing to study human behavior. You can use its methods to help solve human problems. I have outlined the behavioral strategy for doing so. The heart of this approach involves five tactics. First, you create a behavioral definition of the problem behavior. Second, you use a method of direct observation to gather information about the behavior. Third, you check the reliability and social validity of your observations. Fourth, you use a single-subject experiment to test the treatment. Fifth, you do a visual analysis of your data. This method can produce dramatic successes. Used by behavior analysts, it has spawned many new fields of scientific inquiry.

## Notes

### Note #1

Baer, Wolf, and Risley (1968), propose a set of practices that characterize applied behavior analysis. They asserted that applied behavior analysis research studies applied problems, defines them behaviorally, analyzes their causes, specifies the treatment so others can use it, states the principle underlying the treatment, makes effective changes, and has generality. This article is often referred to as the classic definition of the science. See also the follow up (Baer, Wolf, & Risley, 1987).

## Helpful Hints

### Helpful Hint #1

You can review the entire unit by working through the Practice Review that follows the Glossary. It has questions similar to those in a Programmed Reading. But it has many more questions than do the Programmed Reading sections. Also, it has a wide variety of questions from all of the lessons in this unit. Answering them all is an excellent way to study for the review exam covering these lessons.

3. An excellent way to study for the review exam over Unit 1 is to answer the questions in the _____ Review.

### Helpful Hint #2

The definitions of all terms introduced in this unit of the book are presented below. You can review the unit and prepare for your exam by testing yourself on the definitions and correlated facts presented for each term. You might use a piece of paper to mask the definition, leaving only the term exposed. See if you can formulate a reasonable definition and produce any other facts about that term. Then, move the paper and check on yourself.

## Glossary

You can review the ideas taught in this unit by reading the following definitions. As you review the terms, see if you can define them before looking at the definition (see hint #2 above). See if you can think of an example for each term.

**baseline** The period of an experiment without the treatment.

**behavior** Anything that a person does.
- This implies that the activity is physical.
- This includes obvious, subtle, internal, and private events.

**behavior analysis** The study of environmental events that change behavior.
- The founder of behavior analysis is Skinner.
- Behavior analysis exploded in popularity in 1970.
- Behavior analysis studies thoughts and feelings as behavior.
- Behavior analysis sees most behavior as voluntary behavior.

**behavioral definition** A statement that specifies exactly what behavior to observe.
- Creating a behavioral definition is the first step in studying behavior.
- It makes communication clearer; it maintains consistency of observations.

**behavioral strategy** The strategy of defining human problems as behavioral problems.
- It involves five tactics:
  1. Specify the behavior with a behavioral definition.
  2. Gather information using the approach of direct observation.
  3. Check the reliability and social validity of your observations.
  4. Use a single-subject experiment to test your treatment.
  5. Do a visual analysis of your data.

**comparison design** An experimental design comparing the baseline condition with the treatment condition.

- It rules out individual differences but not time coincidences.

**convincing differences** Every pair of adjacent conditions must be divided; every condition must be stable.

**direct observation** The observer personally sees and immediately records the behavior.

**divided conditions** The ranges of the last three points of two conditions are mutually exclusive.

**event recording** You record a response when you see an instance of the behavior.
- You use this method when the instances of the behavior are regular or uniform.

**interval recording** You record a response if the behavior occurs in one of a series of continuous intervals.

**multiple-baseline design** An experimental design that introduces the treatment at different times for two or more behavioral variables.
- This design rules out alternative explanations.

**outcome recording** You record a response when you see the result of the behavior.

**principle of direct observation** Using trained observers for the **direct observation** of behavior.
- When a person observes their own behavior with a behavioral definition and immediately records it, behavior analysts regard this approach as direct observation.

**principle of public events** Seeking the causes of behavior in environmental events.
- The problem with using private events to explain behavior is that you still must explain the private events.

**principle of single-subject experiments** To expose the same person to the baseline and treatment.

**principle of visual analysis** Finding differences that look convincing.

- Differences are convincing if conditions are <u>divided</u> and <u>stable</u>.

**reliability** The percentage of <u>agreement</u> between two independent observers.
- Both observers must observe the same <u>responses</u> and use the same <u>behavioral definition</u>.
- The formula for reliability is <u>100%x A/(A+D)</u>.
- Trial reliability is where you compare each <u>observation</u>. You can always use trial reliability with interval and time sample recording. You can only use trial reliability with outcome or event recording of complex behaviors with a checklist.
- Frequency reliability is where you compare overall <u>frequencies</u>. You can use frequency reliability with outcome or event recording of simple behaviors.
- Old definitions should reach <u>90%</u> while new definitions only <u>80%</u>.

**reversal design** An experimental design that looks at a behavior during <u>baseline</u>, <u>treatment</u>, and <u>reversal</u>.
- It can rule out alternative explanations.

**ruling out alternative explanations** Showing that events other than the treatment are unlikely to have <u>caused</u> an observed difference.
- One alternative is that any effect is caused by <u>individual differences</u>.
- Another alternative is that the effect is caused by <u>time coincidences</u>.

**self-report observations** The observer relies on their <u>memory</u> of the behavior.
- The problem with self-reports such as questionnaires and interviews is that they are usually <u>inaccurate</u> or of unknown accuracy.

**social validity** The <u>correlation</u> between ratings by outside judges and observations by trained observers.

**stable conditions** The last three numbers of one condition are <u>not moving closer</u> to the numbers in the other condition.

**time sample recording** You record a response if the behavior occurs within one of a series of <u>discontinuous</u> intervals.
- This method is also used to observe <u>multiple behaviors</u> of one person or <u>multiple people</u> performing one behavior.

**treatment** The method introduced to <u>modify</u> the rate of a behavior.

## Additional Readings

Bachrach, A. J. (1962). *Psychological research: An introduction.* New York: Random House. This book is an easily read introduction to the philosophy of behavioral research.

Bernard, C. (1957). *An introduction to the study of experimental medicine.* New York: Dover. Claude Bernard is often called the father of experimental medicine. This book is a modern release of his century-old classic. It advocates an experimental method similar to single-subject experimentation. Because the logic is applied to medical problems, it may help you understand the same logic applied to behavioral problems.

Skinner, B. F. (1958). *Cumulative record.* New York: Appleton-Century-Crofts. This book is an excellent introduction for the advanced student to Skinner's approach to the methods of behavioral science.

## Practice Review I

The following material covers every concept studied in Unit 1. By answering the questions and checking your answers, you can prepare yourself for the Review Exam. The Review Exam will contain questions from all the lessons in Unit 1. This section has a long module to give you plenty of review for the exam.

### 1. Some Review Questions

23. Pre-test: During the first week, Wade observed Tom's smiling and making positive comments. Starting the second week, Wade gave Tom frequent pep talks on the importance of smiling. He said nothing about positive comments. Starting the third week, Wade also gave frequent

pep talks about the importance of positive comments. He continued to give frequent pep talks about the importance of smiling. Tom is a changed person because of those pep talks. What experimental design did Wade use to investigate the effect of his pep talks on Tom's two behaviors of smiling and making positive comments?_____ design

28. Pre-test: You watch four children to see their writing behavior. You divide the one-hour writing period into 240 intervals of 15 seconds each. You watch the first child for the first 15 seconds, the second child during the next 15 seconds, and so on. Thus, you observe each child's writing for one 15-second period per minute. Your method of observing is _____ _____ recording.

25. Pre-test: Suppose that Diane developed a behavioral definition of assertiveness. She had an outside group rate the assertiveness of individuals observed by means of a videotape in which some individuals exhibited a high level of what she defined as assertive behavior and others exhibited a low level. If she compared the ratings made by the outside group with her own observations to see whether they were using a similar definition of assertiveness, she would be determining the _____ _____ of her definition.

27. Pre-test: Two observers are counting the number of times a person smiles. One counts 8, while the other counts 10. What is the reliability? _____% Is it acceptable? _____

27. Pre-test: A group of students in the sixties tried using sit-ins to desegregate a northern suburb. Before starting their protests, however, they sent 10 black students into three restaurants every day for a week to test whether the owner would serve them. None were served. They began a sit-in at Restaurant A. The testers continued going to two other restaurants during this time. After 10 days, Restaurant A changed its policy and served the testers. The students then repeated the procedure first with Restaurant B and then Restaurant C. The design they used is an example of a(n) _____ design.

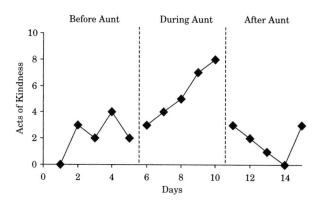

***Figure 7-2.*** An experimental analysis of kindness.

24. Pre-test: May observed Professor Brainbuster on Thursday to see how many chauvinistic comments he made. She counted 18. April observed Professor Brainbuster on Friday and found that he made 20 such comments. Can you conclude that May and April were making reliable observations of Professor Brainbuster's chauvinistic comments? _____ (yes, no)

26. Pre-test: The statement that "assertive behavior consists of making eye contact, speaking loud enough to be clearly heard, and asking the other person to change his or her behavior" is called a(n) _____ _____ of assertiveness.

21. Pre-test: Figure 7-2 shows how many acts of kindness Dale emitted each day when her favorite aunt did and did not try to convince her to emit more acts of kindness. Divided? _____ Stable? _____ Convincing? _____ Cause? _____ (yes, no)

1. A formal description of what to observe is called a(n) _____.

14. Ken was intensely interested in nervousness. He observed his professor's displays of nervous pacing during lectures by breaking the lecture period down into 150 consecutive 20-second periods of time and recording whether any nervous pacing occurred during each 20-second period. Ken was using _____ recording.

37. The method of observation that involves observing someone's behavior for 10 seconds at several randomly scheduled times is called _____ recording.

12. In the science of behavior analysis, any procedure designed to change the rate of a behavior is called a(n) _____.

33. The behavioral strategy is to define human problems as _____ problems.

10. If Dave observed the amount of studying that Pam did for three weeks, then started urging her to study more while continuing to observe the amount of studying she did for another three weeks, and then finally stopped urging her to study but observed her studying for another three weeks, he would be using what experimental design? _____ design

5. Behavior analysis was founded by _____.

49. What method of observation involves observing a behavior during a series of discontinuous intervals? _____ recording

16. Mr. Warren, a high school teacher, was quite negative in his class. Several of his students decided to observe him to find out how much of the time he was negative. They made their observations in consecutive 15-second blocks throughout the day. They found out that he was negative 75% of the time. What method of observation did they use? _____ recording

34. The correlation of ratings by outside judges with observations by a trained observer using a behavioral definition is called determining the _____ of the behavioral definition.

42. The problem with using private events to explain behavior is that we must still _____ them.

41. The principle of visual analysis is to seek differences in graphical data that look _____.

31. Suppose a behavior is observed for a period before treatment and then a period during treatment to see whether the treatment has any effect. What single-subject experimental design is used? _____ design

43. The simplest form of the time sample method of observation involves observing behavior during a series of _____ time intervals.

7. Defining human problems as <u>behavioral</u> problems is called the _____ strategy.

40. The principle of single-subject experiments is to experiment with the _____ person in all conditions.

45. The widespread publication of behavior analysis results began in what year? _____

38. The principle of direct observation is using a trained observer for the _____ _____ of behavior.

46. Two requirements of reliability are that both observers must observe the same _____ and must use the same _____.

50. When Damon counts the number of times that Janice compliments him, he is using what method of observation? _____ recording

11. If John observes Mary's smiling during 75 consecutive time periods, each of 15 seconds duration, he is using what method of observation? _____ recording

18. Observing a behavior during one brief interval at several times of the day would be called _____ recording.

32. The basic formula for computing reliability is _____.

13. John was a pretty good golfer, scoring an average of 85. He decided to see what effect daily practice would have on his score. After five weeks of practice, his scores had decreased to an average of 78. He stopped practicing when school started again and noticed that his scores slowly crept up until he was averaging about 83. What single-subject experimental design was John inadvertently using? _____ design

4. Behavior analysis studies _____ events that _____ behavior.

39. The principle of public events is to seek the causes of behavior in _____ events.

3. A single-subject experimental design in which treatment is introduced at different times for two or more behaviors is called a(n) _____ design.

35. The instructor decided to count the number of times that Dale spoke in class. She found that Dale spoke 20 times during one class period. However, another observer counted only 15 times. Compute their reliability: _____%. If this is a new behavioral

definition, is the reliability acceptable? _____

19. One criterion for sound observations is that they be based on what the observer can personally see and immediately record. Any procedure that incorporates those features conforms to the principle of _____ .

15. Mary's teacher and another observer made the following observations of Mary's nearness to other children (N=near; F=far). Teacher:
F N F F F F F N F F F F F N F F N N F F;
Another observer:
F N F N F F F N N F F F F F F F N N F F. What is the reliability of these observations? _____ %. Is this an acceptable level if the behavioral definition is a new one? _____ (yes, no)

36. The method of observing that counts occurrences of behavior is called _____ _____ recording.

17. Name a specific single-subject experimental design that rules out both time coincidences and individual differences as alternative explanations of any observed change in behavior: _____ .

44. The tactics in using the behavioral strategy: first, specify the behavior with a behavioral definition; second, gather information using the approach of direct observation; third, check the reliability and social validity of your observations; fourth, use a single-subject experiment to test your treatment; fifth, do a(n) _____ analysis of the data.

9. If a behavior is observed during many consecutive short periods of time, the method of observation is called _____ _____ recording.

2. A good experimental design is one that can rule out _____ explanations of any observed behavior change.

48. Vera kept a record of the number of kisses from James before she started to use musk oil to increase his rate of kissing. The period before she started to use musk oil would be called the _____ condition.

29. Professor Mills made up a checklist of behaviors that a good teaching assistant should perform every time that a student came up to obtain a quiz form. The check-

list included such behaviors as greeting the student by name, asking the student if he or she has a question, and so on. The professor then watched every new assistant when students came to get a quiz. He recorded each behavior as it occurred. He was using _____ recording.

6. Behavior analysts regard thoughts and feelings as physical activities that people do. Therefore, they call them _____ _____ .

47. Two young black men were observing a policeman as he covered his beat to see how many times he called another black man "boy." They wrote their observations down immediately. What method of direct observation were they using? _____ _____ recording

30. Reliability for <u>new</u> behavioral definitions should equal or exceed _____%.

8. Exposing one person at a time to the baseline and treatment is called the principle of _____ experiments.

## Practice Review II

This section contains one short module.

### 1. Programmed Examples

7. Pre-test: Figure 7-4 shows how many conversations Luis started when Laura was around to praise him and when she was not. Divided? _____ Stable? _____ Convincing? _____ Cause? _____ (yes, no)

10. Pre-test: Figure 7-5 shows the results for two observers. Compute their reliability: _____ %. Is it acceptable? _____

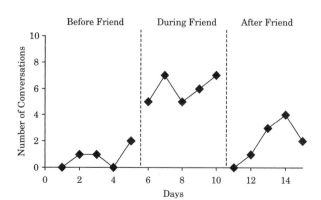

***Figure 7-4.*** An experimental analysis of conversing.

| Observer #1 | Y | N | Y | Y | Y | Y | Y | Y | N | Y |
|---|---|---|---|---|---|---|---|---|---|---|
| Observer #2 | Y | N | Y | Y | Y | N | Y | Y | Y | Y |

**Figure 7-5.** Observations by two observers.

| Teacher | Y | Y | N | N | N | N | N | N | Y | N |
|---|---|---|---|---|---|---|---|---|---|---|
| Another | N | Y | N | N | N | N | N | N | Y | Y |

**Figure 7-6.** Observations by a teacher and another observer.

8. Pre-test: Suppose that Behavior A is observed for 12 weeks before any procedure is used to change its rate. Suppose that Behavior A is observed for 24 weeks after the procedure is introduced. Suppose Behavior B is observed for 24 weeks (instead of 12 weeks) before the same procedure is used and then 12 weeks after. The name of the experimental design is ———————————— design.

6. Pre-test: About one student per week joined the new compact disc–buying cooperative. Then, the cooperative decided to try a newspaper advertisement. As a result, about 20 students joined each week. The members concluded that advertising pays because the ad succeeded in attracting many new members. This is not a good experimental design because it doesn't rule out ———————————— explanations of the increase (such as the approach of Christmas).

9. Figure 7-6 shows the result of observations made by a teacher and another observer after developing a behavioral definition of the amount of time that John was studying. Since they weren't able to make continuous observations, they checked John every half hour and noted whether he was studying. What is the reliability? ——— % Is this acceptable? ——— (yes, no)

1. An experimental design that studies a behavior before, during, and after the treatment is called a(n) ———————————— design.

12. The percentage of agreement between two observers is called ————————————.

16. What science studies environmental events that modify what people do? ———————

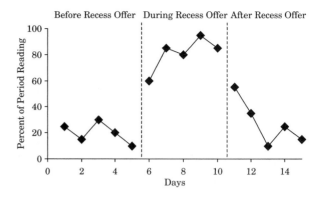

**Figure 7-7.** An experimental analysis of reading.

13. The period of time when behavior is observed prior to an attempt to change the rate of that behavior is called the ——————— ——————— condition.

4. Jenny decided to record the number of pieces of junk that her slobbish roommate piled on her desk and bed for two weeks and then confront her roommate with this information. At the end of the two weeks, she showed her roommate the data proving that an average of 12 objects per day had been left in Jenny's part of the room. Her roommate was surprised by the data, apologized, and promised to stop. If this is considered a behavioral experiment, what is Jenny's talking with her roommate called? ———————————

2. Behavior analysts call anything that a person does ————————————.

5. Name a single-subject experimental design that does not rule out all alternative explanations of any observed change in behavior: ————————————.

3. Figure 7-7 shows what percentage of study hall Harry devoted to reading when his teacher did or did not offer early recess if he read most of the period. Teacher used a(n) ———————————— design.

14. Vera wasn't getting anywhere with James during an initial period of knowing him. He hadn't even kissed her yet. She decided to wear musk oil perfume to see if that would increase his kissing behavior. James now kisses Vera on every date. What type of single-subject experimental design is this? ————————————

11. The method that observes a result of behavior is called ———————————— recording.

17. When you do a visual analysis, you check to see if the conditions are both _____ and _____ _____ before concluding that the differences are convincing.

15. Using the behavioral strategy involves: first, specifying the behavior with a(n) _____; second, gathering information using the approach of direct observation; third, checking the reliability and social validity of your observations; fourth, using a(n) _____ ____ experiment to test your treatment; fifth, visually analyzing the data.

# Reinforcement of Everyday Behaviors

## Reading Section

### Introduction to Unit 2

This unit and the rest of the units in the book introduce you to what behavior analysis has learned about environmental influences on behavior. Unit 2 teaches you about reinforcement and the reinforcement strategy for solving human problems. The first lesson in this unit introduces *reinforcement*, a concept that lies at the heart of environmental influences that create and maintain behavior. Subsequent lessons explain related concepts. Unit 3 explains how reinforcement influences *cognitive behavior*. Finally, Unit 4 explains the term *punishment*, which is the opposite of reinforcement. It reduces and destroys behavior. Units 2 through 4 present what you might call the behavioral theory of everyday human behavior. Thus, they present an introduction to what behavior analysts have learned by using the methodology outlined in Unit 1.

Reinforcement expresses the idea that people learn behaviors that work. That is, they learn through experience. Usually, such learning helps people become happier and more productive. However, such learning can misfire, producing the opposite effect. Behavior analysts have found that reinforcement holds the key to understanding both results.

In this lesson, you will learn the first tactic of the reinforcement strategy, which is to increase desired behavior through <u>reinforcement</u>.

1. The first tactic in using the reinforcement strategy is to increase desired behavior through _____ .

## Definition of Reinforcement

A **reinforcer** is any event that (1) <u>follows</u> a behavior and (2) <u>increases</u> the rate of that behavior. The first part of the definition stresses that a reinforcer must be a consequence. It must come after the behavior. The second part of the definition stresses that a reinforcer must be effective. It must cause the person to emit more of the behavior. In other words, the reinforcer itself is a proven reward.

2. A **reinforcer** is any event that (1) _____ _____ a behavior and (2) _____ ____ the rate of that behavior.

**Reinforcement** is the <u>procedure</u> of using a reinforcer to increase the rate of a behavior. The procedure is to ensure that the reinforcer follows the behavior. Be sure you understand the difference between *reinforcer* and *reinforcement*. One is an event, the other is a procedure. This is an important distinction. You will run into it throughout the book, so be sure you understand it.

3. **Reinforcement**: Using a reinforcer to increase the rate of a behavior is not an event; it is a(n) _____ .

I can illustrate these terms with respect to an obvious behavior. Suppose that Mom gives Tommy a dessert for eating spinach. If Tommy eats spinach more often in the future, you call the dessert a reinforcer. You call the procedure of giving Tommy dessert after he eats spinach reinforcement.

Notice that Mom doesn't reinforce Tommy. She gives the dessert to Tommy, but she doesn't

**Figure 8-1.** A touchdown probably reinforces the obvious football behavior that produces it. (Source: Jim Cummins/CORBIS)

reinforce him. She reinforces Tommy's *behavior* of eating spinach. She doesn't strengthen her son, she strengthens a specific behavior he exhibits. The rule for talking about reinforcement is simple. You do not reinforce a person, you reinforce their behavior (Baer, 1976).

You must carefully look to see if both elements of reinforcement exist in every example. Suppose that Mom gave Tommy a bagel whenever he ate his spinach. Suppose that Tommy didn't eat his spinach any more often because of the bagel. Notice that giving Tommy the bagel for eating his spinach did not produce an increase in his rate of eating spinach. Therefore, the bagel would not be an example of a reinforcer. We will call an event that follows a behavior but does not increase its rate an *unknown* in this book.

Remember, you must carefully look to see if both elements of reinforcement exist in every example. Suppose that Mom told Tommy he had to eat his spinach from now on. Tommy might eat his spinach more often after that. Notice that the event "Mom told Tommy he had to eat his spinach" does not follow Tommy's behavior of eating spinach. It precedes it. It should be obvious to you that Mom would tell

Tommy to eat his spinach before he has eaten it, not after. Therefore, her demand would not be an example of a reinforcer. We will call an event that does not follow a behavior but does increase its rate an *unknown* in this book until a later lesson.

An event must have two elements to be a reinforcer. It must <u>follow</u> the behavior of interest. It must also cause that behavior to <u>increase</u> in rate. If an event does not have both elements, it is not a reinforcer. I will call events that have one but not both elements an *unknown*. I will slip in examples of events that have one but not both elements in order to teach you to look very carefully for both elements before calling an event a reinforcer.

Notice that the definition of reinforcer does not require that the event be "pleasant." For example, suppose that Tommy burped at the table and Mom yelled at him, "That's disgusting!" Tommy might react like many little boys and burp more often as a result of Mom's reaction. Her yelling follows his burping and increases the rate of burping. Even though you might think of her yelling as unpleasant, it is still a reinforcer.

The term *reinforcer* may seem similar in meaning to the everyday word *reward*. However, the meaning is very different. <u>Reward</u> refers to an event that the speaker feels another person *should* like. But the feeling of the speaker does not *prove* that the event really is a reinforcer. In fact, your own biases may lead you to totally misjudge what another person should like. The following example illustrates the relation between reward and reinforcer with respect to a subtle behavior. Don might reward his daughter Mary for admitting that she broke a dish. Don might reward Mary with a trip to a movie that Don really likes. Don hopes that rewarding Mary with the movie will make her more likely to tell the truth in the future. It may not. Mary may not like that particular movie! Only if the movie is a reinforcer will Mary be more likely to tell the truth in the future.

A reinforcer is proven to modify the behavior of the person receiving it. You might think of a reinforcer as a <u>proven reward</u>.

Students often get mixed up between *reinforcer* and *reinforcement*. A reinforcer is an <u>event</u>. It is giving a piece of candy, seeing a sunset, or receiving a thank you. Of course, the event has to follow the response and increase its future rate. A reinforcement is a <u>procedure</u>. It is a rule or repeated pattern of giving a reinforcer for a particular behavior. It is giving dessert whenever Tommy eats his spinach.

4. Students often get mixed up between *reinforcer* and *reinforcement*. A reinforcer is a(n) _____. A reinforcement is a(n) _____.

## The Variety of Reinforcers

A limitless variety of events can serve as reinforcers. Social reinforcers might consist of a smile, a word of praise, agreement, or attention. Edible reinforcers might consist of candy, snacks, or beer. Play reinforcers might consist of toys, airplanes, or Frisbees. Activity reinforcers might consist of dancing, skydiving, or jogging. Generalized reinforcers might consist of money or points. Rare and sublime events can be reinforcers, as the box on the The Case of the Glass Meadow illustrates. Some events are reinforcers for almost everyone. Sex, money, and food are examples. On the other hand, some events may be reinforcers only for small groups or even single individuals. Rare art or the study of Latin might be examples. In fact, some reinforcers may even be painful. Some people like others to spank or whip them.

People may deliberately contrive reinforcement, or nature may deliver it (see Skinner, 1982). Teachers may deliberately praise the studying of their pupils. Nature may produce a beautiful sunset that increases the rate at which you go outside in the evening.

---

### *Reinforcers Can Be Magic, Too: The Case of the Glass Meadow*

You may think that *reinforcer* applies only to events like money, praise, or candy. Perhaps you think they miss the magic of life. One mom and dad went night-sledding with their children after a freezing rain. "I will never forget the unbelievably beautiful sight that met our eyes when we reached the meadow. The moon and stars, shining brilliantly in the clear, cold night, had turned the meadow into a lake of glass. . . . We left most of the sledding to our children and stayed absorbed in the dreamlike magic of this night." They learned from this magic night to go with their children to other special moments. "We have gone with them to glimpse the moment—a new calf, a robin on the lawn, a butterfly or bug" (Carpenter, 1993).

5. Because these magic moments are <u>events</u>, and not procedures, that follow going with their children and these events increase the rate of going, we call them _____ (reinforcements, reinforcers).

**Figure 8-2.** A beautiful scene may reinforce the subtle behavior involved in looking at it. (Source: © Charles Krebs/CORBIS)

**"Boy! What do you do with all that swell stuff?"**

© 1972 McNaught Synd., Inc.          7-10

**Figure 8-3.** A reinforcer for one person is not necessarily a reinforcer for another person. (Source: Cartoon copyright 1972 McNaught Syndicate, Inc. Used by permission.)

You should carefully limit your use of the term *reinforcer*. Suppose you find that an event follows a behavior and increases the rate of that behavior. You should call that event a reinforcer only for that person and that behavior. You cannot be sure that the event would reinforce other behaviors of that person, although it might. Nor can you be sure that the event would reinforce the same behavior of another person. The cartoon in Figure 8-3 makes this point eloquently. Remember the old hippie motto "Different strokes for different folks"? Be sure to limit your use of the term reinforcer to an event proven for a particular person. Do not depart from this very precise use of the term. It represents the very essence of the meaning of *reinforcer*. Applied researchers have found that this precision is essential to helping people in many situations (e.g., Lindauer, Zarcone, Richman, & Schroeder, 2002; Mason, McGee, Farmer-Dougan, & Risley, 1989; Vollmer & Iwata, 1991).

## Uses of Reinforcement

Reinforcement is a concept that applies to all human behavior. Behavior analysts use the concept to guide their help for people. They deliberately arrange reinforcing events to follow desirable behaviors. Behavior analysts aren't alone in using reinforcement. We all use reinforcement in our everyday lives. We sometimes deliberately use it. More often we use it without deliberate plan.

Behavior analysts have introduced the use of reinforcement to teach a variety of desirable behaviors. For example, the staff of a home for elderly people taught residents to choose healthy foods by praising them when they did so (Stock & Milan, 1993). Basketball coaches improved players' foul-shooting performance by providing immediate feedback on proper shooting form (Kladopoulos & McComas, 2001). Therapists taught people with retardation simple language skills by giving them candy when they made correct responses (e.g., Garcia, Guess & Byrnes, 1973). Therapists taught people to relax (e.g., Budzynski & Stoyva, 1969). Coaches improved swimming warm-ups by following them with music (Hume &

Crossman, 1992). A cooperative dorm increased the amount of cleaning by giving residents rent reductions (Feallock & Miller, 1976). Coaches have improved blocking by giving football players immediate feedback (Komaki & Barnett, 1977). Researchers improved oral reading fluency among elementary students with reading problems (e.g., Eckert, Ardoin, Daly, & Martens, 2002). Reinforcement helps many types of people improve their behavior.

Everyday people often make intuitive use of reinforcement. Madeline Cartwright used reinforcement to make an inner city school into a dynamic learning center. See the box on Blaine School.

## Basic Building Block

The significance of reinforcement extends far beyond helping people improve their behavior. Behavior analysts claim that reinforcement is the basic building block of all human behavior. People are more likely to repeat behavior that produces reinforcement. They are less likely to repeat behavior that does not. Ultimately, people usually do that which

**Figure 8-4.** Meditation leads to normalizing body functions. Muscles relax, heart rate slows down, blood pressure decreases, hands warm. These changes may reinforce the internal behaviors involved in meditation. (Source: Frederick Palmer/Stock Boston)

produces reinforcement. Thus, reinforcement is the basic motor that drives all human learning and hence everything that we are and do.

Reinforcement plays a central role in children's development. Suppose Danny cleans his room thoroughly. His parents might praise, hug, and otherwise pay increased attention to him. Danny may be more likely to clean his room in the future. If so, then attention is a reinforcer for room cleaning. Behavior analysts believe that children learn many behaviors because of parental attention. Attention may reinforce talking clearly, using new words, studying in school, bathing, wearing clean clothes, saying "thank you," and so on. The results shape the child's personality.

## Misuse of Reinforcement

Of course, the use of attention doesn't always work out so nicely. Danny might pester Mom around dinnertime for a snack. She might

---

### Even Presidents Can Misuse Reinforcement

Former president Nixon and Henry Kissinger were sitting in the Oval Office discussing policy matters. King Timahoe, Nixon's Irish setter, came in and began chewing on the rug. The president commanded him to stop. King Timahoe kept right on chewing. The president commanded again. More chewing. Finally, Nixon opened his desk drawer, took out a dog biscuit, and gave it to King Timahoe. "Mr. President," said Kissinger, "you have taught that dog to chew the rug." (Based on Roberts & Santogrossi, 1976.)

7. If King Timahoe chewed on the rug more often as a result of Nixon giving him a dog biscuit, we would say that Nixon used the behavioral procedure called _____ (reinforcer, reinforcement).

---

### Oops!

Our young daughter had adopted a stray cat. To my distress, he began to use the back of our new sofa as a scratching post. "Don't worry," my husband reassured me. "I'll have him trained in no time." I watched for several days as my husband patiently "trained" our new pet. Whenever the cat scratched, my husband deposited him outdoors to teach him a lesson. The cat learned quickly. For the next 16 years, whenever he wanted to go outside, he scratched the back of the sofa. (Based on Wyatt, 1990.)

8. You would call the event "being put out" a(n) _____ (reinforcer, reinforcement) for scratching the back of the sofa!

---

reprimand or lecture him about not eating just before dinner. Such attention, although unpleasant, may be reinforcing to Danny. This is even more likely if Mom pays little attention otherwise. Misused parental attention can lead to many problem behaviors in children.

Behavior analysts find that parents aren't the only people who misuse their attention. Teachers attend to disruptive behavior. They do so almost three times more frequently than they attend to constructive behavior (Thomas, Presland, Grant, & Glynn, 1978; White, 1975). This may account for the rise of violent and disorderly behavior in public schools. Friends often express sympathy for complaints of pain. This may cause some people to develop chronic pain behaviors (White & Sanders, 1986). Mental hospital aides often attend to the "crazy" behavior of patients (e.g., Ayllon & Michael, 1959). This may cause much of the crazy behavior in mental hospitals. Nurses may show "understanding" whenever children with autism hurt themselves (Lovaas & Simmons, 1969). This may cause much of the self-injurious behavior that is so common among hospitalized people.

Parents of delinquents frequently give in to the aggressive behavior of their children (e.g., Patterson, 1977). Many well-meaning people accidentally reinforce unpleasant behavior by the attention they give to it (e.g., Thompson & Iwata, 2001).

## What Behaviors Can Be Reinforced?

Behavior analysts have studied the impact of reinforcement on many types of behavior. I have given a wide range of examples in this lesson. These examples span the range of activities constituting behavior. They include obvious, subtle, internal, and private behaviors.

You have seen how reinforcement might apply to obvious behaviors as varied as eating spinach, going to school, cleaning your room, choosing healthy foods, warming up before swimming, cleaning co-op dorms, and performing football-blocking assignments. And you have also seen how reinforcement can mistakenly increase undesirable behaviors. Pestering of parents, disrupting classrooms, and exhibiting crazy, delinquent, or even self-injurious behavior are all examples of obvious behaviors that are the result of misapplied reinforcement.

You have seen how reinforcement might apply to subtle behaviors such as telling the truth and sharing rare moments within a family and how it can increase subtle behaviors such as language skills among people with retardation. I will give an extended description later in this lesson of increasing the subtle behavior of creative word use.

Finally, you have seen how reinforcement can increase internal behaviors such as relaxation. The whole field of biofeedback suggests that therapists can reinforce many internal behaviors. In fact, behavior analysts have reinforced individual brain cell activation (Stein, Xue, & Belluzzi, 1994)! These authors suggest that they may have found "atoms" of behavior!

In fact, as noted earlier, reinforcement by well-meaning friends may even increase the private behavior of feeling pain. Skinner has argued that the form of thought called *problem*

***Figure 8-5.*** Passing your test tomorrow may reinforce the private behaviors involved in understanding the assignment. (Source: Gary Conner/PhotoEdit)

*solving* helps us control our world in ways that are reinforcing (Skinner, 1953). I will provide other examples of how reinforcement can affect private behavior in future lessons.

Thus, behavior analysts have shown that all forms of human activity are affected by reinforcement. It applies not only to obvious behaviors but to subtle behaviors, internal behaviors, and private behaviors. It affects the entire range of human activity!

## Unknown: What Is Not a Reinforcer

You are now learning about your first behavioral procedure. In studying reinforcement, learning about what it *is not* is just as important as learning what it *is*. In fact, you won't really understand reinforcement until you also clearly understand what it is not!

To test your understanding of what is not reinforcement I will give you examples of procedures that are similar in some ways to reinforcement but that are not reinforcement. I will ask, "What procedure does this example illustrate?" I will ask you the same question when I give you an example of reinforcement. To ask you a different question would soon give away the answer. When developing the book, I asked myself, "What answer should students give if the example doesn't illustrate reinforcement?" Instead of requiring that they answer, "It's not reinforcement," I decided on a simpler approach. They should simply reply, "Unknown."

23. For example, suppose that last week, Joe started smiling every time Wanda looked at him. Wanda doesn't look at him any more often since he started smiling. What behavioral procedure is Joe using? Obviously, Joe's smiling follows Wanda's looking at him and is therefore like reinforcement. But also notice that Wanda's looking at Joe doesn't increase. Therefore, Joe's smiling when Wanda looks is an example of what behavioral procedure? _____

Here's a formal definition of **unknown**: Any behavioral procedure (1) that is <u>unsuccessful</u> in changing behavior or (2) for which a name and definition are <u>untaught</u>. Clearly, the procedure that Joe used by smiling when Wanda looked at him was unsuccessful in changing behavior.

## Summary

The first tactic in using the reinforcement strategy is to increase desired behavior through reinforcement. Reinforcement can modify behavior, causing both desirable and undesirable outcomes. Incompetent or unscrupulous persons can use it in dangerous ways. They might try to reinforce conformity, exploitation, or even criminal behavior. Behavior analysts can help people in safe ways. The key to safety is to consult with others about when and how to use reinforcement. Behavior analysts can teach teachers to reinforce their pupils for studying. They can teach parents to reinforce their children for desirable behavior. They can teach clients important skills that will produce reinforcement. They can teach members of groups to reinforce other members to work for the common good.

## Behavior Analysis Examples

### Helping Athletes

Two researchers used music to help teenage swimmers make better use of their warm-up time (Hume & Crossman, 1992). Typically these swimmers failed to stretch, run, do push-ups, or help other swimmers. Instead, they ate, talked, played practical jokes, or even left practice. Kevin is a good example of this pattern. He made good use of about 10% of his time. The coach then announced that he would play music if the swimmers made better use of their time. Specifically, he set the goal of increasing good use of the warm-up period by 15%. Kevin increased his use of the warm-up period to about 45%. The other members of the team made comparable improvements. The swimmers liked the procedure so much that they voted to continue using it.

9. Behavior analysts call the procedure of playing music only when team members make good use of the warm-up period _____.

### Creative Word Use

Researchers studied the creative use of words by fourth- and fifth-grade students (Glover & Gary, 1976). To do so, they created a game by putting the name of a new object on the blackboard every day. Suppose they wrote the word *football* on Monday. They would then give students 10 minutes to list all the uses they could think of for footballs. Brad might respond with "throwing it, sitting on it, flinging it, and giving it to a friend." Suppose that they wrote the word *video* on Tuesday. Brad might respond "watching it, looking at it, writing an English paper about it, and giving it as a gift."

The researchers counted four aspects of Brad's responses. First they counted the number of <u>different responses</u>. This is any use not identical to a use for another object. On

Monday, Brad listed four uses for a football: throwing it, sitting on it, flinging it, and giving it to a friend. He would get a score of four different responses. Notice that even though throwing and flinging are similar, he used a different word. On Tuesday, Brad listed four uses for a video: watching, looking, writing, and giving it as a gift. He would clearly get credit for suggesting watching, looking, and writing because these are different from the uses of a football. Although he suggested giving the football as a gift, he did not word his giving of the video identically, so he gets credit for all four uses.

Second, the researchers counted the number of different <u>verb forms</u>. Brad's list included watching, giving, looking, and writing about the video. They did not give him credit for watching and looking, since they have the same meaning. He would get a count of three verb forms.

Third, the researchers counted the number of <u>words per response</u>. This was the number of words used by the students in explaining each use of the object for that day. Brad used 17 words to explain four uses of video or an average of 4.33.

Fourth, the researchers counted the number of <u>infrequent verb forms</u>. This was the number of verb forms students used that they had never used before. For Tuesday Brad used watching, looking, giving, and writing. He had not used watching or writing before (for football), but he had used giving before and looking was a duplicate form of watching. So he got a score of two for novel verb forms.

The researchers observed the baseline frequency of each of these behaviors daily. During treatment, the experimenter picked one behavior such as verb forms. Each student earned a point for each new verb form. The researchers divided the group into two teams that competed against each other for the highest score. The team with the highest point total went to recess early. However, both teams could win if the lower team got 80% of the points earned by the higher team.

Figure 8-6 shows the results. During treatment, the number of different responses increased from 10 to 13. The number of different verb forms increased from 1 to 5 per day. The number of words per response increased from 3 to 13. The number of infrequent verbs

increased from 1 to 3. Each behavior decreased when the researchers removed treatment. Thus, for each aspect of creativity, when researchers awarded points, the behavior increased.

10. These data show that the event "going to recess early" was a(n) _____ _____ for the students' creative responses.

The researchers wished to find out whether these behaviors would increase the children's creativity. They used a popular standardized test of creativity, which they gave before and after the experiment. The students' scores increased about 13% after their training. This suggests that these behaviors relate to what other psychologists consider creativity. Thus, the researchers' definition of creativity was socially valid.

## Notes

### Note #1
The definition of the term *reinforcer* requires the rate of the behavior to increase. You should be able to answer two questions about that increase. First question: "The rate increases compared to what?" The answer is, "With respect to its baseline." In other words, the rate increases above the period when the event was not delivered. Second question: "The rate increases when?" The answer is, "For the duration of the treatment period"—in other words, when the event follows the behavior.

11. A reinforcer should increase the rate of the behavior compared to its _____ ___ and it should increase for the duration of the _____ period.

### Note #2
I will give you many examples in which people accidentally reinforce others for talking about their problems. Don't conclude that talking with people about their problems is harmful. Don't conclude that listening to their complaints is harmful. Behavior analysts always start by talking with their clients. It is the major component of many treatments.

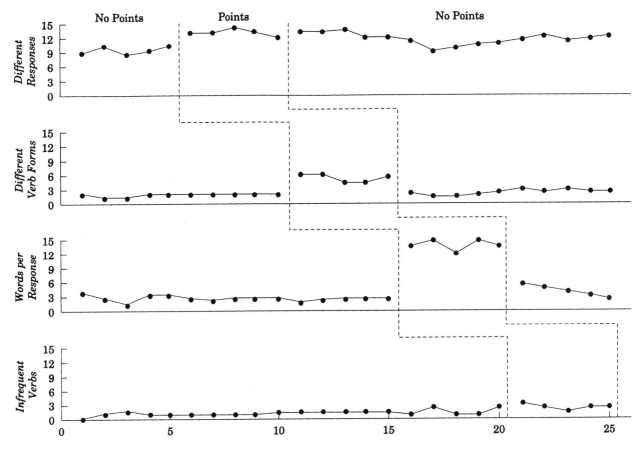

***Figure 8-6.*** This graph shows four behaviors used in a multiple-baseline program to increase creative word usage. The panels show the number of different responses, the number of different verb forms, the number of words, and the use of infrequent verb forms. (Adapted from "Procedures to increase some aspects of creativity," by J. Glover and A. Gary, *Journal of Applied Behavior Analysis*, 1976, 9, 79–84. Copyright 1976 by the Society for the Experimental Analysis of Behavior, Inc. Used by permission.)

However, talking with people is like any other application of reinforcement. It can harm people if misapplied as a form of treatment.

12. If talking with people about their problems actually increased the rate of their complaining, the procedure of "delivering" talking with them would be called _____.

### Note #3

The definition of a reinforcer requires that you observe an increase in behavior caused by the event. Suppose you observe that the rate of a particular response increases. Suppose the increase occurs after you start delivering some event following the response. This does not prove that the event caused the increase. Alternative events could have caused the

increase. For example, suppose the teacher gives John an M & M each time he raises his hand instead of just blurting out his question. Suppose John raises his hand more often. Without further research, the new behavior pattern doesn't prove that the teacher caused this increase by delivering the M & Ms. John's mother might have just previously told him always to raise his hand in class—or else!

The most rigorous way to prove that an event is a reinforcer is to use a reversal design. You observe the rate of a behavior during a baseline condition. Then, you observe the rate of the behavior during the reinforcement condition. Suppose that it increases. Finally, you observe the rate of the behavior during a reversal-to-baseline condition. If it decreases, then you have firm evidence that the event is a reinforcer.

A slightly less rigorous way is to use a multiple-baseline design across behaviors. Suppose the rate of three behaviors increases only after each is followed by reinforcement. This is evidence that the event is reinforcing. Likewise, you could use a multiple-baseline design across different situations or different individuals.

13. To scientifically prove that an event is a reinforcer requires the researcher to use either a(n) _____ design or a(n) _____ design.

For convenience, the book assumes that an increase from baseline to treatment proves that the treatment was a reinforcer. That is, the book requires only a comparison design to prove that an event is a reinforcer. You should assume that if an event follows a behavior and increases its rate from baseline to treatment, the event is a reinforcer. However, remember that this is a convention in this book. You should not make that assumption in your everyday life.

14. You should assume that if an event follows a behavior and increases its rate from baseline to treatment, the event is a(n)

_____ .

### Note #4

The term *contingent* is useful when talking about reinforcement. *Contingent* means that something is dependent on something else. Suppose you get a good grade on psychology tests only when you study. You can describe this by using the term *contingency*. Getting a good grade is <u>contingent</u> on studying. That is, you will get the good grade only if you study. A <u>contingency</u> is a relationship between the behavior and the reinforcer. This term is commonly used in behavior analysis to label this relationship. I will not use it as a technical term until a later lesson. I will often use it to refer to the relationship.

15. When I write that a reinforcer is contingent on a behavior, I mean that you won't get the reinforcer unless you perform the

_____ .

### Note #5

A person's <u>history of reinforcement</u> often explains their current behavior. If they have a history of reinforcement for working math problems, they are likely to use math skills now. If they have a history of reinforcement for assertive behavior, they are likely to act assertively now. Many aspects of a person that we call personality stem from their history of reinforcement.

16. A person's current behavior can often be explained by their past experience in receiving reinforcement for that behavior, which is called their _____ of reinforcement.

### Note #6

Please understand that you must observe whether an event increases behavior to be sure it is a reinforcer. One study showed that even teachers have trouble predicting what events will reinforce their own students (Dyer, Dunlap, & Winterling, 1990). Another study showed that caregivers can't predict what will reinforce people with retardation who are in their care (Green, Reid, Canipe, & Gardner, 1991). Numerous studies confirm that casual observation does not lead to accurate predictions.

17. To be sure an event that follows a behavior is a reinforcer, you must <u>observe</u> whether it produces a(n) _____ in that behavior.

## Helpful Hints

I designed the remainder of this lesson to teach you how to apply the term *reinforcer*. You may often have difficulty deciding whether or not one exists.

### Helpful Hint #1

Perhaps the most difficult examples to analyze in terms of reinforcement involve <u>instructions</u> to perform a behavior. An instruction usually precedes the behavior that it influences. It usually does not follow the behavior that it influences. You tell someone to do something, and they do it. In these cases, an instruction is not an event that follows a behavior.

To give someone an instruction may mean more than explaining to them how to do something. It may also mean instructing them to do something. Thus, you might "tell" them, "ask" them, "remind" them, or "demand" of them. If someone "tells," "asks," "reminds," or "demands" that another person do something, this is just another form of instruction.

The situation is murkier when an instruction follows a low-rate behavior and leads to an increase. You usually won't go wrong if you remember that an instruction can't be a reinforcer. Until later chapters, an instruction will be labeled an unknown because it does not follow the behavior that it affects. Any verbal behavior is an instruction if it implies that a positive or negative consequence will follow the behavior. However, verbal behavior that follows a behavior and is not an instruction may be a reinforcer if it increases the rate of the behavior.

18.  An instruction usually _____ (can, can't) be a reinforcer. If you are asked to identify an instruction in the examples, you should label it a(n) _____.

### Helpful Hint #2

An unpleasant event may follow a behavior and, surprisingly, the behavior may increase in probability. A person may engage in stupid arguments and be put down. Instead of shutting up, the person may start more stupid arguments. Remember that the unpleasant event is a reinforcer because it follows the behavior and increases its probability.

19.  If an unpleasant event follows a behavior and increases the probability of that behavior, then the event would be termed a(n) _____.

### Helpful Hint #3

Sometimes an event will occur concurrently with the behavior, and the rate of the behavior will increase. A teacher may watch while a child works a problem, and the rate of working problems may increase. The attention would be a reinforcer, because *follows* can refer to following the start of the behavior as well as its end. An event can qualify as a reinforcer if it follows the end of the behavior or if it follows the start of the behavior.

20.  In other words, you should call an event that occurs at the same time as the behavior (and increases the rate of the behavior) a(n) _____.

### Helpful Hint #4

I will extend use of *unknown* to examples of events as well as procedures. The stories on the following pages provide many examples of events that have both elements defining a reinforcer. However, other stories provide examples of events that have only one of the defining elements. For example, a story may tell you that the event follows the behavior while not telling you that it increases the behavior. For that matter, the story may even tell you that the behavior does not change! Another story may tell you that an event increases the behavior but not that it follows the behavior. You should label such events as an unknown.

21.  If you know only that an event follows a behavior, you should label it as a(n) _____ in this book. If you know only that an event increases the behavior, you should label the event as a(n) _____.

### Helpful Hint #5

The book will ask you to distinguish between *reinforcer* and *reinforcement* throughout the rest of the book. Remember that a reinforcer is an event that follows a behavior and increases the rate of the behavior. Reinforcement is the procedure of delivering that event following the behavior. For example, suppose the rate of a behavior increases after an event follows it. The book may ask two kinds of questions. It might ask you "What is the event called?" In this case, you should label the event a *reinforcer*. The book might ask, "What behavioral procedure did Mom use to increase the behavior?" In this case, you should label the procedure *reinforcement*.

22.  If an event follows a behavior and increases the rate of the behavior, you should call it a(n) _____. The procedure of delivering that event following a behavior is called _____.

# Additional Readings

Allen, K. E., Hart, B. M., Buell, J. S., Harris, F. R., & Wolf, M. M. (1964). Effects of social reinforcement on isolate behavior of a nursery school child. *Child Development, 35,* 511–518. The teacher used her attention effectively to reinforce a shy child for playing with other children.

Homme, L. E., DeBaca, P. D., Devine, J. V., Steinhorst, R., & Rickert, E. J. (1963). Use of the Premack principle in controlling the behavior of nursery school children. *Journal of the Experimental Analysis of Behavior, 6,* 554. This article discusses an interesting use of reinforcement. It illustrates the Premack principle for finding reinforcers. "Suppose Behavior B is more likely than Behavior A. You can reinforce Behavior A by making permission to engage in Behavior B depend upon it." The authors noted that preschool children ran and screamed at a high rate. They did not often sit and look at the blackboard. The authors gave permission to run and scream only after the children sat and looked at the blackboard. The rate of sitting and looking increased dramatically. Another reinforcing event was kicking the wastebasket. The most reinforcing event was pushing the instructor around the room in a chair. Who said reinforcement had to be serious?

McEvoy, M. A., Nordquist, V. M., Twardosz, S., Heckaman, K. A., Wehby, J. H., & Denny, R. K. (1988). Promoting autistic children's peer interaction in an integrated early childhood setting using affection activities. *Journal of Applied Behavior Analysis, 21,* 193–200. These researchers used affection to help integrate children with retardation into a normal classroom. They prompted the children to show affection through hugs, smiles, and words. After this show of affection, the normal children and children with retardation interacted many times more often.

Osborne, J. G. (1969). Free time as a reinforcer in the management of classroom behavior. *Journal of Applied Behavior Analysis, 2,* 113–118. This article reports the effective use of free time as a reinforcer. The researcher studied children in a normally rowdy classroom. He got the teacher to let them have extra free time if they stayed in their seats during study time. The number of children staying seated increased.

# Programmed Reading

## *1. How to Increase Behavior*

41. Pre-test: Because Freddie's school attendance increased when he got new, clean clothes following attendance, the event of getting clothes would be called a(n) _____.

59. Pre-test: Teacher awarded points for a creative behavior by Ali, and her creative behavior increased. Teacher used the procedure of _____ for Ali's creative behavior.

48. Pre-test: If you deliver an event after a behavior and the rate of the behavior increases, you are using the procedure called _____.

38. Pre-test: A reinforcer is an event that is timed to _____ a behavior and that _____ the rate of the behavior.

39. Pre-test: An event that follows a behavior and increases its rate is a(n) _____.

75. This module teaches you to define the behavioral procedure of reinforcement. It teaches you the difference between the procedure called reinforcement and the single event called a reinforcer. I will start by teaching you about the events called _____.

11. Any event that is timed to <u>follow</u> a behavior and that <u>increases</u> the probability of that behavior is called a(n) _____.

2. A reinforcer is any event that is timed to <u>follow</u> a behavior and that _____ (decreases, increases) the probability of that behavior.

3. A reinforcer is any event that is timed to _____ (follow, precede) a behavior and that <u>increases</u> the probability of that behavior.

4. A reinforcer is any <u>event</u> that is timed to _____ a behavior and that _____ the probability of that behavior.

74. The term *reinforcement* is used to refer to the <u>procedure</u> of arranging for an event to follow a behavior that will increase the rate of the behavior. Therefore, if I tell you that an event follows a behavior and increases the rate of the behavior and ask you to name the procedure, you would answer _____ _____.

73. The <u>procedure</u> of delivering a reinforcer is called _____. An <u>event</u> that follows a behavior and increases its rate is called a(n) _____.

29. If Davey eats spinach in the future because he was given dessert after eating spinach in the past, then giving him the dessert is an <u>event</u> called a(n) _____.

31. If the rate of eating spinach is increased by delivering a dessert after spinach is eaten, then this <u>procedure</u> is called _____.

66. Studies have shown that even teachers who know their students well often cannot predict what events will be reinforcers. You cannot guess about what is a reinforcer. To be sure that an event that follows a behavior is a reinforcer, you must <u>observe</u> whether it produces a(n) _____ in that behavior.

34. Minor point: An event can qualify as a reinforcer if it follows the end of the behavior or if it follows the start of the behavior. In other words, you should call an event that occurs at the same time as the behavior (and increases the rate of the behavior) a(n) _____.

9. An event that follows a behavior and increases the rate of the behavior is called a(n) _____. The procedure of delivering that event whenever a behavior occurs is called _____.

10. An example might tell you that Tom praised Ann every time she asked a question at the Greenpeace meeting. It might tell you that Ann's rate of questions increased. It might then ask what a single instance of Tom's praise is called. This is like asking what the event is called. You should answer that a single occurrence of Tom's praise following Ann's questioning is a(n) _____.

## 2. Events That Precede Behavior

44. Pre-test: Coach told Juan to be sure and stretch before basketball practice. Juan's rate of stretching increased. Coach used the procedure of _____.

42. Pre-test: Coach delivered music to Jane following her stretching during a warm-up period. Jane's rate of stretching increased. Coach's procedure is called _____.

35. Not all events are reinforcers. For now you may label an event that is not a reinforcer an unknown. Later I will teach you specific labels for many of these events. If an event follows a behavior and increases the rate of that behavior, you should call it a reinforcer. However, if it does not both follow and increase the behavior, then you should label it a(n) _____ (reinforcer, unknown).

19. Here is one way an event can be similar to a reinforcer but still not be a reinforcer. If an event <u>precedes</u> a behavior and increases the rate of the behavior, you should call it a(n) _____ (reinforcer, unknown).

83. You must distinguish closely related examples. First example: Suppose you smile every time that Tim looks at you. Suppose Tim looks at you more often. Because your smile follows his looking and his looking increases, you call your smile a(n) _____ (reinforcer, unknown).

63. Second example: Suppose you whisper "psst" and Tim looks at you. Suppose you whisper "psst" often so that the rate of Tim's looking at you increases. Because your "psst" <u>precedes</u> his looking, even though his looking increases you call your "psst" a(n) _____ (reinforcer, unknown).

## 3. Events That Don't Increase Behavior

55. Pre-test: Suppose Jan got new, clean clothes after she came to school but her attendance did not increase. Giving Jan new, clean clothes is an event called a(n) _____.

45. Pre-test: Dad gave Nixon a big hug every time he smiled. Nixon smiled more and more often. What behavioral procedure did Dad use? _____

43. Pre-test: Coach delivered music to Jane following her stretching during a warm-up period. Jane stretched about as much after Coach started giving her music. His procedure is called _____ _____.

82. You just learned that an event can increase the rate of a behavior and not be a reinforcer because it precedes the behavior rather than follows it. Here is the other way an event can be similar to a reinforcer but still not be a reinforcer. If an event follows a behavior and <u>doesn't increase</u> the rate of the behavior, is it a reinforcer? _____

7. Again, you must distinguish closely related examples. First example: You're a little kid who has never thrown horseshoes before. You throw for a while but can't quite get the hang of it. Then, you throw a "ringer," the best throw possible. Your rate of throwing goes up! The event "throwing a ringer" is called a(n) _____.

64. Second example: You're a different little kid. You've never thrown horseshoes before. You throw for a while but can't quite get the hang of it. Then, you throw a ringer, the best throw possible. Your rate of throwing doesn't change. The event "throwing a ringer" is called a(n) _____.

18. Here are a few practice examples. Suppose that Mom gave Tommy a bagel whenever he ate his spinach, but Tommy didn't eat his spinach any more often after that. Because the bagel did not increase the rate of eating spinach, call the event of giving the bagel a(n) _____ in this book.

70. Suppose that Mom told Tommy he had to eat his spinach from now on. Tommy might eat his spinach more often after that. Because Mom's demand did not follow Tommy's spinach eating, call the event "Mom told Tommy he had to eat his spinach" a(n) _____ (until a later chapter).

77. Tommy burped at the table, and Mom yelled at him, "That's disgusting!" Tommy burped more often as a result of Mom's reaction. Label the event of Mom's yell a(n) _____.

17. Every time that Tommy burped at the table, his mom calmly said, "Don't do that at the table young man!" Tommy burped no more often as a result of Mom's reaction. Label the event of Mom's calm comment as a(n) _____.

12. Be careful about this one. As they sat down to dinner, Mom said, "I know your stomach is upset. You can burp at the table tonight." Tommy burped at the table much more than usual that night. You should label the event of Mom's comment as a(n) _____.

26. If an unpleasant event follows a behavior and increases the probability of that behavior, then the event would be termed a(n) _____.

69. Suppose George makes a terrible face every time that Wendy serves steamed broccoli for dinner. If Wendy's rate of serving steamed broccoli increases, George's terrible face would be called a(n) _____.

68. Suppose George gives Wendy an extra dollar for fun money whenever she serves chicken for dinner. If Wendy's rate of serving chicken stays the same, the dollar would be called a(n) _____.

### 4. Desirable Events

53. Pre-test: Mrs. Jones made Willie stay after school any time he mouthed off in class. Willie mouthed off more often. By making Willie stay after school, Mrs. Jones used the procedure of _____.

51. Pre-test: Mary kissed Tom any time he bought her a gift. Mary used the procedure of _____.

54. Pre-test: Rich John paid Butch $100 whenever he read a book! Butch read about the same number of books. The event "paid $100" is called a(n) _____.

21. Here's a variation that many students have trouble with. Suppose that Tommy apologizes for one of his burps and his dad gives him $5. Many students seem to assume that money will always be a reinforcer for everyone. They forget to look to see if the money increases the rate of the behavior. Would you call the $5 a reinforcer if Tommy's rate of apologizing did not increase? _____ (yes, no)

33. Johnny's Dad gave him $5 for apologizing for a burp at the dinner table. Johnny's rate of apologizing increased after that. What is the $5 called? _____

78. Tommy's Dad gave him $5 for apologizing for a burp at the dinner table. Tommy's rate of apologizing didn't change after that. What is the $5 called? _____

62. Remember, no matter how desirable an event may seem to you, if it doesn't increase the rate of a behavior that it follows, it _____ (is, isn't) a reinforcer.

8. An event must have two elements to be a reinforcer. It must be timed so that it _____ (when) the behavior of interest. It must also cause that behavior to _____ in rate.

65. So remember, if an event has one, but not both, elements of a reinforcer, I will call it a(n) _____ in this book.

36. One last point on this issue. If an example tells you only that an event increases a behavior, you should call it a(n) _____ because you don't know if it followed the behavior.

79. We will assume in the examples given in this book that any event that follows the behavior and the behavior increases is actually a(n) _____, even without scientific proof.

### 5. Telling Someone What to Do

56. Pre-test: Suppose that Ben fails to make his bed and Mom tells him to make it from now on. Suppose that Ben's rate of making his bed increases. You should label "Mom's telling" as a(n) _____.

57. Pre-test: Suppose that Ben makes his bed and Dad gives him a driving lesson. Suppose that Ben's rate of making his bed increases. You should label "Dad's driving lesson" as a(n) _____.

22. I want to teach you about a special type of event that precedes behavior and increases their rate. The event "Bob tells Mary to take out the garbage" may increase the rate of Mary taking out the garbage. However, such an instruction will usually _____ (follow, precede) actually taking out the garbage.

14. Because the event "Bob tells Mary to take out the garbage" increases the rate of Mary taking out the garbage but does not follow it, you _____ (can, can't) call "Bob's telling" a reinforcer.

15. Because the event "Bob tells Mary to take out the garbage" increases the rate of Mary taking out the garbage but does not follow it, you would call "Bob's telling" a(n) _____.

80. When do you usually tell someone to do something? Do you tell them following their behavior of doing it, or do you tell them preceding their behavior of doing it? _____ (following, preceding)

13. Because instructions generally precede the behavior that they influence, they generally would be called a(n) _____ rather than a reinforcer.

1. "Instructions" refer to any talk that lets another person know you want them to do something. You might "tell" them, "ask" them, "remind" them, or "demand" of them. If Jim demands that Jack study and Jack studies, is the event "Jim demands" likely to be a reinforcer? _____

27. If Ann asks that Larry make his bed every day and he does, I want you to call this a(n) _____ until I teach you about instructions in a later chapter.

28. If Ann thanks Ben for cooking dinner and he cooks dinner more often, I want you to call Ann's thanks a(n) _____.

30. If Pablo reminds Eduardo to eat brown rice for lunch and he does, you would label Pablo's procedure as _____.

20. Here's a twist on what you just learned. Suppose an instruction follows an <u>incorrect</u> performance of a behavior. Suppose you observe an increase in the <u>correct</u> performance of the behavior. The instruction can't be a reinforcer for correct behavior because it did not follow the _____ (correct, incorrect) behavior.

67. Suppose at breakfast George asks Wendy to serve potatoes for dinner more often. If Wendy's rate of serving potatoes increases, George's request would be called a(n) _____.

### 6. Another Tactic

58. Pre-test: Tactic #1 in using the reinforcement strategy to solve human problems is

to increase desired behavior through
_____.

72. Tactic #1 in using the reinforcement strategy to solve human problems is to increase desired behavior through _____ _____.

### 7. Review

49. Pre-test: Ken told Wanda to work harder. She did. The event of Wanda working harder is called a(n) _____.

52. Pre-test: Mom started spanking Mary whenever she cried. Mary's crying increased. Mom used the procedure of _____.

50. Pre-test: Kevin expressed sympathy every time Rhonda complained about one of her friends. Rhonda's rate of complaining about her friends remained the same. What procedure did Kevin use when delivering sympathy? _____

60. Pre-test: The first tactic in the reinforcement strategy is to increase desirable behavior through _____.

46. Pre-test: Dr. Glover awarded points to Julie for creative responses. Her rate of creative responses increased. The points would be called a(n) _____; awarding the points to increase creativity would be called _____.

40. Pre-test: Any behavioral procedure that (1) is unsuccessful in changing behavior, or (2) for which a name and definition are untaught is called a(n) _____.

47. Pre-test: If an unpleasant event follows a behavior and increases the probability of that behavior, then the event would be termed a(n) _____.

61. Pre-test: You know only that an event increases a behavior. You should label it in this book as a(n) _____.

37. Pre-test: A reinforcer is any event timed to _____ a behavior and that _____ the probability of that behavior.

71. Tactic #1 in the reinforcement strategy enables you to increase the rate of desired behavior through _____.

6. After every statement that Rhonda made to Kevin about her problems, Kevin expressed sympathy. If Rhonda started telling Kevin more about her problems,

the procedure of delivering sympathy for her statements of problems would be called _____.

76. To be sure that an event is a reinforcer, you must observe to see if it actually results in a(n) _____ in behavior.

23. If an event follows a behavior and results in an increase in the behavior, that event is called a(n) _____.

5. A researcher must use either a(n) _____ _____ design or a(n) _____ _____ design to scientifically prove that an event is a reinforcer.

25. If an instruction follows an <u>incorrect</u> performance of a behavior and leads to an increase in the <u>correct</u> performance of the behavior, it would be called a(n) _____ _____. (Think carefully about this one.)

24. If an event occurs while someone is making a response, it is considered to be the same as an event following the response. Therefore, if the event also increases the probability of the behavior, we would call the event a(n) _____.

16. Dad gave Jeremy a dime whenever he spelled and defined a new word. Dad used the procedure of _____.

81. Whenever Maggy waved at him, Tom gave her one of those wonderful smiles. Maggy started waving at him more often. What is a single smile called? _____

32. If you deliver an event following a behavior and the rate of the behavior doesn't change, the book will always label the procedure as _____.

## Programmed Examples

### 1. Programmed Examples

16. Pre-test: Larry sometimes commented that he liked long hair. His friends always agreed with him, and they frequently discussed how stupid was the reaction of many older people to long hair. Larry's rate of commenting about long hair remained unchanged. What behavioral procedure did his friends' agreement exemplify? _____

18. Pre-test: Stuart spontaneously trimmed the front hedge around his home one day. His parents were delighted and took him out for a steak dinner to thank him

for his spontaneous helping around the house. His spontaneous helping increased. What behavioral procedure did his parents use? _____

15. Pre-test: Dollie was really turned off by Jim's table manners, so she asked him to request food rather than just grabbing it. To her surprise, Jim started asking her to pass food. Dollie's asking Jim to request food is an example of what behavioral procedure? _____

17. Pre-test: Professor Reynolds was dissatisfied with the rate of participation by his students in his discussion class, so he announced that he would award all students who presented good ideas during discussion with a bonus point toward their grade, and they would know they got it because he would write it in his book as soon as it happened. Professor Reynolds was disheartened to discover that none of his students participated more often as a result of his new rule. What procedure did he use? _____

4. Carla sometimes smiled at men whom she passed on campus. One day she smiled at a guy who then came right up and asked her for a date. Carla now smiles at many of the guys whom she passes on campus and frequently gets asked out for interesting dates. Check for both elements of reinforcement. First, when Carla smiled, getting a date _____ (followed, preceded). Second, after she started getting dates, the rate at which Carla smiled _____ (decreased, increased, steadied). In this example, "getting a date" is an event that follows smiling and that increases the rate of smiling. Therefore, "getting a date" is a(n) _____.

1. Alma liked Grant a lot. However, he rarely did favors for her like opening doors or helping her put her coat on. So she started saying "thank you" immediately after a favor. After a month, Alma found that Grant still rarely did favors for her. Check for two elements. First, when Grant did a favor, Alma's thanks _____ (followed, preceded). Second, his rate of doing favors _____ (decreased, increased, steadied). Because the "thank you" followed the behavior but did not

increase the rate of doing favors, it should be labeled a(n) _____.

9. Joe's TV set went on the blink during the NFL playoffs, so he tapped it with the palm of his hand. Immediately, the picture cleared up. Now, whenever the picture goes bad, he taps the set. Check for two elements. First, when Joe tapped, picture clearing _____ (followed, preceded). Second, Joe's rate of tapping the set _____. Therefore, the event of the picture clearing up is an example of a(n) _____.

19. Sam was a fourth grader who liked to wander around town after school. His mother worried about him, especially after he described what the underside of a train looked like. She therefore told him to come straight home from school. Sam started coming home earlier after his mother told him to. Check for both elements. First, Mom told Sam to come straight home following not coming home. Therefore, Mom's telling Sam to come straight home didn't follow coming home. When Sam started coming straight home, Mom's telling _____ (followed, preceded)! Second, the rate of Sam's coming right home after school _____ after his mother told him to. You should label Mom's telling as a(n) _____. You could also have guessed that this cannot be an example of a reinforcer because of the rule "An instruction _____ (can, can't) be a reinforcer."

6. Dave was a slob; he would rip off his clothes at night and just throw them down. Shawn, his roommate, didn't like living with the resulting mess, so she asked Dave to please hang up his stuff. No result. She then started looking carefully for any time that Dave did hang up even one article of clothing. When he did so, she gave him a special hand-printed ticket that read: "This ticket good for one special gift of your choosing." Dave started picking up all his clothes! Check for both elements. First, when Dave picked up, Shawn's ticket giving was timed to _____. Second, the rate of Dave's picking up _____. Therefore, you would call the event of giving a ticket a(n) _____.

20. Verna decided that her child Tom interrupted her too often. She tried to punish

him every time he interrupted by giving him a good spanking. She was disappointed, however, because Tom seemed to interrupt much more often than before. She concluded that punishment just doesn't work with some children. Check both elements. First, when Tom interrupted, Verna's spanking was timed to _____ it. Second, Tom's interrupting _____ in rate. Therefore, the spanking is an unpleasant event that a behavior analyst would label a(n) _____.

7. Elvis used to be a safe and sane driver. One day he was in a hurry to get to a movie that supposedly had a torrid opening love scene, so he drove fast. He noticed that as soon as he increased his speed, his girlfriend appeared frightened and leaned on him much more than usual. Elvis frequently drove fast after that. Check both elements. First, in this example, Elvis's girlfriend leaned on him while he was still speeding. You could say that her leaning followed the beginning of his speeding. Thus, the moment that Elvis started to speed, his girlfriend's leaning was timed to _____. Second, the rate of Elvis's speeding _____. Therefore, you should label the event "leaning on" in relation to Elvis's speeding a(n) _____.

2. As usual, Francie didn't do her homework Thursday night. The teacher firmly told Francie to start doing her homework. From then on, Francie did her homework all the time. Be sure to check for both elements of reinforcement. First, did the teacher's demand follow doing the homework? Second, did Francie's rate of homework increase? Therefore, the event "teacher demanded" is called a(n) _____.

13. Marty was in second grade. One day during spelling he laid his head on the desk. The teacher asked him what was the matter, and he said, "Teacher, I have a terrible head hurt." The teacher, a kind woman, soothed him by saying, "That's too bad, Marty. Why don't you just lay your head down until it feels better?" It was noted that Marty frequently complained about headaches after that, even though he had never had any in the previous year. Marty's schoolwork became much poorer. First, did the teacher's permission to rest follow Marty's complaint of a headache?

Second, did Marty's rate of complaining about headaches increase? Therefore, the teacher's permission to rest is an event called a(n) _____. The procedure of giving permission following a complaint is called _____.

12. Linda didn't talk with her roommate Priscilla very often. However, whenever Priscilla complained about how badly life was going for her, Linda would reassure her that everything would be okay. After several months, Priscilla was talking about how awful life was even more often than before. Check: Does the reassurance follow the complaining? Does the complaining increase? Therefore, Linda's procedure of reassuring complaints would be an example of _____. The event "reassurance" is an example of _____.

14. May came home from school on Monday and told her parents that she had finally beaten up the little boy who had been tormenting her every day. On Friday, May's father took her out for ice cream and told her it was a special treat for beating up the awful little boy. May now beats up the little boy more often. What is the ice cream an example of? _____

3. Bill almost never welcomed Jane home when she finished her late evening class. So Jane decided on a new approach. When Bill did welcome her, she kissed him. Naturally, Bill's rate increased. What behavioral procedure did Jane use? _____

8. Gail felt that her 6-year-old son Jimmy did not hug her often enough. She started giving him a special treat every time that he spontaneously hugged her. She found that Jimmy gradually hugged her more often. Gail used what behavioral procedure? _____

11. Leslie had long regretted being so remote from her parents. She had tried talking with them about it to no avail. So she decided that she would give them a really nice compliment any time they shared something intimate with her. Their rate slowly increased. One of Leslie's compliments would be an example of a(n) _____.

5. Carla sometimes went to the club for a little dancing. The trouble was she was a

super dancer and was bored dancing with most of the guys who usually hung out there. One day Steve asked her to dance, and she found out that he was also a super dancer. She started dancing a lot more after Steve started asking her. One dance with Steve is a(n) _____.

10. John complained of problems every once in a while. One day his friend had a long talk with him. After that, John complained more often of his problems and thus had more talks with his friend. His friend inadvertently used what procedure to increase John's rate of complaining? _____

# Extinction of Everyday Behaviors

## Reading Section

In the last lesson, you learned about reinforcement. It is a procedure that <u>increases</u> the rate of a behavior. In this lesson, you will learn about extinction. It is a procedure that <u>decreases</u> the rate of a behavior.

You can use extinction to help solve human problems. It is very useful because it is a gentle way to decrease the rate of a behavior. You will see that you do not need to hurt, coerce, or punish people to help them reduce their unpleasant or harmful behaviors. With extinction, you simply stop delivery of the reinforcers that were maintaining that behavior. Tactic #2 in using the reinforcement strategy for solving human problems is to decrease undesired behavior through <u>extinction</u>.

1. Tactic #2 in using the reinforcement strategy for solving human problems is to decrease undesired behavior through _____.

## Definition of Extinction

**Extinction** is the procedure in which an event that follows a behavior is <u>stopped</u> and the rate of the behavior <u>decreases</u>. You should call a procedure *extinction* only if it has both of these elements. Behavior analysts call the act of using extinction <u>extinguishing</u> the behavior.

2. Extinction is the procedure in which an event that follows a behavior is _____ and the rate of the behavior _____.

The definition of extinction requires that the event being stopped is a reinforcer. Why this connection between reinforcement and extinction? If the event is a reinforcer, then its delivery must have increased the rate of the behavior. Therefore, stopping its delivery must decrease the rate of the behavior. Here is another connection. Remember that using a reversal design is the best way to find out if an event is a reinforcer. You find the rate of the behavior during baseline. Baseline is when the event does not follow the behavior. You observe the rate again during treatment. The event now follows the behavior. Finally, you observe the rate during reversal. That is when you stop delivery of the event. Therefore, we call that an <u>extinction condition</u>. Note that extinction and reinforcement include each other in their definition.

Two elements must be present for a procedure to be labeled extinction. First, the delivery of a reinforcer must be <u>stopped</u>. Second, you must observe a <u>decrease</u> in the behavior. For example, suppose that Mom accidentally reinforces Tommy's burping by yelling, "That's disgusting!" Tommy starts burping often during meals. Mom might realize her mistake and stop the reinforcer. Tommy's rate of burping might then decrease. In this case, Mom would stop the reinforcer and the behavior would decrease. Since both elements are present, we would label this extinction. We would say that Mom extinguished Tommy's burping.

If only one element is present, then you should not label the procedure as extinction. For example, suppose Mom told Tommy before he sat down for his next meal that he mustn't burp at the table any more. Tommy might stop burping at the table. However, Mom's instruction cannot be a reinforcer. Therefore, in this case, the behavior decreased but Mom did not stop the reinforcer. Since only one element of reinforcement was present, we would not label this extinction. I will follow the convention of calling such a procedure an unknown.

Of course, either element might be missing. For example, suppose Mom stopped yelling, "That's disgusting!" whenever Tommy burped at the table. Tommy might not stop burping at the table. In this case, Mom stopped a reinforcer but the behavior did not decrease. Since only one element was present, we would not label this extinction. You should also label this procedure as an unknown.

Before you label any procedure as extinction, be sure that both elements required in the definition are present. An event following the behavior must be stopped. The behavior must decrease. If either element is missing, do not label the procedure as extinction. Label it as unknown.

## Uses for Extinction

In the prior lesson, I described some cases in which people often reinforce very undesirable behaviors. Extinction gives us a gentle but effective method for dealing with undesirable behavior. For example, most of us assume that children with retardation who hit themselves are crazy or stupid. But Lovaas and Simmons (1969) guessed that this behavior was a method to get attention from the children's attendants. To check this guess, they picked the most active self-hitting children from among several thousand in local hospitals.

John was an 8-year-old with an IQ of 24. John struck his forehead with his fists and knuckles, giving himself bruises and contusions. Whenever John struck himself, the hospital attendants put him in restraints. They did this to keep him from hurting himself. However, notice that they had to give him lots of attention to get him into the restraints. To test whether this attention reinforced John's behavior of hitting himself, the researchers took the restraints off John and did not put

them on again. By abandoning the restraints, the researchers stopped giving John the attention involved in putting them on. At first, their approach seemed to fail. John struck himself at the rate of once every two seconds for a total of more than 2,500 times during the first 1.5 hours. Over the next 10 days, John struck himself almost 9,000 times. However, during this time, his rate gradually decreased and finally dropped to zero. By the end of 10 days, they could permit John to sit in the room without the restraints. John was a bit more normal and certainly a lot freer.

This case exemplifies extinction. The researchers stopped the delivery of a reinforcer—attention—for hitting. They saw a decrease in the rate of hitting. The example contains both elements of extinction.

This case also illustrates another aspect of extinction called the extinction burst. An *extinction burst* is a temporary increase in responding as soon as extinction begins (see, e.g., Thackeray & Richdale, 2002). John illustrated this increase when he initially hit himself once every two seconds at the beginning of extinction! It is almost as if he couldn't believe that no one would pay attention when he was hitting himself. The occurrence of an extinction burst may discourage people who try to use extinction. If this ever happens to you, the solution is simply to persist until the person finishes with their extinction burst.

An extinction burst is a temporary increase in responding as soon as extinction begins.

Another researcher used a very clever way to decrease self-injury (Luiselli, 1991). She put mittens on the patient's hands so that their blows would not cause injury. This gradually reduced hitting. If feeling the injury (or the attention that it produced) was the reinforcer, then the mittens eliminated the injury and any attention it might have produced. Researchers used a similar procedure to extinguish a child's repetitive hair twirling (Deaver, Miltenberger, & Stricker, 2001), a response that often led to hair pulling and scalp injury.

Behavior analysts rarely use extinction of self-injurious behavior (SIB) by itself. People can seriously hurt themselves during an

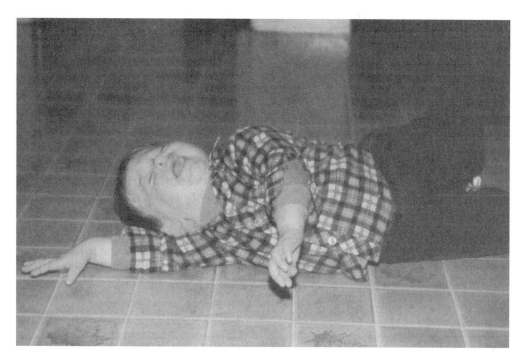

***Figure 9-1.*** Many small children throw temper tantrums. This behavior is often reinforced by busy parents who pay attention only when their child throws a tantrum. Tantrums can often be extinguished by teaching parents to stop giving attention to their child when it emits this behavior. (In later lessons you will learn procedures that produce even greater benefits for the children.) (Source: Myrleen Ferguson/PhotoEdit)

extinction burst before they stop. Therefore, behavior analysts often use punishment initially. That way, they can reduce SIB quickly before it causes much injury (e.g., Linscheid, Iwata, Ricketts, Williams, & Griffin, 1990). They often combine punishment with extinction (e.g., Lerman, Kelley, Vorndran, & Van Camp, 2003). Behavioral methods are the only effective way to reduce SIB (see Yang, 2003). There is little scientific evidence that either medical or psychodynamic methods can reduce SIB (Favell et al., 1982).

Williams (1959) described an example of extinction with a normal 2-year-old child living with its parents. The parents reinforced the child's behavior by comforting him anytime he cried after being put to bed. As a result, the child cried and raged whenever his parents put him to bed. He typically took several hours to go to sleep. Williams advised the parents to put the child to bed and then firmly ignore the crying. Figure 9-2 graphs the resulting crying. On the first day, the child cried for a total of 45 minutes before quitting and going to sleep.

This is typical of an extinction burst. It might have discouraged the parents had the researchers not warned them to expect it. The second day the child did not cry at all. On successive days the child cried only a few minutes, finally stopping on the seventh day. An unexpected reversal (not shown on the graph) occurred when the child's aunt took care of him one night. His aunt comforted him when he cried. The next night the parents ignored the child's crying, which again showed an extinction burst. His crying lasted for almost an hour. The crying rapidly decreased and stopped in the following days.

Williams's (1959) use of ignoring is a clear case of extinction. The parents stopped their comforting, which had reinforced crying. The crying decreased. Other similar studies with crying at night also report success (e.g., France & Hudson, 1990; Seymour, Bayfield, Brock, & During, 1983). Several studies have used graduated extinction (Durand & Mindell, 1990; Lawton, France, & Blampied, 1991). The parents wait longer

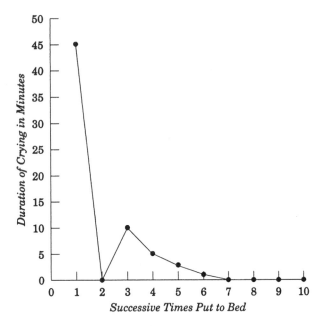

**Figure 9-2.** Number of minutes a chronic crier cried after being put to bed and ignored on 10 successive nights. The parent previously comforted the child if he cried. (Adapted from "The Elimination of Tantrum Behavior by Extinction Procedure," by C. D. Williams, *Journal of Abnormal and Social Psychology*, 1959, 59, 269. Copyright 1959 by the American Psychological Association. Reprinted by permission.)

---

### Outpsyching Crazy Drivers

We hear many stories about crazy drivers these days. You try to pass them, they speed up, you speed up more, they take out a gun and shoot you! We all have encountered crazy drivers. Maybe the most common kind is tailgaters. A car comes up behind you, can't pass, and stays dangerously close. Why do drivers do that? What is the reinforcer? Such drivers may be reinforced by your own behavior, which indicates that they are influencing you. The National Safety Council suggests two ways you may be doing that. You may be responding by slowing down or by making eye contact (in the rearview mirror). What's the best defense if you can't let them pass? Stop delivering eye contact, and stop slowing down. (Based on Rodgers, 1993.)

3. If their tailgating decreases, then behavior analysts would call your procedure _____ (extinction, reinforcement, unknown).

---

and longer before attending to crying. The crying gradually stops. The only alternative to behavioral management of crying is drugs (France & Hudson, 1990). Drugs are not an acceptable alternative to most parents.

I noted in the prior lesson that public school teachers pay far more attention to undesirable than to desirable behaviors. The widespread disruptive behavior in schools may result from this pattern of teacher attention. Researchers studied a child who had frequent tantrums lasting 5 minutes apiece (Allen, Turner & Everett, 1970). They guessed that the teacher unwittingly reinforced the tantrums with attention. They convinced her to start ignoring them. From that point only two more tantrums occurred. The first one showed a typical extinction burst lasting over 25 minutes! Many classroom studies have shown similar results. When teachers stop attending to undesirable behaviors, those behaviors decrease sharply (e.g., Moore, Mueller, Dubard, Roberts, & Sterling-Turner, 2002).

Researchers have used extinction to help reduce adults' fear of social situations (Turner, Beidel, Long, & Greenhouse, 1992). They found that pulse rate and subjective fear decreased as a result.

Most of us could react more constructively to disruptive behavior in many everyday situations. For example, we may laugh when one member of our group rudely interrupts another member. Ignoring that rudeness would likely reduce it. This would be a sound use of extinction in everyday situations. The box on Outpsyching Crazy Drivers gives a more serious use of extinction.

## Misuses of Extinction

People can use extinction, like reinforcement, incorrectly. Parents may ignore a child's desirable behavior because they are "too busy." By doing so they may decrease the probability of that behavior. Many of us have a fit of shyness and act embarrassed at compliments. By doing so, we will decrease the rate at which we get compliments. Parents may not take time to talk with their teenage child. By doing so, they may create a "communication problem" in later years. They may have extinguished conversational behavior with that child.

Similar problems may arise in the business world as well. Employers may not praise good work behavior of their employees. They may feel that they should not have to "baby" the worker. The worker "should want to do a good job." Perhaps that is true, but they may be extinguishing good work behavior anyway. You might guess that the worker's pay reinforces the behavior, but pay usually only reinforces showing up. You don't get more pay for doing a good job. Praise from the employer is the major reinforcer for good work!

Similar problems may arise even in government. A government's employees and politicians may ignore the legitimate complaints of its citizens. By doing so, they may extinguish communication. They may later face open rebellion and an inability to communicate with those same citizens.

Extinction, then, is a powerful tool with which to change behavior. Like reinforcement, people can use it wisely or unwisely.

# Summary

Tactic #2 in using the reinforcement strategy for solving human problems is to decrease undesirable behavior through extinction. Extinction can modify behavior. If a response no longer produces reinforcement, the person will probably stop emitting it. Behavior analysts use extinction to eliminate undesirable behavior. Everyone can use extinction to change behavior. We often do so without even being aware of what we are doing. Often the result is desirable and helpful. However, extinction can be used incorrectly. We can end up extinguishing valuable behavior from other people. This can sometimes have tragic results. You can be sure you do not produce such results by learning about extinction. If you are aware when you are using extinction, you may avoid eliminating desirable behavior from others.

# Behavior Analysis Examples

## *Helping the Elderly Communicate*

Elderly people often communicate negative messages to their loved ones. They may make bizarre statements and angry accusations. We often explain this behavior as the inevitable result of growing old. Mr. Ford, a 63-year-old man who had a stroke, spent several hours a day making wild accusations at his wife. He accused her of hiding men, staying out all night, and being a whore. Researchers found that Mrs. Ford discussed or denied the accusations 95% of the time and ignored them only 5% of the time. As a result, Mr. Ford spent over an hour a day making accusations. The researchers then taught her to ignore this behavior. She discussed or denied 14% of the time and ignored 82% of the time. This changed Mr. Ford's talk until he spent almost no time making accusations. A reversal to baseline resulted in increased accusations. (Based on Green, Linsk, & Pinkston, 1986.)

4. Mrs. Ford stopped the delivery of a reinforcer when she stopped arguing. Mr. Ford's rate of making accusations decreased. Therefore, behavior analysts would call her procedure _____ (extinction, reinforcement, unknown.)

## *Aggression in Young Children*

Pinkston, Reese, LeBlanc, and Baer (1973) studied Cain, a 3½-year-old child of well-educated parents. Cain was bright and often had long discussions with the teachers in his preschool. However, playing with other children was a disaster. The researchers noticed that he often stood on the edge of the play area with his fists clenched. After a few minutes, he attacked other children without reason. He bit, scratched, struck, and yelled "I hate you" at any teacher who tried to stop him.

The researchers defined aggression so that it included both physical and verbal aggression. Physical aggression was any negative behavior directed toward peers. It could also be directed at materials the peers used. They gave specific definitions for eight categories of physical aggression. These included choking, head pushing, biting, pinching, pushing, poking, hitting,

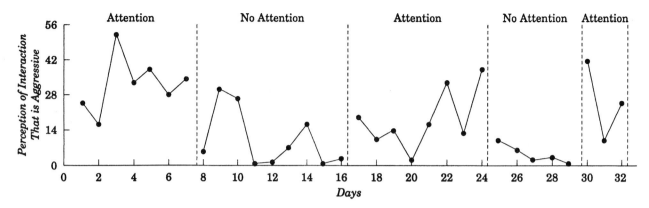

**Figure 9-3.** The effects of attention and elimination of attention on the percentage of aggressive behavior of Cain. (Adapted from "Independent Control of a Preschool Child's Aggression and Peer Interaction by Contingent Teacher Attention," by E. M. Pinkston, N. M. Reese, J. M. LeBlanc, and D. M. Baer, *Journal of Applied Behavior Analysis*, 1973, 6, 115–124. Copyright 1973 by the Society for the Experimental Analysis of Behavior, Inc. Used by permission.)

and kicking. They also defined verbal aggression, which included threatening or ordering someone to stop an activity, and making negative judgments about persons, their relatives, or their property. The researchers made observations during consecutive 10-second intervals. They found that reliability was 92%.

Figure 9-3 shows the results of this experiment. During baseline teachers tried to stop aggression. Aggression averaged almost 30% of all interactions with other children during that time, indicating that attending to aggression by trying to stop it was reinforcing. During treatment, the teachers used extinction by ignoring all aggression. Aggression decreased to an average of only 6% of all interactions. During reversal, teachers again tried to stop aggression. The rate of aggression once again rose. During the last three days, it averaged about 30% again. Subsequent withdrawal of attention and reinstatement of it produced similar results. In a long period of observation not shown on this figure, the teachers continued to ignore aggressive acts. Aggression remained between 0% and 5% for 30 days.

5. The Pinkston study shows that the teachers eliminated Cain's aggressive behaviors by ignoring them. Therefore, the teachers were using the behavioral procedure of _____ .

## Notes

### Note #1

You will find examples where someone ignores another person's complaining behavior. Don't conclude that behavior analysts solve problems by ignoring them. They use extinction only when the complaining behavior *is* the problem—that is, when it is not justified. I noted in Lesson 8 that behavior analysts often listen to clients talk as part of the treatment. This lesson should lead you to be careful about this practice. Extinguishing a client's talk is sometimes necessary.

6. Behavior analysts ignore a person's complaints only when the complaining behavior _____ (is, isn't) the problem.

### Note #2

A person's history of reinforcement for a behavior may be that they never got any. That is, their history is extinction. A person's parents may never have reinforced them for complaining. They are less likely to be chronic complainers than someone with a history of receiving reinforcers for complaining.

7. If in the past a person's parents never reinforced them for complaining, then we say that their history of reinforcement for complaining is _____ .

## Helpful Hints

You might confuse two types of situations in which the rate of a response decreases with extinction.

### Helpful Hint #1

Someone may stop giving an instruction to perform a behavior. The rate of the behavior may decrease. This would not be an example of extinction. The reason is that instructions do not usually act as reinforcers. Therefore, the delivery of a reinforcer is not being stopped. Just remember: <u>stopping an instruction cannot be extinction</u>. You should label the stopping of instructions as unknown.

8. If an instruction to perform a behavior is stopped and the rate of the behavior decreases, this illustrates what procedure?

   _____

To *stop giving instructions* refers to more than to stop explaining how to do something. To stop giving instructions to a person can also mean to stop instructing that person to do something. Therefore, you might stop "telling" or "asking" or "reminding" or "requesting" that the person do something. However, even if the behavior to which you are referring decreases, you are not stopping a reinforcer. You are stopping a request. This sort of example is tricky. Many students notice the stopping of a behavior and jump to the conclusion that you are stopping a reinforcer. They incorrectly label the procedure extinction. Be on the lookout for this kind of example, and be sure to label the procedure as unknown.

9. If someone stops "instructing," "telling," "asking," or even "reminding" another person to do something and their rate of doing it decreases, you should label their procedure as _____.

### Helpful Hint #2

Someone may tell another person to stop performing a behavior. Or they may threaten to stop some event if the other person does not stop the behavior. In neither situation does the person actually stop an event that had been following the behavior. Therefore, these are not examples of extinction. You should label these situations as unknown.

10. If a threat is made that an event will be stopped if a behavior is not decreased, and the behavior decreases, using the threat is an example of what procedure?

    _____

### Helpful Hint #3

I will give you many examples in which a reinforcer is stopped but the rate of the behavior does not change. I might not explicitly say it doesn't change. I might say that you stopped praising Martha for eating a good diet but that she kept eating a good diet. Look very carefully to see whether the rate of the behavior actually changes in examples where a reinforcer is stopped. If it does not, then you should label the procedure as unknown.

11. Suppose that you stop praising someone for eating a good diet and they keep on eating a good diet. What behavioral procedure is this an example of? _____

### Helpful Hint #4

Remember, call the act of applying extinction to a behavior extinguishing the behavior.

12. The act of applying extinction to a behavior is called _____ the behavior.

## Additional Readings

Ayllon, T., & Michael, J. (1959). The psychiatric nurse as a behavioral engineer. *Journal of the Experimental Analysis of Behavior, 2,* 323–334. This article consists of a series of case studies. They show how behavioral principles can improve the behavior of mental patients. One case involves Lucille, a person with retardation. Lucille continually entered the nurses' office and disrupted their work. The nurses had in the past usually taken her by the hand led her out of the office. This reaction seemed only to increase the rate of office entering. When the nurses totally ignored Lucille's visits, she stopped entering their office.

Wolf, M. M., Birnbrauer, J., Lawler, J., & Williams, T. (1970). The operant extinction, reinstatement, and re-extinction of vomiting behavior in a retarded child. In R. Ulrich, T. Stachnik, & J. Mabry (Eds.), *Control of human behavior* (Vol. 2). Glenview, IL: Scott, Foresman. This article shows how you can use extinction to eliminate severe behavior problems in children with retardation. A girl with retardation vomited most days when she was in a class, and when she did so, the teacher immediately sent her to her residence. The teacher then began to keep the child in in class regardless of her vomiting behavior. Not giving the child attention and not allowing her to get out of class eliminated the vomiting behavior. This case shows again how easy it is to reinforce disruptive behaviors accidentally.

## Programmed Reading

This section includes the following modules: (1) Reducing the Rate of Behavior, (2) Telling the Difference, (3) What Happens Right after Starting Extinction, (4) Another Tactic, and (5) Review.

### 1. Reducing the Rate of Behavior

35. Pre-test: Extinction is defined as the procedure in which an event that followed a behavior is _____ and the rate of the behavior _____.

45. Pre-test: The act of applying extinction to a behavior is called _____ the behavior.

47. Pre-test: The procedure of stopping a reinforcer for a behavior and seeing the behavior decrease is called _____.

67. You learned in the last lesson that <u>reinforcement</u> is a procedure that _____ the rate of a behavior. You learned in this lesson that a procedure that decreases the rate of a behavior is _____.

12. Extinction is defined as (a) stopping the delivery of a reinforcer that has followed a behavior in the past and (b) causing a(n) _____ in the rate of that behavior.

13. Extinction is defined as (a) the delivery of an event that has followed a behavior is _____ (started, stopped) and (b) the rate of that behavior decreases.

14. Extinction is defined as (a) the delivery of an event that has followed a behavior is _____ (started, stopped) and (b) the rate of that behavior _____ _____.

1. <u>Extinguishing</u> a behavior is the term used when what procedure is applied to the behavior? _____

54. Students often misspell *extinguishing*, so I want you simply to copy the word to see how it is spelled: _____.

62. The act of applying extinction to a behavior is called _____ the behavior.

15. Extinction is defined as <u>stopping</u> the delivery of a certain kind of event. The certain kind of event follows a behavior and increases the rate of that behavior. The label for the event that is stopped is _____.

66. When Deb stopped laughing at Bob's rudeness and it decreased, we say that Deb was _____ his rude behavior.

24. Mom grabbed Don whenever he hit Bev. Don's rate of hitting increased. What procedure did Mom use to increase Don's hitting? _____

10. Deb used to laugh at Bob's rudeness. She has stopped laughing, and his rudeness has decreased. Deb used the procedure of _____ to reduce rudeness.

68. You might use a reversal design to prove that an event is a reinforcer. You would initially observe the rate of the behavior during a baseline in which the event did not follow the behavior. Then, you would observe the rate during a treatment condition in which the event did follow the behavior. Finally, you would observe the rate during a reversal condition. During the reversal condition, you would <u>stop</u> delivery of the event. If you observed that the rate of the behavior <u>decreased</u>, you would label the reversal condition as the procedure of _____ (extinction, reinforcement).

### 2. Telling the Difference

38. Pre-test: Maria stopped telling Jimmy to bring out the garbage after dinner. Jimmy's rate of bringing out the garbage decreased. Maria used the procedure of _____.

39. Pre-test: Maria stopped praising Jimmy for bringing out the garbage after dinner. Jimmy continued to bring out the garbage. Maria used the procedure of _____ _____.

40. Pre-test: Maria stopped praising Anthony for making his bed. Anthony did not make his bed as often after that. Maria used the procedure of _____.

11. Extinction can easily be confused with similar procedures. If you stop an instruction to perform a behavior (rather than stopping a reinforcer) and the rate of the behavior decreases, your procedure would be similar to extinction. Both cause a decrease in behavior. But you did not stop a reinforcer. Therefore, stopping an instruction _____ (would, wouldn't) be an example of extinction.

7. As with reinforcement, you can label a procedure similar to extinction but missing one of its elements as unknown. If you stop telling another person to do something and their rate of doing it decreases, you should label the procedure as _____.

19. If you make a threat to stop a reinforcer if a behavior is not decreased and the behavior decreases, this is similar to extinction. Both decrease behavior. But you are not stopping the reinforcer, only threatening to do so. Therefore, this _____ (would, wouldn't) be an example of extinction.

58. Suppose that you threaten to stop giving Penny dessert if she doesn't stop drinking colas and she stops. What behavioral procedure is this an example of? _____

16. Finally, you might stop giving someone a reinforcer for performing a behavior and their rate might not change. This is similar to extinction in that it stops a reinforcer. However, the rate doesn't change. Therefore, this _____ (is, isn't) an example of extinction.

56. Suppose that Kim stops giving Johan, her spouse, a kiss after he does a favor and his rate of doing favors stays the same. What behavioral procedure is Kim using? _____

30. One final unknown. Suppose you know only that someone stopped a reinforcer but you don't know if the behavior decreased. You can't be sure that the behavior decreased, so you _____ (can, can't) label this situation as extinction.

8. Barbara stopped apologizing to Billy when he complained about her playing with Marty. Barbara used the procedure called _____.

69. You should apply the term *extinction* only when two elements are present. First, you must _____ delivery of a reinforcer. Second, you must observe a(n) _____ in the rate of the behavior.

22. Mom accidentally reinforces Tommy's burping by yelling, "That's disgusting!" She might realize her mistake and stop the reinforcer. Tommy's rate of burping might then decrease. In this case, Mom would have stopped the reinforcer and would have seen the behavior decrease. If so, since both elements are present, you would label her procedure as _____.

28. Mom told Tommy before he sat down for his next meal that he mustn't burp at the table any more. Tommy stopped burping at the table. Because the behavior decreased but Mom did not stop a reinforcer, you would label this procedure as _____.

27. Mom stopped yelling, "That's disgusting!" whenever Tommy burped at the table. Tommy did not stop burping at the table. Because Mom stopped a reinforcer but the behavior did not decrease, you should label this situation as a(n) _____.

9. Before you label any situation as extinction, be sure that both elements required in the definition are present. The reinforcer must be _____. The behavior must _____.

55. Suppose Percy stopped crying when Butch hit him. If Butch liked to see Percy cry, Percy used the procedure of _____ _____ to decrease Butch hitting him.

57. Suppose that Mrs. Jones had told Mr. Jones that she was no longer going to discuss his accusations. Suppose his rate of accusations decreased to almost none. This would be an example of _____.

18. If Mrs. Jones no longer discussed her husband's accusations with him and if Mr. Jones accusations dropped to almost none, Mrs. Jones is using the procedure called _____.

### 3. What Happens Right after Starting Extinction

41. Pre-test: Peggy used to give in to Petey's demands for a snack just before dinner. Today she did not give in. Petey's rate of demands increased sharply from yesterday. This increase is called a(n) _____ _____.

32. Pre-test: A temporary <u>increase</u> in responding as soon as extinction begins is called a(n) _____.

34. Pre-test: An extinction burst is a temporary _____ in responding as soon as extinction begins.

31. One of the unexpected effects of extinction is that the person often increases rather than decreases their responding for a short time. This effect is called an extinction burst. An extinction burst is a temporary _____ (decrease, increase) in responding as soon as extinction begins.

2. A temporary <u>increase</u> in responding as soon as extinction begins is called a(n) _____ burst.

3. A temporary <u>increase</u> in responding as soon as extinction begins is called a(n) _____.

21. John was a severely self-destructive child who hit himself over 2,500 times in the first hour and a half of extinction. Behavior analysts call this temporary increase a(n) _____ burst.

29. No one attended to John's self-destructive acts. He completely stopped hitting himself within 10 days. Removal of attention is an example of what behavioral procedure: _____.

6. Ann never decreased her rate of self-hitting when she stopped getting delivery of attention. You should then label the procedure of stopping attention as _____.

23. Mom comforted Juanita anytime that she cried after being put to bed. By doing so, Mom inadvertently increased crying by using the procedure of _____.

25. Mom stopped comforting Juanita when she cried. Juanita cried more than ever the first night, but her crying decreased in following nights. The extra crying the first night is called a(n) _____.

26. Mom stopped comforting Juanita when she cried. The rate of crying decreased. Mom used what procedure to decrease crying? _____

17. If Mom had stopped comforting Juanita but her crying had not decreased, you would say Mom used what procedure? _____

53. Researchers often find that right after teachers stop paying attention to undesirable behaviors, the rate of those behaviors _____ sharply.

20. Jane, a preschool teacher, stopped grabbing Don when he hit Bev. If the rate of Don's hitting stayed about the same, Jane was using the procedure of _____ _____.

### 4. Another Tactic

48. Pre-test: The second tactic in using the reinforcement strategy for solving human problems is to decrease undesired behavior through _____.

61. Tactic #2 in using the reinforcement strategy for solving human problems is to decrease undesired behavior through _____ (reinforcement, extinction).

### 5. Review

46. Pre-test: The act of applying extinction to a behavior is called _____ the behavior.

42. Pre-test: Suppose that you stop telling your roommates to clean the room and they stop. This would be an example of what behavioral procedure? _____

36. Pre-test: Extinction is the procedure in which an event that has followed a behavior in the past is _____ and the rate of the behavior _____.

33. Pre-test: A temporary increase in responding as soon as extinction begins is called a(n) _____.

49. Pre-test: When a preschool teacher stopped paying attention to Cain's aggressive behavior and the behavior decreased, what behavioral procedure did the teacher use? _____

44. Pre-test: Tactic #2 in using the reinforcement strategy for solving human problems is to decrease undesired behavior through _____.

50. Pre-test: You give John a bonus of $100 each time he sells a sports car. John sells just as many sports cars now as before you started giving him the bonus. By giving John the bonus of $100, you are using the behavioral procedure of _____ _____.

37. Pre-test: If you ignore Sara's behavior of interrupting others and her interruptions continue, this would illustrate what behavioral procedure? _____

43. Pre-test: Suppose you tell people to perform a certain behavior and they do it. Suppose you stop telling them to do it and they stop. You decreased their behavior with the procedure of _____.

65. When complaining behavior is ignored but the behavior does not decrease, what behavioral procedure is being used? _____

59. Tactic #1 in using the reinforcement strategy for solving human problems is to increase the desired behavior through reinforcement. Tactic #2 is to decrease undesired behavior through _____ _____.

63. The definition of extinction is "an event that followed a behavior is _____, which produces a(n) _____ in the rate of that behavior."

4. A temporary increase in responding as soon as extinction begins is called a(n) _____.

51. Preschool teachers stopped paying attention to Cain's aggressive behavior, resulting in a decrease of that behavior. Their procedure is an example of _____.

70. You tell Fred to stop scowling. If he stops scowling, you would be using what procedure? _____

52. Remember, if you use a procedure to increase someone's behavior and it does not increase, the book will always label the procedure as _____. Likewise, if you use a procedure to decrease someone's behavior and it does not decrease, the book will always label the procedure as _____.

60. Tactic #1 in using the reinforcement strategy for solving human problems is to increase the desired behavior through _____. Tactic #2 is to decrease the undesired behavior through _____ _____.

64. The procedure of stopping a reinforcer for a behavior and seeing the behavior decrease is called _____.

5. An extinction burst is a temporary _____ in responding as soon as extinction begins.

## Programmed Examples

### 1. Programmed Examples

17. Pre-test: Whenever Pam took Clara with her in the car, Clara would continually ask, "How long until we get there?" At first Pam would explain carefully, but later she decided that Clara was just pestering her so she did not answer these questions. Clara continued to ask the question afterwards. What procedure was Pam using? _____ _____

15. Pre-test: Pat teased Carol incessantly about her weight. At first, Carol made defensive comments. When she realized that her comments increased Pat's teasing, she stopped making them. Instead, she just laughed the teasing off. Pat stopped teasing her. What behavioral procedure did Carol use? _____

18. Pre-test: Willie was unhappy with the slow pace at which Sonny was carrying rocks for the wall. So he started asking Sonny to carry the rocks faster, and sure enough Sonny did. What behavioral procedure did Willie use to increase Sonny's rate of carrying rocks? _____

16. Pre-test: Tom liked compliments a lot. Anytime he got one he beamed and profusely

thanked the person for the compliment. Tom noticed that this increased the number of compliments that he got from each person he had thanked. What behavioral procedure did Tom use by thanking people? _____ _____

12. Martha's 5-year-old son Paul frequently pinched his mother for no apparent reason. When Paul pinched Martha, she explained that pinching was not nice and asked Paul why he had pinched her. He usually said, "I don't know," and later pinched her again. Martha finally started to ignore the pinches no matter how irritating they were. She did this for several weeks and noticed that the pinching stopped. Check for two elements if you think this is extinction. First, did Martha eventually stop an event that could be a reinforcer? _____ (yes, no) (Note that her explanations could be a reinforcer because they followed the pinching.) Second, did the frequency of Paul's pinching decrease? _____ (yes, no) (Note that the fact that the behavior decreased when Martha stopped explaining provides evidence that explaining was a reinforcer.) Because Martha stopped paying attention to the pinches and the rate of pinching decreased, ignoring pinching is called _____.

11. Lora was taking a biology course from a rather conservative professor. Each class period she would ask one silly question, such as, "Why do dogs mate only twice a year? Don't they like it?" The professor usually got mad, turned red, and said, "That will be enough, Miss Smith." After talking with a behavior analyst, the professor started handling Lora's questions differently. He didn't get mad or turn red, he just followed her question with, "Are there any other questions?" After 12 class periods of the professor's new technique, Lora was still asking one silly question every class period. Check for both elements of the behavioral procedure. First, did the professor stop an event that could be a reinforcer? _____ (yes, no) (He no longer "got mad and turned red" after a silly question.) Second, did the rate of Lora's behavior decrease? _____ (yes, no) Because the professor stopped an event that could be a reinforcer but the rate of silly questions did not change, you should label the procedure used by the

professor to decrease Lora's silly questions as _____.

5. Bobby often whispered to his friends in English class. To stop his behavior the teacher told the class, "I will tolerate no more whispering in this class. I want it stopped as of today!" Bobby never whispered in class again after that. Check for both elements of the behavioral procedure First, did the teacher stop an event that could be a reinforcer? _____ (yes, no) (Note that the teacher's demand could not be a reinforcer.) Second, did the rate of a behavior decrease? _____ (yes, no) In this example the teacher did not stop a reinforcer. Therefore, the teacher's procedure is called _____.

13. Mary had spent Wednesday nights with her friends for the past few months. She enjoyed their company, and they liked hers except for one habit: she interrupted the conversation (particularly when Sally was talking). She always had something interesting to say, however, so they would pay attention to her interruptions. Sally finally became angry with Mary for interrupting her all the time. She asked Mary to stop doing it, and Mary apologized and said she would stop. But she didn't, so Sally told her feelings to the other members of the group. They all agreed to ignore Mary whenever she interrupted Sally. Sally would continue to talk, and the other members would continue to pay attention to her and to ignore Mary. After several Wednesday nights of this procedure, Mary had completely stopped interrupting. Check for both elements of the behavioral procedure: First, did the group stop an event that could be a reinforcer? _____ (yes, no) Second, did the rate of a behavior decrease? _____ (yes, no) In this example, the group stopped a reinforcer and an undesirable behavior decreased. Therefore, the group's procedure is called _____.

10. Jimmy and his dad had trouble getting along with each other. Whenever his dad would ask him how things were, Jimmy always explained at great length how bad his life was. Not wanting to make the boy's sad state worse, his dad always paid attention to him and tried to comfort him. One evening Jimmy's mother suggested that perhaps Dad should stop all the attention to such sad talk.

Dad stopped the attention, and Jimmy's rate of sad talk decreased. Check for both elements of the behavioral procedure. First, did Dad stop an event that could be a reinforcer? Second, did the rate of a behavior decrease? _____ (yes, no) In this example, Dad's procedure is called _____.

9. James would often say things to Don, thereby interrupting his studying. When James would say something, Don would answer. Eventually, Don did not answer James any longer. James continued to say things to Don. Check for both elements of the behavioral procedure: Did Don stop an event that could be a reinforcer? Did the rate of the behavior decrease? In this case, Don's refusal to answer James is an example of what procedure? _____

3. At the beginning of the semester, Gary, the new instructor of philosophy, told his students that he would give them a bonus if they handed their weekly papers in by Thursday. Everyone in the class did so. After several weeks, Gary figured that the problem of late papers was solved and stopped giving bonuses. The students stopped handing their papers in on time. Check for two elements: stopped reinforcer and decreased behavior. In this example, Gary's procedure is called _____.

4. Ben, the star pledge in his fraternity, was in charge of vacuuming the pledge dormitory. As long as Skoog, the frat president, asked him every Saturday to do it, Ben did an excellent job. However, Skoog finally stopped asking Ben to do it, feeling that Ben should be responsible enough to do it without being asked. Ben's rate of vacuuming the dorm dropped to nearly zero. Check for two elements: stopped reinforcer and decreased behavior. In this case, Skoog's stopping his requests is an example of what procedure? _____

14. Mr. Smith wanted to get his students to turn their papers in on time each week, so he reminded them on Thursday to be sure to have them in by Friday. Everyone did so. Midway through the semester, he stopped reminding them, and to his surprise, they stopped handing them in on time. Check for both elements of the behavioral procedure. What procedure did he use when he stopped reminding them? _____

2. At first Mary tried to be nice to Fred. But she did not like the kind of attention that he gave her, so she finally just totally ignored his attention and he stopped paying attention to her. What behavioral procedure was she using by ignoring him? _____

◆ **Very Important** ◆

I will start mixing in examples of reinforcement. Check first whether you think the example illustrates reinforcement or extinction. Then, check for the elements appropriate to your guess as to the correct term. (Remember, it may be unknown!) Connie was becoming extremely irritated with her husband's habit of throwing his clothes around. She had asked and entreated him repeatedly about this habit, but the chair in the bedroom was still his favorite storage place. One morning Connie saw him actually hanging up his clothes, so she fixed him a large breakfast (his usual breakfast was oatmeal and toast). Connie thought this was such a good idea that she made a rule to fix a large breakfast whenever the clothes were hung up. She noticed that they were hung up most of the time from then on. What procedure did Connie use?

_____

8. Galen had finally gotten fed up with the teasing that he was getting from Ben for going to church. So he decided to totally ignore all teasing. Ben continued teasing as much as before. What behavioral procedure did Galen use? _____

7. Darwin, a publicity-seeking student posing as a radical, came up with a sensational new tactic for disrupting the campus. The disruption was followed by the news media, and Darwin was interviewed on TV. He used that same tactic frequently thereafter. What behavioral procedure were the news media unwittingly applying to Darwin?

_____

20. Ward liked Bev a lot and so he went out of his way to find things about her to compliment. At first Bev liked this and smiled and thanked him. However, after she got engaged to Tom she felt embarrassed by Ward's compliments. As a result, she invariably ended up ignoring them. Ward doesn't compliment her anymore. What behavioral

procedure did Bev use when she ignored Ward's compliments? _____

6. Dan had a fantastic smile. Anyone who did a favor for him and received a "thank–you" accompanied by that smile was much more likely to do another favor for him in the future. One of Dan's smiles is termed a(n) _____.

19. Professor Jones disrupted faculty meetings with insane ideas. His colleagues used to argue vehemently with him. However, the chairman finally convinced them to simply ignore Jones. Soon, Jones wasn't disrupting meetings anymore. The faculty's ignoring Jones's insane ideas is an example of what behavioral procedure? _____

# 10 Differential Reinforcement of Everyday Behavior

## Reading Section

You have learned two tactics in using the reinforcement strategy to solve human problems. First, when you want to increase a single behavior, you can use tactic #1. You can increase the desired behavior through reinforcement. Second, when you want to decrease a single behavior, you can use tactic #2. You can decrease the undesired behavior through extinction. However, there will be times when you may want to increase one behavior while decreasing other related behaviors. As you might guess, you can combine the two procedures of reinforcement and extinction to change the relative rate of two behaviors. You will learn in this lesson that this combined procedure is called *differential reinforcement*. Tactic #3 in using the reinforcement strategy to solve human problems is to increase a desired behavior relative to undesired behaviors through differential reinforcement.

1. Tactic #3 in using the reinforcement strategy to solve human problems is to increase a desired behavior relative to an undesired behavior through differential _____
   _____.

## Defining Differential Reinforcement

Differential reinforcement refers to a procedure in which one behavior is reinforced while other behaviors are extinguished. The ultimate goal is to increase the rate of that behavior relative to the others. **Differential reinforcement** is a procedure involving two or more physically different behaviors; One

behavior is reinforced, and all other behaviors are extinguished. All three elements must be present before the procedure can be called differential reinforcement.

2. The term **differential reinforcement** is applied to any procedure involving two or more physically _____ behaviors; One behavior is _____, and all other behaviors are _____.

Here is an example in which all three elements are present. Suppose Dad wants to get Lulu to eat more vegetables and drink less pop during lunch at home. He might praise Lulu when she eats vegetables. He might ignore Lulu when she drinks pop. If Lulu starts to eat more vegetables and drink less pop, then this example has all three elements of differential reinforcement. First, it has two physically different behaviors: eating vegetables and drinking pop. They occur in one location: home. Second, Dad uses praise to reinforce eating vegetables. Third, Dad uses ignoring to extinguish drinking pop. This is an example of differential reinforcement because all three elements are present.

Many situations might look like differential reinforcement but be missing one element. For example, suppose Dad wants Lulu to eat with the family more often and to eat by herself less often. He might praise Lulu when she eats with the family but ignore her when she eats alone. If Lulu starts to eat with the family at home more often, then this example is similar to differential reinforcement. It involves reinforcement and extinction, but it does not involve two different behaviors. Lulu could pick up the same food with the same fork held in the same way with the same hand and

***Figure 10-1.*** Suppose Dad comforts Jenny whenever she's unhappy. He may end up paying lots of attention to Jenny when she's crying. He may figure Jenny doesn't need help when she is happy. Which face do you think Jenny would make most often? (Source: Bob Daemmrich/Stock, Boston)

chew it in the exact same way with the family and alone. Her eating behavior might remain exactly the same. So Dad is not praising one kind of eating behavior and ignoring another kind. Rather he is praising eating behavior in one situation and ignoring the same eating behavior in a second situation. This example has one behavior in two different situations. It does not have two different behaviors in one situation.

Other situations might look like differential reinforcement while missing other elements. For example, Dad might praise Lulu when she eats slowly and ignore her when she eats fast. If Lulu continues to eat fast just as often as before, then Dad is not using reinforcement on one of the behaviors. Thus, this would not be an example of differential reinforcement. Likewise, he might also tell her to eat slowly, but ignore her eating fast. She might start eating slowly. But this too would not be an example of differential reinforcement, because he used an instruction instead of reinforcement.

Be sure to read every example very carefully to see if it is similar to differential reinforcement but missing one element. I will include many examples both of differential reinforcement and of procedures very similar to differential reinforcement. You will not truly understand differential reinforcement until you can tell not only when it is present but also when it is not. As in past lessons, I will label procedures that miss one element of differential reinforcement as *unknown*.

## Uses of Differential Reinforcement

Two researchers applied differential reinforcement to coaching a junior high girl in tennis (Buzas & Ayllon, 1981). The tennis coach previously coached Debbie by first explaining how to make the strokes. He then watched her try the strokes and pointed out her errors. She couldn't seem to get the hang of basic tennis strokes. She made forehand, backhand, and service strokes correctly only 13% of the time. The researchers convinced the coach to ignore errors and praise correct strokes. Debbie improved until she was making 58% of these strokes correctly. The researchers had similar success with Sherry and Kristen.

We met up with a good example of the application of differential reinforcement in

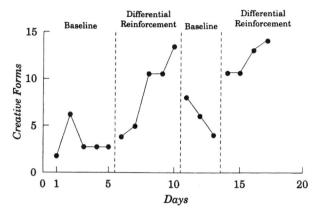

**Figure 10-2.** This graph shows that the creativity of Mary's block building increased when her teacher gave enthusiastic, approving attention to creative new structures and ignored repetitive structures. (Adapted from "Social Control of Form Diversity and the Emergence of New Forms in Children's Blockbuilding," by E. M. Goetz and D. M. Baer, *Journal of Applied Behavior Analysis*, 1973, 6, 209–217. Copyright 1973 by the Society for the Experimental Analysis of Behavior, Inc. Used by permission.)

Unit 1. Goetz and Baer (1973) differentially reinforced the behavior of Mary, a preschool child, for creative block building. They did this in two ways. They praised any form that she had not previously built, and they ignored those forms that she had previously built. Figure 10-2 shows the result of that experiment. During the periods marked *differential reinforcement*, Mary was given social attention only when she built a new, creative structure with her building blocks. During the reversal period, Mary was reinforced only when she built noncreative forms similar to ones that she had already built. As you can see, Mary built many new forms when they were differentially reinforced. She built few new ones when they were not. This experiment suggests that creative behavior can be nurtured by using differential reinforcement.

I gave other examples of differential reinforcement in Unit 1. For example, Komaki and Barnett (1977) improved the coaching skills on a little-league football team. They taught the coaches to differentially reinforce the young players for doing their part of the play. All team members increased correct play. Budzynski and Stoyva (1969) used biofeedback to differ-

entially reinforce relaxation. This led to a decrease in forehead tension. Wilder, White, and Yu (2003) used attention to differentially reinforce socially appropriate talk exhibited by an adult diagnosed with schizophrenia. Differential reinforcement of relaxation may produce meditation skills (Karlins & Andrews, 1972). Thus, differential reinforcement can teach such diverse skills as creativity, football plays, socially appropriate talk, and relaxation. It has even helped a great-grandmother cure an alleged case of possession by demons (Murphy & Brantley, 1982)!

Differential reinforcement may explain how people teach many behaviors in everyday life. For example, a skillful singing teacher might use differential reinforcement to teach her student to sing middle C. The teacher would reinforce singing middle C. She would extinguish singing notes close to middle C but not close enough. Similarly, a skillful Mom might use differential reinforcement to teach Bobby how to say "television." Jose might use differential reinforcement to teach you how to say "carrumba." A coach might use differential reinforcement to teach

---

> ### *Even Carl Rogers Used Differential Reinforcement*
>
> Carl Rogers rejected behavior analysis in a famous series of debates with Skinner (Rogers & Skinner, 1956). He asserted that psychotherapists could help clients most if they expressed positive regard for them no matter what they did. Charles Truax, a colleague of Rogers, studied whether Rogers did this with his own clients (Truax, 1966). He found that Rogers expressed positive regard when his client showed insight, but not when his client showed negative feelings. As a result, insight increased and negative feelings decreased.
>
> 3. Truax concluded that Rogers used the procedure of differential _____ on constructive behavior and ignored nonconstructive behavior.

a young pitcher how to throw a curve ball. Dad might use it to teach Sue how to shift gears. He might praise pushing on the clutch while letting up on the accelerator. He might ignore letting the clutch up on the accelerator too fast.

People often are not aware when they use differential reinforcement. One researcher showed that the father of humanistic psychology, Carl Rogers, unwittingly used it to help people. The box on Carl Rogers explains this interesting development.

## Misuses of Differential Reinforcement

In earlier lessons, I pointed out that people often use reinforcement to increase problem behavior and extinction to decrease desired behavior. You won't be surprised to learn that people often misuse differential reinforcement. For example, researchers studied children with chronic skin problems (Gil, Keefe, Sampson, McCaskill, Rodin, & Crisson, 1988). They had skin problems that covered about 13% of their body. The children made the problem worse by scratching. The researchers found that parents paid attention to the children when they scratched. The parents were less likely to pay attention when the children were not scratching. Thus, the

parents differentially reinforced scratching. See the box How a Therapist Taught Unhappiness for a description by one psychologist of how his psychoanalyst taught him to be unhappy (Kaufman, 1991).

Differential reinforcement may also explain how people often fail to teach the desired behavior. It may explain how they sometimes even teach problem behaviors. For example, an unskillful singing teacher might ignore notes close to C. She might react with criticism only to those notes that differ from C. If the pupil rarely gets any kind of attention, the criticism might be reinforcing. Their singing might get worse and worse. An unskillful Mom might show great sympathy when Bobby refuses to try saying "television." He might start refusing to even try saying difficult words. An unskillful teacher of Spanish might become annoyed when your pronunciation is wrong. If he boasted what a good teacher he is, you might delight in annoying him. An unskillful coach or Dad might ignore your attempts to perform well. They might react only when you don't follow their instructions. Your goofs might be reinforced by these reactions. Granted, many people might not react this way. Even so, the approach of focusing on mistakes instead of good attempts often involves the unwitting use of differential reinforcement for undesirable behavior.

---

### How a Therapist Taught Unhappiness

Kaufman tells this story about his psychoanalysis. "During some early sessions I moaned and groaned, incriminating myself and protesting the actions of others. As I walked toward the door in the concluding moments, the therapist often put his arm on my shoulder parentally and said 'you're really working on it. Good session. Just stay with it.' However, on other rare occasions, I talked effusively about seeing my life as moving productively ahead. When those sessions terminated, the analyst walked me to the door and said 'maybe next time you'll

get down to it and really work.' His message was clear. Be anxious, uncomfortable, fearful and frustrated and the session would be deemed productive and useful; be cheerful and optimistic and I would be seen as avoiding issues, the session not helpful or meaningful." (From Kaufman, 1991.)

4. By calling some sessions "good" and not others, the therapist differentially _____ unhappy talk by Kaufman.

# Reducing Behavior with Differential Reinforcement

Differential reinforcement has two effects. One effect is to increase the rate of a desirable behavior. Another effect is to decrease the rate of a competing undesirable behavior. Therefore, you can use differential reinforcement to reduce problem behavior rather than to increase desired behavior.

Researchers applied this method to Stan, a kindergarten student (Madsen, Becker, & Thomas, 1968). Stan was wild. He pushed, hit, and grabbed. He swore, stole, and broke things. He didn't do any work. The teacher tried what anyone would to control his behavior. She scolded and reprimanded, but as you might expect, this simply reinforced Stan's wildness. She then tried another common approach: she told Stan "the rules." This didn't do any good. The researchers then suggested that the teacher ignore the wild behavior. But this didn't do any good either. Finally, they had the teacher praise Stan when he followed the rules and ignore him when he was wild. As a result, appropriate behavior increased and wild behavior dropped from 80% of the time to around 30%. The researchers found similar effects with two other second-grade children. This approach has become the foundation for the behavioral approach to classroom management.

Sometimes, you need to quickly decrease problem behaviors. This is particularly true when the problem behaviors are dangerous. Yet these behaviors may be very resistant to change. Perhaps the behavior analyst cannot eliminate their reinforcing consequences. For example, suppose Tom is a very aggressive preschool child. He likes to use the swing but other children often won't let him. Tom might punch Carl to convince him to turn it over. If punching works, then it may increase in frequency. Teachers can't withdraw the reinforcer. They also may find such punching difficult to catch. One solution is to differentially reinforce a behavior that is incompatible with hitting. They might teach Tom to tell the teacher when he asked nicely. The teachers could then check with the other child. If Tom told the truth, they could give him a strong reinforcer.

Researchers used differential reinforcement to stop the aggression of a youth with severe retardation (Mace, Kratochwill, & Fiello, 1983). The 19-year-old youth hit, scratched, and butted others with his head. The researchers reinforced him for complying with instructions. He could not comply with the instructions and aggress at the same time. During baseline, he aggressed 16 times per 10 minutes. During treatment, he aggressed twice in eight months. His compliance increased from 0% to over 60% of all requests.

Differential reinforcement offers a positive approach to reducing problematic and dangerous behaviors. It provides an alternative to punishment.

## Summary

Tactic #3 in using the reinforcement strategy to solve human problems is to increase a desired behavior relative to an undesired behavior through differential reinforcement. Differential reinforcement can alter the relative rates of two or more behaviors. You can exert a powerful effect on the behavior of others with this process. Behavior analysts use it to help people develop more functional behavior. People often use differential reinforcement to help others even when they are not aware of it. However, they can also damage others because of a lack of awareness. You can avoid this danger by being very aware when you are using it.

## Behavior Analysis Examples

### *Helping the Elderly Communicate*
Elderly people often have trouble with communicating positively. They may say things that don't make sense. They may fail to say anything. We often explain this behavior as the result of medical conditions or the inevitable result of growing old. Such was the case with Mr. Orr. He was 67 years old and had suffered a stroke. He correctly responded to questions about 30% of the time. He spoke spontaneously about once every two hours. Researchers taught Mrs. Orr to praise, smile,

and touch him when he answered questions and spoke spontaneously. She ignored him when he incorrectly responded to questions. Mr. Orr's correct answers increased to about 85%. Mrs. Orr could again talk meaningfully to her husband of many years. Even his spontaneous talk increased to about three times per hour! (Based on Green, Linsk, & Pinkston, 1986.)

5. Mrs. Orr improved Mr. Orr's ability to talk by using what behavioral procedure? differential _____

### Safe Garbage

One of the most unpleasant jobs in a modern urban society is that of garbage collector. The job is made worse by the lack of citizens' cooperation in packaging their trash carefully. Stokes and Fawcett (1977) investigated the possibility of improving the packaging of trash by the citizens of one city. The city ordinance specified a number of rules to be followed by citizens when they put out their garbage. These rules were designed to make the work of the sanitation personnel safer and more pleasant. These rules included the following: place containers conveniently near curb; don't overfill the containers; tie plastic bags and use only untorn ones; don't use containers that fall apart when wet; tie yard trimmings into easily manageable bundles; and pick up loose litter at collection point. Stokes and Fawcett developed behavioral definitions that would permit the observation of violations of these standards. They measured reliability on four days and found it to be 95%. Their observations suggested that almost half of all residences violated the standards before treatment.

They then developed a simple treatment procedure in which the households being studied were notified of the standards and told that only trash correctly packaged would be collected. In addition, the sanitation crews wrote out a ticket to be placed on any container not collected and that explained the reason(s) that it was not being collected. In other words, those packaging behaviors that met the city standards were followed by

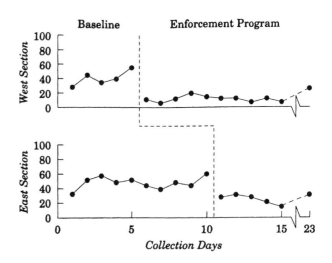

**Figure 10-3.** Percentage of residences in the middle-class and the working-class neighborhoods violating the trash packaging standards of a midwest city. (From "Evaluating Municipal Policy: An Analysis of a Refuse Packaging Program," by T. F. Stokes and S. B. Fawcett, *Journal of Applied Behavior Analysis*, 1977, 10, 391–398. Copyright 1977 by the Society for the Experimental Analysis of Behavior, Inc. Used by permission.)

collection of the trash while those packaging behaviors that did not meet city standards were followed by no collection.

The experiment was conducted by studying two neighborhoods, one middle class and the other working class. Figure 10-3 shows that in the middle-class neighborhood, the percentage of households violating one or more of the standards was about 40% under normal conditions. After five days, the noncollection policy was implemented and the percentage of households making one or more violations fell to about 12%. In the working-class neighborhood, the percentage of violating households was about 45% under normal conditions. After 10 days, the noncollection policy was implemented and the percentage fell to 23%. Thus, for both neighborhoods, the effect of the noncollection policy was a sharp drop in packaging behaviors that violated the standards.

To determine whether the packaging standards were relevant to the sanitation crews, they were asked to rate the neighborhoods before and after the new policy was put into effect. These ratings indicated that the packaging was considered by the crews to be much better done after the start of the policy and that the collections were easier and safer to make. This study suggests that differential reinforcement may be relevant not only to individual skill acquisition but also to the broader societal process of social change.

6. The process of collecting trash when packaged properly and not collecting improperly packaged trash would be called _____.

## Notes

### Note #1

A <u>history of reinforcement</u> may describe the differential reinforcement a person has received in the past. Suppose Tom's parents reinforced reading books and discouraged watching TV. This reinforcement could have turned Tom into a bookworm, and the history of such reinforcement would help to explain bookworm behavior.

7. In order to explain current behavior, it may be necessary to describe the differential reinforcement a person has received in the past, which is called the person's _____ of reinforcement.

### Note #2

Behavior analysts label several types of differential reinforcement. When they use it to increase a desirable behavior among other less desirable behaviors, they simply call it differential reinforcement. When they use it to reinforce behavior incompatible with an undesirable behavior, they call it <u>differential reinforcement of incompatible</u> behavior, or DRI (e.g., Olson & Houlihan, 2000). When they use it to reinforce any behavior that is an alternative to undesirable behavior but not incompatible, they call it <u>differential reinforcement of alternative</u> behavior, or DRA (e.g., Ringdahl, Kitsukawa, Andelman, Call, Winborn, Barretto, & Reed, 2002). They call differential reinforcement of behavior other than undesirable behavior <u>differential reinforcement of other</u> behavior, or DRO (e.g., McCord, Iwata, Galensky, Ellingson, & Thomson, 2001).

8. When differential reinforcement is used to reinforce behavior that is <u>incompatible</u> with an undesirable behavior, the procedure is abbreviated as *DRI*, which stands for "differential reinforcement of _____" behavior.

## Helpful Hints

### Helpful Hint #1

To apply the term *differential reinforcement* to everyday situations, you must first determine whether there are at least two different behaviors involved. If not, then you can rule out differential reinforcement. This step is particularly important because there is another behavioral procedure to be introduced in a later lesson that involves the reinforcement and extinction of one behavior in differing situations. Thus, determining whether there are at least two behaviors will permit you to easily make a very difficult distinction. Examples of this other procedure will be introduced in this lesson to help you learn how to tell the difference. If the example involves a <u>single</u> behavior that is reinforced in one situation and extinguished in a different situation, you should label it as unknown.

Here is the best rule to remember. If one behavior is reinforced and a different behavior is extinguished in the same situation, then this might be differential reinforcement (if the behavior changes). If a single behavior is reinforced in one situation and the same behavior is extinguished in a different situation, then this cannot be differential reinforcement. If a procedure involving reinforcement and extinction is applied to two behaviors in one situation, the procedure might be differential reinforcement. However, if a procedure involving reinforcement and extinction is applied to one behavior in two situations, the procedure cannot be differential reinforcement. Call the second procedure unknown.

9. Therefore, if a <u>single</u> behavior is reinforced in one situation and extinguished in a different situation, you should label this procedure as ⸻ .

### Helpful Hint #2

To determine whether an example contains two or more different behaviors you must analyze whether the individual makes different physical movements of his or her muscles. If the same muscles are moved in the same way, then only one behavior is involved no matter what else may differ in the surrounding situation.

10. You should conclude that a person emits two different behaviors only if they make different movements of their ⸻ ⸻ .

The following are some common examples in which there is only one behavior.

• <u>Making and not making a response</u>. Not making a response is the absence of behavior. So it cannot be considered to be a second behavior.

11. Hitting and not hitting someone ⸻ (are, aren't) two different behaviors.

• <u>The same muscles in two locations</u>. Digging a hole in the front yard does not require different muscular movements than digging a hole in the back yard. You don't shovel differently just because you are in the back yard.

12. Are playing tennis in Kansas and playing tennis in Florida two different behaviors? ⸻ (yes, no)

• <u>The same muscles at different times</u>: Pointing at a cardinal does not require a different movement of the finger muscles than pointing at a robin.

13. Is touching a wall and touching a door a single behavior? ⸻ (yes, no)

• <u>Reading different materials</u>. Your eyes focus in the same way and scan from left to right no matter what you are reading. Although there may be slight differences in line length, print

size, illustrations, and even type arrangement (as in a comic book), the minor variations in movement required usually do not justify regarding the behaviors as different.

14. Reading the front page and reading the editorial page ⸻ (are, aren't) two different behaviors.

• <u>Saying the same word to different people</u>. Your vocal cords, lips, tongue, and lungs move in the same way to say "stop" to John as to Sam.

15. If John talks about the weather with Mary and says the same thing about the weather to Bob, is John emitting two different behaviors? ⸻

The following are examples of different behaviors.

• <u>The same muscles at different speeds</u>. Sprinting and running involve similar movements of the leg muscles. However, the greater speed of sprinting clearly requires a different length stride, a stronger push-off, and even landing on a different portion of the foot.

16. Is walking up the hill a different behavior from walking down the hill? ⸻ (yes, no)

• <u>The same muscles at different strengths</u>. Whispering "stop" exerts the vocal muscles differently than screaming it. Driving a nail with one blow requires a longer backswing, more wrist action, and a stronger pull than driving it with ten blows.

17. Slamming a tennis ball ⸻ (is, isn't) the same behavior as tapping a tennis ball.

• <u>Talking about different topics</u>. Talking about different topics requires the use of different words that in turn involve different movements of the vocal apparatus. Talking about poetry would be a different behavior than talking about cars.

18. Is talking about a sunny day the same behavior as talking about a hurricane? ⸻ (yes, no)

• <u>Pronouncing a word correctly and incorrectly</u>. This would be the same as saying two or more different words since differing pronunciation will result in differing sounds.

19. If a person imitates the way a New Yorker says "you all" and the way a southerner says "you all," he/she _____ (is, isn't) performing a single behavior.

### Helpful Hint #3

Verbal behavior can present problems in analysis (see Salzinger, 2003). If two individuals are talking, it is helpful to focus on <u>one</u> individual's talking as a series of responses whose rate might be increased or decreased. Then, the talking of the other individual can be analyzed as a possible reinforcing event for the first person. For example, if Jean talks about how tough her job is and Larry listens sympathetically, he could well be reinforcing her. That is, each comment that Jean makes about her job (the response) may be followed by comments from Larry such as "Gee, that's too bad!" or "You ought to do something about that." If these comments by Larry increase the rate of Jean's negative job statements, they can be viewed as reinforcing events because they follow and increase the rate of Jean's comments. When you read examples involving conversations, be sure to read into the example this type of dyadic interaction between the two individuals.

20. When analyzing a discussion, it is helpful to focus on the talking of _____ (one, both) individual(s) as a behavior whose rate may be increased or decreased by the response of the other individual.

### Helpful Hint #4

Here's another way you can decide whether a procedure is differential reinforcement. Differential reinforcement teaches a person <u>what</u> response to make. It teaches them to eat vegetables instead of drink pop, to stroke the tennis ball correctly, to build new instead of repeated block patterns, to answer questions correctly, to carry out their football assignments, or to package their garbage correctly. A procedure is likely to be differential reinforcement if it teaches someone <u>what</u> response to make.

Here's how to decide if a procedure is not differential reinforcement. Differential reinforcement does not teach a person <u>when</u> to make a response. If the procedure teaches a baby to call its father "dada" but not any other male, then it is teaching the baby when to say "dada." If it teaches Lulu to eat with the family rather than alone, it is teaching her when to eat. If a procedure teaches someone when to make a response, label it as unknown.

21. If a procedure teaches someone <u>when</u> to make a response, label it as _____ _____. If a procedure teaches someone <u>what</u> behavior to make, the procedure is likely to be _____.

### Helpful Hint #5

If the teacher reinforces the student <u>only</u> for a particular behavior, then the teacher must be extinguishing the student for all other behaviors. Therefore, the teacher is using differential reinforcement. Please note the use of *only* in descriptions of examples.

22. If the teacher is reinforcing the student only when he emits a particular behavior, then the teacher must be applying what procedure to all other behaviors? _____ _____

Suppose you read that a teacher reinforces the student for a particular behavior. If the example does not say the student was reinforced only for that behavior, do not assume that it means "only." Thus, the teacher would be using reinforcement instead of differential reinforcement.

23. The procedure that the teacher would be using if she reinforces a student for a particular behavior is called _____ _____.

### Helpful Hint #6

I will ask questions about examples that illustrate differential reinforcement and examples that don't. I will ask what behavioral procedure is involved.

24. If the example contains some of the elements of differential reinforcement but

not all of them and it is not an example of another procedure that you've already learned, you should answer that the example illustrates what procedure? _____

_____

### Helpful Hint #7

Here is a hint about how to use *unknown*. When you try to explain why *unknown* fits the example, you must remember that the keywords contain an "or" between them. *Unknown* applies if the procedure is either "unsuccessful" or "untaught." Thus, your explanation need only show that the example fits one or the other (but not both) keywords.

25. Suppose an example applies reinforcement to one behavior and extinction to another but produces no change in behavior. Is your explanation correct if you note that "no change" means "unsuccessful" but don't comment on "untaught"? _____ (yes, no)

### Helpful Hint #8

I will sometimes simplify a question by referring to Behavior A and Behavior B, rather than some specific behaviors. You should assume that the two behaviors are physically different.

26. Thus, if you reinforce Behavior A and extinguish Behavior B, you will be using the behavioral procedure called _____

_____.

## Additional Readings

Green, G. R., Linsk, N. L., & Pinkston, E. M. (1986). Modification of verbal behavior of the mentally impaired elderly by their spouses. *Journal of Applied Behavior Analysis*, *19*, 329–336. This paper reports two case studies of wives using differential reinforcement to help elderly spouses communicate meaningfully.

Schwartz, G. J. (1977). College students as contingency managers for adolescents in a program to develop reading skills. *Journal of Applied Behavior Analysis*, *10*, 645–655. Schwartz organized a tutorial program for 260 seventh-grade students with important reading deficits. She used 42 college students as the tutors. They gave the grade schoolers special remedial materials. They wrote contracts with the grade schoolers to complete agreed upon amounts of work. They awarded points to the students based on carrying out the contracts. The grade schoolers advanced about two school years on a reading test. The tutors differentially reinforced the grade schoolers for making positive comments about reading, the learning process, and their abilities. The ratio of positive to negative comments changed from 50% positive before the program to about 85% afterwards. Differential reinforcement and effective training of reading skills improved the attitudes of the students toward reading and also toward themselves.

## Programmed Reading

I will teach you the practical use of this lesson's concepts in the following sections: (1) The Elements of Differential Reinforcement, (2) Are the Behaviors Different? (3) Use of the Word *Only*, (4) Practice Identifying Differential Reinforcement, (5) Another Tactic, and (6) Review.

### 1. The Elements of Differential Reinforcement

61. Pre-test: Jen praised Billy's studying physics but ignored her studying Spanish. Billy continues to study each subject at the same rate. Jen used the procedure of _____.

48. Pre-test: A situation might involve two or more different behaviors in one situation. Reinforcement might be used to increase one behavior and extinction used to decrease one or more other behaviors. If all three elements are present, then you should label this procedure as _____

_____.

51. Pre-test: Differential reinforcement has three elements. (1) It must involve at least two _____ behaviors in the same situation. (2) It must increase one behavior through the procedure of _____. (3) It must

decrease other behaviors through the procedure of _____.

53. Pre-test: Fred praised May's pencil drawings but ignored her watercolor drawings. May started drawing mostly pencil drawings. Fred used the procedure of _____ _____.

94. You will be called on to write the word *differential* many times in this lesson. Focus on spelling it correctly. Copy the word now: _____. Notice that you will sometimes be asked to write *differentially*. Copy that word now: _____ _____.

1. <u>Differential reinforcement</u> has the following three elements: (1) two or more physically <u>different</u> behaviors occur in one <u>situation</u>; (2) one behavior is <u>reinforced</u>; and (3) all other behaviors are <u>extinguished</u>. Any procedure that has all three of these elements is called _____.

45. Notice that the term *differential reinforcement* starts with the word *different*. That can remind you that one characteristic of differential reinforcement is that two or more physically _____ behaviors are involved.

83. The different behaviors occurring in an example of differential reinforcement must occur in _____ (many, one) situation(s).

92. Whenever you find an example that you don't know how to label because it doesn't meet any definition, you should label it as unknown. For example, if a <u>single</u> behavior is reinforced in one situation and extinguished in a different situation, you should label this procedure as _____ _____.

16. Dad praises Lulu when she eats with the family but ignores her when she eats alone. Suppose Lulu starts to eat with the family more often. Notice that she could eat exactly the same way whether she is eating with the family or alone. Therefore, this is an example of a single behavior in two different situations. It is not an example of differential reinforcement because it does not involve two different behaviors. Therefore, it is a(n) _____ procedure.

2. A second characteristic of differential reinforcement is that one behavior is increased through use of the procedure of _____.

77. So far you have learned two tactics for altering the rate of a single behavior. They are the procedures of (1) _____ and (2) _____.

85. The third characteristic of differential reinforcement is that another behavior is decreased through use of the procedure of _____.

11. Dad might praise Lulu when she eats with a fork and ignore her when she eats with her fingers. Lulu might continue to eat with her fingers just as often as before. Because praise doesn't increase the rate of eating with a fork, Dad isn't using reinforcement. Because ignoring doesn't decrease eating with her fingers, Dad isn't using extinction. Therefore, we say that Dad is using what procedure? _____

12. Dad might tell Lulu to eat with a fork, while he ignores eating with her fingers. She might start eating with a fork. Because telling Lulu to eat with a fork does not involve delivering a reinforcer, Dad changed the rate of using a fork by the procedure of _____.

44. Mrs. Orr used praise, smiles, and touch to reinforce her elderly husband's correct answers. She ignored incorrect answers. Her husband's rate of answering questions correctly did not change relative to answering them incorrectly. What procedure did she use? _____ _____

84. The Millers' trash-packaging behaviors that met the city standards were followed by collection and those packaging behaviors that did not meet the standards were followed by no collection. If the Millers' correct packaging increased and incorrect packaging decreased, the city used the procedure of _____.

17. Dad praises Lulu when she eats vegetables but ignores her when she drinks pop at home. Lulu starts to eat more vegetables and drink less pop. Notice that Dad works with two different behaviors (drinking, eating) in one situation (home). He increases

eating vegetables by praise. He decreases drinking pop by ignoring it. Because his procedure has these three elements to it, this is an example of what procedure?

_____

3. An example might involve two or more different behaviors in one situation. Reinforcement might be used to increase one behavior and extinction used to decrease one or more other behaviors. If all three elements are present, then you should label this procedure as _____
_____.

28. In summary, to be an example of differential reinforcement, an example must have three elements. (1) It must involve at least two _____ behaviors in the same situation. (2) It must increase one behavior through the procedure of _____. (3) It must decrease other behaviors through the procedure of _____.

## 2. Are the Behaviors Different?

62. Pre-test: Making and not making a response _____ (are, aren't) two different behaviors.

63. Pre-test: Reading about conservation and reading about weather _____ (is, isn't) a single behavior.

59. Pre-test: Are giving a high five on the football field and giving a high five at dinner two different behaviors? ____ (yes, no)

79. Students have a great deal of trouble telling whether an example involves a single behavior or different behaviors. This is the biggest cause of student errors. I am going to give you a whole series of examples describing same and different behaviors so you can practice telling which is which. If a procedure doesn't involves two different behaviors, it can't be the procedure of _____.

86. To determine whether a person emits two different behaviors, you must examine the movements they make with their muscles for each behavior. Only if a person makes different movements with his/her muscles should you conclude that the person emits two _____ behaviors.

25. If you do not make a response, then you are not performing any behavior. Therefore, making and not making a response _____ (are, aren't) two different behaviors.

31. Is moving a muscle fast a different behavior from moving the same set slowly? (yes, no) _____ (Warning: Many students miss similar questions because they don't realize that you have to move a muscle differently to move it at a different speed. If you were moving the muscle in exactly the same way, the muscle would be moving at the same rate. Thus, moving the muscle slowly involves doing something different than when moving it fast.)

4. Are using a set of muscles in Location A and using the same muscles in Location B different behaviors? _____ (yes, no)

89. Using a set of muscles to move a heavy object _____ (is, isn't) the same behavior as using the same set to move a light object. (Warning: This question is similar to moving the same muscles fast or slowly. You must move the muscles differently in order to move heavy or light objects.)

37. Is using a set of muscles when X happens and using the same muscles when Y happens a single behavior? _____ (yes, no)

36. Is talking about one topic the same behavior as talking about a different topic? _____ (Warning: This kind of item is often missed. If you talk about a different topic, you must use different words. If you use different words, you must use your speech, tongue, and mouth muscles differently. For example, you must move your lip muscles so your lips touch when saying "bear" but not when saying "air.")

72. Reading Novel A and reading Novel B _____ (is, isn't) a single behavior. (Warning: Again many students miss the fact that you read books in the same way no matter what the words are. You start at the beginning of one line, sweep along it, then start at the beginning of the next line. More specifically, you focus on the first word (or phrase), move the focal point of your eyes slightly to focus on the next word (or phrase), repeat until you've finished a line, then move the focal point of your eyes to the beginning of the next line and

repeat. Reading lines of words involves the same muscles moving in the same way.)

22. If individuals pronounce a word one way and then another way, they _____ (are, aren't) performing a single behavior.

34. Is saying the same word to Person A and then to Person B two different behaviors? _____ ( yes, no)

30. Is jogging a different behavior from walking? _____ (yes, no)

76. Smiling and not smiling at someone _____ (are, aren't) two different behaviors.

71. Reading about conservation and reading about weather _____ (is, isn't) a single behavior.

35. Is talking about Fred the same behavior as talking about Jane? _____ ( yes, no)

33. Is saying "that's one" when you see a jet and saying "that's one" when you see a car a single behavior? _____ ( yes, no)

75. Screaming "No!" _____ (is, isn't) the same behavior as whispering "No."

29. Are giving a "high five" on the football field and giving a high five at dinner two different behaviors? _____ ( yes, no)

27. If you say "buenas dias" with a learner's accent and "buenas dias" with a perfect Spanish accent, you _____ (are, aren't) performing a single behavior.

32. Are saying "hello" to Mary and saying "hello" to Bob two different behaviors? _____ ( yes, no)

### 3. *Use of the Word* **Only**

65. Pre-test: Suppose that a singing teacher praises only notes sung close to C. If your rate of singing close to C increases, then what procedure has your singing teacher used by praising only when you sing close to C? _____

58. Pre-test: If the teacher is reinforcing the student only when he emits a particular behavior and that behavior increases, can you conclude that the teacher is using differential reinforcement? _____ (yes, no)

66. Pre-test: Suppose the teacher reinforces Behavior A and extinguishes Behavior B. Suppose that Behavior A increases and Behavior B decreases. Is the teacher using differential reinforcement? _____ (yes, no)

26. If you reinforce someone only when they engage in Behavior A, you must not be reinforcing that person when they engage in any other behavior. Therefore, the situation involves at least two behaviors: Behavior A and every other behavior. You are increasing Behavior A through reinforcement. You are decreasing all other behaviors through extinction. Therefore, you are using what behavioral procedure by reinforcing only Behavior A? _____

91. When you read that a teacher gives a reinforcer to a student only when they perform a certain behavior, you know that the teacher also decreases other behavior through the procedure called _____.

80. Suppose that a singing teacher praises only notes sung close to C. That means that he ignores notes sung far from C. If your rate of singing close to C increases, then what procedure has your singing teacher used by praising only when you sing close to C? _____

24. If the teacher is reinforcing the student only when he emits a particular behavior and that behavior increases, can you conclude that the teacher is using differential reinforcement? _____ (yes, no)

74. Remember that the word *only* is an important word in describing differential reinforcement. It permits me to keep examples short. If you know that only one behavior is reinforced, then you also know that all other behaviors are subjected to what procedure? _____

19. Differential reinforcement can sometimes produce the wrong result. Remember that an unpleasant event can sometimes serve as a reinforcer. Suppose a singing teacher criticizes only those notes that differ from C. If the student's singing gets worse, the procedure used by criticizing only mistakes is called _____.

73. Remember also if an example states that a teacher reinforces a student for a particular behavior, that's what it means. Do not assume that it means "only." The teacher might also be reinforcing many other behaviors. If a teacher reinforces

a student for a particular behavior, the teacher is using what behavioral procedure? _____

13. Dad praises John only when he rides his bike but not when he watches TV. If John's rate of bike riding increases and his TV watching decreases, Dad's procedure is _____.

15. Dad praises John when he rides his bike. If John's rate of bike riding increases, Dad's procedure is _____.

14. Dad praises John only when he rides his bike. If John's rate of bike riding increases, Dad's procedure is _____.

39. Jim praises Erin when she asks for what she wants. Erin's rate of asking for what she wants increases. Jim is using the procedure of _____.
Actually, Jim praises Erin for everything she does because he wants a date.

### 4. Practice Identifying Differential Reinforcement

54. Pre-test: Howard praised Alice when she built taller structures, but ignored shorter structures. If Alice built the same number of tall structures compared to short structures, then Howard used the procedure of _____.

60. Pre-test: Jane praised John when he was reading English but ignored him when he was reading physics. If John starts to read more English and less physics, Jane used the procedure of _____?
(Explanation: Reading involves the same behavior—moving your eyes left to right— no matter what you are reading. Jane's praise is not simple reinforcement because John's reading of physics decreases.)

64. Pre-test: Ruby smiled at Tommy when he used crayons and ignored him when he used watercolors. Pretty soon, Tommy used crayons more and watercolors less. Ruby's procedure is an example of _____.

69. Pre-test: To teach the correct pronunciation of a difficult English word to a child while eliminating the incorrect pronunciation, one could use the behavioral procedure of _____.

50. Pre-test: Coach praised little-league football player Clem when he carried out his assignments and ignored him when he didn't. If the procedure did not improve the correct carrying out of assignments, you would label the procedure _____ _____.

68. Pre-test: The Millers' correct packaging of trash increased when it was followed by City trash collection. We can conclude that the city used the procedure of _____.

49. Pre-test: Chou told Gerry to build taller structures while he ignored shorter structures. If Gerry built more tall structures compared to short structures, then Chou used the procedure of _____.

6. Bob the tennis coach ignored errors by a junior high student and praised correct strokes. If the rate of correct strokes increased and the rate of errors decreased, the coach used what procedure? _____ _____

23. If an example describes a teacher praising Behavior A, you should not assume that the teacher is not praising other behaviors. You must limit your analysis to Behavior A. If praising Behavior A increases its rate, then you should label the use of praise as the procedure called _____.

7. Bob the tennis coach yelled at Kim whenever she made incorrect strokes. Her rate of incorrect strokes increased. Since you don't know if the coach ignored correct strokes, you don't know if his procedure included extinction. Therefore, you cannot conclude that he was using differential reinforcement. You can only analyze what he did with the errors. The coach unwittingly used what procedure to increase errors? _____

10. The Coach praised little-league football player Butch when he carried out his assignments and ignored him when he carried out the wrong assignment. The procedure improved the correct carrying out of assignments. Label the procedure _____.

5. Betty the preschool teacher praised Bob when he built novel structures and ignored him when he built repeated structures. Bob built more creative structures

and less repeated structures. The procedure is an example of _____
_____.

8. Brett, another preschool teacher, simply told Fred to build more creative structures while he ignored repeated structures. If Fred built more creative structures compared to repeated structures, then Brett used the procedure of _____
_____.

40. Karen the teacher scolded and reprimanded Willie for wild behavior. Willie increased his wild behavior. Karen inadvertently uses the procedure of _____ _____ to increase his wild behavior.

41. Mary used a feedback device to learn how to relax her forehead muscles. The device made a soothing sound when her forehead was relaxed. It made no sound when her forehead muscles were tense. Mary's rate of relaxed muscles increased, and her rate of tensed muscles decreased. Mary used the procedure of _____.

9. Carl Rogers expressed positive regard when his client said insightful things, but not when she said negative things. The client's insight increased relative to her negative feelings. Carl Rogers used the behavioral procedure of _____.

42. Mom paid attention to Bruce when he scratched himself but she did not pay attention when he engaged in behavior other than scratching. Bruce scratched more often. By her attention, Mom accidentally used what procedure to increase scratching? _____

18. Dad usually pays attention if baby says "dada" to him, but he ignores when baby says "dada" to other males. Baby will quickly come to say it only to Dad. Before you jump to conclusions about the procedure that Dad uses, ask "Does baby move different muscles when saying "dada" to Dad than when she says it to other males?" You should label the procedure that Dad uses as _____.

21. His psychoanalyst praised Dan for unhappy talk and ignored him for happy talk. Dan's talk became unhappy more

often and happy less often. The psychoanalyst used what procedure? _____

38. Jane praised John when he was reading English but ignored him when he was reading physics. John started to read English more than physics. Decide whether reading different books is different behavior. What procedure did Jane use? _____

93. You react with excitement when Tom talks about sports but not when he talks about school. If Tom starts talking with you a lot more about sports, you have used what procedure? _____

43. Mom praises Abdullah when she sees him reading about biology but not when she sees him reading about sports. If Abdullah starts reading more biology and less sports, Mom used what procedure? _____

### 5. Another Tactic

70. Pre-test: You can use tactic #3 of the reinforcement strategy to increase one behavior relative to another behavior through _____.

81. Tactic #3 in using the reinforcement strategy to solve human problems is to increase a desired behavior relative to an undesired behavior through _____ _____.

### 6. Review

56. Pre-test: If a single behavior is reinforced in one situation and extinguished in a different situation, you should label the procedure as _____.

67. Pre-test: Tactic #3 in using the reinforcement strategy to solve human problems is to increase a desired behavior relative to an undesired behavior through _____ _____.

57. Pre-test: If Fred praises May only when she works on her computer and she starts working more on her computer and less on other activities, then Fred is using what procedure? _____

55. Pre-test: If a baby says "mama" to other females besides the mother and the parents ignore these occurrences but pay attention to the "mama" said to the

mother, what procedure are they using?
_____

52. Pre-test: Differential reinforcement involves three elements. First, the example must involve one situation with at least two behaviors that are _____ from each other. Second, the example must increase one behavior through the procedure of _____. Third, the example must decrease one or more behaviors through the procedure of _____.

47. One of the characteristics of differential reinforcement is that one behavior is increased by using _____.

90. When one behavior is reinforced and any others are extinguished in the same situation, this is termed _____.

87. To use the reinforcement strategy for solving human problems you may follow these tactics: (1) increase the desired behavior through reinforcement; (2) decrease the undesired behavior through extinction; (3) increase a desired behavior relative to an undesired behavior through _____.

20. Dr. Stokes observed the Millers' correct trash-packaging behaviors increased and their incorrect behaviors decreased when only correctly packaged trash was collected. The behavioral procedure used was: _____.

88. Two behavioral procedures that are involved in differential reinforcement are: _____ and _____.

46. One characteristic of differential reinforcement is that one or more behaviors are decreased by using the method of _____.

78. Stokes and Fawcett (1977) studied the effect on packaging behavior of collecting properly packaged trash and not collecting improperly packaged trash. Does the example involve two (or more) different behaviors? _____

82. Tactic #3 in using the reinforcement strategy to solve human problems is to increase a desired behavior relative to an undesired behavior through _____.

## Programmed Examples

### 1. Programmed Examples

16. Pre-test: Faith has learned about radical politics from her friend Imamu. After she had read parts of *Das Kapital*, Imamu would talk with her excitedly about it. After she had read parts of *The Rise and Fall of the Roman Empire*, however, he was very quiet. Faith came to read *Das Kapital* more and more often. What behavioral procedure was Imamu using? _____

19. Pre-test: Kurt wanted to learn to speak German really well, but he was having trouble in his language class learning to say "ch" as the Germans do. He found that it was a gutteral sound that combined some aspects of the English "k" and the English "ch." His instructor praised him strongly when he got it right but ignored him the rest of the time. If Kurt's pronunciation of "ch" improved, what procedure was his instructor using?
_____

18. Pre-test: If a child starts to read the comics out loud, his or her parents usually make a big fuss about this suddenly displayed reading skill. What behavioral procedure would account for any increase in the child's reading from the comics? _____

17. Pre-test: Gary found that if he smiled when he was with Jane, she would pay a lot of attention to him. However, if he smiled when he was with Gloria, she would ignore him. Naturally, Gary started smiling a lot when he was around Jane and hardly at all when he was around Gloria. Getting attention from Jane and ignoring from Gloria for smiling is what behavioral procedure?
_____

2. A baby boy makes many vocalizations such as "behavior analysis," "glub," "goo-goo," and eventually "da" or "da-da." When parents first hear a vocalization similar to "da," they immediately pay a lot of attention to the child, pet him, hold him, make nice sounds back at him and generally ignore "behavior analysis," "glub," and "goo-goo." As a result, the child starts saying "da" more often. Check for the elements of differential reinforcement. First, is "da" a different behavior from "behavior analysis" and "glub"? _____ (yes,

no) Second, is one behavior increased with use of reinforcement? ____ (yes, no) Third, are one or more other physically different behaviors decreased with use of extinction? ____ (yes, no) Since the example involves two or more different behaviors, one of which is being reinforced and the other extinguished, the parents are using what procedure? _____ They were teaching baby what sound to make, not when to make it.

3. A baby boy may say "mama" to many females other than his mother. His parents, by reserving their attention for those occasions when the child says "mama" to its mother, will eventually teach the child not to say "mama" to any other females. Check for the elements of differential reinforcement. First, does saying "mama" to the mother involve a behavior that is physically different from saying "mama" to other females? ____ (yes, no) Because the parents are reinforcing a behavior in one situation and extinguishing the same behavior in another situation, you should label the procedure that the parents use to teach their baby to call its mother "mama" _____. They are teaching the baby when to say "mama," not what sound to make.

20. Roger watched everything on TV from cartoons to *Sesame Street*. However, his father started praising him when he watched *Sesame Street* and started ignoring him when he watched cartoons. Soon Roger was watching only *Sesame Street*. Check for the elements. First, do Roger's eyes focus differently while watching cartoons than while watching *Sesame Street*? ____ (yes, no) Therefore, you should label father's procedure as _____. Father was teaching Roger when to watch TV, not what behavior to emit.

9. Frank's dad noticed that his son's habit of tuning the radio had changed considerably. At first, his son would usually twirl the knob very quickly and then complain about not being able to find his favorite radio station. As time went on, Roger's rapid twirling of the dial decreased. However, the few times that he turned it slowly, he was able to find the station. As time went on, Frank turned the knob slowly more often. Check for elements. First, does turning the knob quickly constitute a different behavior from turning it slowly? ____ (yes, no) Second, does the example state any evidence that turning the knob slowly was reinforced by Frank's finding his favorite radio station? ____ (yes, no) Third, is turning the knob quickly extinguished by failure to find his favorite radio station? ____ (yes, no) The procedure being followed by the natural operation of the tuner on the radio would be called _____. The radio was teaching him what behavior to emit, not when to emit it.

4. Billy was pretty good at using a hammer and screwdriver. However, his mother saw him sometimes hammer a screw in rather than use the screwdriver. Mom decided to help Billy by praising him whenever he used the screwdriver on the screw. She ignored him when he used the hammer on the screw. Soon, Billy was using the screwdriver for the screw. Check: First, are there two or more different behaviors? ____ (yes, no) Second, is one behavior increased through reinforcement? ____ (yes, no) Third, are one or more other behaviors decreased through extinction? ____ (yes, no) Therefore, by praising using the screwdriver on screws and ignoring using the hammer on screws, Mom was using what procedure? _____ She was teaching him what behavior to emit, not when to emit it.

8. Faith was learning the language of radical politics. For some reason she had trouble pronouncing "imperialism." So her boyfriend Imamu delighted in helping her learn the correct pronunciation. When she was right, he praised her; when she was wrong, he didn't. She soon learned to pronounce it correctly. Check for different behaviors, reinforcement of one and extinction of others, before answering the following question: "What procedure is Imamu using in this example?" _____ _____ He was teaching Faith what behavior to emit.

10. Garvey liked the meetings of the Red Riders, and he also liked the meetings of the Humanists' Club. But he found that if he made his speech about the dignity of all humans,

including poor people, the Red Riders didn't seem too interested. However, when he made the same speech to the Humanists, they seemed overjoyed. Without even noticing it, Garvey found himself giving his speech less to the Red Riders and more to the Humanists. Check the elements of reinforcement. Between them, these organizations unintentionally applied what procedure to Garvey's speech about dignity? _____
They were teaching him when to talk about dignity, not what to talk about.

14. Marcie was tired of Dave watching the baseball game on TV every weekend. She told him about her feelings and asked him to stop watching it. He agreed and now no longer watches the weekend game. Check, then answer the following question: "What procedure did Marcie use to reduce Dave's rate of watching the game"? _____

1. (I will start mixing in examples of other procedures. Start by deciding what term you think may be involved. Then, check for the elements of reinforcement appropriate to that term. Remember, the procedure may be unknown.) Gary's parents talked incessantly about the "yuppies" who attended college. During his freshman year, they made about three put-downs an hour. During his sophomore year, any time his parents put down yuppies, he started explaining to them why students need to buy the latest fashion. Gary's parents' rate of put-downs increased to nine an hour. What behavioral procedure did Gary unintentionally use to increase the parents' put downs? _____

12. John and Darrin were in the cafeteria having an important discussion about their social action meeting that night. Lee came over and sat down with them. John and Darrin both said "hello" and immediately included Lee in their conversation. After this incident, Lee sat with John and Darrin more often during lunchtime, and they always included him in their conversations. What behavioral procedure is at work determining how often Lee sat with John and Darrin? _____

5. Bob's coach helped him to improve his hitting. Prior to every at-bat, he would

remind Bob to keep his eye on the ball. Bob usually did. Then, the coach decided that Bob now could do it on his own, so he stopped reminding him. Bob does not keep his eye on the ball very often now. What procedure did the coach use that resulted in the decrease in Bob keeping his eye on the ball? _____

7. David Jaynes was the new psychiatrist for Mrs. Brooke. She became annoyed at Jaynes's habit of describing his own problems but never asking what help Mrs. Brooke needed. So Mrs. Brooke started ignoring all descriptions of his problems and paid attention only when he asked what she needed. He quickly changed to ask her more often what she needed and to describe his own problems less often. What behavioral procedure was Mrs. Brooke using? _____

15. Mr. Howard taught a ninth-grade geography class. It was his conviction that the students would learn more about geography if they participated in class discussion. For the most part, the students appeared to enjoy the discussion classes and to willingly enter into discussions. However, one boy, Ben, said very little. Mr. Howard decided that, rather than continue to put him on the spot by constantly asking him questions, he would compliment him profusely whenever he did say anything. Pretty soon Ben was talking a lot during class. Mr. Howard changed Ben's behavior by using what behavioral procedure? _____

11. Grace wanted desperately to learn how to do the new dance, but she didn't know the steps. Patty showed her the whole dance step. Then, Grace copied it. She had learned the dance just like that. By showing her how the dance went, what method did her roommate use? _____

13. Many new parents are unhappy that their baby cries so often. For example, they may change a baby's diapers, attend to all his or her physical needs, and put him or her to bed for the night. However, they will then answer the baby's cries for hours even though there is nothing wrong with the child. They would be advised by a behavior analyst to ignore all crying after the baby is put to bed properly cared for. The

child will cry a lot for the first part of a few nights but will gradually stop crying. This method of decreasing the baby's crying after he or she is put to bed is called what?

_____

6. Carol had a friend who was helping her learn to jog. Whenever she took a long smooth stride, her friend praised her; when she took a shorter stride or a rougher stride, her friend made no comment. She was soon the smoothest runner around. What procedure is her friend using to teach Carol how to jog? _____

# Shaping Everyday Behaviors

## Reading Section

You have now learned the basics of reinforcement. Any behavior that produces reinforcement will increase. That's how you and I have learned the many useful everyday skills that we have. Behavior analysts can use reinforcement to help people learn particular skills. You can use reinforcement to increase desired behavior of other people.

Of course, reinforcement can also cause undesirable behavior to increase. However, if undesirable behavior is no longer followed by reinforcement, then it will decrease. That's called *extinction*. Most of us don't have lots of undesirable behavior because other people have extinguished it. They have also punished it, but that's a story for later in the book. Behavior analysts can use extinction to help people get rid of some of the remaining undesirable behavior. You can use extinction to decrease the undesirable behavior of others.

As you know, most of our behavior is the result of the combined effect of reinforcement and extinction. The world usually reinforces one behavior while it extinguishes many other behaviors. Behavior analysts, you, and I can use these procedures to help ourselves and others. They are powerful procedures. However, as powerful as they are, they only work on existing behavior. They can't create new behavior—such as that displayed by a skillful ballerina.

Behavior analysts can use these procedures to teach children creative block building. However, notice that the children must already know how to build with blocks. Teachers can use these procedures to teach creative word use, but the students must already know how to speak and write those same words. The

point is that reinforcement can only increase the frequency of an existing behavior. Critics often point to this limitation. They claim that behavior analysts cannot explain the origin of "new" behaviors (see Shahan & Chase, 2002). However, this criticism in no way detracts from the effectiveness of reinforcement as a behavioral strategy. In this lesson, you will

***Figure 11-1.*** Many psychologists wonder how reinforcement could account for such a rare accomplishment as ballet dancing. After all, you can't reinforce such behavior if it doesn't exist. You learn how in this lesson! (Source: Bruno Vincent/Getty Images)

learn how simple it is to *shape* behavior to create <u>new</u> behavior. You will learn tactic #4 in using the reinforcement strategy to solve human problems: to create new behavior through <u>shaping</u>.

1. Tactic #4 in using the reinforcement strategy to solve human problems is create new behavior through ———————————.

## Some Examples of Shaping

The easiest way to introduce you to *shaping* is to give an example. Suppose Danny, your 3-year-old son, fears the dark. He insists on sleeping with the light on all night. You want to teach him a new behavior. You want him to turn the light off. Suppose you ask him to turn it off but he refuses. If he never turns the light off, you can't reinforce that response. What do you do? You <u>shape</u> the new behavior of turning off the light.

The first thing you might do is to install a light dimmer. This light dimmer has 10 gradations of dim. When it is on 10, the light is fully on; when it is on 0, it is fully off. The dimmer permits Danny to dim the light a little bit. Now you can ask him at bedtime to dim the light to 9. If he turns it to 9 and leaves it there all night, you can praise him the next morning. If he leaves it on 10, you can ignore his behavior and say good night. If he sometimes turns it to 9, your praise may increase the rate. You can then ask him to turn it to 8. You can repeat this process until he turns it all the way off. You will have created the new behavior of turning off the light. Researchers taught the parents of six children to use this procedure. It worked with all six (Giebenhain & O'Dell, 1984).

Notice the pattern here. You first pick a starting point for the shaping. In this case, the starting point was any dimming of the light. The starting point must be a behavior that the child can now do. You pick the starting point because it is related to your goal of turning the light off. You then differentially reinforce that starting behavior. At the same time, you extinguish behavior that is not related to the goal. You thereby increase the rate of the behavior that is related to the goal compared to that which is not. Once you have increased your starting point, you find the next step: a behavior that moves you closer to the goal. (According to the example, this step would be to move from a setting of 9 to a setting of 8.) In other words, you shift your criterion for the behavior, reinforcing it incrementally so that you move more closely to your goal. Step by step you get closer and closer. Finally, you reach it. You have "shaped" an entirely new behavior!

Here's another example. Suppose Ann, your infant, makes the usual baby vocal sounds. She coos, cries, gurgles, and babbles. Suppose she makes vowel sounds like "ah," "uh," "oh," and "eeh." Suppose you want to teach her to say "Dada." The hard part is the "duh" sound because she is already saying the "ah" sound. You start shaping by picking any sound that is remotely like the "duh." When you hear it you smile at her and praise her immediately. You might also hug, pat, and even feed her. You want to reinforce that sound. You ignore all the others, seeking to increase the occurrence of "d" sounds. When she makes more "d" sounds, you start listening for "da" sounds. Again, reinforce those sounds and ignore all other sounds, including the simple "d" sounds. When she makes lots of "da" sounds, start working on repeats of "da." You might hear "da" and a second later another "da." Reinforce that. Keep going this way until she says "Dada." Depending on how skillful you are, you might take a few minutes or a few hours. You will have shaped an entirely new behavior! Two researchers used this method to teach a mute 4-year-old child to say "eat" (Blake & Moss, 1967).

Parents often use shaping to develop language skills of normal children (Moerk, 1990). In fact, we all use this method to help children learn many important skills. The advantage of shaping is that it does not rely on <u>language</u>. People can use it to teach new behaviors to babies, infants, and individuals with retardation. Of course, once a person can speak, you can use other methods. I will teach you some of those other methods in Unit 3. However, even after we develop exquisite language skills, we continue to learn through shaping. You might be surprised just how much of your own behavior is influenced by the procedure of shaping. I will give some examples later in this lesson.

## Definition of Shaping

**Shaping** is the <u>differential reinforcement</u> of a series of <u>successive approximations</u> to a <u>target behavior</u>. Normally the person doing the shaping specifies the target behavior or goal of the shaping. However, you can also use the term *shaping* when no one has intentionally specified a target behavior. You need only observe that the successive approximations move toward some end result. You can think of that end result as an *unintentional target behavior.*

2. Use the term *shaping* for the differential reinforcement of a series of successive _____ to a target behavior.

**Target behavior** is the ultimate <u>goal</u> of shaping. In the earlier example, it is "Dada." The target behavior is any behavior that you seek to produce through shaping. It is also any behavior that the world unintentionally moves a behavior toward.

3. The ultimate goal of shaping is called the _____ behavior.

**Successive approximation** is any behavior that is <u>similar</u> to a target behavior for a program of shaping. Its similarity is what permits it to serve as a step toward the target behavior. In the example, "duh," "da," and "da . . . da" were successive approximations to "Dada."

The shaping procedure rests on successive approximations. It involves selecting an initial approximation to the target behavior and differentially reinforcing that approximation until it occurs frequently. You then select a second, closer approximation and differentially reinforce that behavior until it occurs at a high rate—and then a third, fourth, and so on. You repeat the process until you reach the target behavior. Each behavioral approximation to the target behavior is called a successive approximation.

4. You should use the term successive _____ to refer to any behavior similar to a target behavior for a program of shaping.

## Shaping Shooting an Arrow

For example, suppose that you wished to teach your son, Fred, how to shoot an arrow into the target from 25 feet. You teach him the first approximation. That might be how to draw the bow with the arrow in it. You praise him when he does it right. You overlook his mistakes. When he can do it, you move on to the second approximation. You teach how to sight the target and release the arrow from 5 feet. You praise him when he hits the target. You overlook his goofs. When he can hit the target every time, you are ready to find a third approximation. Perhaps it is to shoot from 10 feet. Again

---

### *How Skinner Shaped a Critic's Behavior*

Skinner told this story. A committee he was on brought in Eric Fromm as a guest. "All morning long he had easy explanations for everything. And after lunch it was the same thing. We were all seated at a big table, a couple of dozen of us. He was sitting across the table from me and he started in. 'Pigeons aren't people you know,' he told me. 'You have to realize that man is different.' He went on and on. I wrote a note saying, 'Watch Fromm's left hand. I'm going to shape a chopping motion.' I passed the note down to the chairman. I just turned toward [Fromm] and every time his hand went up, I nodded. Pretty soon he was chopping and chopping the air with his left hand as he spoke. I thought, 'Why does he say this doesn't work with people?' " (Cited in Snyder, 1990: p. 4).

5. Skinner's goal was to get Fromm to make a chopping motion. The chopping motion would be considered the _____ (approximation, shaping, target) behavior of a shaping procedure.

***Figure 11-2.*** When using shaping to teach someone a new skill, you should start by differentially reinforcing behavior that the individual can do successfully. (Source: Cartoon copyright 1973 King Features Syndicate. Reproduced by permission.)

you praise and ignore. You continue this process until he can shoot accurately from 25 feet, the target behavior. Figure 11-2 illustrates how a concerned father might start with a very easy first approximation.

## Overcoming Shyness and Other Problems

Intentional shaping involves the deliberate effort of a behavior analyst to create a new behavior. A good example is the program devised by Jackson and Wallace (1974), who set out to teach a very shy 15-year-old girl to speak loudly enough to be heard. Alice had been diagnosed as extremely withdrawn since age 7. She had no social skills, no friends, and learned little in school. She spoke in such a soft whisper that no one could hear her.

The researchers used very sensitive electronic equipment. They gave Alice a list of 100 simple words. They asked her to read them. They set the equipment to detect when she did so in a soft whisper but not in a very soft whisper. They used the equipment to immediately deliver a reinforcer for soft whispers but not for very soft whispers. Thus, they differentially reinforced Alice for softly whispering the words on their list. Once she was doing that, they required a louder whisper for reinforcement. They continued to slowly increase the loudness requirement as she mastered each stage. Eventually, she was reading the words in a normal tone of voice. The researchers then went through a series of additional steps. They

reinforced her for reading words of more than one syllable in a normal voice. They reinforced her for saying things to other people. Finally, they reinforced her for talking in a classroom. After this training, Alice changed quite dramatically. She talked with other kids. She did quite well in a normal classroom. She even got a job as a waitress.

Here's another example of intentional shaping. Researchers helped children accept insertion of contact lenses (Mathews, Hodson, Crist, & LaRoche, 1992). For example, they helped the parents of 2-year-old Charles. They broke insertion down to eight steps. The first step was teaching Charles to accept touching his face. Second was accepting pulling open the eyelid. Third was having the child pull open the eyelid. Fourth was accepting drops in the eye. Fifth was accepting approaching the eye with a finger. Sixth was accepting touching the eye with the finger. Seventh, accepting touching the eye with a soft lens. The target behavior was accepting touching the eye with a hard lens. That permitted insertion. The researchers reinforced Charles' acceptance of each step with praise, bubbles, food, and access to toys. They ignored nonacceptance. Charles learned to accept each step. Eventually, he accepted insertion.

Horner (1971) gives another example of intentional shaping. He taught Dennis, a 5-year-old child with moderate retardation, to walk with crutches. Dennis had moderate retardation, with a birth defect that left his legs paralyzed. His muscles functioned at the level of a 10-month-old child. He could sit up. He could pull himself along the floor with his arms. Horner differentially reinforced Dennis for a series of approximations to using the crutches. The first step was to have Dennis place the crutch tips on two dots on the floor. The next step was to place the crutch tips on the dots and swing his body to an erect crutch-supported position. The very gradual increase in the behavior required for differential reinforcement occurred through ten steps. Dennis finally learned to walk unassisted with the crutches. He learned to walk to and from all programs and activities in the hospital within 15 days. The treatment permitted Dennis the dignity of controlling when and where he went.

Researchers have used shaping to develop complex behaviors. They have used it where normal psychiatric or medical procedures had not worked. For instance, researchers have used shaping to teach electively mute psychotics to resume talking. They started by first reinforcing eye contact. They then reinforced nodding in response to questions. Then, they moved to grunting. Finally, they reinforced verbal behavior (Isaacs, Thomas, & Goldiamond, 1960). Others have used similar procedures (e.g., Sherman, 1963).

Behavior analysts have used shaping to teach many of the skills of verbal communication to children with retardation. They have shaped the correct use of plurals (Guess, Sailor, Rutherford, & Baer, 1968). They have shaped the correct use of adjectives (Baer & Guess, 1971). They have shaped the appropriate asking of questions (Twardosz & Baer,

1973). They have used similar procedures in natural settings (Cavallaro & Poulson, 1985). These studies hold promise for teaching children with retardation improved language skills. They may also help us understand normal language acquisition.

A rather unusual example of shaping involves helping individuals with retardation to quit smoking. Ream and Williams (2002) had Chuck exhale into a smoking detection device each day to determine if he had smoked within the previous 24 hours. Chuck usually exhaled into the device for only 5 seconds. However, the device could measure Chuck's recent smoking only if he exhaled for at least 20 seconds. Since Chuck did not have sufficient language skills to understand the necessity for a longer exhale, the researchers shaped his exhales until they were 20 seconds long. The feedback from this measurement helped many individuals quit smoking.

Karen Pryor used shaping to train porpoises to perform many kinds of behavior. Perhaps the most heartwarming is the story of Hou. Pryor helped Hou to develop a much more creative personality. See the box Giving Hou a New Personality for the whole story.

Behavior analysts have also used shaping as a humane way to train animals. In one case, horses had been abused by the previous owner: "all 5 horses had been forced into trailers in the past through whips and ropes." Ferguson and Rosales-Ruiz (2001) used shaping to successfully train these horses to enter a trailer voluntarily.

### Giving Hou a New Personality

Hou was a female porpoise at the Sea Life Park in Hawaii who showed little initiative. Karen Pryor, a veteran porpoise trainer, set out to teach Hou initiative by reinforcing novel tricks. During the first sessions, Pryor did not reinforce Hou's existing tricks. Hou engaged in the highly repetitive tricks of leaping and circling. Pryor broke the pattern by differentially reinforcing successive approximations to the novel trick of "tail walking." That got Hou started. She added a tail slap on her own. She did back flips,

somersaults, figure 9's, and spins. Hou's novel tricks became so complex and rapid that Pryor could not react fast enough. Pryor taught Hou wonderful initiative. (Pryor, Haag, & O'Reilly, 1969)

6. By differentially reinforcing successive approximations to "tail walking," Pryor used what behavioral procedure to teach Hou this novel trick? _____ _____ (differential reinforcement, reinforcement, shaping)

## What Shaping Is Not

Do not apply the term *shaping* to all gradual changes related to a person's behavior. It is not shaping when response rate gradually increases as a result of reinforcement. Nor is it shaping when a person's behavior changes without differential reinforcement. For example, suppose that Mary were to gradually buy more expensive books, yet her actual buying behavior might not change. That is, she might still pick out the book, carry it to the counter, and write a check. Be sure that some physical aspect of the person's behavior changes through a series of approximations.

## Natural Shaping

You can't overestimate the importance of shaping. Shaping is responsible for much complex human behavior. We acquire many of our skills through natural shaping. We are shaped into playing a musical instrument, writing poetry, making a speech, building a house, speaking a foreign language, or pleasing a sweetheart. Virtually everything we do builds on a simple starting behavior. Shaping helps build on that behavior until we have a complex skill. Much of the building occurs through shaping without explicit verbal instruction.

The normal functioning of your environment may produce natural shaping. You might find that a light tap restores the picture on your TV. As the TV gets worse, you may find yourself pounding on it harder and harder. The normal functioning of a failing TV shaped you into beating on it. You might find that a computer is very useful to you. You start by learning the basics of one program. Pretty soon you learn many programs. Eventually, you may learn operating systems, utilities, and even how to program. The advantages of computer use shaped you into acquiring a very complex skill. You might start out jogging a few times a week. Then, you might train for a short race. Pretty soon, you are running marathons. You've been shaped into running farther and harder. No one intentionally shaped any of these behaviors. The normal benefits of aerobic health plus the admiration of others shaped you into a marathon runner. No one intended to shape any of these target behaviors. The normal operation of your physical and social environment shaped your behavior.

People often use shaping without awareness. They often talk about it in nontechnical words. For example, Barry Neal Kaufman and his wife Samahria use words of love to describe their use of shaping. They discovered that their infant son had severe retardation and autism. When the doctors "encouraged institutionalization, we suggested love. When they advised realism, we countered with hope. . . . We turned to God more fervently than ever. . . . We decided to be happy with our son and rather than push him to come to us and conform to our world, we joined him in his. Since

---

### Overcoming Autism through Shaping

Doctors told the Kaufmans that their infant son, Raun, had incurable autism. He lived in an alien world devoid of human contact. The Kaufmans worked with his existing behaviors. When he rocked, they rocked. When he flapped his fingers, they flapped theirs. When he screeched, they treated it like a song and tried to learn it. They report that, "Slowly we reached into the darkness and . . . built bridges of words and affection. . . . By taking thousands of painstakingly tiny steps with him, we taught him how to speak, interact with people and master self-help skills." They worked with him 12 hours a day, seven days a week, for three years. He "blossomed into a highly verbal, extroverted, expressive and loving youngster" with a near-genius I.Q. and graduated from college. (Based on Kaufman, 1991.)

7. Behavior analysts call the "painstakingly tiny steps" successive _____ (approximations, targets) to the target behavior.

we did not judge his autistic behaviors as "bad" or "sick" but saw them as the best he could do for now, we used them as vehicles to communicate acceptance and to teach him about the world" (Kaufman, 1991: pp. 15–16). Read the box on overcoming autism to see what they actually did. See if you don't agree that their miraculous efforts are actually an inspiring example of shaping.

## Misuse of Shaping

Shaping can be misused just like any other behavioral procedure. For example, mothers often shape very obnoxious pestering behaviors in their children. Often a mother will give her sweet young child a cookie just before dinner the first few times that he or she asks. Later, the mother may decide that it isn't such a good idea to do that and will refuse to give the cookie. But the child may persist and pretty soon the mother gives him a cookie to shut him up. At a later time, the mother may again resolve to stop this pattern, whereupon the child may raise his voice and continue nagging, perhaps breaking down the mother's resolve. In such a situation, the mother's natural, unprogrammed response is to differentially reinforce first sweet requests, then persistent requests, then loud and obnoxious requests—each being a successive approximation to some unintended target behavior that might best be described as "brat" behavior.

## Summary

Tactic #4 in using the reinforcement strategy to solve human problems is to create new behavior through shaping. Shaping involves picking a target behavior; selecting successive approximations to the target behavior; and differentially reinforcing those approximations. Researchers have used shaping to help people with many kinds of problems. They helped a normal teenager speak loud enough so others could hear her. They helped a youngster use crutches. They helped many individuals with retardation improve their language skills. Our normal environment may naturally shape many of our skills with no "intentional"

direction. People may unintentionally shape obnoxious behavior. But overall, shaping offers the magic of creating new behavior.

Belief in the "magic" of shaping has made many behavior analysts into radical egalitarians. Some believe that any skill can be taught through shaping. Shaping specific skills requires sound behavioral definitions of the successive approximations. It also requires discovery of effective reinforcers (Skinner, 1948a). We may find someday that everyone has vastly greater potential than we now assume. Perhaps no one need be inferior.

## Behavior Analysis Examples

### *Proper Use of Asthma Therapy Equipment*

Renne and Creer (1976) investigated the possibility of using behavior analysis methods to help young asthmatic children learn how to use inhalation therapy equipment properly. When properly used, the equipment gave the children immediate relief from asthma symptoms. If the children did not use the equipment properly, they frequently required additional medication that relieved their symptoms more slowly, or sometimes they even required hospitalization. Although simple instructions from a nurse usually sufficed to teach the children to use the equipment properly, a small percentage did not learn in this way. This description will focus on one of the children helped by Renne and Creer, whom we shall call David.

Renne and Creer identified three behaviors that were involved in successful use of the equipment: (1) eye fixation, which consisted of looking at the pressure gauge indicating air pressure; (2) facial posture, which consisted of holding the mouthpiece at the right angle and keeping the lips motionless and secured to the mouthpiece; and (3) deep breathing, which consisted of extending the stomach when inhaling and contracting when exhaling.

Prior to teaching David proper eye fixation, Renne and Creer observed him during three baseline trials, each consisting of 15 breaths. They counted the number of breaths during which he looked at the air pressure dial for the full duration of each breath. They found that he looked at the dial during 4, 4, and 3 breaths for these baseline trails. They then explained to him that he could earn tickets that could be applied toward a surprise gift. To earn the first ticket, he had to look at the dial without interruption for the duration of at least 4 breaths—his best baseline score. They then followed the rule that if he surpassed the criterion, they would increase it to his new best score. As you can see from Figure 11-3, he surpassed his best baseline score of 4 by looking at the dial for all 15 breaths. He looked at the dial for all 15 breaths on most subsequent trials.

By the end of the sixth trial, it was clear that eye fixation had been taught. Renne and Creer turned their attention to teaching David correct facial posture. Prior to trial #7, they told him that to earn a ticket he now had to do two things. First, he had to maintain his eye fixation performance; second, he had to at least match his best baseline performance of the correct facial posture. That was easy, because his best baseline performance was that he maintained the correct posture only one breath out of 15. He maintained it 13 out of 15 breaths on the next trial, so they changed the criterion, requiring that he maintain correct facial posture for 13 out of 15 breaths. As you can see, he improved in several trials, to the point where he was maintaining the correct facial posture and eye fixation for virtually every breath.

At the end of the twelfth trial, Renne and Creer told David he could now earn tickets by maintaining his performance on eye fixation and facial posture and by matching his best baseline performance for deep breathing. The figure shows that it was somewhat harder to develop correct deep breathing responses, but there was a notable improvement, to an average of about 13 out of 15 breaths correct.

The social validity of the behavioral definition was obtained in an interesting way for this experiment. When David did not use the equipment properly, he often needed supplementary medication within two hours of the inhalation treatment. In fact, sometimes he would have to be hospitalized as a result. Renne and Creer used the occurrence of such a situation as an indication that under normal, nonexperimental conditions David was using the equipment incorrectly. They found that he used the equipment incorrectly about 60% of the time prior to training but only 20% after training. This

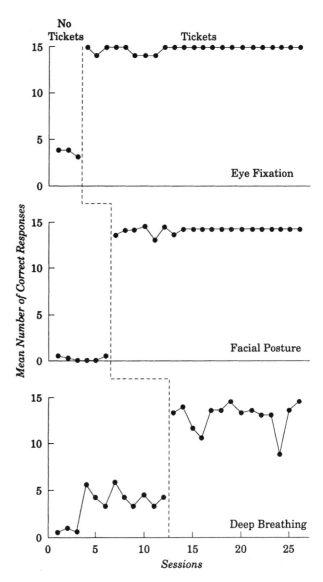

**Figure 11-3.** Training asthmatic children in the correct use of inhalation therapy equipment by training the needed behaviors of correct eye fixation, facial posture, and deep breathing. This figure is based on the average of David and three other children. (Adapted from "Training Children with Asthma to Use Inhalation Therapy Equipment," by C. M. Renne and T. L. Creer, *Journal of Applied Behavior Analysis,* 1976, 9, 1–11. Copyright 1976 by the Society for the Experimental Analysis of Behavior, Inc. Used by permission.)

development suggests that the trained behaviors were those needed to use the equipment properly. The behavior analysts first required proper eye fixation to earn a prize. Then, they required eye fixation and facial posture. Finally, they added deep breathing.

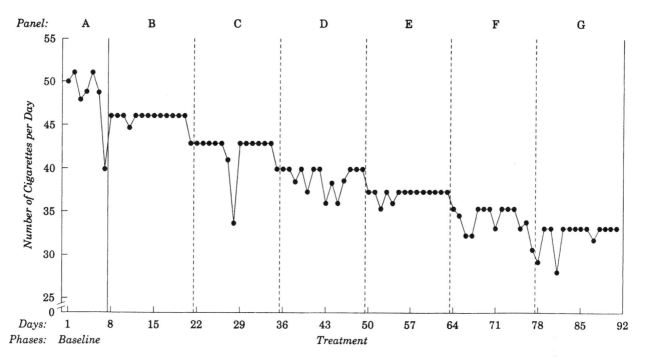

**Figure 11-4.** Number of cigarettes smoked per day in a shaping program designed to reduce smoking. (From "The Changing Criterion Design," by D. P. Hartmann and R. V. Hall, *Journal of Applied Behavior Analysis,* 1976, 9, 527–532. Copyright 1976 by the Society for the Experimental Analysis of Behavior, Inc. Used by permission.)

8. Proper eye fixation is behavior similar to the target behavior of correct use of the equipment. It would be considered an example of a(n) _____ _____ (successive approximation, target behavior).

### *Reducing Cigarette Smoking*

Hartmann and Hall (1976) developed a behavioral procedure to help a heavy smoker, whom we shall call Paul, reduce his rate of smoking. The first step was to determine Paul's initial rate of smoking. His rate averaged 46 cigarettes per day. They then imposed a monetary contingency that paid Paul $0.10 for smoking one less, $0.20 for two less, $0.30 for three less, and so on. In addition, a fine was imposed for smoking more than 46 cigarettes per day. After Paul's rate had held steady at 46 or fewer cigarettes per day, Hartmann and Hall changed the criterion to 43 cigarettes per day and used the same payment schedule. They continued to reduce the criterion through

a series of 21 steps until the rate was under 15 per day. Figure 11-4 shows the gradual decrease in smoking through the first six criteria. Paul's smoking decreased from 46 cigarettes smoked per day to less than 15 per day. The entire course of treatment extended over a period of one year.

9. The procedure of reinforcing successive approximations to smoking under 15 cigarettes per day is called _____ _____ (differential reinforcement, shaping).

## Notes

### *Note #1*

Martin and Pear (1999) suggest several guidelines for effective application of shaping. First, select a target behavior that is as specific as possible and that will be maintained by naturally occurring reinforcers after it has been shaped. Second, select an appropriate reinforcer that is readily available, that can be delivered immediately after the behavior, that can be consumed quickly, and that the person won't tire of rapidly. Third, select an initial behavior that occurs at least once during the observation period and that resembles the target behavior as closely as possible. Fourth, if possible, explain to the person the goals of shaping, move from one approximation to the next after it has been performed correctly 6 out of 10 times, and, if the person has difficulty with a step, reassess your program, because if the program is properly designed you can produce the new behavior.

10. Among the suggested guidelines for shaping are the following: (1) Select as your ultimate goal a target behavior that is as specific as possible, and (2) select an event that can be delivered immediately after the behavior as your _____.

### Note #2

Shaping complex behaviors with many components is sometimes referred to as *chaining* (see Lesson 20) because, for example, teaching a child to walk with crutches involves a number of discrete steps that are joined together into a smoothly functioning unit. This book will not employ this term but rather will conform to general usage and refer to such a procedure as shaping.

11. Teaching a child to walk with crutches involves a number of components that are joined together into a smoothly functioning unit. This book will not refer to such a procedure as *chaining* but rather will conform to general usage and refer to such a procedure as _____.

## Helpful Hints

### Helpful Hint #1

When I give examples of shaping, I will often not explicitly state the extinction component. However, if the example states that a person is reinforced <u>only</u> when she makes a particular response, you should assume that extinction is being applied for all other responses and that, therefore, the procedure is differential reinforcement. It saves many words to present examples in this way, so I will use this wording often. If you fail to realize that when someone only reinforces one behavior, they also extinguish all other behaviors, you will often get the wrong answer!

12. If the teacher reinforces <u>only</u> when the student emits a particular behavior, you can assume that the teacher is using what procedure to increase that behavior and decrease all other behaviors? _____

If an example states that Tom is reinforced when he makes a particular response, you should not assume that all other responses are extinguished. You should make that assumption if the example states that the person is reinforced <u>only</u> for that response. You should not make that assumption otherwise.

13. If a teacher reinforces a person when he makes a particular response, the teacher is using what procedure? _____

### Helpful Hint #2

Many students incorrectly shorten the answer of "target behavior" to "target" by itself. When a question asks you to name the ultimate goal of a shaping procedure, you should answer "target behavior," not "target." Only "target behavior" will be considered a correct response.

14. When a question asks you to name the ultimate goal of a shaping procedure, you should give the full answer of _____.

### Helpful Hint #3

You may shorten the very long answer "successive approximation" to simply "approximation."

15. Remember, you can shorten "successive approximation" to _____.

### Helpful Hint #4

When answering a question asking you to name a procedure described in an example, you may be tempted to answer "successive approximation" when several steps are involved. Do not do so. Successive approximation is an element in the procedure of shaping. It is not itself a procedure. For instance, a teacher may set "correctly counting to 100" as the target behavior. The teacher may set successive approximations of counting to 10, then to 20, and so on, until the student can count to 100. If I ask you to name the procedure, do not name "successive approximation." The best rule is this: Successive approximation is not a procedure. The teacher uses the *procedure of shaping* to reach the target behavior of counting to 100.

16. Remember that successive approximation is not a <u>procedure</u>. It is merely an element in the procedure called _____.

### Helpful Hint #5

Identifying the procedure involved in an example is often quite complex. First, you have to decide if it is a procedure taught in a prior lesson. Second, you must consider whether it resembles a procedure from a prior lesson but is actually unknown. Third, you have to decide whether it is the new procedure being taught in this lesson. Fourth, you must consider whether it is similar to the new procedure but is actually unknown. At first, you will have to consider each of these possibilities rather carefully. While that will take time at first, very soon you will be able to perform the process of elimination almost automatically.

17. Remember, when determining what procedure is involved in an example, do not jump to conclusions and name an old procedure before you have read the whole example. Be sure to consider the possibility that the example is illustrating a(n) _____ (new, old) procedure.

18. For example, suppose the example has a Dad teaching a child to count to 100. The Dad may give the child pennies for correctly counting to 10 but not if she uses an incorrect number or fails to reach 10. When she can count to 10, her Dad may require that she count to 20 and then to 30 and so forth. You should consider both past and new procedures. First, the procedure involves reinforcement with pennies. But

you can rule out simple reinforcement because the procedure also involves extinction by not giving pennies for incorrect numbers. The procedure might be differential reinforcement because it involves both reinforcement and extinction. But the requirement for reinforcement changes from 10 to 20 and so forth. So finally, you realize the procedure involves the differential reinforcement of approximations to counting to 100. The procedure is therefore

_____.

## Additional Readings

Baer, D. M., Peterson, R. F., & Sherman, J. A. (1967). The development of imitation by reinforcing behavior similarity to a model. *Journal of the Experimental Analysis of Behavior, 10,* 405–416. This classic article demonstrates the use of shaping for training children with severe retardation to imitate progressively more complex behaviors demonstrated by others. Such imitation makes it possible for the children to learn new skills by observing the people around them.

Hingtgen, J. N., Sanders, B. J., & DeMeyer, M. K. (1965). Shaping cooperative responses in childhood schizophrenics. In L. Ullman & L. Krasner (Eds.), *Case studies in behavior modification* (pp. 130–183). New York: Holt, Rinehart, and Winston. Six subjects diagnosed as early childhood schizophrenics were taught to engage in cooperative responses through shaping. At first, either of two children was permitted to push a button for coins whenever he or she wanted, then only when the signal light was on, then only when the one member of the pair turned on the signal light for the other. This procedure resulted in a simple cooperative response between the two children.

Isaacs, W., Thomas, J., & Goldiamond, I. (1960). Application of operant conditioning to reinstate verbal behavior in psychotics. *Journal of Speech and Hearing Disorders, 25,* 8–12. This article illustrates the use of shaping procedures to get mute mental patients to begin talking. The patients were reinforced with a stick of gum, first when they moved their lips, then only when they made a noise, and finally only when they imitated a word. As a result, the patients quickly learned to engage in conversation.

Iversen, I. H. (2002). Response-initiated imaging of operant behavior using a digital camera. *Journal of the Experimental Analysis of behavior, 77,* 283–300. This article illustrates in images how response topography successively and systematically changes during shaping.

Keenan, M., & Dillenburger, K. (2000). Images of behavior analysis: The shaping game and the behavioral stream. *Behavior and Social Issues, 10,* 19–38. This article provides some simple classroom exercises and demonstrations on shaping. It also raises issues of discriminative control and the role of private events in the analysis of behavior.

Skinner, B. F. (1948). *Walden Two.* New York: Macmillan. This is a Utopian novel based on the principles of behavior analysis. The novel presents a vision of how people can control their own behavior and develop a more perfect community. The use of shaping to develop new behavioral skills plays a prominent part in the novel.

Wolf, M. M., Risley, T. R., & Mees, H. L. (1964). Application of operant conditioning procedures to the behavior problems of an autistic child. *Behavior Research and Therapy, 1,* 305–312. This paper reports the use of shaping to teach a child with severe autism to wear corrective glasses, thereby permitting him to see. The problem was that the child would not wear the glasses, would not permit anyone to touch him, and would throw the glasses down if handed them. Shaping this response proceeded from picking them up, holding them, carrying them about, and bringing them toward his eyes. Food was used as the reinforcer.

# Programmed Reading

This section includes the following modules: (1) A Procedure for Creating New Behavior, (2) Examples of Shaping, (3) Tactic #4 in the Reinforcement Strategy, and (4) Review.

## 1. A Procedure for Creating New Behavior

33. Pre-test: Shaping has two elements. First, the teacher must specify the ultimate goal, which is called the _____. Second, the teacher must differentially reinforce a series of behaviors similar to the ultimate goal. Those behaviors are called _____ to that target behavior.

35. Pre-test: Shaping involves applying what procedure to a behavior that approximates the target behavior? _____ _____

39. Pre-test: The second element of shaping is that the teacher must differentially reinforce each of a series of behaviors that are progressively more similar to the target behavior. Each behavior in this series is called a(n) _____.

You will learn in this module how to define shaping. Shaping is important because it offers a way to teach new behavior through reinforcement. Shaping can be used even where language can't be used. Shaping involves the technical terms of *differential reinforcement, successive approximations,* and *target response.*

17. From the last lesson, you learned that reinforcing an infant for making a desired sound and ignoring all other sounds is an example of _____.

56. The term *shaping* should be used only when both a target behavior has been specified and differential reinforcement has been applied to a series of successive _____ _____.

59. Use the term *shaping* only when you have differentially reinforced a series of successive approximations and when you have specified a(n) target _____.

54. The term *shaping* has two elements. First, there must be an ultimate goal called the target _____. Second, differential reinforcement must be applied to a series of increasing similar behavior called successive _____ to that target behavior.

64. You may shorten *successive approximation* by omitting *successive.* The second element of shaping is the differential reinforcement

of a series of (omit *successive*) _____ _____ to the target behavior.

49. The first element of shaping is the existence of a new behavior that is the ultimate goal of the shaping program. This new behavior is called the _____. (Be sure to enter both words.)

41. Remember, if the teacher reinforces <u>only</u> Behavior A, you should assume that the teacher is using what procedure for all the other behaviors of that person? _____

44. Suppose the teacher reinforces <u>only</u> Behavior A. Since you can assume that the teacher extinguishes all other behaviors, what procedure is the teacher using to increase the relative rate of the desired behavior? _____

2. A teacher may establish "correctly counting to 100" as the target behavior. The teacher may then establish successive approximations to that goal of counting to 10, then to 20, and so forth until the student can count to 100. If asked what procedure the teacher used, be sure not to answer "successive approximations." Remember that successive approximation is not a <u>procedure</u>! It is merely an element in the procedure called _____.

43. Students often confuse differential reinforcement with shaping. Shaping involves a series of steps during which differential reinforcement is used to increase an approximation. If an example does not involve a series of approximations, then it _____ (can, can't) be shaping.

18. If someone reinforces one approximation and extinguishes all other behavior, then the procedure used is not shaping. Instead, it is _____.

19. If someone reinforces one approximation and extinguishes all other behavior, and then repeats the process with a new approximation, the procedure is _____.

20. If someone reinforces one approximation and extinguishes all other behavior, then the procedure used is _____.

### 2. Examples of Shaping

28. Pre-test: Dr. Jackson differentially reinforced first soft whispers, then louder and louder whispers, in order to teach Maria, a girl with retardation, to talk loudly enough to be heard. What is the name of the procedure in which he differentially reinforced successively louder talking until she "talked loudly enough"? _____

29. Pre-test: Dr. Jackson used shaping to teach Maria to talk loudly enough to be heard by others. Talking loudly enough to be heard by others would be called a(n) _____. (Use both words.)

30. Pre-test: Dr. Jackson selected "barely audible whispering" to start teaching Maria to talk loudly. Such whispering would be called his first _____ to talking loudly enough.

31. Pre-test: Dr. Jackson selected "barely audible whispering" by Maria as his first approximation to talking loudly. What behavioral procedure did he use when he reinforced barely audible whispers and extinguished inaudible whispers? _____

42. Shaping proceeds in a series of steps. First, you apply differential reinforcement to a first approximation to the target behavior. Once the rate of that approximation has increased, you then take a second step. You apply differential reinforcement to a second, closer approximation to the _____. (Use both words of the whole term.)

21. If you wanted to teach someone to shoot a bow and arrow accurately from a distance of 30 feet, you might differentially reinforce her for shooting accurately from 5 feet on the theory that shooting from 5 feet is a first _____ to the target behavior of shooting from 30 feet.

61. When Dr. Mathews selected accepting the insertion of contact lenses as the ultimate goal of his shaping program, he was specifying what is known as his _____ behavior.

5. By differentially reinforcing a series of successive approximations to walking with crutches, Dr. Horner used the behavioral procedure of _____.

9. Dr. Horner developed a procedure to teach Dennis how to walk with crutches. The ultimate goal of having Dennis walking

with crutches would be called Horner's
_____.

10. Dr. Horner first differentially reinforced David for placing the tips of the crutches on two circles on the floor while they were attached to Dennis's hands. This would be called the first _____ to walking with crutches.

51. The procedure of differentially reinforcing approximations to novel behavior in order to teach spontaneity to a dolphin would be termed _____.

24. Many procedures that do not involve the differential reinforcement of approximations to a target behavior produce a gradual change in people's behavior. Therefore, if you are asked to name a procedure that produces a gradual change in a person's behavior, you _____ (can, can't) assume that it is shaping.

53. The term *shaping* can sometimes be applied even if no "teacher" has deliberately established a target behavior. Someone may be unintentionally acting as a teacher. Without planning to do so, or even knowing that they are doing so, they may differentially reinforce successive approximations that will lead to an ultimate behavior. You might call the ultimate behavior an *unintentional* target _____.

6. Can the term *shaping* ever be applied to situations in which no target behavior has been intentionally defined in advance? _____ (yes, no)

48. The everyday world often produces approximations to a target behavior that no individual consciously planned. The differential reinforcement of approximations to such an unintentional target behavior would still be called _____.

3. Beating on a failing TV, acquiring complex computer skills, and becoming a marathon runner may be unintentional target behaviors that _____ (can, can't) be acquired through natural shaping.

50. The Kaufmans helped their son overcome autism by approaching his treatment as a series of painstakingly tiny steps of development. These tiny steps would be called _____.

25. Mom taught Jane the unintended target behavior of loudly and obnoxiously demanding a snack by differentially reinforcing a series of _____ to that behavior.

15. Dr. Renne taught David, an asthmatic child, the correct use of inhalation equipment. He did so by differentially reinforcing approximations to correct use. The correct use of the equipment would be called the _____ _____ in their experiment.

14. Dr. Renne identified three behaviors that could be taught in steps leading up to the goal of proper use of inhalation equipment. Those three behaviors are called _____ _____ to the target behavior.

11. Dr. Renne at first gave David a ticket good for a prize only if he looked at the dial for at least 4 breaths out of 15. David earned a ticket only if he looked at the dial but not if he looked elsewhere. David's rate of looking at the dial increased as a result. This was one step toward the target behavior of correct use of the inhalation equipment. *Shaping* is the name of the overall procedure used on all the steps, but what is the name of the procedure that they used on this step? _____

13. Dr. Renne gave David a prize only if he looked at the dial 4 or more times out of 15. His ultimate target behavior is for David to look at the dial for all 15 breaths, and this requirement would be called a(n) _____ _____ to that ultimate goal.

23. Later, Dr. Renne required David to breathe deeply at least 7 of 15 times (and to also look at the dial and maintain the correct facial posture). This would be a more advanced _____ _____ to using the equipment properly.

60. When David did not use the inhalation therapy equipment correctly, he often required medication or even hospitalization. You might say that the doctors judged whether David had used the equipment properly. The correlation between the researchers' observations based on their behavioral definition of

correct use and the doctors' decision to medicate or hospitalize confirms the _____ (reliability, social validity) of the behavioral definition of correct use of the equipment.

8. Dr. Hartmann helped Paul reduce his rate of smoking from 46 cigarettes per day during baseline to 15 after treatment. In this example, 15 cigarettes per day is called the _____.

16. For the first step, Dr. Hartmann paid Paul only when he smoked less than 46 cigarettes a day. For the second step, Dr. Hartmann paid him only when he smoked less than 43 per day. Dr. Hartmann continued with many additional steps until paying him only when he smoked less than 15 per day. Dr. Hartmann used what overall procedure to get from first to last step? _____

### 3. Tactic #4 in the Reinforcement Strategy

38. Pre-test: The reinforcement strategy to solve human problems is to create new behavior through the procedure called _____.

36. Pre-test: Tactic #4 states that you can use shaping to create _____ behavior.

22. In prior lessons, you learned that the procedure of reinforcement is used to _____ (decrease, increase) desired behavior.

63. You also learned that when you stop reinforcing an undesirable behavior, the behavior decreases. The procedure is called _____.

52. The procedures of reinforcement and extinction can only work on _____ (new, old) behavior.

4. Behavior analysts use shaping to create _____ (new, old) behavior.

45. Tactic #4 in using the reinforcement strategy to solve human problems is to create new behavior by using the behavioral procedure called _____.

### 4. Review

34. Pre-test: Shaping has two elements. First, the teacher must specify the ultimate goal, which is called the _____.

Second, the teacher must differentially reinforce a series of increasingly similar behaviors called _____ to that target behavior.

27. Pre-test: Dad started by surprising Luis with $5 only when he scored over 60% on his English quizzes. Then, he surprised Luis only when he scored over 70%. Eventually, he surprised him only when he scored over 90%. Dad was using the procedure of _____.

32. Pre-test: If the teacher reinforces only when the student emits a particular behavior, you can assume that the teacher is using what procedure to increase that behavior and decrease all other behaviors? _____

26. Pre-test: An approximation is a behavior that is similar to the _____ of a shaping procedure.

40. Pre-test: The shaping process begins with the selection of an ultimate goal called a(n) _____.

37. Pre-test: Tactic #4 in using the reinforcement strategy to solve human problems is to create new behavior through _____.

55. The term *shaping* is used to denote the repeated use with approximations of what behavioral procedure that you have already studied? _____

62. When one behavior is reinforced and all others are extinguished, then another behavior that more closely approximates the target behavior is reinforced while others are extinguished, the overall process is called _____.

12. Dr. Renne defined for David the goal of correct use of inhalation equipment. That goal would be called the _____ of their experiment.

1. A behavior that is similar to a target behavior is called a(n) _____.

57. To use the reinforcement strategy to solve human problems is to (1) increase desirable behavior through reinforcement; (2) decrease undesirable behavior through extinction; (3) increase a desirable behavior relative to undesirable behavior through _____;

(4) create new behavior through _____
_____.

47. The differential reinforcement of successive approximations to a target behavior is called _____.

7. David's looking at the dial 4 out of 15 breaths is called a(n) _____ _____ to looking at it for all 15 breaths.

58. Two conditions that must be met for a situation to involve shaping: (1) The teacher must specify the _____ _____, and (2) the teacher must differentially reinforce a series of _____.

46. Tactic #4 in using the reinforcement strategy to solve human problems is create new behavior through _____ _____.

## Programmed Examples

### 1. Programmed Examples

16. Pre-test: Her new Mom pays close attention to Betty's complaints of illness, BUT Mom ignores other things that Betty says. Betty complains of illness much more since she got her new Mom. What behavioral procedure has her new Mom used to make Betty a hypochondriac? _____

15. Pre-test: Five-year-old John was a loner. He never played with the other children. He preferred to play alone in a far corner of the room. Mr. Smith, John's teacher, decided to get John to play with other children. At first, Mr. Smith attended to John only when he looked toward other children. Next, he attended to him only if he moved toward other children. Finally, he attended to John only if John were actually playing with another child. After a few weeks of this special teacher attention, John was playing with other children. Name the procedure employed by the teacher in modifying John's play behavior: _____.

17. Pre-test: James decided to teach his best friend to do the new disco step, the Twirling Chicken. He always praised her when she did it correctly and said nothing when she did it incorrectly. She started

doing it much better. James's procedure would be an example of _____.

14. Pre-test: At first, Dave swam the 100 in about 75 seconds. His coach praised him only when he swam it in under 75 seconds. Then, his coach praised him only when he swam it in under 70 seconds. Using this same approach, the coach eventually got Dave swimming the 100 in under 50 seconds. What behavioral procedure did his coach use? _____ _____

(Many students have difficulty telling shaping from differential reinforcement. Therefore, in addition to helping you identify the elements of shaping, I will also give examples of shaping. I will give examples of shaping with questions about differential reinforcement. I will give examples of differential reinforcement alone. Look for the differences between shaping and differential reinforcement in the following examples.)

4. Dean taught his son Jason how to play badminton. Jason learned the rules quickly and developed a good stroke. However, he kept hitting the shuttle right to Dean instead of challenging him. To change this, Dean started praising Jason anytime that he hit the shuttle at least one step away from him. The intermediate goal of hitting the shuttle at least one step away from Dean is called the first _____ _____ to the target behavior. By praising Jason only when he hit the shuttle one step away (but not praising him when he didn't), Dean was using what procedure? _____ _____. When Jason was hitting the shuttle one step away, Dean started praising Jason only when he hit the shuttle two steps away from him. Pretty soon Jason was hitting his shots away from Dean as often as possible. The ultimate goal of hitting the shuttle as far away as possible is called the _____ _____. Dean's total procedure is called _____.

2. Charlie Brown wants the little red-headed girl to sit by him. He decided to stop being wishy-washy and to try to get her to sit near him at lunch. At first, each time she looked in his direction, he smiled at her. After a while, he smiled only when she sat within

5 feet of him. Then, he smiled only when she sat within 2 feet of him. Finally, the little red-headed girl sat right next to Charlie Brown at lunch. You should call the behaviors of having her look at him, sit within 5 feet, and sit within 2 feet _____ to his ultimate goal. The ultimate goal of having the little redheaded girl sit next to him would be an example of a(n) _____ _____. Reinforcing her only when she sat within 5 feet is called _____ _____. The behavioral procedure used in this example is called _____ _____.

13. Mr. Baker had taken on the job of teaching Tone Deaf Tony to sing on key. He decided to start by teaching Tony to hum within half a note of middle C. He first played the note on the piano and asked Tony to hum the same note. Mr. Baker praised him when he came within a half tone of middle C. He ignored Tony and simply played the note over again when he missed it. Pretty soon Tony could sing within a half tone of middle C. Mr. Baker used what behavioral procedure? _____

18. Ralph was helping his brother learn to hit a fast-pitched ball. He started by throwing not-so-fast pitches. Each time that Bob got a hit, Ralph gave him a quarter. After many hits, Ralph threw medium-fast pitches and continued to give Bob a quarter after each hit. Finally, Ralph threw fast pitches and still gave Bob a quarter after every hit. Bob learned to hit a fast ball pretty well in the process, but further practice had to be put off, because after 100 hits Bob's pockets were getting heavy and Ralph was running out of quarters. Hitting a fast-pitched ball in this example would be called the _____. Giving Bob a quarter only after he got a hit increased the rate of good swings and decreased the rate of poor swings. Therefore, Ralph was using what behavioral procedure? _____ _____ Hitting medium-fast pitches is a(n) _____ to hitting fast pitches. What procedure did Ralph use to teach his brother to hit a fast pitch? _____

7. Janice's parents wanted her to be more assertive, so they talked with her about it and found that she too wished to be more assertive.

They decided to teach her through role playing to be able firmly to say "No, thank you" if a boy asked her to go to a movie she wasn't interested in. Initially, they praised her if she simply said "No, thank you" even if they could barely hear it. They did not reinforce her if she said nothing or shook her head. Later, they praised her only if she said "No, thank you" firmly. Being able to say "No, thank you" firmly would be called the _____ _____. Simply saying "No, thank you" even if they could barely hear it would be called a(n) _____ _____ to saying it firmly. What procedure did Janice's parents use by praising her only when she first whispered "No, thank you" and later firmly said "No, thank you"?_____ _____

19. Tad wanted to take up jogging. He decided to slowly build up to running a mile a day in under 6 minutes. He set as his goal during the first week to run the mile under 12 minutes. When he made it, he bought himself a Super Sundae. The next week he tried to run it under 11 minutes and again rewarded himself when he made it. Each week he lowered his goal until he was running the mile under 6 minutes. Tad's first goal of running the mile in under 12 minutes would be termed a(n) _____ _____ to running it in under 6 minutes. What behavioral procedure was Tad using to get in condition to run the mile in under 6 minutes? _____ _____

6. His mother told Sammy to take out the garbage every night, and he did so. When he was 12, she stopped telling him to take out the garbage, and he quit doing it. What behavioral procedure did she inadvertently employ to reduce his rate of taking out the garbage? _____

9. John lived in a coed living group with eight other people. He complained to Mary about how his teachers treated him. Mary agreed that they treated him unfairly. She listened with endless patience to his complaints. John complained more and more often. What behavioral procedure is Mary using? _____

10. Kerr went to the New West Freedom Preschool, where he was the brat of the

school. He yelled, he broke things, he pushed into line, he spilled paint, he even wet his pants. The staff had a meeting and decided that instead of paying attention to him as they had done, they would henceforth ignore Kerr's brat behavior. Unfortunately, he kept doing it. What behavioral procedure did they use? _____

3. Clarence is a skilled carpenter. One day he was reminiscing about how he had learned to hammer in a 16-penny nail with one thump. At first, his father had praised him only when he hit the nail with each tiny tap—making many taps to drive the nail in. His father had then praised him only when he drove it in with several rough raps. Finally, his father had praised him only when he drove it in with one thunderous thump. What behavioral procedure was his father using? _____

20. Yancey wanted Fran to smile more often. So every time that she smiled, he told her how good she looked. Fran didn't smile any more often even after a month of compliments. What behavioral procedure was Yancey using? _____

1. Bobby was a pretty good chess player who liked to win. When he played with Dan, he won most of the time, and as a result, he started playing with Dan more often. But when he played with Shelly, he lost most of the time even when he made the same moves! As a result, he almost completely stopped playing with Shelly. What behavioral procedure

accounts for Bobby playing more with Dan and less with Shelly (remember to check the elements)? _____

11. Marie helped Fred learn to not get angry over a minor annoyance. She taught him to count to 10 if an annoying event occurred. She continued to praise him whenever he counted to 10 during annoyances until he was doing it all the time. Next, she would praise him only when he counted to 20, which he soon mastered. In this way, she finally got him to count to 100, at which time he was no longer angry. What is the goal of getting Fred to count to 100 called? _____

8. Jean wanted Sam to help more often so she wouldn't have to do all the work. Every time that he helped, she made sure to get him a cold beer immediately. As a result, he started helping more often. What procedure did she use? _____

2. Mary wanted to teach John how to do really good, fast dancing. She decided to start by teaching him some very slow steps. Slow dancing would be a(n) _____ to fast dancing.

5. Frank was a pretty inattentive boyfriend. Finally, Marsha told him to start opening doors for her. From then on, he always opened the door for Marsha. What behavioral procedure did Marsha employ? _____

# LESSON 12

# Reinforcer Effectiveness

## Reading Section

Reinforcers are events that cause an increase in the rate of a behavior that they follow. You already know that an event that is a reinforcer for one person may not be a reinforcer for another person. You will learn in this lesson that the same event may be a reinforcer when it is delivered in one way but not in another. Behavior analysts have learned quite a lot about how to make reinforcers effective. I will consider an event effective when it <u>increases</u> the rate of the behavior.

There are four main factors that cause events to be more effective, rather than less. You must deliver an event <u>contingent</u> on the behavior. That means delivering it only when the desired behavior occurs. You must deliver it <u>immediately</u> after the behavior has occurred. You must ensure that the <u>size</u> (or amount) of the event is worthwhile. You must ensure that the person is <u>deprived</u> of the event. That means you use a reinforcer that the person hasn't had too much of.

Tactic #5 in using the reinforcement strategy to solve human problems is to use the principles of <u>reinforcer effectiveness</u>.

1. Tactic #5 in using the reinforcement strategy to solve human problems is to use the principles of _____ effectiveness.

## The Effect of Contingency on Effectiveness

The first factor in effectiveness is *contingency*. Let's define the **principle of contingency**: The more consistently the reinforcer is delivered <u>only</u> for the desired behavior, the more effective the reinforcer. You must never deliver a reinforcer for an undesired behavior. Consider why this is so. Suppose you repeatedly deliver the event for an undesired behavior. The rate of that behavior will increase, which will decrease the time available for the desired behavior. In fact, it may totally crowd out the desired behavior. You may reinforce undesired behaviors when you deliver events sloppily. Stealing an object is a classic example of an undesired behavior. If you permit a person to steal something, why would they work for it? Figure 12-1 suggests that stealing is a very attractive option.

2. The principle of contingency states that you must deliver the event _____ when a desired behavior occurs.

Notice that the principle of contingency does not state that you are restricted to delivering the reinforcer for only <u>one</u> desired behavior. Most of the time, a reinforcer will be delivered for only one desired behavior at a time. However, you can deliver the reinforcer for several desired behaviors. You cannot, however, repeatedly deliver it for even one undesired behavior. To do so would undermine the effect of the reinforcer on the desired behaviors. Thus, you will see examples in which the reinforcer is delivered for several desired behaviors.

You would still be observing the principle of contingency if you deliver the reinforcer for more than one desired behavior. You could give your brother chocolate-covered raisins for vacuuming your room, for playing nicely with his toys, and for just being a sweet kid. You just have to ensure that he can't get them without doing the behaviors that you desire.

**Figure 12-1.** This man may have tried to steal money rather than working for it. Reinforcers like money will be effective only to the extent that their delivery is contingent on desired behaviors like work. (Source: Richard Hutchings/Photo Researchers)

You must ensure that he can't steal them, lie about his behaviors, or otherwise "trick" you into giving him the candy.

Consider an everyday example. Suppose you ask Sam, your little brother, to vacuum your room while you are at a dance. You might come home, glance at the room, and conclude that he has vacuumed it. You might give him a box of chocolate-covered raisins, his favorite candy, as thanks. But perhaps your quick glance didn't evaluate his job very well. He might have picked up your room without vacuuming it. Clearly your gift would teach him the wrong lesson. He would learn that you are satisfied with a partial job. Your gift certainly would not be very effective in increasing his rate of vacuuming. Thus, the principle of contingency warns you to take care that you deliver the event only when the desired behavior occurs. You must

be sure not to deliver it for undesirable responses like stealing, lying, or doing only part of the job.

Behavior analysts are careful to deliver reinforcers only when desired behavior occurs (e.g., Bourgeois, 1990). They know that if they deliver reinforcers whether or not the behavior occurs, the behavior <u>decreases</u>.

Behavior analysts can sometimes use the principle of contingency to understand behavioral problems (e.g., Borreo, Vollmer, & Wright, 2002). One team of researchers examined the case of Brenda (Vollmer, Iwata, Zarcone, Smith, & Mazeleski, 1993). Brenda was a 42-year-old woman with profound retardation who often deliberately banged her head very hard. The researchers found that aides usually paid no attention to her except when she banged her head. Anytime she banged her head, the aides would tell her she would hurt herself. Without realizing it, the aides were attending to Brenda <u>only</u> when she banged her head. This attention was an effective reinforcer because it was <u>contingent</u> on Brenda banging her head.

The researchers were able to use the principle of contingency in reverse to solve the problem. They instructed each aide to give Brenda attention as often as possible. They continued to express their concern about hurting herself when she banged her head. However, they often attended to her when she wasn't banging her head. Her rate of head banging decreased from one every second to almost none at all! This shows how much noncontingent reinforcement can weaken the effect of a reinforcer based on lack of contingency. Initially, the undesired behavior increased when attention paid to the client was contingent on that very behavior— the attention responded to and effectively reinforced a negative behavior. However, the undesired behavior decreased when the attention was not contingent on head banging. In many cases, you will be seeking to increase a desired behavior rather than decrease a negative one (as in this example). You will be more successful if you are contingent with your reinforcement.

To decide whether the principle of contingency was followed in a specific case, ask, "Was the event given <u>only</u> for a desired behavior?"

3. To decide whether the principle of contingency was followed in a specific case, ask, "Was the event given _____ for a desired behavior?"

## The Effect of Immediacy on Effectiveness

The second factor in effectiveness is *immediacy*. Immediacy is a very powerful determinant of an event's effectiveness. Here's how we define the **principle of immediacy**: The more immediate the delivery of the reinforcer after the behavior, the more effective the reinforcer. That is, the faster you deliver it, the stronger the effect. Remember that you wanted to shape Ann into saying "Dada." Your praise would be most effective if you gave it the instant she first said "da." In fact, you would be most successful with each successive approximation if you reinforced it immediately.

4. The **principle of immediacy**: The more _____ the delivery of the reinforcer after the behavior, the more effective.

Consider an everyday example. You want to get Sam to vacuum your room. Suppose, miracle of miracles, he did vacuum your room. You should reinforce his vacuuming immediately after he does it to have the greatest effect. For the greatest effect, give Sam his chocolate-covered raisins just as he is finishing the job. If you wait until you get home from the dance, or maybe even until tomorrow, the gift will have less effect. In general, the event should be delivered as soon after the behavior as possible. Delivering it within seconds is the most effective timing. (I will describe two exceptions to this principle in a moment.)

Behavior analysts usually are very careful to give reinforcers immediately. For example, one researcher sought to help Alzheimer's patients to engage in meaningful conversations (Bourgeois, 1990). You may remember that she gave them a picture book to help them remember important topics. She taught husbands to immediately praise their wives when they talked about the pictures. The number of on-topic statements for one patient increased from a few per day to about 45. Immediacy is a powerful factor in reinforcer effectiveness.

Behavior analysts have found two exceptions to the principle of immediacy. The first exception is that a delayed reinforcer can be effective if you immediately signal the later reinforcement (see Stromer, McComas, & Rehfeldt, 2000). (In fact, this is not a true exception because the signal itself becomes a reinforcer. I will describe this procedure in a later lesson.) The second exception is that a delayed reinforcer can be effective if the person can describe the relation between behavior and delayed reinforcer (e.g., Bryne, McNulty, Babcock, Connors, et al., 2000). For example, employers give you your paycheck many days and even weeks after you put in your work. Yet you continue to work, even with this delay. Clearly, you can describe the relation between work and pay. If I asked you what the relation was, you would say, "No work, no pay!" For the rest of the book, do not assume that the characters in an example can describe a relation unless the example clearly states they can. If the example does not state the relation, then assume that the principle of immediacy holds true.

To decide whether the principle of immediacy was followed, ask, "Was the event delivered within a minute of the behavior (or while the behavior was still occurring)?" This rule will hold true unless the recipient can describe the relation between their behavior and a delayed reinforcer.

5. To decide whether the principle of immediacy was followed, ask, "Was the event delivered within a _____ of the behavior (or while the behavior was still occurring)?"

## The Effect of Size on Effectiveness

The third factor in effectiveness is *size*. The amount of the event is an important determinant of the event's effectiveness. According to the **principle of size**: The more worthwhile the amount of a reinforcer, the more effective the reinforcer. That is, the more you deliver at one time, the more effect it will have. Your goal is to deliver just enough of the event to be effective. You don't want to give so much that the person never has to emit the desired behavior again. This optimum amount will vary depending on such factors as the difficulty of the behavior, the amount of behavior required, and competing opportunities for reinforcement.

6. The **principle of size**: The more worthwhile the _____ of a reinforcer, the more effective the reinforcer.

Consider an everyday example. If Sam vacuumed your room, one chocolate-covered raisin probably wouldn't be effective. Maybe even a handful wouldn't be enough. But a small box of the candy might be. To decide just how many raisins might be effective, you need to decide what amount would be worthwhile. This will depend on how hard it is for him to operate the vacuum, how long it takes, and whether Mom just offered him a slice of chocolate cake. In any event, this principle is based on the fact that the more of an event that you deliver, the more effective it will be.

Behavior analysts have found that the amount of reinforcement is very important in helping people. For example, one study examined chronic smokers (Stitzer & Bigelow, 1984). I will call the average smoker among them "Fred." The researchers found that the more they paid Fred, the more he reduced his smoking. During baseline, Fred smoked about 12 cigarettes a day. When they paid Fred $1.50 for reducing his smoking, he smoked about 10 cigarettes. When they paid him $12, he smoked only about 5 cigarettes. Another researcher tried to help mental patients keep their teeth clean (Fisher, 1979). He found that about 60% of the patients brushed their teeth during baseline. When he gave them one reinforcer for brushing their teeth, the percentage increased to 76%. When he gave them five reinforcers, the percentage increased to 91%. The amount of reinforcement is clearly an important factor in effectiveness.

To decide whether the principle of size was followed, ask, "Was the amount of the event used <u>worthwhile</u>?"

7. To decide whether the principle of size was followed, ask, "Was the amount of the event used _____?"

## The Effect of Deprivation on Effectiveness

The final principle involves the opposite terms *deprivation* and *satiation*. **Deprivation** is the <u>frequency</u> with which the person has received a particular reinforcer in the recent past. A person is more deprived the less often they have received the event. If you have not had ice cream for a month, you are more deprived of it than if you have had it recently. **Satiation** is the <u>opposite</u> of deprivation. If you have just had a quart of ice cream, you are more satiated on ice cream than if you had not had it for a month.

8. **Deprivation** refers to the _____ with which a person has received a reinforcer in the recent past. **Satiation** refers to the _____ of deprivation.

The state of deprivation of the person with respect to a particular event is a powerful determinant of the event's effectiveness. Thus, we get the **principle of deprivation**: The more <u>deprived</u> the person, the more effective the reinforcer.

9. The **principle of deprivation**: The more _____ the person is of a reinforcer, the more effective the reinforcer.

This principle plays an important role in everyday behaviors. For example, suppose that Sam has not had any chocolate-covered raisins for a week. The raisins will be more effective than if he just had a box of them half an hour ago. Two researchers found such an effect with young children (Gewirtz & Baer, 1958). They reinforced with praise children's performance of a simple task. They deprived some children of attention by not interacting with them before the experiment. Those children responded faster. The researchers concluded that even this short deprivation increased the effectiveness of the praise. In a second study, they satiated some children with attention by interacting with them before the experiment (Gewirtz & Baer, 1958). Those children responded more slowly. The researchers concluded that even this small amount of satiation decreased the effectiveness of the praise. You should carefully examine the level of deprivation for any event you hope to use as a reinforcer.

Behavior analysts make careful use of satiation and deprivation. For example, one researcher used satiation to reduce a man's hallucinations (Glaister, 1985). The man was a chronic mental patient who frequently hallucinated voices. The researcher urged the patient to sit quietly and listen to them. He instructed the patient to record what the voices said, how long he heard them, and so on. After 16 months, the patient was sick of hearing the voices. He stopped hearing them! The researcher suggested that by listening to the voices, the patient satiated on them.

A team of researchers studied the effects of satiation and deprivation on Rich, a man with severe retardation (Vollmer & Iwata, 1991). Rich liked to listen to music. To create satiation, they played taped music for him while he sat for 30 minutes in a waiting room. To create deprivation, they played no music while he sat for 30 minutes in the waiting room. After the 30 minutes, the researchers asked Rich to do a simple task. Every time that he made six responses they played taped music for four seconds. If he responded fast enough, he could hear music continuously. He made 10 responses per minute when he was deprived. He made only about 2 per minute when he was satiated. Thus, he responded much faster when deprived than when satiated on music. The researchers found similar results for investigations of food and social reinforcers.

To decide whether the principle of deprivation was followed, ask, "Has the reinforcer rarely been delivered?"

10.   To decide whether the principle of deprivation was followed, ask, "Has the reinforcer _____ been delivered?"

## Comparison of the Four Principles

You might easily confuse the principle of immediacy and the principle of contingency. If you deliver an event immediately after the desired behavior occurs and only after it occurs, you have used both principles. However, you can deliver the event so that you use only one of the principles. For example, suppose that you deliver the event within a minute after a behavior, but it is undesirable behavior. You will have used the principle of immediacy but not the principle of contingency. Your reinforcement won't increase the desired behavior. Likewise, suppose you deliver the event for the desired behavior, but long after it occurs. You will have used the principle of contingency but not the principle of immediacy. Your reinforcement probably won't increase the desired behavior.

You might also easily confuse the principle of size and the principle of deprivation. If you deliver a worthwhile amount of the event to someone who hasn't had any recently, you have used both principles. However, you can deliver the event so that you use only one of the principles. For example, suppose you deliver a worthwhile amount to someone who recently had lots of the event. You will have used the principle of size but not the principle of deprivation. Your reinforcement probably won't work. Likewise, you might rarely deliver the event to someone, but in too small an amount. You will have used the principle of deprivation but not the principle of size. Again, your reinforcement probably won't work.

The principle of size refers to whether the amount of the reinforcer on any <u>one</u> given delivery is large enough to be worthwhile. The principle of deprivation refers to whether the reinforcer has rarely been delivered so the person has not had too much of the reinforcer. Thus, the distinction is between the amount of a single delivery and the timing of deliveries.

These four principles can make the difference between success and failure. You can fail if you don't deliver reinforcers contingently and immediately. You can also fail if you use too little reinforcement or give the other person something they already have too much of. All four factors are important tools for improving the effectiveness of a reinforcer.

You should take several other factors into account when selecting reinforcers. For example, the reinforcers should be convenient to dispense, inexpensive, and not simultaneously available from another source. In addition, they should not generate behaviors that are incompatible with the behavior that is being reinforced. For example, you shouldn't give gum for saying words clearly.

# Summary

Tactic #5 in using the reinforcement strategy to solve human problems is to use the principles of reinforcer effectiveness. Reinforcers can have powerful effects on our behavior. Their effectiveness depends on four factors: the more contingent, immediate, large, and rare the reinforcement, the more effective. Whenever your use of a reinforcer is not effective, you may find that you failed to use one or more of the principles of reinforcer effectiveness.

# Behavior Analysis Examples

Basic research with animals discovered the importance of the four principles of reinforcer effectiveness. In research using human subjects, the complexity of applied situations often obscures their importance. However, I have been able to find the following examples in applied behavior analysis to give you an idea of their practical value.

### Teaching Handwriting

Researchers taught kindergarten children beginning handwriting. They developed a set of materials for the children to use. However, the children made only about 50% correct responses during baseline observation. The investigators decided to give the children tokens good for a variety of fun activities. They first tried giving them tokens at the beginning of the session with no respect to accuracy of work. The children's accuracy decreased to around 40% correct. When they gave the tokens to the children only for accurate responses; the children's accuracy increased until it was over 60%. Thus, when tokens were given regardless of accuracy, the accuracy decreased below baseline. When they were given only for accurate responses, accuracy increased. (Based on Brigham, Finfrock, Bruenig, & Bushell, 1972.)

11. Giving tokens only for accurate responses is following the principle of _____ (contingency, deprivation, immediacy, size).

### Wearing an Orthodontic Device

Researchers consulted with the mother of an 8-year-old boy who needed a removable orthodontic device to straighten his teeth. Despite spending about $3,000 with four dentists over a period of eight years, Jerry's teeth were not any better because Jerry did not remember to wear the device. Observations during baseline indicated that he was wearing it during only 25% of the five times that he was checked each day.

Hall and his colleagues suggested that the mother give Jerry a quarter for each time he was wearing the device during those five checks. A record was kept of the money owed, which was to be paid at the end of the month. This procedure increased the rate of wearing the device to about 60%. The rate increased to nearly 100% when Jerry was given the money immediately after any check during which he was wearing it. Thus, you can see that when money was given at the end of the month, the rate was better than baseline but not nearly as good as when the money was given as soon as the desired behavior was observed. Eight months after the study was initiated, the dentist indicated that there had been great progress in Jerry's mouth structure. (Based on Hall, Axelrod, Tyler, Grief, Jones, & Robertson, 1972.)

12. Immediate payment for wearing an orthodontic device is an example of the principle of _____ (contingency, deprivation, immediacy, size).

### Towel Hoarding

A patient whom we will call Doris had been a resident in a mental hospital for nine years. One of her behaviors was particularly bothersome to the staff: she hoarded towels. This required the staff to enter her room twice a week and remove some of the towels, which were needed for the rest of the hospital. During a period of baseline observation lasting seven weeks, researchers observed that the patient had about 25 towels in her room even though they were continually removed.

In an attempt to solve the problem, Doris was given all the towels she wanted. Within four weeks, she was keeping more than 600 towels in her room. At first she patted the towels, folded, and stacked them.

During the first week of this treatment, when the nurses brought her some towels, she said, "Oh, you found it for me, thank you." The second week, she said, "Don't give me no more towels. I've got enough." The third week, she said, "Take them towels away . . . I can't sit here all night and fold towels." The fourth week, she said, "Get these dirty towels out of here." The sixth week, she had started to remove the towels from her room herself, and she told the nurse, "I can't drag any more of these towels, I just can't do it." Within the 16 weeks, Doris had removed all the towels from her room and no longer kept them. This observation was followed for more than a year, during which time the towel hoarding never reappeared.

The nurses had felt that hoarding towels reflected a deep-seated need for love and security and guessed that this approach would not work because it did not treat that underlying need. Not only did it work, but no other problems were observed to develop that might have replaced hoarding. This example deliberately violates a principle of effectiveness in order to reduce the effectiveness of towels as reinforcers. They reduced the effectiveness of towels as reinforcers for hoarding behavior by not giving them <u>rarely</u> but rather by giving them freely. (Based on Ayllon, 1963.)

13. Giving Doris as many towels as she wanted is an example of violating the principle of _____ (contingency, deprivation, immediacy, size).

## Notes

### Note #1
Jack Michael (1982) has proposed the term *establishing operations* to label a broad range of events that increase reinforcer effectiveness. Michael defines *establishing operation* in part as any operation that increases (or establishes) the effectiveness of an event as a reinforcer. Thus, the operation of depriving someone of an event may establish it as an effective reinforcer. As you learned in this lesson, food is more effective as a reinforcer if access to it has been restricted. Bar owners engage in a different kind of establishing operation when they supply their customers with lots of salty nuts and pretzels. This makes the customers thirsty and may establish beer as an effective reinforcer. Business owners engage in yet another type of establishing operation when they advertise to establish their goods as reinforcers.

## Helpful Hints

### Helpful Hint #1
When asked a question about which principle is involved when a reinforcer is given frequently, you may be tempted to answer "satiation." That would be wrong. The name of the principle is the principle of deprivation. However, if a person has recently received a lot of a reinforcer, we say that the person is satiated with that reinforcer.

14. So remember, the name of the principle concerned with how frequently a reinforcer has been given is not satiation. Rather it is called the principle of _____.

### Helpful Hint #2
I have given you a major hint in this lesson. If I want you to consider the principles of contingency, immediacy, size, and deprivation, I ask you, "What <u>principle</u> is involved?" If I want you to consider the procedures of reinforcement, extinction, differential reinforcement, or shaping, I ask you, "What <u>procedure</u> is involved?" Remember, when I ask you, "What principle is involved?" don't even think about the procedures you have learned in prior lessons.

15. When answering questions that ask you to name a <u>principle</u> of reinforcer effectiveness, remember to think in terms of the principles of _____, _____, _____, and _____.

16. When asked to name a behavioral <u>procedure</u> that is involved, do not select from the list of <u>principles</u> of effectiveness. Rather, think in terms of the procedures learned in prior lessons that increase or decrease behaviors: _____, _____, _____, and _____.

### *Helpful Hint #3*

Judging whether the size of a reinforcer is worthwhile can be very difficult. I will give you clues in the examples. The clues will be whether the person receiving the reinforcer acts as though they "like" it. This might be an expression of wanting or liking it. It might be simply that it works to maintain their behavior. It might be that they were thrilled with it. Look for these clues to judge whether a reinforcer is worthwhile.

17. If an example states (or implies) that the person liked the reinforcer, you can conclude that the principle of size has been used and that the amount of the reinforcer is _____.

### *Helpful Hint #4*

Later in this lesson, I will give you many examples of people using reinforcers. I will ask you what principles of reinforcer effectiveness, if any, are being violated. If you find any being violated, you should write the name of those principles in the blank. If none are being violated, you should enter "none" in the blank. I will mix in some questions asking what procedure from prior lessons is involved, some of which may have the answer "unknown." Many students end up getting confused between "none" and "unknown."

18. Remember, if a procedure is not one that you have already learned, then you should answer _____. If an example violates no principle of reinforcer effectiveness, then you should answer _____.

## Additional Readings

Iwata, B. A., Smith, R. J., & Michael, J. (2000). Establishing operations in applied behavior analysis [Special issue]. *Journal of Applied Behavior Analysis, 33*, 401–651. Establishing operations are procedures that increase the strength of a reinforcer. Deprivation is one example of such a procedure. This issue defines and gives examples of many additional types of establishing operations. It also describes empirical investigations of the use of establishing operations in applied behavior analysis.

Ayllon, T., & Michael, J. (1959). The psychiatric nurse as a behavioral engineer. *Journal of the Experimental Analysis of Behavior, 2*, 323–334. Several mental patients who hoarded magazines were treated through satiation by giving them as a many as they would accept. Within a few weeks, they were no longer hoarding magazines.

Olson, R., Laraway, S., & Austin, S. (2001). Unconditioned and conditioned establishing operations in organizational behavior management. *Journal of Organizational Behavior Management, 21*(2), 7–36. This article analyzes workplace motivation in the field of organizational behavior management in terms of establishing operations. Specifically, it addresses the nature of establishing operations and how such operations could be applied to shape and maintain effective workplace behaviors.

Schroeder, S. R. (1972). Parametric effects of reinforcement frequency, amount of reinforcement, and required response force on sheltered workshop behavior. *Journal of Applied Behavior Analysis, 5*, 431–441. This article reports a study in which the amount of money paid to people with retardation for a job was increased. Unlike the expected finding that they would work harder for the larger amount, they actually worked less. No satisfactory explanation was offered for this contradictory finding.

Schwartz, M. L., & Hawkins, R. P. (1970). Application of delayed reinforcement procedures to the behaviors of an elementary school child. *Journal of Applied Behavior Analysis, 3*, 85–96. This article reports the use of delayed feedback to teach a 12-year-old girl to use more socially acceptable behavior. The authors taught her to stop slouching and picking at her face and to start talking loudly enough to be heard. They showed her videotape records of her behaviors in class five hours later. In spite of the lack of immediacy, they were very effective at improving her behaviors. In addition, her self-image soared as a result. The delayed consequences may have worked in this case because of the powerful impact of videotaping.

Sulzer, B., & Mayer, G. R. (1972). *Behavior modification procedure for school personnel*. Hinsdale, IL.: Dryden Press. This book contains many practical tips for teachers wishing to use behavior modification procedures. Chapter 2, "Reinforcement," reviews some of the principles covered in this lesson.

## Programmed Reading

I will help you practice applying your reading about the principles of reinforcer effectiveness in the following sections: (1) The Principle of Contingency, (2) The Principle of Immediacy, (3) The Principle of Size, (4) The Principle of Deprivation, (5) Telling the Principles Apart, (6) Tactic #5 in the Reinforcement Strategy, and (7) Review.

### 1. The Principle of Contingency

35. Pre-test: Of which principle do you ask, "Was the reinforcer given only if a desired behavior occurred?" The principle of _____ _____.

38. Pre-test: The principle of contingency states that the more consistently the reinforcer is delivered _____ for the desired behavior, the more effective the reinforcer.

63. The first principle of reinforcer effectiveness is the principle of contingency. Saying that there is a contingency between the particular Reinforcer A and the particular Behavior A means that Reinforcer A will be delivered <u>only</u> if Behavior A occurs. You might guess that the principle of contingency is the general rule that the reinforcer is delivered to the person _____ if they emit the desired behavior.

83. What principle states that the reinforcer must be delivered to people <u>only</u> if they emit a desired behavior? The principle of _____ (contingency, deprivation, immediacy, size).

68. The principle of contingency states that the reinforcer will be more effective, the more consistently it is delivered _____ _____ for the desired behavior.

69. The principle of contingency states that the effectiveness of an event will be maximized if it is delivered when a desired behavior occurs and it _____ (is, isn't) delivered when an alternative behavior occurs.

56. Suppose you give chocolate-covered raisins to Sam because you think, based on only a quick glance, that he did a good job of vacuuming your room. What principle of effective reinforcement may you have neglected? _____

7. Behavior analysts observe that if people don't have to perform the behavior to get the reinforcer, they won't. Therefore, behavior analysts have concluded that if a reinforcer is delivered whether or not the behavior actually occurs, the behavior _____ (decreases, increases) in rate.

8. Brenda, an adult with retardation, banged her head because she only received attention when she did so. The attention was a(n) _____ for banging her head.

59. The aides used to give Brenda attention <u>only</u> when she banged her head. Then, they started giving Brenda attention at other times as well. Her head banging decreased. This is an example of deliberately violating the principle of _____ to weaken attention as a reinforcer for head banging.

66. The important message of the principle of contingency is that you should never give the reinforcer for an undesired behaviors. Does the principle of contingency imply that you are restricted to delivering a particular event for only one desired behavior? _____ (yes, no)

25. Of which principle do you ask, "Was the reinforcer given only if a desired behavior occurred?" The principle of _____ _____.

78. To determine whether the principle of contingency is being used, ask, "Was the reinforcer given _____ if a desired behavior occurred?"

### 2. The Principle of Immediacy

28. Pre-test: Ask the question, "Was the reinforcer delivered within one minute of the behavior (or while the behavior was still

occurring)?" to determine whether the principle of _____ was used.

47. Pre-test: To determine whether the principle of immediacy was used, ask, "Was the reinforcer delivered within one _____ _____ of the behavior (or while it was still occurring)?"

72. The second principle of reinforcer effectiveness is the principle of immediacy. You can easily guess it states that the more _____ (delayed, immediate) the delivery of a reinforcer, the more effective that reinforcer will be.

1. According to the principle of immediacy, a reinforcer should be delivered as _____(quickly, slowly) after the behavior as possible (or even during the behavior).

18. Fred immediately praised Wanda, his wife who has Alzheimer's, when she talked about pictures in a book designed to help her remember important topics. This treatment caused a(n) _____ in the number of on-topic statements made by his wife.

26. One exception to the principle of immediacy is that a delayed reinforcer can be effective if you immediately signal that there will be a delayed _____ _____.

3. Another exception to the principle of immediacy is that a delayed reinforcer can be effective if the person is able to describe the relation between their _____ and the delayed reinforcer.

5. Ask the question, "Was the reinforcer delivered within one minute of the behavior (or while the behavior was still occurring)?" to determine whether the principle of _____ was used.

79. To determine whether the principle of immediacy was used, ask, "Was the reinforcer delivered within one _____ _____ of the behavior (or while it was still occurring)?"

22. If an event is delivered to a person while he or she is performing a behavior (in other words, after he or she started performing it), the principle of immediacy _____ _____ (would, wouldn't) be followed.

### 3. The Principle of Size

50. Pre-test: You ask, "Was the amount of the reinforcement used worthwhile" to detect the principle of _____ _____.

45. Pre-test: To decide whether the principle of size was followed, ask, "Was the amount of the reinforcement used _____ _____?"

73. The third principle of reinforcer effectiveness is the principle of size. If you give a worthwhile amount of the reinforcer, you are using the principle of _____ _____.

19. How much of the reinforcer should you give to be effective? You should give a worthwhile amount according to the principle of _____.

20. How much of the reinforcer should you give to be effective? According to the principle of size, you should give a(n) _____ _____ (minimal, reasonable, worthwhile) amount.

87. You ask, "Was the amount of the reinforcement used worthwhile" to detect the principle of _____ _____.

75. To decide whether the principle of size was followed, ask, "Was the amount of the reinforcement used _____ _____?"

80. To help you decide whether the amount of a reinforcer is "worthwhile," examples will give clues about whether the person _____ (disliked, liked) it.

24. If the person liked the reinforcer, then you can conclude it was a _____ amount.

17. Every time that Jan argued with him, Jim smiled at her. She liked those smiles. Can you conclude that Jim is using the principle of size? _____ (yes, no)

54. Researchers paid Fred, a chronic smoker, for not smoking. When they paid him only $1.50 for reducing smoking, he didn't change much. When they paid him $12.00, he reduced by more than half. Was $1.50 a worthwhile amount to endure the agony of reducing smoking? _____ (yes, no) Clearly, that amount violates the principle of size. Was $12.00 a worthwhile amount to endure the agony

of reducing smoking? _____ (yes, no) Clearly, that amount follows the principle of size.

### 4. The Principle of Deprivation

43. Pre-test: The principle stating that the more deprived a person is of the reinforcer, the more effective it will be, is called the principle of _____.

37. Pre-test: The principle of deprivation states that the more _____ a person is of the reinforcer, the more effective it will be.

46. Pre-test: To determine whether the principle of deprivation was followed, ask, "Has the reinforcer _____ been delivered?"

65. The fourth principle of reinforcer effectiveness is the principle of deprivation. You violate this principle if you use a reinforcer that you have repeatedly given to someone recently. We say that the person to whom you have repeatedly given that reinforcer is _____ (deprived, satiated) of that reinforcer.

23. If someone has received the reinforcer rarely, we say that he or she is _____ (deprived, satiated) of that reinforcer.

67. The more rarely a person has received the reinforcer, the more _____ they are.

71. The principle stating that the more deprived a person is of the reinforcer, the more effective it will be is called the principle of _____.

70. The principle of deprivation states that the more _____ a person is of the reinforcer, the more effective it will be.

76. To determine whether the principle of deprivation was followed, ask, "Has the reinforcer _____ (rarely, frequently) been delivered?"

4. Ask the question, "Has the reinforcer rarely been delivered?" to determine whether the principle of _____ was followed.

77. To determine whether the principle of deprivation was followed, ask, "Has the reinforcer _____ been delivered?"

13. Dr. Gewirtz scheduled a period of time before Alice was to perform a simple task. He withheld attention from Alice during that period of time. Once he permitted Alice to start performing the task, he praised her. Making attention rare by withholding it for a period of time increases the effectiveness of the attention as a reinforcer through the principle of _____.

85. When John listened as often as possible to the voices he hallucinated, the voices became a less effective reinforcer for listening. The instructions to listen to the voices deliberately violated a principle in order to weaken their effectiveness. By making the voices anything but rare, the researchers were instructing the patient to violate the principle of _____ _____.

86. When the patient listened to his "voices" so often, he eventually became _____ _____ with them.

16. Dr. Vollmer used taped music to reinforce a simple task performed by Rich, a man with severe retardation. He played no music while Rich sat for 30 minutes in the waiting room prior to starting work on the task. Because the taped music was rare (in fact, so rare it was absent) during the initial 30 minutes, we would say that Rich was _____ of music.

53. Remember, the question to ask to confirm that an example uses the principle of deprivation is, "Has the reinforcer been delivered _____?" If so, then the principle has been followed.

84. When asked a question about which principle is concerned when a reinforcer is given frequently, you should not answer "the principle of satiation." Rather, answer "the principle of _____."

51. Remember, satiation is the _____ _____ of deprivation.

### 5. Telling the Principles Apart

31. Pre-test: If a person is reinforced within a minute of his or her response, the principle of _____ is being used.

32. Pre-test: If a reinforcer is given only when a particular desired behavior is made, the principle of _____ is being used correctly.

33. Pre-test: If the amount of a reinforcer was worthwhile, then the principle of _____ _____ was being used correctly.

34. Pre-test: If the reinforcer has rarely been delivered, then the principle of _____ _____ was being used correctly.

39. Pre-test: The principle of size is being used if the amount of a reinforcer was _____.

40. Pre-test: The principle of deprivation is being used if the reinforcer has _____ _____ been delivered. If you got this one wrong, be sure to memorize it, because you will use it often throughout the book.

41. Pre-test: The principle of contingency is being used if a reinforcer is given _____ _____ when a particular desired behavior is emitted.

42. Pre-test: The principle of immediacy is being used if a person is reinforced within one _____ of the response.

10. Dr. Brigham delivered tokens to April whether or not she made accurate responses. He delivered the tokens within a minute of the response. The tokens bought April a worthwhile amount of activities that she enjoyed. She got the tokens rarely enough because she could trade them for many enjoyable activities. This example clearly violated which principle of effective reinforcement? The principle of _____

11. Dr. Brigham delivered tokens during treatment contingent on accurate handwriting. He then delivered them during reversal noncontingent on correct handwriting. Which procedure do you think produced a higher rate of accurate behaviors? _____ (contingent, noncontingent)

14. Dr. Hall gave Jerry 25 cents at the end of the month for each time during the month he wore his braces. He got money only for the times when he was wearing his braces. He got a worthwhile amount of money because he could buy things he wanted. He certainly got the money rarely enough. What principle of effective reinforcement, if any, did Hall violate? _____ _____

15. Dr. Hall tried two procedures for giving Jerry 25 cents for each time that he was observed wearing his braces. The first procedure involved observing him every day and paying him at the end of the month.

The second procedure involved observing him every day and paying him within a minute of observing that he was wearing them. Which procedure would you guess produced the higher rate of wearing the braces—paying him daily or monthly? _____ (daily, monthly)

9. Doris had hoarded towels for nine years. During those nine years, the attendants constantly took towels back from Doris. Dr. Ayllon violated one of the principles in order to reduce the effectiveness of towels as a reinforcer for Doris's hoarding behavior. Instead of taking towels away from her, he flooded her with as many as 600 towels so they were anything but rare! She started taking them out of her room herself. Dr. Ayllon violated what principle of effective reinforcement to reduce the reinforcing effectiveness of towels? _____ _____

### 6. Tactic #5 in the Reinforcement Strategy

48. Pre-test: To use the reinforcement strategy to solve human problems (5), use the principles of (use two words) _____ _____.

60. The effectiveness of an event as a reinforcer is defined as the extent to which it _____ (decreases, increases) the rate of the behavior.

61. The extent to which a reinforcer increases the rate of a behavior is called its _____ (effectiveness, ineffectiveness).

74. This lesson is about the principles of reinforcer effectiveness. Notice that the principles are not directed at making the procedure more effective but rather at making the event more effective. Thus, it is called the principle of _____ _____ effectiveness.

57. Tactic #5 in using the reinforcement strategy to solve human problems is to use the principles of reinforcer _____ _____ (effectiveness, ineffectiveness).

62. The fifth tactic in using the reinforcement strategy to solve human problems is to use the principles of _____ _____ effectiveness.

81. When using tactic #5 of the reinforcement strategy to solve human problems, use the principles of _____ _____.

### 7. Review

29. Pre-test: Doris had hoarded towels for nine years. Dr. Ayllon started giving her towels only when she was in her room. After she had been given 600 towels, she started removing them from her room. Ayllon reduced the reinforcing properties of towels for Doris by the principle of _____.

47. Pre-test: When a reinforcer is delivered only when a desired behavior occurs, the principle of _____ is being followed.

44. Pre-test: The principle that states that a reinforcer should be delivered as soon after the behavior has occurred as possible is the principle of _____.

30. Pre-test: Dr. Hall gave Jerry 25 cents for each time he wore braces during the month. Jerry got paid only for the times he was wearing braces. Jerry got the money at the end of the month. He liked the money because it permitted him to buy things that he wanted. He got money rarely enough to always appreciate it. What principle of effective reinforcement, if any, was violated? _____

27. Pre-test: According to the principle of contingency, the reinforcer should not be delivered after any undesired behavior. Rather it should be delivered _____ after a desired behavior.

36. Pre-test: The fifth tactic in using the reinforcement strategy to solve human prob-lems is to use the four principles of _____.

21. If a person has recently received a lot of a particular reinforcer, that person is said to be _____ with respect to the reinforcer.

12. Dr. Brigham delivered tokens to Anna whether or not she wrote a letter correctly. If delivering tokens is meant to be a way to reinforce the accuracy of writing, this procedure violates what, if any, principle of effective reinforcement? _____

64. The four factors that contribute to the effectiveness of a reinforcer are: _____ _____, _____ _____, _____, and _____.

82. To use the reinforcement strategy to solve human problems, (1) increase desirable behavior through reinforcement, (2) decrease undesirable behavior through extinction, (3) increase a desirable behavior relative to undesirable behavior through differential reinforcement, (4) create new behavior through _____, and (5) use the principles of _____.

52. Remember, the opposite of deprivation is _____.

2. According to the principle of size, enough of the reinforcer should be given to the person to be _____.

55. Selecting a reinforcer according to whether the person has rarely had a lot of that reinforcer is making use of the principle of _____.

6. Asking whether enough of the reinforcer has been delivered to be worthwhile tests the principle of _____.

58. Tactic #5 in using the reinforcement strategy to solve human problems is to use the principles of _____.

## Programmed Examples

### 1. Programmed Examples

18. Pre-test: Professor Brainbuster asked his students to formulate literary criticisms of the novel that they had just read. The moment that Fred made a good point, the professor praised him lavishly, hoping to reward such critical thinking. Little did the good professor know that Fred was simply parroting the notes from his frat brother. Fred, knowing that his grade was going up, was very pleased about each occurrence of praise. He certainly only rarely received praise. What principle of effective reinforcement, if any, did the professor not follow in this example? _____

17. Pre-test: Mary didn't like the way that Vera treated her—Vera was usually very unpleasant. But Mary had heard about

reinforcement and decided to try it. She kept track of any pleasant behavior that Vera engaged in for a week and then mentioned those things to her on Sunday night. She never praised Vera for unpleasant behaviors. You can be sure that Vera did not get too much praise. Vera seemed genuinely delighted at the praise. However, Vera did not get any nicer as a result. If you could talk with Mary, what principle of effective reinforcement would you tell her she was neglecting in her method? _____ (Ask questions. Don't assume that the clues are in the order you learned them.)

16. Pre-test: Hal did not invite Dana to parties very often. On those occasions when Hal did extend an invitation, Dana would immediately say, "Thank you very much" as enthusiastically as he knew how. He did not say "Thank you very much" when Hal failed to invite him to a party. Hal did not seem very receptive to Dana's thank you. Dana thanked Hal rarely enough to not overdo it. Hal did not invite Dana to parties any more often. What principle of effective reinforcement, if any, did Dana ignore in his attempt to get Hal to invite him to more parties? _____ (Keep asking questions, but I'm no longer going to put the clues in the order you learned them.)

15. Pre-test: Dave didn't like Timmy to play with his model cars because Timmy usually played too rough and damaged them. One day Dave had the idea that he would reinforce Timmy for playing nicely with the models by giving him several M & M's. He only gave Timmy M & M's for playing nicely. He gave him the M & M's right after or while Timmy played nicely. Timmy loved M & M's. The procedure worked really well for several hours, but finally Timmy started getting too rough again. What principle of effective reinforcement, if any, would you guess had finally been violated after several hours? _____

12. Lora gave Mary one cookie for reading each of the first 99 pages. When Mary read the hundredth page, Lora gave her a cookie only when she had read that page. She gave her the cookie immediately after finishing the page. Clearly Mary considered each of the first 99 cookies worthwhile. Yet Mary stopped reading. Did Lora deliver the hundredth cookie for the hundredth page according to the principles of effective reinforcement? First, the principle of contingency: "Was the hundredth reinforcer given _____ when a desired behavior occurred? Yes!" Second, the principle of immediacy: "Was the hundredth reinforcer given within a(n) _____ of reading a page? Yes!" Third, the principle of size: "Was the amount of the 100th reinforcer _____ _____? Yes!" Finally, the principle of deprivation: "Was the reinforcer delivered _____ (frequently, rarely) by the hundredth page? No!" What principle, if any, was violated with the 100th cookie? _____ (Write just the key word for the principle violated, if any: *contingency, deprivation, immediacy, none,* or *size.*)

19. Sarah tried to help her friend John overcome his shyness by signaling him with a wink only when he acted assertively during a social gathering. She winked at him as soon as he acted assertively. John was elated each time that she winked at him. He never tired of earning a wink in the sense that he got them too often. For the principle of contingency you should ask, "Was the reinforcer given only when a desired behavior occurred? _____ (yes, no) For the principle of immediacy you should ask, "Was the reinforcer given within a minute of the desired behavior? _____ (yes, no) For the principle of size, you should ask, "Was the amount of the reinforcer given worthwhile? _____ (yes, no) (Answer "yes" if he seemed to like it.) For the principle of deprivation you should ask, "Had the reinforcer rarely been delivered? _____ (yes, no) What principle, if any, was ignored by Sarah when she was helping John become more assertive? _____ (Remember, write either the key word or "none.")

11. Judy encouraged her son Tom to read by bringing him a delicious snack. She gave him a snack only when he was reading, never when he was not. She gave them while he was reading. Tom appreciated the snacks immensely, as they were always his favorite foods. Judy was careful never to give the snacks too often. Tom's rate of reading increased. Decide whether Judy gave the snacks only for reading: _____ (yes, no). Decide whether Judy delivered the snacks within a minute of the behavior: _____ (yes, no). Decide

whether Judy's snacks were worthwhile: _____ (yes, no). Decide whether Judy rarely used the snacks: _____ (yes, no). What principle of effective reinforcement, if any, did Judy fail to employ? _____ (Write "none" if she used them all.)

3. Ben and Hal usually went fishing all day every Saturday. They usually would catch a fish every 20 casts or so. This Saturday they went to an artificial lake that had been stocked with fish, and they caught a fish almost every cast. Each cast took less than a minute. They quit by lunchtime after each had caught dozens of fish. Clearly their casting was reinforced at the beginning by catching a fish. But what principle was violated that led them to quit early? Ask, "Did they catch fish only by casting?" _____ (yes, no) "Did they catch the fish right after a cast occurred (less than a minute)?" _____ (yes, no) "Was the amount of each reinforcer worthwhile?" _____ (yes, no)" Did they rarely catch a fish on this Saturday?" _____ (yes, no) What principles, if any, were violated this Saturday by the end of their fishing that led to a decrease in the effectiveness of catching fish as a reinforcer? _____

14. Members of Utopian Village rely on expressions of respect to maintain work behaviors in their community. These expressions of respect were given only for work behavior but on no other occasion. They were given during or right after work behavior. Members did not seem too thrilled when they got them, but the expressions of respect were not given too often. (Ask the four questions to decide whether any of the principles were violated.) What principle of effective reinforcement, if any, is being ignored by this community when they used "expressions of respect" as a reinforcer? _____

2. Barb had been really thoughtful of Ken. Every time that he complained about how poorly his relationship with friends was going, she had listened and asked questions, hoping to help him. She listened only to his complaints. She asked questions after each complaint. However, he had gotten to complaining more and more often. So she decided to just plain quit listening—in fact, she would get up and walk away when the complaining started. Barb was disappointed to find that Ken just kept right on complaining as frequently as ever.

What behavioral <u>procedure</u> did Barb use? _____ (Note that the question is not about a principle but about a procedure.)

10. Jerry told his mother that he wanted to learn how to sew. His mother did not have a stereotyped view of children's sex roles, so she welcomed Jerry's interests. She patted him on the head but only when he was sewing. She patted him during his sewing or right afterwards. Jerry didn't seem too thrilled to get a brief pat on the head. His mom rarely patted Jerry on the head. As a result, Jerry lost interest in sewing very quickly. What principle of effective reinforcement, if any, did his mother fail to employ (remember to ask the four questions)? _____ (Remember to answer "none" if she used them all.)

6. Chester took his children for an ice cream treat only on the Sunday of any week, during which they brought home a good school paper for him to see. They loved the ice cream treat, which they got rarely. (Ask questions!) Not using what principle probably accounts for the fact that this is not an effective reinforcer for schoolwork? _____

8. Dave got interested in meditation. To try it out he began very brief (five-minute) meditation periods during the day. He felt so good afterward that he started doing more of them during the day. "Feeling good" as an event would be called a(n) _____ for meditating.

7. Dad wanted to help Bobby improve his math skills, so Dad gave Bobby problems orally ("What is 4 times 9?"). For every correct answer, Dad gave Bobby a potato chip. Bobby could not earn potato chips during this session in any other way. Dad gave the chips immediately after the correct answer. Bobby loved potato chips when he was hungry. Dad always scheduled these sessions for right after dinner. Dad's procedure didn't work too well. What principle of effective reinforcement, if any, did Dad ignore? _____

1. Alice liked Rich very much, but he was a bit backward. So she was very warm and friendly only when he at least held her hand. Then, she was warm and friendly only when he held her hand and kissed her. Next, she was warm and friendly only when he held

her hand, kissed her, and embraced her passionately. You can guess what Alice's target behavior was. She reached her goal of getting him to propose marriage! What procedure was she using to get there? _____

20. Senor Jimenez taught 4-year-old Janice to say his name by telling her one day, "Say 'hee-may-nayz.'" From then on, she said it correctly. What behavioral <u>procedure</u> did he use? _____

9. Mr. Good was every employee's dream. He praised you only when you did your work well (no matter what your past mistakes had been). He praised you during or right after doing good work. You always appreciated his praise. He didn't load you down with praise too often. What principle of effective reinforcement, if any, did Mr. Good neglect? _____

4. Bob had two really tough classes that were required for his degree. One day he went up to Professor Barnes and asked him a question after his lecture. The professor was very friendly and encouraged Bob to ask his question. Bob frequently did so in the future and was always greeted warmly by Professor Barnes. Bob tried the same thing with Professor Mead, but he was not at all friendly or encouraging. Bob didn't ask questions of Professor Mead very often. What behavioral procedure would be used to explain why Bob asked more questions of Professor Barnes and fewer of Professor Mead? _____

(Most students get this wrong—it would pay to ask the questions you learned in earlier lessons about your first guess!).

13. Marvin was determined to teach his daughter Bee how to do math problems. He bought a math workbook and insisted that every morning she do all the problems in one chapter before being allowed to play. He then graded her problems and had her correct the ones that were wrong. When she was done, she could play for the rest of the day. She could soon do the problems very rapidly but still didn't seem to know any more than before. It was then that he noticed the correct answers listed in the back of the book. If Bee was copying the answers, then the delivery of the opportunity to play would violate what principle of effective reinforcement? _____

5. Carey had Dave, the star football tackle, compose poems and hand them to her during class. She read them and wrote praise only for the good aspects of his poems. She returned them the next day during class. Surprisingly, her praise was very important to Dave. She was careful not to give him too much praise. However, in spite of her careful procedure, Dave's poetry writing did not improve. What principle of effective reinforcement, if any, did Carey fail to use? _____
(Students have been getting this wrong because they are not asking the four questions.)

## Reading Section

This lesson introduces you to <u>schedules of reinforcement</u>. In previous lessons, you learned about two generic schedules of reinforcement. In one of them, the delivery of a reinforcer is scheduled for every occurrence of the behavior. Behavior analysts call that a <u>continuous schedule of reinforcement</u>. In the other one, the delivery of a reinforcer is scheduled to be withheld after occurrences of the behavior. Behavior analysts call this an <u>extinction schedule</u>. You will learn about four additional schedules in which a reinforcer is scheduled to follow only some occurrences of the behavior. Behavior analysts call them by the generic name of <u>intermittent schedules</u>.

1. When the delivery of a reinforcer is scheduled for every occurrence of the behavior, behavior analysts call that a _____ _____ (continuous, extinction, intermittent) schedule of reinforcement.
2. When the delivery of a reinforcer is scheduled to be withheld following the behavior, behavior analysts call that a(n) _____ _____ (continuous, extinction, intermittent) schedule.
3. When a reinforcer is scheduled to follow only some occurrences of the behavior, behavior analysts call these types of schedules by the generic name of _____ (continuous, extinction, intermittent) schedules.

In this lesson, you will learn about the sixth tactic in using the reinforcement strategy to solve human problems. Sometimes, you may want a person to respond more rapidly than is possible when you give them a reinforcer after every response. Tactic #6 is to increase response rate with a <u>ratio schedule</u> of reinforcement.

4. In this lesson, you will learn about the sixth tactic in using the reinforcement strategy to solve human problems. Tactic #6 is to increase response rate with a(n) _____ _____ schedule of reinforcement.

## Fixed-Ratio Schedules

Two common intermittent schedules of reinforcement are based on counting. They count the number of responses that have occurred since the last reinforcement. A **fixed-ratio** schedule is a schedule for reinforcing the first response after a <u>fixed number</u> of responses. For example, if Dan is on a fixed-ratio of 3, then reinforcement occurs for every third response. A common example of this schedule is the piece-rate system of wage payments sometimes used in factories. The employer pays the worker for making a fixed number of responses. Thus, the employer might pay an assembly line worker a quarter for making five spot welds on an auto body. Behavior analysts call this a "fixed-ratio of 5." They abbreviate it "FR-5."

5. A **fixed-ratio** schedule: Reinforcing the first response after a _____ number of responses.

Notice that a continuous schedule involves reinforcement for every single response. Thus, it is a fixed-ratio schedule involving, specifically, a fixed-ratio of 1. You can abbreviate it as FR-1. All other fixed-ratio schedules (FR-2 and greater) are intermittent schedules.

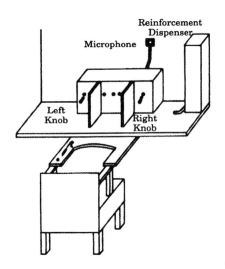
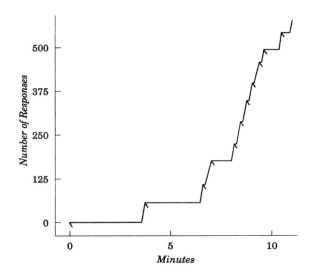

***Figure 13-1.*** This graph shows an experiment with a fixed-ratio schedule. A high school boy made vocal responses into the microphone. These responses are shown on the cumulative record graph on the right. When he was responding rapidly, the graph went up; when he was pausing, the graph went to the right. The boy earned nickels by pulling either the right or the left knob. The right knob required an effortful pull of many pounds. If he made 50 vocal responses, he was permitted to switch for one minute to pulling the left knob. The left knob required an easy pull of only one pound. Thus, the researcher reinforced his vocal responses by permitting him to pull the easier knob on a fixed-ratio schedule of 50. Notice that he emitted vocal responses at a high rate until he got the reinforcement (indicated by the slash mark). Then, he paused his vocal responses for a while. (Adapted from "Escape from an Effortful Situation," by L. K. Miller, *Journal of the Experimental Analysis of Behavior,* 1968, 11, 619–627. Copyright 1968 by the Society for the Experimental Analysis of Behavior, Inc. Used by permission.)

People tend to work rapidly on fixed-ratio schedules. Fixed-ratio schedules of 2 or above generate a higher rate of responding than do intermittent reinforcement schedules. The pattern of responding involves rapid responding prior to reinforcement. After reinforcement, people tend to <u>pause</u>. Thus, the fixed-ratio schedule is characterized by alternating periods of responding and periods of rest.

6. The pattern of responding with fixed-ratio schedules involves rapid responding prior to reinforcement. After reinforcement, people tend to _____.

This pattern of rapid responding followed by rest is best displayed in a *cumulative record* graph. Figure 13-1 shows an example (Miller, 1968). The graph shows the response pattern of a high school boy whose vocal responding was reinforced after every 50 responses. Usually the boy made 50 vocal responses in less than 20 seconds to earn his reinforcer. Then after he used his reinforcer, he paused for up to three minutes before starting to make the vocal responses that would earn him another reinforcer. This alteration between responding and pausing forms what looks like a "stair-step" pattern.

People respond faster as you increase the ratio requirement (e.g., Cohen, Chelland, Ball, & LeMura, 2002). Thus, they respond faster when you increase the ratio from 1 to 5. They will respond even faster if you increase the ratio from 5 to 10. They will continue these increases until you reach some upper limit. At that point, they will start to respond more slowly.

Stephens, Pear, Wray, and Jackson (1975) found this effect when they studied the rate of learning for Sidney, a child with severe retardation. The researchers studied the rate at which Sidney learned to name objects shown in pictures. The researchers used a complex procedure because Sidney had trouble learning. First, they taught Sidney to look at the picture of a table. When he could do that, they said "table" and taught him to repeat it. Second, they required him to say "table" without help. Third, they required him to say "table" when they showed the picture among other already known pictures. The researchers reinforced Sidney's responses on different ratios. When

### Is Attention Behavior? Part 2

In Lesson 4, I told you how Jim Holland approached attention as a behavior. He let Navy men press a button to light a dial for 0.07 seconds. He told them to report the moment they saw the pointer on the dial deflect. His behavioral definition of *attention* was pressing the button to look for deflections. He found that the pointer deflection was a reinforcer for looking. Further, the pattern of looking was controlled by the schedule of reinforcement. When the men saw a deflection only after a fixed number of looks, they worked at high rates. They often paused after a deflection. We see this pattern with fixed-ratio schedules. (Holland, 1958)

7. Thus, he found that attention would come and go according to the pattern found with a(n) _____ (continuous, extinction, fixed-ratio, variable-ratio) schedule.

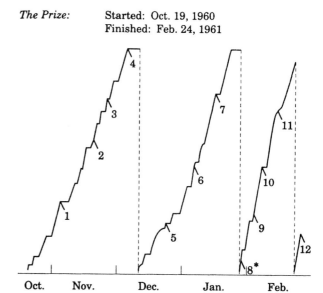

The Prize:    Started: Oct. 19, 1960
              Finished: Feb. 24, 1961

***Figure 13-2.*** This is a cumulative graph of the number of pages written by Irving Wallace on his novel *The Prize*. He gathered the data himself, using his own self-recording diary. The number of written pages was too much for the size of the graph, so it had to be started over again. Without this formatting convention the graph would be three times as high. (Adapted from "Self Control Techniques of Famous Novelists," by I. Wallace and J. Pear, *Journal of Applied Behavior Analysis*, 1977, 10, 515–525. Copyright 1977 by the Society for the Experimental Analysis of Behavior, Inc. Used by permission.)

they increased his ratio from 1 response per reinforcement to 5 responses per reinforcement, he learned faster. His rate increased with ratios of 10, 15, and 20, but it decreased when they increased his ratio to 25. Similar findings were obtained with four other children. This example shows the usual finding in this area of research, but other variables affect the relationship. The Added Readings section lists several studies that illustrate some of the complexities of the area.

### Novel Writing: A Case of Fixed-Ratio Scheduling?

Irving Wallace had to write 1,100 pages to complete his novel. Figure 13-2 shows a cumulative graph of the number of pages he wrote each day for his novel *The Prize*. The graph shows that he wrote less than 10 pages a day when he started but increased to over 20 pages a day near the completion of the novel. Suppose that writing a page is one response. Suppose that completing the whole book of 1,100 pages is a reinforcer. If Wallace must write 1,100 pages to get the reinforcer, then the specific schedule he would be on is called a fixed-ratio schedule.

It took him over four months to complete the book. How would you like to be on such a huge schedule? (Based on Wallace & Pear, 1977.)

8. Suppose that writing a page is one response and completing the whole book of 1,100 pages is a reinforcer. If Wallace must write 1,100 pages to get the reinforcer, then the specific schedule he would be on is called a(n) _____ (fixed-ratio, variable-ratio) schedule.

Pear has suggested that writing one chapter in a book may serve as a fixed ratio within the overall book. The graph shows a pause in writing after many of the chapters were completed (for example, Chapter 1). Furthermore, the author's records indicate that he stopped writing for the day after completing all but one of the 12 chapters (the missed one is Chapter 8, indicated by an asterisk). This pattern suggests that each chapter served as a fixed-ratio schedule. Thus, the laws of behavior extend even into that most creative and "subjective" process of writing a novel.

## Variable-Ratio Schedules

Behavior analysts use another common intermittent schedule based on counting. They call it a *variable-ratio* schedule. The **variable-ratio** schedule involves reinforcing the first response after a <u>variable number</u> of responses. The number of responses required for reinforcement <u>varies</u> every time. For example, suppose you reinforce Ann after three responses, then after one more response, then after two more responses. You reinforced her according to a variable-ratio schedule that <u>averages</u> a reinforcer after two responses (the average of 3, 1, and 2).

9. **Variable-ratio** schedule: Reinforcing the first response after a _____ number of responses.

Many situations involve delivering reinforcers after varying numbers of responses. "Looking for something" is a common example. Looking for friends among a crowd of pedestrians is an example of variable-ratio reinforcement. You might look at 50 faces to find one friend, 35 to find another, and 65 to find a third. Your looking is on a variable-ratio schedule of 50.

Variable-ratio schedules can be useful in business situations. One lumber company found that beavers were damaging their trees. They paid employees for trapping the beavers. They compared the productivity of employees paid $1 for every beaver versus the productivity of employees paid an average of $4 for every four beavers. Even though the pay per beaver is the same, the employees paid on the variable-ratio-of-4 schedule trapped 11% more beavers. Both schedules were more effective than an hourly rate. Other business-related studies show a similar effect (Latham & Huber, 1992).

Two researchers used a variable-ratio schedule to increase exercise (DeLuca & Holborn, 1992). Overweight kids pedaled an exercise bicycle. The bicycle counted turns of the pedal. The equipment awarded points on a variable-ratio schedule. The kids could turn in the points for prizes after their exercise. They greatly increased their exercise, improved their physical appearance, and enjoyed exercising.

Two other researchers used a variable-ratio schedule to increase the attention of Jamie, a deaf child (Van Houten & Nau, 1980). The teacher observed whether Jamie attended to her for each five-minute interval. If he did, then the teacher let him draw one block out of a bag. One of the eight blocks was blue. Every time Jamie drew a blue block, he got a small toy. This method put Jamie on a variable-ratio of 8. His rate of attending increased from about 60% of the intervals to about 90%!

Variable-ratio schedules produce the highest overall rate of responding of any schedule considered in this book. However, you should note that people respond as fast on a fixed-ratio schedule <u>when they are responding</u>! The absence of pausing on variable-ratio schedules gives it the advantage over fixed-ratio schedules. The lack of a pause may be caused by the fact that the very next response might produce a reinforcer. Later in this lesson, a behavior analysis example includes a graph that illustrates responding on a variable-ratio schedule.

Here is a summary. The fixed-ratio schedule delivers a reinforcer after a fixed number of responses. It produces a high rate of responding prior to reinforcement and a pause after reinforcement. The variable-ratio schedule delivers a reinforcer after a variable number of responses. It produces a high rate of responding with no pauses. Overall, the variable-ratio schedule produces a higher rate of responding because of the absence of pauses (e.g., Van Houten & Nau, 1980).

## Advantages of Ratio Schedules

Ratio schedules have a number of advantages for behavior analysts, which I outline below.

### *Resistance to Extinction*

Behavior analysts may use ratio schedules to increase a person's resistance to <u>extinction.</u> By resistance, I mean the number of responses that the person makes <u>without reinforcement</u>. For example, suppose Mary has a history of receiving a reinforcer for every response. She will stop responding pretty quickly after her responses no longer produce reinforcement. That is, she will stop responding quickly during extinction. Suppose that Alice has a history of receiving a reinforcer only after some of her responses but not after all of them. She will continue responding much longer than Mary. The basic fact is that a person will continue to respond longer during extinction if they have a history of reinforcement from an intermittent schedule.

10. Behavior analysts may use ratio schedules to increase a person's resistance to _____.

This approach can be very useful. Often, the behavior analyst knows that a person's behavior will result in extinction at some point. For example, the behavior analyst may be teaching Fred to be more assertive. After this training period ends, Fred will take his new skill to his usual environment. Fred's new assertiveness may not pay off as often as in the training period. The behavior analyst may anticipate this transition by using an intermittent schedule during the last part of the training period. Instead of praising Fred for every assertive act, the behavior analyst may shift to praising only an average of one in three assertive acts. With this history, Fred is likely to persist with many more assertive acts even if they don't always work. The result is that his usual environment has longer to accidentally reinforce his new skill. This gives him a greater chance of obtaining enough reinforcement to keep him using the skill.

Koegel and Rincover (1977) provide a dramatic illustration of this effect. They taught children with severe retardation to imitate behaviors that a therapist demonstrated—quite an accomplishment when the children's IQs were so low that they were untestable! They then had another adult, in a different setting, demonstrate the same behavior but provide no reinforcement for imitation. They found that the children stopped imitating after 20 trials if they had a history of continuous reinforcement. The children stopped after 60–100 trials if they had a history of reinforcement on every other response (FR-2). However, the children showed no signs of stopping if they had a history of reinforcement on every fifth correct response (FR-5). They were still responding after as many as 500 trials. The use of a ratio schedule resulted in the children maintaining the behavior in the natural environment even with no one reinforcing that behavior.

An experiment by Kazdin and Polster (1973) also confirmed this effect. They worked with two adults with retardation who were social isolates. They reinforced every social conversation by Ted with another person in his workplace. They reinforced only 1 of 3 conversations by John. When they stopped reinforcement, Ted decreased interactions to less than 1 per day. John maintained the high rate of about 10 interactions per day.

Here is one explanation for the greater resistance to extinction produced by intermittent schedules. People can easily recognize the change from every response producing a reinforcer to no responses producing a reinforcer. When they can be sure that their responses are not going to produce reinforcers, they are likely to quit responding. On the other hand, people may have more difficulty recognizing the change from some responses producing reinforcers to no responses producing reinforcers. Since they can't be as sure that their responses are not going to produce reinforcers, they are less likely to quit responding.

This theory leads to other predictions. For example, people may more readily recognize the change from reinforcers after a fixed number of responses to extinction than from a variable number to extinction. Indeed, research indicates that variable-ratio schedules produce <u>greater</u> resistance to extinction than do fixed-ratio schedules.

For example, Goltz (1992) suggests that a person's history of reinforcement with investments may determine whether they persist when they should stop investing. She examined people who have a history of successful investments on a fixed-ratio schedule. She compared them with people who have a history of successful investments on a variable-ratio schedule. Those with the fixed-ratio history reduced or stopped their investments during extinction faster than did those with a variable-ratio schedule. In fact, many of those with a variable-ratio history actually increased the amount of their investment during extinction.

### Decreased Satiation

Ratio schedules also have the advantage that behavior analysts can use fewer reinforcers to generate the same amount of behavior. For instance, suppose that a behavior analyst is delivering 1 reinforcer for 10 responses (FR-10 or VR-10). That means they will use 10 reinforcers for a 100 responses. With continuous reinforcement, 100 reinforcers would have to be delivered. As a result, ratio schedules may be used to reduce the problem of the person becoming satiated on the reinforcer and then no longer responding. Both fixed-ratio and variable-ratio schedules of the same size are equally good at opposing satiation.

11. Ratio schedules also have the advantage that behavior analysts can use fewer reinforcers to generate the same amount of behavior, resulting in decreased _____.

## The Disadvantages of Ratio Schedules

### Continuous Schedule for Shaping

When shaping a new response, you must consistently reinforce each approximation. The fastest way to increase its rate compared to nonapproximations is to reinforce it every time that it occurs. Thus, behavior analysts use continuous reinforcement during shaping.

12. Behavior analysts use continuous reinforcement during _____.

### Ratio Strain

If a person's behavior is reinforced too infrequently, the behavior may fall apart and become very irregular. Normally, a ratio schedule is introduced by small steps. First, the person is reinforced for every response, then for every other one, then for one of five, and so on. Using this gradual approach, behavior analysts can gradually build up very sizable ratios. However, at some point, no matter how gradually the schedule is changed, the ratio simply becomes too large to maintain responding. There is no predictable point at which this happens because it depends on how effortful the response is, how valuable the reinforcer is, how much is delivered, and how gradually the behavior analyst increased the ratio requirement. Thus, at some point *ratio strain* occurs. Here's the definition. **Ratio strain**: Requiring so many responses for a reinforcer that the behavior slows or even totally stops.

13. When people are placed on such a large ratio that they aren't reinforced often enough to maintain responding, ratio _____ occurs.

## Summary

Tactic #6 in using the reinforcement strategy for solving human problems is to increase response rate with a ratio schedule of reinforcement. You are using a ratio schedule when you reinforce varying numbers of responses. Ratio schedules are intermittent schedules. You are using an intermittent schedule when you do not reinforce every response. You are using a fixed-ratio schedule when you deliver reinforcement for a fixed number of responses. This schedule produces a pattern of pausing after reinforcement followed by a high rate until reinforcement. You are using a variable-ratio schedule when you deliver reinforcement for a varying number of responses. This schedule produces a pattern of high and uniform responding. You would use ratio schedules to increase resistance to extinction and to reduce problems from satiation. You would not use them for shaping or when you are concerned about ratio strain.

# Behavior Analysis Examples

### Pay for Performance

Businesses usually pay workers by the hour. A few companies pay workers for each piece of work completed. Economists call this *piece-rate* wages. Lincoln Electric uses piece rates to manufacture welding equipment and electrical motors. It has been in business since 1895 (Handlin, 1992). You can think of piece rate as a fixed-ratio of 1. Some research demonstrates that workers are more productive with the piece rate than with hourly pay (e.g., Bucklin & Dickinson, 2001; Latham & Huber, 1992).

14. Because it continuously reinforces whenever there is a response, fixed-ratio of 1 is also known as the generic schedule called a(n) _____ (continuous, extinction, intermittent) schedule of reinforcement.

### Teaching Reading

Staats, Finley, Minke, and Wolf (1964) developed a behavioral approach to teaching reading under controlled conditions so that the process could be carefully studied. They first attempted to analyze the process of reading acquisition from a behavioral point of view. They determined that to acquire a reading response meant that people could name the word that they were looking at. In order to acquire it, they had to begin by looking at the word. Next, they had to either hear how that word sounded or sound it out for themselves. They then had to repeat that sound. Finally, they had to discriminate that word from other words and say its name. Each step involves a response on the part of the learner. Staats could increase the probability of each response by reinforcing it. He developed an apparatus based on this analysis that permitted the observation of each component response. It also permitted reinforcement of the total reading acquisition response.

Figure 13-3 shows the apparatus that Staats developed to study the children's reading acquisition behaviors. It consisted of a working area facing the child and a reinforcer area to the right.

Here is how a child named Sally might proceed. Sally would begin learning a word by

***Figure 13-3.*** The Staats apparatus for studying the reading acquisition process. (From "Reinforcement Variables in the Control of Unit Reading Responses," by A. W. Staats, J. R. Finley, K. A. Minke, and M. M. Wolf, *Journal of the Experimental Analysis of Behavior,* 1964, 7, 139–149. Copyright 1964 by the Society for the Experimental Analysis of Behavior, Inc. Used by permission.)

pressing a button on the table. The apparatus then projected the word onto the square window. The experimenter said the word. Sally then named that word out loud while pressing that window. Pressing the window ensured that she looked at the word. The press also provided a way to observe her looking response. Next, Sally repeated the word and pressed the rectangular windows below that contained the same word. This step required her to practice naming the word without the help of the experimenter. It also required her to notice the difference between that word and other similar words.

If Sally made the wrong response, the experimenter required her to repeat the sequence. If Sally made the correct response, she received a marble from the dispenser on the right. She could apply that marble toward the purchase of any of the toys on the right by placing it in the tube below her choice. When the tube was filled, she earned the toy.

Staats and his colleagues have undertaken many experiments to investigate the development of reading behavior. These studies included an examination of different schedules of reinforcement. Figure 13-4 shows a cumulative graph of responding under two conditions. The bottom record shows the rate of responding when Staats reinforced Sally for every correct response. The top record shows the rate when he reinforced her on a variable-ratio schedule of

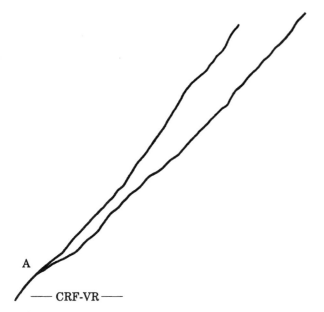

A

—— CRF-VR ——

*Figure 13-4.* A cumulative graph of reading acquisition responses in the Staats experiment. The line on the left shows the rate of reading responses when every fifth correct response on the average was reinforced; the one on the right shows the rate of reading responses when every correct response was reinforced. (From "Reinforcement Variables in the Control of Unit Reading Responses," by A. W. Staats, J. R. Finley, K. A. Minke, and M. M. Wolf, *Journal of Experimental Analysis of Behavior,* 1964, 7, 139–149, Copyright 1964 by the Society for the Experimental Analysis of Behavior, Inc. Used by permission.)

five correct responses (VR-5). This experiment demonstrates that Sally's rate of responding was more rapid with <u>variable-ratio</u> than with continuous reinforcement. The series of experiments illustrates that as complex a human behavior as the acquisition of reading behavior occurs according to behavioral principles.

15. Under which schedule of reinforcement was Sally's rate of responding more rapid? The _____ (continuous, extinction, fixed-ratio, variable-ratio) schedule.

## Notes

### Note #1
Notice that the number of responses for a reinforcer and the size of the reinforcer

interact. Suppose your boss pays you $10 to load 5 trucks. You can view this as a fixed ratio of 5. Suppose that your boss pays you $2 for each truck you load. That is continuous reinforcement. In terms of the amount of work you have to do for each dollar, you earn the same either way. You can vary the amount of work per dollar either by changing the size of each reinforcement or by changing the size of the ratio. Behavioral economics calls the relation between amount of work and amount of monetary reinforcement the *unit price* (e.g., Bickel, DeGrandpre, Hughes & Higgins, 1991). This concept unifies the two separate concepts of reinforcer size and ratio size.

## Helpful Hints

### Helpful Hint #1
When asked what schedule describes a situation, always use the most specific name. If a person is reinforced every five responses, describe the situation as a fixed-ratio, not an intermittent, schedule.

16. If a person is reinforced for every 30 responses, would the book label it as an intermittent schedule or as a fixed-ratio schedule? _____.

### Helpful Hint #2
Do *not* abbreviate any of the schedules of reinforcement except when also giving its numerical value. If you want to show off, you may abbreviate a fixed ratio of 10 responses as FR-10 and variable ratio of 15 response as VR-15. These abbreviations are widely used by behavior analysts. Always spell out the words if you are not identifying a specific numerical value.

17. If you read that Jose was praised for every five math problems he got correct, you may abbreviate the schedule as _____. If you read that Katrina the beggar scored money from an average of only one passerby in 53, then you may abbreviate the schedule as _____.

### Helpful Hint #3

You can assume that if the reinforcer is delivered after an <u>average</u> of 14 responses, that it is delivered after varying numbers of responses. This will point to a variable-ratio schedule.

18. You can assume that if the reinforcer is delivered after an <u>average</u> of 14 responses, that it is delivered after _____ (fixed, varying) numbers of responses.

### Helpful Hint #4

If every response is reinforced, then the response is on a "continuous" schedule of reinforcement. That is the answer the book will prefer. However, the book will also list "FR-1" as a correct answer. But it will not list "fixed-ratio." That is too general for this case.

19. If a response is reinforced every time it occurs, then the book will not list as the answer the general response of "fixed-ratio." The best answer is that it is the generic schedule called a(n) _____ schedule.

### Helpful Hint #5

I have again narrowed the possibilities you have to consider in answering a question. In past lessons, I used "what procedure?" to ask about reinforcement, extinction, differential reinforcement, and shaping. I used "what principle?" to ask about contingency, immediacy, size, and deprivation. During this lesson I will continue using those words. In addition, I will use "what schedule?" to ask about continuous, variable-ratio, and fixed-ratio reinforcement schedules and sometimes extinction. I will never use "what procedure?" to ask about a schedule.

20. If I ask you, "What procedure was used?" can the answer ever be "variable-ratio"? _____ (yes, no)

### Helpful Hint #6

I will often use the word *generic* to refer to continuous reinforcement, extinction, and intermittent reinforcement. If I ask for the generic schedule, I am asking for one of these three schedules. However, if the context makes it clear, I will not always refer to them as generic. If I do not ask for the generic schedule, you should not rule out these three schedules.

21. If I ask you for a generic schedule you know I am asking you about _____ _____, _____ _____, or _____.

## Additional Readings

Ferster, C. B., & Skinner, B. F. (1957). *Schedules of reinforcement*. New York: Appleton-Century-Crofts. This advanced book is the original and most comprehensive source of information on schedules. It is the "bible" of behavior analysis.

Lovitt, T. C., & Esveldt, K. A. (1970). The relative effects on math performance of single versus multiple ratio schedules: A case study. *Journal of Applied Behavior Analysis, 3*, 261–270. This study involved a disturbed child having problems learning math. The researchers found that his response rate did not increase when the schedule was changed from an FR-5 to an FR-20.

Schroeder, S. R. (1972). Parametric effects of reinforcement frequency, of reinforcement, and required response force on sheltered workshop behavior. *Journal of Applied Behavior Analysis, 5*, 431–441. Schroeder found that people with retardation made more electrical components per hour when reinforced on a higher fixed-ratio or variable-ratio schedule (up to FR-600), but only if the effort required in making the response was easy. If the effort was great, then they worked more slowly the higher the ratios.

## Programmed Reading

I have programmed questions to help you review and practice using the ideas in this lesson in the following sections: (1) Generic Schedules, (2) Fixed-Ratio Schedules, (3) Variable-Ratio Schedules, (4) Response Patterns in Ratio Schedules, (5) Resistance to

Extinction, (6) Two Drawbacks, (7) Another Tactic, and (8) Review

### 1. Generic Schedules

51. Pre-test: If I ask you which generic schedule involves reinforcing no responses, the answer will be _____ schedule.

52. Pre-test: If I ask you which generic schedule involves reinforcing every response, the answer will not be a specific schedule, such as "fixed-ratio" schedule, it will be a(n) _____ schedule.

53. Pre-test: If I ask you which generic schedule involves reinforcing only some responses, the answer will not be a specific schedule (e.g., fixed-ratio or variable-ratio), it will be _____ schedule.

90. The goal of this module is to teach you what I mean by a *generic* schedule. The generic schedule of reinforcement in which a reinforcer is delivered after every response is called a(n) _____ (continuous, extinction, intermittent) schedule of reinforcement.

87. The generic schedule of reinforcement in which the delivery of a reinforcer is stopped for responses is called a(n) _____ (continuous, extinction, intermittent) schedule.

88. The generic schedule of reinforcement in which a reinforcer is delivered after only some of the responses is called a(n) _____ (continuous, extinction, intermittent) schedule of reinforcement.

21. If I ask you which generic schedule involves reinforcing only some responses, the answer will not be a specific schedule (e.g., fixed-ratio or variable-ratio), it will be _____ schedule.

22. If I ask you which generic schedule involves reinforcing no responses, the answer will be _____ schedule.

23. If I ask you which generic schedule involves reinforcing every response, the answer will not be a specific schedule, such as "fixed-ratio" schedule, it will be _____ schedule.

20. If I ask you for a generic schedule you know I am asking you about a(n) _____ _____ schedule, a(n) _____ _____ schedule, or a(n) _____ schedule.

### 2. Fixed-Ratio Schedules

49. Pre-test: If Dwayne is praised after every 10 spelling words learned, his response is on a(n) _____ schedule.

56. Pre-test: If you deliver a reinforcer after a fixed number of responses, then the schedule is called a(n) _____ -ratio schedule.

44. Pre-test: A fixed-ratio schedule causes people to respond at a high rate prior to reinforcement, but they tend to _____ _____ immediately after reinforcement.

45. Pre-test: A fixed-ratio schedule requires reinforcement for the first response after a(n) _____ number of responses.

98. The topic of this module is fixed-ratio schedules. A fixed-ratio schedule requires reinforcement for the first response after a(n) _____ number of responses.

28. If you deliver a reinforcer after a <u>fixed</u> number of responses, then the schedule is called a(n) _____ -ratio schedule.

71. Since the continuous schedule involves reinforcement for every single response, it is also known as a fixed- _____ schedule of 1.

92. The name of the schedule in which a reinforcer is delivered after a fixed number of responses is a(n) _____ _____ schedule.

24. If Jose is reinforced after every five responses, he is said to be on a fixed-ratio schedule of 5. When answering a question to identify this schedule, you could answer either spelled out as _____ or abbreviated as "FR-5."

86. The book lists the most specific label for a schedule as the answer to questions. If a person is reinforced for every 30 responses, would the book label it as an *intermittent* schedule or as a *fixed-ratio* schedule? _____

75. Suppose that every fifth response of Jim's is reinforced. If I ask you what <u>generic</u> schedule Jim is on, you know the

answer must be *continuous, extinction,* or *intermittent.* Since every response is not reinforced but some are, Jim is on what generic schedule of reinforcement? _____

77. Suppose that every tenth response of Eric's is reinforced. If I ask you what schedule Eric is on, you should give me the specific, not the generic, intermittent schedule. Eric is on what schedule of reinforcement? _____ schedule

76. Suppose that every seventh response of Kathy's is reinforced. If I ask you what generic schedule Kathy is on, you should not give me the specific schedule of fixed-ratio (or FR-7). Kathy is on what generic schedule of reinforcement? _____ schedule

### 3. Variable-Ratio Schedules

50. Pre-test: If Dwayne is praised after an average of 13 responses, he is on a(n) _____ schedule.

64. Pre-test: The schedule that delivers reinforcement for the first response after a variable number of responses is called a(n) _____ schedule.

54. Pre-test: If Karen is praised after every 17 responses, she is on a(n) _____ schedule.

55. Pre-test: If someone is on a variable-ratio schedule, reinforcement is given for their first response after a(n) _____ number of responses.

99. The topic of this module is variable-ratio schedules. What schedule delivers reinforcement after a <u>variable</u> number of responses? _____ (fixed-ratio, variable-ratio) (Notice that the names of both schedules are always hyphenated.)

4. A variable-ratio schedule produces reinforcement after a(n) _____ (fixed, variable) number of responses.

95. The schedule that delivers reinforcement after a variable number of responses is called a(n) _____ schedule.

25. If Jose is reinforced after an average of five responses, he is said to be on a

variable-ratio schedule of 5. When answering a question to identify this schedule, you could spell out the schedule with two words as _____, or you could abbreviate with numerical value as _____.

16. Fixed-ratio of 5 may be abbreviated as _____. Variable-ratio of 10 may be abbreviated as _____.

32. In learning to distinguish between fixed-ratio and variable-ratio schedules, it is very important that you note whether an example states that the schedule produces the reinforcer after <u>every</u> 7 responses or whether it produces it on the <u>average</u> of 7 responses. If it produces reinforcement on the average of every 7 responses, then it might first produce reinforcement after 6 responses and then after 8, for an average of 7. If a schedule produces reinforcement on the average of every 7 responses, should you assume that it produces reinforcement after every 7 responses? _____ (yes, no)

114. You can assume that if the reinforcer is delivered after an <u>average</u> of 14 responses, that it is delivered after _____ _____ (fixed, varying) numbers of responses.

17. If a reinforcer is delivered after seven responses on the average, the schedule would be a(n) _____-ratio schedule. If the reinforcer is delivered after every seventh response, then the schedule is a(n) _____-ratio schedule.

27. If the reinforcer is delivered after every eleventh response, then the schedule is a(n) _____-ratio schedule. If a reinforcer is delivered on the average of seven responses, then the schedule is a(n) _____-ratio schedule.

29. If you look at 50 faces to find one friend, 35 to find another, and 65 to find a third, your looking is on a(n) _____ _____ schedule. (Remember, if you abbreviate you must give numerical value.)

41. One group of lumber company employees was paid $4 for varying numbers of beavers, averaging four. What schedule

were they on? A(n) _____
_____ schedule.

42. Overweight kids pedaled an exercise bicycle. They earned points after varying numbers of pedal responses. The schedule of reinforcement is known as a(n) _____ schedule (DeLuca & Holborn, 1992).

110. When Jamie drew a blue block (good for a prize) out of the bag on the average of one out of every eight times, he was on a(n) _____ schedule (Van Houten & Nau, 1980).

73. Suppose that an average of one in five of Jim's responses is reinforced. If I ask you what <u>generic</u> schedule Jim is on, you know the answer must be "continuous," "extinction," or "intermittent." Since every response is not reinforced but some are, Jim is on the generic schedule of reinforcement called _____.

78. Suppose that on the average Eric must make 10 responses for reinforcement. If I ask you what schedule Eric is on, you should give me the specific, not the generic, intermittent schedule. Eric is on what schedule of reinforcement? The _____ schedule.

79. Suppose that on the average every seventh response of Kathy's is reinforced. If I ask you what generic schedule Kathy is on, you should not give me the specific schedule of fixed-ratio (or FR-7). Kathy is on what generic schedule of reinforcement? The _____ schedule.

80. Suppose that on the average every fifteenth response of Ken's is reinforced. Ken is on what specific schedule of reinforcement? The _____ schedule.

18. If a response is reinforced every time it occurs, then the book will not list as the answer the general response of "fixed-ratio." The best answer is that it is the generic schedule called a(n) _____ _____ schedule.

### 4. Response Patterns in Ratio Schedules

59. Pre-test: Let's summarize. Which schedule produces the higher and more uniform rate? The _____ schedule.

Which schedule produces the stair-step pattern of working and pausing? The _____ schedule. Which generic schedule produces the slowest rate? The _____ schedule.

6. An important characteristic of each schedule of reinforcement is the rate and pattern of responding that it produces. You might guess that the rate and pattern of responding produced by variable-ratio and fixed-ratio schedules is _____ (different, identical).

94. The pattern of responding for fixed-ratio and variable-ratio is easily described. The fixed-ratio produces a stair-step pattern of responding. The person works really hard until reinforcement and then pauses afterwards. The variable-ratio schedule produces a uniform rate of responding in which the person works really hard all the time. Guess which schedule produces the higher rate of responding? _____

3. A fixed-ratio schedule causes people to respond at a high rate prior to reinforcement, but they tend to _____ _____ (pause, work) immediately after reinforcement.

26. If Ken is reinforced for every 50 responses, he might make the responses in less than 20 seconds. Then, after he had consumed the reinforcer, he would _____ _____ for a while.

93. The pattern of pausing after reinforcement is associated with the _____ _____ schedule. (Spell out the whole phrase. Hint: Only use the abbreviation whenever you can also give the numerical size of the ratio.)

7. Behavior analysts usually find that people's response rates _____ _____ as the ratio requirement increases (up to some limit).

72. So, a fixed ratio of 5 usually produces a _____ (higher, lower) rate of responding than does a continuous schedule.

15. Dr. Stephens found that May, a child with retardation, learned to name pictures. He reinforced her on schedules of continuous reinforcement and fixed-ratio reinforcement. On which schedule

did she respond more rapidly? _____
_____

8. Does a variable-ratio schedule usually produce a pause after reinforcement? _____ (yes, no)

43. People do not pause after reinforcement with the variable-ratio schedule. They do pause after reinforcement with the fixed-ratio schedule. Which of these two schedules produces the highest rate of responding? _____

100. The variable-ratio schedule produces a uniform and _____ (high, low) rate of responding.

31. In general, the more responses you require before delivering a reinforcer, the faster the person works. How would you guess the rate of a person working on a continuous schedule, also known as a fixed-ratio of 1, will compare with the rate of a person working on a fixed-ratio of 10? The continuous schedule will produce a _____ (higher, lower) rate.

36. Let's summarize. The schedule that produces the higher and more uniform rate is the _____ schedule; the schedule that produces the stair-step pattern of working and pausing is the _____ schedule; the generic schedule that produces the slowest rate is the _____ schedule.

### 5. Resistance to Extinction

69. Pre-test: Which of the following schedules produces the greatest resistance to extinction? _____
(continuous, fixed-ratio, variable-ratio)

63. Pre-test: Remember, intermittent schedules produce greater resistance to _____, and they combat the decrease in reinforcer effectiveness due to _____.

101. This module teaches two benefits of ratio schedules. I will start with increased resistance to extinction. Ratio schedules may be used to reduce satiation and also increase a person's resistance to _____.

5. After a behavior analyst has helped change a client's behavior, the client must return to their everyday life. If they don't receive reinforcement for the new

behavior, it will extinguish. Behavior analysts often create greater resistance to extinction in their client by shifting them to the generic schedule called a(n) _____ (continuous, extinction, intermittent) schedule near the end of training.

10. Dr. Koegel found that, at the request of an adult who never reinforced them, children with retardation would imitate for much longer when they had been trained on what type of schedule—continuous or fixed-ratio? _____
_____

9. Dr. Kazdin found that an individual who was reinforced for one in three interactions maintained a high rate of interaction when reinforcement was discontinued, compared to another individual who had been reinforced for every interaction. Thus, they found that intermittent reinforcement leads to greater resistance to _____.

81. Suppose that you have been reinforcing someone for every response she makes. Suppose you then stop reinforcing any of her responses. The change from a reinforcer after every response to no reinforcers after any responses is obvious. She could notice after only one response. Therefore, you would expect her rate of responding to decrease _____ (quickly, slowly).

82. Suppose that you have been reinforcing someone for every tenth responses. Suppose you then stop reinforcing any of his responses. He would take some time to notice the change from a reinforcer after every tenth response to no reinforcers after any responses. The quickest he could notice would require at least 10 responses instead of the minimum of only one response for continuous reinforcement. Therefore, you would expect the rate of responding to decrease for fixed-ratio compared to continuous reinforcement more _____ (quickly, slowly).

83. Suppose that you have been reinforcing someone for every tenth response on the average. Suppose sometimes you reinforced her after only 3 responses, most of

the time for 5 to 15 responses, but sometimes only after 30 responses! Suppose you then stop reinforcing any of her responses. The quickest she could be sure of the change would be after the largest ratio, in this case 30 responses, instead of the 10 for a fixed-ratio of 10. Therefore, you would expect the rate of responding during extinction to decrease for variable-ratio compared to fixed-ratio even more _____ (quickly, slowly).

112. Which of the following schedules produces the <u>greatest</u> resistance to extinction? _____ (continuous, fixed-ratio, variable-ratio)

74. Suppose that Daddy Warbucks often emits the response of making a financial investment. Suppose that his investment response is reinforced by making money. Suppose that he makes money on a fixed-ratio schedule. Now compare his resistance to extinction with Little Annie who makes money on a variable-ratio schedule. How would Daddy Warbucks's investment responding extinguish compared to Little Annie's? _____ (faster, slower)

40. One benefit of ratio schedules is that they increase resistance to extinction. Here is a second benefit from ratio schedules. Ratio schedules produce more responses per reinforcement than continuous schedules. Therefore, using them reduces the number of reinforcers you have to give someone. In other words, reinforcers occur more rarely. This fact makes them useful in combating the <u>decrease</u> in reinforcer effectiveness due to _____ (deprivation, satiation).

89. The generic schedule that produces greatest resistance to extinction and that combats the decrease in reinforcer effectiveness due to satiation is a(n) _____ schedule.

70. Remember, intermittent schedules produce greater resistence to _____, _____ and they combat the decrease in reinforcer effectiveness due to _____.

## 6. *Two Drawbacks of Ratio Schedules*

67. Pre-test: What type of schedule should be used when shaping a new response? _____

57. Pre-test: If you make the ratio of responses to reinforcers too large, then you risk reducing responding in what is called _____.

102. This module will next cover two drawbacks to ratio schedules. The generic continuous schedule of reinforcement is the most effective schedule when shaping a(n) _____ (new, old) response.

113. You are shaping a new response. You are differentially reinforcing the first approximation to the target behavior. This first approximation doesn't happen very often. Do you think the person would learn to make that approximation more quickly if he were reinforced only some of the time or if he were reinforced every time he performed it? He would learn more quickly if he were reinforced _____ (every time, sometime).

106. Using a ratio schedule for shaping new responses does not produce good results. What type of schedule should be used when shaping a new response? _____ _____

108. When a person stops responding because the ratio has become very high, you might say that the "ratio" has "strained" her ability to respond. You might call such an event by the name ratio _____.

109. When a ratio is made so high that the person receives few reinforcers, his or her responding may be so strained that it breaks down. This occurrence is not extinction because reinforcers are still delivered. Rather this occurrence is known as _____.

2. A drawback to ratio schedules called *ratio strain* comes if you make the ratio too _____ (big, small).

30. If you make the ratio of responses to reinforcers too large, then you risk reducing responding in what is called _____.

105. Two drawbacks of ratio schedules are that they don't work very well when you are _____ new behavior and you can set a ratio so large that you

decrease behavior in what is called _____.

107. Using a ratio schedule for shaping doesn't work very well. What generic schedule is best? _____

35. Let's summarize. The benefits of ratio schedules are that they combat the decrease in reinforcer effectiveness from _____ and they increase resistance to _____.

37. More summary. The drawbacks to ratio schedules are that they are not very effective for _____ new behavior and you can set the ratio so high that you weaken behavior through _____.

34. Let's summarize from the earlier material on rates. Which schedule produces the higher and more uniform rate? The _____ schedule Which schedule produces the stair-step pattern of working and pausing? The _____ schedule Which generic schedule produces the slowest rate? The _____ schedule

111. When you do not deliver reinforcement for every response, you are using which schedule? A(n) _____ (continuous, intermittent) schedule. When you deliver reinforcement for a fixed number of responses (including those greater than one), you are using a(n) _____ schedule. When you deliver reinforcement for a variable number of responses, you are using a(n) _____ schedule.

33. Intermittent schedules produce an increased resistance to _____. They also help combat the decreased effectiveness of reinforcers due to _____.

1. Piece-rate wages are defined as giving a set amount of money for each repetition of a job completed. For example, you might be paid 50 cents for each sales prospect you call and tell about a special sale. Every response (such as a phone call) produces a set reinforcer. Piece-rate wages are the same as the generic schedule called a(n) _____ schedule.

13. Dr. Staats sometimes delivered reinforcers to Ben after every response and sometimes after an average of five responses. Name which these two schedules would have been least likely to satiate Ben: _____ _____ schedule.

### 7. *Another Tactic*

65. Pre-test: The sixth tactic in using the reinforcement strategy for solving human problems is to increase response rate with a(n) _____ schedule of reinforcement.

84. Tactic #6 in using the reinforcement strategy for solving human problems is to increase response rate with a(n) _____ (extinction, ratio) schedule of reinforcement.

96. The sixth tactic in using the reinforcement strategy for solving human problems is to increase response rate with a(n) _____ schedule of reinforcement.

### 8. *Review*

68. Pre-test: When a reinforcer is delivered after every response, the schedule is referred to by the generic label: a(n) _____ schedule. When a reinforcer is delivered after only some responses, the schedule is referred to by the generic label: a(n) _____ _____ schedule. When a reinforcer is never delivered after a response, the schedule is referred to by the generic label: a(n) _____ _____ schedule.

48. Pre-test: If a student is complimented every 13 times she just says "no," what schedule of reinforcement are the student's "no's" on? _____ _____

60. Pre-test: Name a ratio schedule that produces alternating periods of responding and pausing: _____ schedule. Name the schedule that produces a high and uniform rate of responding: _____ schedule.

61. Pre-test: One advantage of ratio schedules is that they produce greater resistance to _____. They also use fewer reinforcers, so they combat

decreased reinforcer effectiveness due to
_____.

46. Pre-test: A person whose responses are never reinforced is on a(n) _____ _____ schedule.

58. Pre-test: If you use too high a ratio, the person often stops responding in the middle of a ratio or responds erratically. This is known as _____.

47. Pre-test: Dr. Staats delivered a reinforcer to Ben after a varying number of reading acquisition responses that averaged 5. What is the name of the schedule? _____

66. Pre-test: The specific schedule in which you deliver a reinforcer after different numbers of responses each time is called a(n) _____ schedule of reinforcement.

62. Pre-test: One disadvantage of ratio schedules is that they are not as good as a continuous schedule when _____ a new response. Another disadvantage is that if you use too high a ratio you may produce _____.

103. To use the reinforcement strategy for solving human problems: (1) increase the desired behavior with reinforcement; (2) decrease undesired behaviors with extinction; (3) increase desired behavior relative to undesired behaviors through differential reinforcement; (4) create new behavior through shaping; (5) use the principles of effective reinforcement; (6) increase the rate of responses through a(n) _____ schedule.

11. Dr. Staats defined an attending response as "pressing a window with a word displayed on it." This statement of what to observe would be called a(n) _____ of "attending."

104. To use the reinforcement strategy for solving human problems: (1) increase the desired behavior through reinforcement; (2) decrease undesired behaviors through extinction; (3) increase desired behavior relative to undesired through differential reinforcement; (4) create new behavior through shaping; (5) use the principles of reinforcer _____; (6) increase the rate of response through a(n) _____ schedule.

38. Name the generic schedule of reinforcement usually used with shaping: a(n) _____ schedule.

97. The specific schedule on which reinforcement is delivered after different numbers of responses each time is called the _____ schedule. The specific schedule on which reinforcement is delivered after the same number of responses each time is called the _____ schedule.

91. The highest and most uniform rate of responding is produced by the _____ _____ schedule.

39. Name the schedule of reinforcement that most increases the length of time for a response to be extinguished after reinforcement is stopped: _____ _____.

14. Dr. Staats studied the rate of Ben's reading acquisition responses for two schedules: (a) when Ben got a reinforcer after every response and (b) when he got a reinforcer after varying numbers of responses that averaged 5. Which schedule would you guess produced the highest rate of responding? ____ (a or b)

19. If Hal receives reinforcers for an average of one out of three responses, then he is on the generic schedule called a(n) _____ schedule.

85. Tactic #6 in using the reinforcement strategy for solving human problems is to increase response rate with a(n) _____ schedule.

12. Dr. Staats found that Ben's reading acquisition responses could be increased in rate by delivering a marble after every response. What generic schedule of reinforcement did he use? _____

## Programmed Examples

### 1. Programmed Examples

12. Pre-test: In Dr. Smith's course, each student used to take a daily quiz that had six questions on it. Any student who got all six questions correct advanced one step toward an A. What is this schedule an example of? _____

11. Pre-test: Bob lived near the phone in the dorm, so he had to answer it much of the time. Furthermore, most of the dorm members didn't bother to thank him for answering it. He found that, on the average, he got thanked once in every four times that he answered the phone. His phone answering is on what schedule of reinforcement? _____

14. Pre-test: Professor Brainbuster required Ken to turn in an essay every week on ancient history. Professor Brainbuster never returned any of Ken's essays. Nor did he tell Ken what his grade was. Ken's essay-writing behavior is on what schedule of reinforcement? _____

13. Pre-test: Mr. Potts couldn't decide whether to reinforce his son's behavior every time that he took out the trash or only after every five times. Under which of these two schedules would his son continue longest to take out the trash if he was never again reinforced? _____ (continuous, fixed-ratio)

7. Johnny found that if he did enough favors for his mother, she would eventually give him a cookie. Sometimes, she gave it to him only after 20 favors, but other times, she gave it to him after the first favor. Mom reinforces Johnny's favors on a(n) _____ schedule of reinforcement. Would Johnny's rate of favors be higher (a) if she continued to give him a cookie after varying numbers of favors or (b) if she gave him a cookie every time he did a favor? ___ (a or b) If his mother wanted Johnny to continue doing favors after she ran out of cookies, should she (c) give him a cookie after varying numbers of favors or (d) after every time that he did a favor? ___ (c or d)

19. When Mr. James was reinforcing Carol's studying after every five problems, he was using what schedule? _____ Would Carol work her problems faster (a) when praised after every problem or (b) when praised after every five problems? ___ (a or b) Father wants Carol to continue working longer when he is not around to praise her. Should he (c) praise her after every problem or (d) praise her after every five problems? ___ (c or d) When Father is praising Carol's work after every five problems, what would she do right after the praise for the fifth problem? _____ (pause, work) Suppose that Mr. James checked Carol's problems after different numbers of problems averaging five. Would Carol work faster on this schedule compared to the one described in the example? _____ (yes, no)

1. Angie seemed to have a hearing problem. She never answered a question the first time it was asked of her. She always said "What?" to the questioner and then would answer the question the second time it was asked. Because Angie answered every second question, what schedule of reinforcement did she put the questioner on? _____

20. When Tom got home from work, he would always check to see if there was any mail for the day because he loved to receive mail. He found that there was mail on the average of 1 day in 3. What schedule of reinforcement is he on for finding mail? _____ If he started finding mail only once in 30 days, his looking might become somewhat strained. What is the name for this phenomenon? _____

6. John praised and hugged his infant daughter Lou when she tried to say "Dada." At first, he praised her only when she said something that started with "da," later only when she said both the "da" and a following "da." Teaching her to say "Dada" is called the _____. By teaching her through a series of steps, John is using what procedure to get Lou to say "Dada"? _____ What schedule of reinforcement would you recommend that John use when he tries to teach Lou to say "Dada"? _____

5. Jeanie was a 6-month-old baby. She was just learning to feed herself with a spoon. Since she was a bit clumsy, she dropped an average of three out of four spoonfuls. Fortunately, Jeanie kept trying. What intermittent schedule of reinforcement was Jeanie on for operating her spoon? _____ (Ask yourself if the reinforcement occurred after a fixed number of spooning responses or after a varying number of spooning responses.)

9. Marge let little Timmy earn some money by pulling weeds. She paid him a penny for each weed that he told her he pulled. She gave

him the money as soon as he told her how many weeds he had pulled that day. Timmy never had any money so his earnings were welcome to him. The pay of one penny per weed seemed to add up fast enough so that Timmy wanted to tell her he had pulled a lot of weeds. However, one day his mother looked at Timmy's weeding and found that he had not done as much as he had told her! The effectiveness of Mom's reinforcer was undermined because Marge ignored the principle of _____.

18. When Don was 14, he was always reading science fiction stories. His father was also a science fiction fan, so when Don had finished reading a chapter, he would immediately go to his father and describe all the interesting events in that chapter of the story. Don's father seemed to have endless interest in hearing about the latest adventures in Don's books. Assuming that father's attention is a reinforcer and that one chapter is one response, what generic schedule of reinforcement is Don on? _____ Suppose that Don's father started listening to Don's accounts of the science fiction stories only when Don had completed a whole book. Because the books contain different numbers of chapters, Don's chapter reading would be on a(n) _____ schedule of reinforcement.

15. Rich had talked Fran into washing the windows of their house, but Fran needed encouragement. At first, Rich made it a point to come by every window Fran completed. Soon, however, Rich just didn't have the time, so he came by after Fran had completed 3, 1, 8, and 4 windows. Fran seemed to finish the windows faster then. What schedule was Fran on for her last 16 windows? _____

17. Walter's mother was teaching him to sew. At first, she praised him for any kind of job that he did. After that, she praised him only when he made the right kind of stitch and made it well. Finally, she praised him only when he cut his own pattern and then sewed it properly. What behavioral procedure is this an example of? _____

4. Jake always says "Sure" when his friends suggest that he have a beer. His friends buy him a beer after 2, 5, 4, 6, or 3 (an average of 4) agreements. On what schedule of reinforcement is his saying "Sure"?

16. Sam thanked his roommate for taking a phone message. His roommate's message taking increased as a result. What behavioral procedure did Sam use to increase message taking? _____

2. At first, Horace's teacher praised him lavishly whenever he wrote a short poem. He wrote several poems one stanza long. Later, she praised him only when he wrote a poem two stanzas long and paid no attention to his shorter poems. By this method, the teacher eventually got him writing 20-stanza poems. What behavioral procedure did the teacher use to teach Horace to write 20-stanza poems?

_____

3. Have you ever played The Dozens? The game involves insulting someone's mother in a funny way. After you say something such as, "You know, Joe is the ugliest person I ever saw," the other person says, "Who's Joe?" You answer, "Joe (your) Momma." The reinforcer is that everyone laughs. Then, it's the other person's turn to trick you into getting an insult. After playing for a while, everyone gets tired of getting laughs this way. Getting tired of the laughs just means that the effectiveness of laughs has decreased as a result of _____.

10. One criticism of the idea that most behavior is caused by reinforcement is that most people are constantly doing all kinds of things without it. One possible explanation for why they do things without reinforcement lies in the idea of resistance to extinction. In other words, perhaps they are doing things without reinforcement because, in the past, they were on the generic schedule called a(n) _____ schedule of reinforcement.

8. Many people try to use reinforcement without success. One reason is that they may deliver their reinforcer long after the response has occurred. If they delay their reinforcer, then they are violating the principle of _____.

# LESSON 14

# Interval Schedules of Reinforcement

## Reading Section

The last lesson described two *intermittent schedules of reinforcement* based on counting—the fixed-ratio and the variable-ratio. These schedules count a person's responses to determine when to deliver the reinforcer.

This lesson describes two intermittent schedules based on the passage of time. Behavior analysts call them *interval schedules*. Tactic #7 in using the reinforcement strategy for solving human problems is to reduce reinforcer frequency with an <u>interval schedule</u>.

1. Tactic #7 in using the reinforcement strategy for solving human problems is to reduce reinforcer frequency with a(n) _____ ___ schedule.

## Definition of Fixed-Interval Reinforcement

The simplest interval schedule is a *fixed-interval* schedule. A **fixed-interval** schedule is a schedule for reinforcing the first response after a <u>fixed period of time</u> since the prior reinforcement.

2. A schedule that reinforces the first response after a fixed period of time is called the _____ schedule.

For example, suppose we reinforce Tom for the first response after five minutes. Suppose we continue to reinforce him for the first response after each additional five minutes. We say that Tom is on a fixed-interval-of-five-minutes schedule. Tom could wait for the

passage of five minutes without making any responses at all. He could then make a single response for the reinforcement. Of course, Tom would have to know in advance how long the interval was, and he would have to time it accurately. This is seldom possible. Be sure to notice that Tom will not receive a reinforcer simply for the passage of the five minutes. He must make a response after the five minutes has passed.

Behavior analysts find that the fixed-interval schedules produce a *scallop* pattern of responding (e.g. Ferster & Skinner, 1957; Weiner, 1969). <u>Scallop</u> refers to a pause after reinforcement followed by a gradual increase in rate prior to the next reinforcement.

3. A pause after reinforcement followed by a gradual increase in rate prior to the next reinforcement is called a _____.

Tom would probably show a scallop pattern during his five-minute fixed-interval. He would probably work at an increasing rate as the five minutes passed. He would end up working at a high rate at the moment of reinforcement. Then, after reinforcement, he would pause for a while. The pattern is similar to a fixed-ratio pattern. Both patterns alternate between responding and resting. However, the overall rate of a fixed-interval schedule is lower. This is because the fixed-interval shows a gradual increase in rate. It does not show the abrupt increase of the fixed-ratio schedule.

Waiting for a friend might be on a fixed-interval schedule. Suppose that every day Jean arrives in the student union at 12:50. Suppose she waits for Bill, who always arrives at 1:00 P.M. If Jean is reading a book, she will probably stop reading and look for Bill from time to time. Furthermore, if Jean is like most of us, she will look up only infrequently at first (say until 12:55). After that, she will start looking more often. If Bill is on time, the first look that Jean takes after 1:00 will be reinforced by the sight of Bill.

In this example, Jean's looking will not be reinforced by the sight of Bill until the 10-minute period of time has passed. Bill's arrival will reinforce her first look after that time.

Note that this is not an example of a fixed-ratio schedule. No fixed number of looks will somehow produce the sight of Bill. She cannot cause Bill to appear sooner by looking more often. She must wait for 10 minutes to pass.

This schedule occurs frequently in the natural environment. Behavior analysts don't have to arrange for it to happen. For example, one researcher studied the betting behavior of chronic horse-racing gamblers (Dickerson, 1979). He found that they tended to place their bets in the last two minutes before a race started. He argued that this was a clear case of fixed-interval scalloping.

Figure 14-1 shows another example of a naturally occurring fixed-interval schedule. It graphs the legislation passed by Congress. The researchers interpret the resulting scallop as the product of a fixed-interval schedule of reinforcement.

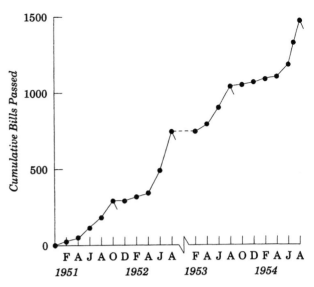

**Figure 14-1.** The cumulative number of bills passed by Congress in two years. The diagonal deflections indicated adjournment of Congress, the presumed reinforcer. (Adapted from "Fixed Interval Work Habits of Congress," by P. Weisberg and P. B. Waldrop, *Journal of Applied Behavior Analysis,* 1972, 5, 93–97. Copyright 1972 by the Society for the Experimental Analysis of Behavior, Inc. Used by permission.)

This schedule is sometimes used by behavior analysts to help people. For example, two researchers studied how to help obese children to exercise more (DeLuca & Holborn, 1985). They reinforced pedaling an exercise bicycle on a fixed-interval schedule.

---

### Even Congress Obeys the Laws of Behavior

Two researchers investigated the rate at which Congress passed bills. Congress passes very few bills at the beginning of a legislative session. Their rate gradually increases as they approach adjournment. Figure 14-1 shows this pattern on a cumulative graph for the years 1951, 1952, 1953, and 1954. The researchers suggested that finishing the legislative session and going home was the reinforcer. They can do this by passing the last bill before them by the last day of the session. Since the interval between the first and last days is always the same, Congress is on a fixed-interval schedule of reinforcement. This schedule should produce a pattern of passing bills that starts out at a low rate. The rate of passing bills should then increase as the interval passed. This is exactly what happens! Note that this same pattern occurs for pigeons responding for food reinforcement. (Based on Weisberg & Waldrop, 1972.)

4. Since the interval between the first and last days is always the same, Congress is on a(n) _____ interval schedule of reinforcement.

The first rotation of the pedal after the end of the interval resulted in a reinforcer. This schedule resulted in increased exercise for the children.

## Definition of Variable-Interval Schedule

Behavior analysts call the other common interval schedule a *variable-interval* schedule. A **variable-interval** schedule is for reinforcing the first response after a <u>varying period of time</u> from the prior reinforcement. For example, suppose we reinforce the first response after three minutes. We might then reinforce the first response after seven minutes. We might reinforce the first response after five minutes. Ann's responding would be on a variable-interval schedule averaging five minutes. Theoretically, Ann could wait for the passage of each of these differing intervals. She could then make only one response per interval and receive reinforcement. Of course, she would have to know in advance how long each interval was. She would also have to accurately time it. Clearly, this would not usually happen. Note that Ann will not receive the reinforcer simply after the passage of time. She must respond after the time has passed.

5. **Variable-interval**: A schedule for reinforcing the first response after a _____ <u>period of time</u> from the prior reinforcement.

Typically, people on a variable-interval schedule work at a <u>uniform</u> rate. They do not stop working after reinforcement, so the next interval may be very short. Thus, any response may produce reinforcement. Similarly, they do not work faster as they near the end of the interval. They can't because the end of the interval is not predictable. The rate of responding is considerably lower than for a variable-ratio schedule.

6. Typically, people on a variable-interval schedule work at a _____ rate.

I described how Jean's looking for Bill might be reinforced on a fixed-interval schedule. Actually, looking for a friend is more likely to be reinforced on a variable-interval schedule. For example, suppose Ted waits for Jen in the student union every day from 12:50 on. Suppose Jen arrives after 5 minutes the first day. Ted may look up from his paper from time to time to see if Jen is coming. He will probably look up fairly often right from the beginning. After all, Jen could show up at any time. But on this day, only his first look after 5 minutes

---

### *Is Attention Behavior? Part 3*

Jim Holland found that the deflection of a pointer reinforced Navy men for looking at a dial. When deflections of a pointer on the dial occurred after a fixed number of looks, they looked steadily. When deflections never occurred, they stopped looking. Holland also studied the effect of deflections for the first look after a fixed time. He found that the Navy men seldom looked during the start of the interval. But they looked often toward the end. This is the pattern typical of fixed-interval schedules. When the deflections occurred after variable periods, the men's attention was on a variable-interval schedule. On this schedule, they looked steadily. Holland showed that the schedule of reinforcement increases the private behavior called attention just like any other behavior He took the idea of attention out of the mysterious realm of the mind. It is just something that people do. It is behavior! (Based on Holland, 1958).

7. When the deflections occurred after variable periods, the men's attention was on a(n) _____-interval schedule. On this schedule, they looked steadily.

will see her. Suppose that on the next days Jen arrives after 1, then 10, then 8 minutes. Ted is on a variable-interval schedule that averages 6 minutes.

Note that this is an example of a variable-interval schedule, not a variable-ratio schedule. Ted cannot cause Jen to appear sooner by looking more often. On the first day, he must wait for 5 minutes to see her. No amount of looking will cause her to arrive sooner.

This schedule occurs in the natural environment. The box on attention describes how it affects attention. The box Is Attention Behavior? describes more of the research by Jim Holland on human attending. He showed that seeing what you are looking for can reinforce the looking. If what you are looking for appears on a fixed- or variable-interval schedule, looking will show the patterns typical of those schedules. When the deflections appeared on a fixed-interval schedule, the rate of looking scalloped. When the deflections occurred on a variable-interval schedule, the rate of looking was uniform.

Behavior analysts sometimes use a variable-interval schedule to help people change. For example, researchers used variable-interval reinforcement with Dan, a fourth grader who didn't study very much during class (Martens, Lochner, & Kelly, 1992). During baseline, he studied about 45% of the time. They praised Dan according to a variable-interval schedule. When they praised his first academic responses after an average of two minutes, his studying increased to 94% of the time. His rate of studying was quite uniform during the school period.

## Advantages and Disadvantages of Interval Schedules

Interval schedules have advantages similar to ratio schedules. You can use them to reduce the problem of <u>satiation</u>. You can use them to produce increased <u>resistance to extinction</u>. They also have similar disadvantages. You will not find them to be useful in <u>shaping</u> a new response. You may find that they deliver too little reinforcement to maintain

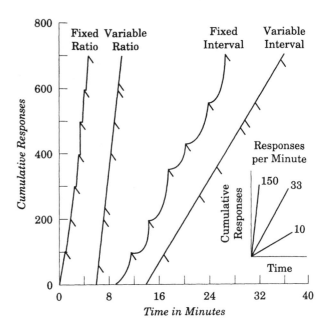

**Figure 14-2.** Stylized cumulative graph of the patterns of responding produced by the four simple schedules of reinforcement. The diagonal slash marks indicate the delivery of reinforcement. (From *Operant Learning: Procedures for Changing Behavior*, by J. L. Williams [Brooks/Cole, 1972]. Reprinted with permission.)

responding. This results in a breakdown of responding similar to <u>ratio strain</u>.

## Comparison of Basic Intermittent Schedules

Figure 14-2 illustrates the patterns and comparative rates of the four simple schedules of reinforcement. As you can see, variable-ratio produces the fastest rate of responding, and fixed-ratio somewhat less. The two interval schedules produce response rates that are lower than the ratio schedules. Notice that the variable-interval and variable-ratio schedules both produce uniform rates of responding. The fixed-ratio and fixed-interval both produce pauses after reinforcement. However, the fixed-interval schedule tends to produce a brief pause that switches very gradually to high-rate responding, This pattern is called a *scallop*.

Researchers have confirmed these comparisons. For example, researchers reinforced reading acquisition on interval and continuous schedules (Staats et al., 1964). The interval schedule produced response rates below that of continuous reinforcement. Other researchers reinforced pedaling an exercise bicycle according to fixed-interval and fixed-ratio schedules (DeLuca & Holborn, 1990). They found that the fixed-ratio schedule produced faster pedaling. These same researchers reinforced pedaling on a variable-ratio schedule (DeLuca & Holborn, 1992). This produced the highest overall rates that they observed. Thus, these comparisons apply to common everyday behavior.

## Laws of Behavior

The unique patterns of responding associated with each schedule are immensely important to behavioral science. They provide powerful examples that behavior is <u>lawful.</u> In fact, behavior analysts describe these patterns as behavioral laws applicable to many species and many behaviors. As you have seen, these laws apply to many complex forms of human behavior. They may even apply to passing congressional legislation and novel writing.

## Summary

Tactic #7 in using the reinforcement strategy for solving human problems is to reduce reinforcer frequency with an <u>interval schedule.</u> Interval schedules are another kind of intermittent schedule that is based on time rather than counting. You are using *a fixed-interval* schedule when you reinforce the first response after a fixed period of time. This procedure produces a scallop pattern of pausing after reinforcement and then a gradual increase in rate leading up to reinforcement. You are using a *variable-interval* schedule when you reinforce the first response after variable periods of time. This procedure produces a uniform pattern of responding. Note the four following characteristics of interval schedules: (1) they produce lower response rates than ratio schedules; (2) they increase resistance to extinction and reduce problems from satiation; (3) they are not useful for shaping; (4) they may lead to too little reinforcement and thus something like ratio

strain. The patterns produced by ratio and interval schedules are basic laws of behavior. They control many kinds of behavior. They control private behavior. They even control the behavior of Congress!

## Behavior Analysis Examples

### *Study Behavior*
One research team taught a class in which the reading material was available to be checked out only in a library room. They kept track of the total amount of time that each student had the material for study in that room. At first, they scheduled a test for each day of the class. As the cumulative graph in Figure 14-3 shows, during this portion of the semester the students studied the material roughly an equal amount of time each day. The researchers then shifted to a schedule of testing every three weeks. The students studied very little for the first part of the three-week period but gradually started studying more and more as the time of the test approached. They next reversed to daily tests and found equal studying each day. And finally, they once again tried a three-week testing period and, although there was a less dramatic effect, they once again found little studying at the beginning of the period and an increasing rate as the test date approached.

8. Because the researchers' testing was based on time rather than counting, this would be an example of a(n) _____ (interval, ratio) schedule.

This experiment produced a pattern of responding that is like that in fixed-interval studies. It is possible to view the test as a reinforcing event that can be scheduled in different ways. When the test is scheduled daily, it approximates a continuous schedule of reinforcement. A continuous schedule produces uniform responding. When the test is scheduled after long intervals, it is similar to a fixed-interval schedule. A fixed-interval produces a scalloped rate of responding. These results indicate that even the complex intellectual behavior involved in studying follows predictable and lawful patterns observed in other

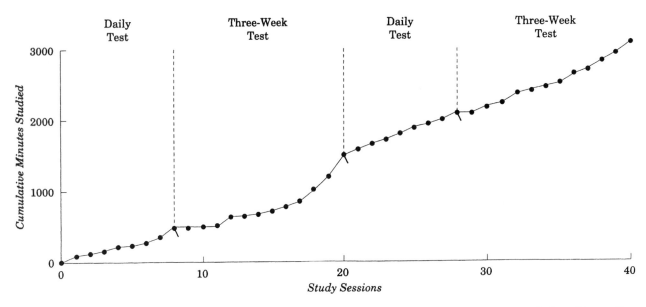

*Figure 14-3.* The cumulative study hours of college students. The experiment compared the effects of testing on a fixed-interval, one-week schedule versus testing on a fixed-interval, three-week schedule. (Adapted from "A Comparison of Students' Studying Behavior Produced by Daily, Weekly, and Three-Week Testing Schedules," by V. T. Mawhinney, D. E. Bostow, D. R. Laws, G. J. Blumenfeld, and B. L. Hopkins, *Journal of Applied Behavior Analysis,* 1971, 4, 257–264. Copyright 1971 by the Society for the Experimental Analysis of Behavior, Inc. Used by permission.)

behaviors. (Based on Mawhinney, Bostow, Laws, Blumenfeld, & Hopkins, 1971.)

9. When the researchers tested every three weeks, they were using a(n) _____ (fixed, variable) -interval schedule.

## Notes

### Note #1

If a person is reinforced after a fixed period of time no matter what he or she is doing at the time, then the situation would be called superstitious reinforcement. This situation was named by Skinner (Skinner, 1948a), who delivered food to pigeons for 5 seconds every 15 seconds no matter what the pigeons were doing. The pigeons developed a variety of superstitious behavior—such as turning in a full circle, swaying the body like a pendulum, and hopping from one foot to the other. These behaviors were called superstitious because the pigeons acted as if their behavior caused the reinforcement even though it did not. People display many superstitious behaviors—like swearing at their cars when they won't start— that may well be caused by the same kind of coincidental reinforcement (e.g., see Aeschleman, Rosen, & Williams, 2002). Superstitious reinforcement differs from fixed-interval reinforcement in that it is delivered after a fixed period of time regardless of whether the person emits a specified behavior.

10. If a person is reinforced after a fixed period of time no matter what he or she is doing at the time, would this be an example of a fixed-interval schedule? _____ (yes, no)

### Note #2

The scalloping of Congress may be due to many factors in addition to the fixed-interval schedule. Other factors include instructions, history, time-correlated stimuli, observation of response, other schedules, response cost and effort, limited-hold, interval duration, and aversive consequences (Poppen, 1982).

## Helpful Hints

### Helpful Hint #1

This section is intended to teach you how to distinguish between interval and ratio schedules when they occur in everyday situations.

Distinguishing between them when a behavior analyst is arranging the delivery of a reinforcer according to a predetermined schedule is quite simple. You must find out his or her rule and determine whether it requires the person to make a number of responses before it is delivered or whether it requires the passage of time before the reinforcer is delivered for the next response.

In everyday situations, however, the distinction is a lot harder to make because we do not have someone to put the rule into words. Suppose, for example, that you are operating a slide projector and you are looking at slides that you took (only a few of which are interesting and therefore reinforcing). What type of schedule is your slide-advance response on? Some responses will be reinforced when you see one of the few interesting slides, most will not be. Is your advancing of the slides reinforced after the passage of time? Or is it reinforced as a function of making a number of responses?

Here's how you should analyze this situation You must realize that the slides are in some unknown sequence in which you may have to advance many slides before coming to an interesting one. Suppose the first interesting one occurs after seven slides. Waiting some amount of time before your next advancing response will not suddenly produce the interesting slide. In fact, if you make no responses for a fixed period of time, you will be no closer to the interesting slide than you were when you started. Thus, the passage of time is not involved in getting to the reinforcer. Rather you must advance the slide projector past seven slides before you get to the reinforcer. You must make those responses before the interesting slide arrives. Because the number of uninteresting slides until the next interesting slide will vary, your slide advancing behavior is on a variable-ratio schedule.

If you think that an example involves an interval schedule, you may check your conclusion by asking the question, "If the person makes no response at all, will there eventually arrive a time at which <u>one response</u> will produce the reinforcer?"

If you think that an example involves a ratio schedule, you may check your conclusion by asking, "If the person makes the

responses very rapidly, will the next reinforcer arrive <u>sooner</u> (than if the responses are made slowly)?" In other words, the rapidity of reinforcement for an interval schedule is <u>time-controlled</u> (although you still must make at least one response), while for a ratio schedule it is <u>response-controlled</u>.

11. When you are advancing slides to find an interesting one, the passage of time does not determine when you get to the reinforcer. Furthermore, if you advance them quickly, you will get to the next interesting one sooner. Therefore, your slide-advancing behavior would be on a(n) _____ (interval, ratio) schedule.

12. To summarize, then, you can ask two questions to decide if an example involves a ratio or if it involves an interval schedule. If you think that an example involves a ratio schedule, you can check your conclusion by asking, "If the person makes the responses very rapidly, will the next reinforcer arrive _____ (later, sooner) (than if the responses are made slowly)?"

13. If you think that an example involves an interval schedule, you can check your conclusion by asking the question, "If the person makes no response at all, will there eventually arrive a time at which _____ (how many?) response(s) will produce the reinforcer?"

### *Helpful Hint #2*
The slide projector example can also be analyzed from the point of view of people watching slides that are being advanced by someone else. In that case, their looking response would be reinforced by the sight of an interesting slide only after the passage of the amount of time that it takes the operator to get around to advancing the projector seven slides. Thus the viewer, unlike the operator, is on a variable-interval schedule. Remember to determine whether the person's response advances the slide or whether it involves looking at a slide whose delivery depends on someone else.

Watching a slide show where someone else is advancing the slides is also like watching a movie, or TV, or any event controlled by someone else. You can't change when anything happens. All you can do is act at the right time. Thus, all of these examples involve interval schedules.

Operating a slide show is like turning the pages of a book to read, flipping through photographs, or sorting slides. They are like any activity in which you are in charge of the pace. The faster you advance slides or pages, the faster you flip photos or sort slides, the sooner you find the reinforcers. Thus these activities all involve ratio schedules.

14. When watching slides being advanced by someone else, you as the viewer, unlike the operator, are on a(n) _____ (interval, ratio) schedule.

### Helpful Hint #3

You may *not* abbreviate the schedule of reinforcement unless you also give its numerical value. If you want to show off, you can enter the exact schedule including the time. If the schedule is fixed-interval, you write *FI* and state the amount of time until the next response produces the reinforcer. If the schedule is variable-interval, you write *VI* and state the average time until the next response produces a reinforcer. These abbreviations are widely used by behavior analysts. If you do show off, be sure to abbreviate the schedule with the length of time. However, do not include whether the unit of time is seconds, minutes, or hours. The book will show two correct answers. For example, if the average interval is two minutes, the book will show "variable-interval" as one answer and "VI-2" as an alternative answer. It will not show "variable-interval of 2," or "VI-2 minutes," or "VI" as answers.

15. If you are labeling a fixed-interval schedule where the first response after three minutes will be reinforced, the correct answer for the full name would be _____ schedule, or abbreviate it as _____.

### Helpful Hint #4

If the book tells you that the first response after an average of 2 minutes will be reinforced,

you can assume that each interval will be variable. It might be 2, 3, 1, and 2 minutes long, but it will average 2 minutes. Thus, the schedule will be a variable-interval, not a fixed-interval schedule.

16. If the first response is reinforced after intervals that average two minutes in length, then you should conclude that the schedule is not a fixed-interval but rather a(n) _____-interval schedule.

### Helpful Hint #5

Throughout the book I have introduced various "helper terms" that refer to a group of terms. The terms include *method* for the methods of observation and *schedule* for the generic and the specific schedules of reinforcement. Students sometimes confuse the interval method of observation with the fixed-interval schedule of reinforcement. If you notice whether a question asks for a method or a schedule, you can avoid this mistake.

17. If an example refers to "intervals every five minutes" and then asks, "What method of observation was used?" you might guess which of the following—"time sample" or "fixed-interval"? _____

## Additional Readings

Bentall, R. P., & Lowe, C. F. (1987). The role of verbal behavior in human learning: III. Instructional effects in children. *Journal of the Experimental Analysis of Behavior, 47*, 177–190. This article shows how instructions affect the pattern of fixed-interval responding for young children. It raises the issue of how reinforcement and verbal behavior interact to determine behavior.

Holland, J. G. (1958). Vigilance. *Science, 128*, 61–67. Also reprinted in R. Ulrich, T. Stachnik, & J. Mabry (Eds., 1966), *Control of human behavior* (Vol. 1). Glenview, IL: Scott, Foresman. This article reports one of the earliest demonstrations of schedule effects with human subjects. Holland showed that the "looking response" is one that is influenced by its consequences (that is, seeing a reinforcing scene) and that, depending on the schedule of seeing what one is looking for, the pattern of looking will vary.

Reese, E. P. (1978). *Human behavior: Analysis and application*. Dubuque, IA: William C. Brown. This book is a fine introduction to operant psychology applied to the analysis of human behavior. It contains an excellent description of schedule effects and many citations to research illustrating these effects.

# Programmed Reading

I have programmed questions to help you master the following topics: (1) Elements of Fixed-Interval Schedules, (2) Elements of the Variable-Interval Schedule, (3) Advantages and Disadvantages of Interval Schedules, (4) Another Tactic, and (5) Review.

### 1. Elements of Fixed-Interval Schedules

34. Pre-test: A scallop is the typical pattern for which schedule? The _____ _____ schedule.

33. Pre-test: A fixed-interval schedule is one in which the person must (1) wait for a(n) _____ period of time to pass and then (2) make a(n) _____ after that time.

55. Pre-test: Will a person on a fixed-interval schedule be reinforced at the end of the fixed-interval even if he or she does not respond? _____ (yes, no)

36. Pre-test: Behavior analysts call the pattern whereby someone pauses and then their rate of responding gradually increases a(n) _____.

51. Pre-test: The name of the schedule on which the person must (1) wait for a fixed period of time to pass and then (2) make a response is called a(n) _____ schedule.

38. Pre-test: Dr. Mawhinney tested James every three weeks. If passing a test is a reinforcer, then James's study behavior was on what schedule of reinforcement? _____

70. The topic of this module is interval schedules. The fixed-ratio and variable-ratio schedules that you learned about in the prior lesson deliver reinforcers based on _____ (counting, timing) responses.

59. The fixed-interval and variable-interval schedules that you learned about in this lesson deliver reinforcers based on _____ (counting, timing) responses.

84. When the behavior of someone is being reinforced on a fixed-interval schedule, not every response is reinforced. Therefore, the person is being reinforced according to the generic schedule called a(n) _____ (continuous, intermittent) schedule.

61. The most important fact about fixed-interval schedules is that the simple passage of time does *not* produce a reinforcer. The person must do more than wait, she must also make a <u>response</u>. So remember, a fixed-interval schedule is one in which the person must (1) wait for a fixed period of time to pass and then (2) make a(n) _____ after that time.

2. A fixed-interval schedule is one in which the person must wait for a fixed period of time to pass. Is it true that (a) the person automatically gets the reinforcer at the end of the period or (b) the person has to make a response after the period is over to get the reinforcer? _____ (a or b)

3. A fixed-interval schedule is one in which the person must make a response after a(n) _____ period of time has passed.

72. Theoretically, a person on a fixed-interval schedule of reinforcement could wait for the passage of the fixed-interval without making any responses. However, they would then have to make one _____.

86. Will a person on a fixed-interval schedule be reinforced at the end of the fixed-interval even if he or she does not respond? _____ (yes, no)

4. A fixed-interval schedule is one in which the person must (1) wait for a(n) _____ period of time to pass and then (2) make a(n) _____ after that time.

62. The name of the schedule on which the person must (1) wait for a fixed period of time to pass and then (2) make a response is called a(n) _____ schedule.

16. If Jose is reinforced for the first response after every five minutes, he is said to be on a fixed-interval schedule of 5. In answering a question to identify this schedule, two forms of answer are correct. First, you can spell out the whole name (but omit the actual time): _____. Or, second, you can "show off" with the abbreviation (with the actual time): _____.

80. Typically, the behavior of someone on a fixed-interval schedule of reinforcement *scallops*. That means they pause just after reinforcement and then as the time for reinforcement nears, their rate of responding _____ (decreases, increases).

79. Typically, someone on a fixed-interval schedule of reinforcement pauses just after reinforcement, and then as the time for reinforcement nears, their rate of responding increases. Behavior analysts call this pattern a(n) _____ (reinforcer, scallop).

6. A scallop is the typical pattern for which schedule? The _____ schedule.

10. Behavior analysts call the pattern where someone pauses and then their rate of responding gradually increases a(n) _____.

60. The fixed-interval schedule produces a pausing and working pattern. Another schedule that you learned about in the lesson on <u>ratio</u> schedules also produces a pausing and working pattern. The name of that schedule is the _____ _____ schedule.

26. Jean arrives in the student union at 12:50 every day and waits for Bill. She must always wait 10 minutes because Bill arrives at 1:00. What schedule is Jean on if seeing Bill is a reinforcer? A(n) _____ schedule.

24. It is easy to confuse interval and ratio schedules. A schedule is a ratio schedule if responding rapidly produces the reinforcer sooner. A schedule is an interval schedule if the person can wait without responding until a time comes when _____ (how many?) response(s) will produce the reinforcer.

15. If Jean looks more often while waiting for Bill, she will not see him any sooner. He will get there at 1:00 no matter what she does. However, at 1:00 she must make the single response of looking for him to see him. Therefore, she is not on a(n) _____ (interval, ratio) schedule.

11. Dickerson found that George, a horse-racing gambler, did not place his bets right after the last race. Rather, his probability of placing the bets slowly increased. He usually placed his bet in the last two minutes before a race started. The reinforcer was the chance to win the bet. Dickerson argued that this pattern was the result of a fixed-interval schedule. Therefore, the pattern of gradual increase should be labeled as a(n) _____.

81. Weisberg pointed out that Congress passes legislation during the 10-month-long period of time set for a legislative session, and that their behavior is then reinforced by adjournment. If legislative sessions are always of the same length, passing legislation is on what schedule of reinforcement?

_____

82. When DeLuca compared not reinforcing versus reinforcing obese children for pedaling an exercise bicycle on a fixed-interval, the result was a(n) _____ (increase, decrease) in exercise.

57. Remember this. Suppose a person is on a fixed-interval of three minutes. If at the end of three minutes they do not make a response, they _____ (will, won't) get a reinforcer.

## 2. Elements of the Variable-Interval Schedule

52. Pre-test: The name of the schedule in which a person (1) waits for a varying period of time and then (2) makes a response is the _____ schedule.

40. Pre-test: If you can make the reinforcer arrive <u>sooner</u> by responding rapidly, then the schedule is a(n) _____ schedule; if you simply have to wait for passage of time until <u>one</u> response will produce the reinforcer, then the schedule is a(n) _____ schedule.

39. Pre-test: If Jose is reinforced for responding after an average of five minutes, he is said to be on a variable-interval schedule

of 5. When answering a question to identify this schedule, two forms of answer are correct. First, you can spell out the full name (without the time): _____ or, second, you can abbreviate (and include the time): _____.

35. Pre-test: A variable-interval schedule is one in which the person must (1) wait for a(n) _____ period of time to pass and (2) make a(n) _____ after that time.

53. Pre-test: Typically, people on a variable-interval schedule work at a(n) _____ rate for the entire period of time that the schedule is in effect.

71. The topic of this module is to learn about variable-interval schedules. Remember, with a fixed-interval schedule a person must wait for a fixed period of time before they can earn the reinforcer. With a <u>variable</u> interval schedule a person must wait for a(n) _____ period of time before they can earn the reinforcer.

14. If a person's behavior is being reinforced according to a variable-interval schedule, not every response is reinforced. Therefore, the behavior is being reinforced according to the generic schedule called a(n) _____ (continuous, intermittent) schedule.

7. A variable-interval schedule is one in which the person must (1) wait for a(n) _____ period of time to pass and (2) make a(n) _____ after that time.

73. Theoretically, if a person's responses are reinforced on a variable-interval schedule, they could wait for the passage of the time without responding and then be reinforced for making _____ (how many?) response(s) after that time.

87. Will a person on a variable-interval schedule be reinforced at the end of the different-length intervals even if he or she doesn't respond? _____ (yes, no)

63. The name of the schedule in which a person (1) waits for a varying period of time and then (2) makes a response is the _____ schedule.

17. If Jose is reinforced for responding after an average of five minutes, he is said to be

on a variable-interval schedule of 5. In answering a question to identify this schedule, two forms of answer are correct. First, you can spell out the full name (without the time): _____ or, second, you can abbreviate (and include the time): _____.

30. On what schedule do people typically work at a <u>uniform</u> rate for the entire period of time that the schedule is in effect? _____

78. Typically, people on a variable-interval schedule work at a(n) _____ rate for the entire period of time that the schedule is in effect.

67. The pattern of uniform responding for the variable-interval schedule is similar to the pattern for a ratio schedule you studied in a prior lesson (not counting continuous reinforcement): _____.

18. If Ted waits in the student union every day from 12:50 on to see Jen, who arrives within an average of six minutes, what schedule of reinforcement is Ted on if seeing Jen is a reinforcer? _____

25. It is essential that you tell the difference between ratio and interval schedules. In the previous example, Ted cannot cause Jen to appear sooner by looking more often. He must wait until the interval passes, and then he must make one response. Therefore, his looking response is on a(n) _____ (interval, ratio) schedule.

89. You can tell the difference by asking two questions. One question is, "If the person makes no response at all, will there eventually arrive a time at which one response will produce the reinforcer?" If the answer is "yes," then the schedule is based on time, and you can be sure that the schedule is a(n) _____ (interval, ratio) schedule.

65. The other question you can ask is, "If the person makes the responses very rapidly, will the next reinforcer arrive sooner (than if the responses are made slowly)?" If the answer is "yes," then the schedule is based on counting, and the schedule is a(n) _____ (interval, ratio) schedule.

19. If you can make the reinforcer arrive <u>sooner</u> by responding rapidly, then the schedule is a(n) _____ schedule; if you simply have to wait for passage of time until <u>one</u> response will produce the reinforcer, then the schedule is a(n) _____ schedule.

74. These questions are the key to telling the difference between ratio and interval schedules. So remember that the schedule is an interval schedule if you simply have to wait for the passage of time until _____ (how many?) response(s) will produce the reinforcer; but the schedule is a ratio schedule if you can respond rapidly and make the reinforcer arrive _____.

12. Dr. Holland found that when deflections of a pointer used to reinforce John appeared on a fixed-interval schedule, the rate of looking showed a(n) _____ (scallop, uniform) pattern as reinforcement approached. When the deflections occurred on a variable-interval schedule, the rate of looking was more of a(n) _____ (scallop, uniform) pattern.

64. The Navy men looked at a steady, uniform rate when deflections of a pointer occurred on a(n) _____ schedule.

13. Dr. Martens found that variable-interval reinforcement helped increase study time for a fourth grader from 45% to 94%. Under this interval schedule, his rate of studying showed a(n) _____ (scallop, uniform) pattern.

### 3. Advantages and Disadvantages of Interval Schedules

41. Pre-test: Interval schedules can be used to combat the decrease in reinforcer effectiveness due to _____. They can also increase resistance to _____.

42. Pre-test: Is the responding rate higher in a variable-ratio schedule or a variable-interval schedule? The _____ schedule.

44. Pre-test: Pauses after reinforcement and then faster response rates are characteristic of the response pattern produced by what two schedules of reinforcement? _____ and _____

69. The topic of this module is the advantages and disadvantages of interval schedules. Interval schedules don't deliver reinforcers after every response. They therefore have many of the advantages of ratio schedules. Interval schedules can be used to combat the decrease in reinforcer effectiveness due to _____. They can also increase resistance to _____.

21. Interval schedules also have many of the disadvantages of ratio schedules. Interval schedules are not suitable for use when _____ a new response. Interval schedules may not maintain responding when, as in ratio strain, they deliver too few _____.

32. People can control how rapidly they earn a reinforcer on a ratio schedule, unlike on an interval schedule. People usually earn reinforcers as fast as possible. Therefore, when they are on a ratio schedule, they work _____ (faster, slower) than when on an interval schedule.

23. Is the responding rate higher in a variable-ratio schedule or a variable-interval schedule? A _____ schedule.

88. Would you guess that the overall rate of responding is higher for a fixed-interval schedule or a fixed-ratio schedule? _____

31. Pauses after reinforcement and then faster response rates are characteristic of the response pattern produced by what two schedules of reinforcement? _____ and _____

66. The pattern of responding that is produced by a fixed-interval (pause after reinforcement and then a gradually increasing response rate) is called a(n) _____.

22. Interval schedules produce _____ _____ (higher, lower) response rates than ratio schedules.

1. A common feature of fixed <u>interval</u> and fixed <u>ratio</u> schedules is that not every response is reinforced. Therefore, both schedules are examples of the generic schedules called _____ schedules.

85. When you are advancing slides to find an interesting one, the passage of time does not determine when you get to the

reinforcer. Therefore, you would be on a(n) _____ (interval, ratio) schedule.

### 4. Another Tactic

48. Pre-test: Tactic #7 in using the reinforcement strategy for solving human problems is to reduce reinforcer frequency with a(n) _____ schedule.

68. The seventh tactic in using the reinforcement strategy for solving human problems is to reduce reinforcer frequency with a(n) _____ (interval, ratio) schedule.

58. Tactic #7 in using the reinforcement strategy for solving human problems is to reduce reinforcer frequency with a(n) _____ schedule.

### 5. Review

47. Pre-test: Sally kept reading *True Romances* hoping that a really exciting scene or passage would soon come along. Such a scene occurred on the average of only once in 20 pages. Because Sally can control how fast she finds these scenes by her reading rate, her reading behavior is on what specific schedule: a(n) _____ schedule. (Warning: Many students get this wrong!).

54. Pre-test: Which intermittent schedule studied in this or in prior lessons produces the highest sustained rate of responding?

    _____

46. Pre-test: Red was learning to soft-boil eggs. If he took an egg out before three minutes, it was runny. If he took it out after three minutes, it was firm. Red was on a(n) _____ schedule of reinforcement.

43. Pre-test: Name the interval schedule in which people respond at a gradually increasing rate called a *scallop* as the time for the reinforcement approaches: _____.

50. Pre-test: The climactic scenes in *A Football Season* occurred on pages 75, 351, and 501. Horace often quit reading for days at a time even though he really enjoyed the climactic scenes when they arrived. He found himself on a rather large ratio schedule. His erratic reading is an example of _____.

56. Pre-test: You have learned three generic schedules in which responding is reinforced always, never, or sometimes. They are the _____, _____, and _____ schedules.

45. Pre-test: People maintain a uniform but low rate of responding in which interval schedule? _____ schedule. (Give full name of schedule.)

37. Pre-test: Billie Bob didn't like most of the music on KROK. He waited 10 minutes for the first good song, then 2 minutes, then 6 minutes. He was on a(n) _____ schedule of reinforcement.

49. Pre-test: Tactic #7 in using the reinforcement strategy for solving human problems is to reduce reinforcer frequency with a(n) _____ schedule.

76. To use the reinforcement strategy for solving human problems: (6) increase response rate with a ratio schedule; (7) reduce reinforcer frequency with a(n) _____ schedule.

27. Mawhinney and associates (1971) might have given tests unannounced but occurring either (a) on the average of every three weeks or (b) exactly every three weeks. Which schedule of test giving would result in a more uniform pattern of studying? _____

75. To determine whether an example involves an interval schedule, you should ask, "If the person makes no response at all, will there eventually arrive a time at which _____ response(s) will produce the reinforcer?"

77. To use the reinforcement strategy for solving human problems, increase response rate with a(n) _____ schedule and reduce reinforcer frequency with a(n) _____ schedule.

28. Mawhinney and associates (1971) observed students' study patterns in relation to tests. Suppose that passing a test is a reinforcer. Then Mawhinney used two schedules of reinforcement: (a) students were tested daily and (b) student were tested at consistent three-week intervals. If the professor suddenly stopped reinforcing

studying with tests but didn't tell the students, which schedule would lead to students studying longer on their own? ___

83. When determining if an example involves a ratio schedule, ask, "If the person makes the response very rapidly, will the next reinforcer arrive? _____ (yes, no)

29. Name two types of intermittent schedules that produce a tendency for people to stop responding after reinforcement (scallop or stair-step): _____ and _____.

8. A variable-interval schedule of reinforcement is one in which the person is reinforced for the first response after _____ periods of time.

5. A fixed-interval schedule is one in which the person is reinforced for the first response made after a(n) _____ period of time passes.

20. If you can make the reinforcer arrive sooner by responding rapidly, then the schedule is a(n) _____ schedule; if you simply have to wait for the passage of time until one response will produce the reinforcer, then the schedule is a(n) _____ schedule.

9. Although only an average of 1 in 10 jokes in a joke book is hilarious, most people rapidly read through all the jokes, looking for the good ones. What schedule of reinforcement is the joke reader on? _____ (Ask if the person can make the reinforcer arrive sooner!)

## Programmed Examples

### 1. Programmed Examples

15. Pre-test: Tillie was difficult to engage in a conversation, and in particular, she was difficult to get started talking about herself. Frank found out that if you asked her enough questions about herself she would eventually open up. Sometimes it took only a couple of questions, but other times it took many more. What schedule of reinforcement is Frank's questioning on if "opening up" is the reinforcer? _____

16. Pre-test: Willis was fascinated by comets. He watched patiently to catch sight of Alpha 13, which was visible at 4 A.M. on August 24 every two years. What schedule of reinforcement was his watching for Alpha 13 on? _____

13. Pre-test: Kay was always thrilled when she saw a deer. She used to sit for hours on her favorite hill waiting to see one. What schedule of reinforcement is her deer-looking behavior on? _____

14. Pre-test: The Kramers had a light switch that didn't work right. The first time you moved the switch, the lights did not come on. In fact, you had to turn the switch three times before the lights would come on. Operating the light switch was on what schedule of reinforcement? _____

6. Dave met Doris for lunch at the corner of Market and Fifth every day. Doris was supposed to show up at 1:00, but she came anywhere from 10 minutes early to 10 minutes late. Suppose Dave looks at each passerby to see if he or she is Doris. Suppose that seeing Doris reinforces his looking. Guess what schedule his looking behavior is on? Suppose you guessed that this was a ratio schedule. You could check your guess by asking, "If Dave looks more often at people, will Doris arrive sooner?" (Notice the question doesn't address whether he will see her sooner but whether she will arrive soon.) The answer is _____. (yes, no) Because his response does not speed up the reinforcer, you know it's not a ratio schedule. You might then guess that the schedule was an interval schedule. You could check this by asking, "If Dave does not look at all, will there eventually arrive a time when one looking response will sight Doris?" The answer is _____. (yes, no) Because one response is ultimately all that's needed, you know it's an interval schedule, but which one? Because Doris comes at different times each day, you can conclude that Dave's looking is on a(n) _____ schedule.

17. Ron and Betty were watching a movie containing a few scenes showing dancing. Since they were interested in learning some new steps, these scenes were the only ones that were of interest to them. Suppose that the scenes were 2 minutes long and the first one occurred after 15 minutes had elapsed, the second after another 5 minutes, the third after another 25 minutes, and the last after

another 15 minutes. Suppose that you guess that this may be a ratio schedule. To check your guess you should ask, "If Ron and Betty look at the movie more often, will the dancing scenes arrive <u>sooner</u>?" The answer is _____. (yes, no) You would now change your guess to an interval schedule. You should again check your answer. Ask, "If Ron and Betty do not look for a time, will there eventually arrive a time when making <u>one</u> looking response will result in seeing the dancing?" The answer is _____. (yes, no) Since the time between scenes varies from 5 to 25 minutes, this example illustrates a(n) _____ schedule.

10. Martha worked on an assembly line at the Ford plant. It was her job to tighten 13 nuts on each car frame. She got to rest until the next frame came along every time she tightened the nuts on the current frame. To determine whether this is a ratio schedule, ask, "If Martha makes the response very fast or very often, will the next reinforcer arrive <u>sooner</u>?" The answer is _____. (yes, no) It is usually wise to also check to see whether this might be an interval schedule by asking, "If Martha makes no response at all, will there eventually arrive a time at which one response will produce the reinforcer?" The answer is _____. (yes, no) Because Martha must make 13 responses per reinforcer, her work is on a(n) _____ schedule of reinforcement.

7. George worked in a factory. His supervisor came by to check on him every 30 minutes. (Assume that the supervisor reinforces his working.) To check whether this is a ratio schedule, ask, "If George works faster will the supervisor arrive <u>sooner</u>? The answer is _____. (yes, no) To check whether this is an interval schedule, first ask, "If George does not work at all for a time, will there eventually arrive a time when one response will result in the supervisor seeing him working?" The answer is _____. (yes, no) Since the supervisor comes by every 30 minutes, this is an example of a(n) _____ schedule.

20. When reading a book, one might find many passages or scenes that are boring. However, most people keep reading with the hope that a really exciting passage will come along soon. Such a scene may occur on the average of only once every 20 pages. This can be a confusing example because you might think it is like watching a movie. However, the movie goes on whether or not you look. Unless you are going to skip pages, which will destroy the plot and make no passages exciting, you must read on. If you were to guess that it is an interval schedule, you should check by asking, "If the person does not read for a period of time (and does not turn pages), will there arrive a time when reading only one page will produce the reinforcer (the exciting passage)?" The answer to this question for reading a book must be _____. (yes, no) If you change your guess to a ratio schedule, ask, "If you read fast, will the reinforcer arrive sooner?" The answer is _____. (yes, no) Therefore, reading a book for exciting passages is on a(n) _____ schedule.

9. John was very clothes conscious. He liked to have on his hip clothes whenever anyone stopped by his room to visit. On an ordinary day, John had a visitor on the average of once every 93 minutes. The visitors came between 7:00 and 11:00 P.M. Having a visitor when he had his hip clothes on reinforced wearing hip clothes. After determining whether John makes the response more often (for example by staying in his hip clothes for the full four hours), ask, "If John does not make the response for a time, will there arrive a time when he could dress in his hip clothes and produce the reinforcer?" With this question you can determine whether this is a(n) _____ schedule. In this example, John's dressing in hip clothes is being reinforced according to a(n) _____ schedule. (Name the specific schedule.)

11. Marty's teacher wanted him to do more math problems for less reinforcement. She decided to reinforce him an average of once every five times that he completed a problem. She kept track of where he started and then complimented him after he completed 3, 8, 5, and 4 problems. The teacher was giving out compliments on a(n) _____ _____ schedule. (Check your answer by asking both questions.)

2. Gloria has a crush on her neighbor Dave but is too shy to make his acquaintance. She starts watching his door at 5:50 every evening just to catch a glimpse of him. Dave

comes home at exactly 6:00, even on weekends. What schedule of reinforcement is Gloria's watching behavior on? _____ _____ (Check your answer by asking both questions.)

8. John has been trying to teach his son to bring his plate into the kitchen and put it in the sink immediately after dinner. During the first month, John gave his son an ice cream dessert each time he brought his plate into the kitchen. In the second month, John started giving his son an ice cream dessert when he brought his plate to the kitchen for several meals in a row, averaging four. What schedule of reinforcement is the son on during the second month? _____

1. Alice was a radar scanner in Alaska. She was supposed to scan the radar screen continually for an eight-hour period looking for unidentified (and possibly hostile) planes. Alice spotted an average of two unidentified planes per night. Usually they were American planes that were off course. What schedule of reinforcement is Alice's scanning on: _____. (Be sure to ask the relevant questions.)

3. Chester took his children for an ice cream treat only when they brought home a good school paper for him to see. He gave them the treat on the Sunday of any week that they brought home a good paper. It seemed like they would do anything for such a treat. They did not get ice cream treats too often. What principle of effective reinforcement accounts for the fact that Chester's treat did not result in higher grades for his children? _____

5. Darlene's clock radio always woke her at exactly 6:45. As she dressed, she would listen to see if the 7:00 news had come on yet.

What schedule of reinforcement is her listening behavior on? _____

4. Daisy continued to cry every night after being put to bed. Her parents would go into her room to see what was the matter, and they always spent some time comforting her. They never found any physical problems such as wet diapers. After some months, they decided that they should simply ignore the crying. They found that within several days Daisy no longer cried after being put to bed. What generic schedule of reinforcement did her parents place her crying on by ignoring her crying? _____

18. Stan wanted everyone around him to be happy and cheerful. Anytime that Susan said something cheerful, he was happy and smiled. Anytime that she said something down, he was unhappy and glum. Susan began saying cheerful things more often. What behavioral procedure did Stan unconsciously apply to Susan's behavior to increase happiness relative to unhappiness? _____

12. Pete had reduced the writing of romance books to a science. He had a chart that told him how many pages to wait before creating one of the steamy scenes for which he was famous. He made his reader wait for 1 page to get to the first one, then 11, then 5, then 23 more, and so on. If reading a page is one response, what schedule of reinforcement is that response on? _____

19. Timmy discovered that if you hold a magnifying lens between an ant and the sun and focus it properly, the ant will burn up with a popping sound. Timmy's rate of focusing the magnifying glass on ants increased dramatically after this discovery. The event "frying ants" is called a(n) _____.

## Reading Section

This unit focuses on reinforcement. The lessons point to many reinforcers, most of which stem directly from the behavior of other people. Such reinforcers include attention, encouragement, and compliments. The lessons have also pointed to many desirable and undesirable behaviors that may result from reinforcement. Such behavior includes studying, talking about problems, and nagging.

## Reinforcement Can Help

Reinforcement is a very social concept. Most reinforcement arises from how people treat each other. Under the best of circumstances, the behaviors of two people are mutually reinforcing. Mutual reinforcement is ideal whether the two people be married, friends, or just roommates. The benefits to each person help maintain the relationship. Read the box on Larry and Jo Ann. Reinforcement can be magic!

## Reinforcement Can Harm

Sometimes we don't fully understand the term *reinforcement*. So we may engage in self-defeating behaviors. We give in to the nagger to stop the nagging. We thereby ensure that the nagger will keep nagging. We listen to complainers to avoid confronting them. We thereby ensure that the complainers will continue to complain. We let shirkers have the same privileges as those who do their share of the work. We thereby increase the probability that the shirkers will continue to avoid doing their share. We may even teach people to be unhappy! Read the box to see how Santa taught a little girl to scream for what she wants! Furthermore, by reinforcing the little

---

### Positive Reinforcement Is Magic!

Here is a love story about the power of reinforcement. Larry and Jo Ann were an ordinary couple who fought and complained about each other until one day Larry thanked Jo Ann for washing his socks! Naturally, Jo Ann suspected that Larry wanted something. A few days later, he thanked Jo Ann for recording the checks in their ledger. She wondered what had gotten into him. But she became more careful of recording check numbers! Then, he thanked her for the great dinner and cleaning the house. Then, gadzooks, he complimented their teenage daughter's appearance. Another day, he washed the dishes. She started to get used to the praise. She even liked it. One day Jo Ann surprised herself. She thanked Larry for bringing home a paycheck! Positive reinforcement from one person led to positive reinforcement from the other. Maybe if we all used a little more, the world would be a better place! (From Larsen, 1991.)

1. The procedure Larry used is _____
_____.

---

### Santa Didn't Save the Day

Barry Kaufman tells the following story. He was waiting in the check-out line of a grocery store during the Christmas season. A two-year-old girl wanted to eat snacks her mother had put in the cart. The mother refused. The girl screamed. Still the mother refused. Other shoppers demanded the mother do something. Suddenly Santa Claus appeared saying, "Ho! Ho! Ho!" He gave her a red and white striped candy cane. She immediately stopped crying and smiled through her tears. One shopper exclaimed, "Santa saved the day." Kaufman's 13-year-old daughter laughed and said, "Santa didn't save the day. He just taught that little girl that unhappiness pays. If you scream and cry, you get candy. I'll bet she does the same thing in the next store." (From Kaufman, 1991.)

2. If she's right, what would you call the candy: a(n) _____ .

girl's screaming, Santa ensured that the mother will have to deal with the screaming in the future. When we misuse reinforcement, we create problems for other people (e.g., Progar et al., 2001).

## Reinforcement Is Everywhere

Reinforcement occurs endlessly in personal interactions. I have recounted numerous anecdotes about it. Larry thanked Jo Ann for being a loving wife. Santa gave candy to a screaming child. A special family shared a magic ice storm. The wonderful principle provided clothes, praise, and hope to children in an inner city school. A president gave his dog a biscuit for chewing on the rug! A husband taught his cat to scratch up the furniture! I have described studies showing that teachers inadvertently reinforce disruptive behavior. Friends reinforce pain behaviors. Mental hospital aides, nurses, and parents teach people to act crazy, to hit themselves, and to engage in violence. None of these people planned to use reinforcement in those ways. They used it naturally. But they used it without understanding it. Surely they would not reinforce undesirable behavior if they understood what they were doing!

Psychologists often make deliberate use of reinforcement to help people. They help students, elderly people, adults, and individuals with retardation. They help swim teams, dorms, and football teams. They help people become more creative, healthier, cooperative, smarter, and even happier! Behavior therapists use reinforcement to help individuals solve their own problems (e.g., Reid, Parsons, Green, & Browning, 2001). Behavioral sociologists use reinforcement to set up more cooperative dorm

### Behavioral Momentum in College Basketball

Behavior analysts find that people generate a high rate of responding if they have recently been reinforced frequently. They call this "behavioral momentum." Researchers extended this to understanding college basketball games. They recorded three types of events for seven games. First, they recorded events that were probably reinforcers. These included scoring baskets and having the other team turn the ball over to them. Second, they recorded adversities. These included fouls, missed shots, and turning the ball over to the other team. Third, they recorded responses to adversities. This was the outcome of the first possession after an adversity. They found that teams responded more favorably to adversities if they had received more reinforcers during the prior three minutes. (Based on Mace, Lalli, Shea, & Nevin, 1992.)

3. This "behavioral momentum" is the result of the delivery of many recent and frequent _____ .

***Behavioral Principles Are
Universal Laws!***

Sociologist John Kunkel studied 17th century Venice and modern day Peruvian Indians. He concluded that: "Behavioral principles . . . operate in the open society of other cultures and historical epochs. These principles are not the reflections [solely] of 20th century America." (Kunkel, 1985b: p. 457)

meetings (Welsh, Miller, & Altus, 1994). Psychologists use reinforcement to teach individuals to apply behavioral procedures to solving their own problems (Watson & Tharp, 1997). Behavior analysts use reinforcement to teach safer driving behaviors (e.g., Ludwig & Geller, 2000). Behavior therapists have even used reinforcement to help people manage such inner behavior as "thoughts," "feelings," and "urges" (e.g., Kostewicz, Kublina, & Cooper, 2000).

Reinforcement is a powerful part of any social system (see Vollmer & Hackenberg, 2001). When group members reinforce desirable behavior and extinguish undesirable behavior, they help to create a happy and comfortable situation. Skinner's novel *Walden Two* illustrates how people might use reinforcement to create a better community. The novel emphasizes how we can use reinforcement to modify our own behavior in ways agreeable to all. Behavior analysts have analyzed how reinforcement affects college basketball teams. See the box on behavioral momentum.

## Reinforcement Works in Every Age and Culture

The effect of reinforcement is not restricted to the United States. It is not even restricted to modern Western Civilization. Researchers have shown that reinforcement influenced ancient cultures. The liberal use of reinforcers sharply increased the musical activities of orphans in 17th century Venice. This resulted in world famous orchestras and performers (Kunkel, 1985). Other researchers found that reinforcement helped reduce disruptive behavior in African second graders (Saigh & Umar, 1983). Anthropologist Allan Holmberg changed the centuries old behavioral patterns of 1,700 Peruvian peasants (Kunkel, 1985). They became very hard workers, adopted new agricultural practices, and even went to school! One researcher has shown the value of reinforcement in Latin America and Indonesia (Elder et al., 1991; Elder et al., 1992). John Kunkel summarizes what we know about the generality of reinforcement in the box on universal laws.

---

***Is "Attention" Behavior? Part 4***

Jim Holland found a way to study "attention" as a behavior. Navy men lit a dial to look for deflections. Their pattern of looking was a function of the schedule on which deflections occurred. The attention of radar observers is vital to our national defense around the world, 24 hours a day. They look for unexpected planes, ships, or missiles. When they pay attention, we are safer. When they don't, we are more vulnerable! Holland's work suggests that we must reinforce them for continuing to attend. The military could supply false signals to the radars on an intermittent schedule. If the observers report the false signals promptly, the computer could thank them. If they fail to report them, the computer could let them know it (Holland, 1958).

4. If the military used schedules of reinforcement to maintain attending by vital radar operators, which schedule would produce a constant rate of attending: _____ (fixed-interval, variable-interval).

# Reinforcement Works with All Behavior

Behavior analysts have used reinforcement to modify all types of behavior. They have used it to modify such obvious behavior as playing tennis and making football plays. They have used it to modify subtle behavior such as studying or relaxing. They have used it to modify internal behavior such as brain waves characteristic of meditation. They have used it to modify private events such as attention. The box at the bottom of the previous page is the last of a series on understanding "attention" as a behavioral event. Reinforcement is not some mechanical and trivial part of life. It is the very foundation on which human beings learn to conduct their lives.

## The Reinforcement Strategy

In Unit 1, you learned how to use the behavioral strategy to solve a human problem. The essence of the behavioral strategy is to view a human problem as a behavioral problem. You can then use one or more of the five tactics. You can define it behaviorally, observe it, check your reliability and social validity, design an experiment, and/or visually analyze the results. You may find that just defining it behaviorally will be enough to solve the problem. The solution may be obvious once it is clearly defined. Or you may have to use other tactics. The essence of the behavioral strategy is that it allows you to react to a problem in a pragmatic, nonmystical way. Many problems will require more specific treatment than that.

If the behavioral strategy does not solve the problem, you can try the next strategy. In Unit 2, you learned about the reinforcement strategy. The essence of this strategy is to change the way reinforcers follow desirable and undesirable behaviors. Doing so lets you change the rate of those behaviors. You learned seven tactics that let you apply this strategy in various ways.

The first tactic is to increase desirable behavior through reinforcement. If the problem is simply that a desirable behavior is not occurring often enough, then all you have to do is find a way to reinforce it. Often, simply paying attention to the behavior is all that is required. However, you may need more powerful reinforcers if the behavior is very difficult or if other factors are discouraging it. You can be sure, however, that if you do find a reinforcer, the behavior will occur more often.

The second tactic is to decrease undesirable behaviors through extinction. If the problem is that an undesirable behavior is occurring too often, then all you have to do is identify the reinforcer and stop delivery of it. Very often the reinforcer will be the ill-advised attention of yourself or others to that behavior. You can be sure that this approach will work if you can find and stop all the reinforcers for the undesired behavior. However, often the reinforcers are controlled by other people who will not stop delivering them. Often, they are controlled by the physical world. Drugs like alcohol and nicotine are always going to produce potentially reinforcing effects. As long as the person can get them, you can't stop those effects.

The third tactic is to increase a desirable behavior relative to undesirable behavior through differential reinforcement. If the problem is more complex than a single desirable or undesirable behavior, then you may need to use this tactic. You reinforce the desirable behavior, and at the same time, you extinguish the undesirable behavior. For this tactic to work, you must find an effective reinforcer for the desirable behavior. You must also identify and stop the reinforcers for the undesirable behaviors. If you can do both parts of the tactic, then you can be sure that the desirable behavior will increase in rate compared to the undesirable behavior.

The fourth tactic is to create new behavior through shaping. If the problem is the total absence of a desirable behavior, then you will never get a chance to reinforce the behavior. The solution is to differentially reinforce an approximation to the desired target behavior. You then define successive approximations to that target behavior and continue differentially reinforcing them until you reach the desired behavior. You must find workable successive approximations. You must find reinforcers for them. If you do, you will be able to shape the new behavior.

The fifth tactic is to use the principles of reinforcer effectiveness. If the problem is that the reinforcer is simply not doing the job, then one possibility is that you are not using it in an effective manner. To do so, you must ensure that the reinforcer is delivered contingent on the desired behavior. You must ensure that it is delivered immediately. You must ensure that the amount of the reinforcer is worthwhile. You must ensure that the delivery of the reinforcer is rare enough to maintain interest. If you use these principles, then your reinforcer should work.

The sixth tactic is to increase response rate with a ratio schedule of reinforcement. If the problem requires more behavior per reinforcement, then you can deliver fewer reinforcers per response. With ratio schedules, you deliver the reinforcer after you have counted some number of responses. The fixed-ratio schedule will produce a pause after reinforcement and then a high rate of responding. The variable-ratio schedule will produce a high and steady rate of responding. The most serious problems with these schedules are that they may lead to ratio strain and they are not suitable for shaping.

The seventh tactic is to reduce reinforcer frequency with an interval schedule of reinforcement. If the reinforcer occurs on a time basis, then you will have to use this schedule. The fixed-interval schedule produces a scalloped pattern of responding. The variable-interval schedule produces a uniform but moderate rate of responding.

These seven tactics provide you with many tools to solve human problems. If the problem stems from inadequate or misplaced reinforcement, then one or more of these tactics should be able to solve the problem.

You may find that the behavioral problem is more complex than can be solved with these tools. For example, the problem may be that the desired behavior does not occur in the proper locations. The infant may say "Dada" to all males, not just its father. The person may not follow instructions very well even though they are capable of doing so. Someone may reinforce undesired behaviors. These problems involve what behavior analysts call "stimulus control." You will learn the stimulus control strategy in the next unit.

You may find that the behavioral problem presents dangers that must be eliminated more quickly than is possible with reinforcement procedures. You would then turn to the use of punishment. You will learn about this in Unit 4, which presents the aversive control strategy.

If the behavioral strategy does not work, then you can try the reinforcement strategy. If that doesn't work, then you can try the stimulus control strategy. If that doesn't work, then you can try the aversive control strategy as a last resort.

## The Ethics of Reinforcement

You need not only help others to use reinforcement. You can use reinforcement to change your own behavior. Usually you should arrange the program through a second person. Otherwise, you might find it more immediately reinforcing simply to adjust the rules for giving yourself reinforcement rather than change your behavior. Democratic groups can also use reinforcement to establish a successful social system.

To be sure, you can use reinforcement to manipulate others. For instance, suppose that someone will not voluntarily change a behavior that is annoying to you. You are then faced with a decision. You can tolerate the behavior, avoid the person, leave the situation, or attempt to modify the behavior. Or suppose that an enemy tries to control your behavior. By understanding the principles of reinforcement, you have a better chance of not being controlled.

Reinforcement always involves the problem of "counter control." Counter control occurs when one person resists the control of another person. For example, if the owner of a factory uses reinforcement principles to make workers work harder and faster, how can workers fight that control? The traditional tool of the worker has been unions. Yet unions are sometimes weak and incapable of resisting the control of owners. One possibility is that workers might use behavioral principles to develop a stronger resistance. Thus, a knowledge of behavioral principles can potentially aid any group to resist control by another group (Skinner, 1953).

Behavior analysis is not manipulative; people are manipulative. Reinforcement is simply a tool. People and groups can use it to modify their social environment. They may be able to create with it a happier and more productive life.

## Summary

Sometimes people use reinforcement to help others. Other times they misuse it to harm others, usually by accident. Reinforcement is involved in everything we do. It works in all ages and cultures. It works with all behaviors from obvious to private. Six tactics will help you design a successful program. Specify the target behavior. Discover a reinforcer. Use the principles of effectiveness. Shape new behavior. Select a schedule. Evaluate the result. Reinforcement is not itself good or bad.

## Helpful Hints

### Helpful Hint #1

In past lessons, I have introduced "helper words" that help you know which group of terms I am selecting from. I have used "methods" to refer to the methods of observation. I have used "designs" to refer to the experimental designs. I have used "procedures" to refer to the ways of increasing or decreasing the rate of a behavior (e.g., reinforcement). I have used "principles" to refer to the principles of effective reinforcement. I have used "schedules" to refer to the generic schedules and the specific ratio and interval schedules. When I start a question with a phrase like "What principle," be sure to notice. You can narrow the terms that you must consider to answer the question. Be sure to notice whether a question has a helper term in it like *principle, procedure, method,* or *schedule.*

5. If the question asks for a method, which of the following terms might be the correct answer? (a) *fixed-interval,* (b) *reinforcement,* or (c) *interval recording*? _____ (a, b, or c)

### Helpful Hint #2

The definitions of all terms introduced in this unit of the book are presented in the Glossary. You can review the unit and prepare for your exam by testing yourself on the definitions and correlated facts presented for each term. You might use a piece of paper as a mask and leave only the term exposed. See if you can formulate a reasonable definition and the facts about that term. Then move the mask and check on your answer.

## Glossary

**approximation (successive)** Any behavior <u>similar</u> to a target behavior.
- It is usually one of a series of behaviors differentially reinforced in a program of shaping toward the goal of producing the target behavior.

**continuous reinforcement** A generic schedule of reinforcement in which <u>every response</u> is reinforced.
- This schedule is usually used when a person is first learning a behavior, particularly in shaping procedures.

**deprivation** The <u>frequency</u> with which a person has received a particular reinforcer in the recent past.
- The less frequent the reinforcer, the more deprived the person.

**differential reinforcement** A procedure involving two or more physically <u>different</u> behaviors: one behavior is <u>reinforced</u>, and all others are <u>extinguished</u>.

**extinction** The procedure in which an event that followed a behavior is <u>stopped</u>, and the rate of the behavior <u>decreases.</u>
- When you use the procedure of extinction, you would say that you are "extinguishing" the behavior.
- An extinction burst is a temporary <u>increase</u> in responding as soon as extinction begins.

**fixed-interval** A schedule for reinforcing the first response after a <u>fixed period of time</u> has passed since the prior reinforcement.

- This schedule usually produces a <u>scallop</u> pattern of responding where people tend to pause after a reinforcer and then to gradually increase their response rate until they are working at a high rate at the moment they receive the next reinforcer.

**fixed-ratio** A schedule for reinforcing the first response after a <u>fixed number</u> of prior responses.
- This schedule usually produces a "stair-step" pattern where people pause after reinforcement and then work at a very high rate until the next reinforcer.
- The overall rate is higher than continuous reinforcement but lower than variable-ratio.

**intermittent reinforcement** A generic schedule of reinforcement in which only <u>some responses</u> are reinforced.
- Ratio and interval schedules are common examples.
- A person trained on an intermittent schedule of reinforcement will have greater <u>resistance to extinction</u> as they will continue making a response during extinction for a longer period of time than a person trained on a continuous schedule.
- Intermittent reinforcement also produces more responding for fewer reinforcers, thus reducing the problem of satiation.

**principle of contingency** The more consistently the reinforcer is delivered <u>only</u> for the desired behavior, the more effective the reinforcer.
- To decide whether this principle has been followed, ask the question, "Was the reinforcer given <u>only</u> when the desired behavior occurred?"

**principle of deprivation** The more <u>deprived</u> the person is, the more effective the reinforcer.
- To decide whether the principle has been followed, ask, "Has the reinforcer <u>rarely</u> been delivered?"

**principle of immediacy** The more <u>immediate</u> the delivery of the reinforcer, the more effective the reinforcer.

- To decide whether this principle has been followed, ask the question, "Was the reinforcer delivered within one <u>minute</u> of the behavior (or while the behavior was still occurring)?"

**principle of size** The more worthwhile the <u>amount</u> of a reinforcer, the more effective the reinforcer.
- To decide whether the principle has been followed, ask the question, "Was the amount of reinforcement <u>worthwhile?</u>"

**ratio strain** Requiring so many responses for a reinforcer that the behavior slows or even totally <u>stops</u>.

**reinforcement**: The <u>procedure</u> of using a reinforcer to increase the rate of a behavior.

**reinforcement strategy** Changing the contingency between behavior and <u>reinforcement</u>.
- It consists of seven tactics:
  1. Increase desirable behavior through <u>reinforcement</u>.
  2. Decrease undesirable behavior through <u>extinction</u>.
  3. Increase a desirable behavior relative to undesirable behavior through <u>differential reinforcement</u>.
  4. Create new behavior through <u>shaping</u>.
  5. Use the principles of <u>reinforcer effectiveness</u>.
  6. Increase response rate with a <u>ratio schedule</u>.
  7. Reduce reinforcer frequency with an <u>interval schedule</u>.

**reinforcer** Any event that <u>follows</u> a behavior and <u>increases</u> the rate of that behavior.

**satiation** The <u>opposite</u> of deprivation.
- The more frequently a person has received a particular reinforcer in the recent past, the more satiated he or she is.

**shaping** The use of <u>differential reinforcement</u> on a series of <u>successive approximations</u> to a <u>target behavior.</u>

**target behavior** The ultimate <u>goal</u> of a program of shaping.

**unknown** Any behavioral procedure (1) that is <u>unsuccessful</u> in changing behavior or (2) for which a name and definition are <u>untaught</u>.
• Some examples:
  1. Any instruction occurring prior to the behavior.
  2. Any attempt to use a method that is unsuccessful.
  3. When a person is reinforced for emitting a behavior in one situation and extinguished for emitting the same behavior in another situation.

**variable-interval** A schedule for reinforcing the first response after a <u>varying period of time</u> from the prior reinforcement.
• This schedule usually causes a person to respond at a uniform rate.

**variable-ratio** A schedule for reinforcing the first response after <u>varying number</u> of prior responses.
• This schedule usually causes people to work at a high and uniform rate of speed.
• It produces the highest rate of responding of the simple schedules.

## Additional Readings

Wheeler, H. (Ed., 1973). *Beyond the punitive society*. San Francisco: W. H. Freeman. This book is a collection of writings by economists, philosophers, and social scientists on the social and political aspects of behavior analysis.

## Practice Review I

The following material has questions over every term studied in Unit 2 as well as review questions from Unit 1. By answering the questions and checking your answers, you can prepare yourself for the Review Exam. The Review Exam will contain questions from both units. This section contains two long modules to provide plenty of review for the exam over this unit.

### 1. A Set of Review Questions

33. Pre-test: If a person is reinforced for emitting a behavior in one situation and is

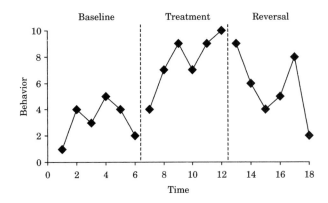

**Figure 15-2.** An experimental analysis of an unspecified behavior.

extinguished for emitting it in another situation, his behavior is being modified by what behavioral procedure?_____
_____

45. Pre-test: Timmy's Dad helped him become strong. At first, Dad praised Timmy only when he picked up a rock. Then, Dad praised him only when he picked up a brick. Finally, Dad praised him only when he picked up a building block. Timmy was now strong. Dad got Timmy strong by using the procedure of _____
_____.

35. Pre-test: Jim and Pete had trouble getting along even though they were brothers. Jim kept teasing Pete, and Pete would get upset and cry. One day, Pete realized that his brother was simply trying to get him to cry. So he decided he would never again cry when he was teased. Jim teased Pete just as often. What behavioral procedure did Pete use on Jim? _____

30. Pre-test: Figure 15-2 shows Tushi's behavior during baseline, treatment, and reversal. Divided? ____ Stable? ____ Convincing? ____ Cause? ____ (yes, no)

44. Pre-test: The swallows come back to Capistrano on exactly March 21st of every year. Mr. Peterson watches all year round for their return. What schedule of reinforcement is his swallow-watching behavior on: _____.

47. Pre-test: Willa helped her friend Sarah learn to be more assertive by providing her with feedback during parties. Anytime that Sarah was properly assertive, Willa nodded her head so that Sarah could see. She nodded her head immediately after

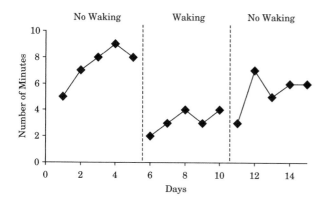

**Figure 15-3.** An experimental analysis of waking-up behavior.

Sarah was assertive and only when she was assertive. Sarah seemed to like the nods and certainly never got too many nods from Willa. What principle of reinforcement, if any, did Willa neglect in her procedure? _____

32. Pre-test: Dave found that he could get a date for dancing if he asked enough single women outside the discotheque. Sometimes the first woman he asked agreed to go dancing, other times he asked as many as 30 before having success. What schedule of reinforcement is his date-asking behavior on? _____ _____

56. To use the reinforcement strategy to solve human problems: (1) Increase desirable behavior through reinforcement. (2) Decrease undesirable behavior through extinction. (3) Increase a desirable behavior relative to undesirable behavior through differential reinforcement. (4) Create new behavior through shaping. (5) Use the principles of reinforcer effectiveness. (6) Increase response rate with a ratio schedule. (7) Reduce reinforcer frequency with a(n) _____ schedule.

24. Intermittent schedules of reinforcement reduce the probability of satiation and create a greater resistance to _____ _____ than do continuous schedules.

3. An event that follows a behavior and leads to no change in the rate of that behavior is always called a(n) _____ _____.

57. To use the reinforcement strategy to solve human problems: (4) Create new behaviors through _____.

| Observer 1 | X | O | X | O | O | O | O | O | O | X |
| Observer 2 | O | O | X | O | O | O | O | O | O | X |

**Figure 15-4.** Observations by two observers.

51. The record of a behavior prior to the treatment is called the _____.

11. Figure 15-3 shows the number of minutes that Doug had to wait for Lynn to get up in the morning when he was not and when he was waking her. Divided? _____ Stable? _____ Convincing? _____ Cause? _____ (yes, no)

9. Figure 15-4 shows the observations of two independent observers. Compute the reliability of these two sets of observations. _____% Is it acceptable? _____ (yes, no)

16. If a behavior produces a reinforcer every second time that it occurs, the behavior is said to be reinforced on a(n) _____ schedule (name the specific schedule).

49. The behavioral procedure of extinction is being used if the delivery of a reinforcing event is _____ and the rate of the behavior _____.

21. If people are reinforced only when they emit a specified behavior, which principle of reinforcer effectiveness is being followed? The principle of _____.

5. Ben and Sue were building up their endurance for the disco marathon. They began by setting the goal of dancing continuously for 3 hours. When they got so they could do that, they set their goal at 4 hours. They were aiming for 35 hours. Dancing for 3 hours straight is called a(n) _____ to dancing for 35 hours.

58. To use the reinforcement strategy to solve human problems: (5) Use the principles of reinforcer _____.

64. What specific schedule of reinforcement produces the highest average rate of responding? _____ _____

6. Ben and Sue were building up their endurance for the dancing marathon. They began by setting the goal of dancing for 3 hours. When they could do that, they set their goal at 4 hours. They were aiming at 35 hours. Dancing for 35 hours would be called the _____ _____.

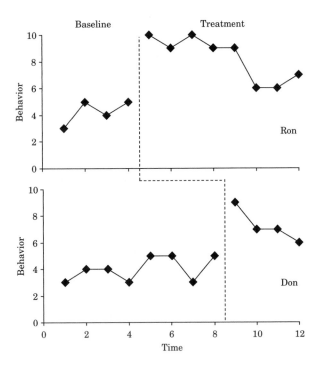

**Figure 15-5.** An experimental analysis of an unspecified behavior.

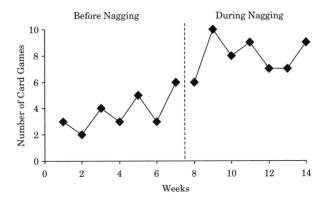

**Figure 15-6.** An experimental analysis of playing cards.

65. What two intermittent schedules produce a uniform rate of responding rather than pausing, then responding? _____ and _____

1. Figure 15-5 shows the number of behaviors emitted by Ron and Don during baseline and treatment. Divided? ____ Stable? ____ Convincing? ____ Cause? ____ (yes, no)

50. The overall name for any one of the many procedures such as reinforcement, extinction, or shaping that is used in an experiment to either increase or decrease a behavior is called a(n) _____.

4. Behaviors that successively approximate a target behavior are differentially reinforced in the procedure called _____.

29. One factor that increases the effectiveness of a reinforcer is having the reinforcer occur as soon as possible after a response has been made. This is called the principle of _____.

25. Interval recording involves observing a behavior during a series of continuous intervals. Time sample recording, on the other hand, involves observing a behavior during a series of _____ intervals.

48. Figure 15-6 shows the number of card games that Joe played with Sheila with and without her nagging him to play. Divided? ____ Stable? ____ Convincing? ____ Cause? ____ (yes, no)

### 2. Another Set of Review Questions

42. Pre-test: Suppose that someone fails to do something that he or she has agreed to do. If you then tell the person to do it and he or she does, what behavioral procedure are you using? _____

40. Pre-test: Sam's teacher tried to come by his desk after different periods of time to see if he was working on his spelling lesson. If it was reinforcing for Sam to be found working, what schedule was his studying on? _____

36. Pre-test: John was interested in finding out whether he would get more compliments if he reinforced those compliments that he got. So he observed the rate of compliments that he got for several weeks when he did not reinforce them. He then started reinforcing compliments from Mary while still not reinforcing them from Bev. After 2 more weeks he started reinforcing them from Bev also. He found large increases after he had started using reinforcement. What experimental design did he use? _____ design

46. Pre-test: Two observers developed a definition of aggression and used it to count the

number of times that Fearsome Freddy hit another child. Observer 1 counted 8 hits, while Observer 2 counted 10 hits. Compute their reliability: _____%. Is this acceptable if it is a new definition? _____ (yes, no)

34. Pre-test: If only some responses are reinforced, then the behavior is said to be on the generic schedule called a(n) _____ _____ schedule of reinforcement.

31. Pre-test: Alice was a third grader who liked to take long bike rides after school. Her father worried about this, particularly after Alice described how she almost got run over by a heavy truck. He therefore told her to come straight home after school. She started coming straight home after that. What behavioral procedure did her father use to increase her rate of coming right home? _____ _____

39. Pre-test: Professor Clark wanted her students to turn in a two-page essay every Friday, so for the first part of the semester she reminded them every Thursday to hand in an essay by Friday. Midway through the semester she stopped reminding them, and to her surprise, they stopped handing them in on time. What behavioral procedure did she use to decrease their rate of handing their essays in on time? _____ (Think about this one!)

43. Pre-test: The correlation between the ratings by outside judges of a behavior and the observations of a trained observer is called _____.

37. Pre-test: One way to increase the effectiveness of a reinforcer is to make sure the person doesn't receive any of that type of reinforcer for a long time. This technique involves the principle of _____ _____.

20. If one behavior is extinguished and another behavior is reinforced, we say that the procedure of _____ _____ is being used.

7. Bernie told Professor Jacobs that he studied so hard in sociology because he was terribly interested in social problems, although he had never explained it that way before. The professor nodded in agreement and then spent a long time discussing social problems with Bernie. After that, Bernie always explained his extensive studying of sociology as resulting from his interest in it. What behavioral procedure did the professor use, probably without realizing it, to increase Bernie's rate of explaining his studying as resulting from a strong interest in sociology: _____.

17. If a person is reinforced after differing numbers of responses, he or she is on a(n) _____ schedule of reinforcement.

55. To determine whether the principle of deprivation was followed, ask, "Has the reinforcer _____ been delivered?"

26. Interval recording involves dividing the observation period into a series of _____ _____ time intervals.

59. To use the reinforcement strategy to solve human problems: (6) Increase response rate with a(n) _____ schedule.

27. John counted the number of times that Professor Brainbuster said the word "orthogonal" because he was interested in the professor's tendency to use big words that his students did not understand. What method of observation was he using? _____ _____ recording.

8. Claire was interested in whether ignoring complaints would reduce complaining behavior. She observed the rate of complaints uttered by Bill for 3 weeks during which she tried to appear sympathetic. She then totally ignored complaints for 3 weeks. And finally, she again appeared sympathetic to his complaints for three weeks. She noted a substantial drop during the time when she ignored them. What experimental design was she using? _____ _____ design.

63. What schedule of reinforcement produces a "stair–step" pattern with a pause after reinforcement and then very rapid responding until the next reinforcement? _____

15. If a behavior is reinforced every time that it occurs, what generic schedule of

reinforcement is it on? _____
_____

60. To use the reinforcement strategy to solve human problems: (1) Increase desirable behaviors through _____.

2. An event is called a reinforcer only if it is timed to _____ a behavior and if it also _____ the rate of the behavior.

23. In Unit 1, you learned the _____ _____ strategy for solving human problems. In Unit 2, you learned the _____ control strategy.

10. Differential reinforcement involves two basic behavioral procedures. They are _____ and _____.

14. If a behavior becomes erratic, or even stops, after it has been placed on a very high ratio of responses to reinforcers, we say that _____ _____ has occurred.

28. One experimental design involves determining the effect of a treatment on two or more behaviors at different times. This is called a(n) _____ _____ design.

22. If you stop telling someone to do something and he stops, what behavioral procedure is this an example of? _____ _____

54. Time sample recording involves observing whether a behavior is occurring during each of a series of _____ _____ intervals.

62. Two intermittent schedules of reinforcement that produce a high rate of responding prior to reinforcement and a pause just after reinforcement are _____ _____ and _____ _____.

19. If an event that usually follows a behavior is stopped and there is no change in the rate, the procedure involved is _____ _____.

52. The term used to refer to the procedure of delivering an event following a behavior that will increase the rate of the behavior is _____; the term used to refer to the event itself is _____ _____.

66. When Damon was first learning to play Ping-Pong, he hit many shots too hard. Those shots didn't hit the table. He also hit a few shots softly. Those shots hit the table. If the rate of his hard shooting decreased while the rate of his soft shooting increased, what behavioral procedure would this be an example of? _____ _____

53. The use of a second observer to determine if your observations are in agreement is called _____; correlating the ratings of outside judges with the observations of trained observers is called determining the _____ of your behavioral definition.

18. If a person is reinforced for many responses in a row, the effectiveness of the reinforcer may decrease because the person has been _____ with respect to that reinforcer.

13. Harvey (the con man) Miller once told Jim a fantastic story about how he could arrange for Jim to buy a small jet airplane worth $100,000 for only $5,000 if he could just get the money this hour. Jim believed him and got the money. Naturally, Harvey took the money and left town, never to be heard of again. He told many stories to other suckers in the future. The money is clearly a(n) _____ _____ for Harvey's con jobs.

61. To use the reinforcement strategy to solve human problems: (3) Increase a desirable behavior relative to undesirable behavior through _____ _____.

12. Fran tried to increase the amount of study time put in by her daughter. She looked in on Melanie often. She gave Melanie a snack at bedtime if she had been studying more than a half hour. She gave her a snack only if she was sure that Melanie had been studying all that time. Melanie loved the snack and never seemed to get too much of it. But she didn't increase her studying. What principle of effective reinforcement, if any, did Fran fail to employ? _____ _____

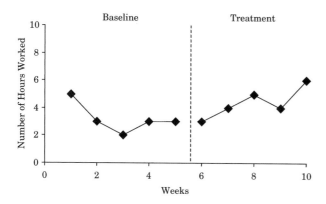

**Figure 15-7.** An experimental analysis of practicing.

## Practice Review II

This section contains one moderate length module.

### 1. Programmed Examples

11. Pre-test: At first, little Janie called everyone "Mama." But her parents hugged and petted her when she called her mother "Mama" and ignored her when she called anyone else "Mama." Gradually, Janie called only her mother "Mama." What behavioral procedure did her parents use to teach her to call only her mother by the name "Mama"? _____
(Warning, most students get this wrong so ask your questions.)

13. Pre-test: Mr. Davis helped his daughter with her homework by checking her work after every seven problems. If having her homework checked is a reinforcer, what schedule is doing homework on: _____
_____.

12. Pre-test: Can you name all of the tactics based on the reinforcement strategy to solve human problems? (1) Increase desirable behaviors through _____.
(2) Decrease undesirable behaviors through _____. (3) Increase a desirable behavior relative to undesirable behavior through _____.
(4) Create new behavior through _____
_____. (5) Use the principles of _____
_____. (6) Increase response rate with a(n) _____

_____ schedule. (7) Reduce reinforcer frequency with a(n) _____ schedule.

17. Figure 15-7 shows the hours each week that Ted worked on his tennis serve during baseline and treatment. Divided? _____ Stable? _____ Convincing? _____ Cause? _____ (yes, no)

19. Pre-test: To use the reinforcement strategy to solve human problems: (2) Decrease undesirable behaviors through _____
_____.

18. The principle of size states that you must give a worthwhile _____ of a reinforcer.

2. At the Freedom Food Co-op, the bookkeeper's work was observed by auditing his books. Assuming that his entries in the books are the results of the behavior of interest, what method of observation is this? _____ recording

22. What generic schedule of reinforcement should be used when shaping a new response? _____

8. Les had long regretted that he was so distant from his parents. He had tried talking with them about the problem to no avail. So he decided to give them a really nice compliment anytime that they shared something intimate with him. Their rate of intimacy did not change. What behavioral procedure was Les using? _____

5. If the old reinforcer for a behavior is no longer delivered and the rate of the behavior decreases, what generic schedule is the behavior on? _____

6. If you reinforce the first response that occurs after varying periods of time, the behavior is on a(n) _____
_____ schedule.

9. Most researchers aim for a reliability figure that is _____%.

4. Differential reinforcement involves two or more physically _____ behaviors.

20. To use the reinforcement strategy to solve human problems: (7) Reduce reinforcer frequency with a(n) _____ schedule.

1. At first Kevin liked to have Alice hang around him all the time, and he always tried to be friendly. Finally, however, it got to be a

drag, so he stopped being friendly to her. To his surprise, she kept hanging around him anyway. What behavioral procedure did Kevin use to decrease Alice's hanging around? _____

3. Computing the agreement between two independent observations results in a measure of the _____ _____ of the observers.

23. What schedule of reinforcement produces very rapid, uniform responding? _____

21. Wanda rarely did any work at the Freedom Food Co-op. If you worked at the Co-op, your hours were immediately recorded on the bulletin board; if you had 5 hours a month, you could buy the food at wholesale price. Wanda needed the financial savings and could never get enough money. However, anyone could just write up the number of hours he or she worked, and many people cheated. Wanda found that she could work an hour and record 5 hours. What principle of effectiveness was at work weakening the privilege of buying at wholesale as a reinforcer for working for the Co-op? _____

16. Suppose that you wanted to engineer a classroom in which ghetto children learned basic skills more effectively. If they didn't possess those skills at all, you might find some skills they did possess that were related to your target skills. You could then differentially reinforce these simpler skills. You might gradually progress to the more difficult skills. This behavioral procedure would be called _____ the complex skills.

7. If you reinforce the first response that occurs after a fixed amount of time has passed, you are following a(n) _____ _____ schedule.

10. One experimental design involves studying a behavior before the treatment has been introduced and while the treatment is in effect. This single subject design is called a(n) _____ design.

14. Shaping involves the differential reinforcement of a series of behaviors that are _____ to a target behavior.

15. Shaping involves the differential reinforcement of a series of behaviors that are successive approximations to a(n) _____ .

# LESSON 16

# Stimulus Discrimination and Everyday Behavior

## Reading Section

### Introduction to Unit 3

This unit looks at the principles describing how stimulus situations affect behavior. These principles govern the development and maintenance of stimulus control. What is stimulus control? Let me contrast it with *reinforcement*, the major factor controlling behavior. In Unit 2, you learned that reinforcement control is the increase in behaviors from an event that <u>follows</u> the behavior. By contrast, stimulus control is the increase in behavior from an event that <u>precedes</u> the behavior. Some events that might precede a behavior and influence the person's behavior include questions, commands, the sight of a person or object, or being present in a room or at a football game. Behavior analysts call the effect of such events on behavior *stimulus control*. Sidman suggests that *cognition* refers to behavior under stimulus control (Sidman, 1978).

The emphasis in this unit changes from looking at what happens after you behave—reinforcement or extinction—to looking at what happens before you behave. The term *stimulus* is central. A **stimulus** is anything that affects the person's <u>behavior</u>. The plural of stimulus is *stimuli*. Stimuli might refer to objects such as doors, windows, other people, parts of one's own body, clothing, or hair. It might refer to vocal sounds such as words, sighs, or laughter. It might refer to visible configurations such as words on a page, colors, length, and width. It also refers to broader situations such as an entire room. In that case, we then often use the term *stimulus situation*. As you can see from this definition, reinforcers

***Behavioral Approach to Cognition***

"Behavior under <u>stimulus control</u> is essentially the field of cognition. . . . Terms like <u>cognition</u> or <u>knowledge</u> refer to the control of behavior by its environmental context, by events which, unlike consequences, precede or accompany the behavior; here, it is sometimes said that our behavior expresses <u>meaning</u> or <u>comprehension</u>" (Sidman, 1978: p. 265).

1. The field of cognition is behavior under _____ (reinforcement, stimulus) control.

are also stimuli. A reinforcing stimulus is one that follows a behavior. This unit will deal primarily with stimuli that precede a behavior.

2. A **stimulus**: Anything that affects the person's _____.

This unit deals with how people learn to behave in ways that work for their current stimulus situation. The lessons in this unit teach concepts relating to the influence of the stimulus situation on behavior. This lesson deals with distinguishing among different situations, a process known as *discrimination*. The next lesson deals with grouping similar situations into general categories, a process known as *generalization*. Future lessons deal with simple aspects of verbal behavior. In general, this unit describes a behavioral approach to <u>intellectual behavior</u>.

Stimulus control is present in everyday situations. By understanding stimulus control, you can better understand your own behavior. You can also better understand the behavior of friends, family, and coworkers.

Behavior analysts use stimulus control to solve people's problems. They turn to it when the behavioral strategy and the reinforcement strategy aren't enough. They may be able to define the problem in behavioral terms. They may be able to differentially reinforce desirable behavior, but the behavior may not occur in the appropriate situations. They may then turn to the stimulus control strategy. The order of our discussion of these three basic strategies in this book reflects the order in which behavior analysts use them.

This unit will describe five tactics in using the stimulus control strategy: They include using discrimination training, generalization training, fading/programming, imitation/instruction, or conditioned reinforcement. This lesson introduces tactic #1 in using the stimulus control strategy: to narrow stimulus control through <u>discrimination training</u>.

3. The first tactic in using the stimulus control strategy is to narrow stimulus control through _____ training.

## Discrimination Training

People act differently in the presence of different stimulus situations. They act differently toward the friendly professor than they do toward the pompous one. They act differently in a library than in a car. They act differently when driving toward a red light than toward a green light. There is a basic process at work in developing these behavioral differences. The process involves reinforcement of a behavior in the presence of one stimulus. It involves extinction of the same behavior in the presence of another stimulus. Behavior analysts call this procedure *discrimination training*.

Here's our definition. **Discrimination training** is a procedure where a behavior is <u>reinforced</u> in the presence of one stimulus

and <u>extinguished</u> in the presence of another stimulus. Examples of discrimination training in everyday life are common. Consider the story of Sam, a professor's 6-year-old son. Sam visits his mom in the large campus building where she teaches. He often leaves without his mom so he can get home for dinner. How did he learn to get out of the building? Each time Sam went through a door with the sign "Exit" over it, he got out. Each time he went through doors marked with signs such as "Women," "Library," or "223," he did not. He soon learned to look for doors with exit signs over them. In this example, Sam's response of going through doors with an exit sign was reinforced by being able to leave the building. His response of going through other doors was extinguished. Therefore, this is an example of discrimination training.

4. Discrimination training is a procedure where a behavior is _____ in the presence of one stimulus and _____ _____ in the presence of another stimulus.

Behavior analysts call the stimulus associated with reinforcement the *discriminative stimulus*. They abbreviate it *SD*. Obviously, the *D* stands for "discriminative" and the *S* stands for "stimulus" (although not so obviously, you'll notice, the words they stand for are reversed). A **discriminative stimulus** (or SD) is a stimulus that precedes the behavior and is present only if reinforcement will occur for that behavior. For example, the sign "Exit" indicates that the behavior of going through the door will be reinforced by getting out of the building.

5. A stimulus that precedes a behavior and is present only if reinforcement will occur for that behavior is called a _____ _____.

Behavior analysts call the stimulus associated with extinction the *S-delta*. An **S-delta** is a stimulus that precedes the behavior and is present only if extinction will occur for that behavior. For example, the sign "Library" would indicate that the behavior of going through that door will not be reinforced by getting out of the building.

6. A stimulus that precedes the behavior and is present only if extinction will occur for that behavior is called the _____.

If discrimination training is successful, it will cause a behavior to occur more frequently in the presence of the SD than in the presence of the S-deltas. Behavior analysts call that behavior *discriminated behavior*. **Discriminated behavior** is a behavior that is <u>more likely</u> to occur in the presence of the SD than in the presence of the S-delta. Sam's behavior of going through doors marked "Exit" is discriminated behavior. Before he learned to go through exit doors, his behavior was not discriminated behavior. We would call a single instance of the behavior a *discriminated response*. Thus, when Sam went through the exit door last Sunday, he made a discriminated response.

7. A behavior that is more likely to occur in the presence of the SD than in the presence of the S-delta is called a(n) _____ behavior.

Behavior analysts refer to the effect of the SD on the behavior as *stimulus control*. **Stimulus control** is the <u>increased probability</u> of a discriminated behavior produced by a stimulus (SD). Thus, behavior analysts call the increased probability that Sam will go through a door marked "Exit" stimulus control. The exit sign literally controls his behavior. We usually say that the stimulus <u>exerts</u> stimulus control over the behavior.

8. **Stimulus control** is the _____ _____ (decreased, increased) probability of a discriminated behavior produced by a stimulus.

Thus, if you wish to refer to the <u>behavior</u> that results from discrimination training, you would designate it as discriminated behavior. A single instance of the behavior is a discriminated response. If you wish to talk about the effect of the <u>stimulus</u> involved in discrimination training, you would call it stimulus control.

## Simple Examples of Discrimination Training

Many everyday examples of discrimination training are easy to analyze. For example, history teachers use discrimination training to increase the probability of their students giving the correct answers. They will reinforce students for answering, "December 7, 1941," when asked, "When did the Japanese bomb Pearl Harbor?" However, they will attempt to extinguish that response when asking, "When did the Japanese formally surrender in World War II?" Behavior analysts call the question "When did the Japanese bomb Pearl Harbor?" the discriminative stimulus (SD), or <u>cue,</u> for "December 7, 1941." They call most other questions the S-delta for that response. They call the correct answer a discriminated behavior. If a student is more likely to answer December 7, 1941, in response to the question, then they say that the question exerts stimulus control over that answer.

Here are some other simple examples based on discrimination training. You might learn to call the blonde person Laverne but not the brunette person. The blonde person reinforces you by looking at you when you call her Laverne. She is a discriminative stimulus, or SD, for that name because she will reinforce you for calling her by that name. The brunette person ignores you if you call her Laverne. She is an S-delta for that name because she will extinguish you if you call her Laverne. When you learn the difference, your use of "Laverne" is a discriminated response. Your increased probability of calling the blonde person Laverne is called stimulus control. You might say that the blonde person exerts stimulus control over your use of her name.

You might learn to yell at a football game but not in a library. Other people join you when you yell at the football game but not when you yell in the library. If having others yell with you is reinforcing, then what would you call the stimulus situation of the football game? You would call it an SD because yelling is reinforced at the game. If having others not yell with you is extinguishing, what would you call the stimulus situation of the library? You would call it an S-delta because yelling is extinguished in the library. Thus, the library is the S-delta and the game is the SD. What would you call the process of having yells reinforced at the game and extinguished in the library? Discrimination training, because yelling is reinforced at the game and extinguished in the library. What would you call the effect of being at the game on your probability of yelling? Stimulus control. What would you call the behavior of yelling? Discriminated behavior, because it is more likely to occur at the game than in the library.

Suppose that the question "What is 9 x 9?" has come to exert stimulus control over your behavior. That means that you are more likely to answer "81" when the teacher asks you that question than when she asks you another question. Other questions, such as "What is 8 x 8?," will serve as S-deltas for that answer. You will be less likely to answer "81" when asked, "What is 8 x 8?" The answer has become a discriminated behavior. Presumably this happens because the teacher uses a form of discrimination training to teach you the difference. She may smile and say "that's right" when you answer 81 to "What is 9 x 9" but not when you answer 81 to "What is 8 x 8?"

These examples share two basic components. First, the training is for only one behavior (Laverne, yelling, or 81). Second, the behavior is reinforced in the presence of only one stimulus situation (the blonde person, a football game, or "What is 9 x 9?"). It is not reinforced in the presence of other stimulus situations (brunette people, libraries, or other questions).

You may feel a bit overwhelmed by the strange new terminology that I have introduced. I have done so because I need the new terms to talk about the elements of discrimination training and the behavior that results from it—what behavior analysts call *discriminated behavior*. I need to talk about the stimulus associated with reinforcement for the discriminated behavior—the *discriminative stimulus,* or, more simply, the SD. I need to talk about the stimulus associated with extinction for the discriminated behavior—what behavior analysts call the *S-delta*. Finally, I need to talk about the whole process by which some stimuli increase the probability of certain behaviors: *stimulus control*. I need each and every term. So hang in there. You will soon find using them as natural as using *reinforcement* and *extinction*.

Sometimes you may be tempted to confuse the behavior with the stimulus. For example, reading Freud's *Interpretation of Dreams* may seem like a different behavior from reading Skinner's *Walden Two*. However, reading is the same behavior no matter what you read. You hold a book open, look at the page, and move your eyes to the next word or phrase. Therefore, learning to read historical novels instead of science fiction is an example of developing a discriminated behavior. Reading behavior is occurring in the presence of one kind of book but not the other. The same analysis applies to watching TV or movies. The same looking behavior occurs in the presence of different stimulus situations.

## Realistic Examples of Discrimination Training

Discrimination training is usually more complex than the prior examples imply. It usually involves some modification of the stimuli. Suppose you show Nan two pictures. The one on the right is a cat, and the one on the left is a dog. If you always ask Nan to point to the cat, all she has to remember is to point to the picture on the right. She doesn't even have to look at it. However, if you switch the sides on which the cat and dog appear, Nan must look at the pictures to point to the cat. Even simple discrimination training requires that you switch the order of the stimuli.

Discrimination training usually involves even more than switching the order of the stimuli (e.g., Conners, Iwata, Kahng, Hanley, Worsdell, & Thompson, 2000). It usually involves learning multiple discriminations at the same time (e.g., Conyers, Doole, Vause, Harapiak, Yu, & Martin, 2002). For example, the teacher wants you to answer "81" to "What is 9 x 9?" But she wants you to do more than not answer "81" to the other question. She wants you to give the correct answer to every question. You learn the whole times table, not just one correct answer. Likewise, you not only learn the blonde person's name, you also learn other people's names. Similarly, you not only learn not to yell in the library, you learn what to do there.

One study provides a behavior analysis example. Two researchers taught a 4-year-old child to discriminate four industrial objects

(Mann & Baer, 1971). The researchers named one object and asked the child to point to it. When correct, the child earned chips that she could later exchange for a toy. When wrong, the child lost a chip. The researchers did not repeatedly name one object. Rather, they randomly named each of the four objects. Thus, the child was learning the name of four objects rather than just one. She was undergoing four discrimination training programs at the same time. When the researchers named object #1, it became an SD for that name. But it was also an S-delta for the other three names. Thus, this training situation was no longer a simple discrimination training procedure. Even so, the child learned the four discriminations in about 300 trials.

Researchers have used similar methods to teach other discriminations. They have taught 4-year-old children to discriminate letters (Tawney, 1972). They have taught teachers to discriminate correct use of behavior analysis in their teaching (Koegel, Russo, & Rincover, 1977). They have taught baseball players to discriminate curve balls and thus hit them better (Osborne, Rudrud, & Zezoney, 1990). They have even taught individuals with severe retardation to discriminate complex forms (e.g., Laarhoven, Johnson, Repp, Karsh, & Lenz, 2003; Rodgers & Iwata, 1991). In each case, the researchers taught multiple discriminations at the same time.

Two researchers taught male trainees to discriminate females' level of interest (Azrin & Hayes, 1984). They trained the males with films of couples conversing. They might show a conversation in which the female later said she was "very interested." They asked the trainee to guess her level of interest. They then informed the trainee of her true level of interest. Presumably, if the trainee guessed "very interested," the feedback that she was indeed "very interested" would reinforce his guess. If he guessed "uninterested," the feedback that she was "very interested" would extinguish his guess. The training consisted of 24 conversations. The trainees improved in the accuracy of their guesses by 50% as a result of the feedback. They thus became more socially "sensitive." Using your new terminology, you could say that this sensitivity has become discriminated behavior. The subtle cues of the females were now exerting stimulus control over the males' guesses about the females' level of interest.

Researchers have taught several health-related discriminations. One researcher taught a woman to discriminate the temperature of her hand (Gainer, 1978). A lower temperature is a warning of an impending migraine headache. This training led to a marked reduction in migraine headaches. Another research team taught college students to discriminate their blood pressure (Cinciripini, Epstein, & Martin, 1979). The researchers asked the students to guess their blood pressure. They then measured it and gave them feedback. This feedback led to

---

### Helping Batters Discriminate Curve Balls

Researchers guessed that a batter must discriminate the spin of a pitched baseball for effective batting. Seeing the spin allows batters to adjust the speed and location of their swing. "Different types of pitches have differing rates and directions of spin. A curve ball spins in a downward direction. . . . A batter must decide whether or not to swing within 0.13 seconds after the delivery of the pitch." The researchers taught hitters to discriminate the spin on a curve ball by adding ¼-inch-wide orange highlighting to the seams of the ball. This made it easier for the hitters to see the spin on the ball. The percentage of well-hit curve balls increased from about 40% to about 50% with the addition of the orange highlighting. (Based on Osborne, Rudrud, & Zezoney, 1990.)

9. When a batter adjusts his or her swing depending on the spin of the ball, we say that the spin is exerting _____ _____ (reinforcement, stimulus) control over their swing.

improved guesses. The researchers suggest that this skill might improve the ability of individuals with high blood pressure to manage their disease better. Another team taught diabetics to discriminate their blood sugar level (Gross, Wojnilower, Levin, Dale, & Richardson, 1983) by asking them to guess their level and then providing feedback. This experiment may help diabetics everywhere to manage their disease better. The two examples illustrate that internal events can become SDs for people.

Behavior analysts often use discrimination training. They use it with educational behaviors, particularly in programmed instruction (e.g., Perez-Gonzalez, Spradlin, & Saunders, 2000). They use it to teach simple skills to children with retardation and autism (e.g., Mithaug & Mithaug, 2003). These skills include imitation and following instructions. They use it to get behaviors to occur outside the training situation. The methods used to teach these skills involve the basic discrimination-training procedure. Hence, I will describe them in greater detail in succeeding lessons.

## Establishing Stimulus Control

Sometimes behavior analysts can create stimulus control without explicit training. In this case, they use procedures that seek to establish a "right" time and place to emit problematic behaviors. When their efforts are successful, the behaviors become discriminated behaviors. The behaviors occur at a more functional rate in this more restricted situation. The "right" situation becomes the SD that controls the behavior.

For example, researchers helped a group of worriers decrease their worrying (Borkovec, Wilkinson, Folensbee, & Lerman, 1983). They told the worriers to note but otherwise ignore their worries during most of the day. The worriers were then to do all their worrying during a half-hour Worry Period once a day. The worriers reported considerably less worrying as a result.

Researchers helped overweight people lose weight (Carroll & Yates, 1981). They told these people to eat in only one room, to use only one chair, and to eat at the same times each day. They told them to do nothing else while eating, such as reading or watching TV. They told them to keep food out of sight—no fruit or candy in bowls, for instance. They even told them to store food in the refrigerator in opaque bowls. These rules greatly reduced the stimuli that would lead to eating. They helped the control group lose weight and led to better maintenance of weight loss.

Researchers have used similar methods to improve insomnia (Espie, Lindsay, Brooks, & Hood, 1989). Other researchers have helped normal adults maintain exercise programs (Keefe & Blumenthal, 1980).

---

### *Improving Supervision with Marked Items*

Cities often hire youths to pick up the litter in an area. They pay them for each bag of trash they turn in. Unfortunately, their supervisor can't tell whether the youths picked up the trash from the ground or from a garbage can. One solution is to place marked pieces of trash on the ground in the target area. If the youths don't know which items are marked, then they must pick up all litter to be sure of getting the marked items. Three researchers tried this procedure. They paid the youths 25 cents for each marked item. This approach reduced litter as much as 90%, resulting in a much cleaner neighborhood. The marked items permitted the supervisors to discriminate when the youths were actually picking up litter from the area. (Based on Hayes, Johnson, & Cone, 1975.)

10. Because seeing a marked item comes <u>before</u> paying the youth, a marked item is called a(n) _____ (reinforcer, SD) for the supervisor to pay the youth.

## Summary

Every day people frequently use discrimination training. Behavior analysts often use it to help people. It involves reinforcing a behavior in the presence of one stimulus and extinguishing it in the presence of other stimuli. Behavior analysts call the stimulus associated with reinforcement a discriminative stimulus, or SD. They call the stimulus associated with extinction the S-delta. When the behavior occurs with the SD but not the S-delta, they call it *discriminated behavior*. They say the SD exerts stimulus control. Tactic #1 of the stimulus control strategy is to narrow stimulus control through discrimination training.

## Behavior Analysis Examples

### *Teaching Reading to a Culturally Deprived Chicano*

Carlos was a 14-year-old Chicano boy. He read at a second-grade level. He had a long history of school failure. He had <u>never</u> passed a course in school. He was a persistent behavioral problem for his teachers.

Staats and Butterfield (1965) used behavior analysis to help Carlos learn to read. They gave him training consisting of four stages. First, they taught him new words. Second, they had him read stories out loud using those words. Third, they had him read the same stories to himself and then answer questions about them. Fourth, they reviewed his new words every twenty lessons.

The researchers used a set of stories starting at the first-grade reading level and progressing to a higher level. Each story ended with a set of test questions. They reinforced reading behavior with toys, special events, and money.

For stage one, they taught Carlos any new words appearing in the next story. They gave him a reinforcer when he read a new word correctly. They corrected him when he did not read it and gave him another chance.

For stage two, they had Carlos read the story out loud after he had mastered the new words. They gave him a reinforcer each time he read a paragraph with no errors. They corrected him when he made an error and gave him another chance later.

For stage three, they gave him the whole story on a single page along with the test questions. They instructed him to read it silently and answer the questions. They reinforced him on a variable-interval schedule averaging 15 seconds when he was looking at the story. They gave him a reinforcer when he completed the questions. They told him of his errors and let him reread the story.

---

### *Intelligence Can Be Taught*

Educators test for "intelligence" by giving students analogies, jumbled sentences, and verbal math problems. Recently, educators have begun teaching "intelligence" by teaching the behaviors involved in solving such problems. Xavier, a small black college, has increased their graduates going to medical school from 5 to 74 a year by teaching what they called intelligence behaviors. Washington, D.C., schools increased their Merit Scholars from none in 1988 to four in 1995 by teaching the steps in solving problems. Intelligence can be defined as knowing how to take these steps when faced with a problem. Being faced with a problem is the SD for taking the steps. Taking the steps when faced with a problem constitutes a discriminated behavior. Ultimately, being able to treat "low intelligence" as a "behavioral problem" may mean that we don't have to "condemn the educationally disadvantaged to a life of wretchedness." (Based on Cose, 1995.)

11. The increased probability of taking the problem-solving steps when faced with a problem is called _____ _____ (reinforcement, stimulus) control.

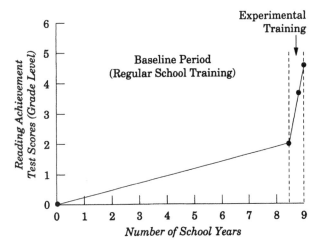

**Figure 16-1.** The reading achievement level of Carlos with regular school training and using discrimination training methods. (Adapted from "Treatment of Non-Reading in a Culturally Deprived Juvenile Delinquent: An Application of Reinforcement Principles," by A. W. Staats and W. H. Butterfield, *Child Development*, 1965, 36, 925–942. Copyright 1965 by the Society for Research in Child Development, Inc. Used by permission.)

For stage four, they presented him with a review of all his newly learned words after every 20 stories. They gave him a reinforcer for each correct answer on the review.

The training resulted in remarkable improvements in his reading. Figure 16-1 shows the results of reading-achievement tests given to him. Carlos had attained a second-grade reading level after 8½ years in public school. In just 6 months of special training, he improved to a grade level of 4.3. Further, during that term he passed all of his courses–the first time that he had passed even one course! Also, his misbehavior in the classroom had decreased to near zero. Behavior analysis helped Carlos more in 40 hours than had public school methods in over 8 years.

I mentioned before that Skinner guessed that at least 50,000 responses must be reinforced to learn basic arithmetic. Carlos made a total of about 65,000 oral responses to words during his training period. This experiment shows that Carlos was not stupid. He couldn't read simply because his parents and teachers had not reinforced enough reading responses. When behavior analysts reinforced his reading responses, he learned to read.

12. The first stage of teaching Carlos involved showing him a written word and asking him to say that word. For example, if Carlos said "car" when they showed him the word *car*, they reinforced him. If he said "car" when they showed him the word *cat*, they did not reinforce him. Instead, they corrected him. Because they reinforced a behavior in the presence of one stimulus and extinguished it in the presence of another stimulus, the researchers were using discrimination _____ (behavior, training).

### The Effects of Different Adults on a Child's Behavior.

Redd and Birnbrauer (1969) studied the effects of Bill and Bob on the cooperative play behavior of Paul, a 14-year-old boy with retardation. The researchers selected Paul because he did not engage in cooperative play. They had Bill reinforce cooperative play but not Bob. They studied whether Paul would play differently around Bob than around Bill.

The researchers brought Paul and four other children into a playroom containing a wide variety of toys. Two observers sat behind a one-way mirror. They recorded whether Paul engaged in cooperative play every 2½ seconds. With no adults in the room, Paul engaged in no cooperative play.

Bill then proceeded to shape cooperative play. He gave Paul reinforcers contingent upon approximations to cooperative play. The reinforcers consisted of saying "good boy" plus an M & M, a bite of ice cream, or a sip of Coke. Paul learned to play cooperatively. Bill then gradually reduced the reinforcement to a fixed-interval schedule of 45 seconds. That schedule maintained cooperative play.

Bob came into the room at times when Bill was not there. He gave as many reinforcers as did Bill, but they were not contingent on cooperative play.

Paul very soon adopted a very distinctive pattern of cooperative play. If neither adult was in the room, he did not engage in cooperative play. If Bill came into the room, he immediately started playing cooperatively. He continued as long as Bill remained. If Bill left the room, Paul stopped playing cooperatively.

When Bob came into the room, Paul did not play cooperatively. Thus, Bill became an SD.

The researchers wanted to make sure that this finding was not the result of some personality difference between Bill and Bob. So they had them exchange roles. Bob now awarded reinforcers contingently for cooperative play. Bill did not. With this reversal, Paul started to play cooperatively the moment that Bob entered the room. He stopped when Bill entered the room.

This study shows that the cooperative play behavior of Paul underwent only a very limited change. Paul's behavior changed only in the presence of the adult who reinforced him. It did not change more generally than that. Paul had not learned to play cooperatively with other children in general. The next lesson will discuss procedures for producing such general changes.

This study has everyday implications for all of us. Suppose that your friend Stanley never compliments you. Suppose he often compliments Kay. You might conclude that he doesn't like you very much or that he isn't a very positive person. But it may be that you simply don't reinforce his compliments. You may act shy. You might look embarrassed. Receiving compliments is like any other behavior. If you stop reinforcing others for giving you compliments, they will stop the behavior.

13. If Bob's presence prompted Paul to play cooperatively, then his presence exerts _____ (reinforcement, stimulus) control over his cooperative play.

## Notes

### *Note #1*
The ability of humans to use language may explain our extraordinary success as a species. Sidman may have discovered the behavioral foundation for language. He found that *stimulus equivalence* may emerge from discrimination training (Sidman, 1971). It works this way. A discrimination based on a visual stimulus may become equivalent without specific training to one based on an auditory stimulus. For example, suppose you teach Pat to point to the picture of a "cat"

when you say the word. Suppose you then teach Pat to point to the written word *cat* when she sees the picture. Without further training, she may also point to the written word *cat* when you say the word. Further, she may even say the word when you show her the written word. Numerous experiments have demonstrated that spoken and written words and the objects or pictures that they stand for become equivalent with the right kind of training (e.g., Sidman & Tailby, 1982; Saunders & Spradlin, 1990; Hayes, Kohlenberg, & Hayes, 1991).

14. *Stimulus equivalence* refers to people responding as though one stimulus is _____ (different, equivalent) to another unrelated stimulus.

### *Note #2*
The SD, or discriminative stimulus, is sometimes confused with a reinforcer. For any specific response these two elements are different. The SD is present <u>before</u> the response is made. It is associated with reinforcement, but it is not reinforcement. You should view it as a cue to what behavior will be reinforced. To hear "Please pass the butter" is not a reinforcer. It is a discriminative stimulus (SD) that indicates that you will be reinforced (thanked) for passing the butter but not for passing anything else. The request is the SD, and the "thanks" is the reinforcer. The SD always occurs <u>before</u> the behavior. The reinforcer always occurs <u>after</u> the behavior.

15. The SD always occurs _____ _____ (after, before) the behavior.

### *Note #3*
Dinsmoor (1995) argues that discrimination between two stimuli is the result of increased observing responses. That is, people learn to look more frequently for the discriminative stimulus because that tells them when to make the response leading to reinforcement. He argues that this can happen even when the S-deltas have never been extinguished. This is a fascinating area for further research. I have used the established definition of discrimination training in this lesson pending the outcome of that research.

# Helpful Hints

### *Helpful Hint #1*

As you have probably guessed by now, *discrimination training* is the name for the procedure mentioned in an earlier lesson that is easy to confuse with differential reinforcement. At the time, the book had you label the undefined procedure as unknown. From this lesson on, you should label it as discrimination training. Remember, differential reinforcement involves two or more different behaviors, one of which is reinforced and the other extinguished. These differential consequences occur in the presence of one stimulus. Discrimination training involves two or more different stimuli and one behavior, which behavior is reinforced in the presence of one stimulus and extinguished in the presence of the other stimulus. Therefore, you should also label complex cases involving two or more stimuli and two or more behaviors as discrimination training.

16. If you reinforce a behavior in one situation and extinguish it in others, then the name of the procedure is _____ _____.

# Additional Readings

Barrett, B. H., & Lindsley, O. R. (1962). Deficits in acquisition of operant discrimination and differentiation shown by institutionalized children with retardation. *American Journal of Mental Deficiency, 67,* 424–436. Also reprinted in L. P. Ullman & L. Krasner (Eds., 1965), *Case studies in behavior modification.* New York: Holt, Rinehart, and Winston. This article reports the use of operant psychology to measure the ability of children with retardation to rapidly form a variety of discriminations.

Dinsmoor, J. A. (1995). Stimulus control: Part 1. *The Behavior Analyst, 18,* 51–68. This is an excellent introduction for the advanced student to current issues in stimulus control. It contains an excellent discussion of the role of observing responses in discrimination training.

Hayes, S. C., & Wilson, K. G. (1993). Some implications of a contemporary behavior-analytic account of verbal events. *The Behavior Analyst, 16,* 283–301. Presents a behavior analytic theory of verbal behavior called *relational frame theory* that is based on stimulus equivalence. This article is for the advanced student who wishes to understand how the meaning of language arises from discrimination processes.

Neale, D. H. (1963). Behavior therapy and encopresis in children. *Behaviour Research and Therapy, 1,* 139–149. Discrimination training was used as part of the procedure for treating four disturbed children with encopresis (the children defecated in their pants rather than in the toilet). The success of the procedure permitted the children to be released from the hospital and develop normal lives.

Rodgers, T. A., & Iwata, B. A. (1991). An analysis of error-correction procedures during discrimination training. *Journal of Applied Behavior Analysis, 24*(4), 775–781. The standard discrimination training procedure simply ignores errors made by the trainee. This study compares the effect of the standard procedure with a variation. The variation is to present the same discrimination problem to the person until they get the right answer. The study found that this variation improved the performance of some trainees.

Simmons, M. W., & Lipsitt, L. P. (1961). An operant discrimination apparatus for infants. *Journal of the Experimental Analysis of Behavior, 4,* 233–235. Chimes were used as a reinforcer to teach a 10-month-old girl a simple discrimination.

Staats, A. W., Staats, C. K., Schutz, R. E., & Wolf, M. M. (1962). The conditioning of textual responses using "extrinsic" reinforcers. *Journal of the Experimental Analysis of Behavior, 5,* 33–40. This article describes a procedure to systematically teach young children to discriminate written words from one another through a complex discrimination training procedure. This procedure provides a systematic way to teach young children to read.

# Programmed Reading

This Programmed Reading section covers the following topics: (1) Narrowing Stimulus Control, (2) Stimuli Associated with Reinforcement, (3) Stimuli Associated with Extinction, (4) Discriminated Behavior, (5) Summary of Discrimination Training, (6) Discrimination Training versus Differential Reinforcement, (7) Complex Examples of Discrimination Training, (8) Research Examples of Discrimination Training, (9) Another Tactic, and (10) Review.

### *1. Narrowing Stimulus Control*

68. Pre-test: If Ann's boyfriend calls her "honey bunch" when they are alone, she responds. If he calls her "honey bunch" when others are around, she ignores him. If he calls her "honey bunch" more when they are alone than when others are around, Ann would be using the procedure of _____ _____.

62. Pre-test: Discrimination training: A behavior is _____ in the presences of one stimulus and that same behavior is _____ _____ in the presence of another stimulus.

61. Pre-test: Behavior analys00ts call the procedure of extinguishing a behavior in the presence of one stimulus and reinforcing it in the presence of another stimulus _____ _____.

36. I will start this module by introducing the idea of stimulus control. The increase in a behavior caused by an event that follows it is called reinforcement control. The increase in behavior from a preceding event is called _____ (reinforcement, stimulus) control.

38. If an event like a question influences someone's behavior, then it is called a(n) _____.

164. You will need to know that *stimuli* is the plural of _____.

148. To explain stimulus control I must define *stimulus*. Any physical event or object in a person's environment that is related to his behavior is termed a(n) _____.

135. The plural of *stimulus* is _____ _____.

143. The topic of this module is discrimination training. Behavior analysts call the procedure of <u>reinforcing</u> a behavior in the presence of one stimulus and <u>extinguishing</u> it in the presence of another stimulus, _____ _____ training.

20. Discrimination training consists of reinforcing a behavior in the presence of one stimulus and _____ _____ that same behavior in the presence of another stimulus.

16. Behavior analysts use the term *discrimination training* to refer to the procedure of extinguishing a behavior in the presence of one stimulus and _____ it in the presence of another stimulus.

14. Behavior analysts call the procedure of extinguishing a behavior in the presence of one stimulus and reinforcing it in the presence of another stimulus _____.

112. Suppose Mom praises Benny when he calls his father "Dada" but ignores him when he calls his uncle "Dada." Benny may learn to call his father Dada but no one else. Mom is reinforcing Benny for saying "Dada" in the presence of his father and extinguishing saying the same word in the presence of his uncle. She is using the procedure called _____ _____.

50. Mom uses discrimination training by using the procedure of reinforcement to increase Benny's saying "Dada" in the presence of his father and using the procedure of _____ to decrease saying the same word in the presence of his uncle.

157. When Mom reinforces "Dada" in one situation and extinguishes in another, she is working with how many behaviors? _____ The presence of Benny's father is one situation. The presence of his uncle is another situation. Mom is using reinforcement and extinction with how many situations? _____

## 2. Stimuli Associated with Reinforcement

69. Pre-test: If Ann's boyfriend calls her "honey bunch" when they are alone, she responds. If he calls her "honey bunch" when others are around, she ignores him. If he calls her "honey bunch" more when they are alone than when others are around, you would call the stimulus situation of being alone with her a(n) _____.

100. Pre-test: You might say the SD "signals" that a particular behavior will be _____.

67. Pre-test: If an event occurs before the behavior and increases the rate of the behavior, it is a(n) _____ _____, while if it occurs after and increases the rate of the behavior, it is a(n) _____.

90. Pre-test: The abbreviation for a stimulus that precedes the behavior and is present only if reinforcement will occur for that behavior is the two letters: _____.

134. The next few modules teach several technical terms for different parts of the procedure of discrimination training. I will start with *discriminative stimulus*. Any <u>stimulus</u> that precedes the behavior and is present only if reinforcement will occur for that behavior is called a discriminative _____ _____.

52. Notice that the name of the procedure *discrimination training*, ends with the suffix *-ion* but the name of the stimulus, *discrimina<u>tive</u> stimulus*, ends with the three-letter suffix _____.

163. You will be reading and writing the word *discriminative* many times in the rest of the book. Many students have trouble spelling it at first. Practice spelling *discriminative* right now. I would suggest that you try to memorize it with your eyes closed, check to see if you are right, and if so, then enter it without looking at this page: _____.

9. Any stimulus that precedes the behavior and is present only if reinforcement will occur for that behavior is called a(n) _____ stimulus.

45. Let's go back to Mom and Benny. Mom reinforces Benny's saying "Dada" in the presence of his father. The father is a stimulus in the presence of which saying "Dada" is reinforced. Thus, it is a stimulus that is "discriminative" of reinforcement for that response. Therefore, behavior analysts call the father a(n) _____ (give the full term, do not use the abbreviation).

15. Behavior analysts define a discriminative stimulus as "any stimulus that precedes the behavior and is present only if reinforcement will occur for that behavior." In what sense does the father <u>precede</u> the behavior? In the sense that the father must already be present in the room for Benny to call him "Dada." Thus, the father is a stimulus that _____ (follows, precedes) the behavior, and only if he is present will Mom reinforce that behavior.

139. The term *discriminative stimulus* is a mouthful. Behavior analysts abbreviate it. They abbreviate it in an unusual way. They abbreviate it as though the term were *stimulus, discriminative*. They abbreviate it with the first letter of each of those words, in that order. Thus, the abbreviation is the two letters: _____.

1. *SD* is a widely used abbreviation for the term _____ *stimulus*.

121. The abbreviation for a stimulus that precedes the behavior and is present only if reinforcement will occur for that behavior is _____.

21. Don't confuse *SD* with *reinforcer*. Both are stimuli and both increase the rate of a behavior. If an event occurs before the behavior and increases the rate of the behavior, it is a(n) _____ _____, while if it occurs after and increases the rate of the behavior, it is a(n) _____.

43. In the case of Mom and Benny, Mom's praise is delivered after Benny says "Dada" in the presence of the father. If the stimulus called "praise" increases the rate of "Dada," then you should call it a(n) _____. Mom praises Benny's "Dada" only if

the father was already in the situation. If the praise is a reinforcer, then you should call the father a(n) _____ _____ (you may abbreviate).

33. Here's another way to look at an SD. We know that an SD (discriminative stimulus) is a stimulus that precedes a behavior. We know that this stimulus is associated with reinforcement for a particular behavior. When father is there, Benny knows that saying "Dada" will be reinforced. You might say that the SD "signals" that the particular behavior will be _____.

### 3. Stimuli Associated with Extinction

70. Pre-test: If Ann's boyfriend calls her "honey bunch" when they are alone, she responds. If he calls her "honey bunch" when others are around, she ignores him. If he calls her "honey bunch" more when they are alone than when others are around, you would call the stimulus situation consisting of other people a(n) _____.

101. Pre-test: You must be vigilant about the difference between a reinforcer and an SD. Both are stimuli. Both increase the rate of the behavior. If the stimulus occurs after the behavior, it is called a(n) _____, while if it occurs before the behavior, it is called a(n) _____.

95. Pre-test: The name of the procedure of reinforcing a behavior in the presence of one stimulus and extinguishing it in the presence of another stimulus is _____. The full name of the stimulus associated with reinforcement is _____ stimulus. It is abbreviated as _____. The name of the stimulus associated with extinction is _____.

60. Pre-test: Any stimulus that precedes a behavior and is present only if extinction will occur for that behavior is called a(n) _____.

8. Another term you will need to know is called an "S-delta." Whereas SD stands

for a stimulus that increases behavior because it is associated with reinforcement, S-delta stands for a stimulus that decreases behavior because it is associated with _____ (extinction, reinforcement).

10. Any stimulus that precedes a behavior and is present only if extinction will occur for that behavior is called a(n) _____.

12. Back to Mom and Benny again. Benny's father is an SD. Benny's uncle is an S-delta. Mom extinguishes Benny's saying "Dada" in the presence of his uncle. The uncle is a stimulus in the presence of which Mom reduces saying "Dada" by applying the procedure of _____ to saying "Dada."

48. Mom extinguishes Benny's saying "Dada" in the presence of his uncle. Because his uncle is a stimulus in the presence of which Mom extinguishes saying "Dada," behavior analysts call the uncle a(n) _____ for saying "Dada."

149. To tell the difference between SD and S-delta, you have to find out what response we are talking about. So read past the blanks. Because Benny is reinforced for saying "Dada" only when his father is around, his father is a(n) _____ for saying "Dada." Because Benny is extinguished for saying "Dada" when only his uncle is around, his uncle is a(n) _____ for saying "Dada."

102. Quick summary of terms so far. The name of the procedure of reinforcing a behavior in the presence of one stimulus and extinguishing it in the presence of another stimulus is _____. The full name of the stimulus associated with reinforcement is _____ stimulus. It is abbreviated as _____. The name of the stimulus associated with extinction is _____.

162. You must be vigilant about the difference between a reinforcer and an SD. Both are stimuli. Both increase the rate of the behavior. If the stimulus occurs after the behavior, it is called a(n)

_____, whereas if it occurs before the behavior, it is called a(n) _____.

17. Benny may never say "Dada" during the day when his father is at work. But when his father comes home from work and Benny sees him, he is likely to say "Dada" a bunch of times. He sees his father before saying "Dada." Seeing his father increased his rate of saying "Dada." Therefore, father is a(n) _____ for saying "Dada."

37. If a stimulus precedes a behavior and increases the rate of the behavior, the stimulus is a(n) _____; if a stimulus follows a behavior and increases the rate of the behavior, the stimulus is an event called a(n) _____.

### 4. Discriminated Behavior

71. Pre-test: If Ann's boyfriend calls her "honey bunch" when they are alone, she responds. If he calls her "honey bunch" when others are around, she ignores him. If he calls her "honey bunch" more when they are alone than when others are around, you would call his calling her "honey bunch" a(n) _____ behavior.

65. Pre-test: If a behavior has a higher probability of occurring in the presence of an SD than it does in the presence of an S-delta, then it is called _____ behavior.

58. Pre-test: A single instance of a discriminated behavior is called a discriminated _____.

144. This module covers another term you will need to apply discrimination training. Discriminated behavior is the name of behavior that has a higher probability of occurring in the presence of an SD than it does in the presence of an S-delta. Notice that the name of the behavior ends with the two-letter suffix: _____.

161. You learned about discrimination training. Then, you learned about discriminative stimulus. Now, you are learning about discriminated behavior. Memorize these endings. If a behavior

has a higher probability of occurring in the presence of an SD than it does in the presence of an S-delta, then that behavior is called _____ behavior.

44. Let's find out how discriminated behavior applies to Mom and Benny. We would call the behavior of saying "Dada" discriminated behavior" once Benny was _____ (less, more) likely to say "Dada" in the presence of his father than in the presence of his uncle.

55. Once Benny is more likely to say "Dada" in the presence of his father than in the presence of his uncle, we would call the behavior of saying "Dada" _____ behavior. You could now say that Benny has learned to call his father "Dada."

53. Notice that the name of the procedure (discrimination training) ends with the three-letter suffix: _____. The name of the stimulus (discriminative stimulus) ends with the three-letter suffix: _____. And the name of the behavior (discriminated behavior) ends with the two-letter suffix: _____.

147. Time to remember the exact terms with the right endings! If a behavior has a higher probability of occurring in the presence of an SD than it does in the presence of an S-delta, then it is called _____ behavior.

11. Any stimulus that precedes the behavior and is present only if reinforcement will occur for that behavior is called a(n) _____ stimulus. (Don't use the abbreviation.)

136. The procedure in which a behavior is reinforced in the presence of one stimulus and extinguished in the presence of another stimulus is called _____.

31. Here is a small variation on one of these new terms. You learned in an earlier lesson that behavior analysts call a single instance of a behavior a response. Thus, they call a single instance of a discriminated behavior a discriminated _____.

47. Let's say that Benny's father comes home from work on Thursday evening.

Benny might see his father and say "Dada." Because this is a single instance of discriminated behavior, you should call it a discriminated _____.

### 5. Summary of Discrimination Training

76. Pre-test: If the brunette person ignores you when you call her "Laverne," she is considered a(n) _____ _____ for that name.

66. Pre-test: If a brunette person smiles at you when you call her "Sally," she is considered a(n) _____ _____ for that name.

94. Pre-test: The increased probability of a discriminated behavior that is produced by the stimulus (SD) is called _____ control.

96. Pre-test: The name of a behavior that is more likely to occur after the SD than after the S-delta is a discriminated _____. The name of a single instance of that behavior is a discriminated _____.

99. Pre-test: When being present at a football game exerts stimulus control over your yelling behavior, yelling has become a(n) _____.

77. Pre-test: If the question "What is 9x9?" results in a greater probability that you will answer "81," it is said to exert _____ over your answering behavior.

97. Pre-test: The name of the procedure where a behavior is reinforced in the presence of one stimulus and extinguished in the presence of another stimulus is _____.

93. Pre-test: The full name of the stimulus associated with reinforcement is _____ _____, which is abbreviated as _____. The name of the stimulus associated with extinction is _____.

30. Here is a review of a term learned at the beginning of the lesson. Remember that **stimulus control** refers to the _____ (decreased, increased) probability that a discriminated behavior is evoked by the SD.

128. The increased probability of a discriminated behavior that is produced by the stimulus (SD) is called _____ control.

158. When referring to the effect of the stimulus on a behavior (as a result of discrimination training), we say that the stimulus <u>exerts</u> stimulus _____ _____ over the behavior. When referring to the behavior that occurs more frequently in the presence of the SD than the S-delta, we call it _____ behavior.

122. The behavior that results from discrimination training is _____ behavior. A single instance of the behavior is a(n) discriminated _____ _____, and the effect that a stimulus exerts on the behavior is called _____ control.

34. I want to emphasize how important it is to not confuse reinforcer and SD. If an event that increases behavior occurs before the behavior, you should call it a(n) _____ _____; if it occurs after the behavior, you should call it a(n) _____.

133. The next few items summarize the terms you need in order to apply discrimination training to everyday situations. To firm up your mastery of each term, I will have you write out the whole term. The increased probability that a discriminated behavior will occur in the presence of the SD is called _____.

127. The full name of the stimulus associated with reinforcement is _____ _____, which is abbreviated as _____. The name of the stimulus associated with extinction is _____ _____.

130. The name of a behavior that is more likely to occur after the SD than after the S-delta is _____ _____. The name of a single instance of that behavior is _____ _____.

131. The name of the procedure where a behavior is reinforced in the presence of one stimulus and extinguished in

the presence of another stimulus is
_____.

35. I will give you a bunch of examples of the terms you have just learned. This will help you master those terms for use throughout this unit. Suppose Mrs. Jones teaches American history. Her lesson today is Important Dates in World War Two. She wants to teach when the war started. In case you don't remember, December 7, 1941, is the day that the Japanese bombed Pearl Harbor. Suppose she asks two questions: "When did the Japanese bomb Pearl Harbor" (and start the war), and "When did Franklin Roosevelt die (near the end of the war). If she reinforces you for answering December 7, 1941, for the first question but extinguishes you for the same answer to the second question, she would be using what procedure? _____

138. The question "When did the Japanese bomb Pearl Harbor?" would be called a(n) _____ (use the abbreviation!) for the answer "December 7, 1941."

13. Be sure to read to the end of the sentence or you may get this one wrong. The question "When did President Franklin Roosevelt die?" would be called a(n) _____ with respect to answering "December 7, 1941."

160. When you are more likely to give the answer "December 7, 1941" when asked about Pearl Harbor and less likely when asked about Roosevelt, we would call your answer _____ behavior.

159. When the question "When did the Japanese bomb Pearl Harbor?" evokes the response "December 7, 1941," we say that the question exerts _____ _____ control over the behavior.

154. Tom's reading historical novels more often than science fiction is an example of developing a(n) _____ behavior.

### 6. Discrimination Training versus Differential Reinforcement

63. Pre-test: Fred reinforces Marci's laughing but ignores her crying when they are

out on a date. He is using the procedure called _____.

64. Pre-test: Fred reinforces Marci's laughing when he makes a joke but ignores her laughing when he makes a point. He is using the procedure called _____ _____.

81. Pre-test: If you reinforce a desirable behavior in one situation and ignore the same desirable behavior in another situation, you are using the procedure called _____.

82. Pre-test: If you reinforce desirable behavior and ignore undesirable behavior in the same situation and if the rate of desirable behavior increases, you are using what procedure? _____

83. Pre-test: If you reinforce desirable behavior in one situation and ignore undesirable behavior in the same situation and if the rate of desirable behavior increases, you are using what procedure? _____

123. The biggest difficulty for most students is telling the difference between discrimination training and differential reinforcement. One behavior might be reinforced and one or more other behaviors extinguished in one stimulus situation. The name of that procedure is _____. (Check your answer!)

56. One behavior might be reinforced in one situation and extinguished in a second situation. You should label the procedure as _____.

108. So, if reinforcement and extinction are applied to one behavior in two situations, the procedure is called _____ _____; but if reinforcement and extinction are applied to two or more behaviors in one situation, the procedure is called _____ _____. (Notice that the key is in the number of situations.)

40. If reinforcement and extinction are applied to behaviors in one situation, the procedure is _____ _____; if in two situations, the procedure is _____ _____.

54. Now that you know that some of those "unknown" examples in earlier lessons illustrated discrimination training, you can finish learning how it differs from differential reinforcement. Dad praises Lulu when she eats vegetables but ignores her when she drinks pop at home. Lulu starts to eat more vegetables and drink less pop. Because Dad was increasing the rate of one behavior and decreasing the rate of another in the same situation, you know that Dad used the procedure called _____ .

19. Dad praised Lulu when she waited until after eating her vegetables to have dessert but ignored her when she had her dessert first. Pretty soon Lulu waited until after eating her vegetables before having her dessert. Because Dad was increasing the rate of eating dessert in one stimulus situation (after eating veggies) and decreasing the same behavior in another stimulus situation (before eating veggies), you know that this time Dad was using the behavioral procedure called _____ .

110. Suppose Dad praised Lulu when she called their big loud vehicle "truck" but ignored her when she called their smaller vehicle "truck." If Lulu came to call only the big loud one a truck, what procedure was he using? _____

111. Suppose Dad praised Lulu when she called the picture of the airplane "airplane" but ignored her when she called it a "truck." If Lulu came to call the picture an "airplane," what procedure was he using? _____

41. If you praise Timothy when he drinks pop but ignore him when he drinks whiskey, and if his rate of drinking pop increases, you would be using what procedure? _____

42. If you praise Timothy when he puts on a suit to go to a business meeting but ignore him when he puts on a suit to eat dinner at home, then what procedure have you used? _____ _____

39. If Mr. Jones looks pleased when Martha says "I don't like that idea" about physics but ignores her when she says "I don't like that idea" about the way he grades the class, he is using what procedure? _____

### 7. Complex Examples of Discrimination Training

88. Pre-test: Mrs. Jones praised Velma for saying "one" but not "two" when asked what world war started in 1914. She praised Velma for saying "two" but not "one" when asked what war started in 1939. Mrs. Jones used the procedure of _____ .

84. Pre-test: If you reinforce behavior #1 and ignore behavior #2 in Situation A and you reinforce behavior #2 and ignore behavior #1 in Situation B, you are using the procedure called _____ .

142. The topic of this module is complex discrimination training. When discrimination training involves only one behavior in two stimulus situations, I will call it simple discrimination training. When discrimination training involves two behaviors in two stimulus situations, I will call it complex _____ training. I will also call discrimination training involving more than two behaviors and/or more than two stimuli complex. You do not have to learn *complex*, just recognize it when you see it.

107. Simple discrimination training involves learning only one discriminated behavior. Complex discrimination training involves learning multiple _____ behaviors at the same time.

114. Suppose that you reinforce one response in the presence of stimulus #1 and extinguish it in the presence of stimulus #2. Suppose you reinforce a second response in the presence of stimulus #2 and extinguish it in the presence of stimulus #1. Notice that this is discrimination training that involves two behaviors and two stimuli. Would this be an example

of complex discrimination training? _____ (yes, no)

150. To understand complex discrimination training, let's go back to Mom and Benny. Suppose Mom starts reinforcing Benny for calling his uncle "Unk" and extinguishing calling his father "Unk." Mom is now using a second instance of what procedure? _____ _____

49. Mom is now applying discrimination training to the behavior "Dada" at the same time that she is applying it to the behavior of "Unk." What she is doing is a perfect example of _____ (complex, simple) discrimination training.

132. The next few items cover what is a very difficult and very arbitrary point. Suppose Mom reinforces Benny for calling his father "Dada" and extinguishes him for calling his father "Unk." Because this example involves using reinforcement and extinction with two different behaviors in the same situation, you would properly call Mom's procedure _____.

115. Suppose the example is more complicated. Mom reinforces Benny for calling his uncle "Unk" but extinguishes him for calling his uncle "Dada." But she also reinforces Benny for calling his father "Dada" and extinguishes him for calling his father " Unk." Another way of describing what's going on here is that Mom reinforces Benny for calling his uncle "Unk" but extinguished Benny for calling his father "Unk." She also reinforces Benny for calling his father "Dada" but extinguishes him for calling his uncle "Dada." Because in both cases Mom is using reinforcement and extinction with one behavior in two situations, you could properly call either case the procedure of _____.

146. This simple distinction (of number of behaviors versus number of situations) also applies to complex discrimination training. In complex discrimination training, reinforcement and extinction are applied to behaviors in two or more stimulus situations. So anytime reinforcement and extinction are applied in more

than two stimulus situations, the name of the procedure is always _____ _____.

29. Finally, I can get to the point! Mom is working with a complex procedure involving two behaviors and two situations. Behavior analysts have pretty much arbitrarily decided not to call such a complex combination *differential reinforcement* and instead they call it _____.

113. Suppose that Dad praises Tommy when he puts plastic in the recycling bin for plastic but ignores him when he puts paper in the same bin. Suppose that Tommy's rate of putting in plastic increases while putting in paper decreases. Because this involves reinforcing one behavior and extinguishing another in the same stimulus situation, you would label the procedure _____ _____.

18. Dad might later add a recycling bin for paper. Suppose that Dad continues to praise Tommy when he puts plastic in the recycling bin for plastic and to ignore him when he puts paper in the bin for plastic. But now suppose that, in addition, Dad praises Tommy when he puts paper in the bin for paper but ignores him when he puts plastic in the bin for paper. Suppose that Tommy's rate for both correct responses increases relative to mistakes. We now have a situation that is more complex. What should you label Dad's procedure now? _____

116. Suppose you reinforce Timothy for wearing a suit to a business meeting but ignore him if he wears casual clothing to a business meeting. Suppose you reinforce him for wearing casual clothing to eat dinner at home but ignore him for wearing a suit to eat dinner at home. What procedure are you using? _____

117. Suppose you thank Bev for telling you to "lighten up" when you are looking very tense but you ignore her for telling you to "lighten up" when you are simply looking busy. If she starts saying it only when you look tense, what procedure

are you using? _____

118. Suppose you thank Bev for telling you to "lighten up" when you are looking very tense but you ignore her for telling you "it will be ok" when you look tense. If she starts saying "Lighten up" when you look tense, what procedure are you using? _____

119. Suppose you thank Bev for telling you to "lighten up" when you are looking very tense but you ignore her when she asks "Can I help?" when you look tense. Suppose you also thank Bev for asking "Can I help?" when you are looking busy, but ignore her if she tells you to "lighten up" when you look busy. If she starts saying "Lighten up" when you look tense, and "Can I help?" when you look busy, what procedure are you using? _____

155. When a child is learning the names of four objects rather than just one, the situation is an example of complex discrimination training. The teacher must use discrimination training for each of the four objects versus the other three. Thus, the child is undergoing four _____ training procedures at the same time.

### 8. Research Examples of Discrimination Training

86. Pre-test: Increasing the probability of a behavior in one situation through reinforcement and decreasing the probability of a second behavior in the same situation through extinction is called _____.

87. Pre-test: Increasing the probability of a behavior in one situation through reinforcement and decreasing its probability in another situation through extinction is called _____.

145. This module reviews the application of *differential reinforcement* and *discrimination training* to actual behavioral research examples. Researchers devised a discrimination training procedure based on an orange highlighting that helped batters see the spin on a pitched

ball. Increased hits by a batter indicated that the spin had come to exert greater _____ over the batter's hitting.

120. Teaching Fred to discriminate his blood pressure involves reinforcing his guess when it matches the measurement his actual blood pressure and extinguishing his guess it doesn't. Teaching this behavior is a health-related example of the procedure of _____.

57. Placing marked pieces of trash into the target area helped supervisors to tell when youths hired to pick up trash were actually picking up litter from the area. A marked item was a(n) _____ for the supervisor to pay the youth.

109. Sometimes behavior analysts can create stimulus control without explicit training by establishing a "right" time and place to emit problematic behaviors. When successful, the "right" situation becomes a stimulus in whose presence the behavior leads to reinforcement. Behavior analysts call that stimulus the _____.

106. Researchers told overweight people to eat in only one room, use only one chair, and to eat at the same times each day. They also were to do nothing else while eating and to keep food out of sight. This "right" situation reduced eating and led to reinforcers in the form of weight losses. You can say that the right situation came to exert _____ over their eating.

25. Dr. Staats presented Carlos with the written word *whenever*. He gave him a token if he said that word. The written word *whenever* would be called a(n) _____ for the spoken word "whenever"; it would be called a(n) _____ for any other spoken word.

27. Dr. Staats repeatedly presented any written word to Carlos that he got wrong until he could say its name correctly. Of course, he had to also not say that word when some other word was on the card. The increased probability of

saying the written word would be called
_____ control.

26. Dr. Staats reinforced the behavior of saying the name of the word on the card. If that behavior was more likely to occur in the presence of the word on the card than it was in the presence of some other word, then we would call the behavior _____ behavior.

24. Dr. Staats gave Carlos a token when he said "inspect" if that was the word on the card. He gave him nothing when he said "inspect" if any other word was on the card. What procedure was he employing? _____

32. Here's a review question. Bill gave Paul reinforcers contingent upon approximations to cooperative play. By differentially reinforcing closer and closer approximations to the target behavior of cooperative play, he was using the behavioral procedure called _____ _____.

22. Dr. Redd studied the results of having one behavior analyst give a child with retardation edibles when he played cooperatively with other children, while a second behavior analyst did not. The child learned to play cooperatively when the adult who reinforced him was present but not when the other adult was present. What procedure accounts for this result? _____ _____

124. The child with retardation is observed to play cooperatively in the presence of an adult who reinforced him for such play but not play cooperatively in the presence of a second adult. We say that the first adult exerts _____ _____ over the child's play behavior.

156. When Bob gave praise and edibles to Paul for cooperative play, his presence became a(n) _____ _____ for cooperative play.

4. A child with retardation was observed to play cooperatively in the presence of an adult who reinforced such play but not in the presence of a second adult who did not. We say that cooperative

play has become _____ behavior.

### 9. Another Tactic

89. Pre-test: Remember that the third strategy for solving human problems is called the _____ strategy.

91. Pre-test: The first tactic in using the stimulus control strategy for solving human problems is to narrow stimulus control through _____ _____.

85. Pre-test: In past units, you have learned some tactics that are part of the behavioral strategy and the reinforcement control strategy. The third strategy for solving human problems is called the _____ strategy.

98. Pre-test: To use the stimulus control strategy for solving human problems (1) narrow stimulus control through _____.

3. A brief introduction to the third strategy. When behavior does not occur in the appropriate situations, behavior analysts turn to the _____ _____ (behavioral, reinforcement control, stimulus control) strategy.

140. The third strategy for solving human problems is called the stimulus _____ strategy.

105. Remember that the third strategy for solving human problems is called the _____ strategy.

51. Narrowing stimulus control through discrimination training is the first tactic in the _____ _____ strategy.

151. To use the stimulus control strategy for solving human problems, (1) narrow stimulus control through discrimination _____.

152. To use the stimulus control strategy for solving human problems, (1) narrow stimulus control through _____ _____ training.

125. The first tactic in using the stimulus control strategy for solving human problems is to narrow stimulus control through _____.

### 10. Review

80. Pre-test: If Tom usually answers the question "7 x 15 = ?" with "105," then we say that the question exerts _____ over his response.

92. Pre-test: The first tactic in using the stimulus control strategy for solving human problems is to narrow stimulus control through _____ _____.

78. Pre-test: If the teacher praises John when he answers "105" to the question "7 x 15 = ?" the question is called a(n) _____ with respect to "105."

73. Pre-test: If Mrs. Smith praises John when he answers "one hundred and five" to the question "7 x 15 = ?" and ignores him when he answers "hunnerty five," and if John starts to answer "one hundred five" more often, then Mrs. Smith is using the procedure of _____ _____.

79. Pre-test: If the teacher ignores John when he answers "15" to the question "7 x 15 = ?" then the question is called a(n) _____ with respect to "15."

59. Pre-test: A stimulus occurring before a behavior that increases the rate of the behavior is called a(n) _____ _____; a stimulus occurring after a behavior that increases the rate of the behavior is called a(n) _____.

74. Pre-test: If Mrs. Smith praises John when he answers "105" to the question "7 x 15 = ?" and ignores him when he answers "105" to the question "6 x 15 = ?" then she is using the procedure called _____.

75. Pre-test: If reinforcement and extinction occur with different stimuli (i.e., two or more stimuli), then the procedure is called _____, but if reinforcement and extinction occur with the same stimulus (i.e., one stimulus), then the procedure is called _____.

72. Pre-test: If John usually answers "105" to the question "7 x 15 = ?" then his answer

is called a(n) _____ behavior.

46. Let's review an important distinction you have learned in this lesson. If a stimulus increases the probability of a behavior and occurs before the behavior, that stimulus is called a(n) _____. If a stimulus increases the probability of a behavior and occurs after the behavior, the stimulus is called a(n) _____.

28. Dr. Staats showed Carlos a card with the word *love* on it. Dr. Staats gave him a token if he said "love" but nothing if he said any other word. He repeated this for about 700 new words. What procedure did he use? _____

129. The increased probability of a discriminated behavior produced by a stimulus (SD) is called _____.

7. An SD (discriminative stimulus) is a stimulus that precedes a behavior. It "signals" that the behavior will produce _____.

137. The question "What is 2 + 2?" always gets Ward to say "four." Therefore, the question exerts _____ over his behavior.

5. A particular behavior that is more likely to occur in the presence of the <u>SD</u> than in the presence of the S-delta is called a(n) _____.

2. "What does 2 + 2 equal?" is called a(n) _____ for the answer "four."

126. The first tactic in using the stimulus control strategy for solving human problems is to narrow stimulus control through _____.

103. Reinforcing one behavior while extinguishing a second behavior in the presence of one stimulus and extinguishing the first behavior while reinforcing the second behavior in the presence of a second stimulus is considered to be an example of what procedure? _____ _____

104. Reinforcing one behavior while extinguishing a second behavior in the presence of one stimulus and seeing a relative increase in the reinforced

behavior is the procedure labeled _____.

23. Dr. Redd studied the results of having one behavior analyst give a child with retardation edibles when he played cooperatively with other children while a second behavior analyst did not. The child learned to play cooperatively when the first adult was present but not when the second adult was present. The behavioral procedure that accounts for this result is called _____ _____.

6. A stimulus that precedes a behavior and is associated with extinction is called a(n) _____.

153. To use the stimulus control strategy for solving human problems, (1) narrow stimulus control through _____ _____.

141. The third strategy for solving human problems is called the _____ strategy.

## Programmed Examples

### 1. Programmed Examples

12. Pre-test: Bob tried to boogie with Alice every chance that he had because she was such a good dancer. She easily followed any complicated turn that Bob tried, which increased his rate of complicated turns. However, she often missed the dips that he tried, thus decreasing his dips. He gradually came to perform many complicated turns but no dips when dancing with Alice. What procedure accounts for the increase in turns and decrease in dips? _____ _____

11. Pre-test: Barb showed little Wanda a picture of a dog and praised her when she said "doggy," but not when she said "kitty." Of course, Barb also showed Wanda pictures of cats, snakes, and Gila monsters and followed the same procedure. What procedure did Barb use to teach Wanda the names of the animals? _____

13. Pre-test: Doris usually acted in a happy mood around Fran because Fran got into the spirit and they had a good time together. Doris usually did not act in a happy

mood around Kay because Kay remained serious and did not get into the happy mood. In this situation, we would say that Fran exerted _____ over Doris's happy behavior.

14. Pre-test: Martha had two teachers in her kindergarten class. Ms. Smith praised Martha any time she was appropriately assertive around the other children whereas Mrs. Warner ignored Martha's assertive behavior. Pretty soon Martha was assertive when Ms. Smith was around but was not when Mrs. Warner was around. The two teachers were unwittingly using what procedure with respect to Martha's assertive behavior? _____

10. Ms. Yablonski asks Ward "What does 2 + 2 equal?" and praises him when he says "four." When she asks "What does 2 + 3 equal?" she ignores him when he answers "four." Ward learns to say "four" to answer the first question but to not say "four" to answer the second question. Clearly, this example involves reinforcement and extinction. However, both discrimination training and differential reinforcement involve reinforcement and extinction. Differential reinforcement would require that one behavior be reinforced while a second behavior be extinguished. It requires that there be two behaviors and one stimulus situation. This example talks about the answer "four". How many behaviors are there? _____ (1, 2) The relevant stimuli are the questions that might call forth his answer. How many stimuli are there? _____ (1, 2) Because the response "four" is reinforced with one stimulus and extinguished with the other, this example must involve what procedure? _____

15. Sammy had trouble pronouncing dates in his American history class. He just couldn't seem to say "1492" clearly. When the teacher asked him, "When did Columbus discover America?" Sammy would answer "forty nineteen two," "forty-nine two," or "fourteen nineteen two." The teacher ignored Sammy when he made these responses. Sometimes Sammy answered "fourteen ninety-two," and the teacher immediately praised him. Sammy soon learned to say the date correctly. This procedure involves reinforcement of one behavior and extinction of all others. Again, the relevant

stimulus is the question that calls forth his answers. How many stimuli (not behaviors) are reinforcement and extinction used with? _____. How many answers, correct and incorrect, does Sammy give at different times? _____ (1, 2, 3, 4, or 5) Because the example involves reinforcement of one answer and extinction of all other answers in a single stimulus situation, the procedure involved is _____.

4. Jeff swears by saying "X#!" a lot around the dorm, and his friends pay a lot of attention to it. When Jeff goes home, his parents ignore his "X#!." As a result, Jeff does not say "X#!" much at home. In this example, the relevant stimuli are the locations where he says "X#!." How many stimuli does this example involve? _____ (1, 2) How many types of behaviors occur in the example? _____ (1, 2) Because his swearing is reinforced in one situation but not the other, what procedure is being applied to him? _____

18. When Jeff was around Gerry, he often loudly and angrily said "gosh" and "X#!." Gerry ignored "gosh" but paid attention when he said "X#!." Gradually, Jeff said "X#!" more often than "gosh." Be careful not to think of the words "X#!" and "gosh" as stimuli. They are words that Jeff said, not stimuli that set the stage for the words. How many stimulus situations are there in which Jeff could swear? _____ (1, 2) How many behaviors does this example involve? _____ (1, 2) Because one word is reinforced in the dorm but the other word is extinguished in the same situation, this is an example of what procedure? _____

8. Mr. Campbell frequently asked Dave multiplication questions. When Mr. Campbell asked "What does 7 x 8 equal?" he praised Dave for answering "fifty-six" but ignored him for saying "eighteen." When Mr. Campbell asked Dave "What does 3 x 6 equal?" he praised Dave when he said "eighteen" but ignored him when he said "fifty-six." In this example, how many stimuli call forth Dave's answers? _____ (1, 2) How many behaviors did Dave perform as answers? _____ (1, 2) Since Mr. Campbell praised Dave when he answered "fifty-six" but not "eighteen" to the first question and also praised Dave when he answered "eighteen,"

but not "fifty-six" to the second question, Mr. Campbell was using what procedure? _____ I hope you remembered that this was a complex situation.

5. Johnny's parents ignored most of the "baby noises" he made when they were around. However, when Johnny first said "Dada," his parents paid a lot of attention to him, but they ignored "goo-goo." As a result, Johnny said "Dada" at a much higher rate than "goo-goo." How many stimulus situations does this example involve? _____ (1, 2) How many of Johnny's behaviors does this example involve? _____ (1, 2) What procedure are the parents using to increase "Dada" compared to "goo go"? _____

19. When Johnny first said "Mama," his father showered him with attention. Soon afterwards, father praised him when he said "Mama" to his actual mother and ignored his when he said "Mama" to anyone else. As a result, he started saying "Mama" only to his mother. The relevant stimuli in this case are those that signal him that he's going to get reinforced or extinguished for saying "Mama." If his mother is there, will father reinforce him for saying "Mama"? _____ (yes, no) Thus, the presence of his mother is one relevant stimulus. If his mother is not present, will his father reinforce him for saying "Mama"? _____ (yes, no) You could count mother as one relevant stimulus and then many additional people as additional stimuli. Therefore, this is an example of what procedure? _____

6. Johnny's parents paid a lot of attention when he called his mother "Mama" but ignored him when he called his mother "Dada." They, of course, paid a lot of attention when he called his father "Dada" but ignored him when he called his father "Mama." Count how many stimuli are associated with reinforcement and extinction. What procedure were Johnny's parents using? _____ (Check your answer on this one!)

7. Mary's father started going into her room after coming home from the university to see what she was reading. If she was reading archeology books, he got very interested and held long discussions with her. If she was reading anything else, he usually went off to

read the paper. She started reading many more archeology books than other kinds of books. Since reading occurred more frequently in the presence of archeology books, we would say that archeology books exert _____ _____ over Mary's reading behavior.

17. When Frank started hanging around with the gang, he found that the tall red-headed guy answered when called "Bob" but didn't if called "Jim," "Ken," or "Dave." Similarly, the short muscular dude answered when called "Jim" but not when called anything else. If the guys' answering is a reinforcer, what procedure is at work affecting Frank's choice of names for each person? _____

16. When Flora first moved into the sorority, she found that she could get to the bathroom by going down her hall and turning left at the corner. If you consider the corner of the hall to be a stimulus, then it would be considered a(n) _____ for turning left to get to the bathroom.

20. When Karen was learning how to use this book, she discovered that the answers to the Behavior Analysis questions could be found by looking under the heading Programmed Reading in the Answer Key section rather than under Programmed Examples. If looking up an example answer under Programmed Reading produced reinforcement whereas looking up an example answer under Programmed Examples produced extinction, then the book is applying what procedure to where Karen looks up example answers? _____

3. If Carol smiled at Lenny, you would guess that this would be a(n) _____ _____ for asking her out for a date; but if Carol frowned at Lenny, you would guess that this would be a(n) _____ _____ for asking her out for a date.

2. Frank always stops his car at any red, octagonal sign that says "Stop." He does this because his Dad praises him when he stops at this sign and ignores him when he stops at other signs. Behavior analysts say that the stop sign exerts _____ over his stopping behavior.

9. Mrs. Niles praised her son Larry for using unusual words when describing events. Unfortunately, his friends ignored him when he used unusual words around them. In this situation, we would call Mrs. Niles a(n) _____ for using such words and Larry's friends a(n) _____ for using such words.

1. Dennis was sometimes out past the 11:00 P.M. curfew. A few times he was stopped by a policeman. He learned to act courteously and apologize for losing track of time. When he did that, the policeman would let him go. He did not act this way at other times. His polite behavior was more likely to occur when talking to a policeman, so it is therefore referred to as _____ behavior.

# Generalization Training of Everyday Behaviors

## Reading Section

Discrimination training increases behavior in one situation and decreases it in other situations. In a sense, it draws a boundary between two situations so that the behavior does not spread from one to the other. The person involved learns the <u>difference</u> between situations. This lesson introduces *generalization training*, which does just the opposite: it eliminates boundaries between situations, and the behavior spreads from one situation to the other. The person involved learns the <u>similarity</u> between situations. Thus, discrimination training and generalization training are related but opposite procedures (Stokes, 1992). Tactic #2 of the stimulus control strategy is to broaden stimulus control through <u>generalization training</u>.

1. Tactic #2 of the stimulus control strategy is to broaden stimulus control through _____ training.

## Definition of Generalization Training

Suppose that Dad teaches Kay to call animals of a certain shape *dogs.* Dad might point to Bowser and ask her to say "dog." Of course, he would reinforce her when she says it. Suppose Kay learns to call Bowser a dog. How does Dad get her to do the same with all dogs? Obviously he doesn't want to repeat his lesson for every single dog in the world! What he needs is a way to "give her the idea." He can do so by teaching her to label a few animals dogs. From there, her naming can spread to all dogs without

further teaching. Behavior analysts use generalization training to accomplish this goal.

**Generalization training** is reinforcing a behavior in a <u>series</u> of situations until it <u>generalizes</u> to other members of that <u>stimulus class</u>. This book is full of examples of this procedure. For example, I wanted you to "get the idea of extinction." I presented a series of stories exemplifying extinction. I taught you with the first stories to label the procedure as extinction. Then, I asked you to identify added stories as extinction on your own. Right now, you could probably correctly label any new story I give you as extinction. You would not need further generalization training to do so. By using this procedure, the book has eliminated the boundaries between examples of extinction so that your labeling spreads to most of them.

2. **Generalization training** is reinforcing a behavior in each of a <u>series</u> of situations until it generalizes to other members of that same _____.

A key term in defining generalization training is **generalization,** which refers to the occurrence of a behavior in the presence of a <u>novel</u> stimulus. A novel stimulus would be any stimulus in whose presence the person's behavior has not been reinforced. With this book, new stories of extinction are novel stimuli because you had not already been reinforced for identifying them as extinction.

3. The occurrence of a behavior in the presence of a <u>novel</u> stimulus is called _____.

Another key term in the definition of generalization training is **stimulus class,** which is a set of <u>related stimuli</u>. For example, stories of extinction are all related because they conform to the definition of extinction. Other examples of related stimuli would be red objects, behavior analysts, differential equations, or students.

5. A **stimulus class** is a set of _____ _____ stimuli.

I can't overemphasize the importance of generalization and generalization training. Without generalization, you would have to learn whether every possible story was or was not extinction. You would not fully understand the concept. You would only memorize individual instances of it. Without generalization, human behavior would come to a virtual standstill. We would always be helpless in the face of constant bombardment by novel stimuli.

Don't get me wrong. Generalization is not magic. You won't always be reinforced when your behavior generalizes to a novel situation. You might call someone's infant a pretty girl just because it is wrapped in a pink blanket. That might be very embarrassing if the parents are particularly proud of their handsome little baby boy! This sort of response is sometimes called *overgeneralization*. It is a real, but undesirable, instance of generalization that can be counteracted through discrimination training. Thus, behavior analysts often use the procedures of discrimination training and generalization training together.

Generalization of behavior change is an important issue in behavior analysis. Suppose Jim wishes to become more assertive. A behavior analyst may present Jim with situations requiring assertive behavior and praise him for behaving assertively. However, Jim's assertiveness may remain subject to extinction by his friends and family. Jim might learn to discriminate when others will reinforce him for behaving assertively instead of becoming more assertive when he needs to in his everyday life. His new behavior may occur with increased frequency only with the behavior analyst, a result that wouldn't be worth much. What Jim needs and wants to learn is how to be effectively assertive in everyday situations. Many behavior analysts have studied this problem. After treatment, they measure assertive behavior in the person's normal situations. They measure if the behavior has generalized to people and situations outside training.

Behavior analysts have developed many strategies to obtain generalization (Stokes & Baer, 1977). I will review several commonly used strategies.

## The Train-and-Hope Method

The most frequent approach to generalization by behavior analysts has been dubbed by Stokes and Baer (1977) *train and hope*. The behavior analyst trains the desired behavior

---

### *The Importance of Generalization*

"A child who is learning to talk may speak his first words in the presence of his mother, who usually has more opportunities than other people to reinforce this behavior. He soon 'speaks' to other members of the family and to strangers. When he is taken to a strange place, speaking usually generalizes to the new surroundings. All of which is fortunate. Without generalization, we would probably spend most of our time relearning the same few skills in each new situation, and be able to develop only the most limited behavioral repertoires." This

quote is about <u>generalization</u>, the occurrence of a behavior in the presence of a novel stimulus. (Reese, 1978: p. 26)

4. Suppose Kenny has been reinforced for speaking to his parents. If Kenny has never been reinforced for speaking to Jim, then Jim is a novel stimulus. Therefore, the occurrence of Kenny speaking to Jim for the first time is an example of _____ (generalization, generalization training).

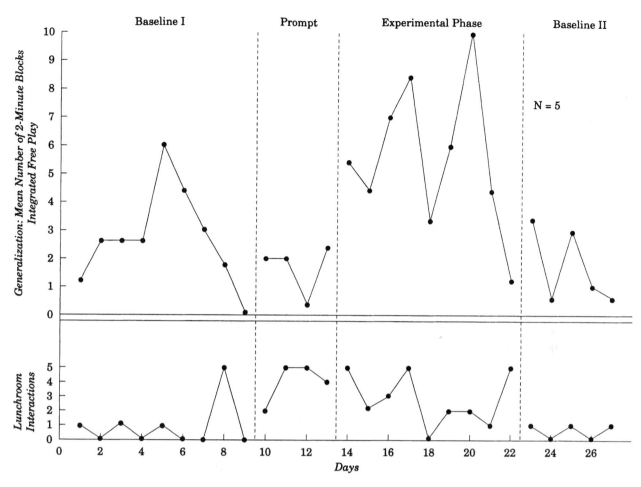

***Figure 17-1.*** The bottom panel shows the number of the 5 black first graders who had at least one of the 25 white first graders sitting with them in the lunchroom. The researchers gave snacks to any child sitting with "new friends" in the lunchroom during "prompt" and "experimental" phases. The top panel shows generalization to free play in the classroom by showing the number of two-minute intervals of integrated free play by the children. Children were not reinforced for playing together during any condition. (Adapted from "Reinforced Racial Integration in the First Grade: A Study in Generalization," by N. Hauserman, S. R. Walen, and M. Behling *Journal of Applied Behavior Analysis,* 1973, 6, 193–200. Copyright 1973 by the Society for the Experimental Analysis of Behavior, Inc. Used by Permission.)

and hopes it generalizes to everyday situations. The train-and-hope approach usually results in failure to produce generalization. Sometimes it produces limited success.

A successful example of the train-and-hope method occurred when researchers studied racial integration in a first-grade classroom (Hauserman, Walen, & Behling, 1973). They measured social contacts between 5 black children and 20 white children. Then, they reinforced any child who sat with a new friend (of any race) during lunch. The first panel of Figure 17-1 shows that this increased the rate of integrated seating in the lunchroom from about 20% to about 60%. The second panel of Figure 17-1

shows the surprising result that reinforcing the children for sitting together in the lunchroom also increased the amount of playing together on the playground. More playing together on the playground is an example of generalization because such playing was not reinforced. Unfortunately, this generalization stopped when sitting together in the lunchroom was no longer reinforced. Thus, this study showed generalization of the reinforcement effect from the lunchroom to the playground for only a limited time.

Other studies have also shown some limited success with the train-and-hope approach. Researchers treated four couples with

### *Reducing Video Game Stress*

Believe it or not, playing video games can stress you out. Your heart beats faster, your blood pressure goes up, and your hands get clammy. Researchers gave some kids biofeedback to lower their heart rate when they played video games. The children's heart rate remained lower when they played video games after termination of the biofeedback procedure. It also stayed low during the novel-stimulus situation of mental arithmetic! (Larkin, Zayfert, Abel, & Veltum, 1992).

6. Because the kids had not been reinforced to lower their rate during mental arithmetic, its occurrence in the presence of that novel stimulus is called _____ (generalization, generalization training).

distressed marriages (Behrens, Sanders, & Halford, 1990). They taught the couples communication and problem-solving skills. They assessed the couples' skills by observing them discussing difficult issues. They found that negative comments decreased sharply. They scored audiotapes of the couples discussing touchy issues at home. They found that the couples also made few negative comments at home after training. Thus, the improved communications generalized to the home.

Researchers reinforced nondepressed behavior emitted by depressed individuals (Hersen, Eisler, Alford, & Agras, 1973). Several of them continued emitting a small amount of nondepressed behavior even after the reinforcement program was stopped. Thus, the nondepressed behavior generalized to the everyday situation without reinforcement.

Sturgis, Tollison, and Adams (1978) showed that biofeedback training reduced migraine headaches (and that the reduction continued after biofeedback training was stopped. The researchers also observed decrements in headaches at home even though the training occurred in a psychological clinic. Thus, the headache reduction generalized to the home.

I have reviewed several studies in which the train-and-hope-method produced generalization. These studies are in the minority, however, because most studies using this approach show little or no generalization (e.g., Brobst & Ward, 2002). In general, researchers must use some systematic approach to produce generalization if they are to produce it with any consistency.

## Generalization Training

Generalization training appears to be the most effective method for producing generalization (Horner, McDonnell, & Bellamy, 1986). In fact, it may be the underlying principle in other generalization methods (Kirby & Bickel, 1988). In one case, researchers used this approach to teach a child with retardation to greet people (Stokes, Baer, & Jackson, 1974). They taught the child to greet one experimenter. That training did not cause the child to greet others, but after they taught the child to greet a second experimenter, the behavior generalized. The child greeted other staff members and even visitors without having been trained to do so.

Remember the researchers who taught males how to discriminate females' interest level? They showed the males videotape scenes of conversations involving several females (Azrin & Hayes, 1984). As you may recall, the males learned to discriminate interest indicated by these females. The researchers then observed the males in role-playing situations with new females. They found improvements in the males' ability to discriminate the interest level of these new females. Thus, the males' sensitivity generalized to new (i.e., novel) females.

Another researcher taught two children with retardation to converse (Garcia, 1974). The children readily learned to converse in the presence of the trainer. However, conversing did not generalize until a second trainer also reinforced them for conversing. The behavior analysts produced generalization by training the children across trainers.

Two researchers used a slightly different approach (Griffiths & Craighead, 1972).

***Figure 17-2.*** Trevor Stokes and Don Baer wrote the "classic" article on generalization. They convinced applied behavior analysts that studying and producing generalization are important. They described a number of strategies for producing generalization. (Source: Courtesy of Elise Pinkston and Trevor Stokes)

Training her in a special classroom setting, they reinforced a 30-year-old woman with retardation to speak clearly. She continued to speak unclearly in other settings. Next, they also reinforced her speaking clearly at her residence. She then began to speak clearly in all situations. The researchers in this study produced generalization by training the woman across settings.

You might think that the important skills learned by intelligent adults would generalize by themselves, but they often don't. For example, a researcher taught two fourth-grade teachers to give "specific praise" to their pupils during reading instruction (Horton, 1975)— that is, to tell them specifically what they were doing right. The teachers readily learned to use specific praise. They understood how this helped the children learn. However, they did not begin to use specific praise in math and language arts until they were trained to do so. Even then, they did not use specific praise in health or social science.

## The Similar-Stimuli Method

Behavior analysts use other methods to increase generalization. One common method is the *similar-stimuli* strategy. This method ensures that stimuli similar to those present in the training situation are also present in the everyday situation. Reinforcement always occurs in the presence of one or more specific stimuli. For example, suppose that Kay learned to say "dog" in a situation involving many stimuli. Bowser was one stimulus, and Dad was another. Others might include the lawn, the house, Dad's clothing, and the doghouse. The presence of any of those stimuli might increase the chances that Kay would label a second animal a "dog." In general, a response reinforced in the presence of one stimulus will tend to occur spontaneously in the presence of similar stimuli (Skinner, 1953). Those stimuli common to both situations assist generalization.

The similar-stimuli method involves trying to maximize the similarity between the training situation and the everyday situation. One way to do this is by training in the everyday situation. Another is to structure the training situation so that it is similar to the everyday situation. For example, two researchers worked with severely disruptive elementary school children (Walker & Buckley, 1972). They trained them in a special classroom to engage in appropriate behavior. These children increased their rate of appropriate behavior from about 40% in their regular classroom to about 90% in the special classroom. The researchers arranged for some elements of the regular classroom to be similar to the training classroom for half the children. They did not do so for the others. The children who were returned to similar classrooms maintained over 50% of their improved behavior. The other children maintained only about 30% of their improvement.

Football practice has many similarities to an actual game. The similarities include wearing padded uniforms, making running plays, and engaging in frequent contact. Researchers investigated the effects of self-set goal and public posting on athletic performance of five collegiate football players during practice (Ward & Carnes, 2002). They found an immediate increase in the practice performance. Correspondingly, they found an increase in game performance. Thus, increased performance generalized from practice to game settings.

## Generalization of Extinction

Generalization training may be used in connection with many behavioral procedures other than reinforcement. Thus, an undesirable behavior could be extinguished in a series of situations to produce generalized extinction. For example, one researcher used this approach to reduce 8-year-old Ben's "penguin talk" (Allen, 1973). Ben fantasized about penguins for up to 8 hours a day. While at summer camp, Ben talked constantly about penguins. He frequently talked about his imaginary pet penguins, "Tug-Tug," "Junior Polkado," and "Super Penguin." The researcher used a multiple-baseline analysis. He told the camp counselors to ignore Ben's penguin talk while walking on a trail. Ben

---

### Beating Up Black Bears

In the middle of his vacation in Canada Kenneth Markley was awakened by a noise. Discovering a huge black bear raiding the refrigerator in his cabin, he grabbed a lawn chair and hit the bear over the head. "That made him mad and he started snapping. His old teeth was just a-popping. He was growling and swinging his head and coming right at me. I hit him two or three times on the head, but the last time I got him on the nose." The hit on the nose caused the bear to bolt out the door! (Based on a story in the *Lawrence Journal World* on September 1, 1995.)

7. If Ken had won fights before taking on the bear by hitting several big humans, the bear might simply be a novel stimulus for hitting. If so, Ken's hitting the bear would be an example of _____ (discrimination, generalization).

---

stopped his penguin talk on the trail, but he didn't talk about penguins less in other settings. The counselors next ignored Ben's penguin talk in the dining hall. Ben immediately talked less about penguins there. At this point, Ben stopped talking about penguins in his cabin and in his classroom. Thus, extinguishing the behavior in two settings produced generalized extinction in other settings.

## Concept Formation

A particularly important behavioral process occurs when discrimination training is generalized so that a person can discriminate whether a stimulus is within or outside of a stimulus class. The outcome of this process is called *concept formation*. It is one basis of complex intellectual activity. Any type of understanding beyond memorizing must involve this process. Miller and Weaver (1974) showed how this book's use of discrimination and generalization produced concept formation.

***You Don't Generalize, Your Responses Generalize!***

"Generalization is not an activity of the organism; it is simply a term which describes the fact that the control [over a behavior] acquired by a stimulus is shared by other stimuli with common properties" (Skinner, 1953: p. 134). Thus, don't say, "You generalized." Rather say, "Your behavior generalized."

8. A behavior analyst wouldn't say, "You generalized." Rather, they would say, "Your _____ generalized."

## Summary

Generalization is the occurrence of a response in a novel situation. The train-and-hope method sometimes produces generalization, but generalization training is more certain to do so. Behavior analysts have used generalization training to increase greeting behavior and speech clarity among individuals with retardation. They have used it to increase social sensitivity and use of specific praise with normal adults. Teaching people to emit these behaviors in enough situations leads to them generalizing to many similar situations. Such generalization is crucial to human behavior. Without it, we would be endlessly learning the same few behaviors in new situations. Tactic #2 of the stimulus control strategy is broadening stimulus control through generalization training.

## Behavior Analysis Examples

### Teaching Assertiveness

Researchers sought to help Jane, a very passive 8-year-old girl (Bornstein, Bellack, & Hersen, 1977). She had difficulty relating to her peers. She didn't express anger even when it was appropriate. She was unable to refuse unreasonable requests. She was oversensitive to criticism. Finally, she rarely volunteered in class.

The researchers taught Jane three assertive behaviors. They defined <u>eye contact</u> as looking at the other person while speaking. They defined <u>loudness of speech</u> on a scale of 1 to 5, where normal was 5. They defined <u>requests for new behavior</u> as asking the other person to change their behavior. They computed reliability for each measure. It ranged from 85% to 100%.

The researchers used a role-playing scene to teach Jane the assertive behaviors. They told Jane to imagine the following scene. "You are part of a small group in science class. Your group is trying to come up with an idea for a project to present to class. You start to give your idea when Amy begins to tell hers also." Then, an actor pretended to be Amy. She said, "Hey, listen to my idea." The researchers asked Jane to react to Amy's interruption. Afterwards, they gave Jane feedback for one target behavior. For example, they might say "Jane, you failed to look at Amy for the whole time!" Then, they discussed the situation with Jane and modeled the correct behavior for her. Finally they instructed Jane how to perform the target behavior. They replayed the scene with Jane performing the target behavior. Training continued until Jane correctly performed the target behavior. The researchers used six different everyday scenes during training.

For the experiment, the researchers used three novel scenes. Figure 17-3 shows the results with those scenes. Jane's eye contact increased from near zero to 100% after training. Her loudness increased from very low to close to normal. Her requests increased from zero to two out of three. Jane maintained her new assertive behaviors two and four weeks later.

Two independent judges rated Jane's behavior as very unassertive before treatment. Figure 17-3 shows the results. They rated it slightly higher after Jane learned to make eye contact. They rated it slightly higher after she increased her loudness. Finally, they rated it much higher when she started to request changes in the other person's behavior. The final ratings were "moderately" to "very" assertive.

The researchers replicated these results with three other unassertive children. The results indicate that behavioral training can

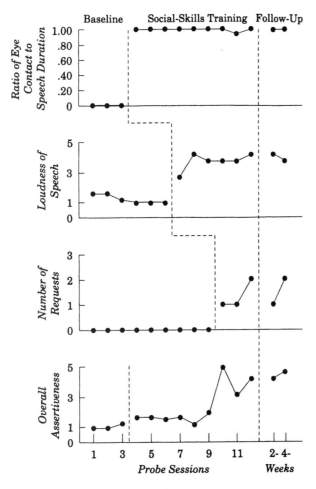

**Figure 17-3.** These graphs show the results of teaching Jane the social skills called "assertiveness." The first panel shows the ratio of eye contact to speech duration. The second shows the loudness of her talking. The third shows the number of requests she made. The bottom panel shows how outside judges rated Jane's overall assertiveness throughout the training. (Adapted from "Social Skills Training for Unassertive Children: A Multiple-Baseline Analysis," by M. R. Bornstein, A. S. Bellack, and M. Hersen, *Journal of Applied Behavior Analysis*, 1977, 10, 183–196. Copyright 1977 by the Society for the Experimental Analysis of Behavior, Inc. Used by permission.)

increase assertive behaviors in untrained situations. The judges' ratings suggest that everyday people call these three target behaviors assertive.

9. Behavior analysts call the increase in assertive behaviors in the novel scenes _____.

### Understanding

Hal Weaver and I studied the effect of an early version of this book as a generalization training program (Miller & Weaver, 1974). We observed whether readers' responses generalized from examples in the book to other novel stories. We made a test with 48 novel stories unrelated to any examples in the book. The test had four parts. Each part defined a baseline for each unit of the book. We gave this test at the beginning of every week during the semester. We computed the percentage of correct responses for each baseline.

We used a multiple-baseline design. The reading material in each unit was the treatment condition for each of the four baselines.

Figure 17-4 shows the results of the experiment. After reading the unit on Research Methods, scores for that baseline increased. However, they did not increase at that time for the other three baselines. After reading the unit on Reinforcement Control, only scores for that baseline increased. The same effect was present for each baseline.

10. The book reinforces responses to a series of similar stories. For example, it reinforces the response "satiation" to stories about too frequent reinforcement. These stories about frequent reinforcement are members of the same stimulus class. This research suggests that the response generalized to novel stories about satiation. Thus, the reinforcement of the response to many stories of satiation would be an example of _____ training.

### Notes

#### Note #1

Behavior analysts use other strategies to produce generalization (Stokes & Baer, 1976). They facilitate control by the everyday contingencies. They train loosely with varying stimuli so that discrimination doesn't occur. They use contingencies in training that can't be discriminated from everyday contingencies. They teach people to talk about the generalization. They train a generalized skill of *generalizing*.

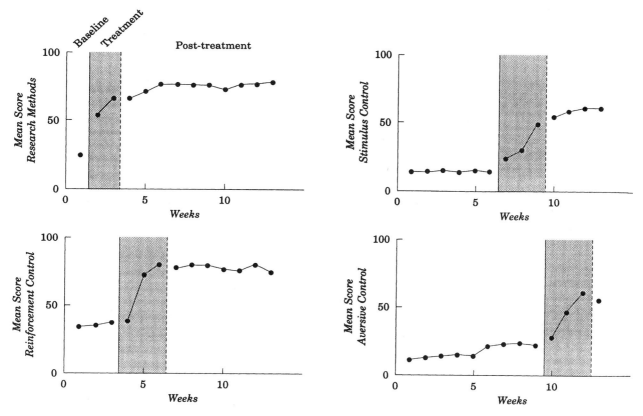

***Figure 17-4.*** A multiple-baseline experiment to see whether the first edition of this book produced generalization to examples not taught in the book. The researchers gave 50 students a weekly test containing novel examples from each unit of the book. Each graph shows the average scores for a different unit of the book. Each shaded bar shows when the students studied the unit associated with that graph. (From "The Use of 'Concept Programming' to Teach Behavioral Concepts to University Students," by L. K. Miller & F. H. Weaver. In J. Johnston (Ed.), *Behavior Research and Technology in Higher Education.* Copyright 1974 by Charles C. Thomas, Publisher. Reprinted by permission.)

11. Each method is a strategy for promoting _____ to novel stimuli.

### Note #2
Reports concerning generalization have become standard in applied behavior analysis. For example, almost 50% of all studies of child and adolescent therapy from 1978–1979 reported whether generalization occurred (Allen, Tarnowski, Simonian, Elliott, et al., 1991). Seventy percent of all studies of social skill training with children between 1976 and 1990 reported on generalization (Chandler, Lubeck, & Fowler, 1992).

12. Almost 50% of all studies of child and adolescent therapy from 1978–1979 reported whether _____ to novel stimuli occurred (Allen et al, 1991).

### Note #3
Generalization may also occur among behaviors. For example, when teaching someone to make positive statements to other people, one might begin by teaching first one positive statement, then another, and another. At some point, the individual will generalize to the class of all positive statements. This process is often referred to as *induction* or *response generalization.*

13. Generalization occurring among behaviors, such as making positive statements, is often referred to as induction or response _____.

# Helpful Hints

### Helpful Hint #1

When you are asked to identify instances of generalization and generalization training, remember the following: Generalization is a process, and generalization training is a behavioral procedure. Therefore, you would identify "reinforcing a behavior in each of a series of situations until it generalizes to other members of that same stimulus class" as the procedure of generalization training. You would identify "the occurrence of a behavior in the presence of a novel stimulus" as the process of generalization.

14. Remember that one of the terms refers to a procedure and one refers to a process. Which term refers to a process? _____ _____ Which term refers to a procedure? _____

### Helpful Hint #2

Students often mix up discrimination training and generalization training. Here's how you can always tell the difference. If the procedure increases the behavior in the presence of one stimulus but not in the presence of another stimulus, then it is discrimination training. The person is learning to discriminate between the situations. If the procedure increases the behavior in the presence of many related stimuli, then it is generalization training. The person is learning to generalize to novel stimuli. So you can tell whether an example is discrimination training or generalization training by asking if it uses reinforcement in the presence of one stimulus or in the presence of many stimuli.

15. If the procedure increases the behavior in the presence of many related stimuli, then it is _____ training, but if the procedure increases the behavior in the presence of one stimulus but not in the presence of another stimulus, then it is _____ training.

### Helpful Hint #3

Remember to always consider the possibility that a complex example is differential reinforcement (or shaping). I will give you many such examples so that you can learn to tell the difference between differential reinforcement, discrimination training, and generalization training. You can tell the difference by asking whether the example involves two behaviors and one stimulus or one behavior and two stimuli.

16. Always ask whether a complex example involves differential reinforcement. You can tell whether it does by asking if it involves _____ (1, 2) behaviors and _____ (1, 2) stimulus/stimuli.

# Additional Readings

Boyce, T. E., & Geller, E. S. (2001). Applied behavior analysis and occupational safety: The challenge of response maintenance. *Journal of Organizational Behavior Management, 21*(1), 31–56. This article reviews a sample of occupational safety research published from 1974 to 1996. It examines the success of four methods suggested by Stokes and Baer (1977) to produce generalization of safety behavior over long periods of time.

Chandler, L. K., Lubeck, R. C., & Fowler, S. A. (1992). Generalization and maintenance of preschool children's social skills: A critical review and analysis. *Journal of Applied Behavior Analysis, 2*(2), 415–428. This review reports on generalization with a select set of studies. It examines only studies of children learning social skills. The article examines the success of different strategies in producing generalization of those skills.

Houchins, N., & Boyce, T. E. (2001). Response generalization in behavioral safety: Fact or fiction? *Journal of Organizational Behavior Management, 21*(4), 3–11. This article discusses the definition and use of the term *generalization* in the behavioral safety literature.

Houlihan, D. D., Sloane, H. N., Jones, R. N., & Patten, C. (1992). A review of behavioral conceptualizations and treatments of child noncompliance. *Education and Treatment of Children, 15*(1), 56–77. This article reviews studies of how to modify child noncompliance from 1968 to 1990. The review examines methods used to increase compliance. It reports how effectively these methods promote generalization of the increased compliance to everyday situations.

Osnes, P. G., & Lieblein, T. (2003). An explicit technology of generalization. *The Behavior Analyst Today, 3*, 364–374. This article addresses the status of generalization promotion by behavior analysts. It reviews both conceptual and empirical articles published in behavior analytic journals between the years 1990 and 2000.

Stokes, T. F., & Baer, D. M. (1977). An implicit technology of generalization. *Journal of Applied Behavior Analysis, 10*, 349–367. This is the "classic" treatment of generalization in applied behavior analysis. It reviews 270 behavior analysis studies to establish what was known about generalization. The authors suggest nine strategies for promoting generalization. The article has been widely influential. It led to a great increase in attempts to produce generalization.

## Programmed Reading

This Programmed Reading is arranged into the following topics: (1) Elements of Generalization Training, (2) Generalization, (3) Generalization Training versus Discrimination Training, (4) Tactic #2 in the Stimulus Control Strategy, and (5) Review.

### 1. Elements of Generalization Training

38. Pre-test: Dave praises Bruiser for calling "praise" a reinforcer if it increases behavior that it follows. He then praises Bruiser for calling "smiles" a reinforcer. Eventually, Bruiser calls "agreeing" a reinforcer if it increases behavior. Dave taught Bruiser to call any event that increases behavior (that it follows) a reinforcer by using the procedure of _____.

47. Pre-test: The three elements of the procedure of generalization training are that you reinforce the same behavior (1) in a(n) _____ of situations until (2) the behavior _____ to (3) other members of the same _____.

49. Pre-test: What is the name of the procedure in which you reinforce the same behavior (1) in a series of situations until (2) the behavior generalizes to (3) other members of the same stimulus class?
_____

30. Let's start this module with the difference between discrimination training and generalization training. Remember Mom and Benny from an earlier lesson? Mom praised Benny for saying "Dada" in the presence of his father but not in the presence of his uncle. She was teaching Benny to draw a "boundary" for whom to call "Dada." Discrimination training _____ (draws, eliminates) boundaries between two or more stimulus situations.

84. Unlike discrimination training, generalization training _____ (draws, eliminates) boundaries between stimulus situations.

16. Dad teaches Kay to call Bowser a dog. He then teaches her to label Rover, Spot, and Blackie as dogs. From there, he wants her naming to spread to all dogs with a minimum of further teaching. Dad's procedure is an example of generalization training because it _____ (draws, eliminates) boundaries between different dogs.

60. The first goal is to learn to define and apply the term *generalization training*. What is the name of the procedure that has these three elements: it reinforces the same behavior (1) in a <u>series</u> of situations until (2) the behavior <u>generalizes</u> to (3) other members of the same <u>stimulus class?</u> _____ training.

78. To talk about the first element of generalization training, I refer to a <u>series</u> of situations. Because you must reinforce the same behavior in more than one situation, I refer to a(n) _____ (instance, series) of situations.

14. Dad reinforces Kay for calling first Bowser and then Rover, Spot, and Blackie "dog." Dad is reinforcing the same behavior of saying _____, in the *series* of situations involving the _____ (how many?) dogs.

76. To produce generalization with the procedure of generalization training, you must reinforce the same behavior in a(n)

_____ of situations until it generalizes to other members of that stimulus class.

79. To talk about the second element, I refer to the process when the behavior <u>generalizes</u> to other stimuli. Because your goal is for the behavior to occur in the presence of novel stimuli in the same stimulus class, I talk about when the behavior _____ (discriminates, generalizes).

8. After Dad reinforces Kay for calling Bowser, Rover, Spot, and Blackie "dog," Kay then calls Prince "dog." Kay's behavior of saying "dog" generalizes when she calls _____ (which dog?) a dog.

77. To produce the process of generalization with the procedure of generalization training, you must reinforce the same behavior in a series of situations until it _____ to other members of that stimulus class.

13. Dad is teaching Kay to perform the same behavior in the presence of all members of the stimulus class called _____ .

80. To talk about the third element, I refer to a <u>stimulus class</u>. Because you want the behavior to generalize only to relevant stimuli, I talk about other members of the same _____ class.

86. What is the name of the procedure in which you reinforce the same behavior (1) in a series of situations until (2) the behavior generalizes to (3) other members of the same stimulus class? _____

73. The three elements of the procedure of generalization training are that you reinforce the same behavior (1) in a <u>series</u> of situations until (2) the behavior <u>generalizes</u> to (3) other members of the same _____ .

74. The three elements of the procedure of generalization training are that you reinforce the same behavior (1) in a <u>series</u> of situations until (2) the behavior _____ to (3) other members of the same _____ .

75. The three elements of the procedure of generalization training are that you reinforce the same behavior (1) in a(n) _____ of situations until

(2) the behavior _____ to
(3) other members of the same _____
_____ .

15. Dad reinforces Kay for calling first Bowser and then Rover, Spot, and Blackie "dog." Kay then calls Prince a dog. Dad taught Kay to call Prince and other new dogs "dog" by the procedure of _____ _____ .

### 2. Generalization

35. Pre-test: Dad reinforces Kay for calling first Bowser and then Rover, Spot, and Blackie "dog." Kay then sees a new dog whose name is Prince and calls him a dog. Kay's labeling Prince a dog is an example of the process of _____ _____ .

36. Pre-test: Dad reinforces Kay for calling first Bowser and then Rover, Spot, and Blackie "dog." Kay then sees a new dog whose name is Prince and calls him a dog. The collection of all these dogs and other dogs is called a(n) _____ _____ .

37. Pre-test: Dad reinforces Kay for calling first Bowser and then Rover, Spot, and Blackie "dog." Kay then sees a new dog whose name is Prince and calls him a dog. Because Dad had never reinforced Kay for calling Prince a dog Prince is called a(n) _____ stimulus.

31. Pre-test: A set of related stimuli is called a(n) _____ .

32. Pre-test: A stimulus class is a set of _____ stimuli.

44. Pre-test: The process of generalization is the occurrence of a behavior in the presence of a(n) _____ stimulus.

50. Pre-test: Which one of the two terms *generalization* and *generalization training* refers to a process? _____ _____ Which term refers to a procedure? _____ _____

67. The process of generalization is the key to the procedure of generalization training. Notice that I will always refer to generalization training as a(n) _____ (procedure, process) and generalization as a(n) _____ (procedure, process).

64. The procedure of generalization training involves generalization. The process of generalization involves making a response in the presence of a <u>novel stimulus</u>. A novel stimulus is a stimulus in whose presence a particular response _____ (has, hasn't) previously been reinforced.

24. Everyday speech would use the term "novel stimulus" to refer to a stimulus that the person has never seen or heard before. In this book, I will use the term in a slightly more specific way. I will call any stimulus in whose presence the person's behavior has not been reinforced a(n) _____ stimulus.

66. The process in which a behavior occurs in the presence of a novel stimulus is called _____ (generalization, generalization training).

68. The process of generalization is the occurrence of a behavior in the presence of a(n) _____ stimulus.

1. A child who is learning to talk may be reinforced for speaking to her mother. There may be a time when she has spoken to her mother but not to her father. Naturally, she will not yet have been reinforced for speaking in the presence of her father. Therefore, speaking to her father for the first time is an example of the behavioral process called _____.

65. The procedure of generalization training involves creating conditions in which a behavior will generalize to other members of a stimulus class. A stimulus class is a set of _____ (related, unrelated) stimuli.

6. A set of stimuli that are <u>related</u> by some common element like color, species, or name is called a(n) stimulus _____.

9. All those animals we call dogs form a stimulus class because they are a set of stimuli that are _____ by common elements like barking, four legs, and a tail.

11. Because cats are a set of stimuli related by such common elements as meowing, fur, and claws, they are called a(n) _____.

58. Suppose Kay learns to call Bowser "dog." When she sees Prince for the first time, she calls him "dog." Because she has never

been reinforced for calling Prince "dog," Prince would be called a(n) _____ stimulus.

12. Because Prince is a novel stimulus in the same stimulus class as Bowser, having Kay call Prince a dog, would be an example of the process called _____.

4. A set of related stimuli is called a(n) _____. When a behavior occurs in the presence of a novel stimulus, the process is called _____.

7. A stimulus class is a set of _____ stimuli. Generalization occurs in the presence of a(n) _____ stimulus in the same stimulus class.

26. Generalization is the process whereby a behavior occurs in the presence of a(n) _____ stimulus. A set of related stimuli is called a(n) _____.

72. The three elements of the procedure called generalization training are that you reinforce the same behavior (1) in a(n) _____ of situations until (2) the behavior _____ to (3) other members of the same _____.

## 3. Generalization Training versus Discrimination Training

33. Pre-test: Bob nods when Katrina calls wearing a baseball cap backward "cool" but ignores her when she calls wearing a cap forward "cool." After several tries, Katrina comes to always call the backward cap "cool" but not the forward cap. Bob taught Katrina which way of wearing your cap was cool by the procedure of _____.

34. Pre-test: Bob nods when Katrina calls a backward cap "cool." He nods when she calls knees sticking out of jeans "cool." He nods when she calls untied sneakers "cool." Katrina finally calls cut-off t-shirts "cool." Bob has been teaching Katrina the American meaning of "cool" by the procedure of _____.

41. Pre-test: If a procedure increases the behavior in the presence of many related stimuli, then call it _____, but if the procedure increases the behavior in the presence of one stimulus but not in the presence of another stimulus, then it is _____.

88. You may find it easy to confuse generalization training with discrimination training. As you recall, discrimination training consists of reinforcing a behavior in the presence of a particular stimulus and _____ it in the presence of another stimulus.

85. We saw how generalization training might help Kay call both Bowser and Blackie "dog." Dad might also reinforce Kay for calling their dog "Bowser" but extinguish her for calling the neighbor's dog "Bowser." Dad would be using what behavioral procedure? _____ _____

56. Suppose Dad praised Kay whenever she called their cat, Fluffy, "cat." If Kay's rate of calling Fluffy "cat" increased, what procedure would Dad be using? _____ _____ .

57. Suppose Dad praised Kay whenever she called a series of four cats that they saw around the neighborhood "cat." If Kay then called a fifth cat "cat," what procedure would Dad be using? _____ _____

59. Suppose Kay then called a big dirty rat "cat." Suppose Dad ignored her when she called the rat a cat and reinforced her when she called Fluffy a cat. If Kay came to call only Fluffy "cat," then Dad used what behavioral procedure? _____ _____

87. When Dad reinforced Kay for making the same response in the presence of more and more cats, he was using what behavioral procedure? _____ _____ However, when he was reinforcing Kay for making the response in the presence of one cat but (through extinction) not a rat, he was using what behavioral procedure? _____

51. Researchers gave some kids biofeedback for their heart rates while playing video games. The biofeedback lowered their heart rates. Their heart rates also stayed low during mental arithmetic. What behavioral process occurred? _____ _____

54. Researchers showed that biofeedback training reduced migraine headaches at the clinic. They also observed decrements in headaches at home. Thus, the headache reduction _____ to the home.

52. Researchers reinforced Henry when he guessed that Jane was highly interested in conversing with Bob shown in Videotape A. They extinguished him when he guessed Jane was highly interested in talking to Mortimer shown in Tape B. Pretty soon Henry guessed "high" for Tape A but not for Tape B. The researchers used the procedure of _____ training.

53. Researchers reinforced Henry when he correctly guessed the interest level of Jane shown in a series of videotaped conversations. They then found that Henry more often correctly guessed the interest level of Karen in role-playing situations. What behavioral procedure accounts for this result? _____ training.

83. Two children with retardation readily learned to converse in the presence of one trainer. However, a second trainer had to reinforce them for conversing before this response _____ to other people.

19. Dr. Griffiths reinforced a 30-year-old woman with retardation for speaking clearly in a special classroom setting. They also reinforced her speaking clearly at her residence. She then began to speak clearly in all situations. What behavioral procedure did the researchers use to get her to speak clearly in all situations? _____ _____

55. Researchers taught two fourth-grade teachers to use specific praise with their pupils during reading instruction. The teachers did not begin to use specific praise in math and language arts until they were trained to do so. The researchers had to reinforce the use of specific praise in math and language arts because the praise did not _____ to those subjects without further training.

2. A person does not generalize. Rather his _____ generalizes.

17. Dr. Bornstein taught Jane to be assertive in response to being interrupted by another person. He then taught her to be assertive in several other types of situations. When he tested her assertiveness in three other untrained situations, he

found her to be quite assertive. What behavioral procedure did he use? _____

18. Dr. Bornstein used six teaching situations and three testing situations. Because he had never reinforced Jane for being assertive during the three test situations, the test situations would be called _____ stimuli.

20. Dr. Miller reinforced students for correctly labeling the examples contained in this book. He then observed that the students could correctly label examples they had not seen before. The occurrence of the students' labeling behavior in the presence of the new examples would be called _____ .

21. Dr. Miller reinforced students for correctly labeling successive examples of extinction in this book. He then observed that the students could correctly label examples that he had not seen before. What behavioral procedure did he use to produce this result? _____

23. Dr. Miller showed students a series of examples of extinction. Because the examples are related by virtue of all being examples of extinction, the collection of examples would be termed a(n) stimulus _____ .

### 4. Tactic #2 in the Stimulus Control Strategy

45. Pre-test: The second tactic in using the stimulus control strategy is to broaden stimulus control through _____ .

3. A procedure in which a behavior is reinforced in each of a series of situations until it generalizes to other members of that stimulus class is called _____ .

69. The second tactic in using the stimulus control strategy is to broaden stimulus control through generalization _____ .

70. The second tactic in using the stimulus control strategy is to broaden stimulus control through _____ training.

71. The second tactic in using the stimulus control strategy is to broaden

stimulus control through _____ _____ .

### 5. Review

42. Pre-test: Reinforcing Kay for saying "four" when asked "What is 2 plus 2?" and extinguishing her for saying "four" when asked "What is 8 plus 3?" would be the procedure of: _____ _____ .

39. Pre-test: Dr. Bornstein taught Jane to be assertive in response to being interrupted by another person. His team of researchers then taught her to be assertive in several other types of situations. When they tested her assertiveness in three novel situations, they found her to be quite assertive. What behavioral procedure did the researchers use? _____

43. Pre-test: The collection of stimuli that share being tall, woody, and leafy would be an example of a(n) _____ .

46. Pre-test: The second tactic in using the stimulus control strategy is to broaden stimulus control through _____ .

40. Pre-test: I may ask you what <u>process</u> is involved when a behavior occurs in the presence of some stimulus not previously associated with reinforcement. Because I used the word *process*, you can guess that the answer is _____ .

48. Pre-test: The three elements of generalization training are that you reinforce the same behavior (1) in a(n) _____ of situations until (2) the behavior _____ to (3) other members of the same _____ .

63. The procedure in which a behavior comes to occur more frequently in the presence of one stimulus but less frequently in the presence of other stimuli is called _____ .

29. If a person's behavior is changed in one situation, the procedure for ensuring that the change appears in other situations would be _____ .

5. A set of related stimuli is called a(n) _____ .

81. To use the stimulus control strategy, (1) narrow stimulus control through discrimination training; (2) broaden stimulus

control through _____
_____.

61. The increased probability of a discriminated behavior that is produced by a stimulus is called _____.

25. Generalization is defined as a behavior occurring in the presence of a(n) _____ _____ in the same stimulus class.

28. Here's a review from an earlier lesson. The statement "Eye contact is looking the other person in the eye while speaking" would be an example of a(n) _____.

10. Any stimulus in whose presence a behavior has not previously been reinforced is called a(n) _____ stimulus.

62. The occurrence of a behavior in the presence of a novel stimulus is called _____ _____.

27. Generalization training is defined as reinforcing a behavior in each of a series of situations until it _____ to other members of that same stimulus class.

22. Dr. Miller reinforced students for correctly labeling the examples contained in this book. He then observed that the students could correctly label examples that they had not seen before. What process is responsible for the students' labeling behavior in the presence of the new examples? _____

82. To use the stimulus control strategy to help people, (1) narrow stimulus control through _____ and (2) broaden stimulus control through _____.

## Programmed Examples

### 1. Programmed Examples

13. Pre-test: Dr. Feelgood reacted positively when Felix thanked him for a compliment but ignored him when he deferred the compliment. Gradually, Felix learned to thank Dr. Feelgood for his compliments. What behavioral procedure did Dr. Feelgood employ to teach Felix to thank him for compliments? _____

16. Pre-test: The taxonomy class was interesting but terribly difficult for Clara. She got a correct score when she remembered to apply the label "invertebrate" to a crab but not to a rat. Likewise, she got a correct score for applying the label "vertebrate" to a rat but not to a crab. The course instructor is applying what behavioral procedure to her behavior? _____

14. Pre-test: Grant was usually pretty stingy with his favors. However, every time that he did something nice for Alma, she immediately thanked him and often did something even nicer for him. His rate of doing favors for Alma gradually increased. One day he did a very nice thing for Karen, and she was so surprised that she thanked him profusely. This same pattern occurred with several other of Grant's friends. He gradually started doing favors for many people. What behavioral procedure was being unknowingly employed by Grant's friends to increase his favor doing for everyone? _____

15. Pre-test: Janice learned to call a picture of the biggest planet "Jupiter." Behavior analysts say that the picture exerted _____ _____ over her planet-naming behavior.

17. Professor Brainbuster had a talent for bringing students into his discussions. He was so successful that he even managed to get Sweet Sue to talk in class and express her opinions. Ken thought that this was great, that the professor was making an important change in Sue's behavior. Lisa disagreed, however, pointing out that Sue still didn't express her opinions in other classes. If Sue's talking occurred in other classes after Professor Brainbuster had reinforced her, this would be an instance of what behavioral process? _____. All university classes would be called a(n) _____ because they are related stimuli. If someone had wanted badly enough to change Sweet Sue's talking behavior in all classes, he or she could have tried arranging for several professors to reinforce talking in class. What procedure would be used by the combined group to increase her talking in all classes? _____

20. Steve began speaking poetically with a beautiful rhythm and sound to his words when he was around Marcia, and she loved it. When Steve was around Ken, he started

to speak the same way, but Ken looked at him really funny and split. Eventually, Steve spoke poetically around Marcia but not around Ken. The first instance of poetic speaking in the presence of Ken would be an example of the process of _____.
Because Steve's poetic speaking was reinforced in the presence of Marcia but extinguished in the presence of Ken, the combined reaction of Ken and Marcia is an example of what procedure? _____ If Ken had praised poetic speaking instead of splitting, then the combined reaction of Ken and Marcia would have been an example of what procedure to produce poetic talking in Ken for many situations? _____

5. Dave showered Bad Bertha with attention when she was being nice to him. He ignored her when she was bad. Dave mentioned to several friends how nice Bertha was. They thought Dave was crazy since they showered her with attention only for her tough behavior. Because in Dave's presence gentle behavior was reinforced, what kind of stimulus would he be for her acting gently? _____ In his friends' presence, Bertha's gentle behavior was extinguished. What kind of stimulus would their presence be for gentle behavior? _____ Between them, Dave and his friends were using what behavioral procedure to encourage Bertha to act gently in one place and tough in the other? _____ If Dave convinced all his friends to change their reaction to Bertha and to reinforce gentleness, they would be using what behavioral procedure to make Bertha into a gentle person? _____

3. Arnie Smith teased the family's dogs. He chased them and sprayed them with water. This behavior upset Mrs. Smith. She yelled at her son. She pleaded with him to stop. Arnie continued to tease the dogs. Finally, in desperation, Mrs. Smith listened to the advice of a behavior analyst. He told them to totally ignore Arnie's behavior. After a month, Mrs. Smith discovered that Arnie had indeed stopped teasing their dogs. She bragged about this one night at a cocktail party given by Mrs. Jones, a neighbor. Mrs. Jones told Mrs. Smith that Arnie hadn't stopped teasing her dogs even though she had chased him away and pleaded with him. The Jones had inadvertently reinforced Arnie's teasing with attention, whereas the Smiths had extinguished it. The combination of reinforcement from the Jones and extinction from the Smith's for Arnie's teasing is an example of what procedure? _____
The Smiths should have arranged for a series of families to extinguish Arnie's behavior until it generalized to everyone's pet. In that case, they would have been using what behavioral procedure? _____

4. Calvin was undergoing training as a salesperson for a company that makes and sells encyclopedias. After explaining to him the virtues of their product and how to be a good salesperson, the trainers had him enter a special room at their factory that looked like someone's living room. A trainer played the role of the homeowner, and Calvin was to use what he had learned to try to "sell" the trainer a set of encyclopedias. The trainer had a checklist of behaviors that Calvin was supposed to perform, which he quietly checked off as they went along. Calvin was told about any steps he might have forgotten. This training was repeated until Calvin did it right three times in a row. Then, another different trainer was brought in, one who was a "harder sell." Again, the training was repeated until Calvin got it right. Several other trainers were then brought in as the final part of the process. The training room was made to look like a living room to increase the probability that Calvin's selling ability would _____ to real living rooms. What procedure was the company using by employing a series of trainers? _____

18. Professor Forsyth taught his classes that *imperialism* was when one country intervened in the affairs of another country. He gave as an example the intervention in Lithuania by the Soviet Union in 1939. He then asked John to give three other examples. John delighted the professor by citing the Soviet Union's intervention in Czechoslovakia in 1948. He also won approval from the professor for citing North Korea in 1945. But then he suggested that American intervention

in Vietnam was imperialism. The professor ignored John. The occurrence of labeling the Vietnam intervention as imperialistic would be an example of what behavioral process? _____ The professor reinforced John for labeling as imperialism any intervention by the Soviet Union. He did not reinforce John for using the label when the United States intervened. By reinforcing John when he labeled communist intervention as imperialism and extinguishing him when he labeled U.S. intervention as imperialism, the professor was using what behavioral procedure? _____

11. Ms. Lucci is an eighth-grade English teacher. She taught her students the meaning of the word *alliteration*—the repetition of a sound that begins several words in a row. She asked Michael of what the sentence "Peter Piper picked a peck of pickled peppers" is an example. She praised him profusely when he said "alliteration." Several days later she asked Michael of what poetic concept Poe's line "In the clamor and the clangor of the bells!" is an example. He said "alliteration." Michael's second response is an example of what behavioral process? _____ If his behavior had not generalized after one reinforcement, Ms. Lucci could have introduced more examples and reinforced his behavior many times. She would then be using what behavioral procedure? _____

10. Margo complained when Danny wouldn't go out because he was studying, and she complained when Danny wouldn't go out because he was going to a football game. Danny decided that she had a right to complain when he put football ahead of her, but not when he put studying ahead of her. He explained his conclusions to her. Thereafter, every time that she complained that he wouldn't go out with her because of a football game, he canceled plans to attend the game and went out with her instead. However, when she complained about his studying, he totally ignored her. After six months, Margo was complaining about his putting football ahead of her, but she was not complaining of his putting studying ahead of her. By going along with her when she complained about football

but ignoring her when she complained about studying, what procedure did Danny use? _____

1. A self-control procedure for studying used by many students is to set aside a specific place to do schoolwork. They make sure that no other behavior is reinforced there. Thus, they never bring magazines, food, a radio, or other potential reinforcers to their study area. By ignoring nonstudying behavior in the study area, the study area becomes a stimulus associated with extinction for nonstudying behavior. Such a stimulus is called a(n) _____. By restricting the study area to studying, you would hope that the student's study behavior gets reinforced. Thus, the study area becomes a stimulus associated with reinforcement for studying. Such a stimulus is called a(n) _____. If study behavior began to occur in the study area and nowhere else, we would say that the study area exerted _____ over study behavior.

12. One day Corbin complained of his unhappiness to his mother. She listened sympathetically and told him that he didn't have to do his chores that day. Corbin frequently complained of his unhappiness to his mother after that, and she let him stop any chores that he was doing. Corbin complained to his teacher one day that he was unhappy. What behavioral process describes Corbin's complaining about his unhappiness to his teacher? _____

19. Raney was in second grade. One day during spelling, she laid her head on the desk. The teacher asked her what was the matter, and she said, "Teacher, I have a terrible head hurt." The teacher soothed her by saying, "That's too bad, Raney, why don't you just lay your head down until it feels better?" Raney frequently complained of head hurts after that. She also complained of head hurts to her third-grade teacher the next year. That teacher didn't buy it. She gave Raney a glass of water and told her to get back to work. These two teachers were combining to apply what procedure to Raney's complaints of head hurts? _____

6. Diane has many friends: Ann, Mary, Fred, Kenny, David, Helen, and John, to

mention a few. If we consider Diane's friends as stimuli, then the collection consisting of all her friends would be called a(n) _____ _____.

9. Janice swears in the presence of her friends at school but not in the presence of her parents. Because her swearing behavior occurs more often with her friends, it would be called _____ behavior.

7. Frank made a joke when asked by his English teacher to define *noun,* and everyone in class laughed uproariously. As a result, he made a joke in his social studies class the next hour where he had never been reinforced for telling a joke. The occurrence of his joking behavior in the second class is an example of what behavioral process? _____

8. Janice carefully typed a course paper for the first time in college. She received her first A ever for that paper. She then typed a paper for another course and got another A. This happened in several other courses. What procedure are those course instructors unknowingly applying to Janice's typing behavior to increase its occurrence in many other courses? _____

2. After much trial and error, Janice learned to call the big planet Jupiter and the little one Venus, but not vice versa. Her behavior of calling the big planet Jupiter but not the little one would be called _____ behavior.

## Reading Section

This lesson introduces the two behavioral procedures of *fading* and *programming*. Behavior analysts turn to these two procedures to develop stimulus control with a novel stimulus when the person they are training never responds to that stimulus. Because the person does not respond to the novel stimulus, behavior analysts can never reinforce them for doing so. Both procedures temporarily use an added stimulus whose control is already established to evoke responding in the presence of the novel stimulus.

Fading and programming add to the novel stimulus an existing discriminative stimulus that already exerts control over the desired response. They call this added stimulus a *prompt*. They call it a prompt because it prompts the person to make the desired response. The behavior analyst then slowly eliminates the prompt until the person is responding to the novel stimulus alone. The temporary use of the prompt produces new discriminated behaviors.

Behavior analysts turn to fading and programming as they sometimes turn to shaping. They use shaping when the target behavior does not exist. Likewise, they use fading and programming when the discriminated behavior they want to work with does not exist.

Fading uses an added prompt to produce a single discrimination. Programming uses many added prompts to produce generalization. Tactic #3 in using the stimulus control strategy is to create new stimulus control by temporarily using <u>prompts</u>.

1. Tactic #3 in using the stimulus control strategy is to create new stimulus control by temporarily using _____.

## Prompts

Both procedures introduced in this lesson temporarily add a prompt to a novel stimulus. For example, you want to teach Baby Jane to say "da-da" when you point to her father. If she never spontaneously says "da-da" when you point to her father, you can't reinforce her for saying it. Now suppose that Baby Jane will imitate "da" if you say it. In the language of discrimination training, your saying "da" is an existing SD in whose presence she will say "da." It can therefore serve as a prompt.

The procedures used in this lesson depend upon being able to withdraw the prompt in such a way that the father becomes the SD. The tactic is to point to her father and say "da." If that gets her to start saying "da" you can reinforce her for saying "da" when you point to her father <u>plus</u> say your prompt. You then try to gradually withdraw your prompt. For example, she may still say "da" even if you only make the "d" sound. If so, you would reinforce her "da." She may then say "da" if you only whisper the "d" sound. Again you reinforce her "da." You may then be able to mouth "d" silently. Eventually Baby Jane will be saying "da-da" when you point to her father without the prompt. You have taught her to respond correctly to her father alone so you no longer have to give her the prompt. A **prompt** is an <u>added stimulus</u> that increases the probability that a person will make the correct response in the presence of a novel stimulus. It is usually withdrawn as soon as is practical.

2. A **prompt** is an added _____ that increases the probability that a person will make the correct response in the presence of a novel stimulus.

# Fading

The first procedure that uses a prompt is called *fading*. Behavior analysts use fading when the person never makes the desired response in the presence of a novel stimulus.

**Fading** is the temporary use of a <u>prompt</u> to establish a specific <u>discrimination</u>. You gradually <u>withdraw</u> the prompt. Your goal is for the person to discriminate without the prompt. Fading solves a problem that may arise when teaching a discrimination. The problem is that the behavior may never occur in the presence of the SD. When that happens, you can never reinforce the behavior to begin discrimination training. However, you may be able to get the behavior to occur by using a prompt. You can prompt the behavior in the presence of the SD so that you can reinforce it. By gradually eliminating the prompt, you shift stimulus control solely to the SD.

3. The temporary use of a prompt that is gradually withdrawn to establish a specific <u>discrimination</u> is the procedure of _____.

For example, you might use a prompt to teach Patty to label colors. You might show her a red spot and ask, "What color is this?" If she can't answer, you might give her a hint such as "Is it red?" or "Say red." You would use a prompt to get the behavior started. Then, you can reinforce it. Since you don't want to have to give her hints all the time, you would gradually withdraw the hint.

You must understand that fading is a particular kind of discrimination training—a kind that involves the use of a prompt. Everything else about the discrimination training procedure remains the same. However, stimulus control may develop more rapidly.

## Examples of Fading

Examples of prompts and fading abound in everyday life. Each time parents give a hint to a child and then gradually withdraw it, they are using prompting and fading. For example, they may show Suzie a picture of a cow. Then they may ask, "What is this, Suzie? You know, moo." "Moo" is a prompt. They may show Suzie a picture of a dog. Then they ask, "What is this, Suzie? You know, bow-wow." They are again using a prompt. They use these prompts to help Suzie make the discrimination between the cow and the dog.

Once the initial discrimination is established, the parents may start to eliminate the prompts. For example, the next time they show Suzie the picture of the cow, they may only say "moo." The time after that, they may silently mouth the "moo" sound. Finally, they may eliminate the prompt so that the child responds solely to the visual stimulus of the cow. The gradual elimination of the "bow-wow" prompt for the dog is also an example of fading. Although it is not spelled out in either example, you should understand that the parents must reinforce the prompted behavior.

---

*Helping Hitters Discriminate Curve Balls, Part 2*

Remember the team of sports psychologists who helped batters discriminate curve balls? They added a 1/4-inch wide stripe of orange to the seams of pitched curve balls. This helped batters hit better. But how could this help the batters learn to hit unmarked balls better? The team used fading to help the batters learn. They faded the width of their stripe from a fourth of an inch to an eighth of an inch. The batters hit almost as well with the narrower stripe. Unfortunately, the season ended at that point. Could the researchers fade the stripe out altogether while maintaining the improved hitting? You'll have to wait until next year, sports fans! (Based on Osborne, Rudrud, & Zezoney, 1990.)

4. Because it is an added stimulus, behavior analysts call the orange stripe a(n) _____ in a fading procedure. (Hint: The answer starts with the letter *p*.)

Notice that the parents used prompts to establish a discrimination between two distinct pictures. They used prompts to establish a discrimination.

Fading will be ineffective if a prompt is used with a single stimulus. If the parents always show Suzie the dog, she would not need a prompt. She could just remember to say "dog." However, if they alternate the dog with the cow, remembering only "dog" would not work. The hint then helps the child learn which animal is which. The general rule is to always use at least two stimuli when trying to teach a child to label an object. In fact, you should always use at least two stimuli when teaching any discriminated behavior.

Researchers used a fading procedure to overcome children's fear of the dark (Giebenhain & O'Dell, 1984). "BL," an 11-year-old, would not sleep unless his parents left his lights on all night. They could never get him to sleep in the dark, so could never reinforce him for doing so. They approached the dark as a novel stimulus and the light as an added stimulus. The researchers put a dimmer on BL's bedside light so he could control the amount of light. They marked the dial of the dimmer from full illumination of 11 to no illumination of 0. BL set the dimmer at about 8 during baseline, which provided lots of light. The parents started playing a fear reduction game at bedtime. They encouraged BL to relax and make positive statements such as "I am brave when I'm in the dark." They suggested to BL that he set the dimmer lower. They reinforced staying the whole night with the dimmer one-half number lower than the prior night. They gave him praise, hugs, toys, and treats. He faded the light to 0 in less than three weeks! He now sleeps without the light on. Now he <u>is</u> brave when he's in the dark!

Researchers used fading to teach not-shy preschoolers to play with shy children (Odom, Chandler, Ostrosky, McConnell, & Reaney, 1992). I will describe their procedure with Pete, one of the not-shy children. Pete made virtually no initiations to the shy children. To change this, the teacher first taught Pete five ways to initiate play. He could share his play with the other child, ask to share the other child's play, organize play, assist the other in their play, or simply persist in his efforts. Next, whenever Pete did not initiate to the other child, the teacher prompted him to use one of the methods every 30 seconds. The teacher also posted a happy face every time Pete initiated. Pete's rate of initiating increased to 20 initiations every five minutes. Next, the teacher faded her prompts. She changed from prompting a specific method to prompting Pete to get the other child to play. She stopped prompting but kept the happy face. Finally, she stopped the happy face. Pete continued to initiate about 15 times in five minutes. Both Pete and the shy child benefitted.

Researchers use fading to teach other skills as well. They teach arithmetic skills (e.g., Paine, Carnine, White, & Walters, 1982). They teach nearsighted people to see better (Pbert, Collins, Smith, Sharp, et al, 1988). They

---

### Throw Away Your Glasses and See!

Most nearsighted people wear glasses. Without glasses, their eyes bring an image into focus <u>in front of</u> the retina rather than <u>on</u> the retina. This is because their muscles make the eyeball too long. Evidence suggests that this reflects a history of reinforcement for close work. Making the eyeball long produces the reinforcer of clear focus on their close work. Many studies now indicate that discrimination training with fading can change that habit. Case studies show that some people no longer need glasses after such training. Behavior analysts regard the muscular response of making the eyeball a different length depending upon the distance of the SD as a "behavior." (Rosen, Schiffman, & Cohen, 1984)

5. Because that behavior becomes more likely after fading, behavior analysts call the behavior a(n) _____. behavior (Hint: The answer is one word that starts with *d* and ends with *–ated*.)

teach children with feeding disorder to eat better (e.g., Patel, Piazza, Kelly, Ochsner, & Santana, 2001). They teach children with insomnia to go right to sleep when they go to bed (Piazza & Fisher, 1991). They teach smokers to gradually change to low-tar-and-nicotine cigarettes (Prue, Krapfl, & Martin, 1981).

## Programming

Programming involves a more complex use of prompts. **Programming** is the temporary use of <u>prompts</u> to establish a <u>generalization</u>. You gradually withdraw the prompts. Your goal is for the behavior to generalize without the prompts.

6. **Programming** is the temporary use of prompts to establish a _____ _____.

Programming is necessary when you teach a generalization, but the behavior never occurs in the presence of the novel stimulus. You can use a prompt to start the behavior. Once the behavior is started, you can reinforce it in the presence of the novel stimulus. Then you can begin to withdraw the prompt. The result is that the person learns to perform the behavior solely in response to the (once novel) stimulus. The procedure becomes programming if you reinforce the same behavior in the presence of a series of novel stimuli until it generalizes to other members of the stimulus class (see Cuvo, 2003).

For example, suppose that Suzie calls a big round object, but nothing else, a ball." You might use a prompt to start her generalization to other round objects. You might hold up a golf ball and ask, "What is this?" If you get no response, you might ask, "Is it a ball?" or you might say, "Say 'ball.' " You must, of course, reinforce the resulting response. By slowly withdrawing the prompt, you may get Suzie to call the golf ball a "ball" with no prompting. You might do this with several other balls until she generalizes to all balls.

Programming occurs often in everyday life. Remember the parents' teaching Suzie to discriminate between a cow and a dog? Suppose they used several pictures of each animal. The cows might differ in color, size, and location. The parents could use prompts to establish the label "cow" or "dog" for each picture. They would then gradually withdraw the prompts. If they used different cows and dogs, they would be using programming. If they used enough different animals, this procedure might produce generalization to all cows (or dogs).

Picking a prompt and programming its withdrawal are largely unspecified and artistic processes at this time. You must withdraw the prompt so that the novel stimulus gradually develops stimulus control (e.g., Mueller, Moore, Tingstrom, & Doggett, 2001). Transferring stimulus control from the prompt to the SD is the hardest aspect of withdrawing the prompt. You must get the person to gradually shift his or her attention from the prompt to the SD. If the prompt is totally unrelated to the SD, this can be even more difficult (Schreibman, 1975).

You should understand that programming is a particular kind of generalization training. It is a kind that employs prompts. Everything else is the same about the two procedures.

Be sure you know the difference between fading and programming. Fading uses prompts to establish a <u>discrimination</u> between two specific stimuli. Programming uses prompts to teach <u>generalization</u> to a class of stimuli.

7. Programming uses prompts to teach generalization to a class of stimuli. Fading uses prompts to establish a _____ _____ between two specific stimuli.

Figures 18-1 through 18-3 illustrate an innovative program designed to teach German by reading short stories written by Edgar Allen Poe. The program simply replaces some English words with the German word of the same meaning. The program uses the nearby English words to make it easy to guess at the meaning of the German words. The English words are prompts for translating the German words into the correct English words. The program gradually withdraws the prompts over the three stories. English words make up 90% of the words in the first story, 75% in the second story, but only 30% in the third story. This is a "program" because the student learns to recognize each word in many novel contexts. For example, the German word *ich* appears in five different

True!—nervous, very very dreadfully nervous, *ich*, had been, and am; but why will you say that *ich* am mad? The disease had sharpened *mein* senses—not destroyed, not dulled them. Above all was *der* sense of hearing acute. *Ich* heard all the things in *dem* heaven and *der* earth. I heared many things in hell.

**Figure 18-1.** A paragraph from the first story modified by Schaefer to teach German. He changed it into a program to teach skeletal German words such as those for "I," "my," and "the." The program uses the English words of a short story by Poe as prompts to help the reader guess at the meaning of the italicized German words. Almost 90% of the words are English. (From "A Vocabulary Program Using 'Language Redundancy,' " by H. H. Schaefer, *Journal of Programmed Instruction,* 1963, 2, 9–16.)

*Der* second *und* third day went by *und* yet showed him self *mein* tormenter *nicht.* Again could *ich* as a free man breathe. *Das* monster was apparently in great terror ran away! Never again would *ich es* see!

**Figure 18-2.** A paragraph from the second story modified by Schaefer to teach German. He has further withdrawn the prompts from English words to about 75% of the words. He has also eliminated the prompts from English word order by using German word order. Thus, the student learns more German words and also learns German word order. (From "A Vocabulary Program Using 'Language Redundancy,' " by H. H. Schaefer, *Journal of Programmed Instruction,* 1963, 2, 9–16.)

contexts in these illustrations. Thus, recognition of *ich* may generalize to other contexts.

8. Refer to Figure 18-1. For example, you can guess that *ich* means ____. You can guess that *mein* means ____. (Be careful.) And you can guess that *der* and *dem* are different forms of the word ____. Most readers learn these skeletal words by the end of the first story.

9. Look carefully at the last three sentences in Figure 18-2. Note the position of the verbs *breathe, ran away,* and *see.* You learn that for these common sentences that the

*Die* slope *seiner* Wande *wurde von Moment zu Moment smaller, und der* bottom *der Vortex* seemed *sich* gradually *zu* lift. *Der* sky *war klar, die Winde Hatten sich* died, *und der* moon went brightly *im Westen* down, *als ich mich auf dem* surface *des Ozeans* facing *die* coast *von Lofden* found, exactly *uber der* place, . . .

**Figure 18-3.** A paragraph from the third story modified by Schaefer to teach German. He has further withdrawn the prompts from English words to only 30%. If you had read the first two stories all the way through, you would be able to read this passage with many German words in the German word order. Students can learn a lot of German by simply reading three interesting short stories. (From "A Vocabulary Program Using 'Language Redundancy,' " by H. H. Schaefer, *Journal of Programmed Instruction,* 1963, 2, 9–16.)

German verbs often come at the ____ ____ (end, middle, start) of the sentence.

10. These stories use many strategies to teach German. The first story uses German for little words whose meaning you can guess. The second puts English words in German word order. The third uses German for words very similar to English. For example, look at Figure 18-3 and guess what German word means "oceans": ____.

Programmed instruction is a common form of programming. It consists of a series of statements requiring a written response. Typically, these statements are sentences with one word left out. Sometimes longer units of reading are used (such as a paragraph) before the fill-in sentence occurs. Skinner suggests that three features are particularly important. (1) Programmed instruction requires a <u>written response</u>. This response tells the author if the student understands the statement. (2) Programmed instruction provides <u>immediate feedback</u> on the accuracy of each response. This feedback may serve as a reinforcement for correct responses. (3) Programmed instruction uses <u>small steps</u>. The program asks the student to learn only a small amount of new information at one time. Programmed instruction usually teaches complex verbal behavior. Teachers have used it to teach children

| | |
|---|---|
| no | Is that a pig in the bag?    yes<br>no |
| ba**g** | That is Ann in the ba__ . |
| b**ag** | It is a big b __ __ . |
| **b**ag | The sandman has a __ag. |
| bag | His __ __ __ has sand in it. |

***Figure 18-4.*** Five items from a sequence designed to teach children to read the word *bag*. Children use this program covering the answers on the left with a mask. They then circle either "yes" or "no" to answer the first question, slide the mask down far enough to reveal the answer to that question, and then proceed to the next question. This sequence is taken from the second of 23 books designed to teach children with no prior reading ability how to read. The last book involved reading complete stories at the sixth-grade level. (From *Programmed Reading, Book 2* (3rd ed.), by C. D. Buchanan. New York: McGraw-Hill, 1973. Copyright 1973 by McGraw-Hill, Inc. Reprinted by permission.)

reading, arithmetic, and writing. Professors have used it to teach college students foreign language, algebra, history, and psychology (e.g., Martin, Pear, & Martin, 2002b).

11. Programmed instruction (1) requires a written _____, (2) provides immediate _____ on the accuracy of each response, and (3) uses small _____.

Figure 18-4 shows a simple sequence from *Programmed Reading* (Buchanan, 1973). This sequence teaches children to write the word *bag*. Initially, it gives the children the prompt "ba_" to draw their attention to the "g". Then, it shortens the prompt to "b_ _." Next, it omits the "b" so the children write out the whole word. Of course, they can still see the complete word in previous questions so that part of the prompt still remains. At a later stage, they will fill in the whole word with no prompts. By then, they will have a pretty good grasp of the word and its meaning.

*Programmed reading* has the features of programmed instruction. The children must make a <u>written response</u>. They can obtain <u>immediate feedback</u> by looking at the correct answer on the left. They learn only the amount contained in each of the <u>small steps</u>. Your first reaction might be that they will never learn very much with such a method. In fact, the program takes them from no reading skill to a sixth-grade reading level. It teaches reading faster than alternative teaching methods. For example, it can produce gains in low-income children that are equivalent to or even greater than those attained by middle-class children using conventional instructional materials. Interestingly, this method works extremely well even with children who have severe learning disabilities.

Figure 18-4 would be an example of fading if it showed a picture of a bag and stated "This is a ba_" and later "This is a ___." In such a simplified situation, the children's reading of *bag* might not generalize to other sentences or other pictures of bags. They would be learning a simple discrimination (labeling this picture "bag" and not other pictures). The example shown in Figure 18-4, since it does teach a generalized response, would be an example of programming.

The implications of fading and programming are revolutionary, not only for our educational system but also for our society. One implication is that specific intellectual skills can now be taught to segments of society that seemed incapable of learning by standard teaching methods. For example, these methods have been used to teach new skills to preschool children (Moore & Goldiamond, 1964), children with retardation (Birnbrauer, Bijou, Wolf, & Kidder, 1965), and low-income children (Miller & Schneider, 1970).

## Summary

Fading uses an existing SD as a prompt to teach a discrimination. The prompt is added to a novel stimulus that has no effect on behavior. Then the prompt is slowly withdrawn until the novel stimulus has become an SD. The influence exerted by the prompt has then been transferred to the novel stimulus. This teaches the person the discrimination. Behavior analysts use this very powerful teaching technique to teach very difficult discriminations. Programming also uses an existing prompt. But its goal is to teach a generalization rather than a discrimination. Tactic #3 of the stimulus control strategy is to create new stimulus control by temporarily using prompts.

## Behavior Analysis Examples

### *Teaching Toddlers Triangles*

Researchers used fading to teach 3-year-old Sarah to match triangles (Moore & Goldiamond, 1964). The researchers showed Sarah a sample triangle. They then showed her three other triangles. One of the triangles was oriented exactly as the sample triangle. The other two were rotated to different angles. If Sarah pressed the button below the matching triangle, she was given an edible treat. If she pressed the button below the other two triangles, she was given nothing.

The researchers tried two ways of teaching Sarah to find the matching triangle. One

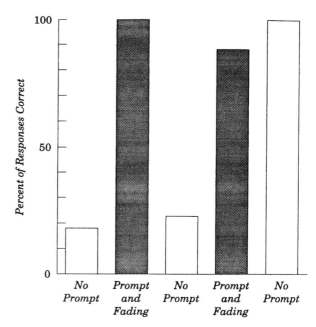

*Figure 18-5.* Sarah's accuracy in matching triangles when no prompt was given and when a prompt was given and then gradually faded out. The last bar shows her accuracy after the prompt had been completely faded out. Without prior use of the prompt and fading, this last bar would have been only about 20% accurate. (Adapted from "Errorless Establishment of Visual Discrimination Using Fading Procedures," by R. Moore and I. Goldiamond, *Journal of the Experimental Analysis of Behavior,* 1964, 7, 269–272. Copyright 1964 by the Society for the Experimental Analysis of Behavior, Inc. Used by permission.)

approach involved trial and error learning similar to that used in all discrimination training. If she was correct, she received a reinforcer; otherwise, she received nothing. The other was fading. They lit up the matching triangle as a prompt. They did not light up the nonmatching triangles. Sarah always picked the lit triangle. The researchers then faded this prompt by lighting the two nonmatching triangles. At first they lit them slightly. They then gradually increased the light until the wrong triangles were as bright as the matching triangle.

Figure 18-5 is a graph of the results. When they first used trial and error with no prompt, Sarah got the correct answer about 20% of the time. When they used the prompt, she got the correct answer 100% of the time. They then partially faded the prompt until the nonmatching triangles were 60% as bright as the matching triangle. Sarah continued picking the matching triangle. They then returned to the trial and error condition with no prompt. Sarah got less than 20% correct. They returned to the prompt. Again Sarah got mostly right answers. They then completely faded the prompt, and this time Sarah continued to get the correct answer 90% of the time. Finally, they eliminated the prompt. Because of the training with the prompt, Sarah could now always pick the correct triangle. She made many errors while learning poorly through trial and error. She made almost no errors while learning through fading.

12. Refer to Figure 18-5. Notice that Sarah's accuracy was 20% for the first and second No Prompt conditions. However, during the third No Prompt condition, after the Prompt and Fading condition, Sarah's accuracy shot up to _____%.

These results are similar to other results often obtained when using fading or programming procedures. They suggest that learning can be both faster and almost error free when prompts are used to assist learning.

13. Behavior analysts call lighting up the correct triangle a(n) _____. (Hint: The answer is a short word that starts with the sixteenth letter of the alphabet.)

## Notes

### Note #1
Programmed instruction has a rather unfortunate history. It was first developed by B. F. Skinner in the mid-1950s. It showed great promise of improving educational technology. Skinner wrote a series of articles promoting its use (e.g., Skinner, 1954). The idea, particularly in the form of teaching machines, was picked up by book publishers. Many psychologists and educators who did not understand behavior analysis developed programmed instruction books. The publishers promoted these books without ensuring that they were properly developed (Sulzer & Mayer, 1972). The results were disastrous. Many educators exposed to these products concluded that programmed instruction was boring and ineffective. It may

be many years before the ill effects of this history are overcome.

14. What behavioral procedure did B. F. Skinner invent in the mid-1950s to help students learn but that had an unfortunate history? _____ instruction.

### Note #2
The book will ask you to identify several examples of programmed instruction. In these cases, you may label the example either as *programmed instruction* or simply as *programming*, since programmed instruction is a type of programming.

15. You may label an example of programmed instruction either as *programmed instruction* or simply as *programming,* since programmed instruction is a type of _____ _____ (fading, programming).

## Helpful Hints

### Helpful Hint #1
Students often have trouble telling the difference between fading and programming. Both procedures involve the use of prompts added onto an underlying procedure. Fading is the use of prompts with discrimination training. Programming is the use of prompts with generalization training. So, to tell whether an example involves fading or programming, first decide whether the underlying procedure is discrimination training or generalization training.

16. If a prompt is used with generalization training, the procedure is called _____ _____; if a prompt is used with discrimination training, the procedure is called _____.

### Helpful Hint #2
Shaping and fading are sometimes confused. Shaping involves gradually changing <u>behavior</u>. The stimulus situation remains the same, but the rules of reinforcement, and therefore the behaviors, are changed. Fading involves gradually changing the <u>stimulus</u>. The behavior stays the same, but the prompt is gradually withdrawn, and the stimulus situa-

tion is changed. Fading is used to gradually change the <u>stimulus;</u> shaping is used to gradually change the <u>behavior.</u>

17. Shaping is a behavioral procedure that involves the gradual changing of the _____; fading is a behavioral procedure that involves the gradual changing of the _____.

### Helpful Hint #3

You are now learning about many behavioral procedures that are quite complicated. Within each lesson, I have given you hints to help you distinguish between the procedures covered by that lesson. But you must also distinguish between the procedures covered in different lessons. I will ask you from now on about differential reinforcement, discrimination training, generalization training, fading, and programming. You must keep all of them separate.

18. Remember to read each example to find out whether it involves reinforcing one behavior and extinguishing other behaviors in the same situation. If so the procedure is called _____.

## Additional Readings

Birnbrauer, J. S., Bijou, S. W., Wolf, M. M., & Kidder, J. D. (1965). Programmed instruction in the classroom. In L. P. Ullman and L. Krasner (Eds.), *Case studies in behavior modification.* New York: Holt, Rinehart, and Winston. This article describes the use of programmed instruction to advance the academic scores of children with retardation who had no previous record of academic achievement. Gains were made in the children's writing, reading, and math skills.

Cox, B. S., Cox, A. B., & Cox, D. J. (2000). Motivating signage prompts safety belt use among drivers exiting senior communities. *Journal of Applied Behavior Analysis, 33,* 635–638. This article demonstrates the effectiveness of prompts on increasing safety belt used among senior citizen drivers. This article offers a simple and cost-effective way to prompt and promote safety belt use.

Holland, J. G. (1960). Teaching machines: An application of principles from the laboratory. *Journal of the Experimental Analysis of Behavior, 3,* 275–287. This article is an early description of the principles of teaching machines and programmed instruction.

Lumsdaine, A. A., & Glaser, R. (1960). *Teaching machines and programmed learning.* Washington, DC: National Education Association. This book is a collection of early articles that discuss programmed instruction.

Markle, S. (1969). *Good frames and bad: A grammar of frame writing.* New York: Wiley. This is a programmed how-to-do-it book. It explains in simple language how to write programmed materials, gives many examples, and then requires the reader to try his or her knowledge.

Miller, L. K., & Schneider, R. (1970). The use of a token system in Project Head Start. *Journal of Applied Behavior Analysis, 3,* 213–200. An early study using fading procedures to teach low-income children simple printing skills.

Newsom, C. D., & Simon, K. M. (1977). A simultaneous discrimination procedure for the measurement of vision in non-verbal children. *Journal of Applied Behavior Analysis, 10,* 633–644. Psychotic children with severe retardation often do not receive proper vision testing and needed eyeglasses because they don't follow the instructions necessary in such testing. To adequately test such children, a procedure was devised in which they were reinforced with an edible (such as an M & M) for selecting one of two cards that could be discriminated only if their vision at that level was adequate. A fading procedure was used to initially train them to select one type of card.

Schreibman, L. (1975). Effects of within-stimulus and extra-stimulus prompting on discrimination learning in autistic children. *Journal of Applied Behavior Analysis, 8,* 91–112. This study demonstrates that it is possible to teach severely psychotic children to make very fine discriminations without errors through the use of fading. However, the prompts must be integrally related to the discriminative stimuli rather than simply unrelated prompts.

Skinner, B. F. (1954). The science of learning and the art of teaching. *Harvard Educational Review, 24,* 99–113. Also reprinted in the Lumsdaine and Glaser (1960) book referenced above. This is the earliest statement by Skinner of the concepts lying behind programmed instruction.

Vargas, E. A., & Vargas, J. S. (1991). Programmed instruction: What it is and how to do it. *Journal of Behavioral Education, 1*(2), 235–251. This paper describes the current state of programmed instruction.

Wulbert, M., Nyman, B. A., Snow, D., & Owen, Y. (1973). The efficacy of stimulus fading and contingency management in the treatment of elective mutism: A case study. *Journal of Applied Behavior Analysis, 6,* 435–441. This study concerns a 6-year-old child who did not speak or follow instructions in kindergarten. However, she reacted normally at home in the presence of her mother. The mother was used as a prompt to maintain normal responding, and an experimenter was faded into the situation in gradual steps until the child responded normally in her presence. This was repeated with five experimenters until the child responded normally to the sixth and to her teacher. At this point, the mother's presence was not required, and the child became a well-adjusted student in her class.

## Programmed Reading

I will present questions about the following six topics: (1) Prompts for Discrimination, (2) Prompts for Generalization, (3) Using Prompts in Education, (4) Fading versus Programming, (5) Another Tactic, and (6) Review.

### 1. Prompts for Discrimination

25. Pre-test: Mom asked Harry to point to the cow. She then pointed at the cow but not the horse. She gradually decreased how distinctly she pointed at the cow. Mom used the procedure of _____ .

30. Pre-test: The behavioral procedure of fading is used to establish a specific _____ between two distinct stimuli.

21. Pre-test: An added stimulus that increases the probability that a behavior will occur in the presence of a novel stimulus is called a(n) _____ .

36. Pre-test: When you add a temporary prompt and gradually withdraw it to assist with discrimination training, you are using the procedure called _____ .

63. The goal of this module is to teach about fading. Fading is the use of a temporary prompt to establish a specific discrimination. The gradual withdrawal of that prompt is called _____ (fading, programming).

2. An introductory point. Fading is a procedure that uses a <u>prompt</u> to develop _____ (new, old) discriminated behaviors.

1. An added stimulus that increases the probability that a behavior will occur in the presence of a novel stimulus is called a(n) _____ .

11. Fading is teaching a specific discrimination by the gradual withdrawal of an added stimulus called a(n) _____ .

16. If the correct behavior never occurs in the presence of the SD during discrimination training, then you can try to increase its probability by using a(n) _____ .

58. Suppose when you ask Patty the question "What color is this?" she never answers correctly. If you give her the hint "Is it red?" when asking the question, this added stimulus would be an example of a(n) _____ .

10. Fading is a particular kind of _____ (discrimination, generalization) training that employs prompts.

56. Suppose that you show a young child a picture of a dog and ask her, "What is this? You know, bow-wow!" "You know, bow-wow" would be called a(n) _____ .

65. The gradual elimination of a prompt such as "bow-wow" while teaching a discrimination between a cow and a dog is called _____ .

60. The behavioral procedure of fading is used to establish a specific _____ _____ between two distinct stimuli.

57. Suppose that you show Debby a picture of a dog (interspersed with pictures of a cat) many times during the day. You ask her what it is. You reinforce her when she calls this picture "dog" but ignore her when she calls the cat "dog." What behavioral procedure would you be using if you first add "You know, bow-wow," next add it more softly, then only silently mouth the "bow-wow," and finally omit it altogether? _____

68. The orange stripe added to baseballs to help batters discriminate curve balls is an example of a(n) _____.

6. Dr. Giebenhain helped "BL" to overcome his fear of the dark. His parents praised him when he slept in the dark but ignored him when he slept with his light on all night. They used a dimmer to permit low light as a prompt for sleeping in less than full light. They encouraged him to gradually dim this light from full light of 11 to no light of 0. Gradually reducing this "prompt" to teach him to sleep in the dark is an example of what behavioral procedure? _____

8. Dr. Odom helped a preschooler named Pete to play with shy children. He praised Pete when he played with shy children and ignored him when he played with normal children. Part of the procedure involved the teacher suggesting one of five ways of playing every 30 seconds. Each suggestion would be called a(n) _____.

76. When you add a temporary prompt and gradually withdraw it to assist with discrimination training, you are using the procedure called _____.

12. Fading is the use of a temporary prompt that you gradually withdraw to assist with _____ training.

77. When you use fading, you gradually withdraw a prompt. You might say that fading changes the stimulus. When you use shaping, you successively approximate the target behavior. So you might say that shaping, unlike fading, changes the _____.

80. When you use shaping, you successively approximate the target behavior. You might say that shaping changes the behavior. When you use fading, you gradually withdraw the added stimulus called a prompt. So you might say that fading changes the _____.

54. Shaping is a behavioral procedure that involves the gradual changing of the _____; fading is a behavioral procedure that involves the gradual changing of the _____.

## 2. Prompts for Generalization

38. Pre-test: You show Craig a series of pictures of cars, some red, some black. To get him started you say, "What is this? You know, VROOM," and praise him when he says, "car." Suppose you gradually eliminate the "VROOM" for all of the pictures. What behavioral procedure are you using to teach Craig to call even novel pictures of cars "car"? _____

28. Pre-test: Programming is using a prompt to establish a(n) _____.

37. Pre-test: When you use prompts to help in training a generalization, you are using what procedure? _____

33. Pre-test: Using a prompt to establish a generalization is called _____; using a prompt to establish a specific discrimination is called _____.

64. The goal of this module is to teach about programming as a kind of generalization training. For review, remember that reinforcing a behavior in each of a series of situations until it generalizes to novel stimuli from that same stimulus class is the procedure called _____ training.

62. The goal of generalization training is for the behavior to occur in the presence of _____ stimuli from the same stimulus class.

67. The occurrence of a response in the presence of a novel stimulus is the process called _____.

66. The gradual withdrawal of prompts to establish a specific discrimination behavior analysts call *fading*. The gradual withdrawal of prompts to establish a

generalization they call _____
_____ (fading, programming).

45. Programming is the gradual withdrawal of prompts during generalization training to establish a(n) _____ (discrimination, generalization).

17. If the correct behavior never occurs in the presence of a novel stimulus during generalization training, then you can try to get it to occur by using a(n) _____.

79. When you use prompts to help in training a generalization, you are using what procedure? _____

59. Suppose you are ready to praise Suzie when she calls a basketball a ball, but she never does. You might then use a prompt to get her to call it a ball and praise her lavishly when she does. You might gradually withdraw your prompt until she calls the basketball a ball without any prompting. Suppose you use, and then withdraw, a prompt to teach her to call a golf ball a ball. If she now calls a novel ball a ball, her *behavior* illustrates the process called _____.

55. Suppose parents show Peggy a series of pictures of dogs, some big, some small. To get her started, they say, "What is this? You know, bow-wow," and praise her when she says, "dog." Suppose they gradually eliminate the "bow-wow" for all of the pictures. What behavioral procedure are they using to teach Peggy to call even novel pictures of dogs "dog"? _____

78. When you use programming, your goal is to have the behavior continue to occur in the presence of the novel stimulus even after you have completely withdrawn the _____.

14. Generalization training that temporarily employs prompts is called _____.

47. Programming is using a prompt to establish a(n) _____.

73. Using a prompt to establish a generalization is called _____; using a prompt to establish a specific discrimination is called _____.

48. Programming is using a prompt to establish a(n) _____; fading is using a prompt to establish a(n) _____.

53. Schaeffer (1963) used the German word ich to replace the English *I* in several short stories by Poe. The context of redundant sentences was enough to serve as an effective prompt for correct translation. Presumably understanding the sentence and ultimately the story was the reinforcer. Schaeffer withdrew this kind of prompt by selecting a series of sentences that were not as redundant. By seeing *ich* in a series of different sentences, students learned to translate that word in many novel sentences. What behavioral procedure did Schaeffer use to teach the meaning of ich? _____

### 3. Using Prompts in Education

26. Pre-test: Programmed instruction involves three important features: (1) It makes the student give a written _____; (2) it gives immediate _____; and (3) it uses small _____.

34. Pre-test: What form of programming has these three characteristics: (1) It requires a written response; (2) it gives immediate feedback; and (3) it uses small steps? _____

39. Programmed instruction involves three important features: (1) It requires a written response; (2) it provides immediate feedback about whether the response is correct; and (3) it requires the student to take only one _____ (large, small) step at a time.

40. Programmed instruction: (1) requires a written response, (2) provides immediate feedback, and (3) requires the student to take only a small _____ at a time.

41. Programmed instruction: (1) requires a written response, (2) provides immediate _____ about whether the response is correct, and (3) requires the student to take only small steps.

42. Programmed instruction: (1) requires a written _____, (2) gives immediate feedback, and (3) uses small steps.

43. Programmed instruction involves three important features: (1) It makes the student give a written _____; (2) it gives immediate _____; and (3) it uses small _____.

74. What form of programming has these three characteristics: (1) It requires a written response; (2) it gives immediate feedback; and (3) it uses small steps? Programmed _____.

18. In <u>Programmed reading</u>, the child is shown a picture of a bag and is then required to fill in a blank like "That is Ann in the ba_." Showing one or more letters contained in the correct answer would be called a(n) _____.

61. The book called *Programmed Reading* has the following characteristics: (1) The children must make a written response. (2) They can obtain immediate feedback by looking at the correct answer on the left. (3) They learn only the amount contained in each of the small steps. This program is an example of what type of programming? _____ instruction

49. Programming may contain fading within it. As part of teaching the child to call any bag "bag," the child might be shown a picture of a bag with the statement "This is a ba_" and later "This is a b_ _" and still later "This is a _ _ _." The procedure of teaching the child to label the same picture "bag" by using the added stimulus of the word and then gradually showing fewer letters in the word is called _____.

### 4. Fading versus Programming

35. Pre-test: When you add a temporary prompt and gradually withdraw it to assist with generalization training, you are using the procedure called _____; when you add a temporary prompt and gradually withdraw it to assist with discrimination training, you are using the procedure called _____.

27. Pre-test: Programming is using a prompt to establish a(n) _____; fading is using a prompt to establish a(n) _____.

20. In an earlier lesson, you learned that behavior analysts can teach <u>physical</u> skills to many people who seemed incapable of learning with conventional teaching methods by using shaping. In this lesson, you learned that behavior analysts can teach specific <u>intellectual</u> skills to many people who seemed incapable of learning by conventional teaching methods by using the procedures of _____ and _____.

9. Fading and programming both add an existing SD to a novel stimulus. Behavior analysts call an existing SD added to the novel stimulus a(n) _____. Then, the prompt is slowly withdrawn until the novel stimulus alone evokes the correct response. Because it is a stimulus in the presence of which the correct response will be reinforced, the novel stimulus will have become a(n) _____.

46. Programming is using a prompt to establish a(n) _____; fading is using a prompt to establish a(n) _____.

75. When you add a temporary prompt and gradually withdraw it to assist with generalization training, you are using the procedure called _____; when you add a temporary prompt and gradually withdraw it to assist with discrimination training, you are using the procedure called _____.

7. Dr. Moore made the correct answer light up while the incorrect answers remained dark. He then gradually increased the brightness of the incorrect answers until they were as bright as the correct answer. The brightness of the correct answer is an example of a(n) _____.

52. Sarah made many errors when trying to match the unlit triangles through trial-and-error learning. She made _____ _____ (few, many) errors while learning through fading.

51. Research results suggest that learning can be both faster and almost error free when prompts are used to assist learning with the two behavioral procedures of _____ or _____.

### 5. Another Tactic

31. Pre-test: The third tactic in using the stimulus control strategy suggests that when you must create new stimulus control, you try temporarily using _____ _____.

4. Creating new stimulus control by temporarily using <u>prompts</u> is the third tactic in using the stimulus _____ strategy for solving human problems.

69. The third tactic in using the stimulus control strategy for solving human problems is to create new stimulus control by temporarily using _____ ____ (prompts, shaping).

70. The third tactic in using the stimulus control strategy suggests that when you must create new stimulus control, you try temporarily using _____ _____.

### 6. Review

24. Pre-test: Mary was shown a figure for several seconds and then shown three similar figures. The apparatus lit up the identical figure while leaving the incorrect figures dark. After Mary could reliably pick the identical figure, the apparatus gradually increased the brightness of the incorrect figures until they were as bright as the correct one. What behavioral procedure did the apparatus use by changing the brightness to teach this specific discrimination? _____

32. Pre-test: The third tactic in using the stimulus control strategy for solving human problems is to create new stimulus control by temporarily using _____.

22. Pre-test: Behavior analysts call the procedure that involves the gradual withdrawal of a prompt to establish a specific discrimination: _____.

23. Pre-test: Hans read several short stories in which the German word *ich* was inserted in place of *I*. The context of redundant sentences was enough to serve as an effective prompt for proper translation. By placing the German word in many different sentences, Hans learned to always recognize the word even where the sentence was not an effective prompt. Hans learned the meaning of *ich* by means of the behavioral procedure of _____.

29. Pre-test: Programming is the temporary use of a prompt during generalization training to establish a(n) _____.

71. To use the stimulus control strategy: (1) Narrow stimulus control through discrimination training; (2) broaden stimulus control through generalization training; (3) create new stimulus control by temporarily using _____ as in fading or programming.

50. Programming temporarily uses prompts to be able to reinforce the same response in the presence of a series of stimuli from the same stimulus class. Therefore, programming is a particular kind of _____ training that temporarily employs prompts.

5. Discrimination training that temporarily employs prompts to establish a specific discrimination is called _____.

13. Fading is the use of a temporary prompt to help _____ training, whereas programming is the use of a temporary prompt to help _____ training.

44. Programmed instruction requires a written response, provides immediate feedback for the response, and uses small _____.

19. In *Programmed Reading,* the child is shown a picture of a girl in a bag and then required to fill in the blank: "That is Ann in the ba_." Showing one or more letters from the correct answer is called a(n) _____.

3. Behavior analysts call an added stimulus that increases the probability of making the correct response a(n) _____.

15. Gradually eliminating a prompt during discrimination training is called _____.

72. To use the stimulus control strategy: (1) Narrow stimulus control through discrimination training; (2) broaden stimulus control through _____; (3) create new stimulus control by temporarily using _____.

## Programmed Examples

### Programmed Examples

11. Pre-test: A special tutor was used to teach Bruiser Bob, not the smartest of students, to learn his blocking assignments for the power sweep and end run. At first, the tutor let Bob read from a crib sheet "power sweep—block

opposing tackle to left." Later, he had him use a crib sheet that had only "power sweep—tackle" and later, no crib sheet. The tutor praised him when he said he was supposed to block the tackle if the play was a power sweep. The tutor ignored him if he gave the same answer if the play was flea flicker. Bruiser learned his assignment perfectly. What behavioral procedure did the tutor employ? _____

13. Pre-test: Ray was a loner, never playing with the other preschool children. Ms. Gray started praising Ray whenever he was playing with Jane. After several days, he started playing quite a bit with Jane. Then, she started praising Ray when he was playing with Billy. In a few days, he was playing with Billy and Jane. In addition, without further praise, Ray started playing with Mary. What behavioral method had Ms. Gray used to produce this result? _____

12. Pre-test: Mrs. Livermore taught her kindergarten pupil, Francie, to label a large circular line as a "circle" by asking, "Francie, what is this? You know, a circle" and praising her when she said "circle." Next, she gave as a hint only, "You know, a cirk" but did not say the "l." Pretty soon, Francie could label the drawing as a circle with no hint. Then, Mrs. Livermore showed Francie a small solid circle and used the same procedure. Mrs. Livermore had used a hint to help Francie label a series of circles correctly until she could label new circular patterns as circles. What behavioral procedure did Mrs. Livermore use to teach that skill?

_____

14. Pre-test: The coach praised Bruiser Bob for tackling the practice dummy low but ignored him when he tackled it high. Soon, Bob only tackled it low. What behavioral procedure was the coach using? _____ (Ask questions to identify what procedure was used. Note that many students get this one wrong.)

18. Professor Smith was trying to teach 18-month-old Tracey the concepts of "above" and "below." She placed her hand over the table and asked, "Where is my hand? You know, above," and gave Tracey a spoonful of applesauce if she repeated it. Next time, she asked, "Where is my hand? You know, abuh," not pronouncing the "v" sound. Again she reinforced Tracey for saying "above." She

gradually taught Tracey to say "above" without hints. (She ignored anytime Tracey said "above" when the hand was below the table.) In several days, Tracey could answer the question correctly with no hints. The phrase "You know, above" is an added stimulus that is called a(n) _____. Because the prof was using a prompt to teach Tracey to say "above" when her hand was over the table but not when it was under the table, her procedure is called _____.

17. Professor Smith wanted Tracey to learn to use "above" correctly for any situation. So she next placed her hand over a dish and asked Tracey, "Where is my hand? You know, above," and gave Tracey a bite if she repeated "above," She then gradually eliminated the hint. Next, she put a ball over the dish and asked Tracey, "Where is the ball?" To her surprise, before she could give the hint, Tracey blurted out "above." Professor Smith tried placing the dish on top of the ball and asking where it was. Again, Tracey said "above." Tracey could always tell you whether an object was above or below from then on. When Tracey saw the ball over the plate for the first time, it was a novel stimulus. Saying "above" for the new situation where the ball was over the plate is an example of what process? _____ Because the prof is using a prompt to teach Tracey to tell when one object is over another in a series of situations until she could tell even with a new situation, she is using the behavioral procedure called _____.

8. Mr. Franklin had just about given up on teaching his ninth-grade students the principles of algebra. Then, he heard about a new type of book that required the students to write answers, gave them immediate feedback on their responses, and presented one small step at a time. He tried it and found that his students really started to learn algebra well. The new type of book is an example of programming called _____.

20. Terry looked up the definition of every unknown word that she came across. First, she referred to the full definition while writing several sentences using the word. Second, she referred to a shortened version of the definition while writing several sentences. Third, she looked at a definition consisting only of

a synonym or key word. Finally, she wrote sentences with no help from a definition. After this process, she could use the word fluently in both speech and writing. Terry's goal was to be able to use the new word in any novel situation that might come along. Her production of the word in a novel situation is an example of the process called _____. The written definition served as a(n) _____ for correct use of the new word. Next, decide whether this temporary use of prompts is fading or programming. To do so, decide whether she was using discrimination training or generalization training with each word. Because Terry is using prompts to learn the word's use in a series of sentences until she can use it in novel sentences, this is an example of what behavioral procedure?

_____

7. Mom showed Mary a card with the word *rejoice* on it. She said, "What is this word, you know, rejoice." She praised Mary if she said "rejoice." Mom then said "rejoice" more and more softly until Mary said "rejoice" just from looking at the word alone. Mom also used the same procedure with the word *exhaust*. Mom praised Mary when she said "rejoice" when that was the word on the card but ignored her when the word on the card was *exhaust*. Because Mom was using a prompt to teach Mary to read the word on each card, her procedure is called _____.

1. Can you tell the difference between programming and generalization training? James held up a tennis ball for his sister to see and asked her what it was. When she said "ball," he gave her a big smile and praised her. After she had learned to call the tennis ball "ball," he showed her a basketball and asked her what it was, again repeating the same procedure used on the tennis ball. After she had learned to call it a ball, he showed her a golf ball, and she immediately said "ball." Note that he used no prompts. His procedure involved reinforcing the word *ball* for a series of many different balls until his sister applied the "ball" to novel types of balls. You call his procedure: _____.
If he had given her a hint that he gradually withdrew for each ball, what behavioral

procedure would he have been using?

_____

5. Fred learned the definition of *reinforcer* from a specially designed book. In the book, he was first given a specific definition of *reinforcer*. The first question had the same words but gave a hint with two possible answers in parentheses: "An event that follows a behavior and increases its probability is called a(n) _____ (reinforcement, reinforcer)." When this question was presented again, the choices in parentheses were left out. Fred was asked a second version of the question using different words that meant the same: "An event that occurs after a behavior such that its frequency increases is called a(n) _____ (reinforcement, reinforcer)." Next time the parentheses were left out. The book reinforced him for using the word reinforcer with a series of different versions of the question. Fred was able after that to correctly label the definition of a *reinforcer* whenever the wording had the same meaning even if he had never seen that wording before. What behavioral procedure did the book use to develop this skill?

_____

6. Here's another review example to help you keep terms from past lessons distinct from current terms. Ken's goal was to get Roger to say "television" correctly. At first, Ken reinforced Roger only when he said the "tel" part of "television" correctly. Then, Ken reinforced him only if he got the "e" sound also. Then, he reinforced him only when he added "viz." Finally, Ken reinforced Roger only when he also said the "ion" distinctly. Notice that Ken is not gradually changing a prompt but rather gradually changing the behavior that he will reinforce. Therefore, Ken used what behavioral procedure to teach Roger to say "television" correctly? _____

3. Darlene held up the picture of a crow, asked her daughter, "What is this?" and then said, "This is a large bird." Later she simply said "large," still later she made a movement with her hands to indicate "large;" and finally she did nothing. If the child said "crow," Darlene praised her lavishly. However, if Darlene held up the picture of a blackbird and the child said "crow," Darlene ignored her. The daughter quickly learned to call the larger bird a crow but

not the smaller one. What behavioral procedure was Darlene using? _____
If Darlene did not provide the hint about size, what procedure would she be using?

_____

9. Mr. Janes taught Robert to draw a map of Kansas by first praising any rectangle that was twice as long as it was high. He then praised the map only if the Missouri River was shown, and finally he praised the map only if Wichita, Kansas City, and Topeka were shown. The behavioral procedure by which Mr. Janes taught Robert to draw a map with all the basic features of Kansas on it is called

_____.

15. Professor Smart pointed to a complex differential equation and asked Mary, "What is that?" Mary immediately said, "That is a differential equation," and was rewarded with a broad smile from the professor. In the presence of the differential equation, the response "That is a differential equation" is reinforced. Therefore, it is called a(n) _____ for that response. But an algebraic equation where that same response would be extinguished would be called a(n) _____ for that response.

16. Professor Smart pointed to a linear equation (12x+7=y) that no one had seen before. He asked Jane what kind of equation it was. She said, "That is a linear equation." The occurrence of her correct response in the presence of this novel equation is the process called _____.

10. Mr. Jones, Pete's dad, tutored Pete in the identification of football plays. He showed Pete diagrams of many kinds of plays and asked him to name them. He praised Pete for calling the first one a "power sweep" but not

a "flea flicker." He praised Pete for calling the second diagram a "flea flicker" but not for calling it a "power sweep". Because Dad reinforced Pete for applying each name to the corresponding diagram but not to other diagrams, this procedure is an example of complex _____. If his dad used temporary prompts, what behavioral procedure would he be using? _____

_____

2. Carol was taught to add by a teacher who let her see two sets of matchsticks that corresponded to the addition problem. When he asked, "How much is 4+7?" the teacher would arrange a pile of four matches and a pile of seven matches. He praised her when she said "eleven" for this problem but ignored her if she said "eleven" for other problems. As Carol learned to answer the question, the teacher would gradually move the match piles out of sight. Eventually, Carol could add 4+7 without the help of the matches. What behavioral procedure did the teacher use?_____

_____

4. Eleanor praised her daughter for saying "dog" when shown a picture of a dog and ignored her for saying "dog" when shown a picture of a cat. What behavioral procedure was she using? _____

19. Suppose Dad asked Lulu what to call their big loud vehicle and made a loud "VROOMMM" to help her. If she said "truck," he praised her. If she called their smaller vehicle "truck," he ignored her. After she learned to say "truck" for the big vehicle and a loud "VROOMMM," he made the sound more quietly and then quit altogether. If Lulu came to call only the big loud one a truck, what procedure was Dad using?

_____

# Imitation and Instructions

## Reading Section

This lesson introduces two widely used procedures for modifying behavior: imitation training and instructional training. Imitation training involves demonstrating to another person how to perform a behavior. Instructional training involves describing to another person how to perform a behavior. In everyday life, both procedures can be very complex. The Quakers' path of "bearing witness" to their faith through exemplary behavior may be a very complex example of imitation training. Academic courses are an everyday example of complex instructional training.

Tactic #4 in the stimulus control strategy is creating complex stimulus control through imitation training and instructional training.

1. Tactic #4 in the stimulus control strategy is creating complex stimulus control through _____ training and instructional training.

## Definition of Imitation Training

**Imitation training** is when (1) the teacher demonstrates the imitative stimulus, (2) the learner emits the imitative behavior, and (3) the teacher reinforces it. Put another way, the teacher shows the student the desired behavior by performing it; the learner copies the desired behavior; and the teacher reinforces it. For example, a teacher says "gut," the German word for "good," pronounced "goot." That is the imitative stimulus. The learner copies the teacher's "gut." That is the imitative behavior. The teacher reinforces the correct response.

2. **Imitation training**: (1) The teacher demonstrates the _____ stimulus. (2) The learner emits the _____ behavior. (3) The teacher _____ it.

Notice that imitation training is a specific type of discrimination training. The teacher reinforces the learner for saying "gut" only when the imitative stimulus is "gut." The teacher does not reinforce the learner for saying "gut" when the imitative stimulus is "der." The teacher saying "gut" becomes an SD for the learner saying "gut." The teacher saying other German words becomes an S-delta for the learner saying "gut."

People frequently use imitation training in everyday situations. When Dad shows Debby how to hold a football, has her hold it, and praises correct holding, he uses imitation training. When Mom shows Paul how to sauté onions, has him do it, and praises good sautéing, she uses imitation training. People who do not fully understand behavioral principles may use only part of the procedure. They may show Debby how to hold the football, the imitative stimulus, but not have her hold it. Thus, Debby won't be reinforced for actually making the response. This short form of imitation training is not as sure to work. Behavior analysts sometimes call this short form *modeling* (e.g., Marcus, Swanson, & Vollmer, 2001) and, when it works, *observational learning*.

## Uses of Imitation Training

Behavior analysts use imitation to help change many behaviors. Researchers have used imitation to increase spontaneous speech

(Ingenmey & VanHouten, 1991) as well as social peer interaction (e.g., Garfinkle & Schwartz, 2002) by children with autism. Japanese researchers used it to increase conversations by a child with autism (Inoue & Kobayashi, 1992). Researchers used it to overcome phobias in children (Love, Matson, & West, 1990). Behavior analysts often use imitation training with individuals who have little or no language (e.g., Ross & Greer, 2003). They can demonstrate more effective behaviors even if the learner can't understand instructions or explanations. Research suggests that imitation training is the most acceptable treatment for persons with developmental disabilities (Davis & Russell, 1990).

Researchers often use very complex imitation training. For example, researchers sought to change the food-buying habits of 20 Blacksburg, Virginia, families (Winett, Kramer, Walker, Malone, & Lane, 1988). They showed the families a videotape of a family changing its food habits. This family modeled discussing the issues and then modeled making a healthy shopping list, shopping, and preparing more nutritious meals. The researchers presented a complex set of imitative stimuli in this videotape. They obtained shopping reports from the families, and they gave them feedback about the nutrition of their choices. As a result, the families changed their buying habits. For example, they reduced fat calories by 7%.

## Teaching How to Imitate

You might imagine that everyone knows how to imitate. You might even feel that imitating another person is "human nature." Unfortunately, many people do not naturally imitate others. People with developmental disabilities, autism, and other disabilities often do not imitate. Psychologists have difficulty influencing the behavior of people who neither speak nor imitate. If you can't talk to them and you can't show them, how can you help them? Therefore, behavior analysts have tried to learn how to teach the general skill of imitating.

Researchers taught the skill of imitating to Fran, a child with profound retardation (Baer, Peterson, & Sherman, 1967). Bob trained Fran at mealtime by reinforcing her imitations with bites of the meal. Bob first taught Fran to imitate him when he raised his left arm. Bob said, "Do this," and then raised his arm. Initially, Bob had to prompt Fran by raising her arm for her. He then gave her a bite of her meal. He gradually faded his help until, when he raised his arm, Fran raised her arm by herself. This required about 60 meals.

Bob next taught Fran to imitate his tapping the table with his left hand. Fran learned this second imitation more quickly than the first. Bob proceeded to teach additional imitations. Bob noticed that Fran gradually started imitating some behaviors on the first trial. In fact, she gradually came to imitate behaviors with no reinforcement. Fran had learned how to imitate. Bob gave her a basic skill that he and others could use to help her. Bob had taught Fran how to imitate in general by teaching her to imitate many specific behaviors. Bob's procedure is an example of generalization training. The complete analysis of this procedure involves generalization to the class of responses called *imitative*, a process that we will not study in this book (Baer & Deguchi, 1985).

Other studies have used generalized imitation to develop language skills in several individuals with developmental disabilities (Goldstein & Mousetis, 1989). Researchers have noted both gestural imitation (Poulson & Kymissis, 1988) and vocal imitation (Poulson, Kymissis, Reeve, Andreatos, & Richards, 1991) in infants. These studies suggest that generalized imitation leads to human language learning (Kymissis & Poulson, 1990). It seems that generalized imitation is a common process in the everyday development of children.

## Definition of Instructional Training

**Instructional training** is defined as follows: (1) The teacher gives a <u>verbal description,</u> (2) the learner emits the <u>instructed behavior,</u>

and (3) the teacher <u>reinforces</u> it. Put simply, the teacher describes the desired behavior, the student emits it, and the teacher reinforces it. For example, Mr. Jones says to Leo, "Pass the butter." Leo passes the butter. Mr. Jones says, "Thank you," or gives an even stronger reinforcer.

3. The procedure that consists of these three parts—(1) the teacher gives a verbal description, (2) the learner emits the instructed behavior, and (3) the teacher reinforces it—is called _____ _____ training.

The training procedure for teaching by instruction is also usually a discrimination training procedure. The teacher reinforces the learner for putting the ball on the table only if the instruction was "put the ball on the table." The teacher does not reinforce the learner for putting the ball on the table if the instruction was "put the ball on the floor." Thus, the instruction is an SD for the described behavior.

People frequently use instructional training in everyday situations. When Dad tells Jane how to start the car, has her do it, and praises correct starting, he uses instructional training. When Mom tells Pete how to change channels with the remote control, has him do it, and praises correct changing, she uses instructional training. People who do not fully understand behavioral principles may use only part of the procedure. They may tell Jane how to start the car but not have her try starting it. Thus, Jane won't be reinforced for actually making the response. This short form of instructional training is not as sure to work.

## Uses of Instructional Training

Behavior analysts use instructional training as part of almost all treatment programs. One widely adopted procedure increases the rate at which patients keep medical appointments (Ross, Friman, & Christophersen, 1993). Researchers had the staff at a clinic mail reminders to patients one week before their appointments. They then called the day

before. These patients were more likely to cancel rather than simply not show up than patients not reminded. The researchers did not reinforce keeping appointments. Presumably, the patients had a history of intermittent reinforcement sufficient to maintain following instructions.

Instructional training is probably the most widely used form of behavior modification employed in everyday settings. We are all constantly engaged in talking, telling people what to do, when to do it, how to do it, and why to do it. Unfortunately, the non–behavior analyst frequently fails to follow through by observing the instructed behavior and then supplying reinforcement. As a result, following instructions is frequently placed on a schedule of extinction.

Researchers showed the importance of reinforcement for following instructions (Ayllon & Azrin, 1964). Figure 19-1 shows that long-term psychotics rarely bothered to use eating implements during baseline, even when eating soup. The researchers tried instructing the patients to use implements. About one-third of the patients complied. The researchers then awarded tokens to those patients following the instructions. Virtually all patients started following the instructions to use implements at that point. The researchers found that reinforcement can be crucial for maintaining instruction following.

Behavior therapists have explored an interesting implication of instructional training. Normal adults with "problems" frequently report repeating the same instructions to themselves. For example, they may constantly tell themselves that they must have something to eat. They may literally instruct themselves to become fat. Such instructions may be implicated in alcoholism, depression, anxiety, drug dependence, and many other problems. Behavior therapists regard these self-instructions as behavior. Looking at them as behavior suggests that they can be influenced by reinforcement, extinction, and punishment (e.g., Matsumoto & Okouchi, 2001). Modifying self-instructions with these procedures is often very successful—perhaps more successful than looking for the causes in the person's childhood.

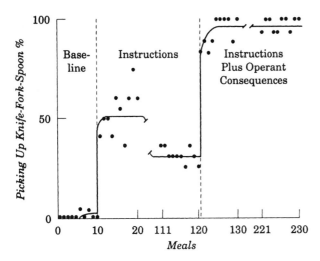

**Figure 19-1.** Chronic schizophrenic patients in many hospitals eat their food with their hands (including soup!). This figure shows the tiny number of patients who picked up a knife, fork, and spoon during a baseline period. More patients picked them up during a period when they were instructed to do so. Finally, most patients picked them up during a period when they were instructed plus reinforced for doing so. Notice that the instructions helped at first but tended to lose their effect over time. Also notice that when reinforcement was added, almost all the patients always picked up the implements. This example shows the necessity of using reinforcement along with instructions in many situations. (Adapted from "Reinforcement and Instructions with Mental Patients," by T. Ayllon and N. H. Azrin *Journal of the Experimental Analysis of Behavior,* 1964, 7, 327–331. Copyright 1964 by the Society for the Experimental Analysis of Behavior, Inc. Used by permission.)

## Generalized Instruction-Following

Most people readily follow instructions unless their source is dubious for some reason. You might think that this common pattern is just human nature. But again, as with imitating, following instructions is not a natural skill but one that probably develops similarly to generalized imitation. An idealized pattern for learning to follow instructions might start with a parent teaching a child to follow one instruction. She gives the instruction and then reinforces the child for following it. When that is learned, he teaches a second, then a third. The child's instruction-following behavior starts to generalize to all instructions. She will then follow most instructions as long as some of them are reinforced. She will also learn some conditions under which instructions do not lead to reinforcement. She will learn to resist such instructions (Riegler & Baer, 1989).

## Imitation and Instructions Combined

Many researchers use both procedures combined. For example, researchers used both procedures in a public health project. They wanted to encourage "safe sunning" at swimming pools (Lombard, Neubauer, Canfield, & Winett, 1991). They used signs and flyers to inform swimmers about the connection between sunburn and skin cancer. They described how swimmers could protect themselves. They had lifeguards model safe sunning (that is, they provided an imitative stimulus). The lifeguards wore t-shirts, sunglasses, hats, zinc oxide, and sun screen. In addition, they equipped lifeguard stands with an umbrella for shade. Imitation and instructions increased the number of swimmers protecting themselves from the sun. Other researchers used the combined procedures to teach cooperative play to children (e.g., Jahr & Eldevik, 2002).

## Imitation and Instructional Training Are Efficient

Instructional training is simpler and more direct than relying on reinforcement alone. For example, a teacher may wish to increase students' talking in class. Telling them to talk more is faster than waiting for them to talk and reinforcing them. Telling people to hit their ping-pong shots softly is quicker than reinforcing soft shots and extinguishing hard shots. Perhaps most important, instructional training is an alternative to shaping. You may be able to instruct someone to do something in a brief time that would take an extended period to teach by shaping.

You cannot use instructional training with people who lack basic verbal skills. For example, you may not be able to use it with infants, people with retardation, or children with autism. Their verbal skills often do not permit instructions. Singing provides a different type of exception. You cannot describe behaviors like singing well enough to teach them to another person using only verbal instructions. You can often use imitation training with such behaviors.

## Summary

Imitation training and instructional training are forms of discrimination training. You can use them to modify many behaviors easily. They are most effective with people who have generalized skills of imitating or following instructions. These generalized skills can themselves be taught through generalization training. Imitation may be basic to learning language. Tactic #4 of the stimulus control strategy is to create complex stimulus control through imitation training and instructional training.

## Behavior Analysis Examples

### *Teaching a College Graduate How to Get a Job*

Researchers have used imitation and instructional training to teach people how to interview for jobs (Hollandsworth, Glazeski, & Dressel, 1978). For example, they helped Herbert, an extremely nervous college graduate, to obtain a position. Herbert had not found a job five months after graduating with a general business degree. He participated in more than 60 job interviews without a single offer. In desperation, he finally accepted a part-time sales job in a men's clothing store at minimum wage.

The researchers guessed that Herbert was extremely nervous when being interviewed. His speech was incoherent, he lost his train of thought, and he silently stared into space for long periods. They therefore specified three behaviors that would improve his interview performance: (1) focused responses to the interviewer's questions, (2) coping statements, such as "Excuse me" and "Let

me start over," to be made when he goofed, (3) asking questions to request additional information, feedback, or clarification.

The researchers designed a role-playing situation to teach these three skills. One of them played the role of an interviewer while another observed the interview. Herbert's baseline performance level for each of the three interviewing behaviors was very poor.

After session 6 the researchers taught Herbert a simple method for making focused answers to an interviewer's questions. They started with instructions. First, they defined *clear responses* and explained their importance. Then, they explained how to make clear responses, using a pause-think-speak paradigm. *Pause* referred to breaking eye contact and pausing when the interviewer asked him a question. *Think* referred to picking out one or two key words in the question and then deciding on one or two key words for his answer. Finally, *speak* referred to making eye contact and stating a clear answer to the interviewer's question.

Next, the researchers used modeling. They showed Herbert a videotape of an actor using the pause-think-speak method for making focused responses to interview questions. They then asked Herbert to practice what he had learned. The interviewer asked him five questions commonly asked by job interviewers. The trainer provided feedback on his performance. After practice, Herbert appeared very natural using pause-think-speak. Herbert's performance improved dramatically after training for focused responses.

Next, the researchers used a similar procedure to teach Herbert how to make coping statements. They taught this behavior prior to session 12, and he made a modest improvement in his use of coping statements. Finally, prior to session 17, the researchers taught him how to ask questions. This behavior produced a dramatic increase in performance. Figure 19-2 shows that all three behaviors increased convincingly after treatment and remained stable. The multiple-baseline design ruled out alternative interpretations, so the researchers concluded that the imitation training caused Herbert to engage in the behaviors more often.

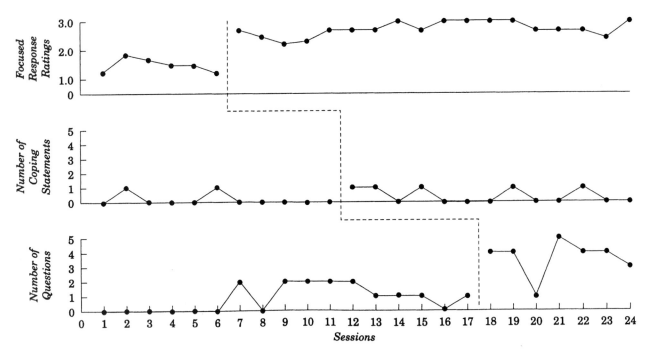

*Figure 19-2.* The effect of modeling and feedback on Herbert's interview skills. The graph shows the effect on focused responding to interviewer's questions, coping statement, and asking questions. (From "Use of Social Skills Training in the Treatment of Extreme Anxiety and Deficient Verbal Skills in the Job Interview Setting," by J. G. Hollandsworth, R. C. Glazeski, and M. E. Dressel *Journal of Applied Behavior Analysis,* 1978, 11, 259–269. Copyright 1978 by the Society for the Experimental Analysis of Behavior, Inc. Used by permission.)

4. Refer to Figure 19-2. Notice the *highest* rating during baseline was ___, while the *lowest* rating during treatment was ___.

The researchers gathered additional data during the experiment. They measured the number of stutters that Herbert made during each role-playing session. This served as an indication of nervousness. Stutters decreased from a baseline level of about 20 per session to about 2 or 3.

The most important outcome of the experiment was that Herbert went for three interviews after training and was offered three jobs. He took one as an administrative assistant in a hospital for about triple the minimum wage.

After much practice with feedback, Herbert became quite natural with the pause-think-speak behavior. Interview questions became an SD for pause-think-speak behavior. When that happened, behavior analysts would call pause-think-speak behavior discriminated behavior.

5. The researchers produced the appropriate behavior by showing Herbert a videotape of an actor demonstrating pause-think-speak behavior, asking him to role-play the behavior, and giving him praise for engaging in the behavior. The researchers used _____ (imitation, instructional) training.

## Notes

### Note #1
Imitation training sometimes appears to be differential reinforcement. Such cases arise when the teacher reinforces the learner for Imitative Behavior A but extinguishes the learner for Imitative Behavior B in the presence of Imitative Stimulus A. However, teachers rarely present imitative stimuli singly. Rather, they teach the learner several imitative stimuli. In that case, they reinforce the learner for Imitative Behavior A in the presence of Imitative Stimulus A but not in

the presence of Imitative Stimulus B. At the same time, they reinforce the learner for Imitative Behavior B in the presence of Imitative stimulus B but not in the presence of Imitative Stimulus A.

6. In the case of complex situations like this, the procedure could be interpreted either as differential reinforcement or discrimination training. As I have noted before, behavior analysts have arbitrarily agreed to call the procedure in such complex cases

_____ .

### Note #2
Programming and fading may involve imitation training prior to the withdrawal of the prompt. For example, if a fading sequence involves asking the question, "What is this, (a tree)?" the person can simply imitate the word "tree." However, since that imitative stimulus is eventually withdrawn, this would not be classified as an example of imitation training. So in any example involving the withdrawal of an imitative stimulus used as a prompt, the only acceptable answer is programming or fading.

7. When teachers use an imitative stimulus as a temporary prompt during discrimination training, you should not label the procedure as imitation training but rather as _____ .

### Note #3
People often use imitation training and instructional training in everyday situations. Parents often praise their children when they imitate a word or phrase. Employers often tell employees how to perform a task and thank them when they do. Teenagers often say a hip new word and act impressed when others repeat it. People often describe how to use a new electronic device and congratulate a friend on following their instructions. People often use either imitation training or instructional training accidentally or casually.

You can use the term *imitation training* as long as the learning situation includes a demonstration, imitative behavior, and reinforcement. Likewise, you can use the term *instructional training* as long as the learning

situation has a verbal description, instructed behavior, and reinforcement.

8. If someone "accidentally" demonstrates a behavior, another person copies it, and the first person praises them for copying it, you can refer to the procedure as an everyday example of _____ training.

## Helpful Hints

### Helpful Hint #1
Students sometimes confuse imitation training and instructional training. In both cases the teacher engages in some form of behavior designed to influence another person. The distinction lies in whether the teacher's behavior is identical to the desired behavior. If it is identical, then the teacher is using imitation training. If the teacher's behavior is different but somehow describes the desired behavior, then the teacher is using instructional control. For example, if the teacher says "Guten Tag" and reinforces the student for saying "Guten Tag," then the technique used is imitation training. If the teacher says "Say the German phrase for hello" and reinforces the student for saying "Guten Tag," the technique used is instructional training. Usually you can clarify which type of training is involved by asking one of two questions. If you think the example is instruction, ask, "Did the teacher <u>describe</u> the correct behavior? If you think it is imitation, ask, "Did the teacher <u>demonstrate</u> the correct behavior?"

9. If you think an example is imitation training, you may check your analysis by asking the question, "Did the teacher _____ the correct behavior?"

### Helpful Hint #2
Be careful to use the correct forms of imitation when labeling the procedure and its respective parts. <u>Imitation</u> training is the procedure that consists of the teacher providing an <u>imitative</u> stimulus and then reinforcing the student for performing the <u>imitative</u> behavior.

10. Practice this terminology now by filling in the appropriate terms in the blanks: The procedure in which the teacher demonstrates the desired behavior is _____ _____ training. The teacher provides the _____ stimulus and the learner performs the _____ behavior.

### Helpful Hint #3

Be careful to use the correct forms of instruction when labeling the procedure and its respective parts. Instructional training is the procedure that consists of the teacher providing a verbal description and then reinforcing the student for performing the instructed behavior.

11. Practice this terminology now by filling in the appropriate terms in the blanks: The procedure in which the teacher describes the desired behavior is called _____ training. The teacher gives a verbal description and the learner performs the _____ behavior.

### Helpful Hint #4

With this lesson, your task of identifying the procedure in an example becomes harder. You must still decide if the example involves differential reinforcement. If it doesn't, you must consider two more stimulus control procedures. The examples now may be discrimination training, generalization training, programming, fading, imitation training, or instructional training. Your job will be to figure out which procedure the example is based on. You will increase your chances of picking the correct label if you analyze the example systematically.

The first step is to decide whether the example is based on differential reinforcement or whether it involves a stimulus control procedure. If the example involves one stimulus and two or more behaviors, then it must involve differential reinforcement. Be sure to consider whether the differential reinforcement involves successive approximations. If so, then the procedure is shaping. If the example involves two (or more) stimuli and one behavior, then you know that you are dealing with a form of stimulus control such as discrimination training. You must decide what type of stimulus control procedure is involved. If you think the example involves stimulus control, you need to ask questions to label the specific procedure.

First, ask if the example involves either an imitative stimulus or a verbal description. If it does, you know that the procedure involves either imitation training or instructional training. You already know how to tell the difference.

Second, ask if the procedure involves a prompt. If it does not involve a prompt, then you can label the procedure as discrimination training or generalization training. You already know how to tell the difference. If it involves a prompt, then the procedure is either fading or programming. You can check this conclusion by asking if the prompt is gradually withdrawn. If the example involves a prompt that is withdrawn, then you already know how to tell whether it is fading or programming.

In summary, if you think the procedure involves stimulus control, you can ask two questions. First, ask if the procedure involves an imitative stimulus or a verbal description. Second, ask whether the procedure uses prompts. These two questions will help you pinpoint the procedure used in the example.

12. If the example involves one stimulus and two or more behaviors, then it must involve _____.

### Helpful Hint #5

People sometimes use both imitation and instructional training at the same time. For example, Mom might tell Jimmy: "What is the name of that animal? Say 'cat.'" She verbally describes what she wants Jimmy to say. But she also says the word so that Jimmy can copy it. Since her description is really only an imitative stimulus, I will always label this type of example as imitation training.

13. Mom might tell Jimmy: "What is the name of that animal? Say 'cat.'" I will always label this type of example as _____ training.

### *Helpful Hint #6*

People sometimes use either an imitative stimulus or a verbal description as a prompt in fading or programming. You have encountered examples in which Mom points to the cat and says, "What is that? Say 'cat.'" If she then fades out "cat" by saying "ca" and then "c," she is using an imitative stimulus. However, because she eventually fades it out, I will consider this an example of fading, not imitation training. In general, if a procedure uses either an imitative stimulus or a verbal description as a temporary prompt, I will consider the correct label for the procedure to be either fading or programming.

14. If a procedure uses an imitative stimulus as a temporary prompt to train a specific discrimination, I will consider the correct label for the procedure to be _____ _____.

## Additional Readings

Bandura, A. (1971). *Psychological modeling: Conflicting theories.* Chicago: Aldine-Atherton. This is an excellent source book for a broader understanding of imitation training and various psychological theories of imitation.

Brawley, E. R., Allen, K. D., Fleming, R. S., & Peterson, R. F. (1969). Behavior modification of an autistic child. *Behavioral Science, 14,* 87–97. Systematic reinforcement procedures were used to strengthen appropriate behaviors, such as talking and following instructions. Extinction was used to weaken inappropriate behaviors, such as the child's hitting himself and throwing a tantrum. These procedures were used with effectiveness in therapy sessions three times a week. Generalization was programmed by involving ward personnel in the reinforcement and extinction procedures.

Garcia, E., Guess, D., & Byrnes, J. (1973). Development of syntax in a retarded girl using procedures of imitation, reinforcement, and modeling. *Journal of Applied Behavior Analysis, 6,* 299–310. This article describes the effectiveness of using imitation training for developing complex speech patterns in a person with severe retardation.

Kennedy, D. A., & Thompson, I. (1967). The use of reinforcement techniques with a first grade boy. *Personality and Guidance Journal, 46,* 366–370. In this case report, a child taught to pay attention in a counselor's office also paid attention more closely in the classroom. This example involved spontaneous generalization because the behavior modifier did not have to reinforce the child for paying attention in the classroom.

## Programmed Reading

I will present questions over the following six topics: (1) Copying Behavior, (2) Following Instructions, (3) Imitation Training versus Instructional Training, (4) Research on Use of Instructions, (5) Another Tactic, and (6) Review.

### 1. Copying Behavior

51. Pre-test: When Sally copies Ted's demonstration of how to start the computer program, you call Sally's behavior the _____.

45. Pre-test: Ted shows Sally how to start the computer program. Call his demonstration of how to start the program the _____.

37. Pre-test: After Ted demonstrates for Sally how to start the program and Sally copies the demonstration by starting it herself, Ted must _____ Sally's moves.

48. Pre-test: The three elements of imitation training are: (1) The teacher provides the _____, (2) the student produces the _____, and (3) the teacher then _____ the imitative behavior (assuming it is correct).

49. Pre-test: What procedure has the teacher demonstrate a behavior, the learner copy the demonstration, and the teacher reinforce correct copies? _____

63. The goal of this module is to teach imitation training. You call the act of showing a learner how to perform a behavior the

*imitative stimulus*. You then ask them to perform the behavior. You call their behavior the *imitative behavior*. You then reinforce their imitative behavior, if they perform it. You call the procedure that presents an imitative stimulus, looks for an imitative behavior, and reinforces it _____ training.

97. You need to learn about each of the three elements of imitation training. The first element involves showing a person how to do something. You call the behavioral demonstration the _____ (imitation, imitative) stimulus.

81. When the teacher demonstrates how to do something, the teacher's behavior becomes a <u>stimulus</u> for the learner. That is why you call the teacher's behavior the imitative _____.

82. When the teacher demonstrates how to do something, you call the teacher's demonstration the _____ stimulus.

11. Dad shows Jimmy how to throw a curve ball. Call his demonstration of how to throw the curve ball the _____ _____.

92. You have now learned the first element of imitation training. It involves: (1) demonstrating a behavior to the learner. You call this demonstration the _____ _____. (2) The learner then copies the demonstration. You call that copy the imitative behavior. (3) The teacher then reinforces the correct behavior.

65. The second element of imitation training is the learner's copying of the teacher's demonstration. You call the learner's copying of the demonstration the _____ (imitation, imitative) behavior.

88. You call the demonstration of how to perform a behavior during imitation training the imitative _____; you call the copying of that performance by the learner the imitative _____.

76. When Jimmy copies Dad's demonstration of how to throw a curve ball, you call Jimmy's behavior the _____.

93. You have now learned both elements of imitation training. (1) It involves demonstrating a behavior to the learner. You

call this demonstration the imitative stimulus. (2) The learner then copies the demonstration. You call that copy the _____. (3) The teacher then reinforces the correct behavior.

68. The third element of imitation training is reinforcement. After the teacher provides the imitative stimulus and the student provides the imitative behavior, the teacher then _____ the imitative behavior (and the student provides the correct imitative stimulus).

3. After Dad demonstrates for Jimmy how to throw a curve ball and Jimmy copies the demonstration by throwing a curve ball himself, Dad must _____ Jimmy's throw.

94. You have now learned the third element of imitation training. It involves: (1) demonstrating a behavior to the learner. You call this demonstration the imitative stimulus. (2) The learner then copies the demonstration. You call that copy the imitative behavior. (3) The teacher then _____ the correct behavior.

71. What procedure has the teacher demonstrate a behavior, the learner copy the demonstration, and the teacher reinforce correct copying? _____

18. Here is a summary of the three elements. (1) The teacher provides the _____ _____, (2) the student produces the _____, and (3) the teacher then _____ the imitative behavior (assuming it is correct).

56. Suppose that the learner is reinforced for producing imitative behavior #1 in the presence of imitative stimulus #1 but not in the presence of imitative stimulus #2. This form of imitation training would be an example of what behavioral procedure? _____ (discrimination, generalization) training.

72. When a father demonstrates to a child how to hold a football in order to throw it, the father is producing a(n) _____ _____ stimulus.

32. Notice that the two elements of imitation training start with *–imatat"* and end with *–ive*, whereas the name of the procedure ends with _____.

16. Dr. Winett showed families a videotape of a family changing its food habits in hopes of changing the viewers' food-buying habits. The family on videotape made a healthy shopping list, went shopping, and prepared more nutritious meals. Because the videotape demonstrates how to eat healthily, it would be called a(n) _____.

55. Suppose Mom shows Jimmy how to fry an egg and reinforces him when he does it correctly but ignores him when he does not. Suppose she also shows Jimmy how to soft-boil an egg and reinforces him when he does it correctly but ignores him when he does not. Clearly Mom is using imitation training in this example. However, would behavior analysts label this complex procedure as *differential reinforcement* or *discrimination training*? _____

### 2. Following Instructions

35. Pre-test: After Sally explains how to integrate a function, Ted might integrate X to get X-squared. His integration would be called _____.

44. Pre-test: Sally explains to Ted how to integrate a function. Sally's explanation is called a(n) _____.

36. Pre-test: After Sally explains to Ted how to integrate a function and he correctly integrates X, Sally must be sure to _____ his response.

42. Pre-test: Instructional training involves explaining to someone how to perform a behavior. You call the explanation a(n) _____. You call the learner's correct performance the _____. The teacher then must _____ the instructed behavior.

52. Pre-test: When you explain to someone how to perform a behavior and then reinforce her if she does so, you are using the behavioral procedure of _____.

64. The goal of this module is to teach instructional training. When you explain to someone how to perform a behavior and then reinforce him if he does so, you

are using the behavioral procedure of instructional _____.

29. Instructional training has three elements. First, you describe the behavior. You call this description the <u>verbal description</u>. Second, the learner performs the behavior. You call their performance <u>instructed behavior</u>. Third, you <u>reinforce</u> correct instructed behavior. You call this procedure _____ (imitation, instructional) training.

58. The first element of instructional training involves describing to someone how to do something. Because the teacher gives a <u>description</u> of the desired behavior, you call the first element a verbal _____.

83. When the teacher explains how to do something, the teacher's behavior is <u>verbal</u>. That is why you call the teacher's explaining behavior the _____ description.

10. Dad explains to Jimmy how to square a number: "You multiply the number by itself." Dad's explanation is called a(n) _____.

95. You have now learned the first element of instructional training. (1) The teacher provides a(n) _____. (2) The learner performs the <u>instructed behavior</u>. (3) The teacher <u>reinforces</u> correct instructed behavior.

66. The second element of instructional training is the person following the instructions correctly. His instruction-following behavior is called instructed _____.

6. After the teacher provides the verbal instructions, the student performs the _____ behavior.

4. After Dad explains how to square a number, Jimmy then might square 8 to get 64. His squaring of the number would be called _____.

96. You have now learned the second element of instructional training. (1) The teacher provides a <u>verbal description</u>. (2) The learner performs the _____. (3) The teacher <u>reinforces</u> correct instructed behavior.

57. The explanation of how to perform a behavior in instructional training is

called the _____ description. The performance of that behavior by the learner is called _____ behavior.

67. The third element in instructional training is reinforcing the student for correct instructed behavior. After giving the verbal description, a trainer using instructional training must be sure to _____ the person's correct responses.

5. After Dad explains to Jimmy how to square a number and Jimmy correctly squares 8, Dad must be sure to _____ _____ Jimmy's response.

30. Instructional training involves explaining to someone how to perform a behavior. You call the explanation a(n)_____ _____. You call the learner's correct performance the _____. _____ The teacher then must _____ the instructed behavior.

86. When you explain to someone how to perform a behavior and then reinforce them if they do so, you are using the behavioral procedure of _____.

### 3. Imitation versus Instructional Training

50. Pre-test: When May starts the computer program the way Phil explained to her, you should label what she did to start the program as the _____.

41. Pre-test: Imitation training involves demonstrating a behavior to the learner. You call this demonstration the _____ _____.

43. Pre-test: Mom shows Timmy how to tie his shoes by tying her own, watching him tie his shoes, and praising him when he does a good job. You should label Mom's tying her own shoes as _____ _____.

84. When you demonstrate how to perform a behavior and then reinforce your student for correctly copying your demonstration, you are using what behavioral procedure? _____ When you explain to someone how to perform a behavior and then reinforce that person for doing so, you are using what behavioral procedure? _____

17. Here are a few items to sharpen your ability to tell the difference between imitation training and instructional training. Mom explains to Pete how to use the TV remote control and then reinforces him when he does it correctly. She is using what procedure? _____ training

33. Pete shows Mom how to draw a box with the computer mouse and then reinforces her for correctly doing it. What procedure is Pete using? _____ training

79. When Pete shows Mom how to grill a marshmallow and then reinforces her for doing it, he is using what procedure? _____ training

78. When Mom tells Pete how to fry an egg and then reinforces him for frying a beautiful egg, she is using what procedure? _____ training

75. When Bob tells Ann how to outline a chapter, you should label his description as a(n) _____.

77. When Karen writes out the solution to the same set of differential equations as Professor Brainbuster had demonstrated on the blackboard, you should label what she writes as the _____.

25. Imitation training involves demonstrating a behavior to the learner. You call this demonstration the _____.

80. When Professor Brainbuster shows how to solve a set of differential equations on the blackboard, you should label what he writes on the blackboard as a(n) _____.

74. When Ann outlines a chapter the way that Bob had told her to, you should label her outlining as the _____.

73. When a teacher provides an imitative stimulus, a learner emits an imitative behavior, and the teacher reinforces the correct behavior, the teacher is using what procedure? _____

31. Notice that behavior analysts refer to the teacher's behavior in imitation training as a stimulus. That is because the behavior serves as a stimulus for the student. Notice that behavior analysts refer to the copying by the student of the teacher's behavior as imitative _____.

26. In imitation training, then, the teacher's behavior is called the imitative _____, whereas the student's behavior is called the imitative _____.

27. In the presence of verbal description #1, the learner will be reinforced for performing instructed behavior #1. In the presence of verbal description #2, the learner will be extinguished for performing instructed behavior #1. This is a kind of discrimination training. In discrimination training, you would call verbal description #1 what kind of a stimulus? It is a(n) _____ for instructed behavior #1.

22. If you think that an example is instructional rather than imitation training, you may check your analysis by asking the question, "Did the teacher _____ (demonstrate, describe) the correct behavior?"

### 4. Research on Use of Instructions

53. Pre-test: When you show someone how to perform a behavior and then reinforce him if he copies you, you are using the behavioral procedure of _____ training.

40. Pre-test: If you describe to someone how to perform a behavior and then reinforce her if she follows your instructions, you are using the behavioral procedure of _____ training.

19. Here's a question based on a prior lesson: If the teacher describes to learners how to do something, watches them try to do it, but fails to reinforce them, what schedule of reinforcement is the learner's instructed behavior on if their rate of imitating decreases? _____

12. Dr. Ayllon instructed long-term mental patients to pick up and use eating utensils at meals. This was largely ineffective until they gave tokens for following instructions. Most patients then began using utensils. Because giving tokens increased the rate of instructed behavior, the token is called a(n) _____.

7. Behavior therapists have diagnosed many of the problems experienced by "normal" adults as resulting from faulty self-instructions that they repeat to themselves. Since telling yourself what to do is itself doing something, behavior analysts regard self-instructions as _____.

8. Behavior therapists regard self-instructions as verbal behavior. Therefore, they assume that ignoring undesirable self-instructions will reduce their frequency as an example of the behavioral procedure called _____.

1. Parents teach a child to follow one instruction. They give the instruction and then reinforce the child for following it. When the child learns that first instruction, they teach a second instruction, then a third, and so on. The child soon starts to follow most new instructions even without immediate reinforcement. Because the parents have reinforced instruction following in a series of situations until it occurs with a novel instruction, the parent has used what procedure? _____

15. Dr. Lombard told swimmers how they could protect themselves from sunburn. You would label the explanation as giving a(n) _____. The lifeguards demonstrated how to avoid sunburn by wearing t-shirts, sunglasses, hats, zinc oxide, and sun screen. You would label their demonstration as a(n) _____.

9. Both imitation training and instructional training increase the probability that learners will perform the desired behavior by including as the third element, the procedure of _____ for correctly performed behavior.

24. Imitation training and instructional training are forms of _____ training. These procedures are most effective with people who imitate novel imitative stimuli and follow novel verbal instructions. People can be taught to imitate novel imitative stimuli and to follow novel verbal instructions through _____ training.

87. When you show people how to perform a behavior and then reinforce them if they copy you, you are using the behavioral procedure of _____ training.

85. When you describe to someone how to perform a behavior and then reinforce her if she follows your instructions, you are using the behavioral procedure of _____ training.

13. Dr. Hollandsworth provided a verbal description to Herbert of how to make

clear responses to interview questions. Dr. Hollandsworth then observed his performance in a simulated interview session and reinforced correct performance. Dr. Hollandsworth used the behavioral procedure of _____ _____.

14. Dr. Hollandsworth showed Herbert how to ask questions designed to clarify interview questions. Dr. Hollandsworth watched Herbert ask questions in a simulated interview situation and reinforced correct performance. Dr. Hollandsworth use the behavioral procedure of _____.

### 5. Another Tactic

46. Pre-test: The fourth tactic in using the stimulus control strategy to help solve human problems is to create complex stimulus control through _____ training and _____ training.

59. The fourth tactic in using the stimulus control strategy to help solve human problems is to create complex stimulus control through imitation training and instructional _____ (stimuli, training).

60. The fourth tactic in using the stimulus control strategy to help solve human problems is to create complex stimulus control through imitation training and _____ training.

61. The fourth tactic in using the stimulus control strategy to help solve human problems is to create complex stimulus control through _____ training and _____ training.

62. The fourth tactic involves two procedures. The first procedure this lesson presented for modifying behavior involves demonstrating to another person how to perform a behavior. You call this procedure _____ (imitation, instructional) training. The second procedure this lesson presented involves describing to another person how to perform a behavior. You call that procedure _____ training.

### 6. Review

39. Pre-test: If an instructor provides a behavioral demonstration of what another person is supposed to do, the instructor's behavior is called the _____.

38. Pre-test: Demonstrating to other people how to perform a behavior, watching them do it, and then reinforcing successful performance is using what behavioral procedure? _____

47. Pre-test: The fourth tactic in using the stimulus control strategy to help solve human problems is to create complex stimulus control through _____ training or _____ training.

34. Pre-test: A teacher describes a behavior that he or she would like a learner to produce; this description would be called a(n) _____.
(Hint: It is not called an instruction.)

90. You can use the stimulus control strategy to help solve human problems by (3) creating new stimulus control by temporarily using prompts and by (4) creating complex stimulus control through _____ training and _____ training.

21. If a learner produces a behavior that someone else describes verbally, the learner's behavior would be an example of _____ behavior.

54. Remember that imitation training is a type of discrimination training. Because an imitative stimulus is associated with reinforcement for the imitative behavior, the technical term for that imitative stimulus is _____.

23. Imitation training and instructional training will be effective only if the person's imitative or instructed behavior is _____.

20. If a learner copies the behavior of another person, you call the learner's behavior _____ behavior.

2. A person can learn from a lecture in two ways: (1) by doing what the lecturer tells him to do, which would be an example of _____ training, and (2) by repeating arguments and information contained in the lecture, which would be an example of _____ training.

69. The three parts of imitation training are the _____, the _____, and reinforcement.

89. You call the use of verbal descriptions of behavior and reinforcement to teach a new behavior _____.

28. Instructional training is a particular kind of discrimination training. Because the verbal description is associated with reinforcement for the instructed behavior, the technical term for a verbal description is _____.

70. The three parts of instructional training are a(n) _____, the _____, and reinforcement.

91. You can use the stimulus control strategy to help solve human problems by (3) creating new stimulus control by temporarily using _____; and by (4) creating complex stimulus control through imitation training or _____ training.

## Programmed Examples

### 1. Programmed Examples

13. Pre-test: Ada had a lot of trouble teaching Billy to field the ball. He kept taking his eyes off the ball. Ada hit several balls right to him. When he kept his eyes on the ball, she praised him. When he took his eyes off the ball, she did not praise him. Billy started keeping his eyes on the ball more and more often. What procedure did Ada use by praising Billy when he kept his eyes on the ball and ignoring him when he did not? _____

15. Pre-test: Sam was the best pitcher on the team, but he tended to take his eye off the catcher's mitt when he was throwing. This behavior often led to his missing the strike zone. So Ada patiently explained to Sam exactly where to look when he was pitching. She then had him throw several pitches while she was watching and praised him when he did it right. What procedure did Ada use by explaining where to look and praising him when he did? _____

16. Pre-test: Tiny Tim's mother often showed him a picture of a sailboat and asked him, "What is that?" She praised him when he said "boat." She later showed him a picture of

the Queen Mary and asked him what it was. She praised him when he said "boat." Later, she showed him a picture of many novel boats, and he always labeled them as "boats." What behavioral procedure had she used? _____

14. Pre-test: Mrs. Price asked Gladys, "What does 'eight squared' equal?" She also asked, "What does 'four squared' equal?" She praised Gladys when she answered "sixty-four" to the first question but ignored her when she said "sixty-four" to the second question. To help her, she showed Gladys a set of eight rows of eight dots. Over time, Mrs. Price permitted Gladys to look at dots that were harder and harder to see. Eventually Gladys "knew" that 8 x 8 equaled 64 even without looking at the dots. What behavioral procedure did Mrs. Price use to teach Gladys the value of 8 to the second power? _____

12. One night at dinner, Tiny Tim's father said, "Pass the salt." Since Tiny Tim did not yet speak very well, his father was surprised when Tim passed the salt. Father managed to say "Thank you" and act pleased enough to make Tim feel like a hero. After that, Tiny Tim always passed the salt when asked to and he always looked very grown up and pleased about doing so. When Father said, "Pass the salt," he gave a verbal _____ of the desired behavior. By passing the salt, Tim performed the instructed _____. His father's pleased reaction clearly served as a(n) _____ for Tim. This is clearly an example of instructional training because Father _____ (demonstrated, described) the desired behavior.

18. Tiny Tim got a wooden puzzle involving different geometric shapes. However, he wasn't able to put the shapes into the right holes, so his mother showed him where to put each piece. She took the piece from Tim, put it into the right hole, and then gave it back to Tim. Tim put the right piece into the right hole immediately. Mother beamed at him, gave him a kiss, and said "Good, Timmy." She continued this procedure with each piece. This example of imitation training consists of three parts. (1) Mother shows Tim where to put the puzzle

piece—called the _____ stimulus. (2) Tim's putting the puzzle piece in correctly—called the _____ behavior. (3) Tim's mother beaming, kissing, and praising—called the _____. This is clearly an example of imitation training because Mom _____ _____ (demonstrated, described) the desired behavior.

17. The first time Tom heard Judy say "cool," he didn't pay any attention. But after she said "cool" a few more times, he started saying "cool" and found that she listened to him a lot more closely. When Judy said "cool," she demonstrated a new behavior. Tom copied her behavior. Judy then listened more closely when he said "cool." Therefore, you would call Judy's saying "cool" a(n) _____ _____ for Tom's copying behavior. You would call Tom's saying "cool" an example of _____. The fact that Judy started listening more closely to Tom might be a(n) _____ for saying "cool." Judy accidentally used what behavioral procedure to teach Tom to say "cool"? _____ _____ (Did Judy <u>demonstrate</u> the behavior, or did she <u>describe</u> it?)

10. Marcia came from a small rural farm to start college. She looked square and never got any dates. Amy, her roommate, gave Marcia informal instructions about what clothing styles were "in" and how to apply makeup. Marcia followed Amy's instructions by buying some new clothes and putting on makeup. She looked much more collegiate. Amy told her how nice she looked. Marcia had succeeded in changing her look to fit college. She got many dates. Amy's instructions would be called a(n) _____ of the hipper new behavior. Marcia's behaviors of buying some new clothes and applying makeup are examples of _____. Amy's compliment and getting dates would be an example of two _____ that kept Marcia following her Amy's instructions. Amy accidentally used what procedure to change Marcia's behavior? _____

4. Dr. Morris always worked an example of the latest type of math problem on the board before she asked her class to work any problems. By doing this, she taught them how to organize their work—where to write the different parts of the answer and how much of

the answer to show. She then gave the children an assignment of similar problems to work in class. As they worked, she walked around the room and indicated to them whether they were doing the problems correctly. This procedure of teaching the children how to organize their answers would be called _____. (Hint: Did she demonstrate or describe how to work the problems?) The children's behavior is called _____.

19. Tiny Tim's mother showed him a picture of a robin and asked him, "What is that? Is it a bird?" Tim agreed and said, "bird," to his mother's obvious delight. She showed him the picture of the robin later and repeated the question but said "bird" much more softly. Tim said, "That's a bird." He could still identify the picture as a bird after his mother stopped saying "bird." She then showed him a picture of a bluejay and repeated the same procedure. After she had stopped giving the hint, Tim could still identify the bluejay as a bird. His mother then showed him many other pictures of birds, and he always labeled them as birds. Tiny Tim's mother used temporary hints to teach him to label a series of birds as birds. She reinforced him for his response until he labeled novel birds as birds. Because she used prompts to teach him, you should name her procedure _____.

9. John had never used the table saw. John asked his father if he could use it to make a doghouse for his new collie. His father cut the first piece of wood for him. In the process, his father demonstrated how to measure the wood, how to set the saw blade at the right height, how to guide the wood through safely, and several other aspects of correct use of the saw. John then cut a piece with his father watching. His father praised John's efforts and left him to cut the rest of the wood. By showing John how to use the table saw, father used what procedure to train John to use the power saw? _____ _____ (Ask whether Dad demonstrated or described.)

8. Jan wanted some new clothes for her vacation trip. She asked her mother to show her how to use the sewing machine. Her mother didn't have time to show her but did explain in some detail how to use it. Jan followed

her mother's explanation and sewed several articles of clothing for her vacation. What procedure did Jan's mother use to change Jan's behavior with respect to the sewing machine? _____ Successfully sewing the clothing would probably be a(n) _____ for Jan's following her mother's explanation. The mother's explanation would be called a(n) _____.

6. Henry was writing a book. He typed a rough draft of each chapter himself and then gave that copy to a typist to produce a polished copy. However, he found that the polished copy wasn't always perfect. If he left any abbreviations in the copy that he gave the typist, she did not complete the abbreviation (as a whole word) but, rather, just copied it. Thus, he found that he had to type the entire word if he wanted it to appear in the final copy. Henry started typing the entire word and stopped using abbreviations. Because the typist did not type the full word when Henry used an abbreviation, and his rate of using abbreviations decreased, you would say that Henry's use of abbreviations was on what schedule of reinforcement? _____ Because his typing full words led to full words in his polished copy, and his rate of typing full words increased, you would say that Henry's typing full words was on what schedule? _____ Henry's typing behavior changed in that he started typing whole words and stopped typing abbreviations. What behavioral procedure accounted for this change? _____

3. Children often learn cursive writing by seeing examples of the properly formed letters and words. Then, the children are required to copy these letters over and over again. The teacher usually praises correct copies. The examples of properly formed letters that the children copy would be called _____. Showing the children examples and praising good copies is an example of what procedure for teaching writing?_____

7. I am going to give you some complex examples to help you tell the difference between all the procedures. This will help you on your test. Here's the first complex example. Ada was a little-league baseball coach. She had the children hit ground balls

to her while she demonstrated the essential elements of fielding them. These elements included getting her body in front of the ball, kneeling, and keeping her eye on the ball. Then, she hit some ground balls and had the children try to field them. When they fielded the ball correctly, she praised them. What procedure was Ada using when she showed them how to field ground balls and then praised them when they fielded correctly? _____

5. Gordie was a good hitter, but Ada felt that he could be much better. His main problem was that he swung at bad pitches—pitches that were not thrown over the plate. So Ada got out on the mound and threw several pitches. Sometimes she threw pitches right over the plate, and sometimes she threw bad pitches. She had Gordie stand at the plate and call "strike" for the good ones. She praised him when he called "strike" in the presence of a good pitch and ignored him when he called strike in the presence of a bad pitch. She hoped this procedure would teach him which pitches were worth swinging at. What procedure was she using to teach Gordie to call "strike" only for the good pitches? _____

2. Ann took Billy to the zoo and showed him an owl and a chicken. She pointed to first one, then the other, and asked him, "What is that?" She praised him when he said "owl" when looking at the owl but ignored him when he said "chicken" while looking at the owl. She also praised him when he said "chicken" while looking at the chicken but ignored him when he said "owl" while looking at the chicken. You call the owl a(n) _____ for Billy's behavior of calling it an "owl." However, you call the chicken a(n) _____ for Billy's behavior of calling it an "owl."

11. Mrs. Price praised Gladys for saying "eighty-one" when asked, "What does nine to the second power equal?" but not for saying anything else. She also praised Gladys for saying "forty-nine" when asked, "What does seven times seven equal?" but not for saying anything else. What complex behavioral procedure did Mrs. Price use? _____

1. After Gladys had learned the value of 7, 8, and 9 squared, Mrs. Price asked her, "What is ten squared?" Gladys thought

a moment, realized that she had simply multiplied 7x7 to get the value of 7 squared and that she had done the same for 8 and 9, and simply multiplied 10x10 to get 100. The occurrence of Gladys multiplying the number by itself to find its square for a new number would be an example of what behavioral process? _____

20. Turning around while on skis can be a very complicated process unless you know how to do it. Debby showed Felix how to do it. First, you take your right ski and kick it in the air right in front of you with the back end dug into the snow. Then, you pivot it to the right so that the tip is pointing backwards and you are standing with your right foot pointed backwards. Then, you simply bring your left ski around and place it parallel to your right ski, and you are turned around. Felix tried it. Turning around so easily reinforced using this method. Debby used what behavioral procedure to train Felix to turn around on skis? _____ (This is a situation in which imitation training is far superior to instructional training, as you now realize!)

# Conditioned Reinforcers and Everyday Situations

## Reading Section

Reinforcing events rooted in our biological nature influence our behavior from birth. Behavior analysts call these events *primary reinforcers*. They include food, water, sex, and reasonable temperatures. The events that serve as primary reinforcers tend to be pretty much the same for everyone.

Reinforcing events other than primary reinforcers also influence our behavior. These events grow out of our experience. Behavior analysts call these events *conditioned reinforcers*. They might include such events as our mother's smile, the opportunity to wear blue jeans, or first prize in a contest. The list of such events varies enormously from person to person and society to society. Many behavioral problems result from the absence of appropriate conditioned reinforcers. Behavior analysts solve this problem by creating conditioned reinforcers. This lesson introduces you to three behavioral procedures designed to create them.

Tactic #5 in the stimulus control strategy is making reinforcement more practical by creating <u>conditioned reinforcers</u>.

1. Tactic #5 in the stimulus control strategy is making reinforcement more practical by creating _____ reinforcers.

## Definition of Primary and Secondary Reinforcer

A **primary reinforcer** is any reinforcer that loses its effectiveness only temporarily through <u>satiation</u>. In other words, a primary reinforcer is any event that is always

reinforcing unless someone has had too much of it recently. The effectiveness of such reinforcers is not based on learning. Rather it is based on the unlearned biological effects they produce in us.

2. Any reinforcer that loses its effectiveness only temporarily through <u>satiation</u> is known as a(n) _____ reinforcer.

Behavior analysts often use primary reinforcers to teach new skills. For example, researchers used food to teach children to hold still for brain scans (Slifer, Cataldo, Cataldo, Llorente, & Gersen, 1993). Researchers taught teenagers with retardation to name a snack item by giving them bites of that item (Schussler & Spradlin, 1991). Food is the most common primary reinforcer used by behavior analysts.

Behavior analysts observe that the reinforcing effect of some events is less durable than primary reinforcers. These events start out as "neutral" events, events without reinforcing power. They become reinforcers after being paired with other reinforcers. If mother always smiles at her baby before feeding him, her smile may become as effective as the milk itself. Basic researchers have not fully established the necessary and sufficient conditions that create these reinforcers (Kelleher & Gollub, 1962; Williams, 1994). One hypothesis is that any event that "signals" the delivery of another reinforcer will become reinforcing itself (Rachlin, 1976). In any event, the pairing of an existing reinforcer and a neutral event is a necessary part of the process. They call these events conditioned reinforcers.

A **conditioned** reinforcer is a reinforcer that loses its effectiveness permanently through <u>unpaired</u> presentations. Earlier you learned about an experiment designed to treat a woman who hoarded towels (Ayllon, 1963). Why did the towels reinforce hoarding behavior? The researchers guessed that the towels were paired with attendants coming to take them back. They knew that the attendants rarely gave the patients any attention otherwise. They solved the problem by instructing the attendants to give the woman all the towels she wanted. They no longer picked them up. This stopped the pairing of attention and towels. Hoarding towels was no longer reinforcing. This is a good example of the mechanism underlying the establishment and elimination of events as conditioned reinforcers.

3. A **conditioned reinforcer**: A reinforcer that permanently loses its effectiveness through _____ presentations.

A **backup reinforcer** is any reinforcer that makes a <u>conditioned</u> or <u>generalized</u> reinforcer effective. As its name indicates, it "backs up" the conditioned reinforcer, strengthening it. The effectiveness of the towels as conditioned reinforcers depended on being "backed up" by the attention of the attendants. Often you can think of "spending" the conditioned reinforcer to "buy" the backup reinforcer. While talking about the towel hoarder spending her towels to buy attention from the attendants is strained, you will encounter many examples for which the analogy is quite helpful. (You will learn about generalized reinforcers in the next section.)

4. Behavior analysts call the reinforcer that makes a conditioned or generalized reinforcer effective, a(n) _____ reinforcer.

Behavior analysts usually use conditioned reinforcers when reinforcing desirable behavior. They often use conditioned reinforcers based on gestures, timers, and verbal statements that they can give immediately after the desired response (e.g., Lalli, Mauro, & Mace, 2000). Probably the most common conditioned reinforcers are social. For example, researchers used immediate praise to teach naming snack items to children (Schussler & Spradlin, 1991).

They then gave a bite of the snack item itself. The bite served as the backup reinforcer for the praise. Other researchers praised children whenever they sounded out the spelling of words (Gettinger, 1993). They used no specific backup reinforcers. Other researchers used points to teach Chris to maintain eye contact (Koegel & Frea, 1993). Chris could spend his points to buy the right to play video games. You can see that conditioned reinforcers can be backed up with primary or other conditioned reinforcers. They may also be used without backups.

The effectiveness of a conditioned reinforcer is affected by the person's deprivation with respect to the backup reinforcer. If the person is not deprived of the backup reinforcer, the conditioned reinforcer won't work. For example, suppose the attendants gave attention to the towel hoarder for many other behaviors. Hoarding towels would not be the only response that led to more attention. The woman would be relatively satiated with attention. Thus, the towels would not be as effective a reinforcer.

Conditioned reinforcers are often events that occur immediately after the person has made a response. Often they are not very powerful events. However, they are associated with the delivery of delayed events that are powerful. Thus, they can be effective because of their immediacy. Behavior analysts take advantage of this immediacy by creating conditioned reinforcers that help bridge the gap to delayed reinforcers (e.g., Grindle & Remington, 2002). For example, a behavior analyst may give praise immediately after a desired behavior and deliver the more valuable backup reinforcer when it is convenient.

Surprisingly, sometimes primary reinforcers are not as effective as conditioned reinforcers. Researchers have used conditioned reinforcers to solve two types of eating problems (see Patel, Piazza, Martinez, Volkert, & Santana, 2002). In one type of eating problem, children refuse food to the point of suffering weight problems. Researchers used praise to teach children to swallow food (Greer, Dorow, Williams, McCorkle, & Asnes, 1991). In another type of eating problem, children refuse to eat some kinds of foods. Researchers taught parents to use contingent attention to teach their children to eat foods they had to chew (Werle, Murphy, & Budd, 1993). In both types of eating problems, behavior analysts used conditioned reinforcers to teach children to consume primary reinforcers. In other words, the conditioned reinforcers were stronger than the primary reinforcers!

In other cases, the very strength of primary reinforcers is the problem. Psychoactive drugs presumably are effective reinforcers because of their biological effects. Researchers worked with two cocaine addicts (Budney, Higgins, Delaney, Kent, & Bickel, 1991). They tested these men for drug use weekly. When they were "clean," the researchers reinforced them with purchased items. These included movie tickets, sporting goods, and dinner certificates. This procedure produced evidence of stopping cocaine use five months after treatment. It is ironic that the researchers used conditioned reinforcers to overcome the effects of primary reinforcers.

# Definition of Generalized Reinforcers

Behavior analysts create and use very powerful reinforcers called *generalized reinforcers*. A **generalized reinforcer** is a conditioned reinforcer that is associated with <u>many</u> other reinforcers. A generalized reinforcer depends for its effectiveness on its backup reinforcers. It would lose it effectiveness if it were no longer paired with those backups. It would also lose its effectiveness for a person who is satiated on all of its backups. Money is the most obvious example of a generalized reinforcer. It is backed up with any reinforcer that can be purchased. If you could no longer purchase desired items, it would permanently lose its effectiveness. Such a calamity occurred when the money issued by the southern Confederacy lost its value after the Civil War. As with simple conditioned reinforcers, you can always talk about spending a generalized reinforcer to buy its backup reinforcers.

5. A **generalized reinforcer**: A conditioned reinforcer that is associated with _____ _____ (many, one) backup reinforcer(s).

Generalized reinforcers are more uniformly effective than other conditioned reinforcers. You usually remain deprived of at least one backup reinforcer. As long as you are deprived of at least one backup, the generalized reinforcer will remain effective. Even if you satiate on food after dinner at a restaurant, you might still buy a drink, a movie, or a new car. Generalized reinforcers differ in this respect from primary reinforcers. You can easily satiate on any primary reinforcer. You will not be reinforced by it again until you are deprived of it. Generalized reinforcers differ in the same way from other conditioned reinforcers. You can satiate on the backup reinforcer for a conditioned reinforcer. You will not again be reinforced by it until you are deprived. You are less likely to become satiated on all of the reinforcers backing up a generalized reinforcer—thus the saying that "you can't have too much money!"

Social approval is a more subtle example of a generalized reinforcer. If someone approves of you, you can expect a wide variety of favors from that person. These might include loans of money, invitations to parties, general assistance, and even dates. Because social approval is associated with so many backup reinforcers, it is a generalized reinforcer. In a way, you spend some of the person's approval to buy specific favors from them. If you ask for too much, you may find that you haven't built up *that* much good will.

Another advantage of generalized reinforcers is that they can be delivered immediately after the behavior occurs. The various backup reinforcers usually cannot be delivered immediately. Therefore, the generalized reinforcer can enhance the effectiveness of the backup reinforcers by utilizing the *principle of immediacy*.

Behavior analysts frequently use token systems. A token system is a local monetary system backed up by available reinforcers. For example, a token system was used by a teacher to increase the number of difficult math problems completed in class by students poor in math (e.g., Martens, Ardoin, Hilt, Lannie, Panahon, & Wolfe, 2002). The teacher gave the student tokens for completing the problems. When they had earned enough tokens, they could obtain candy, shopping, file folders, or a

**Figure 20-1.** Ted Ayllon developed the most influential token economy in the early 1960s. His work led to the use of token economies by numerous other behavior analysts. (Source: Courtesy of Ted Ayllon)

"good work" certificate. The students completed far more problems when reinforced by tokens. In another example, researchers used a token system to encourage boys to exercise on a stationary bicycle (DeLuca & Holborn, 1992). By exercising, the boys earned points that they could spend on a kite, flashlight, model car or plane, puzzle, or comic books. Their rate of exercise doubled because of this system.

Behavior analysts have used token systems to solve many behavioral problems. Researchers used tokens to help 8-year-old deaf children to improve their social skills (Rasing & Duker, 1992). They used them to assist chronic mental patients in learning self-care and productive work behaviors (Ayllon & Azrin, 1965). They used them in settings such as institutions for children with severe retardation (Birnbrauer, Bijou, Wolf, & Kidder, 1965). They have used them to help poor people remain involved in self-help groups (Miller & Miller, 1970).

Point systems are like a credit-card economy. No actual token changes hands, but someone records points earned and spent. They maintain a running balance for each person. Point systems have been used in a variety of settings, such as Achievement Place, a family-style alternative to reform school for delinquent youths (Phillips, 1968). Figure 20-2 outlines the point system used by Achievement Place. Youths who watched the news on TV (300 points), read 20 pages of a book (200 points), and did their homework (500 points) earned points. They could then spend the

---

### A Point System in the Nineteenth Century

Alexander Maconochie used a point system to run a nineteenth-century British penal colony. He found the penal colony "a hell but left it an orderly and well regulated community." Each prisoner started his time owing a number of points based on the seriousness of his crime. He earned points for good behavior while losing them for breaking prison rules. When he paid off what he owed, he went free. As Maconochie put it: "When a man keeps the key of his own prison, he is soon persuaded to fit it into the lock." Maconochie's superiors were disturbed by his unorthodox method and openly repudiated his successes, soon replacing him as head of the penal colony. Because the points would lose their effectiveness if prisoners could not spend them to buy release from prison, they are not primary reinforcers. (Based on Pitts, 1976.)

6. Because the points were backed up by only one reinforcer, they are _____ _____ (conditioned, generalized) reinforcers.

| A POINT SYSTEM FOR DELINQUENT YOUTHS | | | |
|---|---|---|---|
| How to earn points | | How to spend points | |
| 300 | Watching/reading news | 1000 | Get allowance |
| 500 | Clean room | 1000 | Use bicycle |
| 500 | Cleaning self | 1000 | Watch TV |
| 5 | Reading book | 500 | Play games |
| 20 | Help Houseparents* | 500 | Use tools |
| 500 | Doing dishes* | 1000 | Eat snacks |
| 100 | Dressing for dinner* | 1000 | Go uptown |
| 500 | Homework* | 1000 | Stay up |
| 500 | Good report card* | 1000 | Come home late |

*Minimum points shown, maximum up to 1000.

***Figure 20-2.*** The Achievement Place point system. Youths go to Achievement Place instead of reform school. The home is run by *teaching parents*, who live in the home and who award points to the youths for basic behaviors such as doing well in school, keeping themselves clean and neat, and helping around the home. The youths can use those points to buy privileges such as an allowance, snacks, staying up late, and watching TV. (Based on Phillips, 1968.)

points to buy a privilege, such as permission to come home late from school (1,000 points). Numerous experiments have shown that this system encourages the delinquent youths to engage in a wide range of constructive behaviors. Delinquents treated with this system did well in school, stayed out of trouble, and got jobs that led to a constructive and law-abiding role in the community (e.g., Fixsen, Phillips, Phillips, & Wolf, 1976; Kirigin, Braukmann, Atwater, & Wolf, 1982).

Systems of generalized reinforcers are an extremely powerful tool for producing behavioral change. The tokens or points maintain their effectiveness as reinforcers because they can buy a wide range of other reinforcers. They are simple to use with large numbers of individuals. They can be backed up with enough different events to ensure that almost everyone in the group will remain deprived of some potential reinforcer.

Groups can use a system of generalized reinforcement to develop a structure for their social environment. Groups can use this tool to develop behavior that they themselves define as desirable. They can thereby create democratically controlled systems of reinforcement. For example, welfare recipients have used tokens to pay people to attend meetings and to help themselves (Miller & Miller, 1970).

Students have used a point system to create cooperative residences that really work. They used points to pay members to prepare food, clean the house, and keep it repaired (Miller & Feallock, 1975). They used points to pay members to participate in managing the residence (Johnson, Welsh, Miller, & Altus, 1991). They used points to pay members to participate in democratic meetings that members like and use (Welsh, Johnson, Miller, Merrill, & Altus, 1989; Welsh, Miller, & Altus, 1994).

---

### You're Sending Me to the Principal's Office? Great!

Can you imagine a high school student saying "Great!" to that news? Well, they do at Pequea Valley High School in Kinzers, Pennsylvania. Teachers look for students who spontaneously pick up trash, help others carry books, or do other commendable activities. They write down the student's name and send it to the office. The teachers also send the names of students making outstanding academic achievements. These students are then "sent to the principal's office." But instead of punishment they receive praise. In addition, on a variable-ratio schedule, they get athletic tickets, McDonald's coupons, and other free prizes. (Based on Stein, 1990.)

7. The teachers tell the students, "I'm sending you to the principal's office." Because this comment is backed up by many reinforcers rather than just one, we call it a(n) _____ (conditioned, generalized, primary) reinforcer.

## Comparison of Different Types of Reinforcers

The book has already asked you to classify points in a penal colony. It will ask you to classify many more examples of reinforcers. You need to know how to classify these examples to fully understand the three kinds of reinforcers. Here are some considerations in the proper use of the three labels: conditioned reinforcer, generalized reinforcer, and primary reinforcer.

Primary reinforcers are pretty easy to spot. We all react to pretty much the same primary reinforcers. If you wish to classify an event that you think is a primary reinforcer, ask if it has a biological base. Ask if that event is likely to always be a reinforcer except when the person has had too much of it too recently. If you are pretty sure that it will always be a reinforcer because of its biological function, then it probably is a primary reinforcer.

Generalized reinforcers are also pretty easy to spot. They rely for the power on their pairing with more than one other reinforcer. I have mentioned several generalized reinforcers. Obviously money can buy many different reinforcers. Social approval usually leads to many other reinforcers. Token or point systems usually permit a person to trade for many backup reinforcers. If you think an event is a generalized reinforcer, just make sure that it is paired with many backup reinforcers.

The trickiest label to use may be conditioned reinforcer. The definition requires that a conditioned reinforcer lose its effectiveness if it is no longer paired with its backup reinforcer. Accordingly, a ticket to a football game is a reinforcer as long as you can go to the game (or sell the ticket). If you slept through the time of the game, the ticket is no longer worth anything, and it is no longer backed up with being able to attend the game. Therefore, the ticket is a conditioned reinforcer only while it is still valid. If the ticket had more than one backup, then you would call it a generalized reinforcer. When I ask you to classify an event as to type of reinforcer, I will always use the label *generalized reinforcer* for an event backed up by many reinforcers. I will always use the label *conditioned reinforcer* for an event backed up by only one reinforcer.

## Stimulus/Response Chains

Up to this point in the book, I have analyzed the occurrence or nonoccurrence of responses. However, most of our behavior is far more complex. We usually make many related responses in some kind of sequence. We don't take just one step; we walk somewhere. We don't say just one word; we engage in conversations. We don't just hit a baseball; we hit the ball, run toward first base, watch where the ball goes, and maybe try for second base. Thus, in most situations we don't engage in just one response over and over again. We engage in a series of responses, each one of which is influenced by the prior response.

Behavior analysts call sequences of related responses *stimulus/response chains* (often shortened to just *chains*). A **stimulus/response chain** is a sequence where each behavior produces an SD for the next behavior and the last behavior is reinforced. Suppose that Pam reads a verbal math problem. She translates it into an equation by writing *2 + 2 =*. Then she writes *4*. The first response in the chain is reading the verbal problem. This is the SD for writing the second response of *2 + 2 =*. Writing *2 + 2 =* is the SD for writing the third response of *4*. The *4* may produce praise from the teacher.

8. A sequence where each behavior produces an SD for the following behavior and the last behavior is reinforced is called a stimulus/response _____.

Virtually all verbal behavior consists of long chains of individual responses. An example might be singing "The Star Spangled Banner." If Ted sings, "Oh say can you . . .," these words serve as an SD for the next word, "see." These words may be an effective SD for "see" because they start at the beginning. A word picked out of the middle may not be as effective. For example, do you immediately know what word comes right after "early" in "The Star-Spangled Banner?" Most people have to go back and start from an earlier point to remember.

Many other types of behavior are chains also. For example, walking is a chain of individual steps. Each step serves as an SD for

***Figure 20-3.*** One dancer's role in a ballet is a very long and complex stimulus/response chain. (Source: Jerry Brendt/Stock Boston)

the next step. If you get off course, your next step may correct the error. Getting someplace serves as the reinforcer. Another example is the movements a ballet dancer makes in a particular dance.

Each response in a chain produces an effect on the environment that acts as a conditioned reinforcer for that response. Getting closer to where you are going reinforces each step you take. Each response moves you closer to the final response that produces the reinforcer. Thus, each response is reinforced by its increasing nearness to the goal. For example, opening a refrigerator, taking out a bottle of milk, filling a glass, and drinking constitute a four-response chain. The last response in the chain, drinking, is obviously reinforced by consumption of the milk. However, you can't drink the milk unless the milk is in the glass. Therefore, the full milk glass is a discriminative stimulus for drinking. But it is also a conditioned reinforcer for the filling response, because it brings you a step closer to drinking the milk.

## Summary

Many kinds of reinforcers influence people's behavior. Behavior analysts classify some as primary reinforcers. They define them as reinforcers that weaken only temporarily because of satiation. They classify other events as conditioned reinforcers. They define them as reinforcers that can weaken because of satiation and because they are no longer being paired with other reinforcers. They call the paired reinforcer a backup reinforcer. They classify still other events as generalized reinforcers, which are conditioned reinforcers that are paired with many backup reinforcers. Finally, behavior analysts define a stimulus/response chain as a sequence of two or more behaviors. Each response in such a chain produces conditioned reinforcement for the prior response. It also produces a discriminative stimulus for the next response. Tactic #5 in the stimulus control strategy is to make reinforcement more practical by creating conditioned reinforcers.

## Behavior Analysis Examples

### *Modifying Teacher Behavior*

The personalities of students and teachers often clash. Researchers worked with Jean, an eighth-grade student (Polirstok & Greer, 1977). Her Spanish teacher, who had an M.A. degree and 15 years of experience,

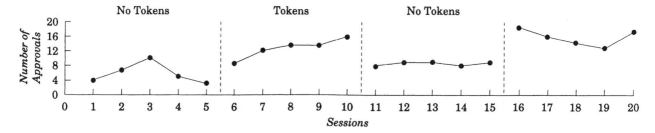

***Figure 20-4.*** The number of approvals Jean gave to her Spanish teacher. Jean was given tokens during two experimental conditions to reinforce her approvals. As a result, the teacher was much more approving (and less disapproving) of Jean. (Adapted from "Remediation of Mutually Aversive Interactions between a Problem Student and Four Teachers by Training the Student in Reinforcement Techniques," by S. Polirstok and R. D. Greer *Journal of Applied Behavior Analysis,* 1977, 10, 707–716. Copyright 1977 by the Society for the Experimental Analysis of Behavior, Inc. Used by permission.)

regarded Jean as a discipline problem. Jean came from a poor family. The teacher sent her to the principal for disciplinary action about five times per week. He referred her for more serious offenses on an average of twice a month. Her achievement level was about a year behind her grade placement.

The researchers taught Jean to approve the teacher's desirable behaviors. They hoped to increase those behaviors. They taught Jean how to do this in two steps. They asked Jean what were desirable teacher behaviors. She then role-played approving of them. They gave Jean a tape player that frequently cued her to show approval. The researchers gave her tokens each day after class based on how many approvals she gave out. She could spend the tokens for popular music tapes, extra gym, lunch with a favorite teacher, and extra English credit.

Figure 20-4 shows the results. Prior to the tokens, Jean averaged about 6 approvals per class. After tokens, Jean averaged 13 approvals per class. When they stopped giving her tokens, Jean's rate of approval fell to a little more than 8 per day. When tokens were again awarded, Jean averaged 13 approvals per class once again.

9. Refer to Figure 20-4. Are Jean's data convincing that there is a difference? _____

The researchers also taught Jean to withhold disapproval of the Spanish teacher. Her rate of disapproval decreased. At the same time, the Spanish teacher's behavior also changed radically. He showed more approval

and less disapproval of Jean. The researchers had Jean use this same procedure on three other teachers with similar results. After the experiment, Jean often commented on how nice her teachers had become. Her teachers indicated that they were pleased with her remarkable socialization and newfound maturity. They referred her for discipline only once after the experiment. The researchers concluded that they had broken a mutually unpleasant interaction pattern and created a mutually pleasant one. The nicer teacher behavior then sustained Jean's behavior even after the experiment was over. (This final phase is not shown on the graph.)

10. Jean could spend the tokens for many backups such as popular music tapes, extra gym, lunch with a favorite teacher, and extra English credit. Because the tokens had many backup reinforcers instead of just one backup, behavior analysts call the tokens _____ (conditioned, generalized, primary) reinforcers.

### *A Token Economy for Self-Control*

Researchers used a token economy to help a student control his own behavior (Whitman & Dussault, 1976). James was a 21-year-old undergraduate who had trouble organizing his time. He had a part-time job, a full class load, and a girlfriend. He began spending more time on his job and with his girlfriend at the expense of school. This led him to feel "guilty and depressed." He lost 20 pounds in six months. His personal habits, such as bathing, were deteriorating.

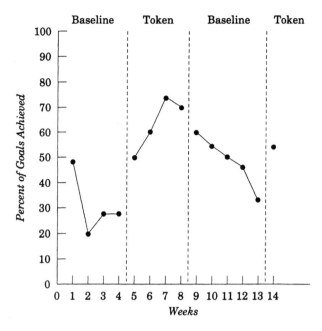

**Figure 20-5.** The percentage of personal goals earned by James, who was having trouble maintaining studying habits, class attendance, and personal cleanliness. He used a token system to balance these goals with seeing his girlfriend and other reinforcing activities. (From "Self Control through the Use of a Token Economy," by T. L. Whitman and P. Dussault *Journal of Behavior Therapy and Experimental Psychiatry,* 1976, 7, 161–166. Copyright 1976, Pergamon Press, Ltd. Reprinted by permission.)

The researchers suggested that James use a token system to organize his own behavior. James specified a large number of desirable behaviors. He assigned them points depending on how important they were. He earned 20 points by studying for one of his courses at least four to six hours a week. He earned 20 points for attending classes for all his courses. He earned 20 points for writing home. He earned 5 points for washing dishes once a day. He earned 10 points for washing his hair once a week. He could buy a visit to his girlfriend for 25 points per day, watching TV for 10 points, and walking for pleasure for 5 points. James recorded all points as he earned them. He agreed not to obtain any reinforcers unless he had previously earned sufficient points to afford them. Figure 20-5 shows that James achieved about 30% of his goals during a baseline period of observation. However, once the token system was introduced, he steadily

improved until he was achieving about 70% of his goals. A reversal to baseline and subsequent reversal to the token economy confirmed the impact of the token economy on his behavior.

James formulated his personal goals in terms of how many points he should earn for achieving them. He formulated his reinforcing activities in terms of how much they were worth to him. He could then keep records that permitted him to more judiciously balance these two aspects of his life.

11. James spent his points for many backups such as visiting his girlfriend, watching TV, and walking. Therefore, behavior analysts would classify the points as _____ _____ (conditioned, generalized, primary) reinforcers.

## Notes

### Note #1

Token economies have sometimes been criticized because they do not always lead to permanent behavioral change. Without the tokens, the behavioral change does not generalize to other situations or even to the same situation (Levine & Fasnacht, 1974). This, of course, is built into the very concept of reinforcement of any kind. If you stop reinforcing a behavior and there is no other source of reinforcement, the behavior will eventually disappear. A token economy may help to teach someone a desired behavior. If the everyday environment reinforces the behavior, then removal of the token system will not stop the behavior. If the everyday environment does not reinforce the behavior, you should reconsider whether the behavior is socially significant. If not, then a socially significant target behavior should be selected. However, if the behavior is socially significant and the everyday environment does not maintain it, then that environment must be redesigned. One way to redesign it is to make the token economy a permanent part of that environment.

### Note #2

Stopping the delivery of the backup reinforcer while continuing the delivery of the conditioned reinforcer <u>isn't</u> an example of extinction. Stopping the delivery of both the backup and the conditioned reinforcer <u>is</u> an example of extinction.

12. Can you label stopping the delivery of a backup reinforcer but not stopping the delivery of the conditioned reinforcer *extinction*? _____ (yes, no)

### Note #3

Some behavior analysts argue that it is futile to classify reinforcers in terms of their biological origins or other causes (Schoenfeld, 1978). The student should note that the classifications of primary, conditioned, and generalized are purely descriptive. Behavior analysts classify reinforcers as "primary" purely in terms of whether they permanently lose their effectiveness. They do this whether or not the reinforcer has a biological origin. They classify reinforcers as conditioned solely in terms of whether they permanently lose their effectiveness when unpaired from their backups. The distinctions between primary, conditioned, and generalized reinforcers made in this lesson are widely accepted by applied behavior analysts. These distinctions appear to help them select or create reinforcers that are useful in solving practical problems.

## Helpful Hints

### Helpful Hint #1

Students sometimes confuse *generalization* and *generalized reinforcer*. Remember that the occurrence of a behavior in a novel situation is called generalization. A reinforcer that is paired with <u>many</u> other reinforcers is called a generalized reinforcer. Be sure to carefully distinguish between these two terms.

13. Would it be correct to refer to a reinforcer that is paired with many backup reinforcers as a generalization? _____ (yes, no) What is the correct label for such a reinforcer? _____ reinforcer.

### Helpful Hint #2

Students sometimes fail to distinguish properly between a conditioned reinforcer and a generalized reinforcer. When I ask you a question concerning one of these terms, be sure to give the most specific answer. If I ask you the name of a reinforcer that is paired with many other reinforcers, use the more specific label of *generalized reinforcer*, rather than the more general label of *conditioned reinforcer*. If I ask you the name of a reinforcer that is paired with only <u>one</u> other reinforcer, you can answer "conditioned reinforcer." If the example <u>does not specify</u> that it is paired with many reinforcers, then you should answer "conditioned reinforcer." The book will consider your answers wrong if you answer in any other way.

14. If praise is used as a reinforcer that is backed up by a ticket to a KU basketball game, the praise is what type of reinforcer? _____ If praise is used as a reinforcer that is backed up by tickets, food, and other privileges, praise is what type of reinforcer? _____

### Helpful Hint #3

Students often have trouble figuring out which event is the conditioned reinforcer and which event is the backup reinforcer. The simplest difference is that the conditioned reinforcer comes first and the backup reinforcer comes later. Thus, you earn the money and then you buy the goodies. The goodies are the backups because you can't get them until you get the money. You get the praise then you get the favors. You can't get the favors until you've gotten on someone's good side by earning their praise.

15. First you get the _____ (backup, conditioned) reinforcer, then you get the _____ (backup, conditioned) reinforcer.

## Additional Readings

Ayllon, T., & Azrin, N. H. (1965). The measurement and reinforcement of behavior of psychotics. *Journal of the Experimental Analysis of Behavior, 8,* 357–383. This classic article describes the first token economy. It reports experiments using a token system to develop self-help behaviors among chronic psychotics.

Ayllon, T., & Azrin, N. H. (1968). *The token economy.* New York: Appleton-Century-Crofts. Designed as a token economies handbook, this book contains a great deal of practical information. It gives rules for how to select and define target behaviors and for how to select reinforcers. It discusses other important aspects of designing and using a token economy.

Glynn, S. M. (1990). Token economy approaches for psychiatric patients: Progress and pitfalls over 25 years. Special Issue: Recent developments in the behavioral treatment of chronic psychiatric illness. *Behavior Modification, 14*(4), 383–407. This article reviews what is known about token economies to date. It suggests that use of token economies has declined and discusses why.

Kazdin, A. E. (1977). *The token economy: A review and evaluation.* New York: Plenum Press. This book reviews what is known about token economies. It expands and updates the Ayllon and Azrin book.

Kelleher, R. T., & Gollub, L. R. (1962). A review of positive conditioned reinforcement. *Journal of the Experimental Analysis of Behavior, 5,* 543–597. This article is a highly technical review of the concept of conditioned reinforcement. It discusses many of the theories about the conditions necessary to turn an event into a conditioned reinforcer.

Stromer, R., McComas, J. J., & Rehfeldt, R. A. (2000). Designing interventions that include delayed reinforcement: Implications of recent laboratory research. *Journal of Applied Behavior Analysis, 33,* 359–371. This article examines the nature of stimulus/response chains. It integrates the findings from basic laboratory research to the design and analysis of durable, applied interventions in everyday situations.

## Programmed Reading

This Programmed Reading section presents questions on the following topics: (1) Unlearned Reinforcers, (2) Learned Reinforcers, (3) Reinforcers That Usually Work, (4) Responses That Occur Together, (5) Another Tactic, and (6) Review.

### 1. Unlearned Reinforcers

60. Pre-test: Mom made sure that Willie Mae got a cookie whenever she said a new word. The cookie was always a reinforcer for Willie Mae unless she had just eaten. The cookie is a(n) _____ reinforcer for Willie Mae.

50. Pre-test: A primary reinforcer is a reinforcing event that loses its effectiveness only temporarily through _____ _____.

63. Pre-test: One kind of reinforcer gains its power from its biological function for people, not from being paired with other reinforcers. What is the name of that kind of reinforcer? _____ reinforcer.

88. The first goal is to learn about primary reinforcers. Reinforcing events that are rooted in our biological nature influence our behavior from birth. They lose their effectiveness only through satiation. Behavior analysts call these events _____ (conditioned, generalized, primary) reinforcers.

100. We call a reinforcer primary because it comes first in a person's life. *Primary* means "first." Some biological events, such as food, air, water, and warmth, are present at birth. They come before you can learn any other reinforcers. An event that is one of your first reinforcers is called a(n) _____ reinforcer.

5. A primary reinforcer is a reinforcing event that loses its effectiveness only temporarily through _____.

23. Behavior analysts frequently use food to reinforce children and severely impaired persons. Food only loses its effectiveness if a person has had too much too recently. What kind of reinforcer is food? A(n) _____ reinforcer.

45. One kind of reinforcer gains its power from its biological function for people, not from being paired with other reinforcers. What is the name of that kind of reinforcer? _____ reinforcer.

### 2. Learned Reinforcers

62. Pre-test: Mr. Jones made a special little mark on Janie's paper whenever she accomplished something for the first time. That mark meant she could go out early for recess. Although the mark was usually effective, it didn't work on cold, rainy days when Janie didn't want to go out. The mark is a(n) _____ reinforcer; going out early to recess is a(n) _____ reinforcer.

58. Pre-test: Any reinforcer that loses its effectiveness permanently if repeatedly presented unpaired with established reinforcers is called a(n) _____ reinforcer.

47. Pre-test: A conditioned reinforcer will no longer be effective if the person has had so much of the backup reinforcer recently that the primary reinforcer has temporarily lost its effectiveness because of the person being _____ with it.

64. Pre-test: One kind of reinforcer is always effective unless the person has had too much of it recently. The name of that kind of reinforcer is a(n) _____ reinforcer.

56. Pre-test: An established reinforcer that is paired with a conditioned reinforcer to make the conditioned reinforcer effective is called a(n) _____ reinforcer.

48. Pre-test: A conditioned reinforcer is any reinforcer that loses its effectiveness permanently if it is repeatedly presented _____ with backup reinforcers.

96. This module teaches about conditioned reinforcers. A conditioned reinforcer _____ (does, doesn't) gain its effectiveness by being paired with other established reinforcers that back it up.

13. A time sequence will help you understand conditioned reinforcers. First, someone performs a desirable behavior. Second, you give them a conditioned reinforcer to increase the rate of the desirable behavior. Third, you back up that conditioned reinforcer by giving the person an established reinforcer. The established reinforcer that you give as a back up comes _____ (after, before) the conditioned reinforcer.

76. Since many students confuse which is the conditioned and which is the backup reinforcer, I will emphasize the point. When you see a desired behavior, you immediately deliver a conditioned reinforcer. You then maintain the effectiveness of the conditioned reinforcer by pairing it with an established reinforcer delivered afterwards. Because it comes later and backs up the conditioned reinforcer, you call this established reinforcer a(n) _____ reinforcer.

1. A <u>conditioned</u> reinforcer is an event that depends for its effectiveness upon being paired with an established reinforcer that you deliver later and that backs it up. You might say that pairing with the backup reinforcer is a *condition* for the newfound effectiveness of the event. That is why behavior analysts call the newly effective event a(n) _____ reinforcer.

102. When a neutral event is paired with an established reinforcer delivered later, it may make the neutral event into an effective reinforcer. The event is effective because it is "backed up" by the established reinforcer. In this case, we call the newly effective event a conditioned reinforcer. Because you deliver it after the conditioned reinforcer, you call the established reinforcer the _____ reinforcer.

43. Notice that any established reinforcer can back up a conditioned reinforcer. The established reinforcer can be another conditioned reinforcer, a generalized reinforcer, or a primary reinforcer. Does the established reinforcer that backs up a conditioned reinforcer have to be a primary reinforcer? _____ (yes, no)

81. Suppose I tell you only two things. I will give you Reinforcer A if you study. When you have 10 Reinforcer As, I will give you one Reinforcer B. Which reinforcer is the backup reinforcer? _____ (A or B)

91. The name for all reinforcers that gain their effectiveness by being <u>paired</u> with one backup reinforcer is _____ reinforcer.

103. Which comes first, the backup reinforcer or the conditioned reinforcer? The _____ reinforcer.

2. A conditioned reinforcer is any reinforcer that loses its effectiveness permanently if it is repeatedly presented <u>unpaired</u> with established reinforcers called _____ reinforcers.

15. An effective conditioned reinforcer must be paired with a backup reinforcer. However, a conditioned reinforcer loses its effectiveness permanently if it is repeatedly presented _____ with its backup reinforcers.

16. An established reinforcer that is paired with a conditioned reinforcer to make the conditioned reinforcer effective is called a(n) _____ reinforcer.

32. For example, the towels were no longer hoarded by the woman in the Ayllon and Michael study when they were no longer paired with attention from the attendants. Because the towels came first and led to attention, which came second, attention was the backup reinforcer. The towels were the _____ reinforcer.

73. Remember, a conditioned reinforcer is any reinforcer that loses its effectiveness permanently if it is repeatedly presented _____ with backup reinforcers.

26. Behavior analysts use conditioned reinforcers much more often than primary reinforcers. However, they often make the conditioned reinforcers effective by pairing them with a primary reinforcer. They pair them by first giving the conditioned reinforcer and then later giving the primary reinforcer. When they pair a primary reinforcer with a conditioned reinforcer, you would call the primary reinforcer a(n) _____ reinforcer.

41. Note that a conditioned reinforcer will no longer be effective if the person has had so much of the backup reinforcer recently that the primary reinforcer has temporarily lost its effectiveness because of the person being _____ with it.

105. You can often create a conditioned reinforcer to deliver as soon as the behavior occurs. This gives you the advantage of delivering the reinforcer according to which principle of reinforcer effectiveness? The principle of _____.

33. For example, you may want to give your daughter a lesson riding her new bike for correctly saying "refrigerator." But you would have to get her dressed, bring her outside, and give the lesson. This may take five minutes between saying the word and getting to the bike. A better idea is to first say, "You just earned a lesson on your new bike!" If you back your words up with the lesson, the words will be an effective conditioned reinforcer. The advantage of the words is that you can deliver your reinforcer _____.

74. Researchers often use conditioned reinforcers to teach eating. What is odd about this is that eating is reinforced by the primary reinforcer of food. For some children, however, that primary reinforcer does not maintain eating. In these cases, other nonfood conditioned reinforcers are stronger than the _____ reinforcer of food.

28. Dr. Budney helped John get off cocaine. When John tested "clean," he got movie tickets, sporting-goods gift certificates, and dinner certificates. Because the tickets and certificates could be exchanged for pleasant activities, they would be labeled _____ reinforcers.

38. It often helps to think of "spending" the conditioned reinforcers, after you get enough of them, to "buy" the backup reinforcer. With this analogy, the reinforcer that you can buy is called the _____ reinforcer.

### 3. Reinforcers That Usually Work

61. Pre-test: Mom smiled whenever Judy washed the dishes. Judy often washed the dishes because when Mom smiled Judy got hugs, extra privileges, and even cool new clothes! Mom's smile is a(n) _____ reinforcer.

70. Pre-test: You call a reinforcer that you can spend to buy only one backup a(n) _____ reinforcer; you call a reinforcer that you can spend to buy many backups a(n) _____

reinforcer; and you call the reinforcers that you can buy _____ reinforcers.

49. Pre-test: A generalized reinforcer is a reinforcer that is paired with _____ (many, one) backup reinforcers.

65. Pre-test: One reason that a generalized reinforcer is so effective is that the person is likely to be _____ of at least one of the backup reinforcers.

53. Pre-test: A reinforcer that is paired with either a conditioned reinforcer or a generalized reinforcer by being delivered afterwards is called a(n) _____ reinforcer.

89. The goal of this module is to teach you about generalized reinforcers. A generalized reinforcer is one type of conditioned reinforcer because it would lose its effectiveness if it were presented to a person _____ (paired, unpaired) with already established reinforcers.

37. In other words, a generalized reinforcer would lose its effectiveness if you could no longer "buy" what behavior analysts call the _____ reinforcers.

3. A generalized reinforcer is a reinforcer that is paired with _____ (many, one) backup reinforcers.

8. A reinforcer that is paired with either a conditioned reinforcer or a generalized reinforcer by being delivered afterwards is called a(n) _____ reinforcer.

21. Because you can use it to get food, a new car, a place to live, and so many other backup reinforcers, what is the most obvious example of a generalized reinforcer? _____

6. A primary reinforcer loses its effectiveness when you are satiated with it. A conditioned reinforcer loses its effectiveness when you are satiated with its one backup reinforcer. But a generalized reinforcer doesn't lose its effectiveness until you are satiated with _____ (all, some) of its many backup reinforcers.

82. Taking into account the probability of satiation, which of the following reinforcers is most likely at any given time to be effective: primary, conditioned, or generalized? _____

39. Let me put the same idea in another way. A primary reinforcer will be effective as long as the person is deprived of it. A conditioned reinforcer will be effective as long as the person is deprived of its backup. But a generalized reinforcer will be effective as long as the person is <u>deprived</u> of at least _____ (how many?) backup reinforcer(s).

46. One reason that a generalized reinforcer is so effective is that the person is likely to be _____ of at least one of the backup reinforcers.

77. Since social approval is paired with many other backup reinforcers, it should be considered a(n) _____ reinforcer.

20. Because they can be delivered right after the behavior occurs, generalized reinforcers can enhance the effectiveness of the backup reinforcers by utilizing the principle of _____.

24. Behavior analysts frequently use a local monetary system of reinforcement called a(n) _____ system.

92. The points in a point system are not always generalized reinforcers. Maconochie ran a penal colony that used a point system for prisoners to earn their freedom. Prisoners could use the points for only one backup: to get out of prison. In this case, the points were a(n) _____ reinforcer.

14. Achievement Place youths can earn points for doing homework, washing dishes, watching news, or getting a good report card. They could spend points for an allowance, watching TV, riding a bike, or staying up late. The points are what kind of reinforcer? A(n) _____ reinforcer.

25. Behavior analysts frequently use *token systems* or *point systems* to reinforce desired behaviors. The points or tokens are usually what type of reinforcer? _____ reinforcers. (Be specific.)

34. Groups of poor people and students have created democratically controlled systems of reinforcement using token economies. The tokens are usually effective reinforcers because they are paired with _____ (many, one) backup reinforcer(s).

75. Sarah was "sent to the principal's office" because she got her first 100% on a spelling test! She got a McDonald's coupon. Because

the stimulus of being "sent to the principal's office" is paired with getting a coupon, you would call the coupon a(n) _____ _____ reinforcer.

72. Remember that you call a reinforcer that you can spend to buy only one backup, a(n) _____ reinforcer; you call a reinforcer that you can spend to buy many backups, a(n) _____ reinforcer; and you call the reinforcers that you can buy _____ reinforcers.

10. A reinforcer that is paired with many backup reinforcers is a(n): _____ _____ reinforcer. The occurrence of a behavior in the presence of a novel stimulus illustrates the process of _____.

### 4. Responses That Occur Together

55. Pre-test: A stimulus/response chain is defined as a sequence of two or more behaviors. Each response in the chain is a(n) _____ for the next response. The last response is followed by the procedure of _____.

59. Pre-test: Any sequence of two or more responses in which each response serves as an SD for the next response and whose last response is followed by reinforcement is called a(n) _____ _____. (You may abbreviate.)

68. Pre-test: The first element of a chain is that it is a(n) _____ of behaviors.

90. The goal of this module is to teach you about *stimulus/response chains*. Behavior analysts call a <u>sequence</u> of two or more responses in which each response produces an <u>SD</u> for the next response and the last response leads to a <u>reinforcement</u> a stimulus/response _____.

17. An example of a stimulus/response chain is singing "The Star Spangled Banner." Each word appears in a <u>sequence</u> from beginning to end. Each word is an <u>SD</u> for the next word. The last word leads to the <u>reinforcement</u> of applause. Thus, singing "The Star Spangled Banner" is called a stimulus/_____ chain.

18. Another example of a stimulus/response chain is walking from Point A to Point B.

Each step occurs in a <u>sequence</u> starting with the step at Point A and ending with the step at Point B. The first step puts you at a location where you must make a step in the right direction to continue on to Point B. This location is an <u>SD</u> for the step in the exact direction. Finally, the last step leads to the <u>reinforcement</u> of arriving at Point B. These three elements define a(n) _____ /response chain.

80. Suppose a behavior has the following three elements: (1) It is composed of a <u>sequence</u> of responses. (2) Each response in the sequence is an <u>SD</u> for the next response. (3) The last response leads to <u>reinforcement</u>. The behavior that has those three elements is called a(n) _____. (Don't forget the "/.")

104. You can abbreviate the term *stimulus/ response chain* by the last word as simply a(n) _____.

84. The first element of a stimulus/response chain is that it is a <u>sequence</u> of responses. A stimulus/response chain involves more than one response that follow one another in a specific order, or _____.

94. "The Star Spangled Banner" is a chain because singing it involves singing many words in a specific _____.

93. The second element of a chain is that each response in the sequence is an SD for the word that follows. For example, when you sing "Oh" to start "The Star Spangled Banner," that word is a stimulus associated with reinforcement for the correct next word, "say." If you sang "can" next, that would be the wrong word and you would not get reinforced. Because "Oh" is a stimulus in whose presence "say" with be reinforced, we call "Oh" a(n) _____ for "say."

42. Notice that "Oh" is both the initial *response* in the chain and also a *stimulus* that precedes the second response. It is a stimulus that is discriminative for the correct response of "say." Because each response in a chain is both a stimulus and a response, the whole unit of behavior is called a(n) _____ /_____ chain.

85. The first element of a chain is that it is a <u>sequence</u> of two or more behaviors. The second element is that each response is a(n) _____ for the next response.

95. The third element of a chain is that the last response is followed by the procedure of _____.

40. Let's review. The first element of a chain is that it is a(n) _____ of behaviors.

86. The first element of a chain is that it is a sequence of two or more behaviors. The second element of a chain is that each response in the chain is a(n) _____ for the next response.

87. The first element of a chain is that it is a sequence of two or more behaviors. The second element of a chain is that each response in the chain is an SD for the next response. The third element is that the last response leads to the procedure of _____.

78. Singing "The Star Spangled Banner" is a chain because: (1) Two or more responses form a(n) _____; (2) each response is a(n) _____ for the next response; (3) the last response is followed by the procedure of _____ _____.

19. Any sequence of two or more responses in which each response serves as an SD for the next response and whose last response is followed by reinforcement is called a(n) _____.
(You may abbreviate.)

71. Probably the hardest part for students to remember is that a chain is a <u>sequence</u> of responses in which the last response leads to reinforcement and each response produces a(n) _____ for the following response.

101. What does saying "Each response produces an SD for the following response" really mean? It usually means that you _____ (can, can't) do the second response until you have done the first one.

31. For example, popping the top of a brew is one response. The opened can makes it possible to pour the brew into the mouth. Pouring the brew into the mouth is the following response. Pouring the brew into the mouth leads to tasting and relaxing. Popping the top is the first response. The opened can is a stimulus in whose presence pouring the brew into the mouth will lead to reinforcement. Therefore, you would call the opened can a(n) _____ for pouring.

44. Notice that the opened can is likely to be a reinforcer for popping the top. The open can must be full of brew to be a reinforcer. You can think of the can full of brew as a backup reinforcer for the stimulus of the open can. Thus, the open can is what kind of reinforcer? A(n) _____ reinforcer.

106. You need not write the full name of the term *stimulus/response chain*. You may use the last word only. So when asked what you call any "sequence of responses where each response produces an SD for the following response and the last response produces reinforcement," you need write only _____.

99. Walking is an example of a chain of individual steps. Each step serves as a(n) _____ for the next step.

79. So, you can call the recitation of "The Star Spangled Banner" without looking at the words a(n) _____.

22. Behavior analysts define primary reinforcers as reinforcers that weaken only temporarily because of _____. Conditioned reinforcers are defined as reinforcers that weaken through satiation and through being _____ with backup reinforcers. Conditioned reinforcers that are paired with many backup reinforcers are classified as _____.

12. A stimulus/response chain is defined as a sequence of two or more behaviors. Each response in the chain is a(n) _____ for the next response. The last response is followed by the procedure of _____ _____.

29. Dr. Polirstok gave Jean a token for each approval she directed at her teachers.

She could use tokens to buy music tapes, extra gym, lunch with a favorite teacher, or extra credit in English. These tokens would be _____ _____ reinforcers.

30. Dr. Whitman helped James set up a point system in which he earned points by such behaviors as studying and attending class, and he spent them on such activities as visiting his girlfriend and watching TV. Because he could spend his points on visits to his girlfriend and on watching TV, these activities are _____ reinforcers for the points.

### 5. Another Tactic

66. Pre-test: The fifth tactic in using the stimulus control strategy is to make reinforcement more practical by creating _____ reinforcers.

35. I want you to get familiar with the wording of the fifth tactic. The fifth tactic in using the stimulus control strategy is to make reinforcement more practical by creating _____ (conditioned, primary) reinforcers.

83. The fifth tactic in using the stimulus control strategy is to make reinforcement more practical by creating _____ _____ reinforcers.

### 6. Review

57. Pre-test: Any reinforcer that loses its effectiveness permanently through being presented unpaired with other reinforcers is called a(n) _____ reinforcer.

69. Pre-test: What kind of reinforcer is most likely to always be effective even after you have earned many reinforcers? _____ reinforcer.

51. Pre-test: A reinforcer that is paired with a conditioned reinforcer and that is responsible for the conditioned reinforcer's effectiveness is called a(n) _____ _____ reinforcer.

54. Pre-test: A sequence of responses in which the results of one response serve as an SD for the next response and in which the last response leads to a reinforcer is called a(n) _____.

52. Pre-test: A reinforcer that loses its effectiveness only temporarily through satiation is called a(n) _____ _____ reinforcer.

67. Pre-test: The fifth tactic in using the stimulus control strategy is to make reinforcement more practical by creating _____ reinforcers.

7. A reinforcer paired with only one backup reinforcer is called a(n) _____ _____ reinforcer.

97. To use the stimulus control strategy: (4) create complex stimulus control through imitation training and instructional training; and (5) make reinforcement more practical by creating _____ reinforcers.

36. If a conditioned reinforcer remains associated with a backup reinforcer, a decrease in the conditioned reinforcer's effectiveness will happen when the person has received too much of the backup reinforcer too recently and is _____ with respect to the backup reinforcer.

9. A reinforcer that is associated with many other reinforcers is called a(n) _____ _____ reinforcer.

11. A sequence of responses that leads to reinforcement and in which each prior response is a discriminative stimulus for the following response is called a(n) _____.

98. When using tactic #4 of the stimulus control strategy, create complex stimulus control through imitation training and _____ training. When using tactic #5, make reinforcement more practical by creating _____ reinforcers.

27. Conditioned reinforcers have one major advantage over their backups with respect to their effectiveness as reinforcers. Conditioned reinforcers can easily be delivered according to the principle of _____.

4. A generalized reinforcer is one that is associated with _____ other reinforcers.

## Programmed Examples

### 1. Programmed Examples

13. Pre-test: When a person has been reinforced to make a response in the presence

of a series of similar stimuli, he or she will sometimes emit that same response in the presence of a novel stimulus. This is known as the process called _____.

10. Pre-test: Flora was careful to always thank anyone who did her a favor. Unlike many people, however, she was extremely careful to ultimately back her thank you with any one of a number of return favors. Therefore, we would refer to her "thank you" as what kind of a reinforcer? _____

11. Pre-test: For every 15 minutes of chores, Calvin was given 1 point by his mother. At the end of the week, Calvin could turn the points in for allowance at the rate of 25 cents per point. What type of reinforcer are the points? _____ (Check your answer carefully.)

12. Pre-test: Martin wore a wrist counter to count the number of times he said something positive to someone. On any day that he counted at least 15 positive statements, he permitted himself to have a beer with dinner. The counts on the counter would probably be a(n) _____ reinforcer, and the beer would be a(n) _____ reinforcer.

18. When Harry did something pleasant for the family, his father awarded him Reinforcer A. Harry could trade in Reinforcer A for cookies later on. If Reinforcer A is unpaired with cookies, it permanently loses its effectiveness (until again paired with cookies). Since Reinforcer A loses its effectiveness permanently when unpaired with cookies, call it a(n) _____ reinforcer. Call the cookies _____ reinforcers for Reinforcer A. You should be aware that the effectiveness of Reinforcer A would also temporarily decrease if Harry were to eat many cookies and become _____ with them.

19. When Harry read the daily news or read a good book, his father delivered Reinforcer B, which could be traded in by Harry for a trip to the movies, allowance, a late-night snack, or a game of Frisbee with his father. Since Reinforcer B is paired with so many reinforcers, call it a(n) _____ reinforcer. Call such events as a trip to the movies or a game of Frisbee _____ reinforcers for Reinforcer B.

One advantage of Reinforcer B is that Harry is likely at any given time to be _____ of at least one of its backup reinforcers. Another advantage of Reinforcer B is that Dad can deliver it right after Harry has done some reading. Thus, it will be more effective due to the principle of _____ than its backup reinforcers.

17. When Harry did household chores, his father gave him Reinforcer C. Reinforcer C was always an effective reinforcer for Harry except temporarily when he got too much of it. Since Reinforcer C lost its effectiveness only when Harry got too much of it, call it a(n) _____ reinforcer.

9. Marla signed her checks *Marla Petty Jones.* If each of her names is a response, then is her whole name a sequence? _____ (yes, no) When she has written *Marla,* that name is all that is on the paper. If she looked away to answer a question, when she looked back the *Marla* would tell her that the correct next response is *Petty.* Therefore, *Marla* is called a(n) _____ for *Petty.* When she makes the final response of writing *Jones,* the signature on her check is valid and will allow her to take home the new briefcase. If that increases the probability of her signing her name correctly to checks, then you would call the event of taking home the new briefcase a(n) _____. What is the name of the behavior of signing her name to a check called ? _____

2. Bobby was a menace to the preschool because he always left his toys strewn around after he was through playing with them. The teachers got together to figure out how to teach Bobby to pick up his toys. They decided to give him a poker chip each time he picked up a toy after playing with it. Bobby could use poker chips to buy a snack, to have a teacher tell him a story, or to go for a long walk outside. Bobby learned to pick up his toys within a week. The poker chips seemed to always be reinforcing to Bobby. Because the poker chip is associated with many other reinforcers, call the poker chip a(n) _____ reinforcer. The poker chip was effective because it could buy many other events called _____ reinforcers. The poker chip is likely to be an effective reinforcer most of the time because

Bobby will probably be in a state of _____ with respect to at least one of the reinforcers associated with it. The poker chips would probably lose their effectiveness if they were not _____ with the backup reinforcers.

14. Six-year-old Sarah was a big eater. She always ate at a rapid rate for the first 10 minutes of a meal. Then she would relax, as though she knew she would get enough to eat that night, and finish the meal slowly. As Sarah ate a meal, she gradually stopped making eating responses. This decrease in response rate occurred because she had become _____ with respect to food. Because food lost its reinforcing ability only temporarily through satiation and always regained the effectiveness that it lost, food would be classified as a(n) _____ _____ reinforcer.

3. Carey had not learned to read at the fourth-grade level during the regular school year. To avoid Carey's repeating the grade, her parents volunteered to get her to finish three books in the Sullivan Reading Series during the summer. Her parents gave Carey 1 point for each page she completed. Carey could exchange 10 points for an ice cream cone. Carey read about five pages a day in her reading book, averaging 1 ice cream cone every other day. The points might become ineffective in two ways. Her parents might no longer let her exchange them for their backup of ice cream. If her parents gave Carey so many points that she could have 10 ice cream cones a day, her reading might decrease because she would become _____ on the ice cream. Because the points in this example could be exchanged only for ice cream, they would be an example of a(n) _____ reinforcer. If her parents allowed Carey to exchange the points for ice cream, watching TV, or visiting a friend, the points would be an example of a(n) _____ reinforcer.

15. Sociology 71 was a unique course. Instead of working for a grade, the students earned "credits" by reading materials for the course. The credits could be exchanged for a variety of learning experiences, including movies, guest speakers, discussions, field trips, parties, and special meetings with the instructor. The instructor found that 50% of the students earned enough credits to "buy" several learning experiences. Because the "credits" are paired with many fun learning experiences, you call the credits _____ _____ reinforcers. The events, such as movies, guest speakers, and discussions, back up the credits and make them effective. Therefore, you call them _____ reinforcers.

8. Kim decided to hike along the railroad track to the old abandoned station five miles away. She thought that she might find interesting old artifacts at the station, and it seemed like an interesting way to spend a slow summer day. To keep track of her progress, she wore a pedometer, which measured the distance she walked. Walking (by itself) usually isn't too reinforcing. However, walking to go somewhere interesting can be reinforcing. In this case, the pedometer measured the rate at which Kim was walking somewhere interesting. Clicks of the pedometer were an effective reinforcer, because they indicated to Kim that she was getting closer to the abandoned station. You might say that Kim was "buying" the event of "getting to the abandoned station" by taking steps that made the pedometer click. You would call "getting to the station" a(n) _____ reinforcer for the pedometer clicks. The pedometer clicks would be an example of what type of reinforcer? _____

16. Teachers give grades for a course long after the students have studied. Teachers even give grades for tests days after the students have studied for it. Teachers can help overcome these long delays by arranging for conditioned reinforcers to occur immediately after the behavior. For example, teachers sometimes give students study guides with questions that they can answer as soon as they finish studying. Getting the correct answer to a question on a study guide may be a conditioned reinforcer. If the student can get the correct answer to the study guide question, they will probably get the correct answer to a similar test question. Thus, the correct answer on the study guide is paired with the correct answer on the test. Therefore, you call getting the correct answer to the study guide question a(n) _____

_____ reinforcer. Because it comes after getting the correct answer on the study guide, you call the correct answer on the test the _____ reinforcer. Getting the correct answer to the study guide question probably is effective due to the principle of _____.

20. Willie's mother, Fay, encouraged Willie to do at least one thoughtful act a day. When she noticed him doing something particularly thoughtful, she would immediately say "thank you" and, as soon as possible, give him an M & M. Willie did many thoughtful things each day with this kind of reinforcement. One week, however, disaster struck. The grocery store was out of M & Ms, and there were no more at home. Fay decided to continue reinforcing thoughtful acts by saying "thank you." She noticed that Willie gradually did fewer and fewer thoughtful things around the house so that by the end of the week he was doing almost none. Because the M & M is paired with the "thank you," you call the M & M a(n) _____ reinforcer (does it come first or second). The effectiveness of the "thank you" decreased due to the fact that it was presented _____ with the M & Ms. Therefore, the "thank you" is considered to be a(n) _____ reinforcer.

5. Here's a review. John found that if he talked about politics when he was with Mary, she would get involved in a conversation with him, but if he talked about politics with Carol, she ignored him. Pretty soon he talked about politics a lot when he was with Mary but not at all when he was with Carol. What behavioral procedure did Mary and Carol unwittingly use to effect when John talked politics? _____
(Remember to ask some questions.)

1. Berry's teacher asked him to complete the sentence "Any event that follows a response and increases the future probability of that response is called what?" She reinforced him when he answered "reinforcer." Because the sentence signals that "reinforcer" is the correct answer, this sentence would technically be called a(n) _____ for the response "reinforcer."

4. Claire wanted to learn to study every afternoon after getting home from high school from four to six. So she made a giant sign for her room that said "If you study from 4 to 6, you can take a bike ride." She reinforced studying with the bike ride and extinguished nonstudying. She left her giant sign up until she was studying every day from four to six. Then, she made a smaller sign for her desk saying the same thing. When she found that she was still studying from four to six, she took all signs away and found that she still studied from four to six. What behavioral method was involved in the use of the signs and their gradual elimination? _____

7. It took a long time for Ed to learn how to shift smoothly. First, he had to take his foot off the accelerator at the same time that he pushed the clutch in. Second, he had to move the lever from one gear position to the next. Third, he had to let the clutch out while he again depressed the accelerator. What is the name of the sequence of behaviors that he learned? _____

6. If a chronic stutterer were reinforced by his best friend for saying complete words and sentences without stuttering, his "cure" might carry over to other friends and acquaintances. We would call the process by which his nonstuttering behavior with his best friend carried over to others _____.

# Review of Stimulus Control

## Reading Section

You have learned in this unit about stimulus control. The unit has described ways in which stimulus situations come to influence a person's behavior. This influence is often extremely complex, subtle, and difficult to observe. Further, the influence is based on past events that led to reinforcement or extinction of the behavior so that the cause of the influence can no longer be observed. In the absence of easily observed causes, many people attribute the cause to inner events (see Marr, 2003). Thus, they explain attention by inventing possible mental mechanisms (see the box Does the Mind Control Attention?). Likewise, they attribute language, complex sequences of behaviors, and intellectual behavior to mental and cognitive events.

Behavior analysts have rejected explanations of cognitive behavior based on private events. They have rejected the idea of the mind as a kind of gatekeeper (see O'Donohue,

Ferguson, & Naugle, 2003). Rather they have sought public causes of cognitive behavior, and they gain an important advantage once they find them. They can use their findings to help people become more skilled. This unit has presented numerous examples of using public events to change cognitive behavior. It is hard to imagine how anyone could gain control over private events, like the hypothetical gatekeeper, in order to help people improve their cognitive behavior.

Take the "concentrated attention" that a baseball player must give to a pitched curve ball (Osborne, Rudrud, & Zezoney, 1990). The researchers did not somehow improve the behavior of a mental gatekeeper who eliminated distractions, yet they did improve the hitters' concentration, as evidenced by their improved hitting. Their strategy was to use discrimination training assisted by coloring the seams of the baseball. Simply noting the way in which the training was set up with the colored seams, they explained their results

---

### Does the Mind Control Attention?

"We can listen to a particular instrument . . . in part by suppressing our responses to the other instruments and we are said to do so with various mental mechanisms; . . . [The mind is considered] a kind of gatekeeper—a loyal servant who admits wanted stimuli and defends his master against unwanted [stimuli]. . . . We have not explained anything, of course, until we have explained the behavior of the gatekeeper. . . . [Behavior analysis explains attention by] the contingencies underlying the process of

discrimination. We pay attention or fail to pay attention to a lecturer or a traffic sign depending upon what has happened in the past under similar circumstances. Discrimination is a behavioral process: the contingencies, not the mind, make discriminations" (Skinner, 1974: 116–117).

1. Discrimination results from reinforcing a response in one situation and _____ _____ (extinguishing, reinforcing) it in another.

directly without reference to causes arising from private events. However, they could still refer to improved concentration—private behavior whose existence is best proven by the players' improved hitting. The training procedure caused both the improved concentration and the better hitting.

Take the "sensitivity" of male clients to women's interest in talking with them (Azrin & Hayes, 1984). Researchers did not change some inner mechanism that you might call sensitivity to help these clients. Instead, they showed the clients videotapes of females talking with other males. They trained their clients to discriminate interest from disinterest. They did so in a way that would generalize to real females in real conversations with them. The training was sufficient to explain the increased ability of the clients to guess when females are interested in talking with them. No mental mechanism was needed.

Take the children who learned how to "identify" and name industrial objects (Mann & Baer, 1971). You do not need to assume some "deep structure" of language to explain their learning. The use of discrimination training seems to explain the learning fully.

Take the teachers who learned how to use specific praise (Horton, 1975). You need not point to a better "understanding of praise" to explain the results. The teachers used specific praise at first only with the students for whom they were trained to use it. After they were trained to use it with additional subjects, their use generalized. Generalization training enabled the teachers to expand their usage of specific praise. Although they may have achieved greater understanding, this private event is not the cause of more specific praise. Rather, both the use of specific praise and the better understanding are the result of generalization training.

Take the kid who overcame "fear" of the dark (Giebenhain & O'Dell, 1984). He did so because of a fading program that let him earn reinforcement for tiny steps toward sleeping in the dark. His parents did not change a cognitive structure in their son that made him a braver person. Rather, they reinforced his approximations of sleeping in the dark. As a result, he may now have a feeling that he identifies as "braveness," but if so, that feeling is not the cause of him sleeping in the dark. Rather, sleeping in the dark and feeling brave are the result of the fading program.

These examples may help you understand how behavior analysts see private behavior. They do not deny that feelings of fear exist. They do not deny the existence of understanding, sensitivity, or attention. They simply regard thoughts, feelings, and cognitive processes as private behavior. They often find that environmental events cause this private behavior just as it causes the observable behavior that is more accessible to us. In fact, the same environmental event that causes the batter to pay better attention to the curve ball also accounts for the batter hitting the ball better. Behavior analysts claim that trying to explain the observable behavior by the private behavior does not lead to an understanding of all the causes. Nor does it lead to the identification of causal events that people can use to change their behavior.

Behavior analysts repeatedly find that the most powerful procedures for changing cognitive behaviors depend on reinforcement. For example, researchers found that psychotics do not follow instructions unless reinforced for doing so (Ayllon & Azrin, 1964). All of these examples, from improving vision to learning how to talk, depend on reinforcement. Remember that the reinforcement need not be continuous. Just because you observe many instances in which behavior is not immediately followed by reinforcement does not mean that reinforcement is not involved. For example, you read about one study in which intermittent reinforcement of some imitations was enough to maintain all imitations.

Also, you learned how conditioned reinforcers can permit immediate reinforcement. Because tokens, praise, and other conditioned reinforcers can be delivered immediately, they aid learning.

All of these processes occur naturally in our everyday lives. They account for most of the influence that complex situations have on our behavior. They may well be the source of cognitive behavior (see Mahadevan, Malone, & Bailey, 2002). Behavior analysts use these processes to actively help people solve their problems. Their first strategy is to define the problem in terms of behavior. Sometimes that alone solves the problem. Their second strategy is to differentially reinforce the desired behavior. If these strategies don't solve the problem, then the next strategy they try is stimulus control.

## The Stimulus Control Strategy

Stimulus control is the basis for the third strategy of applied behavior analysis. The stimulus control strategy is to ensure that the person emits the target behavior when it will produce reinforcement. We want Mary to act assertively when Dave interrupts her. We don't want Mary to act assertively toward a defensive boss who then fires her!

The first tactic in developing stimulus control is discrimination training. Discrimination training is the basic behavioral process that teaches people when to emit a particular behavior. It occurs everywhere we turn. Behavior in one situation produces reinforcement. The same behavior in another situation does not. The stimuli in the first situation become SDs for that behavior. The stimuli in the second situation become S-deltas.

The second tactic is generalization training. Generalization training enlarges the situations in which people emit the target behaviors. Generalization occurs throughout all aspects of our life. If a particular behavior in one situation produces reinforcement, it is likely to produce reinforcement in similar situations. But we can't afford to teach the person to emit that behavior in every one of those other situations. Therefore, we teach the person to emit it in enough of them so that it generalizes to all of them.

The third tactic is using extra prompts to make learning easier. Fading and programming make it possible to teach discrimination and generalization quickly and with few errors. Behavior analysts use these procedures to teach material that people might not otherwise learn. They have used these procedures to teach children in normal schools, and they have also used them to teach children with behavioral and cultural deficits. In addition, they have used them to teach college students everything from foreign languages to English composition to behavior analysis (e.g., Martin, Pear, & Martin, 2002b).

### Improving Study Behavior with Stimulus Control

Bev felt sleepy every time she tried to study. The researcher set out to make her desk an SD for studying. He told her to install a brighter light for her desk. He told her to turn her desk so she could not see her bed while studying. He told her to do nothing but study at her desk. If she wished to write letters, do it at her dining table. If she wished to read a comic book, do it in her kitchen. If she wished to daydream, do it away from her desk. By the end of the semester she had been studying three hours a day for four weeks. Presumably her newfound success with studying was the reinforcer. (Based on Goldiamond, 1965.)

2. The desk became an SD for studying. Other places became S-deltas for studying. Because studying was more likely at her desk, you call it a(n) _____ behavior.

The fourth tactic is to use imitation and instructional training. These two methods are also important tools for behavioral change. For example, behavior analysts have taught children with severe retardation how to imitate other people (Baer, Peterson, & Sherman, 1967). By being able to imitate, those children can learn new behaviors much more easily and will have gained an important skill for surviving in a normal environment. Similarly, behavior analysts have taught oppositional children to follow instructions (Baer, Rowbury, & Baer, 1973), and they have taught adult schizophrenics to follow instructions (Ayllon & Azrin, 1965). Being able to follow instructions is a crucial step toward helping people operate in a normal environment. Undoubtedly people need many other skills to function in a reasonably normal manner. However, being able to imitate and being able to follow instructions are certainly of great importance.

The fifth tactic is to use conditioned reinforcement to improve learning. Conditioned reinforcement permits behavior analysts to use reinforcement more effectively. Most of our everyday behavior does not produce immediate primary reinforcers. In fact, most of our behavior does not even produce immediate conditioned reinforcers of major importance. We work at least a week for our paycheck. We scheme many hours to get a date with a special person. We work for years to graduate from high school or college. We buy groceries on Friday to get a meal on Sunday.

Instead of being influenced by delayed major reinforcers, we are often motivated by immediate but less important reinforcers. We watch TV instead of study. We get tasty snacks from a vending machine instead of nutritious food. We enjoy a cigarette instead of avoiding lung cancer. A major task of behavior analysts is to counteract the lure of immediate reinforcers so that important but delayed reinforcers influence desired behaviors. Conditioned and generalized reinforcers are powerful tools for this purpose.

## Stimulus Control and Other Cognitive Behaviors

The premise of this unit has been that the concept of stimulus control is the basis for a behavioral approach to cognitive behavior. The lessons have given a wide array of examples of what this concept means. For example, most people would regard listening to music as a cognitive behavior. Skinner (1974) suggested that listening to music is a discriminated response. If we have been reinforced for listening to a particular kind of music in the past, then we are more likely to listen to it now. Of course, the reinforcement may arise from the structure of the music itself, or it may arise from the reaction of our parents to our listening. In either event, the complex stimulus that we call music has come to exert control over our listening behavior.

You have read much more concrete examples of the stimulus control approach to cognitive behavior. By manipulating stimuli and reinforcement, behavior analysts have been able to help people improve their cognitive functioning. The mechanism has been similar. In one instance, curve balls came to exert more control over batters' hitting (Osborne, Rudrud, & Zezoney, 1990). We would say that the batters' concentration improved. In another case, how females reacted to males came to exert more control over what guys said to them (Azrin & Hayes, 1984). We would say that the guys' sensitivity improved. Finally, pupils' reaction came to exert control over teachers' use of specific praise (Horton, 1975). We would say that the teachers' understanding improved.

Recently, behavior analysts have extended the stimulus control approach to cognitive behavior even further (see Dymond & Rehfeldt, 2000; Hayes, Barnes-Holmes, &

---

### *The Family Contract Game*

When Timmy and his mother discussed chores, they attacked one another. To reduce antagonistic behavior, they tried playing a board game. The first square told Mrs. Smith to draw a problem card stating, "Timmy never washes dishes." The next square told her to tell Timmy to "wash the dishes every Monday and Tuesday." The next square told Mrs. Smith to "contract" for how she would reinforce Timmy. She might allow him to "stay up an extra half hour." The next square asked Timmy if he agreed. He might or might not. Other squares told Timmy and Mom to draw humorous bonus cards if they reached agreement or risk cards if they didn't. Timmy's antagonism decreased from 60% during baseline to 10% during treatment. It increased to 40% during reversal. Mom's antagonism showed an even greater change. (Based on Blechman, Olson, & Hellman, 1976.)

3. Because Mom and Timmy tended to ignore each other's antagonistic behavior during the game, the game became a(n) _____ (SD, S-delta) for antagonistic behavior.

Roche, 2001; Mahadevan, Malone, & Bailey, 2002; Sidman, 2000). For example, Donahoe and Palmer (1994) have presented detailed analyses of very complex cognitive behaviors. They show how behavioral concepts related to stimulus control can account for problem solving, verbal behavior, and memory. I will illustrate their approach as it applies to memory.

The researchers distinguish between two types of remembering. The simplest is based on the functioning of SDs. When you respond because of an SD, you might say that the stimulus "reminded" you to perform the behavior. Your roommate writes you a note that a friend called. You stick the note in your pocket. When you see the note later, it reminds you to call your friend. The note is a stimulus in whose presence you will be reinforced for calling your friend. Seeing it again "reminded" you to call. This is clearly a simple example of how remembering responds to stimulus control. Another example might be trying to remember how to get to a friend's house. You can't remember whether to turn right or left. Suddenly, you see the huge oak tree on the street to the left. Last time all you had to do was follow the street with the oak tree, and you were there. The oak tree exerts control based on its leading you to your friend's house last time. The oak tree "reminded you to turn left." You can probably think of many instances in which stimulus control exerted through simple SDs reminded you of the correct behavior.

However, we also remember in much more active ways as well. Not only do stimuli <u>remind</u> us to behave, but we also actively <u>remember</u> as well. The box on A Behavioral Approach to Remembering illustrates how even this kind of memory may be viewed as a behavioral process. Although an interpretation of this sort does not prove that behavior analysis can be usefully extended even into the highly cognitive arena of memory, it certainly suggests that it can. Donahoe and Palmer have done a service by showing us this possibility. Indeed we may be seeing the extension of behavior analysis to the study of cognitive phenomena.

## Summary

Stimulus control is the influence that a stimulus situation has on a behavior. The cause of this influence lies in environmental events. Environmental causes are just as important for cognitive as any other behavior. Procedures based on environmental events in general and reinforcement in particular make the stimulus control strategy possible. That strategy is to ensure that people emit target behavior when it will produce reinforcement. We have outlined five relevant tactics. The first tactic is teach people basic discriminations about when the behavior will produce reinforcement. The second tactic is to teach additional similar situations

---

### A Behavioral Approach to Remembering

Suppose someone asks you what you had for breakfast. You might actively behave in ways that increase the likelihood that you will contact SDs reminding you what you ate. You might look at the dishes in your sink for clues that suggested you had eggs and toast. If your sink is clean, you might say, "I can see myself rinsing egg yolk and crumbs off the plate, so I must have had eggs and toast." You might call such active behaviors as visualizing your dirty dishes and talking about them "remembering behaviors." They are behaviors that have

been reinforced in the past by producing reminders that aid your memory. They suggest that memory is a behavioral process that might even be improved by behavioral intervention. (Based on Shull, 1995.)

4. If the question "what did you have for breakfast" increases the probability of such "remembering behaviors," we would say that the question exerted _____ over those behaviors.

until generalization occurs. The third tactic is to use prompts to improve teaching. The fourth tactic is to use imitation and instructional training. The fifth tactic is to use conditioned reinforcers to overcome delayed delivery of important reinforcers.

## Helpful Hints

### *Helpful Hint #1*

The definitions of all terms introduced in this unit of the book are presented below. You can review the unit and prepare for the exam by testing yourself on the definitions and correlated facts presented for each term. You might use a piece of paper as a mask and leave only the term exposed. Then see if you can formulate a reasonable definition of and assemble any other facts about that term. Finally, remove the mask and check on yourself.

## Glossary

**backup reinforcer** Any reinforcer that makes a conditioned or generalized reinforcer effective.
- When a person obtains a conditioned or generalized reinforcer, he or she can exchange it for other reinforcers. These reinforcers are called backups.

**chain (stimulus/response chain)** A sequence where each behavior produces an SD for the next behavior and the last behavior is reinforced.

**conditioned reinforcer** A reinforcer that loses its effectiveness permanently through unpaired presentations.
- An unpaired presentation is the presentation of the event without its being associated with any other reinforcers.
- Behavior analysts generally assume that conditioned reinforcers are caused by a previously nonreinforcing event being frequently paired with a reinforcing event. This pairing may occur when the nonreinforcing event serves as a discriminative stimulus.

**discriminated behavior** A behavior that is more likely to occur in the presence of the SD than in the presence of the S-delta.
- Discriminated behavior occurs as a result of discrimination training.

**discrimination training** A behavior is reinforced in the presence of one stimulus and extinguished in the presence of another stimulus.
- Discrimination training is also used to label more complex situations. Complex situations may be viewed as two or more occurrences of simultaneous discrimination training. One behavior is reinforced during Stimulus A and extinguished during Stimulus B. Another behavior is extinguished during Stimulus A and reinforced during Stimulus B. Be careful—it is easy to misidentify such complex situations as differential reinforcement.

**fading** The temporary use of a prompt to establish a simple discrimination.

**generalization** The process whereby a behavior occurs in the presence of a novel stimulus.
- A novel stimulus is any stimulus in whose presence the person's behavior has not been reinforced. Usually, the novel stimulus is similar to the SD in a discrimination training procedure.

**generalization training** Reinforcing a behavior in a series of stimulus situations until it generalizes to other members of that stimulus class.

**generalized reinforcer** A conditioned reinforcer that is associated with many other reinforcers.
- This kind of reinforcer is effective because the person is usually deprived of at least one of the backup reinforcers.

**imitation training** (1) The teacher demonstrates the imitative stimulus. (2) The learner emits the imitative behavior. (3) The teacher reinforces it.
- The imitative stimulus is an SD for the imitative behavior. All other imitative stimuli are S-deltas for the imitative behavior.

**instructional training** (1) The teacher gives a verbal description. (2) The learner emits the instructed behavior. (3) The teacher reinforces it.

- The verbal description is an SD for the instructed behavior. Other verbal descriptions are an S-delta for the instructed behavior.

**primary reinforcer** Any reinforcer that loses its effectiveness only temporarily through satiation.

**programming** The use of prompts to establish a generalization.

- Programmed instruction is a form of programming involving three features: (1) It requires a written response, (2) it gives immediate feedback, and (3) it uses small steps.

**prompt** An added stimulus that increases the probability that a person will make the correct response in the presence of a novel stimulus.

**SD (discriminative stimulus)** A stimulus that precedes a behavior and is present only if reinforcement will occur for that behavior.

**S-delta** A stimulus that precedes a behavior and is present only if extinction will occur for that behavior.

**stimulus** Anything that affects the person's behavior.

**stimulus class** A set of related stimuli.

**stimulus control** The increased probability of a discriminated behavior produced by a stimulus (SD).

**stimulus control strategy** The strategy of teaching people when to emit the desired behavior.

- The strategy includes five tactics:
  1. Narrow stimulus control through discrimination training.
  2. Broaden stimulus control through generalization training.
  3. Create new stimulus control by using temporary prompts.
  4. Create complex stimulus control through imitation training and instructional training.
  5. Make reinforcement more practical by creating conditioned reinforcers.

# Practice Review I

The following material has questions over every term studied in Unit 3 as well as review questions from Unit 1 and Unit 2. By answering the questions and checking your answers, you can prepare yourself for the Review Exam. The Review Exam will contain question from all three units. The review is contained in one fairly long module.

### 1. Some Review Questions

28. Pre-test: Martha's mother frequently explained how to do chores around the house. If Martha did them, her mother always reinforced her. Describing how to do the chores and then reinforcing the doing of them is an example of what behavioral procedure? _____

33. Pre-test: Maria listened to Lefkowitz when he referred to female persons as "women" but ignored him when he called them "chicks." However, she listened to him when he referred to baby chickens as "chicks" and ignored him when he called them "women" (naturally). What behavioral procedure was she using? _____

29. Pre-test: Figure 21-1 displays the number of Jean's guitar playing practice sessions with and without Carol nagging her. Divided? _____ Stable? _____ Convincing? _____ Cause? _____ (yes, no) (Remember to spell out your answer.)

35. Pre-test: What two types of intermittent schedules produce a tendency for people to work at a uniform rate? _____ _____ and _____

27. Pre-test: Kay didn't give compliments to people very often. One day, however, she complimented Alice. She was delighted by Alice's positive response. As a result, she frequently complimented Alice in the future. A bit later she complimented Norma. The occurrence of Kay's complimenting behavior around a new person,

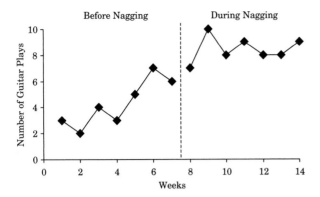

**Figure 21-1.** An experimental analysis of guitar practice.

Norma, would be an example of what behavioral process? _____

30. Pre-test: If Gloria watches Todd only when Todd comes home in the evening, then we say Todd's arrival home exerts _____ over Gloria's watching him.

32. Pre-test: In the process of teaching Marty to say "one," Danny would show Marty how to say "one" by saying it himself. Danny would then reinforce Marty if he correctly said "one." The method that Danny used to teach Marty to say "one" is called _____ training.

13. Generalization training involves reinforcing a behavior in each of a series of situations until _____ occurs to other members of that same stimulus class.

14. Harold's mother praised him when he was good. When he had been praised many times in a day, she would arrange for a special event, such as a trip to the zoo or ice cream. Mother's praise is a generalized reinforcer. Therefore, these special events are called _____ reinforcers for the praise.

47. When you reinforce one behavior in one stimulus situation and extinguish the same behavior in another stimulus situation, you call the procedure _____ _____. When you reinforce one behavior and extinguish another in the same stimulus situation, you call the procedure _____ _____.

15. If a behavior occurs more frequently in the presence of the SD than the S-delta, it is called _____ behavior.

45. When analyzing an example, always check to see if it involves two behaviors in only one stimulus situation. If it does, then the procedure is _____.

26. One reason that a generalized reinforcer is so effective is that the person is likely to be _____ with respect to at least one of the backup reinforcers.

39. Tactic #1 of the stimulus control strategy is to narrow stimulus control through _____.

3. A reinforcer that is paired with a conditioned reinforcer and that is responsible for the conditioned reinforcer's effectiveness is called a(n) _____ reinforcer.

9. Danny held up one object and gave Marty an M & M when he said "one;" Danny held up two objects and ignored Marty when he said "one." What behavioral procedure was Danny using? _____

11. Fading is a method of gradually changing the _____ in a situation. Shaping is a method of gradually changing the _____ in a situation.

19. If an event follows a behavior and the rate of the behavior _____, the event is called a reinforcer.

17. If a person learns a certain behavior in one situation and later emits that behavior in a new situation without being trained to do so, _____ is said to have occurred.

40. To use the tactic #1 of the stimulus control strategy, narrow stimulus control through discrimination training; to use tactic #2, broaden stimulus control through _____.

46. When dealing with a sequence of two responses, if the result of the first response serves as a discriminative stimulus for the second and if the last response is reinforced, we have what is called a(n) _____.

18. If a teacher starts the semester by making class attendance optional and later makes it required to see what difference it makes, he or she would be using a(n) _____ design.

25. One procedure for attempting to produce generalization of a behavior involves the temporary use of prompts. You use generalization training and use a prompt to get the behavior started in a new stimulus situation. The use of temporary prompts with generalization training is called _____.

23. Kay didn't give compliments to people very often. One day, however, she complimented Alice. She was delighted by Alice's positive response. As a result, she frequently complimented Alice in the future. A bit later she complimented Norma. The occurrence of Kay's complimenting behavior around a new person, Norma, would be an example of what behavioral process? _____

38. Suppose you stop all of the many backup reinforcers for tokens. Suppose the rate of responding previously maintained by the tokens declines. What kind of conditioned reinforcers are the tokens? A(n) _____ reinforcer. (Use the most specific term.)

43. What two types of intermittent schedules produce a tendency for people to work at a uniform rate? _____ and _____

41. To use tactic #2 of the stimulus control strategy, broaden stimulus control through generalization training; to use tactic #3, create new stimulus control by using temporary _____.

37. Suppose you are not sure whether a specific example is imitation training or instructional training. If the teacher described what to do, then it is _____ training; if he demonstrated what to do, then it is _____ training.

36. Suppose a teacher touches the top of her head, Danny touches the top of his head, and the teacher reinforces him. You call the teacher's touching the top of her head the _____ stimulus.

44. When a discriminated behavior is more likely to occur in the presence of a discriminative stimulus, you say that the SD exerts _____.

16. If a person is required to make a high number of responses for each reinforcement, his or her responding may become erratic

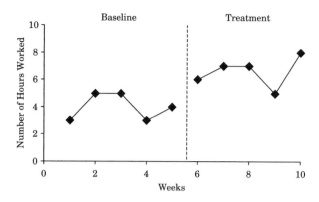

***Figure 21-2.*** An experimental analysis of practicing fly casting to catch fish.

or decrease because of what is called _____.

5. A stimulus associated with extinction for a particular response is called a(n) _____.

22. Figure 21-2 shows the hours that Joe worked on his fly-casting skills. Divided? ____ Stable? ____ Convincing? ____ Cause? ____ (yes, no)

7. An added stimulus used by behavior analysts to increase the probability that a person will make the correct response in the presence of a novel stimulus is called a(n) _____.

20. If Gloria watches Todd only when he arrives home, then we say that Todd's arrival home exerts _____ over Gloria's watching.

42. To use tactic #3 of the stimulus control strategy, create new stimulus control by using temporary prompts; to use tactic #4, create complex stimulus control through _____ training and _____ training.

12. Figure 21-3 shows when Fran and Will observed someone playing a game in the lounge. They used 60-second intervals. Compute their reliability: ____%. Is it acceptable if this is a new behavioral definition? _____

21. In the process of teaching Marty to say "one," Danny would show Marty how to say "one" by saying it himself. Danny would then reinforce Marty if he correctly said "one." The method that Danny used to teach Marty to say "one" is called _____ training.

| Fran | X | X | X | O | X | X | O | X | X | X | X | X | O | O | X | X | O | O | X | X |
|------|---|---|---|---|---|---|---|---|---|---|---|---|---|---|---|---|---|---|---|---|
| Will | X | O | X | O | X | X | X | X | X | X | O | X | O | O | O | X | O | O | X | X |

*Figure 21-3.* Observations by Fran and Will.

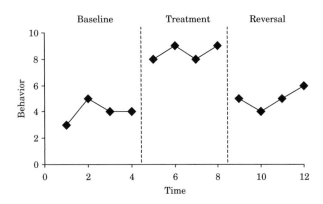

*Figure 21-4.* An experimental analysis of an unspecified behavior.

6. A stimulus/response chain is several related responses in which the results of one response serve as a(n) _____ for the <u>next</u> response.

4. A set of related stimuli is called a(n) _____.

8. Listening to music can put Dour Dan in a good mood. Sometimes it only takes one song, but other times it takes 2, 3, or 4; once it took 47 before his mood changed! If experiencing a good mood is a reinforcer, what specific schedule is Dour Dan's music listening on _____.

1. Figure 21-4 graphs Tina's behavior without and with treatment. Divided? _____ Stable? _____ Convincing? _____ Cause? _____ (yes, no)

24. Many people can say the Lord's Prayer from beginning to end. Because in this sequence each word is the SD for the next word and the last word leads to reinforcement, you call such a verbalization a(n) _____.

10. Every time that Tabby came up to them, Sally asked her baby son, Marty, "What is that? Is that a kitty?" and praised him if he said "kitty." Each time she said the word "kitty" a bit softer until Marty could identify Tabby as a kitty with no help. She then followed the same procedure with a series of cats until Marty could identify any new cat that happened to come up to them. What behavioral procedure did Sally use?

_____

2. A primary reinforcer is a reinforcing event that loses its effectiveness only through _____.

## Practice Review II

This section presents another set of review questions. It contains one short module.

### 1. Programmed Examples

5. Pre-test: "Yassou" means "Hi" in Greek. When Eli said "Yassou" to Lou, he wanted Lou to answer "Hi." He praised Lou when he replied "Hi" to "Yassou" and ignored him when he replied "Hi" to any other word. So when Eli said "Yassou," he also waved at him. Adding the waving to "Yassou" got Lou to say "Hi." So then Eli gradually withdrew the wave by delaying it for a longer period until Lou said "Hi" before he waved. What behavioral procedure was Eli using, by gradually delaying his waving, to teach Lou to say "Hi" when greeted with "Yassou"? _____

7. Pre-test: Listening to music can put Dour Dan in a good mood. Sometimes it only takes one song, but other times it takes 2,3, or 4; once it took 47 before his mood changed! If experiencing a good mood is a reinforcer, what specific schedule is Dour Dan's music listening on? _____

8. Pre-test: If the tall guy will answer you only when addressed as "Marvin" and the short guy will not answer you when addressed as "Marvin," we would call the tall guy a(n) _____ for the response "Marvin."

6. Pre-test: Believe it or not, Shecky counted every step that Tom took while jogging and praised him after every hundredth step. What schedule of reinforcement was Tom's running on? _____

9. Pre-test: When Mrs. Keller held up two marbles and asked "How many?" she gave Janie a cookie if she said "two." When Janie could answer the question every time, Mrs. Keller did the same training with two pencils and a series of two objects. Finally, without reinforcement, Janie could answer the same question when Mrs. Keller held up two books. From then on, she could answer that question no matter what kind of objects were held up. What behavioral procedure did Mrs. Keller use? _____

11. To use tactic #4 of the stimulus control strategy, create complex stimulus control through imitation training and instructional training; to use tactic #5, make reinforcement more practical by creating _____ reinforcers.

13. Two procedures for modifying behavior that use discriminative stimuli (SDs) in the form of demonstrations or descriptions produced by another person are _____ training and _____ training.

1. A generalized reinforcer is a reinforcer that is associated with _____ other reinforcers.

14. When a person copies the demonstration of a behavior, his or her copying behavior is called _____ behavior.

4. If Kelly answers "five" when asked "four plus one equals?" but not when asked "four minus one equals?" then we call her behavior of answering "five" _____ behavior.

10. The stimulus control strategy includes five tactics: (1) narrow stimulus control through _____ training, (2) broaden stimulus control through _____ training, (3) create new stimulus control by using temporary _____, (4) create complex stimulus control through imitation training and _____ training, (5) make reinforcement more practical by creating _____ reinforcers.

3. Danny asked Marty to say "elephant." Every time Marty said "elephant," Danny immediately said "very good." Danny's praise obviously pleased Marty very much. Danny praised him only when Marty said "elephant." At first, Marty said "elephant" over and over again. Then, he slowed down, and finally he quit altogether. Marty probably quit because by using praise so often Danny violated what principle of effective reinforcement, if any? _____

15. Which type of reinforcer gains its effectiveness through pairings with one other reinforcer? A(n) _____ reinforcer.

16. You call an added stimulus that increases the probability of a person's making the correct response in the presence of a novel stimulus a(n) _____.

2. A reinforcing stimulus occurs _____ (after, before) the response; a discriminative stimulus occurs _____ (after, before) the response.

12. Tom was teaching Mona to play the guitar. He first praised her only when she held it correctly, next only when she strummed it correctly, and finally only when she strummed a particular cord. What behavioral procedure was Tom using? _____

## Reading Section

### Introduction to Unit Four

The last unit of this book discusses the topic of aversive control. Aversive control refers to the use of what behavior analysts call punishment and negative reinforcement. The unit's three lessons will examine punishment, escape, and avoidance. These behavioral procedures have a profound influence on daily behavior. Your understanding of them is important to your understanding of everyday behavior.

People make extensive use of aversive control in everyday life. Parents spank and withhold privileges from their children. Employers reprimand, dock the pay of, and even fire employees. Teachers scold pupils and keep them after school. Police arrest criminals. Judges sentence them to prison or even death. People punch each other out. The military makes war on whole countries. Aversive

control is all around us. Skinner asserts that "it is the commonest technique of control in modern life" (Skinner, 1953: p. 182).

Aversive control often stops undesirable behavior immediately. However, it does so at a price, often producing unwanted side effects (Sidman, 1988). It may cause the person to dislike and perhaps avoid the person giving the punishment. It may cause them to try to exert countercontrol through violent means (see Delprato, 2002; Mace, 1994). It may cause a variety of negative emotional responses (see Parsons, Hinson, & Sardo-Brown, 2001). Further, when the punishment stops, the behavior often resumes. For that matter, if people can "get away with" the behavior without being detected, they will. The immediate beneficial effects of aversive control are balanced by these undesirable long-term effects.

Skinner felt that the discovery of reinforcement makes aversive control less necessary (Skinner, 1972). He felt that parents could reinforce children for cleaning their room rather

---

### Progress from Punishment to Reinforcement

"Civilized man has made some progress in turning from punishment to alternative forms of control. Avenging gods and hell-fire have given way to an emphasis upon heaven and the positive consequences of the good life. In agriculture and industry, fair wages are recognized as an improvement over slavery. The birch rod has made way for the reinforcements naturally accorded the educated man. Even in politics and government the power to punish has been supplemented by a more positive support of the behavior

which conforms to the interests of the governing agency. But we are still a long way from exploiting the alternative explanations. . . . Direct positive reinforcement is to be preferred because it appears to have fewer objectionable by-products." (Skinner, 1953: p. 192)

1. You might infer that Skinner defines civilization in part as reducing the use of punishment or aversive control and increasing the use of positive _____.

than hurting them for not doing so. Employers could praise workers for good work rather than complaining about shoddy work. Teachers could give privileges for studying rather than withholding them for making noise.

Skinner did not believe that we could completely eliminate aversive consequences. The physical world will certainly continue to deliver them. Close your eyes, and you will bump into a wall. Step off a cliff, and you'll fall. Speed, and you may drive off the road. We cannot replace these consequences with reinforcement. He simply proposed that people can influence each other through reinforcement rather than through punishment. His ideas may be of value in an increasingly violent world.

Behavior analysts turn to aversive control as a last resort (Iwata, 1988). They do so when they fail to make positive procedures work and the behavior endangers the person or those around them (see Lerman & Vorndran, 2002). Consider behaviorally disturbed individuals in institutions. These people often hit themselves repeatedly. They sometimes break bones, cause bleeding, blind themselves, or knock out teeth. They sometimes die. Psychologists call this *self-injurious behavior*, or SIB. Sometimes behavior analysts rely on punishment to stop SIB (e.g., Linscheid, Iwata, Ricketts, Williams, & Griffin, 1990).

I have placed the unit on aversive control at the end of the book to emphasize that it is a last resort. The first tactic in using this fourth strategy for changing behavior, the aversive control strategy, is to decrease undesirable behavior through <u>punishment.</u>

2. The first tactic in using the aversive control strategy is to decrease undesirable behavior through _____ as a last resort.

## Definition of Punishment

People usually think of punishment as doing something unpleasant to others to stop some behavior they dislike. This is not a scientifically useful definition because people often disagree on what is unpleasant. Behavior analysts define punishment more technically.

***Figure 22-1.*** Nathan Azrin conducted a brilliant series of experiments on punishment in the 1950s and 1960s. He examined the type of punishing stimulus, its intensity and frequency, and the schedule maintaining behavior as well as many side effects of punishment. (Source: Courtesy of Nathan Azrin)

**Punishment** is the <u>procedure</u> of following a behavior with a punisher. A **punisher** is any event that <u>follows</u> a behavior and <u>decreases</u> the rate of that behavior. It is the opposite of a reinforcer (Azrin & Holz, 1966). An event that you consider unpleasant may <u>not</u> be a punisher for someone else. An event that you consider pleasant may be a punisher for someone else.

3. A <u>punisher</u> is an event that _____ a behavior and _____ the rate of that behavior. It is the opposite of a reinforcer.

There are two types of punishment. You can deliver an aversive event or you can take away a reinforcer. This lesson will deal only with the delivery of an aversive stimulus contingent on behavior. Behavior analysts refer to this form of punishment as *punishment by contingent*

"Now I know why a gentleman shouldn't hit a lady."

*Figure 22-2.* Teaching little gentlemen to stop hitting ladies is an excellent example of the use of punishment. (Source: Cartoon copyright 1973 by Cartoon Features Syndicate. Reproduced by permission.)

*stimulation.* The next lesson will deal with punishment by taking away a reinforcer.

You can use both punishment and extinction to reduce the rate of a behavior. These two methods are easily distinguished. You are using punishment by contingent stimulation when you deliver an aversive event contingent on a behavior. You are using extinction when you stop delivering a reinforcing event.

For example, suppose that Bobby throws a tantrum if his mom won't give him a cookie just before dinner. His mother has reinforced this behavior in the past by eventually giving him the cookie. She might decide to eliminate his behavior by spanking him each time he throws a tantrum. This would be an example of contingent punishment—she would be delivering an aversive event after the behavior. She also might decide to eliminate the behavior by never giving him a cookie at that time. This would be an example of extinction because she has stopped delivery of the reinforcing event.

Another example of punishment might occur if Tommy often hits Sally. Sally might turn around and give Tommy a black eye. The results are shown in Figure 22-2.

## The Use of Punishment

The everyday world punishes much of our physical behavior (see Horner, 2002). For example, if you forgot to take your finger out of the door, closing the door will serve as a punisher. If you don't look where you're going, an approaching wall might deliver a punisher.

Behavior analysts resort to strong punishment to eliminate dangerous behaviors. For example, researchers treated Diane for head banging (Linscheid, Iwata, Ricketts, Williams, & Griffin, 1990). Diane was a 22-year-old with severe retardation and autism. She had an extensive medical history

---

### Stopping Diane from Injuring Herself

Diane Grant was a woman with autism. She often hit her face and head hard enough to break bones. Once she almost severed an ear. No treatment of her head banging seemed to work. Finally, her parents built an electronic helmet that sensed head banging and delivered an immediate tiny shock. The helmet rapidly eliminated Diane's head banging, but it was heavy and uncomfortable to wear. The Grants asked a research team at the Johns Hopkins Applied Physics Laboratory to build a lighter helmet. The helmet

helped Diane live a more normal life. It may help many others who injure themselves and for whom present treatments based on positive reinforcement fail. Nevertheless, the inventors remain committed to searching for improved approaches based on positive reinforcement. (Based on Iwata, 1988.)

4. Behavior analysts call the procedure of delivering shock to reduce head banging _____ (punishment, reinforcement).

of trauma to her head, face, and shoulders. She hit her head hard enough to detach a retina and produce cataracts. Doctors gave her numerous drugs to reduce her head banging without success. Other treatments included dance, music, and play therapy, and physical restraint. Behavioral treatments included extinction and differential reinforcement. Even with these treatments, she continued head banging. Further, she injured attendants by aggressively striking them with her head. Her physician felt that continued head banging would produce loss of eyesight.

Researchers resorted to punishment with Diane. They used a device called SIBIS, which stands for *self-injurious behavior inhibiting system*. The device consisted of a helmet worn by Diane that electronically sensed when she banged her head. It instantly gave her a brief, tiny electric shock. These shocks quickly eliminated almost all of her head banging. As a further benefit, Diane began to participate in social activities. (See the previous box.)

Behavior analysts can often eliminate dangerous behaviors with milder punishers. For example, researchers treated a 7-year-old boy with severe retardation (Bailey, Pokrzywinski, & Bryant, 1983). This boy bit his hands. The researchers treated hand biting by spraying a fine mist of water in his face. This mild treatment completely stopped his self-injurious behavior. Other researchers used lemon juice to stop a child from throwing up meals and eating them again (Glasscock, Friman, O'Brien, & Christophersen, 1986).

Behavior analysts also use punishment to eliminate behaviors that endanger others. For example, researchers used electric shock to eliminate severely aggressive behavior (Foxx, McMorrow, Bittle, & Bechtel, 1986). Other researchers used mild punishment to treat a 4-year-old fire setter (Carstens, 1982). They required him to do one hour of hard labor for each fire-setting episode. This produced immediate and complete elimination of fire setting. Other researchers treated convicted child molesters with mild shock (Quinsey, Chaplin, & Carrigan, 1980).

Behavior analysts have used strong punishers to help people change harmful behavior. For example, some clients have volunteered to have their smoking behavior shocked in an attempt to quit smoking (Azrin & Powell, 1968). Since this early study, however, researchers have turned toward much milder approaches to reducing smoking (e.g., Axelrod, 1991; Singh & Leung, 1988).

Behavior analysts use mild forms of punishment in many situations. For example, one researcher treated absenteeism of employees at a mental hospital with feedback (Ford, 1981). Each employee was required to report their sick leave to a supervisor. The supervisor simply described to the employee the number of other sick leaves and the number of staff left to meet work responsibilities for that day. This procedure reduced sick leave hours by about 50%! Other researchers punished hyperactivity in a girl with mild retardation by distorting the TV picture she was watching (Green & Hoats, 1969).

## Everyday Use of Punishers

People will probably continue to use punishment to counteract strong reinforcement that they can't control. For example, stealing may produce very strong reinforcers. By its very nature, we usually cannot observe stealing. Therefore, we can't stop thieves from obtaining reinforcers by stealing. One option is to deliver a very strong punisher whenever we can prove stealing has taken place. Society uses prison. Most of us use more direct and immediate punishment for stealing.

Punishment also plays a role in everyday discussions. Proving a person wrong through logical argument and even presenting facts to a person may all be punishing. Despite their punishing aspect, we will undoubtedly continue to have discussions, complaining, logical arguments, disagreements, and unpleasant facts.

A related example can arise when discussing your friends' problems with them. Often discussion can help them. During your discussion, you might ask your friend a few careful questions, which may help him or her see the problem differently. Robert might suddenly realize that he was thinking about the problem incorrectly. Harriet may discover that it is not as serious as she thought or that she had overlooked an obvious solution. Jake may realize that he had a silly hang-up and might even come to laugh at the problem. Much good can come from a gentle and loving discussion of your

pulled a knob over 100 times per minute when the effort to pull it was very low (Miller, 1970). The rate at which the adults pulled the knob decreased as the effort increased. When the effort was very high, the rate decreased to under 5 per minute. The experiment showed that effort is a punishing stimulus. Thus, every response we make has a punishing element to it. Punishment is always with us!

## Giving Punishment Is Reinforcing

One of the dangers of punishment is that its use is also reinforcing. It can be very reinforcing to the person administering it, If you punish Bert for nagging, he is likely to stop immediately. Your punishment would have produced instant reinforcement for you in the form of no more nagging. Its effectiveness is enhanced through the principle of immediacy. The positive results of punishment are immediate. Furthermore, the negative results, such as Bert not liking you as much, are delivered later. It is a wonder indeed that we are not all punishers.

Contrast this immediacy of effectiveness with the delayed effects of reinforcement. Suppose you praise Bert for playing nicely instead of nagging. Bert continues playing nicely. His behavior does not change immediately and thereby reinforce your praise. No obvious event reinforces praising him. In fact, since you have to take time away from whatever you were doing, praising creates a slight negative

---

### Why Do Battered Women Stay with Their Abusers?

Domestic violence occurs in 28% to 55% of all marriages in any given year. A puzzling question is "why do battered women remain in the marriage?" Here is one possible explanation. Basic researchers have shown that a punisher can sometimes increase behavior. If the punisher is paired with the delivery of a reinforcer, then punishment can become a conditioned reinforcer. It can then increase the behavior that produces it. Thus, it is possible that abuse could reinforce staying with the abuser if the abuse leads to reinforcement. Typically, after an abusive incident, the abusers apologize, buy gifts, and generally offer love and affection. (Based on Long & McNamara, 1989.)

5. Because of its pairing with gifts, love, and affection, abuse can become a _____ (primary, conditioned, generalized) reinforcer.

---

friends' problems. By asking a few questions you may eliminate their complaints about the problem. However, in spite of the gentleness of your questions, you have used punishment!

In fact, every response has its own built-in punisher. One researcher showed that adults

---

### The Ancient Greeks Understood Behavior Analysis

Thales was the "Father of Greek Mathematics." He may have understood the principle of punishment long before the time of Skinner (or Christ, for that matter), as the following account illustrates. One day Thales was carrying several large sacks of salt by donkey to a nearby town. The donkey slipped and fell when crossing a shallow river. Some of the salt dissolved in the water, resulting in a lighter load. When the donkey came to a second river, it purposely fell to further lighten its load. Thales noticed this and bought a load of sponges to load on the donkey's back. When the donkey went into its stumbling act at the next water crossing, the sponges soaked up water. The donkey then had a much heavier load of water-laden sponges to carry. Needless to say, it did not stumble at any more water crossings. (From Talsma, 1976.)

6. Because the heavier load of water soaked-sponges followed stumbling and reduced stumbling, it is an event called a(n) _____ (punisher, reinforcer).

outcome. No wonder so few people learn to reinforce desired behavior rather than punishing undesired behavior.

## Social Validity of Punishment

Researchers have examined the social validity of various punishment procedures. They generally find physical punishment least acceptable. For example, researchers found that adults rated mild punishment procedures most acceptable (Blampied & Kahan, 1992). They rated reprimands and physical punishment as least acceptable. Other researchers found that mothers rated reinforcement and time out as more acceptable than spanking or drugs (Heffer & Kelley, 1987). Researchers found that staff preferred to be managed through education and reinforcement rather than punishment (Davis, Rawana, & Capponi, 1989; Davis & Russell, 1990). These results are consistent with restricting the use of strong punishment to a last resort.

## Analogues between Punishment and Reinforcement

Many of the concepts associated with reinforcers have analogues with punishers. Some punishers seem to have a biological basis for their effectiveness. These include shock, hitting, pinching, and extreme heat or cold. Some punishers seem to gain strength from association with other punishers. And there are even punishers that seem to gain strength from association with <u>many</u> other punishers. The effects of punishment may or may not generalize. If you punish Bert's nagging in the kitchen, he may still nag in the dining room.

A primary punisher is a punisher that loses its effectiveness only through satiation. Behavior analysts commonly call this "adaptation" when referring to punishment. This effect is temporary. Primary punishers include events such as a spanking, an electric shock, or a beating. These events are effective for most people most of the time. However, if a person is subjected to these stimuli frequently in a short period of time, the stimuli may lose part of their effectiveness. The effectiveness can be regained, however, after a period of time without the punishment. This effect is analogous to the effects of satiation and deprivation with reinforcing stimuli. This book will refer to the temporary loss of effectiveness by a primary punisher as *satiation* to highlight the parallel between punishers and reinforcers.

7. A punisher that loses its effectiveness only through satiation is called a(n) _____ _____ punisher.

A **conditioned punisher** is a punisher that loses its effectiveness permanently through <u>unpaired</u> presentations. Unpaired presentations occur when the conditioned punisher is not paired with another punisher. The loss of effectiveness is permanent. One example of a conditioned punisher is saying "no!" when Bert starts to tease his sister. Saying "no!" is a conditioned punisher that gets its strength by being paired with a spanking or other established punisher. The word "no" will permanently lose its effectiveness if it is never paired with another punisher. It may also temporarily lose its effectiveness if you repeat it too often in a short time.

8. A **conditioned punisher**: A punisher that loses its effectiveness permanently through repeated _____ presentations.

A **generalized punisher** is a conditioned punisher that is associated with <u>many</u> other punishers. Generalized punishers are events, such as social disapproval, in which the person stands to have many punishing things happen as a result of the disapproval. Generalized punishers are effective as punishers because usually one or more of the "backup" punishers will be effective for the person.

9. A conditioned punisher that is associated with <u>many</u> other punishers is known as a(n) _____ punisher.

Punishment can also enter into discriminative processes. It is possible for a stimulus to be consistently associated with punishment so that it becomes a discriminative stimulus for punishment. I will refer to such a stimulus as a *discriminative stimulus for punishment*, or SP for short (cf. O'Donnell, 2001). An **SP** is a stimulus that precedes a behavior and is present only if <u>punishment</u> will occur for the behavior. The function of an SP in discrimination training is similar to that of the S-delta. They both produce a low rate of responding as compared with the SD, which produces a high rate of responding.

10. A stimulus that is consistently associated with punishment is called a discriminative stimulus for punishment, or _____ for short.

Discriminative stimuli for punishment can be used in a punishment-based form of instructional training. A teacher may describe an undesirable behavior. If the teacher punishes that behavior each time it occurs, this would be an example of instructional training. In fact, people will often stop making a response just on the basis of the description. This may result from a long history of reinforcement for following instructions and punishment for not following them. For example, you might tell Bert to stop nagging. If you then punish nagging, your instruction can become an SP.

Verbal stimuli can act as instructions or, more generally, as SPs. They can also act as punishers. The phrase "Don't talk" could be either an SP or a punisher, depending on when the phrase occurs. If you said it <u>before</u> a behavior that will be punished, it is an SP. If you said it right <u>after</u> the behavior and the rate of the behavior decreases, it is a punisher. Researchers have used signs to decrease illegal parking in handicapped parking spaces (Cope, Allred, & Morsell, 1991). These signs are paired with police action for violation. Thus, they are SPs.

Finally, the principles of effective reinforcement also apply to punishment. A punisher will be more effective if it is <u>contingent</u> on the behavior (Gibbs & Luyben, 1985). It will be more effective if it follows the response <u>immediately</u> (Abramowitz & O'Leary, 1990). It will be more effective if the person is <u>deprived</u> of the punisher. It will be more effective the greater the <u>size</u> (i.e., the intensity) of the punisher.

# Summary

The fourth strategy for modifying behavior is the **aversive control strategy**, the strategy of using <u>aversive</u> control if positive control fails. It is the strategy of last resort. The first tactic in using the aversive control strategy is to use punishment—that is, a procedure designed to reduce the rate of a behavior. The stimulus used in the procedure is a *punisher*. Punishment is very common in everyday situations. In fact, in the form of effort, it is a part of every response we make. Behavior analysts resort to strong punishers to reduce dangerous behaviors when other methods do not work. They sometimes use mild punishers such as feedback or reprimands. Some punishers are primary, some conditioned, and some generalized. Punishment can be used in differential reinforcement and discrimination training. Punishment is most effective when it is contingent, immediate, rare, and strong.

# Behavior Analysis Examples

### Self-Injury

One researcher developed a very mild method to punish self-injury (Van Houten, 1993). He helped Tom, a 10-year-old boy with severe developmental disabilities and autism. Tom slapped his face hard enough to bruise it. He slapped his face an average of about five times per minute. The problem became severe enough that he was forced to wear a protective helmet. Functional analysis ruled out social reinforcement for face slapping. The researcher treated this behavior by making it more effortful for Tom to slap his face. The treatment was to put 1.5-pound wrist weights on each wrist. Tom had to lift the weights in order to slap himself. This totally eliminated the face slapping. It did not affect his playing with toys or engaging in other desirable behaviors.

11. The greater effort required when wearing wrist weights is a stimulus that has been used to affect a child's slapping response. Because it reduced that response, the stimulus of greater effort is called a(n) _____ (punisher, reinforcer).

### Classwork

Strong punishment is usually used only as a last resort with dangerous behavior. Mild punishment is often used with undesirable behavior, and it is often combined with reinforcement of desirable behavior. Researchers helped underachieving first through third graders to increase their on-task behaviors (Pfiffner & O'Leary, 1987). They started with positive reinforcement, including praise, comic books, work breaks, and toys. They gave the reinforcement contingent on the kids being on task. They found that the kids worked about half the time. They then added brief, firm specific reprimands for off-task behavior. They found that this decreased off-task behavior to 20%. They were then able to fade the reprimands so that they were very rare. On-task behavior remained high.

12. Because the reprimands followed the off-task behavior and decreased its frequency, behavior analysts call the procedure of delivering the reprimands _____ _____ (punishment, reinforcement).

### Shoplifting

Shoplifting is a major problem. In 1973, shoplifting cost the average American family $150 in hidden costs. Researchers developed a way to reduce its occurrence (McNees, Egli, Marshall, Schnelle, & Risley, 1976). They invented an ingenious system for counting the number of women's pants being shoplifted. The system involved stapling a yellow tag on the back of the price tags for every pair of women's pants in stock. The store clerks then tore off the yellow tags when they sold an item. The researchers counted the yellow tags in stock at the end of every day to find out how many were missing. They then compared the number missing with the number that store clerks tore off upon selling a pair of pants. The difference was the number stolen. They used the same system for women's tops.

The researchers observed the number of women's pants and the number of women's tops stolen. Figure 22-3 shows the results of these observations. Tops were taken at the rate of 0.66 per day, whereas pants were taken at the rate of 0.50 per day. After 34 days, a

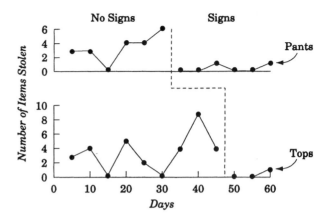

**Figure 22-3.** The effect of warning signs on the number of items shoplifted. (Adapted from "Shoplifting Prevention: Providing Information through Signs," by M. P. NcNees, D. S. Egli, R. S. Marshall, J. F. Schnelle, and T. R. Risley, *Journal of Applied Behavior Analysis,* 1976, 9, 399–406. Copyright 1976 by the Society for the Experimental Analysis of Behavior, Inc. Used by permission.)

sign was posted in the clothing department stating, "Attention shoppers and shoplifters. The items you see marked with a red star are items that shoplifters frequently take." Stars were about 5 inches across; six were mounted on the pants racks. After 47 days, six red stars were also posted on racks containing young women's tops. The rate of shoplifting dramatically decreased for both items.

You may have difficulty labeling the treatment in this study. The researchers did not directly apply punishment to shoplifting. Rather they posted a warning. Shoppers probably had a history of similar warnings leading to punishment when ignored.

13. Behavior analysts call the posted warning a discriminative stimulus for _____ _____ (punishment, reinforcement) which is abbreviated as _____.

## Notes

### Note #1

Punishment can be used in place of extinction in many procedures. For example, it might be used in differential reinforcement. A desirable behavior might be reinforced whereas an undesirable behavior is punished. The use of punishment can speed up the reduction in the undesirable behavior. Doing so would ordinarily be a last resort.

Punishment can also be used in place of extinction in discrimination training. A behavior might be reinforced in one situation whereas it is punished in another situation. Again, the use of punishment in the second situation may speed up the reduction in the behavior in that situation.

You can discriminate between the procedures in the same way you did when extinction was used to reduce the behavior. If you note that reinforcement and punishment are being used with two behaviors in one situation, you know it is differential reinforcement. If you note that reinforcement and punishment are being used with one behavior in two situations, you know it is discrimination training. We call the use of reinforcement and punishment with two behaviors in two situations discrimination training.

14. If you reinforce a desirable behavior while punishing an undesirable behavior, you would be using the procedure of _____ _____.

## Helpful Hints

### *Helpful Hint #1*
You will be given many examples of procedures that decrease the rate of a behavior. You will be asked to figure out what procedure is being used. The first question you need to ask is whether the procedure involves an event that immediately precedes the behavior. If an event decreases behavior and precedes the behavior, then the event must be a discriminative stimulus for punishment. Do not confuse it with a punisher.

You may be given an example in which the behavior decreases, but the event does not immediately precede the behavior. You must then distinguish between punishment and extinction. To tell the difference, you must ask a second question: Does some usually reinforcing event no longer follow the behavior? If an event no longer follows the behavior, the behavioral procedure involves extinction. If an event does follow the behavior, then

the procedure is punishment by contingent stimulation.

To summarize, if an example involves a decrease in behavior, ask two questions. First, does the procedure involve an event that precedes the behavior? If so, then the event is a discriminative stimulus for punishment. If the event does not precede the behavior, then you need to ask a second question: Does the procedure involve no longer delivering a reinforcer? If so, then the procedure is extinction. If it involves delivering a punisher, then it is punishment.

15. If an example involves a decrease in behavior and the delivery of an event that follows the behavior, the procedure is _____.

### *Helpful Hint #2*
A discriminative stimulus for punishment will often be an instruction not to perform a behavior. Such an instruction is usually not a punisher. I will revise the general rule suggested for reinforcers and instructions to apply to punishers. The new rule is as follows: An instruction (usually) cannot be either a reinforcer or a punisher. The only exception is when an instruction quickly follows a behavior and decreases its rate. For example, suppose that Jimmy pushes his brother and Dad says, "Don't push your brother." If Jimmy stops, then you should label Dad's statement as a punisher. This distinction should be clear if you ask your first question: Does the procedure involve an event that immediately precedes or follows the behavior? If it precedes the behavior, it is definitely not a punisher.

16. An instruction usually cannot be either a reinforcer or a(n) _____.

### *Helpful Hint #3*
Remember, a punisher is an event (or stimulus) whereas punishment is a procedure. The distinction is exactly the same as that between a reinforcer and reinforcement.

17. If a question asks for a procedure whereby a stimulus follows a behavior and decreases its rate, you know from the word *procedure* to answer _____.

If a questions asks for an event that follows a behavior and decreases its rate, you know from the word *event* to answer

_____.

### Helpful Hint #4

As with previous lessons, when an example describes an event or procedure that does not change the rate of a behavior, it should be labeled *unknown*.

18. If I give you an example in which a spanking follows a behavior and the rate of the behavior does not change, you should label the event as a(n) _____.

### Helpful Hint #5

Suppose that Dad spanks Jerry when he talks back to him. Suppose that Jerry's rate of talking back *increases*. You might be tempted to call this an unknown because Dad's spanking did not decrease Jerry's talking back. In other words, you might argue that Dad tried to punish Jerry but it didn't work, so it's an unknown. The trouble with that argument is that regardless of what Dad wanted to do, Dad's spanking did increase Jerry's rate of talking back. You learned in a prior lesson to call any event that <u>follows</u> a behavior and that <u>increases</u> the rate of that behavior a reinforcer. Continue applying that label. Dad's intention to punish Jerry does not in any way change what Dad actually achieved.

19. Call an event like a spanking that <u>follows</u> a behavior and that <u>increases</u> the rate of that behavior a(n) _____.

## Additional Readings

Alford, G. S., & Turner, S. M. (1976). Stimulus interference and conditioned inhibition of auditory hallucinations. *Journal of Behavior Therapy and Experimental Psychiatry, 7*, 155–160. A 32-year-old woman who was hospitalized because she frequently heard voices and responded to them was given an apparatus with which she could give herself a shock when she heard the voices. This procedure resulted in the woman no longer reporting hearing the voices and no longer responding to them. She was dismissed from the hospital and has lived a normal life since.

Flanagan, B., Goldiamond, L., & Azrin, N. H. (1958). Operant stuttering: The control of stuttering behavior through response contingent consequences. *Journal of the Experimental Analysis of Behavior, 1,* 173–177. Chronic stutterers read from a book into a microphone while an observer counted the number of stutters. When every stutter was followed by a blast of noise delivered to the stutterers through earphones, their rate of stuttering decreased markedly.

Green, R. J., & Hoats, D. L. (1969). Reinforcing capabilities of television distortion. *Journal of Applied Behavior Analysis, 2,* 139–141. A hyperactive girl of 18 with mild retardation was seated in a room watching TV. Her hyperactivity was observed, and during baseline, it averaged about 22 responses per minute. During treatment, the TV picture was mildly distorted contingent on her hyperactive behavior. Her rate decreased to an average of about 3 responses per minute. Thus, the distortion served as a successful punisher of hyperactive responding.

Holz, W. C., & Azrin, N. H. (1966). Punishment. In W. K. Honig (Ed.), *Operant behavior: Areas of research and application.* New York: Appleton-Century-Crofts. This article provides an excellent overview of the concept of punishment, the side effects of using punishment, a comparison of punishment with other methods for reducing behavior, and the ethical considerations involved in using punishment.

McFadden, A. C., Marsh, G. E., Price, B. J., & Hwang, Y. (1992). A study of race and gender bias in the punishment of school children. *Education and Treatment of Children, 15,* 140–146. This article reports the effects of race on the use of punishment in one school district. The authors found that blacks received more physical punishment and were more often suspended from school. Further, the referral rate for blacks was disproportionately higher than for whites.

Powell, J., & Azrin, N. H. (1968). The effect of shock as a punisher for cigarette smoking. *Journal of Applied Behavior Analysis, 1*, 63–71. Individuals who wished to stop smoking were given a harness device that was hooked up to a special cigarette case. Each time they opened the pack, they were shocked. This procedure decreased their smoking, but the individuals began to wear the harness for only short periods of time.

Risley, T. R. (1968). The effects and side effects of punishing the autistic behaviors of a deviant child. *Journal of Applied Behavior Analysis, 1*, 21–34. A hyperactive child with autism frequently engaged in climbing behaviors that resulted in falls and serious physical damage to the child (such as knocking out teeth). To eliminate such behaviors, shock punishment was used at the start of each climbing episode. This eliminated the dangerous climbing behavior.

Tate, B. G., & Baroff, G. S. (1966). Aversive control of self-injurious behavior in a psychotic boy. *Behavior Research and Therapy, 4*, 281–287. A psychotic boy engaged in such serious head-banging behavior that he was in danger of losing his eyesight. The use of electric shock contingent on the head-banging response quickly eliminated this self-injurious behavior.

Wilson, G. T., Leaf, R. C., & Nathan, P. E. (1975). The aversive control of excessive alcohol consumption by chronic alcoholics in the laboratory setting. *Journal of Applied Behavior Analysis, 8*, 13–26. Shock was used to punish the consumption of alcohol by chronic alcoholics. The alcoholics were permitted to drink as much as they wished. During baseline, they drank over 20 ounces of alcohol per day. During treatment, they were shocked each time they took a drink. This resulted in nearly complete elimination of drinking.

## Programmed Reading

This section provides questions over the following topics: (1) Aversive Control, (2) Another way to Reduce Behaviors, (3) When Is a Procedure Punishment? (4) Types of Punishment, (5) Discriminative Stimuli for Punishment, (6) Similarities with Other Procedures, (7) Another Tactic, and (8) Review.

### *1. Aversive Control*

55. Pre-test: The use of punishment and negative reinforcement are two types of _____ control.

45. Pre-test: Label the procedure in which an unpleasant event follows a behavior as _____.

97. This whole unit is about aversive control. The use of punishment and negative reinforcement to control behavior is called _____ (aversive, reinforcement, stimulus) control.

96. The use of punishment and negative reinforcement are two types of _____ control.

14. Be very careful not to equate *unpleasant* with *aversive* or *punisher*. You learned with reinforcers that events you consider unpleasant, if they follow behavior and increase the rate of that behavior, are called _____. People often work to earn events that other people consider unpleasant.

72. Skinner labels aversive control as the _____ (least, most) common technique of control in modern life.

12. Aversive control may cause a person to try to exert countercontrol over another person through violence. It may cause a person to experience a variety of negative emotional responses. These are two examples of possible _____ (desirable, undesirable) side effects of aversive control.

3. A dream of behavior analysts is to create a world in which the need for _____ (aversive, reinforcement, stimulus) control is minimized.

70. Skinner asserted that the behavioral procedure that "is to be preferred because appears to have fewer objectionable by-products" is positive _____.

71. Skinner did not believe that we could completely avoid aversive consequences. He simply proposed that people can influence each other through reinforcement rather than through _____.

104. When institutionalized people hit themselves repeatedly and break bones, cause bleeding, blind themselves, or knock out teeth, psychologists call this *self-injurious behavior*, which they abbreviate, using the first letter of those three words, as _____.

### 2. *Another Way to Reduce Behaviors*

41. Pre-test: Behavior analysts call delivering a punisher following a behavior the procedure of _____.

47. Pre-test: Suppose Mom delivered the "unpleasant" event of yelling "Don't!" at Baby Ann after she spit her applesauce, but the rate of Baby Ann's spitting did not decrease in the future. You should label this procedure as _____.

38. Pre-test: A punisher is an event that (1) _____ a behavior and (2) _____ the frequency of that behavior.

46. Pre-test: Should you assume that an "unpleasant" event delivered contingent on a behavior must be a punisher? _____ (yes, no)

89. The first goal of this quiz is to teach you about punishers. A punisher is an event that (1) follows a behavior and (2) _____ (decreases, increases) the frequency of that behavior.

6. A punisher is an event that (1) _____ a behavior and (2) _____ the frequency of that behavior.

77. Suppose Baby Ann spits her applesauce on the floor. Mom might yell, "Don't!" The event of yelling "Don't!" follows Baby Ann's spitting. You should call it a punisher if the rate at which Baby Ann spits out her food in the future _____.

13. Baby Ann spits her applesauce. Mom yells, "Don't!" Baby Ann spits her applesauce less often after that. If you wish to label the <u>procedure</u> that Mom uses you should label it as punishment. If you wish to label the <u>event</u> "Mom yells, 'Don't!'" you should label it as a(n) _____.

21. Every time that Baby Ann spits her applesauce, Mom yells, "Don't!" Baby Ann spits her applesauce less often after that. If you wish to label the <u>procedure</u> that Mom uses you should label it as _____.

91. The greater effort of wearing wrist weights is a stimulus that occurs following the start of the slapping response, resulting in a reduction of that response. Therefore, that stimulus is called a(n) _____.

17. Behavior analysts call an event that (1) follows a behavior and (2) decreases the frequency of that behavior a(n) _____.

18. Behavior analysts call delivering a punisher following a behavior the <u>procedure</u> of _____.

64. Punishment is the <u>procedure</u> in which a(n) _____ is administered contingent on some undesired behavior.

85. Suppose you read about an event that (1) follows a behavior and (2) doesn't change the frequency of that behavior. Such an event is not a punisher because a punisher decreases the rate of the behavior. Such an event is not extinction because extinction decreases the rate of the behavior. If you are asked about an event that doesn't meet the definition of any terms you have learned about, you should call that event a(n) _____.

79. Suppose Mom delivered the "unpleasant" event of yelling "Don't!" at Baby Ann after she spit her applesauce. This unpleasant event clearly follows spitting. However, it would be a punisher *only* if it also _____ the rate of spitting.

78. Suppose Mom delivered the "unpleasant" event of yelling "Don't!" at Baby Ann after she spit her applesauce, but the rate of Baby Ann's spitting did not decrease in the future. You should label this procedure as _____.

68. Should you assume that an "unpleasant" event delivered contingent on a behavior must be a punisher? _____ (yes, no)

76. Suppose Baby Ann smiles sweetly at Mom. Suppose Mom delivers a spoonful of applesauce to Baby Ann. Suppose Baby Ann's rate of smiling decreases. Because delivery of the spoonful of applesauce follows the smile and decreases its rate, you have no choice but to label this apparently "pleasant" event as a(n) _____.

69. Should you assume that a "pleasant" event delivered contingent on a behavior cannot be a punisher? _____ (yes, no)

23. If a question asks for a procedure whereby a stimulus follows a behavior and <u>decreases</u> its rate, you know from the word *procedure* to answer _____ _____ . If a question asks for an event that follows a behavior and <u>decreases</u> its rate, you know from the word *event* to answer _____ .

### 3. When Is a Procedure Punishment?

48. Pre-test: Suppose that any hyperactivity from Lulu is followed by distorting the TV picture she was watching, resulting in no change in her hyperactivity. Then the procedure of using the distortion is _____ .

58. Pre-test: Two procedures for reducing the rate of a behavior are _____ _____ and _____ .

49. Pre-test: Suppose that Mom ignores Lulu's hyperactivity. If Lulu's hyperactivity decreases, Mom is using the procedure called _____ .

50. Pre-test: Suppose that any hyperactivity from Lulu is followed by distorting the TV picture she was watching, resulting in a decrease in her hyperactivity. Then the procedure of using the distortion is a form of mild _____ .

93. The procedure of extinction _____ _____ (decreases, increases) the rate of a behavior.

94. The procedure of punishment _____ _____ (decreases, increases) the rate of a behavior.

103. Two procedures for reducing the rate of a behavior are _____ and _____ .

27. If Mother spanks Bobby each time he pesters her for a cookie and his rate of pestering decreases, then the use of spanking would be an example of what behavioral procedure? _____ .

28. If Mother spanks Bobby each time he pesters her for a cookie and his rate of pestering doesn't change, then the use of spanking would be an example of what behavioral procedure? _____ _____ .

29. If Mother spanks Bobby each time he pesters her for a cookie and his rate of pestering increases, then the use of spanking would be an example of what behavioral procedure? _____

82. Suppose Mother ignores, rather than pays attention to, Bobby each time he pesters her for a cookie. If his rate of pestering decreases, then ignoring him would be an example of what behavioral procedure? _____

74. Students sometimes interpret "Mom ignores Bobby" as a punisher. They assume that ignoring someone is an insult. They are assuming that ignoring can be considered an event because it is doing something. When I tell you Mom ignores Bobby, I mean that Mom does nothing. There is no event. Thus, even if her ignoring decreases Bobby's pestering, it _____ (can, can't) be an event call a punisher.

105. When you learn that "Mom ignores Bobby," you should interpret ignoring as not giving him the attention that he got before. Thus, if Bobby's rate of pestering decreases, Mom is using the procedure of _____ .

80. Suppose Mom used to look annoyed every time that Bobby pestered her. But now she maintains a neutral look when he pesters. If his pestering decreases, what procedure is she using? _____ _____

66. Remember, when someone ignores another person, maintains a neutral look, doesn't reinforce them, and that person's behavior decreases, this is not an example of punishment. Such examples usually tell you that the person ignores instead of paying attention, looks neutral instead of annoyed or pleased, doesn't reinforce instead of does reinforce. Thus, such examples involve stopping delivery of a reinforcer and therefore use the procedure called _____ .

19. Behavior analysts often need to eliminate dangerous or self-injurious behaviors more quickly than is possible with extinction. In such a case, they may resort to the procedure of _____ .

75. Suppose a behavior analyst delivered a very brief and mild shock each time that a severely disturbed child with autism

attempted to injure themselves. If the rate of such self-injury decreased, what behavioral procedure would the administration of shock be an example of? _____

83. Suppose that when the behavior analyst delivers the shock, the rate of self-injury doesn't change. What behavioral procedure is the shock an example of? _____

30. If the delivery of immediate, brief shock following dangerous head banging reduces that behavior, the delivery of shock is an example of what behavioral procedure? _____

15. Behavior analysts can often eliminate dangerous behaviors by delivering events following those behaviors that are milder than shock. These milder events are called _____.

67. Researchers required a 4-year-old fire setter to do one hour of hard labor for each fire-setting episode. The fire setting was eliminated. Behavior analysts would label this procedure _____.

84. Suppose that you required the 4-year-old fire setter to do one hour of hard labor following a fire-setting episode. Suppose that the rate of fire setting did not change. You would label this procedure _____.

106. When you prove Barry wrong in a discussion, your proof follows his assertion. If your proof reduces the rate at which he makes that assertion, then you have used what behavioral method? _____

109. You discuss a putdown with Kay. She helps you see that labeling it as your problem is incorrect and even laughable—it's the other person's problem. Your rate of labeling the putdown as your problem decreases. Kay's gentle help is an example of what behavioral procedure? _____

### 4. Types of Punishment

37. Pre-test: A primary punisher is a punisher that loses its effectiveness only through _____.

56. Pre-test: Three types of punishers are _____ punishers, _____ punishers, and _____ punishers.

35. Pre-test: A conditioned punisher may develop when an event is repeatedly paired with another punisher. Therefore, a conditioned punisher loses its effect permanently through _____ presentations.

36. Pre-test: A generalized punisher is a punisher that is associated with _____ _____ other punishers.

5. A primary punisher is a punisher that loses its effectiveness only through _____.

73. Spanking will always be a punisher unless it has been used too often recently. Therefore, behavior analysts classify it as a(n) _____ punisher.

2. A conditioned punisher may develop when an event is repeatedly paired with another punisher. Therefore, a conditioned punisher loses its effect permanently through _____ presentations.

33. Initially, when Mom tells Jimmy "no" immediately after he does something dangerous, he may stop. Suppose she unpairs "no" from its backup of spanking (by never giving him a spanking after she says "no") and "no" permanently loses its effect. You should classify her "no" as a(n) _____ punisher.

4. A generalized punisher is a punisher that is associated with _____ other punishers.

26. If Dad tells May "no" every time she pinches him, she may stop pinching him for a time. Sometimes he backs up his "no" with a light swat, other times by pushing her away, and still other times by grabbing her roughly. Because he pairs his "no" with three other punishers, you should classify his "no" as a(n) _____ punisher.

10. After an abusive incident, the abusers apologize, buy gifts, and generally offer love and affection. Because of its pairing with gifts and love, the physical abuse could become a(n) _____ reinforcer.

98. Three types of punishers are _____ punishers, _____ punishers, and _____ punishers.

### 5. *Discriminative Stimuli for Punishment*

39. Pre-test: A stimulus that decreases the rate of a response that it <u>precedes</u> is called a(n) _____; a stimulus that decreases the rate of a response that it quickly <u>follows</u> is called a(n) _____.

42. Pre-test: If a teacher explains that the student should not perform an undesirable behavior and then punishes that behavior each time it occurs, this would be an example of _____ training.

40. Pre-test: A stimulus associated with punishment for a particular behavior is called a(n) _____ stimulus for punishment and abbreviated as _____.

16. Behavior analysts call a stimulus associated with reinforcement for a particular behavior a <u>discriminative</u> stimulus for reinforcement. They call a stimulus associated with punishment for a particular behavior a(n) _____ stimulus for punishment.

1. A <u>stimulus</u> associated with punishment for a particular behavior is called a discriminative _____ for punishment.

7. A stimulus associated with punishment for a particular behavior is called a(n) _____ stimulus for punishment and abbreviated as _____.

81. Suppose Mom warns Davey, "Don't go near the edge," and then spanks him whenever he does. Behavior analysts call the phrase "Don't go near the edge" a discriminative stimulus for _____.

110. You have learned in prior lessons that instructional training can be used to increase a desirable behavior by describing the behavior and then reinforcing instances of that behavior. You can also decrease undesirable behavior by describing the behavior and then using what procedure when the person performs that behavior? _____ training.

24. If a teacher explains that the student should not perform an undesirable behavior and then punishes that behavior each time it occurs, this would be an example of _____ training.

20. Dr. McNees posted stars identifying clothing items that were often stolen. Customers stole much less after the posting than before. Because the star is present before anyone steals rather than after and because it decreased the rate of stealing, it is called a(n) _____.

111. You must look carefully to find out whether an event precedes or follows a behavior. You learned to do this for reinforcers. Now you must learn to do it for punishers. If an event <u>follows</u> a behavior and decreases it, then call that event a(n) _____.

25. If an event <u>precedes</u> a behavior and decreases it, then call that event a(n) _____ stimulus for punishment. You may abbreviate it in the rest of the book as _____.

8. A stimulus that decreases the rate of a response that it <u>precedes</u> is called a(n) _____; a stimulus that decreases the rate of a response that it quickly <u>follows</u> is called a(n) _____.

### 6. *Similarities with Other Procedures*

60. Pre-test: You can make a punishment most effective by observing four principles: the principle of _____, the principle of _____, the principle of _____, and the principle of _____.

65. Punishment will generally be most effective if it follows the same principles governing reinforcers: contingency, immediacy, size, and _____.

100. To have maximum effectiveness, when should a punisher occur in relation to the behavior? It should occur _____ after it. This would be called the principle of _____.

101. To have maximum effectiveness, for what behavior should a punisher be delivered? It should be delivered _____ for the undesirable behavior. This would be called the principle of _____.

92. The principle of size is a little different for reinforcement than for punishment.

Usually for punishment, you talk about the strength of the punishing stimulus rather than the amount—how hard is the spank, how loud is the yell, how much is the effort, and so forth. To have maximum effectiveness, how strong should the punisher be? It should be of _____ _____ strength.

102. To have maximum effectiveness, how often should the punisher be delivered? It should be delivered _____ (frequently, rarely). This would be called the principle of _____.

108. You can make a punishment most effective by observing four principles: the principle of _____, the principle of _____, the principle of _____, and the principle of _____.

34. Mild punishment is sometimes used in differential reinforcement in place of extinction. In this form of differential reinforcement, you combine the procedure of reinforcement of desirable behavior with the procedure of mild _____ of undesirable behavior.

32. If you reinforce a desirable behavior while punishing an undesirable behavior in one situation, you would be using the procedure of _____.

31. If you reinforce a behavior in one situation while punishing it in another situation, you would be using the procedure of _____.

### 7. Another Tactic

52. Pre-test: The fourth strategy for changing human behavior is the _____ control strategy.

51. Pre-test: Tactic #1 in using the aversive control strategy is to decrease undesirable behavior through _____ as a last resort.

53. Pre-test: The fourth strategy for changing human behavior is the _____ (aversive, reinforcement, stimulus) control strategy.

86. Tactic #1 in using the aversive control strategy is to decrease undesirable behavior through _____ as a last resort.

107. Which strategy is the last resort for changing behavior? The _____ _____ control strategy.

90. The fourth strategy for changing human behavior is the _____ control strategy.

87. Tactic #1 in using the aversive control strategy is to decrease undesirable behavior through _____ as a last resort.

### 8. Review

57. Pre-test: To use the aversive control strategy, (1) decrease undesirable behavior through _____ as a last resort.

59. Pre-test: When a behavior is punished, it will decrease in that situation. The name for the process in which the same behavior decreases in other situations without punishment is _____.

44. Pre-test: Ken gave Jan a withering look every time that she suggested that he go on a diet. Jan is still suggesting that Ken go on a diet. Ken's withering look is an event called a(n) _____.

43. Pre-test: If an event follows a behavior and reduces the future probability of that behavior, it is called a(n) _____.

54. Pre-test: The fourth strategy for changing human behavior is the _____ control strategy.

88. Tactic #1 in using the aversive control strategy is to decrease undesirable behavior through _____ as a last resort.

99. Three types of punishers are: (1) _____, (2) _____, and (3) _____.

63. Punishment is most effective when the following four principles are followed: _____, _____, _____, and _____.

11. An event that decreases the rate of a behavior that it follows is called a(n) _____.

61. Punishers and reinforcers are events that differ in one way but that are similar in another. They differ in that punishers decrease behaviors while reinforcers increase behaviors. They are similar in

that both must be timed to _____
_____ a behavior.

9. A stimulus that occurs before the behavior and is associated with punishment of the behavior is called a(n) _____

_____ .

62. Punishment and extinction both affect a behavior in the same way. They both produce a(n) _____ in the frequency of the behavior.

22. If a punisher's effectiveness is permanently eliminated when no longer paired with another punisher, what type of punisher is it? _____

95. The use of punishment to control behavior is called _____ control.

## Programmed Examples

### 1. Programmed Examples

15. Pre-test: Yvonne told everyone in class that she didn't think President Bush should have gotten us into the 1991 Persian Gulf War unless we were going to completely defeat Iraq. Several people immediately gasped, "Yvonne, you can't mean that!" Yvonne never mentioned her feelings about the war again in class. The reactions of Yvonne's classmates to her remark would be an example of what behavioral procedure? _____

12. Pre-test: Gladys sometimes spanked Danny for bothering her, but she immediately felt sorry for him. She gave him an ice cream cone to stop his tears. If Danny started bothering her more, rather than less, we might guess that the ice cream cone was more reinforcing than the spanking was punishing. Furthermore, whenever Danny got spanked, he knew that Gladys would then give him an ice cream cone. Therefore, a spanking by Gladys was backed up with ice cream. The spanking could actually become a(n) _____ (conditioned, generalized, primary) reinforcer.

13. Pre-test: Jason grabbed for whatever he wanted at dinner. Dad started giving him a lecture on manners each time Jason grabbed. Jason continues to grab for what he wants. Dad used the procedure of _____ .

14. Pre-test: Terry was the newest member of the food co-op's staff. During the regular Thursday staff meetings, Terry would frequently launch into a discourse on the evils of the local merchants. Needless to say, this subject had nothing to do with what order the food co-op was going to place next week or who was going to work what hours. Consequently, the other staff members paid no attention to Terry's irrelevant rhetoric. After a month, he had stopped it. What behavioral procedure was at work decreasing Terry's rate of rhetoric? _____

20. Tom's rate of teasing his sister decreased when Mom spanked him every time he teased her. Ask, "Did Mom's spanking precede, not follow, Tom's teasing behavior?" ____ (yes, no) The spanking is not an SP. Ask, "Did she stop delivering a reinforcer for teasing his sister?" _____ (yes, no) The spanking is not extinction. Since Mom's spanking followed the teasing and decreased its rate, it is an example of the procedure called _____ .

10. Mary got very hungry during the afternoon. By the time her mother was fixing dinner, Mary thought that she would die of hunger, so she would beg her mother for a snack. Her mother would tell her she couldn't have a snack because it would spoil her dinner. Then Mary would nag her mother. Soon her mother would scream "No!" every time Mary asked for a snack. Her mother thought that a scream would punish Mary for asking. However, Mary continued to beg and nag for a snack even when her mother screamed at her for asking. Before you start asking questions, decide whether the example involves a decrease in behavior, this time Mary's. Does it decrease? ____ (yes, no) Is Mom's screaming "No!" an example of punishment? ____ (yes, no) One way Mary's mother could have made her "No!" an effective punisher of Mary's request would be for her to always follow her "No!" with another, more powerful _____ .

7. Fred's repeated racial slurs were annoying to the other members of the Harmony Group. They simply ignored his comments, but the comments didn't decrease. One day he commented to Dick, another member, "Look at that black boy! He's the tallest guy I've ever seen." Dick rebuked Fred by saying, "It's disrespectful of black people to call them 'boys'." Fred looked surprised, but he never used that word again around other group members. Make sure there's a decrease. Ask, "Did Dick's

rebuke precede, not follow, Fred's saying 'boy'?"
_____ (yes, no) Ask, "Did Dick stop delivering a
reinforcer for saying 'boy'?" _____. Since Dick's
rebuke followed and decreased use of "boy," it
is an example of what procedure? _____
_____

11. Mr. Tubbs was mad at Jerry for whispering with his friend yesterday. So before
class the next day, Mr. Tubbs told him not to
whisper to his friend anymore. Jerry never
whispered in Mr. Tubbs's class again. To analyze this example, notice that Mr. Tubbs's
instruction did not follow Jerry's whispering
right away. Did Mr. Tubbs's instruction
precede the next chance of Jerry's whispering?
_____ (yes, no) Is his instruction a punisher?
_____ (yes, no) You could also remember the
following rule: An instruction usually is neither a reinforcer nor a(n) _____.
If Mr. Tubbs's instruction was really a warning that Jerry would be punished for any whispering, the warning would technically be
called a(n) _____.

16. Professor Brainbuster wanted his students to discuss only really important ideas.
As a result, he would immediately ridicule
most comments from them. Most students
stopped making comments in the class discussion within two weeks. Make sure there's
a decrease in comments. Ask, "Did the ridicule
precede the comments?" If not, did he stop
delivering a reinforcer for making comments?
Since Brainbuster's ridicule followed comments and decreased them, it is an event
called a(n) _____. One semester,
Brainbuster gave everyone an A at the beginning of the semester. To his surprise, he found
that the students no longer shut up after he
ridiculed them. Many argued back, and some
even ridiculed him! The fact that his ridicule,
when unpaired with the potential for poor
grades, no longer decreased comments indicates that ridicule is what kind of a punisher?
A(n) _____ punisher.

9. Lou frequently insulted people with
comments such as "That was a dumb idea" or
"That is a terrible-looking shirt." Lou's friends
apparently reinforced his insulting behavior
by looking annoyed when he issued his
insults. One day, several of Lou's friends
decided that they had enough of his insults.
They agreed to not look annoyed when Lou

insulted them. Lou's rate of insults decreased
quite rapidly when his insults no longer produced looks of annoyance. Ask, "Was there a
decrease?" "Did the friends' reaction precede
Lou's insults?" "Did they stop delivering a
reinforcer for his insults?" "Were Lou's friends
delivering a punisher or stopping delivery of
a reinforcer after his insults?" When Lou's
friends stopped looking annoyed after his
insults, what behavioral procedure were they
using? _____

19. The cooperative dorm had a written
rule: No complaining about dinner during
the dinner period. Bob complained one
night about the dinner, and Lou immediately
responded by saying, "Hey, stop that." Bob
never broke that rule again. To figure out
what procedure Lou used to decrease his complaining, ask, "Was there a decrease?" "Did
Lou's reaction precede Bob's complaints?"
"Did Lou stop delivering a reinforcer for the
complaints?" "Was Lou delivering a punisher
or stopping delivery of a reinforcer after the
complaints?" Once you answer those questions, you can see that Lou used the behavioral procedure called _____.

1. Barbara broke the rule "No complaining about dinner during the dinner period."
Another member immediately responded by
saying, "Stop complaining, Barbara." Barbara
continued to break the rule from time to time.
Several members became annoyed enough
with Barbara's complaining to bring the problem up at the next dorm meeting. Someone
suggested that the "reminder" that the other
members were giving Barbara when she
complained wasn't strong enough and that
Barbara (or any other complainer) should be
fined $1 whenever she complained during
dinner. If the reminder served as a punisher
when it was associated with the $1 fine but
quickly lost its effectiveness when it was not
paired with the fine, it would be classified as a
_____ punisher.

3. Carol told her little son, Lenny, not
to touch the steering wheel while she was
driving. The next time that he touched the
wheel, she spanked him. He rarely touched
the wheel after that and always got a spanking when he did. Spanking is an event
that followed touching the steering wheel
and decreased its rate. This event is called

a(n) _____. The procedure of giving a spanking after touching the steering wheel is called _____.

8. Jane was teaching Queenie to count to 10. Queenie said, "one, two, three, five." Jane said, "No, that's wrong." Queenie never made that mistake again. Jane said "No, that's wrong" right after Queenie said "five" instead of "four." Therefore, Jane used what behavioral procedure to decrease saying "five" after "three"? _____ Notice that although this procedure stops Queenie from making that specific error again, she still might make other errors. Notice that punishment does not directly encourage her to repeat any of the correct responses. To increase the rate of correct responses, Jane should also use _____ _____ for correct responses.

6. Frank ran a red light one day when he was in a hurry to get to class. A police officer caught him and gave him a ticket. Frank didn't go through a red light again after that. By asking the right questions, you can see that the event of getting the ticket was an example of a(n) _____. Getting the ticket may help make the red light a(n) _____ for driving through the intersection.

2. Bob's father usually greeted his ideas with encouragement. But when Bob mentioned to his Dad that poor people in this country are treated badly, his father ignored him. Bob never brought the subject up again. Bob's decreased rate of talking about the problems of poor people is the result of what behavioral procedure? _____

17. Professor Young encouraged his sociology students to express ideas about U.S. social problems, but he ridiculed them if they talked about abstract theory. Professor Old encouraged his students to express ideas about abstract sociological theory and scolded them if they expressed ideas about actual social problems. Dan was a student of both professors. He soon learned to talk about social problems in Professor Young's class and not to talk about them in Professor Old's class. The changes in Dan's behavior would be the result of what behavioral procedure?

_____

4. Donny frequently made disparaging remarks about Dale's figure in front of their friends. As soon as they were alone, Dale always became very angry at Donny's remarks. However, Donny continued to make such remarks in front of their friends. What principle of punishment may have reduced the effectiveness of Dale's anger as a punisher?

_____

5. Donny was always arguing. Donny's friends started paying attention when he made reasonable arguments but ignored unreasonable arguments. Donny's rate of unreasonable arguments decreased drastically; his rate of reasonable arguments increased. What behavioral procedure accounts for the relative increase in reasonable arguments? _____

18. Sam hit Bobby a few months ago because Bobby was being a terrible pest. Bobby immediately started acting nice to Sam. Since then, Sam's rate of hitting Bobby whenever he was being a pest has increased. (Hint: For the following question focus on Sam's behavior, not Bobby's.) The increase in the rate of Sam's hitting response is a result of what behavioral procedure? _____

# LESSON

# 23 | Punishment by Contingent Withdrawal

## Reading Section

This lesson introduces a second type of punishment: a reinforcer for some behavior other than the undesirable behavior is taken away from someone each time they emit an undesirable behavior. For example, treating a pinball machine too roughly will cause a "tilt" light to go on. This takes away the privilege of playing the machine any longer. Yelling at your mother may cause her to "ground" you. You can't leave the house. Behavior analysts call this form of punishment *punishment by contingent withdrawal*.

## Definition of Punishment by Contingent Withdrawal

**Punishment by contingent withdrawal** is an event withdrawal that <u>follows</u> a behavior and <u>decreases</u> the rate of that behavior. I have used the unusual phrasing *event withdrawal* to emphasize that the withdrawal takes place following the behavior. The event that is withdrawn does not have to occur following the behavior. For example, Judge Evans might punish Mary for speeding by taking away $100 of her money in the form of a fine. Mary's $100 was in her pocket before she speeded, but the $100 withdrawal occurred following her speeding. You should notice that this definition of punishment by contingent withdrawal is exactly the same as the definition for punishment by contingent stimulation with a crucial difference: For one punishment, the event is withdrawn; for the other it is produced. I will not test you on the two different types of punishment.

1. **Punishment by contingent withdrawal**: Event withdrawal that _____ a behavior and _____ the rate of that behavior.

Behavior analysts may withdraw an event permanently or only temporarily. One example of a permanent loss is the judge who fines a person for speeding. The person permanently loses $50. Another example is the parent who requires the child to pay to replace a window that they broke through careless use of their BB gun. Another example is the person who breaks off a friendship after learning that the other person was lying to them. These examples involve permanent losses. They would be examples of punishment if speeding, careless shooting, and lying decrease.

One example of a temporary loss is when Mom won't let Gwen go out to play after school today because she ate ice cream without permission. Another might be if the teacher makes Jack sit in the corner five minutes because he pulled Ann's pigtail. If Gwen's eating of ice cream without permission and Jack's pigtail pulling decrease, then these procedures would be punishment by contingent withdrawal. Behavior analysts frequently call this form of punishment *time out*. The name comes from making the person take time out from a reinforcing activity.

I will not ask you to distinguish between permanent and temporary forms of punishment by contingent withdrawal. I will ask you to use the label *time out* in some examples.

## Uses of Punishment by Contingent Withdrawal

Punishment by contingent withdrawal is not as severe as physical punishment. Therefore, behavior analysts prefer it to punishment by contingent stimulation when they need to use punishment as a last resort. Sometimes they use it in combination with reinforcement (e.g., Cicero & Pfadt, 2002). They then fade out the punishment if possible (see Lerman & Vorndran, 2002).

Behavior analysts often use fines as part of a token or point system. For example, one researcher used fines as part of a token system for chronic mental hospital patients (Winkler, 1970). He observed rates of physical violence during baseline. This approach included attacks on staff. Sometimes these attacks were so violent that staff required medical care. The baseline rate decreased by about half solely as a result of using tokens to reinforce desirable behaviors. Using token fines for aggression reduced the rate much further. Because they withdrew the tokens (through fines) contingent on aggression and the aggression decreased, the fines are punishment by contingent withdrawal. The nurses reported that the ward was a much nicer place to work as a result.

Other researchers withdrew tokens when teenagers interrupted a class (Sprute, Williams, & McLaughlin, 1990). This approach produced a large reduction in interruptions. Other researchers punished teenagers for coming late to dinner by taking away points (Phillips, Phillips, Fixsen, & Wolf, 1971). The teenagers' lateness decreased. In both these cases, the token withdrawals were contingent on a behavior that decreases. They were therefore examples of punishment by contingent withdrawal.

Researchers used a similar approach to help a 65-year-old man quit smoking (Belles & Bradlyn, 1987). He agreed to donate money to an organization he didn't like at the end of any week during which he failed to reduce smoking. Over a two-year period he managed to reduce his smoking from 82 cigarettes a day to 5. Other researchers have found this same approach to be effective (Singh & Leung, 1988). Another researcher used a similar approach to reduce eating (Mann, 1972). One participant lost more than 100 pounds. This procedure is punishment by contingent withdrawal because people lost money contingent on a behavior and the behavior decreased. It is a clever approach because the participants not only lost money but they gave it to causes that they disliked.

Figure 23-1 gives an interesting example of an everyday use of punishment by withdrawal. The phone company began charging customers 20 cents each local call for information that was made in Cincinnati in 1973. Because the charge followed the call and the rate of such calls decreased, this is an example of punishment.

## Uses of Time Out

Behavior analysts often use time out from a reinforcing activity to punish behavior. Researchers used a brief time out to get children to hold still for brain scans (Slifer, Cataldo, Cataldo, Llorente, & Gersen, 1993). Any slight motion of their head interrupted a cartoon for three seconds. The interruption is a brief withdrawal of the cartoon presentation. Because the children's movements decreased, this would be an example of punishment by contingent withdrawal. Another researcher reduced thumb-sucking behavior in young children by interrupting a cartoon when the children sucked their thumbs (Baer, 1962). Other researchers reduced whining, crying, and complaining in a 5-year-old by withdrawing attention (Hall, Axelrod, Tyler, Grief, Jones, & Robertson, 1972).

Another type of time out involves making the person watch but not participate in a reinforcing activity. For example, researchers helped the teacher of fourth-and-fifth grade physical education classes (White & Bailey, 1990). The kids didn't obey, they hit each other, and they threw things. The teacher briefly removed disruptive children from the activity, permitting them only to watch it. This brief withdrawal of the right to participate resulted in a 95% reduction of disruptive behavior.

Another form of time out involves removing people from the reinforcing environment when they emit the undesirable behavior.

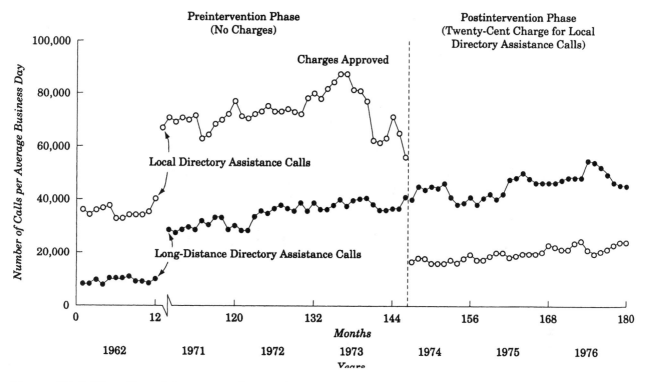

**Figure 23-1** The effect of charges on the number of local and long-distance directory assistance calls made in Cincinnati from 1962 to 1976. The graph compares calls made before and after introduction of a 20-cent charge for such calls. The charges amount to withdrawing an amount of money for the behavior. Therefore, they are punishment by contingent withdrawal. (From "The Effects of Response Cost on the Behavior of a Million Persons: Charging for Directory Assistance in Cincinnati," by A. J. McSweeney, *Journal of Applied Behavior Analysis,* 1978, 11, 47–51. Copyright 1978 by the Society for the Experimental Analysis of Behavior, Inc. Used by permission.)

For example, parents used this approach to reduce the aggressive behavior of a child. They simply removed him from the room. They placed him in a specially modified room that had no toys in it (Zeilberger, Sampen, & Sloane, 1968). They kept the child in the time-out room for two minutes. If he continued screaming, they kept him there for an added two minutes. This type of isolation may seem unusually harsh. However, the child's aggressive behavior was also extreme. It consisted of hitting, kicking, throwing, biting, and scratching.

Behavior analysts pick the duration and form of time out depending on the behavior. They needed only a brief time out from cartoons to change weak behavior like head movement or thumb sucking but needed a longer time out to change children's disruptive play behaviors. They needed to actually remove a very aggressive child from the room to reduce aggression. Other studies have

looked at the length of time out, showing that moderate time out is often effective (Roberts & Powers, 1990).

## Problems with Punishment

Behavior analysts are sometimes faced with individuals who resist time out. Researchers tried several methods to deal with the resistance of oppositional children (Roberts & Powers, 1990). In this research, the mothers gave their children explicit instructions to do some tasks. The mothers praised their children when they complied and warned them when they did not. The mothers confined their children to a chair for two minutes whenever they disobeyed. They required their children to remain sitting for the full two minutes. Some children mildly resisted this time out by crying. The mothers punished this resistance by not releasing their children until they were quiet for 15 seconds. Other children resisted more strongly by leaving the chair before the time was up. The mothers punished this resistance by either putting them in another room for 60 seconds or spanking them. Both forms of punishment eliminated resistance to the time out.

Behavior analysts may also be faced with individuals for whom time out is reinforcing. Researchers found that the inappropriate behavior of two children actually increased when followed by time out (Plummer, Baer, & LeBlanc, 1977). Other researchers replicated this finding (e.g., Magee & Ellis, 2001; Solnick, Rincover, & Peterson, 1977). This result reminds us that the same events can be reinforcing for some people and punishing for others. We must never assume that an event that we think is unpleasant must be a punisher for another person. We must always see whether it decreases behavior.

## Adding Punishment to Reinforcement

Some studies suggest that adding punishment to reinforcement can improve performance. In the last lesson, I described a study testing this theory (Pfiffner & O'Leary, 1987). The researchers showed that punishment helped teach kids to reduce off-task behavior. They found that they could fade out the punishment once they had reduced the off-task behavior. Another researcher found that token fines reduced violent behavior more than token reinforcement of desirable behavior alone (Winkler, 1970). Other research is confirming the benefits of supplemental punishment (e.g., Keeney, Fisher, Adelinis, & Wilder, 2000; Sullivan & O'Leary, 1990). Often you can stop punishment once desirable behaviors have replaced undesirable behaviors (e.g., Rapp et al., 2000).

Be very careful when you think about these results. They do not mean that we should punish more. Punishment does not itself create desirable behavior. It only eliminates undesirable behavior. We usually help individuals more if we teach them more desirable behaviors that produce reinforcement. For example, two researchers worked with children with retardation who emitted challenging behavior

toward their teachers (Durand & Carr, 1992). Analysis suggested that teachers reinforced these behaviors by attending to them. The researchers punished challenging behavior for some children with time out. The researchers taught other children how to ask for attention. They were taught to say, "Am I doing good work?" Both methods reduced challenging behavior. However, the children treated by time out reverted to challenging behavior with new teachers. The children who knew how to ask for attention did not. These children had learned a more desirable way to produce reinforcement. The others had not.

## Punishment Applies to Making a Response

One final point about punishment should be made. Behavior analysts do not speak of "punishing" someone for not making a response. For example, suppose Mom spanks Tommy when he forgets to let the dog out. Can you label the spanking (if it reduces Tommy's failures to let the dog out) as punishment? The answer is no. Tommy is not making the response of letting the dog out. You might be tempted to say that Tommy's response is "forgetting" to let the dog out. But forgetting is not itself a response. It is the absense of a response. Behavior analysts are very precise on this point. You will get very confused in the next lesson if you label spanking Tommy for forgetting to let the dog out as punishment. Behavior analysts label this as an *avoidance* schedule. I will introduce this term in the next lesson. For now just remember the rule: Do not speak of *punishing* someone for not making a response.

2. Behavior analysts do not speak of "punishing" someone for _____ (making, not making) a response.

## Who Decides What Is Undesirable Behavior?

The concept of punishment raises ethical issues. You may have wondered what gives behavior analysts the right to decide what behavior is undesirable. That's an excellent question. In my opinion, they have no more right than anyone else to decide what behavior is undesirable. In fact, they usually don't decide. People consult with them about practical behavioral problems. Doctors ask them how to stop persons with retardation from injuring themselves. Parents ask them how to stop their child from throwing tantrums in public places. Teachers ask them how to stop underachieving students from wasting their time. If behavior analysts agree to help solve a problem and can ethically do so, they help these people. They do not decide on their own what behavior is so undesirable that it warrants punishment.

Here's a related question. What gives a behavior analyst the right to actually punish someone's behavior? I have simplified most of the examples in this book to imply that the researchers administer the punishment. Actually, they rarely do. They simply advise the doctor, parent, or teacher how and when to do it. They rarely punish anyone's behavior.

## Summary

Punishment can occur by withdrawing a reinforcing event contingent on an undesirable behavior. The withdrawal can be permanent, as with a fine. Or it can be temporary, as in loss of a privilege or time out. One problem with punishment is that people may resist it. This may require further punishment to control the behavior. Also, time out may be reinforcing for some people. Punishment by withdrawal is often used as a very mild corrective procedure. It may even be used temporarily and then faded out. Behavior analysts do not assume the right to punish people. They consult with others. They may advise punishment when nothing else seems to work.

## Behavior Analysis Examples

### Tantrums
Children often misbehave when in public with their parents, some developing extreme behaviors. This sort of misbehavior and extreme behavior can develop when parents

don't apply punishment because other people are around. Two researchers invented a way to eliminate tantrums in public (Rolider & Van Houten, 1985). Michael was a 10-year-old child who threw tantrums while taking the taxi to school with his mother. He screamed demands, cried loudly, and threw himself on the floor yelling and screaming. He engaged in this behavior 39% of the time.

During treatment, the mother tape-recorded Michael's tantrums. She played the recording of one of his tantrums at home with the father present. The parents then placed Michael in a very restrictive time out. They made him stand in the corner without moving for 20 seconds. His rate of tantrums in the taxi decreased to 8% of the time. They repeated this treatment in a multiple-baseline design for the bus and for the bus station. In each situation, the baseline level decreased sharply when the treatment was started. The tape recorder helped bridge the delay between the tantrum and the treatment. Standing in the corner followed the tantrums. (Based on Rolider & Van Houten, 1985.)

3. Standing in the corner followed the tantrums. The tantrums decreased in frequency. Therefore, standing in the corner is a(n) _____
(punisher, reinforcer).

### Rule Following in a Recreation Center
Researchers found a way to increase rule following in an urban youth center (Pierce & Risley, 1974). Young black men aged 7 to 25 went to this center, which offered pool, Ping-Pong, and table games for a couple of hours at night. The youth did not keep the center clean. They broke pool cues, fought, and threw trash around.

The director posted a list of rules. Each rule specified a group penalty consisting of closing the center 1–15 minutes early per violation. The director strictly enforced the more severe violations. Problems like fighting, breaking equipment, and crowding into line stopped. However, the director did not consistently enforce less severe violations. He explained, "I'm here to help the kids. I want to show them that I'm a nice guy." Three weeks later he agreed that the rules involving lesser violations had to be enforced also.

The director enforced rule violations by walking through the center every 15 minutes and looking for violations. For every violation that he observed, he noted it and a penalty on the blackboard. He then followed through by closing the center by the number of minutes of accumulated penalties indicated on the blackboard. Thus, the individuals attending the center lost the privilege of using the center when one or more of their group violated the rules.

An observer walked through the center every 30 minutes to count violations. The observer never enforced the rules or showed his observations to the director. At various times, a second observer recorded rule violations at the same time but independently of the primary observer. Reliability averaged 96%.

Figure 23-2 shows the results of the study. When the rules were only enforced occasionally, each rule was broken most of the time. After the director consistently enforced rules, violations decreased dramatically. The amount of time lost in penalties averaged 10 minutes. The number of participants did not change over the period of the experiment.

The group contingency used was well suited to this situation. It did not require personal and possibly abrasive confrontations between director and participants. Instead, the older participants prompted the younger ones not to break the rules. The result of the procedure was a cleaner, better-operating recreation center. It left the director more time to plan constructive activities and to improve the facility.

4. When a participant broke a rule or let someone else break a rule, he lost time in the center. This contingency reduced the rate of violations. The event of losing time is a(n) _____.

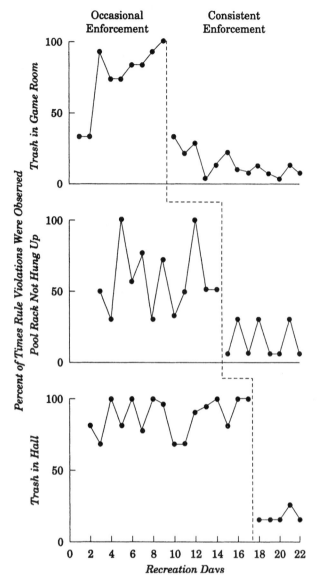

**Figure 23-2** The effect of consistent rule enforcement on neatness in an inner-city recreational facility. (Adapted from "Recreation as a Reinforcer: Increasing Membership and Decreasing Disruptions in an Urban Recreation Center," by C. H. Pierce and T. R. Risley, *Journal of Applied Behavior Analysis,* 1978, 7, 403–411. Copyright 1974 by the Society for the Experimental Analysis of Behavior, Inc. Used by permission.)

## Helpful Hints

### *Helpful Hint #1*

It is not necessary to use the full label describing which type of punisher or punishment is involved. Simply label the procedure as *punishment* and the event as a *punisher*.

5. If you decide that a procedure is punishment by contingent stimulation or punishment by contingent withdrawal, you should label it as _____.

### Helpful Hint #2

Do not confuse punishment by withdrawal with extinction. Extinction is stopping the delivery of the reinforcer that caused the behavior. Punishment by withdrawal is the withdrawal of any reinforcer that did not cause the behavior. When Mom stops giving in to Tommy's pestering her for a snack, she is no longer reinforcing his pestering. She has stopped the reinforcer that caused his pestering in the first place. Therefore, Mom is using extinction. However, when Mom sends Tommy to his room for pestering her, she is not using extinction. She is using punishment because she is sending him away from many reinforcers, such as toys, TV, and Mom. These are not the reinforcers that caused his pestering.

6. If you think a procedure that decreases the rate of a behavior might be extinction, ask if it stops the reinforcer that caused the behavior. If it does, then the procedure is _____.

7. Remember, a procedure that decreases the rate of a behavior is extinction, only if it stops the reinforcer that _____ _____ the behavior in the first place.

8. If you think a procedure that decreases the rate of a behavior is punishment (by withdrawal), ask, "Does it withdraw a reinforcer that probably did not _____ the behavior in the first place?"

### Helpful Hint #3

Remember to distinguish between punishment and punisher in all questions. If you are asked about a procedure, the answer is punishment. If you are asked about an event, the answer is punisher.

9. The procedure of using a punisher should be labeled _____.

### Helpful Hint #4

I will continue to give you examples that do not include all elements required for a behavioral term. You can continue to refer to the procedure in these examples as *unknown*. For example, you may find examples of events whose withdrawal follows the behavior but does not decrease it. However, if the behavior increases, it is reinforcement, not unknown.

You may find examples of the withdrawal of an event following the non-occurrence of a behavior that decreases the non-occurrence of the behavior. Behavior analysts do not call this procedure punishment. They use a term that I will introduce in the next lesson. Until then, you should label the procedure as unknown.

10. You may find examples of the withdrawal of an event following the non-occurrence of a behavior that decreases the non-occurrence of the behavior. Behavior analysts do not call this procedure "punishment." They use a term that I will introduce in the next lesson. Until then, you should label the procedure as _____.

## Additional Readings

Baer, D. M. (1962). Laboratory control of thumb sucking by withdrawal and representation of reinforcement. *Journal of the Experimental Analysis of Behavior, 5,* 525–528. Thumb-sucking children were shown a cartoon movie. Whenever they sucked their thumb, the movie was interrupted for as long as they sucked their thumb. When they pulled their thumb from their mouth, the cartoon was turned on again. The rate of thumb sucking was drastically reduced by this procedure.

Clark, H. B., Rowbury, T., Baer, A. M., & Baer, D. M. (1973). Time-out as a punishing stimulus in continuous and intermittent schedules. *Journal of Applied Behavior Analysis, 6,* 443–455. Time out was used to suppress the rate of extremely disruptive behaviors (including physical aggression) in a child with retardation. The article also contains references to many other studies using time-out procedures.

Hall, R. V., Axelrod, S., Tyler, L., Grief, E., Jones, F. C., & Robertson, R. (1972). Modification of behavior problems in the home with a parent as observer and experimenter. *Journal of Applied Behavior Analysis, 5,* 53–64. Elaise, a 5-year-old girl, took an average of more than three hours to get dressed in the morning during baseline. Treatment consisted of withdrawing

TV-watching privileges if she took longer than 30 minutes. This reduced her dressing time to an average of 23 minutes.

Winkler, R. C. (1970). Management of chronic psychiatric patients by a token reinforcement system. *Journal of Applied Behavior Analysis, 3,* 27–55. Chronic psychiatric patients were fined by loss of tokens for throwing tantrums, screaming, and engaging in acts of violence. These behaviors increased rather sharply when the fines were discontinued.

# Programmed Reading

This Programmed Reading section will permit you to practice applying what you have just learned to the following topics: (1) Decreasing Behavior by Withdrawing Events, (2) Temporary Withdrawal, (3) Non-occurrence and Non-punishment, (4) Punishment by Contingent Withdrawal versus Extinction, (5) Another Tactic, and (6) Review.

### 1. Decreasing Behavior by Withdrawing Events

47. Pre-test: Punishment by contingent withdrawal involves the same two elements as punishment by contingent stimulation. An event withdrawal must <u>follow</u> an undesirable behavior. The rate of the behavior must then _____.

51. Pre-test: Suppose Tom stops talking whenever Ann disagrees. Suppose Ann's disagreements decrease in the future. The event of stopping talking is an example of a(n) _____; by stopping talking following Ann's disagreements, Tom is using the procedure of _____.

42. Pre-test: If you withdraw a reinforcer contingent on an undesirable behavior and the rate of the behavior decreases, then you are using what behavioral procedure? _____

88. Your goal in this module is to learn about punishment by contingent withdrawal. Behavior analysts call the form of punishment in which a reinforcer is withdrawn each time someone emits an undesirable behavior punishment by contingent _____ (stimulation, withdrawal). (Be sure to spell your answer correctly.)

5. Behavior analysts call decreasing the rate of a behavior by withdrawing an event when a person emits the behavior _____ (punishment, reinforcement) by contingent withdrawal.

56. Punishment by contingent withdrawal is a procedure that decreases the rate of a behavior by the _____ (presentation, withdrawal) of an event contingent on the occurrence of the behavior.

57. Punishment by contingent withdrawal involves the same two elements as punishment by contingent stimulation. An event must be withdrawn <u>following</u> an undesirable behavior. The rate of the behavior must then _____.

65. Suppose Mom won't let Karen use her bicycle for a day because she broke the rules. If Karen's rule breaking decreases in the future, you should call Mom's procedure _____ by contingent withdrawal.

59. Remember to label a procedure that doesn't work as unknown. Suppose Mom won't let Karen use her bicycle for a day because she broke the rules. If Karen's rule breaking does not change in the future, you should call Mom's procedure

_____.

58. Punishment by contingent stimulation involves the presentation of an event following an undesirable behavior. Punishment by contingent <u>withdrawal</u> involves the _____ of an event following an undesirable behavior.

87. You learned in the last lesson that behavior analysts refer to punishment by contingent stimulation by the single word <u>punishment</u>. You will probably not be surprised to learn that they also refer to punishment by contingent withdrawal with the single word _____.

66. Suppose Mom yells at Karen for riding her bicycle in the street. If Karen's street riding decreases in the future, you should call Mom's procedure by the single word

_____.

67. Suppose Mom yells at Karen for riding her bicycle in the street. If Karen's street riding doesn't change in the future, you should call Mom's procedure by the single word _____.

14. I will use the same convention I have used before. If I ask you what <u>procedure</u> Mom used to decrease Karen's street riding, you should answer "punishment." If I ask you to name the <u>event</u> of Mom's not letting Karen ride her bike for a day, you should answer _____.

63. Suppose Ken looks away whenever Alice puts down recycling. Suppose Alice's put-downs decrease in the future. The event of looking away is an example of a(n) _____; by looking away following Alice's put downs, Ken is using what procedure? _____

64. Suppose Ken looks away whenever Alice puts down recycling. Suppose the rate of Alice's put-downs doesn't change in the future. By looking away following Alice's put-downs, Ken is using what procedure? _____

30. Mom tape-recorded Tommy's tantrums in public places and played them at home with Dad present. Dad then made Tommy stand in the corner without moving for 20 seconds. His rate of tantrums decreased. The procedure used by Dad is called _____.

86. You have learned to classify punishers depending upon how they arise. You learned to call events that arise from biological factors and lose their effectiveness only temporarily _____ punishers. You learned to call events that are paired with another punisher and may lose their effectiveness permanently _____ punishers.

11. Dr. Pierce posted the number of minutes that a recreation center would close early each time a rule violation was observed. This procedure reduced rule violation dramatically. If these posted numbers were no longer paired with the actual early closing of the center, they would probably lose their effect. If they did, what type of punisher would they have been? A(n) _____ punisher.

10. Dr. Pierce posted a list of rules with the penalties for breaking them but did not always enforce the penalties. Because he was lax in applying the procedure of contingent withdrawal, the rate of rule-violating behavior _____ (did, didn't) decrease.

12. Dr. Pierce withdrew the privilege of playing in the recreation center when a rule was violated. The rule-violating behavior decreased dramatically. He used the behavioral procedure of _____.

25. If you withdraw a <u>reinforcer</u> contingent on an undesirable behavior and the rate of the behavior decreases, then you are using what behavioral procedure? _____

85. You can punish an undesirable behavior by withdrawing a(n) _____ contingent on that behavior.

## 2. Temporary Withdrawal

48. Pre-test: Suppose Mr. Jones keeps Mabel after school when she whispers to Lamar. Suppose that Mabel never whispers again. What form of punishment is "keeping Mabel after school for whispering"? _____

36. Pre-test: Decreasing an undesirable behavior by interrupting a cartoon temporarily when the behavior occurs is an example of what <u>form</u> of punishment by contingent withdrawal? _____

49. Pre-test: Suppose Mr. Jones keeps Mabel after school when she whispers to Lamar. Suppose that Mabel does not whisper as often. What procedure is Mr. Jones using? _____

50. Pre-test: Suppose Mr. Jones keeps Mabel after school when she whispers to Lamar. Suppose that Mabel still whispers often. What procedure is Mr. Jones using? _____

78. The goal of this module is to learn about the form of punishment called *time out*. A judge fines a person $50 for speeding. A fine is an example of a withdrawal that is a(n) _____ (permanent, temporary) loss.

29. Mom grounds Jenny for the day. In other words, Mom withdraws from Jenny the

privilege of playing with her friends. Grounding is an example of a withdrawal that is _____ (permanent, temporary).

83. When punishment by withdrawal is temporary, the person is taken <u>out</u> of a reinforcing situation for a <u>time</u>. This form of punishment is called time ____.

15. If a person is taken <u>out</u> of some reinforcing situation for a <u>time</u> when he or she emits a behavior and the rate of the behavior decreases, this is a form of punishment by contingent withdrawal that is called _____.

3. Always keep in mind that time out is a form of the procedure called _____ _____.

74. Suppose that Mom won't talk to Jimmy for 10 seconds whenever he interrupts her. Suppose the rate of his interruptions decrease. Because Mom temporarily denied Jimmy access to talking with her when he interrupted her, this is the form of punishment called _____ _____.

9. Dr. Belles helped Frank, a 65-year-old man, quit smoking. Any week in which Frank failed to reduce his smoking, he permanently lost money by donating it to an organization that he didn't like. His smoking decreased from 82 cigarettes per day to 5. The behavioral procedure used in this case was _____. (Hint: You don't have to specify whether it involves stimulation or withdrawal.)

33. Phone company customers permanently lost 20 cents for each local call for information made in Cincinnati starting in 1973. The charge followed each call, and the rate of such calls decreased. This is an example of the procedure of _____.

6. Behavior analysts do not have a special name for the form of punishment in which people permanently lose a reinforcer. They refer to this form simply as punishment because it aptly describes the procedure. However, behavior analysts do have a special name for the form of punishment in which people temporarily lose a reinforcer. When asked what <u>form</u> of punishment involves a temporary loss, the best answer is _____ (punishment, time out).

60. Sometimes I will want you to identify the specific procedural technique *time out* and sometimes only the general procedure *punishment*. When I ask what behavioral <u>procedure</u> is involved when the rate of a behavior is decreased through the temporary withdrawal of a reinforcer, do not answer "time out." Rather, label the behavioral procedure as _____.

7. Behavior analysts use two terms to refer to the temporary withdrawal of a reinforcer contingent on a behavior that decreases the rate of that behavior. When they refer to the general name of the <u>procedure</u>, they call it _____. When they refer to the specific <u>form</u> of punishment, they call it _____.

8. Decreasing an undesirable behavior by interrupting a cartoon temporarily when the behavior occurs is an example of what <u>form</u> of punishment by contingent withdrawal? _____

82. When a child plays too roughly with other children, a teacher might use a very mild form of time out. The teacher might let the child watch the other children play but not let the child participate. If this reduced the child's rough play, the teacher would be using what <u>procedure</u>? _____ _____.

2. A stronger form of punishment by withdrawal involves removing people from the reinforcing environment when they emit the undesirable behavior. If doing so decreases the behavior, then the specific name for this <u>form</u> of punishment is _____.

80. The following questions give us an overview. Suppose Mr. Jones yells at Mabel when she whispers to Lamar. Suppose that Mabel continues whispering just as often. What procedure is Mr. Jones using? _____

68. Suppose Mr. Jones keeps Mabel after school when she whispers to Lamar. Suppose that Mabel never whispers again. What do you call the event of keeping Mabel after school? _____

69. Suppose Mr. Jones keeps Mabel after school when she whispers to Lamar. Suppose that Mabel never whispers again. What form of punishment is "keeping

Mabel after school for whispering?"

_____

70. Suppose Mr. Jones keeps Mabel after school when she whispers to Lamar. Suppose that Mabel still whispers often. What procedure is Mr. Jones using?

_____

71. Suppose Mr. Jones keeps Mabel after school when she whispers to Lamar. Suppose that Mabel does not whisper as often. What procedure is Mr. Jones using?

_____

### 3. Non-Occurrence and Non-Punishment

46. Pre-test: Mom spanked Nancy when she did not watch over Baby Annie. Nancy's rate of not watching decreased. Mom used the procedure of _____
_____ .

40. Pre-test: If you punish someone for not performing a behavior and their rate of not performing it decreases, you are using the procedure called _____
_____ .

13. Here is a very important point. Behavior analysts label the procedure whereby they follow the occurrence of a behavior with a punisher as punishment. However, you should be very clear that they _____ (do, don't) label the procedure of following the *non-occurrence* of a behavior with a punisher as punishment.

72. Suppose that a researcher decreases the non-occurrence of a behavior by interrupting a cartoon temporarily when the behavior fails to occur. Until the next lesson, you should label that procedure as _____ .

18. If mother grounds Tommy for kicking the dog and the rate of kicking the dog decreases, mother's grounding would be an example of what behavioral procedure?

_____

24. If mother spanks Tommy for the non-occurrence of brushing his teeth and the rate of not brushing his teeth decreases, mother's spanking is an example of what behavioral procedure? _____

19. If mother grounds Tommy for throwing the ball in the house and the rate of throwing the ball in the house decreases,

mother's grounding would be what form of punishment? _____

20. If mother grounds Tommy for not feeding the dog and the rate of not feeding the dog decreases, mother's grounding of Tommy would be an example of what behavioral procedure? _____

21. If mother sends Tommy to his room for teasing his sister and teasing his sister increases, mother's sending him to his room would be an example of what behavioral procedure? _____

22. If mother sends Tommy to his room for not studying and the rate of not studying decreases, mother's sending him to his room would be an example of what behavioral procedure? _____

73. Suppose that Mom sends Tommy to his room for "forgetting to study." That _____ (is, isn't) just another way of saying that she sent him to his room for not studying.

23. If mother sends Tommy to his room for forgetting to study and the rate of forgetting decreases, mother's sending him to his room would be an example of what behavioral procedure? _____

### 4. Punishment by Contingent Withdrawal versus Extinction

41. Pre-test: If you stop delivering a reinforcing event that causes an undesirable behavior and the rate of the behavior decreases, then you are using the procedure called _____ .

52. Pre-test: Suppose you withdraw any reinforcer other than the one that causes the undesirable behavior when the person makes the response. If the rate of the behavior decreases, what procedure is involved? _____

43. Pre-test: Jan always flirted with Vince. John is jealous, so he decided to do something. Now, John ignores her for about five minutes any time she flirts with Vince. Jan has stopped flirting with Vince. What behavioral procedure is John using? _____

44. Pre-test: Jan always flirted with Vince. Vince knew John is jealous, so he decided to do something. Now, he has stopped flirting back. Jan has stopped flirting

with Vince. What behavioral procedure is Vince using? _____

77. The goal of this module is to learn how to discriminate punishment by contingent withdrawal from extinction. If you stop delivering a reinforcing event that used to cause an undesirable behavior and the rate of the behavior decreases, then you are using the procedure called _____.

62. Suppose every time Baby Annie throws her vegetables you have been giving her some fruit because you know she won't throw it. You may be reinforcing throwing her vegetables. If you stop giving her fruit when she throws her veggies, she may stop throwing them. If so, you have used what procedure? _____

75. Suppose you withdraw any reinforcer other than the one that causes the undesirable behavior when the person makes the response. If the rate of the behavior decreases, what procedure is involved? _____

61. Suppose Baby Annie throws her vegetables. Perhaps you don't have a clue why she throws them. One way to stop her throwing involves finding some reinforcer for any of her behaviors. It doesn't have to be connected with throwing her veggies. Maybe she looks at you often when you are smiling. Her looking is reinforced by your smiling. You may be able to decrease her throwing by withdrawing that reinforcer following her throwing. When she throws vegetables, you stop smiling and look away for a few seconds. If this procedure decreases her throwing, then you should call it _____.

28. Mom can't concentrate on her bill paying because Tommy is banging on a pot. Mom yells at him to stop. He does for a moment and then starts again. Suppose one day Mom stops yelling at him and his rate of banging gradually decreases. Because she has stopped reinforcing him with her yelling, you would call her procedure _____.

81. Tommy is banging on that pot again. Ignoring him by no longer yelling at him doesn't work today. Suppose you notice

that he stays downstairs. Events like getting a soda from the refrigerator, reading the Sunday funnies, and watching TV, all reinforce his behavior of staying downstairs. Suppose any time that he bangs you send him up to his room for 15 minutes. You are temporarily removing him from all those reinforcers. If his rate of banging decreases, you have used what procedure? _____

84. With extinction, you are stopping the delivery of the reinforcer that is causing the undesirable behavior. With punishment by withdrawal, you are temporarily withdrawing reinforcers that _____ (are, aren't) causing the undesirable behavior.

32. Mr. Jones asks David a question about the American history homework. David makes a wisecrack. Mr. Jones keeps him after school making him miss football practice. David never makes a wisecrack again to Mr. Jones. What procedure did Mr. Jones use? _____

27. Kenny pouts when no one asks how his day was. This got started because whenever Dad saw Kenny pout he would immediately ask Kenny how his day was. Starting a week ago, Dad no longer asks the question when Kenny pouts. Kenny rarely pouts now. What procedure did Dad use to decrease Kenny's pouting? _____

26. Kenny often pouted. Mom ignored his pouting. After a week, Kenny was still pouting. What procedure did Mom use? _____

### 5. Another Tactic

53. Pre-test: Tactic #1 of the aversive control strategy is to decrease undesirable behavior through _____ as a last resort.

76. Tactic #1 of the aversive control strategy is to decrease undesirable behavior through _____ as a last resort.

### 6. Review

37. Pre-test: If an event follows a behavior and decreases the rate of that behavior, then you call the event a(n) _____ _____; if an event

precedes a behavior and decreases the rate of that behavior, then you call the event a(n) _____ _____.

45. Pre-test: Kay doesn't talk to Kevin when he gets drunk and makes a fool of himself. Kevin gets drunk and makes a fool out of himself just as often as before. What behavioral procedure did Kay use? _____

39. Pre-test: If Pierce and Risley (1974) ignored all rule-violating behavior and the rate of such behavior decreased, what procedure would they have been using? _____

55. Pre-test: The first tactic in using the aversive control strategy is to use _____ _____ as a last resort.

38. Pre-test: If delivering an aversive event when a person does <u>not</u> emit a particular behavior causes the rate of not emitting the behavior to decrease, the procedure is called _____.

35. Pre-test: A form of punishment by withdrawal that involves the temporary loss of a privilege contingent on the occurrence of a particular behavior is called _____.

54. Pre-test: Tactic #1 of the aversive control strategy is to decrease undesirable behavior through _____ as a last resort.

1. A <u>punisher</u> is any produced or withdrawn event that is timed so that it _____ a behavior and _____ the rate of the behavior.

79. The procedure of withdrawing an event following a behavior, resulting in a decrease in the rate of the behavior is called _____.

4. Ask, "Did the procedure stop the reinforcer that caused the behavior?" If so, then the procedure is _____.

17. If Mom told Kenny he couldn't have dessert tonight because of his pestering and his rate of pestering lessened, what procedure did Mom use? _____

16. If any reinforcer in a person's environment is taken away whenever the person emits a particular behavior and if the rate of that behavior decreases, the

procedure would be an example of _____.

34. Pierce and Risley (1974) withdrew the privilege of playing in the recreation center when a rule was violated. The rule-violating behavior decreased dramatically. What behavioral procedure did they use? _____

31. Mr. Barnes docked Joe's pay $5 because he forgot to lock the money drawer. Joe never forgot again. Mr. Barnes used what behavioral procedure to decrease Joe's forgetting? _____ (Be careful with your answer here.)

## Programmed Examples

### 1. Programmed Examples

18. Pre-test: Little Kathy sometimes threw temper tantrums when she couldn't stay up late. Her parents, wanting to be kind, would usually let her stay up late. However, lately, they have ignored her temper tantrums. Kathy has stopped throwing them. What behavioral procedure did her parents use to eliminate temper tantrums? _____

19. Pre-test: Little Kathy sometimes threw a temper tantrum if she could not have a cookie when she wanted it. When she threw a temper tantrum, her father carried her upstairs to her room and made her stay there until well after she had finished her tantrum. Kathy no longer throws temper tantrums when she can't have a cookie. What behavioral procedure did her father use? _____

17. Pre-test: Dr. Brunner met with Tim three times a week to help him learn to stop forgetting to study. Whenever Tim forgot to study, Dr. Brunner asked him, "Why did you forget to study?" Tim never had an answer. Tim's rate of forgetting to study decreased. What behavioral procedure did Dr. Brunner use to decrease the rate of Tim's forgetting to study? _____

16. Pre-test: Bob used to flirt with all the other women that he met. This greatly angered Barb, who finally decided to withhold all affection from him on any day that he flirted with someone else. Bob no longer flirts with other women. The event of Barb withholding all affection is called a(n) _____

3. Bobby treated his toys roughly. He would make his toy soldiers have war and break them into little pieces or break his toy cars by crashing them into one another. Bobby's parents decided to teach Bobby to stop being destructive. Every time Bobby played too roughly with his toys, his parents took the toys away for about 15 minutes and would explain why. After 15 minutes, Bobby would get his toys back again. Bobby had almost stopped his destructive play within two weeks. If you think his parents used extinction, ask if the toys were the reinforcers that caused his destructive behavior: _____ (yes, no) Therefore, because the toys were not the cause of Bobby's destructive behavior but their removal decreased his destructive behavior, this is an example of what procedure? _____ by contingent withdrawal.

6. Dora was mean to her little brother Rickie all the time. She grabbed toys away from him and wouldn't let him have them back. She called him names and humiliated him in front of other children. Dora's parents were upset about her behavior. They felt that her meanness was harmful to Rickie, so they decided to put a stop to it. Each time they caught her being mean to her brother, they took away her "outside play" privilege by keeping her inside for an hour. Soon Dora had almost stopped being mean to her little brother. If you think that Dora's parents used extinction, ask if her outside play privilege caused her to be mean to Rickie: _____ (yes, no). Because her parents took away her outside play privilege and Dora's rate of being mean decreased, they were using what procedure?

_____

11. John's gripes about bad food were gross. When the fraternity served a meal that he didn't like, he complained that it contained every undesirable form of organic material he could think of. Naturally, this had a terrible effect on everyone's appetite. One day several members decided that they were reinforcing John's obnoxious griping by their outraged reactions. They decided not to act outraged any more. John's rate of griping gradually decreased over a period of about six weeks so that members could eat their meals in peace

again. If you think the group might be using extinction, ask if "acting outraged" caused his griping: _____ (yes, no) Because they stopped delivering the reinforcer that caused his griping, the members of the group were using what procedure? _____

7. Every time Tad pouted, his parents took away some of his play time by immediately sending him to his room for 10 minutes. At the end of the 10 minutes, they would go to his room and tell him his time was up. They usually had a useful discussion about Tad's pouting at that time. Tad's pouting went on at about the same rate for the next few months. In this case, because their procedure did not decrease Tad's pouting, his parents used the procedure called _____.

15. Mary frequently burped at the dinner table. Usually when Mary burped, her parents admonished her and explained that it wasn't polite to burp at the dinner table. Recently, however, Mary's parents decided that they were encouraging Mary's burping behavior by paying attention to her when she burped. Mary has been burping less and less since her parents instituted their new policy of not admonishing her. If you think that this procedure might be extinction, ask if admonishing Mary caused her burping. Once you can answer that question, then you will know that they used what procedure? _____

5. Clarence frequently gossiped about the other members of the group—which ones got drunk, who was sleeping with whom, and who didn't like whom. At first, the members of the group listened to Clarence and took his gossip seriously. Later, however, they decided that it was creating bad feelings in their group. They therefore decided to suspend him from membership for a week each time he gossiped. Clarence gossiped just as much as before. What behavioral procedure is this an example of? _____ (If necessary, ask the question about what caused the behavior.)

8. Fran argued that technology would save the world from global warming. Marcie disagreed with Fran's argument so convincingly that Fran stopped making it. The decrease in Fran's rate of proposing that technology will save the world is the result

of what behavioral procedure? _____

2. Barbara was both the school artist and the school bully. She did beautiful art, but she tended to beat up her schoolmates whenever she felt like it. The teachers felt that Barbara's behavior severely disrupted the recesses and class periods, so they decided to take action. Every time they caught Barbara fighting, they immediately told her that she could not take part in the art period that day. They observed that Barbara's rate of fighting decreased. What procedure did the teachers use to decrease Barbara's fighting behavior? _____

4. Bud had the bad habit of griping about the evening meal almost every night no matter what food was served. The other members of the cooperative dorm became increasingly annoyed by this behavior and tried to explain to Bud why his griping was bad for the group (especially the cooks). But Bud persisted in his griping. Finally, everyone decided to stop explaining to Bud why he shouldn't gripe. So each time Bud started to gripe about the food, everyone just acted as though he hadn't said anything. Bud's griping gradually disappeared. The decrease in Bud's griping is an example of what behavioral procedure? _____

10. Fred was a radical, and Ruth was a liberal. Both of them were very aggressive in arguing their points of view. In spite of their differences, however, Fred and Ruth got along beautifully. One rule that helped them get along was that they never talked about politics. Right from the first Ruth obeyed the rule all the time, but Fred frequently broke it. Ruth taught Fred to obey the rule by getting mad at him whenever he started a political harangue or made a political joke. Within two weeks, Fred was obeying the "no-politics" rule also. The decrease in Fred's political talk is the result of what behavioral procedure? _____

12. Larry often took extreme positions just for the sake of an argument. When he did so, Jim gave him a certain kind of look that made Larry feel very uncomfortable. The rate at which he took extreme positions decreased as a result of Jim's looks.

What behavioral procedure did Jim use? _____

13. Larry took extreme positions with Frank just for the sake of an argument. Later, Frank just ignored all such arguments. Larry's rate of taking extreme positions for the sake of an argument decreased. What behavioral procedure did Frank use? _____

14. Larry took extreme positions with Teresa just for the sake of an argument. Teresa always broke off the conversation in a very gentle way as soon as this started to happen. Larry's rate of taking extreme positions with Teresa decreased soon afterwards. What behavioral procedure did Teresa use? _____

9. Fred decreased Larry's rate of argumentative behavior with him by stopping any conversation as soon as Larry started arguing. Tom was the next one to reduce Larry's arguing by stopping conversations. Finally, Mary also reduced Larry's rate of arguing in the same way. After Mary, Larry stopped being argumentative with other people. This is an example of using punishment (instead of reinforcement) in a series of situations until the lack of arguing spreads to other situations in the same stimulus class. What procedure involving punishment did Fred, Tom, and Mary collectively use to make this lack of arguing occur in the presence of other people who had not punished Fred? _____

20. When Steve and Maria were talking, Maria usually looked directly at Steve with a nice little smile. However, anytime that Steve talked about Maria's belief in God, she stopped looking at him for at least a minute. Pretty soon Steve stopped talking about Maria's beliefs. What behavioral procedure did Maria use? _____

1. Anytime that Steve criticized socialism, Maria argued with him. However, recently she decided that she would not argue with Steve. She would just ignore his comments until he changed topics. Steve does not bring up that issue much any more. What behavioral procedure did Maria use to reduce Steve's rate of discussing socialism? _____

# LESSON

# 24 Escape and Avoidance

## Reading Section

This lesson introduces a new kind of reinforcer—the negative reinforcer. Negative reinforcers require a person to engage in some behavior to get rid of an event. It is a form of aversive control. Negative reinforcement exists widely in everyday life. Examples include brushing your teeth to avoid cavities, closing a window to avoid disturbances in body temperature, drinking alcohol to tune out your problems. Behavior analysts often use negative reinforcement to get someone to emit a behavior when positive reinforcement has failed. Negative reinforcement is a component of the aversive control strategy. Tactic #2 of the aversive control strategy is to increase desirable behavior through <u>negative reinforcement</u> as a last resort.

1. Tactic #2 of the aversive control strategy is to increase desirable behavior through _____ reinforcement as a last resort.

## Definition of Negative Reinforcement

**Negative reinforcement** is the <u>procedure</u> of following a behavior with a negative reinforcer. A **negative reinforcer** is any event that, when terminated or prevented by a behavior, increases the rate of that behavior. We call it negative because you take the event away rather than give it. In this case, *negative* means that a person will try to terminate or prevent the event. We call the event a *reinforcer* because any behavior that is followed by its termination or prevention

will increase. A simple example would be closing your eyes to terminate the sight of a gruesome accident. Another would be wearing a rain hat to prevent rain from wetting your head. Our everyday lives are full of negative reinforcers.

2. **Negative reinforcement** is the <u>procedure</u> of following a behavior with a negative reinforcer. A **negative reinforcer** is any event that meets two criteria: (1) It is terminated or _____ by a behavior. (2) It causes the rate of that behavior to _____.

A more complex example of a negative reinforcer might be the crying of a child who doesn't stop until his mother picks him up. The mother's behavior of picking him up terminates the crying. The crying would be a negative reinforcer if the mother picks him up more often for crying in the future. The crying is called the negative reinforcer.

You should be able to distinguish a negative reinforcer from a positive reinforcer. A positive reinforcer is any event whose <u>delivery</u> following a response increases the rate of that behavior. A negative reinforcer is any event whose <u>termination</u> or <u>prevention</u> following a response increases the rate of that behavior. In everyday terms, people usually think of a positive reinforcer as a pleasant event. They think of a negative reinforcer as an unpleasant event. However, as I have warned you many times, an event that seems pleasant to you may function as a punisher for someone else. The reverse is also true! Both positive and negative reinforcers are reinforcers because they increase the rate of a behavior that they follow.

People who are not behavior analysts sometimes speak of "punishing" another person for not emitting a desired behavior. The other person can terminate or prevent the "punishment" by emitting that behavior. Behavior analysts reserve the term *punishment* for events that decrease behavior. However, the effect of "punishing not emitting behavior" is to increase the rate of the desired behavior. Therefore, they refer to this arrangement as a form of reinforcement. Reinforcement, including negative reinforcement, increases behavior.

For example, suppose a mother spanks Tommy because he didn't clean up his room. She is creating a situation in which Tommy can prevent such a spanking by cleaning his room next time. If Tommy's rate of room cleaning increases because it prevents the spanking, the spanking would be a negative reinforcer. Thus, what many people refer to as *punishing* the non-occurrence of a behavior, behavior analysts call negatively reinforcing the occurrence of that same behavior.

Here is a way that you can decide whether an event that follows a behavior is a punisher or a negative reinforcer. Ask, "Did the rate of the behavior increase, or did it decrease?" If it increased, you are dealing with a reinforcer. If it decreased, you are dealing with a punisher.

Remember, a negative reinforcer is not a punisher. Many psychologists equate *negative reinforcer* with *punisher*. They are emphasizing the *negative* in *negative reinforcer*. Behavior analysts, however, emphasize the *reinforcer* in *negative reinforcer*. The central term here is *reinforcer*. Whether modified by *positive* or *negative*, it always refers to an event that increases the rate of a behavior.

## Uses of Escape and Avoidance

Behavior analysts distinguish between two forms of negative reinforcers. They name the form in which the person <u>terminates</u> a negative reinforcer *escape*. They call the response an *escape response*. **Escape** is a behavior that <u>terminates</u> a negative reinforcer. Behavior analysts name the form in which someone <u>prevents</u> a negative reinforcer *avoidance*. They call the response an *avoidance response*. **Avoidance** is a behavior that <u>prevents</u> a negative reinforcer.

3. Behavior analysts call the form in which the person <u>terminates</u> the negative reinforcer: *escape*. The term "avoidance" refers to the form in which someone _____ the negative reinforcer from occurring.

With an escape response, the negative reinforcer is physically present in the environment until the response is made. Thus the response terminates the negative reinforcer. For example, if Dad lends his son $5 but Jim fails to thank him, Dad might scowl until Jim thanks him. As soon as Jim says "thanks," Dad stops scowling. Jim escapes the dirty look.

Researchers taught a dentist to use escape with uncooperative children (Allen, Loiben, Allen, & Stanley, 1992). For example, 4-year-old Jenny engaged in excessive disruptive behavior during dental treatments. She pulled away from the dentist, cried, moaned, and complained about 70% of the time during baseline. Jenny's behavior was maintained by escaping from the dental work. The dentist modified Jenny's behavior with a behavioral treatment based on escape. The treatment was for the dentist to stop letting Jenny escape when she engaged in disruptive behavior. Instead the dentist taught her to cooperate in order to escape! He told her, "When you are calm, and quiet, and lying still, I will stop for a rest break." Her rate of disruptive behavior fell from 70% to about 10%. The dentist rated her as "cooperative," giving social validity to the technical behavioral definition. The dentist got equally good results with three additional children.

Researchers used escape to increase the frequency of taking pills at the right time (Azrin & Powell, 1969). They developed a timed pill holder that caused a loud buzzer to sound when it was time to take a pill. The buzzer could be turned off by turning a handle that dispensed a pill. The patients usually took the pills if dispensed in this manner. Thus, the patient could terminate the buzzer by dispensing the pill—a good example of escape behavior.

**Figure 24-1.** "Work" is a negative reinforcer for some people. Notice the avoidance response! (Source: Cartoon copyright 1973, King Features Syndicate. Reproduced by permission.)

With an avoidance response, the negative reinforcer is not physically present at the time of the response. However, if the person fails to make the response, it will occur. Thus, the response prevents the negative reinforcer from occurring. For example, suppose Jim immediately thanked Dad for the $5. His "thanks" would be an avoidance response because it prevents Dad from scowling. Of course, we must have some knowledge that Dad would have scowled if Jim had not thanked him. Figure 24-1 shows a more humorous example of avoidance, as Beetle Bailey executes a brilliant avoidance response to avoid work.

Researchers devised a treatment for three severe burn victims (Hegel, Ayllon, Vanderplate, & Spiro-Hawkins, 1986). Severe burn victims must actively practice stretching to prevent the burned areas from contracting.

Otherwise they will lose a great deal of flexibility in their everyday movements. The problem is that stretching burned areas is extremely painful. Thus, stretching is punished by the pain of moving. The three victims were losing flexibility in burned joint areas before the treatment, which involved setting up a highly structured rehabilitation program. The victims could avoid that program by complying with a very flexible self-exercise program. The treatment was very successful. The trends were reversed, and the patients had the chance to resume normal lives.

Researchers used avoidance to increase the social interaction skills of chronic schizophrenics (Fichter, Wallace, Liberman, & Davis, 1976). I will call one of the patients whom they helped "Joe." Joe spoke too softly to be easily heard, made the briefest possible

---

### Side Effects of Using Negative Reinforcement

You have seen that many behavior analysts have argued against the use of punishment or negative reinforcement as treatment procedures. A major reason is that their use produces harmful side effects. These include negative emotions, escape from the treatment procedure, and dislike of the therapist. Fichter and his colleagues found exactly this reaction when they used nagging to increase one patient's social skills. They noted that Joe's "last interaction before [leaving the treatment] unit was to tell one staff member

how much he disliked the unit and the staff" (Fichter et al., 1976, pp. 384–385). Iwata (1987) points out that this dislike means Joe probably did not continue to use his improved social skills. He didn't like his teachers or the way they taught him. Such is the danger of using aversive control.

4. If Joe sought to escape from the unit, then you can guess that the unit was a(n) _____ (negative, positive) reinforcer.

---

### *Do Efforts to Help Sometimes Hurt?*

"It is important for us to identify how environments that we create may provide negative reinforcement for undesirable behaviors. When faced with situations in which our students and clients are disruptive, we should immediately examine the antecedent as well as the consequent conditions. . . . If we conclude that our clients and students exhibit bizarre and potentially dangerous behaviors to terminate instruction, we might question whether or not our well-intentioned efforts to teach are in our clients' best interest; at the very least we must question one or more aspects of our teaching technique" (Iwata, 1987).

5. If a person responds to terminate a lesson, then the lesson is called a(n) _____ (negative, positive) reinforcer.

---

comments, and bit his fingernails. They taught him better social skills by having simple conversations with him. They nagged him if he failed to engage in more skillful behaviors. The nagging consisted of instructing him to engage in those behaviors. They didn't nag him if he engaged in those behaviors during the conversations. Thus, Joe could prevent the occurrence of the nagging by speaking louder and more briefly while not biting his fingernails. This result would be a good example of avoidance behavior.

Researchers used avoidance to treat children with cystic fibrosis (Stark, et al. 1993). These children were very underweight because they did not eat enough. To change this pattern, the researchers had the parents help the children set calorie goals for each meal. Children lost privileges when they did not meet these goals. The children soon started meeting the goals for most meals. They made substantial improvements in eating and body weight as a result.

Escape and avoidance are often combined to produce a more powerful effect. Researchers used such a procedure to teach improved posture to normal adults (Azrin, Rubin, O'Brien, Ayllon, & Roll, 1968). People wore a simple device that detected slouching during their normal daytime activities. They could prevent the device from sounding a loud buzzer by keeping good posture. Thus, keeping good posture was an avoidance behavior. If, however, a person slouched, the buzzer sounded. They could terminate it only by adopting good posture. Thus, adopting good posture was also an escape behavior. The result was that these people looked better to others. They also reduced the probability of back problems that often result from slouching.

## How to Respond to Coercive Behavior

All of us are often faced with unpleasant and coercive behavior by others. We often unintentionally maintain such behavior when we seek to escape or avoid it. Our escape or avoidance response may reinforce the use of such behavior by our tormentor. If we escape their unpleasant behavior by giving in to their demands, they are likely to repeat their unpleasant behavior. What should we do? How should we respond to coercive behavior? How can we best help people who use coercive behavior?

For example, Kim might cry at bedtime unless we comfort her. Kim is controlling us through negative reinforcement. If we comfort her, she will stop crying. Thus, if we comfort her, we escape from her crying. She is using negative reinforcement to get us to comfort her. Unfortunately, by comforting her, we are teaching her to control us and others through crying. We may even be teaching a generalized behavior of controlling others by coercive behavior. While we may think we are being kind and loving, we may in fact be creating a lifetime problem. What are we to do? You may remember that I described an example in the lesson on extinction in which the parents ignored their child's crying for a few nights and it stopped (Williams, 1959). We help our children, our family, and even our community by extinguishing coercive behavior whenever possible.

Earlier in the book, I described studies showing that many unpleasant behaviors are maintained by others trying to escape from them. This includes teachers who pay attention to disruptive student behavior (Thomas, Presland, Grant, & Glynn, 1978; White, 1975). This teacher attention often involves aversive control. The teacher attention may involve demands, reprimands, or even sending the student to the principal. The teacher may be intending to punish the disruptive behavior but only unintentionally reinforcing it. Further, the attention may terminate the disruptive behavior for the moment, but it is likely to make the problem worse in the future. What should teachers do? Often they cannot ignore the behavior until it extinguishes. It may be disruptive to other students. Behavior analysts generally advise solving this problem by reinforcing desirable behaviors (e.g., Hall, 1991). The idea is to increase the rate of desirable behaviors, leaving less time and motivation for disruptive behaviors (e.g., McComas, Hoch, Paone, & El-Roy, 2000). Reinforcing desirable behaviors gives the disruptive student an alternative way to get attention. We help people by noticing when they behave in desirable ways.

You may remember that the staff of mental hospitals often pay attention to patients only when they act "crazy" (Ayllon & Michael, 1959). The staff teach the patients many of their crazy behaviors. This is another case in which hospital staff could make a huge difference by reinforcing desirable behavior. By doing so, they could teach the patients alternative ways to get social attention from the staff.

Teachers of persons with retardation often let them skip difficult tasks if they act aggressively (Carr, Newsom, & Binkoff, 1980). The teachers unintentionally teach the person with retardation that coercion pays. In this case, the teachers are trying to help the person with retardation learn life skills, but in the process, the person with retardation fails so often that the situation becomes aversive. They react by finding ways to terminate it. Behavior analysts are pioneering many ways to make the learning situation for persons with retardation more positive. One way is to teach the person with retardation more acceptable ways to ask for a break in the training (e.g., Reichle & Wacker, 1993). Another way includes increasing the rate at which the person with retardation succeeds at the task, thereby making it less aversive. Another way is to start with very easy tasks and only gradually increase their difficulty (Iwata et al., 1994). Researchers are currently exploring the use of *establishing operations* (see Notes in Lesson 12) to enhance the effectiveness of positive reinforcers in such situations (see Iwata, Smith, & Michael, 2000a).

---

### Parents Teach Delinquents That Coercion Works!

For 30 years, Gerry Patterson has observed hundreds of families in their own homes. He concludes that children learn coercive behavior through thousands of similar episodes that can be broken down into three steps. First, the parent intrudes. Mom might complain about Dave not doing his chores. Second, the child counterattacks. Dave argues, yells, whines, or claims that Mom always picks on him. Third, Mom withdraws. Dave's counterattack punished Mom's parenting. By withdrawing, Mom reinforced Dave's coercion. Patterson suggests that by repeating this process many times, Mom teaches Dave to control her behavior coercively. Similar experiences with other relatives and with friends will put Dave well on his way toward bullying and violent behavior. (Based on Patterson, 1993.)

6. Mom could extinguish Dave's coercive behavior by not withdrawing. She could also increase his desirable behavior through _____ (punishment, reinforcement).

Current research has focused on very careful assessments of exactly what parents, teachers, or caregivers are doing to reinforce coercive behavior. They call it *functional analysis* (Iwata, Dorsey, Slifer, Bauman, & Richman, 1982). Functional analysis provides a further way to help parents trapped by children who control them through severe aggressive behavior. For example, Hagopian and his colleagues helped Preston, a child with autism and retardation (e.g., Hagopian, Wilson, & Wilder, 2001). Preston was quite a case. He hit, kicked, scratched, head-butted, threw things, screamed, broke things, and spit. Shockingly, Preston sometimes emitted such behavior as often as once every 10 seconds. A functional analysis showed that Preston engaged in such behavior when adults paid attention to him or failed to give him a toy. To change the behavior, the researchers simply taught Preston to ask to "play by himself" to eliminate unwanted attention or to ask for "toy, please." His aggressive behavior quickly decreased to near zero. Preston's parents no longer had to give in to Preston's aggression.

Piazza and colleagues dealt with a similar example in which the child was unable to ask for anything (Piazza, Patel, Santana, Goh, Delia, & Lancaster, 2002). Brad was an 8-year-old boy with severe retardation. His mother reported that he screamed, cried, hit himself, and ultimately spit out any food other than chips and chicken skins. After trying without success to feed Brad other foods combined with chips or skins, the researchers tried another procedure. They repeatedly, for up to 60 minutes at a time, gave Brad any food that he spit out. They had to repeat this for 10 hours before Brad's spitting extinguished. He eventually accepted most food without spitting it out. The researchers were able to greatly help Brad's nutrition by extinguishing his food refusal. They also helped Brad's parents by showing them another way to respond to Brad's coercive behavior.

Behavior analysts have much to teach us about how to respond to coercive behavior (see Perone, 2003). The most important rule is to not reinforce it. But also important is to find alternative behavior that lets the person obtain the controlling reinforcer in socially acceptable ways. Finally, seek to make the situation less aversive for the person by making it easier or by making them succeed more often. You might say that such an approach combines toughness with having a heart!

# Analogues between Positive and Negative Reinforcement

You can use negative reinforcement in place of positive reinforcement in any of the procedures that you studied earlier in the book. For example, <u>stopping</u> the termination or prevention of a negative reinforcer and observing a <u>decrease</u> in the rate of the behavior is an example of extinction. If you will remember that positive and negative reinforcement are both reinforcement, then it should be clear that any procedure or principle that applies to positive reinforcement will also apply to negative reinforcement. There follows a brief review of the major reinforcement procedures from the point of view of negative reinforcement.

### Extinction of Behavior Maintained by a Negative Reinforcer

<u>Stopping</u> the withdrawal or termination of an event following a behavior and observing a <u>decrease</u> in the behavior is called extinction. For example, if a father persists in scowling when his son borrows $5 and thanks him so that the son ceases to thank his father when he borrows the money, the son's thanking behavior is subject to extinction.

### Differential Reinforcement Using Negative Reinforcement

Behavior analysts call the procedure in which one behavior is followed by a negative reinforcer, while other behaviors are not, *differential reinforcement*. For example, suppose Dad stops scowling only if Jim says "Thank you, sir" but not if thanked in any other way. Dad is differentially reinforcing the behavior of saying "Thank you, sir."

### Shaping with the Use of Negative Reinforcement

If each of a series of successive <u>approximations</u> to a <u>target behavior</u> is <u>differentially reinforced</u> with a negative reinforcer, then behavior analysts call the procedure *shaping*. For example, Dad might be the kind of person who wants a very formal thank you for lending Jim some money. Suppose Dad terminated his scowl initially only if Jim said "Thanks." Dad might ignore other comments such as "I sure need the money." Jim would eventually learn to thank his father. Dad might then stop scowling only if Jim said "Thank you." Finally, he might stop scowling only if Jim said "Thank you, sir." Dad would be shaping.

The researchers who taught Jenny to cooperate with dental work used shaping (Allen, Loiben, Allen, & Stanley, 1992). The dentist started by giving her a rest break if she cooperated for 1–3 seconds. He differentially reinforced longer periods of cooperation until she was cooperating for 10–20 seconds.

### Intermittent Negative Reinforcement

If only some instances of a behavior terminate or prevent an event, then they are on an *intermittent* schedule of reinforcement. For example, if Jim has to say "thanks" three times before Dad stops scowling, Dad is (negatively) reinforcing the response on a fixed-ratio schedule. If Jim has to say "thanks" a differing number of times averaging three, then Dad is (negatively) reinforcing the response on a variable-ratio schedule. If Jim can eliminate the scowl only by the first response after 10 seconds, then Dad is (negatively) reinforcing the response on a fixed-

interval schedule. If Jim can eliminate the scowl, with the first response averaging 10 seconds, then Dad is (negatively) reinforcing the response on a variable-interval schedule.

The pattern of responding for different schedules is the same for positive and negative reinforcement. For example, a fixed-ratio schedule of negative reinforcement will produce a pause after reinforcement followed by a rapid rate of responding. The longer scalloping effect of fixed-interval schedule will be the same. The more uniform rates produced by variable-interval and variable-ratio schedules will also be produced by negative reinforcement, with variable-ratio schedules producing the highest rate of responding.

Likewise, resistance to extinction will be greater with an intermittent schedule. Satiation will be less likely. Ratio strain may occur if the ratio is too high. Shaping will work more quickly if the teacher uses a continuous schedule of negative reinforcement.

### Principle of Contingent Negative Reinforcement

The termination or prevention of an event will be more effective if it occurs <u>only</u> when the behavior is emitted. For example, Dad's scowl will be most effective if it is terminated only when Jim says, "Thank you, sir." If Dad sometimes stops scowling for a "thank you," it will be less effective in reinforcing the desired behavior of "Thank you, sir."

### How Not to Supervise Employees

Aubrey Daniels is a business consultant. He argues that "A manager using negative reinforcement says 'Do it or else!' The 'or else' is clearly something distinctly aversive or undesirable for the employee. The employee complies in order to avoid the negative consequence. As soon as the heat is off, the employee's pace slackens. The employee is motivated to do only enough work to reduce pressure from the boss. Typically, there are no consequences to doing more work than that. Thus, negative reinforcement teaches

people to do just enough work to 'get by' (Daniels, 1985). Daniels teaches managers to use positive reinforcement to improve productivity and quality. He claims employees will work to get as much positive reinforcement as possible, thereby doing more than just enough to get by.

7. According to Daniels, managers will increase productivity and profit more if they use _____ (negative, positive) reinforcement.

### Principle of Immediate Negative Reinforcement

The more <u>immediately</u> the behavior terminates or prevents the event, the more effective it will be as a negative reinforcer. For example, if Dad stops scowling only several minutes after Jim said "Thank you, sir," the negative reinforcement will not be as effective.

### Principle of Size of a Negative Reinforcer

The larger the <u>amount</u> (or intensity) of a negative reinforcer, the more effective it will be. If Dad makes only a slight grimace when not thanked, it will not be as effective as if he makes a very obvious scowl. Scowling and yelling might be even more effective. Of course, a behavior analyst would not recommend doing that. In fact, most behavior analysts would question Dad's target behavior. They would probably advise father and son to adopt a more mutually reinforcing pattern of behavior.

### Principle of Deprivation of a Negative Reinforcer

The less recently an event has been terminated or prevented, the more effective it will be. Thus, if Dad scowls only very rarely, he will have more of an effect than if he scowls frequently.

### Discrimination Training Using Negative Reinforcement

If a behavior leads to the termination or prevention of an event in one situation but not another, then the procedure being used is called *discrimination training*. Thus, saying "Thank you, sir" may terminate the scowl after borrowing money, but not after Dad has said, "Son, it is your turn to do the dishes."

## Summary

Tactic #2 of the aversive control strategy is to increase desirable behavior through negative reinforcement as a last resort. Negative reinforcement is a form of reinforcement in which the desired behavior is followed by termination or prevention of an event. If this strengthens the behavior, then the event is a negative reinforcer. The procedure of using a negative reinforcer is negative reinforcement. Negative reinforcement comes in the form of escape and avoidance. Behavior analysts have used them to improve cooperation, social skills, and recovery from burns. Much coercive behavior is caused by negative reinforcement. Many people learn that others will do what they want in order to stop the coercive behavior. Behavior analysts have found that by giving in, you reinforce coercive behavior. They recommend reducing coercive behavior by reinforcing more desirable alternative behavior. No matter who uses it, negative reinforcement is analogous to positive reinforcement. It can be delivered according to the same schedules. Its effectiveness can be enhanced by the same principles of effectiveness, and it can be used in shaping.

## Behavior Analysis Examples

### Taking Pills on Time

Doctors regard the failure of patients to take their pills as a major medical problem. This failure can undermine the medical treatment of a wide range of illnesses. Studies have estimated that as many as 35% of all patients fail to take their medication correctly. Doctors reviewed about 1,400 medical research articles studying 34 different strategies for improving pill taking. None of the strategies was based on behavior analysis. None showed much effect.

Behavior analysts tried a behavioral approach. Researchers analyzed the pill taking of 20 patients with a 100-mg dose of vitamin C four times a day (Epstein & Masek, 1978). They approached compliance as a behavioral problem. They devised a simple method for observing whether the patients took the pills as scheduled. They added a small amount of a "tracer" medicine to 3 of the 28 pills for one week. The tracer pills looked and tasted just like the regular vitamin C pills. The tracer pills caused the patient's urine to turn bright red within 12 hours of taking them. The researchers placed all 28 pills in a dispenser so that they would be taken in a fixed order. The tracer pills were placed in a random order known only to the doctors.

The patients reported any time that they noticed red urine. Researchers found

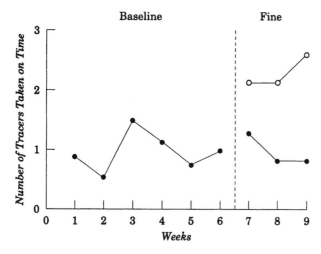

***Figure 24-2.*** Number of pills taken at the prescribed time. The filled circles represent patients operating with no special circumstances. The open circles represent patients fined a dollar for failing to take at least 2 out of 3 tracer pills on time. (From "Behavioral Control of Medicine Compliance," by L. H. Epstein and B. J. Masek, *Journal of Applied Behavior Analysis,* 1978, 11, 1–9. (Copyright 1978 by the Society for the Experimental Analysis of Behavior, Inc. Used by Permission.)

whether reports of red urine occurred within 12 hours of when they had scheduled a tracer pill. The patients did not know which pills contained the tracer medicine. They could not taste or see the difference. As a result, their report could be correct only if they took their pills on time and observed the red urine.

Figure 24-2 shows the results of observations during baseline. The patients took about 33% of their 3 tracer pills at the correct time. The doctors then required half of the patients to pay $1 if they did not take at least 2 of the 3 tracer pills on time. The patients who had to pay the fine started taking about 70% of their pills on time. This result rose to 90%. The other patients who did not have to pay the fine continued at baseline level.

8. In this case, a correct report of red urine prevented the doctors from levying a fine of $1. The procedure increased the rate of correct reports from 33% to 90%. Therefore, you would label the event called a fine as a negative _____.

## Notes

### Note #1

Some behavior analysts argue that the distinction between positive and negative reinforcement is often impossible to make objectively (Michael, 1975). For example, suppose a teacher lets kids play if they stay in their seats for 15 minutes (Osborne, 1969). You might argue that this is positive reinforcement for staying seated. However, it also might be viewed as negative reinforcement. If staying seated is aversive, then playing could be viewed as terminating an aversive situation (Iwata, 1987). Michael also provides an interesting description of the history of the distinction. Michael suggested that the distinction between positive and negative reinforcement be abandoned. Behavior analysis continues to make the distinction. But if you sometimes have a problem figuring out whether an event is a positive or a negative reinforcer, be assured you are not alone.

## Helpful Hints

### Helpful Hint #1

The key to discriminating between escape and avoidance is whether the negative reinforcer is present when you make the response. To escape from an event means to get away from it. You can get away from an event by terminating contact with it. You might do so by stopping the event or by moving away from it. You can only terminate an event that is present. Therefore, if your behavior terminates a negative reinforcer that is present when you make the response, you are making an *escape* response. If your behavior prevents a negative reinforcer that is not present, then you are making an avoidance response. You can tell whether a behavior is escape by asking, "Was the negative reinforcer <u>present</u> at the moment of responding?" If present so that the person's response terminated it, then the behavior is escape. If not present so that the person's response prevented it, then the behavior is an avoidance response.

9. If a negative reinforcer is present at the moment of responding so that the person's

response terminates it, then the behavior is escape. If not present at the moment of responding so that the person's response prevents it, then the behavior is a(n) _____ response.

For example, the $1 fine had not been levied when the patient took the tracer pill. It was not present. The patient prevented the fine from occurring. Therefore, you would label the behavior as avoidance.

10. Since the dental work was present when Jenny engaged in cooperative behavior, and her cooperative behavior terminated the dental work, you call the behavior a(n) _____ response.

11. So when the negative reinforcer is not present and the person responds to prevent it from occurring, you call the behavior a(n) _____ response. When the negative reinforcer is present and the person responds to terminate it, you call the behavior a(n) _____ response.

### Helpful Hint #2
You do not have to name an event involving aversive control a negative reinforcer.

12. Behavior analysts refer to both positive and negative reinforcers with the single word _____.

### Helpful Hint #3
Sometimes you can view a procedure as either punishment or negative reinforcement. For example, if Mom spanks Ron for being dirty, you would normally label the spanking as punishment. That assumes that the spanking is for getting dirty. However, you might assume that the spanking is for Ron not cleaning up. Ron can avoid such spankings by cleaning up. On this assumption, you would label the spanking as negative reinforcement. This problem can arise whenever the person must make one of two responses. In such cases, be sure to answer the question as it is stated. Suppose the question is "What do you call spanking a child for getting dirty if the result is a decrease in getting dirty?" The correct answer is "punishment." Suppose the

question is "What do you call spanking a child for failing to clean up if the result is increased cleaning behavior?" The correct answer is reinforcement (or negative reinforcement). Your answer will be considered incorrect if you do not answer the question as stated.

13. Suppose the question is "What do you call increasing the frequency of cleaning up by spanking a child for failing to clean up?" The correct answer is _____ _____.

14. Even if you can't figure out anything else about the question, don't make the mistake of calling a procedure that increases behavior punishment or a procedure that decreases behavior _____.

Let's look at a situation involving punishment. For example, suppose that Holly has a bad habit of nail biting. Her mother decides to make her wear gloves for the rest of the day each time that she catches Holly biting her nails. After a few weeks of this treatment, Holly rarely bites her nails.

15. Because the rate of her nail biting decreased, the procedure involved would be _____.

Now let's look at a situation that involves negative reinforcement. Stan does not like to clean up his room, but he loves to ask friends over to his house. Whenever his friends come over, they complain to Stan about how messy his room is. Consequently, Stan now cleans his room before inviting friends over to his house.

16. Because the rate of Stan cleaning his room has increased, the procedure involved is _____.

### Helpful Hint #4
Be sure that all of the elements of negative reinforcement are described in any example. If one is missing, then the procedure is unknown.

17. For example, suppose that whenever your roommate leaves dirty dishes in the sink you complain. If you are asked what

procedure your complaining involves, you should answer _____.

### Helpful Hint #5

To simplify this lesson I will not ask you about escape or avoidance as a procedure. I will only ask you about escape behavior or avoidance behavior. If I ask you to label a negative-reinforcement procedure, you can be sure the answer will not be escape or avoidance.

18. For example, Baby Annie cries to get Mom's attention. Mom picks Baby Annie up, which terminates her crying. She picks up Baby Annie more and more often. What procedure is Annie using to increase Mom's rate of picking her up?

## Additional Readings

Ayllon, T., & Michael, J. (1959). The psychiatric nurse as a behavioral engineer. *Journal of the Experimental Analysis of Behavior, 2*, 323–334. Two psychiatric patients who refused to feed themselves and thus required spoon feeding by a nurse were exposed to avoidance. The researchers observed that both patients were extremely concerned about their appearance, so the nurse continued to feed both patients but now dropped a bit of food on the patients' clothing. The patients soon learned to feed themselves in order to avoid the spilled food.

Iwata, B. A. (1987). Negative reinforcement in applied behavior analysis: An emerging technology. *Journal of Applied Behavior Analysis, 20*, 361–378. This article provides an overview of negative reinforcement in applied behavior analysis. It discusses the current conceptualization of it. It discusses how undesirable behavior is learned through negative reinforcement. It discusses many methods for treating negatively reinforced behavior. Finally, it discusses using negative reinforcement as a treatment itself. He suggests that behavior analysts examine any environment that they create to see whether it provides negative reinforcement for undesirable behavior.

Lovaas, O. I., Schaeffer, B., & Simmons, J. Q. (1965). Building social behavior in autistic children by use of electric shock. *Journal of Experimental Research in Personality, 1*, 99–109. This study deals with two children with autism. Psychiatric treatment had been totally ineffective in bringing them into contact with other individuals, so a program was started in which they were shocked for any self-stimulating behaviors. The shock was turned off if they approached the therapist (escape). This procedure rapidly increased the social behaviors of the children and provided a starting point for further behavioral therapy.

## Programmed Reading

The Programmed Reading section provides you with the chance to apply the terms of this lesson to the following topics: (1) Using the Termination or Prevention of Events, (2) Negative Reinforcement versus Punishment, (3 Behaviors That Terminate or Prevent, (4) Coercive Behavior, (5) Analogues to Positive and Negative Reinforcement, (6) Another Tactic, and (7) Review.

### 1. Using the Termination or Prevention of Events

57. Pre-test: Behavior analysts call an event that increases the rate of a behavior that terminated or prevented it a negative _____. They call the procedure that uses a negative reinforcer negative _____.

71. Pre-test: The loud TV used to bother Pam when she studied. One day Pam closed the door to her room, which stopped the sound of the TV from bothering her. Now she always closes the door when she studies. The sound of the TV is called a(n) _____.

54. Pre-test: A negative reinforcer is any event that increases the rate of a behavior that _____ or _____ that event.

90. The first goal of this section is to teach you about negative reinforcers. I will teach you about escape and avoidance a

little later. Any event that is <u>terminated</u> or <u>prevented</u> by a behavior and that causes the rate of that behavior to increase is called a(n) _____ reinforcer (notice that I did not ask for the procedure.)

82. Suppose mother picks up Liz when she is crying and Liz's crying stops. Suppose mother picks her up more often in the future. Notice that the termination of Liz's crying <u>follows</u> mother picking her up. Also, the rate at which mother picks her up when she is crying <u>increases</u>. Crying is an event called a(n) _____ _____ for mother's picking up Liz.

11. Be careful to distinguish between <u>events</u> that function as negative reinforcers and the <u>procedure</u> of using those events. The procedure of using a negative reinforcer is called negative _____.

83. Suppose mother picks up Liz to <u>terminate</u> or <u>prevent</u> her crying. If mother picks her up more often in the future, what procedure is Liz using without knowing it?_____ _____

84. Suppose mother picks up Liz to terminate or prevent her crying. If mother picks her up more often in the future, what do you call the event of crying? _____

28. I will continue to follow the convention about *event* and *procedure*. Behavior analysts call an <u>event</u> that increases the rate of a behavior that <u>terminated</u> or <u>prevented</u> it a negative _____ _____. They call the <u>procedure</u> that uses a negative reinforcer negative _____.

48. Key words in understanding the idea of negative reinforcer are <u>terminates</u> and <u>prevents.</u> A negative reinforcer is any event that increases the rate of a behavior that terminates or _____ that event.

1. <u>Terminates</u> and <u>prevents</u> are key words because both of them help define *negative reinforcer*. A negative reinforcer is any event that increases the rate of a behavior that _____ or prevents that event.

29. If a behavior <u>terminates</u> or <u>prevents</u> an event and the rate of that behavior does not change, then you would label the event a(n) _____.

96. Three key words help define *negative reinforcer*. One of them is *increase*. The other two are _____ and _____.

14. Both a positive reinforcer and a negative reinforcer have a similar effect. When either of them follows a behavior, they _____ the rate of that behavior.

6. A positive reinforcer is any event that follows a behavior and increases its rate. A negative reinforcer is any event that increases the rate of a behavior that _____ or _____ that event.

## 2. Negative Reinforcement versus Punishment

62. Pre-test: Fran used to complain all the time. One day, Ted told Fran to stop complaining. She immediately stopped. Now whenever Fran complains, Ted tells her to stop, and she does. Ted's rate of not telling Fran to stop has decreased. Fran is decreasing Ted's not telling her to stop by the procedure called _____ _____.

55. Pre-test: A punisher leads to a(n) _____ in the rate of a behavior; a negative reinforcer leads to a(n) _____ in the rate of behavior.

63. Pre-test: Fran used to complain to Ted all the time. One day Ted told Fran her complaining was bumming him out, and she immediately stopped. Now Ted frequently tells Fran her complaining is bumming him out. Fran is increasing the rate of Ted's "You're bumming me out" statements by the procedure called _____.

92. The next important goal is to teach you the relation between negative reinforcement and punishment. Should you ever label the procedure of negative reinforcement as the *punishment* of *not* making a response? _____ (yes, no)

86. Suppose that when Joe does not turn off the TV during advertisements, he is

exposed to loud advertisements that he hates. Suppose his rate of not turning off the TV during advertisements decreases. Because his not turning off the TV during advertisements is followed by loud advertisements and the rate of not turning it off decreases, you might incorrectly label the procedure as _____.

12. Behavior analysts describe Joe's situation differently. They describe it as a situation in which his behavior of turning off the TV can terminate an event—the loud ad. If the behavior increases in rate, then they label the procedure as _____.

27. Here is the rule. Behavior analysts always define behavior as an act of doing something. They never define behavior as the absence of doing something. This distinction avoids the confusion of calling a procedure either punishment or negative reinforcement, depending upon your point of view. Thus, behavior analysts _____ (do, don't) consider *not* doing something as a behavior.

37. If Mom spanks Tommy when he fails to clean his room and his rate of room cleaning doesn't change, what procedure has mother used? _____.

42. Tommy's mother spanks him for forgetting to clean his room, and his rate of room cleaning increases. Note the wording of the example and the fact that "forgetting to clean" is the same as "not cleaning." That distinction enables you to rephrase the example as doing something, as opposed to not doing something. Now, if Tommy cleans his room to prevent a spanking, you would call the procedure _____.

41. If Tommy cleans his room to prevent a spanking, you would call the event of the spanking a(n) negative _____.

43. If Tommy's rate of swearing decreases because his mother spanks him when he does, then call the procedure _____.

7. A punisher leads to a(n) _____ in the rate of a behavior; a negative reinforcer leads to a(n) _____ in the rate of behavior.

49. Many psychologists equate the two terms *punisher* and _____ *reinforcer*; behavior analysts do not.

### 3. Behaviors That Terminate or Prevent Events

61. Pre-test: For escape behavior a negative reinforcer is present in the environment until a response is made that _____ the negative reinforcer.

58. Pre-test: Dad glares disapprovingly at Nancy when she wears her short shorts. Nancy can stop the glares by changing to regular shorts. Because it terminates the glaring, changing to regular shorts is a(n) _____ behavior.

59. Pre-test: Dad grounds Nancy when she comes home late. Nancy can head off the grounding by coming home on time. Because it prevents the grounding, coming home on time is a(n) _____ behavior.

68. Pre-test: Remember, when a response prevents delivery of a negative reinforcer, you call the behavior _____ behavior; when a response terminates delivery of a negative reinforcer, you call the behavior _____ behavior.

93. The next major goal is to teach you about avoidance and escape. Behavior analysts distinguish between terminating the negative reinforcer and preventing it. They name the behavior in which the person terminates the negative reinforcer *escape*. They name the behavior in which the person prevents the negative reinforcer from occurring _____.

13. Behavior analysts' usage of *escape* and *avoid* is consistent with everyday usage outside their field. We speak of avoiding something that has not yet happened. We avoid having to talk with Judith by crossing the street. Avoidance means _____ (prevention, termination). We speak of escaping from something that is already present. We escape from a boring conversation. Escape means _____ (prevention, termination).

106. You call the response to terminate a negative reinforcer an escape response. You call the response to prevent a negative reinforcer a(n) _____ response.

30. If a behavior <u>terminates</u> a negative reinforcer, you call it a(n) _____ response.

26. For escape behavior, a negative reinforcer is present in the environment until a response is made that _____ (prevents, terminates) the negative reinforcer.

52. Mom yells at Nancy when she doesn't clean her room. Nancy can prevent being yelled at by cleaning her room. Because it prevents being yelled at, cleaning her room is a(n) _____ behavior.

51. Mom complains to Nancy until she washes the dishes. Nancy can terminate the complaints by washing the dishes. Because it terminates the complaining, washing the dishes is a(n) _____ behavior.

16. Dad yells at Nancy when she grabs her food. Nancy doesn't get yelled at when she asks the closest person to pass the dish she wants. To figure out whether asking is avoidance or escape, you must decide whether it prevents or terminates the yelling. Because the yelling isn't going on when she asks, asking _____ (prevents, terminates) the yelling. Therefore, asking is _____ behavior.

15. Dad sulks when Nancy doesn't say hello to him when he comes home. Nancy can stop the sulking by saying hello. To figure out whether saying hello is avoidance or escape, you must decide whether it prevents or terminates the sulking. Because the sulking is going on when she says hello, saying hello _____ (prevents, terminates) the sulking. Therefore, saying hello is _____ behavior.

18. Dr. Allen advised a dentist to tell uncooperative children that when they were acting calm, he would give them a brief break from the dental work. This resulted in an increase in cooperative behavior. If the children cooperated in order to briefly terminate the dental treatment, their behavior would be called _____ behavior.

19. Dr. Azrin developed a pill dispenser that sounded a buzzer at the prescribed time for taking a pill. The buzzer could be turned off only by dispensing a pill. To decide whether this is avoidance or escape, figure out whether dispensing the pill terminates or avoids the buzzer. The behavior of dispensing the pill would be an example of a(n) _____ _____ behavior.

10. Avoidance is behavior in which a negative reinforcer will be delivered in the future if a response is not made that _____ (prevents, terminates) that stimulus from occurring.

24. Dr. Hegel devised a treatment for severe burn victims. The patient could prevent being sent to a highly structured rehabilitation program by complying with a very flexible self-exercise program. Because stretching in the self-exercise program prevents the structured program, it is an example of _____ _____ behavior.

23. Dr. Fichter nagged Joe anytime that he failed to engage in acceptable social behavior. Because engaging in acceptable social behavior prevents being nagged, the acceptable social behavior would be a(n) _____ _____ behavior.

36. If Joe seeks to escape from a therapy unit that uses nagging to increase social skills, nagging as an event is a(n) _____.

20. Dr. Azrin developed an apparatus that sounded a loud buzzer any time that a person slouched. Because maintaining good posture prevents the buzzer, it would be an example of a(n) _____ behavior. If the person did slouch, he or she could turn the buzzer off only by adopting good posture. Because adopting good posture terminates the buzzer, it would be an example of a(n) _____ behavior.

34. If clients and students attempt to prevent or terminate instruction, it is likely that the environment created by the

teacher is providing _____ reinforcement.

79. Remember, when a response prevents delivery of a negative reinforcer, you call the behavior _____ behavior; when a response terminates delivery of a negative reinforcer, you call the behavior _____ behavior.

47. Just a reminder. I will not ask you to tell the difference between escape and avoidance procedures, only escape and avoidance behaviors. Suppose Joe swats a mosquito to terminate its biting his arm. Suppose Joe's swatting increases. If I ask you what procedure nature is applying to Joe, which would be the correct answer: (a) escape or (b) negative reinforcement? _____

97. To decide whether a behavior is an escape behavior, ask, "Was the negative reinforcer present at the moment of responding?" If it was present so that the behavior terminated it, then the behavior is a(n) _____ behavior.

105. When the negative reinforcer is not present and the person responds to prevent it from occurring, you call the behavior a(n) _____ response. When the negative reinforcer is present and the person responds to terminate it, you call the behavior a(n) _____ response.

45. If you decided that a procedure involves the termination or prevention of an event following a behavior and the rate increases, you should label it as _____.

39. If terminating or preventing an event that follows a behavior results in an <u>increase</u> in the behavior, the procedure involved is _____. When an event that follows a behavior results in a <u>decrease</u> in the behavior, the procedure involved is _____.

### 4. Coercive Behavior

60. Pre-test: Dad is always lecturing Paul about his homework. One day, Paul yelled at Dad to mind his own business. Dad immediately stopped his lecture. Now Paul often yells at him whenever Dad starts a lecture. Dad changed Paul's rate of yelling by using the procedure of _____.

72. Pre-test: The most important rule about how to respond to coercive behavior is to not give in to it because giving in will increase its rate through the behavioral procedure of _____.

102. When faced with unpleasant and coercive behavior by others, we often inadvertently reinforce such behavior by giving in to it. If giving in to it terminates the coercive behavior and our rate of giving in increases, then our giving in is what kind of behavior? _____ behavior.

44. If we allow Kim to control us by crying at bedtime until we comfort her, then our comforting behavior is _____ behavior.

101. When attention by teachers reinforces disruptive behavior rather than punishing it, behavior analysts advise using attention to _____ the rate of constructive behaviors.

50. Mental hospital staff could reduce patients' crazy behavior by only paying attention to their desirable behavior. What behavioral procedure are they using? _____

85. Suppose Mr. Jones asks Sam, a person with retardation, to brush his teeth. Suppose Sam starts acting aggressive toward Mr. Jones. Mr. Jones might cancel the lesson on tooth brushing. Suppose Sam terminates acting aggressive and the rate at which Mr. Jones lets Sam out of tooth brushing increases. You would call Sam's aggressive action what kind of an event? A(n) _____.

91. The most important rule about how to respond to coercive behavior is to not give in to it because giving in will increase its rate through the behavioral procedure of _____.

81. Suppose Mom withdraws her parenting attempt when Dave punishes it. If Dave's

punishing behavior increases, we would say Mom unintentionally used the procedure of _____.

## 5. Analogues between Positive and Negative Reinforcement

76. Pre-test: When termination of a negative reinforcer no longer follows a behavior and the rate of the behavior decreases, you label the procedure _____.

78. Pre-test: If one behavior terminates an event but other behaviors do not and the relative rate of the first behavior increases, then what is the name of the total behavioral procedure? _____

65. Pre-test: If an event is prevented by a varying number of responses, then the behavior is on what generic schedule of reinforcement? A(n) _____ schedule.

73. Pre-test: The principle of immediacy states that in order to be most effective, a negative reinforcer should be terminated _____ (when) after the behavior occurs.

74. Pre-test: The procedure being used when a behavior leads to the termination or prevention of an event in one situation but the same behavior does not have that effect in another situation is called _____.

9. Any procedure or principle that applies to positive reinforcement will also apply to _____ reinforcement.

103. When termination of a negative reinforcer no longer <u>follows</u> a behavior and the rate of the behavior <u>decreases</u>, you label the procedure: _____.

38. If one behavior terminates an event while other behaviors do not and the relative rate of the first behavior increases, then what is the name of the total behavioral procedure? _____

35. If each of a series of successive approximations to some target behavior terminates a negative reinforcer (while non-approximations do not), the procedure is called _____.

33. If an event is prevented by a varying number of responses, then the behavior is on what generic schedule of reinforcement? A(n) _____ schedule.

99. What intermittent schedule of negative reinforcement produces the highest rate of responding? _____

8. An intermittent schedule of negative reinforcement will reduce satiation and have greater resistance to _____ (not satiation).

4. "The termination or prevention of an event will be more effective if it occurs only when the behavior is emitted" is the principle of _____.

94. The principle of immediacy states that in order to be most effective, a negative reinforcer should be terminated _____ (when) after the behavior occurs.

2. "The larger the amount (or intensity) of a negative reinforcer, the more effective it will be" is the principle of _____.

3. "The less often and the less recently an event has been terminated or prevented, the more effective it will be" is the principle of _____.

95. The procedure being used when a behavior leads to the termination or prevention of an event in one situation but does not have that effect in another situation is called _____.

31. If a behavior is followed by the termination or prevention of an event and the behavior is strengthened, the event is a(n) _____.

104. When the behavior terminates a negative reinforcer, call it a(n) _____ response; when it prevents a negative reinforcer, call it a(n) _____ response.

21. Dr. Epstein required that Bob pay a $1 fine if he failed to take his medication at the prescribed time. Bob's rate of taking his medication at the correct time increased to prevent the fine. Taking the medication at the prescribed time is called a(n) _____ response.

22. Dr. Epstein required Bob to pay a $1 fine if he did not take the medication at the prescribed time. Bob's rate of taking his medication at the prescribed time increased as a result. The $1 fine is called a(n) _____.

### 6. Another Tactic

70. Pre-test: Tactic #2 of the aversive control strategy is to increase desirable behavior through _____ (negative, positive) reinforcement as a last resort.

87. Tactic #2 of the aversive control strategy is to increase desirable behavior through _____ as a last resort.

100. When all else has failed to start someone emitting a behavior, you can use tactic #2 of the aversive control strategy. Tactic #2 is to increase desirable behavior through negative _____.

88. Tactic #2 of the aversive control strategy is to increase desirable behavior through _____ as a last resort.

### 7. Review

66. Pre-test: If every fifth response is followed by the termination of a negative reinforcer, that behavior is on what schedule of intermittent reinforcement? _____

64. Pre-test: If a behavior terminates an event and the rate of the behavior increases, the behavior is called a(n) _____ response.

75. Pre-test: To use the aversive control strategy, (1) decrease undesirable behavior through _____ as a last resort, and (2) increase desirable behavior through _____ as a last resort.

56. Pre-test: Avoidance behavior is any behavior that _____ the occurrence of a negative reinforcer.

69. Pre-test: Suppose that every time a person emits a particular behavior another person removes one of their reinforcers. If the rate of that behavior decreases, then what behavioral procedure is the

other person using? _____ _____

67. Pre-test: Jim used to complain all the time. You have stopped arguing with his complaints, and his complaints have decreased. You used the procedure of _____.

77. Pre-test: You fine Tommy for not cleaning his room. He now cleans his room most of the time. You used the procedure of _____.

98. To use the aversive control strategy, (1) decrease undesirable behavior through punishment as a last resort, and (2) increase desirable behavior through _____ as a last resort.

40. If the rate of a behavior increases when it is followed by the termination of an event, the event is called a(n) _____.

17. Do behavior analysts equate negative reinforcers and punishers? _____ (yes, no)

53. Positive reinforcers and negative reinforcers are both events that result in a(n) _____ in the rate of a behavior.

32. If a behavior prevents an event from occurring and the rate of the behavior increases, the behavior is called a(n) _____ response.

46. If you think that an example involves negative reinforcement, be sure to check to see if the rate of the behavior increases. If the rate decreases, then the procedure _____ (can, can't) be negative reinforcement.

25. Escape behavior is behavior that _____ _____ a negative reinforcer.

5. A negative reinforcer is any event that is _____ or _____ by a behavior and that causes the rate of the behavior to increase.

89. The second tactic of the aversive control strategy is to increase desirable behavior through _____ as a last resort.

80. Sometimes students decide whether a procedure is punishment or negative reinforcement by looking only at the "unpleasant" event. If they think of it

as a punisher, then they label the procedure as punishment. For example, a fine can be used as a punisher. You fine them when they do something. If doing so decreases the behavior, then the fine is a punisher. But a fine can also be used as a negative reinforcer. If you fine someone for not emitting a behavior and the rate of the behavior <u>increases</u>, then what procedure are you using?

_____

## Programmed Examples

### 1. Programmed Examples

12. Pre-test: Kip had the bad habit of talking in the weekly dorm meetings without putting up his hand. Marianne, the chairperson of the meeting, finally started yelling at him each time he failed to raise his hand. Kip soon started to raise his hand. Kip's behavior of raising his hand would be called _____ behavior.

11. Pre-test: Jane hated it when Bob put his cigarette out on his dinner plate. Finally, she expressed her feelings to him. He usually did not put his cigarette out that way in the future, and when he did, Jane again expressed her dislike for the practice. Eventually, Bob completely stopped doing it. Because Jane's expressions followed Bob's putting his cigarette out on his plate and his rate decreased, what behavioral procedure did Jane use? _____

_____

14. Pre-test: When Dad says "Stop it" to Tommy for pestering him, Tommy stops immediately. Dad's "Stop it" follows the pestering and decreases it. His command is a punisher. Dad is likely to say "Stop it" more often in the future because it terminated the pestering. Dad's saying "Stop it" is an example of _____ behavior.

13. Pre-test: The students at a big midwestern university were angry that their administration had refused to immediately hire more female faculty members while a special committee was "studying the problem." They decided to sit in the president's office until he changed his mind. They sat there for three days, but the president still would not agree to immediately hire any female faculty members. Finally, they gave up and went home. What behavioral procedure did the students use? _____

20. When 4-year-old Mary got out of bed on a cold morning, she "froze" her feet. One morning she put on her slippers when her feet felt a cold floor. Putting on her slippers stopped her feet from feeling the cold floor. Because Mary did not put on her slippers before feeling the cold but only after feeling the cold, you would say that Mary _____ (prevented, terminated) the cold feeling by putting on her slippers. From then on, she put on her slippers any morning that her feet felt a cold floor. Mary's behavior of putting on slippers when she felt a cold floor _____ in rate after that first time. Because Mary terminated the cold feeling by putting on the slippers and because Mary's rate of putting on the slippers increased in frequency, the event of feeling the cold floor would be classified as a(n) _____. (Remember, you don't have to write both words of the possible two-word answer.)

9. One day Mary put on her slippers before she put her feet on the floor. On that day, the coldness never reached her feet. From that day on, Mary put on her slippers before getting out of bed. Because she put her slippers on before her feet ever felt cold, she _____ (prevented, terminated) the cold feeling. The rate of Mary's putting on the slippers before getting out of bed _____. Therefore, the procedure she was reacting to is called _____ _____.

18. The residents of Corbin Hall dorm used to complain about the meals all the time. They then imposed a fine on anyone who complained about the food. Needless to say, you rarely hear any complaints about the food anymore. You might not be sure whether the fining procedure is negative reinforcement or punishment. Even if you think you know, check your guess by asking if the procedure increases or decreases the behavior. In this case, imposing a fine decreases complaining. Therefore, the fine is an example of what behavioral procedure?

_____

4. Hamm and Carey had been dating for quite a while. But Hamm had a bad habit. Somehow he would just lose track of time when talking with one of his friends and, as a result, would show up late for his dates with Carey. When Hamm was late, Carey looked sad. When Hamm was on time, Carey looked happy. By showing up on time, Hamm could keep Carey from looking sad. Soon, Hamm noticed the difference in Carey's look when he was on time and when he was late, so he started showing up on time. By showing up on time, Carey's looking sad was _____ (prevented, terminated). The rate of Hamm's showing up on time _____. Carey's sad look is an event called a(n) _____.

15. Sally never did her homework for Ms. Mann's social studies class, so Ms. Mann started keeping Sally after class every day she failed to do her homework. Of course, Sally could get out of having to stay after school by simply doing her homework. Ms. Mann found after two months that Sally still never did her homework. Sally could _____ (prevent, terminate) being kept after school by doing her homework. The rate of Sally's doing her homework during the two months that Ms. Mann tried keeping her after school _____ (decreased, increased, stayed same). What procedure did Ms. Mann use with Sally? _____

3. Gene had a beautiful Siamese cat that would run around the apartment knocking over furniture and climbing up curtains. Gene started putting his cat in the basement to keep him out of trouble. After several weeks, the cat started to howl and cry when locked in the basement. Gene found that he could stop the cat's howling by letting him out of the basement. Gene now lets the cat out of the basement as soon as the cat howls. By letting the cat out of the basement as soon as he howls, Gene _____ (prevents, terminates) the howling. The rate at which Gene let the cat out of the basement, after discovering that this would stop the howling, _____. The event "stopping the howling" is an example of a(n) _____. Gene's behavior of letting the cat out of the basement" is called a(n) _____ response. (Ask, "Is the howling present when Gene lets the cat out of the basement?")

7. Ken wasn't doing well in his sixth-grade math class. When his mother and father had their regular conferences with the teacher, she told them that Ken handed in fewer than half of his homework assignments. Ken's parents started sending him to bed early as a "punishment" when he didn't do his homework. Ken handed in all of his homework assignments from then on. Ken could _____ (prevent, terminate) his parents from sending him to bed early by handing in his homework. Ken's behavior of doing his homework would be classified as _____ behavior. What behavioral procedure produced Ken's increased rate of doing his homework? _____

2. Eight-year-old Dan had trouble pronouncing "refrigerator." His parents always said, "No, Dan, that's wrong!" when he said it incorrectly. After a while, Dan got so he always pronounced "refrigerator" correctly. By pronouncing "refrigerator" correctly the first time, Dan could _____ (prevent, terminate) his parent's "no." Because telling him "no" increased the rate of correct pronunciation by Dan, his parents used what procedure? _____ Dan's correct pronunciation of "refrigerator" is an example of what type of behavior? _____

6. Jerry didn't do his homework often enough in his social studies class. His teacher, Mr. Johnson, decided that he would embarrass Jerry every day until he started to do his homework. The first day after this change in procedure, he called on Jerry first for every question on the assignment. Naturally, Jerry didn't know the answers to any of them. Mr. Johnson repeated this same pattern every day for a week. Jerry got called on an average of 10–15 times each day, and he never had the correct answer. Finally, Jerry did his homework, so the teacher didn't ask him any questions. From then on, Jerry usually did his homework. On the few days that he didn't, the teacher again asked him many questions in class. The increase in Jerry's homework behavior is due to the teacher's use of what behavioral procedure? _____

16. The children on the corner frequently got into arguments with Mr. Ryker, the candy store owner. Mr. Ryker yelled that they were

killing his business by standing there and bothering people who walked by. The children replied that they were among his best customers, and they had a right to stay there. One day, Mr. Ryker got angrier than usual. In spite of his outburst, the children remained on the corner, so Mr. Ryker called the police. The children left before the police arrived, but they were angry. As a result, they threw a rock through one of his windows. Mr. Ryker never called the police again. What procedure did the children use to decrease Mr. Ryker's police-calling behavior? _____

17. The dorm, like all cooperative dorms, had a problem with getting its members to do the work needed to keep the house going. To solve the problem, the membership voted to fine any members who didn't do their share of the work during a given week. After this rule was instituted, everyone started doing their share of the work. Because working prevented a fine and the rate of work increased, what procedure is fining members who don't do their share? _____

5. In some courses, if students don't score high enough on the daily quiz, they must take it over again. If this procedure gets the student to work hard to pass the quiz on the first try, the quiz repetition would be an example of what procedure? _____

8. Mrs. Marlowe often reprimanded Ken for not doing his daily chores, but she usually waited many hours to give her reprimand. Ken's rate of doing his daily chores did not increase. The reprimand probably had little effect because did not occur _____ after his failure to respond.

1. Dave didn't like waiting for Carol to come home at dinnertime when she had not called him. Finally, one day when she came home late without calling, he explained his feelings to her. From then on, Carol prevented Dave's complaint by calling when she was going to be late. Carol's calling behavior would be called _____ behavior.

10. People learn to use negative reinforcement and punishment procedures more rapidly and more easily than they learn to use reinforcement procedures. When a person uses either negative reinforcement or punishment, the change in another person's behavior is likely to occur immediately. When a person uses reinforcement techniques, he or she reinforces a behavior that has already happened and that may not be appropriate again for a long time. Thus, any change resulting from the reinforcement can't be seen until that later time. Which principle of reinforcer effectiveness suggests that such a long delay may radically reduce the reinforcing effectiveness of any resulting behavioral change? _____

19. Todd was a very careful driver: he looked carefully at side streets, parked cars, and moving cars to prevent being hit; he stopped at traffic lights and signs to prevent accidents. He concluded that most of his driving should be classified as _____ behavior.

# LESSON

# 25 | Review of Aversive Control

## Reading Section

This unit introduced aversive control. Aversive control involves either withdrawing a reinforcer or delivering a punisher. Most people report "not liking" aversive control. Thus, aversive control is sharply different from positive reinforcement control. Aversive control and reinforcement control operate using four types of contingencies.

## Four Types of Contingencies

The table in Figure 25-1 reviews the four types of contingencies and related procedures that you have learned in previous lessons. Behavior analysts call the procedure in which an event follows and increases a behavior reinforcement. They call it *positive* reinforcement if it presents a stimulus. They call it *negative* reinforcement if it withdraws a stimulus. They call both procedures reinforcement because the event follows and increases a behavior. Behavior analysts call the procedure in which an event follows and decreases a behavior punishment. They call it punishment by contingent stimulation if it *presents* a stimulus. They call it punishment by contingent withdrawal if it

| Four types of contingencies | | |
|---|---|---|
| Rate | Presentation | Withdrawal |
| Increase | Positive Reinforcement | Negative Reinforcement |
| Decrease | Punishment by stimulation | Punishment by withdrawal |

*Figure 25-1.* The four basic procedures for delivering contingent stimuli.

*withdraws* a stimulus. They call both procedures punishment because the event follows and decreases a behavior. Thus, the distinction between punishment and reinforcement is whether the behavior decreases or increases. Only positive reinforcement is <u>not</u> a form of aversive control.

## The Aversive Control Strategy

This unit described three types of aversive contingencies. Aversive contingencies are pervasive because they are a natural part of the physical world and they are widely used by the people around us (see Vollmer, 2002). Their widespread use springs from the immediate and obvious results that their use produces. A major task of behavior analysts is to find ways to get the same results from positive reinforcement. Behavior analysts use them only as a last resort when they can't get positive reinforcement to work. Each contingency defines a technique for using the aversive control strategy.

Tactic #1 in using the aversive control strategy is to decrease undesirable behavior through <u>punishment</u> as a last resort. One procedure would be to use <u>punishment by contingent stimulation</u>, which involves delivering an event that reduces the rate of a behavior that it follows. Primary punishers include spanking, restraint, and shock. Behavior analysts use these events only as a last resort for dangerous behaviors that they can't control through positive reinforcement. Conditioned punishers include reprimands and feedback. Behavior analysts often use conditioned punishers for short periods while they attempt to start a person using desirable behaviors.

Another procedure would be to use <u>punishment by contingent withdrawal</u>. This involves withdrawing an event so that the rate of the behavior it follows is reduced. Good examples include fines, suspending privileges, and time out. These examples are mild forms of punishment that are widely acceptable.

Tactic #2 in using the aversive control strategy is to increase desirable behavior through <u>negative reinforcement</u> as a last resort. This procedure involves a response that terminates or prevents an event and that increases the rate of the response. This procedure is often used to get someone to start behaving when we don't know how to get positive procedures to work. It may then be stopped and positive reinforcement applied to the behavior.

Behavior analysts usually view all of these procedures as a last resort.

## Reducing the Need for Aversive Control

Early behavior analysts saw the awesome power of positive reinforcement. Even before they applied it to human problems, they imagined its potential for helping people. They predicted that its use would make it possible to abandon aversive control. They foresaw a world in which the science of human behavior could greatly reduce human suffering.

You realize by now that positive reinforcement is the most important discovery of behavior analysis. You have read many examples of positive reinforcement. They give you a good idea of the enormous range of behaviors influenced by positive reinforcement. This range includes obvious behavior such as football, subtle behavior such as looking, internal behavior such as muscle tension, and private behavior such as pain. It includes both normal behavior and abnormal behavior. It includes both manual and cognitive behavior.

You have read about the effect of positive reinforcement on the behaviors of normal people in everyday situations. These behaviors include creating, relaxing, laboring, learning, talking, taking care of one's health, and running a business. I have shown how these behaviors often start and continue because

they lead to reinforcement; that is, they are reinforced. When they do not occur at an optimal rate, I have tried to show you how they can often be improved through positive reinforcement. We can help people by teaching them how to get more positive reinforcement. We can help by improving their environment.

You have read earlier in this book about the misuse of positive reinforcement that causes abnormal behaviors. These behaviors include self-injury, acting crazy, aggression, complaining, crying, and even hallucinating. I have shown how these behaviors are often the result of misuses of reinforcement. The first step in eliminating them is to help the person learn more appropriate behaviors that produce reinforcement. But eliminating the abnormal behaviors entirely usually requires removing the misplaced reinforcement. Sometimes behavior analysts use aversive procedures to ensure elimination.

As you have seen throughout this book, applied behavior analysts often use positive reinforcement to help people change inappropriate behaviors. However, they sometimes fail to find ways to change disruptive and dangerous behavior with positive reinforcement alone. This sometimes leaves them with no alternative but to use primary punishment when self-injury and aggression are life threatening (see Lerman & Vorndran, 2002). Most of the time the inability to find ways to change disruptive behavior through positive reinforcement leads behavior analysts to use mild punishment on a wide range of behaviors, but this approach is usually temporary and used in conjunction with positive reinforcement. Many behavior analysts view the application of aversive control as a failures of the science (Sidman, 1989). Others view them as practical solutions to heart-wrenching problems (Baer, 1970).

The new approach of *functional analysis* mentioned in the last lesson emerged rapidly in the closing years of the twentieth century (Carr, 1977; Iwata, Dorsey, Slifer, Bauman, & Richman, 1982). In many ways it is a return to the vision of the early behavior analysts. The use of functional analysis and other tools has greatly reduced the failures that lead to the use of aversive control (see Kahng, Iwata, & Lewin, 2002a).

# Functional Analysis of Undesirable Behavior

Undesirable behavior often permits a person to avoid or escape from a situation. We saw that with Jenny's disruptive behavior. By pulling away and crying, she could stop the dentist from working on her teeth. We saw it with the burn victims. By not stretching, they could avoid the pain of stretching the burned areas on their bodies. Remember the slouchers. By slouching, they could avoid the effort of standing up straight. In all cases, the undesirable behavior avoided or escaped some aversive stimulus. Notice that these behaviors are not irrational or "crazy." They produce a reduction in immediate pain or discomfort.

On the face of it, these undesirable behaviors make sense, but each of these people stood to lose some important positive reinforcers by responding the way they did. Jenny would not get clean, pain-free teeth. The burn victims would not regain the ability to move freely. The slouchers would not enjoy a smoothly functioning back free of pain. Helping all of these people learn more useful behaviors permitted them to gain additional reinforcers.

Although some undesirable behaviors may "make sense" at some level, do all of them? Self-injury, refusing to eat, and even aggression are cases in point. One research team has analyzed the causes of self-injury (Iwata, et al., 1994).

The team found that misused positive social attention can explain 26% of the cases of self-injury. Such cases stem from the misuse of positive reinforcement by parents and other caregivers who may not have given attention unless the subjects injured themselves. Once we have established that this dynamic was the source of the person's self-injury, we can use positive reinforcement to modify it. The caregiver must withhold attention for self-injury and give it instead in response to more desirable behaviors. The person still gets the attention, but in the process he or she learns new and more functional behaviors.

The same team of researchers found that escape from a task or other demands caused 38% of the cases of self-injury. Such cases stem from caregivers giving in to obnoxious behaviors. They resemble the case of Jenny, who was so disruptive that dentists had let her escape dental treatment. In such cases, something about the caregiver's behavior is aversive to the person. Perhaps the caregiver treats them roughly or insists on teaching something that is too hard for the person to learn. The person has no way besides self-injury to stop the caregiver's behavior. Again, once we understand the dynamic at work, we can alter it. That is, we can reduce the demands made by the caregivers and teach the person more acceptable ways to stop the caregiver's behavior (Carr & Durand, 1985; Durand & Carr, 1992). In the case of moderate retardation, subjects may be able to learn a phrase like "Please stop" or "I would like a rest." In the case of severe retardation, subjects may be taught to press a button that signals the caregiver to give them a rest. The individuals get the same rest they got emitting obnoxious behaviors, but now have learned a more acceptable way to get it.

Finally, the team of researchers found that sensory stimulation caused 26% of the cases of self-injury. These cases are perhaps the hardest to understand intuitively. They represent people who found the pain, sound, or other sensation involved in self-injury to be reinforcing. The reason for this sort of response is still unclear. Perhaps such persons are so totally lacking in ways to produce reinforcers that this is the best they can do and/or basic neurological mechanisms may play a role. However, once we know that sensory reinforcement is causing the self-injury, we can devise ways to eliminate the sensory stimuli. Earlier in the book you read about an example in which the person inflicting self-injury was required to wear mittens (Luiselli, 1991). This cushioned the self-directed blows enough to make them no longer reinforcing. Such methods might be combined with teaching the person some simple skills with which to produce other reinforcers. As a result, the person would get reinforcement and would also have gained some useful skills.

The kinds of analyses outlined above permit individualized treatment for each case, allowing for modification of the specific aspect of the individual's environment that caused the abnormal behavior in the first place. This

***Figure 25-2.*** Brian Iwata developed SIBIS, an effective method for reducing self-injury based on aversive control At the same time, he pioneered functional analysis to increase the effectiveness of positive reinforcement to control self-injury. His work illustrates the way in which behavior analysis can pursue its founders' dream of a world whose people do not rely on aversive control. (Source: Courtesy of Brian Iwata)

individualized approach has been astonishingly successful. Iwata's team succeeded with about 85% of the cases. They resorted to punishment in the form of spraying a water mist in only seven cases. They treated the rest of the cases using positive reinforcement, extinction, or differential reinforcement. This sort of approach marks a major shift in the field of applied behavior analysis—a shift away from having to use aversive control because nothing else works. It is also a shift toward finding ways to make positive reinforcement work (see Kahng, Iwata, & Lewin, 2002b)! It is a shift toward the dream of a world without coercion, as envisioned by the founders of behavior analysis.

## Freedom

Skinner argues that the word *freedom* usually refers to the absence of aversive control. When we behave under the influence of positive reinforcement, we usually call ourselves free. We are not free of environmental influence, but rather, we are free of coercive influence. When our behavior leads to positive reinforcement, we act in our own interest. We behave because doing so helps us attain our own goals. The history of civilization has in many ways been the history of our struggle to throw off coercive control, whether it be from the king, the church, or the paternalistic family. "Movements for freedom . . . are in essence escape behaviors" (Richelle, 1993).

---

### *Reducing the Use of Aversive Control*

Does not behavior analysis "clearly stand out among other sciences by frequently claiming that wars can be prevented, prisoners can be rehabilitated, children can be taught . . . without resort to aversive contingencies? A few of these claims have been documented, but there is much to be learned, demonstrated, and applied. How will we acquire that learning? We will use every encounter with an aversive contingency . . . to learn more about the behavior in question, its controlling events, and ways in which

reinforcement and extinction schedules may be used to bring about the behavioral displacement. Through these experiences, we may not only solve the immediate problem, but also acquire the skills necessary to deal with the really tough cases in our culture—the drug dealers, the murderers." (Iwata, 1988: p. 151)

1. Iwata claims that behavior analysis can use reinforcement and extinction instead of _____ control.

Behavior analysts see their science as providing the understanding and the tools by which civilization can increase the speed and sureness of its march toward a society based on positive reinforcement (see Commentaries, 2001).

## Helpful Hints

### Helpful Hint #1

The definitions of all terms introduced in this unit of the book are presented below. You can review the unit and prepare for your exam by testing yourself on the definitions and correlated facts presented for each term. You might use a piece of paper as a mask and leave only the term exposed; see if you can formulate a reasonable definition and any other facts about that term. Then move the mask and check on yourself.

## Glossary

**aversive control strategy** The strategy of using <u>aversive</u> control if positive control fails.

- This strategy consists of two tactics:
  1. Decrease undesirable behavior through <u>punishment</u> as a last resort.
  2. Increase desirable behavior through <u>negative reinforcement</u> as a last resort.

**avoidance** Behavior that <u>prevents</u> a negative reinforcer from occurring.

**conditioned punisher** A punisher that loses its effectiveness through <u>unpaired</u> presentations.

**discriminative stimulus for punishment (SP)** A stimulus that precedes a behavior and is present only if <u>punishment</u> will occur for the behavior.

**escape** Behavior that <u>terminates</u> a negative reinforcer.

**generalized punisher** Any conditioned punisher that is associated with <u>many</u> other punishers.

**negative reinforcement** The <u>procedure</u> of following a behavior with a negative reinforcer.

- Any procedure or principle that applies to positive reinforcement may also be applied to negative reinforcement.

**negative reinforcer** Any event that, when <u>terminated or prevented</u> by a behavior, increases the rate of that behavior.

- A negative reinforcer is simply another form of a reinforcer and thus can be used in shaping, discrimination training, and conditioned reinforcement.
- Both positive and negative reinforcers increase the rate of a behavior, but a positive reinforcer is an event that is delivered, whereas a negative reinforcer is an event that is terminated or prevented.

**primary punisher** Any punisher that loses its effectiveness only through <u>satiation</u>.

- Primary punishers are usually basic physical events such as hitting, shock, pinching, and so on.

**punishment** The <u>procedure</u> of following a behavior with a punisher.

- <u>Punishment by contingent stimulation</u> involves delivery of a <u>punisher</u> and producing a decrease in the rate of the behavior.
- <u>Punishment by contingent withdrawal</u> involves withdrawal of a reinforcing event and producing a decrease in the rate of the behavior.
- When a person is removed from a reinforcing activity, that form of punishment by contingent withdrawal is called <u>time out</u>.

**punisher** Any event that <u>follows</u> a response and <u>decreases</u> the rate of that behavior.

- This definition of a punisher also applies to the withdrawal of an event following a behavior such that the rate of the behavior decreases—for instance, fining people or "timing them out" of a reinforcing activity.

## Practice Review I

The following material includes questions on every term studied in this unit as well as review questions from all prior units. By answering the

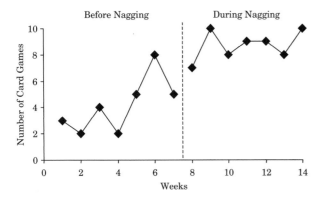

***Figure 25-3.*** An experimental analysis of card playing.

questions and checking your answers, you can prepare yourself for the Review Exam, which will contain questions from all four units. Because this is your last review for the final exam, it is composed of three long modules.

### 1. *Some Review Questions*

87. Pre-test: Tom frequently looks in his rearview mirror so that he won't have an accident. If having an accident is a negative reinforcer, then looking in his rearview mirror is an example of a(n) _____ behavior.

82. Pre-test: Figure 25-3 shows the number of card games that Ron played when Kelsey did not and did nag him. Divided? _____ Stable? _____ Convincing? _____ Cause? _____ (yes, no) (Remember to spell out your answer.)

84. Pre-test: Suppose Brad is praised for saying "nine" when asked "What is the sum of five plus four?" but ignored for saying anything else. Suppose he is praised for saying "twelve" when asked "What is the sum of eight plus four?" but ignored for saying anything else. Behavior analysts call this complex procedure _____.

81. Pre-test: If a behavior analyst reinforces someone for chewing gum but not for smoking cigarettes and if his rate of chewing gum increases, the behavior analyst would be using what procedure? _____

85. Pre-test: The person who is consistently nice to other people may be reinforced by the smile of the other person. If the smile is usually associated with many other reinforcers from that other person, it would be an example of what type of reinforcer? _____ reinforcer

83. Pre-test: Mr. Cosgrove explained to his eighth graders exactly how to find the square of a number. He then asked them to find the square of the number. He praised each student who got the right answer. What behavioral procedure was he using? _____ training

78. Pre-test: Barb used to throw tantrums often. Then Mom started making her go to her room for a half hour when she threw one. Her rate of throwing tantrums decreased. What procedure did Mom use to decrease Barb's rate of throwing tantrums? _____

43. If a behavior analyst reinforces a particular behavior, she becomes associated with reinforcement for it. The behavior analyst then becomes a stimulus that influences that behavior. The name of that kind of stimulus is a(n) _____ for that behavior.

53. If a teacher shows students how to do something, observes to see whether they do it the same way, and then reinforces them, we say that the teacher is using the method of _____ _____ training.

115. The use of punishment and negative reinforcement to control behavior is called _____ control.

61. If you stop delivering a reinforcer for an unrelated behavior whenever the person makes an undesirable response and the rate of the undesirable behavior decreases, you are using the procedure of _____. If you stop delivering a reinforcer following an undesirable response and the rate decreases, you are using what procedure? _____

63. Instructional training involves explaining to someone how to do something. That explanation is called a(n) _____ _____ description.

101. The attention that one person pays to another is frequently associated with many other reinforcers. What kind

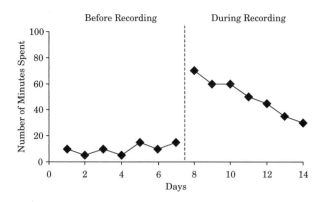

**Figure 25-4.** An experimental analysis of Daniel's playing with his son.

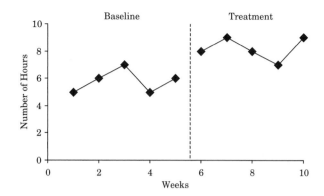

**Figure 25-5.** An experimental analysis of piano practice.

of conditioned reinforcer is it? A(n) _____ reinforcer.

98. Tactic #1 in using the aversive control strategy is to decrease undesirable behavior through _____ as a last resort.

48. If a reinforcer is produced by the first response that occurs after a fixed period of time, we say that it is being reinforced according to a(n) _____ schedule.

9. A stimulus associated with reinforcement for a particular response is called a(n) _____.

13. A stimulus/response chain is a sequence of responses in which the occurrence of one response serves as the _____ for the <u>next</u> response. (Note carefully the order of events implied by this question.)

126. What principle of effective reinforcement is determined by asking, "Was the amount of the event used worthwhile?" The principle of _____.

1. A conditioned reinforcer is one that is weakened permanently by _____ presentations.

28. Figure 25-4 shows the minutes that Daniel spent playing with his son when he self-recorded his playing time. Divided? _____ Stable? _____ Convincing? _____ Cause? _____ (yes, no)

76. People will continue to imitate the behavior of someone else only if they are _____ for doing so.

109. The method of observation based on dividing the observational period into many continuous intervals and observing during each interval whether the behavior occurs is called _____ recording.

51. If a response prevents a negative reinforcer, it is termed a(n) _____ response.

4. A primary reinforcer is one that is weakened only temporarily by _____.

102. The baseline is a record of a behavior before the _____ condition.

68. Mr. Cosgrove displayed on the blackboard how to find the square of a number. He then erased his example and asked his students to find the square of that same number. He examined each student's work and praised him or her if it was correct. What behavioral procedure did he use? _____ training.

6. A punisher is defined as any event that (1) _____ a response and (2) _____ the rate of that response.

49. If a response is reinforced after a fixed number of occurrences of the response, this procedure is an example of a(n) _____ schedule.

27. Figure 25-5 shows the number of hours that Dan practiced on the piano per week: Divided? _____ Stable? _____ Convincing? _____ Cause? _____ (yes, no)

19. Any conditioned reinforcer that is paired with many backup reinforcers is called a(n) _____ reinforcer.

44. If a behavior occurs more frequently in the presence of one stimulus and less frequently in the presence of another stimulus, we call it _____ behavior.

127. When civil rights groups measure the number of shoppers at a store prior to undertaking a boycott, the resulting data are called a(n) _____.

120. To decide whether the principle of immediacy was followed, ask, "Was the event delivered within a(n) _____ _____ of the behavior (or while it was still occurring)?"

58. If Tommy has learned to call the funny little car a "beetle" but not the long sleek car, we say that the funny little car exerts _____ over his behavior of calling it a "beetle."

42. Husbands and wives often point out one another's thoughtless acts right after they occur. If pointing them out decreases the rate of thoughtless acts, it would be an example of what behavioral procedure? _____

95. Shaping involves applying the procedure of _____ to a series of successive _____ to some target behavior.

56. If people have not received a particular reinforcer for a while, we say that they are _____ with respect to that reinforcer.

125. Two kinds of experimental designs that rule out both kinds of alternative explanations are the _____ _____ design and the _____ _____ design.

65. Larry wondered if Kevin's stuttering was decreasing, so he recorded each time that Kevin emitted a stuttered word in his presence. What method of direct observation was he using? _____ recording.

11. A stimulus event that occurs <u>prior</u> to a response and increases the frequency of that response is called a(n) _____; a stimulus event that occurs <u>after</u> a response and increases the frequency of that response is called a(n) _____.

110. The more immediate the delivery of an event after the occurrence of the desired behavior, the more effective the reinforcer, according to the principle of _____ _____.

8. A snerkel is a card that can be exchanged for a wide range of privileges in the fraternity house. A reinforcer of this type is effective because at least one of the back-up reinforcers is likely to be an effective reinforcer at any given time due to what principle? _____

55. If one behavior is reinforced while another behavior is extinguished in the presence of one stimulus and if the first behavior is extinguished while the second is reinforced in the presence of a second stimulus, we label this complex procedure _____.

114. The single-subject design in which a behavior is observed during baseline and then during treatment would be called a(n) _____ design.

57. If the delivery of the reinforcer for a behavior is stopped and the rate of that behavior decreases, then this procedure is called _____.

38. Fred and Charlie observed Murray's study behavior using the same definition but on different days. Is their agreement a measure of the reliability of their observations? _____ (yes, no)

37. Frank is one of those guys who starts arguments with everyone around him. One day he argued long and loud against the idea that only co-op members should be allowed to buy at reduced prices. If no one paid any attention to him, it is likely that this verbal behavior (arguing) would decrease. What procedure would be involved? _____

## 2. Some More Review Questions

80. Pre-test: A chance to quit review. Do you wish to skip this review module? _____ (yes, no)

◆ **Very Important** ◆

Both "yes" and "no" are correct answers. You are being given the chance to decide whether to complete this module or skip to the next.

129. When you arrange to deliver an event after each instance of a behavior, thereby increasing the rate of behavior, you refer to the procedure as _____ _____ and the event as a(n) _____.

3. A positive reinforcer must have two characteristics: It must be timed so that it _____ a behavior, and it must _____ the frequency of the behavior.

91. Reinforcing a behavior in the presence of one stimulus and extinguishing that same behavior in the presence of another stimulus is called _____ _____.

124. Tom's only problem was that he was always griping about the food at the frat. When he griped, people argued with him. The more they argued, the more he griped. What behavioral procedure did the other frat members use to increase his rate of griping? _____ _____.

14. An escape response is any response that _____ a negative reinforcer.

52. If a stimulus signals the contingent withdrawal of a reinforcer, that stimulus is called a(n) _____ _____.

5. A procedure for gradually changing a behavior is called _____.

15. An experimental design in which two behaviors are observed over baselines of different length prior to the introduction of the treatment is called a(n) _____ design.

45. If a person is reinforced after varying numbers of responses, what schedule of reinforcement is being used? _____ _____.

75. Outcome recording involves observing some relatively lasting _____ of the response.

105. The differential reinforcement of a series of successive approximations to some target behavior is called _____.

40. Generalization training consists of reinforcing a behavior in each of a series of situations until it _____ to other members of that same stimulus class.

106. The funny-shaped little car is not a plane. Therefore, "plane," as part of the questions about what the objects would be called, is a(n) _____.

99. Tactic #2 in using the aversive control strategy is to increase desirable behavior through _____ reinforcement as a last resort.

18. Any behavior that prevents a negative reinforcer is called a(n) _____ behavior.

31. Differential reinforcement is a procedure in which one response is _____ _____ and other responses are _____.

67. May studied the child-rearing practices of college graduates by asking a random sample of 25 of them to answer such questions as "How many times last week did you tell your child to finish the rest of the food on his or her plate?" Since the parents did not record the observations when they occurred, the approach they used is an example of _____ _____ observation.

123. Tom's goal was to teach Mona how to play a particular chord on the guitar step by step. He first praised her only when she held it correctly, next only when she strummed it correctly, and finally only when she strummed a particular chord. Tom's goal of Mona playing a particular chord is called the _____ _____ that he was trying to teach.

69. Mr. Jackson observed five students to determine whether they were studying. He first observed Diane for 12 seconds, then shifted to Ken and observed him for 12 seconds, and so on for the other three students. He started over again with Diane after having observed the others. What method of observation is he using to observe Diane? _____ recording

10. A stimulus associated with extinction for a particular response is called a(n) _____.

117. Time sample recording involves observing whether or not a behavior occurs during each of a series of _____ _____ intervals.

32. Dr. Gold observed Maria's assertiveness prior to assertiveness training and then during assertiveness training. What experimental design was he using? _____

50. If a response is reinforced every time it occurs, it is said to be on what generic schedule? A(n) _____ schedule of reinforcement.

73. Name the four principles of effective reinforcement: (1) _____, (2) _____, (3) _____, (4) _____.

97. Suppose Bob Behaviorist found that any time Ruby wasn't shocked for taking a cigarette, she smoked at her normal rate. This discovery would indicate that the effect of the shock on her rate of smoking did not _____ to situations in which she wasn't shocked.

112. The principle of effective reinforcement that states "the more deprived a person is with respect to the event, the more effective it will be" is called the principle of _____.

33. Event recording involves recording each _____ of a behavior.

59. If Tommy has learned to call the funny-shaped little car a "beetle" but not other cars, then we would call his behavior of calling it a "beetle" _____ behavior.

93. Reliability is a measure of the _____ between two independent observers.

47. If a reinforcer is delivered to people for their first response after differing periods of time, they are said to be on what specific schedule? A(n) _____ schedule.

34. Extinction involves stopping the delivery of a reinforcer for a behavior and observing a(n) _____ in the rate of that behavior.

17. An S-delta is a stimulus that is associated with the _____ of a particular response.

39. Fred felt that it was important to determine whether the behaviors that he was observing and calling studying would be regarded by others as studying. He had a panel of individuals observe several students who were studying according to his definition and several who were not studying according to his definition to see if the panel would agree with his definition. Fred is attempting to determine the _____ of his definition of studying.

121. To decide whether the public areas of a building are clean enough, you might make up a checklist of things that should be clean (floors, ashtrays, trash baskets, etc.) and check once a day to see whether they are clean. You would be using what method of direct observing? _____ recording

16. An observation that is seen (or heard) by the observer and promptly recorded uses what approach to observation? _____ observation

60. If you show someone how to do something, watch his behavior, and reinforce it when it is correct, your behavior is called the _____ stimulus.

30. Differential reinforcement involves two basic behavioral procedures. They are _____ and _____.

116. The weakness of a simple comparison design is that it does not rule out _____ explanations of an observed change in the behavior.

88. Programming is the temporary use of a prompt to produce _____ of behavior to a novel situation

104. The design in which a behavior is observed during a baseline, during a treatment condition, and, finally, during a return to baseline, is called a(n) _____ design.

96. Students listening to a lecture are often regarded as being "attentive" if their eyes are open and their heads are pointed toward the speaker. If this statement were used to describe attentive behavior, it would be called what? _____

24. Brad was helping Carol change several of her behaviors. He started by doing baseline observations on her interrupting and arguing behaviors for one month. During the second month, he gave her a wrist counter and asked her

to count interrupting but not arguing. During the third month, he gave her a second wrist counter and asked to also count arguing behaviors. The two were happy to find that both behaviors decreased. What single subject experimental design was Brad using? _____ design

41. Henry was particularly interested in pictures of birds. When he looked through a book of photos, he skipped the those that did not include birds. What specific schedule of intermittent reinforcement was his picture-looking behavior on? _____ _____

### 3. Some More Review Questions

79. Pre-test: Another chance to quit review. Do you wish to skip this review module and go to Lesson Quiz B? _____ (yes, no)

♦ **Very Important** ♦
Both "yes" and "no" are correct answers. You are being given the chance to decide whether to complete this module or skip to the next.

35. Fading is a procedure used to help teach a specific _____ that involves gradually withdrawing a stimulus called a prompt. (Hint: The answer is not "behavior" or "response"!)

46. If a person's behavior occurs in the presence of a novel stimulus, we call this the process of _____.

64. Interval recording involves recording whether or not a behavior occurs during each of a series of _____ intervals.

70. Mr. James awarded Tom a token for every 10 multiplication problems he got correct. What schedule of intermittent reinforcement is Mr. James using? _____

74. Observation based on some physical <u>result</u> of a response rather than observation of the response itself is called _____ recording.

119. To decide whether the principle of deprivation was followed rather than violated, ask, "Has the reinforcer _____ _____ been delivered?"

71. Mr. Warren, a high school teacher, was always negative in his class. Several of his students decided to observe him to find out how much of the time he was negative. They made their observations in consecutive 15-second blocks throughout the day and found that he was negative 75% of the time. What method of direct observation did they use? _____ recording

113. The procedure of having an event follow a behavior and increase its rate is called _____.

20. Any time a response is not reinforced after every occurrence, we say that the response is on what generic schedule? A(n) _____ schedule.

26. Correlating ratings by outside judges with observations by observers trained to use a particular behavioral definition is called determining the _____ of the definition.

7. A response will take longer to extinguish if it has been on what generic schedule? A(n) _____ schedule.

94. Remember, if you tell people to do something and they do, this _____ _____ (is, isn't) an example of reinforcement.

108. The longer the delay in providing reinforcement for a response, the _____ _____ (less, more) effective the reinforcer.

111. The observation of a behavior prior to introducing a treatment is called the _____ condition.

36. Four basic methods of observation of behavior are _____ recording, _____ recording, _____ recording, and _____ recording.

92. Reinforcing one response while extinguishing a different response is called _____.

2. A generalization may occur when a response has been reinforced in the presence of a stimulus so that the person emits the same response in the presence of a(n) _____ stimulus.

12. A stimulus that consistently signals the occurrence of punishment is called a(n) _____.

29. Danny was trying to teach Marty to say "one." Every time Marty said something like "one," Danny said, "Very good." At first, Marty had a high rate of saying something close to "one." Then he slowed down, and finally, he quit altogether. Marty probably quit because Danny was saying "Very good" too often. What principle of effective reinforcement did Danny violate? _____

122. Tom was teaching Mona to play the guitar. He first praised her only when she held it correctly, next only when she strummed properly, and finally only when she struck a particular chord. Holding the guitar properly is called a(n) _____ to playing it correctly.

107. The goal of shaping is to produce a specified behavior called a(n) _____.

21. Avoidance behavior prevents an event called a(n) _____ from occurring.

54. If an event follows a behavior and increases its rate, it is called a(n) _____.

118. To decide if the principle of contingency was followed, ask, "Was the event given _____ if the desired behavior occurred?"

89. Recording whether or not a behavior occurs during each of a series of discontinuous intervals is called _____ _____ recording.

23. Bob really liked Kay when she acted assertively, so he always made it a point to praise such behavior. After a while, Kay always acted assertively around Bob, but for some reason her assertiveness did not spill over into her other relationships. However, after David also started reinforcing assertiveness, Kay began acting assertively with everyone she knew. What behavioral procedure did this series of friends use to change Kay's behavior in this way? _____ training

25. Clearly stating what behavior to observe is called a(n) _____.

90. Reinforcing a behavior in the presence of a series of situations until it generalizes to novel members of that same stimulus class is called _____.

103. The collection of all works of art would be considered a(n) _____.

100. The agreement between the observations of two independent observers is called the _____ of those observations.

72. Mrs. Whalen observed Penny's study behavior prior to praising it, while she praised it, and after she had stopped praising it. What experimental design was she using? _____ design

62. If you withdraw a reinforcer (unrelated to an undesirable behavior) every time that particular undesirable behavior occurs and the undesirable behavior decreases, you are using what procedure? _____

128. When Thurmond moved up north, no one paid any attention to his racially prejudiced statements. However, his statements did not decrease in rate. What behavioral procedure was being applied to his prejudiced behavior? _____

22. Behavior analysis looks at _____ events that _____ behavior.

66. Lenny's mother was very interested in increasing his rate of comments reflecting a positive outlook on life. Therefore, she watched very carefully for such comments to occur and noted them to herself. She then would praise Lenny for each comment at a special meeting that they held every Sunday. She never praised comments that were not positive. Her praise was very important to Lenny, and he never seemed to get too much of it. What principle of effective reinforcement, if any, did his mother neglect? _____

# Practice Review II

This section provides additional review questions covering every chapter in the book. It includes two modules of moderate length.

### *1. Some Review Questions*

30. Pre-test: Pete designed the world's best token system for his third-grade pupils. They could trade tokens for snacks, TV lessons, meeting with the principal, having a story read, and lots of agreeable things. Pete never gave them so many tokens that they didn't want them any more. And he always gave the tokens immediately after the behavior that he desired. When he tried to reinforce his pupils for pronouncing difficult words accurately, however, he had little success because he was hard of hearing. Thus, he gave them tokens for both right and wrong pronunciation. What principle of effective reinforcement, if any, did he neglect? _____

23. Pre-test: Eleanor learned to read the word *dog* from a special book. The book reinforced her when she pronounced *d-o-g* "dog" but not when she pronounced another word "dog." The book started out by showing a picture of a dog when the word was first presented but gradually showed the dog less and less frequently—until Eleanor had to read the word without the help of the picture. What behavioral procedure did the book use? _____

32. Pre-test: Writing the date, the store's name, and the amount on a check usually precedes the signing of the check and the receiving of the store's merchandise. If signing the check is reinforced by receiving the merchandise, the sequence of writing behaviors is what is called a(n) _____ .

27. Pre-test: Mary was observed by the primary observer to talk with other children in her class 8 times. A reliability observer noted 10 instances of talking. Compute the reliability of these observations: _____%. Is it acceptable? _____ (yes, no)

24. Pre-test: If observers check for 5 seconds every 14 minutes to see if a certain behavior is occurring, what method of direct observation are they using? _____ recording.

21. Pre-test: A set of related stimuli is called a(n) _____ .

26. Pre-test: Is a generalized reinforcer defined as an event that can be used to reinforce a response as it generalizes to new situations? _____ (yes, no)

38. The effectiveness of an event will be maximized if it is delivered only when the desired behavior occurs, according to the principle of _____ .

42. The temporary use of a prompt to produce a generalization is called _____ .

15. Each of a series of behaviors that are similar to some target behavior is called a(n) _____ .

43. Tommy's mother wanted to teach him the idea of "boy," so she showed him a picture of Ken and asked, "What kind of person is this—you know, like Daddy?" and reinforced him when he said "boy." She then gave him the hint less and less frequently until Tommy always said "boy" when showed a picture of Ken. She then repeated the procedure with a picture of Joe until he learned to call Joe a boy. Eventually, Tommy could label any picture of a young male as a boy. By adding the hint to the basic procedure, what procedure did his mother use? _____

41. The reliability of a new behavioral definition should be at least _____%.

8. An added stimulus, used to help learn a discrimination or generalization, is called a(n) _____ .

45. What two schedules of reinforcement produce low rates of responding right after reinforcement and a higher rate as the time for the next reinforcement approaches? _____ and _____

7. A stimulus class consists of a set of _____ stimuli.

37. Schedules of reinforcement based on time are called _____ schedules; schedules based on number of responses are called _____ schedules.

3. A negative reinforcer is any event that is terminated or _____ by a behavior and that causes the rate of the behavior to _____ .

36. Satiation, extinction, and punishment all have the effect of _____ the rate of a response.

35. Reinforcing one response and extinguishing a different response is called _____; reinforcing a response in one situation and extinguishing the same response in a different situation is called _____ _____.

4. A procedure used to help teach a specific discrimination that involves gradually withdrawing a prompt is called _____ _____.

9. An intermittent schedule of reinforcement will reduce satiation and also produce a greater resistance to _____ _____ than will a continuous schedule.

39. The principle of effective reinforcement that states "The more worthwhile the amount of an event that is delivered after the desired behavior, the more effective it will be" is called the principle of _____ _____.

2. A method of direct observation based on counting instances of a behavior is called _____recording.

16. Escape is a procedure in which a negative reinforcer is _____ _____ following a response.

6. A sequence of responses in which the prior response serves as the discriminative stimulus for the succeeding response is called a(n) _____.

## 2. Some More Review Questions

31. Pre-test: Figure 25-6 shows the observations of two observers who have developed a definition of nervous behavior. They recorded the occurrence of nervous looks by witnesses at the congressional hearings (where "N" stands for "nervous" and "C" stands for "calm"). Compute the reliability: _____% Is the reliability acceptable? _____ (yes, no)

22. Pre-test: Any event that follows a response and reduces the probability of that response's occurring is called a(n) _____.

25. Pre-test: If people are reinforced only every 500 responses, their responding may

| First observer | N | N | N | N | N |
| Second observer | N | N | C | N | N |

***Figure 25-6.*** Observations by two observers.

become erratic and slower. This consequence is known as _____.

28. Pre-test: Mike's parents "punished" him by sending him to bed early on any day that he hadn't done his homework for school. Mike started doing his homework. What procedure increased Mike's rate of doing homework? _____ _____

29. Pre-test: Ms. Whalen wanted to increase the amount of studying in her fourth grade so that the children would learn faster. She decided that she would walk through the room while the children were working on their math and would grade their work right then and there. Each child would then be allowed to play outside for 10 minutes after he or she had completed 10 problems correctly. She found that the rate of work in the class went up dramatically as a result of this approach. The grade in this example is probably a(n) _____ (conditioned, generalized, primary) reinforcer. Because you can earn it with 10 correct problems, the right to play would be a _____ reinforcer for the grade.

17. If you make a negative reinforcer most effective in increasing the rate of a response by removing it right after the response, you are using what principle of reinforcer effectiveness? The principle of _____.

5. A punisher that loses its effectiveness through unpaired presentations is called a(n) _____ _____ punisher.

20. People will continue to follow instructions only if they are _____ _____ for doing so.

46. What two schedules of reinforcement produce uniform rates of responding? The _____ schedule and the _____ _____ schedule.

44. What is the best generic schedule of reinforcement to use when attempting to

shape a new behavior? _____ reinforcement.

34. Reinforcing events that make conditioned reinforcers and generalized reinforcers effective as a result of being paired with them are called _____ reinforcers.

19. In order for punishment to be most effective, it should follow the undesirable response _____.

33. Quite frequently, we can't use a particular reinforcer immediately after the behavior we would like to encourage. The important thing about a conditioned reinforcer, such as a smile or a thank you, is that it can be delivered _____ _____, which enhances its effectiveness.

10. An SD is a stimulus that precedes a behavior and is present only if that behavior will be _____; an S-delta is a stimulus that precedes a behavior and is present only if that behavior will be _____ _____.

14. Carol didn't like football, but she did like the interviews with the players. So she tuned in exactly at the start of half time. The interviews always started five minutes after the start of half time. What schedule of reinforcement is her TV viewing on? A(n) _____ schedule

11. Any reinforcer that is weakened permanently by unpaired presentations is called a(n) _____ _____ reinforcer.

40. The procedure of reinforcing a desired behavior that has been verbally described to a person is called _____ _____.

1. A generalized reinforcer is any conditioned reinforcer that is paired with _____ _____ backup reinforcers.

18. If you withdraw an event contingent on a behavior and if the rate of that behavior decreases, the procedure is called _____.

12. Any reinforcer that is weakened temporarily only by satiation is called a(n) _____ reinforcer.

13. Behavior analysts don't consider negative reinforcement and _____ _____ to be the same.

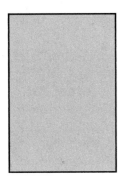

# References

ABRAMOWITZ, A. J., & O'LEARY, S. G. (1990). Effectiveness of delayed punishment in an applied setting. *Behavior Therapy, 21*, 231–239.

AESCHLEMAN, S. R., ROSEN, C. C., & WILLIAMS, M. R. (2002). The effect of non-contingent negative and positive reinforcement operations on the acquisition of superstitious behaviours. *Behavioural Processes, 61*, 35–65.

AHLES, T. A., COOMBS, D. W., JENSEN, L., STUKEL, T., et al. (1990). Development of a behavioral observation technique for the assessment of pain behaviors in cancer patients. *Behavior Therapy, 21*, 449–460.

ALFORD, G. S., & TURNER, S. M. (1976). Stimulus interference and conditioned inhibition of auditory hallucinations. *Journal of Behavior Therapy and Experimental Psychiatry, 7*, 155–160.

ALLEN, G. J. (1973). Case study: Implementation of behavior modification techniques in summer camp settings. *Behavior Therapy, 4*, 570–575.

ALLEN, J. S., TARNOWSKI, K. J., SIMONIAN, S. J., ELLIOTT, D., et al. (1991). The generalization map revisited: Assessment of generalized treatment effects in child and adolescent behavior therapy. *Behavior Therapy, 22*, 393–405.

ALLEN, K. D., LOIBEN, T., ALLEN, S. J., & STANLEY, R. T. (1992). Dentist-implemented contingent escape for management of disruptive child behavior. *Journal of Applied Behavior Analysis, 25*, 629–626.

ALLEN, K. D., & STOKES, T. F. (1987). Use of escape and reward in the management of young children during dental treatment. *Journal of Applied Behavior Analysis, 20*, 381–390.

ALLEN, K. E., HART, B. M., BUELL, J. S., HARRIS, F. R., & WOLF, M. M. (1964). Effects of social reinforcement on isolate behavior of a nursery school child. *Child Development, 35*, 511–518.

ALLEN, K. E., TURNER, K. D., & EVERETT, P. M. (1970). A behavior modification classroom for Head Start children with problem behaviors. *Exceptional children, 37*, 119–127.

ALLPORT, G. W., & POSTMAN, L. F. (1945). The basic psychology of rumor. *Transactions of the New York Academy of Sciences*, Series II, 61–81.

ANDERSON, G., & KIRKPATRICK, M. A. (2002). Variable effects of a behavioral treatment package on the performance of inline roller speed skaters. *Journal of Applied Behavior Analysis, 35*, 195–198.

ANDRZEJEWSKI, M. E., KIRBY, K. C., MORRAL, A. R., & IGUCHI, M. Y. (2001). Technology transfer through performance management: The effects of graphical feedback and positive reinforcement on drug treatment counselors' behavior. *Drug & Alcohol Dependence, 63*(2), 179–186.

APPELBAUM, K. A., BLANCHARD, E. B., NICHOLSON, N. L., RADNITZ, C., et al. (1990). Controlled evaluation of the addition of cognitive strategies to a home-based relaxation protocol for tension headache. *Behavior Therapy, 21*, 293–303.

ARAUJO, J., & BORN, D. G. (1985). Calculating percentage agreement correctly but writing its formula incorrectly. *The Behavior Analyst, 8*, 207–208.

ARDOIN, S. P., & MARTENS, B. K. (2000). Testing the ability of children with attention deficit hyperactivity disorder to accurately report the effects of medication on their behavior. *Journal of Applied Behavior Analysis, 33*, 593–610.

AXELROD, S. (1991). Smoking cessation through functional analysis. *Journal of Applied Behavior Analysis, 24*, 717–718.

AYLLON, T. (1963). Intensive treatment of psychotic behavior by stimulus satiation and food reinforcement. *Behavior Research and Therapy, 1*, 53–61.

AYLLON, T., & AZRIN, N. H. (1964). Reinforcement and instructions with mental patients. *Journal of the Experimental Analysis of Behavior, 7*, 327–333.

AYLLON, T., & AZRIN, N. H. (1965). The measurement and reinforcement of behavior of psychotics. *Journal of the Experimental Analysis of Behavior, 8*(6), 357–383.

AYLLON, T., & AZRIN, N. H. (1968). *The token economy: A motivational system for therapy and rehabilitation.* Englewood Cliffs, NJ: Prentice Hall.

AYLLON, T., & MICHAEL, J. (1959). The psychiatric nurse as a behavioral engineer. *Journal of the Experimental Analysis of Behavior, 2*, 323–334.

AZRIN, N., RUBIN, H., O'BRIEN, F., AYLLON, T., & ROLL, D. (1968). Behavioral engineering; Posture control by a portable operant apparatus. *Journal of Applied Behavior Analysis, 1*, 99–108.

AZRIN, N. H., & HOLZ, W. C. (1966). Punishment. In W. K. Honig (Ed.), *Operant behavior: Areas of research and application* (pp. 380–447). New York: Appleton-Century-Crofts.

AZRIN, N. H., & POWELL, J. (1968). Behavioral engineering: The reduction of smoking behavior by a conditioning apparatus and procedure. *Journal of Applied Behavior Analysis, 1*, 193–200.

AZRIN, N. H., & POWELL, J. (1969). Behavioral engineering: The use of response priming to improve prescribed self-medication. *Journal of Applied Behavior Analysis, 2*, 39–42.

AZRIN, R. D., & HAYES, S. C. (1984). The discrimination of interest within a heterosexual interaction: Training, generalization, and effects on social skills. *Behavior Therapy, 15*, 173–184.

BACHRACH, A. J. (1962). *Psychological research: An introduction.* New York: Random House.

BACON, D. L., FULTON, B. J., & MALOTT, R. W. (1982). Improving staff performance through the use of task checklists. *Journal of Organizational Behavior Management, 4*, 17–25.

BAER, A. M., ROWBURY, T., & BAER, D. M. (1973). The development of instructional control over classroom activities of deviant preschool children. *Journal of Applied Behavior Analysis, 6*, 289–298.

BAER, D. M. (1962). Laboratory control of thumb sucking by withdrawal and representation of reinforcement. *Journal of the Experimental Analysis of Behavior, 5*, 525–528.

BAER, D. M. (1970). A case for the selective reinforcement of punishment. In C. Neuringer & J. L. Michael (Eds.), *Behavior modification in clinical psychology* (pp. 243–249). New York: Appleton-Century-Crofts.

BAER, D. M. (1976). The organism as host. *Human Development, 19*, 87–98.

BAER, D. M. (1977a). Perhaps it would be better not to know everything. *Journal of Applied Behavior Analysis, 10*, 167–172.

BAER, D. M. (1977b). Reviewer's comment: Just because it's reliable doesn't mean that you can use it. *Journal of Applied Behavior Analysis, 10*, 117–119.

BAER, D. M. (1987). Do we really want the unification of psychology? A response to Krantz. *New Ideas in Psychology, 5*, 356–359.

BAER, D. M., & DEGNCHI, H. (1985). Generalized imitation from a radical-behavioral viewpoint. In R. Bootzin & S. Reiss (Eds.), Theoretical issues in behavior therapy (pp. 179–217). Orlando, FL: Academic Press.

BAER, D. M., & GUESS, D. (1971). Receptive training of adjective inflections in mental retardates. *Journal of Applied Behavior Analysis, 4*, 129–140.

BAER, D. M., PETERSON, R. F., & SHERMAN, J. A. (1967). The development of imitation by reinforcing behavioral similarity to a model. *Journal of the Experimental Analysis of Behavior, 10*, 405–416.

BAER, D. M., WOLF, M. M., & RISLEY, T. R. (1968). Some current dimensions of applied behavior analysis. *Journal of Applied Behavior Analysis, 1*, 91–97.

BAER, D. M., WOLF, M. M., & RISLEY, T. R. (1987). Some still-current dimensions of applied behavior analysis. *Journal of Applied Behavior Analysis, 20*, 313–327.

BAER, R. A., & DETRICH, R. (1990). Tacting and manding in correspondence training: Effects of child selection of verbalization. *Journal of the Experimental Analysis of Behavior, 54*, 23–30.

BAILEY, J. S., & BURCH, M. R. (2002). *Research methods in applied behavior analysis.* Thousand Oaks, CA: Sage.

BAILEY, S. L., POKRZYWINSKI, J., & BRYANT, L. E. (1983). Using water mist to reduce self-injurious and stereotypic behavior. *Applied Research in Mental Retardation, 4*, 229–241.

BANDURA, A. (1969). *Principles of behavior modification.* New York: Holt, Rinehart and Winston.

BANDURA, A. (1971). *Psychological modeling: Conflicting theories.* Chicago: Aldine-Atherthon.

BARLOW, D. H., HAYES, S. C., & NELSON, R. O. (1984). *The scientist practitioner: Research accountability in clinical and educational settings.* New York: Pergamon.

BARLOW, D. H., & HERSEN, M. (1984). *Single case experimental designs: Strategies for studying behavior change.* New York: Pergamon.

BARRETT, B. H., & LINDSLEY, O. R. (1962). Deficits in acquisition of operant discrimination and differentiation shown by institutionalized retarded children. *American Journal of Mental Deficiency, 67*, 424–436.

BASS, R. F. (1987). Computer-assisted observer training. *Journal of Applied Behavior Analysis, 20*, 83–88.

BASS, R. F., & ASERLIND, R. (1984). Interval and time-sample data collection procedures: Methodological issues. In K. V. Gadow (Ed.), *Advances in learning and behavioral disabilities* (Vol. 3, pp. 1–39). Greenwich, CT: JAI Press.

BECKMAN, P. J., & KOHL, F. L. (1987). Interactions of preschoolers with and without handicaps in integrated and segregated settings: A longitudinal study. *Mental Retardation, 25*, 5–11.

BEHRENS, B. C., SANDERS, M. R., & HALFORD, W. K. (1990). Behavioral marital therapy: An evaluation of treatment effects across high and low risk settings. *Behavior Therapy, 21*, 423–433.

BELLES, D., & BRADLYN, A. S. (1987). The use of the changing criterion design in achieving controlled smoking in a heavy smoker: A controlled case study. *Journal of Behavior Therapy and Experimental Psychiatry, 18*, 77–82.

BENTALL, R. P., & LOWE, C. F. (1987). The role of verbal behavior in human learning: III. Instructional effects in children. *Journal of the Experimental Analysis of Behavior, 47*, 177–190.

BEREITER, C., & MIDIAN, K. (1978, March 30). *Were some follow through models more effective than others?* Paper presented at American Educational Research Association, Toronto, Canada.

BERNARD, C. (1957). *An introduction to the study of experimental medicine.* New York: Dover.

BICKEL, W. K., DEGRANDPRE, R. J., HUGHES, J. R., & HIGGINS, S. T. (1991). Behavioral economics of drug self-administration: II. A unit-price analysis of cigarette smoking. *Journal of the Experimental Analysis of Behavior, 55*, 145–154.

BIJOU, S. W., PETERSON, R. F., & AULT, M. H. (1968). A method to integrate descriptive and experimental field studies at the level of data and empirical concepts. *Journal of Applied Behavior Analysis, 1*, 175–191.

BIRNBRAUER, J. S., BIJOU, S. W., WOLF, M. M., & KIDDER, J. D. (1965). Programmed instruction in the classroom. In L. P. Ullman & L. Krasner (Eds.), *Case studies in behavior modification.* New York: Holt, Rinehart and Winston.

BLAKE, P., & MOSS, T. (1967). The development of socialization skills in an electively mute child. *Behavior Research and Therapy, 5*, 349–356.

BLAMPIED, N. M., & KAHAN, E. (1992). Acceptability of alternative punishments: A community survey. *Behavior Modification, 16*, 400–413.

BLECHMAN, E. A., OLSON, D. H., & HELLMAN, I. D. (1976). Stimulus control over family problem-solving behavior: The Family Contract Game. *Behavior Therapy, 7*, 686–692.

BORKOVEC, T. D., WILKINSON, L., FOLENSBEE, R., & LERMAN, C. (1983). Stimulus control applications to the treatment of worry. *Behaviour Research and Therapy, 21*, 247–251.

BORNSTEIN, M. R., BELLACK, A. S., & HERSEN, M. (1977). Social-skills training for unassertive children: A multiple-baseline analysis. *Journal of Applied Behavior Analysis, 10*, 183–195.

BORRERO, J. C., VOLLMER, T. R., & WRIGHT, C. S. (2002). An evaluation of contingency strength and response suppression. *Journal of Applied Behavior Analysis, 35*, 337–347.

BOSCH, S., & FUQUA, R. W. (2001). Behavioral cusps: A model for selecting target behaviors. *Journal of Applied Behavior Analysis, 34*, 123–125.

BOURGEOIS, M. S. (1990). Enhancing conversation skills in patients with Alzheimer's disease using a prosthetic memory aid. *Journal of Applied Behavior Analysis, 23*, 29–42.

BOURGEOIS, M. S. (1993). Effects of memory aids on the dyadic conversations of individuals with dementia. *Journal of Applied Behavior Analysis, 26*, 77–87.

BOYCE, T. E., & GELLER, E. S. (2001a). Applied behavior analysis and occupational safety: The challenge of response maintenance. *Journal of Organizational Behavior Management, 21(1)*, 31–56.

BOYCE, T. E., & GELLER, E. S. (2001b). A technology to measure multiple driving behaviors without self-report or participant reactivity. *Journal of Applied Behavior Analysis, 34*, 39–55.

BRANDT, R. M. (1972). *Studying behavior in natural settings.* New York: Holt, Rinehart and Winston.

BRAWLEY, E. R., HARRIS, F. R., ALLEN, K. E., FLEMING, R. S., & PETERSON, R. F. (1969). Behavior modification of an autistic child. *Behavioral Science, 14*, 87–97.

BRICKMAN, L. (1972). Environmental attitudes and actions. *Journal of Social Psychology, 87*, 223–224.

BRIGHAM, T. A., FINFROCK, S. R., K., BRUENIG, M. K., & BUSHELL, D. (1972). The use of programmed materials in the analysis of academic contingencies. *Journal of Applied Behavior Analysis, 5*, 177–182.

BROBST, B., & WARD, P. (2002). Effects of public posting, goal setting, and oral feedback on the skills of female soccer players. *Journal of Applied Behavior Analysis, 35*, 247–258.

BRY, B. H. (1991). B. F. Skinner for behavior therapists. *The Behavior Therapist, 14*, 9–10.

BRYNE, T., MCNULTY, S., BABCOCK, Q., CONNORS, D., & Al, E. (2000). Verbal behavior and initial exposure to delayed reinforcement. *The Analysis of Verbal Behavior, 17*, 129–141.

BUCHANAN, C. D. (1973). *Programmed reading*. New York: McGraw-Hill.

BUCKHOUT, R. (1980). Nearly 2,000 witnesses can be wrong. *Bulletin of the Psychonomic Society, 16*, 307–310.

BUCKLIN, B. R., & DICKINSON, A. M. (2001). Individual monetary incentives: A review of different types of arrangements between performance and pay. *Journal of Organizational Behavior Management, 21(3)*, 45–137.

BUDNEY, A. J., HIGGINS, S. T., DELANEY, D. D., KENT, L., & BICKEL, W. K. (1991). Contingent reinforcement of abstinence with individuals abusing cocaine and marijuana. *Journal of Applied Behavior Analysis, 24*, 657–665.

BUDZYNSKI, T. H., & STOYVA, J. M. (1969). An instrument for producing deep muscle relaxation by means of analog information feedback. *Journal of Applied Behavior Analysis, 2*, 231–237.

BURGESS, R. L., & BUSHELL, D. J. (1969). *Behavioral sociology*. New York: Columbia University Press.

BURGIO, L. D., BURGIO, K. L., ENGEL, B. T., & TICE, L. M. (1986). Increasing distance and independence of ambulation in elderly nursing home residents. *Journal of Applied Behavior Analysis, 19*, 357–366.

BURGIO, L. D., WHITMAN, T. L., & REID, D. H. (1983). A participative management approach for improving direct-care staff performance in an institutional setting. *Journal of Applied Behavior Analysis, 16*, 37–53.

BUSHELL, D., JR. (1978). An engineering approach to the elementary classroom: The Behavior Analysis Follow Through Project. In A. C. Catania & T. A. Brigham (Eds.), *Handbook of applied behavior analysis: Social and instructional processes* (pp. 525–563). New York: Irvington Press/Halstead Press.

BUZAS, H. P., & AYLLON, T. (1981). Differential reinforcement in coaching tennis skills. *Behavior Modification, 5*, 372–385.

CALKIN, A. B. (2002). Inner behavior: Empirical investigations of private events. *The Behavior Analyst, 25*, 255–259.

CAMPBELL, D. T., & STANLEY, J. C. (1963). *Experimental and quasi-experimental designs for research*. Chicago: Rand McNally.

CARPENTER, C. (1993, November). In the glass meadow. *Reader's Digest*, 63–64.

CARR, E. G. (1977). The motivation of self-injurious behavior: A review of some hypotheses. *Psychological Bulletin, 84*, 800–816.

CARR, E. G., & DURAND, V. M. (1985). Reducing behavior problems through functional communication training. *Journal of Applied Behavior Analysis, 18*, 111–126.

CARR, E. G., NEWSOM, C. D., & BINKOFF, J. A. (1980). Escape as a factor in the aggressive behavior of two retarded children. *Journal of Applied Behavior Analysis, 13*, 101–117.

CARROLL, L. J., & YATES, B. T. (1981). Further evidence for the role of stimulus control training in facilitating weight reduction after behavioral therapy. *Behavior Therapy, 12*, 287–291.

CARSTENS, C. (1982). Application of a work penalty threat in the treatment of a case of juvenile fire setting. *Journal of Behavior Therapy and Experimental Psychiatry, 13*, 159–161.

CARSTENSEN, L. L. (1988). The emerging field of behavioral gerontology. *Behavior Therapy, 19*, 259–281.

CARTWRIGHT, M., & D'ORSO, M. (1993). For the children. *Reader's Digest, 143*, 169–208.

CATANIA, A. C. (1998). *Learning*. (4th ed.). Upper Saddle River, NJ: Prentice Hall.

CAVALLARO, C. C., & POULSON, C. L. (1985). Teaching language to handicapped children in natural settings. *Education and Treatment of Children, 8*, 1–24.

CHANDLER, L. K., LUBECK, R. C., & FOWLER, S. A. (1992). Generalization and maintenance of preschool children's social skills: A critical review and analysis. *Journal of Applied Behavior Analysis, 25*, 415–428.

CHAPLIN, J. P. (1985). *Dictionary of psychology*. New York: Dell.

CICERO, F. R., & PFADT, A. (2002). Investigation of a reinforcement-based toilet training procedure for children with autism. *Research in Developmental Disabilities, 23*, 319–331.

CINCIRIPINI, P. M., EPSTEIN, L. H., & MARTIN, J. E. (1979). The effects of feedback on blood pressure discrimination. *Journal of Applied Behavior Analysis, 12*, 345–353.

CLARK, H. B., ROWBURY, T., BAER, A. M., & BAER, D. M. (1973). Timeout as punishing stimulus in continuous and intermittent schedules. *Journal of Applied Behavior Analysis, 6*, 443–455.

COHEN, S. L., CHELLAND, S., BALL, K. T., & LEMURA, L. M. (2002). Effects of fixed ratio schedules of reinforcement on exercise by college students. *Perceptual and Motor Skills, 94*, 1177–1186.

Commentaries. (2001). Commentaries on "the design of cultures." *Behavior and Social Issues, 11*, 14–30.

CONNERS, J., IWATA, B. A., KAHNG, S., HANLEY, G. P., WORSDELL, A. S., & THOMPSON, R. H. (2000). Differential responding in the presence and absence of discriminative stimuli during multielement functional analyses. *Journal of Applied Behavior Analysis, 33*, 299–308.

CONYERS, C., DOOLE, A., VAUSE, T., HARAPIAK, S., YU, D. C. T., & MARTIN, G. L. (2002). Predicting the relative efficacy of three presentation methods for assessing preferences of persons with developmental disabilities. *Journal of Applied Behavior Analysis, 35*, 49–58.

COPE, J. G., ALLRED, L. J., & MORSELL, J. M. (1991). Signs as deterrents of illegal parking in spaces designated for individuals with physical disabilities. *Journal of Applied Behavior Analysis, 24*, 59–63.

COSE, E. (1995 August). Teaching kids to be smart. *Newsweek, 21*, 58, 60.

COX, B. S., COX, A. B., & COX, D. J. (2000). Motivating signage prompts safety belt use among drivers exiting senior communities. *Journal of Applied Behavior Analysis, 33*, 635–638.

CRITCHFIELD, T. S., & PERONE, M. (1990). Verbal self-reports of delayed matching to sample by humans. *Journal of the Experimental Analysis of Behavior, 53*, 321–344.

CUVO, A. J. (2003). On stimulus generalization and stimulus classes. *Journal of Behavioral Education, 12*, 77–83.

DAHLQUIST, L. M., & GIL, K. M. (1986). Using parents to maintain improved dental flossing skills in children. *Journal of Applied Behavior Analysis, 19*, 255–260.

DANIELS, A. C. (1985). Performance management: The behavioral approach to productivity improvement. *National Productivity Review*, 225–236.

DANSKIN, D. G., & CROW, M. A. (1981). *Biofeedback: An introduction and guide*. Palo Alto, CA: Mayfield.

DAVIDSON, D. (1974). Psychology as philosophy. In S. C. Brown (Ed.), *Philosophy of psychology* (pp. 41–52). London: MacMillen.

DAVIS, J. R., RAWANA, E. P., & CAPPONI, D. R. (1989). Acceptability of behavioral staff management techniques. *Behavioral Residential Treatment, 4*, 23–44.

DAVIS, J. R., & RUSSELL, R. H. (1990). Behavioral staff management: An analogue study of acceptability and its behavioral correlates. *Behavioral Residential Treatment, 5*, 259–270.

DEAVER, C. M., MILTENBERGER, R. G., & STRICKER, J. M. (2001). Functional analysis and treatment of hair twirling in a young child. *Journal of Applied Behavior Analysis, 34*, 535–538.

DELPRATO, D. J. (1977). Observing covert behavior ("mind-reading") with Chevreul's pendulum. *Psychological Record, 27(2)*, 473–478.

DELPRATO, D. J. (2002). Countercontrol in behavior analysis. *The Behavior Analyst, 25*, 191–200.

DELUCA, R. V., & HOLBORN, S. W. (1985). Effects of a fixed interval schedule of token reinforcement on exercise in obese and non-obese boys. *Psychological Record, 35*, 525–533.

DELUCA, R. V., & HOLBORN, S. W. (1990). Effects of fixed interval and fixed ratio schedules of token reinforcement on exercise in obese and non-obese boys. *Psychological Record, 40*, 67–82.

DELUCA, R. V., & HOLBORN, S. W. (1992). Effects of a variable-ratio reinforcement schedule with changing criteria on exercise in obese and non-obese boys. *Journal of Applied Behavior Analysis, 25*, 671–679.

DERENNE, A., & BARON, A. (2002). Behavior analysis and the study of human aging. *The Behavior Analyst, 25*, 151–160.

DERRICKSON, J. G., NEEF, N. A., & CATALDO, M. F. (1993). Effects of signaling invasive procedures on a hospitalized infant's affective behaviors. *Journal of Applied Behavior Analysis, 26*, 133–134.

DICKERSON, M. G. (1979). FI schedules and persistence at gambling in the U.K. betting office. *Journal of Applied Behavior Analysis, 12*, 315–323.

DINSMOOR, J. A. (1995). Stimulus control: Part 1. *The Behavior Analyst, 18*, 51–68.

DONAHOE, J. W., & PALMER, D. C. (1994). *Learning and complex behavior*. Boston: Allyn and Bacon.

DURAND, V. M., & CARR, E. G. (1992). An analysis of maintenance following functional communication training. *Journal of Applied Behavior Analysis, 25*, 777–794.

DURAND, V. M., & MINDELL, J. A. (1990). Behavioral treatment of multiple childhood sleep disorders: Effects on child and family. *Behavior Modification, 14*, 37–49.

DUSH, D. M., & SPOTH, R. L. (1988). Comprehensive behavioral medicine in community mental health: A needs assessment that needs assessment. *Evaluation and Program Planning, 11*, 297–306.

DYER, K., DUNLAP, G., & WINTERLING, V. (1990). Effects of choice making on the serious problem behaviors of students with severe handicaps. *Journal of Applied Behavior Analysis, 23*, 515–524.

DYMOND, S., & REHFELDT, R. A. (2000). Understanding complex behavior: The transformation of stimulus functions. *The Behavior Analyst, 23*, 239–254.

ECKERT, T. L., ARDOIN, S. P., DALY, E. J., III, & MARTENS, B. K. (2002). Improving oral reading fluency: A brief experimental analysis of combining an antecedent intervention with consequences. *Journal of Applied Behavior Analysis, 35*, 271–281.

ELDER, J., BODDY, P., & BARRIGA, P. (1991). Training Honduran health workers and mothers in infant acute respiratory infection control. *Boletin de la Official Sanitaria Panamericana, 110*, 29–40.

ELDER, J. P., LOUIS, T., SUTISNAPUTRAS, O., SULAEIMAN, N. S., WARE, L., SHAW, W., MOOR, C., & GRAEFF, J. (1992). The use of diarrhoeal management counseling cards for community health volunteer training in Indonesia: The HealthCom Project. *Journal of Tropical Medicine and Hygiene, 95*, 301–308.

ELLIOTT, A. J., & FUQUA, R. W. (2002). Acceptability of treatments for trichotillomania. *Behavior Modification, 26*, 378–399.

EPSTEIN, L. H., & MASEK, B. J. (1978). Behavioral control of medicine compliance. *Journal of Applied Behavior Analysis, 11*, 1–9.

ESPIE, C. A., LINDSAY, W. R., BROOKS, D. N., HOOD, E. M., et al. (1989). A controlled comparative investigation of psychological treatments for chronic sleep-onset insomnia. *Behaviour Research and Therapy, 27*, 79–88.

ESPOSITO, B. G., & KOORLAND, M. A. (1989). Play behavior of hearing impaired children: Integrated and segregated settings. *Exceptional Children, 55*, 412–419.

FAVELL, J. E., et al. (1982). The treatment of self-injurious behavior. *Behavior Therapy, 13*, 529–554.

FAWCETT, S. B., & MILLER, L. K. (1975). Training public-speaking behavior: An experimental analysis and social validation. *Journal of Applied Behavior Analysis, 8*, 125–135.

FEALLOCK, R., & MILLER, L. K. (1976). The design and evaluation of a worksharing system for experimental group living. *Journal of Applied Behavior Analysis, 9*, 277–288.

FELDMAN, M. A., CONDILLAC, R. A., TOUGH, S., HUNT, S., & GRIFFITHS, D. (2002). Effectiveness of community positive behavioral intervention for persons with developmental disabilities and severe behavior disorders. *Behavior Therapy, 33*, 377–398.

FERGUSON, D. L., & ROSALES–RUIZ, J. (2001). Loading the problem loader: The effects of target training and shaping on trailer-loading behavior of horses. *Journal of Applied Behavior Analysis, 34*, 409–424.

FERSTER, C. B., & SKINNER, B. F. (1957). *Schedules of reinforcement*. East Norwalk, CT: Appleton-Century-Crofts.

FICHTER, M. M., WALLACE, C. J., LIBERMAN, R. P., & DAVIS, J. R. (1976). Improving social interaction in a chronic psychotic using discriminated avoidance ("nagging"): Experimental analysis and generalization. *Journal of Applied Behavior Analysis, 9*, 377–386.

FISCH, G. S. (2001). Evaluating data from behavioral analysis: Visual inspection or statistical models? *Behavioural Processes, 54*, 137–154.

FISHER, E. B. (1979). Overjustification effects in token economies. *Journal of Applied Behavior Analysis, 12*, 407–415.

FIXSEN, D. L., PHILLIPS, E. L., PHILLIPS, E. A., & WOLF, M. M. (1976). The teaching-family model of group home treatment. In W. E. K. Craighead, A. E. Ka-div, and M. J. Mahoney, (Eds.), *Behavior Modification*. Boston: Houghton Mifflin.

FLANAGAN, B., GOLDIAMOND, I., & AZRIN, N. (1958). Operant stuttering: The control of stuttering behavior through response-contingent consequences. *Journal of the Experimental Analysis of Behavior, 1*, 173–177.

FLOOD, W. A., WILDER, D. A., FLOOD, A. L., & MASUDA, A. (2002). Peer-mediated reinforcement plus prompting as treatment of off-task behavior in children with attention deficit hyperactivity disorder. *Journal of Applied Behavior Analysis, 35*, 199–204.

FORD, J. E. (1981). A simple punishment procedure for controlling employee absenteeism. *Journal of Organizational Behavior Management, 3*, 71–79.

FOSTER, L. H., WATSON, T. S., & YOUNG, J. S. (2002). Single-subject research design for school counselors: Becoming an applied researcher. *Professional School Counseling, 6(2)*, 146–154.

FOXX, R. M., MCMORROW, M. J., BITTLE, R. G., & BECHTEL, D. R. (1986). The successful treatment of a dually-diagnosed deaf man's aggression with a program that included contingent electric shock. *Behavior Therapy, 17*, 170–186.

FRANCE, K. G., & HUDSON, S. M. (1990). Behavior management of infant sleep disturbance. *Journal of Applied Behavior Analysis, 23*, 91–98.

FUQUA, R. W., & SCHWADE, J. (1986). Social validation of applied behavioral research. In A. Poling & R. W. Fuqua (Eds.), *Research methods in Applied behavior analysis: Issues and advances* (pp. 265–292) New York: Plenum.

GAINER, J. C. (1978). Temperature discrimination training in the biofeedback treatment of migraine headache. *Journal of Behavior Therapy and Experimental Psychiatry, 9*, 185–187.

GALLAGHER, S. M., & KEENAN, M. (2000). Independent use of activity materials by the elderly in a residential setting. *Journal of Applied Behavior Analysis, 33*, 325–328.

GARCIA, E. (1974). The training and generalization of a conversational speech form in nonverbal retardates. *Journal of Applied Behavior Analysis, 7*, 137–149.

GARCIA, E., GUESS, D., & BYRNES, J. (1973). Development of syntax in a retarded girl using procedure of imitation, reinforcement, and modeling. *Journal of Applied Behavior Analysis, 6*, 299–310.

GARFINKLE, A. N., & SCHWARTZ, I. S. (2002). Peer imitation: Increasing social interactions in children with autism and other developmental disabilities in inclusive preschool classrooms. *Topics in Early Childhood Special Education, 22(1)*, 26–38.

GETTINGER, M. (1993). Effects of invented spelling and direct instruction on spelling performance of second-grade boys. *Journal of Applied Behavior Analysis, 26*, 281–291.

GEWIRTZ, J. L., & BAER, D. M. (1958a). Deprivation and satiation of social reinforcers as drive conditions. *Journal of Abnormal and Social Psychology, 57*, 165–172.

GEWIRTZ, J. L., & BAER, D. M. (1958b). The effect of brief social deprivation on behaviors for a social reinforcer. *Journal of Abnormal and Social Psychology, 56*, 49–56.

GIBBS, J. W., & LUYBEN, P. D. (1985). Treatment of self-injurious behavior: Contingent versus noncontingent positive practice overcorrection. *Behavior Modification, 9*, 3–21.

GIEBENHAIN, J. E., & O'DELL, S. L. (1984). Evaluation of a parent-training manual for reducing children's fear of the dark. *Journal of Applied Behavior Analysis, 17*, 121–125.

GIL, K. M., KEEFE, F. J., SAMPSON, H. A., MCCASKILL, C. C., et al. (1988). Direct observation of scratching behavior in children with atopic dermatitis. *Behavior Therapy, 19*, 213–227.

GLAISTER, B. (1985). A case of auditory hallucination treated by satiation. *Behaviour Research and Therapy, 23*, 213–215.

GLASSCOCK, S. G., FRIMAN, P. C., O'BRIEN, S., & CHRISTO-PHERSEN, E. R. (1986). Varied citrus treatment of ruminant gagging in a teenager with Batten's disease. *Journal of Behavior Therapy and Experimental Psychiatry, 17*, 129–133.

GLENN, S. (1986). Behavior: A gene for the social sciences. Presented at poster session, American Psychological Association, Washington, DC, 1–6.

GLOVER, J., & GARY, A. L. (1976). Procedures to increase some aspects of creativity. *Journal of Applied Behavior Analysis, 9*, 79–84.

GLYNN, S. M. (1990). Token economy approaches for psychiatric patients: Progress and pitfalls over 25 years. *Behavior modification, 14*, 383–407.

GOETZ, E. M., & BAER, D. M. (1973). Social control of form diversity and the emergence of new forms in children's blockbuilding. *Journal of Applied Behavior Analysis, 6*, 209–217.

GOLDIAMOND, I. (1965). Self-control procedures in personal behavior problems. *Psychological Reports, 17*, 851–868.

GOLDSTEIN, H., & MOUSETIS, L. (1989). Generalized language learning by children with severe mental retardation: Effects of peers' expressive modeling. *Journal of Applied Behavior Analysis, 22*, 245–259.

GOLTZ, S. M. (1992). A sequential learning analysis of decisions in organizations to escalate investments despite continuing costs or losses. *Journal of Applied Behavior Analysis, 25*, 561–574.

GOODALL, K. (1972 November). Shapers at work. *Psychology Today*, 53–63.

GRAHAM, S. R. (1990). Citation for outstanding lifetime contribution to psychology: Presented to B. F. Skinner, August 10, 1990. *American Psychologist, 45*, 1205.

GREEN, C. W., REID, D. H., CANIPE, V. S., & GARDNER, S. M. (1991). A comprehensive evaluation of reinforcer identification processes for persons with profound multiple handicaps. *Journal of Applied Behavior Analysis, 24*, 537–552.

GREEN, G. R., LINSK, N. L., & PINKSTON, E. M. (1986). Modification of verbal behavior of the mentally impaired elderly by their spouses. *Journal of Applied Behavior Analysis, 19*, 329–336.

GREEN, R. R., & HOATS, D. L. (1969). Reinforcing capabilities of television distortion. *Journal of Applied Behavior Analysis, 2*, 139–141.

GREER, R. D., DOROW, L., WILLIAMS, G., MCCORKLE, N., & ASNES, R. (1991). Peer-mediated procedures to induce swallowing and food acceptance in young children. *Journal of Applied Behavior Analysis, 24*, 783–790.

GRIFFITHS, H., & CRAIGHEAD, W. E. (1972). Generalization in operant speech therapy for misarticulation. *Journal of Speech and Hearing Disorders , 37*, 485–494.

GRINDLE, C. F., & REMINGTON, B. (2002). Discrete-trial training for autistic children when reward is delayed: A comparison of conditioned cue value and response making. *Journal of Applied Behavior Analysis, 35*, 187–190.

GROSS, A. M., & DRABMAN, R. S. (1990). *Handbook of behavioral pediatrics*. New York: Plenum Press.

GROSS, A. M., et al. (1983). Discrimination of blood glucose levels in insulin-dependent diabetics. *Behavior Modification, 7*, 369–382.

GUESS, D. (1969). A functional analysis of receptive language and productive speech: Acquisition of the plural phoneme. *Journal of Applied Behavior Analysis, 2*, 55–64.

GUESS, D., SAILOR, W., RUTHERFORD, G., & BAER, D. M. (1968). An experimental analysis of linguistic development: Productive use of the plural morpheme. *Journal of Applied Behavior Analysis, 1*, 297–306.

HAGGBLOOM, S. J., WARNICK, R., WARNICK, J. E., JONES, V. K., YARBROUGH, G. L., RUSSELL, T. M., & Al, E. (2002). The 100 most eminent psychologists of the 20th century. *Review of General Psychology, 6*, 139–152.

HAGOPIAN, L. P., WILSON, D. M., & WILDER, D. A. (2001). Assessment and treatment of problem behavior maintained by escape from attention and access to tangible items. *Journal of Applied Behavior Analysis, 34*, 229–232.

HALL, R. V. (1991). Behavior analysis and education: An unfulfilled dream. *Journal of Behavioral Education, 3*, 305–316.

HALL, R. V., AXELROD, S., TYLER, L., GRIEF, E., JONES, F. C., & ROBERTSON, R. (1972). Modification of behavior problems in the home with a parent as observer and experimenter. *Journal of Applied Behavior Analysis, 5*, 53–64.

HANDLIN, H. C. (1992). The company built upon the Golden Rule: Lincoln Electric [Special issue: Pay for performance: History, controversy, and evidence]. *Journal of Organizational Behavior Management, 12*, 151–163.

HARDYCKE, C. D., PETRINOVICH, L. F., & ELLSWORTH, D. W. (1966). Feedback of speech muscle activity during silent reading: Rapid extinction. *Science, 154*, 1467–1468.

HARRIS, M. (1979). *Cultural materialism: The struggle for a science of culture*. New York: Random House.

HARROP, A., FOULKES, C., & DANIELS, M. (1989). Observer agreement calculations: The role of primary data in reducing obfuscation. *British Journal of Psychology, 80*, 181–189.

HARTMANN, D. P., & HALL, R. V. (1976). The changing criterion design. *Journal of Applied Behavior Analysis, 9*, 527–532.

HARTMANN, D. P., & PETERSON, L. (1975). A neglected literature and an aphorism. *Journal of Applied Behavior Analysis, 8*, 231–232.

HATCH, J. P. (1990). Growth and development of biofeedback: A bibliographic update. *Biofeedback and Self-Regulation, 15*, 37–46.

HATCH, J. P., FISHER, J. G., & RUGH, J. D. (Eds.). (1987). *Biofeedback: Studies in clinical efficacy*. New York: Plenum.

HAUSERMAN, N., WALEN, S. R., & BEHLING, M. (1973). Reinforced racial integration in the first grade: A study in generalization. *Journal of Applied Behavior Analysis, 6*, 193–200.

HAYES, S. C. (1988). Contextualism and the next wave of behavioral psychology. *Behavior Analysis, 23*, 7–22.

HAYES, S. C., BARNES-HOLMES, D., & ROCHE, B. (2001). *Relational frame theory: A post Skinnerian account of human language and cognition*. New York: Kluwer Academic Plenum.

HAYES, S. C., JOHNSON, V. S., & CONE, J. D. (1975). The marked item technique: A practical procedure for litter control. *Journal of Applied Behavior Analysis, 8*, 381–386.

HAYES, S. C., KOHLENBERG, B. S., & HAYES, L. J. (1991). The transfer of specific and general consequential functions through simple and conditional equivalence relations. *Journal of the Experimental Analysis of Behavior, 56*, 119–137.

HAYES, S. C., & WILSON, K. G. (1993). Some implications of a contemporary behavior-analytic account of verbal events. *The Behavior Analyst, 16*, 283–301.

HEFFER, R. W., & KELLEY, M. L. (1987). Mothers' acceptance of behavioral interventions for children: The influence of parent race and income. *Behavior Therapy, 18*, 153–163.

HEGEL, M. T., AYLLON, T., VANDERPLATE, C., & SPIRO-HAWKINS, H. (1986). A behavioral procedure for increasing compliance with self-exercise regimens in severely burn-injured patients. *Behavior Research and Therapy, 24*, 521–528.

HERSEN, M., EISLER, R., ALFORD, G., & AGRAS, W. S. (1973). Effects of token economy on neurotic depression: An experimental analysis. *Behavior Therapy, 4*, 392–397.

HINELINE, P. N. (1992). A self-interpretive behavior analysis. *American Psychologist, 47*, 1274–1286.

HINGTGEN, J. N., SANDERS, B. J., & DEMEYER, M. K. (1965). Shaping cooperative responses in childhood schizophrenics. In L. K. Ullman, and L. Kasner (Eds.), *Case studies in behavior modification* (pp. 130–183). New York: Holt, Rinehart and Winston.

HOELSCHER, T. J., LICHSTEIN, K. L., & ROSENTHAL, T. L. (1984). Objective vs subjective assessment of relaxation compliance among anxious individuals. *Behaviour Research and Therapy, 22,* 187–193.

HOGBEN, L. T. (1957). *Statistical theory: The relationship of probability, credibility, and error. An examination of the contemporary crisis in statistical theory from a behaviourist viewpoint.* New York: W. W. Norton.

HOLLAND, J. G. (1958). Human vigilance. *Science, 128,* 61–67.

HOLLAND, J. G. (1960). Teaching machines: An application of principles from the laboratory. *Journal of the Experimental Analysis of Behavior, 3,* 275–287.

HOLLAND, J. G. (1965). Research on programming variables. In R. Glaser (Ed.), *Teaching machines and programming learning II: Data and directions.* Washington, DC: National Education Association.

HOLLANDSWORTH, J. G., Glazeski, R. C., & Dressel, M. E. (1978). Use of social-skills training in the treatment of extreme anxiety and deficient verbal skills in the job interview setting. *Journal of Applied Behavior Analysis, 11,* 259–269.

HOMME, L. E., DEBACA, P. C., DEVINE, J. V., STEINHORST, R., & RICKERT, E. J. (1963). Use of the Premack Principle in controlling the behavior of nursery school children. *Journal of the Experimental Analysis of Behavior, 6,* 544.

HOPKINS, B. L., & HERMANN, J. A. (1977). Evaluating interobserver reliability of interval data. *Journal of Applied Behavior Analysis, 10,* 121–126.

HORNER, R. D. (1971). Establishing use of crutches by a mentally retarded spina bifida child. *Journal of Applied Behavior Analysis, 4,* 183–189.

HORNER, R. H. (2002). On the status of knowledge of using punishment: A commentary. *Journal of Applied Behavior Analysis, 35,* 465–467.

HORNER, R. H., MCDONNELL, J. J., & BELLAMY, G. T. (1986). Teaching generalized skills: General case instructions in simulation and community settings. In L. H. Meyers & H. D. Fredericks (Eds.), *Education of learners with severe handicaps: Exemplary service strategies* (pp. 289–314). Baltimore: Paul H. Brookes.

HORTON, G. O. (1975). Generalization of teacher behavior as a function of subject matter specific discrimination training. *Journal of Applied Behavior Analysis, 8,* 311–319.

HOUCHINS, N., & BOYCE, T. E. (2001). Response generalization in behavioral safety: Fact or fiction? *Journal of Organizational Behavior Management, 21(4),* 3–11.

HOULIHAN, D. D., SLOANE, H. N., JONES, R. N., & PATTEN, C. (1992). A review of behavioral conceptualizations and treatments of child noncompliance. *Education and Treatment of Children, 15,* 56–77.

HUME, K. M., & CROSSMAN, J. (1992). Musical reinforcement of practice behaviors among competitive swimmers. *Journal of Applied Behavior Analysis, 25,* 665–670.

HURSH, S. R. (1984). Behavioral economics. *Journal of the Experimental Analysis of Behavior, 42,* 435–452.

INGENMEY, R., & VAN-HOUTEN, R. (1991). Using time delay to promote spontaneous speech in an autistic child. *Journal of Applied Behavior Analysis, 24,* 591–596.

INGHAM, P., & GREER, R. D. (1992). Changes in student and teacher responses in observed and generalized settings as a function of supervisor observations. *Journal of Applied Behavior Analysis, 25,* 153–164.

INOUE, M., & KOBAYASHI, S. (1992). Conversation skill training through videotape modeling in an autistic child. *Japanese Journal of Behavior Therapy, 18,* 22–29.

IRWIN, D. M., & BUSHNELL, M. M. (1980). *Observational strategies for child study.* New York: Holt, Rinehart and Winston.

ISAACS, W., THOMAS, J., & GOLDIAMOND, I. (1960). Application of operant conditioning to reinstate verbal behavior in psychotics. *Journal of Speech and Hearing Disorders, 25,* 8–12.

IVERSEN, I. H. (2002). Response-initiated imaging of operant behavior using a digital camera. *Journal of the Experimental Analysis of Behavior, 77,* 283–300.

IWATA, B. A. (1987). Negative reinforcement in applied behavior analysis: An emerging technology. *Journal of Applied Behavior Analysis, 20,* 361–378.

IWATA, B. A. (1988). The development and adoption of controversial default technologies. *The Behavior Analyst, 11,* 149–157.

IWATA, B. A., DORSEY, M. F., SLIFER, K. J., BAUMAN, K. E., & RICHMAN, G. S. (1982). Toward a functional analysis of self-injury. *Analysis and Intervention in Developmental Disabilities, 2,* 3–20.

IWATA, B. A., PACE, G. M., DORSEY, M. F., ZARCONE, J. R., et al. (1994). The functions of self-injurious behavior: An experimental–epidemiological analysis. *Journal of Applied Behavior Analysis, 27,* 215–240.

IWATA, B. A., SMITH, R. G., & MICHAEL, J. (2000a). Current research on the influence of establishing operations on behavior in applied settings. *Journal of Applied Behavior Analysis, 33,* 411–418.

IWATA, B. A., SMITH, R. G., & MICHAEL, J. (Eds.). (2000b). Establishing operations in applied behavior analysis [Special issue]. *Journal of Applied Behavior Analysis, 33.*

JACKSON, D. A., & WALLACE, R. F. (1974). The modification and generalization of voice loudness in a fifteen-year-old retarded girl. *Journal of Applied Behavior Analysis, 7,* 461–471.

JAHR, E., & ELDEVIK, S. (2002). Teaching cooperative play to typical children utilizing a behavior modeling approach: A systematic replication. *Behavioral Interventions, 17,* 145–157.

JAMES, J. E., RICCIARDELLI, L. A., HUNTER, C. E., & ROGERS, P. (1989). Relative efficacy of intensive and spaced behavioral treatment of stuttering. *Behavior Modification, 13,* 376–395.

JOHNSON, S. P., WELSH, T. M., MILLER, L. K., & ALTUS, D. E. (1991). Participatory management: Maintaining staff performance in a university housing cooperative. *Journal of Applied Behavior Analysis, 24,* 119–127.

JONES, F. H., FREMOUW, W., & CARPLES, S. (1977). Pyramid training of elementary school teachers to use a classroom management "skill package." *Journal of Applied Behavior Analysis, 10,* 239–253.

JONES, R. R., WEINROTT, M. R., & VAUGHT, R. S. (1978). Effects of serial dependency on the agreement between visual and statistical inference. *Journal of Applied Behavior Analysis, 11,* 277–283.

KAGEL, J. H., & WINKLER, R. C. (1972). Behavioral economics: Areas of cooperative research between economics and applied behavioral analysis. *Journal of Applied Behavior Analysis, 5,* 335–342.

KAHNG, S., IWATA, B. A., & LEWIN, A. B. (2002a). Behavioral treatment of self-injury, 1964 to 2000. *American Journal on Mental Retardation, 107,* 212–221.

KAHNG, S., IWATA, B. A., & LEWIN, A. B. (2002b). The impact of functional assessment on the treatment of self-injurious behavior. In M. L. Oster-Granite, S. R. Schroeder, & T. Thompson (Eds.), *Self-injurious behavior: Gene-brain-behavior relationships* (pp. 119–131). Washington, DC: American Psychological Association.

KARLINS, M., & ANDREWS, L. H. (1972). *Biofeedback.* New York: Lippencott.

KAUFMAN, B. N. (1991). *Happiness is a choice.* New York: Fawcett Columbine.

KAZDIN, A. E. (1975). Characteristics and trends in applied behavior analysis. *Journal of Applied Behavior Analysis, 8,* 332.

KAZDIN, A. E. (1977a). Assessing the clinical or applied importance of behavior change through social validation. *Behavior Modification, 1,* 427–452.

KAZDIN, A. E. (1977b). *The token economy: A review and evaluation.* New York: Plenum Press.

KAZDIN, A. E. (1980). Acceptability of time out from reinforcement procedures for disruptive child behavior. *Behavior Therapy, 11*, 329–344.

KAZDIN, A. E., & POLSTER, R. (1973). Intermittent token reinforcement and response maintenance in extinction. *Behavior Therapy, 4*, 386–391.

KEEFE, F. J., & BLUMENTHAL, J. A. (1980). The life fitness program: A behavioral approach to making exercise a habit. *Journal of Behavior Therapy and Experimental Psychiatry, 11*, 31–34.

KEENAN, M., & DILLENBURGER, K. (2000). Images of behavior analysis: The shaping game and the behavioral stream. *Behavior and Social Issues, 10*, 19–38.

KEENEY, K. M., FISHER, W. W., ADELINIS, J. D., & WILDER, D. A. (2000). The effects of response cost in the treatment of aberrant behavior maintained by negative reinforcement. *Journal of Applied Behavior Analysis, 33*, 255–258.

KELLEHER, R. T., & GOLLUB, L. R. (1962). A review of positive conditioned reinforcement. *Journal of the Experimental Analysis of Behavior, 5*, 543–597.

KELLER, J. J. (1991). The recycling solution: How I increased recycling on Dilworth Road. *Journal of Applied Behavior Analysis, 24*, 617–619.

KELLY, M. B. (1977). A review of the observational data-collection and reliability procedures reported in the *Journal of Applied Behavior Analysis. Journal of Applied Behavior Analysis, 10*, 97–101.

KENNEDY, C. H. (2002). The maintenance of behavior change as an indicator of social validity. *Behavior Modification, 26*, 594–604.

KENNEDY, D. A., & THOMPSON, I. (1967). The use of reinforcement techniques with a first-grade boy. *The Personality and Guidance Journal, 46*, 366–370.

KIRBY, K. C., & BICKEL, W. K. (1988). Toward an explicit analysis of generalization: A stimulus control interpretation. *The Behavior Analyst, 11*, 115–129.

KIRIGAN, K. A., BRAUKMANN, C. J., ATWATER, J. D., & WOLF, M. M. (1982). An evaluation of Teaching-Family (Achievement Place) group homes for juvenile offenders. *Journal of Applied Behavior Analysis, 15*, 1–16.

KLADOPOULOS, C. N., & MCCOMAS, J. J. (2001). The effects of form training on foul-shooting performance in members of a woman's college basketball team. *Journal of Applied Behavior Analysis, 34*, 329–336.

KLATT, K. P., & MORRIS, E. K. (2001). The Premack principle, response deprivation, and establishing operations. *The Behavior Analyst, 24*, 173–180.

KOEGEL, R. L., & FREA, W. D. (1993). Treatment of social behavior in autism through the modification of pivotal social skills. *Journal of Applied Behavior Analysis, 26*, 369–377.

KOEGEL, R. L., & RINCOVER, A. (1977). Research on the difference between generalization and maintenance in extra-therapy responding. *Journal of Applied Behavior Analysis, 10*, 1–12.

KOEGEL, R. L., RUSSO, D. C., & RINCOVER, A. (1977). Assessing and training teachers in the generalized use of behavior modification with autistic children. *Journal of Applied Behavior Analysis, 10*, 197–205.

KOHLER, F. W., & GREENWOOD, C. R. (1986). Toward a technology of generalization: The identification of natural contingencies of reinforcement. *The Behavior Analyst, 9*, 19–26.

KOHLER, F. W., & GREENWOOD, C. R. (1990). Effects of collateral peer supportive behaviors within the classwide peer tutoring program. *Journal of Applied Behavior Analysis, 23*, 307–322.

KOMAKI, J., & BARNETT, F. T. (1977). A behavioral approach to coaching football: Improving the play execution of the offensive backfield on a youth football team. *Journal of Applied Behavior Analysis, 10*, 657–664.

KOSTEWICZ, D. E., KUBLINA, R. M., & COOPER, J. (2000). Managing aggressive thoughts and feelings with daily counts of non-aggressive thoughts and feelings: A self-experiment. *Journal of Behavior Therapy and Experimental Psychiatry, 31*, 177–187.

KRANTZ, P. J., & MCCLANNAHAN, L. E. (1993). Teaching children with autism to initiate to peers: Effects of a script-fading procedure. *Journal of Applied Behavior Analysis, 26*, 121–132.

KRATOCHWILL, T. R., & BRODY, G. H. (1978). Single subject designs: A perspective on the controversy over employing statistical inference and implications for research and training in behavior modification. *Behavior Modification, 2*, 291–307.

KULIK, J., KULIK, C., & COHEN, P. A. (1979). A meta-analysis of outcome studies of Keller's personalized system of instruction. *American Psychologist, 34*, 307–318.

KUNKEL, J. H. (1975). *Behavior, social problems, and change: A social learning approach*. Englewood Cliffs, NJ: Prentice-Hall.

KUNKEL, J. H. (1985a). The Vicos Project: A cross-cultural test of psychological propositions. *The Psychological Record, 36*, 451–466.

KUNKEL, J. H. (1985b). Vivaldi in Venice: An historical test of psychological propositions. *The Psychological Record, 35*, 445–457.

KYMISSIS, E., & POULSON, C. L. (1990). The history of imitation in learning theory: The language acquisition process. *Journal of the Experimental Analysis of Behavior, 54*, 113–127.

LA PIERRE, R. T. (1934). Attitudes vs actions. *Social Forces, 13*, 230–237.

LAARHOVEN, T. V., JOHNSON, J. W., REPP, A. C., KARSH, K. G., & LENZ, M. (2003). Discrimination training: A comparison of two procedures for presenting multiple examples within a fading and non-fading paradigm. *Research in Developmental Disabilities, 24*, 1–18.

LALLI, J. S., MAURO, B. C., & MACE, F. C. (2000). Preference for unreliable reinforcement in children with mental retardation: The role of conditioned reinforcement. *Journal of Applied Behavior Analysis, 33*, 533–544.

LAMAL, P. A. (2000). The philosophical terrain of behavior analysis: A review of B. A. Thyer (Ed.), *The philosophical legacy of behaviorism. Journal of the Experimental Analysis of Behavior, 74*, 255–264.

LARKIN, K. T., ZAYFERT, C., ABEL, J. L., & VELTUM, L. G. (1992). Reducing heart rate reactivity to stress with feedback: Generalization across task and time. *Behavior Modification, 16*, 118–131.

LARSEN, J. A. (1991, January). A story for Valentine's Day. *Reader's Digest*, 7–8.

LATHAM, G. P., & HUBER, V. L. (1992). Schedules of reinforcement: Lessons from the past and issues for the future [Special issue: Pay for performance: History, controversy, and evidence]. *Journal of Organizational Behavior Management, 12*, 125–149.

LAVELLE, J. M., HOVEL, M. F., WEST, M. P., & WAHLGREN, D. R. (1992). Promoting law enforcement for child protection: A community analysis. *Journal of Applied Behavior Analysis, 25*, 885–892.

LAVIE, T., & STURMEY, P. (2002). Training staff to conduct a paired-stimulus preference assessment. *Journal of Applied Behavior Analysis, 35*, 209–211.

LAWTON, C., FRANCE, K. G., & BLAMPIED, N. M. (1991). Treatment of infant sleep disturbance by graduated extinction. *Child and Family Behavior Therapy, 13*, 39–56.

LERMAN, D. C., KELLEY, M. E., VORNDRAN, C. M., & VAN CAMP, C. M. (2003). Collateral effects of response blocking during the treatment of stereotypic behavior. *Journal of Applied Behavior Analysis, 36*, 119–123.

LERMAN, D. C., & VORNDRAN, C. M. (2002). On the status of knowledge for using punishment: Implications for treating behavioral disorders. *Journal of Applied Behavior Analysis, 35*, 431–464.

LEVINE, F. M., & FASNACHT, G. (1974). Token rewards may lead to token learning. *American Psychologist, 29*, 816–820.

LICHSTEIN, K. L., & JOHNSON, R. S. (1991). Older adults' objective self-recording of sleep in the home. *Behavior Therapy, 22*, 531–548.

LINDAUER, S. E., ZARCONE, J. R., RICHMAN, D. M., & SCHROEDER, S. R. (2002). A comparison of multiple reinforcer assessments to identify the function of maladaptive behavior. *Journal of Applied Behavior Analysis, 35*, 299–303.

LINDSLEY, O. R. (1968). A reliable wrist counter for recording behavior rates. *Journal of Applied Behavior Analysis, 1*, 77.

LINSCHEID, T. R., IWATA, B. A., RICKETTS, R. W., WILLIAMS, D. E., & GRIFFIN, J. C. (1990). Clinical evaluation of the self-injurious behavior inhibiting system (SIBIS). *Journal of Applied Behavior Analysis, 23*, 53–78.

LLOYD, K. E. (1980). Do as I say, not as I do. *New Zealand Psychologist, 9*.

LLOYD, K. E. (1985). Behavioral anthropology: a review of Marvin Harris' Cultural Materialism. *Journal of the Experimental Analysis of Behavior, 43*, 279–287.

LOMBARD, D., NEUBAUER, T. E., CANFIELD, D., & WINETT, R. A. (1991). Behavioral community intervention to reduce the risk of skin cancer. *Journal of Applied Behavior Analysis, 24*, 677–686.

LONG, G. M., & MCNAMARA, J. R. (1989). Paradoxical punishment as it relates to the battered woman syndrome. *Behavior Modification, 13*, 192–205.

LOOS, F. M., WILLIAMS, K. P., & BAILEY, J. S. (1977). A multi-element analysis of the effect of teacher aides in an "open style" classroom. *Journal of Applied Behavior Analysis, 10*, 437–448.

LOSHORCONES. (1986). News from now-here, 1986: A response to "News from Nowhere, 1984." *The Behavior Analyst, 9*, 129–132.

LOVAAS, O. I., SCHAEFFER, B., & SIMMONS, J. Q. (1965). Experimental studies in childhood schizophrenia: Building social behavior in autistic children by the use of electric shock. *Journal of Experimental Research in Personality, 1*, 99–109.

LOVAAS, O. I., & SIMMONS, J. (1969). Manipulation of self-destruction in three retarded children. *Journal of Applied Behavior Analysis, 2*, 143–157.

LOVE, S. R., MATSON, J. L., & WEST, D. (1990). Mothers as effective therapists for autistic children's phobias. *Journal of Applied Behavior Analysis, 23*, 379–385.

LOVITT, T. C., & ESVELDT, K. A. (1970). The relative effects on math performance of single versus multiple ratio schedules: A case study. *Journal of Applied Behavior Analysis, 3*, 261–270.

LUDWIG, T. D., & GELLER, E. S. (2000). Intervening to improve the safety of delivery drivers: A systematic behavioral approach. *Journal of Organizational Behavior Management, 19(4)*, 1–124.

LUISELLI, J. K. (1991). Assessment-derived treatment of children's disruptive behavior disorders [Special issue: Current perspectives in the diagnosis, assessment, and treatment of child and adolescent disorders]. *Behavior Modification, 15*, 294–309.

LUMSDAINE, A. A., & GLASER, R. (1960). *Teaching machines and programmed learning*. Washington, DC: National Education Association.

MACE, F. C. (1994). Basic research needed for stimulating the development of behavioral technologies. *Journal of the Experimental Analysis of Behavior, 61*, 529–550.

MACE, F. C., KRATOCHWILL, T. R., & FIELLO, R. A. (1983). Positive treatment of aggressive behavior in a mentally retarded adult: A case study. *Behavior Therapy, 14*, 689–696.

MACE, F. C., LALLI, J. S., SHEA, M. C., & NEVIN, J. A. (1992). Behavioral momentum in college basketball. *Journal of Applied Behavior Analysis, 25*, 657–663.

MADSEN, J. C. H., BECKER, W. C., & THOMAS, D. R. (1968). Rules, praise, and ignoring: Elements of elementary classroom control. *Journal of Applied Behavior Analysis, 1*, 139–150.

MAGEE, S. K., & ELLIS, J. (2001). The detrimental effects of physical restraint as a consequence for inappropriate classroom behavior. *Journal of Applied Behavior Analysis, 34*, 501–504.

MAGER, R. F. (1962). *Preparing instructional objectives*. Belmont, CA: Fearon.

MAHADEVAN, R., MALONE, J. C., & BAILEY, J. (2002). Radical behaviorism and exceptional memory phenomena. *Behavior and Philosophy, 30*, 1–13.

MANN, J., TEN HAVE, T., PLUNKETT, J. W., & MEISELS, S. J. (1991). Time sampling: A methodological critique. *Child Development, 62*, 227–241.

MANN, R. A. (1972). The behavior-therapeutic use of contingency contracting to control an adult behavior problem: Weight control. *Journal of Applied Behavior Analysis, 5*, 99–109.

MANN, R. A., & BAER, D. M. (1971). The effects of receptive language training on articulation. *Journal of Applied Behavior Analysis, 4*, 291–298.

MARCUS, B. A., SWANSON, V., & VOLLMER, T. R. (2001). Effects of parent training on parent and child behavior using procedures based on functional analysis. *Behavioral Interventions, 16(2)*, 87–104.

MARKLE, S. (1969). *Good frames and bad: A grammar of frame writing*. New York: Wiley.

MARKS, I. M., & GELDER, M. G. (1967). Transvestism and fetishism: Clinical and psychological changes during faradic aversion. *British Journal of Psychiatry, 113*, 711–729.

MARR, M. J. (2003). The switching and the unswitching: What can behavior analysis have to say about creativity? *The Behavior Analyst, 26*, 15–27.

MARTENS, B. K., ARDOIN, S. P., HILT, A. M., LANNIE, A. L., PANAHON, C. J., & WOLFE, L. A. (2002). Sensitivity of children's behavior to probabilistic reward: Effects of a decreasing-ratio lottery system on math performance. *Journal of Applied Behavior Analysis, 35*, 403–406.

MARTENS, B. K., LOCHNER, D. G., & KELLY, S. Q. (1992). The effects of variable-interval reinforcement on academic engagement: A demonstration of matching theory. *Journal of Applied Behavior Analysis, 25*, 143–151.

MARTIN, G., & PEAR, J. (1999). *Behavior modification: What it is and how to do it*. (6th ed.). Upper Saddle River, NJ: Prentice Hall.

MARTIN, T. L., PEAR, J. J., & MARTIN, G. L. (2002a). Analysis of proctor marking accuracy in a computer-aided personalized system of instruction course. *Journal of Applied Behavior Analysis, 35*, 309–312.

MARTIN, T. L., PEAR, J. J., & MARTIN, G. L. (2002b). Feedback and its effectiveness in a computer-aided personalized system of instruction course. *Journal of Applied Behavior Analysis, 35*, 427–430.

MASON, S. A., MCGEE, G. G., FARMER-DOUGAN, V., & RISLEY, T. R. (1989). A practical strategy for ongoing reinforcer assessment. *Journal of Applied Behavior Analysis, 22*, 171–179.

MATHEWS, J. R., HODSON, G. D., CRIST, W. B., & LAROCHE, G. R. (1992). Teaching young children to use contact lenses. *Journal of Applied Behavior Analysis, 25*, 229–235.

MATHEWS, R. M., & DIX, M. (1992). Behavior change in the funny papers: Feedback to cartoonists on safety belt use. *Journal of Applied Behavior Analysis, 25*, 769–775.

MATSUMOTO, A., & OKOUCHI, H. (2001). Establishing self-instructional control by differential reinforcement of a verbal-nonverbal behavioral chain. *Japanese Journal of Behavior Analysis, 16*, 185–196.

MAWHINNEY, V. T., BOSTOW, D. E., LAWS, D. R., BLUMENFELD, G. J., & HOPKINS, B. L. (1971). A comparison of students studying-behavior produced by daily, weekly, and three-week testing schedules. *Journal of Applied Behavior Analysis, 4*, 257–264.

MAYFIELD, K. H., & CHASE, P. N. (2002). The effects of cumulative practice on mathematics problem solving. *Journal of Applied Behavior Analysis, 35*, 105–123.

MCCOMAS, J., HOCH, H., PAONE, D., & EL-ROY, D. (2000). Escape behavior during academic tasks: A preliminary analysis of idiosyncratic establishing operations. *Journal of Applied Behavior Analysis, 33*, 479–493.

MCCORD, B. E., IWATA, B. A., GALENSKY, T. L., ELLINGSON, S. A., & THOMSON, R. J. (2001). Functional analysis and treatment of problem behavior evoked by noise. *Journal of Applied Behavior Analysis, 34*, 447–462.

MCEVOY, M. A., NORDQUIST, V. M., TWARDOSZ, S., HECKAMAN, K. A., WEBBY, J. H., & DENNY, R. K. (1988). Promoting autistic children's peer interaction in an integrated early childhood setting using affection activities. *Journal of Applied Behavior Analysis, 21*, 193–200.

MCFADDEN, A. C., MARSH, G. E., PRICE, B. J., & HWANG, Y. (1992). A study of race and gender bias in the punishment of school children. *Education and Treatment of Children, 15*, 140–146.

MCNEES, M. P., EGLI, D. S., MARSHALL, R. S., SCHNELLE, J. F., & RISLEY, T. R. (1976). Shoplifting prevention: Providing information through signs. *Journal of Applied Behavior Analysis, 9*, 399–405.

MCSWEENY, A. J. (1978). Effects of response cost on the behavior of a million persons: Charging for directory assistance in Cincinnati. *Journal of Applied Behavior Analysis, 11*, 47–51.

MELAMED, B. G., & BENNETT, C. G. (1985). Behavioral dentistry. In L. J. Siegel & C. Twentyman (Eds.), *Prevention and Treatment in Behavioral Medicine.* New York: Springer.

MERTZ, W., TSUI, J. C., JUDD, J. T., REISER, J., HALLFRISCH, J., MORRIS, E. R., STEELE, P. D., & LASHLEY, E. (1991). What are people really eating? The relation between energy intake derived from estimated diet records and intake determined to maintain body weight. *American Journal of Clinical Nutrition, 54*, 291–295.

MICHAEL, J. (1974). Statistical inference for individual organism research: Mixed blessing or curse? *Journal of Applied Behavior Analysis, 7*, 647–653.

MICHAEL, J. (1975). Positive and negative reinforcement, a distinction that is no longer necessary; or a better way to talk about bad things. *Behaviorism, 3*, 33–44.

MICHAEL, J. (1982). Distinguishing between discriminative and motivational functions of stimuli. *Journal of the Experimental Analysis of Behavior, 37*, 149–155.

MILLER, L. K. (1968a). Determinancy versus risk: A critique of contemporary statistical methodology in sociology. *Kansas Journal of Sociology, 4*, 71–78.

MILLER, L. K. (1968b). Escape from an effortful situation. *Journal of the Experimental Analysis of Behavior, 11*, 619–627.

MILLER, L. K. (1970). Some punishing effects of response-force. *Journal of the Experimental Analysis of Behavior, 13*, 215–220.

MILLER, L. K., & FEALLOCK, R. A. (1975). A behavioral system for group living. In E. A. S. Ramp, G. Semb (Eds.), *Behavior analysis: Areas of research and application* (pp. 73–96). Engelwood Cliffs, NJ: Prentice-Hall.

MILLER, L. K., & MILLER, O. L. (1970). Reinforcing self-help group activities of welfare recipients. *Journal of Applied Behavior Analysis, 3*, 57–64.

MILLER, L. K., & SCHNEIDER, R. L. (1970). The use of a token system in Project Head Start. *Journal of Applied Behavior Analysis, 3*, 213–220.

MILLER, L. K., & WEAVER, F. H. (1974). The use of "concept programming" to teach behavioral concepts to university students. In J. Johnston (Ed.), *Behavior research and technology in higher education.* Springfield, IL: Charles C. Thomas.

MILLER, W. C. (1976). Brainwaves and the creative state. *Behavioral Engineering, 3*, 73–75.

MINKIN, N. M., BRAUKMANN, C. J., MINKIN, B, L., TIMBERS, G. D., TIMBERS, G. D., FIXSEN, D. L., PHILLIPS, E. L., & WOLF, M. M. (1976). The social validation and training of conversational skills. *Journal of Applied Behavior Analysis, 9*, 127–139.

MITHAUG, D. K., & MITHAUG, D. E. (2003). Effects of teacher-directed versus student-directed instructions on self-management of young children with disabilities. *Journal of Applied Behavior Analysis, 36*, 133–136.

MOERK, E. L. (1990). Three-term contingency patterns in mother-child verbal interactions during first-language acquisition [Special issue: The experimental analysis of human behavior]. *Journal of the Experimental Analysis of Behavior, 54*, 293–305.

MONTESINOS, L., FRISCH, L. E., GREENE, B. F., & HAMILTON, M. (1990). An analysis of and intervention in the sexual transmission of disease. *Journal of Applied Behavior Analysis, 23*, 275–284.

MOORE, J. (1975). On the principle of operationism in a science of behavior. *Behaviorism, 3*, 120–138.

MOORE, J. (1980). On behaviorism and private events. *Psychological Record, 30*, 459–475.

MOORE, J. (2000). Thinking about thinking and feeling about feeling. *The Behavior Analyst, 23*, 45–56.

MOORE, J. W., MUELLER, M. M., DUBARD, M., ROBERTS, D. S., & STERLING-TURNER, H. E. (2002). The influence of therapist attention on self-injury during a tangible condition. *Journal of Applied Behavior Analysis, 35*, 283–286.

MOORE, R., & GOLDIAMOND, I. (1964). Errorless establishment of visual discrimination using fading procedures. *Journal of the Experimental Analysis of Behavior, 7*, 269–272.

MORAN, D. J., & TAI, W. (2001). Reducing biases in clinical judgment with single subject design methodology. *The Behavior Analyst Today, 2(3)*, 196–203.

MORRIS, E. K. (1988). Contextualism: The world view of behavior analysis. *Journal of Experimental Child Psychology, 46*, 289–323.

MORRISON, R. S., SAINATO, D. M., BENCHAABAN, D., & ENDO, S. (2002). Increasing play skills of children with autism using activity schedules and correspondence training. *Journal of Early Education, 25*, 58–72.

MUELLER, M. M., MOORE, J. W., TINGSTROM, D. H., & DOGGETT, R. A. (2001). Increasing seating opportunities using a behavioral prompt. *Journal of Organizational Behavior Management, 21(2)*, 99–109.

MURPHY, J. K., & BRANTLEY, P. J. (1982). A case study reportedly involving possession. *Journal of Behavior Therapy and Experimental Psychiatry, 13*, 357–359.

NEALE, D. H. (1963). Behavior therapy and encopresis in children. *Behavior Research and Therapy, 1*, 139–149.

NEEF, N. A., NELLES, D. E., IWATA, B. A., & PAGE, T. J. (2003). Analysis of precurrent skills in solving mathematic story problems. *Journal of Applied Behavior Analysis, 36*, 21–33.

NEWSOM, C. D., & SIMON, K. M. (1977). A simultaneous discrimination procedure for the measurement of vision in nonverbal children. *Journal of Applied Behavior Analysis, 10*, 633–644.

NINNESS, H. C., FUERST, J., RUTHERFORD, R. D., & GLENN, S. S. (1991). Effects of self-management training and reinforcement on the transfer of improved conduct in the absence of supervision. *Journal of Applied Behavior Analysis, 24*, 499–508.

ODOM, S. L., CHANDLER, L. K., OSTROSKY, M., MCCONNELL, S. R., & REANEY, S. (1992). Fading teacher prompts from peer-initiation interventions for young children with disabilities. *Journal of Applied Behavior Analysis, 25*, 307–317.

O'DONNELL, J. (2001). The discriminative stimulus for punishment or SDp. *The Behavior Analyst, 24*, 261–262.

O'DONNELL, J., CROSBIE, J., WILLIAMS, D. C., & SAUNDERS, K. J. (2000). Stimulus control and generalization of point-loss punishment with humans. *Journal of the Experimental Analysis of Behavior, 73*, 261–274.

O'DONOHUE, W., & BUCHANAN, J. A. (2001). The weakness of strong inference. *Behavior and Philosophy, 29*, 1–20.

O'DONOHUE, W., FERGUSON, K. E., & NAUGLE, A. E. (2003). The structure of the cognitive revolution: An examination from the philosophy of science. *The Behavior Analyst, 26*, 85–110.

O'LEARY, K. D. (1979). Behavioral assessment [Special issue]. *Journal of Applied Behavior Analysis, 12*, 489.

OLSON, L., & HOULIHAN, D. (2000). A review of behavioral treatments used for Lesch-Nyhan syndrome. *Behavior Modification, 24*, 202–222.

OLSON, R., LARAWAY, S., & AUSTIN, S. (2001). Unconditioned and conditioned establishing operations in organizational behavior management. *Journal of Organizational Behavior Management, 21(2)*, 7–36.

O'NEILL, G. W., BLANCK, L. S., & JOYNER, M. A. (1980). The use of stimulus control over littering in a natural setting. *Journal of Applied Behavior Analysis, 13*, 379–381.

OSBORNE, J. G. (1969). Free-time as a reinforcer in the management of classroom behavior. *Journal of Applied Behavior Analysis, 2,* 113–118.

OSBORNE, K., RUDRUD, E., & ZEZONEY, F. (1990). Improved curve-ball hitting through the enhancement of visual cues. *Journal of Applied Behavior Analysis, 23,* 371–377.

OSBORNE, M. L., & HIMADI, B. (1990). Evaluation of a shaping procedure with the changing-criterion design. *Behavioral Residential Treatment, 5,* 75–81.

OSNES, P. G., & LIEBLEIN, T. (2003). An explicit technology of generalization. *The Behavior Analyst Today, 3,* 364–374.

PAINE, S. C., CARNINE, D. W., WHITE, W. A., & WALTERS, G. (1982). Effects of fading teacher presentation structure (covertization) on acquisition and maintenance of arithmetic problem-solving skills. *Education and Treatment of Children, 5,* 93–107.

PALMER, M. H., LLOYD, M. E., & LLOYD, K. E. (1977). An experimental analysis of electricity conservation procedures. *Journal of Applied Behavior Analysis, 10,* 665–671.

PAPATHEODOROU, T. (2000). Management approaches employed by teachers to deal with children's behaviour problems in nursery classes. *School Psychology International, 21(4),* 415–440.

PARSONS, R. D., HINSON, S. L., & SARDO-BROWN, D. (2001). *Educational psychology: A practitioner-researcher model of teaching.* Belmont, CA: Wadsworth/Thomson Learning.

PARSONSON, B. S., & BAER, D. M. (1978). The analysis and presentation of graphic data. In T. R. Kratochwill (Ed.), *Single-subject research: Strategies for evaluating change* (pp. 101–165). New York: Academic Press.

PATEL, M. R., PIAZZA, C. C., KELLY, M. L., OCHSNER, C. A., & SANTANA, C. M. (2001). Using a fading procedure to increase fluid consumption in a child with feeding problems. *Journal of Applied Behavior Analysis, 34,* 357–360.

PATEL, M. R., PIAZZA, C. C., MARTINEZ, C. J., VOLKERT, V. M., & SANTANA, C. M. (2002). An evaluation of two differential reinforcement procedures with escape extinction to treat food refusal. *Journal of Applied Behavior Analysis, 35,* 365–374.

PATTERSON, G. R. (1977). A performance theory for coercive family interaction. In R. Cairns (Ed.), *Social interaction: Methods, analysis, and illustrations.* Chicago: Society for Research in Child Development Monograph.

PATTERSON, G. R. (1993). Coercion as a basis for early age of onset for arrest. In J. McCord (Ed.), *Coercion and punishment in long-term perspective* (pp. 1–50). Cambridge: Cambridge University Press.

PATTISHALL, E. G., JR. (1989). The development of behavioral medicine: Historical models. *Annals of Behavioral Medicine, 11,* 43–48.

PAVLOV, I. P. (1927). *Conditioned reflexes: An investigation of the physiological activity of the cerebral cortex.* London: Oxford University Press.

PBERT, L. A., COLLINS, F. L., SMITH, S., SHARP, B., et al. (1988). Visual acuity improvement following Fading and Feedback training: II. Relationship to changes in refractive error. *Behaviour Research and Therapy, 26,* 467–473.

PENNYPACKER, H. S., & JOHNSTON, J. M. (1993). *Strategies and Tactics of Behavioral Research.* (2nd ed.). Hillsdale, NJ: Erlbaum.

PÉREZ–GONZÁLEZ, L. A., SPRADLIN, J. E., & SAUNDERS, K. J. (2000). Learning-set outcome in second-order conditional discriminations. *Psychological Record, 50,* 429–442.

PERONE, M. (2003). Negative effects of positive reinforcement. *The Behavior Analyst, 26,* 1–14.

PFIFFNER, L. J., & O'LEARY, S. G. (1987). The efficacy of all-positive management as a function of the prior use of negative consequences. *Journal of Applied Behavior Analysis, 20,* 265–271.

PHILLIPS, E. L. (1968). Achievement Place: Token reinforcement procedures in home-style rehabilitation setting for "pre-delinquent" boys. *Journal of Applied Behavior Analysis, 1,* 213–223.

PHILLIPS, E. L., PHILLIPS, E. A., FIXSEN, D. L., & WOLF, M. M. (1971). Achievement Place: Modification of the behaviors of pre-delinquent

boys within a token economy. *Journal of Applied Behavior Analysis, 4,* 45–59.

PIAZZA, C. C., & FISHER, W. W. (1991). Bedtime fading in the treatment of pediatric insomnia. *Journal of Behavior Therapy and Experimental Psychiatry, 22,* 53–56.

PIAZZA, C. C., PATEL, M. R., SANTANA, C. M., GOH, H., DELIA, M. D., & LANCASTER, B. M. (2002). An evaluation of simultaneous and sequential presentation of preferred and nonpreferred food to treat food selectivity. *Journal of Applied Behavior Analysis, 35,* 259–270.

PIERCE, C. H., & RISLEY, T. R. (1974). Recreation as a reinforcer: Increasing membership and decreasing disruption in an urban recreation center. *Journal of Applied Behavior Analysis, 7,* 403–411.

PINKSTON, E. M., REESE, N. M., LEBLANC, J. M., & BAER, D. (1973). Independent control of a preschool child's aggression and peer interaction by contingent teacher attention. *Journal of Applied Behavior Analysis, 6,* 115–124.

PITTS, C. E. (1976). Behavior modification—1887. *Journal of Applied Behavior Analysis, 9,* 146.

PLACE, U. T. (1993). A radical behaviorist methodology for the empirical investigation of private events. *Behavior and Philosophy, 20,* 25–35.

PLAUD, J. J., GILLUND, B., & FERRARO, F. R. (2000). Signal detection analysis of choice behavior and aging. *Journal of Clinical Geropsychology, 6,* 73–81.

PLUMMER, S., BAER, D. M., & LEBLANC, J. M. (1977). Functional considerations in the use of procedural timeout and an effective alternative. *Journal of Applied Behavior Analysis, 10,* 689–705.

POLIRSTOK, S. R., & GREER, R. D. (1977). Remediation of mutually aversive interactions between a problem student and four teachers by training the student in reinforcement techniques. *Journal of Applied Behavior Analysis, 10,* 707–716.

POPPEN, R. (1982). The fixed-interval scallop in human affairs. *The Behavior Analyst, 5,* 127–136.

POULSON, C. L., & KYMISSIS, E. (1988). Generalized imitation in infants. *Journal of Experimental Child Psychology, 46,* 409–415.

POULSON, C. L., KYMISSIS, E., REEVE, K. F., ANDREATOS, M., et al. (1991). Generalized vocal imitation in infants. *Journal of Experimental Child Psychology, 51,* 267–279.

POWELL, J., & AZRIN, N. (1968). The effects of shock as a punisher for cigarette smoking. *Journal of Applied Behavior Analysis, 1,* 63–71.

PROGAR, P. R., NORTH, S. T., BRUCE, S. S., DINOVI, B. J., NAU, P. A., EBERMAN, E. M., et al. (2001). Putative behavioral history effects and aggression maintained by escape from therapists. *Journal of Applied Behavior Analysis, 34,* 69–72.

PRUE, D. M., KRAPFL, J. E., & MARTIN, J. E. (1981). Brand fading: The effects of gradual changes to low tar and nicotine cigarettes on smoking rate, carbon monoxide, and thiocyanate levels. *Behavior Therapy, 12,* 400–416.

PRYOR, K. (1984). *Don't shoot the dog.* New York: Bantam Books.

PRYOR, K. W., HAAG, R., & O'REILLY, J. (1969). The creative porpoise: Training for novel behavior. *Journal of the Experimental Analysis of Behavior, 12,* 653–661.

QUINN, J. M., SHERMAN, J. A., SHELDON, J. B., QUINN, L. M., & HARCHIK, A. E. (1992). Social validation of component behaviors of following instructions, accepting criticism, and negotiating. *Journal of Applied Behavior Analysis, 25,* 401–413.

QUINSEY, V. L., CHAPLIN, T. C., & CARRIGAN, W. F. (1980). Biofeedback and signaled punishment in the modification of inappropriate sexual age preferences. *Behavior Therapy, 11,* 567–576.

RACHLIN, H. (1976). *Introduction to modern behaviorism.* San Francisco: Freeman.

RAPP, J. T., MILTENBERGER, R. G., GALENSKY, T. L., ELLINGSON, S. A., STRICKER, J., GARLINGHOUS, M., et al. (2000). Treatment of hair pulling and hair manipulation maintained by digital-tactile stimulation. *Behavior Therapy, 31,* 381–393.

RASING, E. J., & DUKER, P. C. (1992). Effects of a multifaceted training procedure on the acquisition and generalization of social behaviors in language-disabled deaf children. *Journal of Applied Behavior Analysis, 25,* 723–734.

REAM, J., & WILLIAMS, D. (2002). Shaping exhale durations for men with mild retardation. *Journal of Applied Behavior Analysis, 35,* 415–418.

REDD, W. H., & BIRNBRAUER, J. S. (1969). Adults as discriminative stimuli for different reinforcement contingencies with retarded children. *Journal of Experimental Child Psychology, 7,* 440–447.

REESE, E. P. (1978). *Human behavior analysis and application.* (2nd ed.). Dubuque, IA: William C. Brown.

REICHLE, J., & WACKER, D. P. (1993). *Communicative alternatives to challenging behavior: Integrating functional assessment and intervention strategies.* Baltimore: Paul H. Brookes.

REID, D. H., PARSONS, M. B., GREEN, C. W., & BROWNING, L. B. (2001). Increasing one aspect of self-determination among adults with severe multiple disabilities in supported work. *Journal of Applied Behavior Analysis, 34,* 341–344.

RENNE, C. M., & CREER, T. L. (1976). Training children with asthma to use inhalation therapy equipment. *Journal of Applied Behavior Analysis, 9,* 1–11.

REPP, A. C., ROBERTS, D. M., SLACK, D. J., REPP, C. F., & BERKLER, M. S. (1976). A comparison of frequency, interval, and time-sampling methods of data collection. *Journal of Applied Behavior Analysis, 9,* 501–508.

RICHELLE, M. N. (1993). *B. F. Skinner: A reappraisal.* Hillsdale, NJ: Erlbaum.

RIEGLER, H. C., & BAER, D. M. (1989). A developmental analysis of rule-following. In H. W. Reese (Ed.), *Advances in child development and behavior* (Vol. 21). New York: Academic Press.

RINGDAHL, J. E., KITSUKAWA, K., ANDELMAN, M. S., CALL, N., WINBORN, L., BARRETTO, A., & REED, G. K. (2002). Differential reinforcement with and without instructional fading. *Journal of Applied Behavior Analysis, 35,* 291–294.

RISLEY, T. R. (1968). The effects and side effects of punishing the autistic behaviors of a deviant child. *Journal of Applied Behavior Analysis, 1,* 21–34.

RISLEY, T. R., & WOLF, M. M. (1972). Strategies for analyzing behavioral change over time. In J. R. H. Nesselroade (Ed.), *Life-span developmental psychology: Methodological issues.* New York: Academic Press.

ROANE, H. S., FISHER, W. W., & MCDONOUGH, E. M. (2003). Progressing from programmatic to discovery research: A case example with the overjustification effect. *Journal of Applied Behavior Analysis, 36,* 21–33.

ROBERTS, M. C., & SANTOGROSSI, D. A. (1976). Behavior analysis in the White House (communication). *Journal of Applied Behavior Analysis, 9,* 334.

ROBERTS, M. W., & POWERS, S. W. (1990). Adjusting chair timeout enforcement procedures for oppositional children. *Behavior Therapy, 21,* 257–271.

RODGERS, M. A. (1993, September). How to handle a hostile driver. *Reader's Digest,* 85–87.

RODGERS, T. A., & IWATA, B. A. (1991). An analysis of error-correction procedures during discrimination training. *Journal of Applied Behavior Analysis, 24,* 775–781.

ROGERS, C. R., & SKINNER, B. F. (1956). Some issues concerning the control of human behavior. *Science, 124,* 1057–1066.

ROLIDER, A., & VAN-HOUTEN, R. (1985). Suppressing tantrum behavior in public places through the use of delayed punishment mediated by audio recordings. *Behavior Therapy, 16,* 181–194.

ROSEN, R. C., SCHIFFMAN, H. R., & COHEN, A. S. (1984). Behavior modification and the treatment of myopia. *Behavior Modification, 8,* 131–154.

ROSENTHAL, R., & ROSNOW, R. L. (1969). *Artifact in behavioral research.* New York: Academic Press.

ROSS, D. E., & GREER, R. D. (2003). Generalized imitation and the mand: Inducing first instances of speech in young children with autism. *Research in Developmental Disabilities, 24,* 58–74.

ROSS, L. V., FRIMAN, P. C., & CHRISTOPHERSEN, E. R. (1993). An appointment-keeping improvement package for outpatient pediatrics: Systematic replication and component analysis. *Journal of Applied Behavior Analysis, 26,* 461–467.

RYAN, S., ORMOND, T., IMWOLD, C., & ROTUNDA, R. J. (2002). The effects of a public address system on the off-task behavior of elementary physical education students. *Journal of Applied Behavior Analysis, 35,* 305–308.

SACKETT, G. P., RUPENTHAL, G. C., & GLUCK, J. (1978). Introduction: An overview of methodological and statistical problems in observational research. In G. P. Sackett (Ed.), *Observing behavior: data collection and analysis methods* (Vol. 2, pp. 1–14). Baltimore: University Park Press.

SAGAN, C. (1989, September 10). Sagan on science. *Parade,* 6–7.

SAIGH, P. A., & UMAR, A. M. (1983). The effects of a Good Behavior Game on the disruptive behavior of Sudanese elementary school students. *Journal of Applied Behavior Analysis, 16,* 339–344.

SALZINGER, K. (2003). Some verbal behavior about verbal behavior. *The Behavior Analyst, 26,* 29–40.

SAMELSON, F. (1985). Organizing for the kingdom of behavior: Academic battles and organizational policies in the twenties. *Journal of the History of Behavioral Science, 21,* 33–47.

SANDERS, M. R., & PARR, J. M. (1989). Training developmentally disabled adults in independent meal preparation: Acquisition, generalization, and maintenance. *Behavior Modification, 13,* 168–191.

SAUNDERS, K. J., & SPRADLIN, J. E. (1990). Conditional discrimination in mentally retarded adults: The development of generalized skills [Special issue: The experimental analysis of human behavior]. *Journal of the Experimental Analysis of Behavior, 54,* 239–250.

SCHAEFER, H. H. (1963). A vocabulary program using language redundancy. *Journal of Programmed Instruction, 2,* 9–16.

SCHOENFELD, W. N. (1978). "Reinforcement" in behavior theory. *The Behavior Analyst, 18,* 173–185.

SCHREIBER, J., & DIXON, M. R. (2001). Temporal characteristics of slot machine play in recreational gamblers. *Psychological Reports, 89,* 67–72.

SCHREIBMAN, L. (1975). Effects of within-stimulus and extra-stimulus prompting on discrimination learning in autistic children. *Journal of Applied Behavior Analysis, 8,* 91–112.

SCHROEDER, S. R. (1972). Parametric effects of reinforcement frequency, amount of reinforcement and required response force on sheltered workshop behavior. *Journal of Applied Behavior Analysis, 5,* 431–441.

SCHUSSLER, N. G., & SPRADLIN, J. E. (1991). Assessment of stimuli controlling the requests of students with severe mental retardation during a snack routine. *Journal of Applied Behavior Analysis, 24,* 791–798.

SCHWARTZ, B. (1977a). Studies of operant and reflexive key pecks in the pigeon. *Journal of the Experimental Analysis of Behavior, 27,* 301–313.

SCHWARTZ, G. J. (1977b). College students as contingency managers for adolescents in a program to develop reading skills. *Journal of Applied Behavior Analysis, 10,* 645–655.

SCHWARTZ, I. S., & BAER, D. M. (1991). Social-validity assessments: Is current practice state-of-the-art? *Journal of Applied Behavior Analysis, 24,* 189–204.

SCHWARTZ, M. L., & HAWKINS, R. P. (1970). Applications of delayed reinforcement procedures to the behaviors of an elementary school child. *Journal of Applied Behavior Analysis, 3,* 85–96.

SECAN, K. E., EGEL, A. L., & TILLEY, C. S. (1989). Acquisition, generalization, and maintenance of question-answering skills in autistic children. *Journal of Applied Behavior Analysis, 22,* 181–196.

SEYMOUR, F. W., BAYFIELD, G., BROCK, P., & DURING, M. (1983). Management of night waking in young children. *Australian Journal of Family Therapy, 4,* 217–223.

SHAHAN, T. A., & CHASE, P. N. (2002). Novelty, stimulus control, and operant behavior. *The Behavior Analyst, 25,* 175–190.

SHERMAN, J. A. (1963). Reinstatement of verbal behavior in a psychotic by reinforcement methods. *Journal of Speech and Hearing Disorders, 28,* 398–401.

SHULL, R. L. (1995). Interpreting cognitive phenomena: A review of Donahoe and Palmer's *Learning and complex behavior. Journal of the Experimental Analysis of Behavior, 63,* 347–358.

SIDMAN, M. (1960). *Tactics of scientific research.* New York: Basic Books.

SIDMAN, M. (1971). Reading and auditory-visual equivalences. *Journal of Speech and Hearing Research, 14,* 5–13.

SIDMAN, M. (1978). Remarks. *Behaviorism, 6,* 265–268.

SIDMAN, M. (1988). *A behavior analyst's view of coercion.* Paper presented at a meeting of the Eastern Psychological Association.

SIDMAN, M. (1989). *Coercion and its fallout.* Boston, MA: Authors Cooperative.

SIDMAN, M. (2000). Equivalence relations and the reinforcement contingency. *Journal of the Experimental Analysis of Behavior, 74,* 127–146.

SIDMAN, M., & TAILBY, W. (1982). Conditional discrimination vs matching to sample: An expansion of the testing paradigm. *Journal of the Experimental Analysis of Behavior, 37,* 5–22.

SIMMONS, M. W., & LIPSITT, L. P. (1961). An operant discrimination apparatus for infants. *Journal of the Experimental Analysis of Behavior, 4,* 233–235.

SINGH, N. N., & LEUNG, J. P. (1988). Smoking cessation through cigarette-fading, self-recording, and contracting: Treatment, maintenance and long-term follow up. *Addictive Behaviors, 13,* 101–105.

SKINNER, B. F. (1945). The operational analysis of psychological terms. *Psychological Review, 52,* 270–277.

SKINNER, B. F. (1948a). "Superstition" in the pigeon. *Journal of Experimental Psychology, 38,* 168–172.

SKINNER, B. F. (1948b). *Walden two.* New York: Macmillan.

SKINNER, B. F. (1950). Are theories of learning necessary? *Psychological Review, 57,* 193–216.

SKINNER, B. F. (1953). *Science and human behavior.* New York: Macmillan.

SKINNER, B. F. (1954). The science of learning and the art of teaching. *Harvard Educational Review, 24,* 99–113.

SKINNER, B. F. (1958). *Cumulative record.* New York: Appleton-Century-Crofts.

SKINNER, B. F. (1972). *Beyond freedom and dignity.*

SKINNER, B. F. (1974). *About behaviorism.* New York: Vintage Books.

SKINNER, B. F. (1982). Contrived reinforcement. *The Behavior Analyst, 5,* 3–8.

SKINNER, B. F. (1986). Is it behaviorism? *Behavioral and Brain Sciences, 9,* 716.

SKINNER, B. F. (1989). The place of feelings in the analysis of behavior. In B. F. Skinner (Ed.), *Recent issues in the analysis of behavior* (pp. 3–11). Columbus, OH: Merrill.

SLIFER, K. J., CATALDO, M. F., CATALDO, M. D., LLORENTE, A. M., & GERSEN, A. C., (1993). Behavior analysis of motion control for pediatric neuroimaging. *Journal of Applied Behavior Analysis, 26,* 469–470.

SMITH, L. D., BEST, L. A., STUBBS, D. A., ARCHIBALD, A. B., & ROBERSON-NAY, R. (2002). Constructing knowledge: The role of graphs and tables in hard and soft psychology. *American Psychologist, 57,* 749–761.

SMITH, L. D., BEST, L. A., STUBBS, D. A., JOHNSTON, J., & ARCHIBALD, A. B. (2000). Scientific graphs and the hierarchy of the sciences: A Latourian survey of inscription practices. *Social Studies of Science, 30,* 73–94.

SNYDER, G. (1990). Burrhus Frederic Skinner—The man behind the science. *The Applied Behavior Analysis Newsletter, 13,* 3–5.

SOLNICK, J. V., RINCOVER, A., & PETERSON, C. R. (1977). Some determinants of the reinforcing and punishing effects of timeout. *Journal of Applied Behavior Analysis, 10,* 415–424.

SPRUTE, K. A., WILLIAMS, R. L., & MCLAUGHLIN, T. F. (1990). Effects of a group response cost contingency procedure on the rate of classroom interruptions with emotionally disturbed secondary students. *Child and Family Behavior Therapy, 12,* 1–12.

STAATS, A. W., & BUTTERFIELD, W. H. (1965). Treatment of non-reading in a culturally deprived juvenile delinquent: An application of reinforcement procedures. *Child Development, 36,* 925–942.

STAATS, A. W., FINLEY, J. R., MINKE, K. A., & WOLF, M. (1964). Reinforcement variables in the control of unit reading responses. *Journal of the Experimental Analysis of Behavior, 7,* 139–149.

STAATS, A. W., STAATS, C. K., SCHULTZ, R., & WOLF, M. M. (1962). The conditioning of textual responses using "extrinsic" reinforcers. *Journal of the Experimental Analysis of Behavior, 5,* 33–40.

STARK, L. J., ALLEN, K. D., HURST, M., NASH, D. A., RIGNEY, B., & STOKES, T. F. (1989). Distraction: Its utilization and efficacy with children undergoing dental treatment. *Journal of Applied Behavior Analysis, 22,* 297–307.

STARK, L. J., KNAPP, L. G., BOWEN, A. M., POWERS, S. W., et al. (1993). Increasing calorie consumption in children with cystic fibrosis: Replication with 2-year follow-up. *Journal of Applied Behavior Analysis, 26,* 435–450.

STEIN, B. (1990). "I'm Going to the Principal's Office – Great!" *Behavior Analysis Digest, 2*(1), 4.

STEIN, L., XUE, B. G., & BELLUZZI, J. D. (1994). In vitro reinforcement of hippocampal bursting: A search for Skinner's atoms of behavior. *Journal of the Experimental Analysis of Behavior, 61,* 155–168.

STEPHENS, C. E., PEAR, J. L., WRAY, L. D., & JACKSON, G. C. (1975). Some effects of reinforcement schedules in teaching picture names to retarded children. *Journal of Applied Behavior Analysis, 8,* 435–447.

STITZER, M. L., & BIGELOW, G. E. (1984). Contingent reinforcement for carbon monoxide reduction: Within-subject effects of pay amount. *Journal of Applied Behavior Analysis, 17,* 477–483.

STOCK, L. Z., & MILAN, M. A. (1993). Improving dietary practices of elderly individuals: The power of prompting, feedback, and social reinforcement. *Journal of Applied Behavior Analysis, 26,* 379–387.

STOKES, T. (1992). Discrimination and generalization. *Journal of Applied Behavior Analysis, 25,* 429–432.

STOKES, T. F., & BAER, D. M. (1976). Preschool peers as mutual generalization-facilitating agents. *Behavior Therapy, 9,* 549–556.

STOKES, T. F., & BAER, D. M. (1977). An implicit technology of generalization. *Journal of Applied Behavior Analysis, 10,* 349–367.

STOKES, T. F., BAER, D. M., & JACKSON, R. L. (1974). Programming the generalization of a greeting response in four retarded children. *Journal of Applied Behavior Analysis, 7,* 599–610.

STOKES, T. F., & FAWCETT, S. B. (1977). Evaluating municipal policy: An analysis of a refuse-packaging program. *Journal of Applied Behavior Analysis, 10,* 391–398.

STROMER, R., MCCOMAS, J. J., & REHFELDT, R. A. (2000). Designing interventions that include delayed reinforcement: Implications of recent laboratory research. *Journal of Applied Behavior Analysis, 33,* 359–371.

STURGIS, E. T., TOLLISON, C. D., & ADAMS, H. E. (1978). Modification of combined migraine-muscle contraction headaches using BVP and EMG feedback. *Journal of Applied Behavior Analysis, 11,* 215–223.

SULLIVAN, M. A., & O'LEARY, S. G. (1990). Maintenance following reward and cost token programs. *Behavior Therapy, 21,* 139–149.

SULZER, B., & MAYER, G. R. (1972). *Behavior modification procedures for school personnel.* Hinsdale, IL: Dryden Press.

TALSMA, T. (1976). Thales on behavior modification. *Journal of Applied Behavior Analysis, 9,* 178.

TATE, B. G., & BAROFF, G. S. (1966). Aversive control of self-injurious behavior in a psychotic boy. *Behavior Research and Therapy, 4,* 281–287.

TAWNEY, J. W. (1972). Training letter discrimination in four-year-old children. *Journal of Applied Behavior Analysis, 5,* 455–465.

THACKERAY, E. J., & RICHDALE, A. L. (2002). The behavioral treatment of sleep difficulties in children with an intellectual disability. *Behavioral Interventions, 17,* 211–231.

THOMAS, J. D., PRESLAND, I. E., GRANT, M. D., & GLYNN, T. L. (1978). Natural rates of teacher approval and disapproval in Grade-7 classrooms. *Journal of Applied Behavior Analysis, 11,* 91–94.

THOMPSON, R. H., & IWATA, B. A. (2001). A descriptive analysis of social consequences following problem behavior. *Journal of Applied Behavior Analysis, 34,* 169–178.

THYER, B. A. (1988). Social work as a behaviorist views it: A reply to Nagel. *Social Work, 33,* 371–372.

TRUAX, C. B. (1966). Reinforcement and nonreinforcement in Rogerian psychotherapy. *Journal of Abnormal Psychology, 71,* 1–9.

TUDOR, R. M., & BOSTOW, D. E. (1991). Computer-programmed instruction: The relation of required interaction to practical application. *Journal of Applied Behavior Analysis, 24,* 361–368.

TURNER, S. M., BEIDEL, D. C., LONG, P. J., & GREENHOUSE, J. (1992). Reduction of fear in social phobics: An examination of extinction patterns. *Behavior Therapy, 23,* 389–403.

TWARDOSZ, S., & BAER, D. M. (1973). Training two severely retarded adolescents to ask questions. *Journal of Applied Behavior Analysis, 6,* 655–661.

TWOHIG, M. P., & WOODS, D. W. (2001). Evaluating the duration of competing response in habit reversal: A parametric analysis. *Journal of Applied Behavior Analysis, 34,* 417–520.

ULLMAN, L. P., & KRASNER, L. (1965). *Case studies in behavior modification.* New York: Holt, Rinehart and Winston.

VAN HOUTEN, R. (1993). The use of wrist weights to reduce self-injury maintained by sensory reinforcement. *Journal of Applied Behavior Analysis, 26,* 197–203.

VAN HOUTEN, R., & NAU, P. A. (1980). A comparison of the effects of fixed and variable ratio schedules of reinforcement on the behavior of deaf children. *Journal of Applied Behavior Analysis, 13,* 13–21.

VAN HOUTEN, R., & RETTING, R. A. (2001). Increasing motorist compliance and caution at stop signs. *Journal of Applied Behavior Analysis, 34,* 185–193.

VARGAS, E. A., & VARGAS, J. S. (1991). Programmed instruction: What it is and how to do it. *Journal of Behavioral Education, 1,* 235–251.

VAUGHAN, W., JR. (1984). Giving up the ghost. *The Behavioral and Brain Sciences, 7,* 501.

VOLLMER, T. R. (2002). Punishment happens: Some comments on Lerman and Vorndran's review. *Journal of Applied Behavior Analysis, 35,* 469–473.

VOLLMER, T. R., & HACKENBERG, T. D. (2001). Reinforcement contingencies and social reinforcement: Some reciprocal relations between basic and applied research. *Journal of Applied Behavior Analysis, 34,* 241–253.

VOLLMER, T. R., & IWATA, B. A. (1991). Establishing operations and reinforcement effects [Special Issue: Social validity: Multiple perspectives]. *Journal of Applied Behavior Analysis, 24,* 279–291.

VOLLMER, T. R., IWATA, B. A., ZARCONE, J. R., SMITH, R. G., et al. (1993). The role of attention in the treatment of attention-maintained self-injurious behavior: Noncontingent reinforcement and differential reinforcement of other behavior. *Journal of Applied Behavior Analysis, 26,* 9–21.

VON BOZZAY, G. D. (1984). *Projects in biofeedback: A text/workbook.* Dubuque, IA: Kendall/Hunt.

WAINER, H., & VELLEMAN, P. F. (2000). Statistical graphics: Mapping the pathways of science. *Annual Review of Psychology, 52,* 305–335.

WALKER, H. M., & BUCKLEY, N. K. (1968). The use of positive reinforcement in conditioning attending behavior. *Journal of Applied Behavior Analysis, 1,* 245–250.

WALKER, H. M., & BUCKLEY, N. K. (1972). Programming generalization and maintenance of treatment effects across time and across settings. *Journal of Applied Behavior Analysis, 5,* 209–224.

WALLACE, I. (1977). Self-control techniques of famous novelists. *Journal of Applied Behavior Analysis, 10,* 515–525.

WARD, P., & CARNES, M. (2002). Effects of posting self-set goals on collegiate football players' skill execution during practice and games. *Journal of Applied Behavior Analysis, 35,* 1–12.

WATSON, D. L., & THARP, R. G. (1997). *Self-directed behavior: Self-modification for personal adjustment.* (7th ed.). Monterey, CA: Brooks/Cole.

WATSON, J. B. (1914). *Behavior.* New York: Holt.

WEAVER, F. H., & MILLER, L. K. (1975). Teaching students how to proctor in a PSI course by means of a role-playing procedure. In J. Johnston (Ed.), *Behavior research and technology in higher education.* Springfield, IL: Charles C. Thomas.

WEINER, H. (1969). Controlling human fixed-interval performance. *Journal of the Experimental Analysis of Behavior, 12,* 349–373.

WEISBERG, P., & WALDROP, P. B. (1972). Fixed interval work habits of Congress. *Journal of Applied Behavior Analysis, 5,* 93–97.

WELLS, G. L., & OLSEN, E. A. (2003). Eyewitness testimony. *Annual Review of Psychology, 54,* 277–295.

WELSH, T. M., JOHNSON, S. P., MILLER, L. K., MERRILL, M. H., & ALTUS, D. E. (1989). A practical procedure for training meeting chairpersons. *Journal of Organizational Behavior Management, 10,* 151–166.

WELSH, T. M., MILLER, L. K., & ALTUS, D. E. (1994). Programming for survival: A meeting system that survives 8 years later. *Journal of Applied Behavior Analysis, 27,* 423–433.

WERLE, M. A., MURPHY, T. B., & BUDD, K. S. (1993). Treating chronic food refusal in young children: Home-based parent training. *Journal of Applied Behavior Analysis, 26,* 421–433.

WHEELER, H. (1973). *Beyond the punitive society.* San Francisco, CA: W. H. Freeman.

WHITE, A. G., & BAILEY, J. S. (1990). Reducing disruptive behaviors of elementary physical education students with Sit and Watch. *Journal of Applied Behavior Analysis, 23,* 353–359.

WHITE, B., & SANDERS, S. H. (1986). The influence on patients' pain intensity ratings of antecedent reinforcement of pain talk or well talk. *Journal of Behavior Therapy and Experimental Psychiatry, 17,* 155–159.

WHITE, M. A. (1975). Natural rate of teacher approval and disapproval in the classroom. *Journal of Applied Behavior Analysis, 8,* 367–372.

WHITEHEAD, W. E., RENAULT, P. F., & GOLDIAMOND, I. (1975). Modification of human gastric acid secretion with operant-conditioning procedures. *Journal of Applied Behavior Analysis, 8,* 147–156.

WHITMAN, T. L., & DUSSAULT, P. (1976). Self control through the use of a token economy. *Journal of Behavior Therapy and Experimental Psychiatry, 7,* 161–166.

WICKER, A. W. (1969). Attitudes versus actions: The relationship of verbal and overt behavioral responses to attitude objects. *Journal of Social Issues, 25,* 41–78.

WILDER, D. A., WHITE, H., & YU, M. L. (2003). Functional analysis and treatment of bizarre vocalizations exhibited by an adult with schizophrenia: A replication and extension. *Behavioral Interventions, 18,* 43–52.

WILLIAMS, B. A. (1994). Conditioned reinforcement: Experimental and theoretical issues. *The Behavior Analyst, 17*(2), 261–285.

WILLIAMS, C. D. (1959). The elimination of tantrum behavior by extinction procedures. *Journal of Abnormal and Social Psychology, 59,* 142–145.

WILLIAMS, J. A., HURST, M. K., & STOKES, T. F. (1983). Peer observation in decreasing uncooperative behavior in young dental patients. *The Behavior Modification, 7,* 225–242.

WILLIS, J., & GILES, D. (1976). *Great experiments in behavior modification.* Indianapolis: Hackett.

WILSON, G. T., LEAF, R. C., & NATHAN, P. E. (1975). The aversive control of excessive alcohol consumption by chronic alcoholics in the laboratory setting. *Journal of Applied Behavior Analysis, 8,* 13–26.

WINETT, R. A., KRAMER, K. D., WALKER, W. B., MALONE, S. W., & LANE, M. K. (1988). Modifying food purchases in supermarkets with modeling, feedback, and goal-setting procedures. *Journal of Applied Behavior Analysis, 21,* 73–80.

WINKLER, R. C. (1970). Management of chronic psychiatric patients by a token reinforcement system. *Journal of Applied Behavior Analysis, 3,* 47–55.

WOLF, M. M. (1978). Social validity: The case for subjective measurement or how applied behavior analysis is finding its heart. *Journal of Applied Behavior Analysis, 11,* 203–214.

WOLF, M. M., BIRNBRAUER, J., LAWLER, J., & WILLIAMS, T. (1970). The operant extinction, reinstatement, and re-extinction of vomiting behavior in a retarded child. In R. Ulrich, T. Stachnik, & J. Mabry (Eds.), *Control of human behavior* (Vol. 2 ). Glenview, IL: Scott, Foresman.

WOLF, M. M., RISLEY, T. R., & MEES, H. L. (1964). Application of operant condition procedures to the behavior problems of an autistic child. *Behavior Research and Therapy, 1,* 305–312.

WONG, S. E., SEROKA, P. L., & OGISI, J. (2000). Effects of a checklist on self-assessment of blood glucose level by a memory-impaired woman with diabetes mellitus. *Journal of Applied Behavior Analysis, 33,* 251–254.

WOOLF, H. B. (1977). *Webster's new collegiate dictionary.* Springfield, MA: Merriam.

WRIGHT, H. (1960). Observational child study. In P. Mussen (Ed.), *Handbook of research methods in child development.* New York: Wiley.

WULBERT, M., NYMAN, B. A., SNOW, D., & OWEN, Y. (1973). The efficacy of stimulus fading and contingency management in the treatment of elective mutism: A case study. *Journal of Applied Behavior Analysis, 6,* 435–441.

WYATT, W. J. (1990). Is there a behavior analyst in the house? *Behavior Analysis Digest, 2*(1), 2.

WYATT, W. J., HAWKINS, R. P., & DAVIS, P. (1986). Behaviorism: Are reports of its death exaggerated? *The Behavior Analyst, 9,* 101–105.

YANG, L. J. (2003). Combination of extinction and protective measures in the treatment of severely self-injurious behavior. *Behavioral Interventions, 18,* 109–121.

ZEILBERGER, J., SAMPEN, S. E., & SLOANE, J. H. N. (1968). Modification of a child's problem behaviors in the home with the mother as therapist. *Journal of Applied Behavior Analysis, 1,* 47–54.

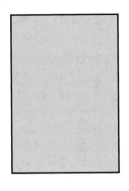

# Answer Key

## Introduction

### Programmed Reading

1. check;   2. check;   3. Exam;
4. problems;   5. learn;   6. underlined;   7. programmed;   8. examples;
9. check;   10. different;   11. every;
12. calculator;   13. review;
14. boldface;   15. read;   16. different;   17. write;   18. check;
19. read; write; check;   20. reading;
examples;   21. read;   22. examples;
23. programmed;   24. Class;
25. behavior;   26. check;   27. reading;   28. review;   29. behavior
analysis;   30. behavior;   31. respond;
32. sections;   33. hints;   34. hints;
35. example

## Lesson 1

### Reading Section and Behavior Analysis Examples

1. behaviorism;   2. facts;   3. applied;
4. everyday;   5. 1970;   6. change;
7. explain;   8. environmental;
9. feelings;   10. yes;   11. behavioral;
12. methods;   13. private;   14. Skinner;   15. different;   16. same;
17. environmental; change [or: modify]

### Programmed Reading

1. environmental;   2. 1970;
3. explain;   4. environmental; change
[or: modify];   5. voluntary;
6. behavior;   7. voluntary;
8. Skinner;   9. no;   10. involuntary;
11. explain;   12. Skinner;   13. analysis;   14. behavior;   15. explain;
16. behavior analysis; Public;
17. Public;   18. environmental;
19. behavioral;   20. explain;
21. 1970;   22. Skinner;   23. environmental [or: external or: public or:
observable]; change [or: modify or: cause];
24. behavior;   25. voluntary;
26. environmental; change [or: modify];

27. behavioral;   28. Public;
29. public;   30. behavior analysis;
31. environmental;   32. environmental
[or: external or: public];   33. explain;
34. behavior analysis;   35. behavioral;
36. behavior analysis [or: applied
behavior analysis];   37. 1970;
38. explain;   39. environmental;
40. private;   41. private;   42. environmental;   43. behavioral;
44. behavioral;   45. change [or: modify
or: cause];   46. behavior analysis;
47. behavior analysis;   48. strategy;
49. 1970;   50. behavior;   51. environmental [or: external];   52. explain;
53. explain;   54. Public;   55. environmental [or: external or: public];
56. 1970;   57. behavioral;   58. voluntary;   59. different;   60. multiple
choice;   61. behavior analysis;
62. Public;   63. Public;   64. Skinner;
65. is;   66. environmental; change;
67. voluntary; behavior;   68. Skinner;
1970; voluntary; behavior;   69. environmental; change [or: modify];
70. voluntary

### Programmed Examples

1. private; explain;   2. behavior
analysis;   3. environmental; change;
behavior analysis;   4. public;
5. environmental; public;   6. behavioral;   7. behavioral;   8. public;
9. behavior analysis;   10. private;
explain

## Lesson 2

### Reading Section and Behavior Analysis Examples

1. does;   2. behavior;   3. behavior;
4. observe;   5. clearer [or: clear];
observations;   6. memory;   7. inaccurate [or: wrong];   8. inaccurate
[or: wrong];   9. direct observation;
10. sees; records;   11. observed;

12. definition;   13. behavior;
14. definition;   15. behavior;
16. isn't;   17. whole;   18. direct
observation;   19. behavioral
definition;   20. direct observation;
21. records;   22. approach

### Programmed Reading

1. behavior;   2. behavioral definition;
3. behavioral definition;   4. observations;   5. behavior;   6. behavioral;
7. clearer [or: clear];   8. direct;
9. self-report [or: self report];
10. direct;   11. behavioral definition;
direct observations;   12. definition;
13. definition;   14. direct;
15. behavior;   16. does;   17. observation;   18. Direct Observation;
19. behavior;   20. internal;
21. private;   22. clearer; observations;
23. clearer; observations;   24. behavioral definition;   25. Behavioral;
26. see;   27. sees; records;
28. record;   29. observe;   30. behavioral definition;   31. does;
32. behavior;   33. self-report [or: self
report], direct;   34. yes;   35. does;
36. internal, private;   37. records;
38. report;   39. self;   40. self-report
[or: self report];   41. observe;
42. clearer; observations;   43. observe;
44. behavioral definition;   45. behavior;   46. behavior;   47. does;
48. internal, private;   49. behavioral
definition;   50. self-report [or: self
report];   51. direct;   52. behavioral;
53. sees [or: hears]; records;
54. behavior analysis;   55. behavioral
definition;   56. direct observation;
57. inaccurate [or: false or: wrong];
58. inaccurate [or: false or: wrong];
59. behavior analysis;   60. direct;
self-report [or: self report];   61. clearer
[or: clear]; observations;   62. self-
report [or: self report];   63. inaccurate
[or: wrong];   64. behavioral;
65. behavioral definition;   66. behavioral definition; direct observation;
67. direct;   68. direct;   69. direct;
70. does;   71. does;   72. does;
73. isn't;   74. does;   75. behavioral
definition;   76. behavioral definition;

77. behavioral; behavior; 78. behavioral; behavior; 79. direct observation; 80. behavior; 81. direct observation; 82. direct observation; 83. inaccurate [or: false or: wrong]; 84. direct; 85. self-report [or: self report]; 86. direct; 87. direct; self-report [or: self report]; 88. behavior; 89. direct observation; 90. al

## *Programmed Examples*

1. behavioral definition; 2. result; behavioral definition; 3. direct; behavior analysis; 4. behavioral; direct; 5. direct; self-report [or: self report]; 6. yes; 7. direct observation; behavior analysis; 8. no; 9. direct observation; 10. direct

# Lesson 3

## *Reading Section and Behavior Analysis Examples*

1. result; 2. outcome; 3. instance; 4. event; 5. event; 6. continuous; 7. 2 [or: two]; 8. discontinuous; 9. aren't; 10. discontinuous; 11. 45; 12. interval; 13. 10 [or: tenth]; 14. event; 15. outcome; 16. replace; 17. time sample [or: time-sample]; 18. response; 19. event; 90 [or: 90%] [or: 88]; 20. event; 21. event; 23. time sample [or: time-sample]; 24. interval; 25. method; 26. interval

## *Programmed Reading*

1. after; 2. behavioral; behavior; 3. event; outcome; 4. event; 5. interval; 6. outcome; 7. outcome; 8. outcome; 9. intervals; 10. intervals; 11. interval, time sample [or: time-sample]; 12. event; interval; outcome; 13. result; 14. instances; 15. continuous; 16. instances; 17. result; 18. instance; 19. is; 20. discontinuous; 21. event; 22. couldn't; 23. response; 24. method; 25. interval; 26. time sample [or: time-sample]; interval; 27. outcome; 28. interval; 29. time sample [or: time-sample]; 30. time sample [or: time-sample]; 31. interval; 32. outcome; 33. event; 34. outcome; 35. interval; outcome; time sample [or: time-sample]; event; 36. continuous; 37. response; behavior; 38. yes; 39. interval; 40. time sample [or: time-sample]; 41. outcome; 42. time sample [or: time-sample]; 43. result; 44. results; 45. discontinuous; 46. non-uniform;

47. event; 48. result; 49. instances; 50. continuous; 51. continuous; 52. interval; 53. time sample [or: time-sample]; 54. outcome; 55. continuous; 56. outcome; 57. time sample [or: time-sample]; 58. event; outcome; 59. outcome; 60. direct observation; 61. direct observation; 62. discontinuous; 63. interval; 64. interval; 65. no; 66. event; 67. behavior; response; 68. interval; 69. result; 70. time sample [or: time-sample]; 71. event; outcome; 72. behavior; 73. wrong; 74. instance; 75. discontinuous; 76. time sample [or: time-sample]; 77. continuous; 78. interval; 79. aren't; 80. outcome; 81. event, interval, time sample [or: time-sample]; 82. no; 83. outcome; 84. behavioral definition; 85. sample [or: time sample or: time-sample]; 86. different; 87. during; 88. direct observation; 89. event; 90. discontinuous; 91. intervals; continuous; results; 92. continuous; 93. direct observation; 94. event [or: event recording]; direct observation; 95. event; 96. no; 97. discontinuous; 98. discontinuous; 99. discontinuous; 100. instance; 101. continuous; 102. e; 103. time sample [or: time-sample]; 104. outcome; 105. interval [or: time sample]; 106. behavioral definition; direct observation; 107. direct observation; 108. can't; 109. time sample [or: time-sample]; 110. instance; 111. event; 112. interval; 113. interval; 114. result; 115. event; 116. continuous

## *Programmed Examples*

1. event; 2. event; 3. yes; yes; interval; 4. yes; yes; interval; 5. event; 6. yes; no; time sample [or: time-sample]; 7. no; no; event; 8. no; yes; outcome; 9. self report [or: self-report]; 10. behavioral definition; 11. yes; yes; interval; 12. interval; 13. direct observation; 14. behavioral definition; 15. time sample [or: time-sample]; 16. yes; no; time sample [or: time-sample]; 17. no; yes; outcome; 18. outcome; 19. outcome; 20. interval

# Lesson 4

## *Reading Section and Behavior Analysis Examples*

1. validity; 2. agreement; 3. reliability; 4. behavioral definition;

responses; 5. each; 6. agreements; 7. disagree; 8. 5 [or: five]; 9. 4 [or: four]; 5 [or: five]; 10. 3 [or: three]; 6 [or: six]; 11. count; 12. 90 [or: 90% or: ninety]; 13. correlation; 14. validity; 15. validity; 16. social; 17. reliability; 18. social validity; 19. reliability; 20. reliability; 21. social validity; 22. social validity; 23. 29 [or: 29%]; 24. old; new; 25. social validity; reliability; 26. 100% x A/(A+D) [or: 100 x A/(A+D)]; 27. didn't; 28. reliability; social validity

## *Programmed Reading*

1. agreement; 2. behavioral definition; responses; 3. 80 [or: 80%]; no; 4. 80 [or: 80%]; yes; 5. can't; 6. no; 7. response; 8. reliability; 9. time sample [or: time-sample]; 10. no; 11. no; 12. 50 [or: 50%]; 13. no; 14. 3 [or: three]; 1 [or: one]; 4 [or: four]; 15. outcome, event; 16. 3 [or: three]; 2 [or: two]; 17. can't; no; 18. response; 19. larger [or: large]; 20. behavioral definitions; 21. .80 [or: 0.80 or: 0.8 or: .8]; 80 [or: 80%]; 22. 3/5; 60 [or: 60%]; 23. social validity; 24. 40; 10; 50; 25. 80 [or: 80%]; 26. 100% x A/(A+D) [or: 100 x A/(A+D)]; 27. low; 28. 100% x A/(A+D) [or: 100 x A/(A+D)]; 29. behavioral definition; responses; 30. no; 31. 90 [or: 90%]; 80 [or: 80%]; 90 [or: 90%]; 32. 80 [or: 80%]; 33. old; 34. no; 35. can't; 36. social validity; 37. reliability; 38. new; 39. 50 [or: 50%]; 40. outcome, event; 41. behavioral definition; responses; 42. reliability; 43. no; 44. 80 [or: 80%]; no; 45. no; 46. social validity; 47. 80 [or: 80%]; no; 48. yes; 49. no; 50. 80 [or: 80%]; yes; 51. agreement; 52. 90 [or: 90%]; 53. correlation; 54. correlation; 55. 67 [or: 66 or: 67% or: 66%]; 56. reliability; 57. behavioral; 58. social validity; 59. 100% x A/(A+D) [or: 100 x A/(A+D)]; 60. responses; 62. 80 [or: 80%]; 64. 67 [or: 67%]; 65. no; 66. 80 [or: 80%]; yes; 67. outcome, event; 68. 80 [or: 80%]; 90 [or: 90%]; 69. interval, time sample [or: time-sample]; 70. behavioral definition; 71. direct observation; 72. reliability, social validity; 73. yes; 74. time sample [or: time-sample]; interval; 75. 3 [or: three]; 5 [or: five]; .6 [or: .60 or: 0.6 or: 0.60]; 60 [or: 60%]; 76. agreement; 77. agreement; 78. behavioral definition; responses; 79. 90 [or: 90%]; 80. agreement; correlation; 81. outcome, event; 82. correlation; 83. no; 84. yes; 85. doesn't; 86. responses; 87. social validity; 88. reliability; 89. can't; 90. no;

91. yes;   92. yes;   93. 80 [or: 80%]; no;   94. social validity;   95. reliability;   96. behavioral;   97. social validity;   98. 100%;   99. A; D; 100. social validity;   101. behavior analysis;   102. 2 [or: two]; 103. 1+1 [or: 2];   104. A/(A+D); 105. 8 [or: eight]; 10 [or: ten]; 8/10 [or: 4/5]; 80 [or: 80%];   106. behavioral definition;   107. direct observation;   108. reliability; social validity;   109. behavioral definition; direct observation; reliability; social validity;   110. no;   111. can't; 112. 80 [or: 80%]; 90 [or: 90%]; 113. no; 114. behavioral definition; 116. can;   117. 80 [or: 80%]; no; 118. can;   119. reliability, social validity;   120. 100% x A/(A+D) [or: 100 x A/(A+D)];   121. 90 [or: 90%]; 80 [or: 80%]

## Programmed Examples

1. time sample [or: time-sample]; 2. a;   3. yes; 9; 1; 10; .90 [or: 0.90 or: .9 or: 0.9]; 90 [or: 90%];   4. no; no; 5. social validity;   6. yes; 90 [or: 90%]; yes;   7. 80 [or: 80%]; no;   8. 90 [or: 90%]; yes;   9. 80 [or: 80%]; yes; 11. 80 [or: 80%]; no;   12. no; 13. yes; 8 [or: eight]; 2 [or: two]; 10 [or: ten]; .8 [or: 0.8 or: .80 or: 0.80]; 80 [or: 80%];   14. yes; 60 [or: 60%]; 80 [or: 80%]; no; c;   15. yes; 90 [or: 90%]; yes; 16. behavioral definition;   17. 80 [or: 80%]; no;   18. event;   19. 90 [or: 90%]; yes;   20. social validity

# Lesson 5

## Reading Section and Behavior Analysis Examples

1. experiment;   2. modify;   3. treatment;   4. baseline;   5. cause; 6. alternative;   7. same;   8. treatment;   9. comparison;   10. reversal; 11. reversal;   12. alternative; 13. different;   14. baseline; 15. multiple baseline;   16. 18; 17. reversal;   18. 27;   19. comparison;   20. notes;   21. experiment; 22. group;   23. alternating; 24. treatment;   25. different

## Programmed Reading

1. alternative;   2. didn't;   3. cause; 4. reversal;   5. comparison; 6. treatment;   7. different;   8. alternative;   9. baseline, treatment; 10. multiple;   11. reversal;

12. baseline;   13. alternative; 14. alternative;   15. treatment; 16. alternative;   17. single; 18. treatment;   19. single subject; 20. Tony;   21. girlfriend;   22. two [or: 2];   23. comparison;   24. alternative;   25. treatment; 26. multiple baseline; reversal; 27. comparison; multiple baseline; 28. comparison;   29. treatment; 30. treatment;   31. reversal, multiple baseline;   32. comparison, reversal, multiple baseline;   33. reversal; 34. comparison;   35. multiple baseline; 36. comparison;   37. cause; 38. multiple baseline;   39. different; 40. single subject;   41. multiple baseline;   42. reversal;   43. 2 [or: two];   44. comparison;   45. comparison;   46. reversal;   47. reversal; 48. comparison;   49. multiple baseline; 50. comparison;   51. comparison; 52. reversal;   53. comparison; 54. alternative;   55. backward; 56. alternative;   57. comparison; 58. 100% x A/(A+D) [or: 100 x A/(A+D)]; 59. treatment;   60. baseline; 61. reliability, social validity; 62. modify;   63. behavioral definition; direct observation; reliability; social validity; single subject;   64. backward; 65. multiple baseline;   66. reversal; 67. comparison;   68. treatment; 69. alternative;   70. multiple baseline; 71. multiple baseline;   72. reversal; 73. comparison;   74. cause; 75. single subject;   76. treatment; 77. reliability; social validity; 78. doesn't;   79. comparison; multiple baseline;   80. 2 [or: two];   81. 1 [or: one];   82. alternative; 83. comparison;   84. backward; 85. treatment;   86. can't;   87. reversal;   88. alternative;   89. can't; 90. alternative;   91. yes; multiple baseline;   92. multiple baseline; 93. yes; multiple baseline;   94. no; reversal;   95. comparison; 96. multiple baseline;   97. comparison; 98. 2 [or: two];   99. treatment; 100. alternative;   101. reversal; 102. alternative;   103. baseline; treatment;   104. treatment; 105. different;   106. alternative; 107. modify;   108. modify [or: change]; 109. comparison;   110. multiple baseline;   111. comparison, reversal, multiple baseline;   112. reversal, multiple baseline;   113. baseline; 114. behavioral definition;   115. direct observation;   116. reliability, social validity;   117. single subject; 118. single subject;   119. treatment; 120. modify [or: change];   121. yes; 122. can't;   123. backward; 124. treatment;   125. treatment; 126. discontinuous;   127. treatment; 128. different;   129. different;

130. treatment;   131. multiple baseline;   132. reversal;   133. multiple baseline;   134. reversal; 135. comparison;   136. treatment; 137. same;   138. comparison; reversal

## Programmed Examples

1. alternative;   2. reversal; 3. baseline; treatment; baseline; no; yes; no; reversal;   4. 80 [or: 80%]; no; 5. baseline;   6. reliability; 7. treatment;   8. treatment; comparison;   9. event;   10. no; no; yes; comparison;   11. social validity; 12. multiple baseline;   13. comparison;   14. reversal;   15. behavioral definition;   16. baseline; treatment; no; no; yes; comparison;   17. yes; multiple baseline;   18. multiple baseline;   19. 87 [or: 87%]; no; 20. alternative

# Lesson 6

## Reading Section and Behavior Analysis Examples

1. didn't;   2. convincing;   3. exclusive;   4. closer;   5. divided; stable; 6. divided; stable;   7. outside; 8. aren't;   9. away from; 10. aren't;   11. are;   12. are; are; 13. comparison;   14. no; yes; no; no; 15. yes; no; no; no;   16. yes; yes; yes; no;   17. visual;   18. yes; yes; yes; yes;   19. yes; no; no; no;   20. no; yes; no; no;   21. Analysis;   22. yes; yes; yes; yes;   23. yes; no; no; no; 24. experiments;   25. no;   26. convincing; caused;   27. identical; 28. 3 [or: three];

## Programmed Reading

1. are;   2. no;   3. no;   4. yes; 5. yes;   6. yes;   7. no;   8. yes; 9. yes;   10. no;   11. yes; 12. no;   13. yes;   14. no; 15. no;   16. yes;   17. yes; 18. yes; yes;   19. no;   20. yes; 21. yes; yes; yes;   22. no; yes; no; 23. no;   24. yes;   25. yes; 26. no;   27. yes; no; no; no; 28. divided, stable;   29. visual; 30. visual;   31. yes; yes; yes; no; 32. yes; yes; yes; yes;   33. visual; 34. divided, stable;   35. yes; no; no; no;   36. yes; no; no; no;   37. yes; no; no; no;   38. no; yes; no; no; 39. 3 [or: three];   40. no; yes; no; no; 41. divided;   42. divided; stable; convincing; cause [or: caused]; 43. divided; stable; convincing; cause [or: caused];   44. divided; stable;

convincing; cause [or: caused];
45. yes; 46. can't; 47. no; yes;
no; no; 48. yes; no; no; no;
49. yes; no; no; no; 50. yes; no; no;
no; 51. yes; yes; yes; no; 52. 3
[or: three]; 53. yes; yes; yes; no;
54. yes; yes; yes; yes; 55. yes; yes;
yes; yes; 56. no; yes; no; no;
57. yes; 58. no; 59. yes;
60. no; 61. no; 62. yes; no; yes;
63. yes; 64. yes; no; no; no;
65. no; yes; no; no; 66. no; yes; no;
no; 67. yes; yes; yes; no;
68. Visual; 69. yes; no; no; no;
70. yes; yes; yes; yes; 74. yes; no;
no; no; 75. yes; yes; yes; yes;
76. no; yes; no; no; 77. yes; yes; yes;
no; 81. divided; stable; convincing;
cause [or: caused]; 82. visual;
85. yes; yes; yes; yes; 86. 3 [or:
three]; 87. aren't; 88. no;
89. are; 90. divided; 91. divided;
92. stable; 93. stable; 94. convincing; 95. cause [or: caused];
96. alternative; 97. aren't;
98. convincing; 99. 100% x A/(A+D)
[or: 100 x A/(A+D)]; 100. single
subject; 101. behavior analysis;
behavioral definition; 102. yes; yes;
yes; no; 103. convincing;
104. aren't; 105. aren't;
106. aren't; 107. aren't;
108. divided; stable; convincing;
cause [or: caused]; 109. visual;
110. visual; 111. visual;
112. single subject; visual; 113. yes;
114. yes; 115. yes; 116. no;
117. convincing; 118. yes; no; no;
no; 119. 3 [or: three];
120. can't

### *Programmed Examples*

1. alternative; comparison; 2. divided;
stable; convincing; cause [or:
caused]; 3. yes; yes; yes; yes;
4. yes; yes; yes; yes; 5. interval;
6. yes; yes; yes; yes; 7. behavioral
definition; 8. yes; no; no; no;
9. baseline; treatment; reversal;
reversal; alternative; 10. baseline;
11. yes; no; no; no; 12. yes; yes; yes;
no; 13. yes; yes; yes; yes; 14. no;
yes; no; no; 15. multiple baseline;
16. time sample [or: time-sample];
17. yes; yes; yes; yes; 18. no; yes; no;
no; 19. no; yes; no; no; 20. yes;
yes; yes; no; 21. yes; no; no; no

## Lesson 7

### *Reading Section*

1. time sample [or: time-sample];
2. unexpected; 3. Practice

### *Practice Review I*

1. behavioral definition; 2. alternative; 3. multiple baseline;
4. environmental [or: external or:
public]; change [or: modify or: cause];
5. Skinner; 6. behaviors [or: private
event]; 7. behavioral; 8. single
subject; 9. interval;
10. reversal; 11. interval;
12. treatment; 13. reversal;
14. interval; 15. 85 [or: 85%]; yes;
16. interval; 17. reversal [or:
multiple baseline]; 18. time sample
[or: time-sample]; 19. direct
observation; 20. multiple baseline;
21. yes; no; no; no; 23. multiple
baseline; 24. no; 25. social
validity; 26. behavioral definition;
27. 80 [or: 80%]; no; 28. time sample
[or: time-sample]; 29. event;
30. 80 [or: 80%]; 31. comparison;
32. 100% x A/(A+D) [or: 100 x A/(A+D)];
33. behavioral [or: behavior];
34. social validity; 35. 75 [or: 75%];
no; 36. event; 37. time sample
[or: time-sample]; 38. direct
observation; 39. environmental [or:
external or: public]; 40. same;
41. convincing; 42. explain;
43. discontinuous; 44. visual;
45. 1970; 46. responses; behavioral
definition [or: definition];
47. event; 48. baseline; 49. time
sample [or: time-sample];
50. event

### *Practice Review II*

1. reversal; 2. behavior; 3. reversal; 4. treatment; 5. comparison;
6. alternative; 7. yes; no; no; no;
8. multiple baseline; 9. 80 [or: 80%];
yes; 10. 80 [or: 80%]; no; 11. outcome; 12. reliability; 13. baseline;
14. comparison; 15. behavioral
definition; single subject; 16. behavior analysis; 17. divided; stable

## Lesson 8

### *Reading Section and Behavior Analysis Examples*

1. reinforcement; 2. follows;
increases; 3. procedure; 4. event;
procedure; 5. reinforcers; 6. reinforcers; 7. reinforcement;
8. reinforcer; 9. reinforcement;
10. reinforcer; 11. baseline;
treatment; 12. reinforcement;
13. multiple baseline, reversal;
14. reinforcer; 15. behavior;
16. history; 17. increase;
18. can't; unknown; 19. reinforcer;
20. reinforcer; 21. unknown;

unknown; 22. reinforcer;
reinforcement 23. unknown

### *Programmed Reading*

1. no; 2. increases; 3. follows;
4. follow; increases; 5. reversal;
multiple baseline; 6. reinforcement;
7. reinforcer; 8. follows; increase;
9. reinforcer; reinforcement;
10. reinforcer; 11. reinforcer;
12. unknown; 13. unknown;
14. can't; 15. unknown;
16. unknown; 17. unknown;
18. unknown; 19. unknown;
20. correct; 21. no; 22. precede;
23. reinforcer; 24. reinforcer;
25. unknown; 26. reinforcer;
27. unknown; 28. reinforcer;
29. reinforcer; 30. unknown;
31. reinforcement; 32. unknown;
33. reinforcer; 34. reinforcer;
35. unknown; 36. unknown;
37. follows; increases; 38. follows;
increases; 39. reinforcer;
40. unknown; 41. reinforcer;
42. reinforcement; 43. unknown;
44. unknown; 45. reinforcement;
46. reinforcer; reinforcement;
47. reinforcer; 48. reinforcement;
49. unknown; 50. unknown;
51. unknown; 52. reinforcement;
53. reinforcement; 54. unknown;
55. unknown; 56. unknown;
57. reinforcer; 58. reinforcement;
59. reinforcement; 60. reinforcement; 061. unknown; 62. isn't;
63. unknown; 64. unknown;
65. unknown; 66. increase;
67. unknown; 68. unknown;
69. reinforcer; 70. unknown;
71. reinforcement; 72. reinforcement; 73. reinforcement; reinforcer;
74. reinforcement; 75. reinforcers;
76. increase; 77. reinforcer;
78. unknown; 79. reinforcer;
80. preceding; 81. reinforcer;
82. no; 83. reinforcer

### *Programmed Examples*

1. followed; steadied; unknown;
2. unknown; 3. reinforcement;
4. followed; increased; reinforcer;
5. reinforcer; 6. follow; increased;
reinforcer; 7. follow; increased;
reinforcer; 8. reinforcement;
9. followed; increased; reinforcer;
10. reinforcement; 11. reinforcer;
12. reinforcement; reinforcer;
13. reinforcer; reinforcement;
14. reinforcer; 15. unknown;
16. unknown; 17. unknown;
18. reinforcement; 19. preceded;
increased; unknown; can't;
20. follow; increased;
reinforcer

# Lesson 9

## *Reading Section and Behavior Analysis Examples*

1. extinction;    2. stopped; decreases;
3. extinction;    4. extinction;
5. extinction;    6. is;    7. extinction;
8. unknown;    9. unknown;
10. unknown;    11. unknown;
12. extinguishing

## *Programmed Reading*

1. extinction;    2. extinction;
3. extinction burst;    4. extinction burst;    5. increase;    6. unknown;
7. unknown;    8. unknown;
9. stopped; decrease;    10. extinction;
11. wouldn't;    12. decrease [or: reduction];    13. stopped;    14. stopped; decreases;    15. reinforcer;
16. isn't;    17. unknown;
18. extinction;    19. wouldn't;
20. unknown;    21. extinction;
22. extinction;    23. reinforcement;
24. reinforcement;    25. extinction burst;    26. extinction;
27. unknown;    28. unknown;
29. extinction;    30. can't;
31. increase;    32. extinction burst;
33. extinction burst;    34. increase;
35. stopped; decrease;    36. stopped; decrease;    37. unknown;
38. unknown;    39. unknown;
40. extinction;    41. extinction burst;
42. unknown;    43. unknown;
44. extinction;    45. extinguishing;
46. extinguishing;    47. extinction;
48. extinction;    49. extinction;
50. unknown;    51. extinction;
52. unknown; unknown;    53. increases [or: increased];    54. extinguishing;
55. unknown;    56. unknown;
57. unknown;    58. unknown;
59. extinction;    60. reinforcement; extinction;    61. extinction;
62. extinguishing;    63. stopped [or: stop]; decrease;    64. extinction;
65. unknown;    66. extinguishing;
67. increases; extinction;    68. extinction;    69. stop; decrease;
70. unknown

## *Programmed Examples*

1. reinforcement;    2. extinction;
3. extinction;    4. unknown;    5. no; yes; unknown;    6. reinforcer;
7. reinforcement;    8. unknown;
9. unknown;    10. extinction;
11. yes; no; unknown;    12. yes; yes; extinction;    13. yes; yes; extinction;
14. unknown;    15. extinction;
16. reinforcement;    17. unknown;

18. unknown;    19. extinction;
20. extinction

# Lesson 10

## *Reading Section and Behavior Analysis Examples*

1. reinforcement;    2. different; reinforced; extinguished;    3. reinforcement;    4. reinforced [or: reinforces];
5. reinforcement;    6. differential reinforcement;    7. history;    8. incompatible;    9. unknown;    10. muscles;
11. aren't;    12. no;    13. yes;
14. aren't;    15. no;    16. yes;
17. isn't;    18. no;    19. isn't;    20. 1
[or: one];    21. unknown; differential reinforcement;    22. extinction;
23. reinforcement;    24. unknown;
25. yes;    26. differential reinforcement

## *Programmed Reading*

1. differential reinforcement;
2. reinforcement;    3. differential reinforcement;    4. no;    5. differential reinforcement;    6. differential reinforcement;    7. reinforcement;
8. unknown;    9. differential reinforcement;    10. differential reinforcement;    11. unknown;
12. unknown;    13. differential reinforcement;    14. differential reinforcement;    15. reinforcement;
16. unknown;    17. differential reinforcement;    18. unknown;
19. differential reinforcement;
20. differential reinforcement;
21. differential reinforcement;
22. aren't;    23. reinforcement;
24. yes;    25. aren't;    26. differential reinforcement;    27. aren't;
28. different; reinforcement; extinction;
29. no;    30. yes;    31. yes;
32. no;    33. yes;    34. no;    35. no;
36. no;    37. yes;    38. unknown;
39. reinforcement;    40. reinforcement;    41. differential reinforcement;
42. differential reinforcement;
43. unknown;    44. unknown;
45. different;    46. extinction;
47. reinforcement;    48. differential reinforcement;    49. unknown;
50. unknown;    51. different; reinforcement; extinction;    52. different; reinforcement; extinction;
53. Differential Reinforcement;
54. unknown;    55. unknown;
56. unknown;    57. differential reinforcement;    58. yes;    59. no;
60. unknown;    61. unknown;
62. aren't;    63. is;    64. differential reinforcement;    65. differential

reinforcement;    66. yes;    67. differential reinforcement;    68. reinforcement;    69. differential reinforcement;
70. differential reinforcement;    71. is;
72. is;    73. reinforcement;
74. extinction;    75. isn't;    76. isn't;
77. reinforcement, extinction;
78. yes;    79. differential reinforcement;    80. differential reinforcement;
81. differential reinforcement;
82. differential reinforcement;
83. one [or: 1];    84. differential reinforcement;    85. extinction;
86. different;    87. differential reinforcement;    88. reinforcement, extinction;    89. isn't;    90. differential reinforcement;    91. extinction;
92. unknown;    93. differential reinforcement;    94. differential; differentially

## *Programmed Examples*

1. reinforcement;    2. yes; yes; yes; differential reinforcement;    3. no; unknown;    4. yes; yes; yes; differential reinforcement;
5. unknown;    6. differential reinforcement;    7. differential reinforcement;    8. differential reinforcement;    9. yes; yes; yes; differential reinforcement;
10. unknown;    11. unknown;
12. reinforcement;    13. extinction;
14. unknown;    15. reinforcement;
16. unknown;    17. unknown;
18. reinforcement;    19. differential reinforcement;    20. no; unknown

# Lesson 11

## *Reading Section and Behavior Analysis Examples*

1. shaping;    2. approximations;
3. target;    4. approximations;
5. target;    6. shaping;    7. approximations;    8. successive approximation;
9. shaping;    10. reinforcer;
11. shaping;    12. differential reinforcement;    13. reinforcement;    14. target behavior;    15. approximation;
16. shaping;    17. new;    18. shaping

## *Programmed Reading*

1. approximation [or: successive approximation];    2. shaping;
3. can;    4. new;    5. shaping;
6. yes;    7. approximation [or: successive approximation];    8. target behavior;    9. target behavior;
10. approximation [or: successive approximation];    11. differential

reinforcement; 12. target behavior;
13. approximation [or: successive
approximation]; 14. successive
approximations [or: approximations];
15. target behavior; 16. shaping;
17. differential reinforcement;
18. differential reinforcement;
19. shaping; 20. differential
reinforcement; 21. approximation
[or: successive approximation];
22. increase; 23. approximation
[or: successive approximation];
24. can't; 25. approximations [or:
successive approximations];
26. target behavior; 27. shaping;
28. shaping; 29. target behavior;
30. approximation [or: successive
approximation]; 31. differential
reinforcement; 32. differential
reinforcement; 33. target behavior;
approximations [or: successive
approximations]; 34. target
behavior; approximations [or:
successive approximations];
35. differential reinforcement;
36. new; 37. shaping;
38. shaping; 39. approximation
[or: successive approximation];
40. target behavior; 41. extinction;
42. target behavior; 43. can't;
44. differential reinforcement;
45. shaping; 46. shaping;
47. shaping; 48. shaping;
49. target behavior; 50. approximations [or: successive approxima-
tions]; 51. shaping; 52. old;
53. behavior; 54. behavior;
approximations; 55. differential
reinforcement; 56. approximations;
57. differential reinforcement;
shaping; 58. target behavior;
successive approximations [or: app-
roximations]; 59. behavior;
60. social validity; 61. target;
62. shaping; 63. extinction;
64. approximation

## Programmed Examples

1. unknown; 2. successive
approximations [or: approximations];
target behavior; differential
reinforcement; shaping; 3. shaping;
4. approximation [or: successive
approximation]; differential
reinforcement; target behavior; shaping;
5. unknown; 6. unknown;
7. target behavior; approximation [or:
successive approximation]; shaping;
8. reinforcement; 9. reinforcement;
10. unknown; 11. target behavior;
12. approximation [or: successive
approximation]; 13. differential
reinforcement; 14. shaping;
15. shaping; 16. differential
reinforcement; 17. differential

reinforcement; 18. target behavior;
differential reinforcement; approximation [or: successive approximation];
shaping; 19. successive approximation [or: approximation]; shaping;
20. unknown

# Lesson 12

## Reading Section and Behavior Analysis Examples

1. reinforcer; 2. only; 3. only;
4. immediate; 5. minute;
6. amount; 7. worthwhile;
8. frequency; opposite; 9. deprived;
10. rarely; 11. Contingency;
12. immediacy; 13. Deprivation
[or: Satiation]; 14. deprivation;
15. contingency, immediacy, size,
deprivation; 16. reinforcement,
extinction, differential reinforcement,
shaping; 17. worthwhile;
18. unknown; none

## Programmed Reading

1. quickly; 2. worthwhile;
3. behavior; 4. deprivation;
5. immediacy; 6. size; 7. decreases;
8. reinforcer; 9. deprivation;
10. contingency; 11. contingent;
12. contingency; 13. deprivation;
14. immediacy; 15. daily;
16. deprived; 17. yes; 18. increase;
19. Size; 20. worthwhile; 21. satiated; 22. would; 23. deprived;
24. worthwhile; 25. contingency;
26. reinforcement [or: reinforcer];
27. only; 28. immediacy;
29. deprivation; 30. immediacy;
31. immediacy; 32. contingency;
33. size; 34. deprivation;
35. contingency; 36. reinforcer
effectiveness; 37. deprived;
38. only; 39. worthwhile;
40. rarely; 41. only; 42. minute;
43. deprivation; 44. immediacy;
45. worthwhile; 46. rarely;
47. minute; 47. contingency;
48. reinforcer effectiveness; 50. size;
51. opposite; 52. satiation;
53. rarely; 54. no; yes; 55. deprivation; 56. contingency; 57. effectiveness; 58. reinforcer effectiveness;
59. contingency; 60. increases;
61. effectiveness; 62. reinforcer;
63. only; 64. contingency, immediacy,
size, deprivation; 65. satiated;
66. no; 67. deprived; 68. only;
69. isn't; 70. deprived; 71. deprivation; 72. immediate; 73. size;
74. reinforcer; 75. worthwhile;
76. rarely; 77. rarely; 78. only;

79. minute; 80. liked;
81. reinforcer effectiveness;
82. shaping; reinforcer effectiveness;
83. contingency; 84. Deprivation;
85. deprivation; 86. satiated;
87. Size

## Programmed Examples

1. shaping; 2. unknown;
3. yes; yes; yes; no; deprivation;
4. unknown; 5. immediacy;
6. immediacy; 7. Deprivation;
8. reinforcer; 9. none; 10. Size;
11. yes; yes; yes; yes; none; 12. only;
minute; worthwhile; rarely;
Deprivation; 13. contingency;
14. size; 15. deprivation;
16. size; 17. immediacy;
18. contingency; 19. yes; yes; yes;
yes; none; 20. unknown

# Lesson 13

## Reading Section and Behavior Analysis Examples

1. continuous; 2. extinction;
3. intermittent; 4. ratio; 5. fixed;
6. pause; 7. fixed-ratio; 8. fixed-
ratio; 9. variable; 10. extinction;
11. satiation; 12. shaping;
13. strain; 14. continuous;
15. variable-ratio [or: VR-5];
16. fixed-ratio [or: FR-30]; 17. FR-5;
VR-53; 18. varying; 19. continuous; 20. no; 21. continuous,
intermittent, extinction

## Programmed Reading

1. continuous; 2. big; 3. pause;
4. variable; 5. intermittent;
6. different; 7. increase; 8. no;
9. extinction; 10. fixed-ratio;
11. behavioral definition; 12. continuous [or: FR-1]; 13. variable-ratio
[or: VR-5]; 14. b; 15. fixed-ratio;
16. FR-5; VR-10; 17. variable; fixed;
18. continuous [or: FR-1]; 19. intermittent; 20. continuous, extinction,
intermittent; 21. intermittent;
22. extinction; 23. continuous;
24. fixed-ratio; 25. variable-ratio;
VR-5; 26. pause; 27. fixed;
variable; 28. fixed; 29. variable-
ratio [or: VR-50]; 30. ratio strain;
31. lower; 32. no; 33. extinction;
satiation; 34. variable-ratio; fixed-
ratio; continuous; 35. satiation;
extinction; 36. variable-ratio;
fixed-ratio; continuous; 37. shaping;
ratio strain; 38. continuous [or:
FR-1]; 39. variable-ratio;

40. satiation;    41. variable-ratio [or: VR-4];    42. variable-ratio;
43. variable-ratio;    44. pause;
45. fixed;    46. extinction;    47. variable-ratio [or: VR-5];    48. fixed-ratio [or: FR-13];    49. fixed-ratio [or: FR-10];    50. Variable-ratio [or: VR-13];    51. extinction;    52. continuous;    53. intermittent;    54. Fixed-ratio [or: FR-17];    55. variable [or: varying];    56. fixed;    57. ratio strain;    58. ratio strain;    59. variable-ratio; fixed-ratio; continuous;
60. fixed-ratio; variable-ratio;
61. extinction; satiation;    62. shaping; ratio strain;    63. extinction; satiation;
64. variable-ratio;    65. ratio;
66. variable-ratio;    67. continuous [or: FR-1];    68. continuous; intermittent; extinction;    69. variable-ratio;
70. extinction; satiation;    71. ratio;
72. higher;    73. intermittent;
74. faster;    75. intermittent;
76. intermittent;    77. fixed-ratio [or: FR-10];    78. variable-ratio [or: VR-10];    79. intermittent;    80. variable-ratio [or: VR-15];    81. quickly;
82. slowly;    83. slowly;    84. ratio;
85. ratio;    86. fixed-ratio [or: FR-30];
87. extinction;    88. intermittent [or: variable-ratio or: fixed-ratio];
89. intermittent;    90. continuous [or: FR-1];    91. variable-ratio;
92. fixed-ratio;    93. fixed-ratio;
94. variable-ratio;    095. variable-ratio;    96. ratio;    97. variable-ratio; fixed-ratio;    98. fixed;    99. variable-ratio;    100. high;    101. extinction;
102. new;    103. ratio;    104. effectiveness; ratio;    105. shaping; ratio strain;    106. continuous [or: FR-1];
107. continuous;    108. strain;
109. ratio strain;    110. variable-ratio [or: VR-8];    111. intermittent; fixed-ratio; variable-ratio;    112. variable-ratio;    113. everytime;
114. varying

## Programmed Examples

1. fixed-ratio [or: FR-2];    2. shaping;
3. satiation;    4. variable-ratio [or: VR-4];    5. variable-ratio [or: VR-4];
6. target behavior; shaping; continuous [or: FR-1];    7. variable-ratio; a; c;
8. immediacy;    9. contingency;
10. intermittent [or: variable-ratio or: fixed-ratio];    11. variable-ratio [or: VR-4];    12. fixed-ratio [or: FR-6];
13. fixed-ratio [or: FR-5];    14. extinction;    15. variable-ratio [or: VR-4];
16. reinforcement;    17. shaping;
18. continuous [or: FR-1]; variable-ratio;
19. fixed-ratio [or: FR-5]; b; d; pause; yes;    20. variable-ratio [or: VR-3]; ratio strain

# Lesson 14

## Reading Section and Behavior Analysis Examples

1. interval;    2. fixed-interval;
3. scallop;    4. fixed;    5. varying;
6. uniform;    7. variable;    8. interval;    9. fixed;    10. no;    11. ratio;
12. sooner;    13. one [or: 1];
14. interval;    15. fixed-interval; FI-3;
16. variable;    17. time sample [or: time-sample]

## Programmed Reading

1. intermittent;    2. b;    3. fixed;
4. fixed; response;    5. fixed;
6. fixed-interval;    7. varying; response;    8. varying;    9. variable-ratio [or: VR-10];    10. scallop;
11. scallop;    12. scallop; uniform;
13. uniform;    14. intermittent;
15. ratio;    16. fixed-interval; FI-5;
17. variable-interval; VI-5;    18. variable-interval [or: VI-6];    19. ratio; interval;    20. ratio; interval;
21. shaping; reinforcers;    22. lower;
23. variable-ratio;    24. one [or: 1];
25. interval;    26. fixed-interval [or: FI-10];    27. a;    28. b;    29. fixed-ratio, fixed-interval;    30. variable-interval;    31. fixed-ratio, fixed-interval;    32. faster;    33. fixed; response;    34. fixed-interval;
35. varying; response;    36. scallop;
37. variable-interval;    38. fixed-interval [or: FI-3];    39. variable-interval; VI-5;    40. ratio; interval;
41. satiation; extinction;
42. variable-ratio;    43. fixed-interval;
44. fixed-ratio, fixed-interval;
45. variable-interval;    46. fixed-interval;    47. variable-ratio [or: VR-20];    48. interval;    49. interval;
50. ratio strain;    51. fixed-interval;
52. variable-interval;    53. uniform;
54. variable-ratio;    55. no;
56. continuous, extinction, intermittent;
57. won't;    58. interval;
59. timing;    60. fixed-ratio;
61. response;    62. fixed-interval;
63. variable-interval;    64. variable-interval;    65. ratio;    66. scallop;
67. variable-ratio;    68. interval;
69. satiation; extinction;
70. counting;    71. varying;
72. response;    73. one [or: 1];
74. one [or: 1]; sooner;    75. one [or: 1];
76. interval;    77. ratio; interval;
78. uniform;    79. scallop;
80. increases;    81. fixed-interval [or: FI-10];    82. increase;    83. sooner;
84. intermittent;    85. ratio;
86. no;    87. no;    88. fixed-ratio;
89. interval

## Programmed Examples

1. variable-interval [or: VI-4];
2. fixed-interval [or: FI-10];
3. immediacy;    4. extinction;
5. fixed-interval [or: FI-15];    6. no; yes; variable-interval;    7. no; yes; fixed-interval [or: FI-30];
8. variable-ratio [or: VR-4];    9. interval; variable-interval [or: VI-93];
10. yes; no; fixed-ratio [or: FR-13];
11. variable-ratio [or: VR-5];
12. variable-ratio [or: VR-10];
13. variable-interval;    14. fixed-ratio [or: FR-3];    15. variable-ratio;
16. fixed-interval [or: FI-2];    17. no; yes; variable-interval [or: VI-15];
18. differential reinforcement;
19. reinforcer;    20. no; yes; variable-ratio [or: VR-20]

# Lesson 15

## Reading Section

1. reinforcement;    2. reinforcer;
3. reinforcers [or: reinforcements];
4. variable-interval;    5. c [or: (c)]

## Practice Review I

1. yes; no; no; no;    2. follow; increases;
3. unknown;    4. shaping;
5. approximation [or: successive approximation];    6. target behavior;
7. reinforcement;    8. reversal;
9. 90 [or: 90%]; yes;    10. reinforcement, extinction;    11. yes; yes; yes; yes;    12. immediacy;    13. reinforcer;    14. ratio strain;    15. continuous [or: continuous reinforcement];
16. fixed-ratio [or: FR-2];    17. variable-ratio;    18. satiated;
19. unknown;    20. differential reinforcement;    21. Contingency;
22. unknown;    23. Behavioral; Reinforcement;    24. extinction;
25. discontinuous;    26. continuous;
27. event;    28. multiple baseline;
29. immediacy;    30. no; yes; no; no;
31. unknown;    32. variable-ratio;
33. unknown;    34. intermittent;
35. unknown;    36. multiple baseline;
37. Deprivation;    39. unknown;
40. variable-interval;    42. unknown;
43. social validity;    44. fixed-interval [or: FI-1 or: continuous];    45. shaping;
46. 80 [or: 80%]; yes;    47. none;
48. yes; no; no; no;    49. stopped; decreases [or: decreased];    50. treatment;    51. baseline;    52. reinforcement; reinforcer;    53. reliability; social validity;    54. discontinuous;
55. rarely;    56. interval;    57. shaping;    58. effectiveness;    59. ratio;
60. reinforcement;    61. differential

reinforcement; 62. fixed-interval, fixed-ratio; 63. fixed-ratio; 64. variable-ratio; 65. variable-ratio, variable-interval; 66. differential reinforcement

## Practice Review II

1. unknown; 2. outcome; 3. reliability; 4. different; 5. extinction; 6. variable-interval; 7. fixed-interval; 8. unknown; 9. 90 [or: 90%] [or: ninety]; 10. comparison; 11. unknown; 12. reinforcement; extinction; differential reinforcement; shaping; reinforcer effectiveness; ratio; interval; 13. fixed-ratio [or: FR-7]; 14. successive approximations [or: approximations]; 15. target behavior; 16. shaping; 17. yes; no; no; no; 18. amount; 19. extinction; 20. interval 21. Contingency; 22. continuous; 23. variable-ratio

# Lesson 16

## Reading Section and Behavior Analysis Examples

1. stimulus; 2. behavior; 3. discrimination; 4. reinforced; extinguished; 5. discriminative stimulus [or: SD]; 6. S-delta; 7. discriminated; 8. increased; 9. stimulus; 10. SD; 11. stimulus; 12. training; 13. stimulus; 14. equivalent; 15. before; 16. discrimination training

## Programmed Reading

1. discriminative; 2. SD [or: discriminative stimulus or: prompt]; 3. stimulus control; 4. discriminated; 5. discriminated behavior [or: discriminated]; 6. S-delta; 7. reinforcement; 8. extinction; 9. discriminative; 10. S-delta; 11. discriminative; 12. extinction; 13. S-delta; 14. discrimination training; 15. precedes; 16. reinforcing; 17. SD [or: discriminative stimulus]; 18. discrimination training; 19. discrimination training; 20. extinguishing; 21. SD [or: discriminative stimulus]; reinforcer; 22. discrimination training; 23. discrimination training; 24. discrimination training; 25. SD [or: discriminative stimulus or: prompt]; S-delta; 26. discriminated; 27. stimulus; 28. discrimination training; 29. discrimination training;

30. increased; 31. response; 32. shaping; 33. reinforced; 34. SD [or: discriminative stimulus]; reinforcer; 35. discrimination training; 36. stimulus; 37. SD; reinforcer; 38. stimulus; 39. discrimination training; 40. differential reinforcement; discrimination training; 41. discrimination training; 42. discrimination training; 43. reinforcer; SD [or: discriminative stimulus]; 44. more; 45. discriminative stimulus; 46. SD [or: discriminative stimulus or: prompt]; reinforcer; 47. response; 48. S-delta; 49. complex; 50. extinction; 51. stimulus control; 52. ive; 53. ion; ive; ed; 54. differential reinforcement; 55. discriminated; 56. discrimination training; 57. SD [or: discriminative stimulus or: prompt]; 58. response; 59. SD [or: discriminative stimulus or: prompt]; reinforcer; 60. S-delta. 61. discrimination training; 62. reinforced; extinguished; 63. differential reinforcement; 64. discrimination training; 65. discriminated; 66. SD [or: discriminative stimulus]; 67. SD [or: discriminative stimulus]; reinforcer; 68. discrimination training; 69. SD [or: discriminative stimulus]; 70. S-delta; 71. discriminated; 72. discriminated; 73. differential reinforcement; 74. discrimination training; 75. discrimination training; differential reinforcement; 76. S-delta; 77. stimulus control; 78. SD [or: discriminative stimulus]; 79. S-delta; 80. stimulus control; 81. discrimination training; 82. differential reinforcement; 83. differential reinforcement; 84. discrimination training; 85. stimulus control; 86. differential reinforcement; 87. discrimination training; 88. discrimination training; 89. stimulus control; 90. SD; 91. discrimination training; 92. discrimination training; 93. discriminative stimulus; SD; S-delta; 94. stimulus; 95. discrimination training; discriminative; SD; S-delta; 96. behavior; response; 97. discrimination training; 98. discrimination training; 99. discriminated behavior; 100. reinforced; 101. reinforcer; SD [or: discriminative stimulus]; 102. discrimination training; discriminative; SD; S-delta; 103. discrimination training; 104. differential reinforcement; 105. stimulus control; 106. stimulus control; 107. discriminated; 108. discrimination training;

differential reinforcement; 109. SD [or: discriminative stimulus or: prompt]; 110. discrimination training; 111. differential reinforcement; 112. discrimination training; 113. differential reinforcement; 114. yes; 115. discrimination training; 116. discrimination training; 117. discrimination training; 118. differential reinforcement; 119. discrimination training; 120. discrimination training; 121. SD; 122. discriminated; response; stimulus; 123. differential reinforcement; 124. stimulus control; 125. discrimination training; 126. discrimination training; 127. discriminative stimulus; SD; S-delta; 128. stimulus; 129. stimulus control; 130. discriminated behavior [or: discriminated]; discriminated response; 131. discrimination training; 132. differential reinforcement; 133. stimulus control; 134. stimulus; 135. stimuli; 136. discrimination training; 137. stimulus control; 138. SD; 139. SD; 140. control; 141. stimulus control; 142. discrimination; 143. discrimination; 144. ed; 145. stimulus control; 146. discrimination training; 147. discriminated; 148. stimulus; 149. SD [or: discriminative stimulus]; S-delta; 150. discrimination training; 151. training; 152. discrimination; 153. discrimination training; 154. discriminated; 155. discrimination; 156. SD [or: discriminative stimulus or: prompt]; 157. 1 [or: one]; 2 [or: two]; 158. control; discriminated; 159. stimulus; 160. discriminated; 161. discriminated; 162. reinforcer; SD [or: discriminative stimulus]; 163. discriminative; 164. stimulus

## Programmed Examples

1. discriminated; 2. stimulus control; 3. SD [or: discriminative stimulus]; S-delta; 4. two [or: 2]; 1 [or: one]; discrimination training; 5. 1 [or: one]; 2 [or: two]; differential reinforcement; 6. discrimination training; 7. stimulus control; 8. 2 [or: two]; 2 [or: two]; discrimination training; 9. SD [or: discriminative stimulus or: prompt]; S-delta; 10. 1 [or: one]; 2 [or: two]; discrimination training; 11. discrimination training; 12. differential reinforcement; 13. stimulus control; 14. discrimination training; 15. 1 [or: one]; 4 [or: four]; differential reinforcement; 16. SD [or: discriminative stimulus

or: prompt];    17. discrimination training;    18. 1 [or: one]; 2 [or: two]; differential reinforcement;    19. yes; no; discrimination training;    20. discrimination training

# Lesson 17

## Reading Section

1. generalization;    2. stimulus class; 3. generalization;    4. generalization; 5. related;    6. generalization; 7. generalization;    8. behavior [or: response];    9. generalization; 10. generalization;    11. generalization;    12. generalization; 13. generalization;    14. generalization; generalization training; 15. generalization; discrimination; 16. 2 [or: two]; 1 [or: one]

## Programmed Reading and Behavior Analysis Examples

1. generalization;    2. behavior [or: response];    3. generalization training; 4. stimulus class; generalization; 5. stimulus class;    6. class; 7. related; novel;    8. Prince; 9. related;    10. novel;    11. stimulus class;    12. generalization;    13. dogs; 14. dog; four [or: 4];    15. generalization training;    16. eliminates; 17. generalization training; 18. novel;    19. generalization training; 20. generalization;    21. generalization training;    22. generalization; 23. class;    24. novel;    25. novel stimulus;    26. novel; stimulus class; 27. generalizes;    28. behavioral definition;    29. generalization training;    30. draws;    31. stimulus class;    32. related;    33. discrimination training;    34. generalization training;    35. generalization; 36. stimulus class;    37. novel; 38. generalization training; 39. generalization training; 40. generalization;    41. generalization training; discrimination training; 42. discrimination training; 43. stimulus class;    44. novel; 45. generalization training;    46. generalization training;    47. series; generalizes; stimulus class; 48. series; generalizes; stimulus class; 49. generalization training; 50. generalization; generalization training;    51. generalization; 52. discrimination;    53. generalization;    54. generalized [or: generalizes]; 55. generalize;    56. reinforcement; 57. generalization training;    58. novel; 59. discrimination training;    60. generalization;    61. stimulus control; 62. generalization;    63. discrimination training;    64. hasn't;    65. related; 66. generalization;    67. procedure; process;    68. novel;    69. training; 70. generalization;    71. generalization training;    72. series; generalizes; stimulus class;    73. stimulus class; 74. generalizes; stimulus class; 75. series; generalizes; stimulus class; 76. series;    77. generalizes; 78. series;    79. generalizes; 80. stimulus;    81. generalization training;    82. discrimination training; generalization training; 83. generalized [or: generalizes]; 84. eliminates;    85. discrimination training; 86. generalization training; 87. generalization training; discrimination training; 88. extinguishing

## Programmed Examples

1. S-delta; SD [or: discriminative stimulus or: prompt]; stimulus control; 2. discriminated;    3. discrimination training; generalization training; 4. generalize; generalization training; 5. SD [or: discriminative stimulus or: prompt]; S-delta; discrimination training; generalization training; 6. stimulus class;    7. generalization; 8. generalization training;    9. discriminated;    10. discrimination training;    11. generalization; generalization training;    12. generalization;    13. differential reinforcement;    14. generalization training; 15. stimulus control;    16. discrimination training;    17. generalization; stimulus class; generalization training; 18. generalization [or: overgeneralization]; discrimination training; 19. discrimination training; 20. generalization; discrimination training; generalization training

# Lesson 18

## Reading Section and Behavior Analysis Examples

1. prompts;    2. stimulus;    3. fading;    4. prompt;    5. discriminated [or: prompted];    6. generalization; 7. discrimination;    8. I; my; the; 9. end;    10. ozeans;    11. response; feedback; steps;    12. 100 [or: 100%]; 13. prompt;    14. programmed; 15. programming;    16. programming; fading;    17. behavior; stimulus; 18. differential reinforcement

## Programmed Reading

1. prompt;    2. new;    3. prompt; 4. Control;    5. fading;    6. fading; 7. prompt;    8. prompt;    9. prompt; SD [or: discriminative stimulus]; 10. discrimination;    11. prompt; 12. discrimination;    13. discrimination; generalization;    14. programming;    15. fading;    16. prompt; 17. prompt;    18. prompt; 19. prompt;    20. fading, programming;    21. prompt;    22. fading; 23. programming;    24. fading; 25. fading;    26. response; feedback; steps;    27. generalization; discrimination;    28. generalization; 29. generalization;    30. discrimination;    31. prompts;    32. prompts; 33. programming; fading;    34. programmed instruction [or: programming];    35. programming; fading; 36. fading;    37. programming; 38. programming;    39. small; 40. step;    41. feedback; 42. response;    43. response; feedback; steps;    44. steps;    45. generalization;    46. generalization; discrimination;    47. generalization; 48. generalization; discrimination; 49. fading;    50. generalization; 51. fading, programming;    52. few; 53. programming;    54. behavior; stimulus;    55. programming; 56. prompt;    57. fading; 58. prompt;    59. generalization [or: generalizing];    60. discrimination; 61. programmed;    62. novel; 63. fading;    64. generalization; 65. fading;    66. programming; 67. generalization;    68. prompt; 69. prompts;    70. prompts; 71. prompts;    72. generalization training; prompts;    73. programming; fading;    74. instruction;    75. programming; fading;    76. fading; 77. behavior;    78. prompt; 79. programming;    80. stimulus

## Programmed Examples

1. generalization training; programming; 2. fading;    3. fading; discrimination training;    4. discrimination training; 5. programming [or: programmed instruction];    6. shaping;    7. fading; 8. programmed instruction [or: programming];    9. shaping; 10. discrimination training; fading; 11. fading;    12. programming; 13. generalization training; 14. dif-ferential reinforcement; 15. SD [or: discriminative stimulus or: prompt]; S-delta;    16. generalization; 17. generalization; programming; 18. prompt; fading;    19. fading; 20. generalization; prompt; programming

# Lesson 19

## *Reading Section and Behavior Analysis Examples*

1. imitation; 2. imitative; imitative; reinforces; 3. instructional; 4. 2 [or: two]; 2 [or: two]; 5. imitation; 6. discrimination training; 7. fading; 8. imitation; 9. demonstrate; 10. imitation; imitative; imitative; 11. instructional; instructed; 12. differential reinforcement; 13. imitation; 14. fading

## *Programmed Reading*

1. generalization training; 2. instructional; imitation; 3. reinforce; 4. instructed behavior; 5. reinforce; 6. instructed; 7. behavior; 8. extinction; 9. reinforcement; 10. verbal description; 11. imitative stimulus; 12. reinforcer; 13. instructional training; 14. imitation training; 15. verbal description; imitative stimulus; 16. imitative stimulus; 17. instructional; 18. imitative stimulus; imitative behavior; reinforces; 19. extinction; 20. imitative; 21. instructed; 22. describe; 23. reinforced; 24. discrimination; generalization; 25. imitative stimulus; 26. stimulus; behavior; 27. SD [or: discriminative stimulus or: prompt]; 28. SD [or: discriminative stimulus or: prompt]; 29. instructional; 30. verbal description; instructed behavior; reinforce; 31. behavior; 32. ion; 33. imitation; 34. verbal description; 35. instructed behavior; 36. reinforce; 37. reinforce; 38. imitation training; 39. imitative stimulus; 40. instructional; 41. imitative stimulus; 42. verbal description; instructed behavior; reinforce; 43. imitative stimulus; 44. verbal description; 45. imitative stimulus; 46. imitation, instructional; 47. imitation, instructional; 48. imitative stimulus; imitative behavior; reinforces; 49. imitation training; 50. instructed behavior; 51. imitative behavior; 52. instructional training; 53. imitation; 54. SD [or: discriminative stimulus or: prompt]; 55. discrimination training; 56. discrimination; 57. verbal; instructed; 58. description; 59. training; 60. instructional; 61. imitation, instructional; 62. imitation; instructional; 63. imitation; 64. training; 65. imitative; 66. behavior; 67. reinforce; 68. reinforces; 69. imitative stimulus, imitative behavior; 70. verbal description, instructed behavior;

71. imitation training; 72. imitative; 73. imitation training; 74. instructed behavior; 75. verbal description; 76. imitative behavior; 77. imitative behavior; 78. instructional; 79. imitation; 80. imitative stimulus; 81. stimulus; 82. imitative; 83. verbal; 84. imitation training; instructional training; 85. instructional; 86. instructional training; 87. imitation; 88. stimulus; behavior; 89. instructional training; 90. imitation, instructional; 91. prompts; instructional; 92. imitative stimulus; 93. imitative behavior; 94. reinforces; 95. verbal description; 96. instructed behavior; 97. imitative

## *Programmed Examples*

1. generalization; 2. SD [or: discriminative stimulus or: prompt]; S-delta; 3. imitative stimuli [or: imitative stimulus]; imitation training; 4. imitation training; imitative behavior; 5. discrimination training; 6. extinction; continuous [or: FR-1 or: reinforcement]; differential reinforcement; 7. imitation training; 8. instructional training; reinforcer [or: reinforcement]; verbal description; 9. imitation training; 10. verbal description; instructed behavior; reinforcer; instructional training; 11. discrimination training; 12. description; behavior; reinforcer [or: reinforcement]; described; 13. differential reinforcement; 14. fading; 15. instructional training; 16. generalization training; 17. imitative stimulus; imitative behavior; reinforcer; imitation training; 18. imitative; imitative; reinforcer [or: reinforcement]; demonstrated; 19. programming; 20. imitation training

# Lesson 20

## *Reading Section*

1. conditioned; 2. primary; 3. unpaired; 4. backup; 5. many; 6. conditioned; 7. generalized; 8. chain; 9. no; 10. generalized; 11. generalized; 12. no; 13. no; generalized; 14. conditioned; generalized; 15. conditioned; backup

## *Programmed Reading*

1. conditioned; 2. backup; 3. many; 4. many; 5. satiation; 6. all; 7. conditioned; 8. backup; 9. generalized; 10. generalized; generalization; 11. chain [or: stimulus/response chain]; 12. SD

[or: discriminative stimulus]; reinforcement; 13. after; 14. generalized; 15. unpaired; 16. backup; 17. response; 18. stimulus; 19. chain [or: stimulus/response chain]; 20. immediacy; 21. money; 22. satiation; unpaired; generalized reinforcers [or: generalized]; 23. primary; 24. token [or: point or: token economy]; 25. generalized [or: generalized reinforcer]; 26. backup; 27. immediacy; 28. conditioned [or: generalized]; 29. generalized; 30. backup; 31. SD [or: discriminative stimulus or: prompt]; 32. conditioned; 33. immediately; 34. many; 35. conditioned; 36. satiated; 37. backup; 38. backup; 39. 1 [or: one]; 40. sequence; 41. satiated; 42. stimulus; response; 43. no; 44. conditioned; 45. primary; 46. deprived; 47. satiated; 48. unpaired; 49. many; 50. satiation; 51. backup; 52. primary; 53. backup; 54. chain [or: stimulus/response chain]; 55. SD [or: discriminative stimulus]; reinforcement; 56. backup; 57. conditioned; 58. conditioned; 59. chain [or: stimulus/response chain]; 60. primary; 61. generalized; 62. conditioned; backup; 63. primary; 64. primary; 65. deprived; 66. conditioned; 67. conditioned; 68. sequence; 69. generalized; 70. conditioned; generalized; backup; 71. SD [or: discriminative stimulus or: prompt]; 72. conditioned; generalized; backup; 73. unpaired; 74. primary; 75. backup reinforcers [or: backup]; 76. backup; 77. generalized; 78. sequence; SD [or: discriminative stimulus]; reinforcement; 79. chain [or: stimulus/response chain]; 80. stimulus/response chain; 81. B; 82. generalized; 83. conditioned; 84. sequence; 85. SD [or: discriminative stimulus]; 86. SD [or: discriminative stimulus]; 87. reinforcement; 88. primary; 89. unpaired; 90. chain; 91. conditioned; 92. conditioned; 93. SD [or: discriminative stimulus]; 94. sequence; 95. reinforcement; 96. does; 97. conditioned; 98. instructional; conditioned; 99. SD [or: discriminative stimulus or: prompt]; 100. primary; 101. can't; 102. backup; 103. conditioned; 104. chain; 105. immediacy; 106. chain

## *Programmed Examples*

1. SD [or: discriminative stimulus or: prompt]; 2. generalized; backup; deprivation; paired; 3. satiated; conditioned; generalized; 4. fading;

5. discrimination training;    6. generalization;    7. chain [or: stimulus/response chain];    8. backup; conditioned;    9. yes; SD [or: discriminative stimulus or: prompt]; reinforcer; chain [or: stimulus/response chain];    10. generalized;    11. conditioned;    12. conditioned; backup; 13. generalization;    14. satiated; primary;    15. generalized; backup; 16. conditioned; backup; immediacy; 17. primary;    18. conditioned; backup; satiated;    19. generalized; backup; deprived; immediacy; 20. backup; unpaired; conditioned

# Lesson 21

## *Reading Section*

1. extinguishing;    2. discriminated; 3. S-delta;    4. stimulus control

## *Practice Review I*

1. yes; no; no; no;    2. satiation; 3. backup;    4. stimulus class; 5. S-delta;    6. SD [or: discriminative stimulus or: prompt];    7. prompt; 8. variable-ratio;    9. discrimination training;    10. programming; 11. stimulus [or: prompt or: SD]; behavior [or: response];    12. 80 [or: 80%]; yes;    13. generalization; 14. backup;    15. discriminated; 16. ratio strain;    17. generalization; 18. comparison;    19. increases; 20. stimulus control;    21. imitation; 22. no; yes; no; no;    23. generalization;    24. chain [or: stimulus/response chain];    25. programming; 26. deprived;    27. generalization; 28. instructional training;    29. yes; no; no; no;    30. stimulus control; 32. imitation;    33. discrimination training;    35. variable-ratio, variable-interval;    36. imitative; 37. instructional; imitation; 38. generalized;    39. discrimination training;    40. generalization training; 41. prompts;    42. imitation, instructional;    43. variable-ratio, variable-interval;    44. stimulus control;    45. differential reinforcement;    46. chain [or: stimulus/response chain];    47. discrimination training; differential reinforcement

## *Practice Review II*

1. many;    2. after; before;    3. deprivation;    4. discriminated;    5. fading; 6. fixed-ratio [or: FR-100];    7. variable-ratio;    8. SD [or: discriminative stimulus or: prompt];    9. generalization training;    10. discrimination; generalization; prompts; instructional; conditioned;    11. conditioned; 12. shaping;    13. imitation, instructional;    14. imitative;    15. conditioned;    16. prompt

# Lesson 22

## *Reading Section and Behavior Analysis Examples*

1. reinforcement;    2. punishment; 3. follows; decreases;    4. punishment; 5. conditioned [or: generalized]; 6. punisher;    7. primary; 8. unpaired;    9. generalized; 10. SP;    11. punisher;    12. punishment;    13. punishment; SP; 14. differential reinforcement; 15. punishment;    16. punisher; 17. punishment; punisher; 18. unknown;    19. reinforcer

## *Programmed Reading*

1. stimulus;    2. unpaired;    3. aversive;    4. many;    5. satiation [or: adaptation];    6. follows; decreases [or: reduces];    7. discriminative; SP; 8. SP; punisher;    9. discriminative stimulus for punishment [or: SP]; 10. conditioned [or: generalized]; 11. punisher;    12. undesirable; 13. punisher;    14. reinforcers; 15. punishers;    16. discriminative; 17. punisher;    18. punishment; 19. punishment;    20. discriminative stimulus [or: SP];    21. punishment; 22. conditioned;    23. punishment; punisher;    24. instructional; 25. discriminative; SP;    26. generalized;    27. punishment;    28. unknown;    29. reinforcement; 30. punishment;    31. discrimination training;    32. differential reinforcement;    33. conditioned;    34. punishment;    35. unpaired;    36. many; 37. satiation [or: adaptation]; 38. follows; decreases [or: reduces]; 39. SP [or: discriminative stimulus for punishment]; punisher;    40. discriminative; SP;    41. punishment; 42. instructional;    43. punisher; 44. unknown;    45. unknown; 46. no;    47. unknown; 48. unknown;    49. extinction; 50. punishment;    51. punishment; 52. Aversive;    53. Aversive; 54. Aversive;    55. aversive; 56. primary, conditioned, generalized; 57. punishment;    58. punishment, extinction;    59. generalization; 60. contingency, immediacy, size, deprivation;    61. follow;    62. decrease [or: reduction];    63. contingency, immediacy, size, deprivation;    64. punisher;    65. deprivation;    66. extinction;    67. punishment;    68. no; 69. no;    70. reinforcement; 71. punishment [or: aversive control]; 72. most;    73. primary;    74. can't; 75. punishment;    76. punisher; 77. decreases;    78. unknown; 79. decreased [or: decreases]; 80. extinction;    81. punishment; 82. extinction;    83. unknown; 84. unknown;    85. unknown; 86. punishment;    87. punishment; 88. punishment;    89. decreases; 90. Aversive;    91. punisher; 92. worthwhile;    93. decreases; 94. decreases;    95. aversive; 96. aversive;    97. aversive; 98. primary, conditioned, generalized; 99. primary, conditioned, generalized; 100. immediately [or: right]; immediacy; 101. only; contingency;    102. rarely; deprivation;    103. punishment, extinction;    104. SIB;    105. extinction;    106. punishment; 107. Aversive;    108. contingency, immediacy, size, deprivation; 109. punishment;    110. instructional; 111. punisher

## *Programmed Examples*

1. conditioned;    2. extinction; 3. punisher; punishment;    4. immediacy;    5. differential reinforcement; 6. punisher; SP;    7. no; no; punishment;    8. punishment; reinforcement [or: positive reinforcement];    9. extinction;    10. no; no; punisher;    11. yes; no; punisher; SP [or: discriminative stimulus]; 12. conditioned;    13. unknown; 14. extinction;    15. punishment; 16. punisher; conditioned; 17. discrimination training; 18. reinforcement;    19. punishment;    20. no; no; punishment

# Lesson 23

## *Reading Section and Behavior Analysis Examples*

1. follows; decrease;    2. not making; 3. punisher;    4. punisher; 5. punishment;    6. extinction; 7. caused;    8. cause;    9. punishment;    10. unknown

## *Programmed Reading*

1. follows; decreases [or: reduces]; 2. time out;    3. punishment; 4. extinction;    5. punishment;

6. time out;    7. punishment; time out;
8. time out;    9. punishment;
10. didn't;    11. conditioned;
12. punishment;    13. don't;
14. punisher;    15. time out;
16. punishment;    17. punishment;
18. punishment;    19. time out;
20. unknown;    21. reinforcement;
22. unknown;    23. unknown;
24. unknown;    25. punishment;
26. unknown;    27. extinction;
28. extinction;    29. temporary;
30. punishment;    31. unknown;
32. punishment;    33. punishment;
34. punishment;    35. time out;
36. time out;    37. punisher; SP;
38. unknown;    39. extinction;
40. unknown;    41. extinction;
42. punishment;    43. punishment;
44. extinction;    45. unknown;
46. unknown;    47. decrease;
48. time out;    49. punishment;
50. unknown;    51. punisher;
punishment;    52. punishment;
53. punishment;    54. punishment;
55. punishment;    56. withdrawal;
57. decrease;    58. withdrawal;
59. unknown;    60. punishment;
61. punishment;    62. extinction;
63. punisher; punishment;
64. unknown;    65. punishment;
66. punishment;    67. unknown;
68. punisher;    69. time out;
70. unknown;    71. punishment;
72. unknown;    73. is;    74. time out;
75. punishment;    76. punishment;
77. extinction;    78. permanent;
79. punishment;    80. unknown;
81. punishment;    82. punishment;
83. out;    84. aren't;    85. reinforcer;
86. primary; conditioned;    87. punishment;    88. withdrawal

### *Programmed Examples*
1. extinction;    2. punishment;
3. no; punishment;    4. extinction;
5. unknown;    6. no; punishment;
7. unknown;    8. punishment;
9. generalization training;    10. punishment;    11. yes; extinction;
12. punishment;    13. extinction;
14. punishment;    15. extinction;
16. punisher;    17. unknown;
18. extinction;    19. punishment
[or: time out];    20. punishment

## Lesson 24

### *Reading Section and Behavior Analysis Examples*
1. negative;    2. prevented; increase;
3. prevents;    4. negative;    5. nega-

tive;    6. reinforcement;    7. positive; 8. reinforcer;    9. avoidance;
10. escape;    11. avoidance; escape;
12. reinforcer;    13. reinforcement
[or: negative reinforcement];    14. reinforcement [or: negative reinforcement];
15. punishment;    16. reinforcement
[or: negative reinforcement];
17. unknown;    18. reinforcement
[or: negative reinforcement]

### *Programmed Reading*
1. terminates;    2. size;    3. Deprivation;    4. contingency;    5. terminated [or: terminate], prevented
[or: prevent];    6. terminates, prevents;
7. decrease [or: reduction]; increase;
8. extinction;    9. negative;
10. prevents;    11. reinforcement;
12. negative reinforcement [or:
reinforcement];    13. prevention;
termination;    14. increase;
15. terminates; escape;    16. prevents;
avoidance;    17. no;    18. escape;
19. escape;    20. avoidance; escape;
21. avoidance;    22. reinforcer [or:
negative reinforcer];    23. avoidance;
24. avoidance;    25. terminates;
26. terminates;    27. don't;
28. reinforcer; reinforcement;
29. unknown;    30. escape;
31. negative reinforcer [or: reinforcer];
32. avoidance;    33. intermittent
[or: variable-ratio];    34. negative;
35. shaping;    36. reinforcer [or:
negative reinforcer];    37. unknown;
38. differential reinforcement [or:
negative reinforcement];    39. reinforcement [or: negative reinforcement];
punishment;    40. negative reinforcer
[or: reinforcer];    41. reinforcer;
42. negative reinforcement [or:
reinforcement];    43. punishment;
44. escape;    45. reinforcement [or:
negative reinforcement];    46. can't;
47. b [or: (b.)];    48. prevents;
49. negative;    50. reinforcement
[or: differential reinforcement];
51. escape;    52. avoidance;
53. increase;    54. terminates,
prevents;    55. decrease [or:
reduction]; increase;    56. prevents;
57. reinforcer; reinforcement;
58. escape;    59. avoidance;
60. reinforcement [or: negative
reinforcement];    61. terminates;
62. reinforcement [or: negative
reinforcement];    63. reinforcement
[or: negative reinforcement];
64. escape;    65. intermittent [or:
variable-ratio];    66. fixed-ratio [or:
FR-5];    67. extinction;    68. avoidance; escape;    69. punishment;
70. negative;    71. reinforcer
[or: negative reinforcer];    72. reinforcement [or: negative reinforcement];
73. immediately;    74. discrimination

training;    75. punishment; negative
reinforcement;    76. extinction;
77. reinforcement [or: negative
reinforcement];    78. differential
reinforcement [or: negative reinforcement];    79. avoidance; escape;
80. negative reinforcement [or:
reinforcement];    81. reinforcement
[or: negative reinforcement];
82. negative reinforcer [or: reinforcer];
83. reinforcement [or: negative
reinforcement];    84. negative
reinforcer [or: reinforcer];    85. negative reinforcer [or: reinforcer];
86. punishment;    87. negative reinforcement;    88. negative reinforcement;    89. negative reinforcement;
90. negative;    91. reinforcement [or:
negative reinforcement];    92. no;
93. avoidance;    94. immediately;
95. discrimination training;    96. terminates, prevents;    97. escape;
98. negative reinforcement;
99. variable-ratio;    100. reinforcement;    101. increase;    102. escape;
103. extinction;    104. escape;
avoidance;    105. avoidance; escape;
106. avoidance

### *Programmed Examples*
1. avoidance;    2. prevent; negative
reinforcement [or: reinforcement];
avoidance;    3. terminate; increased
[or: increase]; negative reinforcer
[or: reinforcer]; escape;    4. prevented;
increased; negative reinforcer [or:
reinforcer];    5. negative reinforcement [or: reinforcement];    6. negative
reinforcement [or: reinforcement];
7. prevent; avoidance; negative
reinforcement [or: reinforcement];
8. immediately;    9. prevented;
increased; reinforcement [or: negative
reinforcement];    10. immediacy;
11. punishment;    12. avoidance;
13. unknown;    14. escape;
15. prevent; stayed same; unknown;
16. punishment;    17. negative
reinforcement [or: reinforcement];
18. punishment;    19. avoidance;
20. terminated; increased; reinforcer
[or: negative reinforcer]

## Lesson 25

### *Reading Section*
1. aversive

### *Practice Review I*
1. unpaired;    2. novel;    3. follows;
increase;    4. satiation;    5. shaping;
6. follows; decreases [or: reduces];
7. intermittent;    8. deprivation;

9. SD [or: discriminative stimulus or: prompt]; 10. S-delta; 11. SD [or: discriminative stimulus or: prompt]; reinforcer; 12. discriminative stimulus for punishment [or: SP]; 13. SD [or: discriminative stimulus or: prompt]; 14. terminates [or: terminated]; 15. multiple baseline; 16. direct; 17. extinction; 18. avoidance; 19. generalized; 20. intermittent; 21. negative reinforcer; 22. environmental [or: external or: public]; change [or: modify]; 23. generalization; 24. multiple baseline; 25. behavioral definition; 26. social validity; 27. no; yes; no; no; 28. yes; no; no; no; 29. Deprivation; 30. reinforcement, extinction; 31. reinforced; extinguished; 32. comparison; 33. instance; 34. decrease [or: reduction]; 35. discrimination; 36. outcome, event, interval, time sample [or: time-sample]; 37. extinction; 38. no; 39. social validity; 40. generalizes; 41. variable-ratio; 42. punishment; 43. SD [or: discriminative stimulus or: prompt]; 44. discriminated; 45. variable-ratio; 46. generalization; 47. variable-interval; 48. fixed-interval; 49. fixed-ratio; 50. continuous; 51. avoidance; 52. discriminative stimulus for punishment [or: SP]; 53. imitation; 54. reinforcer; 55. discrimination training; 56. deprived; 57. extinction; 58. stimulus control; 59. discriminated; 60. imitative; 61. punishment; extinction;

62. punishment; 63. verbal; 64. continuous; 65. event; 66. immediacy; 67. self-report [or: self report]; 68. imitation; 69. time sample [or: time-sample]; 70. fixed-ratio [or: FR-10]; 71. interval; 72. reversal; 73. Contingency, immediacy, Size, Deprivation; 74. outcome; 75. result; 76. reinforced; 78. punishment; 79. yes [or: no]; 80. yes [or: no]; 81. differential reinforcement; 82. no; yes; no; no; 83. instructional; 84. discrimination training; 85. generalized; 87. avoidance; 88. generalization; 89. time sample [or: time-sample]; 90. generalization training; 91. discrimination training; 92. differential reinforcement; 93. agreement; 94. isn't; 95. differential reinforcement; approximations; 96. behavioral definition; 97. generalize; 98. punishment; 99. negative; 100. reliability; 101. generalized; 102. treatment; 103. stimulus class; 104. reversal; 105. shaping; 106. S-delta; 107. target behavior; 108. less; 109. interval; 110. immediacy; 111. baseline; 112. Deprivation; 113. reinforcement; 114. comparison; 115. aversive; 116. alternative; 117. discontinuous; 118. only; 119. rarely; 120. minute; 121. outcome; 122. approximation [or: successive approximation]; 123. target behavior; 124. rein-

forcement; 125. reversal, ; 126. Size; 127. baseline; 128. unknown; 129. reinforcement; reinforcer

## *Practice Review II*

1. many; 2. event; 3. prevented; increase; 4. fading; 5. conditioned; 6. chain [or: stimulus/response chain]; 7. related; 8. prompt; 9. extinction; 10. reinforced; extinguished; 11. conditioned; 12. primary; 13. punishment; 14. fixed-interval [or: FI-5]; 15. successive approximation [or: approximation]; 16. terminated [or: terminate]; 17. immediacy; 18. punishment; 19. immediately; 20. reinforced; 21. stimulus class; 22. punisher; 23. fading; 24. time sample [or: time-sample]; 25. ratio strain; 26. no; 27. 80 [or: 80%]; no; 28. negative reinforcement [or: avoidance or: reinforcement]; 29. conditioned; backup; 30. Contingency; 31. 80 [or: 80%]; yes; 32. chain [or: stimulus/ response chain]; 33. immediately; 34. backup; 35. differential reinforcement; discrimination training; 36. decreasing [or: reducing or: decrease]; 37. interval; ratio; 38. Contingency; 39. Size; 40. instructional training; 41. 80 [or: 80%]; 42. programming; 43. programming; 44. continuous; 45. fixed-ratio, fixed-interval; 46. variable-interval, variable-ratio

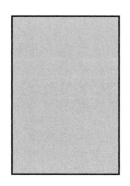

# Class Quizzes

1. Dr. Schmidt consulted with Jimmy. Jimmy wanted to get over being shy. Dr. Schmidt told Jimmy to look other people in the eye, talk loudly, and smile. When Jimmy did so, Dr. Schmidt praised him. Dr. Schmidt was helping Jimmy by using the behavioral science of _____.

2. The person who founded behavior analysis is _____.

3. The science that studies environmental events that change behavior is called _____.

4. Dr. Schmidt consulted with Jimmy. Jimmy wanted to get over being shy. Dr. Schmidt told Jimmy that no one had ever taught him to be direct with other people. Dr. Schmidt explained Jimmy's shyness by using the principle of _____ events.

5. The problem with explaining behavior with private events is that we still must _____ the private events.

6. The first strategy taught in this book is to define your problem as a behavioral problem and to gather information about it. I call this the _____ strategy.

7. Behavior analysts see most behavior as _____ behavior.

8. The principle of public events is to look for the causes of behavior in _____ events.

9. Dr. Schmidt consulted with Jimmy about his shyness. Dr. Schmidt told Jimmy that his shyness was the result of no one teaching him to look others in the eye, talk loud enough, and smile. By defining Jimmy's problem this way, Dr. Schmidt was using the _____ strategy.

10. Applied behavior analysis began widespread publication in _____.

11. Short-answer question A. Define *behavior analysis*:

_____

_____

_____

_____

_____

_____

1. Behavior analysis is the science that studies _____ events that _____ behavior.

2. Behavior analysts study thoughts and feelings as a form of _____.

3. Ken helped Maria overcome her depression. He advised her to view it as staying home and not doing anything. By defining her problem as lack of activity, he was using the _____ strategy.

4. Ken helped Maria overcome her depression by setting up fun things for her to get out and do. He hoped to change her pattern of staying home and not doing anything. Ken helped Maria by using the science of _____.

5. The problem with explaining behavior with private events is that we still must _____ the private events.

6. The behavioral strategy is defining human problems as a _____ problem.

7. Behavior analysts view most behavior as _____ behavior.

8. The principle of public events is to look for the causes of behavior in _____ _____ events.

9. Ken helped Maria understand that her depression was caused by not connecting up with any fun activities away from home. By pointing to the lack of fun activities as the cause of her depression, Ken was using the principle of _____ events.

10. Applied behavior analysis began widespread publication about the year _____.

11. Short-answer question B. Define the *behavioral strategy*:

_____

_____

_____

_____

_____

_____

1. Dr. Fernandez told Anna her problem was that she didn't have an immediate reward for studying. He explained that she wasn't studying because the test was too far off in the future to affect her studying. He was explaining her lack of studying by using the principle of _____ events.

2. Applied behavior analysis exploded on the American scientific scene about _____.

3. Behavior analysis is the science that studies _____ events that _____ behavior.

4. The first strategy for changing behavior is defining problems in behavioral terms. I call this the _____ _____ strategy.

5. Dr. Fernandez told Anna her problem was that she needed some immediate rewards for studying. He got Mr. Held to ask about Anna's studying every evening and to show interest in what she was learning. Dr. Fernandez tried to change Anna's studying by using the science of _____.

6. Seeking the causes of behavior in environmental events conforms to the principle of _____ events.

7. Behavior analysts view most behavior as _____ behavior.

8. Dr. Fernandez told Anna her problem was that she wasn't sitting down and actually studying. Her problem wasn't that she was weak-willed or lazy. By defining her problem as studying, Dr. Fernandez was using the _____ strategy.

9. The problem with private events is that we still must _____ them.

10. Behavior analysis studies thoughts and feelings as a form of _____.

11. Short-answer question C. What is the problem with using private events to explain behavior?

_____

_____

_____

_____

_____

_____

1. Behavior is anything that a person _____.

2. Tom wrote down anytime that Carol made a friendly comment to him as soon as she made it. What approach to observing Carol's friendliness did Tom use? _____ observation

3. Barb defined "studying" the social code as being able to answer the ten questions listed at the end of it. She asked Ann if she could answer those questions. Ann said "yes." Using her answer of "yes" to observe studying the social codes is the approach called _____ observation.

4. To develop a sound behavioral definition, the behavior analyst must clearly describe what behavior he or she will _____.

5. The problem with using private events to explain other behavior is that they must still be _____.

6. Using a behavioral definition makes communication _____ and maintains consistency of _____.

7. When an observer writes down an observation as soon as they see it, we call it _____ observation. When they write it down from memory, we call it _____ observation.

8. Describing joy as "laughing, singing, and dancing" would be called a(n) _____.

9. Maria developed a list to help decide whether Juan was doing his share of household chores. The list included washing dishes, taking out garbage, and shopping for food. Behavior analysts call Maria's list a(n) _____.

10. Barb could multiply any two numbers between 1 and 20 in her head. Behavior analysts view Barb's activity as a form of _____.

11. Short-answer question A. Explain how behavior analysts view thinking. How might thinking be similar to silent reading?

_____

_____

_____

_____

1. The observers in the Goetz and Baer study did not watch children building novel block structures. Because they recorded any resulting block structure as soon as they saw it, this was an example of the approach to observation called _____ observation.

2. Behavior analysts view everything that a person does as _____.

3. John defined *understanding* a word as meaning that the person correctly defined the word on the English test. John asked Mary if she correctly defined the term *reify* on last Friday's test. Mary said "yes." John used what approach to observing her behavior? _____ observations

4. Behavior analysts create a successful behavioral definition by describing exactly what behavior they will _____.

5. The problem with self-reports is that when you ask people to report on their own behavior from memory the results are usually _____.

6. Dr. Parlato studied factors that interfered with John's digestion. Because digestion is something that John does, Dr. Parlato is studying a form of _____ _____.

7. The principle of direct observation requires a trained observer who used _____ of behavior.

8. Dr. Quail tried to explain poor learning by students in terms of a poor attitude. Because the poor attitude must itself be explained, Dr. Quail's explanation shows the problem with _____ events.

9. Professor Rose measured Shelley's studying as "the number of problems she completed and handed in on her calculus homework." The phrase in quotes is a(n) _____ _____.

10. The principle of public events is to seek the causes of behavior in _____ events.

11. Short-answer question B. Give two benefits for creating specific behavioral definitions:

_____

_____

_____

_____

_____

1. Ahles and colleagues (1990) defined pain behavior as patients "guarding, bracing, rubbing, expressing and grimacing." Behavior analysts call the statement in quotes a(n) _____ _____.

2. Dan wrote down each time that Fred did not answer their phone. Dan used the approach of _____ observation.

3. Joan decided that she meant by sensitivity the following: "Chad encouraged her to talk about her feelings." Joan was treating sensitivity as a form of _____.

4. A statement that pinpoints what behavior to observe is called a(n) _____.

5. The problem with using private events to explain other behavior is that they must still be _____.

6. An observer who immediately records any observation that he personally <u>sees</u> (or hears) is using the principle of _____.

7. John asked Mrs. Miller how much trash her family had generated last week. John's approach is called _____ _____ observation.

8. Dr. Casey found that sixth graders studied more if they signed a contract with their teacher. The contract said that they could go to an early recess as soon as they learned their spelling words for the day. Because the contract is part of the students' environment, Dr. Casey was using the principle of _____ _____events.

9. Tom studied whether Marge initiated conversations with men. He meant by the term *initiated conversations* whether she "approached a man and was the first to speak." The phrase in quotes is called a(n) _____.

10. As long as an action is something that a person does and it is physical and produces a result, behavior analysts call the action _____.

11. Short-answer question C. Give one reason why behavior analysts usually rely on direct observation, rather than observations that involve memory, such as those evoked by questionnaires or interviews:

_____
_____
_____
_____
_____

1. The principle of public events is to look for the causes of behavior in _____ events.

2. Counting the occurrence of instances of a behavior is called _____ recording; observing a behavior for a brief time several times a day is called _____ recording.

3. When John counted the number of times during the lecture that his English professor split his infinitives, he was using what method of direct observation? _____ recording.

4. What two methods involve dividing the period of observation into smaller units of time?_____ and _____ recording

5. The checklist covering the results of cleaning behavior used by Feallock and Miller (1976) would be an example of what method of observation? _____ recording

6. A racing heart, racing feet, racing thoughts, and racing words are all activities that people do. Therefore they are all called _____ by behavior analysts.

7. The method of observation that involves the results of behavior rather than the behavior itself is called _____ _____ recording.

8. To discover the level of violence of a TV show, you might note how many 15-second intervals contain some form of violence. You would be using what method of observation? _____ _____ recording.

9. David Lombard observed whether swimmers wore a shirt, got in the shade, wore a hat, sunglasses, zinc oxide, and sun screen lotion. What method of observation did he use?_____ recording.

10. Maria checked on her son 10 times an evening, at randomly selected times, to see whether he was studying. What method of observation was she using? _____ recording

11. Short-answer question A. What questions can you ask to decide the method of observation that is being used?

_____

_____

_____

_____

1. Heddy watched Family A for 15 seconds to see if they dropped litter; she then turned to Family B and watched them for 15 seconds; she also watched Families C and D each for 15 seconds. Every minute she would return to Family A and start the routine over again. To observe Family A, she was using what method of observation? _____ recording

2. Event recording is based on counting _____ of the behavior.

3. When the Bakers checked their son's room each day to see whether it had been cleaned, they were using what method of direct observation? _____ _____ recording

4. Behavior analysis studies _____ _____ events that _____ behavior.

5. The observation of whether or not a behavior occurs during a series of continuous intervals is called _____ recording.

6. If you immediately note the number of times that you say something positive to another person during the day, you are using what method of observation? _____ recording

7. The observation of behavior during a series of discontinuous intervals is called _____ recording.

8. If a mother wanted to find out how much of the class period her child spent studying in math class, she might go to the school and observe whether her child was studying during each 20-second period during the math class. She would be using what method of observation? _____ recording

9. Walker and Buckley (1968) analyzed the study behavior of a fourth grader by writing down anytime he was "looking at the assigned page, working problems, and recording responses." This statement would be called a behavioral definition because it describes what to _____.

10. One of the behavior analysts observed John's study behavior in spelling. He noted when John was studying during a 15-second interval every 5 minutes. The behavior analyst had other chores during the rest of the 5 minutes when he was not observing John. What method of observation was the behavior analyst using? _____ recording

11. Short-answer question B. Define *time sample*. Explain how it differs from *interval recording*:

_____

_____

_____

_____

1. The method that involves observation of behavior during continuous periods of time is called _____ _____ recording.

2. When a teacher gives a written test, he or she is using the method of observation called _____ recording.

3. The problem with using private events to explain behavior is that they must still be _____.

4. Outcome recording, event recording, and interval recording all involve trained observers writing down their observations as they make them. Therefore, they follow the principle of _____ _____.

5. When Dee observed the number of times any child struck another child at the alternative school, she was using what method of observation? _____ _____ recording

6. Outcome recording is based on observing a(n) _____ of behavior, rather than the behavior itself.

7. Lindsley (1968) recommended the use of a simple wrist counter so that people could count the number of cigarettes they smoked, the number of smiles, and so on. These would be examples of _____ recording.

8. Willie observed his political science professor during 30-second intervals over a whole 50 minute period. He noted each 30-second interval during which his professor talked to the pretty blonde. He was using what technique of direct observation? _____ _____ recording

9. Time sample recording involves the observation of behavior during a series of brief intervals that are _____ with one another.

10. Being a bit of a gossip, you want to know what percentage of the time John has his girl friend in his room. To find out, you briefly check once every hour to see whether she is there. You study the rest of the time. You are using what method of observation? _____ _____ recording

11. Short-answer question C. Both outcome recording and event recording observe uniform behavior. Explain the major difference between them:

_____

_____

_____

_____

_____

_____.

| Reliability of Ping-Pong observations | | | | | |
|---|---|---|---|---|---|
| Interval | 1 | 2 | 3 | 4 | 5 |
| Delores | 0 | 0 | 0 | x | 0 |
| Richard | 0 | 0 | 0 | x | 0 |

**Figure 4-7.** Delores and Richard's argument on Ping-Pong observations.

| Reliability: Thumb sucking observations | | | | | |
|---|---|---|---|---|---|
| Interval | 1 | 2 | 3 | 4 | 5 |
| Dr. Baer | Y | N | Y | N | N |
| Robert | Y | N | N | N | N |

**Figure 4-8.** The agreement of Robert's and Dr. Baer's observations of Annie's thumb sucking.

1. Figure 4-7 shows how many of five scheduled observation intervals Delores and Richard found the Ping-Pong table being used. What is their reliability? _____% Is it acceptable? _____ (yes, no)

2. When the doctor weighs Morgan as a measure of eating behavior, he uses what method of observation? _____ _____ recording

3. If two observers agree on their observations, you cannot conclude that their observations are reliable unless they were made on the same _____ _____.

4. Most of us tend to look for the causes of behavior in people's thoughts. The problem with such private events is that we must still _____ them.

5. Dom observed the stories on the evening news one day. He found that 9 of the news items were biased. Jan also watched the evening news on the same day and found that 10 were biased. She decided that Dom's observations were reliable. Do you agree with her conclusion?_____ (yes, no)

6. Marge defined good teaching behavior as having personal contact with students. She observed that Tom had few personal contacts with his students. She suggested that he start having more personal contact with his pupils. She again observed and found that he had many personal contacts with them. Marge then had 10 parents view a videotape of Tom's teaching. They rated Tom's quality of teaching as low when they observed few personal contacts and high when he started having many personal contacts. In other words, the parents' ratings correlated with Marge's observations based on her behavioral definition. This correlation showed that Marge's behavioral definition of good teaching had _____ _____.

7. Figure 4-8 shows Dr. Baer's and Robert's observations of Annie's thumb sucking for five consecutive 20-second intervals. What is their reliability? _____% Is it acceptable? _____ (yes, no)

8. Barb inspected the cleaning jobs according to a 10-item checklist at 8:00 Thursday night. She found that 9 items had been done. Vince inspected the same cleaning jobs according to the same checklist at 8:00 Friday night and found only 3 of them done. Is this evidence that their observations are unreliable? _____ (yes, no)

9. The general formula for calculating reliability is _____.

10. Williams and colleagues developed a behavioral definition of non-cooperation. Two of their observers agreed 83% during simultaneous observations. Is this level acceptable? _____ (yes, no)

11. Short-answer question A. Suppose you define pain behavior as holding the pained area, moaning, and complaining of pain. Suppose observers using this behavioral definition find Mark not

engaging in those behaviors during videotape A. Suppose they find him engaging in those behaviors during videotape B. How would you use five nurses to test the social validity of your behavioral definition?

_____

_____

_____

_____

_____

_____

| Tom | O | T | O | T | T | O | T | O | T | O |
|-----|---|---|---|---|---|---|---|---|---|---|
| Pam | O | T | T | T | T | O | T | O | T | T |

**Figure 4-20.** Observations by Tom and Pam.

| Alice | H | N | H | N | H | H | N | N | N | H |
|-------|---|---|---|---|---|---|---|---|---|---|
| Janet | H | N | H | N | H | H | H | H | H | H |

**Figure 4-21.** Observations by Alice and Janet.

1. Dan counted the number of consecutive 15-second intervals during which his baby sister was smiling. He was using _____ recording.

2. The formula for reliability is: _____ _____.

3. Figure 4-20 shows the first 10 observations when Tom and Pam observed the chairperson of the ecology committee during 10-second intervals to see if he was dominating the meetings (with "T" indicating talking and "O" indicating others talking). What is their reliability? _____% Does the evidence indicate that the observations are reliable? _____ (yes, no)

4. Reliability is a measure of the extent to which there is _____ between two independent observers.

5. Kim and Jose counted shooting stars one night. Kim saw 17, and Jose saw 20. Compute their reliability: _____%; is it acceptable? _____ (yes, no)

6. Tamara observed that Boris watched the news during 59 out of 60 half-minute intervals on Monday. Ann observed that Boris only watched the news during 23 out of the 60 half-minute intervals on Tuesday. Can you conclude that Tamara and Ann's observations are unreliable? _____ (yes, no)

7. Figure 4-21 shows the resulting observations when Alice and Janet watched 10 commercials shown on late-night TV to determine how many of them were advertising products that were ecologically harmful. They developed their own behavioral definition. Their results were (where "H" stands for harmful commercials). Compute their reliability: _____%; would this be acceptable? _____ (yes, no)

8. Suppose you observe three of Willie's behaviors that you think are related to how good he is at having a conversation. Suppose you also have three adults watching the same conversations rate how good he was in the conversation. The correlation between your observations and their ratings gives you a measure of the _____ of your behavioral definition.

9. Eileen checked to see whether her lazy roommate was studying during a short observation made at 19 random times during the day. What method of observation was she using? _____ recording

10. Behavior analysts consider everything that a person does to be _____ _____.

11. Short-answer question B. Explain in words the formula to compute the reliability of two observers using interval recording:

_____
_____
_____
_____
_____
_____

Grade _____

Name _____     Date _____

| Dave | X | X | O | X | O | O | O | O | X | X |
|------|---|---|---|---|---|---|---|---|---|---|
| Pat  | X | X | X | X | O | X | O | O | X | X |

**Figure 4-30.** Observations by Dave and Pat.

| Barb | N | S | S | N | S | N | N | N | N | N |
|------|---|---|---|---|---|---|---|---|---|---|
| Gary | S | S | S | N | N | N | N | N | N | N |

**Figure 4-31.** Observations by Barb and Gary.

1. When we ask people what TV programs they watch, they name educational programs more often than they actually watch them. This is an example of the problem with what approach to observing behavior? _____

2. Figure 4-30 shows the resulting observation when Dave and Pat were assigned to check on the bookkeeper in the food co-op. They used an established checklist of 10 job tasks. What is their reliability? _____%; is their agreement acceptable? _____ (yes, no)

3. Kim wanted to observe how well the typists for large companies typed. She counted the number of errors appearing on a letter from Exxon. She found 6. She is using what method to observe that typist's typing? _____ recording

4. Figure 4-31 shows the resulting observations when Barb and Gary wanted to find out how much time the children at Yellow Brick Road Free School were spending learning to read, write, and do arithmetic. They developed their own behavioral definition and observed in 30-second blocks of time (S = studying; N = not studying). What is their reliability? _____%. Is their reliability acceptable? _____ (yes, no)

5. Reliability can be measured only when two people observe using the same behavioral definition to observe the same _____.

6. Joan counted the number of times Professor Brainbuster said "uh" during Monday's lecture and found that he said it 50 times. If Nel counts 50 "uh's" during Wednesday's lecture, can we conclude that their observations are reliable? _____ (yes, no)

7. Larry observed how often Professor Green encouraged students to make comments in his discussion class. Larry decided to record agreements with the comment by the professor. He also recorded praise of the comment. Larry's decision about what to record would be called a(n) _____.

8. With a new behavioral definition, researchers will accept a reliability figure of _____%.

9. The agreement between two sets of observations is called their _____.

10. Quinn et al. (1992) showed that adults rated accepting criticism as high when roommates kept calm and repeated the criticism and low when they did not. The researchers showed that using those behaviors to define "accepting criticism" has _____.

11. Short-answer question C. Suppose that one observer using event recording counts 25 responses, and a second observer counts 20. What observations do you assume they agree on and what observations do you assume they disagree on? Compute the reliability for this case:

_____

_____

_____

_____

_____

_____

1. If the teacher introduced Old West material to Bernie in his history and literature classes <u>at the same time</u> and compared his performance using Old West material with his performance using the regular material, the teacher would be using which single-subject design? a(n) _____ design

2. Observing Jane's grades on math homework, before, during, and after she has had a tutor is a strong research design because it can rule out _____ _____ explanations of any improvement in her grades during the time she had the tutor.

3. The multiple-baseline design gets its name from the fact that the researcher finds baselines for _____ (how many) or more behaviors. However, be sure to remember that the definition also requires that the treatment be introduced for each baseline at _____ times.

4. The record of a behavior prior to some attempt to change it is called a(n) _____.

5. Suppose that three people have been annoying you. If this week you ask the first one to stop annoying you, next week the second one, and a week later the third one, you would be using a(n) _____ design.

6. Palmer and associates (1977) measured electrical usage for a time period when not giving them cost information, for a period of time while giving it, and for a period of time after no longer giving them the information. They used what single-subject experimental design? _____ _____ design

7. Frank had a behavioral definition for acting sexy. He observed that Bud didn't come close to meeting the definition. He asked five of his girlfriends to rate Bud's sexiness. They rated him low! When Bud complained that he couldn't get any dates, Frank told him how to act. Frank observed that Bud was doing what he suggested. Frank again asked five of his girlfriends to rate the sexiness of the new Bud. They rated him high! Frank was trying to establish the _____ of his behavioral definition for acting sexy.

8. Marie's dorm observed the amount of cleaning that she did for a period of time. They then assigned a specific job to her for another period of time. Finally, they relieved her of that job for a time. They used what single-subject design to study the effect of giving her a specific job? a(n) _____ design

9. In a simple comparison design, we compare the rate of a behavior during two periods of time called the _____ _____ and the _____ _____ conditions.

10. The problem with asking people to tell us about their own behavior is that their reports are often _____ _____ or of unknown accuracy.

11. Short-answer question A. Name the conditions in a reversal design:

_____

_____

_____

_____

_____

_____

1. If two students measure the amount of time that another student, Nate, dominates the discussion before trying to get him to change, their agreement is a measure of the _____ of these data.

2. Comparing a baseline condition with the treatment condition is called a(n) _____ design.

3. Dave observed the cleaning behavior of his children. If he started giving cookies for a clean room to one of them after one week, to the second one after two weeks, and to the third one after three weeks, he would be using what single-subject design? _____ design

4. Professor Brainbuster based his lectures on the text *Moldy History* for five weeks and found most students sleeping. He then based his lectures on the new text called *Hip History* and found that most students stayed awake. He used a(n) _____ design.

5. Steve and Cleo, who were performing in a play, agreed to determine whether their friend was reciting his lines loud enough to be heard in the last row. Since they were also reading their own scripts, they agreed to listen to his loudness at random times throughout his recitation. They were using what method of observation? _____ recording

6. The Cornucopia Food Co-op assigned a clerk to count the number of customers prior to their advertising campaign. They are gathering data during the _____ condition.

7. The strength of a reversal design is that it can rule out _____ explanations of an observed behavior change.

8. The process of exposing the same person to both the baseline and the treatment is the principle of _____ _____ experiments.

9. If you observe the cuddling of 2-year-old Jose before having a half-hour reading time each day, while having the reading time, and after stopping the reading time. You are using a(n) _____ _____ design.

10. You are disappointed with how much studying Cal does. So you start giving him pop quizzes most days. The name for giving him pop quizzes to increase studying is _____.

11. Short-answer question B. Define *baseline* and *treatment* conditions:

_____
_____
_____
_____
_____
_____
_____

1. If parents transfer their two children from a public school to a free school in order to see whether the children will be more willing to go to school, the parents would be using a(n) _____ design.

2. Observing whether math tutoring improves Tom's test scores tells you his behavior rate during the _____ _____ condition.

3. The name of the design in which you measure the behavior for three periods of time, one before, one during, and one after the treatment is what single-subject design? a(n) _____ design

4. Komaki and Barnett (1977) provided feedback for football play performance after 10 sessions for the option play, after 14 sessions for the power sweep, and after 18 sessions for the counter. What experimental design did they use? _____ design

5. Observing how well a student does in math before he or she starts receiving help from a tutor would be called determining the student's rate of behavior during what condition? _____

6. Steve recorded during consecutive 15-second intervals whether his friend was reciting his lines loud enough during play practice to be heard in the last row. What method of observation did Steve use? _____ recording

7. If a teacher makes class attendance optional for one student and then a week later makes it optional for a second student (to see whether it affects their participation), the teacher would be using a(n) _____ design.

| Steve | L | L | L | L | S | L | L | S | L | S |
|-------|---|---|---|---|---|---|---|---|---|---|
| Clare | L | L | S | L | S | L | L | S | L | L |

**Figure 5-9.** Observations by Steve and Clare.

8. The anti-pollution committee observed that Greg, and other members like him, came to their weekly meeting about 15% of the time. They then started scheduling short Greenpeace films at each meeting and found that Greg came about 65% of the time. They later stopped the films and attendance fell back to under 20% for Greg. What single-subject design did they use to study the effects of the films? a(n) _____ design

9. Figure 5-9 shows the results when Steve and Clare recorded during 15-second intervals whether their friend was talking loud enough during his play practice to be heard in the last row (where "L" stands for "loud enough" and "S" for "too soft"). What is the reliability of their observations? _____%. Is it acceptable? _____ (yes, no)

10. To use the behavioral strategy: (1) Create a behavioral definition, (2) use a method of direct observation, (3) check the reliability and social validity of your observations, and (4) design a(n) _____ experiment.

11. Short-answer question C. Explain why the reversal design and the multiple-baseline design are strong designs:

_____

_____

_____

_____

_____

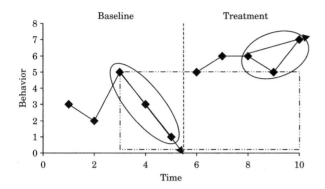

**Figure 6-16.** The results of an experiment.

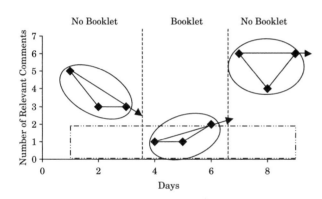

**Figure 6-17.** The results of an experiment.

| Rob | O | O | O | O | X | O | O | X | O | O |
| Jan | O | X | O | O | O | O | O | X | O | O |

**Figure 6-18.** Observations by Rob and Jan.

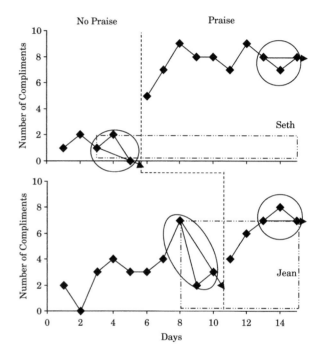

**Figure 6-19.** An experimental analysis of compliments given to Seth and Jean.

1. To decide if differences between conditions are convincing, you must ask if the conditions are _____ and if they are _____.

2. A single-subject experimental design in which two behaviors are subjected to the same treatment at different times is called a(n) _____ design.

3. The principle of visual analysis is to look for differences that are _____.

4. Figure 6-16 shows the results of a simple experiment. Divided? _____ Stable? _____ Convincing? _____ Caused? _____ (yes, no)

5. Figure 6-17 shows the number of relevant comments that Henry made before, during, and after he was given a memory booklet. Divided? _____ Stable? _____ Convincing? _____ Caused? _____ (yes, no)

6. Figure 6-18 shows what happened when Rob and Jan observed Professor Brainbuster to find out whether he was looking at students when he lectured. They did this in 15-second intervals. Compute the reliability: _____%. Is this an acceptable level? _____ (yes, no)

7. Figure 6-19 shows the number of compliments you make to Seth and Jean when Bob did not praise your compliments and when he did. Divided? _____ Stable? _____ Convincing? _____ Caused? _____ (yes, no)

8. If the data in baseline are the low numbers 1, 4, 5, 3 would you conclude that they are stable with respect to higher treatment values? _____ (yes, no)

9. The problem with using private events to explain behavior is that we must still _____ the private events.

10. When determining if conditions are divided, look only at the last _____ data points in each condition.

11. Short-answer question A. Name two criteria for a convincing difference:

_____

_____

_____

_____

_____

_____

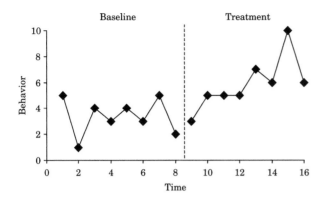

**Figure 6-91.** An experimental analysis of an unspecified behavior.

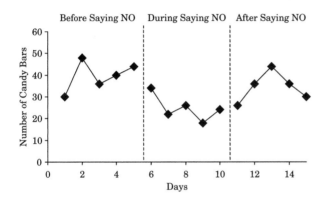

**Figure 6-92.** An experimental analysis of getting candy bars.

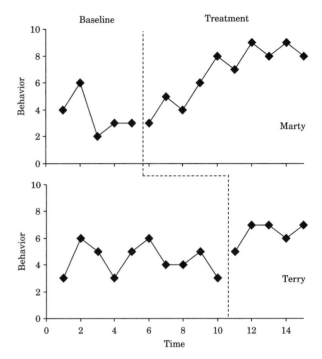

**Figure 6-93.** An experimental analysis of an unspecified behavior.

1. Bonnie used a new technique called *empathy self-actualization* last week with George. This week she asked George to compare how depressed he was before and after the new counseling technique. He said he was a lot less depressed after the counseling. Behavior analysts would call the approach to observation that Bonnie used to find out about his earlier depression _____ observation because he did not record it immediately.

2. You cannot conclude that a treatment caused a difference when using a comparison design because it fails to rules out _____ explanations.

3. Figure 6-91 shows the behavior of Juan during baseline and treatment. Divided? _____ Stable? _____ Convincing? _____ Caused? _____ (yes, no)

4. Figure 6-92 shows the number of chocolate bars that Ken normally ate and the number that he ate when to tried "just saying no." Divided? _____ Stable? _____ Convincing? _____ Caused? _____ (yes, no)

5. Figure 6-93 shows the number of behaviors emitted by Marty and Terry during baseline and treatment. Divided? _____ Stable? _____ Convincing? _____ Caused? _____ (yes, no)

6. Two single-subject experimental designs which rule out alternative explanations are the _____ and _____ designs.

7. The formula for reliability is 100%x _____/(_____).

8. Tommy studied 30% during baseline and 90% when praised. Marie studied 40% during baseline and 70% when praised. To decide if these are convincing

differences you should ask: are the conditions _____ and _____.

9. The method introduced during an experiment to modify the rate of a behavior is called the _____. The period of an experiment without the treatment is called the _____.

10. Here's how you visually analyze any experiment. First, decide whether the conditions are _____. Second, decide if the conditions are _____. Third, decide whether the differences between conditions are _____. Fourth, decide whether the treatment _____ behavior to change.

11. Short-answer question B. Define *visual analysis*:

_____
_____
_____
_____

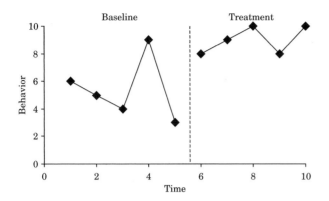

Figure 6-107. An experimental analysis of an unspecified behavior.

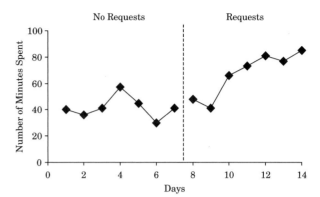

Figure 6-109. An experimental analysis of Terry reading to his daughter.

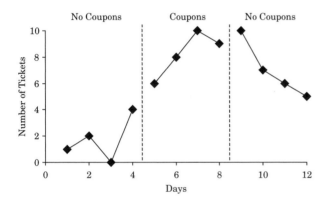

Figure 6-108. An experimental analysis of issuing safety tickets.

1. Data are not convincing if conditions are not both _____ and _____.

2. The reversal design observes for three conditions: _____, _____, and _____.

3. Behavior analysis is the science that studies _____ events that _____ behavior.

4. Figure 6-107 shows the number of responses by Mohammed during baseline and treatment. Divided? _____ Stable? _____ Convincing? _____ Caused? _____ (yes, no)

5. Figure 6-108 shows the number of safety tickets issued by police when they could not and when they could also give coupons permitting violators to go to class to escape the ticket. Divided? _____ Stable? _____ Convincing? _____ Caused? _____ (yes, no)

6. List three single-subject experimental designs that can rule out individual differences: _____ design, _____ design, and _____ design.

7. The problem with using people's observations based on memory is that they are often _____. The problem with explaining behavior with events inside the person is that these events must still be _____.

8. Figure 6-109 shows the number of minutes that Terry spent reading to his daughter Jill when his wife did not request and when she did request Terry to read. Divided? _____ Stable? _____ Convincing? _____ Caused? _____ (yes, no)

9. The extent that the ratings of outside judges correlate with observations based on your behavioral definition is called _____.

10. When you do an experiment, you compare behavior during treatment and baseline. To conclude that the treatment caused the difference, you must find divided and

stable conditions and you must rule out
_____ explanations.

11. Short-answer question C. Explain the
principle of single-subject experiments:

_____

_____

_____

_____

_____

_____

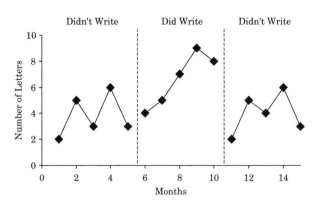

Didn't Write     Did Write     Didn't Write

*Figure 7-1.* An experimental analysis of letter writing.

1. The statement "giving support means to make a positive comment" is an example of a(n) _____.

2. Figure 7-1 shows how many letters Ben received when he didn't write and when he did write letters to others. Divided? ____ Stable? ____ Convincing? ____ Caused? ____ (yes, no)

3. Suppose a teacher observes the amount of studying for two students for a month. Then, for the second month, the teacher gives daily quizzes to one student but not the other. Finally, for the third month, the teacher gives daily quizzes to both students. The teacher is using what single-subject design? A(n) _____ _____ design.

4. If you see a behavior and immediately record it, you are using the principle of _____.

5. Janet applies for a driver's license. The Department of Motor Vehicles gives her a driving manual to bring home and read. Janet returns to the department where they test her over the manual. They are observing her reading of that manual with the method of direct observation called _____ recording.

6. Frank counted the number of times that the president referred to a human rights violation in another country and the number of times that he referred to the mistreatment of American Indians in the United States. He found 123 mentions for other countries and no mention of Indians. He concluded that these data constituted a classic example of hypocrisy. What method of observation was he using? _____ recording

7. About one student per week joined the new compact disc buying co-op. Then the co-op decided to try a newspaper advertisement. As a result, about 20 students per week joined. The members concluded that advertising pays because the ad succeeded in getting new members. This is not a good experimental design because it doesn't rule out _____ explanations.

8. The basic formula for computing reliability is _____.

9. Hineline (1992) discusses when an explanation of behavior by environmental events sounds right or wrong in our culture. The behavioral approach may sound right to you when it points to an external cause to explain a behavior that most people would regard as expected under those circumstances. However, it is likely to sound wrong to you when it points to an external cause to explain a behavior that most people would regard as _____ (expected, unexpected) under those circumstances.

10. Dr. Smith developed a way to observe depressed behavior and a treatment to reduce it. She asked a group of psychiatrists to rate Jake's depression before and after the treatment. If these ratings correlated with her behavioral observations, she would have evidence that her behavioral definition of non-depressed behavior had _____.

11. Short-answer question A. Give one reason why behavior analysts usually do not rely on observations that involve memory, such as questionnaires or interviews:

_____

_____

_____

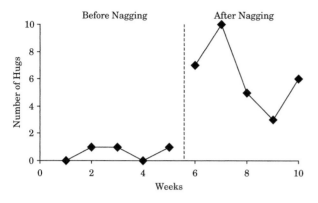

*Figure 7-3.* An experimental analysis of hugging.

1. Figure 7-3 shows how often Tim hugged his sister when his Dad did not and did nag him to hug his sister. Divided? _____ Stable? _____ Convincing? _____ Caused? _____ (yes, no)

2. An experimental design that studies a behavior before the treatment, during the treatment, and after the treatment is called a(n) _____ design.

3. Behavior analysts view thinking and feeling as _____ .

4. Experimenting with one person at a time is called the principle of _____ _____ design.

5. Using the behavioral strategy: first, creating a behavioral definition. Second, using the approach of _____. _____ Third, checking reliability and social validity. Fourth, using single-subject experimental design. Fifth, doing a(n) _____ analysis of the data.

6. Lou took time out from his work to check on his children every little while. He checked to see if Jim was playing nicely outside. Then he went back to work. Then he checked to see if May was playing nicely near the TV. Then he worked. Then he checked again on Jim. He continued this pattern. He was using _____ recording.

7. A measure of the amount of agreement between two observers is called _____ _____ .

8. Behavior analysis is a behavioral science that examines _____ events that _____ behavior.

9. Minkin and his colleagues (1976) investigated the correlation between two measures. First, he observed good conversation skills of teenagers talking to each other using his behavioral definition. Second, he obtained ratings of the conversational skills of the same teenagers made by a cross-section of adults. The researchers were evaluating the _____ _____ of their behavioral definition.

10. Name an experimental design that rules out both time coincidence and individual differences as alternative explanations of any observed change in behavior: _____ .

11. Short-answer question B. Explain why behavior analysts do not use private events to explain behavior:

_____

_____

_____

_____

_____

_____

| Teacher | F | N | F | N | F | F | F | N | F | F |
| Another | F | N | F | F | F | F | F | N | N | F |

**Figure 7-8.** Observations by a teacher and another person.

1. Figure 7-8 shows shows the observations of Mary's nearness to other children made by Mary's teacher and another observer (where "N" stand for "near" and "F" stands for "far"). What is their reliability? _____% Is this an acceptable level of reliability? _____ (yes, no)

2. The principle of public events is to seek the causes of behavior in _____ _____ events.

3. Dave observed the cleaning behavior of his children. He started giving cookies for a clean room to one of them after one week, to the second after two weeks, and to the third one after three weeks. He was using what kind of design? _____ design

4. Name a single-subject experimental design that doesn't rule out both alternative explanations of any observed change in behavior: _____ design.

5. The problem with using private events to explain behavior is that you still must _____ them.

6. The method of observing that counts occurrences of behavior is called _____ recording.

7. The problem with self-reports is that they are usually _____ or can't be checked.

8. You observe John's study behavior during a series of intervals 15 seconds long. You used what method of observation? _____ recording

9. Harry was a poor reader. He read 25%, 15%, 30%, 20%, and 10% of the time during the first week of observation. During the second week, he was told that he could stay at recess for an extra ten minutes on any day that he read more than 70% of the time. That week he read 60%, 85%, 80%, 95%, and 85% of the time. What experimental design was being used to determine the effectiveness of the extra recess time? _____

10. The principle of visual analysis is to look for differences between baseline and treatment that are convincing. To decide if differences are convincing, you must look for conditions that are _____ and _____.

11. Short-answer question C. Explain why a comparison design is a weak design:

_____

_____

_____

_____

_____

_____

_____

1. An event that seems unpleasant but increases the rate of a behavior that it follows would be called a(n) _____ _____.

2. When Sue was a tiny infant, her father had a bright idea. Maybe it would increase her rate of smiling if he followed each adorable smile with a lullaby. It did. Sue's father was using what behavioral procedure? _____

3. Suppose that a person is late to class and the teacher asks him to be on time in the future. If the person starts coming to class on time more often, the teacher's request would be an example of _____.

4. An event is called a reinforcer if it is timed to _____ a behavior and _____ the probability of that behavior.

5. May came home from school and told her parents that she had finally beaten up the little boy who had been tormenting her every day. May's father took her out for a special ice cream treat for beating up the little boy. May has not beaten up the horrible little boy since then. The ice cream treat is an example of a(n) _____.

6. Glover and Gary (1976) delivered points to students after each different function that they listed for an object. If the rate of listing different functions increased, then the procedure of delivering the points would be called _____ _____.

7. When Larry commented that he liked long hair, his friends always agreed. They then frequently discussed how stupid other people's reactions to long hair were. Larry commented on the virtues of long hair more and more frequently. The event consisting of one of his friends saying "yeah, man, that's right" would be an example of a(n) _____.

8. Verna spanked Tom every time he interrupted her. Tom seemed to interrupt even more than usual after she started spanking him. The event consisting of spanking Tom would be called a(n) _____.

9. To prove that an event is a reinforcer, you would have to use a(n) _____ design.

10. Kim complained of problems every once in awhile. One day when Kim complained, his teacher, concerned that the problems might be interfering with school, had a long talk with him. After that, Kim complained more often about his problems and thus had more talks with the teacher. By talking with Kim after a complaint, the teacher was using what behavioral procedure? _____ _____.

11. Short-answer question A. Explain the difference between *reinforcer* and *reinforcement:*

_____
_____
_____
_____
_____

1. Kay was the only person in the group who supported the war. She always said things in favor of the war, and the other group members would always argue with her. She gradually said more and more things supporting the war. When another member of the group said something like "I think that war is immoral," this statement would be an example of a(n) _____ for statements favoring the war.

2. Increasing the rate of a behavior by delivering a reinforcer after it occurs is called _____.

3. Glover and Gary (1976) gave points to students following each word they used in describing functions of an object. Since this procedure increased the number of words they used, you would term the procedure of delivering points _____.

4. Tactic #1 in using the reinforcement strategy to solve human problems is to increase desired behavior through _____.

5. Frank was given $10 by his dad for cleaning the garage. During the next year, Frank's dad asked him to clean the garage again, but he never did. The $10 is an example of what? _____

6. When Priscilla complained about life, Linda tried to cheer her up by talking with her. But the more often she talked with Priscilla about her complaints, the more often Priscilla complained about life. By talking with Priscilla after she complained, Linda was using what behavioral procedure? _____

7. If an event follows a behavior and the frequency of that behavior becomes greater, the event is called a(n) _____.

8. Linda paused after giving a customer his coin change and before giving him the bills. He left without the bills. Linda did not pause more in the future after giving the coin part of someone's change. Having the customer leave without his bills is an example of _____.

9. If an instruction precedes a behavior and increases the rate of the behavior, it is called a(n) _____.

10. Jerome didn't do his share of cleaning, so every time that the apartment became dirty, Bob asked Jerome to help clean it. After he was asked, Jerome would do his share. As a result, Jerome's rate of cleaning increased. Bob's request for help is a(n) _____.

11. Short-answer question B. Define a *reinforcer:*

_____

_____

_____

_____

_____

1. Joe tried tapping his TV set when the picture went out. His tapping restored the picture, but Joe still forgets to tap his TV set when the picture goes out. The restored picture is an example of a(n) _____.

2. The teacher firmly told Francie to start doing her homework. Immediately thereafter, Francie started doing her homework. The teacher's demand is an example of what? _____

3. Any event that occurs after the beginning of a behavior and leads to an increase in the rate of the behavior is called a(n) _____.

4. Four-year-old Tony almost never greeted his father when he came home from work at night. The father then started giving Tony a big kiss every time he greeted his father at the door. Within a week, Tony was greeting his father every night. What behavioral procedure was the father using? _____

5. Suppose that every time Jed fails to do what you want him to do you tell him to do it. If this increases the rate at which Jed does what you want him to do, the arrangement would be called a(n) _____.

6. Janice carefully typed her term paper for the first time. She received an A for the paper. Thereafter, she frequently typed her term papers. The A is an example of what? _____

7. Glover and Gary (1976) gave students one point for each different verb form that they used in describing possible functions of an object. The delivery of points increased the students' rate of using different verb forms. The points would be an example of a(n) _____.

8. Marty complained of a headache, so his teacher let him lay his head on the desk. Marty doesn't complain about headaches anymore. The teacher's permission to put his head down is an example of a(n) _____.

9. Dana didn't kiss his girlfriend very often. One day she bit him just after a kiss. He kisses her quite often now, and she always pinches him just after the kiss. Her pinch is an example of a(n) _____.

10. If you arrange to deliver an event following every instance of a behavior and the rate of the behavior increases, then you would refer to this procedure as _____.

11. Short-answer question C. Explain how a behavioral scientist would prove that an event is a reinforcer and disprove that an alternative event is the cause of the increase in behavior:

_____

_____

_____

_____

_____

_____

_____

1. Joyce started fixing her husband a fancy breakfast whenever he hung up his clothes. She noticed that he started hanging up his clothes most of the time after that. What behavioral procedure did Joyce use? _____

2. During the reversal condition, Pinkston and her colleagues (1973) instructed the preschool teachers to pay attention to Cain's aggressive behavior as they had done during baseline. Cain's aggressive behavior once again increased. An instance of the teacher's attention is an example of a(n) _____.

3. Ben did a good job every week of vacuuming as long as the president asked him first. Ben's rate of vacuuming decreased dramatically when the president no longer asked him. The president's procedure is called _____.

4. The temporary increase in a behavior after it has been put on extinction is called a(n) "_____."

5. Lora asked silly questions that caused the professor to get mad. He tried ignoring the questions and found that Lora kept asking silly questions. Ignoring her questions is an example of what behavioral procedure? _____

6. Mary interrupted Sally while she was with her friends all the time, and her friends paid attention to her interruptions rather than Sally's conversation. Sally finally talked them into ignoring Mary, however, and Mary's rate of interruptions decreased. What behavioral procedure does the group's ignoring of Mary's interruptions illustrate? _____

7. John could be a star swimmer if he would only practice more. The coach had talked with him, praised him when he did swim many laps, but still John did not practice enough. Finally, the coach told him in no uncertain terms to practice. John's rate of practice increased dramatically. The coach's talk is an example of what behavioral concept?_____.

8. Suppose that you have been in the habit of telling people to perform behavior A and they do it. If you now stop telling them to do it and they stop doing it, what behavioral procedure are you using? _____

9. Fritz frequently looked out of the train window as he rode through Switzerland. After sundown, he could no longer see the beautiful countryside. His rate of looking out the window decreased dramatically. Sundown delivered a natural procedure for Fritz's looking out the window called _____.

10. Bull, a regular at the restaurant, was always calling for Ronald's service by yelling, "Hey boy, come here." This annoyed Ronald greatly so he finally decided not to serve Bull when he called him a boy. Pretty soon Bull stopped calling him "boy." What behavioral procedure did Ronald use? _____

11. Short-answer question A. Explain why telling someone to stop doing something is not an example of extinction even if the person stops doing it:

_____
_____
_____
_____
_____
_____

1. Dave always started pestering his mother for a snack just about the time she started cooking dinner. While this irritated her, she tried to be a good mother and explain why he couldn't have a snack at that time. She finally decided that this wasn't working and that she would be better off ignoring his requests. What procedure would she be using if she ignored his requests and he stopped them? _____

2. When Sam was young, he often came home and started talking with his father about his day at school. His father usually listened and asked questions. Sam started talking with his father more often as a result. What behavioral procedure was Sam's father using? _____

3. For five weeks, Professor Johnson told his students to type their weekly take-home exam, and they did. He then forgot to tell them during the rest of the semester, and all of them no longer typed their exams. By forgetting to tell them, Professor Johnson inadvertently used what procedure? _____

4. One day Harry stroked Tabby softly, and the cat started to purr. Harry thereafter frequently stroked Tabby softly. Tabby's purr would be an example of a(n) _____.

5. Karen told John to stop using cocaine immediately. John never used cocaine again. John's change in behavior is an example of what behavioral procedure? _____

6. Ann thought it would be cute to teach her son to swear. So every time that he swore, she laughed and paid a lot of attention. Her son did not swear any more as a result. What behavioral procedure was Ann using? _____

7. If you tell someone to stop a behavior and the behavior decreases, you are using what behavioral procedure? _____

8. Pinkston and her colleagues (1973) instructed the preschool teacher to stop paying attention to Cain's aggressive behavior, which she did. Cain's aggressive behavior decreased. What behavioral procedure did the teacher use? _____

9. Professor Adams disrupted faculty meetings with insane ideas. His colleagues argued vehemently with him. However, the chairman finally convinced them to simply ignore Adams. Soon, Adams wasn't disrupting meetings anymore. The faculty ignoring Adam's insane ideas is an example of what? _____

10. Jimmy's dad asked many questions when Jimmy complained about how bad life was. Later, Dad stopped asking questions, but Jimmy complained as much as before. What behavioral procedure was Dad using when he stopped asking questions? _____

11. Short-answer question B. Define the term *extinction*:

_____
_____
_____
_____
_____
_____

1. Extinction is defined as the delivery of an event following a behavior is _____, thereby producing a(n) _____ in the rate of that behavior.

2. Angela spent little of her time with her classmates, so her fourth-grade teacher started complimenting her whenever she did spend time with them. Soon, Angela spent a lot of time working on class projects with other children. One of the teacher's compliments would be an example of a(n) _____.

3. Mimi asked Gary to help her remember to count calories. For a month, he reminded her. Then he stopped reminding her, and Mimi's rate of counting calories decreased. What behavioral procedure did Gary inadvertently use to produce the decrease? _____

4. Fay used to ask Harry to go to the store. However, since he took up jogging, Harry won't go to the store when Fay asks. After ten weeks of asking with no results, Fay finally gave up asking Harry to go to the store. What behavioral procedure did Harry use to eliminate Fay's requests? _____

5. If Pinkston and her colleagues (1973) had told the preschool teacher to tell Cain to "stop being aggressive" and he had stopped, what behavioral procedure would the teacher have been using? _____

6. Martha's son pinched her all the time, and she invariably asked him not to do it or told him it wasn't nice. Eventually, Martha stopped paying any attention to the pinching, and it stopped. What behavioral procedure did she eventually use? _____

7. Dollie wanted Jim to light her cigarettes for her, so she started kissing him whenever he did light her cigarette. Pretty soon he was lighting it all the time. What behavioral procedure was she using? _____

8. Within six months of starting Happiness House, each member had stopped praising other members for cleaning the house. The result was that the amount of cleaning behavior drastically decreased for each member. This is an example of what behavioral procedure? _____

9. Ben teased Jan about her weight a lot, and she usually protested. Jan decided that she would simply ignore all future teasings. She noticed that Ben's rate of teasing did not change. What behavioral procedure did Jan use? _____

10. Dan wanted Karen to smile more. On one day when she hadn't smiled at all, he worked up his nerve and said to her, "Karen, you have a beautiful smile; I sure would like it if you smiled more." To his delight, Karen smiled more. What behavioral procedure did he use to increase her rate of smiling? _____

11. Short-answer question C. Sometimes when you stop delivering a reinforcer, the person's rate of behavior may briefly increase! Explain why stopping the reinforcer can still be an example of extinction:

_____
_____
_____
_____
_____
_____

1. John and Darrin always welcomed Lee when he sat with them during lunch. One day John and Darrin ignored Lee when he sat down because they were having an important conversation. From then on, John and Darrin ignored Lee when he sat with them. Eventually, Lee stopped sitting with them. What behavioral procedure accounts for Lee's changed behavior? _____

2. Stokes and Fawcett (1977) studied the effect of collecting properly packaged trash and not collecting improperly packaged trash. Does the example involve two (or more) different behaviors? _____

3. When John was 5 years old, he used jerky movements of his fingers to tune his radio, and he could rarely get his favorite station. Sometimes his movements were less jerky by accident, and he could get the station. Gradually, he developed a smooth movement that let him tune his favorite station quite easily. What behavioral procedure built into the way radio tuners work leads to smooth tuning movements? _____

4. One characteristic of differential reinforcement is that all but one behavior should be decreased through the use of _____.

5. Ben was an excellent ski instructor. He made a nice comment when you made your turn smoothly, but said nothing when you goofed it up. He didn't even laugh when you fell down. His students learned smooth turns quickly. What behavioral procedure did he use to teach smooth turning? _____

6. Roger's parents get on his case when he watches TV cartoons but ignore him when he watches educational programs. The rate at which he watches TV cartoons increases. What behavioral procedure did his parents inadvertently use to increase the rate at which he watches TV cartoons but not educational programs? _____.
(Explanation: Watching TV cartoons involves the same behavior of focusing the eyes in the direction of the TV no matter what you watch.)

7. Grannies often spoil a child even when the parents are careful not to. If a child learns to beg for candy from Granny but does not beg from her parents, what procedure is unwittingly being used by the adults? _____

8. When people are learning to drive a car with a manual transmission, they often have trouble learning how to shift. One problem is that, if they take their foot off the accelerator too slowly when they start to shift, the engine races. On the other hand, if they take their foot off the accelerator too rapidly, the car will suddenly slow down. They must learn to let the accelerator off at just the right speed. The process of decreasing responses that are too slow or too fast while increasing responses that are the right speed is the result of what behavioral procedure? _____

9. If a single behavior is reinforced in one situation and extinguished in another situation, the behavioral procedure that is being used is called _____.

10. John's coach, Ms. Davidson, permitted him to leave practice early on any day that he correctly performed a high dive. John's rate of correct high dives increased as a result. The event "time off from practice" is an example of a(n) _____.

11. Short-answer question A: Why is being reinforced for reading about physics while being extinguished for reading about social problems not an example of differential reinforcement?

_____
_____
_____
_____
_____
_____
_____

1. Stokes and Fawcett (1977) asked sanitation workers to rate how safely the trash was packaged before and after the new rules were enforced. They then correlated the ratings with observations made by trained observers using a strict definition of "safe packaging." The researchers were determining the _____ of their behavioral definition of safe packaging.

2. Gary's parents were a problem. They frequently ranted and raved about all the "yuppies" running around the university. Gary decided to change this by ignoring all unfavorable comments about young people and by praising his parents for being so in touch with young people when they made favorable comments. His parents gradually started talking more nicely about young people. What behavioral procedure did Gary use to change his parents comments? _____

3. If one behavior is increased through reinforcement and all others are decreased through extinction, the procedure is called _____.

4. Parents who find their son reading a serious novel will probably ask him questions about his reading. Parents who find their son reading a western will often ignore him altogether. If the son starts reading serious novels more often and westerns less often, what behavioral procedure would account for the change? _____

5. Janice Johnson was a new social-welfare caseworker. Mrs. Brooks, one of her clients, became annoyed at Janice's habit of discussing her own children but never trying to find what welfare help Mrs. Brooks needed. So Mrs. Brooks started ignoring all discussions about Janice's children and paid attention only when her own welfare problems came up. If Janice started talking more about Mrs. Brooks's problems, then this is an example of _____.

6. Mel was new to the ecology club. At first, he talked about how hard it is to sort your garbage into plastics, wet vegetation, cans, and so on, but everyone ignored him. When he talked about how everyone should do their share for the environment, everyone enthusiastically agreed. Pretty soon he was talking about everyone doing their share and not complaining about how hard sorting your garbage is. The members of the ecology club were using what behavioral procedure to change Mel's behavior? _____

7. Gale's teacher watched her while she made a series of connected handwritten *l*'s. The teacher praised her when the loops were smooth and said nothing when they were rough or irregular. Gradually, Gale learned to write smooth and beautiful *l*'s. What procedure did her teacher use? _____

8. Good discussion leaders are remarkably successful in getting everyone into a group discussion. They generally praise anyone who speaks. Even shy people, if praised, will contribute their ideas more often. This increase in the rate of everyone's talking is the result of what behavioral procedure? _____

9. When they were alone, John politely pulled out Mary's chair for her. She thanked him, and he did it more often over time. When they were with friends, John used to politely pull out Mary's chair for her. She did not thank him because she was embarrassed by this old fashioned politeness. He did it less often with friends around. What behavioral procedure did Mary use to increase his politeness when alone and decrease it when with friends? _____

10. One characteristic of differential reinforcement is that one behavior should be increased through the use of _____.

11. Short-answer question B. Explain how you determine whether two behaviors are the same:
_____
_____
_____
_____

1. Mr. Howard taught ninth grade geography class. One boy, Ben, said very little. Mr. Howard decided that, rather than continue to put Ben on the spot by constantly asking him questions, he would compliment him when he said anything. If Ben's rate of talking increased, Mr. Howard would be using what behavioral procedure? _____

2. Stokes and Fawcett (1977) found that correct trash-packaging behaviors increased and incorrect ones decreased when only correctly packaged trash was collected. What behavioral procedure did they use? _____

3. If David always moved his eyes forward even when he had forgotten a prior word, he found that he read much faster. When David frequently stopped to move his eyes backwards to look at a previous word, he found that he read much slower. Gradually, he learned to always move his eyes forward and to stop moving them back. Suppose that reading faster is reinforcing and reading slower is extinguishing. What behavioral procedure caused him to change his reading behavior? _____

4. Gary found that, if he smiled when he was with Jane, she would pay a lot of attention to him. However, if he smiled when he was with Gloria, she would ignore him. Naturally, Gary started smiling a lot when he was around Jane but hardly at all when he was around Gloria. What behavioral procedure is at work changing his pattern of smiling? _____

5. Billy found that he couldn't pound in a nail if he struck with a pushing movement. But he could pound it in if he struck with a swinging movement. He quickly learned to strike with a swinging movement. What behavioral procedure is this an example of? _____

6. Differential reinforcement involves the behavioral procedures of _____ _____ and _____.

7. Manuel smiled broadly and said "bueno" every time that Sara properly trilled her *r*'s in "perro," the Spanish word for dog. He let improper trills just pass by without comment. Gradually, Sara learned to make the correct trill. What behavioral procedure did Manuel use? _____.

8. A baby may say "Dada" to many adult males other than his father. The parents will probably ignore the misdirected "Dada's" and pay attention to the "Dada's" said to the father. If the baby comes to call his father "Dada" more often than other males, what behavioral procedure is this an example of? _____

9. Bernie decided that it would be good for his girlfriend to jog more often, so he told her that she had to do it. She did. What behavioral procedure did Bernie use to increase her rate of jogging? _____

10. Mr. Green, the football coach, made a point of praising Ann when she blocked her opponent away from the runner. He ignored her when she missed her block or blocked her opponent toward the ball. As a result, her blocking away from the ball increased relative to poor blocks. What behavioral procedure was the coach using? _____

11. Short-answer question C. What is the difference between *reinforcement* and *differential reinforcement*?

_____
_____
_____
_____
_____
_____
_____

1. Renne and Creer (1976) gave David a ticket at first for looking at the dial 4 times out of 15 breaths; that would be called a(n) _____ to their ultimate goal of looking at it for all 15 breaths.

2. Kerr's teachers showed interest in his reading during the first month of school. As soon as Kerr finished a reading, they asked him to report on what he had learned. During later months, they lost their enthusiasm and stopped asking him for reports. Kerr gradually stopped reading. What behavioral procedure were they using when they stopped asking him about his reading? _____

3. Dr. Franklin used a portable railing for Bobby to lean on and learn to walk again. She moved this farther and farther away from Bobby until he stood on his own and actually walked. She first reinforced Bobby just for standing with his weight on the railing, then reinforced him only when he leaned just a little, and finally reinforced him only when he stood on his own. She was using what behavioral procedure to change Bobby's behavior? _____

4. For a situation to involve shaping, two conditions must be met: (a) a(n) _____ must be specified; and (b) differential reinforcement must be applied to a series of _____.

5. Marie told Fred to stop swearing whenever a minor annoyance occurred. Fred's rate of swearing decreased as a result. What behavioral procedure did Marie use? _____

6. Bobby was trying to pronounce it correctly, but the best he could say was "refrigelator." June, his mom, praised him for saying it so well. "Refrigelator" would be called a(n) _____ _____ to June's target behavior of "refrigerator."

7. Last week Mary started kissing Dave every time he lit her cigarette in hopes that he would light her cigarette more often. Dave didn't get the message, however, and still doesn't light her cigarette very often. What behavioral procedure did Mary use? _____

8. At first, Mary dreamed about John only after they had been discussing their problems. Later, Mary dreamed about John only after they had a mild fight. Finally, she dreamed about him only after they had a terrible, screaming fight. What behavioral procedure accounts for the increasing severity of John and Mary's fights? _____

9. Dave's coach praised him only when he swam the 100-yard freestyle in under 50 seconds but ignored him when he swam it in over 50 seconds. Dave soon got so he could do it. What behavioral procedure was his coach using? _____

10. Bobby didn't start playing very much chess until after he started winning. Now he plays a lot. Because the event of winning comes after playing well, it is called a(n) _____.

11. Short-answer question A: Explain how you use differential reinforcement within shaping:

_____

_____

_____

_____

_____

_____

1. Mrs. Baker began the process of overcoming the tone-deafness of Toneless Tony by asking him to sing A flat, which she then played on the piano. She praised him when he came within a half tone of it and simply asked him to try again if he did not. It took two lessons to teach him to sing within a half tone of A flat. Mrs. Baker was using what behavioral procedure to teach Tony to sing within a half tone of A flat? _____

2. John's teacher helped him overcome acting like a loner. At first the teacher paid attention to him only when he looked at other children, then only when he was near them, and finally only when he was playing with them. What procedure did the teacher use to modify John's loner behavior? _____

3. Frank never opened a door for Marsha. She decided to kiss him every time that he did so. Pretty soon Frank was opening the door for Marsha all the time. What behavioral procedure did Marsha employ to get him to open doors? _____

4. Sammy's mother praised him every time that he took out the garbage, and he did so regularly. When he was 12, she stopped praising him, feeling that he was old enough to accept responsibility. Sammy's rate of taking out the trash rapidly decreased after that. What behavioral procedure did Sammy's mother inadvertently use to reduce his rate of taking out the garbage? _____

5. The term *shaping* is used to describe a particular use of what behavioral procedure that involves reinforcement? _____

6. Dean taught Jason to hit badminton shots at least three steps away from Dean. Here's how he did it. First, Dean praised Jason only when he hit a shot at least one step away from him. Next, he praised Jason only when he hit a shot two steps from him. Finally, he praised Jason only when he hit a shot three steps away from him. Hitting a shot one step away from Dean is called a(n) _____ _____ to hitting a shot three steps away from Dean.

7. By giving tickets to David only when he looked at the dial 4 out of 15 times, then only when he looked at the dial 5 out of 15, and then changing that criterion until completely correct use developed, Renne and Creer (1976) were using what behavioral procedure? _____ _____

8. Yancey noticed that when he said to Fran, "You look nice today," she smiled and thanked him for his compliment. However, when he said to Dan, "You look nice today," Dan looked slightly embarrassed and ignored the compliment. Soon Yancey was frequently saying, "You look nice today," to Fran but almost never to Dan. What behavioral procedure is involved in changing Yancey's rate of saying this compliment to his two friends? _____

9. Tom smoked only 15 cigarettes yesterday, and Vera praised his willpower mightily. Vera was sure that such praise would help Tom learn to stop smoking altogether. Stopping smoking would be called Vera's _____ _____.

10. Reinforcing one behavior and extinguishing all others and then changing to another behavior that more closely approximates the target behavior and repeating the process is called _____ _____.

11. Short-answer question B. Explain what an *approximation* is:

_____
_____
_____
_____

1. Tactic #4 in using the reinforcement strategy to solve human problems is create new behavior through _____ _____.

2. A behavior that is similar to a target behavior would be called a(n) _____ _____.

3. Tad wanted to run a mile in under 6 minutes. So during the first week, he bought himself a Super Sundae every time that he ran a mile under 12 minutes. During the next week, he bought himself a Super Sundae when he ran the mile in under 8 minutes. He continued this process until he ran a mile under 6 minutes. What behavioral procedure did he use on himself to attain this goal? _____

4. James wanted to teach his best friend to recognize the music to which it was appropriate to do the Twirling Chicken. So he let her initiate the dancing each time and praised her when she did the Twirling Chicken to the right music and didn't say anything when she did the Twirling Chicken to the wrong music. Her ability to do the Twirling Chicken with the right music increased rapidly. What behavioral procedure did James use to help her learn what was the correct music (since almost every student gets this wrong, be sure to check the elements required for your answer)? _____

5. Ralph Radical wanted Bob to be against clear cutting the redwoods. At first, Ralph agreed with Bob whenever he said anything mildly against clear cutting. Then, Ralph agreed only when Bob made strong statements against clear cutting. Pretty soon Bob was often making strong statements against clear cutting. Ralph used what procedure to change Bob's statements about clear cutting? _____ _____

6. Shaping begins with the selection of an ultimate goal called a(n) _____ _____.

7. Clarence's father told him to undertake more projects that involved the use of a hammer, so he did. What behavioral procedure was his father using to increase the rate of using a hammer? _____

8. Renne and Creer (1976) attempted to teach the correct use of inhalation equipment to asthmatic children. The correct use of the equipment would be called the _____ of their experiment.

9. Charlie Brown smiled at the little red-headed girl only when she sat within 5 feet of him at lunch, then only when she sat within 2 feet, and finally only when she sat next to him. Charlie Brown's goal of getting her to sit next to him is called the _____.

10. John often smelled gamey because he usually forgot to put on his underarm deodorant. Barb decided to do something about it. For the next two months she praised John every time that he remembered to put on his deodorant. John eventually remembered to put on his deodorant more often. What behavioral procedure was Barb using? _____

11. Short-answer question C. Define *shaping*:
_____
_____
_____
_____
_____

1. Senor Jimenez taught 4-year-old Janice to say his name right by saying a syllable, "hee," and hugging her only when she said it right. Next, he said "hee-mayn" and hugged her only when she said both syllables right. Finally, he said 'hee-mayn-ays" and hugged her only when she said his whole name right. What procedure did he use to teach her how to say his name?

   _____

2. Reinforcers should be selected according to whether the person has not had a lot of that reinforcer recently. This is known as the principle of _____.

3. Jane's brother wasn't a very warm person. So every time that he acted cold and distant, she would tell him to stand close and touch people. His rate of standing close and touching people increased after she started the procedure. What is the name of her procedure? _____

4. Hal did not invite Dana to parties very often. Dana decided to change this by quickly offering free tutoring only when Hal invited him to a party. Dana made these offers immediately after an invitation. These offers were terribly important to Hal because Dana was the only person who could explain the material well enough to enable Hal to pass the exams. Hal rarely received these offers from Dana. What principle of effective reinforcement, if any, did Dana neglect?

   _____

5. Enough of the reinforcer must be delivered to be worthwhile. This is known as the principle of _____.

6. He was every employee's dream. He praised your work no matter how poorly you did it. He gave it right after you finished a job. He didn't give you too much praise. You felt important afterwards. Still, it wasn't effective—no one improved the quality of his or her work. What principle of effective reinforcement, if any, is he neglecting? _____

7. Kevin lent his truck and his muscles to help Bob move. At first, he carried boxes to the front door, where Bob took them and carried them inside and put them in the right room. Bob always thanked Kevin as soon as he brought a box to the door and at no other time. Bob did not give praise so much or so often that Kevin tired of it. But when Kevin saw Bob drinking a beer without offering him any, he decided that getting thanks didn't justify all the hard work. What principle of effective reinforcement, if any, did Bob neglect? _____

8. Sarah tried to help John overcome his shyness by praising him for being assertive. She conveyed her praise about his assertive behaviors after they returned home from social gatherings. During these conversations, she only praised him for the assertive acts that he had made during the event. John never got too much praise from Sarah during these conversations. Every instance of her praise was very important to him. What principle of effective reinforcement, if any, did Sarah neglect in providing help to John in this way? _____

9. Dr. Ayllon gave Doris towels only when she was in her room; she had hoarded them for nine years, so each one was important to her. By the time that she had been given 600 towels, she started removing them from her room. Ayllon deliberately violated what principle of reinforcer effectiveness to reduce the reinforcing properties of towels for Doris?

   _____

10. Tactic #5 in using the reinforcement strategy is to use the principles of _____.

11. Short-answer question A. State the *principle of immediacy*:

    _____
    _____
    _____
    _____
    _____
    _____

1. Jerry's mother agreed to teach him how to sew. She paid attention to him by pointing out only the good aspects of his sewing skill. She did this while he was sewing. This attention was very important to Jerry. She kept her lessons brief so that Jerry rarely received attention. What principle of effective reinforcement, if any, did Jerry's mother neglect? _____

2. If a person has recently had a lot of a certain reinforcer, the person may no longer be _____ with respect to that reinforcer.

3. Bob usually didn't pay his share of the rent on time. Alice praised him only when he paid his rent on time. She praised him as soon as she learned that he had paid—usually within a week. Alice praised him rarely. Alice's praise was a big deal for Bob. What principle did Alice fail to use, if any, to maximize the effectiveness of her praise? _____ (Many students getthis wrong—ask questions!)

4. Jane's brother wasn't a very warm person. She felt that he would be friendlier if he would just hug people a little bit. She decided to praise him, first only if he stood close. Next, she praised him only if he touched her hand or shoulder briefly. Finally, she praised him only if he hugged her. Getting him to hug her would be termed a(n) _____.

5. Reinforcers should be delivered only when the desired behavior occurs. This is called the principle of _____.

6. John reinforced Marty with an M&M for reading sentences out loud. He gave Marty an M&M as soon as Marty finished reading the sentence. Marty worked eagerly for the M&M's at first. But after about 50 sentences, Marty didn't want to read anymore. Had John continued at that point, he would have violated what principle of effective reinforcement? _____

7. Reinforcers should be delivered as soon after the behavior has occurred as possible. This is called the principle of _____.

8. Kay decided to go out for basketball. She went to practice six days a week, usually putting in three hours of practice. The coach praised her play only when she played well and immediately after good plays. Even with that, she didn't feel that she got praised too often. The coach restricted her praise to "good play," but never gave any other feedback, pointers for improvement, indication of appreciation for efforts, or even a friendly comment. Kay quit after concluding that such mechanical praise just didn't make all that work worth doing. What principle of effective reinforcement did the coach neglect? _____

9. Brigham and his colleagues (1972) delivered tokens to children to get them to work more on their handwriting. The researchers gave tokens immediately after the children first sat down whether or not they had done any handwriting. The tokens could be traded for activities that they enjoyed but did not get to participate in too often. Delivering tokens immediately after sitting down, in order to reinforce the accuracy of writing, violates what principle of effective reinforcement, if any? _____

10. Mrs. Upton allowed Betty to stay home from school whenever she complained of being sick. Mrs. Upton did not let Betty stay home for talking about any other problems. Now Betty complains often about her illnesses but not about other problems. What behavioral procedure accounts for Betty's becoming a hypochondriac? _____

11. Short-answer question B: Name the four principles that govern the effectiveness of a reinforcer:

_____

_____

_____

_____

1. Mr. Mack wanted to teach Ken, his infant son, to sit up before any other children his age. So, when Ken was 4 months old, Mr. Mack designated the half hour after dinner as time to reward Ken for sitting up by giving him a spoon of applesauce. Ken didn't seem interested in the applesauce. A behavior analyst would guess that the applesauce did not work very well because Ken was already _____ on food (use technical term).

2. The principle of contingency states that the reinforcer should be delivered _____ when the behavior occurs.

3. The Spanish Club met for lunch each day. Members passed you the ice cream if you asked for it in Spanish but not if you asked for it in English. Members soon used the Spanish word for ice cream and stopped using the English word. What procedure was the Club using to increase asking for ice cream in Spanish rather than English? _____

4. Judy encouraged Tom to read by patting his head. She patted while he was reading. She patted only when he was reading. Attention was important to Tom because Judy gave him few pats or other attention. However, because each pat lasted about a second, he didn't even seem to notice. Tom soon stopped reading. What principle of effective reinforcement, if any, does Judy's procedure omit?

    _____

5. Hall and his colleagues (1972) gave Jerry 25 cents at the end of the month for each time that he was observed wearing his braces (and only for wearing his braces). The money permitted him to buy things that he wanted, and he never seemed to have too much money. What principle of effective reinforcement, if any, did they violate? _____

6. Mary and Ken played tic-tac-toe in class. Mary was apparently reinforced by the challenge of Ken's responses. He made his mark immediately after she made her mark. He made a mark only when she made a mark. By the twentieth game, they were tired of tic-tac-toe. What principle of effective reinforcement accounts for their getting tired of the game?

    _____

7. Members of the Utopian Village agreed to rely on expressions of love to maintain work behaviors in their community. The members provided each other with these expressions immediately after work behaviors. They also provided these expressions after goofing off behaviors. These expressions of love were extremely important to every member of the group, and no one ever got too many of them. What principle of effective reinforcement, if any, did they neglect? _____

8. Carey tutored Dave, the star football tackle, in poetry by having him compose short poems on a blackboard while she watched. She reserved her praise for the good aspects of his compositions. She gave her praise as soon as he wrote a line. She kept the sessions short so he wouldn't tire of the tutoring. To her surprise, her praise was very important to him. What principles, if any, did she omit in her procedure?

    _____

9. The principle of size states that you must be sure to give the person enough of the reinforcer to be _____.

10. Jane's brother wasn't a very warm person. She decided to praise him only when he stood close to people. Then, she praised him only when he stood close and touched them briefly on the arm. Finally, she praised him only when he also hugged them. Because her goal was to have him stand close and hug people, standing close to someone would be called a(n)

    _____

    to that goal.

11. Short-answer question C. State the *principle of size*:

    _____
    _____
    _____
    _____

Grade _____

Date _____

1. What schedule of reinforcement would you use in order to maximize the length of time that it takes a response to extinguish after reinforcement is stopped? _____

2. If every hundredth response is reinforced, the person may stop responding or start responding irregularly. The effect of such a large ratio is known as _____.

3. Maria's parents put her on a well-designed chore system. She was paid right after correctly doing a chore and only for doing it correctly. She felt the amount of money was plenty for the work. But Maria already earned more money than she could spend by babysitting. They were weakening the money reinforcer by ignoring the principle of _____.

4. Staats and associates (1964) found that reading acquisition responses could be increased by delivering a marble after every response. What is the label for the generic schedule of reinforcement they were using? _____

5. Sarah sold Tupperware to Barbara but Barbara usually would not buy the newest item on the first try. Usually Sarah had to try many times (2, 3, 4 or 5 times), but Barbara always bought the new item eventually. What schedule is Sarah's selling behavior on? _____
_____

6. Rich agreed to paint the house as part of his chores if he could have a rest break after every 100 brush strokes, After he counted 100 strokes, he got a drink of water and took a brief break. What schedule of reinforcement is his painting on? _____

7. Maria's parents had her on a well-designed chore system. They checked carefully to see if she did the chore. They kept a careful record of her chore behavior. They paid her at the end of the week. Maria seemed to like the amount of money they paid her. They weakened the effectiveness of the money by ignoring the principle of _____.

8. Angie seemed to have a hearing problem. She never answered a question the first time it was asked of her. She always said "What?" to the questioner and then would answer the second time it was asked. What is the name of the schedule that the questioner is on? _____
_____

9. Bob lived near the common phone in the dorm, so he had to answer it much of the time. Furthermore, most of the dorm members didn't bother to thank him for answering it. He found that, on the average, he got thanked only once in four times. His phone answering was reinforced according to what schedule? _____

10. A schedule of reinforcement in which the response is never reinforced is called a(n) _____ schedule.

11. Short-answer question A. Describe the rate of responding with a *fixed-ratio* schedule and a *variable-ratio* schedule:

_____
_____
_____
_____
_____
_____

1. Maria earned a portion of her allowance doing chores. The money was given to her right after she told her parents that she had done the chore. The pay was pretty good—for example, 10 cents for taking out the garbage, 25 cents for the dishes. Maria was always broke, so the money was welcome. But the parents hardly ever bothered to check the job after Maria told them it had been completed. As a result, it often wasn't done right, and sometimes it wasn't done at all. They were weakening the effectiveness of their reinforcer by ignoring the principle of _____.

2. When someone is reinforced for every response, he or she is said to be on the generic schedule referred to as the _____ schedule of reinforcement.

3. Don's father used to have an endless interest in hearing about the latest chapter in his science-fiction books. Later, his father listened to Don's account only after Don had read an entire book. If you consider a response to be the reading of one chapter, and three books had 6, 19, and 11 chapters each, what schedule of reinforcement was his father using later to reinforce reading of chapters? _____

4. If a person is reinforced for different numbers of responses each time, he is on the specific schedule called a(n) _____ schedule.

5. Jake is complimented for just saying "no" every 13 times. What schedule of reinforcement are Jake's "no's" on? _____

6. Staats and associates (1964) studied the rate of reading acquisition responses of children when they were given a reinforcer after every response and when they were given a reinforcer after varying numbers of responses that averaged five. Name the schedule that produced the highest rate of responding. _____.

7. When Don came home late at night, the door was always locked. So he would dig out his keys, insert the key in the lock, and turn it. The door never opened, so he would turn it again and it would open. What schedule of reinforcement was his key-turning behavior on? _____

8. Frank wanted to increase the rate at which his infant daughter Alice imitated his behavior when he said, "Can you do this?" So he gave her a bite of ice cream each time she imitated. She usually lost interest after about 15 imitations. If Frank asked you how he could increase the number of times she imitated him while still using ice cream, you should suggest that he switch to what generic schedule? A(n) _____ schedule.

9. The ratio schedule that produces alternating periods of responding and pausing is called a(n) _____.

10. Tactic #6 in using the reinforcement strategy for solving human problems is to increase response rate with a(n) _____ schedule of reinforcement.

11. Short-answer question B. Describe one advantage and one disadvantage of the ratio schedules:

_____

_____

_____

_____

1. Professor Irving often talks with students about what field to major in; she tries to interest them in psychology. She finds that about 1 in 10 on the average end up by becoming psychology majors. If getting majors is a reinforcer for her, what schedule is her talking with students on? _____

2. Maria's parents put her on a well-administered chore system. She earned one chocolate-covered peanut right after completing such chores as washing dishes and mowing the lawn. They gave her the peanut only when they had verified that she did a good job on the chore. Maria never got peanuts too often. Maria didn't do too many of her chores. Her parents weakened the effectiveness of the peanuts by ignoring the principle of _____ _____.

3. Staats and associates (1964) delivered a reinforcer after varying numbers of reading acquisition responses that averaged 5. What is the name of the schedule that they were using? _____ _____

4. If a person is reinforced for some responses but not for every response, he is said to be on what generic schedule: a(n) _____ schedule.

5. Koegel and Rincover (1977) found that children with retardation would imitate without reinforcement for much longer when they had been trained on what schedule, continuous or fixed-ratio? _____

6. In Professor Smith's course, students could start on the next lesson only after they had correctly answered ten questions about the current lesson. If starting on the next lesson is a reinforcer, then having to make ten correct responses would define a(n) _____ schedule of reinforcement.

7. David was very obnoxious in class. His teacher used to tell him to stop, explain why what he was doing was inappropriate, and generally spend a lot of attention on him. She finally decided to totally ignore his obnoxious behavior. David kept right on doing it, however. What procedure did his teacher use to try to decrease his obnoxious behavior? _____

8. What schedule of reinforcement is usually used with shaping? _____ _____

9. Ann worked in a special room on her algebra homework problems. Dr. Otterman could observe through a one-way mirror and tell when she had completed seven problems. He then went in and complimented her on her progress. What schedule is she on for working problems? _____

10. The schedule that produces the highest and most uniform rate of responding is called a(n) _____ _____.

11. Short-answer question C. Name and define two specific types of schedules that involve counting the number of responses:

_____

_____

_____

_____

_____

1. In most joke books, an average of only 1 in 10 jokes is hilarious, and the rest are terrible. But most people will plow through all the jokes looking for the good ones. What schedule of reinforcement is a joke reader on? _____
   _____

2. If you think that an example involves a ratio schedule, ask, "If the person makes the response very rapidly, will the next reinforcer arrive _____?"

3. The author of a behavior analysis textbook sits in his office hour after hour typing new examples. His writing is reinforced by finally finishing the twentieth example for a lesson. If typing out one example is the response, what schedule of reinforcement is his writing on?
   _____

4. What two types of intermittent schedules produce a tendency for people to stop responding after reinforcement? _____
   _____ and _____

5. Bernie's mother used to remind him to start his homework as soon as he got home from school. But she stopped doing it last month, and Bernie almost never starts his homework right after school like he used to. What behavioral procedure did his mother use to produce this disastrous change in behavior?
   _____

6. When Danny gets in the car to go on a trip (no matter how long), he immediately begins asking, "Are we there yet?" Sometimes the trips last just 3 minutes to the corner market, and other times they last 30 minutes to a nearby lake. Assuming that having one of his parents say, "Yes, we are there" is a reinforcer, Danny is on what schedule of reinforcement for his questions? _____
   _____

7. A schedule in which the person is reinforced for the first response that he or she makes after differing periods of time is called a(n) _____
   schedule.

8. If the author of a book were to put his or her climactic scenes too far apart in the book, the readers might quit reading even though they were still being reinforced occasionally. This would be an example of
   _____.

9. Mawhinney and associates (1971) tested students at three-week intervals. Their study behavior would be on what schedule of reinforcement? _____
   _____

10. Tactic #7 in using the reinforcement strategy for solving human problems is to reduce reinforcer frequency with a(n) _____ schedule.

11. Short-answer question A. Explain why being reinforced every 10 minutes isn't necessarily a fixed-interval schedule:
    _____
    _____
    _____
    _____

1. Ken gets credit for one unit of work every time he tightens 18 nuts on the frame of a washing machine. What schedule is he on for getting credit? _____
_____

2. In most books, there are passages or scenes that are boring. However, most people just keep reading with the hope that a really exciting scene or passage will soon come along. Such a scene may occur on the average of only once in 33 pages, yet most people continue reading. Their reading behavior is on a(n) _____
schedule.

3. Of the four intermittent schedules that you have studied, which one produces the highest rate of responding? _____
_____

4. Chester works in a factory in which his supervisor comes by to check on him every 10 minutes. If it is reinforcing for him to be found working, what schedule is his working on? _____
_____

5. Gladys loved rock music. When she drove along in her car, she listened intently when music was being played but stopped listening when the announcer started talking or playing a commercial or reading the news. Music as an event would be called a(n) _____
for Gladys's listening behavior.

6. Mawhinney and associates (1971) might have given tests in either of two ways: (a) after every three weeks or (b) after differing periods of time averaging three weeks. Which schedule would produce the more uniform rate of studying?
_____

7. Do people maintain a uniform rate of responding on (a) fixed-interval or (b) variable-interval schedules? _____
(a or b)

8. Ron and Betty are only interested in the few scenes of the movie showing dancing. These came after 5, 25, 15, and 15 minutes. What schedule of reinforcement is their movie viewing on? _____

9. If you think that an example involves an interval schedule, you should ask, "If the person makes no response at all, will there eventually arrive a time at which _____ response will produce the reinforcer?"

10. Richard is a radar scanner whose job is to look for unidentified planes on his radar screen. He usually sees one on the average of every four hours. What schedule is his looking behavior on? _____
_____

11. Short-answer question B. Name and define the two interval schedules:
_____
_____
_____
_____
_____
_____
_____

1. On which interval schedule do people work at a gradually increasing rate as the time for reinforcement approaches? _____

2. Teachers frequently check on their students' work by walking around the room and looking to see whether or not they are working. The students are being reinforced for working on what schedule? _____

3. Marty's teacher complimented him after he completed 6, 8, 6, and 4 problems. What type of schedule was he on? _____

4. If you think that an example involves an interval schedule ask, "If the person does not emit the behavior for a time, will there eventually arrive a time when emitting _____ response will produce the reinforcer?"

5. A schedule in which the person is reinforced for the first response that occurs after a constant period of time is called a(n) _____ _____ schedule.

6. Sarah wanted her son Dan to become a bookworm, so she encouraged him to read books. Every time that he showed her an interesting fact in the book, she gave him money right then and there. She gave him the money only if he showed her a fact. Dan seemed delighted with the amount. He never seemed to get the money too often. What principle of effective reinforcement, if any, did Sarah fail to employ? _____

7. Mawhinney and associates (1971) studied student study patterns. They used two schedules: (a) They tested the students daily, and (b) they tested them every three weeks. If the professor stopped giving tests without telling the students, which of the two schedules that he used would lead to more enduring studying behavior? _____

8. John stays "properly" dressed in his room expecting visitors (he is a bit pompous). He has a visitor on the average of once every 65 minutes. If he is reinforced by his visitors for being properly dressed, what schedule is he on? _____

9. John's father gives him an extra dessert when John has brought his own plate into the kitchen for four meals. What schedule is John on for bringing his plate into the kitchen? _____

10. Darrel didn't like football, but he sure liked the cheerleaders. So he tuned in at the beginning of half time. Exactly five minutes later, the cheerleaders came on and did a routine. What schedule was Darrel's watching behavior on? _____

11. Short-answer question C. Describe the pattern of responding produced by each of the four schedules:

_____
_____
_____
_____
_____
_____
_____

Grade _____

Name _____    Date _____

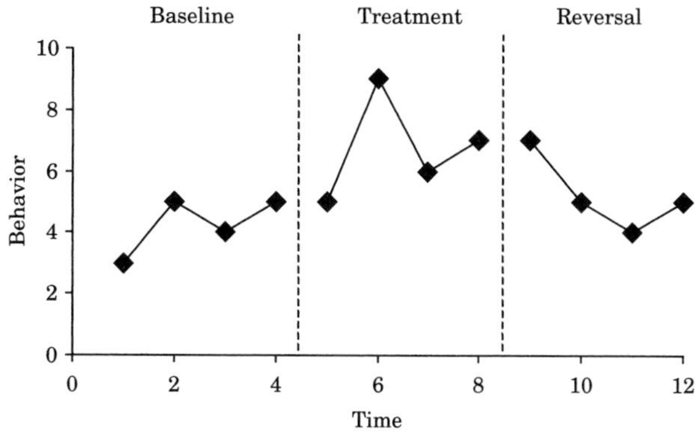

**Figure 15-1.** An experimental analysis of an unspecified behavior.

1. Roy always looked for an insert in the newspaper announcing food sales. He found that inserts occurred sometimes after a week, sometimes after five weeks, but that he found one on the average of every two weeks. If finding an insert reinforced his looking for them, what schedule of reinforcement is his looking on?

   _____

2. Interval recording is a method of observation in which a response is recorded if some part of a behavioral episode is observed within one of a series of _____ intervals. Time sample recording differs only in that the series of intervals are _____ _____.

3. Jason Johnson aspired to become a great poet. But the trouble is that he couldn't sit still long enough to write very much poetry. So he set himself the goal of writing a 25-stanza poem each day. He started by writing a one-stanza poem, then a two stanza poem, and so on until he had worked up to 25 stanzas. Writing a one-stanza poem would be called a(n) _____ to the 25-stanza poem.

4. What level of reliability is considered acceptable for a new behavioral definition? ____%

5. Differential reinforcement involves two basic behavioral procedures. They are _____ and _____ _____.

6. Figure 15-1 shows the number of behaviors that Fran emitted with and without treatment. Divided? _____ Stable? _____ Convincing? _____ Caused? ____ (yes, no) (Don't forget to spell out "yes" and "no" instead of "y" and "n.")

7. Dan was concerned about his son's small vocabulary, so he decided to promote crossword puzzles as a way to build vocabulary. He bought a book of crossword puzzles and paid his son $5 for finishing a complete puzzle. He paid for the puzzle as soon as it was completed. His son seemed always to need money to fix his old dragster and seemed to feel that $5 was good pay for completing a puzzle. When Dan's son didn't seem to have an improved vocabulary after 25 puzzles, Dan got suspicious and checked the puzzle book to find that the answers were listed in the back. What principle of effective reinforcement did the presence of the answers negate? _____

8. The elementary school teacher who grades students' tests as soon as they finish them is enhancing the effectiveness of her grade as a reinforcer by what principle? _____

9. Reliability is computed by the formula _____.

10. Harvey earned money picking pears. He was paid 25 cents for every ten that he picked. What schedule of reinforcement is his pear-picking behavior on? _____ _____

11. Short-answer question A. Explain why being reinforced every 10 minutes isn't necessarily a fixed-interval schedule:

_____

_____

_____

_____

Grade _____

Name _____

Date _____

1. If a response produces reinforcement after differing periods of time, we say that response is being reinforced according to a(n) _____ _____ schedule (two words).

2. Katherine got fed up with Gladys's lack of enthusiasm, so she had a long talk with Gladys one day and told her to act more enthusiastic. Gladys became a changed person, acting much more enthusiastic as a result. What behavioral procedure did Katherine use to increase Gladys's enthusiasm? _____ _____

3. Two observers counted the number of times that Fearsome Freddy hit another child. Observer One counted 15 hits, and Observer Two counted 20 hits. Compute the reliability: _____%. Is it adequate? _____ (yes, no)

4. Karen was into target shooting with a .38 magnum. She found that from 50 feet she could hit a bull's-eye about once in 10 tries, sometimes more, sometimes less. If hitting the bull's-eye is the reinforcer for shooting, what schedule is her shooting on: _____ .

5. If a person is required to make a high number of responses for each reinforcement, his responding may decrease because of what is called _____ .

6. Professor King gave Margo, the star basketball player, the assignment of composing a poem to hand in every day of the semester. He read the poem and returned it with praise for the good aspects of it the next class period. He praised only the good features of the poems. He was careful not to provide too much praise. His praise seemed to be very important to Margo. In spite of his careful procedure, Margo's poetry writing did not improve. What principle of effective reinforcement, if any, did he neglect? _____

7. The Barker Street baby-sitting club awards 10 points to any mother who takes care of another club member's child for an hour and charges 10 points to a mother whose child is cared for. Marge's rate of baby-sitting for other club members increased after she joined the club and was awarded points. The points would be called a(n) _____ .

8. Shaping involves the differential reinforcement of a series of responses that are successive approximations to a(n) _____ .

9. If a person's behavior is no longer reinforced and its rate decreases, what schedule of reinforcement is it said to be on? _____ .

10. Sally tried to teach Harry how to throw a frisbee. She praised him right after every correct throw and only when he threw it well. Harry was very turned on by Sally so her praise was really important to him. He never seemed to get too much of it. What principles of effective reinforcement, if any, did Sally fail to employ? _____

11. Short-answer question B. Name the four principles that govern the effectiveness of a reinforcer:

_____

_____

_____

_____

_____

1. Name the four principles that govern the effectiveness of a reinforcer: _____, _____, _____, and _____.

2. When Flora studied in history class, the teacher praised her efforts. When she studied in English class, the teacher ignored her. Flora soon came to study more in history than in English. What behavioral procedure were these two teachers accidently using to increase studying in one class compared to the other? _____

3. Backward Ben hated the idea that behavioral methods might improve the ease of learning. As he worked through this very book, he rejoiced every time that he missed an answer—saying to himself, "See, behavior analysis isn't so hot after all!" But he found that, try as he might, he could only miss an average of one question in 89. What schedule of reinforcement is his question answering on? _____

4. If you were concerned about the problem of satiating someone by reinforcing them for every instance of behavior that they emit, give the generic name for the kind of schedule that you would use to reduce the problem _____.

5. John's teacher helped him overcome being a loner. At first she paid attention to him only when he looked at other children, then only when he was near them, and finally only when he was playing with them. What procedure did the teacher use to modify John's loner behavior? _____

6. Experimental designs are used to discover exactly why a behavior changed. They are used to rule out _____ explanations based on coincidence.

7. If you reinforce the first response that occurs after a fixed amount of time has passed, you are following a(n) _____ schedule.

8. Clarence had to write a five-page essay for his art history class every week. If a page is one response, what schedule of reinforcement is his essay-writing behavior on? _____

9. When shaping a new behavior, both reinforcement and extinction are used in the procedure of differential reinforcement. What is the best generic schedule to use for the reinforcement part of differential reinforcement? _____

10. Johnny used to be very brave; but one day when he fell down and skinned his knee he cried. His mother immediately rushed over to him and held him. She brought him inside for an ice cream treat to help him forget his pain. Johnny now cries a lot when he hurts himself. His mother always comforts him and gives him an ice cream treat. What behavioral procedure did his mother unintentionally use to increase Johnny's crying? _____

11. Short-answer question C. Explain the relationship between *shaping* and *differential reinforcement*:

_____
_____
_____
_____
_____

1. Kenny had trouble learning how to pronounce 1776, so his teacher praised "seventeen seventy six" and ignored "seventy seventy six." In a few days, Kenny was saying it right. What procedure is the teacher using to teach Kenny the correct pronunciation? _____

2. Adolf had 100 flash cards with German words like *und*, *der*, and *kopf* written on their fronts and the translations written on their backs. Adolf looked at the front of each card and said the English translation. Then, he turned the card over to see if he was right. He was always right after about a month. Suppose when the card reads *"und,"* the English word *and* is reinforced, while other words are extinguished. Suppose when the card reads *"der,"* only *the* is reinforced. What procedure is at work here? _____

3. Professor Tod always made positive comments about statements Gene made. Professor Rose rarely had a reaction. Gene talked a lot to Professor Tod, and he talked only a little to Professor Rose. Professor Rose is what kind of stimulus for talking to him? _____

4. Donna used to be confused about what constituted a straight in poker. Her husband often asked her two questions: "What is 'four-five-six-seven-and-eight' called?" and "What is five hearts called?" He praised her when she said straight to the first question but not when she said straight to the second question. Gradually, she came to say "straight" only when asked the first question. Her <u>behavior</u> of saying "straight" is called _____.

5. Ted ignored Dick when he pronounced Aaron Burr's name as "Brr" and praised him when he said "Bur." Pretty soon Dick always pronounced it as "Bur." What procedure is Ted using? _____

6. After much practice, Xavier had learned the square root of many numbers. If his teacher asked him, "What is the square root of eighty-one?" he promptly said, "Nine." But he did not give "nine" as the square root of any other number. The increased probability of saying "nine" when asked the square root of 81 means that the question has come to exert _____ over that behavior.

7. Jonah has three goldfish. He played a game with his friend Robert to see if Robert could name his goldfish. If he called the big goldfish "whale," Jonah praised him but ignored him if he called the big goldfish "Tiny." If he called the small goldfish "Tiny," Jonah praised him but not if he called the small goldfish "whale". What procedure was Jonah using? _____

8. A stimulus that occurs before a behavior and increases the rate of the behavior is called a(n) _____.
A stimulus that occurs after a behavior and increases the rate of the behavior is called a(n) _____.

9. If a stimulus that precedes a behavior is present only if extinction will occur for that behavior, it is called a(n) _____.

10. Doug got a lot of attention if he was reading a mechanics book, but his father ignored him if he was reading anything else. Doug became an avid reader of mechanics books. What procedure increased Doug's reading of mechanics books? _____

11. Short-answer question A. Define *stimulus control*:

_____
_____
_____
_____
_____
_____

1. Johnny made many baby noises. However, when he said "Dada," his parents paid a lot of attention to him. When he made other sounds, they ignored him. He came to say "Dada" a lot. What procedure accounts for Johnny saying "Dada" a lot? _____ _____

2. If a behavior occurs with increased probability in the presence of an SD, then we say that the stimulus exerts _____ _____ over the behavior.

3. A discriminative stimulus (SD) is a stimulus that precedes a behavior and is present only if what procedure will be applied to the behavior: _____.

4. Jeff swears a lot around the dorm but doesn't swear much at home. His dorm friends encourage swearing; his parents don't. What procedure accounts for the fact that Jeff swears more in the dorm than at home? _____

5. The first tactic in using the stimulus control strategy for solving human problems is to narrow stimulus control through _____ _____.

6. If the question "What is two plus two?" always gets Ward to say "four," then we say that the question exerts _____ _____ over his behavior.

7. Redd and Birnbrauer (1969) had Bill give a child with retardation edibles for playing cooperatively with other children and had Bob not reward the child for cooperative play. Bill would be called a(n) _____ for playing cooperatively while Bob would be called a(n) _____.

8. Staats and Butterfield (1965) showed Carlos 700 cards, each with one word on it. They gave him a token if he said the word on that card but nothing if he said the word on another card. What procedure did they use to teach Carlos to read 700 words? _____.

9. Burris's classmates helped him learn the meaning of *reinforcer* by asking him two questions. The first question was: "If Rose asked for some candy and got it but didn't ask for any more in the future, what is the candy called?" The second question was: "If Rose asked for some candy and got it, and if she asked for more in the future, what is the candy called?" His classmates praised him if he said "reinforcer" in response to the second but not the first question. He soon came to answer the questions correctly. His behavior of answering "reinforcer" is called _____ behavior.

10. The cooperative dorm uses a green tag as a "welcome signal" for anyone who is welcoming visitors. Assume that welcoming a visitor reinforces visiting behavior. If the occupant welcomes visitors only if the green tag is out, the green tag is a(n) _____ for visiting behavior.

11. Short-answer question B. Explain the difference between *discrimination training* and *differential reinforcement*:

_____

_____

_____

_____

_____

_____

_____

_____

1. Adolf asked Gert to help him learn German pronunciation. Gert showed him a card with the German word *der* on it. Gert praised him when he pronounced "der" like "dayrr." Gert ignored him when he pronounced "der" like "dur." After 30 trials, Adolf was always saying "dayrr." What procedure improved Adolph's pronunciation of "der"? _____ _____

2. When a person is more likely to emit a particular behavior in the presence of the SD than in the presence of the S-delta, we call the behavior _____ _____.

3. Sheila was trying to become more assertive around men. When she was assertive with Bill, he responded favorably. When she was assertive with Ken, he ignored her. As a result, Sheila became more assertive around Bill but not Ken. The increased probability of assertive behavior in the presence of Bill means that Bill has come to exert _____ over her assertive behavior.

4. When Charlie Brown smiled at the little redheaded girl, she ignored him. When he smiled at Lucy, she was very nice to him. If Charlie Brown's smiles were reinforced by "niceness," what type of stimulus is Lucy? _____

5. Reinforcing one behavior and extinguishing a different behavior in the presence of the same stimulus is called _____.

6. The third strategy in solving human problems is the _____ _____ strategy.

7. Reinforcing one behavior while extinguishing a second behavior in the presence of stimulus A and extinguishing the first behavior while reinforcing the second behavior in the presence of stimulus B is considered to be an example of what procedure? _____ _____

8. Redd and Birnbrauer (1969) studied the results of having one behavior analyst give a child with retardation edibles when he played cooperatively with other children while a second behavior analyst did not. The child learned to play cooperatively when the first adult was present but not when the second adult was present. What procedure accounts for this result? _____ _____

9. Jeff's dorm friends paid attention when he said "X#!" but not when he said "gosh" or "darn." Jeff gradually said only "X#!" What procedure is at work? _____

10. Dickie's mother taught him to recognize the picture of her favorite candidate, Aaron Burr, by sometimes showing him a picture of Burr and sometimes of Jefferson and asking, "Who is this?" She praised him when he answered correctly. Soon he answered "Burr" to the first picture but not the second. His behavior of calling only the first picture "Burr" is called _____.

11. Short-answer question C. Explain the difference between a *reinforcer* and a *discriminative stimulus*:

_____
_____
_____
_____
_____

1. The occurrence of a behavior in the presence of a novel stimulus is called _____.

2. Generalization training is a procedure in which a behavior is reinforced in each of a series of situations until it _____ _____ to other members of that same stimulus class.

3. Davey looked at the big old elm and said, "That's a tree, mom" to his surprised mother. She praised him for knowing it, and he often told her that the elm was a tree. One day he said, "Hey mom, that is a tree, too, isn't it?" and pointed to a giant oak. Again, she made a big fuss over his knowledge. After several more trees, Davey started referring to all big woody plants as "trees". What behavioral procedure did his mother use? _____

4. A stimulus that precedes the behavior and is present only if the behavior will be reinforced is called a(n) _____ _____; a stimulus that precedes the behavior and is present only if the behavior will be extinguished is called a(n) _____.

5. Dr. Rutherford taught Karen a number of "not shy" behaviors using role playing in his clinic. However, she never could get up enough nerve to apply them anywhere else. So Dr. Rutherford arranged to have another psychologist reinforce Karen for "not shy" behavior also in a role-playing situation. Karen then started to act in not-shy ways at school, on her job, and even among strangers. What behavioral procedure did Dr. Rutherford employ to help Karen? _____

6. Professor Smart always got a big smile whenever she referred to the pretty brunette as "Kay" in class, but she didn't seem to recognize the brunette outside of class. One day, as she was crossing campus, she looked up, saw the brunette, and said, "Hi, Kay" and was rewarded with a giant smile. From then on, she recognized Kay no matter where she saw her. What behavioral procedure did Kay use to teach Professor Smart to recognize her in all places outside of class? _____ _____

7. The collection of all people that you encounter during a day would be called a(n) _____.

8. Miller and Weaver (1974) reinforced students for correctly labeling the examples contained in this book. They then observed that the students could correctly label examples that they had not seen before. The occurrence of the students' labeling behavior in the presence of the new examples would be called _____.

9. Rex praised his daughter for saying "fifteen" when asked "What does eight plus seven equal?" but not when asked "What does nine plus four equal?" What procedure was Rex using? _____ _____

10. Damien helped his little sister learn addition by showing her simple problems that were printed on a series of flash cards. Damien gave her a chocolate-covered peanut after showing her the card "3 + 9 =?" if she said "twelve" but not if she said "twelve" when he showed her the card "8 + 7=?". Damien used the same approach to answers to other cards. What procedure did he use? _____

11. Short-answer question A. Define *stimulus class*:

_____

_____

_____

_____

_____

1. Mr. Wyler worked long and hard to teach Fran to study most of the time when she was in third-grade spelling. However, this did not change her habit of goofing off all the time in other classes. Mr. Wyler suggested to Ms. Green that she also reinforce Fran for studying in third-grade math. Pretty soon, Fran was the champion studier in all of her classes. What procedure had her teachers used to bring about this remarkable change? _____ _____

2. Reinforcing a behavior in each of a series of situations until the behavior generalizes to other members of that same stimulus class, is what procedure? _____

3. Professor Smart always got a big smile whenever she referred to the pretty brunette as "Kay" in class, but she didn't seem to recognize her outside of class. One day, however, as she was walking across campus she looked up, saw the pretty brunette, and said, "Hi, Kay," and was rewarded by a giant smile. The occurrence of the naming behavior outside of class would be an example of what process ? _____

4. If a behavior is more likely to occur in the presence of the SD than the S-delta, the behavior is called a(n) _____ behavior.

5. The grouping of all situations in which Professor Smart might encounter Kay at the University—class, hallway, campus, student union, and so on-would be called a(n) _____.

6. Bornstein and associates (1977) taught Jane to be assertive in response to being interrupted by another person. They then taught her to be assertive in several other types of situations. When they tested her assertiveness in three situations, they found her to be quite assertive. What behavioral procedure did they use? _____

7. Reinforcing a behavior in the presence of a particular stimulus and extinguishing it in the presence of other stimuli is called _____.

8. James usually acted very businesslike around Mr. Smith because he seemed to appreciate it. James usually did not act businesslike around Mr. Clevis because he ignored such behavior and acted in a slower and more relaxed manner. In this situation, we would say that Mr. Smith exerted _____ _____ over James's businesslike behavior.

9. A set of related stimuli is called a(n) _____.

10. Dr. Ford taught Jan a number of "good listening" behaviors using role playing in his clinic. However, she never used them anywhere else. So Dr. Ford arranged to have a colleague reinforce Jan for "good listening" behavior also in another role-playing situation. Jan then used good listening with her English teacher. The occurrence of good listening behavior outside the role-playing situation would be an example of _____.

11. Short-answer question B. Define generalization (not generalization training):
_____
_____
_____
_____
_____

1. Sally was a health food nut. Whenever Ralph ate healthy food at home, she praised his diet. Later, she praised him whenever he ate healthy food at their favorite restaurant. Pretty soon he was eating only healthy foods no matter where he ate. What behavioral procedure did Sally use? _____ _____

2. Miller and Weaver (1974) showed students a series of examples of extinction. If you regard each example as a stimulus, then the collection of all examples of extinction would be termed a(n) _____ _____.

3. Generalization is defined as the occurrence of a behavior in the presence of a(n) _____.

4. Professor Brainbuster usually got a smile when he called the student in the front row "Ted" but not if he called him "Dan." Likewise, he usually got a smile when he called the burly athlete in the back row "Dan" but not if he called him "Ted." What behavioral procedure are these guys unknowingly applying to the prof's behavior? _____ _____

5. If Danny is reinforced for calling the giant old tree in front of his house a "tree," he might see the giant oak down the street and call it a tree also. If he does, the occurrence of his labeling behavior for the second tree is called _____.

6. The second tactic in using the stimulus control strategy to help people is to broaden stimulus control through _____.

7. Peggy never volunteered to answer a question in class. However, a question arose one day in one of her classes concerning her greatest love, classical art, and she got so excited she volunteered. The teacher praised her for having the right answer. She volunteered often in that class in the future. Somewhat later, the same thing happened in another class, and again she volunteered and had the right answer. After that, she started to volunteer in all of her classes. Even though no one was intentionally arranging it, Peggy's behavior changed as a result of what procedure? _____ _____

8. The Klines praised little Sarah when she called their dog "doggy." One day she called the neighbor's dog "doggy" also. What behavioral process occurred? _____

9. The increased probability of a discriminated behavior that is produced by a stimulus is called _____ _____.

10. Any stimulus in whose presence a behavior has not previously been reinforced is called a(n) _____ stimulus.

11. Short-answer question C. Define *generalization training*:

_____

_____

_____

_____

_____

1. Moore and Goldiamond (1964) had the correct answer light up while the incorrect answers remained dark. They always used the same problem with the same correct answer. They reinforced pushing the correct answer but ignored pushing the incorrect answer. They then gradually increased the brightness of the incorrect answers until they were as bright as the correct answer. What behavioral procedure were they using when they gradually made the correct and incorrect answers equally bright? _____

2. Fading is the use of a prompt to establish a specific _____.

3. A method for gradually changing a behavior is called _____; a method for gradually changing one stimulus is called _____.

4. Darlene praised her daughter for saying "crow" when shown a picture of the large black bird and ignored her for saying "crow" when shown the picture of the small black bird. Darlene then gave the child hints for "bigness" when showing the picture of the crow. She gradually withdrew these hints. What behavioral procedure was Darlene using? _____

5. Roger was shown a picture of a red ant and the words *This is a r—d ant* (he had been taught to fill in such a blank). Next he got a picture of a red ant and the words "This is a r— ant." After each problem, Roger was given an M & M if he filled in the blank correctly and was ignored if he got it wrong. As the sequence developed, fewer of the letters in the word *red* were given to him. Those letters would be called a(n) _____.

6. Marvin ignored Sheila when he was using the headphones to listen to his new stereo. Marvin gave her a lot of attention when he was listening to the stereo without headphones. Sheila started sitting next to Marvin only when he did not have the headphones on. What behavioral procedure influenced when Sheila sat next to Marvin? _____

7. Her workbook showed Carol pictures of many red objects: ants, balls, houses, fire engines. It asked her: *What color is this? _____.* The book reinforced Carol for writing *red* for this series of objects. At first, the question had one or more of the letters in *red* attached to the blank as a clue. But the book gradually eliminated these letters. Eventually, Carol could label an object as red even when she had not seen it before and had no prompt. What behavioral procedure did the book use to teach Carol to label red objects as "red"? _____

8. Mr. Hearthstone taught Greg to sing middle C by first playing the note loudly on the piano and asking Greg to copy it, which he could do easily. Mr. Hearthstone then played the note more and more softly until Greg was singing the note without any reminder from the piano. What procedure did Mr. Hearthstone use? _____

9. Suppose that Bev called the baseball a "ball" but she didn't call the bat a "ball." Because the behavior of saying "ball" is higher in the presence of the ball than in the presence of the bat, we call the behavior _____ behavior.

10. The temporary use of a prompt to establish a generalization is called _____.

11. Short-answer question A. Define a *prompt*:

_____

_____

_____

_____

1. Terry was taught to add by a teacher who showed him two piles of blocks, with two and three blocks in each, and who asked the question, "How much is two plus three?" As the training went on, the blocks were moved farther and farther from Terry. The blocks would be called a(n) _____.

2. The book showed Roger a picture of a red ant. It used many repetitions of the question "This is a ____ ant." It reinforced him for the correct answer. Later, the book showed Roger a red mat. The first time he saw the mat, he answered "red" to the question "This is a ____mat." The occurrence of his response to the new example of a red object would be an example of what behavioral process? _____

3. Melba taught Hilda to read the word "dog" by making cards with the word *dog* printed across the head of a picture of a dog. She then made a series of cards with less and less of the dog sketched in. She praised Hilda for saying "dog" when that was the word she was reading but ignored her when it was not. Melba used what procedure to teach Hilda to read the word "dog"? _____

4. Tom gets a ride home after school every day from Carol. He praised Carol every time she made the correct turn. The first day she didn't know the way, so he told her which way to turn at "Five Corners;" the next day he only said "here" at the turn and didn't tell her which way to turn; on following days, he gave no instructions at all. Carol learned the way perfectly in three days. What behavioral procedure did Tom use? _____

5. An added stimulus that increases the probability that a person will make the correct response is called a(n) _____.

6. Mr. Kline taught Roberta to label the kitchen floor as a rectangle by asking her "What shape is that? A rect____?", then "What shape is that? a rrrr____?" and, finally, with no prompt. He praised her when she said "rectangle." Mr. Kline taught Roberta to label the shape of a piece of paper in the same way. Roberta came to label any novel object with parallel sides, with right angles, and length greater than width as a rectangle. What procedure did Mr. Kline use? _____
_____

7. Schaefer (1963) used the German word *ich* to replace the English *I* in several short stories by Poe. The context of redundant sentences was enough to serve as an effective prompt for proper translation. By placing the German word in many different sentences, students learned to always recognize that word. What behavioral procedure did Schaefer use to teach the meaning of *ich*? _____

8. Programmed instruction requires a written response, provides immediate _____ on the correctness of the response, and uses small steps.

9. Programming is the temporary use of a prompt during generalization training to establish a(n) _____.

10. Professor Brainbuster shunned Samantha when she wore jeans, but one of her students, David, didn't mind. Samantha learned to wear jeans around David but not around the prof. What procedure influenced when she wore jeans? _____

11. Short-answer question B. Define the procedure of *fading*:

_____
_____
_____

1. In *Programmed Reading*, the child is shown a picture of a girl in a bag and then required to fill in the blank "That is Ann in the ba—." Showing one or more letters contained in the correct answer is called a(n) _____.

2. To use the stimulus control strategy to help solve human problems, (3) create new stimulus control by temporarily using _____.

3. Fran taught Jimmy to write *P* when shown a *P* but not when shown a *B*. Fran drew some light dashed lines that Jimmy drew over. She made the dashed lines fainter until they were not longer needed. What behavioral procedure did Fran use? _____

4. The teacher praised Juanita if she said "car" when he showed her the word "car," but not when he showed her the word "cat." To help her learn "car," he put a picture of a car next to the word. He gradually made the picture smaller until Juanita could no longer see it. What behavioral procedure was the teacher using? _____

5. The temporary use of a prompt to establish a generalization is called _____.

6. The gradual elimination of a prompt when teaching a discrimination is called _____.

7. Ann pointed to the table and asked Shigura, "What is this?" and then said the word "table" so he could hear it. She praised him when he also said the word "table." Gradually, she said the word more and more softly. What behavioral procedure did Ann use to teach Shigura to label this table correctly? _____

8. A prompt is an added _____ that increases the probability of a person's making the correct response in the presence of a novel stimulus.

9. Darlene praised her daughter for saying "crow" when shown a picture of the large black bird and ignored her for saying "crow" when shown the picture of the small black bird. What behavioral procedure was Darlene using? _____

10. Bob showed Tom a big red ball and asked, "What is this?" When Tom answered "ball," Bob gave him a tiny candy. After many trials, Tom would always say "ball." Next Tom held a little green ball up many times, asked what it was and gave Tom a candy when he said "ball." When Bob held up any kind of ball after that, Tom always called it a ball. What behavioral procedure did Bob use to teach Tom the idea of "ball"? _____

11. Short-answer question C. Define the procedure of *programming*:

_____

_____

_____

_____

1. The fourth tactic in the stimulus control strategy is to create complex stimulus control through _____ training or _____ training.

2. The use of verbal descriptions of behavior and reinforcement to teach a new behavior is called _____.

3. John's father sawed the first board to show John how to use the power saw. He then watched John cut a board and praised him when he followed the father's example. This would be an example of what behavioral procedure? _____

4. Ada patiently explained to Sam exactly where to look when he was pitching. She then had him throw several pitches while she was watching and praised him only when he did it right. What procedure for changing Sam's behavior did Ada use?
_____

5. Tom explained in detail how Frank should operate the chain saw, watched him try, and praised his performance. What behavioral procedure did Tom use?
_____

6. Cursive writing is often taught in school by showing children examples of the properly formed letters and words. The children are required to copy these letters over and over. The teacher praises good copies. This would be an example of what behavioral procedure? _____
_____

7. Mary showed Tommy two blocks and asked, "How many are there? Two?" and praised him when he said "Two." She then repeated the question at various times during the day, each time saying "Two" softer and softer until Tommy answered "Two" without any help. Mary then showed Tommy two toys and repeated the procedure. When she showed him two spoons and asked him how many, he said "Two" without any hint. By reinforcing Tommy's response of "Two" in the presence of a series of stimuli until he could apply it to a novel stimulus, Mary used what behavioral procedure? _____

8. Because the teacher's verbal description concerning what behavior the learner should produce is associated with reinforcement for the instructed behavior, the verbal description would technically be called a(n) _____
_____ for the instructed behavior.

9. Hollandsworth and his colleagues (1978) provided a verbal description to Herbert of how he should make clear responses to interview questions. They then observed his performance in a simulated interview session and reinforced correct responses. The behavior analysts were using what behavioral procedure to teach Herbert to make clear answers? _____
_____

10. Barb showed Kenny a picture of a tree and asked, "What is this? Say 'tree.'" Kenny said, "Tree." Several other times during the week she showed him the same picture and asked him, "What is this, a tree?" but saying "tree" more and more softly until he called it a tree without her hint. Barb was using what behavioral procedure? _____

11. Short-answer question A. Define *instructional training*, referring to its three parts:

_____
_____
_____
_____
_____
_____
_____

1. Buzz explained to Carol how to grip the ball in order to throw a curve. She tried it and threw a perfect curve! What behavioral procedure did Buzz use? _____

2. If a teacher provides a behavioral demonstration of what another person is supposed to do, the teacher's behavior is called the _____.

3. When a teacher describes a behavior that he or she would like a learner to produce, this description would be called a(n) _____.
   (Hint: The answer is not "instruction.")

4. If a learner produces a behavior that someone else describes orally, the learner's behavior would be an example of _____ behavior.

5. Henry found that when he typed out the full word in the rough copy of his book, his typist did, too. However, if he used abbreviations in the rough copy of his book, his typist did not type the full word out but simply copied the abbreviations. Since Henry wanted the full word typed out, he gradually stopped using abbreviations and started typing full words. The change in Henry's typing behavior is the result of what behavioral procedure? _____

6. Shawn showed Sherril several shimmering seashells and asked, "What are these? Are they several shimmering seashells?" Shawn praised Sherril for saying "They are several shimmering seashells." The next time that Shawn asked, he gave as a hint only the phrase "several shimmering sea. . . ." Each successive time he dropped a word from the hint. Finally, Sherril could say the whole thing without any part of the hint. What behavioral procedure did Shawn use? _____

7. Carol explained in detail to Buzz how to sew a buttonhole. He tried it and sewed a perfect hole the first time. What behavioral procedure did Carol use? _____

8. Ada demonstrated the essential elements of fielding. These elements included getting her body in front of the ball, kneeling to one knee, keeping her eye on the ball, and so on. Then, she hit some balls to the children and had them try to field them. When they fielded the ball correctly, she praised them. What procedure increasing correct fielding was Ada using? _____

9. Professor Brainbuster showed his students what a multiple-baseline graph looked like. When his students drew their own graphs in the same way, he praised them and gave them a good grade. What procedure did he use to teach his students to make good multiple-baseline graphs? _____

10. Ada had Gordie stand at the plate and call "strike" for only the good pitches. She praised him when he called a good pitch a "strike" but ignored him when he called a bad pitch a "strike." What procedure is she using to teach Gordie to call "strike" for the good pitches and not for the bad pitches? _____

11. Short-answer question B. Explain what question to ask to differentiate between instructional and imitation training:

_____
_____
_____
_____
_____

1. Frank explained in detail how Felicia should sight the rifle on the target. His explanation would be referred to as a(n) _____ in the behavioral procedure of instructional training.

2. Because the imitative stimulus is associated with reinforcement for the imitative behavior, it is technically known as a(n) _____ for the imitative behavior.

3. Ada hit several ground balls to Billy. If he kneeled with one knee on the ground when fielding a ball, she praised him. If he bent down with his knees straight when fielding the ball, she ignored him. Ada used what procedure to teach Billy to put one knee down when fielding? _____

4. Marcia's roommate explained what clothing to buy and how to put on makeup in order to be in "style." Marcia did these things and found that she got asked out for a lot more dates. Marcia's behavior changed as a result of what behavioral procedure? _____

5. Sometimes a nontalker in a discussion class may learn to use an effective argument simply by listening to another person use it. The nontalker may, in the future, use that same line of argument and be reinforced. Changing the person's behavior in this way would be an example of _____.

6. Imitation training and instructional training will continue to work only if the person's imitative or instructed behavior is _____.

7. If a learner copies the behavior of another person, the learner's behavior is called _____.

8. Hollandsworth and colleagues (1978) demonstrated for Herbert how to ask questions designed to clarify interview questions. They then watched his ability to ask such questions in a simulated interview and reinforced correct performance. What behavioral procedure did they use to teach Herbert how to ask questions of the interviewer? _____

9. Sam can learn from a lecture in two ways. He can do things that the lecturer tells him to do in which case the lecturer would be using what procedure? _____ He can copy arguments contained in the lecture in which case the lecturer would be using what procedure? _____

10. Dr. Feelgood taught Marcia to act assertively toward Howard. He praised her when she acted assertively toward him. He then brought in Felix and praised her when she acted assertively toward him. The good doctor used a series of males until Marcia started acting assertively to new males without reinforcement. What behavioral procedure did Dr. Feelgood and his assistant use to create this result? _____

11. Short-answer question C. Define *imitation training*, referring to its three parts:

_____
_____
_____
_____
_____
_____
_____

1. What type of reinforcer is most likely to always be an effective reinforcer even if you have just had a lot of it? _____ _____ reinforcer

2. When reciting "Mary had a little lamb," you would first say, "Mary," and this response would serve as a discriminative stimulus for the second response, "had," and so on. The entire sequence would be called a(n) _____ _____ (if there were some "final" reinforcement).

3. Everyone at Sunflower House had to earn 100 points a week to be eligible to continue living there. In January, Sunflower House changed that rule so that the members did not have to earn 100 points. They are now on their honor to earn 100 points a week simply to help keep the house running. Sunflower House soon learned that the members earned fewer and fewer points each week. These results suggest that points should be classified as what kind of reinforcer? _____

4. A reinforcer that makes a conditioned reinforcer effective is called a(n) _____ reinforcer.

5. Members of the behavioral dorm gave a ticket worth one point to anyone they saw complimenting another person. These points could be traded for theater or sports-events tickets, a special dessert at dinner, or the loan of a typewriter or other house tools. You call the points a(n) _____ reinforcer; you call the desserts and other privileges a(n) _____ reinforcer for the points.

6. Getting the correct answer on a self-quiz may be a minor reinforcer for a student. However, if getting the correct answer on the self-quiz is associated with doing well on a lesson quiz, it may be a fairly strong reinforcer. What type of reinforcer is getting correct answers on the self-quiz if it is associated with a good grade on the lesson quiz? _____ reinforcer

7. Claire started using "ephemeral" when she was around Dale because he complimented her for having such a good vocabulary. One day Kevin also complimented her for using "ephemeral." After that, she said "ephemeral" in her conversation with many people. What behavioral procedure did Dale and Kevin use to get Claire to say the word with new people who had never reinforced her? _____ _____

8. Every time that Jean made an approving statement to her teachers, Polirstok and Greer (1977) gave her a token. The tokens could be exchanged for music tapes, extra gym time, lunch with a favorite teacher, or extra English credit. These tokens could be considered to be a(n) _____ reinforcer.

9. Melody had been praised very strongly by her father for using the word "gregarious" for the first time one day. After that, Melody used the word in a conversation with her mother. What is the name for the process of using "gregarious" with her mother without ever having been reinforced by her mother? _____ _____

10. A sequence of responses in which the results of one response serve as an SD for the next response and in which the last response leads to a reinforcer is called a(n) _____.

11. Short-answer question A. Define *generalized reinforcer*:

_____

_____

1. Carey earned a point for every page of the SRA Reading Program that she finished. She could trade each point for one cookie. Carey's parents noted that she usually earned a few points early in the morning and then quit working for that day. The points probably lost their effectiveness as a conditioned reinforcer because Carey soon becomes _____ with cookies.

2. The fifth tactic in using the stimulus control strategy for solving human problems is to make reinforcement more practical by creating _____ reinforcers.

3. Larry often forgot to wear safety goggles when using the chain saw. Dad reminded him by putting on his own goggles. Dad later reminded Larry by simply putting his own goggles on his forehead but not slipping them over his eyes. Still later, Dad reminded Larry by simply picking up his goggles without putting them on. Finally, Dad was able to stop giving any hint because Larry always put on his safety goggles when operating the chain saw. What behavioral procedure did Larry's father use to teach him to wear safety goggles? _____

4. One day Mary wore her hair loose. That day, Kevin stopped and talked with her for the first time ever. Don also stopped to talk with her, and he complimented her on her hair. When she went home for Thanksgiving break, she again decided to wear her hair loose. If home is a situation where she has not been reinforced for wearing her hair loose, then occurrence of wearing her hair loose at home is an example of what behavioral _____ .

5. Any reinforcer that loses its effectiveness permanently through unpaired presentations is called a(n) _____ _____ reinforcer.

6. When towels were no longer backed up with social attention by Ayllon and Michael (1963), the towels lost their effectiveness as reinforcers. Thus, towels should be considered to be a(n) _____ reinforcer.

7. A reinforcer associated with <u>many</u> other reinforcers is called a(n) _____ _____ reinforcer.

8. Ms. Whalen walked through the room while the children were working on their math. She marked all correct work with a big, red C. Each child was allowed to play outside for 10 minutes after he or she had gotten ten Cs. She found that the rate of work in the class went up dramatically as a result of this approach. Call "playing outside" a(n) _____ reinforcer for Ms. Whalen's Cs.

9. Marlin's teachers gave him a button every time he picked up his toys after he was finished playing. Marlin could use the button to get a snack, a story, or a long walk. If these three events are reinforcers, you would call the button a(n) _____ reinforcer.

10. Bev learned to cube the number 5 by the sequence of multiplying 5 x 5 to get 25. This 25 was then an SD for multiplying by another 5 to get the answer 125. Her teacher always praised her final answer. Bev's behavior in this example constitutes a(n) _____ .

11. Short-answer question B. Define *stimulus/response chain*:

_____

_____

_____

_____

_____

_____

_____

1. A stimulus/response chain is several related responses in which the results of one response serve as a(n) _____ _____ for the next response.

2. Whitman and Dussault (1976) helped James set up a point system. James earned points by studying and attending class. He spent them on such activities as visiting his girlfriend and watching TV. Visiting his girlfriend and watching TV would be considered _____ reinforcers for the points.

3. Willie's mother reinforced Willie for doing something thoughtful with an immediate "thank you" and later an M & M. Willie's mother decided to reinforce his thoughtful behavior only with a "thank you." He started doing fewer thoughtful things until he eventually stopped altogether. This pattern indicates that "thank you" is what type of reinforcer? _____ _____

4. Suppose the teacher gave Juan two math problems such as "2 + 2 = ?" and "4 + 3 = ?". Juan's responses would not constitute a stimulus/response chain because the response to one problem does not serve as a(n) _____ for the response to the second problem.

5. Any event that loses its effectiveness only temporarily through satiation is called a(n) _____ reinforcer.

6. One major advantage that conditioned reinforcers have over their backups, with respect to their effectiveness as reinforcers, is that conditioned reinforcers can easily be delivered according to the principle of _____.

7. One day Fat Frank was once again teasing Slim Simpson. Simpson gave Frank a look that he had never used before. The look said, "I'm going to hurt you very much if you do that again!" Frank immediately started being very nice. Simpson used that same look many times with Frank in the following days. One day, Heavy Harry started teasing Simpson. Simpson gave Harry the same look he had used with Frank. He had never used the look before with Harry. What is the name of the behavioral process that accounts for Simpson looking at Harry that way: _____.

8. A generalized reinforcer is an event that is associated with _____ other reinforcers.

9. Carol's teacher showed her a picture of a maple tree and asked, "What is this? Is it a tree?" and gave her a token whenever she said "tree." She ignored her when she said the flower was a tree. On subsequent occasions, the teacher said, "Is it a tree?" more and more softly until Carol could identify it as a tree without the hint. When she had succeeded, Carol could identify that maple as a tree. What behavioral procedure had the teacher used? _____

10. In Sociology 71, students had to pay credits if they wanted to come to class. In class, they could see movies, listen to guest speakers, and participate in discussions. The credits would be classified as what kind of reinforcer? _____ _____ reinforcer

11. Short-answer question C. Define *conditioned reinforcer*:

_____

_____

_____

_____

1. Katie showed her son the word *house*. She praised him if he said "house" when shown that word but not when shown other words. To help him, she showed him a picture of a house along with that word. She showed the picture for successively briefer times. Because it helps establish the response of reading the word, the picture would be called a(n) _____ _____.

2. Mary's mother checked every 15 minutes to see if she was cleaning her room. If it was reinforcing for Mary to be found cleaning, what schedule was she on? _____ schedule.

3. Fran praised Melanie when she said she had been studying. Unfortunately, Melanie lied. When Melanie said she had been studying, Fran immediately gave Melanie a special snack. Melanie loved the snacks; in fact, she would do anything to get one. She never got too much of the snack. What principle of effective reinforcement, if any, was Fran failing to employ? _____

4. If a reinforcer is paired with one backup reinforcer, it is called a(n) _____ _____ reinforcer; if it is paired with many backup reinforcers, it is called a(n) _____ reinforcer.

5. During World War II, Colonel Peterson frequently showed a photo of a British Spitfire fighter plane to his Civilian Defense recruits and asked them what it was. To help them, he made a spitting sound. Every time that he showed the outline after that he made a slightly softer spitting sound until everyone could identify the Spitfire with no clue. Later, he showed them a different picture of the Spitfire and repeated the process. He had to teach them four different pictures before they could identify new photos. What behavioral procedure had Colonel. Peterson used? _____ _____

6. If Gloria watches Todd only when he arrives home in the evening, we would call her watching behavior a(n) _____ _____ behavior.

7. Some word processors permit users to see a help panel listing the most common commands above the writing space. When a person can use all the commands, they can eliminate the help panel and gain more writing space. The help panel is an added stimulus called a(n) _____.

8. Davey's friends explained to him how to highlight important points, how to review them, and how to work in an area without distractions. They praised him when he followed their suggestions. Davey tried their suggestions and got all As that semester while his friends got Cs. What behavioral procedure did his friends use to teach him how to study effectively? _____

9. Barb and Carey loved to go window shopping. Barb had undertaken to teach Carey how to dress in the latest hip fashions. When Carey expressed the opinion that some garment looked really hip, Barb would praise her taste. She did it immediately, but only if Carey were correct. Carey was always delighted when Barb told her she had good taste and never seemed to get too much praise of this sort. What principle of effective reinforcement, if any, did Barb overlook? _____

10. Cutting a two-by-four with a table saw required Mary to put on safety goggles, turn on the saw, set guides, and cut it. This sequence of Mary's behaviors is called a(n) _____.

11. Short-answer question A. Define *generalized reinforcer*:

_____

_____

_____

_____

_____

_____

1. A person will follow instructions only if frequently _____ for doing so.

2. If a behavior occurs more frequently in the presence of the SD than the S-delta, we say that the stimulus exerts _____ over that behavior.

3. We often think of people who bubble over with "fun" as having that trait ingrained in their personality. Yet a group could accidentally eliminate this behavior by ignoring it. They would be unintentionally applying the procedure called _____.

4. Flora asked Melody to read "cat" from a card showing the word "cat" with a cat picture as a hint. She praised when Melody said "cat" for this card but ignored her when she said "cat" with any other card. Flora covered the cat picture after shorter times until she stopped showing it at all. What behavioral procedure was Flora using? _____

5. The name for reinforcers that are paired with other events to make them effective conditioned reinforcers is _____ reinforcers.

6. Dr. Coe showed Jeff a photo of an *Amanita muscaria* mushroom with the words "Amanita" underneath. He uncovered a bit of the label until Jeff could name the mushroom. When Jeff said "Amanita," Dr. Coe praised him. He ignored when Jeff called other mushrooms "Amanita." Dr. Coe showed less of the label until Jeff could name it without seeing the label at all. Dr. Coe repeated the process with photos of two different Amanita mushrooms. Jeff was then able to correctly name new Amanitas. What behavioral procedure did Dr. Coe use when he showed less of the label for all three photos until Jeff could identify new photos? _____

7. In the process of teaching Marty to say "elephant," Danny would show Marty how to say "elephant" by saying it himself. Danny would then praise Marty if he correctly said "elephant." You call the method that Danny used to teach Marty to say "elephant:" _____ training.

8. Primary reinforcers lose their effectiveness only temporarily through the process called _____; conditioned reinforcers lose their effectiveness permanently by being _____ _____ from their backups.

9. Any time that Karen used a new word longer than three syllables, her father immediately gave her a quarter and praised her improving vocabulary. Her father never did this unless Karen had used a new word. Karen always needed the money and seemed to think of it as a reasonable payoff for learning a new word. What principle of effective reinforcement, if any, did Karen's father fail to employ? _____

10. Everyone was given a "snerkel" each time he or she said something positive about the food. People could cash the snerkels in for a small amount of money or for privileges in the house (such as the use of games). What kind of reinforcer is the snerkel? _____

11. Short-answer question B: Explain the difference between *discrimination training* and *differential reinforcement:*

_____
_____
_____
_____
_____
_____
_____
_____.

1. Fred kissed Gloria only at the drive-in theater. Assuming Gloria finds it reinforcing to be kissed by Fred, the drive-in is called a(n) _____ for kissing.

2. Olivia explained to John exactly how to do a particular dance, even to drawing out little feet diagraming where John should move his feet. John tried it and Olivia provided feedback to him until he could do it perfectly. What behavioral procedure was Olivia using to teach the dance to John? _____

3. Her parents never listened to Gladys during dinner, preferring to discuss the day's news instead. However, one day Gladys criticized the Republicans, and her father had a long argument with her about politics. As a result, Gladys became an ardent critic of Republicans at home. Later, she criticized Republicans around a series of her parents' friends and similarly got an argument and lots of attention. Gladys now criticizes Republicans whenever she is in the presence of conservative, business-oriented people. What behavioral procedure produced this change in Gladys? _____

4. Mr. Howard pointed to a VW going by and asked little Alicia, "What is that? Vroom, vroom." She said, "Car." Mr. Howard pointed to another Beetle later and said the "vroom, vroom" much more softly. He repeated this until she could identify a VW as a car without the addition of the "vroom, vroom." Mr. Howard then used the same approach on a Mustang. From then on, Alicia could identify any passenger vehicle as a car. What behavioral procedure did Mr. Howard use? _____

5. You define generalization as the occurrence of a behavior in the presence of a(n) _____ stimulus.

6. Generalization training involves reinforcing a behavior in the presence of each of a series of situations until generalization occurs to other members of that same _____.

7. Changing a diaper requires placing baby on her back, removing the old diaper, putting on and pinning a new diaper. This sequence of behaviors is called a(n) _____.

8. Sue frequently told Ken that she couldn't jog with him because she didn't know how to run. To help her learn how, Ken took her out on their lawn and jogged for her, showing her where on the foot to land, how to extend the legs, how to coordinate swinging the arms with the leg movements. Sue then tried, and Ken provided feedback. In a few minutes, Sue was able to run almost as smoothly as Ken. What behavioral procedure did Ken employ to teach Sue how to jog? _____

9. If the probability of a behavior decreases because an event that used to follow it has been stopped, what behavioral procedure is being used? _____

10. Discrimination training is a procedure in which a behavior is _____ _____ in the presence of one stimulus and _____ in the presence of a second stimulus.

11. Short-answer question C: Explain how to differentiate between instructional and imitation training:

_____

_____

_____

_____

_____

_____.

1. One day, Mr. King spanked Marcie in front of the class right after he caught her teasing a friend. Marcie never teased a friend in class again. Her teasing decreased due to what behavioral procedure? _____

2. Punishment and extinction both result in a(n) _____ in the frequency of a behavior.

3. The procedure in which a punisher is administered for the occurrence of a particular behavior and in which it reduces the rate of that behavior, is called _____.

4. Mary nagged her mother for snacks while dinner was being cooked. Mary's mother repeatedly said "no," but Mary nagged even more. Mary's mother finally screamed, "No!" at Mary, and Mary stopped nagging. One of mother's screams would be an example of what behavioral event? _____

5. Punisher A reduced the rate of the behavior as long as it was paired with Punisher B. But when it was no longer paired, its effectiveness gradually diminished. Behavior analysts call Punisher A a(n) _____ punisher.

6. Every time that Tom threw a ball in the house, Paula, his mother, spanked him. For some unknown reason, Tom threw the ball around inside the house even more after that. What behavioral procedure did Paula use to produce this change in Tom's ball throwing? _____

7. Yvonne told everyone in her class that she didn't think that President Nixon should have got us out of Vietnam until the United States had won. Her classmates ignored her, knowing that she liked to get attention by taking controversial positions. They ignored this same statement every time that she made it; pretty soon she stopped saying it. What behavioral procedure had her class members used to reduce her rate of making that statement? _____

8. Steve used to pester Carla for a date. However, Carla completely ignored his requests. Steve no longer pesters Carla for a date. What behavioral procedure did she use to decrease the rate of requests? _____

9. An event that follows a behavior and reduces the future probability of that behavior is called a(n) _____.

10. McNees and his associates (1976) posted stars identifying clothing that was most often stolen. Customers stole much less after the posting than before. If the customer stole less because they had in the past been punished in similar situations for stealing, then the star would technically be called a(n) _____.

11. Short-answer question A. Explain in behavioral terms why people use punishment so often:

_____

_____

_____

_____

_____

_____

1. Three types of punishers are _____ _____, _____ and _____.

2. Tom told his mother several times that disco dancing Saturday night was far more important to him than saving his soul Sunday morning. She simply ignored him each time that he said that. Pretty soon he stopped saying that. The reduction in his frequency of making that statement is the result of what behavioral procedure? _____

3. Here are the principles of effective punishment. A punishing stimulus should be _____ only on the behavior that you want to decrease in frequency. It should follow the behavior _____. The person should be relatively _____ of the punisher. The _____ (or intensity) of the stimulus should be sufficiently large.

4. To use the aversive control strategy, (1) decrease undesirable behavior through _____ as a last resort.

5. Every time that Bob broke the rule about dinner complaints, Paul reminded him that he had broken the rule. Bob's rate of breaking the rule increased. The reminder was an event called a(n) _____ for Bob.

6. A punisher is defined as an event that (1) _____ a behavior and (2) _____ the frequency of that behavior.

7. On the few occasions that Marty swore, his mother told him, "Stop that, I'm going to tell your father," and his father spanked him. Recently, however, she took pity on him and, while still telling Marty "Stop that, I'm going to tell your father," did not tell his father. Pretty soon Marty was swearing all the time. His mother's statement is a(n) _____ punisher.

8. Professor Ann Klein ridiculed Ronnie Republican because he made what she considered to be trivial comments. As a result, Ronnie made even more comments. The increase in Ronnie's comments is a result of what behavioral procedure? _____

9. Bob broke the written rule about dinner complaints. Another member of the group reminded him that he had broken the rule. He never complained at dinner again. If you view the written rule about dinner complaints as a stimulus, what is its technical name? _____

10. Kevin repeatedly said racist things in the presence of members of his frat. One day he made a racist comment, and another member said, "Kevin, please don't say that any more. It was disrespectful." Kevin never repeated that comment again. Kevin's racist comment was eliminated by what procedure? _____

11. Short-answer question B: Define *punisher:*
_____
_____
_____
_____
_____
_____
_____

1. When Ben used to insult his friends, they would argue with him about the insults. Now they no longer argue with him but just pretend that he didn't say anything. Ben's rate of insults has decreased dramatically. What behavioral procedure is at work here? _____

2. Mary tried to teach her child to count by saying, "No, that's wrong" whenever the child made a mistake. The child never repeated those mistakes. Mary's statement would be an example of an event called a(n) _____.

3. Frank ran a red light one day when he was in a hurry to get to class. A police officer caught him and gave him a ticket. Frank didn't go through a red light again after that. The red light would be called a(n) _____ for going through it.

4. The fourth strategy for changing human behavior is the _____ control strategy.

5. *Punisher* and *reinforcer* both refer to events that are timed to _____ a behavior.

6. Gloria hit Lenny every time that he attempted a soul kiss. His rate of attempting a soul kiss increased. What behavioral procedure did Gloria use to bring about this increased rate? _____

7. A stimulus that occurs before the behavior and is associated with the punishment of that behavior would be called a(n) _____.

8. Bob broke the rule about dinner complaints, but a reminder didn't work to stop his complaining. The group members decided to fine him 25 cents in addition to the reminder. The reminder now works for Bob. The reminder is a(n) _____ punisher.

9. Tom was spanked every time he teased his little sister. His rate of teasing increased as a result. Spanking would be called a(n) _____.

10. If a person's behavior is decreased through punishment in one situation, any decrease in other situations without punishment would be called _____ and will not necessarily occur.

11. Short-answer question C. Name four principles that determine the effectiveness of punishment:

_____

_____

_____

_____

_____

_____

_____

1. The procedure in which the failure to make a response is followed by the delivery of an aversive event _____ _____ (should, shouldn't) be labeled *punishment*.

2. If an event is normally in a person's environment but is taken away whenever the person emits a particular behavior and if the rate of that behavior decreases, the procedure would be an example of _____.

3. The temporary loss of a privilege contingent on the occurrence of a particular behavior is a form of punishment by withdrawal called _____.

4. Every time Ted pouted, his parents took away some of his play time by sending him to his room. Afterward, they discussed with him why they had sent him to his room. He pouted more often. What procedure did his parents use? _____

5. Pierce and Risley (1974) withdrew the privilege of playing in the recreation center when a rule was violated. The rule-violating behavior decreased dramatically. What behavioral procedure did they use? _____

6. Hedley was a pool shark who started all sorts of stories about members of the group. They decided to refuse to play pool with him for 24 hours whenever he told such a story. Hedley stopped telling such stories. The decrease in his storytelling is the result of what behavioral procedure? _____

7. The frat members no longer argued with Larry when he griped about the food. Soon he stopped making such comments. This is an example of what behavioral procedure? _____

8. Marge used to cook meals for John. But ever since he started following each meal with "thank you," her rate of cooking meals has decreased. "Thank you" is an event called a(n) _____ for Marge's meal cooking behavior.

9. When Professor Odd made absurd statements to his friends, they would argue with him. Recently, they have stopped arguing with him when he makes absurd statements, and his rate of making absurd statements has decreased. What behavioral procedure did they use? _____

10. One day Ken said something about engineering students that Bob didn't like, and Bob said, "Why don't you shut up, you damned fool; you don't know anything about engineering!" Ken never said anything about engineering students around Bob. The decrease in Ken's comments about engineering students is the result of what behavioral procedure? _____

11. Short-answer question A. Explain how to tell whether a procedure that decreases behavior is extinction:

_____
_____
_____
_____
_____
_____
_____

1. Pierce and Risley (1974) posted the number of minutes early that a recreation center would have to close each time a rule violation was observed. This reduced rule violations dramatically. If these numbers were no longer paired with the actual closing of the center, they would probably lose their effect. If they did, they would be the type of punisher called a(n) _____ punisher.

2. Frank's parents took away his erector set each time he played too roughly with it. If Frank's rate of rough play decreased, this would be an example of what behavioral procedure? _____

3. Previously when Beth burped at the dinner table, her parents argued with her about it. Now they no longer argue with her, and her rate of burping has decreased. What behavioral procedure did her parents use to decrease her burping? _____

4. Tommy hit his little brother frequently and was always spanked. After a while, his mother decided to stop spanking Tommy. She was surprised to see that Tommy rarely hit his little brother after she stopped spanking him. What behavioral procedure accounts for the decrease in Tommy's hitting his brother? _____

5. Tommy hit his little brother frequently. One day Tommy's mother just happened to see Tommy hitting him and immediately ran and spanked Tommy. Tommy hit his brother again, and his mother spanked him. Tommy rarely hit his brother after that, but when he did, he got a spanking. Spanking in this case is an example of what behavioral procedure? _____

6. Tommy hit his little brother frequently. One day Tommy's mother just happened to see Tommy hitting him and immediately ran in and spanked Tommy. Tommy hit his brother again, and his mother spanked him. Tommy hit his brother even more often after that and always got a spanking. The event "spanking" in this case is an example of a(n) _____.

7. When Larry pouted, Carol used to sympathize with him. Since she has stopped sympathizing with his pouting, his rate of pouting has decreased sharply. What procedure did Carol use to decrease Larry's pouting? _____

8. There are two types of punishment. In one, a behavior produces an event, and the rate of the behavior decreases; in the second, a behavior is followed by withdrawal of an event and the rate _____.

9. A <u>punisher</u> is any event (produced or withdrawn) timed such that it _____ _____ a behavior and _____ _____ the rate of the behavior.

10. If an event that is normally in a person's environment is withdrawn following a behavior and the rate of the behavior decreases, then the procedure is called _____.

11. Short-answer question B. Define *time out*, and explain how it conforms to the definition of *punishment*:

_____

_____

_____

_____

_____

1. The procedure of stopping the delivery of a reinforcer that follows a behavior and finding a decrease in the rate of the behavior is called _____.

2. If a stimulus precedes the withdrawal of a reinforcer when a particular behavior occurs, that stimulus would be called a(n) _____.

3. Tactic #1 in using the aversive control strategy for solving human problems is to decrease undesirable behavior through _____ as a last resort.

4. If Pierce and Risley (1974) had ignored all rule-violating behavior and the rate of such behavior had decreased, what procedure would they have been using? _____

5. Lora's parents made her stay inside each time she pinched her little brother. If she stopped pinching him, this would be an example of what behavioral procedure? _____

6. Dave frequently made gross comments about the food, and his friends always acted outraged. His friends then decided to no longer act outraged when he complained. Dave stopped complaining. The decrease in Dave's complaining is the result of what behavioral procedure? _____

7. Alice griped about the dorm food a lot. Every time she made such a comment, she was fined 25 cents. She stopped making such comments quickly. The decrease in griping is the result of what behavioral procedure? _____

8. Tommy hit his little brother frequently. His mother decided that she would send Tommy to his room whenever he hit his little brother. Tommy stopped hitting his little brother after this change in his mother's behavior. Sending Tommy to his room for hitting is an example of what behavioral procedure? _____

9. Frank frequently explained his theory of politics. Melody defeated Frank's theory with her criticism. Soon Frank stopped explaining his theory. The event "Melody defeated Frank's theory," would be called a(n) _____.

10. When Tommy first suggested vigilante action to oppose the liberal government, other conservatives supported his ideas. However, now that they have stopped agreeing with his positions, he is making fewer and fewer vigilante proposals. The group used what procedure to reduce Tommy's violent proposals? _____

11. Short-answer question C. State the two elements that define punishment by contingent withdrawal:

_____
_____
_____
_____
_____
_____

1. Mrs. Norris had become annoyed by Carol's frequent failure to do her homework for her American history course. So she started making Carol do her homework during the outside recess period. Carol soon started doing her homework the night before so she wouldn't miss recess. Mrs. Norris used what behavioral procedure to increase Carol's frequency of doing her homework the night before? _____

2. Avoidance behavior is any behavior that _____ the occurrence of a negative reinforcer.

3. Escape behavior is behavior that _____ a negative reinforcer.

4. A negative reinforcer is any event that is _____ or _____ by a behavior and that causes the rate of the behavior to increase.

5. Epstein and Masek (1978) required their patients to pay a $1 fine if they failed to take their medication at the prescribed time. The patients' rate of taking their medication at the correct time increased as a result. The $1 fine would be an event called a(n) _____.

6. Frank and Jerry used to whisper and giggle a lot in the movie theater. One day, the manager came in and asked them to follow him. He made them miss 5 minutes of the movie because they were bothering other customers. They never whispered and giggled again after that. What behavioral procedure did the manager use to reduce their noise making? _____

7. Karen hated to have work pile up on her to the extent that she had to rush to get her assignments done. As a result, when a term paper was assigned in a class early in the semester, she immediately started to work on it a little each day to keep from being overburdened. Karen's working a little each day would be an example of _____ behavior.

8. Melody didn't really start working hard on her studies until the work piled up. Since she didn't like having work piled up, she would start to work practically day and night to get out from under the burden. Melody's rate of work when work had piled up would be an example of _____ behavior.

9. Billy got up about every 15 minutes to sharpen a pencil. Mrs. Feingold started glaring at Billy. As a result Billy's rate of pencil sharpening decreased. What procedure did Mrs. Feingold use to reduce Billy's frequency of pencil sharpening? _____

10. Barb was on a point system at home. She lost points for teasing her little brother. As a result, Barb soon stopped teasing her brother. What behavioral procedure was used to reduce her rate of teasing her brother? _____

11. Short-answer question A. Explain what "punishing someone for not making the desired response" would be called by a behavior analyst and why:

_____
_____
_____
_____
_____

1. Larry used to argue a lot. But he finally realized that every time that he got into a really intense argument he lost a good friend. So he decided to stop arguing and, in fact, never argued again. What behavioral procedure did his social environment use to reduce his rate of arguing: _____ _____.

2. Azrin and Powell (1969) developed a pill dispenser that sounded a buzzer at the prescribed time for taking a pill. The buzzer could be turned off only by dispensing a pill. The behavior of dispensing the pill would be an example of _____ behavior.

3. If every third response is followed by the termination of a negative reinforcer, that behavior is on what schedule of intermittent reinforcement: _____ _____.

4. The moment that Brad guessed that he might get a cold, he started taking a lot of vitamin C. As a result, he never got a cold. Taking vitamin C would be an example of a(n) _____ behavior.

5. Terry used to come home late from school. Then his mother started scolding him every day that he was not home on time. He started coming home on time. Coming home on time would be an example of _____ behavior for Terry.

6. If the termination of an event increases the rate of a behavior that the termination follows, the event is called a(n) _____.

7. Andy frequently forgot to bring any money along on his dates with Leslie. As a result, she usually paid for the movie or drinks. Finally, Leslie explained that she couldn't afford to pay for all their dates. From then on, Andy brought along money. What behavioral procedure did Leslie use to increase Andy's rate of bringing along money for their dates? _____ _____

8. Tactic #2 of the aversive control strategy is to increase desirable behavior through _____ as a last resort.

9. Penny just hated it when Kenny got fresh with her. So she would always haul off and slap the hell out of him when he did. Kenny no longer is fresh with Penny. What behavioral procedure did Penny use to stop Kenny from acting fresh? _____

10. Anytime that Reginald played with any of his toys in any part of the house outside of his own room, his parents picked them up and kept them for a week before returning them. As a result, Reginald stopped playing with his toys in the rest of the house. What behavioral procedure did his parents use to eliminate the behavior of playing with his toys in the rest of the house? _____

11. Short-answer question B. Define *escape* and *avoidance behavior*:

_____

_____

_____

_____

_____

1. When Lester showed up for a date with Felicia in his grubby clothes, she wouldn't let him put his arm around her in the movie—in fact, she wouldn't let him touch her at all. Lester stopped showing up for dates with Felicia in his grubbies. Felicia used what procedure to reduce his rate of showing up in his grubbies? _____

2. Bev didn't like doing any kind of dirty work at the sorority. On "work Saturdays," she would start working, but after a little while, she would remember a doctor's appointment that she had to leave for immediately. Leaving for a doctor's appointment would be an example of _____ behavior.

3. Everyone at the police station was pretty sure that Paul knew more about the crime than he was admitting. Captain Thomas therefore kept questioning him until he finally "broke" and admitted what he knew. Captain Thomas immediately stopped the questioning. Paul admitted later under similar questioning knowing about a number of other crimes. Paul's "confessions" would be an example of _____ behavior.

4. Epstein and Masek (1978) required their patients to pay a $1 fine if they failed to take their medication at the prescribed time. The patients' rate of taking their medication at the correct time increased. The patients' behavior would be called a(n) _____ response.

5. Positive reinforcers and negative reinforcers are both events that can be used to _____ the rate of a behavior.

6. Larry was a conservationist freak. When he and Fran went for a hike, he would always remind her when she littered by saying something like, "Hey, you dropped something." Pretty soon Fran stopped littering when on a hike with Larry. What behavioral procedure did Larry use to eliminate littering? _____ _____

7. If a behavior terminates a negative reinforcer, the behavior is called a(n) _____ behavior.

8. Frank and Jerry used to whisper and giggle a lot in the movie theater. One day, the manager kicked them out of the theater for being noisy. They never made noise again in the theater. What behavioral procedure did the manager use to decrease their whispering and giggling? _____

9. If a behavior prevents a negative reinforcer from occurring, it is called a(n) _____ behavior.

10. Professor Brainbuster had an uncanny knack for guessing when Meredith had not read the assignment. He would inevitably call on her to answer a question about the material on those days. After having this happen a few times, Meredith always read the assignment. What behavioral procedure did the professor use to increase her frequency of reading the assignment? _____ _____

11. Short-answer question C. Define a *negative reinforcer*, and distinguish it from a *positive reinforcer:*

_____

_____

_____

_____

_____

_____

_____

Grade _____

Date _____

1. The statement that "Shyness is the behavior of avoiding eye contact, speaking so softly that the words cannot be heard, and failing to make one's wishes known" would be an example of a(n) _____.

2. Howard's swearing bothered his friend, Barbara. So every time he swore, she gave him a look designed to singe his eyebrows. Howard's rate of swearing remains unchanged. What behavioral procedure did Barbara use with respect to Howard's swearing? _____.

3. Ken was only interested in those parts of the movie that showed scenes of Hawaii where he had lived as a boy. These scenes came after 13, then another 18, then another 2, and finally another 7 minutes of the movie. What specific schedule of reinforcement was his movie watching on? _____ schedule

4. Two observers, who worked in the same office as Ruby, observed to see whether she was smoking during each 15-minute period of the day.

   First:   S N S N S N N S N N
   Second: S N S N S N N N S N

   What is the reliability of their observations? _____% If this is not a new definition, is it acceptable? _____ (yes, no)

5. For effective use of punishment or reinforcement, it is necessary to deliver them very soon after the behavior has occurred. This is known as the principle of _____.

6. If a book asks a child to read a word like *cat* but shows the child a picture of a cat as a hint and then shows less and less of the cat in subsequent pages where the child must read the word, the picture of the cat would be called a(n) _____.

7. Martin wore a wrist counter to count the number of times that he said something positive to someone. On any day that he counted at least 15 positive statements, he permitted himself to watch TV that night. What kind of reinforcer is the counter: a(n) _____ reinforcer; the TV would serve as a(n) _____ reinforcer for the counts.

8. Flora wanted to teach her daughter to be an opera singer. When the daughter was 2 years old, Flora started devoting the half hour after dinner to singing lessons in which she used ice cream to reinforce singing. Because it was right after dinner, her daughter didn't seem very interested in the ice cream. What principle of effective reinforcement, if any, had Flora neglected in choosing a time right after dinner? _____ _____

9. Claire likes to ride her snowmobile without a hat. If the cold becomes too intense after driving for awhile, she puts on a hat. Putting on a cap after feeling intense cold is an example of _____ _____ behavior.

10. Ruby was using a special cigarette case that counted the number of times that she opened the case to take out a cigarette. Bob Behaviorist recorded the number of such openings for three weeks prior to helping Ruby stop smoking. This three-week period of measurement is called a(n) _____.

11. Short-answer question A. Define a *negative reinforcer*, and distinguish it from a *positive reinforcer*:

_____

_____

_____

_____

_____

_____

_____

1. Wendy agreed to encourage Carol to speak more loudly as a step toward helping her to become more assertive. At first, Wendy praised Carol only if she could hear her; later, only if she could hear her 5 feet away; and still later, only if she could hear her from 10 feet away. Carol speaking loud enough to be heard from 5 feet away would be called a(n) _____ to the ultimate goal.

2. We say that the question "What is the sum of eight and two?" is a(n) _____ for the answer "four."

3. Mr. Levin observed five groundskeepers to determine whether they were working. He first observed Ken for 30 seconds, then shifted to Diane for 30 seconds, and so on for the other three workers. He started over again every two and a half minutes. What method of direct observation is he using? _____ recording

4. If a behavior is reduced in frequency by removing an event usually in the person's environment any time that the behavior occurs, the name of the procedure is _____; if a behavior is reduced in frequency by stopping the delivery of an event that had followed the behavior in the past, the name of the procedure is _____.

5. Judy was curious to find out how much of the time the president was smiling. So she watched several of his news conferences. She divided the conferences into a series of intervals 15 seconds long and recorded whether he was smiling or not during each interval. (He smiled 79% of the time!) What method of direct observation was she using? _____ recording.

6. Jim broke the rule about dinner complaints, but a reminder didn't work to stop him complaining. The group decided to fine him a dollar in addition to the reminder, which worked. What procedure decreased Jim's complaining? _____ _____

7. Gail liked to go dancing, but Harvey almost never took her. She finally started nagging him like the hounds of hell until he would say, "All right, we'll go dancing tonight." Harvey takes her dancing more often now. What procedure did Gail use to increase Harvey taking her dancing? _____

8. To use the aversive control strategy, (1) decrease undesirable behavior through _____ or (2) increase desirable behavior through _____ reinforcement as a last resort.

9. Bob observed Ruby's rate of smoking during three different periods: before the case shocked her, while the case shocked her, and after the case stopped shocking her. Bob used what type of design to study the effect of the shocks on Ruby's smoking? _____ design

10. Sally hated to carry out the garbage at night after dinner. So her father carried the garbage out for her if she studied for at least an hour after dinner. Since he has started doing that, Sally has done a lot more studying. Because studying prevents having to take out the garbage, her study behavior would be an example of _____ behavior.

11. Short-answer question B. Explain in behavioral terms why people use punishment so often:

_____

_____

_____

_____

1. Dr. Brown developed a behavioral definition of generosity. He asked a number of nonbehaviorists to rate the generosity of several individuals appearing in videotape recordings. If he compared their ratings of generosity with the level of generosity according to his behavioral definition, he would be able to determine the _____ of his definition.

2. Customers in grocery stores used to be given trading stamps as incentive to continue buying at a particular store. The trading stamps could later be exchanged for anything from a toaster to a vacation. What kind of reinforcers are trading stamps? _____ reinforcers

3. Jane kept track of her reading rate for two weeks for each homework assignment. She read about 150 words per minute and usually didn't finish her homework. Then she took a speed-reading course. After finishing the course, she observed her reading rate again for two weeks and found that it had increased to 700 words a minute. Her homework was much easier to finish as a result. What kind of design was she using to determine the effect of the course on her reading rate? _____ design

4. If Tommy learns to say "forty-nine" when asked "What is the square of seven?" but not when asked for the square of other numbers, we would say that the question "What is the square of seven?" has come to exert _____ over his behavior of saying "49."

5. Peter used to drink beer after beer immediately upon arriving home from work. His wife begged him for months to stop doing it, but to no avail. Finally, she decided to leave the house anytime that he drank beer, and she would stay gone until the next day. Peter has stopped drinking beer. What behavioral procedure did his wife use to decrease beer drinking? _____

6. A behavior will take longer to extinguish if it has been on what generic schedule? A(n) _____ schedule.

7. Responding to terminate a negative reinforcer is called a(n) _____ response. Responding to prevent a negative reinforcer is called a(n) _____ response.

8. Wendy agreed to encourage Carol to speak more loudly as a step toward helping her to become more assertive. Wendy's goal was to get Carol to speak loudly enough so she could be heard 10 feet away. At first, Wendy praised Carol only if she could hear her from 2 feet; later, only if she could hear her from five feet; finally, only if she could hear her from 10 feet away. Hearing her from 10 feet away would be an example of a(n) _____.

9. Mrs. Franklin taught Jimmy to label a large circular line as a "circle." When he labeled a circle as "circle," she would praise him. When he labeled any other figure a "circle," she ignored him. She helped him learn by adding onto her question "You know, a circle" and praising him when he said "circle." Next, she gave as a hint only "you know, a cirk; leaving the "le" sound off. Finally, she gave no hint at all, and Jimmy could label the circle correctly. What behavioral procedure did Mrs. Franklin use? _____

10. Sue repeatedly said racist things in the presence of members of her group. One day she made a racist comment, and another member said, "Sue, that's ugly talk." She never repeated that comment again. Sue's racist comment was eliminated by what procedure? _____

11. Short-answer question C. Explain how to distinguish between *punishment by contingent withdrawal* and *extinction*:

_____

_____

_____

_____

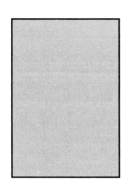

# Name Index

# Subject Index

## A

Abuse, 377, 411
Accuracy, 62
Achievement Place, 378–379
Addiction, 377
Aggressive behavior, 183–184, 197, 428
Agreement, reliability as, 62
Alternative events, 168
Alternative explanations, 85–87, 91, 150, 152
Alzheimer's disease, 121
American Psychological Association (APA), 3
Animal training, 164
Anthropology, behaviorism and, 7
Approaches, for observations, 19–20, 48
Approval, as reinforcement, 377. *See also* Praise
Approximations, successive, 215, 222, 252, 284, 286, 396, 448
Assertiveness training, 325–326
Asthma therapy, 219–221
Attention, as behavior, 24, 249, 267, 283, 376, 447–448, 465
Attitudes, 15, 18–19
Autism, 1, 4, 218, 300, 358, 361, 409
Averaging reinforcers, 250
Aversive control. *See also* Punishment by contingent stimulation; Punishment by contingent withdrawal; Reinforcement, negative
contingencies in, 463
definition of, 407
freedom as absence of, 466–467
functional analysis in, 465–466
glossary on, 467
helpful hints on, 467
reducing need for, 464
review of, 467–477
strategy for, 413, 463–464, 467
Avoidance behavior, 444–446, 451, 467
Awareness, 18

## B

Backup reinforcers, 376, 381, 383–384, 400
Backward comparison experimental designs, 89–90
Backward reversal experimental designs, 121
Baseline, 86–89, 151, 168, 179
Battered women, 411
"Bearing witness," 357
Behavior, 15–34. *See also* Extinction; Observation of behavior; Reinforcement
absence of, 200
aggressive, 183–184, 197, 428
attention as, 24, 249, 267, 283, 376, 447–448, 465
avoidance, 444–446, 451. *See also* Reinforcement, negative
building blocks of, 163–164
causes of, 149
chaining, 222
coaching as, 93
coercive, 446–448
cognitive, 295, 395, 398–399
complex, 39
conservation as, 93–94
constructive, 164
contingencies in, 169. *See also* Contingency, principle of
cooperation as, 198–199
copying, 365–367
creativity as, 25
criminal, 414
definition of, 15–18, 151
discriminated, 297–298, 308–309, 339, 400
driving, 182
eating, 194, 359, 376
of elderly, 121–122, 183, 197–198
escape, 444–446, 451, 466. *See also* Reinforcement, negative
expression of, 295
extinguishing, 296, 347, 448
helpful hints on, 27–28
imitative, 357
incompatible, 197, 199
increasing, 171–172, 171–173
instructed, 358–359, 364

intellectual, 295
laws of, 269
learning as, 25–26
modifying, 18–19
operant, 2, 5, 147
pain as, 26–27
of police, 120–121
programmed reading on, 29–34
reduction of, 418–419. *See also* Punishment by contingent stimulation; Punishment by contingent withdrawal
self-defeating, 281–282
self-injurious, 180–181, 408, 410, 413–414
self-reporting, 19–22
sleeping as, 148
studying, 45, 269–270
supervision, 300, 449
target, 215, 221–222, 284, 287, 448
of teachers, 381–383
tension as, 24–25
undesirable, 430–431
verbal, 201
Behavioral definition, 151
Behavioral gerontology, 147
Behavioral medicine, 4, 147
Behavioral momentum, 282
Behavioral strategy, 7–8, 147–157
definition of, 151
glossary for, 151–152
helpful hints on, 150
practice review of, 152–157
programmed reading on, 32
tactics in, 148–150
Behavior analysis, 1–14
behavioral strategy in, 7–8
behaviorism *versus*, 147
Carl Rogers on, 195
definition of, 5–6, 151
growth of, 3–5
helpful hints on, 8–9
modern behaviorism in, 1–3
private events in, 6
programmed reading on, 10–14
public events in, 6–7